Encyclopedia of
World War II
A Political, Social, and Military History

Encyclopedia of
World War II
A Political, Social, and Military History

VOLUME I: A–C

Dr. Spencer C. Tucker
Editor

Mr. Jack Greene
Col. Cole C. Kingseed, USA Ret., Ph.D.
Dr. Malcolm Muir Jr.
Dr. Priscilla Mary Roberts
Maj. Gen. David T. Zabecki, USAR, Ph.D.
Assistant Editors

Dr. Priscilla Mary Roberts
Editor, Documents Volume

FOREWORD BY
Dr. Allan R. Millett

A B C 🟤 C L I O

Santa Barbara, California   Denver, Colorado   Oxford, England

Library of Congress Cataloging-in-Publication data available from the Library of Congress

ISBN 13: 978-1-57607-999-7   ebook 978-1-57607-095-6

ISBN 1-57607-999-6 (hardcover)   ISBN 1-57607-095-6 (ebook)

10 09 08 07 06   10 9 8 7 6 5 4 3

This book is also available on the World Wide Web as an ebook. Visit abc-clio.com for details.

ABC-CLIO, Inc.
130 Cremona Drive, P.O. Box 1911
Santa Barbara, California 93116–1911

This book is printed on acid-free paper ∞.
Manufactured in the United States of America

This encyclopedia is dedicated to my Father,
Colonel Cary S. Tucker, USAR (1906–1962),
who fought in the Pacific Theater in World War II

About the Editors

Spencer C. Tucker, Ph.D., held the John Biggs Chair of Military History at his alma mater of the Virginia Military Institute, Lexington, for six years until his retirement from teaching in 2003. Before that, he was professor of history for thirty years at Texas Christian University, Fort Worth. He has also been a Fulbright scholar and, as an army captain, an intelligence analyst in the Pentagon. Currently a senior fellow in military history at ABC-CLIO, he has written or edited twenty-three books, including the award-winning *Encyclopedia of the Vietnam War* and the *Encyclopedia of the Korean War,* both published by ABC-CLIO.

Priscilla Mary Roberts received her Ph.D. from Cambridge University and is a lecturer in history and honorary director of the Center of American Studies at the University of Hong Kong. Dr. Roberts has received numerous research awards and was the assistant editor of the *Encyclopedia of the Korean War* published by ABC-CLIO. She spent 2003 as a visiting Fulbright scholar at the Institute for European, Russian, and Eurasian Studies at The George Washington University in Washington, D.C.

Contents

List of Entries

List of Maps

Foreword

I am a child of World War II. The *Anschluss* of Austria was Adolf Hitler's birth gift. The Führer topped that generosity the next year with the Munich Crisis, in which Prime Minister Neville Chamberlain discovered peace in our time, meaning the next eleven months. In the autumn of 1938, my parents and I lived in London, which meant that they became acquainted with gas masks and civil defense air-raid pamphlets. I must have wailed with baby deprivation when I didn't get my own gas mask, too, but there were no gas masks for infants. I have been a fan of appeasement ever since. Of course, I have no memory of the invasion of Poland, but I remember dimly being on the traditional family countryside Sunday drive (soon to be a casualty of war) when NBC told us about Pearl Harbor. My next memory is a radio report about Guadalcanal while living with my grandparents in Bloomington, Indiana. It is hard to believe that their war memories included *their* parents' tales of the Civil War, in which my paternal grandfather had lost three uncles. Guadalcanal was as far away as Antietam.

In our wartime neighborhood in Arlington, Virginia, we fought a proxy war fed by 1945 with enemy souvenirs. My father, an army "emergency" colonel, could provide nothing more interesting than Pentagon papers, but my best friends' fathers were U.S. Army Air Forces (USAAF) pilots, young lieutenant colonels who commanded B-29 squadrons in the Marianas. Colonels Doubleday and Rustow, both of whom retired as Air Force generals, deluged us with Japanese war matériel, less weapons. We subsequently fought Iwo Jima and Okinawa in the woods off South Hayes Street. I do not recall who got to die in agony for the Emperor, but I certainly know who played a heroic Marine lieutenant with a wooden submachine gun. The best my father, an Army Service Forces planner, could do was to awaken me at O-Dark-Hundred to listen to the first broadcasts about D Day. It was enough then and now.

The last year of the war is a blur—Hitler's death, FDR's death, V-E and V-J Days, the first atomic bombs. I recall that we veterans of the South Hayes Street Front were unhappy to see the war end, probably because we wanted even more Japanese souvenirs, courtesy of the USAAF's XX Bomber Command. As 1946 dawned, we were on our way back to my father's real job, teaching public administration at Columbia University. My postwar veteran's readjustment meant entering the third grade at Leonia (New Jersey) Grammar School. My posttraumatic stress syndrome probably involved sinus headaches and learning I needed glasses for infantile myopia, spoiling my BB gun marksmanship and kickball games.

World War II did not disappear from my scope, however, even when important things intruded, like the Yankees-Giants rivalry and the latest $2 box of Britain's toy soldiers. Two of my new friends and I wrote a book for a fifth-grade project, mostly cribbed from *Compton's Encyclopedia*. Its title was "Warfare." Most of the book was about World War II, and I wrote about the war with Japan, all five pages. The word count has gone up considerably since 1948, but my interest has been unchecked for almost 60 years of living with World War II. The world has had equal difficulty putting the war behind it, its memory refreshed daily by political allusions, movies, television series, and more than 4,000 books in print in English alone. The fascination with the war reflects a great human truth: we are all children of World War II.

We are children surrounded by the ghosts of the dead of World War II. The graves of the slain stain the earth around the world, although much less so for the United States. The American cemeteries abroad hold only about half of the American wartime combat dead of 292,131 and 113,842 dead of other causes. According to policy, unique among the belligerents, the United States brought remains back from abroad by family request for reinterment on American soil in national cemeteries like the ones at Arlington, Virginia, or Honolulu, Hawaii. Another option was burial in a private family cemetery, still with a military ceremony and a modest government headstone. For service members for whom no identifiable remains could be found, the largest American cemeteries have memorials that provide the names of the missing in action and unidentified dead, who number 78,955. The largest such memorial is at the National Cemetery of the Pacific ("the Punchbowl"), which lists the names of 18,000 missing in action, most of them airmen and sailors lost forever in the depths of the Pacific Ocean. The cemetery holds 13,000 remains. The two largest American military cemeteries in Europe—Saint-Laurent-sur-Mer, in Normandy, France, and Saint-Avold, in Lorraine, France—contain the graves of 9,079 and 10,338, respectively, and commemorate 1,864 and 595 missing in action and unidentified dead. That I can provide statistics of reasonable certitude about American wartime losses is telling commentary on how relatively few ghosts the United States provides from the world's most awful recorded war.

We will never know just how many people died in World War II, but the estimates are horrific and get worse all the time. When I began my life as a professional historian, the estimates of World War II deaths stood at 40 million, more than half of them civilians. The estimates have now climbed above 50 million and may be as high as 60 million. The death toll between 1937 and 1945, arbitrary dates that could be extended easily into the 1950s, has expanded because of recent revelations on the number of Soviet military deaths and the recalculation of war-related deaths throughout China. The totality and globalization of the war is most apparent in one chilling statistic: for the first time in recorded history, more civilians died from direct enemy action than military personnel. Military deaths number in excess of 20 million, civilian deaths probably 35 million. The Axis civilian deaths from bombing and the Red Army's campaign of revenge from 1944 to 1945 number more than 3 million. Chinese and Russian civilian deaths could be 10 times as many, which explains the enduring hatred of China for Japan and Russia for Germany. By contrast, the deaths of American civilians (excluding Filipinos but not Hawaiians) number 6,200, almost all of whom were merchant seamen.

How does one account for the extent of human suffering among "the innocents" or nonmilitary dead of World War II? Since the warfare of the Napoleonic era, the "civilized" Western nations in practice, national law, and formal international treaty have tried to establish "laws for the conduct of war" or "rules of engagement" that obliged armies to spare nonresisting, nonparticipating civilians caught in the path of warfare. The first difficulty was that the nineteenth-century codes, brought together in the Hague Convention of 1899, were based on the experiences of armies occupying hostile territory, like the Union army in the rebellious American Confederate states from 1861 to 1865 or the German army in France in 1870 and 1871. When civilians became targets, however inadvertent, of aerial bombing and maritime commerce raiding conducted by submarines in World War I, the rules grew more complex and ambiguous in application. One rationalization was that civilian war-workers in munitions factories on "the Home Front," a new Great War usage, were no longer innocents but willing participants in the war. Another problem was a military commander's duty to protect the lives of his men, sometimes called "military necessity." Why should a submarine commander allow a merchant ship's captain to get his crew and passengers into lifeboats before the ship was sunk when the ship's wireless operator could call forth naval assistance that imperiled the submarine? The use of convoys placed escorts nearby, which made surface attacks unattractive. How could a submarine commander risk his crew to pick up survivors? It was one small step to killing enemy merchant mariners in lifeboats and in the water, either with machine guns or by abandonment, a common practice of all submarine forces in World War II.

The growing vagaries of international maritime law do not explain the genocidal nature of World War II. Virulent nationalism, infected with a peculiar brand of racism and religious discrimination, set off the waves of mass murder that characterized the war. By legal definition—regarded as moral standards in some societies—civilians and prisoners of war (POWs) are to be protected from death by the occupying or detaining power. Nazi Germany, Imperial Japan, and the Soviet Union showed how little such standards meant. The Germans still enjoy the dubious distinction of being the most genocidal belligerents of World War II. The Nazi regime divided its victims into three broad categories of exploitation and death: (1) European Jews, 6 million of whom perished as captives in the Holocaust, an exercise in genocide in which almost all European nations participated with some level of complicity; (2) Slavs, broadly defined but especially Poles and Russians, civilians and POWs, whose deaths by murder furthered the "repopulation" and enslavement of eastern Europe required by the *lebensraum* of the Thousand-Year Reich and whose deaths by starvation and disease as slave laborers underwrote the Nazi industrial war effort, numbering an estimated 12 to 15 million; and (3) prisoners of war, resistance fighters, hostages, famine victims, and conscripted laborers from western European nations who died, estimated at around 1 million. Deaths in Great Britain and for the British merchant marine numbered about 100,000. The victims of Imperial Japan were principally other Asians (the Chinese, the Filipinos) and reached an estimated 9 million. Axis civilian deaths numbered an estimated high of 3 million, about equally divided between the fatalities of strategic bombing and the Soviet ethnic cleansing of 1944 and 1945. When deaths are measured against population, the most victimized nation was Poland, attacked and massacred by Germany and the Soviet Union after 1939; 6 million of 34 million Poles died (Jews and gentiles). One of every 3 Poles left Poland; 1 in 10 eventually returned. Only an estimated 100,000 Poles died fighting in uniform in 1939 or in the exile armed forces eventually formed in France, Great Britain, and the Soviet Union. Geographic vulnerability and appeasement politics could not be redressed by fighting heart, ample enough in the Polish armed forces and the urban guerrillas of the Warsaw ghetto uprising (1943) and the Home Army's war in the same city the next year.

The Asia-Pacific war had its horrific novelties. After 1945, Japanese political leaders, now good conservative-capitalists, cultivated the impression that Japan had been a victim of racism, goaded into war and then attacked in "a war without mercy." To save his people, another innocent victim, Emperor Hirohito, shocked by the atomic bombs that leveled Hiroshima and Nagasaki, surrendered his helpless nation. This version of Japan's war—still believed by many Japanese—served the American postwar purpose, which was to make Japan an anti-Communist bastion against Communist China and the Soviet Union. Japan's real victims—China, the Philippines, Malaya, Australia, and Vietnam—never forgot the real war. I witnessed a colonel of the People's Liberation Army thanking Brigadier General Paul W. Tibbets Jr., U.S. Air Force (Ret.), for freeing China. The Chinese colonel only regretted that the United States had chosen peace rather than dropping more atomic bombs.

The Japanese conducted their war against fellow Asians with only a little less sympathy than they showed the hated Europeans—which meant American, British, Dutch, Canadian, French, Australian, and New Zealand military personnel and civilians. Only 65 percent of the 80,000 Europeans held by Japan as POWs or civilian internees survived the war; capricious execution (mostly of Allied airmen), casual murder, and studied neglect of food and medical needs doomed Allied POWs. The Japanese treatment of fellow Asians beggars the imagination, the most egregious example being the month-long orgy of murder, torture, and rapine in Nanjing that took at least 200,000 Chinese lives. The Japanese used Asians for their varied forms of inhumane projects: army brothels, forced labor, bayonet practice, germ-warfare experiments, medical "research" that included vivisection, and the mass murder of hostages and helpless villagers.

For all its atrocious behavior, Japan escaped a reckoning worthy of its crimes against humanity. It lost the war because the United States destroyed its navy and its army and naval air forces. It is true that Japan lost close to 2 million servicemen and probably 500,000 civilians from a population of 72 million, but Germany had more than 3 million service dead and more than 2 million civilian dead from a population of 78 million. When the Asia-Pacific war ended, the Allies took custody of over 5 million overseas Japanese and returned them to Japan. The only Japanese who really paid the loser's price were those captured by the Soviets in Manchuria and Korea; of the 600,000 Japanese and Koreans taken into the Soviet Union as human reparations, only 224,000 survived to return home by 1950. The sudden Japanese surrender, motivated by a frantic effort to save the institution of the emperor, deprived the Soviets of additional revenge for their defeat at the hands of Japan in 1905. Japan may have lost its empire in 1945, but it saved its soul, however unique.

World War II marked the apogee of the military power of the nation-state, the culmination of a process of institutional development that began for Europe in the sixteenth century. To wage war effectively, Prussian General Karl von Clausewitz opined in the 1820s, a nation required the complete commitment and balanced participation of its government, its armed forces, and its people. He might have added its economy to "the holy trinity" he analyzed in *Vom Krieg*. Phrased another way, the 56 belligerent states of World War II could create and sustain an industrialized war effort that in theory left no significant portion of their population or resources untouched. Wartime participation might be voluntary or coerced—usually both—but it was complete, at least in intent. Whatever their prewar political system, the belligerents all came to look like modern Spartas, with their national life conditioned by war-waging.

The authoritarian, police-state character of Nazi Germany and the Soviet Union is familiar enough to be ignored as an example of total mobilization, but the experience of Great Britain, a paragon of individual liberty, dramatizes the depths of wartime sacrifice and dislocation, even for a nominal victor. First of all, Great Britain, with a population of 47 million, put almost 6 million men and women into the armed forces, a level of participation about the same as that of the United States. The raw demographics, however, do not do justice to the British commitment. British male deaths of World War I (900,000) and the male children the dead of the Somme would have sired meant that Great Britain had a limited manpower pool from which to draw. Conscription of able-bodied men (and some not able-bodied or young) became almost complete in theory but still had to deal with the personnel demands of critical occupations: fishing, farming, coal mining, the merchant marine, civil defense and fire fighting, railroads, war material and munitions manufacturing, and health services. Twenty-one million Britons served in war-essential jobs. No sector was adequately staffed, even though almost all British males from teenagers to the elderly who were not in the services found a place in such organizations as the Ground Observer Corps, the Home Guard, and police and fire-fighter auxiliaries. British women filled some of the essential jobs; about half the adult female population of Great Britain took full-time jobs or joined the armed forces. The other part of the female population cared for children and the elderly and did volunteer work that supported the armed forces and the industrial workforce. Male and female, Britons worked more than 50 hours a week, endured German air attacks, and attempted to live on shrinking rations of meat, sugar, eggs, dairy products, and all sugar-dependent condiments like jam and pastries, and tea. Only fish, bread, and vegetables were available in reasonable quantities, thanks to the heroic efforts of the fishing industry and the emergency cultivation of marginal farmlands, inadequately fertilized. As American GIs flooded Great Britain in 1943 and 1944, they redistributed their own imported, ample rations to the British people, sometimes for profit, more often in charity.

There is no reason to doubt that the British war effort represented a voluntary national commitment to survival outside the Axis orbit. Yet behind the stiff upper lips and choruses of "Land of Hope and Glory," a national government of iron will and ample authority ensured that Britons put the war effort first. The British intelligence services and police had broad powers to ferret out spies, dissenters, war profiteers, and civil criminals. The Official Secrets Act could have been written on the Continent. The British Broadcasting Corporation (BBC) and the newspapers became essentially an arm of the Churchill government. Military catastrophes—and there were many from 1940 until 1944—disappeared into a void of silence or received the special spin that the War Office and the Admiralty had perfected since the Napoleonic Wars. In such a world, Narvik became an experiment in countering amphibious operations and the pursuit of the *Bismarck* only a combat test of Royal Navy ship design. At heart a war correspondent as well as a politician, Winston Churchill needed no Josef Goebbels.

For most of the major belligerents, World War II seemed a larger repetition of the challenges of World War I, and many of the political and military leaders between 1939 and 1945 had rich experience in coping with a national mobilization for war. Churchill and Franklin D. Roosevelt had held important administrative positions in a wartime government when Hitler was a *frontsoldat* (front-line soldier) in the advanced rank of corporal and Benito Mussolini was having a similar military experience fighting the Austrians in the Tyrol. The Anglo-American alliance profited from authoritarian leadership that remained answerable to a representative legislative branch. The Allies welcomed European exiles to their war effort, knowing the wide range of talents modern war required. Even Josef Stalin released more than a million political prisoners because he needed their services. Hitler, by contrast, killed 300,000 of his countrymen, imprisoned hundreds of thousands more, and drove thousands into the arms of his enemies.

The lessons of World War I could be interpreted in several ways, and Hitler's "lessons" contributed to Germany's defeat. The Nazis resisted surrendering any managerial power to their talented industrial class, and Hitler refused to embrace long war economic programs until 1943. The German civilian population received ample food supplies while the slave-labor force starved to death, a considerable drag on productivity. Albert Speer, Hitler's favorite architect, did not take control of the German economy until it was about two years too late to win the war with superweapons or mass-produced, simpler tanks, aircraft, trucks, artillery pieces, and tactical communications. The Allies produced 10,000 fighter aircraft in 1940; the Germans did not reach that annual production until 1943. The Germans, in a heroic effort, then produced 26,000 fighters in 1944, but the Allies had already more than doubled this force with 67,000 fighters the same year. Pilot experience and gasoline supplies contributed to the Luftwaffe's demise, but so too did Allied aircraft numbers. The Japanese made a comparable econo-strategic error in handling imported petroleum from the occupied Dutch East Indies. Unlike the British and American navies, tested by the German submarine force in World War I, the Imperial Japanese Navy did too little too late to maintain a tanker fleet and protect it with well-escorted convoys. The Indonesian wells pumped merrily away, but the actual tonnage of crude oil that reached Japan dropped by half in 1944. The U.S. Navy failed to protect the Allied tanker fleet in the Caribbean in 1942, but it then enforced convoy discipline and provided adequate escorts and air coverage. In 1943, the navy checked the U-boats' "happy times" in creating flaming merchant ships. Time and again, the Allies faced problems like maintaining a viable industrial workforce or allocating scarce raw materials. The war managers found the appropriate technical solutions in the World War I experience, and their political leaders found ways to make their people's economic sacrifices acceptable for World War II.

The exploitation of the means of mass communication reflected the war's populist character. Once again, World War I—the poster war—provided precedents that World War II exploited to the fullest. No belligerent government functioned without an office of public information. No military establishment went to war without press officers and morale officers. The Soviets called their officers commissars, the Americans public information officers. The Germans published *Signal*, the Americans *Stars and Stripes.* The civilian populations, however, received the full media blitz. The international motion picture industry went to war, producing eternal images in sound and living color (sometimes) of the wartime leaders and their causes. The newsreels that preceded commercial films brought the war news (in highly selected form) to the home front. Documentary feature films made legends of director-producers like Leni Riefenstahl, Frank Capra, Sir J. Arthur Rank, Sergei Eisenstein, and Watunabe Kunio. Radios reached even more people than movies; by 1939—as a matter of Nazi policy—70 percent of German families had radios, and they were not designed to pick up the BBC. In the United States and Great Britain, 37 million households owned radios. One-third of wartime broadcasts were war news and commentary. Public loudspeaker systems provided the same services in poorer belligerents like the Soviet Union and Japan. The war turned words and images into weapons.

World War II became so lethal because all the major belligerents, even China, had entered the industrial-electronic age by the twentieth century. Technological innovation and mass production worked hand in hand to give the armed forces a capacity for destruction on every type of battlefield that had been demonstrated in World War I and brought to higher levels of destructiveness in the 1940s. Governments and private industry collaborated to institutionalize research and development; to obtain essential raw materials to make steel and rubber; to recruit and train skilled workers; to build factories capable of mass production; and to fabricate munitions, weapons, and vehicles that filled military requirements. The war industries of World War II could even go underground, as they did in Germany and China, or move a thousand miles out of harm's way, as they did in the Soviet Union.

The technology of the war was shaped by two major developments: (1) the evolution of the internal combustion engine fed by fossil fuels, and (2) the exploitation of the electromagnetic spectrum through the development of batteries or generators tied to internal combustion engines, whether they powered aircraft, ships, or vehicles. A parallel development was the ability to make essential parts of engines and radios lighter and more durable by creating components of plastic and alloyed metals and using special wiring, optics, and crystals. The knowledge and skill to pursue these developments was international and uncontrollable. Although one or another national military establishment might become a technological pioneer—like that of the Germans in jet engines and the Anglo-Americans in nuclear weapons—no instrument of war was beyond the technical capability of the principal belligerents, except China.

The air war dramatizes how rapidly aviation technology advanced and how radar (radio direction and ranging) influenced the battle for the skies. The first strategic bombing raids of the war (1939–1940) involved Royal Air Force bombers whose bomb loads were 4,500 to 7,000 pounds maximum and whose range (round-trip) was around 2,000 miles; the German Heinkel He-111 H-6 had similar characteristics. The last strategic bombing campaign (by the USAAF on Japan in 1945) was conducted by the B-29, which had a 5,600 mile maximum range and 20,000 pound maximum bomb load. The earliest bombing raids involved traditional navigation methods of ground sightings, compass headings, and measurements of air speed and elapsed time. The B-29s had all these options (including celestial navigation at night), but they also relied on radio navigation beacons and ground-search radar to measure speed, direction, and altitude. Radar also assisted in the location of target cities. Aerial gunners on first-generation bombers fired light machine guns with visual sights; B-29 gunners fired remote-controlled automatic cannon and machine guns. Of course, radar also made air defenses more formidable. British air early-warning radar reached out 185 miles, German radar 125 miles, Japanese radar 62 miles, and American radar 236 miles. Airborne and surface naval search radars ranged from 3 to 15 miles. The best antiaircraft gun-laying radars could plot targets from 18 to 35 miles distant.

Naval warfare also exploited the new technologies of propulsion, navigation, target acquisition, and ordnance to make war at sea more destructive. For example, the U.S. Navy commissioned 175 *Fletcher*-class destroyers (DD 445–804), the largest single production run of a surface warship by any wartime navy. These ships weighed about 3,000 tons and carried a crew of 300, putting them on the high side of displacement and manning for World War II destroyers. They bristled with weapons designed to destroy aircraft, ships, and submarines. The five 5-inch, 38-caliber dual-purpose main battery guns were mounted in turrets fore and aft, and each gun could fire 12 shells a minute in sustained fire. The *Fletchers* mounted 10 torpedo tubes amidships for the standard Mark XIV electric-turbine-powered, 21-inch-diameter torpedo with a warhead of 600 pounds of explosive. To combat enemy submarines, the

Fletchers had two depth-charge racks bolted to the stern; each rack carried six Mark VII 600 pound depth charges. Each destroyer also employed a K-gun or depth-charge launcher that could propel a 200 pound depth charge out to a range of over 100 yards; the normal pattern of a K-gun attack incorporated nine depth charges. As the war progressed, the depth charges, like the hedgehog system of rocket charges, improved in sinking speed, depth, and detonation systems.

A major mission for a destroyer, probably the dominant mission in the war with Japan, was to serve as an antiaircraft platform in a carrier battle group. The main battery turret guns provided the first layer of defense. They improved their lethality by a factor of five with the deployment of the proximity fuse for shells in 1944. The proximity fuse detonated a shell by radio waves emitted and returned in the shell's nose cone; this miniature radar system gave new meaning to a near miss, as Japanese kamikaze pilots learned. The close-in defense system depended on rapid-firing automatic cannon adopted in 40 mm and 20 mm configurations that could be single, dual-mounted, or quadruple-mounted gun systems. By the end of the war, *Fletchers* had 16 of these antiaircraft artillery (AAA) stations of "pom-poms."

A *Fletcher*-class destroyer could not have fought its tridimensional naval war without the use of the electromagnetic spectrum. The AAA radar suite included the mating of three different radars to provide information on the altitude, speed, distance, and numbers of incoming aircraft up to 40,000 yards distant from the ship. The surface-search system of two radars provided coverage of up to 40,000 yards of ocean around the ship. The radars sent data to the ship's combat information center, where the gunnery director sent data to the gun captains and subordinate fire directors for the main batteries; the turret fire directors often received the same radar returns so that they could order targets engaged as soon as the central fire director assigned priorities to targets.

For antisubmarine warfare, a *Fletcher*-class destroyer employed passive and active acoustical systems to acquire targets. Hydrophone systems, either attached to a ship or deployed in the ocean's depths, listened for undersea noises like a submarine's propeller. The active radio systems—called "asdic" by the British and "sonar" by the Americans—had varied properties for beam strength, range, depth, and degrees of coverage, but the multi-transmitter systems could detect and track a submarine at only about 2 miles, thereby being most useful for target localization. When the radio beams reached out and touched something, experienced sonar operators faced the challenge of differentiating a submarine from a large whale. Electronic displays aboard the destroyer showed the direction, speed, and depth of its underwater target but only briefly and through a sea made dark with noise by the movement of the destroyer itself. Successful attacks on submarines still required a dose of good luck and tactical cunning that could be gained only by experience.

Although the Allies used aircraft (also radar equipped) to attack Axis submarines and submarines also sank submarines, surface warships like the *Fletchers* broke the back of the Axis submarine force. The Germans lost 625 of 871 U-boats, and Japanese submariners went to the bottom in 74 of their 77 submarines.

The blinding acceleration of technological innovations in warfare since 1945 should not devalue the advances between 1914 and 1945, especially in the interwar period from 1919 to 1939. In a brief span of two decades, scientists, inventors, engineers, designers, and military users conceived of a variety of weapons that brought direct, immediate death and destruction to a new level of probability for soldiers and civilians alike. Atomic bombs and the B-29 bombers that carried them had entered the early development phase in the United States before Pearl Harbor, a combination of foresight, fear, and ferocity. Although J. Robert Oppenheimer was referring to the awesome fireball of his test bomb when he quoted the Hindu god Vishnu, "I am become death, destroyer of worlds," his reverie could have applied to the whole World War II arsenal.

Although World War II survives as the most destructive and geographically extensive interstate conflict in history, it also included at least 20 civil wars. These wars within a war often extended beyond 1945, filling the vacuum created by failed occupations and social upheaval. In many aspects, these civil wars repeated a similar phenomenon that followed the collapse of the German, Austro-Hungarian, and Ottoman Empires in the last stages of World War I. As the Bolsheviks had proved in 1917, a great war created the preconditions for a great revolution. The new wave of civil wars came in many forms. The civil war in Spain, from 1936 to 1939, is often interpreted as an opening phase of World War II, as is the Sino-Japanese War that began in 1937. Both of these conflicts are more accurately the first of the new civil wars that attracted foreign intervention. They set the global pattern of combining the Big War with many little wars, little only in their disaggregated nature. All the little wars produced a revolution in world affairs, the era of decolonization.

The civil wars of World War II often began in collaborationism with the Axis occupations and the resistance to those occupations. The Stalinist and Nazi forms of coerced corporatism had global appeal in the chaotic 1930s. Japan enjoyed a modest reputation for its anti-European anti-colonialism and for its economic dynamism and superficial modernity. The Spanish Civil War gave the world the term for internal subversion, "the Fifth Column." Norway provided the word for treacherous politician, "quisling." The collaborators were pro-Fascist, if not pro-German. Many were simple opportunists, adventurers, and minor functionaries. Some were ardent anti-Communists, the ideological glue that joined Belgians and Bulgarians; some were anti-Semitic, the paranoia that unified Frenchmen with Hungarians. Volunteers from every western European nation joined the Waffen SS to exterminate Jews and Bolsheviks. For the Finns and Romanians, Germany was a powerful ally in their continuing war with the Soviets. The Balkans were especially complex. Mouthing memories of the Roman conquest of Thrace and Dacia, Benito Mussolini invaded Moslem Albania in 1939, to which the British responded with a partisan war mounted from Kosovo, Yugoslavia. This war created a hero, Enver Hoxha, a Communist dictator until 1983. When the patchwork monarchy of Yugoslavia came apart with a German occupation in 1941, the Slovenes and Croats used the Germans to wage war on the Serbian Chetnik ultranationalists (the Mihajlović group) and the Communist resistance movement led by Josip Broz, a Croat revolutionary known as Tito. Before the Germans abandoned Yugoslavia in September 1944, more than a million Yugoslavs had died, the majority killed by their fellow countrymen, not the Germans. The Soviets then pillaged all of Yugoslavia, Communist-held areas included.

The Europe of 1943 through 1945 became a kaleidoscope of shifting political loyalties as the German occupations began to collapse. When an Italian royalist coalition deposed Mussolini and surrendered to the Allies in September 1943, Italy split wide open. Hitler rescued Mussolini and supported a rump Fascist regime in the Po Valley. Part of the Italian army stayed with the Germans, part joined the Allies, and most of its troops became German prisoners. The resistance movement, formed by northern Communists, built a solid political base in 1944 and 1945 by killing Germans and other Italians, including devout Catholic villagers and their priests. They also killed Mussolini. The experience of the Poles followed a similar course. When the Germans destroyed the Jewish resistance and the Home Army, the exile Poles inherited the leadership of national liberation. The difficulty was that there were two Polish exile governments, the Catholic Nationalists in London and the Communists in Lublin. By 1945, there were two Polish armies, both bearing the Polish

eagle. The armored division and parachute brigade in France and a two-division corps (with armor) in Italy represented the London Poles. The Communist Poles formed a nine-division force with five additional armored brigades that joined the Red Army in July 1944. When the Soviets rolled through Poland, the Communist Poles took control of Poland and held it for 45 years. The Free Poles joined Europe's 16 million "displaced persons."

As the Soviets battered their way into eastern Europe in 1944 and 1945, they ensured that native Communists, backed by a "people's" police and army, took control of Romania, Bulgaria, Poland, and Hungary. Tito kept the Soviet Union out of Yugoslavia as an extended occupier; the Albanian Communists seized power; the non-Communist Czechs held out until 1948; and the Greek civil war flared between the royalists and Communists almost as soon as a British Commonwealth expeditionary force accepted the Germans' surrender. In France, the Resistance partisans attacked collaborators during the liberation, then held war crimes trials for the Vichyites. The same pattern appeared in Belgium, the Netherlands, and Norway.

The Middle East became a region beset by civil strife during World War II. German agents in Palestine and Iraq encouraged the Arabs to attack the Palestinian Jews, the pro-British Jordanian monarchy, and the pro-British Iraqi monarchy. A revolt actually occurred in Iraq in 1941, and terrorism and guerrilla warfare plagued Palestine. The British forces in Egypt watched the Egyptian army with care because of the pro-Axis sympathies of its officer corps. To the south, Commonwealth forces liberated Ethiopia and Somalia from the Italians, assisted by both Moslems and Coptic Christians. In the Levant, Free French colonial and British forces took Lebanon and Syria away from the Vichyites but found the Moslem nationalists unwilling to accept another French colonial government, setting the stage for the French withdrawal under duress in 1946.

Throughout Asia, the anti-imperialist resistance movements developed a two-phase strategy: (1) fight the Japanese hard enough to attract Allied money and arms, and (2) build a popular political base and native guerrilla army capable of opposing the reimposition of European colonial rule after Japan's defeat. For native Communists, active since the 1920s, the second task offered a chance to replace or challenge the native nationalists, who saw communism as a new form of Soviet or Chinese imperialism. Some Asian resistance movements reflected civil strife between a dominant ethnic majority and an oppressed minority, like the Chinese in Malaya, the Dyaks of Borneo, and the Chin, Kachen, Karen, and Shan hill tribes of Burma. Fighting the Japanese had some appeal to the partisans; fighting each other or preparing to fight each other had equal priority. In China, the Nationalists of Generalissimo Chiang Kai-shek (now Jiang Jieshi) and his Guomindang (Kuomintang) Party conducted minimal operations against the Japanese and improved their American arsenal for the continuing struggle against the Chinese Communists of Mao Zedong, building their own forces in north China. In the Philippines, *americanista* partisans, supplied by General Douglas MacArthur, vied with the Communist *hukbalahap* guerrillas for primacy on Luzon. MacArthur's massive return in 1944 and 1945 swung the balance to the *americanistas* but only temporarily, since the *hukbalahaps* fought for control of the independent Philippines (as of 1946) for years thereafter.

Elsewhere in Asia, the collapse of the Japanese Empire set off more postcolonial civil wars. In Indochina, the Communists (under Ho Chi Minh) already held the field by default since the Japanese had crushed their rivals in a premature uprising in 1944. In Malaya, the resistance movement had formed around the Chinese minority, while the Malay Moslem elite, supported by Great Britain, patiently waited for liberation and a final confrontation with the Malaya Chinese. Modern Malaya and the modern island-state of Singapore are the products of that decades-long struggle that began in 1945. In the Dutch East Indies, the Moslem nationalists (whose most extreme members created today's abu-Sayyid terrorist group) played off collaborationism with the Japanese with guerrilla warfare for the Allies to create a resistance movement that fought a Dutch return from 1945 to 1949. More civil strife continued until the army-led nationalists replaced the charismatic President Achmet Sukarno and destroyed the Indonesian Communists in a civil war in the 1960s that killed at least half a million Indonesians. One neglected aspect of the Japanese hurried surrender—usually explained by the influence of two nuclear weapons and Soviet intervention—is the Imperial peace faction's fear of a Communist-led popular revolt in Japan.

There is no question that the movement of great armies throughout Europe in 1944 and 1945 created social destruction of unimagined proportions, which set the stage for postwar revolutionary changes. In 1945, more than 50 million Europeans found themselves severed from their original homes. Thirteen million orphans wandered across the land. The Allies appeased the Soviet Union by the forced repatriation of 6 million Soviet citizens (defined in Moscow) who had found their way to western Europe as POWs, forced laborers, or military allies of the Germans, like the Ukrainians and varied anti-Bolshevik Cossack clans. Sending these people—most often neither Russian nor Communist—back to the Soviet Union resulted in the death or imprisonment of 80 percent of the repatriates, but it also cut the "displaced persons" population of Europe. To a Europe already plagued with famine and on the brink of epidemic diseases, the Anglo-American forces brought food and medicine, distributed by the United Nations, individual governments, and private relief organizations. The Soviets not only ferreted out former Nazis in their German and Austrian occupation zones but also stripped off food supplies, factories, transportation assets, and raw materials for the USSR's reconstruction. They also imprisoned eastern Europeans who had fought in the Allied armed forces, and former partisans (no matter their politics) faced a similar fate or worse. At war's end, the Soviets had held or still held 3 million Wehrmacht POWs, most of them placed in forced-labor camps in the Urals or Siberia. Only 1 million returned to Germany by the time the last POWs were released in 1955.

Not known for his radical politics, General of the Army Douglas MacArthur recognized the enormity of the war and its revolutionary implications for all mankind. In a postsurrender radio broadcast, MacArthur gave one of his greatest sermons: "We have had our last chance. If we do not now devise some greater and more equitable system, Armageddon will be at our door."

The children of World War II are rapidly becoming the aging men and women of the twenty-first century. Their parents, who lived through the war as young adults, may or may not be "the greatest generation," but they are most certainly a disappearing generation. Will the grip of World War II on the popular culture and politics of Eurasia loosen as the living memory of the war fades? It does not seem likely. Even in Japan, where historical amnesia is institutionalized in the school system, the residual remembrance will continue at the Hiroshima Peace Park, Yasukuni Shrine, and the new "Peace Museum" in Tokyo. Even if Japan still takes refuge in its self-assigned victimization, contact with other Asians (especially the Chinese) and Americans will expose the Japanese to an alternative perspective. As for the Germans, had they not renounced their Nazi past, admitted their criminality, and continued programs to compensate their victims—a process still under way—the Russians and the Jews would be at their collective throats. Yad Vashem in Jerusalem and the Holocaust Museum in Washington, D.C., will keep alive the images of German atrocities for world visitors. Russia is a nation of war memorials, mass graves, and long memories. Few Russians families who lived west of the Urals escaped the war without loss; those whom the Germans didn't kill, Stalin's work camps, factories, and military system did. The American experience—a low number of military deaths by World War II standards and virtually no civilian deaths in the continental United States—was a global anomaly. American cultural gurus—even combat veterans—suffer little embarrassment in calling World War II "the good war," with both moral and existential meaning. Although the Eurasian nations still have collective posttraumatic stress syndrome after 60 years, the United States has finally built a real World War II memorial in Washington and recognized its World War II veterans, who had gratefully used their GI Bill benefits and faded back into the general population. Sixty years later, their children and grandchildren learn in wonderment of their perils, their courage, and their leadership—or lack thereof.

The informal, tribal communication of historical meaning will no doubt preserve the World War II memory in those societies most affected by the war, but the American people will continue to profit from the more formal written word.

Although family tradition can preserve the war as a personal, human experience—as institutionalized in local museums and oral-history projects—World War II demands the continued attention of professional historians who can provide a broader vision of the war's conduct and consequences. As this encyclopedia project shows, the number of topics and international historians such a study requires continues to grow. These volumes represent a giant step forward as a reference work and should encourage more students of the war to continue the search for the effect and meaning of the modern world's most destructive war.

Dr. Allan R. Millett

Maj. Gen. Raymond E. Mason Jr.
Professor of Military History

The Ohio State University

Preface

One might disagree as to which of the two world wars of the twentieth century made a greater impact. World War I had the larger overall influence in changing the course of events, but World War II was certainly the most wide-ranging and costly conflict in human history; it ultimately involved, to some degree, every major power and region of the world.

Wars are preventable, and World War II was no exception. It represented the triumph of inadequate leadership and narrow nationalism over internationalism. Unfortunately, little has changed in that regard. The League of Nations has given way to the United Nations, but we still live in a state of international anarchy in that each nation pursues the course of action it deems most appropriate to further its own interests. This is not the outcome that many who fought in the conflict were seeking.

This encyclopedia treats the causes, the course, and, to some extent, the effects of the war. With the exception of introductory essays, as well as the glossary of terms and the selective bibliography, all entries are arranged alphabetically. These cover the major theaters of war, the campaigns, the individual battles, the major weapons systems, the diplomatic conferences, and the key individuals on all sides of the conflict. We have also included entries on the home fronts and on the role of women in the war, and we have sought to address some of the war's historiographical controversies and major turning points.

Throughout, we have followed the system the Japanese use for expressing their personal names—that is, with the family name followed by the given name. In Chinese proper names and locations, we use both the pinyin system and the older Wade-Giles system. The Wade-Giles system was first devised by British diplomat-linguist Thomas F. Wade in 1859 to help in pronouncing the official Mandarin and/or Putonghua. His work was slightly revised in 1912 by another British consular officer, Herbert A. Giles. This system has its defects, since many Chinese sounds have no exact counterpart in English. For the first consonant in "zero," for example, the Wade-Giles romanization uses "ts" and/or "tz," and for Chen Yi, both "Chen Yi" and "Chen I" are acceptable. Following the establishment of the People's Republic of China (PRC), a new system for expressing Chinese words in the Latin alphabet was adopted in the 1970s, at the same time that the PRC devised and used simplified characters for written Chinese. Known as pinyin, this new system was intended to ensure standardized spelling, with each vowel and consonant having a counterpart in English. Still, variation in pronunciation is inevitable because of the four tones of each Chinese vowel and consonant and because of different Chinese dialects. Throughout this encyclopedia, however, we have endeavored to employ the most recent spelling forms: thus, for instance, we use "Guandong" rather than "Kwantung."

All of us who have labored on this encyclopedia trust that it will be an asset both for scholars and for students of World War II. We hope also that it will contribute to the understanding of how wars occur and that this might help in preventing them in the future. Finally, we seek to preserve the contributions of the many who fought and died in the conflict, no matter the side.

Dr. Spencer C. Tucker

Acknowledgments

Many people contributed to this encyclopedia. I retired as holder of the John Biggs Chair in Military History at the Virginia Military Institute (VMI) in the summer of 2003, and I am grateful to a number of cadet assistants who worked with me on this project in the several years before my retirement. Alex Haseley, Daniel Cragg, Lawton Way, and above all Shelley Cox helped chase down obscure facts and bibliographical citations. I am also appreciative of assistance provided by staff members of the Preston Library at VMI, especially Lieutenant Colonel Janet Holley, for their repeated gracious assistance, even following my retirement.

Of course, I am greatly in the debt of assistant editors Jack Greene; Dr. Malcolm Muir Jr.; Dr. Priscilla Roberts; Colonel Cole Kingseed, USA (Ret.), Ph.D.; and Major General David Zabecki, USAR, Ph.D. Each brought a special expertise to the project, and their reading of the manuscript has helped improve it immeasurably. Dr. Debbie Law of the Hong Kong University Open Learning Institute read all the Chinese entries and assisted with their editing and the pinyin and Wade-Giles spellings. Rear Admiral Hirama Yoichi (Ret.), Ph.D., located Japanese authors for many entries, checked their work, and answered many inquiries.

We are pleased to have a large number of foreign authors in this project, including scholars from such nations as Austria, Australia, Britain, China, France, Germany, Hungary, Italy, Japan, and Russia. We believe that these authors provide unique perspectives and, in many cases, information that is not available in other sources. This reference work has the most complete biographies of Chinese, Japanese, and Soviet individuals of any general encyclopedia of the war to appear in English.

I am also grateful to a number of contributors who took on additional tasks when others dropped out, especially Dr. Priscilla Roberts but also Drs. Timothy Dowling, Eric Osborne, and Ned Willmott. Members of the Editorial Advisory Board suggested changes to the entry list, recommended contributors, and, in most cases, wrote entries. One member of the board, Gordon Hogg, a research librarian by profession but also a linguist, has proved invaluable to this project by assisting in chasing down obscure facts, bibliographical citations, and arcane matters of language.

Finally, I am most especially grateful to Dr. Beverly Tucker for her forbearance in regard to my long hours in front of the computer. She is, in the end, my strongest supporter in everything I do.

Dr. Spencer C. Tucker

General
Maps

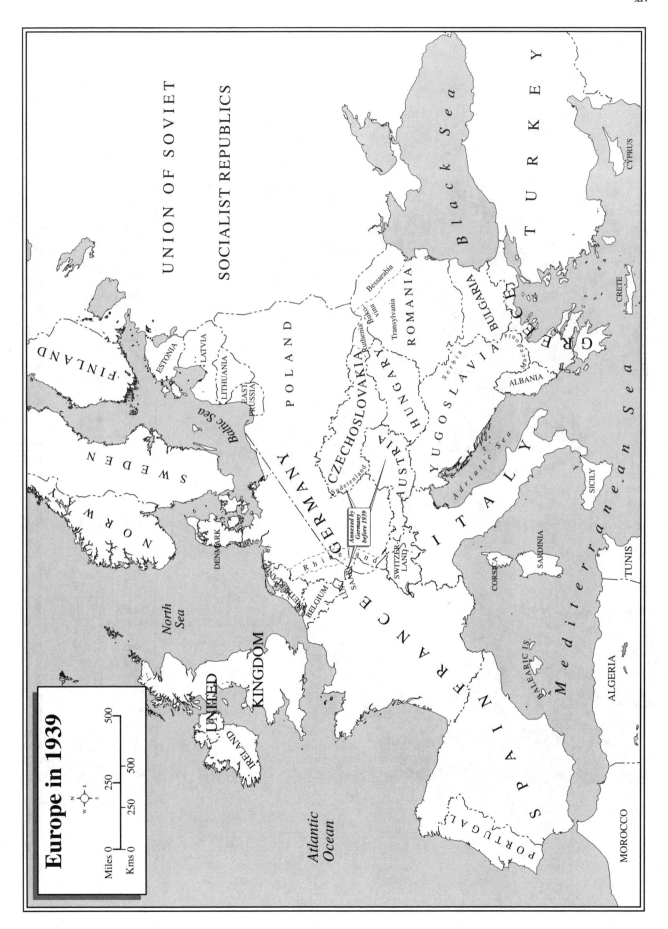

Europe in 1939

UNION OF SOVIET

SOCIALIST REPUBLICS

FINLAND

ESTONIA

LATVIA

LITHUANIA

EAST PRUSSIA

POLAND

Baltic Sea

SWEDEN

NORWAY

GERMANY

CZECHOSLOVAKIA

Sudetenland

Annexed by Germany before 1939

AUSTRIA

HUNGARY

Ruthenia

Bukovina

Bessarabia

Transylvania

ROMANIA

Black Sea

TURKEY

CYPRUS

CRETE

GREECE

BULGARIA

YUGOSLAVIA

Serbia

Macedonia

ALBANIA

Adriatic Sea

ITALY

Mediterranean Sea

SICILY

SARDINIA

CORSICA

BALEARIC IS.

TUNIS

ALGERIA

MOROCCO

SPAIN

PORTUGAL

FRANCE

SWITZER-LAND

SAAR

LUX.

BELGIUM

Rhineland

NETHERLANDS

DENMARK

North Sea

UNITED KINGDOM

IRELAND

Atlantic Ocean

Miles 0   250   500

Kms 0   250   500

N

W   E

S

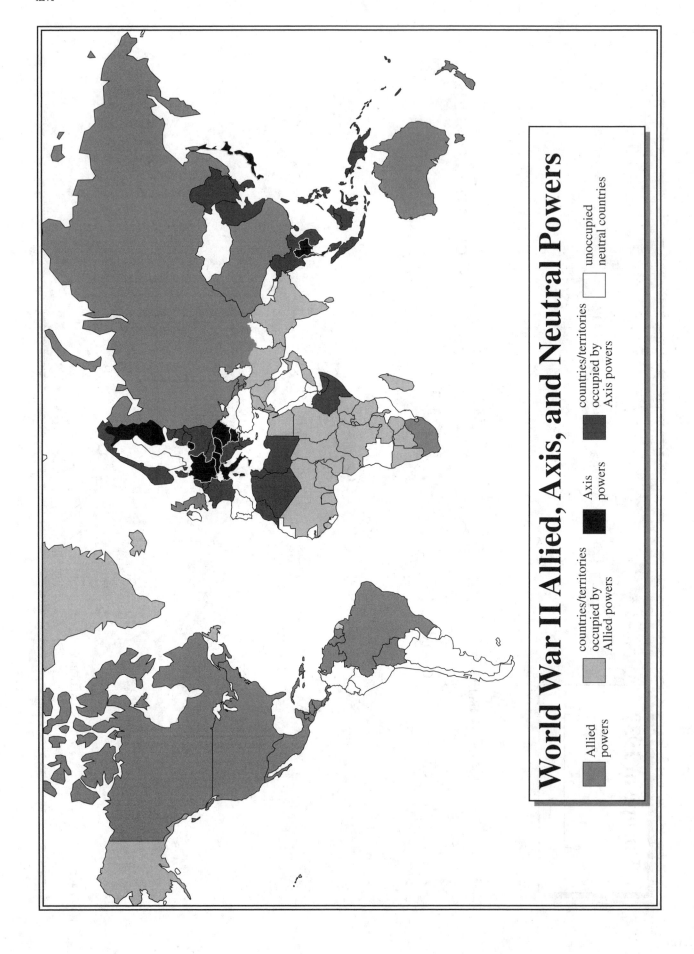

World War II Allied, Axis, and Neutral Powers

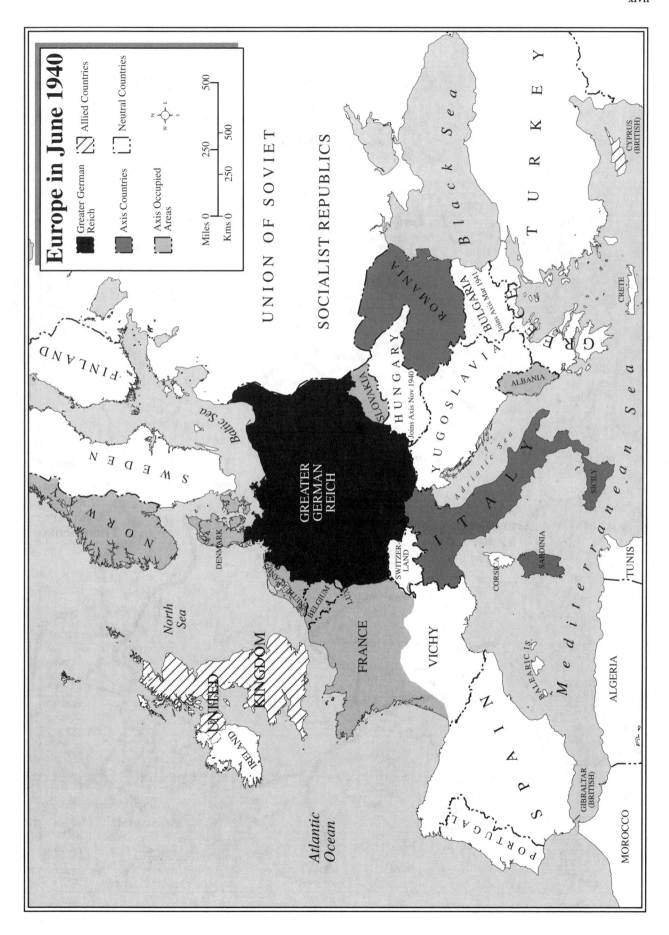

Europe in June 1940

Greater German Reich ■

Axis Countries ▨

Axis Occupied Areas ▨

Allied Countries ▨

Neutral Countries ⬚

Miles 0 — 250 — 500
Kms 0 — 250 — 500

UNION OF SOVIET SOCIALIST REPUBLICS

FINLAND

SWEDEN

NORWAY

Baltic Sea

North Sea

Atlantic Ocean

UNITED KINGDOM

IRELAND

DENMARK

GREATER GERMAN REICH

NETHERLANDS

BELGIUM

LUX.

FRANCE

VICHY

SWITZERLAND

SPAIN

PORTUGAL

GIBRALTAR (BRITISH)

MOROCCO

ALGERIA

TUNIS

BALEARIC IS.

CORSICA

SARDINIA

SICILY

ITALY

Mediterranean Sea

Adriatic Sea

SLOVAKIA

HUNGARY — Joins Axis Nov 1940

ROMANIA

YUGOSLAVIA

BULGARIA — Joins Axis Mar 1941

ALBANIA

GREECE

Black Sea

TURKEY

CYPRUS (BRITISH)

CRETE

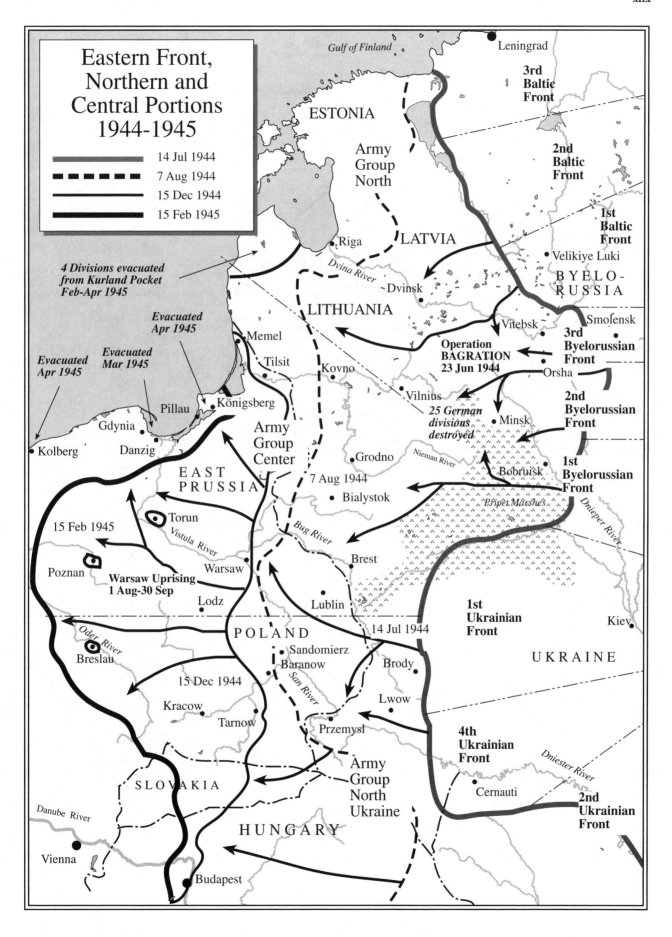

Eastern Front, Northern and Central Portions 1944-1945

	14 Jul 1944
	7 Aug 1944
	15 Dec 1944
	15 Feb 1945

4 Divisions evacuated from Kurland Pocket Feb-Apr 1945

Evacuated Apr 1945

Evacuated Apr 1945

Evacuated Mar 1945

Gulf of Finland

Leningrad

3rd Baltic Front

2nd Baltic Front

1st Baltic Front

ESTONIA

Army Group North

LATVIA

Riga

Dvina River

Dvinsk

LITHUANIA

Memel

Tilsit

Kovno

Königsberg

Pillau

Gdynia

Danzig

Kolberg

Vilnius

Grodno

Nieman River

Vitebsk

Smolensk

Velikiye Luki

B Y E L O - R U S S I A

3rd Byelorussian Front

Orsha

Operation BAGRATION 23 Jun 1944

25 German divisions destroyed

Minsk

Bobruisk

2nd Byelorussian Front

1st Byelorussian Front

Pripet Marshes

Dnieper River

Army Group Center

EAST PRUSSIA

7 Aug 1944

Bialystok

Brest

Bug River

Torun

Vistula River

15 Feb 1945

Poznan

Warsaw Uprising 1 Aug-30 Sep

Warsaw

Lodz

Lublin

1st Ukrainian Front

Kiev

Oder River

P O L A N D

14 Jul 1944

Breslau

15 Dec 1944

Kracow

Tarnow

Sandomierz

Baranow

San River

Przemysl

Brody

Lwow

U K R A I N E

4th Ukrainian Front

Dniester River

Cernauti

2nd Ukrainian Front

Army Group North Ukraine

S L O V A K I A

Danube River

Vienna

H U N G A R Y

Budapest

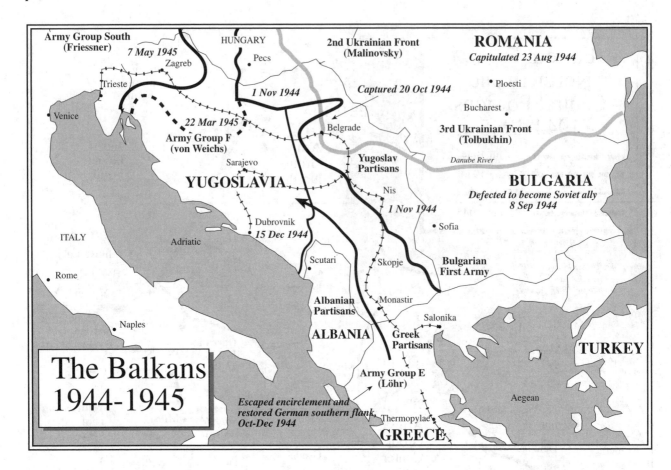

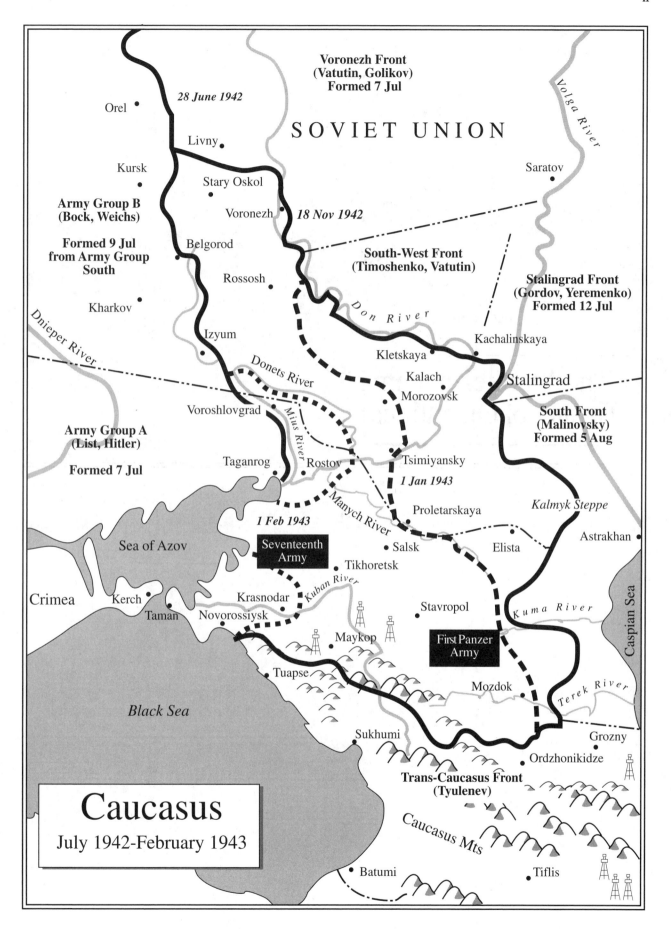

Voronezh Front
(Vatutin, Golikov)
Formed 7 Jul

Orel

28 June 1942

Livny

SOVIET UNION

Kursk

Stary Oskol

Saratov

Army Group B
(Bock, Weichs)

Voronezh

18 Nov 1942

Belgorod

Formed 9 Jul
from Army Group
South

South-West Front
(Timoshenko, Vatutin)

Rossosh

Stalingrad Front
(Gordov, Yeremenko)
Formed 12 Jul

Kharkov

Don River

Izyum

Kachalinskaya

Kletskaya

Dnieper River

Donets River

Kalach

Morozovsk

Stalingrad

Voroshlovgrad

Mius River

South Front
(Malinovsky)
Formed 5 Aug

Army Group A
(List, Hitler)

Taganrog

Rostov

Tsimiyansky

1 Jan 1943

Formed 7 Jul

Manych River

Proletarskaya

Kalmyk Steppe

Astrakhan

1 Feb 1943

Seventeenth Army

Salsk

Elista

Sea of Azov

Tikhoretsk

Crimea

Kerch

Kuban River

Stavropol

Kuma River

Caspian Sea

Taman

Novorossiysk

Krasnodar

Maykop

First Panzer Army

Tuapse

Mozdok

Terek River

Black Sea

Sukhumi

Grozny

Ordzhonikidze

Caucasus
July 1942-February 1943

Trans-Caucasus Front
(Tyulenev)

Caucasus Mts

Batumi

Tiflis

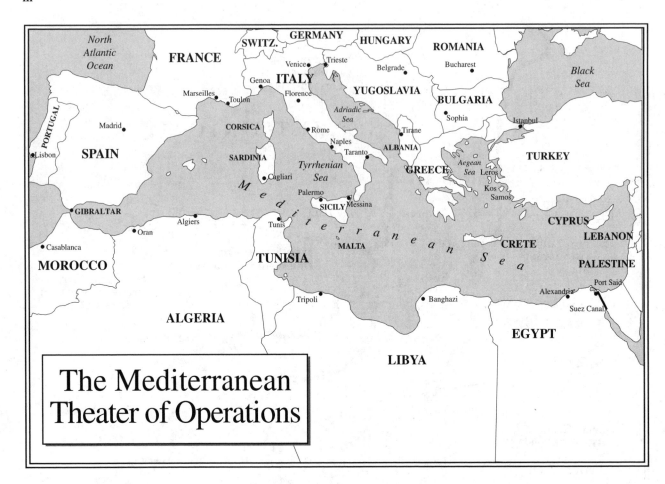

The Mediterranean
Theater of Operations

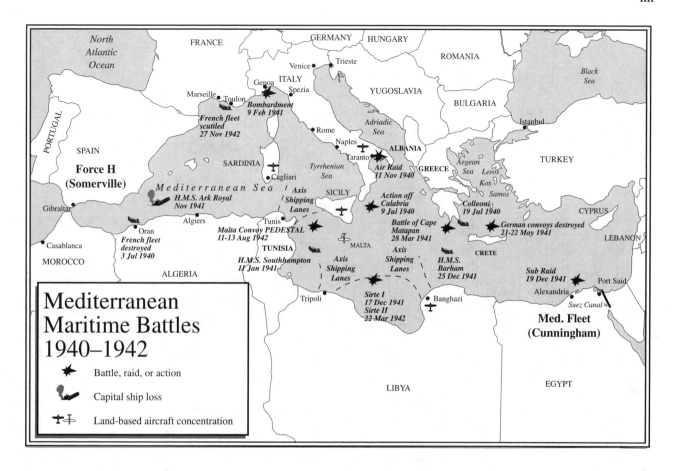

North
Atlantic
Ocean

FRANCE
GERMANY   HUNGARY
ROMANIA

Venice
Trieste

Genoa
ITALY
Spezia
YUGOSLAVIA
*Bombardment
9 Feb 1941*

Marseille
Toulon

PORTUGAL

SPAIN

*French fleet
scuttled
27 Nov 1942*

Rome

Black
Sea

Istanbul

*Adriatic
Sea*

**Force H
(Somerville)**

SARDINIA

Mediterranean Sea

Naples
Taranto
ALBANIA

*Tyrrhenian
Sea*

Cagliari

*Air Raid
11 Nov 1940*
GREECE

*Aegean
Sea*
Leros
Kos
Samos

TURKEY

Gibraltar

*H.M.S. Ark Royal
Nov 1941*

*Axis
Shipping
Lanes*

SICILY

*Action off
Calabria
9 Jul 1940*

*Colleoni
19 Jul 1940*

CYPRUS

Algiers

Tunis

*Battle of Cape
Matapan
28 Mar 1941*

*German convoys destroyed
21-22 May 1941*

LEBANON

Casablanca

Oran
*French fleet
destroyed
3 Jul 1940*

*Malta Convoy PEDESTAL
11-13 Aug 1942*

TUNISIA

MALTA

*Axis
Shipping
Lanes*

CRETE

*H.M.S.
Barham
25 Dec 1941*

*Sub Raid
19 Dec 1941*
Port Said

MOROCCO

ALGERIA

*H.M.S. Southhampton
11 Jan 1941*

*Axis
Shipping
Lanes*

Alexandria

Suez Canal

Tripoli

*Sirte I
17 Dec 1941
Sirte II
22 Mar 1942*

Banghazi

**Med. Fleet
(Cunningham)**

Mediterranean
Maritime Battles
1940–1942

Battle, raid, or action

Capital ship loss

Land-based aircraft concentration

LIBYA

EGYPT

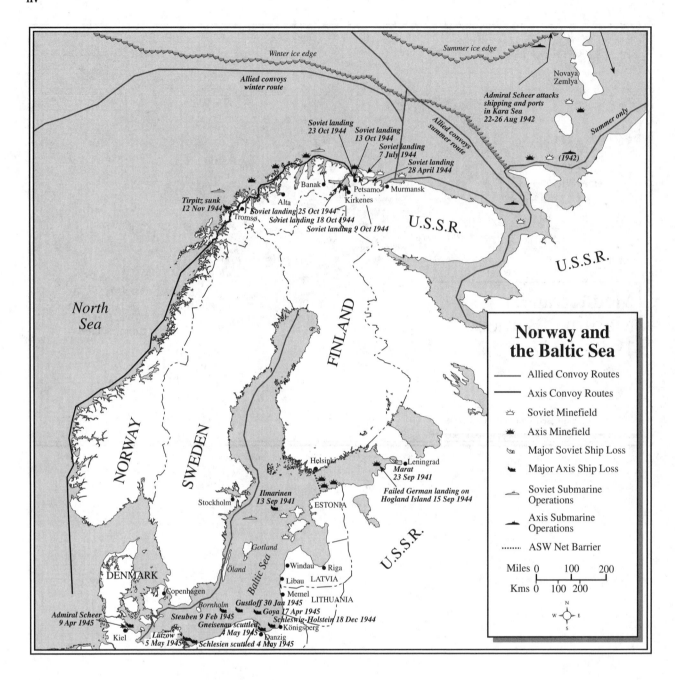

Winter ice edge

Summer ice edge

Allied convoys
winter route

Novaya
Zemlya

Admiral Scheer attacks
shipping and ports
in Kara Sea
22-26 Aug 1942

Summer only

(1942)

Soviet landing
23 Oct 1944

Soviet landing
13 Oct 1944

Allied convoys
summer route

Soviet landing
7 July 1944

Soviet landing
28 April 1944

Banak

Petsamo

Kirkenes

Murmansk

Tirpitz sunk
12 Nov 1944

Alta

Soviet landing 25 Oct 1944

Tromsø

Soviet landing 18 Oct 1944

Soviet landing 9 Oct 1944

U.S.S.R.

North
Sea

U.S.S.R.

FINLAND

NORWAY

SWEDEN

Helsinki

Leningrad

Marat
23 Sep 1941

Failed German landing on
Hogland Island 15 Sep 1944

Ilmarinen
13 Sep 1941

Stockholm

ESTONIA

U.S.S.R.

Gotland

Öland

Windau

Riga

Baltic Sea

Libau

LATVIA

DENMARK

Copenhagen

Memel

LITHUANIA

Bornholm

Gustloff 30 Jan 1945

Admiral Scheer
9 Apr 1945

Steuben 9 Feb 1945

Goya 17 Apr 1945

Schleswig-Holstein 18 Dec 1944

Gneisenau scuttled
4 May 1945

Königsberg

Kiel

Lützow
5 May 1945

Danzig

Schlesien scuttled 4 May 1945

Norway and
the Baltic Sea

———— Allied Convoy Routes

———— Axis Convoy Routes

Soviet Minefield

Axis Minefield

Major Soviet Ship Loss

Major Axis Ship Loss

Soviet Submarine
Operations

Axis Submarine
Operations

.... ASW Net Barrier

Miles 0   100   200

Kms 0   100 200

N
W E
S

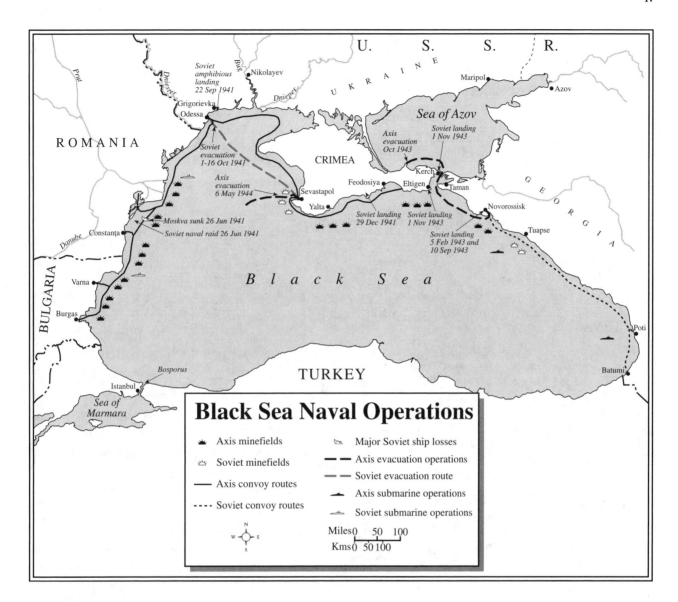

Black Sea Naval Operations

Axis minefields

Soviet minefields

Axis convoy routes

Soviet convoy routes

Major Soviet ship losses

Axis evacuation operations

Soviet evacuation route

Axis submarine operations

Soviet submarine operations

Miles 0   50   100

Kms 0 50 100

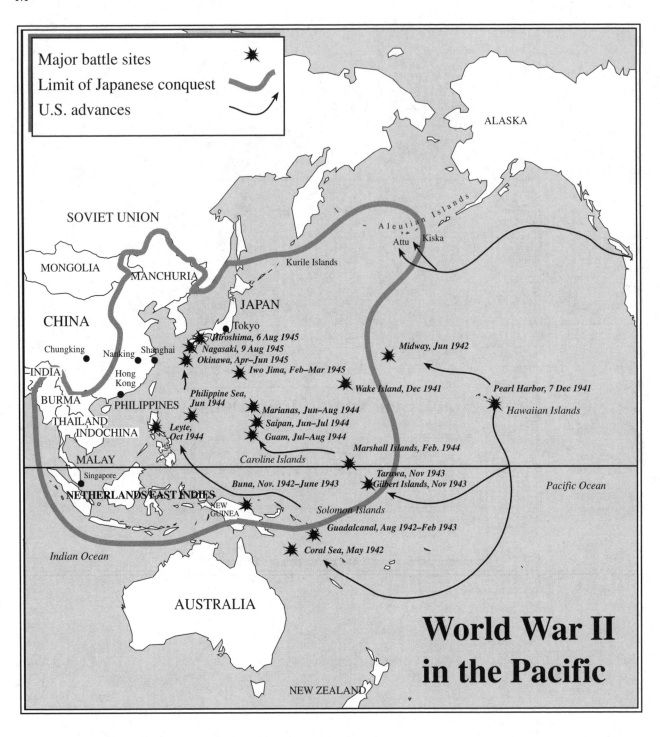

Major battle sites

Limit of Japanese conquest

U.S. advances

ALASKA

SOVIET UNION

MONGOLIA

MANCHURIA

CHINA

Chungking

Nanking   Shanghai

Hong
Kong

INDIA

BURMA

THAILAND

INDOCHINA

PHILIPPINES

MALAY

Singapore

NETHERLANDS EAST INDIES

Indian Ocean

AUSTRALIA

NEW ZEALAND

JAPAN

Tokyo

Hiroshima, 6 Aug 1945

Nagasaki, 9 Aug 1945

Okinawa, Apr–Jun 1945

Iwo Jima, Feb–Mar 1945

*Philippine Sea,
Jun 1944*

Marianas, Jun–Aug 1944

Saipan, Jun–Jul 1944

Guam, Jul–Aug 1944

*Leyte,
Oct 1944*

Caroline Islands

Kurile Islands

Aleutian Islands

Attu   Kiska

Midway, Jun 1942

Wake Island, Dec 1941

Pearl Harbor, 7 Dec 1941

Hawaiian Islands

Marshall Islands, Feb. 1944

Tarawa, Nov 1943

Gilbert Islands, Nov 1943

Buna, Nov. 1942–June 1943

NEW
GUINEA

Solomon Islands

Guadalcanal, Aug 1942–Feb 1943

Coral Sea, May 1942

Pacific Ocean

World War II
in the Pacific

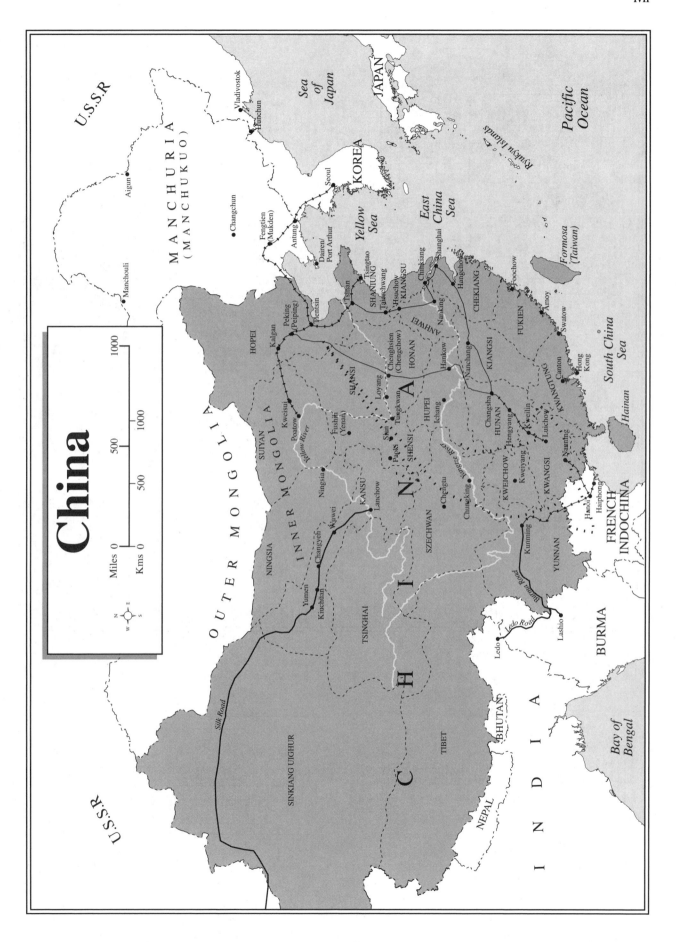

China

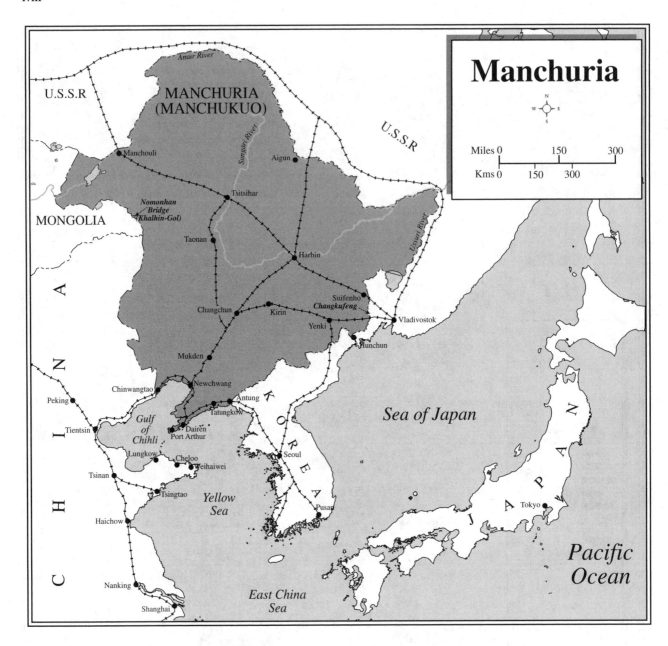

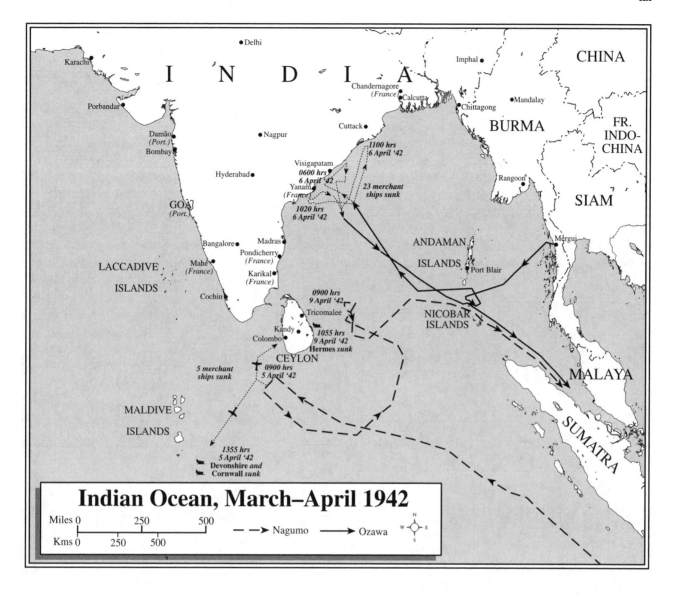

Indian Ocean, March–April 1942

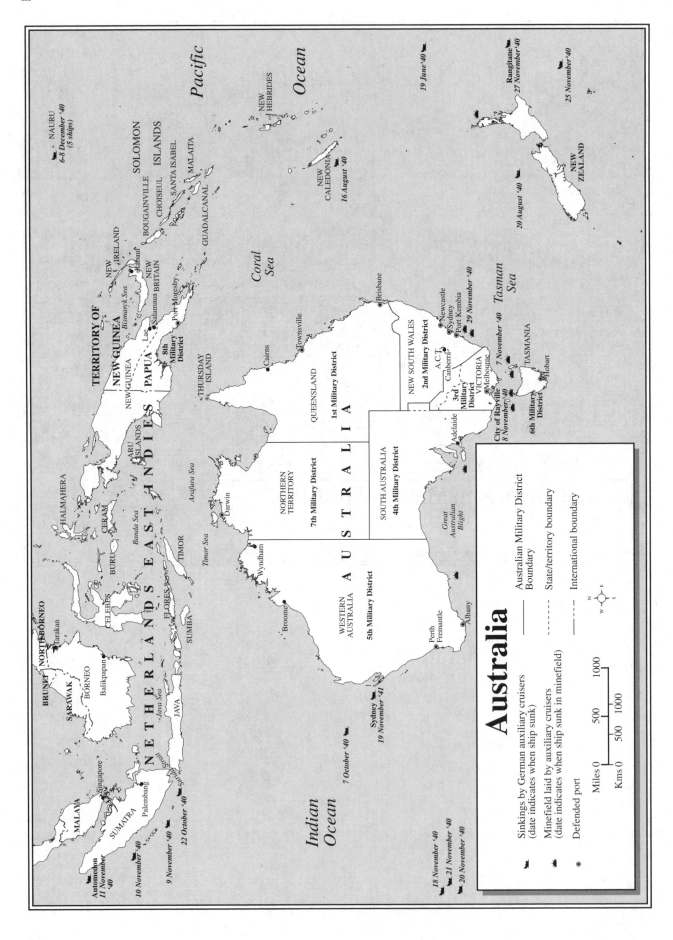

Australia

Pacific Ocean

NAURU
6-8 December '40
(5 ships)

19 June '40

Rangitane
27 November '40

25 November '40

NEW ZEALAND

20 August '40

TERRITORY OF NEW GUINEA

NEW GUINEA

SOLOMON ISLANDS

BOUGAINVILLE
CHOISEUL
SANTA ISABEL
MALAITA
GUADALCANAL

NEW HEBRIDES

NEW CALEDONIA
16 August '40

NEW IRELAND
NEW BRITAIN
Rabaul
Salamaua
Lae
Port Moresby

8th Military District

PAPUA

Coral Sea

Brisbane

Newcastle
Sydney
Port Kembla
29 November '40

7 November '40

Tasman Sea

THURSDAY ISLAND

Townsville

Cairns

QUEENSLAND
1st Military District

NEW SOUTH WALES
2nd Military District

A.C.T.
Canberra
3rd Military District
VICTORIA
Melbourne

TASMANIA

Hobart

6th Military District

City of Rayville
8 November '40

NETHERLANDS EAST INDIES

HALMAHERA
CERAM
BURU
Banda Sea
TIMOR
Timor Sea
Arafura Sea
ARU ISLANDS

NORTHERN TERRITORY
7th Military District

Darwin

SOUTH AUSTRALIA
4th Military District

Adelaide

Great Australian Bight

AUSTRALIA

Wyndham

WESTERN AUSTRALIA
5th Military District

Broome

Perth
Fremantle

Albany

BRUNEI NORTH BORNEO
Tarakan
SARAWAK
BORNEO
Balikpapan
Java Sea
JAVA
SUMATRA
Palembang
SUMBA
FLORES
CELEBES
Singapore
MALAYA

Sydney
19 November '41

7 October '40

Automedon
11 November '40

10 November '40

9 November '40

22 October '40

Indian Ocean

18 November '40

21 November '40

20 November '40

Sinkings by German auxiliary cruisers (date indicates when ship sunk)

Minefield laid by auxiliary cruisers (date indicates when ship sunk in minefield)

● **Defended port**

── Australian Military District Boundary

---- State/territory boundary

── International boundary

N
W E
S

Miles 0   500   1000

Kms 0   500   1000

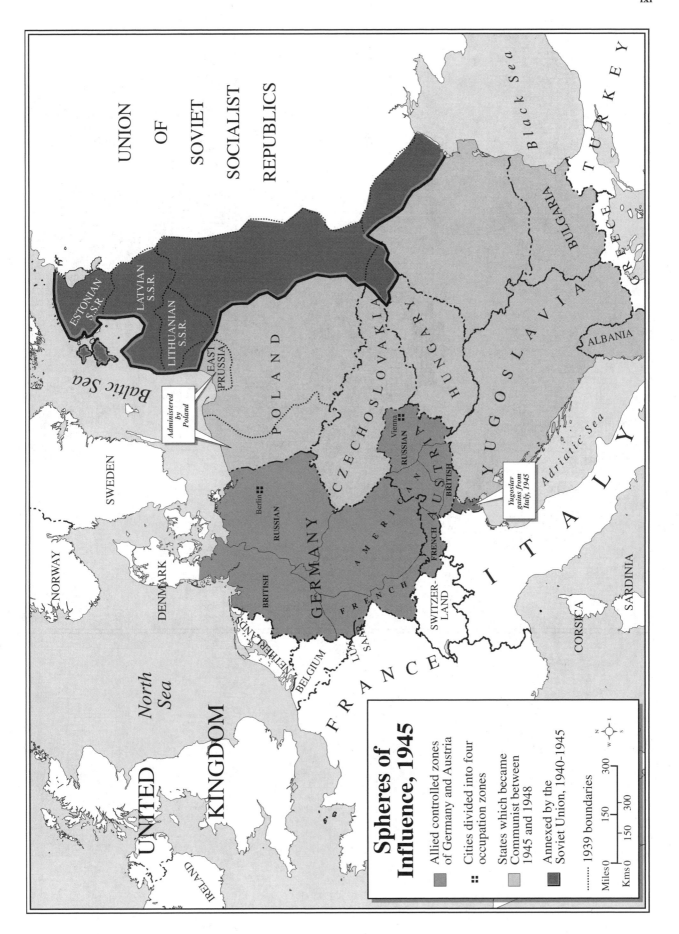

Spheres of Influence, 1945

- Allied controlled zones of Germany and Austria
- Cities divided into four occupation zones
- States which became Communist between 1945 and 1948
- Annexed by the Soviet Union, 1940–1945
- · · · · · 1939 boundaries

Miles 0   150   300
Kms 0   150   300

UNION   OF   SOVIET   SOCIALIST   REPUBLICS

ESTONIAN S.S.R.
LATVIAN S.S.R.
LITHUANIAN S.S.R.
EAST PRUSSIA
Administered by Poland
Baltic Sea
POLAND
CZECHOSLOVAKIA
HUNGARY
AUSTRIA
RUSSIAN
BRITISH
FRENCH
Vienna
Yugoslav gains from Italy, 1945
YUGOSLAVIA
ROMANIA
BULGARIA
ALBANIA
GREECE
TURKEY
Black Sea
Adriatic Sea
ITALY
SARDINIA
CORSICA
SWITZER-LAND
GERMANY
Berlin
RUSSIAN
BRITISH
AMERICAN
FRENCH
SAAR
LUXEMBOURG
BELGIUM
NETHERLANDS
FRANCE
DENMARK
NORWAY
SWEDEN
North Sea
UNITED   KINGDOM
IRELAND

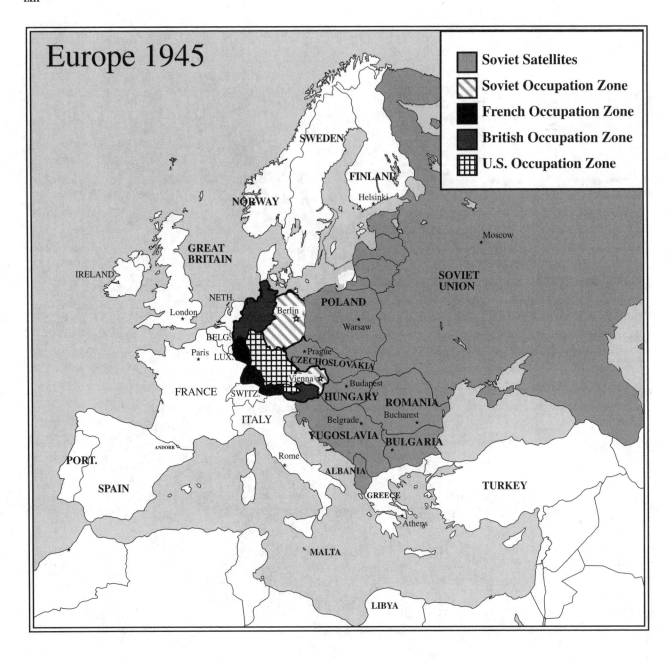

Europe 1945

Soviet Satellites
Soviet Occupation Zone
French Occupation Zone
British Occupation Zone
U.S. Occupation Zone

SWEDEN

FINLAND

Helsinki

NORWAY

Moscow

GREAT
BRITAIN

IRELAND

SOVIET
UNION

NETH.

London

POLAND

Berlin

Warsaw

BELG.

Paris

LUX.

Prague

CZECHOSLOVAKIA

FRANCE

SWITZ.

Vienna

Budapest

HUNGARY

ROMANIA

ITALY

Belgrade

Bucharest

ANDORR

Rome

YUGOSLAVIA

BULGARIA

PORT.

ALBANIA

SPAIN

GREECE

TURKEY

Athens

MALTA

LIBYA

General
Essays

Hitler accepts the ovation of the Reichstag after announcing the annexation of Austria. This action set the stage to annex the Czechoslovakian Sudetenland, largely inhabited by a German-speaking population. Berlin, March 1938. (National Archives)

Origins of the War

On 1 September 1939, German forces invaded Poland. Two days later, Britain and France declared war on Germany, beginning World War II. Some historians date the war from 1937, with the Japanese invasion of China; Japanese official histories, however, start with 1931, when Japan's forces overran Manchuria. But perhaps the most accurate place to begin is with the end of World War I. That conflict exacted horrible human and economic costs, destroyed the existing power structure of Europe, and toppled all the continental empires. It also sowed the seeds for a new conflict.

In January 1919, representatives of the victorious Allied, or Entente, powers met in Paris to impose peace terms on the defeated Central Powers. The centerpiece of the settlement, the Versailles Treaty, was the worst of all possible outcomes—it was too harsh to conciliate but too weak to destroy. It was also never enforced, making a renewal of the struggle almost inevitable.

The Paris peace settlement was drafted chiefly by Britain, France, and the United States. The Germans claimed they had assumed the November 1918 armistice would lead to a true negotiated peace treaty, yet in March and May 1918, when they were winning the war, their leaders had imposed a truly harsh settlement on Russia. In the Treaty of Brest-Litovsk, Russia lost most of its European territory, up to a third of its population, and three-quarters of its iron and coal production. It was also required to pay a heavy indemnity.

Far from being dictated by French Premier Georges Clemenceau, as many Americans still believe, the Paris peace settlement of 1919 was largely the work of British Prime Minister David Lloyd George and U.S. President Woodrow Wilson, who repeatedly blocked proposals advanced by Clemenceau. The irony is that the British and American leaders prevented a settlement that, although punitive, might indeed have brought actual French and Belgian security and prevented war in 1939.

The most novel creation of the conference was undoubtedly the League of Nations. Clemenceau did not place much stock in a league, but if there had to be one, he wanted mandatory membership and an independent military force. The Anglo-American league relied primarily on moral suasion; its strongest weapon was the threat of sanctions.

The most contentious issue at the peace conference—and arguably its most important matter—was that of French and Belgian security. Alsace and Lorraine were returned to France, and for security purposes, Belgium received the two small border enclaves of Eupen and Malmédy. France was granted the coal production of the Saar region for 15 years in compensation for Germany's deliberate destruction of French mines at the end of the war. The Saar itself fell under League of Nations control, with its inhabitants to decide their future at the end of the period.

A storm of controversy broke out, however, over the Rhineland, the German territory west of the Rhine River. France wanted this area to be reconstituted into one or more independent states that would maintain a permanent Allied military presence to guarantee Germany would not again strike west, but Lloyd George and Wilson saw taking the Rhineland from Germany as "an Alsace-Lorraine in reverse." They also wished to end the Allied military presence on German soil as soon as a peace treaty was signed.

These vast differences were resolved when Clemenceau agreed to yield on the Rhineland in return for the Anglo-American Treaty of Guarantee, whereby Britain and the United States promised to come to the aid of France should Germany ever invade. The Rhineland would remain part of the new German Republic but would be permanently demilitarized, along with a 30-mile-deep belt of German territory east of the Rhine. Allied garrisons would remain for only a limited period: the British would occupy a northern zone for 5 years, the Americans a central zone for 10, and the French a southern zone for 15 years. Unfortunately for France, the pact for which it traded away national security never came into force. The U.S. Senate refused to ratify it, and the British government claimed its acceptance was contingent on American approval.

Germany lost some other territory: northern Schleswig to Denmark and a portion of Silesia and the Polish Corridor to the new state of Poland—accessions the Allies justified along ethnic lines. The Polish Corridor allowed Poland access to the sea, but it also separated East Prussia from the remainder of Germany and became a major rallying point for German nationalists. Despite these losses, German power remained largely intact; Germany was still the most powerful state in central and western Europe. Nonetheless, Germans keenly resented the territorial losses.

The Treaty of Versailles also limited Germany in terms of both the size and the nature of its military establishment. The new German army, the Reichswehr, was restricted to 100,000 men serving 12-year enlistments. It was denied heavy artillery, tanks, and military aviation, and the German General Staff was to be abolished. The navy was limited to 6 predreadnought battleships, 6 light cruisers, 12 destroyers, and no submarines. From the beginning, the Germans violated these provisions. The General Staff remained, although clandestinely; moreover, Germany maintained military equipment that was to have been destroyed, and it worked out arrangements with other states to develop new weapons and train military personnel.

Other major provisions of the settlement included Article 231, the "war guilt clause." This provision blamed the war on Germany and its allies and was the justification for reparations, which were fixed at $33 billion in 1920, well after Germany had signed the treaty on 28 June 1919. British economist John Maynard Keynes claimed that reparations were a perpetual mortgage on Germany's future and that there was no way the Germans could pay them, yet Adolf Hitler's Germany subsequently spent more in rearming than the reparations demanded. In any case, Germany, unlike France following the Franco-Prussian War in 1871, was never really forced to pay.

The breakup of the Austro-Hungarian Empire and the peace treaties following the war led to the creation of a number of new states in central Europe, most notably Poland but also Czechoslovakia and Yugoslavia. Resolving the boundaries of Poland proved difficult, especially in the east; it was not until December 1919 that a commission headed by Lord Curzon drew that line. Neither the new Polish government nor Russia recognized it, however. Romania was greatly enlarged with the addition of Transylvania, which was taken from Hungary. Hungary was, in fact, the principal loser at the peace conference, having been left

with only 35 percent of its prewar area. The much reduced rump states of Austria and Hungary were now confronted by Yugoslavia, Czechoslovakia, and Romania. The latter three, the so-called Little Entente, allied to prevent a resurgence of their former masters. They were linked with France through a treaty of mutual assistance between that nation and Czechoslovakia.

The Allied solidarity of 1918, more illusion than reality, soon disappeared. When the peace treaties were signed, the United States was already withdrawing into isolation and Britain was disengaging from the Continent. This situation left France alone among the great powers to enforce the peace settlement. Yet France was weaker in terms of population and economic strength than Germany. In effect, it was left up to the Germans themselves to decide whether they would abide by the treaty provisions, which all Germans regarded as a vengeful diktat. Moreover, the shame of the Versailles settlement was borne not by the kaiser or the army—the parties responsible for the decisions that led to the defeat—but rather by the leaders of the new democratic Weimar Republic.

The new German government deliberately adopted obstructionist policies, and by 1923, it had halted major reparations payments. French Premier Raymond Poincaré acted. He believed that if the Germans were allowed to break part of the settlement, the remainder would soon unravel. In January 1923, Poincaré sent French troops, supported by Belgian and Italian units, into the Ruhr, the industrial heart of Germany. German Chancellor Wilhelm Cuno's government adopted a policy of passive resistance, urging the workers not to work and promising to pay their salaries. The German leaders thereby hoped to secure sufficient time for the United States and Britain to force France to depart. Although that pressure was forthcoming, Poincaré refused to back down, and the result was catastrophic inflation in Germany.

The mark had already gone from 4.2 to the dollar in July 1914 to 8.9 in January 1919. It then tumbled precipitously because of deliberate government policies. By January 1920, its value was 39.5 to the dollar and in January 1922, 191.8. Then came the French occupation of the Ruhr and Cuno's ruinous policy. In January 1923, the value was 17,972, but by July, it was 353,412. In November, when the old mark was withdrawn in favor of a new currency, the mark's value stood at 4.2 trillion to the dollar. The ensuing economic chaos wiped out the German middle class, and many middle-class citizens lost all faith in democracy and voted for Adolf Hitler a decade later.

Germany now agreed to pay reparations under a scaled-down schedule, and French troops withdrew from the Ruhr in 1924. Although the French generally approved of Poincaré's action, they also noted its high financial cost and the opposition of Britain and the United States. These factors helped bring the Left to power in France in 1924, and the new government reversed Poincaré's go-it-alone approach. The new German government of Chancellor Gustav Stresemann, moreover, announced a policy of living up to its treaty obligations. Notions of "fulfillment" and "conciliation" replaced "obstruction" and led to the Locarno Pacts of 1925, by which Germany voluntarily guaranteed its western borders as final and promised not to resort to war with its neighbors and to resolve any disputes through arbitration. For at least half a decade, international calm prevailed.

By the 1930s, national boundaries were still basically those agreed to in 1919. Italy, Germany, and Japan continued to be dissatisfied with this situation, however, and in the 1930s, the economic difficulties resulting from the Great Depression enhanced popular support in those nations for politicians and military leaders who supported drastic measures, even at the risk of war, to change the situation in the "revisionist" powers' favor. The "status quo" powers of France, Great Britain, and the United States saw no advantage in making changes, but at the same time, they were unwilling to risk war to defend the 1919 settlement. They therefore acquiesced as, step by step, the dissatisfied powers dismantled the peace settlement. From the Japanese invasion of Manchuria in 1931 to the outbreak of war in Europe in 1939, those who wanted to overturn the status quo used force—but not those who sought to maintain it.

The Western democracies seemed paralyzed, in part because of the heavy human cost of World War I. France alone had 1,397,800 citizens killed or missing in the conflict. Including the wounded, 73 percent of all French combatants had been casualties. France could not sustain another such bloodletting, and the defensive military doctrine it adopted came to be summed up in the phrase "Stingy with blood; extravagant with steel." In 1929, France began construction of a defensive belt along the frontier from Switzerland to Belgium. Named for Minister of War André Maginot and never intended as a puncture-proof barricade, the Maginot Line nonetheless helped fix a defensive mindset in the French military.

By the 1930s, attitudes toward World War I had changed. German people believed their nation had not lost the war militarily but had been betrayed by communists, leftists, pacifists, and Jews. Especially in Britain and the United States, many came to believe that the Central Powers had not been responsible for the war, that nothing had been gained by the conflict, and that the postwar settlement had been too hard on Germany.

In Britain, there was some sympathy in influential, upper-class circles for fascist doctrines and dictators, who were seen as opponents of communism. British Member of Parliament Winston L. S. Churchill, for example, praised Italian dictator Benito Mussolini. The British government avoided continental commitments, and its leaders embraced appeasement—the notion that meeting the more legitimate demands of the dictators would remove all need for war. Prime Minister Neville Chamberlain (who served in that post from 1937 to 1940) was the principal architect of this policy. There was also great concern in Britain, as elsewhere, over the possible air bombardment of cities in any future war.

The United States had been one of the few powers that actually benefited from World War I. At a modest cost in terms of human casualties, it had emerged from the struggle as the world's leading financial power. Yet Americans were dissatisfied with their involvement in European affairs; they believed they had been misled by wartime propaganda and that the arms manufacturers (the so-called merchants of death) had drawn the nation into the war to assure themselves payment for sales to the Entente side. In the 1930s, the United States adhered to rigid neutrality, and Congress passed legislation preventing the government from loaning money or selling arms to combatants in a war. Unfortunately, such legislation benefited the aggressor states, which were already well armed, and handicapped their victims. Franklin D. Roosevelt, the U.S. president from 1933 to 1945, understood the threat the aggressors posed to the world community, but most Americans eschewed international involvement.

The Soviet Union was also largely absorbed in its internal affairs. Following World War I, Russia experienced a protracted and bloody civil war as the Communist Reds, who had seized control in November 1917, fought off the Whites, who were supported by the Western Allies. When this conflict ended in 1921, efforts by the government to introduce Communist economic practices only heightened the chaos and famine. In the 1930s, Soviet leader Josef Stalin pushed both the collectivization of agriculture, which led to the deaths of millions of Soviet citizens, and the industrialization essential for modern warfare.

In foreign policy, Stalin was a revisionist who did not accept the new frontiers in eastern Europe as final. Particularly vexing to him was the new Poland, part of which had been carved from former Russian territory. Russia had also lost additional lands to Poland following its defeat in the 1920 Russo-Polish War.

After 1933 and Adolf Hitler's accession to power, Stalin became especially disturbed over Germany, for the German Führer (leader) had clearly stated his opposition to communism and his intention of bringing large stretches of eastern Europe under German control, even by the sword.

The German threat led Stalin to turn to collective security and pursue an internationalist course. In 1934, the Soviet Union joined the League of Nations.

Simultaneously, Stalin launched unprecedented purges against his own people, largely motivated by his own paranoia and desire to hold on to power. The number of victims may have been as high as 40 million, half of whom were killed. The so-called Great Terror consumed almost all the old-guard Bolshevik leadership and senior military officers. The consequences of decimating the latter group were felt in 1941 when the Germans invaded the Soviet Union.

By the late 1930s, many Western leaders distrusted the Soviet Union to the point that they hoped German strength could be directed eastward against it and that Nazism and communism would destroy one another. Thus, despite the fact that the Kremlin was willing to enter into arrangements with the West against Germany and Japan, no effective international coalition was forged.

In 1931, Japan seized Manchuria. Japan had been one of the chief beneficiaries of World War I. At little cost, it had secured the German islands north of the equator and concessions in China. Riding the crest of an ultranationalist wave, Japanese leaders sought to take advantage of the chaos of the world economic depression and the continuing upheaval in China after the 1911 Chinese Revolution to secure the natural resources their country lacked. The Japanese attempted to garner these not only in Manchuria but also in Mongolia, China proper, and South Asia.

Although Japan had many of the trappings of a democracy, it was not one. The army and navy departments were independent of the civilian authorities; from 1936 onward, the ministers of war and navy had to be serving officers, giving the military a veto over public policy because no government could be formed without its concurrence. Army leaders had little sympathy for parliamentary rule or civil government, and in the 1930s, they dominated the government and occasionally resorted to political assassinations, even of prime ministers.

On the night of 18 September 1931, Japanese staff officers of the elite Guandong (Kwantung) Army in southern Manchuria set off an explosion near the main line of the South Manchuria Railway near Mukden, an act they blamed on nearby Chinese soldiers. The Japanese military then took control of Mukden and began the conquest of all Manchuria. Tokyo had been presented with a fait accompli by its own military, but it supported the action.

The Japanese held that they had acted only in self-defense and demanded that the crisis be resolved through direct Sino-Japanese negotiation. China, however, took the matter to the League of Nations, the first major test for that organization. The League Council was reluctant to take tough action against Japan, and the Japanese ignored its calls to withdraw their troops and continued military operations. In February 1932, Japan proclaimed the "independence" of Manchuria in the guise of the new state of Manzhouguo (Manchukuo). A protocol that September established a Japanese protectorate over Manzhouguo. In 1934, the Japanese installed China's last Manchu emperor—Aixinjueluo Puyi (Aisingioro P'u-i, known to Westerners as Henry Puyi), who had been deposed in 1911)—as emperor of what was called Manzhoudiguo (the empire of the Manzhus [Manchus]).

A League of Nations investigating committee blamed Japan and concluded that only the presence of Japanese troops kept the government of Manzhouguo in power. On 24 February 1933, the League Assembly approved the report of its committee and the Stimson Doctrine, named for U.S. Secretary of State Henry L. Stimson, of nonrecognition of Manzhouguo. Of 42 member states, only Japan voted against the move. Never before had such a universal vote of censure been passed against a sovereign state. Tokyo then gave notice of its intention to withdraw from the league.

Manzhouguo was larger than France and Germany combined, but in March, Japanese troops added to it the Province of Rehe (Jehol). Early in April, they moved against Chinese forces south of the Great Wall to within a few miles of Beijing (Peking) and Tianjin (Tienstin). In May, Chinese forces evacuated Beijing, then under the authority of pro-Japanese Chinese leaders. The latter concluded a truce with Japan that created a demilitarized zone administered by Chinese friendly to Japan.

Had the great powers been able to agree on military action, Japan would have been forced to withdraw from its conquered territory. Such a war would have been far less costly than fighting a world war later, but the world economic depression and general Western indifference to the plight of Asians precluded a sacrifice of that nature. A worldwide financial and commercial boycott in accordance with Article 16 of the League of Nations Covenant might also have forced a Japanese withdrawal, but this, too, was beyond Western resolve. Other states with similar aspirations took note.

Germany was the next to move. In January 1933, Adolf Hitler became Germany's chancellor, by entirely legitimate means, and in October 1933, he withdrew Germany from both the League of Nations and the international disarmament conference meeting in Geneva. In July 1934, Austrian Nazis, acting with the tacit support of Berlin, attempted to seize power in Vienna in order to achieve Anschluss, or union with Germany. Ultimately, Austrian authorities put down the putschists without outside assistance, although Mussolini, who considered Austria under his influence, ordered Italian troops to the Brenner Pass.

Germany was then still largely unarmed, and Hitler expressed regret at the murder of Austrian Chancellor Engelbert Dollfuss and assured the world that Germany had no role in the failed coup. The Nazis' unsuccessful attempt at a takeover of Austria was clearly a setback for Hitler. Secure in French support, Mussolini met with the new Austrian chancellor, Kurt von Schuschnigg, in Rome that September and announced that Italy would defend Austrian independence. A French pact with Italy rested on agreement with Yugoslavia, but on 9 October 1934 when King Alexander of Yugoslavia arrived at Marseille for discussions with the French government, Croatian terrorists assassinated him and French Foreign Minister Louis Barthou. This event was a great embarrassment for France, although Barthou's successor, Pierre Laval, did secure the pact with Italy. The January 1935 French-Italian accords called for joint consultation and close cooperation between the two powers in central Europe and reaffirmed the independence and territorial integrity of Austria. They also recommended a multilateral security pact for eastern Europe. In secret provisions, Italy promised to support France with its air force in the event of a German move in the Rhineland and France agreed to provide troops to aid Italy if the Germans should threaten Austria. France also transferred land to the Italian colonies of Libya and Eritrea, and Laval promised Mussolini that France would not oppose Italy's efforts to realize its colonial ambitions. Thereafter, Mussolini behaved as if he had France's approval to wage aggressive war.

Only a week later, with Hitler declaring the Saar to be his last territorial demand in Europe (the first of many such statements), Saarlanders voted nine to one to rejoin Germany. On 1 March 1935, the League Council formally returned the Saar to German control. Two weeks later, on 16 March, Hitler proclaimed the rearmament of Germany. Secret rearmament had been under way for some time, including development of an air training center at Lipetsk, a gas warfare school at Torski, and a tank school at Kazan (all in the Soviet Union), but Hitler now announced publicly that the Reich would reintroduce compulsory military service and increase its army to more than 500,000 men, moves he justified on the grounds that the Allies had not disarmed. France, Britain, and Italy all protested but did nothing further to compel Germany to observe its treaty obligations. In April 1935, Laval, Prime Minister J. Ramsay MacDonald of Britain, and Mussolini met at Stresa on Lake Maggiori and formed the so-called Stresa Front, agreeing "to oppose unilateral repudiation of treaties that may endanger the peace" (with the phrase "of Europe" being added at Mussolini's request).

On 2 May, France and the Soviet Union signed a five-year pact of mutual assistance in the event of unprovoked aggression against either power. The French rejected a military convention that would have coordinated their military response to any German aggression, however. On 16 May, the Soviet Union and Czechoslovakia signed a similar mutual-assistance pact, but the Soviet Union was not obligated to provide armed assistance unless France first fulfilled its commitments.

Britain took the first step in the appeasement of Germany, shattering the Stresa Front. On 18 June 1935, the British government signed a naval agreement with Germany that condoned the latter's violation of the Versailles Treaty. In spite of having promised Paris in February that it would take no unilateral action toward Germany, London permitted the Reich to build a surface navy of a size up to 35 percent that of Britain's own navy—in effect, a force larger than the navies of either France or Italy. It also allowed the Reich to attain 45 percent of the Royal Navy's strength in submarines, armaments that Germany was prohibited from acquiring by the Treaty of Versailles. British leaders were unconcerned. The Royal Navy had only 50 submarines, which meant the Germans could build only 23. Moreover, the British were confident that the new technology of asdic, later known as sonar, would enable them to detect submarines at a range of several thousand yards. The Anglo-German Naval Agreement was, of course, another postdated German check. The conclusion of this accord was also the first occasion on which any power sanctioned Germany's misdeeds, and it won Britain the displeasure of its ally France.

On 3 October 1935, believing with some justification that he had Western support, Mussolini invaded Ethiopia (Abyssinia). Long-standing border disputes between Italian Somaliland and Ethiopia were the excuse. Mussolini's goal was to create a great Italian empire in Africa and to avenge Italy's defeat by the Ethiopians at Adowa in 1896. The outcome of the Italo-Ethiopian War was a foregone conclusion, and in May 1936, Italian forces took Addis Ababa and Mussolini proclaimed the king of Italy as the emperor of Ethiopia.

On 7 October 1935, the League of Nations condemned Italy, marking the first time it had branded a European state an aggressor. But behind the scenes, British Foreign Secretary Sir Samuel Hoare and French Foreign Minister Pierre Laval devised their infamous proposals to broker away Ethiopia to Italy in return for Italian support against Germany. Public furor swept both men from office when the deal became known.

Ultimately, the league voted to impose some economic sanctions—but not on oil, which would have brought an Italian withdrawal. In the end, even those ineffectual sanctions that had been voted for were lifted. Italy, like Japan, had gambled and won, dealing another blow to collective security.

Probably the seminal event on the road to World War II occurred in early 1936, when Hitler remilitarized the Rhineland. On 7 March 1936, some 22,000 lightly armed German troops marched into the Rhineland, defying not just the Treaty of Versailles but also the Locarno Pacts, which Germany had voluntarily negotiated. Hitler deliberately scheduled the operation to occur while France was absorbed by a bitterly contested election campaign that brought the leftist Popular Front to power.

Incredibly, France had no contingency plans for such an eventuality. French intelligence services also grossly overestimated the size of the German forces in the operation and believed Hitler's false claims that the Luftwaffe had achieved parity with the French Armée de l'Air (air force). Vainly seeking to disguise its own inaction, Paris appealed to London for support, but Foreign Secretary Anthony Eden made it clear that Britain would not fight for the Rhineland, which was, after all, German territory.

Had the French acted, their forces in all likelihood would have rolled over the Germans, which would probably have meant the end of the Nazi regime. But as it turned out, remilitarization of the Rhineland provided Germany a buffer for the Ruhr and a springboard for invading France and Belgium. That October, it also led Belgian leaders to renounce their treaty of mutual assistance with France and seek security in neutrality.

Almost immediately after the German remilitarization of the Rhineland, another international crisis erupted, this time in Spain, where civil war began on 18 July 1936. The issue centered on whether Spain would follow the modernizing reforms of the rest of western Europe or maintain its existing structure, favored by Spanish traditionalists. When the Republicans won a narrow victory in the Spanish elections of 1936, the traditionalists, who were known as the Nationalists, took to arms.

It is probable, though by no means certain, that the Republicans would have won the civil war had Spain been left alone to decide its fate. Certainly, the conflict would have ended much sooner. But Germany and Italy intervened early, providing critical air support that allowed the airlifting of Nationalist troops and equipment across the Straits of Gibraltar from Morocco to Nationalist-held territory in Spain—in effect, the first large-scale military airlift in history.

Germany even formed an air detachment, the Kondor Legion, to fight in Spain, a key factor in the ultimate Nationalist victory. The Germans also tested their latest military equipment under combat conditions, developed new fighter tactics, and learned about the necessity of close co-ordination between air and ground operations, along with the value of dive-bombing. Italy also provided important naval support and sent three divisions of troops, artillery, and aircraft.

Surprisingly, the Western democracies did not support the Spanish Republic. France initially sent some arms to the Republicans, but under heavy British pressure, it reversed its stance. British leaders devised a noninterventionist policy. Although all the great powers promised to observe that policy, only the Western democracies actually did so. This agreement, which made it impossible for the Republicans to obtain the arms they needed, was probably the chief factor in their defeat.

Only the Soviet Union and Mexico assisted the Spanish Republic. Stalin apparently hoped for a protracted struggle that would entangle the Western democracies and Germany on the other side of the European continent. During the civil war, the Soviet Union sent advisers, aircraft, tanks, and artillery to Spain. Eventually, this Soviet aid permitted the Spanish Communists, who were not a significant political factor in 1936, to take over the Republican government. Finally, in March 1939, Nationalist forces, led by General Francisco Franco, entered Madrid. By April, hostilities ended.

The Western democracies emerged very poorly from the test of the Spanish Civil War. Although tens of thousands of foreign volunteers had fought in Spain, most of these for the Republic, the governments of the Western democracies had remained aloof, and many doubted the West had any will left to defend democracy. Internationally, the major effect of the fighting in Spain was to bring Germany and Italy together. In October 1936, they agreed to cooperate in Spain, to collaborate in matters of "parallel interests," and to work to defend "European civilization" against communism. Thus was born the Rome-Berlin Axis. Then, on 25 November, Germany and Japan signed the Anti-Comintern Pact to oppose activities of the Comintern (the Communist International), created to spread communism. On the same day, Germany and Japan also signed a secret agreement providing that if either state was the object of an unprovoked attack by the Soviet Union, the other would do nothing to assist the USSR. On 6 November 1937, Italy joined the Anti-Comintern Pact. Shortly afterward, Mussolini announced that Italy would not assist Austria against a German attempt to consummate Anschluss. Italy also withdrew from the League of Nations, and it recognized Manzhouguo as an independent state in November 1937 (as did Germany in May 1938).

Japan, meanwhile, continued to strengthen its position in the Far East, asserting its exclusive right to control China. Tokyo demanded an end to the provision of Western loans and military advisers to China and threatened the use of force if such aid continued. In 1935, Japan began encroaching on several of China's northern provinces. The Chinese government at Nanjing (Nanking), headed by Generalissimo Jiang Jieshi (Chiang Kai-shek), initially pursued a policy of appeasement vis-à-vis the Japanese, but students and the Chinese military demanded action. The Chinese Communists declared themselves willing to cooperate with the Nationalist government and place their armies under its command if Nanjing would adopt an anti-Japanese policy. The rapid growth of anti-Japanese sentiment in China and the increasing military strength of the Nationalists alarmed Japanese military leaders, who worked to establish a pro-Japanese regime in China's five northern provinces.

On the night of 7 July 1937, a clash occurred west of Beijing between Japanese and Chinese troops. Later that month, after Nanjing rejected an ultimatum from Tokyo, the Japanese invaded the coveted northern provinces. In a few days, they had occupied both Tianjin and Beijing, and by the end of the year, Japan had extended its control into all five Chinese provinces north of the Yellow River. In mid-December, Japan also installed a new government in Beijing. Tokyo never declared war against China, however, enabling it to evade U.S. neutrality legislation and purchase American raw materials and oil. But by the same token, this situation permitted Washington to send aid to China.

The fighting was not confined to north China, for in August 1937, the Japanese attacked the great commercial city of Shanghai. Not until November, after three months of hard fighting involving the best Nationalist troops, did the city fall. Japanese forces then advanced up the Changjiang (Yangtse) River, and in December, they took Nanjing, where they committed widespread atrocities.

As scholars have since noted, Japan subsequently developed a collective amnesia in regard to its actions at Nanjing and its atrocities in the war through South Asia in general. (According to the Chinese, Japan has a long history and a short memory.) This Japanese evasion of responsibility stands in sharp contrast to German attempts to come to terms with the Holocaust, and it has affected Japan's relations with China and other nations in Asia right up to the present.

On 12 December 1937, while trying to clear the Changjiang River of all Western shipping, Japanese forces attacked a U.S. Navy gunboat, the *Panay*. Other American ships belonging to an oil company were also bombed and sunk, and British vessels were shelled. Strong protests from Washington and London brought profuse apologies from Tokyo. The Japanese, falsely claiming they had not realized the nationality of the ships, stated their readiness to pay compensation and give guarantees that such incidents would not be repeated. Washington and London accepted these amends, and the episode only served to convince Tokyo that it had little to fear from Western intervention.

Again, China appealed to the League of Nations, which once more condemned Japan. Again, too, the West failed to withhold critical supplies and financial credits from Japan, so once more, collective security failed. By the end of 1938, Japanese troops had taken the great commercial cities of Tianjin, Beijing, Shanghai, Nanjing, Hankou, and Guangzhou (Canton), and the Nationalists were forced to relocate their capital to the interior city of Chongqing (Chungking), which Japan bombed heavily. In desperation, the Chinese demolished the dikes on the Huang He (Hwang Ho), known to Westerners as the Yellow River, costing hundreds of thousands of lives and flooding much of northern China until 1944.

Japan was also confronting the Soviet Union. Fighting began in 1938 between Japanese and Soviet troops in the poorly defined triborder area normally referred to as Changkufeng, where Siberia, Manzhouguo, and Korea met. Although no state of war was declared, significant battles were fought, especially at Changkufeng Hill in 1938 and Nomonhan/Khalkhin Gol in 1939. The fighting ended advantageously for the Soviets. A cease-fire in September 1939 preempted a planned Japanese counterattack, and the dispute was resolved by treaty in June 1940. The fighting undoubtedly influenced Stalin's decision to sign a nonaggression pact with Germany in August 1939. It also gave Tokyo a new appreciation of Soviet fighting ability, and in 1941, it helped to influence Japanese leaders to strike not north into Siberia but against the easier targets of the European colonies in Southeast Asia.

In the West, the situation by 1938 encouraged Hitler to embark on his own territorial expansion. Mussolini was now linked with Hitler, and France was experiencing another period of ministerial instability. In Britain, appeasement was in full force, so much so that in February 1938, Anthony Eden, a staunch proponent of collective security, resigned as foreign secretary.

Austria was Hitler's first step. In February 1938, Austrian Chancellor Schuschnigg traveled to Berchtesgaden at the Führer's insistence to meet with the German leader. Under heavy pressure, Schuschnigg agreed to appoint Austrian Nazi Arthur Seyss-Inquart as minister of the interior and other Austrian Nazis as ministers of justice and foreign affairs. On 9 March, however, in an attempt to maintain his nation's independence, Schuschnigg announced that a plebiscite on the issue of Anschluss would be held in only four days, hoping that the short interval would not allow the Nazis to mobilize effectively.

Hitler was determined that no plebiscite be held, and on 11 March, Seyss-Inquart presented Schuschnigg with an ultimatum demanding his resignation and postponement of the vote under threat of invasion by German troops, already mobilized on the border. Schuschnigg yielded, canceling the plebiscite and resigning. Seyss-Inquart then took power and belatedly invited in the German troops "to preserve order" after they had already crossed the frontier. Yet Germany's military was hardly ready for war; indeed, hundreds of German tanks and vehicles of the German Eighth Army broke down on the drive toward Vienna.

On 13 March, Berlin declared Austria to be part of the Reich, and the next day, perhaps a million Austrians gave Hitler an enthusiastic welcome to Vienna. France and Britain lodged formal protests with Berlin but did nothing more. After the war, Austrian leaders denied culpability for their association with the Third Reich by claiming that their country was actually the first victim of Nazi aggression.

The Anschluss greatly strengthened the German position in central Europe. Germany was now in direct contact with Italy, Yugoslavia, and Hungary, and it controlled virtually all the communications of southeastern Europe. Czechoslovakia was almost isolated, and its trade outlets operated at Germany's mercy. Militarily, Germany outflanked the powerful western Czech defenses. It was thus not surprising that, despite his pledges to respect the territorial integrity of Czechoslovakia, Hitler should next seek to bring that state under his control.

In Austria, Hitler had added 6 million Germans to the Reich, but another 3.5 million lived in Czechoslovakia. Germans living there had long complained about discrimination in a state that had only minority Czech, German, Slovak, Hungarian, Ukrainian, and Pole populations. In 1938, however, Czechoslovakia had the highest standard of living east of Germany and was the only remaining democracy in central Europe.

Strategically, Czechoslovakia was the keystone of Europe. It had a military alliance with France, an army of 400,000 well-trained men, and the important Skoda munitions complex at Pilsen, as well as strong fortifications in the west. Unfortunately for the Czechs, the latter were in the Erzegeberge (Ore Mountains) bordering the Bohemian bowl, where the population was almost entirely German. From the German point of view, it could now be said that Bohemia-Moravia, almost one-third German in population, protruded into the Reich. Hitler took up and enlarged the past demands of Konrad Henlein's Sudetendeutsch (Sudeten German) Party to turn legitimate complaints into a call for outright separation of the German regions from Czechoslovakia and their union with Germany.

In May 1938, during key Czechoslovakian elections,

German troops massed on the border and threatened invasion. Confident of French support, the Czechs mobilized their army. Both France and the Soviet Union had stated their willingness to go to war to defend Czechoslovakia, and in the end, nothing happened. Hitler then began to construct fortifications along the German frontier in the west. Known to Germans as the West Wall, these fortifications were clearly designed to prevent France from supporting its eastern allies.

Western leaders, who believed they had just averted war, now pondered whether Czechoslovakia, which had been formed only as a consequence of the Paris Peace Conference, was worth a general European war. British Prime Minister Chamberlain concluded that it was not. In early August, he sent an emissary, Lord Runciman, to Prague as a mediator, and on 7 September, based on Runciman's suggestions, Prague offered Henlein practically everything that the Sudeten Germans demanded, short of independence.

A number of knowledgeable Germans believed that Hitler was leading their state to destruction. During August and early September 1938, several opposition emissaries traveled to London with messages from the head of the Abwehr (German military intelligence), Admiral Wilhelm Canaris, and the chief of the German General Staff, General der Artillerie (U.S. equiv. lieutenant general) Ludwig Beck. They warned London of Hitler's intentions and urged a strong British stand. Beck even pledged, prior to his resignation in mid-August, that if Britain would agree to fight for Czechoslovakia, he would stage a putsch against Hitler. Nothing came of this effort, however, as London was committed to appeasement.

By mid-September, Hitler was demanding "self-determination" for the Sudeten Germans and threatening war if it was not granted. Clearly, he was promoting a situation to justify German military intervention. France would then have to decide whether to honor its pledge to Czechoslovakia. If it chose to do so, this would bring on a general European war.

In this critical situation, Chamberlain asked Hitler for a personal meeting, and on 15 September, he flew to Germany and met with the Führer at Berchtesgaden. There, Hitler informed him that the Sudeten Germans had to be able to unite with Germany and that he was willing to risk war to accomplish this end. London and Paris now decided to force the principle of self-determination on Prague, demanding on 19 September that the Czechs agree to an immediate transfer to Germany of those areas with populations that were more than 50 percent German. When Prague asked that the matter be referred to arbitration, as provided under the Locarno Pacts, London and Paris declared this unacceptable. The Czechs, they said, would have to accept the Anglo-French proposals or bear the consequences alone.

The British and French decision to desert Czechoslovakia resulted from many factors. The peoples of both countries dreaded a general war, especially one with air attacks, for which neither nation believed itself adequately prepared. The Germans also bluffed the British and French into believing that their Luftwaffe was much more powerful than it actually was, and both Chamberlain and French Premier Édouard Daladier feared the destruction of their capitals from the air. The Western leaders also thought they would be fighting alone. They did not believe they could count on the USSR, whose military was still reeling from Stalin's purges. It also seemed unlikely that the United States would assist, even with supplies, given its neutrality policies. Nor were the British dominions of Canada, Australia, New Zealand, and South Africa likely to support Great Britain in a war for Czechoslovakia. In France and especially in Britain, there were also those who saw Nazism as a bulwark against communism and who hoped that Hitler could be diverted eastward and enmeshed in a war with the Soviets in which communism and fascism might destroy one another.

Chamberlain, who had scant experience in foreign affairs, hoped to reconcile differences in order to prevent a general European war. He strongly believed in the sanctity of contracts and could not accept that the leader of the most powerful state in Europe was a blackmailer and a liar. But the West also suffered from a moral uncertainty. In 1919, it had touted the "self-determination of peoples," and by this standard, Germany had a right to all it had hitherto demanded. The transfer of the Sudetenland to the Reich did not seem too high a price to pay for a satisfied Germany and a peaceful Europe. Finally, Hitler stated repeatedly that, once his demands on Czechoslovakia had been satisfied, he would have no further territorial ambitions in Europe.

Under heavy British and French pressure, Czechoslovakia accepted the Anglo-French proposals. On 22 September, Chamberlain again traveled to Germany and met with Hitler, who, to Chamberlain's surprise, demanded that all Czech officials be withdrawn from the Sudeten area within 10 days and that no military, economic, or traffic establishments be damaged or removed. These demands led to the most serious international crisis in Europe since 1918. Prague informed London that Hitler's demands were absolutely unacceptable. London and Paris agreed and decided not to pressure Prague to secure its acceptance. It thus appeared that Hitler might have to carry out his threat to use force and that a general European war might result.

Following appeals by Roosevelt and Mussolini to Hitler, the German leaders agreed to a meeting. Chamberlain, Daladier, and Mussolini then repaired to Munich to meet with Hitler on 29 September. The Soviet Union was not invited, and Czechoslovakia itself was not officially represented. There were no real negotiations, the object being to give Hitler the Sudetenland in order to avoid war.

The Munich Agreement, dated 30 September, gave the Führer everything he demanded, and early on 1 October 1938, German troops marched across the frontier. Other neighboring states joined in. Poland demanded—and received—an area around Teschen of some 400 square miles with a population of 240,000 people, only 100,000 of whom were Poles, and in November, Hungary secured some 4,800 square miles of Czechoslovakia with about 1 million people.

In retrospect, it would have been better for the West to have fought Germany in September 1938. The lineup against Germany might have included the Soviet Union and Poland, but even discounting them, the German army would have been forced to fight against France and Britain, as well as Czechoslovakia. Despite Hitler's claims to the contrary, Germany was not ready for war in September 1938. The Luftwaffe had 1,230 first-line aircraft, including 600 bombers and 400 fighters, but nearly half of them were earmarked for use in the east, leaving the rest too thinly stretched over the Reich frontier to counter any serious offensive by the French air force and the Royal Air Force (RAF). The Luftwaffe was also short of bombs. Worse, only five fighting divisions and seven reserve divisions were available to hold eight times that number of French divisions.

Britain itself was far from ready, its rearmament program having begun only the year before. France had many more artillery pieces than Germany but was weak in the air. According to one estimate, France had only 250 first-quality fighters and 350 bombers out of perhaps 1,375 front-line aircraft, but France also could have counted on 35 well-armed and well-equipped Czech divisions, backed by substantial numbers of artillery pieces and tanks and perhaps 1,600 aircraft.

Later, those responsible for the Munich debacle advanced the argument that the agreement bought a year for the Western democracies to rearm. Winston Churchill stated that British fighter squadrons equipped with modern aircraft rose from only 5 in September 1938 to 26 by July 1939 (and 47 by July 1940), but he also noted that the year "gained" by Munich left the democracies in a much worse position vis-à-vis Hitler's Germany than they had been in during the Munich crisis.

The September 1938 crisis had far-reaching international effects. Chamberlain and Daladier were received with cheers at home, the British prime minister reporting that he believed he had brought back "peace in our time." But the agreement effectively ended the French security system, since France's eastern allies now questioned

French commitments to them. Stalin, always suspicious, was further alienated from the West. He expressed the view that Chamberlain and Daladier had surrendered to Hitler in order to facilitate Germany's *Drang nach Osten* (drive to the east) and a war between Germany and the Soviet Union.

Hitler had given assurances that the Sudetenland was his last territorial demand, but events soon proved the contrary. The day after the Munich Agreement was signed, he told his aides that he would annex the remainder of Czechoslovakia at the first opportunity. Within a few months, Hitler took advantage of the Czech internal situation. In March 1939, he threw his support to the leader of the Slovak Popular Party, Jozef Tiso, who sought complete independence for Slovakia. On 14 March, Slovakia and Ruthenia declared their independence. That same day, Hitler summoned elderly Czech President Emile Hácha to Berlin, where the commander of the Luftwaffe, Hermann Göring, threatened the immediate destruction of Prague unless Moravia and Bohemia were made Reich protectorates. German bombers, he alleged, were awaiting the order to take off. Hácha signed, and on that date, 15 March, Nazi troops occupied what remained of Czechoslovakia. The Czech lands became the Protectorate of Bohemia and Moravia, and Slovakia became a vassal state of the Reich, with little more independence than Bohemia-Moravia.

Thirty-five highly trained and well-equipped Czech divisions thus disappeared from the anti-Hitler order of battle. Hitler had also eliminated what he had referred to as "that damned airfield" (meaning all of Czechoslovakia), and the output of the Skoda arms complex would now supply the Reich's legions. In Bohemia and Moravia, the Wehrmacht acquired 1,582 aircraft, 2,000 artillery pieces, and sufficient equipment to arm 20 divisions. Any increase in armaments that Britain and France achieved by March 1939 was more than counterbalanced by German gains in Czechoslovakia, which included nearly one-third of the tanks they deployed in the west in spring 1940. Between August 1938 and September 1939, Skoda produced nearly as many arms as all British arms factories combined.

Hungarian troops crossed into Ruthenia and incorporated it into Hungary. Later in March, Germany demanded from Lithuania the immediate return of Memel, with its mostly German population. Lithuania, which had received the Baltic city after World War I to gain access to the sea, had no recourse but to comply.

Hitler's seizure of the rest of Czechoslovakia demonstrated that his demands were not limited to areas with German populations but were instead determined by the need for Lebensraum, or living space. His repudiation of the formal pledges given to Chamberlain at Munich did,

however, serve to convince the British that they could no longer trust Hitler. Indeed, Britain and France responded with a series of guarantees to the smaller states now threatened by Germany. Clearly, Poland would be the next pressure point, as the German press orchestrated charges of the Polish government's brutality against its German minority. On 31 March, Britain and France extended a formal guarantee to support Poland in the event of a German attack. At the eleventh hour and under the worst possible circumstances—with Czechoslovakia lost and the Soviet Union alienated—Britain had changed its eastern European policy and agreed to do what the French had sought in the 1920s.

Mussolini took advantage of the general European situation to strengthen Italy's position in the Balkans. In April 1939, he sent Italian troops into Albania. King Zog fled, whereon an Albanian constituent assembly voted to offer the crown to King Victor Emmanuel III of Italy. On 13 April, Britain and France extended a guarantee to defend Greece and Romania.

The Western powers began to make belated military preparations for an inevitable war, and they worked to secure a pact with the Soviet Union. Unfortunately, the guarantee to Poland gave the Soviet Union protection on its western frontier, virtually the most it could have secured in any negotiations.

On 23 May, Hitler met with his leading generals at the Reich Chancellery. He reviewed Germany's territorial requirements and the need to resolve these by expansion eastward. War, he declared, was inevitable, and he announced that he intended to attack Poland at the first suitable opportunity.

The same month, Britain and France initiated negotiations with the Soviet Union for a mutual-assistance pact. Although negotiations continued until August, no agreement was reached. Poland, Latvia, Lithuania, and Estonia were all unwilling to allow Soviet armies within their borders, even to defend against a German attack. Many in these countries feared the Soviets more than the Germans, and Polish leaders refused to believe that Hitler would risk war with Britain and France. But due to the 1920 Russo-Polish War, Poland's eastern border extended almost to Minsk, and the Soviets believed that the French and British wished them to take the brunt of the German attack. The Poles also had an exaggerated sense of their own military power. In any case, the Anglo-French negotiators refused to sacrifice Poland and the Baltic states to Stalin as they had handed Czechoslovakia to Hitler.

While the Kremlin had been negotiating more or less openly with Britain and France, it concurrently sought an understanding with Germany, even to the point of Stalin dispatching personal emissaries to Berlin. On 10 March 1939, addressing the Eighteenth Party Congress of the Soviet Union, Stalin had said that his country did not intend to "pull anyone else's chestnuts out of the fire." He thus signaled to Hitler his readiness to abandon collective security and negotiate an agreement with Berlin. Within a week, Hitler had annexed Bohemia and Moravia, confident that the Soviet Union would not intervene. Another consideration for Stalin was that the Soviet Union potentially faced war on two fronts, owing to the threat from Japan in the Far East. Japanese pressure on Mongolia and the Maritime Provinces may well have played a significant role in predisposing Stalin to make his pact with Hitler.

In early May 1939, Stalin gave further encouragement to Hitler when he dismissed Commissar for Foreign Affairs Maksim Litvinov and appointed Vyacheslav Molotov in his place. Litvinov was both a champion of collective security and a Jew. Hitler later said that the dismissal of Litvinov made fully evident Stalin's wish to transform its relations with Germany. Contacts begun in May culminated in the German-Soviet Non-aggression Pact signed on 23 August in Moscow by Molotov and German Foreign Minister Joachim von Ribbentrop.

The German-Soviet agreement signed that night consisted of an open, 10-year, nonaggression pact, together with two secret protocols that did not become generally known until Rudolf Hess revealed them after the war during the proceedings of the International Military Tribunal at Nuremberg. These secret arrangements, never publicly acknowledged by the Soviet Union until 1990, partitioned eastern Europe between Germany and the Soviet Union in advance of the German invasion of Poland, for which Hitler had now, in effect, received Stalin's permission. Any future territorial rearrangement of the area was to involve its division between the two powers. The Soviet sphere would include eastern Poland, the Romanian Province of Bessarabia, Estonia, Latvia, and Finland. Lithuania went to Germany. A month later, Hitler traded it to Stalin in exchange for further territorial concessions in Poland. In addition, a trade convention accompanying the pact provided that the Soviet Union would supply vast quantities of raw materials to Germany in exchange for military technology and finished goods. This economic arrangement was immensely valuable to Germany early in the war, a point that Churchill later made quite clear to Stalin. Certainly, Stalin expected that Hitler would face a protracted war in the west that would allow the Soviet Union time to rebuild its military. All indications are that Stalin welcomed the pact with Germany, whereas he regarded the subsequent wartime alliance with Britain and the United States with fear and suspicion. His position becomes understandable when one realizes that Stalin's primary concern was with the internal stability of the Soviet Union.

The nonaggression pact had the impact of a thunderbolt on the world community. Communism and Nazism, supposed to be ideological opposites on the worst possible terms, had come together, dumbfounding a generation more versed in ideology than power politics.

On 22 August, Hitler summoned his generals and announced his intention to invade Poland. Neither Britain nor France, he said, had the leadership necessary for a life-and-death struggle: "Our enemies are little worms," he remarked, "I saw them at Munich." British and French armament did not yet amount to much. Thus, Germany had much to gain and little to lose, for the Western powers probably would not fight. In any case, Germany had to accept the risks and act with reckless resolution.

The German invasion of Poland, set for 26 August, actually occurred on 1 September, the delay caused by Italy's decision to remain neutral. Prompted by his foreign minister and son-in-law, Galeazzo Ciano, Mussolini lost faith in a German victory. Ciano proposed that Mussolini tell Hitler that Italy would enter the conflict only if Germany would agree to supply certain armaments and raw materials. On 25 August, the Germans rescinded their plans and engaged in frenzied discussions. The next day, Mussolini asked for immediate delivery of 170 million tons of industrial products and raw materials, an impossible request. Hitler then asked that Mussolini maintain a benevolent neutrality toward Germany and continue military preparations so as to fool the English and French. Mussolini agreed.

On 1 September, following false charges that Polish forces had crossed onto German soil and killed German border guards—an illusion completed by the murder of concentration camp prisoners who were then dressed in Polish military uniforms—German forces invaded Poland. On 3 September, after the expiration of ultimatums to Germany, Britain and France declared war on Germany.

Spencer C. Tucker

See also

Aixinjueluo Puyi; Anti-Comintern Pact; Beck, Ludwig; Canaris, Wilhelm Franz; Chamberlain, Arthur Neville; Churchill, Sir Winston L. S.; Ciano, Galeazzo; Daladier, Édouard; Eden, Sir Robert Anthony; Franco, Francisco; Gamelin, Maurice Gustave; Guandong Army; Hess, Walter Richard Rudolf; Hitler, Adolf; Italo-Ethiopian War; Kondor Legion; Manzhouguo; Molotov, Vyacheslav Mikhailovich; Munich Conference and Preliminaries; Mussolini, Benito; *Panay* Incident; Rhineland, Remilitarization of; Ribbentrop, Ulrich Friedrich Willy Joachim von; Roosevelt, Franklin D.; Schuschnigg, Kurt von; Sino-Japanese War; Spain, Civil War in; Stalin, Josef; Stimson, Henry Lewis; Tiso, Jozef; Victor Emanuel III, King of Italy

References

Bell, P. M. H. *The Origins of the Second World War in Europe.* New York: Longman, 1986.

Bendiner, Elmer. *A Time for Angels: The Tragicomic History of the League of Nations.* New York: Alfred A. Knopf, 1975.

Kee, Robert. *1939: In the Shadow of War.* Boston: Little, Brown, 1984.

Kennan, George F. *From Prague after Munich: Diplomatic Papers, 1938–1940.* Princeton, NJ: Princeton University Press, 1968.

Kier, Elizabeth. *Imagining War: French and British Military Doctrine between the Wars.* Princeton, NJ: Princeton University Press, 1997.

Read, Anthony, and David Fisher. *The Deadly Embrace: Hitler, Stalin, and the Nazi-Soviet Pact, 1939–1941.* New York: W. W. Norton, 1988.

Renouvin, Pierre. *World War II and Its Origins: International Relations, 1929–1945.* New York: Harper and Row, 1969.

Shirer, William L. *20th Century Journey: A Memoir of a Life and the Times.* Vol. 2, *The Nightmare Years, 1930–1940.* Boston: Little, Brown, 1984.

Smith, Gene. *The Dark Summer: An Intimate History of the Events That Led to World War II.* New York: Macmillan, 1987.

Watt, Donald C. *Too Serious a Business: European Armed Forces and the Approach to the Second World War.* New York: W. W. Norton, 1975.

Whaley, Barton. *Covert German Rearmament, 1919–1939: Deception and Misrepresentation.* Frederick, MD: University Publications of America, 1984.

Overview of World War II

World War II was the most destructive enterprise in human history. It is sobering to consider that more resources, material, and human lives (approximately 50 million dead) were expended on the war than on any other human activity. Indeed, this conflict was so all-encompassing that very few "side" wars took place simultaneously, the 1939–1940 Finnish-Soviet War (the Winter War) being one of the few exceptions.

The debate over the origins of World War I had become something of a cottage industry among historians in the 1920s and 1930s. Yet the question of origins rarely arises over World War II, except on the narrow issue of whether U.S. President Franklin D. Roosevelt had advance knowledge of the Japanese attack on Pearl Harbor. Whatever their grievances (certainly minor in comparison to the misery they inflicted on their victims), Germany and Japan are still considered the aggressors of World War II.

World War II is historically unique in that it represents if not necessarily a "crusade" of good against evil at least a struggle against almost pure evil by less evil forces. More than half a century after the end of this war, no mainstream or serious historians defend any significant aspect of Nazi Germany. Perhaps more surprisingly, there are also few if any such historians who would do likewise for militaristic Japan. In practically all previous conflicts, historians have found sufficient blame to give all belligerents a share. For example, no prominent historian takes seriously the Versailles provision that Germany was somehow completely responsible for the outbreak of World War I. German Führer Adolf Hitler and his followers have thus retained mythic status as personifications of pure evil, something not seen since the Wars of Religion of seventeenth-century Europe.

The starting date of World War II, however, can be disputed. Some scholars have gone as far back as the Japanese seizure of Manchuria in 1931. Others date its outbreak to the opening of the full-scale Sino-Japanese War in 1937. But these were conflicts between two Asian powers, hardly global war.

The more traditional and more widely accepted date for the start of World War II is 1 September 1939, with the quick but not quite blitzkrieg (lightning) German invasion of Poland. This action brought France and Great Britain into the conflict two days later in accordance with their guarantees to Poland. (The Soviet Union's invasion of eastern Poland on 17 September provoked no similar reaction.)

The Germans learned from their Polish Campaign and mounted a true blitzkrieg offensive against the Low Countries and France, commencing on 10 May 1940. In this blitzkrieg warfare, the tactical airpower of the German air force (the Luftwaffe) knocked out command and communications posts as integrated armor division pincers drove deeply into enemy territory, bypassing opposition strong points. When all went well, the pincers encircled the slow-moving enemy. Contrary to legend, the armored forces were simply the spearheads; the bulk of the German army was composed of foot soldiers and horses. Further, the French army and the British Expeditionary Force combined had more and usually better tanks than the Germans, and they were not too seriously inferior in the air. The sluggish Allies were simply outmaneuvered, losing France in six weeks, much to the astonishment of the so-called experts. France remains the only major industrial democracy ever to be conquered—and, also uniquely, after a single campaign. It was also the only more or less motorized nation to suffer such a fate; many French refugees fled the rapidly advancing Germans in their private cars. The Germans found that the French Routes Nationales (National Routes), designed to enable French forces to reach the frontiers, could also be used in the opposite direction by an invader. The

Germans themselves relearned this military truth on their autobahns in 1945.

Germany suffered its first defeat of the war when its air offensive against Great Britain, the world's first great air campaign, was thwarted in the Battle of Britain. The margin of victory was small, for there was little to choose between the Hurricane and Spitfire fighters of the Royal Air Force (RAF) and the Luftwaffe's Bf-109 or between the contenders' pilots. The main advantages of the RAF in this battle were radar and the geographic fact that its pilots and their warplanes were shot down over Britain itself; German pilots and aircraft in a similar predicament were out of action for the duration, and they also had farther to fly from their bases. But Great Britain's greatest advantage throughout this stage of the war was its prime minister, Winston L. S. Churchill, who gave stirring voice and substance to the Allied defiance of Hitler.

Nonetheless, by the spring of 1941, Nazi Germany had conquered or dominated all of the European continent, with the exception of Switzerland, Sweden, and Vatican City. Greece, which had held off and beaten back an inept Italian offensive, finally capitulated to the German Balkan blitzkrieg in spring 1941.

Nazi Germany then turned on its erstwhile ally, the Soviet Union, on 22 June 1941, in Operation BARBAROSSA, the greatest military campaign of all time, in order to fulfill Hitler's enduring vision of crushing "Judeo-Bolshevism." (How far Hitler's ambitions of conquest ranged beyond the Soviet east is still disputed by historians.) If he had any introspective moments then, Soviet dictator Josef Stalin must have wished that he still possessed the legions of first-rate officers he had shot or slowly destroyed in the gulag in the wake of his bloody purge of the military in 1937. Stalin's own inept generalship played a major role in the early Soviet defeats, and German forces drove almost to within sight of the Kremlin's towers in December 1941 before being beaten back.

Early that same month, war erupted in the Pacific, and the conflict then became truly a world war, with Japan's coordinated combined attacks on the U.S. naval base at Pearl Harbor and on British, Dutch, and American imperial possessions. With the Soviet Union holding out precariously and the United States now a belligerent, the Axis had lost the war, even though few recognized that fact at the time. America's "great debate" as to whether and to what extent to aid Britain was silenced in a national outpouring of collective wrath against an enemy, in a manner that would not be seen again until 11 September 2001.

But Pearl Harbor was bad enough, with 2,280 Americans dead, four battleships sunk, and the remaining four battleships damaged. Much worse was to follow. As with the Germans in France, more-professional Japanese forces surprised and outfought their opponents by land, sea, and air. Almost before they knew it, British and Dutch forces in Asia, superior in numbers alone, had been routed in one of the most successful combined-arms campaigns in history. (The French had already yielded control of their colony of Indochina, whose rice and raw materials were flowing to Japan while the Japanese military had the use of its naval and air bases until the end of the war.) The course of the Malayan-Singapore Campaign was typical. British land forces could scarcely even delay the Japanese army, Japanese fighters cleared the skies of British aircraft, and Japanese naval bombers flying from land bases quickly sank the new battleship *Prince of Wales* and the elderly battle cruiser *Repulse*. This disaster made it obvious that the aircraft carrier was the capital ship of the day. Singapore, the linchpin of imperial European power in the Orient, surrendered ignominiously on 16 February 1942.

The British hardly made a better fight of it in Burma before having to evacuate that colony. Only the Americans managed to delay the Japanese seriously, holding out on the Bataan Peninsula and then at the Corregidor fortifications until May. The end of imperialism, at least in Asia, can be dated to the capitulation of Singapore, as Asians witnessed other Asians with superior technology and professionalism completely defeat Europeans and Americans.

And yet, on Pearl Harbor's very "day of infamy," Japan actually lost the war. Its forces missed the American aircraft carriers there, as well as the oil tank farms and the machine shop complex. On that day, the Japanese killed many U.S. personnel, and they destroyed mostly obsolete aircraft and sank a handful of elderly battleships. But above all, they outraged Americans, who determined to avenge the attack so that Japan would receive no mercy in the relentless land, sea, and air war that the United States was now to wage against it. More significantly, American industrial and manpower resources vastly surpassed those Japan could bring to bear in a protracted conflict.

And yet—oddly, perhaps, in view of its own ruthless warfare and occupation—Japan was the only major belligerent to hold limited aims in World War II. Japanese leaders basically wanted the Western colonial powers out of the Pacific, to be replaced, of course, by their own Greater East Asia Co-prosperity Sphere (a euphemism for "Asia for the Japanese"). No unconditional surrender demands ever issued from Tokyo. To Japan's own people, of course, the war was presented as a struggle to the death against the arrogant Anglo-Saxon imperialists.

Three days after the Pearl Harbor attack, Hitler decided to declare war on the United States, a blunder fully as deadly as his invasion of the Soviet Union and even less explicable.

But the Nazi dictator, on the basis of his customary "insights," had dismissed the American soldier as worthless, and he considered U.S. industrial power vastly overrated. His decision meant the United States could not focus exclusively on Japan.

The tide would not begin to turn until the drawn-out naval-air clash in the Coral Sea (May 1942), the first naval battle in which neither side's surface ships ever came within sight of the opponent. The following month, the U.S. Navy avenged Pearl Harbor in the Battle of Midway, sinking no fewer than four Japanese carriers, again without the surface ships involved ever sighting each other. The loss of hundreds of superbly trained, combat-experienced naval aviators and their highly trained maintenance crews was as great a blow to Japan as the actual sinking of its invaluable carriers. The Americans could make up their own losses far more easily than the Japanese.

Although considered a sideshow by the Soviets, the North African Campaign was of the utmost strategic importance, and until mid-1943, it was the only continental land campaign that the Western Allies were strong enough to mount. Had North Africa, including Egypt, fallen to the Axis powers (as almost occurred several times), the Suez Canal could not have been held, and German forces could have gone through the Middle East, mobilizing Arab nationalism, threatening the area's vast oil fields, and even menacing the embattled Soviet Union itself. Not until the British commander in North Africa, General Bernard Montgomery, amassed a massive superiority in armor was German General Erwin Rommel defeated at El Alamein in October 1942 and slowly pushed back toward Tunisia. U.S. and British landings to the rear of Rommel's forces, in Algeria and Morocco, were successful, but the raw American troops received a bloody nose at Kasserine Pass. The vastly outnumbered North African Axis forces did not capitulate until May 1943. Four months earlier, the German Sixth Army had surrendered at Stalingrad, marking the resurgence of the Soviet armies. One should, nonetheless, remember that the distance between Casablanca, Morocco, and Cape Bon, Tunisia, is much the same as that from Brest-Litovsk to Stalingrad, and more Axis troops surrendered at "Tunisgrad" than at Stalingrad. (One major difference was that almost all Axis prisoners of the Western Allies survived their imprisonment, whereas fewer than one in ten of those taken at Stalingrad returned.)

By this time, U.S. production was supplying not only American military needs but also those of most of the Allies—on a scale, moreover, that was simply lavish by comparison to all other armed forces (except possibly that of the Canadians). Everything from the canned-meat product Spam to Sherman tanks and from aluminum ingots to finished aircraft crossed the oceans to the British Isles, the Soviet Union, the Free French, the Nationalist Chinese, the Fighting Poles, and others. (To this day, Soviets refer to any multidrive truck as a *studeborkii,* or Studebaker, a result of the tens of thousands of such vehicles shipped to the Soviet Union.) Moreover, quantity was not produced at the cost of quality. Although some the Allies might have had reservations in regard to Spam, the army trucks, the boots, the small arms, and the uniforms provided by the United States were unsurpassed. (British soldiers noted with some envy that American enlisted men wore the same type of uniform material as did British officers.) The very ships that transported the bulk of this war material—the famous, mass-produced Liberty ships ("rolled out by the mile, chopped off by the yard")—could still be found on the world's oceanic trade routes decades after they were originally scheduled to be scrapped.

After the North African Campaign ended in 1943, the Allies drove the Axis forces from Sicily, and then, in September 1943, they began the interminable Italian Campaign. It is perhaps indicative of the frustrating nature of the war in Italy that the lethargic Allies allowed the campaign to begin with the escape of most Axis forces from Sicily to the Italian peninsula. The Germans were still better at this sort of thing. Winston Churchill to the contrary, Italy was no "soft underbelly"; the Germans conducted well-organized retreats from one mountainous fortified line to the next. The Italian Campaign was occasionally justified for tying down many German troops, but the truth is that it tied down far more Allied forces—British, Americans, Free French, Free Poles, Brazilians, Canadians, Indians, and British and French African colonials among them. German forces in Italy ultimately surrendered in late April 1945, only about a week before Germany itself capitulated.

The military forces of World War II's belligerents, as might be expected in so historically widespread a conflict, varied wildly. The French army in 1939, considered by "experts" the world's best, was actually a slow-moving mass that was often supplied with very good equipment and was led by aged commanders who had learned the lessons of World War I. No other such powerful army was so completely defeated in so short a period of time. The French air force and navy likewise had some excellent equipment as well as more progressive commanders than the army, but France fell before they could have any great impact on the course of battle.

It is generally agreed that the German army was superb—so superb, in fact, that some authorities would venture that the Germans traditionally have had "a genius for war." (Then again, it was hardly a sign of genius to provoke the United States into entering World War I or to invade the Soviet Union in World War II while the British Empire still fought on, before declaring war on the United States six months later.) Obviously, Germany's greatest and traditional military failing has been the denigration of the fighting ability of its opponents. But on the ground, at the operational and tactical levels, the combination of realistic training, strict discipline, and flexible command made the German army probably World War II's most formidable foe. One need only look at a map of Europe from 1939 to 1945 and calculate Germany's enemies compared to its own resources. The Luftwaffe had superbly trained pilots, although their quality fell off drastically as the war turned against their nation. German fighters were easily the equal of any in the world, but surprisingly, given that Hitler's earlier ambitions seemingly demanded a "Ural bomber," the Luftwaffe never put a heavy, four-engine bomber into production. Germany led the world in aerodynamics, putting into squadron service the world's first jet fighter (the Me-262), with swept wings, and even a jet reconnaissance bomber (although German jet engines lagged somewhat behind those of the British). The Luftwaffe also fielded a rocket-powered interceptor, but this craft was as great a menace to its own pilots as to the enemy.

The German navy boasted some outstanding surface vessels, such as the battleship *Bismarck,* but Hitler found the sea alien, and he largely neglected Germany's surface fleet. Submarines were an entirely different matter. U-boat wolf packs decimated Allied North Atlantic shipping, and the Battle of the Atlantic was the only campaign the eupeptic Churchill claimed cost him sleep. German U-boats ravaged the Atlantic coast of the United States, even ranging into Chesapeake Bay in the first months of 1942 to take advantage of inexcusable American naval unpreparedness. As in World War I, convoy was the answer to the German U-boat, a lesson that had to be learned the hard way in both conflicts.

The British army on the whole put in a mediocre performance in World War II. As with the French, although to a lesser degree, the British feared a repetition of the slaughter experienced on the World War I Western Front, and except for the elite units, they rarely showed much dash or initiative. Montgomery, the war's most famous British general, consistently refused to advance until he had great superiority in men and material over his enemy. The British Expeditionary Force fought well and hard in France in 1940 but moved sluggishly thereafter. By far the worst performance of the British army occurred in Malaya-Singapore in the opening months of the war.

For all of their commando tradition, moreover, the British undertook few guerrilla actions in any of their lost colonies. Churchill himself was moved to wonder why the sons of the men who had fought so well in World War I on

the Somme, despite heavy losses, suffered so badly by comparison to the Americans still holding out on Bataan. As late as 1943, the Japanese easily repulsed a sluggish British offensive in the Burma Arakan.

This situation changed drastically when General William Slim took command of the beaten, depressed Anglo-Indian forces in Burma. His was the only sizable Allied force not to outnumber the Japanese, yet he inflicted the worst land defeat in its history on Japan and destroyed the Japanese forces in Burma. Unlike so many Allied generals, Slim led from the front in the worst climate of any battle front. He managed to switch his army's composition from jungle fighters to armored cavalry. Slim's only tangible advantage over his enemy was his absolute control of the air, and with this, he conducted the greatest air supply operation of the war. Although the modest Slim, from a lower-middle-class background, achieved the highest rank in the British army and then became one of Australia's most successful governor-generals, he is almost forgotten today. Yet, considering his accomplishments with limited resources and in different conditions, William Slim should be considered the finest ground commander of World War II.

The Royal Navy suffered from a preponderance of battleship admirals at the opening of the war, most notably Admiral Sir Tom Phillips, who was convinced that "well-handled" capital ships could fight off aerial attacks. He was proved emphatically and fatally wrong when Japanese torpedo-bombers rather swiftly dispatched his *Prince of Wales* and *Repulse* on the third day after the opening of war in the Pacific. The Royal Navy was also handicapped by the fact that not until 1937 did it win control of the Fleet Air Arm (FAA) from the RAF, which had little use for naval aviation and had starved the FAA of funds and attention through the years between the world wars. Although the Royal Navy's carriers were fine ships and their armored flight decks gave them a protection that the U.S. Navy envied, albeit at the cost of smaller aircraft capacity, Fleet Air Arm aircraft were so obsolete that the service had to turn to U.S. models. Even so, the FAA made history on 11 November 1940 when its obsolete Fairy Swordfish torpedo-bombers sank three Italian battleships in Taranto harbor, a feat that the Japanese observed carefully but the Americans did not. British battleships and carriers kept the vital lifeline through the Mediterranean and the Suez Canal open through the darkest days of the war, and together with the Americans and Canadians, they defeated the perilous German submarine menace in the North Atlantic. Significant surface actions of the Royal Navy included the sinking of the German battleship *Bismarck* in May 1941 by an armada of British battleships, cruisers, carriers, and warplanes and the December 1943 destruction of the pocket battleship *Scharnhorst* by the modern battleship *Duke of York.*

The Soviet army almost received its deathblow in the first months of the German invasion. Caught off balance and shorn by Stalin's maniacal purges of its best commanders (whose successors were the dictator's obedient creatures), the Soviet army suffered heavier losses than any other army in history. Yet, spurred by the bestiality of the German war of enslavement and racial extermination and by Stalin's newfound pragmatism, the Red Army was able to spring back and, at enormous cost at the hands of the more professional Germans, fight its way to Berlin.

The Red Air Force developed into one of the most effective tactical air powers of the war. (The Soviets constructed very few heavy bombers.) The Shturmovik was certainly one of the best ground-attack aircraft of the time. The Red Navy, by contrast, apparently did little to affect the course of the war; its main triumph may have been in early 1945 when its submarines sank several large German passenger ships crammed with refugees from the east in the frigid Baltic, the worst maritime disasters in history.

The United States emerged from World War II as the only nation since the time of the Romans to be a dominant power on both land and sea, not to mention in the air. In 1945, the U.S. Air Force and Navy could have defeated any combination of enemies, and only the Soviet army could have seriously challenged the Americans on land. In 1939, the U.S. Army was about the size of that of Romania; by 1945, it had grown to some 12 million men and women.

World War II in the Pacific was the great epic of the U.S. Navy. From the ruin of Pearl Harbor, that service fought its way across the vast reaches of the Pacific Ocean to Tokyo Bay. Eventually, it had the satisfaction of watching the Japanese surrender on board a U.S. Navy battleship in that harbor. Immediately after Pearl Harbor, it was obvious that the aircraft carrier was the ideal capital ship for this war, and the United States virtually mass-produced such warships in the Essex-class. The U.S. Navy had much to learn from its enemy, as demonstrated in the Battle of Savo Island, where Japanese cruisers sank three U.S. and one Australian cruiser in the worst seagoing defeat in U.S. naval history. By the end of the war, almost all of Japan's battleships and carriers had been sunk, most by naval airpower. U.S. Navy submarines succeeded where the German navy had failed in two world wars, as absolutely unrestricted submarine warfare strangled the Japanese home islands, causing near starvation. Equally impressive, the U.S. Navy in the Pacific originated the long-range seatrain, providing American sailors with practically all their needs while they fought thousands of miles from the nearest continental American supply base.

The U.S. Marine Corps was a unique military force. Alone among the marine units of the belligerents, it had its own air and armor arms under its own tactical control. The U.S. Marines were the spearhead that stormed the Japanese-held islands of the Pacific, and the dramatic photograph of a small group of Marines raising the American flag over the bitterly contested island of Iwo Jima became an icon of the war for Americans.

The Japanese army was long on courage but shorter on individual initiative. It was a near medieval force, its men often led in wild banzai charges by sword-flourishing officers against machine-gun emplacements. The entire nation of Nippon was effectively mobilized against the looming Americans under the mindless slogan "Our spirit against their steel." But the history of the Japanese army will be stained for the foreseeable future by the bestial atrocities it practiced against Allied troops and civilians alike; untold numbers of Chinese civilians, for example, were slaughtered during Japanese military campaigns in China. Only two-thirds of Allied troops unfortunate enough to fall into Japanese hands survived to the end of the war. Yet the Japanese army was probably the best light infantry force of the war, and it was certainly the only World War II army that, on numerous occasions, genuinely fulfilled that most hackneyed order "Fight on to the last man!"

The Imperial Japanese Navy and the air arms of the army and navy were superb in the early stages of the Pacific war. Both had extensive combat experience in the Chinese war as well as modern equipment. Japanese admirals were the best in their class between 1941 and 1942, and Japanese air and naval forces, along with the Japanese army itself, quickly wound up European colonial pretensions. Only the vast mobilized resources of the United States could turn the tide against Japan. And except for their complete loss of air control, only in Burma were the Japanese outfought on something like equal terms.

The aftermath of World War II proved considerably different from that of World War I, with its prevailing spirit of disillusionment. Amazingly, all of World War II's belligerents, winners and losers alike, could soon look back and realize that the destruction of the murderous, archaic, racialist Axis regimes had genuinely cleared the way to a better world. All enjoyed peace and the absence of major war. Even for the Soviets, the postwar decades were infinitely better than the prewar years, although much of this measure of good fortune might be attributed simply to the death of Josef Stalin. Except for Great Britain, the British Commonwealth nations and even more so the United States emerged from the war far stronger than when they entered it after enduring a decade of the Great Depression. By the 1950s, both war-shattered Western Europe and Japan were well on their way to becoming major competitors of the United States. The uniquely sagacious and foresighted Western Allied military occupations of Germany, Japan, and Austria in many ways laid the foundations for the postwar prosperity of these former enemy nations. (For the most part, similar good fortune bypassed the less developed nations.) Within a few years, former belligerents on both sides could agree that, despite its appalling casualties and destruction, World War II had been if not perhaps "the Good War" at least something in the nature of a worthwhile war.

Stanley Sandler

See also
Aircraft, Bombers; Aircraft, Fighters; Atlantic, Battle of the; BARBAROSSA, Operation; *Bismarck,* Sortie and Sinking of; Churchill, Sir Winston L. S.; Convoys, Allied; Coral Sea, Battle of the; El Alamein, Battle of; Finnish-Soviet War (30 November 1939–12 March 1940, Winter War); France, Battle for; Hitler, Adolf; Jet and Rocket Aircraft; Kasserine Pass, Battle of; Lend-Lease; Liberty Ships; Malaya Campaign; Midway, Battle of; Montgomery, Sir Bernard Law; North Africa Campaign; Pearl Harbor, Attack on; Poland Campaign; *Prince of Wales* and *Repulse;* Rommel, Erwin Johannes Eugen; Roosevelt, Franklin D.; Singapore; Sino-Japanese War; Stalin, Josef

References
Dziewanowski, M. K. *War at Any Price: World War II in Europe, 1939–1945.* New York: Prentice-Hall, 1991.

Keegan, John. *The Second World War.* New York: Viking, 1989.

Liddell Hart, Basil H. *History of the Second World War.* New York: G. P. Putnam, 1970.

Tucker, Spencer C. *The Second World War.* New York: Palgrave Macmillan, 2003.

Weinberg, Gerhard L. *A World at Arms: A Global History of World War II.* New York: Cambridge University Press, 1994.

Willmott, H. P. *The Great Crusade: A New Complete History of the Second World War.* New York: Free Press, 1991.

Legacy of the War

Across the globe, people greeted the end of World War II with a profound sense of relief. By virtually any measurement, the war had been the most devastating conflict in human history. All nations were touched by it to some degree. The war's economic cost alone has been calculated at perhaps five times that of World War I. In human terms, it claimed half again as many military lives: 15 million versus 10 million for World War I. Including civilians, between 41 and 49 million people died in the war, a figure that would have been much higher without the advent of sulfa and penicillin drugs and blood plasma transfusions.

When the war finally ended, vast stretches of Europe and parts of Asia lay in ruins. Whole populations were utterly exhausted, and many people were starving and living in makeshift shelters. Millions more had been uprooted from their homes and displaced; many of them had been transported to the Reich to work as slave laborers in German industry and agriculture. Transport—especially in parts of western and central Europe and in Japan—was at a standstill. Bridges were blown, rail lines were destroyed, and highways were cratered and blocked. Ports, particularly those in northwestern Europe and Japan, were especially hard hit, and many would have to be rebuilt. Most of the large cities of Germany and Japan were piles of rubble, their buildings mere shells.

Some countries had fared reasonably well. Damage in Britain was not too extensive, and civilian deaths were relatively slight; Denmark and Norway escaped with little destruction. The rapid Allied advance had largely spared Belgium, although the port of Antwerp had been badly damaged. The Netherlands, however, sustained considerable destruction, and portions of the population were starving. The situation in Greece was also dire, and Poland suffered horribly from the brutal German and Soviet occupation policies and armies sweeping back and forth across its territory.

Among the major powers, the USSR was the hardest hit. With 27 million of its people killed in the war, national demographics were dramatically impacted, an effect that has persisted even to the present. In 1959, Moscow announced that the ratio of males to females in the Soviet Union was 45 to 55. Aside from the catastrophic human costs, the Germans had occupied its most productive regions, and the scorched-earth policy practiced by both the Soviets and the Germans resulted in the total or partial destruction of 1,700 towns, 70,000 villages, and 6 million buildings, including 84,000 schools. The Soviet Union also lost 71 million farm animals, including 7 million horses. There was widespread destruction in such great cities as Kiev, Odessa, and Leningrad. Perhaps a quarter of the property value of the USSR was lost in the war, and tens of millions of Soviet citizens were homeless. Simply feeding the Soviet population became a staggering task. All of these factors help to explain the subsequent policies, both internal and external, of the Soviet Union.

Efforts in Europe, as well as in Asia, centered for several years on the pressing problems of providing food, housing, and employment. As it turned out, much of the damage was not as extensive as initially thought, and many machines were still operational once the rubble was removed. In one perverse sense, Germany and Japan benefited from the bombing in that they rebuilt with many of the most modern techniques and systems.

With the end of the war, the liberated nations carried out purges of fascists and collaborationists. Many of these individuals were slain without benefit of trial. In France, 8,000 to 9,000 people were so executed; subsequently, 1,500 more were sentenced to death and executed following regular court procedures. The victorious Allies were determined to bring to justice the leaders of Germany and Japan, whom they held responsible for the war. Two great trials were held, in Nuremberg and Tokyo. Afterward, interest in bringing the guilty to justice waned, even in the cases of those responsible for wartime atrocities. Punishment varied greatly according to nation and circumstance, and it proved virtually impossible to work out acceptable formulas that might punish the guilty when so many people had, to some degree, collaborated with the occupiers.

At the end of the war, it appeared as if the idealistic, left-leaning resistance movements might realize their goals of forging new political, economic, and social institutions to bring about meaningful change. Although most people thought a return to prewar democratic structures was impossible, bright hopes for building new structures in the future were soon dashed. Resistance leaders fell to quarreling among themselves, and the fracturing of the Left, as occurred in France and Italy, made room for the return of the old but still powerful conservative elites. The political structures that ultimately emerged from the war, at least in western Europe, were little changed from those that had preceded it. In much of eastern and central Europe, where the Soviet Union now held sway, there was significant change, including land reform, although this was seldom to the real benefit of the populations involved. Soviet rule also brought widespread financial exactions in the form of reparations and the stifling of democracy.

The war did intensify the movement for European unity. Many European statesmen believed that some means had to be found to contain nationalism, especially German nationalism, and that the best vehicle for that would be the economic integration of their nations, with political unification to follow in what some called the "United States of Europe." They believed that a Germany integrated into the European economy would not be able to act alone. Although Europe was slow in taking steps in that direction, such thinking led, a decade after the end of the war, to the European Common Market.

Asia was also greatly affected by the war. In China, the bitter prewar contest between the Chinese Nationalist Party—the Guomindang, or GMD (Kuomintang, or KMT)—and the Chinese Communist Party resumed in a protracted civil war when Nationalist leader Jiang Jieshi (Chiang Kai-shek) sent troops into Manchuria in an effort to reestablish Nationalist control of that important region. The conflict ended in 1949 with a Communist victory. To

the west, British imperial India dissolved into an independent India and Pakistan.

The United States granted the Philippines delayed independence, but in other areas, such as French Indochina and the Netherlands East Indies, the colonizers endeavored to continue their control. Where the European powers sought to hold on to their empires after August 1945, there would be further bloodshed. The French government, determined to maintain the nation as a great power, insisted on retaining its empire, which led to the protracted Indo-China War. Fighting also erupted in many other places around the world, including Malaya and the Netherlands East Indies. Even where the European powers chose to withdraw voluntarily, as Britain did in Palestine and on the Indian subcontinent, there was often heavy fighting as competing nationalities sought to fill the vacuum. Nonetheless, independence movements in Africa and Asia, stimulated by the long absence of European control during the war, gathered momentum, and over the next two decades, much of Africa and Asia became independent.

One of the supreme ironies of World War II is that Adolf Hitler had waged the conflict with the stated goal of destroying communism. In the end, he had gravely weakened Europe, and rather than eradicating his ideological adversary, he had strengthened it. In 1945, the Soviet Union was one of the two leading world powers, and its international prestige was at an all-time high. In France and Italy, powerful Communist Parties were seemingly poised to take power. The Soviet Union also established governments friendly to it in eastern and central Europe. Under the pressure of confrontation with the West, these states became openly Communist in the years after World War II. In 1948, the Communists made their last acquisition in central Europe in a coup d'état in Czechoslovakia. Communists also nearly came to power in Greece.

Indeed, far from destroying the Soviet Union and containing the United States, Germany and Japan had enhanced the international position of both. Western and Soviet differences meant that, although treaties were negotiated with some of the smaller Axis powers, there were no big-power agreements concerning the future of Germany and Japan. Germany, initially divided into four occupation zones, became two states in 1949: the western Federal Republic of Germany and the Communist German Democratic Republic. Korea also had been "temporarily" divided at the thirty-eighth parallel for the purposes of a Japanese surrender. Unlike Germany, which was reunited in 1990, Korea remained divided as of 2004—another legacy of World War II.

Despite the continued importance of secondary powers

such as Britain and France, the year 1945 witnessed the emergence of a bipolar world, in which there were two superpowers: the United States and the Soviet Union. Added to the confrontational mix was the threat of nuclear war as both governments embarked on a new struggle known as the Cold War.

Spencer C. Tucker

See also

Casualties; Cold War, Origins and Early Course of; International Military Tribunal: Far East; International Military Tribunal: The Nuremberg Trials; Jiang Jieshi; Paris Peace Treaties

References

Black, Cyril E., et al. *Rebirth: A History of Europe since World War II.* Boulder, CO: Westview Press, 1992.

Wheeler, John, and Anthony J. Nicholls. *The Semblance of Peace: The Political Settlement after the Second World War.* New York: W. W. Norton, 1974.

Encyclopedia of
World War II
A Political, Social, and Military History

A

AAA

See Antiaircraft Artillery and Employment.

Aachen, Battle of (13 September–21 October 1944)

Located on the western border of Germany, the city of Aix-la-Chapelle, later Aachen, had been the capital of the Holy Roman Empire; Charlemagne was crowned emperor there in the year 800. Since German dictator Adolf Hitler considered Charlemagne to be the founder of the first German Reich, the city held special status for him. Aachen was the first major German city encountered by U.S. troops, and the five-week-long battle for it gave notice to U.S. forces that the war against the Third Reich was far from over. Lieutenant General Courtney Hodges, commander of the American First Army, had hoped to bypass Aachen from the south, quickly break through the German defenses of the West Wall (Siegfried Line), and reach the Rhine River.

In September 1944, Lieutenant General Gerhard von Schwerin's understrength 116th Panzer Division defended Aachen. Schwerin entered the city on 12 September and quickly concluded that Aachen was lost. He halted the evacuation of the city so that the population might be cared for by the Americans. Only local defense forces prevented occupation of the city on the morning of 13 September. Unaware of this fact, the commander of U.S. VII Corps, Major General J. Lawton Collins, elected to continue his attack on the Siegfried Line. Late on 15 September, however, troops of Major General Clarence R. Huebner's 1st Infantry Division began to surround Aachen from the south and southeast.

Hitler ordered the city evacuated, but Schwerin refused

that order and was relieved of command. Up to 145,000 of the population of 160,000 fled the city. Meanwhile, the pause in Allied operations along the Siegfried Line during Operation MARKET-GARDEN allowed the Wehrmacht the chance to reinforce its West Wall defenses. By the end of September with the collapse of MARKET-GARDEN, operations around Aachen resumed.

From 7 to 20 October, elements of the U.S. VII and XIX Corps strengthened their hold around the city, now defended by the I Panzer Korps of the 116th Panzer Division, 3rd Panzergrenadier Division, and 246th Volksgrenadier Division under Colonel Gerhard Wilck.

On 8 October, U.S. forces began their attack on Aachen. On 10 October, Huebner sent a message into the city, threatening to destroy Aachen if the Germans did not surrender. When this demand was rejected, 300 P-38s and P-47s of the Ninth Tactical Air Force dropped 62 tons of bombs on Aachen on 10 October. U.S. artillery also pounded the city.

On 12 October, Wilck assumed command of some 5,000 German defenders in Aachen. The German troops, supported by assault guns and tanks (mostly Mark IVs), held their positions tenaciously. Also on 12 October, the U.S. fighter-bombers returned and dropped another 69 tons of bombs, and U.S. artillery fired 5,000 rounds.

On 13 October, troops of the 26th Infantry Regiment assaulted the city proper. The fighting was bitter, with the U.S. infantry accompanied by tanks and self-propelled artillery to knock out German armor and reduce strong points. Fighting was house-to-house. Infantry blasted holes in the outer walls of buildings with bazookas and then cleared resistance room by room with small arms and hand grenades. Many Schutzstaffel (SS) troops died at their posts rather than surrender. When German troops west of Aachen tried to relieve the siege in hastily organized counterattacks, American artillery beat them back. Aachen was now completely surrounded, and gradually the German defensive position shrank to a small section of the western part of the city. Wilck's efforts to break out of the city on 18 and 19 October failed, and he surrendered Aachen on 21 October.

The Allied rebuff in Operation MARKET-GARDEN and German resistance at Aachen prevented a quick Allied crossing of the Rhine and bought Hitler time to strengthen his West Wall defenses, but the costs were heavy. U.S. forces took some 12,000 German prisoners, and thousands more Germans were killed. Several hundred civilians also died. U.S. losses of 3,700 men (3,200 from the 30th Infantry Division and 500 from the 1st Infantry Division) were also high, particularly among experienced riflemen. Remarkably, amidst all the ruin and destruction, Aachen's magnificent medieval cathedral survived.

Terry Shoptaugh and Spencer C. Tucker

See also
Collins, Joseph Lawton; Huebner, Clarence Ralph; MARKET-GARDEN, Operation; West Wall, Advance to the
References
MacDonald, Charles. *The Siegfried Line Campaign.* Washington, DC: Department of the Army, 1963.
Whiting, Charles. *Bloody Aachen.* New York: Stein and Day, 1976.

Abe Hiroaki (1890–1949)

Japanese navy admiral. Born on 15 March 1890 at Ehima Prefecture, Abe Hiroaki graduated from the Naval Academy in 1911. He held various positions and commands in the 1920s and 1930s and graduated from the Naval Staff College. He commanded the battleship *Fuso* in 1937 and was promoted to rear admiral in 1938. In December 1941, Abe led Cruiser Division 8 in the attack on Pearl Harbor. Later that month, his forces assisted during the attack on Wake Island.

In June 1942, Abe commanded the cruiser and battleship screen in the Battle of Midway; that August, he led the Vanguard Group in the southwest Pacific. This force, consisting of the battleships *Hiei* and *Kirishima* and the cruisers *Kumano, Suzuya,* and *Chikuma,* was involved in the carrier battles off the Eastern Solomon Islands. In late October, the Vanguard Group, augmented by destroyers, fought in the Battle of the Santa Cruz Islands, which was a tactical victory for Japan but at some cost. The *Chikuma* was especially hard hit.

In early November, the Japanese planned a direct assault on Guadalcanal. Abe was ordered to shell the U.S. air base Henderson Field to prepare for an amphibious assault. As his ships moved southward, they met the defending Allied force commanded by U.S. Rear Admiral Daniel Callaghan on the night of 12–13 November 1942. The resulting battle was one of the fiercest in naval history, and although Callaghan lost two cruisers and four destroyers and was himself killed, he forced Abe and 13,000 Japanese troop reinforcements to turn back. Abe lost two destroyers in the battle itself. His flagship, the *Hiei,* was also crippled and succumbed to subsequent U.S. air attack.

Abe took the blame for the unsuccessful mission, was relieved of his command on 20 December 1942, and resigned from the navy in March 1943. He died in Kamakura, Kanagawa Prefecture, on 6 February 1949.

Harold Wise

See also
Callaghan, Daniel Judson; Guadalcanal Naval Campaign; Pearl Harbor, Attack on; Santa Cruz Islands, Battle of; Solomon Islands, Naval Campaign; Wake Island, Battle of
References
Frank, Richard B. *Guadalcanal.* New York: Random House, 1990.
Morison, Samuel Eliot. *History of United States Naval Operations in World War II.* Vol. 5, *The Struggle for Guadalcanal, August 1942–February 1943.* Boston: Little, Brown, 1949.

Abe Koso (1892–1947)

Japanese navy admiral. Born in Yamagata on 24 March 1892, Abe Koso became a career naval officer. Abe specialized in naval gunnery and served as a naval gunnery officer on ships ranging from destroyers to battleships. Later he commanded cruisers and battleships. By the beginning of World War II, Abe was a rear admiral. During Operation MŌ, the planned invasion of Port Moresby, he commanded the Port Moresby Transport Force. It consisted of 12 transports carrying the army's South Seas Detachment and the navy's Kure 3rd Special Naval Landing Force to Port Moresby. Abe's convoy left Rabaul on 4 May 1942.

On 7 May, the first day of the Battle of the Coral Sea, Abe lost his close-air support when U.S. aircraft sank the light carrier *Shoho.* The Transport Force retired to the north while the main forces slugged it out. Although the Japanese won a tactical victory in the battle, Admiral Inouye Shigeyoshi could no longer provide close-air support to Abe and ordered the invasion postponed until 3 July. Later events caused the invasion to be canceled.

Abe was promoted to vice admiral and given command of the Marshall Islands to prepare for an American invasion there. Ten days after Marines landed on Guadalcanal, Carlson's Raiders landed on Makin Atoll. They wiped out its small garrison and then withdrew to the two submarines that had carried them to the island. Nine Raiders did not make it back to the submarines. They were captured on 21 August by the Japanese relief force. The American prisoners were transferred to Kwajalein, where they were well treated.

In early October 1942, Abe met with a staff officer from Truk. The officer informed Abe that a revised policy allowed him to deal with prisoners locally and not transport them to Japan. Abe ordered Captain Obara Yoshio, commander of the Kwajalein garrison, to execute the prisoners. Despite Obara's protests, Abe insisted. The commander ordered four of his officers to perform the executions. Obara selected the day of Japan's annual memorial to departed heroes, the Yasukuni Shrine festival, as the execution date. On 16 October 1942, in the presence of Abe, the nine Americans were led to a large grave and beheaded.

The Japanese attempted to cover up the crime, but after the war, Marshall Islanders told U.S. authorities about the executions. Abe was arrested and tried on Guam for war crimes. Convicted, he was hanged there on 24 June 1947.

Tim J. Watts

See also

Coral Sea, Battle of the; Inouye Shigeyoshi; Makin Island Raid

References

Dull, Paul S. *A Battle History of the Imperial Japanese Navy (1941–1945)*. Annapolis, MD: Naval Institute Press, 1978.

Morison, Samuel Eliot. *History of United States Naval Operations in World War II*. Vol. 4, *Coral Sea, Midway and Submarine Operations, May 1942–August 1942*. Boston: Little, Brown, 1949.

Smith, George W. *Carlson's Raid: The Daring Marine Assault on Makin*. Novato, CA: Presidio Press, 2001.

Abe Nobuyuki (1875–1953)

Japanese army general. Born in Ishikawa on 24 November 1875, Abe Nobuyuki was trained as an artillery officer. As the commander of the 3rd Field Artillery Regiment between 1918 and 1919, Colonel Abe took part in the Siberian Intervention. Promoted to lieutenant general in 1927, Abe held several important posts, including vice war minister (1928–1930), deputy war minister (1930), commander of the 4th Division (1930–1932), and commander in chief of the Taiwan garrison (1932–1933). Promoted to full general in 1933, Abe served as a member of the Military Council until his retirement in 1936.

When Baron Hiranuma Ki'ichirō resigned as prime minister in the political crisis following the surprise conclusion of the German-Soviet Non-aggression Pact in August 1939, Abe was appointed prime minister. Abe tried to change the course of national policy in the direction of rapprochement with Britain and the United States, but in January 1940, army hard-liners brought about the collapse of the cabinet.

Thereafter Abe held diplomatic assignments, including a term as ambassador to the Republic of China (April–December 1940), as a minister of the House of Peers (May 1942–February 1946), and as the last Japanese governor general of Korea (July 1944–September 1945, while retaining his seat in the House of Peers). Abe died in Tokyo on 7 September 1953.

Tohmatsu Haruo

See also

German-Soviet Non-aggression Pact

References

Conroy, Hilary, and Harry Wray, eds. *Pearl Harbor Reexamined: Prologue to the Pacific War*. Honolulu: University of Hawaii Press, 1990.

Morley, James William. *The China Quagmire: Japan's Expansion on the Asian Continent, 1933–1941*. New York: Columbia University Press, 1943.

———. *Deterrent Diplomacy: Japan, Germany, and the USSR, 1935–1940*. New York: Columbia University Press, 1976.

Shillony, Ben-Ami. *Politics and Culture in Wartime Japan*. Oxford: Clarendon Press, 1981.

Abrams, Creighton Williams (1914–1974)

U.S. Army general. Born in Springfield, Massachusetts, on 15 September 1914, Creighton Abrams graduated from the U.S. Military Academy in 1936 and was commissioned in the cavalry. Assigned to Fort Bliss, Texas, Abrams joined the famed 7th Cavalry Regiment.

He was an early convert to the armored force, and during World War II, he commanded the 37th Tank Battalion of the 4th Armored Division in fighting across Europe, earning a battlefield promotion to colonel and two Distinguished Service Orders. Said his division commander Major General William M. Hoge of Abrams, "The brilliant combat record of Colonel Abrams constitutes one of the sagas of this war. His command was first to cross the Moselle River, he led the advance which resulted in the relief of Bastogne, and his was the first element in Third Army to reach the Rhine." Lieutenant General George S. Patton said of Abrams, "I'm supposed to be the best tank commander in the Army, but I have one peer: Abe Abrams. He's the world's champion."

Following the war, Abrams headed the Department of Tactics at the Armor School, Fort Knox, Kentucky. Later, he commanded the 63rd Tank Battalion in Germany and then the 2nd Armored Cavalry Regiment. During the Korean War, he served in succession as chief of staff of all three U.S. Army corps there. He was promoted to brigadier general in 1956 and then served a Pentagon tour before returning to Germany as assistant commander of the 3rd Armored Division.

Promoted to major general in 1960, Abrams soon after commanded the 3rd Armored Division. He became a lieutenant general in 1963 and commanded V Corps in Europe. In 1964, he was named army vice chief of staff and promoted to full general, a rank he held for the last 10 years of his service. In 1967, Abrams went to Vietnam as deputy U.S. commander and in 1968 succeeded to the top command. During four years in that post, he radically revised the way the war was being conducted, discarding body count as a measure of merit and emphasizing security for the rural population.

In 1972, Abrams became chief of staff of an army in need of rebuilding and leadership. He served in that post for two years, stressing combat readiness and taking care of the soldier. He died in Washington, D.C., on 4 September 1974. Subsequently, the U.S. Army named its new main battle tank the "Abrams" in his honor. Former Chairman of the Joint Chiefs of Staff General John W. Vessey Jr. observed that the success of U.S. armed forces in the 1991 Gulf War was largely attributable to reforms initiated by Abrams.

Lewis Sorley

See also
Ardennes Offensive; Armored Warfare; Bastogne, Battle for
References
Sorley, Lewis. *Thunderbolt: General Creighton Abrams and the Army of His Times*. New York: Simon and Schuster, 1992.
———. *A Better War: The Unexamined Victories and Final Tragedy of America's Last Years in Vietnam*. New York: Harcourt, Brace, 1999.

Abrial, Jean Marie Charles (1879–1962)

French navy admiral. Born at Réalmont, Tarn, France, on 17 December 1879, Jean Abrial entered the French Naval Academy in 1896 and commanded an antisubmarine patrol boat during World War I. During the early 1920s, he commanded a squadron of torpedo boats in the Mediterranean. He was promoted to captain in 1925. Abrial studied at the Naval War College, commanded a cruiser, and held various staff positions. He was promoted to rear admiral in 1931 and to vice admiral in 1936. From 1936 to 1938, he commanded the Mediterranean Squadron. On 23 May 1940, shortly after German forces invaded France, he became commander of Northern French Naval Forces.

Five days later, as Allied troops retreated to the French Channel port of Dunkerque, Allied Supreme Commander Maxime Weygand ordered Abrial and his deputy commander, Lieutenant General Maurice Fagalde, to organize a beachhead there. The two French officers believed Dunkerque could be held successfully against German forces, but on 20 May, France's British allies, having decided withdrawal from the Continent was inevitable, began to organize the withdrawal effort. Abrial learned of this decision when the evacuation started on 26 May, and he quickly organized all available French maritime vessels into an evacuation fleet. Requisitioning all private boats in the area, he began to embark both British and French troops on 29 May. He also demanded equal space for beleaguered French troops aboard British vessels. Altogether, by 4 June, British and French ships had taken off some 364,000 troops, including some 140,000 French.

Abrial, one of the last to leave Dunkerque, moved to Cherbourg, and on 19 June, he surrendered that port to German forces. Remaining in France with the Vichy government following the defeat of France, Abrial was governor-general of Algeria from July 1940 to July 1941, and from November 1942 to March 1943, he was secretary of the navy in the Vichy government.

Abrial was charged with collaboration after the liberation, and in August 1946, he was sentenced to "national indignity" and 10 years of hard labor, which was later commuted to 5 years' imprisonment. Released provisionally in December 1947 and amnestied in 1954, Abrial died at Dordogne in the Tarn on 19 December 1962.

Priscilla Roberts

See also
Dunkerque, Evacuation of; France Campaign; France, Navy; France, Vichy; Weygand, Maxime
References
Auphan, Paul, and Jacques Mordal. *The French Navy in World War II*. Trans. A. C. J. Short. Annapolis, MD: Naval Institute Press, 1959.
Crémieux-Brilhac, Jean-Louis. *Les Français de l'an 40*. 2 vols. Paris: Gallimard, 1990.
Gelb, Norman. *Dunkirk: The Complete Story of the First Step in the Defeat of Hitler*. New York: William Morrow, 1989.
Paxton, Robert O. *Parades and Politics at Vichy: The French Officer Corps under Marshal Pétain*. Princeton, NJ: Princeton University Press, 1966.

Absolute National Defense Zone (Zettai kokubō ken)

Plan adopted in September 1943 for a Japanese defensive line in the Pacific against the Allied counteroffensive. At the beginning of 1943, Japan lost Guadalcanal in the Solomon Islands in the southwest Pacific, and in August and September 1943, the United States took back the Aleutian Islands of Attu and Kiska. This situation led Imperial General Headquarters in Tokyo to reexamine the planned defensive perimeter in the Pacific Ocean area. Imperial General Headquarters judged that it would be difficult to hold an overextended front line against an Allied counteroffensive, and it thus decided to withdraw forces from some areas in order to shrink the defensive zone and make better use of available resources.

On 25 September 1943, Imperial General Headquarters drew a line that included the Kurile Islands, Ogasawara Islands, Mariana Islands, Caroline Islands, western New Guinea, and the Sunda Islands to Burma. This area was labeled the *Absolute National Defense Zone.* The new defensive perimeter thus excluded the Marshall Islands, the Solomon Islands, and eastern New Guinea. The army and navy General Staffs planned to reorganize and build up the military and naval forces inside the zone for a future decisive battle with U.S. forces.

On 30 September, the plan was officially declared in effect during a meeting at which Emperor Hirohito was in attendance. The plan called for the following: (1) establish an Absolute National Defense Zone to meet an Allied counteroffensive; (2) improve relations with the Soviet Union; (3) bring the war in China to a victorious conclusion; (4) strengthen relations with Germany; (5) educate the peoples of Japanese-occupied areas and develop the Greater East Asia Co-prosperity Sphere; (6) reorganize the nation for total war; and (7) intensify propaganda against the Allies.

Despite this plan, the Japanese army continued to be preoccupied with China to the detriment of the defense of the Pacific islands, and the navy persisted in holding Truk Island in the central Pacific, which was outside the defense zone. The failure of the army and navy to reach complete consensus regarding the defense zone was of considerable benefit to the Allies in 1944 and 1945.

Kotani Ken

See also

Hirohito, Emperor of Japan; Japan, Role in War; Mariana Islands, Naval Campaign; Marshall Islands, Naval Campaign; Truk

References

Evans, David, and Mark Peattie. Kaigun: *Strategy, Tactics, and Technology in the Imperial Japanese Navy, 1887–1941.* Annapolis, MD: Naval Institute Press, 1997.

Kirby, Woodburn. *The War against Japan.* Vol. 3. London: Her Majesty's Stationery Office, 1958.

Van der Vat, Dan. *The Pacific Campaign.* New York: Touchstone, 1991.

Adachi Hatazō (1890–1947)

Japanese army general. Born in Chiba on 17 June 1890, Adachi Hatazō graduated from the Military Academy in 1910 and the Army War College in 1922. Promoted to major in 1926 and to lieutenant colonel in 1930, he was district commander of the Guandong (Kwantung) Army Railway Unit in 1933. He was promoted to colonel in 1934, and he commanded the 12th Infantry Regiment in 1936.

At the beginning of the Sino-Japanese War in 1937, Adachi commanded the 37th Infantry Division. As chief of staff of the North China Area Army, Adachi played a prominent role in defeating Chinese forces during the CHŪGEN Operation of May 1941. He was promoted to lieutenant general in 1940.

Following the death of Lieutenant General Horii Tomitaro in November 1942, Adachi was appointed commander in chief of the newly formed Eighteenth Army at Rabaul, which was designated for the defense of New Guinea and numbered at peak strength some 140,000 men. The Eighteenth Army's first full-scale landing attempt on New Guinea was shattered in the March 1943 Battle of the Bismarck Sea, when U.S. air attacks sank all of Adachi's eight transports, resulting in the loss of 3,000 men and a great amount of supplies and equipment.

Allied air superiority forced Adachi to bring his troops ashore in scattered small formations along more than 400 miles of the north New Guinea coast. A lack of transport and air cover inhibited the concentration of Eighteenth Army forces and led to the deaths of many of Adachi's men from hunger and disease.

When on 22 April 1944 Allied forces went ashore at Hollandia and Aitape, key strategic points on the north-central New Guinea coast, Adachi skillfully assembled his remaining 60,000 troops and moved them 300 miles overland to contest the Allied forces. Adachi ordered an all-out attack on 10 July 1944, and his forces successfully broke through the Allied front lines in place, but the early attacks soon lost momentum and Adachi had to withdraw. In the struggle for Aitape, Adachi lost more than 10,000 men. Thereafter, the Eighteenth Army simply struggled to survive Australian army mopping-up operations. On 13 September 1945, Adachi surrendered with only about 10,000 of his original force alive.

Although Adachi was an officer of great personal integrity and fighting ability, especially in adversity, his offensive tactics have been called into question and contrasted with those of his superior, General Imamura Hitoshi, commander in chief of the Eighth Area Army at Rabaul. Adachi's repeated attempts to attack superior Allied forces led to unnecessarily heavy casualties. In contrast, Imamura on New Britain Island prepared his men for sustained defensive operations and followed a "force-in-being" strategy throughout the remainder of the war.

After the war, the Australian government prosecuted

Adachi for war crimes, specifically the mistreatment of Allied prisoners of war at Rabaul. He was convicted and was sentenced to life imprisonment. Adachi committed suicide in prison at Rabaul on 10 September 1947.

Tohmatsu Haruo

See also

Bismarck Sea, Battle of; Eichelberger, Robert Lawrence; Hollandia, Battle of; Horii Tomitaro; Imamura Hitoshi; MacArthur, Douglas; New Guinea Campaign; Papuan Campaign

References

Drea, Edward. *In the Service of the Emperor.* Lincoln: University of Nebraska Press, 1998.

Komatsu, Shigeo. *Ai no tōsotsu Adachi Hatazō* (Beloved commander: Adachi Hatazō). Tokyo: Kōjinsha, 1989.

Long, Gavin. *The Final Campaigns.* Canberra: Australian War Memorial, 1963.

Adam, Wilhelm (1877–1949)

German army general. Born in Ansbach in Bavaria on 15 September 1877, Wilhelm Adam joined the German army in 1897. He began his military career in a communications unit but then transferred to the engineers. In 1899 he was commissioned a lieutenant. He won promotion to captain in 1911 and at the end of World War I served as a staff officer in a Bavarian reserve division. Adam won promotion to major in 1919 and to colonel in 1927.

During the interwar period Adam served in staff positions, including chief of staff of the 7th Infantry Division. In 1930 he headed the Truppenamt, the secret German General Staff. That same year he was promoted to Generalmajor (U.S. equiv. brigadier general) and in 1931 he was advanced to Generalleutnant (U.S. equiv. major general). In late 1933, after Adolf Hitler came to power, Adam was assigned to Bavaria as commander of its military district. In 1935, he was promoted to General der Infanterie (U.S. equiv. lieutenant general) and named to command the newly created Wehrmachtakademie (War Academy) in Berlin. He served there until March 1938, when he became commander of Army Group 2, which had headquarters at Kassel and was responsible for the defense of western Germany. Adam expressed concern that German fortifications along the western border were inadequate to protect against a combined British-French attack, a view that brought him into conflict with Hitler.

That summer, at Hitler's insistence, German military planners began preparing an invasion of Czechoslovakia, which necessitated pulling troops from the Rhineland. Adam and others including army Chief of Staff General Ludwig Beck argued strongly against the invasion, fearing it would provoke French and British action. In July, Adam went so far as to characterize the planned attack on Czechoslovakia as a "war of desperation."

Hitler was well aware of these sentiments. Beck was relieved of his command in August 1938 and replaced by General Franz Halder. In November, Adam was also sacked, replaced by General Erwin von Witzleben. Adam retired in December 1938. His removal was part of Hitler's effort to secure complete control of the army. Portions of Adam's unpublished memoirs were used after the war as background information at the International Military Tribunal at Nuremberg. Adam died in Garmisch-Partenkirchen on 8 April 1949.

Laura J. Hilton

See also

Beck, Ludwig; Halder, Franz; Hitler, Adolf; International Military Tribunal: Nuremberg; Munich Conference and Preliminaries; Witzleben, Erwin von

References

Deutsch, Harold C. *Hitler and His Generals: The Hidden Crisis, January–June 1938.* Minneapolis: University of Minnesota Press, 1974.

O'Neill, Robert. *The German Army and the Nazi Party, 1933–1939.* New York: Heinemann, 1966.

Wheeler-Bennett, John. *The Nemesis of Power.* London: Macmillan, 1954.

Admiralty Islands Campaign (29 February–18 May 1944)

Island group off of New Guinea seized by Allied forces in 1944. Located 200 miles north of New Guinea, the Admiralty Islands were an attractive target to the commander of the Southwest Pacific Area, General Douglas MacArthur. Seeadler Harbor, an enclosed harbor formed by Manus and Los Negros Islands, and the airstrips on the islands provided a base complex to support subsequent operations against Japanese strong points in New Guinea and complete the isolation of Rabaul. The latter, a major Japanese air and naval base on New Britain Island, had been the major objective of Allied operations in the South Pacific since the summer of 1942.

MacArthur planned to invade the Admiralties in a division-size operation on 1 April 1944, but air reconnaissance in February 1944 indicated the islands were lightly defended. Ignoring the estimates of his intelligence staff that there were more than 4,000 Japanese troops in the islands who would likely put up stiff resistance, MacArthur decided to gamble and advance the landing to the end of February, even though all the forces earmarked for the operation would not be ready by that point. He planned to land a reconnaissance force on Los Negros and then rush in reinforcements faster than the Japanese could react.

The Admiralties operation began on 29 February with the landing of 1,000 assault troops from the 1st Cavalry Division at Hyane Harbor on the east coast of Los Negros. There were 2,000 Japanese on Los Negros; however, their commander had expected a landing on the other side of the island and placed only a few defenders at Hyane. The cavalrymen quickly captured Momote airfield and set up a defensive perimeter. Over the next days, aided by air support, they beat back piecemeal Japanese counterattacks. MacArthur poured in reinforcements, and by the morning of 4 March, the last Japanese counterattack had been defeated.

On 9 March, U.S. troops went ashore at Salami Plantation on the other side of Los Negros, and in 10 days of heavy fighting, the Americans secured the island. In the meantime, American troops landed on Manus Island west of Lorengau airfield, and with the seizure of the airfield on 18 March, the important part of the island was in American hands.

The last Japanese stronghold in the Admiralties, Pityilu Island, was captured on 31 March. Except for a few stragglers in the jungles of Manus, all of the Japanese defenders in the Admiralties had been wiped out. U.S. casualties were 330 killed and 1,189 wounded. MacArthur's gamble to advance the date of the Admiralties landing had paid off. The initial invaders had fought well even though outnumbered on 29 February, and once MacArthur could bring to bear all of the 1st Cavalry Division, the Japanese were doomed.

With the capture of the Admiralties, MacArthur could now extend his operations. Most important, at a time when the Joint Chiefs of Staff were deliberating future strategy in the Pacific war, the successful Admiralties operation helped convince them to underwrite MacArthur's ambition to liberate the Philippine Islands by an offensive along the north coast of New Guinea.

John Kennedy Ohl

See also
MacArthur, Douglas; New Guinea Campaign; Rabaul; Southwest Pacific Theater

References
The Admiralties: Operations of the 1st Cavalry Division, 29 February–18 May 1944. Washington, DC: Historical Division, U.S. War Department, 1945.

Miller, John, Jr. *Cartwheel: The Reduction of Rabaul.* Washington, DC: Office of the Chief of Military History, Department of the Army, 1959.

Morison, Samuel Eliot. *History of United States Naval Operations in World War II.* Vol. 6, *Breaking the Bismarcks Barrier, 22 July 1941–1 May 1944.* Boston: Little, Brown, 1950.

Taaffe, Stephen R. *MacArthur's Jungle War: The 1944 New Guinea Campaign.* Lawrence: University Press of Kansas, 1998.

Afghanistan

Afghanistan was formally nonaligned during World War II, but there were nonetheless complex diplomatic, political, and military developments of consequence in and around that country. As early as 1907, the British Committee of Imperial Defense had concluded, "The gates of India are in Afghanistan and the problem of Afghanistan dominates the situation in India." This assessment reflected the fact that the country was strategically situated between British India and Russia and of considerable interest to both in the diplomatic and political maneuvering of the nineteenth century known as "the Great Game."

Afghanistan was effectively positioned for neutrality in the years before World War II. The February 1921 Soviet-Afghanistan Treaty of mutual recognition was followed in 1926 by a formal nonaggression pact between the two countries. The government in Kabul clearly saw the Soviet Union as an effective counterweight to British power and influence in the region. The November 1921 Anglo-Afghanistan Treaty had accorded Afghanistan full and formal independence, although Britain remained the most important power in terms of immediate control over territory in South Asia, including India and what would become Pakistan.

The Afghanistan constitution, adopted in April 1923 and not replaced until 1963, declared the country to be free and independent, with a free press and free economy. Other democratic guarantees were made explicit in writing, although they were not always followed in actual practice. A constitutional monarchy governed the country, with Islam the established religion. Moderate rule dating from the 1930s was an advantage in dealing with the turmoil and uncertainty of the period.

With the approach of World War II, Afghan leaders established broader ties with Germany. In 1935, they decided to rely mainly on Germany for economic and military modernization, and the following year Germany hosted the Afghan hockey team as well as visiting senior officials as special guests at the Berlin Olympic Games. Weekly air service between Berlin and Kabul commenced in 1938. The German Todt began construction and improvements of airfields, bridges, roads, and industrial plants. German officers began training the Afghanistan military and introduced modern equipment, techniques, and weapons. In diplomatic and political terms, the government in Kabul saw Germany as a counterweight to both Britain and the Soviet Union. Meanwhile, the British government, irritated by Kabul's partnership with Germany, refused to aid Afghanistan in territorial and related disputes with the Soviet Union. Despite the British attitude, Afghan leaders generally saw Britain in positive terms.

After World War II began, developments pressed

Afghanistan toward the Allied camp. The June 1941 German invasion of the Soviet Union and the August 1941 British-Soviet invasion of Iran meant Afghanistan was virtually surrounded by Allied-controlled territory. In preparation for a possible German invasion, antitank mines were laid in the Khyber Pass, and other defensive measures were taken. At Allied insistence, Afghanistan expelled German and Italian representatives in the country and severed all ties with the Axis powers.

Arthur I. Cyr

See also

BARBAROSSA, Operation; India; Iran; Todt Organization
References
Gregorian, Vartan. *The Emergence of Modern Afghanistan.* Stanford, CA: Stanford University Press, 1969.
Toynbee, Arnold, ed. *Survey of International Affairs, 1939–1946.* London: Oxford University Press, 1952.

Africa

Africa was an important theater of operations in World War II. The continent offered war materials and important routes for air and sea communications. Essential to Allied strategic planning was control of the Suez Canal in Egypt, and during the demands of the Battle of Britain, British Prime Minister Winston L. S. Churchill had to divert scant British military resources there. Had the Axis powers taken that vital waterway, all British shipping to and from India would have been forced to detour around the Cape of Good Hope, doubling the length of the voyage.

Securing the vital oil supplies of the Middle East was another important consideration for Allied planners. From Cairo, the British Middle East Command directed operations to secure the Suez Canal and then to take the offensive against Italian forces invading from Libya and resident in East Africa.

Unlike World War I, World War II saw no fighting in southern Africa. The Union of South Africa, a British dominion, rallied to the British cause and made major contributions to the Allied war effort. The French African empire was another situation entirely. Following the defeat of France, most of the empire remained loyal to the new Vichy regime, although Chad declared early for Free French leader General Charles de Gaulle.

Allied operations occurred at Dakar and Madagascar and in the Horn of Africa in Italian East Africa, but most of the fighting took place in French North Africa and in northeast Africa. The road from Tripoli in western Libya through Benghazi and east to Alexandria, Egypt—the Benghazi

Handicap—was the primary scene of fighting as Allied and Axis ground forces engaged in tactical patterns, advancing and retreating along the narrow coastal band of desert. Benito Mussolini's Italian forces invaded Egypt from Libya in September 1940. The fighting there seesawed back and forth with both sides increasing the stakes. Finally, with the British offensive at El Alamein and simultaneous British and U.S. landings in French North Africa, Axis forces there were caught in a vise. The continent was cleared of Axis troops in the Battle of Tunis in May 1943.

The war had tremendous influence on African nationalism, often because of the role African troops played in the war effort. General Charles de Gaulle acknowledged during the conflict that France owed a special debt of gratitude to its African empire for providing France the base and resources that enabled it to reenter the war in its final phases. It was thanks to the French colonial empire that the independent existence of France was continuously preserved. De Gaulle pledged a new relationship between metropolitan France and its colonies after the conflict.

Although Churchill was very much an imperialist, he could not override the strong anticolonial attitudes expressed by the governments of the United States and Soviet Union. U.S. President Franklin D. Roosevelt had often declared himself opposed to European colonialism, and when he attended the Casablanca Conference in early 1943, Roosevelt denounced French imperial practices. Soviet leader Josef Stalin often denounced Western imperialism, although this stance did not prevent him from practicing it himself in the case of eastern and central Europe, nor did it keep him from requesting bases in Libya.

Nationalism found fertile ground in those African states that had been cut off from the mother countries during the war, especially in the case of the French and Belgian African possessions. Serious uprisings against French rule occurred both in Madagascar and at Sétif in Algeria. French authorities put these down with significant loss of life. Repression only temporarily quieted nationalism, which continued to feed on the lack of meaningful political reform.

After the war, Italy lost its African empire save Italian Somaliland as a mandate; Libya became independent. Nationalism also affected the colonial African empires of Britain, Belgium, France, and Portugal. In 1945, Ethiopia, Egypt (nominally), Liberia, and the Union of South Africa were the only free states in Africa. Over the next two decades, however, most of the African states secured independence. Sometimes this occurred peacefully and sometimes with significant loss of life.

In a very real sense, World War II was a great watershed for Africa. Its outcome led to a fulfillment of the nationalism that had first washed over the continent in World War I. Unfortunately, the governments of many of the newly independent states seemed incapable of managing effectively the development of the continent's vast resources and the education of its people.

Spencer C. Tucker

See also

Casablanca Conference; Dakar, Attack on; de Gaulle, Charles; East Africa Campaign; Egypt; El Alamein, Battle of; North Africa Campaign; Roosevelt, Franklin D.; South Africa, Union of; Stalin, Josef; Tunis, Battle of

References

Albertini, Rudolf von. *Decolonization: The Administraion and Future of the Colonies, 1919–1960.* Trans. Francisca Garvie. Garden City, NY: Doubleday, 1971.

Barbour, Nevill, ed. *A Survey of French North Africa [The Maghrib].* New York: Oxford University Press, 1962.

Osborne, Richard E. *World War II in Colonial Africa: The Death Knell of Colonialism.* Indianapolis, IN: Riebel-Roque Publishing, 2001.

Afrika Korps

The Deutsches Afrika Korps (DAK), better known as the Afrika Korps (Africa Corps), was the name given to the initial two German armor divisions sent to Libya in 1941 as part of Operation SONNENBLUME (SUNFLOWER). Commanded by Major General Erwin Rommel, the Afrika Korps would grow and change in character as Rommel received promotions and as other commanders took over, but its legendary mystique would forever be associated with Rommel, "the Desert Fox."

The DAK's 5th Light Division began to arrive in Libya in February 1941 (in August it was officially reconstituted as the 21st Panzer Division). Elements of the 15th Panzer Division arrived in April. At various times other units were added to, or subtracted from, the Afrika Korps. Thus at the time of Operation CRUSADER (11 November–8 December 1941), the then-nonmotorized Afrika Division was attached,

Axis air equipment and installations took a heavy pounding from bombers of the U.S. Army Air Forces as they pursued Field Marshal Erwin Rommel's retreating Afrika Korps through Libya and Tripoli to the Tunisian coast. This former hangar was located at Castel Benito Airdrome. (Library of Congress)

as was the Italian Savona Division. At the time of the Battle of El Alamein in November 1942, the DAK consisted of the 15th and 21st Panzer Divisions, the 90th and 164th Light Motorized Infantry Divisions, the Ramcke Parachute Brigade, the Italian Giovani Fascisti Regiment, and assorted supporting units. During the Tunisia Campaign, the 10th Panzer Division was added.

Because North Africa was an Italian theater, the DAK was technically subordinate to the Italian High Command and thus affected by the variable winds of coalition warfare. The commanders of the DAK often exceeded their authority and could always (and frequently did) appeal directly to Berlin. The DAK was also largely dependent on supply convoys. Thus the ebb and flow of the naval war in the Mediterranean directly influenced DAK operations, especially fuel supplies. As a consequence of a deteriorating naval situation for the Axis powers in the Mediterranean, most of the officers and men arrived in or departed from Africa by air, especially after 1941.

Joining with the better-trained and better-led Italian units shipped to Libya in early 1941, the DAK went on the offensive, advancing quickly to the Egyptian border and laying siege to Tobruk. It would be involved in British Operations BREVITY, BATTLEAXE, and CRUSADER and in the Battles of Gazala and El Alamein. It formed the core of Axis forces in the retreat across Libya to Tunisia and in the ensuing battles there including Kasserine Pass and El Guettar. The DAK ended the war serving under Italy's best general, Marshal Giovanni Messe, who commanded the First Italian Army. The DAK's last commander, General Hans Cramer, surrendered with the DAK on 13 May 1943.

More than 1 million Axis soldiers served in Africa, and 260,000 of them were German. Although the wisdom of sending German forces to Africa may be questioned, certainly the major mistake Adolf Hitler made was in not sending sufficient resources early. Lieutenant General Wilhelm Ritter von Thoma's study, prepared for Hitler before the dispatch of the DAK, recommended that Germany send four divisions or none to North Africa. This recommendation was based on the difficulty of supplying forces in North Africa and on all that would be required to conquer Egypt in conjunction with Italian forces. Had four divisions been sent at the beginning, Rommel in all probability would have secured the Suez Canal, and his victory would have had a major impact on the course of the war. But Hitler only made a halfhearted effort in a theater he always considered to be secondary. The majority of German forces arrived during the Tunisia Campaign, and only a small percentage of them belonged to the DAK.

In the North African fighting, 18,594 Germans died, with another 3,400 missing in action and presumed lost. Approximately 101,784 Germans became prisoners following the Allied conquest of Tunisia.

Jack Greene

See also
Bastico, Ettore; El Alamein, Battle of; Gazala, Battle of; Hitler, Adolf; Kasserine Pass, Battle of; North Africa Campaign; Rommel, Erwin Johannes Eugen; Thoma, Wilhelm Ritter von; Tobruk, First Battle for, Second Battle for, Third Battle of; Tunisia Campaign

References
Bender, Roger James, and Richard D. Law. *Uniforms, Organization and History of the Afrika Korps.* San Jose, CA: Bender Publishing, 1973.
Greene, Jack, and Alessandro Massignani. *Rommel's North Africa Campaign.* Conshohocken, PA: Combined Publishing, 1994.
Jentz, Thomas L. *Tank Combat in North Africa: The Opening Rounds.* Atglen, PA: Schiffer Military History, 1998.
Watson, Bruce Allen. *Exit Rommel: The Tunisian Campaign, 1942–1943.* Westport, CT: Praeger, 1999.

Ainsworth, Walden Lee "Pug" (1886–1960)

U.S. Navy admiral. Born on 10 November 1886 in Minneapolis, Minnesota, Walden Ainsworth graduated from the University of Minnesota in 1905 and the U.S. Naval Academy in 1910. Ainsworth participated in navy operations against Veracruz, Mexico, in 1914. During World War I, Ainsworth served on transports as a gunnery officer. Commissioned an ensign in 1919, Ainsworth was an ordnance specialist for two years ashore before returning to sea as an executive officer of a transport. Ainsworth was then an inspector of ordnance at Pittsburgh, Pennsylvania. He was an instructor at the Naval Academy (1928–1931), and he served at the New York Navy Yard. He was then stationed in the Panama Canal Zone (1934–1935) and graduated from the Naval War College before returning to sea as executive officer of the battleship *Mississippi*. He headed the Naval Reserve Officers' Training Corps (ROTC) unit at Tulane University from 1938 to 1940.

Promoted to captain, Ainsworth commanded Destroyer Squadron 2 in the Atlantic in 1940 and 1941 and then was assigned to Vice Admiral William F. Halsey's staff. At the end of 1941, Ainsworth took command of the battleship *Mississippi*. Promoted to rear admiral (July 1942), Ainsworth became commander, Destroyers, Pacific Fleet. He took a leading role in the Solomon Islands Campaign, commanding the bombardment of the Japanese airfield at Munda during 4–5 January 1943, long considered a textbook operation.

As commander of Cruiser Division 9 (January 1943–October 1944), Ainsworth commanded three cruisers and five destroyers escorting the U.S. invasion force to New Georgia. He fought in the Battle of Kula Gulf (5–6 July 1943), for which he was awarded the Navy Cross. He also fought in the Battle of Kolombangara (12–13 July 1943) and saw action in the Marianas, Guam, Leyte Gulf, and Peleliu. Ainsworth then commanded Cruisers and Destroyers, Pacific Fleet (October 1944–July 1945).

After the war, Ainsworth commanded the Fifth Naval District (August 1945–December 1948) until his retirement as a vice admiral. He died on 7 August 1960 in Bethesda, Maryland. The destroyer escort *Ainsworth* was named for him.

Gary Kerley

See also

Guam, Battle for; Halsey, William Frederick, Jr.; Kolombangara, Battle of; Kula Gulf, Battle of; Leyte Gulf, Battle of; Mariana Islands, Naval Campaign; New Georgia, Battle of; Peleliu, Battle of; Solomon Islands, Naval Campaign

References

Morison, Samuel Eliot. *History of United States Naval Operations in World War II*. Vol. 5, *The Struggle for Guadalcanal, August 1942–February 1943*. Boston: Little, Brown, 1949.

———. *History of United States Naval Operations in World War II*. Vol. 8, *New Guinea and the Marianas, March 1944–August 1944*. Boston: Little, Brown, 1953.

Airborne Forces, Allied

The concept of airborne forces originated in 1918 during World War I when Colonel William Mitchell, director of U.S. air operations in France, proposed landing part of the U.S. 1st Division behind German lines in the Metz sector of the Western Front. Thus was born the idea of parachuting or air-landing troops behind enemy lines to create a new flank, what would be known as *vertical envelopment*. The concept was put into action in the 1930s.

The U.S. Army carried out some small-scale experiments at Kelly and Brooks Fields in 1928 and 1929, and in 1936 the Soviets demonstrated a full-blown parachute landing during Red Army maneuvers. Some 1,500 men were dropped in the exercise. One observer—Major General A. P. Wavell—commented that the previous year vehicles had also been landed by aircraft.

During World War II, the Soviets maintained an airborne corps and numerous Guards Airborne Divisions. These troops, although elite, were never used for strategic purposes. However, on several occasions the Soviets dropped parachute troops behind German lines to aid partisan operations and to disrupt German lines of communication. Ominously for the paratroopers, there were no operations in which drives of ground troops were coordinated with parachute operations to relieve these troops once they had been committed to battle.

British reaction to the reports from the Soviet Union was one of mild interest only, although some antiparachutist exercises took place in Eastern Command, in which Lieutenant Colonel F. A. M. Browning (commanding the 2nd Battalion of the Grenadier Guards) took part. Browning was later, as Lieutenant General Sir Frederick Browning, to command all British airborne forces in World War II. The matter then rested until the Germans showed how effective parachute and air-landing troops were when they carried out their spectacular landings in 1940 in Norway, Denmark, and the Netherlands.

Although manpower demands in Britain in 1940 were such that it should have been impossible to raise a parachute force of any significance, nevertheless at the urging of Prime Minister Winston L. S. Churchill, by August 1940, 500 men were undergoing training as parachutists. Fulfillment of Churchill's order that the number be increased to 5,000 had to await additional equipment and aircraft.

Gliderborne troops were part of the plan, and various gliders were under consideration as troop-carrying aircraft. Inevitably such a new branch of infantry was beset with problems, mainly of supply, and there was also a body of resistance to the concept itself in the regular units of the British army. This attitude often led battalions to post their least effective men to such new units merely to get rid of them; the best men were jealously guarded by their commanding officers.

The War Office (representing the British army) and the Air Ministry (representing the Royal Air Force [RAF]) had to agree on aircraft. However, because Bomber Command was becoming aggressively conservative of aircraft, the only plane initially available for training and operations was the Whitley bomber. Aircraft stocks available to airborne forces were initially severely limited until a supply of Douglas C-47 and DC-3 Dakota (Skytrain in U.S. service) aircraft was established, whereon the parachute troops found their perfect drop aircraft. Gliders were also developed, and the American Hamilcar design could carry a light tank.

Progress in developing airborne forces was slow; Royal Air Force objections were constant, in view of the pressure on the RAF to carry the continental war to Germany by means of the strategic bombing campaign. There is no doubt, however, that once the United States came into the war, the situation eased enormously, and equipment became readily available from the United States that Britain was unable to manufacture.

To provide more men for the airborne forces, the War Office decided in 1941 that whole battalions were to be transferred en masse, even though extra training would be needed to bring many men up to the standards of fitness for airborne troops. At the same time, the Central Landing Establishment became the main training center for airborne forces. The 1st Parachute Brigade was established under the command of Brigadier General R. N. Gale, consisting of four parachute battalions. Initially three battalions were formed, which exist to this day in the British army as 1st, 2nd, and 3rd Battalions, Parachute Regiment.

The Glider Pilot Regiment, also formed in 1941, was based at Haddenham, near Oxford, having moved from Ringway (now Manchester Airport). Pilots were recruited from among army and RAF volunteers, but they were part of the army once trained. Airborne forces are infantry, but they have to be fitter than the average soldier, and so training was rigorous. Troops were trained to endure in the cold, in wet weather, and in heat. They had to be fit to withstand the impact of the landing and to fight alone with light weapons and without support for some days.

The airborne concept at that time was twofold: to raid, in which case troops would be extracted by land or sea after the operation (such as the attack on the German radar station at Bruneval in northern France) or to land at the rear of the enemy to capture a strategic target. Two examples of the latter are the Orne bridge landing on D day in June 1944 and Operation MARKET-GARDEN (MARKET was the airborne portion) the following September when the 1st Airborne Division tried to capture the bridges across the Rhine at Arnhem in Holland.

Airborne forces were regarded, justifiably, as an elite force, but they were a force of considerable strength by the end of the war. Despite the losses suffered at Arnhem, where the 2nd Battalion of the 1st Parachute Regiment held the northern end of the road bridge for four days against two German Schutzstaffel (SS) panzer divisions, the 1st Airborne Division was again up to strength for the Rhine crossing operation in March 1945.

British airborne forces were also engaged in the Far East, and the 44th Indian Airborne Division came into being there. In the Pacific Theater, airborne operations were on a smaller scale than in Europe because the jungle limited the ability to drop large numbers of troops.

The first U.S. airborne division was the 82nd, a conversion of the 82nd Infantry (all-American) Division, formed in March 1942. Major General Omar N. Bradley commanded the division, with Brigadier General Matthew B. Ridgway as his assistant. Ridgway was appointed divisional commander as a major general in June 1942, and the division became the 82nd Airborne Division that August. The 82nd went to North Africa in April 1943, just as German resistance in the theater was ending. It took part in operations in Sicily and Normandy, and under the command of Major General James M. Gavin, it participated in Operation MARKET in the Nijmegen-Arnhem area and also in the Ardennes Offensive.

The 101st Airborne Division was activated in August 1942 with a nucleus of officers and men from the 82nd Division. The 101st was commanded by Major General William C. Lee, one of the originators of U.S. airborne forces. The division left for England in September 1943. Lee had a heart attack in the spring of 1944, and the division was taken over by Major General Maxwell D. Taylor, who led it through D day and Operation MARKET, when it secured the bridge at Eindhoven. The division distinguished itself in the defense of Bastogne during the German Ardennes Offensive.

Three other U.S. airborne divisions were established: the 11th, which served in the Pacific and jumped into Corregidor Island and fought in the Battle of Manila; the 17th, which rapidly moved to Europe for the German Ardennes Offensive and then jumped in the Rhine Crossing with the British 6th Airborne Division; and the 13th, which, although it arrived in France in January 1945, never saw action.

Cooperation between British and U.S. airborne forces was very close. When the U.S. 101st Airborne arrived in England, it was installed in a camp close to the training area for the British 6th Airborne Division, which had prepared much of the camp in advance. Training and operational techniques were almost identical, and there were common exercises and shoots to create close bonds among troops. There were also frequent personnel exchanges to cement friendship. Similar arrangements were made between the U.S. 82nd Airborne and the British 1st Airborne Division.

Parachute training in the United States was centered at Fort Benning, Georgia, and in 1943, some 48,000 volunteers started training, with 30,000 qualifying as paratroopers. Of those rejected, some were kept for training as air-landing troops. In Britain, Polish troops were also trained as parachutists to form the Polish 1st Parachute Brigade, which fought at Arnhem in Operation MARKET. Contingents from France, Norway, Holland, and Belgium were also trained, many of whom served operationally in the Special Air Service Brigade.

One great contribution made by the United States to the common good was the formation and transfer to England of the U.S. Troop Carrier Command. As noted previously, transport aircraft shortages had bedeviled airborne forces' training and operations from the outset. The arrival of seemingly endless streams of C-47 aircraft (known to the

British as the DC-3 or Dakota) was a major help. Further, the Royal Air Force in 1944 had nine squadrons of aircraft, or a total of 180 planes, dedicated to airborne forces.

The British Commonwealth also raised parachute units. Australian paratroopers (1st Australian Parachute Battalion) served in the Far East, and the Canadian 1st Parachute Battalion served in Europe.

Several small-scale operations had been carried out before 1943 with mixed success, but the big date for airborne forces was 6 June 1944. Plans for D day required the flanks of the invasion beaches to be secured in advance, and only airborne forces could guarantee this objective. In Britain for the invasion were two British airborne divisions (1st and 6th) and two American airborne divisions (82nd and 101st). The plan was to use all the available airborne and gliderborne troops in the initial stages of the operation. Unfortunately, even in June 1944, transport aircraft available were insufficient for all troops to be dropped at once. All aircraft were organized in a common pool, so that either British or American troops could be moved by mainly American aircraft. This was another fine example of the cooperation that existed at all levels within the Allied airborne forces.

Operation OVERLORD began for the paratroopers and gliders in the dark of the early morning of 6 June. To the west, American paratroopers dropped at the base of the Cotentin Peninsula to secure the forward areas of what were to be Omaha and Utah Beaches. Despite many dispersal problems, the troops managed to link up and were soon in action, denying the Germans the ability to move against the beachheads. The troops fought with great gallantry despite their weakened strength (caused by air transport problems), and by the end of the day, contact had been established with the shipborne forces from the beachheads.

In the east, Britain's 6th Airborne Division was tasked with controlling the left flank of the British invasion beaches. Perhaps the most startling operation (for the Germans) was the coup de main attack by gliderborne airlanding troops of 11th Battalion, Oxford and Buckinghamshire Light Infantry, who landed so close to their target that they were able to capture bridges over the Caen Canal and the River Orne. On a larger scale, the 3rd Parachute Brigade was ordered to take out the Merville Battery, which posed a threat to the invasion beaches. The 9th Parachute Battalion, which planned to attack with 700 men, was so spread out on landing that only 150 men were available. With virtually no support, however, the men attacked the battery and captured it. The battalion lost 65 men and captured 22 Germans; the remainder of the German force of 200 were either killed or wounded.

The essence of airborne forces is morale; training inculcates a feeling of superiority among the men, and their dis-

tinctive headgear and equipment marks them as men apart. All Allied parachute and glider troops in the war were of a high standard, and their fighting record bears this out. Even when things went wrong, as often happened when troops were dropped from aircraft, the men made every effort to link up and to carry out the task they had been given.

David Westwood

See also

Airborne Forces, Axis; Aircraft, Transports; Anzio, Battle of; Ardennes Offensive; Bastogne, Battle for; Blitzkrieg; Bradley, Omar Nelson; Browning, Frederick; Churchill, Sir Winston L. S.; Commandos/Rangers; Gavin, James Maurice; Infantry Tactics; Manila, Battle for; MARKET-GARDEN, Operation; Naval Gunfire, Shore Support; Normandy Invasion and Campaign; OVERLORD, Operation; Parachute Infantry; Parachutes; Ridgway, Matthew Bunker; Sicily, Invasion of; Taylor, Maxwell Davenport; Wavell, Sir Archibald Percival

References

Imperial General Staff. *Airborne Operations.* London: War Office, 1943.

Otway, T. B. H. *Official Account of Airborne Forces.* London: War Office, 1951.

Harclerode, Peter. *Para.* London: Arms and Armour, 1992.

Airborne Forces, Axis

An initial German airborne force was formed in the spring of 1936 as an experiment after German observers had watched Soviet airborne troops in an exercise. Set up at Stendhal, the force was made up of men from the General Göring Regiment of the Luftwaffe. Within a year of the establishment of the first parachute regiment, the Schutzstaffel (SS) was also training a platoon, and the army was evaluating parachute troops. Luftwaffe commander Hermann Göring, however, ensured that air force troops only were to form the parachute force.

The first German exercises took place in the autumn of 1937, followed later that year by the first use of cargo gliders. Expansion was rapid, and in 1938, Generalmajor (U.S. equiv. brigadier general) Kurt Student was organizing the first airborne German division to take part in the "liberation" of the Sudetenland of Czechoslovakia. This 7th Flieger (Parachute) Division had two parachute battalions, one airborne infantry battalion and an airborne infantry regiment, three airborne SS battalions, and airborne artillery and medical troops. The division was not needed in 1938, and it was decided that the 7th Parachute Division would be all-parachute, whereas the 22nd Infantry Division would be gliderborne.

In the April 1940 German invasion of Norway, a parachute battalion dropped on Stavanger airfield and secured it in 35 minutes. On 10 May 1940, Germany captured bridges and an airfield in Holland, while gliderborne troops attacked and captured Fort Eben Emael in Belgium, which opened the German route into the Low Countries during the invasion of France. Airborne operations had proved their worth, so much so that the British immediately began to form their own parachute units.

These successes encouraged the German High Command to expand its airborne assets. It formed XI Flieger Korps, which included three parachute regiments of three battalions each plus parachute signals; medical, artillery, antiaircraft, antitank, machine gun, and engineer battalions; and the necessary supply troops. These troops were originally seen as the spearhead of the invasion of Britain, but that operation never took place.

The Germans next employed paratroops in their 1941 Balkan Campaign to capture the island of Crete. Student saw this as the forerunner of other more ambitious airborne operations. The largest airborne operation to that point in history, it involved 9,000 men and 530 Junkers Ju-52 transport aircraft flying from Greece. Thanks to Allied ULTRA intercepts, the defenders knew the drop zones in advance. Although by rushing in reinforcements the Germans were able to secure their objectives, they paid a heavy price. They sustained 6,700 casualties (3,000 killed) and lost some 200 transport aircraft in the operation. Student wanted to go on and try to take Malta, but Hitler refused. Crete was the graveyard of the German airborne forces; henceforth they fought as elite ground troops only, whose fighting abilities were recognized by all who met them in battle.

The Italians started early in their evaluation of airborne forces. Their first experiments occurred in 1927, when 9 men dropped on Cinisello airfield. Some 250 paratroops then began training and took part in a training drop at Gefara in Libya. A training center was set up at Tarquinia in central Italy, and in April 1941, Italian paratroops captured the island of Cephalonia, off the west coast of Greece. Although a small number of parachute troops continued thereafter, the planned Italian assault on Malta never took place, and Italian paratroops fought in a ground role for the rest of the war.

The Japanese began parachute training in 1940 with four training centers in the Japanese home islands. In autumn 1941, they were joined by about 100 German instructors, and soon there were nine training centers and 14,000–15,000 men under training. Both the Japanese army and navy had paratroops, all of whom were ready for operations at the start of the war.

Japanese army paratroops numbered about 6,000 men and were known as raiding units. They were divided into parachute and gliderborne units. Their first operation in February 1942 was to capture Menado airfield in the Celebes Islands. They then attacked the airfield and oil refineries at Palembang. Although the Japanese managed to capture the airfield, the refineries were destroyed before they could take them over. A week later the Japanese successfully struck Timor in coordination with seaborne troops.

Operations after this were mainly tactical, especially an assault on Leyte in December 1944. This attack was virtually a total failure. However, Allied intelligence summaries noted that the Japanese parachute troops were part of a well-organized, well-trained force that could have proved extremely effective had the emphasis in the Pacific war not been on manpower and ships to capture the many islands of this area.

David Westwood

See also

Airborne Forces, Allied; Aircraft, Transports; Crete, Battle of; Eben Emael; Freyberg, Bernard Cyril; Göring, Hermann Wilhelm; Netherlands Campaign; Netherlands East Indies, Japanese Conquest of; Norway, German Conquest of; Signals Intelligence; Student, Kurt

References

MacDonald, Callum. *The Lost Battle: Crete, 1940.* New York: Free Press, 1963.

Otway, T. B. H. *Airborne Forces.* London: Imperial War Museum, 1990.

Whiting, Charles. *Hunters from the Sky: The German Parachute Corps, 1940–1945.* New York: Stein and Day, 1974.

Aircraft, Bombers

Aircraft designed to attack enemy targets including troop concentrations, installations, and shipping. During the 1930s, bomber designs underwent something of a revolution; performance increased to the point that many bombers were faster than the fighters in service. The prevailing wisdom was that "the bomber will always get through." It was assumed that the bomber would be fast enough to evade most defending fighters and that defensive armament could deal with any that did intercept. The bomber was therefore seen as something of a terror weapon. Events in the Spanish Civil War, including the German bombing of Guernica, and early German experience in World War II tended to reinforce this view.

At the start of the war, most combat aircraft were not equipped with self-sealing fuel tanks, and most did not have adequate protective armor. However, operational experience during 1939 and early 1940 led the European powers to retrofit their aircraft with armor and self-sealing fuel tanks. Some aircraft designers took this to extremes: for example, about 15 percent of the weight of the Russian Il-2 Shturmovik (1941) was armor plate. On the other hand, many Japanese aircraft had no protection of any sort until very late in the war; they were known to their crews as "flying cigarette lighters" and were very easy to shoot down.

Other changes also affected bomber capabilities. The Germans embraced dive-bombing, and all their bombers had to be able to dive-bomb. The necessary structural changes greatly added to the bombers' weight and decreased bomb loads. The flying weight of the Ju-88, for example, went from 6 to 12 tons, sharply reducing both its speed and bomb-carrying capacity.

Defensive armament of the majority of bombers in service at the start of the war was inadequate in terms of the number and caliber of weapons and/or their field of fire. This situation came about partly because of the assumption that interceptions at 300-plus mph were difficult and would therefore be rare. The early B-17Cs, for example, were quite vulnerable because their few defensive weapons had several blind spots and were single manually aimed weapons. Later B-17Es had much better defensive armament deployed as multiple weapons in power turrets, making them much more difficult to shoot down. An alternative tactic was to dispense with all defensive weapons and rely on speed and performance to evade the defenses. The De Havilland Mosquito, which carried out many pinpoint attacks from 1942 onward, epitomized this approach.

The following text describes the most significant bombers employed by both sides during World War II. (See also Table 1.)

Germany

The Heinkel He-111 entered service in 1935, and the B model served with distinction in the Spanish Civil War, where it was fast enough to fly unescorted. Nearly 1,000 He-111s were in service at the start of the war; they formed a significant part of the Luftwaffe's medium bomber strength early in the conflict, although they were roughly handled during the Battle of Britain in spite of carrying nearly 600 lb of armor. Later versions had better defensive armament and were used in various roles, including torpedo bombing. Approximately 7,450 He-111s were built before production ended in 1944.

The prototype Junkers Ju-87 Stuka dive-bomber flew in 1935, entering service with the Luftwaffe in spring 1937. Examples sent to Spain with the Kondor Legion in 1938 were able to demonstrate highly accurate bombing under conditions of air superiority. Stukas were highly effective in the invasions of Poland in 1939 and France in 1940. During the Battle of Britain, they suffered such heavy losses from opposing British fighters that they were withdrawn from operations partway through the campaign. However, they con-

tinued to serve in the Mediterranean Theater and on the Eastern Front against the Soviet Union in dive-bombing and close ground-support roles. A total of 5,709 Ju-87s of all versions were built.

The Junkers Ju-88, one of the most effective and adaptable German aircraft of the war, entered Luftwaffe service in September 1939. The Ju-88 had good performance for a bomber, particularly the later versions, which were used as night fighters. Specialized variants were also produced for dive-bombing, antishipping, reconnaissance, and training. Ju-88C fighter variants were used in daylight during the Battle of Britain, but they were unable to cope with attacks by modern British single-engine fighters. A total of 14,980 Ju-88s were built, 10,774 of which were bomber variants.

Italy

The principal Italian bomber, and one of the most capable Italian aircraft of the war, was the trimotor Savoia-Marchetti SM.79 Sparviero (Sparrow). The Italians used it as a bomber, torpedo-bomber, and reconnaissance aircraft. Originally designed by Alessando Marchetti as a high-speed, eight-passenger transport, it had retractable landing gear. The SM.79 entered service in 1936 and first saw service in the Spanish Civil War. A total of 1,217 were produced during World War II. Reconverted to military transports after the war, Sparvieros served with the Italian air force until 1952.

The CANT Z.1007 Allcione (Kingfisher) was Italy's second-most-important bomber of the war. Entering production in 1939, it was both a medium conventional bomber and a torpedo-bomber. It was of largely wooden construction with weak defensive armament. It appeared both in single- and twin-rudder configurations without differing designations and often in the same squadron. The CANT Z.1007 was widely used all over the Mediterranean Theater. Of good design and easy to fly, it was nonetheless poorly defended and suffered heavy losses from Royal Air Force (RAF) fighters. CANT Z.1007s continued in service until the end of the war on both sides after the Italian surrender of 1943. A total of 560 were built.

The Italians had only one 4-engine bomber, the Piaggio P.108. Designed by Giovanni Casiraghi, it entered service in May 1941 and was only intermittently used. It had a crew of 6, a maximum speed of 261 mph, and a range of 2,190 mi. Armed with 8 machine guns, it could carry 7,700 lb of bombs. Only 33 were produced, however, 8 of which went to the Germans for use as transports.

Japan

The Mitsubishi Ki-21 medium bomber ("Sally" in Allied designation) was the winner of a 1936 bomber design

Table 1
Bombers, All Powers—Specifications

Name	Year of Introduction	Crew	Engine	Span	Length	Takeoff Weight (lb)*	Maximum Speed (mph)	Operational Ceiling (ft)	Range (mi)†	Armament/ Payload
Germany										
Junkers Ju-87 B-1 (late 1938)	Early 1937	2	1 × 900-hp Junkers Jumo v-type	45 ft 3.25 in.	36 ft 5 in.	9,370	242 mph at 13,410 ft	26,250 ft	342 mi with 1,102 lb bombs	3 × 7.9-mm machine guns, up to 1,542 lb bombs
Heinkel He 111 H-3 (late 1939)	1935	5	2 × 1,200-hp Junkers Jumo v-type	74 ft 1.75 in	53 ft 9.5 in.	24,912	258 mph at 16,400 ft	25,590 ft	758 mi with maximum bomb load	1 × 20-mm cannon, 5 × 7.9-mm machine guns, 4,409 lb bombs
Junkers Ju-88 A-4 (1942)	Late 1939	4	2 × 1,340-hp Junkers Jumo v-type	65 ft 7.5 in.	47 ft 3 in.	26,700	269 mph at 14,765 ft	26,900 ft	650 mi with maximum bomb load	9 × 7.7-mm machine guns, up to 3,306 lb bombs
Great Britain										
Handley Page Hampden 1 (late 1938)	Late 1938	4	2 × 980-hp Bristol Pegasus radials	69 ft 2 in.	53 ft 7 in.	18,756	265 mph at 15,500 ft	22,700 ft	1,095 mi with maximum bomb load	6 × 0.303-in. machine guns, 4,000 lb bombs
Bristol Blenheim IVL (early 1939)	Early 1939	3	2 × 920-hp Bristol Mercury radials	56 ft 4 in.	42 ft 9 in.	13,500	266 mph at 11,800 ft	27,260 ft	1,950 mi maximum	5 × 0.303-in. machine guns, 1,000 lb bombs
Short Stirling I (late 1940)	Late 1940	7 or 8	4 × 1,590-hp Bristol Hercules radials	99 ft 1 in.	87 ft 3 in.	59,400	260 mph at 10,500 ft	20,500 ft	1,930 mi with 5,000 lb bombs	8 × 0.303-in. machine guns, up to 14,000 lb bombs
Vickers Wellington III (early 1941)	Late 1938	6	2 × 1,500-hp Bristol Hercules radials	86 ft 2 in.	64 ft 7 in.	29,000	255 mph at 12,500 ft	19,000 ft	2,200 mi with 1,500 lb bombs	8 × 0.303-in. machine guns, 4,500 lb bombs
Avro Lancaster B.1 (early 1942)	Early 1942	7	4 × 1,280-hp Rolls Royce Merlin v-type	102 ft	69 ft 4 in.	68,000 maximum	287 mph at 11,500 ft	24,500 ft	1,730 mi with 12,000 lb bomb load	8 × 0.303-in. machine guns, up to 18,000 lb bombs
Handley Page Halifax B.III (late 1943)	Early 1941	7	4 × 1,615-hp Bristol Hercules radials	104 ft 2 in.	71 ft 7 in.	54,400	282 mph at 13,500 ft	24,000 ft	1,985 mi with 7,000 lb bombs	9 × 0.303-in. machine guns, up to 13,000 lb bombs
De Havilland Mosquito B.XVI (early 1944)	Late 1941	2	2 × 1,680-hp Rolls Royce Merlin v-type	54 ft 2 in.	40 ft 6 in.	19,093	408 mph at 26,000 ft	37,000 ft	1,370 mi with 4,000 lb bombs	Up to 4,000 lb bombs
Italy										
Savoia-Marchetti S.M.79-II Sparviero (early 1940)	1937	6	3 × 1,000-hp Piaggio radials	69 ft 6.5 in.	53 ft 1.75 in.	25,133	295 mph at 13,120 ft	27,890 ft	1,243 mi with 2,756 lb bombs	3 × 12.7-mm machine guns, 2 × 7.7-mm machine guns, 2 × 450-mm torpedoes, or 2,756 lb bombs
CANT Z.1007bis (late 1940)	1937	5	3 × 1,000-hp Piaggio radials	81 ft 4.5 in.	60 ft 11 in.	38,206	283 mph at 15,100 ft	26,500 ft	1,243 mi with 2,430 lb bombs	4 × 12.7-mm machine guns, 2,430 lb bombs, or 2 × 450-mm torpedoes
Japan										
Mitsubishi Ki-21-IIb (1942)	1937	5–7	2 × 1,500-hp Mitsubishi Ha-101 radials	73 ft 10 in.	52 ft 6 in.	21,407	302 mph at 15,485 ft	32,810 ft	1,350 mi with maximum bomb load	5 × 7.7-mm machine guns, 1 × 12.7-mm machine gun, 2,205 lb bombs

(continues)

Table 1
Bombers, All Powers—Specifications (continued)

Name	Year of Introduction	Crew	Engine	Span	Length	Takeoff Weight (lb)*	Maximum Speed (mph)	Operational Ceiling (ft)	Range (mi)†	Armament/Payload
Japan (continued)										
Mitsubishi G4M2a Betty (mid-1944)	Early 1941	7	2 × 1,850-hp Mitsubishi Kasei radials	81 ft 8 in.	64 ft 5 in.	33,069 maximum	272 mph at 15,090 ft	29,365 ft	1,497 mi with normal bomb load	4 × 20-mm cannon, 1 × 7.7-mm machine gun, up to 2,205 lb bombs or 1 × 1,764-lb torpedo
Soviet Union										
Ilyushin Il-4 (1940)	1940	3–4	2 × 1,100-hp M-88B radials	70 ft 4 in.	48 ft 6.5 in.	22,046 maximum	255 mph at 21,000 ft	29,530 ft	2,647 mi with 2,205 lb bombs	3 × 7.7-mm or 12.7-mm machine guns, up to 5,512 lb bombs
Petlyakov Pe-2	Early 1941	3	2 × 1,100-hp Klimov v-type	56 ft 3.5 in.	41 ft 6.5 in.	18,734	336 mph at 16,400 ft	28,900 ft	700 mi with maximum bomb load	3 × 7.7-mm machine guns, 2,645 lb bombs
Ilyushin Il-2m3 Shturmovik (late 1942)	Mid-1941	2	1 × 1,770-hp Mikulin v-type	47 ft 11 in.	38 ft 2.5 in.	12,147	251 mph at 4,920 ft	19,685 ft	373 mi with normal load	2 × 23-mm cannon, 2 × 7.62-mm machine guns, 1 × 7.62-mm machine gun, 1,323 lb bombs or 8 rockets
United States										
Douglas A-20 C Havoc (1941)	1940	3	2 × 1,600-hp Wright Cyclone radials	61 ft 4 in.	47 ft 3 in.	24,500 maximum	342 mph at 13,000 ft	24,250 ft	1,050 mi with maximum bomb load	7 × 0.303-in. machine guns, 2,000 lb bombs
Martin B-26 B Marauder (early 1942)	1941	7	2 × 1,920-hp Pratt and Whitney radials	71 ft	58 ft 3 in.	37,000	282 mph at 15,000 ft	21,700 ft	1,150 mi with 3,000 lb bombs	11 × 0.5-in. machine guns, 1 × 0.3-in. machine gun, up to 5,200 lb bombs
Boeing B-17F (mid-1942)	1939	9–10	4 × 1,200-hp Wright Cyclone radials	103 ft 9.5 in.	74 ft 8.75 in.	55,000	299 mph at 25,000 ft	37,500 ft	1,300 mi with 6,000 lb bombs	8 or 9 × 0.5-in. machine guns, 1 × 0.303-in. machine gun, 12,800 lb bombs
North American B-25 J Mitchell (1943)	Late 1940	5	2 × 1,700-hp Wright Cyclone radials	67 ft 7 in.	52 ft 11 in.	33,450	275 mph at 15,000 ft	25,000 ft	1,275 mi with 3,200 lb bombs	13 × 0.5-in. machine guns, up to 4,000 lb bombs
Consolidated B-24J Liberator (1944)	Early 1941	8–12	4 × 1,200-hp Wright Cyclone radials	110 ft	67 ft 2 in.	56,000	290 mph at 25,000 ft	28,000 ft	1,700 mi with 5,000 lb bombs	10 × 0.5-in. machine guns, 5,000 lb bombs
Boeing B-29 Superfortress (mid-1944)	Mid-1944	10	4 × 2,200-hp Wright Cyclone radials	141 ft 3 in.	99 ft	120,000	357 mph at 30,000 ft	33,600 ft	3,250 mi with 10,000 lb bombs	1 × 20-mm cannon, 10 × 0.5-in. machine guns, up to 20,000 lb bombs
Douglas A-26 B Invader (late 1944)	Late 1944	3	2 × 2,000-hp Pratt and Whitney radials	70 ft	50 ft	35,000 maximum	355 mph at 15,000 ft	22,100 ft	1,400 mi with maximum load	10 × 0.5-in. machine guns, up to 4,000 lb bombs

Sources: Brown, Eric. *Wings of the Luftwaffe.* Shrewsbury, UK: Airlife, 1993; Green, William. *Famous Bombers of the Second World War.* 2d ed. London: Book Club Associates, 1979; Jarrett, Philip, ed. *Aircraft of the Second World War.* London: Putnam, 1997; and Munson, Kenneth. *Bombers, Patrol and Transport Aircraft 1939–45.* Poole, UK: Blandford, 2002.

* Weight is normal takeoff weight unless specified otherwise.
† Range is maximum flyable distance, including reserves.

competition run by the Japanese army air force. It entered service in 1937 as the Ki-21-Ia and was replaced shortly afterward by the Ki-21-Ic, which had additional armament and defensive armor as a result of combat experience in China. The Ki-21 was the standard Japanese air force bomber at the end of 1941 and was encountered throughout the Pacific and the Far East. When production ended in 1944, 2,064 had been built by Mitsubishi and Nakajima, as well as about 500 transport versions by Mitsubishi.

The Mitsubishi G4M medium bomber ("Betty") entered service with the Japanese army early in 1941 and was involved in pre–World War II operations in China. It was designed in great secrecy during 1938–1939 to have the maximum possible range at the expense of protection for the crew and vital components, and it was mainly used in the bomber and torpedo-bomber roles. G4M1s were mainly responsible for sinking the British battleship *Prince of Wales* and battle cruiser *Repulse* off Malaya in December 1941. The G4M had an extraordinary range, but more than 1,100 gallons of fuel in unprotected tanks made the aircraft extremely vulnerable to enemy fire. The G4M2 appeared in 1943 and was the major production model, with more-powerful engines and even more fuel. Losses of the aircraft continued to be very heavy, and Mitsubishi finally introduced the G4M3 model late in 1943 with a redesigned wing and protected fuel tanks. A total of 2,479 aircraft in the G4M series were built.

Great Britain

The Bristol Blenheim was developed from the private-venture Bristol 142, and the short-nosed Mk 1 entered service as a light bomber in March 1937, although some were completed as fighters. The Blenheim was an effective bomber, but lacking adequate defensive armament and armor, it was vulnerable to fighter attack. The most numerous versions were the long-nosed Mk IV and V, but their performance suffered from significant weight growth, the Mark V in particular suffering heavy losses. The Blenheim nevertheless filled an important capability gap in time of need, and it was exported to Finland, Romania, Turkey, and Yugoslavia. A total of 5,213 Blenheims of all versions were built.

The Vickers Wellington entered service with the RAF late in 1938 and (with the Whitley and Hampden) bore the brunt of the RAF bomber offensive for the first two years of the war. Its light but strong geodetic structure enabled it to carry a respectable bomb load, and it could withstand a significant amount of battle damage. The Wellington was one of the first monoplane bombers to be fitted with power turrets, but (in common with all early World War II bombers) it was vulnerable to fighter attack when flown unescorted in daylight. The Wellington was mainly employed as a

medium bomber, although some were used for maritime reconnaissance, torpedo-bombing, minelaying, and transport duties. Wellingtons were in production throughout the war, 11,461 being built up to October 1945.

The Handley Page Hampden entered RAF service late in 1938. Of imaginative design, it delivered a reasonable performance on only average engine power, but the cramped fuselage caused crew fatigue, and the defensive field of fire was very limited. Hampdens were used as medium bombers and minelayers until late 1942, and they served as torpedo-bombers and maritime reconnaissance aircraft until the latter part of 1943. A total of 1,430 Hampdens and variants were built.

The Short Stirling, the first of the RAF's four-engine "heavies" to see combat, entered service in late 1940. It was built to specification B.12/36, which unfortunately specified that the wingspan should be less than 100 ft to fit in a standard hangar; this compromised the aircraft's altitude capability to the extent that attacks on Italy required British pilots to fly through the Alps rather than over them. However, the Stirling was outstandingly maneuverable for such a large aircraft. It was used as a bomber, minelayer, glider tug/transport, and (with 100 Group) an electronic countermeasures aircraft. A total of 2,381 Stirlings were built.

The Handley Page Halifax I entered service early in 1941 and was found to be a good bomber, but it lacked adequate defensive armament. The Halifax B.II had a dorsal gun turret but suffered from weight growth and a tendency to spin when fully loaded. Later B.IIs underwent a weight- and drag-reduction program and had larger fins fitted to correct these faults. The B.III version was the most numerous, using more powerful Bristol Hercules engines in place of the Merlins. Although the Halifax's main role was as a bomber, it was also employed as a transport, glider tug, and maritime reconnaissance aircraft. A total of 6,176 Halifaxes were built.

The Avro Lancaster was a successful development of the Rolls-Royce Vulture-powered Manchester, entering operational service with the RAF in early 1942. The Lancaster remained in service until the end of the war and rapidly became the primary strategic bomber for the RAF. It lost fewer aircraft per ton of bombs dropped than either the Halifax or Stirling. The Lancaster had a large bomb bay and was designed to take 4,000 lb bombs; successive modifications enabled it to carry 8,000 lb and 12,000 lb weapons, and the B.I (special) carried a single 22,000 lb "Grand Slam" armor-piercing bomb. The Lancaster participated in several special operations, including the Dambusters raid in May 1943, when specially adapted Lancasters of 617 Squadron attacked dams in the Rhine valley using a skipping bomb designed by Barnes Wallis. A total of 7,366 Lancasters were built.

The De Havilland Mosquito was constructed largely from

a plywood/balsa sandwich and was designed to be fast enough to outrun enemy fighters. It had excellent handling characteristics. It began operations with the RAF in the bomber role early in 1942 and quickly demonstrated that it could carry out extremely accurate attacks, including the daring low-level attack on the Gestapo headquarters in Oslo, Norway, in late 1942. Mosquitoes originally equipped the RAF's pathfinder force, and they were able to roam across Germany largely unmolested. Operationally, the Mosquito had by far the lowest loss rate of any aircraft in Bomber Command (about 0.6 percent), as its speed enabled it to avoid most interception and its structure tended to absorb cannon hits. A total of 6,439 Mosquitoes of all marks were built.

Soviet Union

The Ilyushin Il-4 was the most widely used Soviet medium bomber of the war. Initially designed as the DB-3 in 1935, it entered service in that form in 1938. The updated DB-3F was redesignated Il-4 in 1940, and many examples were built. Following the Soviet entry into the war, a force of Soviet Navy Il-4s carried out the first Soviet attack on Berlin in August 1941. As a result of shortages of strategic materials, parts of the airframe including the outer wing panels were redesigned to use wood instead of metal. The Il-4 was a maneuverable aircraft in spite of its size, and approximately 5,000 were built up to 1944.

The Petlyakov Pe-2 entered service early in 1941. It was originally designed as a fighter and therefore had unusually responsive controls for a bomber. It turned out to be one of the most versatile aircraft produced by the USSR in the war, being used as a heavy fighter, light bomber, dive-bomber, ground-attack, and reconnaissance aircraft. More than 11,000 Pe-2s were built.

The Ilyushin Il-2 Shturmovik was probably one of the most effective ground-attack aircraft of World War II, entering service on the Soviet Front in mid-1941. Initial versions were single-seaters, but the higher-performance Il-2m3 introduced in mid-1942 had a gunner and was highly effective in aerial combat at low altitude, even against single-seat German fighters. Later versions of the Il-2m3 had a more powerful engine and a 37 mm cannon against German Panther and Tiger tanks. The Shturmovik was remarkably tough; about 15 percent of its empty weight was armor plate that protected the engine, fuel systems, and crew, and it had few weak points. Approximately 35,000 Shturmoviks were built.

United States

The Boeing B-17 Flying Fortress was designed in 1934 and sold to Congress as a U.S. Army Air Corps requirement for an offshore antishipping bomber. The B-17B entered service late in 1939; it was fast and had a high operational ceiling, but the initial versions were not particularly capable. The B-17E, which entered service early in 1942, had much-improved defensive armament, including a tail gun turret, and the B-17G (late 1943) introduced an additional chin turret, which was later fitted to some F models. The B-17 E, F, and G models formed the mainstay of the U.S. heavy day-bomber force in Europe and remained in service until the end of the war. There were 8,685 B-17s built.

The Consolidated B-24 Liberator heavy bomber was designed with a high aspect-ratio wing that, together with its Davis high-lift airfoil, gave very good range/payload performance. The first Liberators entered service with RAF Coastal Command in mid-1941, and the type went on to serve with the U.S. Army Air Forces (USAAF) and U.S. Navy. USAAF B-24s conducted the ill-fated raid on the Ploesti oil field on 1 August 1943. The Liberator developed a reputation for fragility in the European Theater and was prone to catch fire when hit, but its long range made it the preeminent strategic bomber in the Pacific Theater. The B-24 was employed as a reconnaissance, antisubmarine, and transport aircraft as well as in its primary strategic bombing role, and it was produced in greater quantities than any other American aircraft, 18,188 being built up to May 1945.

The Douglas Aircraft Company built the A-20 attack bomber as a private venture, albeit with the help of U.S. Army Air Corps technicians at the specification stage. It entered service early in 1940 with the French Armée de l'Air, outstanding orders being transferred to the RAF when France capitulated to the Germans. The A-20 (designated Boston or Havoc, depending on the role) was an excellent airplane. Fast, docile, and pleasant to fly, it had a commendably low loss rate. It was very adaptable and was produced in both solid-nose and transparent-nose versions. Used in many roles including low-level attack, strafing, torpedo-bombing, reconnaissance, and night fighting, it remained in frontline service until the end of hostilities. A total of 7,385 variants were built.

North American was awarded a contract to build the B-25 Mitchell without the usual prototypes, relying instead on experience with the NA-40 design and feedback from the Army Air Corps. Self-sealing fuel tanks and armor protection were incorporated on the production line following combat reports from Europe. The Mitchell had good handling characteristics and was probably the best all-around medium bomber of the war. The B-25 achieved lasting fame when 16 of them attacked Tokyo in April 1942, flying from the carrier *Hornet*. The Mitchell was adapted to multiple missions including ground strafing, torpedo-bombing, antisubmarine work, and reconnaissance, mounting a variety of main armament including up to 18 0.5-inch machine guns in the B-25J and a 75 mm cannon in the B-25H. Mitchells were used by most Allied air forces, and approximately 11,000 were built.

The Boeing B-29 Superfortress, the heaviest bomber of the war, evolved from a 1940 Army Air Corps requirement for a "hemisphere defense weapon." The resulting XB-29, which first flew late in 1942, had several innovative design features including a pressurized fuselage and remote-controlled gun turrets. The B-29 entered service in the first half of 1944 and mounted increasingly heavy attacks against the Japanese mainland from bases in the Mariana Islands. Operationally, the B-29 was successful largely as a result of its speed and altitude capabilities. B-29s forced the Japanese surrender following attacks with atomic bombs on Hiroshima and Nagasaki during August 1945. A total of 3,970 were built.

The Douglas A-26 Invader was a worthy successor to the Douglas A-20 Havoc. It entered service late in 1944. The A-26B had a solid attack nose carrying six .50 caliber machine guns, and the A-26C had a more conventional transparent nose for a bombardier. The A-26 was fast and well armed, and it had a very low loss rate (about 0.6 percent), even allowing for low enemy fighter activity toward the end of the war. A total of 2,446 Invaders were built, and they continued to serve for many years after the war.

The Martin B-26 Marauder entered service early in 1942 and initially gained a reputation as a difficult aircraft to fly, partly because of its weight and high landing and takeoff speeds. Certainly it required skill and practice to master. In later models (B-26F onward), the wing incidence was increased to reduce the landing and takeoff speeds. The B-26 could absorb a lot of damage and was an effective bomber; its final combat loss rate was less than 1 percent. A total of 5,157 Marauders were built.

Andy Blackburn

See also
Aircraft, Naval; Aviation, Ground-Attack; Britain, Battle of; B-29 Raids against Japan; Guernica, Kondor Legion Attack on; Hiroshima, Bombing of; Kondor Legion; Nagasaki, Bombing of; Pathfinders; Ploesti; *Prince of Wales* and *Repulse;* Spain, Civil War; Strategic Bombing; Tokyo, Bombing of (1942); Wallis, Barnes Neville

References
Green, William. *Famous Bombers of the Second World War.* 2d ed. London: Book Club Associates, 1979.
Jarrett, Philip, ed. *Aircraft of the Second World War.* London: Putnam, 1997.
Munson, Kenneth. *Bombers, Patrol, and Transport Aircraft, 1939–45.* Poole, UK: Blandford Press, 1975.

Aircraft, Fighters

Aircraft designed to shoot down other aircraft. World War II was a period of transition for fighters; by 1945 aircraft weight, armament, and performance had increased dramatically, and jet fighters were approaching the speed of sound.

Throughout the 1920s and early 1930s, most air forces were equipped with biplane fighters that were little more advanced than their twin-gunned ancestors that had fought on the Western Front in World War I. By the mid-1930s, aero-engine design and airframe construction techniques had advanced dramatically, and newer prototypes were appearing with stressed-skin construction, retractable undercarriages, and top speeds of over 300 mph. These aircraft entered service in the late 1930s, just in time for World War II.

Many of these new designs had flush-fitting cockpit canopies (e.g., Bf-109, Spitfire), partly for reasons of aerodynamic efficiency but also because it was thought (incorrectly) that the classic World War I dogfight would be impossible at speeds of over 300 mph. Visibility from the cockpit turned out to be very important; about 80 percent of pilots shot down during the war never saw their attackers. Bulged cockpit hoods were fitted to some fighters to alleviate the problem, but later aircraft were fitted with clear Perspex canopies that gave unrestricted rearward vision.

Most fighters are defined by performance and maneuverability. Of the two, performance was probably more important during World War II. A speed advantage over an opponent (ignoring surprise attacks and tactical advantage) enabled a fighter to dictate the terms on which combat was joined and also enabled an easy escape if the fight was not going well. Comparisons tend to be problematic since performance varied dramatically with altitude; an aircraft that had a significant advantage against an opponent at sea level could find the position dramatically reversed at 30,000 ft. In any case, in-service improvements could change performance characteristics, and new aircraft usually had the latest equipment and engine variants, further complicating the issue.

Maneuverability is essentially a measure of the ability of an aircraft to change direction and is dictated to a large extent by the wing loading of the aircraft. Some lightly loaded aircraft (particularly the early Japanese fighters) were capable of remarkably tight turns, but the ability of the aircraft to roll and establish the turn also played a part. Some fighters, such as the Focke-Wulf FW 190, had an excellent rate of roll that to some extent compensated for their average rate of turn. An aircraft's handling qualities degrade to a greater or lesser extent as the weight inevitably increases with each new version, and heavier aircraft tend to be less agile than lighter ones. Twin-engine aircraft are particularly disadvantaged in roll as more mass is distributed around the center-line than with a single-engine aircraft.

Many early fighters had tactical limitations because of control difficulties. There is a relationship between the size and shape of a control surface and the effort required to move it; it becomes progressively more difficult to deflect as speed increases and may in some cases exceed the ability of the pilot to apply sufficient force. For example, the Messerschmitt Bf-109 had very heavy stick forces at normal speeds; Spitfires had metal-covered ailerons fitted late in 1940 to make high-speed rolls easier; and the Mitsubishi Zero had (in common with most other Japanese fighters) huge control surfaces that gave outstanding agility below about 200 mph (as with the F4U Corsair and Tempest) but almost none above 300 mph. Much later in the war, new designs had spring-tabs fitted on control surfaces to balance the extra air resistance at high speeds.

In 1939 few, if any, aircraft had self-sealing fuel tanks or armor. Operational experience in the European Theater showed that aircraft were very vulnerable unless so equipped, and in 1940 crash programs were instituted to retrofit fuel tank liners and armor plate to most aircraft. This added weight reduced performance slightly, but most air arms were prepared to accept the price. However, the Japanese army and navy were not. As a result, most Japanese aircraft, which were lightly constructed anyway, were extremely vulnerable even to machine-gun fire, and cannon hits caused immediate and catastrophic damage. The use of armor and other protection on bombers had already obliged designers to fit heavier weapons, and continuing development encouraged the adoption of cannon. The Messerschmitt Me-262 was probably the ultimate World War II bomber-killer with four 30 mm cannon, only three hits from which were usually required to down a four-engine bomber.

The increased performance of fighters brought compressibility effects into play. As speeds increased at high altitude, airflow over parts of the structure could reach the speed of sound (Mach 1.0) even in quite shallow dives, leading to buffeting, nose-down trim changes, and eventually loss of control of the aircraft. Recovery from the dive was difficult, and reducing power usually led to the nose dropping further! Sometimes the only solution was to wait until the aircraft reached warmer air at lower altitudes and the local speed of sound increased above the critical value. These effects were not well understood at the time and caused tactical limitations to some aircraft: the Lockheed P-38 ran into serious compressibility effects above Mach 0.68, and the Messerschmitt Me-262 could reach its limit of Mach 0.83 only in a very shallow dive.

World War II was a fascinating period for fighter devel-opment; the following aircraft were the most significant fighters of the conflict. (See also Table 1.)

Germany

The Messerschmitt Bf-109 entered service in its earliest form (Bf-109B) in 1937 and remained in service throughout the war. It continued to be modified during the conflict. It received progressively more powerful engines, and in common with many other aircraft, its handling qualities and maneuverability degraded with successive versions. The Bf-109 could not turn tightly (although the 109E and 109F models were better than commonly supposed), but it was a very effective fighter when handled correctly, possessing excellent dive and zoom climb capabilities. The later versions in particular were better at high altitude, but the controls became very stiff at high speeds, and visibility from the cockpit was poor. Approximately 35,000 examples were built.

The Messerschmitt Bf-110 was designed as a long-range escort fighter, entering service with the Luftwaffe in 1939. It had a useful top speed and was well armed, but it could not meet contemporary single-engine fighters on equal terms. It was not a success as an escort fighter, but it was first used as a fighter-bomber during the Battle of Britain, and from 1943 the Bf-110 G-4 enjoyed much success as a radar-equipped night fighter. Approximately 6,150 were built.

The Focke-Wulf FW-190A entered service in mid-1941 and became one of the best low- and medium-altitude fighters of the war. It had light and effective controls and possibly the best rate of roll of any World War II fighter, attaining 160 degrees per second at about 260 mph. It was superior to the contemporary Spitfire Mk V in all areas except turning circle and was generally regarded as a strong and rugged aircraft. The 190F and 190G were similar to the 190A, but they had extra armor for ground-attack missions, and the 190D had a 2,240 hp Junkers Jumo liquid-cooled engine for better high-altitude performance. A total of 20,001 Focke-Wulf FW 190s were built.

Italy

The Fiat CR-42 entered service with the Italian air force in 1939 and was exported to Belgium, Sweden, and Hungary. It was a highly maneuverable fighter with (for a biplane) good dive acceleration. However, it was lightly armed and quite vulnerable to enemy fire and was not really capable of taking on modern fighters on equal terms. A total of 1,781 were built.

The Macchi Mc 200 first entered service during 1940. A well-built and extremely maneuverable fighter with finger-light controls, it could outturn most of its opponents. It was, however, lightly armed with only two machine guns. The

Table 1
Fighters, All Powers—Specifications

Name	Year of Introduction	Engine	Span	Length	Wing Area (sq ft)	Takeoff Weight (lb)*	Maximum Speed (mph)	Combat Ceiling (500 ft/min)†	Range (mi)‡	Armament/ Payload
France										
Dewotine D.520 (early 1940)	Early 1940	1 × 910-hp Hispano-Suiza v-type	33 ft 5.5 in.	28 ft 8.5 in.	171.7 sq ft	6,129 lb	329 mph at 19,685 ft	34,000 ft	620 mi	1 × 20-mm Hispano cannon, 2 × 7.5-mm MAC machine guns
Germany										
Messerschmitt Bf 109 E-1 (early 1939)	Mid-1937	1 × 1,100-hp Daimler-Benz DB601 v-type	32 ft 4.5 in.	28 ft 4 in.	174 sq ft	5,523 lb	354 mph at 12,300 ft	34,000 ft (est)	412 mi	2 × 7.9-mm MG 17 machine guns, 2 × 20-mm MG FF cannon
Messerschmitt Bf 110 C-4 (mid-1939)	Mid-1939	2 × 1,100-hp Daimler-Benz DB601 v-type	53 ft 5 in.	39 ft 8.5 in.	413 sq ft	15,300 lb	349 mph at 22,965 ft	30,000 ft (est)	565 mi	4 × 7.9-mm MG 17 machine guns, 2 × 20-mm MG FF cannon, + 1 × flexible 7.9 mm MG-15 machine gun
Messerschmitt Bf 109 F-3 (early 1941)	Mid-1937	1 × 1,300-hp Daimler-Benz DB601 v-type	32 ft 6.5 in.	29 ft 0.5 in.	174.4 sq ft	6,054 lb	390 mph at 22,000 ft	35,000 ft (est)	440 mi	2 × 7.9-mm MG 17 machine guns, 1 × 15-mm MG 151 cannon
Focke-Wulf FW 190 A-3 (mid-1941)	Mid-1941	1 × 1,700-hp BMW 801 radial	34 ft 5.5 in.	28 ft 10.5 in.	197 sq ft	8,770 lb	408 mph at 21,000 ft	32,000 ft	500 mi	2 × 7.9-mm MG 17 machine guns, 2 × 20-mm MG 151 cannon, 2 × 20-mm MG/FF cannon
Messerschmitt Bf 109 G-6 (mid-1942)	Mid-1937	1 × 1,475-hp Daimler-Benz DB605 v-type	32 ft 6.5 in.	29 ft 8 in.	174.4 sq ft	6,950 lb	387 mph at 22,970 ft	36,500 ft (est)	450 mi	2 × 13-mm MG 131 machine guns, 1 × 20-mm MG 151 cannon
Focke-Wulf FW 190 D-9 (mid-1944)	Mid-1941	1 × 2,240-hp Junkers Jumo v-type	34 ft 5.5 in.	33 ft 5.25 in.	197 sq ft	9,480 lb	426 mph at 21,650 ft	40,500 ft (est)	520 mi	2 × 13-mm MG 131 machine guns, 2 × 20-mm MG 151 cannon
Messerschmitt Bf 109 K-4 (early 1945)	Mid-1937	1 × 1,800-hp Daimler-Benz DB605 v-type	32 ft 6.5 in.	29 ft 4 in.	174.4 sq ft	7,410 lb	440 mph at 24,750 ft	38,000 ft (est)	387 mi	2 × 13-mm MG 131 machine guns, 1 × 30-mm MK 108 cannon
Great Britain										
Hawker Hurricane Mk I (early 1940)	Late 1937	1 × 1,030-hp Rolls-Royce Merlin v-type	40 ft	31 ft 11 in.	257.5 sq ft	6,218 lb	324 mph at 17,800 ft	31,000 ft	425 mi	8 × 0.303-in. Browning machine guns
Supermarine Spitfire Mk IA (early 1940)	Mid-1938	1 × 1,030-hp Rolls-Royce Merlin v-type	36 ft 10 in.	29 ft 11 in.	242 sq ft	6,050 lb	355 mph at 19,000 ft	32,500 ft (est)	425 mi	8 × 0.303-in. Browning machine guns
Bristol Beaufighter IF (late 1940)	Late 1940	2 × 1,590-hp Bristol Hercules radial	57 ft 10 in.	41 ft 4 in.	503 sq ft	20,800 lb	323 mph at 15,000 ft	26,500 ft (est)	1,500 mi	4 × 20-mm Hispano cannon, 6 × 0.303-in. Browning machine guns
Hawker Hurricane Mk IIC (early 1941)	Mid-1940	1 × 1,260-hp Rolls-Royce Merlin v-type	40 ft	32 ft 2.5 in.	257.5 sq ft	7,544 lb	329 mph at 17,800 ft	32,400 ft	460 mi	4 × 20-mm Oerlikon cannon
Supermarine Spitfire Mk VB (early 1941)	Mid-1938	1 × 1,470-hp Rolls-Royce Merlin v-type	36 ft 10 in.	29 ft 11 in.	242 sq ft	6,525 lb	371 mph at 20,000 ft	35,500 ft (est)	470 mi	2 × 20-mm Hispano cannon, 4 × 0.303-in. Browning machine guns

(continues)

Table 1
Fighters, All Powers—Specifications (continued)

Name	Year of Introduction	Engine	Span	Length	Wing Area (sq ft)	Takeoff Weight (lb)*	Maximum Speed (mph)	Combat Ceiling (500 ft/min)†	Range (mi)‡	Armament/ Payload
Great Britain (continued)										
Hawker Typhoon Mk IB (late 1941)	Late 1941	1 × 2,180-hp Napier Sabre H-type	41 ft 7 in.	31 ft 10 in.	279 sq ft	11,400 lb	405 mph at 18,000 ft	32,000 ft (est)	610 mi	4 × 20-mm Hispano cannon
Supermarine Spitfire Mk IX (mid-1942)	Mid-1938	1 × 1,585-hp Rolls-Royce Merlin v-type	36 ft 10 in.	29 ft 11 in.	242 sq ft	7,400 lb	408 at 28,000 ft	38,000 ft	434 mi (later 660 mi)	2 × 20-mm Hispano cannon, 4 × 0.303-in. Browning machine guns
Hawker Tempest Mk V series 2 (early 1944)	Early 1944	1 × 2,200-hp Napier Sabre H-type	41 ft	33 ft 8 in.	302 sq ft	11,400 lb	435 mph at 17,000 ft	34,000 ft (est)	820 mi	4 × 20-mm Hispano cannon
Supermarine Spitfire Mk XIV (early 1944)	Mid-1938	1 × 2,050-hp Rolls-Royce Griffon v-type	36 ft 10 in.	32 ft 8 in.	242 sq ft	8,400 lb	446 mph at 25,400 ft	41,500 ft	460 mi	2 × 20-mm Hispano cannon, 2 × 0.5-in. Browning machine guns
De Havilland Mosquito NF Mk 30 (late 1944)	Mid-1942	2 × 1,710-hp Rolls-Royce Merlin v-type	54 ft 2 in.	40 ft 10.75 in.	454 sq ft	20,000 lb	407 mph at 28,000 ft	36,500 ft (est)	1,300 mi	4 × 20-mm Hispano cannon
Italy										
Fiat C.R.42 (mid-1939)	Mid-1939	1 × 840-hp Fiat A.74 radial	31 ft 10 in.	27 ft 1 in.	240.5 sq ft	5,042 lb	266 mph at 13,120 ft	31,300 ft (est)	482 mi	2 × 12.7-mm Breda-SAFAT machine guns
Macchi Mc202 (mid-1941)	Mid-1941	1 × 1,175-hp Alfa-Romeo R.A.1000 v-type	34 ft 8.5 in.	29 ft 0.5 in.	180.8 sq ft	6,459 lb	370 mph at 16,400 ft	35,750 ft (est)	475 mi	2 × 7.7-mm Breda-SAFAT machine guns, 2 × 12.7-mm Breda-SAFAT machine guns
Japan										
Kawasaki Ki-45 KAIc "Nick" (early 1942)	Early 1942	2 × 1,080-hp Mitsubishi Ha.102 radial	49 ft 5.25 in.	36 ft 1 in.	344.4 sq ft	12,125 lb	340 mph at 22,965 ft	30,000 ft	746 mi	1 × 37-mm Ho-203 cannon, 2 × 20-mm type 2 cannon
Kawasaki Ki-61-Ia "Tony" (early 1943)	Early 1943	1 × 1,160-hp Kawasaki Ha-40 v-type	39 ft 4.5 in.	28 ft 8.5 in.	215.3 sq ft	7,650 lb	348 mph at 16,404 ft	30,500 ft (est)	1,118 mi	2 × 7.7-mm type 89 machine guns, 2 × 20-mm MG 151 cannon
Nakajima Ki-44-IIb "Tojo" (mid-1943)	Late 1942	1 × 1,520-hp Nakajima Ha.109 radial	31 ft	28 ft 9.75 in.	161.4 sq ft	6,107 lb	376 mph at 17,060 ft	34,500 ft (est)	497 mi	4 × 12.7-mm type 1 machine guns
Kawanishi N1K1-J "George" (early 1944)	Early 1944	1 × 1,990-hp Nakajima Homare radial	39 ft 4 in.	29 ft 1.5 in.	252.9 sq ft	9,526 lb	362 mph at 17,715 ft	37,000 ft (est)	888 mi	2 × 7.7-mm type 97 machine guns, 4 × 20-mm type 99 cannon
Nakajima Ki-43-IIb "Oscar" (early 1944)	Late 1941	1 × 1,130-hp Nakajima Ha.115 radial	35 ft 6.75 in.	29 ft 3 in.	232 sq ft	5,320 lb	320 mph at 19,680 ft	34,500 ft (est)	1,006 mi	2 × 12.7-mm type 1 machine guns
Nakajima Ki-84 "Frank" (late 1944)	Late 1944	1 × 1,900-hp Nakajima Ha.45 radial	36 ft 10.25 in.	32 ft 6.5 in.	226 sq ft	7,965 lb	388 mph at 19,680 ft	32,000 ft (est)	1,025 mi	2 × 12.7-mm type 103 machine guns, 2 × 20-mm type 5 cannon

(continues)

Table 1
Fighters, All Powers—Specifications (continued)

Name	Year of Intro-duction	Engine	Span	Length	Wing Area (sq ft)	Takeoff Weight (lb)*	Maximum Speed (mph)	Combat Ceiling (500 ft/min)†	Range (mi)‡	Armament/ Payload
Soviet Union										
Polikarpov I-16 type 24 (1941)	Late 1934	1 × 1,000-hp Shvetsov M-62 radial	29 ft 6.5 in.	20 ft 1 in.	161 sq ft	4,189 lb	326 mph at 14,765 ft	27,500 ft (est)	249 mi	2 × 7.62-mm ShKAS machine guns, 2 × 20-mm ShVAK cannon
Yakovlev Yak-9D (early 1943)	Late 1942	1 × 1,210-hp Klimov M-105 v-type	32 ft 9.75 in.	28 ft 0.5 in.	185.7 sq ft	6,897 lb	373 mph at 11,485 ft	30,000 ft (est)	808 mi	1 × 20-mm MPSh cannon, 1 × 12.7-mm UBS machine gun
Lavochkin La-5FN (mid-1943)	Late 1942	1 × 1,640-hp Shvetsov M-82 radial	32 ft 1.75 in.	27 ft 10.75 in.	188.5 sq ft	7,406 lb	402 mph at 16,405 ft	30,000 ft (est)	435 mi	2 × 20-mm ShVAK cannon
Yakovlev Yak-3 (early 1944)	Early 1944	1 × 1,222-hp Klimov M-105 v-type	30 ft 2.25 in.	27 ft 10.75 in.	176 sq ft (est)	5,684 lb	403 mph at 16,400 ft	33,000 ft (est)	560 mi	1 × 20-mm ShVAK cannon, 2 × 12.7-mm BS machine guns
United States										
Curtiss P-40B (late 1940)	Late 1940	1 × 1,090-hp Allison V-1710 v-type	37 ft 3.5 in.	31 ft 8.5 in.	236 sq ft	7,610 lb	351 mph at 15,000 ft	28,000 ft (est)	606 mi	2 × 0.303-in. and 2 × 0.5-in. Browning machine guns
Bell P-39D Airacobra (mid-1941)	Mid-1941	1 × 1,150-hp Allison V-1710 v-type	34 ft	30 ft 2 in.	213 sq ft	7,650 lb	360 at 15,000 ft	29,000 ft (est)	600 mi	1 × 37-mm M-4 cannon, 4 × 0.303-in. and 2 × 0.5-in. Browning machine guns
Curtiss P-40E (early 1942)	Late 1940	1 × 1,150-hp Allison V-1710 v-type	37 ft 3.5 in.	31 ft 2 in.	236 sq ft	8,515 lb	334 mph at 15,000 ft	27,000 ft (est)	716 mi	6 × 0.5-in. Browning machine guns
Lockheed P-38F-15-LO Lightning (early 1942)	Early 1942	2 × 1,225-hp Allison V-1710 v-type	52 ft	37 ft 10 in.	327.5 sq ft	15,900 lb	395 mph at 25,000 ft	37,000 ft	900 mi	1 × 20-mm Hispano cannon, 4 × 0.5-in. Browning machine guns
North American P-51A-10-NA (early 1943)	Early 1942	1 × 1,200-hp Allison V-1710 v-type	37 ft 0.25 in.	32 ft 2.5 in.	232 sq ft	8,600 lb	390 mph at 20,000 ft	29,000 ft (est)	1,000 mi	4 × 0.5-in. Browning machine guns
Republic P-47B Thunderbolt (early 1943)	Early 1943	1 × 2,000-hp Pratt and Whitney radial	40 ft 9.75 in.	35 ft 3.25 in.	300 sq ft	12,245 lb	429 mph at 27,000 ft	39,500 ft (est)	550 mi	8 × 0.5-in. Browning machine guns
Bell P-39Q-5-BE Airacobra (mid-1943)	Mid-1941	1 × 1,325-hp Allison V-1710 v-type	34 ft	30 ft 2 in.	213 sq ft	7,600 lb	376 mph at 15,000 ft	32,000 ft (est)	525 mi	1 × 37-mm M-4 cannon, 4 × 0.5-in. Browning machine guns

(continues)

Table 1
Fighters, All Powers—Specifications (continued)

Name	Year of Intro- duction	Engine	Span	Length	Wing Area (sq ft)	Takeoff Weight (lb)*	Maximum Speed (mph)	Combat Ceiling (500 ft/min)†	Range (mi)‡	Armament/ Payload
United States (con										
Lockheed P-38J-25-LO Lightning (late 1943)	Early 1942	2 × 1,425-hp Allison V-1710 v-type	52 ft	37 ft 10 in.	327.5 sq ft	17,500 lb	414 mph at 25,000 ft	41,500 ft (est)	1,175 mi	1 × 20-mm Hispano cannon, 4 × 0.5-in. Browning machine guns
Republic P-47D-22-RE Thunderbolt (late 1943)	Early 1943	1 × 2,300-hp Pratt and Whitney radial	40 ft 9.75 in.	36 ft 1.75 in.	300 sq ft	13,500 lb	433 mph at 30,000 ft	37,500 ft (est)	640 mi	8 × 0.5-in. Browning machine guns
North American P-51B-1-NA (early 1944)	Early 1942	1 × 1,620-hp Packard Merlin v-type	37 ft 0.25 in.	32 ft 3 in.	232 sq ft	9,200 lb	440 mph at 30,000 ft	37,500 ft (est)	810 mi	4 × 0.5-in. Browning machine guns
North American P-51D-25-NA (early 1944)	Early 1942	1 × 1,695-hp Packard Merlin v-type	37 ft 0.25 in.	32 ft 3 in.	233 sq ft	10,100 lb	437 at 25,000 ft	37,500 ft (est)	1,300 mi	6 × 0.5-in. Browning machine guns

Sources: Brown, Eric. *Wings of the Luftwaffe.* Shrewsbury, UK: Airlife, 1993; Green, William. *War Planes of the Second World War.* Vol. 1. London: MacDonald, 1960; Green, William. *War Planes of the Second World War.* Vol. 2. London: MacDonald, 1961; Green, William. *War Planes of the Second World War.* Vol. 3. London: MacDonald, 1961; Green, William. *War Planes of the Second World War.* Vol. 4. London: MacDonald, 1961; Green, William. *Famous Bombers of the Second World War.* 2d ed. London: Book Club Associates, 1979; Mason, Francis K. *The Hawker Hurricane.* Bourne End, UK: Aston, 1990; Mason, Francis K. *The British Fighter since 1912.* London: Putnam, 1992; Jarrett, Philip, ed. *Aircraft of the Second World War.* London: Putnam, 1997; Munson, Kenneth. *Bombers, Patrol and Transport Aircraft 1939–45.* Poole, UK: Blandford, 2002; Price, Alfred. *World War II Fighter Conflict.* London: Macdonald and Janes, 1975; and Price, Alfred. *The Spitfire Story.* London: Arms and Armour, 1986.

* Weight is normal takeoff weight unless specified otherwise.

† Combat ceiling is the maximum height at which the aircraft would fight and maneuver. The service ceiling would typically be 2,000 or 3,000 ft higher than this.

‡ Range is maximum flyable distance on internal fuel, including reserves. Combat radius would typically be 30 percent to 35 percent of this value.

Macchi Mc 202 was a Mc 200 airframe with a license-built Daimler-Benz DB601 engine. It was probably the most effective Italian fighter of the war, retaining most of its predecessor's maneuverability, and was able to meet the Spitfire Mk V on at least equal terms. A total of 2,251 Mc 200 and Mc 202 aircraft were built.

Japan

The Nakajima Ki.43 ("Oscar" by the Allied identification system) entered service late in 1941 and was highly maneuverable but not particularly fast (304 mph at 13,120 ft). It had extremely sensitive controls that unfortunately stiffened significantly at speed. Allied fighters found that they could not turn with the Oscar but could outdive and outzoom it. Its armament was weak; pilot armor and self-sealing tanks were introduced with the more powerful Ki.43-IIa late in 1942, but the Oscar remained vulnerable to

enemy fire. It continued to undergo development throughout the Pacific war, 5,751 examples being built.

The Kawasaki Ki.45 ("Nick") was designed to a 1937 specification for a long-range escort fighter and entered service early in 1942. The Ki.45 was increasingly used as a night fighter from early 1944 using two 12.7 mm or 20 mm weapons firing obliquely upward. It was relatively successful against U.S. B-29 night raids, and it later became the first Japanese army air force type to be used on a kamikaze mission. A total of 1,701 were built.

The Nakajima Ki.44 interceptor ("Tōjō") first appeared in service late in 1942, although some of the 10 prototypes were evaluated on operations during 1941 and early 1942. The Tōjō was reasonably maneuverable with a good climb, but its high takeoff and landing speeds made it unpopular with pilots. The Ki.44-IIc appeared in mid-1943; armed with two 40 mm cannon and two machine guns, it was quite effective against high-flying U.S. B-24 and later B-29 bombers. A total of 1,233 were built.

The Kawasaki Ki.61 ("Tony") appeared early in 1943 and was the only Japanese fighter powered by a liquid-cooled engine to see operational service. It carried self-sealing fuel tanks and armor and was more maneuverable than were heavier opponents. Its dive characteristics were also very good indeed, comparable to the best U.S. fighters. The Ki.61 was one of very few Japanese fighters able to engage the U.S. B-29 bombers at high altitude. A total of 3,078 Ki.61s were built. Engine production was slow and the power plant gave problems in service, so early in 1945 many Ki.61 airframes were reengined with a 1,500 hp Mitsubishi Ha 112 radial to produce the Ki.100. Only 272 were built by war's end, but it was the best Japanese fighter during the conflict.

The Kawanishi N1K1-J ("George") evolved from a floatplane and was one of the best fighters of the Pacific Theater. Entering service early in 1944, it had automatic combat flaps and was outstandingly maneuverable, its pilots coming to regard even the F6F Hellcat as an easy kill. Its climb rate was, however, relatively poor for an interceptor, and the engine was unreliable. The later N1K2-J was redesigned to simplify production, and limited numbers entered service early in 1945. A total of 1,435 aircraft of the N1K series were built.

The Nakajima Ki.84 ("Frank") was one of the best Japanese fighters of the war. It entered service late in 1944. The Ki.84 could outmaneuver and outclimb late-model P-51 and P-47 fighters and had excellent maneuverability. It was well armed, strong, and well protected, and it was easy for novice pilots to fly. Production examples were beset with manufacturing faults and engine difficulties, causing performance to suffer, particularly at high altitude. A total of 3,470 Ki.84 aircraft were built.

France

The Dewotine D.520 was designed as a private venture and entered service with the French air force in 1940. It was probably the most effective French-designed fighter of the war, shooting down 100-plus enemy aircraft in exchange for 54 losses during the Battle of France. After the fall of France, the D.520 continued in Vichy French service and was encountered by the Allies in Vichy North Africa. A total of 905 were built.

Great Britain

The Hawker Hurricane entered service in 1937 and was the first monoplane fighter of the Royal Air Force (RAF), serving on all fronts. The Hurricane Mk I was the major RAF fighter during the Battle of Britain. On paper it was average, but it had hidden strengths; it was an excellent gun platform

and was more maneuverable than the Spitfire. Its controls did not stiffen appreciably at high speed, and it was very strong, being able to withstand maneuvers that would literally pull the wings off its contemporaries. Later versions (MK IID, Mk IV) were mainly built as fighter-bombers. A total of 14,233 Hurricanes were built.

The Supermarine Spitfire was a very advanced design when the Mk I entered service in 1938, and it was able to accept progressively more powerful engines and heavier armament as the war progressed, with only a slight reduction in handling qualities. The "Spit" was fast and very maneuverable and was widely regarded as a pilot's aircraft. In performance terms, it was usually considered superior to its direct opponents, although the FW-190 gave Spitfire Mk V pilots a hard time until the Mk IX redressed the balance in mid-1942. The Spitfire was continuously updated and revised with many specialist high- and low-altitude versions, and the late-war marks had a particularly impressive performance. It remained in production until after the war. A total of 20,351 were built.

The Bristol Beaufighter was designed as a private venture using components from the Beaufort torpedo-bomber. The Mk IF entered service as a radar-equipped night fighter late in 1940. It operated successfully in Europe, the Western Desert, the Mediterranean, the Far East, and the Pacific as a night fighter, long-range fighter, ground-attack aircraft, and torpedo-bomber. It was a big, heavy aircraft with a good performance at low level and a very heavy armament. A total of 5,562 Beaufighters were built.

The Hawker Typhoon was rushed into service late in 1941 to combat the German FW-190 menace, but it suffered from teething troubles. Its performance at low altitude was very good, particularly its acceleration and dive, but its performance above about 20,000 ft was poor because of its thick wing. The Typhoon was used later in the war as a ground-attack aircraft. The Hawker Tempest appeared early in 1944 and was an aerodynamically cleaner Typhoon with a thinner, laminar-flow wing. The Tempest was very fast and was one of the best late-war fighters. It could be maneuvered easily at high speed and had outstanding dive acceleration and zoom climb capabilities. It was, however, not easy to fly to its limits. A total of 3,300 Typhoons and 800 Tempests were built.

The De Havilland Mosquito was conceived as a bomber but was also produced in radar-equipped night-fighter and fighter-bomber versions. The NF.II entered service with the RAF in May 1942 and was very successful on night-intruder missions; Mosquito night fighters were used over Germany from late 1944 onward and seriously hampered German night-fighter operations. A total of 1,053 Mosquito night fighters of all versions were built;

the most numerous fighter version was the FB.VI, of which 2,718 were built.

Soviet Union

The Polikarpov I-16 Rata entered service late in 1934, the first of the new generation of monoplane fighters. More than 450 machines were operationally tested in the Spanish Civil War, and I-16s bore the brunt of the initial German assault on the Soviet Union. The Rata was marginally stable at best but was outstandingly maneuverable; it had a very good zoom climb but poor diving characteristics. Approximately 20,000 were built, the type remaining in service until 1943.

The Yakovlev series of fighters began with the Yak-1 in early 1942. It was fast at low altitude, but both the Yak-1 and the more powerful Yak-7 were slightly short on range. The Yak-9 appeared late in 1942 with a more powerful engine and particularly effective ailerons; it was capable of outturning all its opponents at low altitude. The Yak-3 was a specialized low-altitude fighter, entering service early in 1944. It had excellent performance below about 10,000 ft and was the preferred mount of the Normandie-Niemen Groupe de Chasse. Approximately 30,000 Yak fighters were produced, of which 16,700 were Yak-9s.

The Lavochkin La-5 was a very successful adaptation of the problematic LaGG-3 airframe to take a 1,330 hp Shvetsov M-82 radial engine. The La-5 entered service late in 1942 and was an immediate success as a highly maneuverable low-altitude fighter. The more powerful La-5FN appeared in mid-1943; it was faster and lighter with improved controls that gave better handling qualities. It is thought that about 15,000 Lavochkin fighters were built, although the total may well have been nearer 20,000.

United States

The Curtiss P-40 entered service in 1940. The aircraft was based on the Curtiss P-36, which was itself a reasonable fighter; French P-36 variants (Hawk 75A) accounted for approximately 70 percent of French air force kills during the Battle of France. The P-40 had reasonable dive acceleration but a poor ceiling and climb. It was average in most departments, its major attribute being that it was available in numbers when required. It was, however, continuously developed until December 1944, when the last of 13,738 P-40s, a P-40N, rolled off the production line.

The Bell P-39 Airacobra entered service in 1941. It was fast at low altitudes and pleasant to fly, but its performance fell away above 12,000 ft. Together with the P-40, the P-39 bore the brunt of the early fighting in the Pacific until later U.S. types appeared. The P-39 was rejected by the RAF but was used with some success as a low-altitude fighter by the Soviet Union, which took more than half the production total of 9,558 machines. The P-39 was used by at least 20 Soviet aces, including Aleksandr Pokryshkin (59 kills) and Grigorii Rechkalov (56 kills).

The Lockheed P-38 Lightning entered service in numbers early in 1942 and was possibly the ultimate long-range tactical fighter of the war. Its long range and twin engines made it the primary U.S. Army Air Corps fighter in the Pacific Theater. Not as maneuverable as a single-engine fighter, it was fast with very effective armament and an outstanding zoom climb. Compressibility problems handicapped diving maneuvers, however. A total of 9,923 Lightnings were built.

The North American P-51 Mustang was one of the most successful fighters of World War II. Offered to the British Air Purchasing Commission in April 1940 as an alternative to the Curtiss P-40, the P-51A entered service early in 1942. Using the same Allison engine as in the P-40, it was appreciably faster than the P-40 because of its laminar-flow wing and efficient cooling system. It had an excellent dive and zoom climb and was quite maneuverable, but it lacked performance at high altitude. The Mustang's performance was transformed by the substitution of a 1,620 hp Rolls-Royce Merlin engine in the P-51B, increasing the ceiling by nearly 10,000 ft and providing a marked performance advantage over Luftwaffe piston-engine fighters, particularly above 20,000 ft. A total of 15,686 P-51s were built.

The Republic P-47 Thunderbolt was designed for high-altitude combat and was the heaviest single-engine fighter of the war. Entering service early in 1943, the P-47B was at its best at high speed and altitude. Maneuverability was quite good at high speed, but it became ponderous at lower speeds. Although its climb rate was poor, it had exceptional dive acceleration and was very rugged. The major production model was the P-47D, which had provision for bombs and rockets and was a very effective ground-attack aircraft. A total of 15,683 Thunderbolts were built.

Andy Blackburn

See also
Aircraft, Naval; Britain, Battle of; B-29 Raids against Japan; Fighter Tactics; France, Battle for; Jet and Rocket Aircraft; Kamikaze; Radar; Spain, Civil War in

References
Green, William. *Famous Fighters of the Second World War.* 2d ed. London: Book Club Associates, 1979.
Jarrett, Philip, ed. *Aircraft of the Second World War.* London: Putnam, 1997.
Munson, Kenneth. *Fighters, Attack and Training Aircraft, 1939–45.* Poole, UK: Blandford Press, 1975.
Price, Alfred. *World War II Fighter Conflict.* London: Macdonald and Janes, 1975.

Aircraft, Gliders

A glider is an aircraft without an engine that is most often released into flight by an aerial tow aircraft. During World War II, both the Axis and Allied militaries developed gliders to transport troops, supplies, and equipment into battle. This technique had been discussed prior to the war but never implemented. These motorless aircraft would crash-land behind enemy lines, often at night, and the men aboard them would then become infantrymen on the ground.

The Germans were first to recognize the potential of gliders in the war, in large part because of extensive pre–World War II scientific research and sport use of them. The Germans embraced gliding because it did not violate military prohibitions in the 1919 Treaty of Versailles. Soaring clubs, which developed in other countries as well, increased interest in gliding worldwide. Sport gliders used air currents to climb and soar for extended periods, while military gliders descended on release from aerial tows.

By the late 1930s, Germany had developed a military glider, the DFS-230. Built of plywood, steel, and fabric, it had a wingspan of 68 ft 5.5 inches, length of 36 ft 10.5 inches, and height of 8 ft 11.75 inches. It weighed 1,896 lb empty and had a maximum weight loaded with troops and cargo of 4,630 lb. A total of 1,022 were produced. This glider was designed to mount a machine gun, which the crew could use for defense. DFS-230 gliders were employed in the invasion of Belgium and the Netherlands in May 1940, especially in securing Fort Eben Emael, which was the key to securing Belgium. The Germans also used gliders in the invasion of Crete and during fighting in the Soviet Union at Stalingrad.

The Gotha 242 glider was larger than the DFS-230 and could carry more troops. It had a wingspan of 80 ft 4.5 inches, length of 51 ft 10 inches, and height of 14 ft 4.5 inches. It weighed 7,056 lb empty and 13,665 lb fully loaded. A total of 1,528 were built. Some were launched by rockets, but most were simply towed by aircraft. Approximately 1,500 Go-242s were produced, of which 133 which adapted into Go-244s, which had twin engines. The huge Messerschmitt Me-321 glider had a wingspan of 180 ft 5.5 inches, length of 92 ft 4.25 inches, and height of 33 ft 3.4 inches. It weighed 27,432 lb empty and 75,852 lb fully loaded. It could perform level flight after rocket-assisted takeoff. A total of 200 were built. The Me-321 could transport 200 troops but was difficult to launch, and most were transformed into the six-engine Me-323.

Great Britain was the first Allied nation to deploy gliders. The Air Ministry's Glider Committee encouraged the use of the Hotspur to transport soldiers in late 1940. The Hotspur had a wingspan of 61 ft 11 inches, length of 39 ft 4 inches, and height of 10 ft 10 inches. It weighed 1,661 lb empty and 3,598 lb fully loaded. The Hotspur was designed to transport 2 crewmen and 6 soldiers. A total of 1,015 were built.

In 1941, the British developed the Horsa. It had a wingspan of 88 ft, length of 68 ft, and height of 20 ft 3 inches. It weighed 8,370 lb empty and 15,750 lb fully loaded. It was capable of carrying 2 crewmen and 25–28 passengers or 2 trucks. In all, Britain manufactured some 5,000 Horsas. They were employed in Operations OVERLORD and MARKET-GARDEN.

The largest Allied glider was the British Hamilcar. With a wingspan of 110 ft, length of 68 ft 6 inches, and height of 20 ft 3 inches, it weighed 18,000 lb empty and 36,000 lb fully loaded. It could transport 40 troops, a light tank, or artillery pieces. A total of 412 were built. It was employed during Operation OVERLORD.

The Soviet Union introduced the A-7 glider in 1939. It had a wingspan of 62 ft 2 inches and length of 37 ft 7 inches. It weighed 2,000 lb empty and carried a pilot and eight passengers. A total of 400 were manufactured. The Soviets, however, had few aircraft available for glider tows, and following the German invasion of the Soviet Union, their priority was with other weaponry. They used the A-7 chiefly to transport supplies to partisans working behind German lines.

The U.S. Navy explored the possibility of military applications for gliders as early as the 1930s. In February 1941, Chief of the Army Air Corps Major General Henry H. Arnold ordered that specifications be drawn up for military gliders. The Waco Aircraft Company in Troy, Ohio, received the first U.S. government contract to build training gliders, and the army began organizing a glider training program. Constructed of plywood and canvas with a skeleton of steel tubing, the Waco CG-4A had a wingspan of 83 ft 6 inches, length of 48 ft 4 inches, and height of 12 ft 7 inches. Its empty weight was 3,300 lb, and its loaded weight was 7,500 lb. It could carry 15 troops or 3,800 lb of cargo, including artillery pieces, a bulldozer, or a jeep. The Ford Motor Company plant at Kingsford, Michigan, manufactured most of the U.S. gliders, although 15 other companies also produced the Waco. In all 13,908 Wacos were built, making it the most heavily produced glider of the entire war by any power.

Because the gliders were so fragile, soldiers dubbed them "canvas coffins." Men and cargo were loaded through the wide, hinged nose section, which could be quickly opened. Moving at an airspeed of 110–150 mph at an altitude of several thousand feet, C-47s towed the gliders with a 300 ft rope toward a designated landing zone and then descended to release the glider several hundred feet above ground. En route to the release point, the glidermen and plane crew communicated with each other either by a telephone wire secured around the towline or via two-way radios. This glider duty was hazardous indeed; sometimes gliders were released prematurely and did not reach the landing zones, and on occasion gliders collided as they approached their destination.

The U.S. 11th, 13th, 17th, 82nd, and 101st Airborne Divisions were equipped with two glider infantry regiments, a glider artillery battalion, and glider support units. U.S. gliders were sent to North Africa in 1942 and participated in the July 1943 Sicily invasion, accompanied by British gliders. High casualties sustained in that operation led General Dwight D. Eisenhower to question the organization of airborne divisions and to threaten to disband glider units. A review board of officers convinced the military authorities to retain them, however. Improvements were made in structural reinforcement of the glider and personnel training.

By mid-1944, gliders had become essential elements of Allied invasion forces. Occasionally they were used to transport wounded to hospitals. During Operation NEPTUNE, U.S. glidermen with the 82nd and 101st Airborne Divisions flew across the English Channel in 2,100 gliders to participate in the D day attack. Many gliders and crews were lost during that mission. New gliders were manufactured for Operation MARKET-GARDEN, the assault on the Germans in the Netherlands, three months later.

Initially, the military did not distribute hazardous-duty pay to glidermen. These soldiers also did not qualify for wing insignia worn by parachutists. Some of the men created posters; one read: "Join the Glider Troops! No Jump Pay. No Flight Pay. But Never A Dull Moment." By July 1944, glider wings were authorized for glider soldiers, and they received hazardous-duty pay. Also in 1944, the modified Waco CG-15A appeared, offering improved crash absorption. The Waco CG-18A could carry 30 soldiers and was deployed during the 1945 Rhine campaign.

Gliders were also used in the Pacific and China-Burma-India Theaters. The final U.S. glider mission of the war occurred on Luzon Island, the Philippines, in June 1945. In July, IX Troop Carrier Command Commander Brigadier General Paul L. Williams issued an order to grant an Air Medal to Normandy glider pilot veterans. Gliders were gradually phased out of military inventories after the war, although the Soviets retained them through the 1950s.

Elizabeth D. Schafer

See also

Airborne Forces, Allied; Airborne Forces, Axis; Aircraft, Transports; Arnold, Henry Harley; Belgium Campaign; Crete, Battle of; Eben Emael; Eisenhower, Dwight D.; Germany, Air Force; Great Britain, Air Force; MARKET-GARDEN, Operation; Normandy Invasion and Campaign; OVERLORD, Operation; Rhine Crossings; Soviet Union, Air Force; United States, Air Force

References

Devlin, Gerard M. *Silent Wings: The Saga of the U.S. Army and Marine Combat Glider Pilots during World War II.* New York: St. Martin's Press, 1985.

Lowden, John L. *Silent Wings at War: Combat Gliders in World War II.* Washington, DC: Smithsonian Institution Press, 1992.

Masters, Charles J. *Glidermen of Neptune: The American D-Day Glider Attack.* Carbondale: Southern Illinois University Press, 1995.

Mrazek, James E. *The Glider War.* New York: St. Martin's Press, 1975.

———. *Fighting Gliders of World War II.* New York: St. Martin's Press, 1977.

———. *The Fall of Eben Emael: The Daring Airborne Assault That Sealed the Fate of France: May 1940.* Novato, CA: Presidio, 1999.

Seth, Ronald. *Lion with Blue Wings: The Story of the Glider Regiment, 1942–1945.* London: Gollancz, 1955.

Smith, Claude. *The History of the Glider Pilot Regiment.* London: Leo Cooper, 1992.

Aircraft, Jet and Rocket
See Jet and Rocket Aircraft.

Aircraft, Naval

Most naval aircraft fall into one of four main classifications: spotters, patrol aircraft, land-based attack aircraft, and carrier-based aircraft. Battleships and cruisers usually carried catapult-launched spotter aircraft to correct gunfire against enemy vessels or shore targets. Most spotter aircraft tended to be relatively slow floatplanes (e.g., Mitsubishi F1M2 ["Pete" in the Allied identification system] and Vought OS2U Kingfisher), as the design parameters were restricted by the launch and recovery mechanism. These aircraft were also very useful in search and rescue missions.

Patrol aircraft were designed to keep track of enemy ships and (in some cases) to attack small vessels such as submarines. The major performance requirements for patrol aircraft were range and endurance; the sea covers a vast area and an enemy fleet occupied a relatively tiny part of it, so the ability to search large areas and remain on station for a long time was important. Flying boats were widely used as patrol aircraft (e.g., the Consolidated PBY Catalina, Kawanishi H8K, and Short Sunderland), but land-based patrollers with longer ranges (e.g., Lockheed Hudson, Ventura, and Consolidated B-24 Liberator) were used toward the latter part of the war, initially to patrol colder areas such as the Aleutians and Iceland, where flying boats found operation difficult.

Land-based attack aircraft were employed by most combatants and were sometimes successful, provided that they employed specialist antiship attack techniques. Torpedo-bombing was probably the most effective form of attack, but results varied depending on the efficiency of the weapon. American torpedoes suffered from problems and were largely ineffective until the second half of 1943, whereas the Japanese 18-inch "Long Lance" torpedo was extremely effective with a large warhead. Italian, German, and British torpedoes were all moderately effective. Dive-bombing and skip-bombing were also effective, but attacks by high-level bombers were universally unsuccessful against moving ships, as the target had plenty of time to take avoiding action.

Great Britain employed purpose-designed torpedo attack aircraft (the Beaufort and Beaufighter). The United States mainly used conversions of existing aircraft as torpedo carriers (the B-25 Mitchell and B-26 Marauder), but it usually employed skip-bombing in preference to torpedoes. Medium bombers were also used as torpedo-aircraft by Japan (the GM-4 "Betty"), Germany (He-111H), Italy (SM.79), and the Soviet Union (Ilyushin DB-3T/Il-4). German and Japanese bombers were particularly effective.

The following two types of specialist torpedo-bombers were widely used during World War II.

1. The Italian Savoia-Marchetti S.M.79, originally designed as a commercial transport, was adapted to use as a bomber when its excellent performance became known. The SM.79-I entered service in 1936 and was used with some success during the Spanish Civil War. The more powerful SM.79-II was employed throughout World War II in the Mediterranean Theater as a torpedo-bomber (carrying two 17.7-inch torpedoes), medium bomber, reconnaissance aircraft, close-support aircraft, and transport/training aircraft. A total of 1,330 were built between 1936 and 1944.

2. The Bristol Beaufort was the standard British land-based torpedo-bomber until it was replaced by the Bristol Beaufighter TF.X in 1943. Entering service late in 1939, the Beaufort was also used for bombing and minelaying operations. It was reasonably successful, although occasionally let down by malfunctioning torpedoes. A total of 1,429 were built in the United Kingdom, and 700 were built under license in Australia.

Flying an aircraft off and onto an aircraft carrier places many more stresses and strains on the aircraft's structure than comparable activities on land. As a consequence, carrier-based aircraft were generally heavier and more ro-

bust—and thus slower and less maneuverable (at least in theory)—than their land-based counterparts. Parts of their structure usually folded to allow the aircraft to be taken below to the hangar, further increasing the weight. On top of that, landing characteristics had to be superior, which required a light wing loading, large flaps, good stall behavior, and a compliant undercarriage. Combining all of these characteristics in a single aircraft was not easy; many of the aircraft that served on carrier decks during World War II had flaws.

Of the major combatants, only the United States, Japan, and Great Britain had aircraft carriers, and each had a different approach to design of carrier-based aircraft (see Tables 1, 2, and 3 for carrier-based attack aircraft, fighters, and bombers respectively).

United States

In 1941, the United States had several large carriers and well-organized carrier operational procedures; it used scout/dive-bombers (SBD Dauntless), torpedo/level-bombers (TBD-1 Devastator), and fighters (F4F Wildcat). Generally speaking, U.S. carrier aircraft were rugged and quite suitable for maritime use. The Douglas TDB-1 Devastator carrier-based torpedo-bomber entered service late in 1937 and was obsolescent when the United States entered the war. Its combat career was terminated by the Battle of Midway when it proved to be vulnerable to fighter attack while unescorted. A total of 129 TBD-1s were built.

The Douglas SBD Dauntless entered service with the U.S. Marine Corps in mid-1940 and with the U.S. Navy later in 1940. It was the standard navy carrierborne dive-bomber in December 1941 when Pearl Harbor was attacked. Operationally, the Dauntless was very successful and could absorb a lot of battle damage, having the lowest attrition rate of any U.S. carrier aircraft in the Pacific Theater. It played a major part in the 1942 Battles of the Coral Sea and Midway and later flew off escort carriers on anti-submarine and close-support missions. A total of 5,936 Dauntless were built.

The Grumman F4F Wildcat entered service with the Royal Navy late in 1940, and it became operational with the Marine Corps and U.S. Navy at the beginning of 1941. The F4F-3 was the standard navy shipboard fighter when the United States entered the war, and it was generally inferior to the Japanese A6M2 Zero in performance and maneuverability. However, the F4F was very rugged and had good dive performance, giving a good account of itself when using the correct tactics. Later in the war, the Wildcat gave sterling service on escort carriers. Approximately 8,000 Wildcats were built.

The Grumman TBF Avenger first flew in August 1941 and became the standard navy carrier-based torpedo-

Table 1
Carrier-Based Attack Aircraft, All Powers—Specifications

Name	Year of Introduction	Crew	Engine (hp)	Span	Length	Takeoff Weight (lb)*	Maximum speed (mph)	Operational ceiling (ft)	Range (mi)†	Armament/ Payload
Fairey Swordfish Mk 1 (late 1936)	Late 1936	3	1 × 690-hp Bristol Pegasus radial	45 ft 6 in.	36 ft 4 in.	9,250 lb	139 mph at 4,750 ft	10,700 ft	546 mi	2 × 0.3-in. machine guns, 1 × 1,610-lb torpedo
Douglas TBD-1 Devastator (late 1937)	Late 1937	3	1 × 900-hp Pratt and Whitney twin-wasp radial	50 ft 0 in.	35 ft 0 in.	10,194 lb	206 mph at 8,000 ft	19,500 ft	716 mi	2 × 0.3-in. machine guns, 1,000 lb bombs
Nakajima B5N2 "Kate" (late 1940)	Late 1937	3	1 × 1,000-hp Nakajima Sakae radial	50 ft 11 in.	33 ft 9.5 in.	9,039 lb	235 mph at 11,810 ft	27,100 ft	1,237 mi	1 × 7.7-mm machine gun, 1 × 1,764-lb torpedo
Blackburn Skua Mk II (late 1938)	Late 1938	2	1 × 890-hp Bristol Perseus radial	46 ft 2 in.	35 ft 7 in.	8,228 lb	225 mph at 6,500 ft	19,100 ft	761 mi	5 × 0.3-in. machine guns, 740 lb bombs
Fairey Albacore Mk I (early 1940)	Early 1940	3	1 × 1,065-hp Bristol Taurus radial	50 ft 0 in.	39 ft 9.5 in.	10,600 lb	161 mph at 4,000 ft	20,700 ft	930 mi	3 × 0.3-in. machine guns, 1 × 1,610-lb torpedo or 1,650 lb bomb
Douglas SBD-3 Dauntless (early 1941)	Mid-1940	2	1 × 1,000-hp Wright Cyclone radial	41 ft 6 in.	32 ft 8 in.	10,400 lb	250 mph at 14,000 ft	27,100 ft	1,345 mi	4 × 0.3-in. machine guns, 1,200 lb bombs
Aichi D3A1 "Val" (mid-1940)	Mid-1940	2	1 × 1,000-hp Mitsubishi Kinsei radial	47 ft 2 in.	33 ft 5.5 in.	8,047 lb	240 mph at 9,840 ft	30,050 ft	915 mi	3 × 7.7-mm machine guns, 813 lb bombs
Grumman TBF-1 Avenger (mid-1942)	Mid-1942	3	1 × 1,700-hp Wright Cyclone radial	54 ft 2 in.	40 ft	15,905 lb	271 mph at 12,000 ft	22,400 ft	1,215 mi	3 × 0.3-in. machine guns, 1,600 lb bombs or 1 torpedo
Curtiss SB2C-1 Helldiver (early 1943)	Early 1943	2	1 × 1,700-hp Wright Cyclone radial	49 ft 9 in.	36 ft 8 in.	16,616 lb	281 mph at 16,700 ft	25,100 ft	1,110 mi	2 × 20-mm cannon, 2 × 0.3-in. machine guns, 2,000 lb bombs
Yokosuka D4Y1 "Judy" (early 1943)	Early 1943	2	1 × 1,200-hp Aichi Atsura v-type	37 ft 9 in.	33 ft 6.5 in.	9,370 lb	343 mph at 15,585 ft	32,480 ft	978 mi	3 × 7.7-mm machine guns, 683 lb bombs
Fairey Barracuda Mk II (early 1943)	Early 1943	3	1 × 1,640-hp Rolls-Royce Merlin v-type	49 ft 2 in.	39 ft 9 in.	14,100 lb	210 mph at 2,000 ft	21,600 ft	604 mi	2 × 0.3-in. machine guns, 1 × 1,610-lb torpedo or 1,600 lb bomb
Nakajima B6N2 "Jill" (late 1943)	Late 1943	3	1 × 1,850-hp Mitsubishi Kasei radial	48 ft 10.5 in.	35 ft 8 in.	12,456 lb	299 mph at 16,075 ft	29,660 ft	1,892 mi	2 × 7.7-mm machine guns, 1 × 1,764-lb torpedo

Sources: Brown, Eric M. *Duels in the Sky.* Shrewsbury, UK: Airlife, 1989; Jarrett, Philip, ed. *Aircraft of the Second World War.* London: Putnam, 1997; Munson, Kenneth. *Bombers, Patrol, and Transport Aircraft, 1939–45.* Poole, UK: Blandford Press, 1969; and Munson, Kenneth. *Fighters, Attack and Training Aircraft, 1939–45.* Poole, UK: Blandford Press, 1969.

* Weight is normal takeoff weight unless specified otherwise.

† Range is maximum flyable distance including reserves.

Table 2
Carrier-Based Fighters, All Powers—Specifications

Name	Year of Introduction	Engine	Span	Length	Wing Area (sq ft)	Takeoff Weight (lb)*	Maximum speed (mph)	Combat ceiling (500 ft/min)†	Range (mi)‡	Armament/Payload
Mitsubishi A6M2 Zero model 21 (mid-1940)	Mid-1940	1 × 925-hp Nakajima Sakae radial	39 ft 4.5 in.	29 ft 8.75 in.	241.5 sq ft	5,313 lb	332 mph at 16,570 ft	31,000 ft (est)	1,595 mi	2 × 7.7-mm type 97 machine guns, 2 × 20-mm type 99 cannon
Grumman F4F-3 Wildcat (early 1941)	Late 1940	1 × 1,200-hp Pratt and Whitney Twin Wasp radial	38 ft 0 in.	28 ft 9 in.	260 sq ft	7,002 lb	328 mph at 21,000 ft	35,000 ft (est)	845 mi	4 × 0.5-in. Browning machine guns
Hawker Sea Hurricane Mk IIC (early 1941)	Mid-1940	1 × 1,260-hp Rolls-Royce Merlin v-type	40 ft 0 in.	32 ft 2.5 in.	258 sq ft	7,618 lb	317 mph at 17,500 ft	28,000 ft	452 mi	4 × 20-mm Oerlikon cannon
Fairey Fulmar II (early 1941)	Mid-1940	1 × 1,300-hp Rolls-Royce Merlin v-type	46 ft 4.5 in.	40 ft 2 in.	342 sq ft	9,672 lb	272 mph at 7,250 ft	24,500 ft (est)	780 mi	8 × 0.303-in. Browning machine guns
Grumman F6F-3 Hellcat (early 1943)	Early 1943	1 × 2,000-hp Pratt and Whitney R-2800 radial	42 ft 10 in.	33 ft 7 in.	334 sq ft	11,381 lb	376 mph at 17,300 ft	36,000 ft (est)	1,090 mi	6 × 0.5-in. Browning machine guns plus 2 × 1,000-lb bombs or 6 × 5-in. rockets
Supermarine Seafire F.III (early 1944)	Mid-1942	1 × 1,470-hp Rolls-Royce Merlin v-type	36 ft 10 in.	30 ft 2.5 in.	242 sq ft	7,100 lb	352 mph at 12,250 ft	31,000 ft (est)	465 mi	2 × 20-mm Hispano cannon, 4 × 0.303-in. Browning machine guns plus 500-lb bombs
Vought F4U-1D Corsair (early 1944)	Early 1943	1 × 2,250-hp Pratt and Whitney R-2800 radial	40 ft 11 in.	33 ft 4 in.	314 sq ft	12,039 lb	425 mph at 20,000 ft	34,500 ft (est)	1,015 mi	6 × 0.5-in. Browning machine guns plus 2 × 1,000-lb bombs or 8 × 5-in. rockets
Mitsubishi A6M6c Zero model 53c (late 1944)	Mid-1940	1 × 1,130-hp Nakajima Sakae radial	36 ft 1 in.	29 ft 9 in.	229.3 sq ft	6,047 lb	346 mph at 19,680 ft	32,500 ft (est)	1,194 mi	3 × 12.7-mm type 3 machine guns, 2 × 20-mm type 99 cannon

Sources: Brown, Eric M. *Duels in the Sky.* Shrewsbury, UK: Airlife, 1989; Jarrett, Philip, ed. *Aircraft of the Second World War.* London: Putnam, 1997; Munson, Kenneth. *Bombers, Patrol, and Transport Aircraft, 1939–45.* Poole, UK: Blandford Press, 1969; and Munson, Kenneth. *Fighters, Attack and Training Aircraft, 1939–45.* Poole, UK: Blandford Press, 1969.

* Weight is normal takeoff weight unless specified otherwise.
† Combat ceiling is the maximum height at which the aircraft would fight and maneuver. The service ceiling would typically be 2,000 or 3,000 feet higher than this.
‡ Range is maximum flyable distance on internal fuel including reserves. Combat radius would typically be 30% to 35% of this value.

Table 3
Naval Bombers, All Powers—Specifications

Name	Year of Introduction	Crew	Engine	Span	Length	Takeoff Weight (lb)*	Maximum Speed (mph)	Operational Ceiling (ft)	Range (mi)†	Armament/ Payload
Bristol Beaufort Mk 1 (late 1939)	Late 1939	4	2 × 1,130-hp Bristol Taurus radials	57 ft 10 in.	44 ft 3 in.	21,228 lb	263 mph at 6,500 ft	16,500 ft	1,600 mi	4 × 0.303-in. machine guns, 1 × 1,650-lb torpedo, or 2,000 lb bombs
Savoia-Marchetti S.M.79-II Sparviero (early 1940)	1937	6	3 × 1,000-hp Piaggio radials	69 ft 6.5 in.	53 ft 1.75 in.	25,133 lb	295 mph at 13,120 ft	27,890 ft	1,243 mi with 2,756 lb bombs	3 × 12.7-mm machine guns, 2 × 7.7-mm machine guns, 2 × 450-mm torpedoes, or 2,756 lb bombs

Sources: Green, William. *Famous Bombers of the Second World War.* 2d ed. London: Book Club Associates, 1979; Jarrett, Philip, ed. *Aircraft of the Second World War.* London: Putnam, 1997; and Munson, Kenneth. *Bombers, Patrol and Transport Aircraft 1939–45.* Poole, UK: Blandford, 2002.

* Weight is normal takeoff weight unless specified otherwise.
† Range is maximum flyable distance, including reserves.

bomber. It entered service in mid-1942 in time for the Battle of Midway. It could take a lot of punishment and, although it was not very maneuverable, it was easy to land on deck. A total of 9,836 Avengers were built; most served with the U.S. Navy, but 958 were supplied to the British navy.

The Curtiss SB2 Helldiver was the most successful carrier-based dive-bomber in U.S. Navy service, in spite of its handling faults and a reputation for structural weakness. Entering service early in 1943, its first major action was the Rabaul Campaign in November 1943, and it took part in almost every major naval/air action during the remainder of the war. The navy was the major user of the Helldiver, although some were flown by the Marine Corps and the British Royal Navy. A total of 7,200 Helldivers were built in the United States and Canada.

The Vought F4U Corsair entered service with the Marine Corps early in 1943; it was not an easy aircraft to deck-land and was initially rejected by the U.S. Navy in favor of the Hellcat. The gull-winged F4U operated from land bases in the Pacific and flew off Royal Navy carriers from late 1943. The Corsair was a very good fighter, convincingly superior in performance to the Mitsubishi Zero and much better than the P-51B Mustang below about 20,000 ft. Eventually the Corsair matured into a reasonable deck-landing aircraft, and it began to supplant the F6F Hellcat as the standard U.S. Navy carrier fighter by the end of the war. It saw extensive service after the war and continued in production until 1952. A total of 12,571 were built.

The Grumman F6F Hellcat entered service early in 1943. It was the most successful carrier-based fighter of the war,

accounting for 76 percent of the total enemy aircraft destroyed by U.S. Navy carrier pilots. It was extremely rugged and had much better speed and dive capabilities than the Mitsubishi Zero, which it could normally beat in an even fight. Many of the U.S. Navy aces flew Hellcats. The Hellcat was also employed with some success at night; approximately 1,300 of the 12,272 produced were dedicated radar-equipped night-fighter versions.

Japan

The Imperial Japanese Navy (IJN) had several carriers at the start of the war, the air groups of which were weighted toward attack aircraft rather than fighters. Its aircraft were lightly built and had very long range, but this advantage was usually purchased at the expense of vulnerability to enemy fire. The skill of Japanese aviators tended to exaggerate the effectiveness of the IJN's aircraft, and pilot quality fell off as experienced crews were shot down during the Midway and Solomon Islands Campaigns.

The Nakajima B5N ("Kate" in the Allied designator system) first entered service in 1937 as a carrier-based attack bomber, with the B5N2 torpedo-bomber appearing in 1940. The B5N had good handling and deck-landing characteristics and was operationally very successful in the early part of the war. Large numbers of the B5N participated in the Mariana Islands campaign, and it was employed as a suicide aircraft toward the end of the war. Approximately 1,200 B5Ns were built.

The Aichi D3A ("Val") carrier-based dive-bomber entered service in mid-1940, and it was the standard Japanese navy dive-bomber when Japan entered the war. It was a good bomber, capable of putting up a creditable fight after dropping its bomb load. It participated in the attack on Pearl Harbor and the major Pacific campaigns including Santa Cruz, Midway, and the Solomon Islands. Increasing losses during the second half of the war took their toll, and the D3A was used on suicide missions later in the war. Approximately 1,495 D3As were built.

When it first appeared in mid-1940, the Mitsubishi A6M Zero was the first carrier-based fighter capable of beating its land-based counterparts. It was well armed and had truly exceptional maneuverability below about 220 mph, and its capabilities came as an unpleasant shock to U.S. and British forces. It achieved this exceptional performance at the expense of resistance to enemy fire, with a light structure and no armor or self-sealing tanks. Its Achilles heel was the stiffness of its controls at high speed, the control response being almost nil at indicated airspeed over 300 mph. The Zero was developed throughout the war, a total of 10,449 being built.

The Nakajima B6N ("Jill") carrier-based torpedo-bomber entered service late in 1943 and was intended to replace the B5N, but the initial B6N1 was plagued with engine troubles. The B6N2 with a Mitsubishi engine was the major production model, appearing early in 1944. Overall, it was better than its predecessor but not particularly easy to deck-land. It participated in the Marianas Campaign and was encountered throughout the Pacific until the end of the war. A total of 1,268 were built.

The Yokosuka D4Y ("Judy") reconnaissance/dive-bomber entered service on Japanese carriers early in 1943 and was very fast for a bomber. Initially assigned to reconnaissance units, it was intended to replace the D3A, but it was insufficiently armed and protected and suffered from structural weakness in dives. In common with most other Japanese aircraft, it was used for kamikaze attacks, and a D4Y carried out the last kamikaze attack of the war on 15 August 1945. A total of 2,819 D4Ys were built.

Great Britain

During the 1930s, Great Britain had a limited number of air assets with which to patrol a far-flung empire; the Admiralty was therefore obliged to buy multirole aircraft and accept the inevitable compromises in performance. The Royal Navy entered the war with low-performing aircraft, and its efforts to introduce better aircraft were compromised by conflicts in engine supply. In 1943 it was only too pleased to have the use of F4U Corsairs that were surplus to the requirements of the U.S. Navy.

The Fairey Swordfish carrier-based torpedo/spotter/reconnaissance aircraft entered service late in 1936 and participated in the night raid on Taranto, the battle of Cape Matapan, and the sinking of the *Bismarck*. It was very slow but was astonishingly agile with excellent flying qualities. Very easy to deck-land, it was a natural choice for use on Atlantic convoy escort carriers. It remained in service until mid-1945, outlasting its replacement (the Fairey Albacore). A total of 2,391 Swordfish were built.

The Blackburn Skua came on line late in 1938 as a carrier-based fighter/dive-bomber. It was not easy to deck-land and had poor stall characteristics, but it was an effective dive-bomber, sinking the German cruiser *Königsberg* in Bergen harbor during the Norwegian Campaign. A total of 190 were built.

The Fairey Albacore carrier-based torpedo/dive-bomber/reconnaissance aircraft entered service as a replacement for the Swordfish early in 1940 and took part in many of the Middle East operations, including the Battles of Cape Matapan and El Alamein and the Allied landings at Sicily and Salerno. The Albacore had only a slightly better performance than the Swordfish and few redeeming features, and its service with the Royal Navy ended late in 1943. A total of 800 were built.

The two-seat Fairey Fulmar carrier fighter entered service in mid-1940 and was principally designed to combat unescorted bombers and maritime patrol aircraft. It had adequate range, but it was underpowered and its performance was insufficient to deal with contemporary fighters. Nevertheless, it filled a gap until better aircraft became available. A total of 600 were built.

The Hawker Sea Hurricane was first used on catapult-armed merchantmen (CAM) ships during early 1941. Many were conversions of existing land-based fighters. Sea Hurricanes were operational on carriers from late 1941; they were maneuverable and well armed but usually had a lower performance than their adversaries. Approximately 800 Sea Hurricanes were built or converted.

The Supermarine Seafire was an adaptation of the land-based Supermarine Spitfire VB fighter. When it appeared in mid-1942, it was the fastest operational carrier fighter in the world, but it was difficult to deck-land and was not sufficiently robust for use at sea. Later versions were very effective at low altitude, the Seafire LIIC having an outstanding climb and roll performance. Approximately 1,900 were built or converted before the end of the war.

The Fairey Barracuda carrier-based dive/torpedo-bomber entered service early in 1943. It was usually used as a dive-bomber and was not popular with its crews; its performance was mediocre and its defensive armament was poor. It was, however, a reasonably good dive-bomber and was easy to deck-land. A total of 1,718 were built.

Andy Blackburn

See also

Aircraft, Bombers; Aircraft Carriers; Aircraft, Fighters; *Bismarck, Sortie and Sinking of;* Cape Matapan, Battle of; Coral Sea, Battle of the; El Alemain, Battle of; Mariana Islands, Naval Campaign; Midway, Battle of; Pearl Harbor, Attack on; Salerno Invasion; Santa Cruz Islands, Battle of; Taranto, Attack on; Torpedoes

References

Brown, Eric M. *Duels in the Sky.* Shrewsbury, UK: Airlife, 1989.

Jarrett, Philip, ed. *Aircraft of the Second World War.* London: Putnam, 1997.

Munson, Kenneth. *Bombers, Patrol, and Transport Aircraft, 1939–45.* Poole, UK: Blandford Press, 1969.

———. *Fighters, Attack and Training Aircraft, 1939–45.* Poole, UK: Blandford Press, 1969.

Aircraft, Production of

Key aspect of World War II industrial production that tipped the scales of the air war decisively away from the Axis powers in favor of the Allies. Although Germany and Japan had entered the war with initial advantages of aircraft and other war matériel because they had begun military production much earlier than the Allies, the combined industrial potential of the Allies far exceeded that of the Axis nations. Even though Axis aircraft production increased during the course of the war, it paled in comparison to that of the Allies, especially the United States. To the extent that World War II was a total war that depended on industrial output, the Allied advantage in manpower and industry ultimately proved decisive, and aircraft production is a key indicator of that advantage (see Table 1).

Axis Powers

Although Germany had entered the war in September 1939 as the world's leading air power, with 4,840 frontline aircraft and an aircraft industry producing 1,000 airplanes a month, the Luftwaffe's arsenal had serious defects. For one, Germany had never developed a satisfactory long-range bomber, in part because the German military's focus on blitzkrieg (lightning war) emphasized production of medium-range bombers and ground-attack aircraft, which had proven so successful in the Spanish Civil War. Germany's defeat in the Battle of Britain revealed the flaw of this policy from a strategic standpoint, as aircraft such as Heinkel He-111, Dornier Do-17, and Junkers Ju-87 proved ineffective against a technologically well-equipped enemy force. Likewise, Germany's lack of long-range bombers prevented it from conducting long-range air operations at sea or striking Soviet manufacturing centers relocated deep within the Soviet Union. Despite the damage inflicted by the Allied air campaign, the German armaments industry, ably led by Fritz Todt and Albert Speer, not only managed to increase production from 8,295 aircraft in 1939 to 39,807 in 1944 but also introduced the world's first jet fighter, the Messerschmitt Me-262, in the second half of 1944. These successes, however, proved to be too little and too late to make a difference, and the Allies had air supremacy in the last two years of the war.

As with Germany, Japan entered the war with a powerful air arm, which included some 2,900 combat-ready aircraft on 7 December 1941. Yet, Japan's attack on Pearl Harbor was in part a desperate gamble designed to cripple the United States to purchase time for Japan to build a defensive perimeter before U.S. industrial might reached heights that Japan knew it could never equal. Indeed, Japanese industry produced just 5,088 aircraft in 1941, compared with 26,277 for the United States. Failure to destroy the U.S. carriers in the surprise attack on Pearl Harbor ranks as a clear strategic mistake for Japan. Once it lost the Battle of Midway in early June 1942, Japan was forced into a defensive war in which it could not compete with the American war machine. Despite Allied attacks that crippled its shipping industry and weakened its industrial infrastructure, Japan still managed to produce 28,180 aircraft in 1944, a testament to the perseverance of its workers on the home front. That the United States produced 96,318 aircraft during the same year is a testament to the futility of Japan's challenge to American industrial might.

Although Benito Mussolini had built a powerful Italian air force in the late 1920s and early 1930s, by the beginning of World War II in September 1939, Italy's air force had become largely obsolete. This decline was in part a reflection of Italy's weak economy. When Italy joined the war on 10 June 1940, barely half of its 3,296 aircraft were of combat quality. While assistance from Germany (particularly in supplying aircraft engines) allowed the Italian aircraft industry to make modest increases from 2,142 aircraft produced in 1940 to 3,503 aircraft in 1941, Italy's weak industrial sector could not withstand the impact of the Allied bombing campaign, and production dropped to 2,818 aircraft in 1942 and just 967 aircraft by the time Italy surrendered in September 1943.

Allied Powers

Although Germany enjoyed a great lead in the number of its combat-ready aircraft at the start of the war, Great Britain had an advantage in that its industry was in the process of introducing aircraft (such as the Hawker Hurricane and Supermarine Spitfire) more technologically advanced than their German counterparts. This qualitative advantage would prove critical to defeating Germany in the Battle of Britain. Secure from the threat of German invasion, British industry succeeded not only in increasing productive capacity with

Table 1
Aircraft Production in World War II

Year	Germany	Japan	Italy	Axis Totals by Year
1939	8,295	4,467	1,692	14,454
1940	10,826	4,768	2,142	17,736
1941	11,776	5,088	3,503	20,367
1942	15,556	8,861	2,818	27,235
1943	25,527	16,693	967	43,187
1944	39,807	28,180	x	67,987
1945	7,544	8,263	x	15,807
Axis totals (all years)	119,331	76,320	11,122	206,773

Year	Great Britain	Soviet Union	United States	Allied Totals by Year
1939	7,940	10,382	5,856	24,178
1940	15,049	10,565	12,804	38,418
1941	20,094	17,735	26,277	64,106
1942	23,673	25,436	47,836	96,945
1943	26,263	34,845	85,898	147,006
1944	26,461	40,246	96,318	163,025
1945	12,070	20,052	49,761	81,883
Allied totals (all years)	131,550	159,261	324,750	615,561

Source: Wilson, Stewart. *Aircraft of WWII.* Fyshwick, Australia: Aerospace Publications, 1998.

each passing year of the war but also in introducing aircraft such as the Handley Page Halifax and Avro Lancaster that played a critical role in the Allied bombing campaign against Germany. Great Britain's highest annual production total reached 26,461 aircraft in 1944, compared with 39,807 aircraft for Germany that year. Nevertheless, Great Britain's overall production of 131,550 aircraft during the war exceeded that of Germany, which produced 119,331 aircraft.

The Soviet Union possessed large numbers of aircraft at the outbreak of the war, but most of these were inferior to their German counterparts. Making matters worse, when Germany launched its invasion of the Soviet Union on 22 June 1941, it destroyed 1,200 Soviet aircraft in the first nine hours of the attack. The Soviet Union managed not only to sustain this loss but to recover, because of its monumental efforts to transfer industries eastward beyond the reach of the German army and air force. In the first three months after the German invasion, the Soviet Union relocated 1,523 factories. The primary production line for the Yakovlev Yak-1, for example, was moved more than 1,000 miles and returned to production in less than six weeks. The success of these efforts allowed the Soviet Union to exceed German production for each year of the war, including 1941, for a total of 159,261 Soviet aircraft compared with 119,331 German aircraft.

In 1939, the U.S. economy was still suffering from the Great Depression, with 8.9 million registered unemployed workers. However, the success of the German blitzkrieg against western Europe in 1940 spurred the American war machine into action. The Burke-Wadsworth Act of 16 September 1940 introduced peacetime conscription for the first time in American history, and massive military spending got the American economy working again. Unlike Germany and Japan, the United States not only had a large population base and natural resources that could be mobilized for pro-

Long lines of A-20 attack bombers roll ceaselessly off the assembly line, night and day, through the Douglas Aircraft plant at Long Beach, California, ca. October 1942. (Franklin D. Roosevelt Library (NLFDR))

duction but also enjoyed an industrial infrastructure far removed from its enemies. By 1944, a total of 18.7 million Americans, approximately 50 percent of whom were women, had entered the American workforce. Of all of their industrial achievements, none was more spectacular than aircraft production. From just 5,856 aircraft produced in 1939, the United States would reach the staggering total of 96,318 produced in 1944—almost one-third more than that produced by Germany and Japan combined for that year. For the war years as a whole, the United States would produce 324,750 aircraft, compared with a total of 206,773 for Germany, Japan, and Italy. The U.S. output, combined with the output of the British and the Soviet Union, gave the Allies an advantage greater than three to one, with 615,561 aircraft. With such an advantage, it is little wonder that the Allies won the war in the air.

Justin D. Murphy

See also

Aircraft, Bombers; Aircraft, Fighters; Aircraft, Gliders; Aircraft, Naval; Aircraft, Reconnaissance and Auxiliary; Aircraft, Transports; Britain, Battle of; Germany, Air Force; Great Britain, Air Force; Italy, Air Force; Japan, Air Forces; Midway, Battle of; Mussolini, Benito; Pearl Harbor, Attack on; Soviet Union, Air Force; Spain, Civil War; Speer, Albert; Strategic Bombing; Todt, Fritz; United States, Army Air Forces

References

Jarrett, Philip, ed. *Aircraft of the Second World War*. London: Putnam, 1997.

Keegan, John. *The Second World War*. New York: Viking, 1989.

Munson, Kenneth. *Bombers, Patrol, and Transport Aircraft, 1939–45*. Poole, UK: Blandford Press, 2002.

Wilson, Stewart. *Aircraft of WWII*. Fyshwick, Australia: Aerospace Publications, 1998.

Aircraft, Reconnaissance and Auxiliary

Aircraft the purpose of which is to provide support for land, sea, and air forces. From the beginning of military aviation, including the use of balloons during the French Revolutionary wars, air reconnaissance of enemy positions and movements has been crucial not only for defense against attack but also in preparation for offensive action. Just as improvements in aviation technology during the 1920s and 1930s greatly expanded the capabilities of fighters and bombers by the beginning of World War II, the same was true of reconnaissance and auxiliary aircraft. High-altitude photo reconnaissance was crucial to successful planning for military invasions such as the Normandy landings, and long-range reconnaissance was crucial for naval operations in the Atlantic and Pacific.

Three main types of reconnaissance and auxiliary aircraft were used during World War II: land-based aircraft, floatplanes, or flying boats designed to conduct reconnaissance missions; army cooperation aircraft designed for multipurpose roles such as liaison or tactical support; and training aircraft designed to train pilots and crewmen for service.

In addition to aircraft specially designed for reconnaissance or auxiliary service, numerous bombers and fighters were either converted to take on these roles or were relegated to these purposes after becoming obsolete in their intended roles. Such aircraft include the following: France's Bloch 131 and Latécoère Laté 298; Germany's Arado Ar 234 Blitz, Junkers Ju-86, Ju-88, and Ju-188 and the Messerschmitt Me-210; Great Britain's De Havilland Mosquito, Fairey Swordfish, Supermarine Spitfire, and Vickers Wellington; Italy's Cant Z. 506 Airone and Savoia-Marchetti S.M.79; Japan's Yokosuka D4Y Suisei; Poland's PZL P.23 Karas; the Soviet Union's Petlyakov Pe-2; and the U.S. Lockheed Hudson, Martin Maryland, and North American P-51 Mustang.

The following text describes the most significant aircraft employed primarily for reconnaissance and auxiliary purposes by both sides during the war (see also Table 1).

Germany

Entering service in September 1940, the twin-engine, three-seat Focke-Wulf Fw-189 Uhu served as the primary tactical reconnaissance aircraft of the German army, especially on the Eastern Front. Although its maximum range of 584 miles limited it to tactical reconnaissance, its rugged construction enabled it to absorb a heavy amount of punishment from antiaircraft fire, and its armament of three to four 7.9 mm machine guns afforded protection from Soviet fighters. These qualities also allowed it to provide close support for German troops on the ground. A total of 894 were produced.

Introduced in August 1939, the single-engine, two-seat Arado Ar. 196 proved to be one of the most versatile reconnaissance seaplanes in the German navy's arsenal. Designed as a catapult-launched aircraft, it was carried onboard Germany's major capital ships to provide reconnaissance at sea. It also conducted coastal and maritime patrol, antisubmarine hunting, and convoy escort operations in the North Sea, the English Channel, and the Bay of Biscay while operating out of coastal bases. A total of 546 were produced.

Germany relied on three primary flying boats for reconnaissance and auxiliary purposes during World War II. Originally designed for passenger service by Hamburger Flugzeugbau, the three-engine, six-seat Blohm und Voss Bv-138, of which 279 were constructed, entered military service in late 1940. With a maximum range of 2,500 miles, the Bv-138 was capable of remaining aloft for up to 18 hours, enabling it to conduct long-range patrols in the North Atlantic, where it reported the positions of Allied convoys to German U-boats. Designed prior to the war as a trans-Atlantic mail carrier, the twin-engine, four- or five-seat Dornier Do-18, of which 152 were constructed, was quickly adopted for military use when Germany began its rearmament program and was used primarily in the Baltic and North Sea for maritime patrol and air-sea rescue operations. Larger, faster, and possessing greater range than the Do-18, the three-engine, six-seat Dornier Do-24, of which 294 were constructed, entered service in 1937. In addition to maritime patrol and air-sea rescue operations, it also served as a transport and troop evacuation aircraft.

The two-seat Fieseler Fi-156 Storch and Henschel Hs-126 were small light aircraft that served effectively as army cooperation and utility aircraft. Noted for its short takeoff and landing (STOL) capabilities—it required just 213 ft for takeoff and just 61 ft for landing roll—the Fi-156 Storch (Stork) served as a liaison and staff transport, air ambulance, and tactical reconnaissance aircraft. It was also used in the daring German rescue of Benito Mussolini in September 1943. A total of 2,834 were produced by war's end. The Hs-126 had proved its usefulness in the Kondor Legion in the Spanish Civil War in tactical reconnaissance, as an artillery spotter, and for strafing enemy positions. It continued in these roles in the early stages of World War II until it was withdrawn from frontline service by early 1943. A total of 803 were produced.

Introduced in 1939, the two-seat Arado Ar-96 served as the Luftwaffe's primary trainer throughout the war. Its unarmed version served as a basic trainer, while its armed version (with a single 7.9 mm machine gun) served as an advanced trainer. It also performed other auxiliary roles, such as liaison transport, glider towing, and reconnaissance. A total of 11,546 were produced.

Table 1
Reconnaissance and Auxiliary Aircraft, All Powers

Aircraft	Year of Intro- duction	Engine (Primary)	Span	Length	Maximum Speed (mph)	Ceiling (ft)	Range (mi)	Weight (Loaded) (lb)	Crew
Aichi E13A	1941	1 × 1,080-hp Mitsubishi Kinsei 43 14-cylinder radial	47 ft 7 in.	37 ft	234 mph	28,640 ft	1,298 mi	8,818 lb	3
Aichi E16A Zuiun	1944	1 × 1,300-hp Mitsubishi Kensei 51 or 54 14-cylinder radial	42 ft	35 ft 6.5 in.	274 mph	32,810 ft	1,504 mi	10,038 lb	2
Arado Ar 96	1939	1 × 485-hp Argus As 410MA-1 inverted V12	36 ft 1 in.	29 ft 11.5 in.	211 mph	22,965 ft	615 mi	3,858 lb	2
Arado Ar. 196	1939	1 × 900-hp BMW 132K 9-cylinder radial	40 ft 10 in.	36 ft 1 in.	193 mph	22,965 ft	670 mi	8,223 lb	2
Avro Anson	1936	2 × 355-hp Armstrong Siddeley Cheetah IX 7-cylinder radial	56 ft 6 in.	42 ft 3 in.	188 mph	19,500 ft	820 mi	8,500 lb	6
Beechcraft AT-11 Kansan	1940	2 × 450-hp Pratt and Whitney R-985-An-1 Wasp Junior 9-cylinder radial	47 ft 8 in.	34 ft 3 in.	214 mph	20,000 ft	850 mi	8,727 lb	8
Beriev MBR-2 (Be-2)	1931	1 × 860-hp Mikulin Am–34NB	62 ft 4 in.	44 ft 3 in.	171 mph	25,920 ft	650 mi	9,359 lb	5
Blohm und Voss Bv 138	1940	3 × 880-hp Junkers Jumo 205D inline diesel engine	88 ft 4 in.	65 ft 1.5 in	170 mph	18,700 ft	2,500 mi	34,100 lb	6
Boeing-Stearman Kaydet	1936	1 × 220-hp Jacobs R-755 7-cylinder radial	32 ft 2 in.	25 ft 0.25 in.	124 mph	11,200 ft	505 mi	2,717 lb	2
Cant Z. 501 Gabbiano	1934	1 × 900-hp Isotta-Fraschini Asso XI R2 C15 V12	73 ft 10 in.	46 ft 11 in.	171 mph	22,966 ft	1,490 mi	15,542 lb	4–5
Cessna AT-17/ UC-78 Bobcat	1939	2 × 245-hp Jacobs R-755-9 7-cylinder radial	41 ft 11 in.	32 ft 9 in.	195 mph	22,000 ft	750 mi	5,700 lb	2–5
Consolidated PB2Y Catalina	1936	2 × 1,200-hp Pratt and Whitney R-1820-92 Twin Wasp 14-cylinder radial	104 ft	63 ft 10 in.	196 mph	18,100 ft	3,100 mi	34,000 lb	7–9
De Havilland Dominie	1935	2 × 200-hp De Havilland Gipsy Queen 3 6-cylinder inline engine	48 ft	34 ft 6 in.	157 mph	16,700 ft	570 mi	5,500 lb	5–9
De Havilland Tiger Moth	1931	1 × 130-hp De Havilland Gipsy Major 4-cylinder inline engine	29 ft 4 in.	23 ft 11 in.	109 mph	14,000 ft	300 mi	1,825 lb	2
Dornier Do 18	1938	2 × 700-hp Junkers Jumo 205D 6-cylinder diesel engine	77 ft 9 in.	63 ft 7 in.	166 mph	17,200 ft	2,175 mi	23,800 lb	4–5
Dornier Do 24	1937	3 × 1,000-hp Bramo 323R-2 Fafnir 9-cylinder radial	88 ft 7 in.	72 ft 2 in.	211 mph	19,360 ft	2,950 mi	35,715 lb	6
Fiat R.S. 14	1938	2 × 840-hp Fiat A 74 RC38 14-cylinder radial	64 ft 1 in.	46 ft 3 in	254 mph	16,400 ft	1,553 mi	17,637 lb	5
Fiesler Fi 156 Storch	1939	1 × 240-hp Argus As 10C inverted V8	46 ft 9 in.	32 ft 5.75 in.	109 mph	15,090 ft	600 mi	2,910 lb	2
Focke-Wulf Fw 189 Uhu	1940	2 × 465-hp Argus As 410A-1 inverted V12	60 ft 4.5 in.	39 ft 4 in.	221 mph	27,560 ft	584 mi	8,708 lb	3
Grumman J2F Duck	1934	1 × 950-hp R-1820-50 Cyclone 9-cylinder radial	39 ft	34 ft	188 mph	27,000 ft	780 mi	7,700 lb	2–3
Henschel Hs 126	1938	1 × 850-hp Bramo Fafnir 323A-1/Q-1 9-cylinder radial	47 ft 6.75 in.	35 ft 7 in.	193 mph	27,000 ft	534 mi	7,209 lb	2
Kawanishi H6K	1938	4 × 1,000-hp Mitsubishi Kinsei 43 14-cylinder radial	131 ft 2.75 in.	84 ft 1 in.	211 mph	31,365 ft	4,210 mi	47,399 lb	9
Kawanishi H8K	1941	4 × 1,530-hp Mitsubishi MK4B Kasei 12 14-cylinder radial	124 ft 8 in.	92 ft 4 in.	290 mph	28,740 ft	4,460 mi	71,650 lb	10

(continues)

Table 1
Reconnaissance and Auxiliary Aircraft, All Powers (continued)

Aircraft	Year of Intro- duction	Engine (Primary)	Span	Length	Maximum Speed (mph)	Ceiling (ft)	Range (mi)	Weight (Loaded) (lb)	Crew
Lockheed F-4 and F-5 Lightning	1942	2 × 1,150-hp Allison V-1710 V12	52 ft	37 ft 10 in.	389 mph	39,000 ft	975 mi	15,500 lb	1
Mitsubishi F1M	1939	1 × 875-hp Mitsubishi Zuisei 13 14-cylinder radial	36 ft 1 in.	31 ft 2 in.	230 mph	30,970 ft	460 mi	6,294 lb	2
Mitsubishi Ki-46	1941	2 × 1,080-hp Mitsubishi Ha-102 14-cylinder radial	48 ft 2.75 in.	36 ft 1 in.	375 mph	35,170 ft	1,537 mi	12,787 lb	2
Nakajima C6N Saiun	1944	1 × 1,990-hp Nakajima NK9B Homare 21 18-cylinder radial	41 ft	36 ft 1 in.	379 mph	34,236 ft	3,330 mi	11,596 lb	3
North American AT-6 Texan/Harvard	1938	1 × 600-hp Pratt and Whitney R-1340 9-cylinder radial	42 ft 0.25 in.	29 ft 6 in.	208 mph	21,500 ft	750 mi	5,300 lb	2
Piper L-4 Grasshopper	1941	1 × 65-hp Continental O-170-3 4-cylinder	35 ft 3 in.	22 ft	85 mph	9,300 ft	190 mi	1,220 lb	2
Polikarpov U-2/Po2	1928	1 × 100-125-hp Shvetsov M-11 5-cylinder radial	37 ft 5 in. upper; 34 ft 11.5 in. lower	26 ft 9 in.	93 mph	13,125 ft	329 mi	2,167 lb	2–3
Short Sunderland	1938	4 × 1,065-hp Pegasus XVIII 9-cylinder radial	112 ft 9.5 in.	85 ft 4 in.	210 mph	16,000 ft	2,900 mi	45,210 lb	10–13
Supermarine Walrus	1935	1 × 775-hp Pegasus VI 9-cylinder radial	45 ft 10 in.	37 ft 7 in.	124 mph	18,500 ft	600 mi	7,200 lb	4
Tachikawa Ki-26 and Ki-55	1938	1 × 510-hp Hitachi Ha-13a 9-cylinder radial	38 ft 8.5 in.	26 ft 3 in.	216 mph	26,900 ft	659 mi	3,794 lb	2
Vought OS2U Kingfisher	1940	1 × 450-hp Pratt and Whitney R-985-AN-1 Wasp Junior 9-cylinder radial	35 ft 11 in.	33 ft 10 in.	164 mph	13,000 ft	805 mi	6,000 lb	2
Vultee Valiant	1939	1 × 450-hp Pratt and Whitney R-985-AN-1 Wasp Junior 9-cylinder radial	42 ft	28 ft 10 in.	180 mph	21,650 ft	725 mi	4,360 lb	2

Sources: Angelucci, Enzo, ed. *The Illustrated Encyclopedia of Military Aircraft: 1914 to the Present.* Milan, Italy: Arnoldo Mondadori S.p.A., 2001; Fredriksen, John C. *Warbirds: An Illustrated Guide to U.S. Military Aircraft, 1914–2000.* Santa Barbara, CA: ABC-CLIO, 1999; Fredriksen, John C. *International Warbirds: An Illustrated Guide to World Military Aircraft, 1914–2000.* Santa Barbara, CA: ABC-CLIO, 2001; and Wilson, Stewart. *Aircraft of WWII.* Fyshwick, Australia: Aerospace Publications, 1998.

Great Britain

Designed in 1935, the twin-engine Avro Anson entered service with the Royal Air Force (RAF) in 1936 as an armed coastal patrol aircraft. While it continued in that role until 1941, it was as an air crew trainer that it made its primary contribution to the British war effort, training navigators, radio operators, and air gun operators. One variant, the Mk.X, was used for transporting freight or up to eight passengers. A total of 10,996 were produced until 1952, and it remained in service until 1968.

The four-engine Short Sunderland was a maritime patrol and antisubmarine flying boat with a maximum range of 2,690 miles. Nicknamed the "Flying Porcupine" because it came equipped with eight .303 caliber machine guns, the Sunderland was more than capable of defending itself. In addition to its reconnaissance and antisubmarine roles, it was also used for transport and air-sea rescue operations and played an important role in successfully evacuating forces from Norway, Greece, and Crete. A total of 749 were constructed and it remained in service with the RAF until 1959.

First introduced in 1935 by Australia, where it was known as the Seagull V and intended as a maritime patrol and antisubmarine aircraft, the single-engine Supermarine Walrus entered British service in 1936 as an amphibious biplane used for search and air-sea rescue operations. Capable of operating in rough seas, it successfully rescued as many as 5,000 downed pilots around Britain and another 2,500 in the Mediterranean. A total of 771 Walrus aircraft were constructed.

Introduced originally as a passenger liner (the D.H.89 Dragon Rapide), the twin-engine De Havilland Dominie served primarily as a radio and navigator trainer and as a communications aircraft. With the outbreak of the war, civilian versions were pressed into military service in an effort to supply the British Expeditionary Force in France. A total of 730 of all varieties were constructed.

The De Havilland Tiger Moth, a single-engine, open-air-cockpit biplane, served as one of the primary trainers for Allied pilots who flew in World War II. In addition to the 8,796 trainers produced, 420 radio-operated, wooden-constructed versions, known as queen bee drones, were manufactured to serve as antiaircraft gunnery targets.

Italy

Introduced in 1934, the single-engine, four- to five-seat Cant Z. 501 Gabbiano served as Italy's only flying boat during World War II. Intended as an armed reconnaissance/maritime patrol aircraft, the wooden-constructed Gabbiano had set numerous long-distance records in the mid-1930s. With Italy's entry into the war, however, they quickly proved to be extremely vulnerable to enemy fire, so they were relegated primarily to coastal patrol service. By the time Italy surrendered in September 1943, only 40 remained out of the 445 that had been produced.

Introduced in 1941, the twin-engine Fiat R.S. 14 was originally designed as a coastal reconnaissance floatplane Although its performance soon proved to be far better than that of the Cant Z.506 and Savoia-Marchetti SM.79, allowing it to be used as a torpedo-bomber, it came too late in the war to allow mass production. As a result, only 187 were produced.

Japan

In addition to transporting troops and supplies, the four-engine Kawanishi H6K and four-engine Kawanishi H8K flying boats also served important roles as long-range reconnaissance aircraft, with the former having a maximum range of 4,210 miles and the latter having a maximum range of 4,460 miles.

Japan relied on three primary reconnaissance floatplanes during the war. The three-seat Aichi E13A, of which 1,418 were produced, was Japan's most widely used floatplane of the war. Entering service in early 1941, it was employed for the reconnaissance leading up to the attack on Pearl Harbor, and it participated in every major campaign in the Pacific Theater, performing not only reconnaissance but also air-sea rescue, liaison transport, and coastal patrol operations. Introduced in January 1944 as a replacement for the E13A, the two-seat Aichi E16A Zuiun offered far greater performance capabilities but came too late in the war to make a significant difference, primarily because Japan's worsening industrial position limited production to just 256 aircraft. Based on a 1936 design that underwent several modifications, the two-seat Mitsubishi F1M biplane, of which 1,118 were produced, proved to be one of the most versatile reconnaissance aircraft in Japan's arsenal. Operating from both ship and water bases, it served in a variety roles throughout the Pacific, including coastal patrol, convoy escort, antisubmarine, and air-sea rescue duties, and it was even capable of serving as a dive-bomber and interceptor.

The three-seat Nakajima C6N Saiun, of which 463 were produced, was one of the few World War II reconnaissance aircraft specifically designed for operating from carriers. With a maximum speed of 379 mph, a maximum range of 3,300 miles, and service ceiling of 34,236 ft, the C6N proved virtually immune from Allied interception. Unfortunately for Japan, it did not become available for service until the Mariana Islands Campaign in the summer of 1944.

The twin-engine, two-seat Mitsubishi Ki-46, of which 1,742 were produced, served as Japan's primary strategic reconnaissance aircraft of the war. Entering service in March 1941, the Ki-46 was one of the top-performing aircraft of its type in the war with a service ceiling of 35,170 ft, a range of 2,485 miles, and a maximum speed of 375 mph.

Although the two-seat Tachikawa Ki-36 served as an effective army cooperation aircraft against the Chinese when it entered service in November 1938, it proved to be vulnerable against better-equipped Allied forces after the outbreak of war in the Pacific. The Ki-55 was an advanced trainer version that became available in 1940. Both were later used as suicide aircraft toward the end of the war. A total of 2,723 of both types were constructed.

Soviet Union

When it entered service in 1928, the two- to three-seat Polikarpov U-2/Po2 biplane was intended as a basic trainer. By the time of the German invasion of the Soviet Union in June 1941, approximately 13,000 had already been constructed for both military and civil use. The U-2/Po2 performed a wide variety of roles besides training, such as tactical reconnaissance, air ambulance, night artillery spotting, and close ground support. One version, the U-2GN, was equipped with loudspeakers and used for propaganda purposes. Production continued in the Soviet Union until 1948 and in Poland until 1953; more than 33,000 were ultimately produced.

The five-seat Beriev MBR-2 (Be-2) flying boat was first introduced in 1931 for coastal patrol service. Incorporating a wooden hull and metal wings and utilizing a single pusher engine, it proved to be one of the most versatile flying boats of its time. In addition to its reconnaissance role, it was used in air-sea rescue, light transport service, and minelaying operations. More than 1,500 of all varieties were produced.

United States

The single-seat Lockheed F-4 and F-5 Lightning were modified versions of the Lockheed P-38 Lightning, which had cameras and clear panels installed in place of its guns in the nose section. First deployed in the Pacific in early 1942, they proved to be one of the most widely used photoreconnaissance aircraft of the war. Of the 1,400 employed during the war, 500 were new and the remaining were converted from existing stocks of P-38s.

Designed to operate from land or catapulted from a ship, the two-seat Vought OS2U Kingfisher, of which 1,519 were produced, first entered service in August 1940 and served as the U.S. Navy's primary observation aircraft in every theater of the war. In addition to its reconnaissance duties, it performed air-sea rescue, antisubmarine patrol, and liaison transport missions.

Entering service in 1936, the twin-engine, seven- to nine-crew Consolidated PB2Y Catalina proved to be the most widely used flying boat of World War II; a total of 3,290 were produced in the United States, Canada, and the Soviet Union. With a maximum range of 3,100 miles, the Catalina served on all fronts of the war primarily for long-range maritime reconnaissance. Other duties included air-sea rescue, minelaying, and transport.

The two- to three-seat Grumman J2F Duck, of which 641 were produced, was an amphibious biplane that entered service in 1936 with the U.S. Navy and the U.S. Coast Guard as a coastal patrol aircraft. After Pearl Harbor, the Duck was pressed into a variety roles in both the European and Pacific Theaters, including air-sea rescue, target towing, coastal patrol, and maritime reconnaissance.

Utilizing a three-tiered system of training—primary, basic, and advanced—for its pilots, the United States relied on training aircraft that corresponded to each level. The two-seat Boeing-Stearman Kaydet, of which approximately 10,000 were constructed, was an open-air biplane that served the U.S. Army Air Forces (USAAF) and U.S. Navy as

a primary trainer throughout the war. The two-seat Vultee Valiant, of which a total of 11,525 were produced, served as the most important basic trainer for the USAAF and the U.S. Navy. Finally, the two-seat North American AT-6 Texan/Harvard, of which over 17,500 were produced in the United States and Canada, served as the most important Allied advanced trainer of World War II.

Other prominent American auxiliary aircraft included the Cessna AT-17/UC-78 Bobcat, which was used as an advanced trainer and light utility transport; the Piper L-4 Grasshopper, which was used as an artillery spotter, trainer, and liaison transport; and the Beechcraft Kansan, a military version of the Beechcraft Model 18 that served as a navigation, bombing, and gunnery trainer.

Justin D. Murphy

See also
Aircraft, Bombers; Aircraft, Gliders; Aircraft, Naval; Aircraft, Production of; Aircraft, Transports; Kondor Legion; Photographic Reconnaissance
References
Jarrett, Philip, ed. *Aircraft of the Second World War.* London: Putnam, 1997.
Munson, Kenneth. *Bombers, Patrol, and Transport Aircraft, 1939–45.* Poole, UK: Blandford Press, 2002.
Wilson, Stewart. *Aircraft of WWII.* Fyshwick, Australia: Aerospace Publications, 1998.

Aircraft, Transports

Aircraft the primary purpose of which is to transport personnel and supplies. Although fighters, bombers, and reconnaissance aircraft played major roles in World War I, the technology of the time did not allow aircraft to play a meaningful role in transporting troops and supplies. By the early 1930s, however, improvements in aircraft design and, more important, aircraft engines had resulted in the emergence of civil aircraft, such as the Douglas DC-3, for commercial passenger service. Military planners were quick to note these developments, which raised the prospect of rapidly deploying large numbers of men and a large amount of supplies to the battle zone, including behind enemy lines. By the outbreak of World War II, most of the powers that would become involved in the war had either already developed military variants of these civil aircraft or had introduced specially designed military transport aircraft.

Two main types of transport aircraft were used during the war: large multiengine, land-based aircraft or flying boats designed to move many troops or supplies (some of these also served in bombing and reconnaissance roles);

and assault or transport gliders designed to be towed, then released, so they could glide silently to a landing behind enemy lines.

The following are the most significant aircraft employed primarily for transport by both sides during World War II (see also Table 1).

Germany

Designed originally in 1930 as a three-engine passenger carrier for Deutsche Lufthansa, the Junkers Ju-52/3m served as the primary transport aircraft of the German army in World War II. Including the approximately 200 civil models constructed prior to the war, a total of 4,800 Ju-52/3ms were built by the end of 1944. It made its military debut as a bomber and troop transport during the Spanish Civil War. Successive versions of the Ju-52/3m incorporated more-powerful engines that provided greater load capacity (approximately twice its empty weight of 12,600–14,300 lb) and interchangeable wheel, ski, or float landing gear that allowed it to operate in a variety of conditions. In addition to its transport duties, it served as a bomber, air ambulance, glider tug, and paratrooper transport.

Intended as a replacement for the Ju-52/3m, the Junkers Ju-252 Herkules relied on the same three-engine configuration as the Ju-52/3m but featured improved interior and exterior designs and more powerful engines, which not only made it faster and capable of bearing heavier loads but also gave it a range as much as twice that of the Ju-52/3m. Unfortunately for Germany, shortages of resources and manpower forced the Luftwaffe to limit production of the all-metal Ju-252 to just 15 aircraft. A mixed-wood and tube-steel version, the Ju-352 entered service in 1944, but it came too late in the war to make a difference. Just 45 of the Ju-352s were constructed.

Originally designed for Deutsche Lufthansa to serve as a trans-Atlantic flying boat, the six-engine Blohm und Voss Bv-222 Viking was the largest flying boat, and the largest aircraft of any kind, to serve in World War II. Although only 13 were produced, the Bv-222, which could carry up to 110 troops in addition to its 11-man crew, played an important role in transporting troops in the Mediterranean and North African Campaigns.

Germany employed three types of gliders as transports during World War II: the DFS-230, the Gotha Go-242, and the Messerschmitt Me-321 Gigant. Entering service in 1938, the DFS 230 could carry 8 airborne troops and proved to be the standard assault glider used by the Germany army during the war, with approximately 1,500 being constructed. Introduced in late 1941, the Gotha Go-242 could carry up to 23 airborne troops or the equivalent weight in supplies. As one of the largest aircraft of the war, the Messerschmitt Me-321 Gigant was capable of carrying up to 120 troops, 21,500 lb of freight, or 60 wounded soldiers. The Go-242 and Me-321 served primarily on the Eastern Front to bring food and supplies to German soldiers. Powered versions, the Go-244 and Me-323, were also developed for transport service.

Great Britain

Although the twin-engine Bristol Bombay was designed as a troop transport carrier in 1931, the economic conditions of the Great Depression delayed production until early 1939. While only 51 were produced, the Bristol Bombay, which was capable of carrying up to 24 troops or a payload of 7,200 lb, saw significant action for the Royal Air Force (RAF) during the first half of the war, ferrying troops and supplies across the English Channel in 1940, evacuating British forces from Crete in 1941, and dropping paratroopers behind enemy lines in North Africa.

Originally intended as a bomber, the Armstrong Whitworth Albemarle was instead converted to transport service. A total of 310 were used as transports for special operations, such as dropping paratroopers behind enemy lines. An additional 247 served as the standard tug for the Airspeed Horsa assault glider, seeing action in the invasion of Sicily in 1943 and the D day landings in June 1944. At least 10 were shipped to the Soviet Union.

Great Britain produced two primary transport gliders during the war: the Airspeed Horsa and the General Aircraft Hamilcar. The Horsa came in two varieties: the Mk.1, which was configured for carrying up to 25 troops; and the Mk.2, which could carry up to 7,000 lb of freight and featured a hinged nose section for easier loading and unloading. Approximately 3,800 of the Horsa gliders were constructed. The Hamilcar was the largest Allied glider of the war and was capable of carrying a payload of 17,500 lb. It first saw action in the D day landings and proved immensely significant because it could provide heavy equipment, such as the British Tetrarch Mk.IV tank, to airborne troops operating behind enemy lines.

Other British aircraft used in a transport role included those that also served as bombers or reconnaissance aircraft, such as the Handley Page Halifax, the Short Stirling, and Vickers Warwick.

Italy

Although Italy relied on several aircraft for transport duties, such as the Caproni CA 309-316, the Piaggio P.108, and the Savoia-Marchetti S.M.81 Pipistrello, their primary role was as bombers or reconnaissance aircraft. The Savoia-Marchetti S.M.75 and the Savoia-Marchetti S.M.82 Canguru were exceptions. The S.M.75 had originally been

Table 1
Transport Aircraft, All Powers

Aircraft	Year of Introduction	Engine	Span	Length	Maximum speed (mph)	Ceiling (ft)	Range (mi)	Weight (loaded) (lb)
Airspeed Horsa	1941	None	88 ft	67 ft	150 mph	NA	NA	15,500 lb
Armstrong Whitworth Albemarle	1942	2 × 1,560-hp Bristol Hercules XI 14-cylinder radials	77 ft	59 ft 11 in.	265 mph	18,000 ft	1,300 mi	36,500 lb
Beechcraft C-45 Expeditor	1940	2 × 450-hp Pratt and Whitney R-985-An-1 Wasp Junior 9-cylinder radials	47 ft 8 in.	34 ft 3 in.	214 mph	20,000 ft	850 mi	8,727 lb
Blohm und Voss Bv 222 Viking	1940	6 × 1,000-hp BMW Bramo Fafnir 323R 9-cylinder radials or 6 × 980-hp Junkers Jumo inline diesel engines	150 ft 11 in.	121 ft 4.5 in.	242 mph	23,950 ft	3,790	109,026 lb
Bristol Bombay	1940	2 × 1,010-hp Bristol Pegasus XXII 9-cylinder radials	95 ft 9 in.	69 ft 3 in.	192 mph	25,000 ft	2,230 mi	20,000 lb
Consolidated Liberator Transport C-87	1940	4 × 1,200-hp Pratt and Whitney R-1830-43 Twin Wasp 14-cylinder radials	110 ft	66 ft 4 in.	306 mph	31,000 ft	2,900 mi	56,600 lb
Curtiss C-46 Commando	1940	2 × 2,000-hp Pratt and Whitney R-2800-51 Double Wasp 18-cylinder radials	108 ft 1 in.	76 ft 4 in.	269 mph	27,600 ft	1,600 mi	56,000 lb
DFS 230	1938	None	68 ft 5.5 in.	36 ft 10.5 in.	112–130 mph	NA	NA	4,630 lb
Douglas C-47 Skytrain	1942	2 × 1,000–1,200-hp Wright R-1820 Cyclone 9-cylinder or 2 × 1,200-hp Pratt and Whitney R-1830 Twin Wasp 14-cylinder radials	95 ft 9 in.	64 ft 5.5 in.	229 mph	24,000 ft	1,500 mi	29,300 lb
Douglas C-54 Skymaster	1942	4 × 1,350-hp Pratt and Whitney R-2000-7 or -11 Twin Wasp 14-cylinder radials	117 ft 6 in.	93 ft 10 in.	275 mph	22,500 ft	3,900 mi	73,000 lb
General Aircraft Hamilcar	1943	None	110 ft	68 ft	150 mph	NA	NA	21,400 lb
Gotha Go 242	1941	None	80 ft 4.5 in.	51 ft 10 in.	149 mph	NA	NA	15,653 lb
Junkers Ju 252/352 Herkules	1939	3 × 1,410-hp Junkers Jumo 211F inverted V-12s	112 ft 3 in.	79 ft 5 in.	205 mph	19,685 ft	1,852 mi	52,911 lb
Junkers Ju 52/3m	1931	3 × 725-hp BMW 123A-3 9-cylinder radials	95 ft 11.5 in.	62 ft	171 mph	18,000 ft	800 mi	23,149 lb
Kawanishi H6K	1938	4 × 1,000-hp Mitsubishi Kinsei 43 14-cylinder radials	131 ft 2.75 in.	84 ft 1 in.	211 mph	31,365 ft	4,210 mi	47,399 lb
Kawanishi H8K	1941	4 × 1,530-hp Mitsubishi MK4B Kasei 12 14-cylinder radials	124 ft 8 in.	92 ft 4 in.	290 mph	28,740 ft	4,460 mi	71,650 lb
Kawasaki Ki-56	1941	2 × 990-hp Nakajima Ha–25 14-cylinder radials	65 ft 6 in.	48 ft 10.5 in.	249 mph	26,250 ft	2,060 mi	17,692 lb
Lockheed Lodestar	1941	2 × 1,200-hp Pratt and Whitney R-1830 Twin Wasp 14-cylinder radials	65 ft 6 in.	49 ft 10 in.	266 mph	30,000 ft	1,660 mi	18,500 lb
Martin PBM Mariner Flying Boat	1941	2 × 1,700-hp Wright R-2600–12 Cyclone 14-cylinder radials	118 ft	80 ft	198 mph	16,900 ft	2,240 mi	58,000 lb
Messerschmitt Me 321 Gigant	1942	None	180 ft 5.5 in.	93 ft 4 in.	112 mph	NA	NA	48,500 lb

(continues)

Table 1
Transport Aircraft, All Powers (continued)

Aircraft	Year of Intro-duction	Engine	Span	Length	Maximum speed (mph)	Ceiling (ft)	Range (mi)	Weight (loaded) (lb)
Mitsubishi Ki–57	1942	2 × 1,050-hp Mitsubishi Ha-102 14-cylinder radials	74 ft 2 in.	52 ft 10 in.	292 mph	26,250 ft	1,865 mi	18,600 lb
Savoia-Marchetti S.M.75	1939	3 × 750-hp Alfa Romeo A.R. 126 RC 34 9-cylinder radials	97 ft 5 in.	70 ft 10 in.	225 mph	20,500 ft	1,070 mi	28,700 lb
Savoia-Marchetti S.M.82 Canguru	1941	3 × 950-hp Alfa Romeo 128 RC 21 9-cylinder radials	97 ft 4.5 in.	75 ft 1.5 in.	230 mph	19,685 ft	1,864 mi	39,727–44,092 lb
Tupolev TB-3 (ANT-6)	1930	4 × 730-hp M-17F V-12s or 4 × 1,200-hp Am-34FRNV V-12s	132 ft 10.5 in.	82 ft 8 in.	122–179 mph	12,470–25,393 ft	839–1,939 mi	37,920–54,012 lb
Waco CG-4A Hadrian	1942	None	83 ft 8 in.	48 ft 4 in.	150 mph	NA	NA	7,500–9,000 lb

Sources: Angelucci, Enzo, ed. *The Illustrated Encyclopedia of Military Aircraft: 1914 to the Present.* Milan, Italy: Arnoldo Mondadori S.p.A., 2001; Fredriksen, John C. *Warbirds: An Illustrated Guide to U.S. Military Aircraft, 1914–2000.* Santa Barbara, CA: ABC-CLIO, 1999; Fredriksen, John C. *International Warbirds: An Illustrated Guide to World Military Aircraft, 1914–2000.* Santa Barbara, CA: ABC-CLIO, 2001; and Wilson, Stewart. *Aircraft of WWII.* Fyshwick, Australia: Aerospace Publications, 1998.

NA = not applicable

designed for passenger service for Ala Littoria in 1937. Requisitioned for military service when Italy entered the war in June 1940, the S.M.75 could carry up to 30 troops and saw action throughout the Mediterranean until the end of the war. A total of 98 were constructed. The three-engine S.M.82 proved to be one of the best heavy transports available to the Axis powers. It was capable of carrying up to 40 fully equipped troops or almost 9,000 lb of freight. Of approximately 400 S.M.82s constructed between 1941 and 1943, at least 50 entered service with the Luftwaffe in the Baltic area of the Eastern Front. Those that survived the war continued in service with the Italian air force into the 1950s.

Japan
Although Japan employed a variety of multipurpose aircraft, such as the Nakajima G5N Shinzan and the Tachikawa Ki-54, for transporting troops and supplies, it relied primarily on four main transport aircraft during World War II: the Kawanishi H6K flying boat, the Kawanishi H8K flying boat, the Kawasaki Ki-56, and the Mitsubishi Ki-57.

When Japan entered the war, the four-engine Kawanishi H6K served as the navy's primary long-range flying boat. Although used at first primarily for long-range reconnaissance, it was soon relegated to transport duty because of its vulnerability to Allied fighters. Capable of carrying up to 18 troops in addition to its crew, the H6K remained in production until 1943. Of the 217 constructed, 139 were designed exclusively for transport.

The four-engine Kawanishi H8K entered service in early 1942 and gradually replaced the Kawanishi H6K. While it also served in a variety of roles, its transport version, the H8K2-L, of which 36 were built, could carry up to 64 passengers. With a cruising speed of 185 mph and a range of up to 4,460 miles, it was well-suited for the Pacific Theater, and its heavy armament afforded better protection than the H6K.

Ironically, Japan's primary light transport aircraft, the twin-engine Kawasaki Ki-56, was a military version of a license-built American plane, the Lockheed 14 Electra. It was capable of carrying a payload of up to 5,290 lb or 14 passengers and had a range of approximately 3,300 miles. A total of 121 were constructed between 1941 and 1943.

Originally intended for passenger service with Nippon Koku KK, the twin-engine Mitsubishi Ki-57 was quickly adapted for service with both the Japanese army and navy beginning in 1940. After Japan entered the war, the original production series, of which 101 were built, was modified by adding more powerful engines. Between 1942 and early 1945, 406 of the new version (Ki-57-II) were constructed. These were capable of carrying a crew of 4 and up to 11 passengers or a cargo of approximately 7,000 lb to a range of up to 1,835 miles.

Soviet Union

While the Soviet Union relied heavily on American aircraft, such as license-built Douglas C-47 Skytrains, for transport purposes, the four-engine Tupolev TB-3 (ANT-6), originally designed in the early 1930s as a heavy bomber, had been converted primarily for troop and freight transport by the time the Soviet Union entered World War II. Later versions fitted with four 1,200 hp engines were capable of carrying more than 12,000 lb of cargo. In addition to carrying airborne troops and supplies, it also served as a glider tug. Some were even modified to carry a tank or truck between their undercarriage legs.

United States

Of all the powers in World War II, the United States had by far the largest number and variety of transport aircraft, in part because it was conducting simultaneous campaigns in the European and Pacific Theaters.

Without question, the twin-engine Douglas C-47 Skytrain was the most famous transport aircraft of World War II. As the DC-3, it had revolutionized civil air travel before the war. Once the United States entered the war, the Skytrain went into full-scale military production; 10,665 were produced by war's end, including 4,878 in 1944 alone. Of its variants, the C-47 Skytrain (known as the Dakota in British service), accounted for more than 9,000 of the total produced, approximately 1,800 of which were loaned to Great Britain through Lend-Lease. An additional 2,500 were constructed on license by the Soviet Union as the Lisunov Li-2. Even the Japanese built 485 as the Nakajima L2D through a 1938 license. With a range of 1,500 miles and capable of carrying 28 troops or a cargo of 10,000 lb, it saw service in every theater of the war.

The four-engine Consolidated Liberator Transport C-87 was a transport version of the Consolidated B-24 Liberator bomber. A total of 287 C-87s were produced and served with the U.S. Army Air Forces (USAAF) and the RAF as a transport and a tanker. As a transport, it was capable of carrying up to 25 passengers and up to 10,000 lb of freight. As a tanker, it could carry up to 2,400 gallons of fuel, which proved useful in a variety of theaters, but especially in support of Boeing B-29 Superfortresses operating in China.

Originally designed in 1936 as the CW-20 (a 36-passenger pressured airliner), the twin-engine Curtiss C-46 Commando entered service in 1942 after undergoing extensive modifications for military service. These included the installation of a large cargo door, a strengthened floor, and folding troop seats. It was capable of carrying up to 50 troops, 33 wounded soldiers, and up to 10,000 lb of cargo. These characteristics, combined with its excellent climbing ability, made it ideally suited for flying over the Himalayas ("the Hump") from India to China. A total of 3,341 were produced.

As with the Douglas C-47 Skytrain, the Douglas C-54 Skymaster was originally designed for passenger airliner service as the DC-4. After Pearl Harbor, the U.S. military quickly adopted it, with the first C-54 Skymaster entering service in February 1942. With a maximum range of 3,900 miles, Skymasters flew almost 80,000 trans-Atlantic flights during the course of the war with a loss of just three aircraft. It was capable of carrying 50 troops or 28,000 lb of cargo. It would remain in service until 1974 and is famous for its role in the Berlin Airlift of 1948.

The Waco CG-4A Hadrian proved to be one of the most effective transport gliders produced in the war. Designed for mass production, the Hadrian featured fabric-covered wooden wings and a steel tube fuselage, which was easily replicated by the 15 firms involved in constructing the 13,910 Hadrians produced during the war. Its most notable feature was a hinged nose section that raised upward and allowed cargo to be loaded directly into the cabin. It was capable of carrying 15 troops or 3,800 lb of cargo, which could include a jeep or 75 mm howitzer and its crew. It proved effective in landings in Sicily, the D day invasion, and the Rhine crossings, and it would have been an integral part of an Allied invasion of the Japanese mainland had the atomic bomb not ended the war.

Other successful U.S. transport aircraft of the war included the following three aircraft: the twin-engine Lockheed Lodestar, of which 625 were produced, was a military version of the civil Lockheed Model 14 Super Electra; the twin-engine Beechcraft C-45 Expeditor, of which 1,391 were built, was a military version of the civil Beechcraft Model 18 light transport; and the Martin PBM Mariner Flying Boat, of which 1,405 were produced, served in a variety of roles besides transport, including antisubmarine warfare, air-sea rescue, and maritime patrol.

Justin D. Murphy

See also

Airborne Forces, Allied; Airborne Forces, Axis; Aircraft, Bombers; Aircraft, Gliders; Aircraft, Naval; Aircraft, Production of; Aircraft, Reconnaissance and Auxiliary; Airlift; Crete, Battle of; DRAGOON, Operation; Germany, Air Force; Great Britain, Air Force; Hump, The; Italy, Air Force; Japan, Air Forces; MARKET-GARDEN, Operation; Normandy Invasion and Campaign, OVERLORD, Operation; Parachute Infantry; Rhine Crossings; Sicily, Invasion of; Soviet Union, Air Force; Spain, Civil War; United States, Army Air Forces

References

Jarrett, Philip, ed. *Aircraft of the Second World War.* London: Putnam, 1997.
Munson, Kenneth. *Bombers, Patrol, and Transport Aircraft, 1939–45.* Poole, UK: Blandford Press, 2002.
Wilson, Stewart. *Aircraft of WWII.* Fyshwick, Australia: Aerospace Publications, 1998.

Aircraft Carriers

Ships capable of launching and recovering fixed-wing aircraft. Almost without exception, the aircraft carriers commissioned by combatant navies during World War II owed their origins to designs developed between the two world wars. Furthermore, since this warship type itself was so new, most of the first generation of semiexperimental vessels remained in frontline service at the outbreak of hostilities. These included the British carriers *Eagle* (converted from an incomplete ex-Chilean battleship into a flush-deck carrier with an offset island) and *Hermes* (the first vessel constructed as a carrier from the keel up, also flush-decked with an island) and the similar Japanese carrier *Hosho.*

Provisions of the 1922 Washington Treaty also had freed large U.S., British, French, and Japanese hulls for conversion into carriers. The United States and France converted two battle cruisers and a battleship, respectively, into the flush-deck carriers *Lexington, Saratoga,* and *Béarn.* British and Japanese concepts emphasizing rapid aircraft launching led both navies to develop designs incorporating multiple flight deck levels to permit several aircraft to fly off simultaneously. Britain rebuilt the *Furious* (which had served as a fleet carrier since 1917 in two earlier guises) with a three-quarter-length flush deck and a forward flying-off deck at a lower level, and it similarly converted two near-sister ships, the *Courageous* and the *Glorious.* Japan took this idea still further and configured a battleship and a battle cruiser, the *Kaga* and the *Akagi,* as carriers with two forward flying-off decks beneath the main deck. Both navies learned through experience that efficient deck-handling procedures were more effective in increasing launch rates. Japan subsequently rebuilt its two carriers with conventional flush decks and greatly enlarged air groups, but the British ships still served unaltered in the front line at the outbreak of war.

Operational experience with these large converted carriers had a profound influence on subsequent carrier doctrine and designs. Their speed allowed them to operate with the battle fleet, and their size and aircraft capacity gave commanders invaluable opportunities to appreciate the importance of efficient deck-handling procedures, rapid launch and recovery, and concentrated mass attacks. They also served as development platforms for crucial operational equipment, including effective arresting gear using transverse wires, safety crash barriers, hydraulic catapults, and fast elevators to move aircraft between the hangar and the flight deck.

During the 1930s, Japan and the United States added new carriers to their fleets. Although constrained by provisions of the 1922 Washington Treaty, both navies evolved effective designs that became the basis for later construction.

Their first treaty vessels, the Japanese *Ryujo* and the U.S. Navy's *Ranger,* were not entirely satisfactory but formed the bases for the two ships of the Soryu-class and the three-vessel Yorktown-class, respectively. They were ships that combined large flight decks, substantial air groups of 60–80 aircraft, strong defensive armament (for the period), high speed, and long range in vessels suitable for extended oceanic operations.

Britain was a latecomer to new-carrier construction in the 1930s. The *Ark Royal,* commissioned in 1939, incorporated internal hangars, an enclosed bow, and a flight deck that was also the vessel's principal strength deck—all features that characterized subsequent British carrier designs—and embarked a similar size air group to those of its American and Japanese contemporaries.

The large fleet carriers commissioned by Britain, Japan, and the United States during World War II derived from their earlier 1930s designs. Japan commissioned two ships of the enlarged Shokaku-class in 1941 with greater offensive and defensive capabilities, followed by the *Taiho,* a variant incorporating an armored flight deck (although at the cost of a reduced air group). In 1942–1943, Japan laid down the six-ship Unryu-class, which was derived directly from the *Soryu,* although only two of these vessels entered service. The United States standardized on the Essex-class, an expansion of the Yorktown-class. No fewer than 32 units were ordered, of which 24 were completed to serve as the backbone of U.S. carrier forces from 1943. They combined a powerful offensive air group of as many as 100 aircraft, substantially augmented defensive armament, long range, and high speed in hulls the size of which conferred great adaptability to changing operational requirements.

The six British wartime carriers of the Illustrious type introduced armor protection for both flight decks and hangar sides. Incorporating this feature into the basic *Ark Royal* design produced vessels that proved very effective in the confined waters of the Mediterranean and in the face of kamikaze attack, but it also incurred severe penalties. Air-group capacity was slashed substantially (the original design accommodated only 36 aircraft; modified to carry 54, it still fell short of the *Ark Royal*'s embarked 72 machines), hangars were cramped, and it proved very difficult and expensive to upgrade these ships postwar.

Both the U.S. Navy and the British Royal Navy developed a third generation of carrier designs from their wartime experience. These emphasized the importance of large air groups, efficient layout for fast aircraft operation, and strong defensive features—both passive in the form of armor at hangar and flight-deck level and active by means of very large batteries of automatic antiaircraft guns. None of these carriers served during World War II. The U.S. Navy

The U.S. Navy aircraft carrier Lexington. *Commissioned in 1927, it was lost in the May 1942 Battle of the Coral Sea. (The Mariners' Museum/Corbis)*

commissioned the three ships of the Midway-class just after the war, but the Royal Navy's Malta-class was canceled, although two vessels of the intermediate Audacious-class entered service postwar as the *Ark Royal* and *Eagle.*

Both Britain and the United States studied small austere carrier designs before World War II, but only the Royal Navy seriously considered vessels for trade protection (the U.S. Navy's XCV projects envisaged second-line fleet duties). In 1935–1936, the British Naval Staff agreed on sufficiently firm requirements to earmark five specific merchant vessels for conversion should war break out. Nevertheless, no action was taken until December 1940, when work began to create Britain's first escort carrier, the *Audacity,* commissioned in June 1941.

U.S. Navy planning for austere mercantile conversions began in October 1940, resulting in the completion of the *Long Island,* its first escort carrier, also in June 1941. The *Long Island* was converted from a completed diesel C-3 cargo ship, the *Mormacmail,* but 45 subsequent conversions used partially completed hulls and steam turbines rather than the mechanically unreliable diesel plants featured in the first five U.S.-built escort carriers. More than half of these vessels went to Britain under Lend-Lease, and all 50 were in service before the end of 1943.

The United States also converted four fleet tankers into escort carriers. These larger twin-shaft turbine vessels were very successful, but a general shortage of tanker hulls prevented further conversions. Nevertheless, they formed the basis for the U.S. Navy's first purpose-designed escort carriers, the 19 Commencement Bay–class vessels. These were the only escort carriers to continue to operate postwar, since their size and speed suited them for the larger antisubmarine warfare aircraft then entering service.

The 50 Casablanca-class ships, however, formed the

bulk of the U.S. Navy escort carrier force, even though they were outside the mainstream of U.S. Navy design. All came from the Kaiser Vancouver yard and were commissioned within one year starting in July 1943. Their design was by Gibbs and Cox, and their construction was under the auspices of the Maritime Commission. Shortages of both turbines and diesels forced the use of reciprocating machinery, but the ships were faster and more maneuverable than the original C-3 conversions, had longer flight decks, and had larger hangars than even the Sangamon-class converted tankers.

Other than the *Audacity,* Britain completed only five escort carriers of its own, all conversions from mercantile hulls. They were similar to contemporary American C-3 conversions, although generally somewhat larger. Thirty-eight of these, transferred under Lend-Lease, formed the core of the Royal Navy's escort carrier force throughout the war.

Escort carriers, initially conceived as platforms providing air cover for convoys, soon expanded their activities into a wide variety of tasks. In the U.S. Navy, escort carriers formed the core of specialized antisubmarine hunter-killer groups, provided close air support for landings, served as replenishment carriers and aircraft transports, and operated as training flight decks. In addition, during 1942 the Sangamons took on fleet carrier assignments to compensate for shortages of first-line vessels.

The Royal Navy employed its escort carriers in much the same way. Its own shortage of large carriers, however, and its operational responsibilities within more confined waters led it to assign escort carriers additional frontline duties. The small carriers operated in strike roles either within a larger force or as autonomous units in the East Indies, the Aegean, and off the Norwegian coast, including in the attacks on the German battleship *Tirpitz.* Escort carriers also provided night-fighter coverage for the British Pacific Fleet.

To circumvent 1922 Washington Treaty quantitative limitations, Japan designed several fast naval auxiliaries and passenger liners for quick conversion into carriers. Beginning in 1940, conversions from five auxiliaries and three liners joined the Combined Fleet as frontline light fleet carriers. Japan also completed several mercantile conversions similar in capability to the British and American escort carriers. However, unlike the Allied vessels, these were designed and usually were deployed as integral components of Japan's main carrier force. In addition, Japan converted one Yamato-class battleship hull, the *Shinano,* into a huge carrier that never entered operational service, and it commenced conversion of an incomplete cruiser as a light fleet carrier.

The United States, too, deployed converted warships—the nine Independence-class light fleet carriers based on Cleveland-class cruiser hulls formed an integral part of the fast carrier force from early 1943. Although conceived as first-line units, their design owed much to plans for the escort carriers, and their operational limitations made them suitable only for emergency service.

Britain also appreciated the need for smaller, less sophisticated carriers that could enter service more quickly, but it chose to construct new vessels rather than convert existing hulls. The design was similar to that of the larger fleet carriers, but the carrier was unarmored. Britain also deliberately conformed to mercantile rather than naval standards, since the Admiralty contemplated selling these vessels for conversion into passenger liners or fast cargo ships after the war, an interesting reversal of procedures! Four of this Colossus-class of light fleet carriers served with the British Pacific Fleet late in 1945, and they joined six sister ships to form the core of British carrier power into the later 1950s, since they proved very economical to operate.

France's converted carrier *Béarn* remained its only example throughout the war, serving mainly as an aircraft transport because of its low speed. France began building a pair of new carriers, the *Joffre* and the *Painlevé,* just before war began, but the fall of France in 1940 terminated construction. The final design incorporated a flight deck offset to port to minimize superstructure intrusion, a feature that has reappeared in several designs in recent years.

Before and during the war, Germany undertook some carrier construction. Its prewar design, the *Graf Zeppelin,* reached an advanced stage of construction by 1940, but subsequent reductions in priority, design changes, and disputes among the Kriegsmarine, the Luftwaffe, and the Reichs Luft Ministerium (Reich Air Ministry) over provision of aircraft and aircrew combined to prevent carrier completion before the war's end. A similar fate befell several conversion projects from merchant vessels and warships.

Italy evinced little interest in aircraft carriers before the war, subscribing to the position that geography would permit shore-based aircraft to provide entirely sufficient air cover and offensive strike potential for its fleet. Wartime experience led to a change in this view, and the Italian navy began two conversions from mercantile hulls to create the fleet's first carriers. The *Aquila* was a sophisticated nearly total reconstruction of the liner *Roma* that was virtually complete when Italy surrendered in 1943. The Italians sabotaged the *Aquila* to prevent its use by Germany, and the ship subsequently was seriously damaged by Allied bombing and an attack using "chariots" (manned torpedoes) at Genoa. The hulk was scrapped after the war. Conversion of the liner *Augustus* into the *Sparviero,* a more austere vessel similar to Allied escort carriers, began in 1941, but she, too, was never completed.

Air power at sea came of age during World War II. The combination of unprecedented striking power (both in volume of ordnance and range of delivery), mobility, and flexibility of use transformed the aircraft carrier into the world's major fleets' new capital ship, a position it retains today.

Paul E. Fontenoy

See also
Aircraft, Naval; Aviation, Naval; France, Navy; Germany, Navy; Great Britain, Navy; Human Torpedoes; Hunter-Killer Groups; Italy, Navy; Japan, Navy; Kamikaze; United States, Navy

References
Chesnau, Roger. *Aircraft Carriers of the World, 1914 to the Present: An Illustrated Encyclopedia.* 2d ed. London: Arms and Armour Press, 1992.
Friedman, Norman. *U.S. Aircraft Carriers: An Illustrated Design History.* Annapolis, MD: Naval Institute Press, 1983.
———. *British Carrier Aviation: The Evolution of the Ships and Their Aircraft.* Annapolis, MD: Naval Institute Press, 1988.
Jentschura, Hansgeorg, Dieter Jung, and Peter Mickel. *Warships of the Imperial Japanese Navy, 1869–1945.* London: Arms and Armour Press, 1977.

Airlift

Use of aircraft to transport personnel, equipment, and supplies. Airlift provided the capability to move critical resources rapidly and over great distances, providing important support to combat forces in all theaters of operation during the war. However, airlift operations were restricted by practical realities, including the need for airfields and maintenance facilities, restricted capabilities in bad weather, and vulnerability to enemy air defenses. Additionally, the limited payload of aircraft restricted the role of airlift; surface transportation was needed to move and sustain large combat forces. Beyond the limitations, however, the speed and range of transport aircraft made airlift a critical component of military operations. Basic airlift concepts and capabilities existed before World War II, and wartime demands stimulated the rapid growth of airlift forces and the refinement of operational missions.

The first airlift was primarily for liaison purposes, moving key personnel about. As aircraft capabilities grew, air transportation came to include the rapid delivery of logistical support for air and surface forces. Additionally, beginning during World War I, supplies were dropped to ground forces, and agents were inserted by parachute behind enemy lines. Airlift potential grew as aircraft capabilities for payload and range increased during the interwar years because of the development of enhanced bomber designs and improved transports produced for the rapidly growing commercial air transportation industry. Several military experiences illustrated the expanding potential of airlift, including the movement of ground units from North Africa to Spain during the Spanish Civil War, which was critical for the Nationalist side. Additionally, both Germany and the Soviet Union experimented with the use of parachute forces and gliders in airborne assaults and with the air-landing of combat forces and supplies to support rapid-offensive ground operations.

From the early phases of World War II, airlift played an important role—in a mission commonly referred to as *tactical airlift*—by providing routine and emergency logistical support for combat forces in all major theaters of operation. The importance of aerial logistical support for ground forces, tactical air forces, and naval forces in all theaters grew significantly during World War II. This support included the rapid movement of key personnel, delivery of critical equipment and supplies, movement of mail, and evacuation of wounded or ill personnel. The German military demonstrated the exceptional value of airlift during its rapid ground operations, especially in the Eastern Theater in the vast expanses of the Soviet Union. The Soviet Union also used airlift to support its widely dispersed and often isolated and cut-off forces.

U.S. and British forces also relied heavily on airlift support, both in geographically remote locations—such as the China-Burma-India Theater and the southwest Pacific islands—and in support of mobile combat operations. The aerial resupply of China by flying over the Himalayas—"the Hump"—was a high point in large-scale airlift support operations during the war. U.S. and British airlift operations were also important in mobile operations in North Africa and Western Europe. In the drive across France, supplies delivered by British and American transports and bombers were especially important in helping ground forces and tactical air units continue offensive operations under the logistical constraints imposed by limited port facilities.

Tactical airlift also included the rapid movement and air landing of small units, delivery of airborne assault forces, and the rapid reinforcement or resupply of units in isolated locations or in dangerous combat situations. The Germans had a well-developed operational concept at the start of the war, demonstrating remarkable effectiveness in the early seizure from the air of key facilities during the Norwegian Campaign and in securing the fortress of Eben Emael in Belgium in the invasion of France and the Low Countries in May 1940. German landings in Crete the next year also demonstrated the value of aerial envelopment, as well as the inherent dangers and risks of such activities. Later, the Germans also employed aerial logistical support to supply their forces trapped in Stalingrad and under pressure in North Africa. However, these efforts had limited effect; the Germans' airlift capability was restricted and aircraft losses were high in these missions compared with the needs of the forces being supplied.

Soviet doctrinal concepts for airborne and air-landing support of offensive operations were well developed and openly demonstrated in exercises during the 1930s. However, the impact of early losses and German control of the air limited Soviet assault operations. Nonetheless, in the final campaign of the war, the Soviets conducted extensive air assault operations against Japanese forces in Manchuria and Korea, often seizing airfields and key facilities.

In the Pacific Theater, the Japanese employed airborne forces early in the war. U.S. and British forces effectively used airborne landings in Burma and often supplied ground forces that were operating away from fixed supply lines. In the southwest Pacific, airborne assaults and aerial resupply efforts were very important for American operations in the widely dispersed islands of that theater. American and British forces conducted a series of increasingly sophisticated large airborne operations in North Africa, Sicily, Normandy, Southern France, Operation MARKET-GARDEN (the attempt to cross the Rhine at Arnhem), and Operation VARSITY (the final Rhine crossing). Some Allied bombers were also used in September 1944 in an attempt to supply the Polish Home Army in its uprising in Warsaw.

For special missions that supported covert and guerrilla operations, airlift resources were used to insert personnel, deliver supplies, and extract personnel from enemy-occupied territory. The Soviets conducted extensive operations in support of partisan activities in German-held territories. British and U.S. aircraft regularly worked with agents and local resistance organizations in occupied Europe, especially in France and the Balkans. Similar activities were conducted to support local guerrilla bands in the China-Burma-India Theater and observer operations in the Pacific islands. An additional innovative development was the use of helicopters for the first time in rescue roles.

The significant development of tactical airlift during the war was matched by the equally impressive growth of the use of long-distance aerial routes between theaters in a mission that has become known as *intertheater airlift* or *strategic airlift*. The long-distance airlift grew from the prewar commercial transportation systems, including the flying boat services in the Atlantic and Pacific Oceans. Airlift allowed key personnel and critical supplies to be delivered in a timely fashion, especially compared with the time needed for surface travel on a global scale. The most extensive system was the U.S. airlift network that stretched from the con-

tinental United States to every theater of operations, covering all continents except Antarctica. During the early period of the war, the U.S. Army Air Forces (USAAF), in addition to absorbing airline operations under contract, developed its long-range delivery capability in the Ferrying Command. This organization delivered aircraft under the Lend-Lease program and developed operations for passengers and high-value freight.

In June 1942, the USAAF established the Air Transport Command, which had responsibility for all ferrying and air transportation activities to the combat theaters. The American air routes grew into a global web: routes included from the Northeast United States to Canada and across the North Atlantic to England and Europe (paralleled by British routes); to Canada and Alaska and on to the Aleutian Islands and to Soviet Siberia; from Southeast U.S. bases to Brazil and on to Africa and the Middle East, continuing on to the Soviet Union or India and China (the longest leg of the network); and from West Coast bases to Hawaii and on into the Pacific islands and Australia. These flights moved matériel and key personnel to all theaters and allowed the rapid return of wounded personnel and returning combat-experienced aircrew members, who became trainers for new flying personnel. Additionally, senior commanders and staff members were able quickly to visit theaters for on-the-scene assessments and conferences with the theater commanders and staffs. By the end of the war, the Air Transportation Command included approximately 210,000 military and 105,000 civilian personnel. The extensive global coverage provided routine and regular flights, as well as responsive emergency missions, over the entire system.

Air Transportation Command provided the foundation for the Military Air Transport Service, the long-range transport capability of the U.S. Air Force after the war. The evolution of airlift missions during World War II established the patterns of airlift for all major military forces in the postwar period.

Jerome V. Martin

See also

Airborne Forces, Allied; Airborne Forces, Axis; Aircraft, Gliders; Aircraft, Transports; Eben Emael; Hump, The; Lend-Lease; MARKET-GARDEN, Operation; Normandy Invasion and Campaign; OVERLORD, Operation; Parachute Infantry; Parachutes; Rhine Crossings; Sicily, Invasion of; Spain, Civil War; Stalingrad, Battle of; Warsaw Rising (1944)

References

Bickers, Richard Townsend. *Airlift: The Illustrated History of Military Air Transport.* New York: Osprey Publishing, 1998.

Bilstein, Roger E. *Airlift and Airborne Operations in World War II.* Washington, DC: Air Force History and Museums Program, Government Printing Office, 1998.

Craven, Wesley Frank, and James Leg Cate. *The Army Air Forces in World War II.* Vol. 7, *Services around the World.* Office of Air Force History, Washington, DC: Government Printing Office, 1983.

Hardesty, Von. *Red Phoenix: The Rise of Soviet Air Power, 1941–1945.* Washington, DC: Smithsonian Institution Press, 1982.

Mrozik, D. Fritz. *German Air Force Airlift Operations.* U.S. Air Force Historical Studies, No. 167, U.S. Air Force Historical Division, Air University: Maxwell Air Force Base, AL, 1961. Reprinted New York: Arno Press, 1968.

Tunner, William H. *Over the Hump.* New York: Duell, Sloan, and Pierce, 1964. Reprint Office of Air Force History. Washington, DC: Government Printing Office, 1983.

Air-Sea Rescue

The rescue of air crews forced to bail out or ditch their aircraft at sea as well as shipwrecked mariners. With the advent of long-range aircraft, it became apparent that some system was necessary to increase the chances of survival for pilots whose aircraft went down during long-distance flights over water. The development of air-sea rescue (ASR) programs was hampered by technological limitations and interservice rivalries, but the rewards of an air-sea rescue program were apparent, especially with mounting casualties of the air war and a shortage of aircrews. Aside from simple life-saving, rescue meant that rescued personnel could return to the flight line, saving the cost and time of training replacements. Such programs also improved the morale of flight crews.

Sometimes a downed crew could send out a mayday (from the French *m'aidez,* or "help me") radio signal with a location. The crew would either bail out of their aircraft by jumping with parachutes, or the plane would be ditched— meaning that it would crash-land on the water, and the crew would endeavor to get out before it sank. Fighters such as a P-51 Mustang sank almost immediately, but large bombers such as the Boeing B-17 could often stay on the surface for 30 minutes. After leaving their aircraft, aircrew would endeavor to stay afloat in the water using a life preserver or a rubber raft until an airplane or boat could locate them by following a radio signal, seeing a large puddle of dye in the ocean, or spotting the men in the water. Crews needed to be prepared for long waits; especially in the Pacific Theater, it could take a week or more for a downed crew to be rescued.

Germany was the first country to develop an ASR program. In 1936, Seenotdienst (air-sea rescue service) units were organized as part of the Luftwaffe. They employed floatplanes and flying boats for rescues in the North Sea. German aircraft on over-water missions were equipped with collapsible rubber dinghies with radio transmitters. During the 1940 Battle of Britain, Seenotdienst units operated in the English Channel.

The Allies were slower to develop air-sea rescue operations. During the Battle of Britain, downed pilots had only life preservers until they were rescued. Eventually, they were provided with dinghies and dye markers. In 1942, the British introduced a lightweight radio transmitter for downed crewmen, nicknamed a "Gibson Girl," which was based on a captured German model. In addition to aircraft operated by Fighter Command, rescue motor launches (RMLs) operated near the coast.

German and British rescue aircraft were painted white and marked with the large red cross of the International Red Cross. The decks of the RMLs were painted yellow, another sign of neutral craft. Both sides considered their ASR vehicles immune from enemy attack and rescued all downed pilots, regardless of their side in the conflict. But since a rescued pilot would return to duty, both sides frequently shot down ASR aircraft, leading to protests from each side in turn.

In January 1941, the British Air Ministry created the Directorate of Air-Sea Rescue to coordinate operations among the Royal Air Force, Royal Navy, and Coastal Command. In the first six months of 1941, out of 1,200 pilots who ditched, 444 were rescued. The British also assumed primary responsibility for all rescue operations in the European and Mediterranean Theaters, relieving their allies from developing their own programs.

The United States organized ASR operations based on the British system, even using British officers in training. Because the British had taken primary responsibilities for rescue operations in the European and Mediterranean Theaters, as well as for all planes departing India, the Americans were able to concentrate on the Pacific Theater. Such efforts were hampered by interservice rivalries. Each U.S. service went its own way, conducting its own operations and duplicating labor and equipment. This cumbersome arrangement was finally solved with the establishment early in 1944 of the Air-Sea Rescue Agency, which was charged with overseeing all operations. A school for training crews was established in Gulfport, Mississippi, but by the time trained crews began to graduate, the need for them was almost over. The U.S. Navy also played an important role in the rescue of B-29 crews flying from the Mariana Islands late in the war. The navy set up submarines stationed at intervals between the Marianas and Japan that acted as lifeguards for downed crewmen.

Although air-sea rescue saved many lives during World War II, its practices, operations, and equipment were constantly improvised and sometimes inefficient. Lessons learned during the war, however, led to improved air-sea rescue techniques thereafter.

Pamela Feltus

References

Pereira, Wilfred D. *Boat in the Blue: The Wartime Story of an RAF Air Sea Rescue Crew and Their Boats.* Cheltenham, UK: Line One Publishers, 1985.
Air Rescue Association. *USAF Air Rescue.* Paducah, KY: Turner Publishing, 1997.

Aisingioro P'u-i

See Aixinjueluo Puyi.

Aitken, William Maxwell (First Baron Beaverbrook, Lord Beaverbrook) (1879–1964)

Canadian-born British press magnate, friend of Winston L. S. Churchill, and member of Churchill's 1940–1942 cabinet. Born on 25 May 1879 in Maple, Ontario, William Aitken was a gifted writer (author of 11 books) who focused early on amassing a fortune. After making several trips to London, he moved there in July 1910, becoming active in business and politics. Aitken was elected to Parliament on a platform of promoting British Empire trade, serving from 1911 to 1916. He was knighted in 1911 and became Lord Beaverbrook in 1917.

Aitken purchased control of the *Daily Express* newspaper in December 1916 and set about building its circulation. Two years later he began the *Sunday Express,* and he took control of *The Evening Standard* in 1924, giving him morning, evening, and Sunday London papers. This editorial base made him a powerful figure in British political circles.

Lord Beaverbrook was one of Winston Churchill's closest advisers when Churchill became prime minister on 10 May 1940. Churchill gave him a post in the War Cabinet, that of minister of aircraft production. He served just less than a year (from 14 May 1940 to 30 April 1941), but in that crucial period he marshaled Britain's aircraft industry to turn out thousands of fighters and bombers to resist German attacks. His forceful methods naturally made him many enemies in the cabinet, the Air Ministry, and the Royal Air Force (RAF). Beaverbrook attempted to resign

Maxwell Aitken, the first Baron Beaverbrook (Lord Beaverbrook), was a Canadian-born businessman, politician, and newspaperman who became a forceful figure in the political scene of Great Britain. During 1940–1941 he was minister of aircraft production. (Hulton Archive by Getty Images)

several times on grounds of health, but he was dissuaded. Residing at 12 Downing Street, he became a minister of state on 30 April 1941 to continue advising Churchill but without specific ministerial portfolio.

On 22 June 1941, Beaverbrook was named minister of supply to supervise broader wartime production. Here his impact was less sensational than his accomplishments in the aircraft sector. He accompanied Churchill to the Placentia Bay meeting with U.S. President Franklin D. Roosevelt and later to White House meetings in 1941 with Roosevelt. He also traveled as Churchill's emissary to meet with Josef Stalin in October 1941.

Beaverbrook resigned as a minister on 28 February 1942, ostensibly over some of the personnel decisions made in a cabinet reshuffle. He continued to serve as an informal adviser to Churchill for the remainder of the war, often championing Soviet interests. Returning to publishing, he died 9 June 1964 in London.

Christopher H. Sterling

See also
Churchill, Sir Winston L. S.; Placentia Bay; Roosevelt, Franklin D.

References

Chisholm, Anne, and Michael Davie. *Lord Beaverbrook: A Life*. New York: Knopf, 1992.

Taylor, A. J. P. *Beaverbrook*. London: Hamish Hamilton, 1972.

Young, Kenneth. *Churchill and Beaverbrook: A Study in Friendship and Politics*. New York: James Heineman, 1966.

Aixinjueluo Puyi (Aisingioro P'u-i) (1906–1967)

Last emperor of China, more commonly remembered as the puppet ruler of Japanese-controlled Manzhouguo (Manchukuo, formerly Manchuria) from 1932 to 1945. Born in Beijing (Peking) in Hebei (Hopeh) on 14 January 1906 and nicknamed Henry by his English tutor (he was known to westerners as Henry Puyi), Aixinjueluo Puyi (Aisingioto P'u-i) ascended the throne in December 1908, at age three, as Xuan Tong (Hsuan T'ung). During the Chinese Revolution of 1911–1912, the emperor's mother negotiated frantically with General Yuan Shikai (Yuan Shih-k'ai) for a settlement that would guarantee their lives and financial security. Ignoring the claims to the throne of Sun Yixian (Sun Yat-sen), Puyi abdicated in favor of Yuan, who was authorized to create a provisional republic and to establish national unity by embracing all anti-imperial forces.

Briefly restored in 1917 by the intrigues of warlord politics, Puyi was again deposed, and he finally sought refuge in the Japanese concession in Tianjin (Tientsin) in Hebei Province by 1924. In July 1931 his brother visited Japan and met with various rightist politicians. Shortly after the 1931 Mukden (Shenyang) Incident in Liaoning, representatives of the Guandong (Kwantung) Army visited Puyi to discuss the future of Manchuria, assuring him that they were merely interested in helping the people of Manchuria establish an independent nation. The Japanese military was vague about whether the new state would be a monarchy or a republic. Negotiations continued through the fall and winter of 1931–1932, and Puyi finally agreed to be smuggled to Manchuria by sea and to accept the title chief executive of the state of Manzhouguo. Tokyo belatedly recognized the army's creation in August 1932.

In 1934 the Guandong Army allowed Puyi to mount the throne as emperor of Manzhoudiguo (Manchoutikuo), the Manzhu (Manchu Empire), wearing imperial dragon robes sent from the museum in Beijing. As "emperor," Puyi served the Greater East Asia Co-prosperity Sphere loyally until 1945, including making a state visit to Tokyo.

When Soviet forces invaded Manzhouguo in August 1945, Puyi was dethroned and imprisoned. Released to Mao

Aixinjueluo Puyi, pictured here in 1934. (The illustrated London News Picture Library)

Zedong's (Mao Tse-tung's) China in 1950, Puyi was again imprisoned and subjected to reeducation programs until his "rehabilitation" in 1959. He spent his final years as a gardener in Beijing's botanical gardens until his death from cancer on 17 October 1967.

Errol M. Clauss

See also

China, Role in War; Guandong Army; Manzhouguo; Mao Zedong

References

Behr, Edward. *The Last Emperor*. New York: Bantam Books, 1987.

Bergamini, David. *Japan's Imperial Conspiracy*. New York: Morrow, 1971.

Brachman, Arnold C. *The Last Emperor*. New York: Scribner's, 1975.

Power, Brian. *The Puppet Emperor: The Life of Pu Yi, Last Emperor of China*. New York: Universe Books, 1988.

Puyi, Henry (Aixinjueluo, Puyi). *From Emperor to Citizen: The Autobiography of Aisin-Gioro Pu Yi*. Beijing: Foreign Language Press, 1964.

Spence, Jonathan. *The Search for Modern China*. New York: W. W. Norton, 1990.

Alam Halfa, Battle of (31 August–7 September 1942)

North African battle between German Field Marshal Erwin Rommel's Afrika Korps and British Lieutenant General Bernard Law Montgomery's Eighth Army. Fearful that he would permanently lose the initiative to the Eighth Army after his advance was halted at the First Battle of El Alamein in July 1942, Rommel reorganized with the intention of resuming his advance toward Suez. Meanwhile, Montgomery assumed command of the British Eighth Army on 13 August and began planning for the offensive, all the while expecting Rommel to attack first.

Late on the evening of 30 August, Rommel attempted, as at Gazala, to get around Eighth Army's left flank although his force was weak in armor. With diversionary attacks designed to hold British forces along the coast, Rommel ordered the Afrika Korps east and south of Alam Halfa Ridge with the aim of swinging north to the Mediterranean coast behind Montgomery and enveloping the Eighth Army.

The Eighth Army had established a defense in depth, including strong positions on the Alam Halfa and Ruweisat Ridges, and Montgomery rejected any withdrawal. The 10th Armored Division, 22nd Armored Brigade, and 44th Division defended Alam Halfa, while the 7th Armored Division was south of the ridge. Montgomery ordered his armored units to defend from their current positions rather than advancing to meet Rommel's panzers.

Slowed by British minefields and fuel shortages, Rommel's tanks did not reach Alam Halfa until the evening of 31 August. Daylight brought vicious Desert Air Force attacks against the Axis advance, and the 7th Armored Division's placement forced Rommel to swing north prematurely, into the teeth of a tank brigade on Alam Halfa Ridge. Fuel shortages prevented the Afrika Korps from outflanking Alam Halfa to the east, forcing Rommel onto the defensive there.

On 1 September, after a flank assault on the 22nd Armored Brigade failed and having suffered severe losses, Rommel ordered his forces to retire to their original positions. The withdrawal, which began the next day, exposed the Afrika Korps to further devastating British aerial attacks. Rommel repulsed a counterattack by the 2nd New Zealand Division on the evening of 3 September, and Montgomery believed that he lacked the resources to force a general Axis withdrawal, so he decided not to press his advantage for the time being. Certainly Rommel's past successes made Montgomery wary of pushing too far forward.

Montgomery had fought his first battle as commander of Eighth Army with great skill. Rommel now had no choice but to go on the defensive. He established positions between the Mediterranean and the Qattara Depression as both sides prepared for the Eighth Army's upcoming offensive: the Second Battle of El Alamein.

Thomas D. Veve

See also
Afrika Korps; El Alamein, Battle of; Montgomery, Sir Bernard Law; North Africa Campaign; Rommel, Erwin Johannes Eugen

References
Lucas, James. *Panzer Army Africa.* San Rafael, CA: Presidio Press, 1977.

Montgomery, Bernard L. *The Memoirs of Field-Marshal the Viscount Montgomery of Alamein, K.G.* Cleveland, OH: World Publishing, 1958.

Thompson, R. W. *Churchill and the Montgomery Myth.* New York: J. B. Lippincott, 1967.

Alamogordo (16 July 1945)

New Mexico site of the first successful test of an atomic device. By 1945 the MANHATTAN Project had produced sufficient plutonium for several fission bombs, but scientists were unsure of the reliability of the implosion technique required to initiate a chain reaction and an explosion. Small-scale experiments were unrevealing, since nothing below critical mass can explode. Thus, Major General Leslie R. Groves, overall director of the MANHATTAN Project, authorized a full-scale test (known as Trinity) of the implosion technique. The Jornada del Muerto (Dead Man's Trail) near Alamogordo, New Mexico, was chosen as ground zero for the explosion. Isolated and ringed by peaks, the site helped to preserve secrecy and contain radioactive fallout, the effects of which were not yet then fully known.

Secured on top of a 100-ft steel tower, the device exploded at 5:30 A.M. on 16 July 1945. With a predicted minimal yield of 500 tons of trinitrotoluene (TNT) and an optimal yield of 5,000 tons if all parts functioned synergistically, the device actually produced a yield of 20,000 tons of TNT. Accompanied by a powerful shock wave and an awesome roar, the device vaporized the tower, creating a crater 400 yards in diameter. A mushroom cloud rose to 41,000 ft; the explosion was heard from 100 miles away, and the light produced was seen from 200 miles. To allay concerns of local residents, army officials reported that an ammunition dump had blown up.

Scientists were awestruck by the power of the explosion. Julius Robert Oppenheimer famously recalled the god Vishnu's line from the Bhagavad Gita: "I have become death, shatterer of worlds." Groves predicted, "The war's over." A report was quickly passed to President Harry S Truman at Potsdam, whose negotiating stance with Josef

Stalin hardened considerably based on the stunning results of the Trinity test.

The Trinity test site is located on White Sands Missile Range. It is open to the public twice a year: the first Saturday in April and the first Saturday in October.

William J. Astore

See also
Atomic Bomb, Decision to Employ; Bush, Vannevar; Einstein, Albert; Fermi, Enrico; Groves, Leslie Richard; Hiroshima; MANHATTAN Project; Nagasaki, Bombing of; Oppenheimer, Julius Robert; Potsdam Conference

References
Lamont, Lansing. *Day of Trinity*. New York: Atheneum, 1965, 1985.
Storms, Barbara. *Reach to the Unknown: Part 1: Trinity. Special Twentieth Anniversary Edition of the Atom, July 16, 1965*. Los Alamos, NM: Office of Public Relations, 1965.
Szasz, Ferenc Morton. *The Day the Sun Rose Twice: The Story of the Trinity Site Nuclear Explosion, July 16, 1945*. Albuquerque: University of New Mexico Press, 1984.

Alanbrooke, Lord
See Brooke, Sir Alan Francis.

Albania, Role in the War

During World War II, Albania was the springboard for the Italian invasion of Greece and the scene of anti-Axis guerrilla warfare. Having dominated Albania politically and economically for some time, Italian dictator Benito Mussolini planned a formal annexation of Albania in the spring of 1939. Italian troops invaded the small mountainous country on 7 April 1939 and met only light resistance, although a small force led by Colonel Abas Kupi held the Italians at Durazzo for 36 hours, sufficient time for Albanian King Zog and his family to escape. On 16 April 1939, King Victor Emmanuel III of Italy accepted the Albanian crown, and a pro-fascist government was installed. Britain, still hoping to prevent an alliance between Mussolini and Adolf Hitler, acceded to the annexation, but the Greeks prepared to resist an inevitable Italian invasion of their own country, which occurred on 28 October 1940.

Already, earlier in 1940, Britain's Special Operations Executive (SOE) had attempted to create a united-front movement under Abas Kupi and to stimulate a revolt against the Italians in northern Albania. The effort began well, but it faltered after the German conquest of Yugoslavia in April 1941 and the subsequent transfer of Kosovo Province from Yugoslavia to Albania. However, as Axis fortunes waned in 1943, Albanian resistance revived.

In the mountains of southern Albania, the Communists, encouraged by Tito (Josip Broz), leader of the Yugoslav Partisans, coalesced under Enver Hoxha. Liberal landowners and intellectuals formed the Balli Kombetar (National Front) resistance movement. In central and northern Albania, Abas Kupi and various tribal leaders also formed resistance groups. SOE agents Colonel Neil McLean and Major David Smiley were sent into southern Albania, and they subsequently recommended that the British provide aid to both Hoxha's partisans and the Balli Kombetar.

The disintegration of the Italian forces in Albania following the overthrow of Mussolini in September 1943 provided the Albanian guerrillas with arms and other supplies captured from or abandoned by the Italians. The Germans quickly sent in troops to clear out the remaining Italian forces, savagely repressed the local population, and "restored Albanian independence." The Germans created a government under Mehdi Frasheri, but it was able to control only the main towns and coastal plain. The rest of Albania descended into chaos as various guerrilla chieftains fought for power.

The British Balkan Air Force headquarters at Bari controlled the support to anti-Axis guerrillas in the Balkans and was decidedly pro-Partisan, in both Albania and Yugoslavia. The British hoped to use all of the Albanian resistance forces to harass the German withdrawal from Greece, which began in September 1944. But when Hoxha's Communists attacked the Balli Kombetar and Abas Kupi instead, the British cut off aid to the non-Communist resistance groups, thereby ensuring their defeat. Kupi and the Balli Kombetar leaders were evacuated to Italy with the McLean SOE mission, and the Communists were left to take over Albania. With Yugoslav support, Hoxha seized power on 29 November 1944, and the People's Republic of Albania was recognized by the Allies. Albanians subsequently developed anti-Western views and supported an isolated Stalinist regime for nearly half a century.

Charles R. Shrader

See also
Balkans Theater; Mussolini, Benito; Special Operations Executive; Tito; Victor Emmanuel III, King of Italy

References
Fischer, Bernd J. *Albania at War, 1939–45*. West Lafayette, IN: Purdue University Press, 1999.
Swire, Joseph. *Albania: The Rise of the Kingdom*. New York: Arno Press, 1971.

Aleutian Islands Campaign (1942–1943)

Military campaign for a 1,100-mile-long chain of U.S. islands stretching west from Alaska in the Bering Sea toward northern Japan. Though the Aleutians had a negligible population, no useful resources, and extreme climatic conditions that made them unsuitable for major military staging bases, they were nonetheless the scene of bitter fighting between the United States and Canada on the one hand and Japan on the other.

On 7 June 1942, elements of Japanese Vice Admiral Hosogaya Boshiro's Northern Naval Task Force seized the Aleutian islands of Attu and Kiska. The Japanese aim was twofold: to support Japan's advance on Midway Island by luring U.S. forces away from there, and to gain bases in the Aleutians to deter U.S. attacks on the Japanese Kurile Islands. By May 1943 the Japanese had more than 2,500 men on Attu and more than 5,400 on Kiska.

This Japanese foothold on U.S. soil triggered a substantial response from the United States and Canada, which together would eventually commit more than 100,000 troops to this remote region. Rear Admiral Robert A. Theobald commanded Task Force 8, an array of sea, air, and land units charged with expelling the Japanese from the Aleutians. Theobald intended to interdict Japanese lines of communication into Attu and Kiska by isolating the Aleutian waters and engaging Japanese transports and warships where possible.

Initially, the Allies employed submarine attacks in the western Aleutians. When Rear Admiral Thomas C. Kinkaid replaced Theobald in January 1943, he doubled the effort to interdict Japanese supply convoys. On 26 March 1943, a small U.S. Navy task force intercepted and defeated a larger Japanese force of cruisers, destroyers, and transports in the Battle of the Komandorski Islands. This action ended further Japanese surface resupply efforts.

Along with naval interdiction, U.S. and Canadian aircraft harassed the Japanese from bases in Alaska and the eastern Aleutians. In August 1942, U.S. forces established an airfield on Adak Island, from which bombers could strike Japanese in the western Aleutians. By September, Allied aircraft bombed targets on Kiska nearly every day for three weeks. The Japanese were forced to rely on submarines as the most dependable conveyance to ferry minimal subsistence supplies. By April 1943, the Allies had succeeded in tightening an air-sea noose around the Japanese bases.

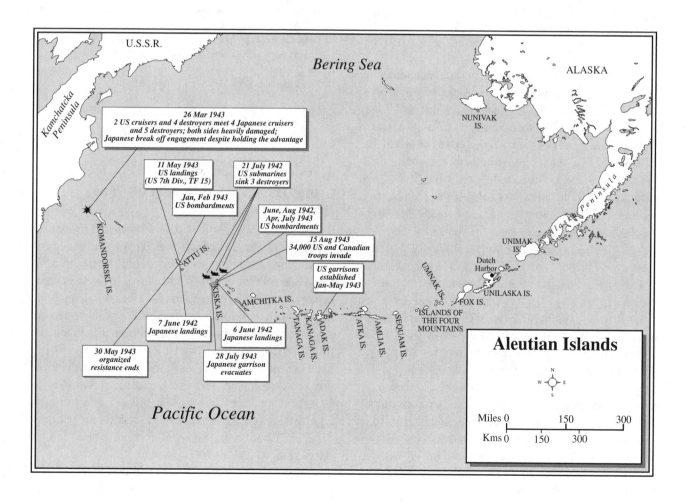

Attu, Aleutian Island, 4 June 1943. U.S. soldiers firing mortar shells over a ridge into a Japanese position. (Library of Congress)

Even so, U.S. commanders determined that an invasion of Attu and Kiska was necessary. One consideration focused on unpredictable weather, especially fog, which could cloak naval activity and allow the Japanese to reclaim control of the seas. The U.S. 7th Infantry Division was designated as the landing force, and it received amphibious warfare training at Fort Ord, California, until April when it deployed north for operations. Attu was chosen as the first objective, because intelligence estimated Japanese troops there to be only 500 men, considerably fewer than on Kiska.

The 7th Division landed on Attu on 11 May 1943 with almost 11,000 men. At first, U.S. commanders thought they had surprised the Japanese when they met no resistance at the shoreline. However, as American troops traversed through mushy tundra and ascended mountains ranging more than 2,000 to 3,000 ft above sea level, they discovered more than 2,500 Japanese waiting in trenches along ridgelines, using the inhospitable terrain to their advantage. The supply-starved Japanese troops conducted a stubborn defense that exacted a heavy toll on the U.S. force. After 19 days of attrition defense, the Japanese conducted a final banzai suicide attack with more than 600 soldiers, many of whom blew themselves up with grenades rather than surrender. U.S. losses were 561 killed and 1,136 wounded. Only 28 Japanese were taken prisoner.

After the loss of Attu, the Japanese decided to evacuate the 5,400 troops remaining on Kiska. On the night of 28 July, while U.S. ships were off refueling in foggy weather, two Japanese cruisers and six destroyers, entered Kiska harbor and in one hour evacuated their troops from the island. Not knowing about the evacuation, on 16 August the Allies conducted the planned amphibious assault on Kiska with more than 34,000 U.S. and Canadian troops. It took the Allies several days to realize the Japanese had departed, but the operation cost some 300 casualties from friendly fire and Japanese booby traps.

The campaign in the Aleutians was an indecisive one that challenged both Japanese and Allied planners. In the end, the Allies removed the Japanese from the two islands, but at great cost in resources committed and for only questionable gain.

Steven J. Rauch

See also
Kinkaid, Thomas Cassin; Komandorski Islands, Battle of the; Midway, Battle of; Theobald, Robert Alfred

References
Chandonnet, Fern, ed. *Alaska at War, 1941–1945: The Forgotten War Remembered: Papers from the Alaska at War Symposium, Anchorage, Alaska, November 11–13, 1993.* Anchorage: Alaska at War Committee, 1995.
Conn, Stetson, et al. *Guarding the United States and Its Outposts.* Washington, DC: Center of Military History, 1964.
Garfield, Brian. *The Thousand-Mile War: World War II in Alaska and the Aleutians.* New York: Doubleday, 1969.

Alexander, Sir Harold Rupert Leofric George (First Earl Alexander of Tunis) (1891–1969)

British army general. Born on 10 December 1891 in London, Harold Alexander was educated at Harrow and Sandhurst and commissioned in the Irish Guards in 1911. He served on the Western Front during World War I and rose to command a battalion and, temporarily, a brigade, ending the war a lieutenant colonel. Following the war he helped organize military forces in Latvia in 1919. He then graduated from the Staff College at Camberley and the Imperial Defence College and held staff assignments, first at the War Office and then in the Northern Command. From 1934 to 1938, he commanded the Nowshera Brigade of the Northern Command in India as a brigadier general. On his return to Britain in 1938, he was advanced to major general and received command of the 1st Division.

Alexander's division was sent to France, where he distinguished himself during the Battle for France by command-

General Sir Harold Alexander (left), *Lieutenant General George S. Patton Jr.* (center), *and Rear Admiral Alan G. Kirk* (right) *inspect invasion task force ships off the coast of North Africa, 1943. (Library of Congress)*

ing the British rear guard to Dunkerque, I Corps, and the Dunkerque perimeter. Promoted to lieutenant general in December 1940, Alexander had charge of Southern Command in Britain. In February 1942, Alexander received command of British forces in Burma. Recalled to Europe, that July he became commander of British forces in the Middle East. There he worked well with Eighth Army Commander General Bernard Law Montgomery as well as other Allied leaders. He undoubtedly played a key role in building up British forces for the Battle of El Alamein in October 1942.

Alexander attended the Casablanca Conference in January 1943, after which he became deputy supreme commander of Allied forces in North Africa and commander of the 18th Army Group. Alexander initially had a low opinion of U.S. Army generals and thought that American forces were poorly trained. He realized that cooperation with the Americans was vital but gave greater latitude to British commanders.

Appointed commander in chief of 15th Army Group for the invasion of Sicily in July 1943, Alexander failed to maintain adequate control over his subordinates, Montgomery and U.S. Major General George S. Patton Jr., each of whom sought the preeminent role. Alexander then directed the Allied invasion of Italy in September. Again the command was hindered by rivalries between his subordinates and grandstanding by Lieutenant General Mark W. Clark. His command in Italy, however, brought Alexander promotion to field marshal in November 1944 and elevation to the position of supreme Allied commander in the Mediterranean.

On 1 May 1945, German forces in Italy surrendered unconditionally, and that October, Alexander handed over his Italian command. In January 1946 he was named Viscount Alexander of Tunis. Not a great general, Alexander was nonetheless regarded as an excellent strategist who never lost a battle.

From 1946 to 1952, Alexander was the appointed governor general of Canada. Named Earl Alexander of Tunis in January 1952, he served from February 1952 to October 1954 as minister of defense in Britain. Alexander died in Slough, England, on 16 June 1969.

Fred R. van Hartesveldt and Spencer C. Tucker

See also

Casablanca Conference; Cassino/Rapido River, Battle for; Clark, Mark W.; Dunkerque Evacuation; El Alamein, Battle of; France, Battle of (1940); Italy Campaign; Leese, Oliver; Montgomery, Bernard Law; Patton, George S., Jr.; Rome, Advance on and Capture of; Salerno, Battle of; Sicily, Invasion of; TORCH, Operation; Tunis, Battle of

References

Alexander of Tunis, Harold Rupert Leofric George Alexander, 1st Earl. *The Alexander Memoirs, 1940–1945.* John North, ed. London: Cassell, 1962.
Jackson, W. G. F. *Alexander of Tunis as Military Commander.* London: Batsford, 1971.
Nicolson, Nigel. *Alex: The Life of Field Marshal Earl Alexander of Tunis.* London: Constable 1956.
Reid, Brian Holden. "Field-Marshal Earl Alexander." In John Keegan, ed., *Churchill's Generals.* New York: Grove Weidenfeld, 1991.

Allen, Terry de la Mesa (1888–1969)

U.S. Army general. Born on 1 April 1888, at Fort Douglas, Utah, Terry de la Mesa Allen grew up in Texas. He entered the U.S. Military Academy in 1907 with the class of 1911, but he was discharged after five years for academic deficiency. He continued his studies at Catholic University, graduated in 1912, and obtained a cavalry commission that November. During World War I, Captain Allen commanded a battalion in the 90th Division in France and was wounded several times. He returned from France as a major and attended army schools, the last being the Army War College in 1935.

In October 1940, Allen was promoted to brigadier general, and in June 1942, he was promoted to major general. He took command of the 1st Infantry Division in August. Allen led his division through the training buildup for Operation TORCH (the invasion of North Africa on 8 November 1942) and in the subsequent campaigns in Tunisia and Sicily. Known as a tough, inspirational commander, Allen was revered by members of the 1st Infantry Division (the "Big Red One"). As a result of his unswerving advocacy of his division and incidents that suggested toleration of lack of discipline, Allen and his assistant division commander, Brigadier General Theodore Roosevelt Jr. were removed from command following the attack on Troina, Sicily, in August 1943.

Major General Allen returned to the United States to organize and train the 104th Infantry Division (Timberwolves).

He took them to France in September 1944, where they fought alongside his beloved Big Red One. In an army in which relief from combat command usually meant no second chance, Allen was restored to division combat command because he was an effective fighter and a distinguished soldier. After successful campaigns in central Europe, Allen took his Timberwolves home in June 1945. Allen retired in August 1946 and died in El Paso, Texas, on 12 September 1969.

John F. Votaw

See also

Kasserine Pass, Battle of; Roosevelt, Theodore, Jr.; Sicily, Invasion of; TORCH, Operation; Tunisia Campaign

References

Atkinson, Rick. *An Army at Dawn: The War in North Africa, 1942–1943.* New York: Henry Holt, 2002.
D'Este, Carlo. *Bitter Victory: The Battle for Sicily, 1943.* New York: E. P. Dutton, 1988.
Society of the First Division. *Danger Forward: The Story of the First Division in World War II.* Washington, DC: Society of the First Division, 1947.

Allied Military Tribunals after the War

Following the conclusion of World War II, leading figures of the German and Japanese governments and armed forces were prosecuted on war crimes charges. The trials of the principal figures took place at Nuremberg in Germany and Tokyo in Japan.

In August 1945, representatives of the British, French, U.S., and Soviet governments, meeting in London, signed an agreement that created the International Military Tribunal and set ground rules for the trial. To avoid using words such as *law* or *code,* the document was named *The London Charter of the International Military Tribunal.* It combined elements of Anglo-American and continental European law. Defendants' rights and the rules of evidence differed in several ways from those in American courtrooms.

The four nations issued indictments against 24 persons and 6 organizations in October 1945. The counts of the charges were as follows: (1) conspiracy to wage aggressive war; (2) waging aggressive war, or crimes against peace; (3) war crimes; and (4) crimes against humanity. Of 22 defendants, 3 were acquitted, 12 were sentenced to death, and the remainder received prison terms. At the conclusion of this trial, 6 Nazi organizations were charged: the Sturmabteilungen (SA), the Reichsregierung (cabinet of the Reich), the General Staff and High Command of the German armed forces, the Schutzstaffel (SS, bodyguard units), the Gestapo, and the Corps of the Political Leaders of the Nazi Party. The first organization was not convicted, and the next two had so few members that the Allies decided simply to deal with the individuals who had belonged to these organizations. The last three organizations were found guilty, making it possible later to convict individuals on the basis of them having belonged to these organizations.

On 9 December 1946, the so-called Doctors´ Trial opened, conducted by the Allies. It dealt with individuals associated with the Nazi euthanasia program. A total of 23 individuals were indicted for their involvement. On 20 August 1947, the court proclaimed 16 of them guilty; 7 were sentenced to death and executed on 2 June 1948. In secondary trials before that, 22 of 31 doctors charged were found guilty and sentenced to death at Buchenwald, the concentration camp where many of their crimes were committed.

The Allied occupying powers also conducted individual war crimes trials in their zones of occupation. The Americans were by far the most fervent in their pursuit of justice, scheduling more than 169,000 trials. Although fewer were actually held, the Americans did sentence 9,000 Germans to prison terms, and others were fined. The British and French were not greatly interested in prosecuting war criminals; the British held 2,296 trials in their zone. The Soviets Union was perhaps the least interested in such legal proceedings.

Trials continued under the Federal Republic of Germany but with little punishment for the guilty. Alfred Krupp served only three years in prison for conscripting slave labor in his industrial enterprises, and on his release his empire was restored to him. The chemical firm of I. G. Farben was not broken up. From 1975 to 1981 the government prosecuted 15 individuals associated with the Majdanek concentration camp. Only 1 person was found guilty of murder, and 5 were acquitted.

In January 1946, General Douglas MacArthur approved a charter to inaugurate the International Military Tribunal for the Far East (IMTFE), which was dominated by the United States. On 3 May 1946, the IMTFE opened with the trial of 28 of 80 Class A Japanese war criminals at Tokyo. The hearings covered crimes that occurred between 1928 and the Japanese surrender in August 1945. The indictments were based on the concept of war crimes that had been stipulated at Nuremberg—that is, crimes against peace, crimes against humanity, war crimes, and aggressive war. However, in the Tokyo proceedings, there was no assumption of collective guilt as in the case of Germany, and thus no organizations were charged. Of the 28 defendants, 19 were professional military men and 9 were civilians. The prosecution team was made up of justices from 11 Allied nations: Australia, Canada, China, France, Great Britain, India, the Netherlands, New Zealand, the Philippines, the Soviet Union, and the United States. Indictments accused the defendants of promoting a plan of conquest and the commission of both war crimes and crimes against humanity.

On 4 November 1948, the sentences were meted out: 2 defendants had died; 1 was considered insane; 7 were sentenced to death; 16 were sentenced to life imprisonment; and the rest were given jail terms. Japanese Emperor Hirohito, in whose name so many war crimes had been committed, was not charged. A second group of 23 men and a third group of 19 men were never brought to trial, and the men were released in 1947 and 1948, respectively. All those sentenced to prison were released over the next several years. No trials of the infamous Japanese Unit 731, which would have been akin to the Doctors' Trial in Germany, were conducted. Prosecution was not pursued because of a bargain struck by the U.S. government to drop prosecution in return for all information on experiments in germ and biological warfare on human guinea pigs, including U.S. prisoners of war.

The British carried out minor war crimes trials of Japanese nationals in Southeast Asia, and other countries also held war crimes trials for individuals guilty of these offenses in their national territories. In China, there were trials in 10 locations.

Thomas J. Weiler

See also
Bataan Death March; Cairo Conference; Germany, Occupation of; Hirohito, Emperor of Japan; Holocaust, The; International Military Tribunal: Far East; International Military Tribunal: The Nuremberg Trials; Japan, Occupation of; MacArthur, Douglas; Potsdam Conference; Prisoners of War; Unit 731, Japanese Army; United Nations, Declaration; United Nations, Formation of

References
Maga, Timothy. *Judgment at Tokyo: The Japanese War Crimes Trials.* Lexington: University Press of Kentucky, 2001.
Marrus, Michael R. *The Nuremberg War Crimes Trial 1945–46: A Documentary History.* The Bedford Series in History and Culture. Bedford, UK: St. Martin's Press, 1997.
Martin, Roy A. *Inside Nürnberg: Military Justice for Nazi War Criminals.* Shippensburg, PA: White Mane Books, 2000.

Alsace Campaign (November 1944–January 1945)

Allied campaign to capture Alsace from German forces. Formidable barriers to the east and west protected the plains of Alsace from invasion; to the east was the Rhine River and to the west the Vosges Mountains. The two primary gaps in the Vosges were the Belfort Gap and the Saverne Gap, with the former defying capture by the German army both in 1870 and 1914. The vaunted Wehrmacht did what past German armies failed to do when Panzer Group Guderian penetrated the Belfort Gap in the French Campaign of 1940. German forces occupied Alsace until the Allied campaign of winter 1944–1945.

The Alsace Campaign was a joint American-French campaign to capture Alsace and reach the Rhine River. Lieutenant General Jacob Devers, commander of the Allied 6th Army Group, exercised overall control of the campaign. His forces consisted of the U.S. Seventh Army under Lieutenant General Alexander Patch and the First French Army under General Jean de Lattre de Tassigny. The VI and XV Corps made up the Seventh Army, and the First French Army consisted of the I and II Corps. Opposing was the German Nineteenth Army under General der Infanterie (U.S. equiv. lieutenant general) Freidrich Wiese. His army consisted of eight infantry divisions, six of which would be nearly destroyed in the campaign. Wiese's most reliable unit was the 11th Panzer Division (known as the Ghost Division for its fighting on the Eastern Front against the Soviet Union).

Ultimate control of the German forces, however, was in the hands of Army Group G Commander General der Panzertruppen (U.S. equiv. lieutenant general) Hermann Balck. Supreme Headquarters, Allied Expeditionary Forces (SHAEF) had low expectations for the campaign in Alsace; its attention was more clearly focused on the battles to the north involving the 12th and 21st Army Groups. General Devers was to clear the Germans from his front and secure crossings over the Rhine River. In the 6th Army Group zone, General Patch's XV Corps, commanded by Major General Wade Haislip, held the left, or northern, flank and was linked up with Lieutenant General George S. Patton's Third Army of the 12th Army Group. Next in line was the VI Corps under Major General Edward Brooks, who took over when Lieutenant General Lucian Truscott was reassigned. Holding the southern flank was the First French Army; this was also the southern flank of the entire Allied line.

The campaign in Alsace was to begin in coordination with the fighting to the north. The XV Corps was to jump off on 13 November 1944 and capture Sarrebourg and the Saverne Gap, then exploit its gains eastward while at the same time protecting Patton's flank. (Patton's offensive started on 8 November.) The VI Corps was scheduled to begin its campaign two days after the XV Corps started, or 15 November. It would attack in a northeasterly direction, break out onto the Alsatian plains, capture Strasbourg, and secure the west bank of the Rhine. Farther south, the First French Army was to commence operations on 13 November. The I and II Corps would force the Belfort Gap, capture the city of Belfort, and exploit its success. There was ample opportunity for spectacular success.

The XV Corps attacked in a snowstorm on 13 November with the 79th and 44th Divisions and the French 2nd Armored Division. The 79th Division captured Sarrebourg on 21 November and advanced so quickly that General Patch directed XV Corps to capture Strasbourg if it could get there before VI Corps. On 23 November, elements of the French 2nd Armored Division liberated Strasbourg, capital of Alsace. The VI Corps began its attack on 15 November with the 3rd, 36th, 100th, and 103rd Divisions and achieved similar success. Crossing the Meurthe River, the 100th Division penetrated the German "Winter Line" on 19 November, a position that quickly crumbled. The attack in the First French Army sector began on 13 November. The French troops successfully breached the Belfort Gap, and elements of the 1st Armored Division of I Corps reached the Rhine on 19 November, the first Allied troops in the 6th Army Group zone to do so.

In the midst of this success in the 6th Army Group zone, Generals Dwight D. Eisenhower and Omar N. Bradley met with Devers and Patch on 24 November. The result was an order for the Seventh Army to turn northward and attack the West Wall (the series of fortifications protecting Germany's western frontier) along with Patton's Third Army. The XV and VI Corps, minus two divisions, were subsequently turned northward while the First French Army and the 3rd and 36th Divisions focused their attention on German troops around the city of Colmar.

The attack northward began on 5 December, with the XV Corps on the left and the VI Corps on the right. After 10 days of heavy fighting, elements of the VI Corps entered Germany on 15 December. The 100th Division's effort around the French city Bitche was so fierce that it was given the sobriquet "Sons of Bitche." The Seventh Army offensive was halted on 20 December to enable it to cooperate with the Allied defense in the Ardennes.

The German troops in the 6th Army Group front planned an offensive for late December 1944, known as Operation NORDWIND. Just before midnight on New Year's Eve, the onslaught commenced. Through much of January 1945, the attack forced Allied troops to give ground. Eisenhower even toyed with the idea of abandoning Strasbourg, but General Charles de Gaulle vehemently opposed such a plan. The city was held, and by 25 January, the German offensive petered out and the German forces withdrew.

With the German attack defeated, the only Wehrmacht troops remaining in Alsace were located around Colmar. The First French Army was assigned the responsibility of reducing the Colmar pocket, and it began this task on 20 January 1945. The I Corps attacked the southern flank of the pocket, while the II Corps assaulted the northern flank.

The plan was for the two forces to meet at the Rhine, enveloping the pocket. On 2 February, the city of Colmar was captured, and by 5 February, German resistance ended. The campaign in Alsace was over. Although overshadowed by the 12th and 21st Army Groups to the north, General Devers's 6th Army Group had contributed an important accomplishment.

Christopher C. Meyers

See also

Ardennes Offensive; Balck, Hermann; Bradley, Omar Nelson; Colmar Pocket, Battle for the; Devers, Jacob Loucks; Eisenhower, Dwight D.; France Campaign (1944); Lattre de Tassigny, Jean Joseph Marie Gabriel de; NORDWIND, Operation; Patch, Alexander McCarrell, Jr.

References

Bonn, Keith E. *When the Odds Were Even: The Vosges Mountains Campaign, October 1944–January 1945.* Novato, CA: Presidio Press, 1994.

Clarke, Jeffrey J., and Robert R. Smith. *United States Army in World War II: European Theater of Operations: Riviera to the Rhine.* Washington, DC: Center of Military History, 1993.

Lattre de Tassigny, Jean M. G. de. *The History of the First French Army.* Trans. Malcolm Barnes. London: Allen and Unwin, 1952.

Weigley, Russell. *Eisenhower's Lieutenants: The Campaign of France and Germany, 1944–1945.* Bloomington: Indiana University Press, 1981.

Wyant, William. *Sandy Patch: A Biography of Lt. Gen. Alexander M. Patch.* New York: Praeger, 1991.

Altmark Incident (16 February 1940)

World War II British navy seizure of a German merchant ship within Norwegian territorial waters. The *Altmark* was a supply ship serving the German pocket battleship *Graf Spee* in the South Atlantic. She also became a prison ship, taking aboard survivors from the nine ships sunk by the *Graf Spee.* Since the outbreak of war, ships of the Royal Navy had been searching for the *Graf Spee* and her supply ships. On 13 December 1939, in the Battle of Río de la Plata, British cruisers located the *Graf Spee* and damaged her. Believing that the British had assembled a superior force, the *Graf Spee*'s captain then scuttled her. The *Altmark,* which had refueled the pocket battleship just prior to her last fight, departed the South Atlantic in late January 1940 for Hamburg. Commanded by Captain Heinrich Dau, she reached the Norwegian coast on 12 February 1940.

On 14 February, the *Altmark* entered Norwegian territorial waters at Trondheim. Although Norwegian naval vessels twice stopped the *Altmark,* Dau hid his ship's guns below and claimed he had no prisoners on board. He resisted any effort to search his vessel on the grounds that she was a German naval ship, immune to search. Despite misgivings and suspecting the nature of the cargo, the Norwegians allowed the *Altmark* to proceed. Norwegian officials did not want to create an incident that might be used to precipitate a German invasion of their neutral country. Word of events, however, reached the British Embassy at Oslo, and the naval attaché there informed the British Admiralty of the situation. On 16 February 1940, after British planes had located the *Altmark,* Captain Philip Vian's destroyer flotilla cornered the *Altmark* near Jössing fjord within Norwegian territorial waters. The Norwegian gunboat *Skarv* hampered the British Navy's efforts to force *Altmark* to sea, and the German supply ship then slipped into the fjord.

In London, meanwhile, the War Cabinet met concerning the situation and the reports that the *Altmark* had on board some 300 British seamen, who were in fact being held below deck in difficult conditions. First Lord of the Admiralty Winston L. S. Churchill personally authorized the boarding and search of the *Altmark* and liberation of her prisoners.

At 11:00 P.M. on 16 February, Vian's flagship, the destroyer *Cossack,* entered the fjord. *Altmark* tried to ram the destroyer, but expert British ship handling saved *Cossack* from damage. As the two ships brushed together, some of the boarding party leaped across to the German ship. *Cossack* then again closed, the remainder of the boarding party followed, and *Cossack* backed clear. In a brief fight, 7 *Altmark* crew members were killed and 299 British prisoners were freed.

The *Altmark* incident was definitely an infringement of Norway's neutrality by Britain. Neutral countries could no longer be certain of their inviolability in this war. This incident caused Hitler on 19 February to order an acceleration in his plans to invade Norway, Operation WESERÜBUNG. After they had conquered Norway, the Germans erected a commemorative marker at Jössing fjord reading (in German), "Here on 16 February 1940 the *Altmark* was attacked by British sea-pirates."

Martin Moll

See also

Churchill, Sir Winston L. S.; Norway, Role in War; Plata, Río de la, Battle of; WESERÜBUNG, Operation

References

Roskill, Stephen W. *White Ensign: The British Navy at War, 1939–1945.* Annapolis, MD: Naval Institute Press, 1960.

Salmon, Patrick, ed. *Britain and Norway in the Second World War.* London: Her Majesty's Stationery Office, 1995.

Wiggan, Richard. *Hunt the Altmark.* London: R. Hale, 1982.

Ambrosio, Vittorio (1879–1958)

Italian army general. Born in Turin on 28 July 1879, Vittorio Ambrosio joined the army in 1901 and served in the cavalry during the 1911–1912 Italo-Turkish War. From 1915 to 1918 he was in charge of the 3rd Cavalry Division. His postwar career advanced steadily, culminating in command of the Second Army in 1939.

Ambrosio commanded Italian occupation forces in Yugoslavia following the German invasion of that country in April 1941. Appointed army chief of staff in January 1942, Ambrosio became involved in efforts to oust Marshal Ugo Cavallero, the inept supreme command chief of staff. In February 1943, Benito Mussolini (Il Duce) finally sacked Cavallero and replaced him with Ambrosio.

As the new chief, Ambrosio set three major goals: to pull back to Italy proper as much of the overextended army as possible, to dig in his heels against the Germans and their demands, and to lighten the top-heavy high command. He failed to achieve any of the three. Although the broken remnants of Italian forces in the Soviet Union were eventually repatriated, Mussolini refused to sanction an Italian withdrawal from North Africa or from the Balkans. Ambrosio's attempts to adopt a firmer posture vis-à-vis the Germans only antagonized Italy's Axis ally, and his attempts to restructure the high command foundered on the firmly embedded military bureaucracy.

Meanwhile, Italy's war effort staggered toward collapse. In May 1943, remaining Axis forces in North Africa surrendered in Tunisia, and in July, the Allies invaded Sicily. Skeptical both of Italy's prospects for victory and of the alliance with Germany, Ambrosio urged Mussolini to stand up to Adolf Hitler and to quit the war. Rebuffed by Il Duce, Ambrosio played a major role in the coup against Mussolini on 24–25 July 1943 by ensuring the army's support. Subsequently, he supported Marshal Pietro Badoglio's attempts to conduct armistice negotiations with the Allies while also trying to persuade the Germans that Italy would remain in the war.

The Allied armistice proclamation on 8 September 1943 forced Ambrosio to flee from Rome with Badoglio. He escaped German vengeance but left the army leaderless. He resigned on 18 November 1943 and became army inspector general until his retirement in November 1944. Ambrosio died in Alessio on 20 November 1958.

John M. Jennings

See also
Badoglio, Pietro; Cavallero, Ugo; Hitler, Adolf; Italy, Army; Mussolini, Benito

References
Ciano, Galeazzo. *The Ciano Diaries, 1939–1943: The Complete, Unabridged Diaries of Count Galeazzo Ciano, Italian Minister for Foreign Affairs.* New York: Doubleday, 1946.
Deakin, Frederick W. *The Brutal Friendship: Mussolini, Hitler, and the Fall of Italian Fascism.* New York: Harper and Row, 1962.

America First Committee (1940–1942)

Leading U.S. anti-interventionist organization prior to the Japanese attack on Pearl Harbor. The America First Committee was established in July 1940 as the presidential election approached. Both Republicans and Democrats nominated pro-Allied candidates, and some prominent Americans were convinced that the United States was in grave danger of being needlessly and foolishly drawn into World War II. The organization's founders included several Midwestern businessmen, including Robert E. Wood of Sears, Roebuck and Robert Douglas Stuart of Quaker Oats, who provided much of the organization's financial support.

Most America First members were Midwestern Republicans, many from the party's conservative wing. Some, though, such as Governor Philip La Follette of Wisconsin and Senator Gerald P. Nye, were political liberals or even radicals. America First also included a contingent of liberal Democrats, such as Chester Bowles and Kingman Brewster of Connecticut, and the radical historian Charles A. Beard. Colonel Charles A. Lindbergh, the famed aviator, was its most celebrated member, and former President Herbert Hoover, although he held aloof so as not to compromise his efforts to feed children in occupied Western Europe, sympathized strongly with the group's stance.

America First members generally united around the belief that the European crisis did not threaten the security of the United States sufficiently to justify American intervention. They also believed that American involvement in war would be highly detrimental to the United States domestically. While supporting measures to strengthen U.S. defenses, they generally opposed, albeit with little success—especially after President Franklin D. Roosevelt's electoral victory in November 1940—many measures the administration introduced. The latter included the establishment of Selective Service (September 1940), the 1940 Destroyers-for-Bases deal, Lend-Lease (March 1941 military aid program to various nations), and the administration's aggressive naval policies against Germany in the Atlantic. America First members opposed these on the grounds that they were moving the United States ever closer to war with Germany. After Pearl Harbor, America First members, despite lingering private misgivings over past administration policies, largely rallied around the wartime president. On 22 April 1942, the organization was officially dissolved.

Priscilla Roberts

See also

Committee to Defend America by Aiding the Allies; Destroyers-Bases Deal; Fight for Freedom; Lend-Lease; Lindbergh, Charles Augustus; Roosevelt, Franklin D.; Selective Service Act

References

Cole, Wayne S. *Roosevelt and the Isolationists 1932–45.* Lincoln: University of Nebraska Press, 1983.

Doenecke, Justus D. *In Danger Undaunted: The Anti-Interventionist Movement of 1940–1941 as Revealed in the Papers of the America First Committee.* Stanford, CA: Hoover Institution Press, 1990.

———. *The Battle against Intervention, 1939–1941.* Malabar, FL: Krieger Publishing, 1997.

———. *Storm on the Horizon: The Challenge to American Intervention, 1939–1941.* Lanham, MD: Rowman and Littlefield, 2000.

Sarles, Ruth, and Bill Kauffman. *A Story of America First: The Men and Women Who Opposed U.S. Intervention in World War II.* Westport, CT: Praeger, 2003.

American Volunteer Group (AVG)

See Flying Tigers.

Amphibious Warfare

The projection of sea-based ground forces onto land. Amphibious warfare was more widely conducted in World War II than in any previous conflict and on a greater scale than ever before or since.

Involving all aspects of naval and military operations—from mine warfare to air and ground combat—amphibious operations are the most complex and risky of all military endeavors. The basic principles had been established in World War I and the postwar period, but the lessons were largely ignored by most military leaders except those in the Soviet Union, the U.S. Marine Corps (USMC), and Germany's Landungspionieren (Landing Pioneers). The Royal Navy concluded that the British Gallipoli operation had demonstrated a successful amphibious assault was impossible in modern war.

Meanwhile, the Japanese navy and army developed separate procedures, forces, and equipment to conduct amphibious operations, and they had the good fortune to carry out their early assaults against undefended beaches in the late 1930s in China and in the early campaigns of the Pacific

war. The German navy had no interest in amphibious operations before the war, but ironically, Germany initiated the war's first large-scale amphibious operation when it invaded Norway in April 1940. It was the Allies, however, who demonstrated true mastery of the amphibious art. In the end, they landed more than 4 million troops in five major amphibious assaults, dozens of tactical landings, and countless raids along German-occupied coasts of Europe. Amphibious operations provided the western Allies with their only means of taking the ground war to the European Axis countries. In the Pacific Theater, there was no Allied victory without amphibious warfare.

Amphibious operations come in three levels—strategic, operational, and tactical—depending on the intended objectives. The Allied landings in France, the Philippines, and Italy and the planned invasion of Japan represent strategic landings intended to have a decisive impact on the war. The North African landings (Operation TORCH), the German assaults on the Dodecanese Islands, and most of the Allied assaults in the Pacific were operational-level landings that supported a specific campaign, each part of an overall strategic effort. Soviet landings and most Allied commando raids were tactical-level operations against limited objectives, although some had a strategic impact (capturing German codes, radars, and so on). The Dunkerque and Crete evacuations are difficult to categorize, but most observers would describe them as operational-level efforts.

Amphibious operations also fall into four types: raids, assaults, evacuations, and administrative (noncombat) landings. The first of these is the most dangerous since it generally occurs in an area of enemy superiority and involves elements of both an assault and an evacuation. An administrative landing is the safest, being conducted in a benign environment with no enemy ground, air, or naval forces present. Assaults and evacuations face varying levels of risk, depending on the defender's strength and support. The German invasion of Norway is an example of an assault, although most of its troops landed under circumstances approaching that of an administrative landing. Britain's Dunkerque evacuation was the war's first major combat evacuation, while Germany's naval evacuation of its forces from the Baltic at the end of the war was the conflict's largest such operation.

The phases of amphibious operations evolved as the war progressed. In 1939 the German army was the only service to recognize the need to rehearse landings and procedures for a specific landing. By 1943, every major military leader realized the necessity to practice for a specific landing. Then, as today, amphibious operations were broken down into five phases: (1) planning, (2) embarkation, (3) rehearsal, (4) movement to the objective area, and (5) the

A Water Buffalo, loaded with Marines, churns through the sea bound for beaches of Tinian Island in the Marianas, July 1944. (Still Picture Records LICON, Special Media Archives Services Division (NWCS-S), National Archives)

assault. Soviet doctrine added a sixth phase, the landing of the follow-on army forces.

Necessarily, the Japanese military was much interested in amphibious warfare in the 1930s. The Japanese pioneered development of ramp front-end landing craft, later copied by other countries including the United States. The Imperial Japanese Army used amphibious landings to outflank British forces in Malaya and to invade the Philippines and other Pacific islands. In Malaya and the Philippines, the army used its own ships and land-based aircraft to support the operations, receiving little or no assistance from the navy other than to have its navy's ships attack those of enemy naval forces. The Japanese navy had its own specialized naval landing troops to execute its amphibious assaults on Wake and other Pacific islands. The assault on the Netherlands East Indies was the only time Japan's two services cooperated in the execution of an amphibious invasion, and there, as in Malaya, the landing beaches were not defended. In cases where the beaches were defended, the Japanese suffered heavy losses, as at Wake.

The Soviet Union had a specialized amphibious force of naval infantry at war's start, but they lacked equipment and training. They were expected to land on the beach using ships' boats or other improvised transport. Soviet doctrine called for naval infantry to conduct amphibious raids and support the army's landing by seizing and holding the beachhead while conventional forces disembarked behind them. Although this approach economized on the number of troops requiring specialized amphibious assault training, it proved costly in combat, as any delays in the follow-on landing left the naval infantry dangerously exposed to counterattack. As a result, Soviet naval infantry suffered heavy casualties in their amphibious assaults but one can argue they led the Allied way in these operations. On 23 September 1941, the Soviet Black Sea Fleet conducted the Allies' first amphibious assault, when Captain Sergei Gorshkov landed a naval infantry regiment against the coastal flanks of the Romanian army besieging Odessa. The action eliminated the Romanian threat to the city's harbor. In fact, amphibious raids and assaults figured prominently in Soviet naval operations along Germany's Black and Arctic Sea flanks, with the Soviets conducting more than 150 amphibious raids and assaults during the war.

However, there was little to no cross-fertilization of ideas or lessons learned among the Allies regarding amphibious landings, particularly between the European and Pacific Theaters. This lack was largely because of antipathy and parochialism among service leaders, but the primary contributing factor was the differing military challenges posed by the Japanese and European Axis countries. The Japanese army had few mechanized units, no heavy tanks, and little artillery, but it was much better at camouflage and improvised defenses than the Germans or Italians. The Germans, conversely, rapidly reinforced their beach defenders with heavily mechanized ("mech-heavy") forces and heavy artillery, and they employed more extensive minefields and beach obstacles than did the Japanese. These differences shaped Allied doctrine and tactics in their respective theaters.

Prime Minister Winston L. S. Churchill forced Britain to develop an amphibious warfare capability with the formation of Combined Operations Command. Beginning in June 1940, this organization conducted amphibious commando raids along the coasts of German-occupied Europe. Gradually, such amphibious raids became more effective as lessons were learned, expertise expanded, and training improved. But, Britain's assault tactics and equipment were driven primarily by lessons learned from the unsuccessful Dieppe raid in August 1942. The beach obstacles, extensive minefield belts, and overlapping antitank and artillery fire proved devastating, suggesting to the British a need for specialized vehicles and equipment. Those "funnies" were ready by the 1944 Normandy landings, but not in time for the earlier Allied landings in North Africa and Italy.

The U.S. Army, present in only a limited capacity at Dieppe, saw little requirement for specialized amphibious equipment, other than landing craft, but it did see a need to remove beach obstacles and isolate the beachhead from enemy reinforcement. The smaller land areas and lack of a mech-heavy counterattack threat obviated the need to isolate Pacific assault beaches from reinforcements. Hence, airborne operations were not endemic to Pacific Theater amphibious assaults, although they were planned for the invasion of Japan.

Operation TORCH in North Africa in November 1942 was the western Allies' first amphibious assault against a defended beach in the European Theater, albeit not a heavily contested one; but it provided the foundations for American amphibious warfare doctrine in Europe. The TORCH landings saw the first employment of underwater demolition teams (UDTs) and the specialized amphibious landing ships that were so critical to getting forces ashore quickly. The tank landing ships were particularly important since they enabled tanks to land directly on the assault beach. Although many mistakes were made in planning and execution of TORCH, it established the basic foundations for all future Allied assaults in the west. All subsequent landings were preceded by special forces, such as UDT and commandos, to remove obstacles and seize key terrain and defensive features before the main assault force approached the beach. Operation TORCH also exposed the need to rehearse the actual landings well in advance of the assault to ensure a smooth and rapid disembarkation. Additional lessons about air and naval support were gained from the Sicily and Salerno landings. More significantly, procedures and equipment were developed to accelerate the pace of force buildup ashore. That it was a successful effort can best be measured by the success of the Normandy landings, which placed six divisions ashore in less than 24 hours and nearly 1 million men and their equipment in France in less than a week—a phenomenal accomplishment.

The almost disastrous Tarawa landing was the pivotal experience that shaped the Navy–Marine Corps team's amphibious warfare doctrine. The failure to chart and survey the offshore waters meant that hundreds of Marines had to wade half a mile in shoulder-deep water under heavy Japanese fire. Casualties in the first wave amounted to more than 85 percent killed or wounded. Naval air and gunfire support was poorly planned and coordinated, leaving the Marines to win by sheer force of will and superior combat cohesion ashore. All subsequent landings enjoyed extensive pre-assault UDT beach surveys. Fire-support plans were refined, and pre-assault advanced-force operations became more extensive and powerful. Firepower for the assaulting troops was substantially increased in terms of automatic weapons, demolitions, and flamethrowers. After Tarawa, as in Europe after Sicily, amphibious assaults in the Pacific enjoyed extensive pre-assault rehearsals and practice landings. Unlike in Europe, the Marines developed specialized amphibious vehicles and equipment to facilitate their movement ashore and to provide some armored-vehicle support to the first landing wave.

Germany did not generate a capacity to land troops against determined opposition until well into 1942. By then, Germany's strategic situation precluded such operations, except in very limited and special circumstances. However, amphibious operations were critical to the Allied war effort. They enabled the Soviets to threaten the Axis powers' extreme flanks throughout the Eastern Campaign. Thus the Soviets were able to divert Axis forces away from the front and facilitate Soviet offensive efforts in the war's final two years. The western Allies could never have contributed to Germany's defeat nor beaten Japan had they not mastered amphibious operations, the most complex of all military activities. The war firmly established the amphibious operations procedures that are used by all Western nations to this day.

Carl O. Schuster

See also

Churchill, Sir Winston L. S.; Crete, Battle of; Dieppe Raid; DRAGOON, Operation; Dunkerque, Evacuation of; Normandy Invasion and Campaign; Norway, German Conquest of; Salerno Invasion; Sicily, Invasion of; Tarawa, Battle of; TORCH, Operation; Wake Island, Battle for

References

Achkasov, V. I., and N. B. Pavlovich. *Soviet Naval Operations in the Great Patriotic War.* Annapolis, MD: Naval Institute Press, 1981.

Clifford, Kenneth J. *Amphibious Warfare Development in Britain and America from 1920–1940.* New York: Edgewood Publishing, 1983.

Miller, Nathan. *War at Sea.* New York: Oxford University Press, 1995.

Morison, Samuel E. *History of United States Naval Operations in World War II.* Vols. 2, 4, 5, 9, 10, and 11. Boston: Little, Brown, 1947–1952.

Roskill, Stephen W. *The War at Sea 1939–1945.* 3 vols. London: Her Majesty's Stationery Office, 1957–1961.

Ruge, Friedrich. *The Soviets as Naval Opponents, 1941–1945.* Annapolis, MD: Naval Institute Press, 1979.

Anami Korechika (1887–1945)

Japanese army general and army minister. Born in Oita on 21 February 1887, Anami Korechika graduated from Military Academy in 1905. He was military aide to Emperor Hirohito from 1926 to 1932. Promoted to colonel in 1930, he commanded the Imperial Guards Regiment during 1933–1934, and he headed the Tokyo Military Preparatory School from 1934 to 1936. He was promoted to major general in 1935 and to lieutenant general in 1938, when he took command of the 109th Division. During 1940–1941, he was vice minister of war. Anami commanded the Eleventh Army in central China from April 1941 to July 1942. He next headed the Second Army in Manchuria and was promoted to full general in 1943.

In December 1944, Anami became inspector general of army aviation. Highly regarded within the army, in April 1945 he became army minister in the government of Prime Minister Suzuki Kantarō. Anami was one of those who urged that Japan continue the war. Even after the atomic bombing of Hiroshima on 6 August 1945 and the Soviet Union's declaration of war on Japan two days later, Anami continued to urge Emperor Hirohito to remain in the war. Anami believed that Japan could negotiate more satisfactory terms if it could inflict heavy losses on Allied forces invading the Japanese home islands. Foreign minister Tōgō Shigenori and Minister

of the Navy Admiral Yonai Mitsumasa opposed Anami's position. In any case, Emperor Hirohito decided to accept the Potsdam Declaration and surrender. Anami and other hawks in the army plotted a military coup d'état, but Anami finally agreed to accept the surrender, and this development led to collapse of plans for a coup. Anami committed suicide in Tokyo on 15 August 1945, shortly before Hirohito's broadcast to the Japanese people.

Kotani Ken

See also

Hirohito, Emperor of Japan; Hiroshima, Bombing of; Japan, Surrender of; Potsdam Conference; Suzuki Kantarō; Tōgō Shigenori; Yonai Mitsumasa

References

Frank, Richard B. *Downfall: The End of the Imperial Japanese Empire.* New York: Random House, 1999.

Oki, Shuji. *Anami Korechika Den* (The life of Anami Korechika). Tokyo: Kodansha, 1970.

Anders, Władysław (1892–1970)

Polish army general. Born to a peasant family in Błonie near Warsaw on 11 August 1892, Władysław Anders graduated from Saint Petersburg Military Academy in 1917. He served in the Polish Army Corps during World War I and, during the Poznan Rising of 1918–1919, as chief of staff in the Poznan army. He commanded a cavalry regiment during the Russo-Polish War of 1919–1920 and studied from 1921 to 1923 at the École Supérieure de Guerre in Paris. An opponent of Józef Piłsudski's coup d'état in 1926, Anders became a general only in 1930.

In September 1939, when Germany invaded Poland, Anders commanded the Nowogródek Cavalry Brigade of the Polish "Modlin" army at the East Prussian border. During his brigade's subsequent withdrawal to southeastern Poland, the Soviet Union invaded Poland from the east and Anders was captured.

Imprisoned in Moscow's Lubianka Prison, Anders was released following an understanding between the Polish government-in-exile and the Soviet Union. On 30 July 1941, General Władysław Sikorski and the Soviet ambassador to Great Britain, Ivan Majskij, agreed to restore diplomatic relations and form a Polish army on Soviet territory. That army was to be composed of Polish soldiers detained in the Soviet Union since 1939. Anders was appointed its commander in chief with the rank of lieutenant general.

Establishing his first headquarters at Buzuluk on the Volga, Anders continued to insist on the liberation of Polish prisoners withheld by Soviet authorities, but he had only limited success. In 1942 he was allowed to move his army to

Yangi-Yul near Tashkent and then to Pahlevi in Persia, where his troops were no longer subordinate to the Soviet Supreme Command. Linking up with the British in Iran, Anders's newly formed II Polish Corps was transferred to North Africa and Italy. There it fought as a part of the British Eighth Army at Monte Cassino in May 1944. Its victory helped open the way to Rome for the Allies.

In the last stages of the war, Anders commanded all Polish forces in the west. After the war, he refused to return to Communist-ruled Poland and became a prominent member of the Polish émigré community. Anders died in London on 12 May 1970.

Pascal Trees

See also

Italy Campaign; Katyń Forest Massacre; Poland, Role in War; Sikorski, Władysław Eugeniusz

References

Anders, Władysław. *An Army in Exile: The Story of the Second Polish Corps.* Nashville, TN: Battery Press, 1981.

Davies, Norman. *God's Playground.* 2 vols. Oxford, UK: Clarendon Press, 1981.

Sarner, Harvey. *General Anders and the Soldiers of the Second Polish Corps.* Cathedral City, CA: Brunswick, 1997.

Żaroń, Piotr. *Armia Andersa* (The Anders army). Toruń, Poland: Adam Marszałek, 2000.

at Regensburg and the ball-bearing plants at Schweinfurt. He also oversaw the massive bombing raids of "Big Week" in February 1944. Although there were heavy losses and disappointments in these raids, adjustments such as shuttle-bombing, twilight raids, and bombing through clouds helped to reduce the loss rate. Promoted to major general in November 1943, Anderson served as deputy commander of operations for Strategic Air Forces, European Theater of Operations, during 1944 and 1945.

After the war, Anderson served as chief of staff for personnel of the Army Air Forces until he retired in 1947. He then worked in investment banking, and he was U.S. ambassador to the North Atlantic Treaty Organization (NATO) during 1952–1953. Anderson died in Houston, Texas, on 2 March 1969.

Pamela Feltus

See also

Arnold, Henry Harley "Hap"; Berlin, Air Battle of; "Big Week" Air Battle; Doolittle, James Harold "Jimmy"; Schweinfurt and Regensburg Raids; Spaatz, Carl Andrew "Tooey"; Strategic Bombing

References

Freeman, Roger A. *The Mighty Eighth: Units, Men, and Machines: A History of the US 8th Army Air Force.* New York: Orion Books, 1989.

Middlebrook, Martin. *The Schweinfurt-Regensburg Mission.* London: Cassell Books, 2001.

Anderson, Frederick Lewis, Jr. (1905–1969)

U.S. Army Air Forces general. Born in Kingston, New York, on 4 October 1905, Frederick Anderson graduated from the U.S. Military Academy in 1928 and was commissioned in the cavalry. He transferred to the Air Corps and graduated from flight school at Brooks Field, Texas, in 1929. He then served in the Philippines and at various posts in the United States, mostly with observation squadrons.

In 1931, Anderson transferred to bombardment aviation and helped to develop strategic bombardment practices and training methods. In 1940, he became the first director of the Bombardiers Instruction School. During that time, he also served as head of the Bombardment Tactics Board.

Following a tour in Britain in 1941 reviewing the Royal Air Force bombing operations, Lieutenant Colonel Anderson became deputy director of bombardment for the Army Air Forces in 1942. Anderson was promoted to brigadier general in February 1943, and that July he was appointed commanding general of the 8th Bomber Command in England, serving under Lieutenant General Carl Spaatz. He oversaw U.S. bombing of German U-boat pens in France and of industrial targets including the Messerschmitt plants

Anderson, Sir Kenneth Arthur Noel (1891–1959)

British army general. Born in India on 25 December 1891, Kenneth Anderson was commissioned in the British army on graduation from Sandhurst in 1911. He served in India and was a captain by 1915. In 1916, Anderson was badly wounded in fighting at the Somme in France. In 1917, he took part in campaigns in Palestine and Syria.

Anderson attended the Army Staff College at Camberley, commanded a regiment on the Northwest Frontier of India, and served in Palestine from 1930 to 1932. Promoted to colonel in 1934, he commanded the 11th Infantry Brigade as part of the 3rd Infantry Division of the British Expeditionary Force (BEF) in France at the beginning of World War II. Toward the end of the withdrawal to Dunkerque, he took command of the 3rd Division. Promoted to major general, he held a variety of posts in the United Kingdom during the next two years, culminating in heading the Eastern Command.

In autumn 1942, Anderson became the senior British officer in Lieutenant General Dwight D. Eisenhower's U.S. headquarters in London. Although unpopular with many

U.S. officers, Anderson was well liked by Eisenhower. Anderson commanded the Eastern Task Force in the Allied invasion of North Africa, Operation TORCH. Anderson's units landed at Algiers, although in respect to French sensibilities, an American, Major General Charles Ryder, commanded the actual landing. Anderson took over the day after the landing, and on 11 November 1942, he became head of the newly constituted British First Army and was concurrently promoted to lieutenant general. Anderson's acerbic nature and dour personality tinged with pessimism did not suit him for command of an Allied force.

Ordered to quickly advance eastward to Tunis, 500 miles away, Anderson had only four brigades at his disposal. Rugged terrain, poor weather, stiffening Axis defenses, and lack of transportation thwarted his offensive, which was stopped 12 miles short of its goal. In January 1943, Eisenhower added to Anderson's command the French XIX Corps and Major General Lloyd Fredenhall's U.S. II Corps. Field Marshal Erwin Rommel and General Hans Jürgen von Arnim then launched a series of counterattacks, most notably at Kasserine Pass during 14–22 February, that threw the Allied armies into disarray. Although there were efforts to replace Anderson, he remained in command of First Army, and his troops entered Tunis in May 1943.

Anderson returned to Britain to take over the British Second Army headquarters in June 1943 and began to plan for the invasion of France. In January 1944, however, Anderson was shifted to Eastern Command. From January 1945 to October 1946, Anderson headed the East Africa Command. During 1947–1952, he was governor and commander in chief of Gibraltar. Promoted to full general in 1949, he retired in 1952. Anderson died at Gibraltar on 29 April 1959.

Dana Lombardy and T. P. Schweider

See also

Arnim, Hans Jürgen Dieter von; Eisenhower, Dwight D.; Fredenhall, Lloyd Ralston; Kasserine Pass, Battle of; Rommel, Erwin Johannes Eugen; TORCH, Operation; Tunis, Battle of; Tunisia Campaign

References

D'Este, Carlo. *Eisenhower, A Soldier's Life.* New York: Henry Holt, 2002.

Howe, George F. *Northwest Africa: Seizing the Initiative.* Washington, DC: Government Printing Office, 1957.

Kelly, Orr. *Meeting the Fox.* New York: Wiley, 2002.

Rolf, David. *The Bloody Road to Tunis.* London: Greenhill Books, 2001.

Andrews, Frank Maxwell (1884–1943)

U.S. Army Air Forces general. Born in Nashville, Tennessee, on 3 February 1884, Frank Andrews graduated from the U.S.

Military Academy in 1906 and was commissioned in the cavalry. He then held routine assignments in the American West, Hawaii, and the Philippines. When the United States entered World War I in 1917, Andrews transferred to the Signal Corps, and in 1918 he qualified as a military aviator, although too late to see active service in France. In mid-1920, Andrews succeeded Brigadier General William Mitchell as the Air Service officer of the American Army of Occupation in Germany.

Returning to the United States in 1923, Andrews then commanded the 1st Pursuit Group. He established several speed and altitude records until transferred to staff assignments. In March 1935, Andrews was promoted to temporary brigadier general and assigned to command General Headquarters (GHQ), Air Force. The new organization placed for the first time all the U.S. Army's air-strike elements under a single commander. He became a strong advocate of the four-engine strategic bomber that became the Boeing B-17 Flying Fortress, and he was certainly one of the leading architects of American military air power in the years before World War II. Andrews molded GHQ, Air Force into the offensive combat arm that became the model for the U.S. Army Air Forces in World War II. GHQ, Air Force was also the model of the Air Force's post–Cold War Air Combat Command.

In 1937, Andrews clashed seriously with elements in the Army General Staff when he forcefully advocated an air force as an independent service during testimony before the House Military Affairs Committee. In 1939, he was reassigned to an insignificant staff position at Fort Sam Houston, Texas, and reduced from his temporary rank of major general to his permanent rank of colonel. But just a few months later, General George C. Marshall became chief of staff of the U.S. Army; Marshall brought Andrews back to Washington and made him assistant chief of staff of the army for training and operations. Andrews was the first aviator to hold that key general staff position.

In 1941, Andrews took over the Caribbean Defense Command, becoming the first American air officer to command a theater. In November 1942, he assumed command of U.S. forces in the Middle East. On 5 February 1943, Andrews became the supreme commander of U.S. forces in the European Theater of Operations (ETO). Three months later, on 3 May, Lieutenant General Andrews died at the controls of a B-24 bomber while attempting a landing at Kaldadarnes, Iceland, during poor visibility.

Andrews's appointment to command the ETO was a tacit recognition that the majority of American forces in Europe at the time were air rather than ground units. However, many contemporary observers at the time of his death considered him rather than Dwight Eisenhower the leading candidate for supreme Allied command of the invasion of the Continent. Andrews had the total confidence of General Marshall, and he possessed an almost ideal balance of intellect, character, courage, and military skill. Andrews Air Force Base in Maryland was later named for him.

David T. Zabecki

See also

Eisenhower, Dwight D.; Marshall, George Catlett; United States, Army Air Forces

References

Copp, DeWitt. *A Few Great Captains: The Men and Events That Shaped the Development of U.S. Air Power.* New York: Doubleday, 1980.

Frisbee, John L., ed. *Makers of the United States Air Force.* Washington, DC: Air Force History and Museums Program, 1987.

McClendon, R. Earl. *The Question of Autonomy for the U.S. Air Arm.* Maxwell Air Force Base, AL: Air University, 1950.

Angelis, Maximilian de (1889–1974)

German army general. Born on 2 October 1889 at Budapest, Hungary, into a military family, Maximilian de Angelis graduated from Theresiani Military Academy in 1910. He was commissioned a second lieutenant in the Austro-Hungarian army. Angelis first served and fought with the 42nd Field Artillery Regiment in 1914 at the beginning of World War I. During 1915–1916, he served on the staff of the Kaiser Jäger Division. From October 1916 to the end of the war, Angelis served in the 2nd Kaiser Jäger Brigade as a staff officer, and he was detached to the 1st Kaiser Jäger Brigade and the 88th Infantry Division.

Taken prisoner by the Italians in November 1918, Angelis was not released until October 1919. He then held a variety of different billets in the Austrian Federal Army. Following the German absorption of Austria in March 1938, Angelis joined the German army. He was promoted to major general in April 1938.

Angelis commanded the 76th Infantry Division from September 1939 to January 1942. In June 1940, he was promoted to lieutenant general. Following the defeat of France, his division participated in the 1941 campaign in the Balkans and the invasion of the Soviet Union. In January 1942, Angelis took command of XLIV Army Corps. He was promoted to general of artillery in March 1942. As chief artillery officer on the Eastern Front, Angelis reported directly to the General Staff. Angelis fluctuated between command of the XLIV Army Corps and the Sixth Army until 1944.

In September 1944, Angelis took command of the Second Panzer Army, and he held this post until the end of the war.

The Second Panzer Army fought Soviet forces at the Battle of Lake Balaton in Hungary in Operation SPRING-AWAKENING. The operation was an attempt to cut off the Red Army and seize Budapest from the rear along with the rest of eastern Hungary. However, the plan failed, and German forces were progressively driven back after each counterattack as the war came to a close.

Taken prisoner by the Americans at the end of the war, Angelis was turned over to Yugoslavia in April 1946. There he was tried and sentenced to prison for 20 years followed by a double sentence of 25 years in prison upon transfer to the Soviet Union in March 1949. He was set free in 1955, and he settled in Graz, Austria, where he died on 6 December 1974.

Keith L. Holman

See also

Balkans Theater; BARBAROSSA, Operation; Budapest, Battle of; France, Battle of (1940)

References

Chant, William Fowler, Richard Humble, and Jenny Shaw. *Hitler's Generals and Their Battles.* New York: Chartwell, 1976.

United States, War Department. *Handbook on German Military Forces. TM-E 30–451.* Washington: Government Printing Office, 1945. Reprint: Gaithersburg, MD: Military Press, 1971.

Animals

During the war, animals fulfilled unique military support roles that humans and machines could not perform. Probably more horses were employed in the war than any other animal. Several were used as cavalry or dragoons by some powers in the war, but chiefly horses were used for transport—to pull artillery or transport supplies. The German army, often thought as being highly mechanized, in fact relied on large numbers of horses: a German infantry division of 1939 required between 4,000 and 6,000 horses, and even the panzer divisions used them. As late as 1944, an estimated 85 percent of German infantry divisions were horse drawn, with very few vehicles. Millions of horses were employed, and died, during the German invasion of the Soviet Union. The Japanese also used horses in Burma, and the Chinese soldiers often traded ponies captured from the Japanese to the Americans.

Many horses were killed for their meat in the Soviet Union and also elsewhere, as in the case of the 26th Cavalry's mounts in the Philippines. After the war, animals deemed in poor shape were destroyed, and their meat was distributed to the local population. Many healthy horses, mules, and oxen that had been captured were sent to countries to help develop agricultural programs for reconstruction.

Mules were also invaluable as pack animals during the conflict, and they saw service on many fronts. Mules could carry one-third of their half-ton weight. The military prized mules for being steady on their hooves despite rocky conditions and for their ability to follow trails even when paths seemed nonexistent. U.S. forces employed mules first in North Africa at the end of 1942 and the next year in Sicily and Italy, where they proved particularly useful in mountainous terrain.

Most U.S. military mules were assigned to the China-Burma-India Theater, however. Shipped to the war zones via Liberty ships, mules were then sent on to base camps via the railroads. Mules transported artillery, crew-served weapons, and ammunition. Mules were distributed among transportation, demolition, communication, and reconnaissance platoons, and some were selected for use by medics and for casualty evacuation.

Mules could often be cantankerous, especially when being loaded into aircraft to fly from India over "the Hump" to China. Mules sometimes kicked soldiers and expressed fear when encountering elephants. Because mules could alert an enemy that Allied troops were approaching, veterinarians sometimes surgically removed their vocal cords to silence them.

Elephants proved useful to Allied and Japanese troops in the China-Burma-India Theater. Elephants could perform heavy work equivalent to that of a dozen people. Elephants were employed to transport supplies and to load cargo planes. One elephant, called Elmer, was often featured in the press and was shown lifting 55-gal fuel drums with his trunk to adjacent airplanes. Elephants were also used to string communication lines, especially in swampy locations where vehicles could not navigate.

Pigeons, cared for by various signal corps, carried messages between units and were essential during periods when radio silence was imposed. Thousands of soldiers, many of them pigeon fanciers, worked in the U.S. Army Pigeon Service, tending to some 54,000 pigeons. The British, Canadians, and Australians also organized pigeon units. Some Allied pigeons were trained to fly messages at night in an attempt to evade enemy fire. The Axis powers also used bird messengers.

Pigeons accompanied ground troops and were also deployed from submarines and seaplanes. Paratroopers often carried pigeons on their jumps. Pigeons flew hundreds of miles over land or water from behind enemy lines to their lofts. Equipped with small cameras, pigeons provided images of enemy troops and ships so officers could determine targets for future air raids. Messages carried by pigeon alerted officers to downed aircraft, grounded ships, and the need for plasma supplies. News pigeons carried timely dispatches from the front written by war correspondents.

War pigeons faced death not only from enemy weapons but also because of disease and birds of prey. Because of difficult jungle climates and high humidity, the militaries bred pigeons in those areas so that the offspring would be accustomed to tropical conditions. Pigeons were essential in some areas where jungle often prevented line and wireless communications from being effective. Many World War II pigeons received ranks and service awards. Some were buried with military honors, while others were mounted for display in museums.

Both Allied and Axis forces mobilized war dogs. British handlers and dogs prepared at the War Dogs Training Schools. The Soviets trained sledge dogs and placed mines on dogs that crawled underneath tanks prior to detonation. After the Japanese attack on Pearl Harbor, dog fanciers in the United States discussed the idea of establishing a system to identify and train war dogs for the military. World War I veteran Harry I. Caesar and poodle breeder Alene Erlanger communicated with quartermaster general Major General Edmund B. Gregory to form Dogs for Defense. This group encouraged patriotic Americans to donate dogs of suitable size and temperament for military service. Newspaper advertisements, posters, and movie reels promoted U.S. war dogs. Regional and state Dogs for Defense representatives recruited and evaluated the animals. Many people donated their dogs because they could not afford to feed them during the war. In any case, donors were not allowed any information as to the disposition of the dogs.

American Kennel Club dog shows sponsored war dog exhibitions and war dog classes to raise funds and identify dogs with qualities the military sought. War dogs were featured at the prestigious Westminster Kennel Club Dog Show. Throughout the country, war dog demonstrations and rallies were held, with themes such as "Back the Attack." On the home front, war dogs guarded prisoner-of-war camps and defended industries from saboteurs. Other breeds, such as beagles, were used to assist in the rehabilitation of wounded veterans.

German-born trainers such as Willy Necker introduced effective training regimens at American war dog training and reception centers. Such facilities were distributed throughout the United States, with significant sites located at Front Royal, Virginia; San Carlos, California; and Fort Robinson, Nebraska. Necker left no doubt about his allegiance, teaching one dog to place its paw over its snout whenever it heard the name "Hitler."

U.S. Marine war dog platoons trained at Camp Lejeune, North Carolina, and Camp Pendleton, California. Their mission was to locate enemy forces, mines, and booby traps.

These dogs, mostly Doberman pinschers, guarded soldiers on patrol and alerted them to approaching enemy soldiers. The Marine dogs also transported supplies and messages. Each Marine division had an attached war dog platoon.

Germany mobilized an estimated 200,000 war dogs. Japan trained war dogs at Nanjing (Nanking) in China, and it had 25,000 trained before its attack on Pearl Harbor. The Japanese used black dogs for night service and white dogs to serve in snow.

After their service was completed, American war dogs were shipped to war dog centers for training to readjust to civilian life before returning to their families. Even after war dogs returned home, their owners did not know where their pets had served. War dog handlers formed closed attachments to their charges, and they often asked the dogs' owners if they could keep the dogs with which they had served. Heroic animals were often praised in newspaper accounts. Chips, perhaps the war's most famous dog, who helped capture Italian soldiers, gained notoriety for biting General Dwight D. Eisenhower. Newspapers reported awards presented to Chips and his handlers.

World War II motivated strange uses of animals. Camels provided the power for mills used to mix mortar. Mice in the Soviet Union chewed through German tank engine wires; the Germans responded by procuring cats to eat the mice. Canaries and mice helped soldiers determine whether poisonous gases were present in tunnels. Among the more bizarre use of animals was a U.S. Army Air Forces plan to place incendiary bombs on bats, which would then be released to fly in kamikaze-style raids against Japanese military sites. Millions of animals and birds served in the war, and numerous memorials around the world testify to their contributions.

Elizabeth D. Schafer

See also
BARBAROSSA, Operation; Burma Road; Cavalry, Horse; China-Burma-India Theater; Eisenhower, Dwight D.; Engineer Operations; Liberty Ships; United States, Home Front

References
Behan, John M. *Dogs of War.* New York: Scribner's, 1946.

Couffer, Jack. *Bat Bomb: World War II's Other Secret Weapon.* Austin: University of Texas Press, 1992.

Downey, Fairfax D. *Dogs for Defense.* New York: Dogs for Defense, Inc., 1955.

Essin, Emmett M. *Shavetails and Bell Sharps: The History of the U.S. Army Mule.* Lincoln: University of Nebraska Press, 1997.

Gilroy, James. *Furred and Feathered Heroes of World War II.* London: Trafalgar Publications, 1946.

Going, Clayton G. *Dogs at War.* New York: Macmillan, 1944.

Osman, W. H. *Pigeons in World War II.* London: Racing Pigeon Publishing Co., 1950.

Putney, William W. *Always Faithful: A Memoir of the Marine Dogs of WWII.* New York: Free Press, 2001.

Antiaircraft Artillery (AAA) and Employment

Antiaircraft artillery (AAA) is ground defense against aircraft. The Germans knew antiaircraft fire by the term *flak* (German acronym for *Flugzeug* [aircraft] *Abwehr* [defense] *Kanonen* [cannon]; the British knew antiaircraft artillery as "ack-ack"). The Americans used these two terms and also "Triple A." In the latter half of the 1930s, new equipment appeared in antiaircraft units around the world. Countries adopted slightly larger-caliber and more-effective guns with higher rates of fire.

Introduced in 1935, the German 88 mm gun became perhaps the most feared artillery weapon of the war. Widely used as a tank gun, it was also a powerful antitank gun and a coast defense and antiaircraft weapon. With a practical ceiling of 35,000 ft, the 88 posed a great threat to enemy bombers. A 105 mm gun also saw widespread use, and in 1942, with Allied bombing intensified, Germany fielded a 128 mm gun as an interim system (pending development of a superheavy 150 mm gun, which, however, never entered service). Lighter German antiaircraft guns ranged from 20 mm to 55 mm. Germany used 20 mm and 37 mm antiaircraft guns in a variety of configurations on several motorized platforms. The effectiveness of German antiaircraft defenses was reduced by a lack of precision radar control (RPC) systems and the fact that its antiaircraft projectiles lacked proximity fuses. The Italians also used a wide range of antiaircraft guns up to 90 mm in size.

Beginning in 1938, the British produced a 3.7-inch gun, which many came to believe was their best gun of the war. It had a ceiling of 28,000 ft. Its effectiveness was greatly increased by the introduction of RPC in 1944. This combination of radar, predictors, and proximity-fused ammunition gave it a high rate of success against German V-1 flying bombs. The U.S. Army began to replace its 3-inch gun with a 90 mm gun in 1940.

The Soviets also employed a wide range of antiaircraft weapons. They reproduced both the Swedish Bofors 25 mm and 40 mm guns, retooling the latter to fire a 37 mm projectile. The largest Soviet field antiaircraft weapon was the 76.2 mm gun; for home defense the Soviets relied on the 85 mm gun. Produced in large numbers, it was the principal Soviet antiaircraft gun of the war. As was the case with the smaller 76.2 mm gun, the 85 mm piece saw widespread service as main tank armament. The Soviets claimed that antiaircraft guns shot down 2,800 Axis aircraft, 40 percent of the total downed.

Operating on the generally held belief in the 1930s that bombers would always get through, the British focused their aviation efforts on developing a strategic bomber force at the expense of air defense. At war's outbreak, antiaircraft artillery was directed by predictors that followed the path of

Antiaircraft Bofors gun on a mound overlooking the beach in Algeria with a U.S. antiaircraft artillery crew in position, 1943. (Library of Congress)

aircraft mechanically; they were useless at night or in poor visibility. Although all major powers experimented with new detection devices, the British made the primary strides in the field of operational radar. This interception device established the height, course, and speed of enemy aircraft. Throwing up shell barrages through which aircraft flew was no more successful as a tactic in World War II than it had been in World War I, but ground-fire threats increased substantially when the speed and height of a bomber stream could be ascertained by radar.

In the autumn of 1939, Britain still had only 540 antiaircraft guns larger than 50 mm. During the Battle of Britain, antiaircraft artillery took second place to fighter aircraft. Most sources place the number of aircraft shot down by antiaircraft artillery at fewer than 300 of the nearly 1,800 Luftwaffe planes destroyed. Yet ground fire forced aircraft to higher elevations, unnerved aircrews, and diminished bombing accuracy.

Flak was the principal defense against night attack. Night fighters were still being developed, although the requisite technology would evolve rapidly. Artillery sighting was largely visual until October 1940, when the British began to equip their forces with gun-laying radar, which increased the accuracy of artillery fire in all weather.

Reliance in Britain on lesser-trained territorial forces for antiaircraft defense foreshadowed personnel difficulties the Axis powers would later encounter in the war. Experienced men usually deployed to distant fronts or to sea, and so air defense depended on women, those too old to qualify for military service, or the physically restricted. During the war about 70,000 women served in British antiaircraft units.

When the Royal Air Force (RAF) and U.S. Army Air Forces (USAAF) strategic bombing campaigns gained impetus in 1942, German flak posed a serious threat. Aircraft coming in below 8,000 ft often suffered grievous losses from ground fire. Damage from flak continued to rise in the air war, and gunfire from the ground shot down more Allied bombers than did fighter aircraft.

Technological developments moved at a staggering pace as the fighting continued. By 1941, German flak units began deploying incendiary shells, gun-laying radar, and grooved projectiles that fragmented into small pieces, causing dreadful damage to aircraft. By 1943, most antiaircraft artillery shells had been converted from powder to mechanical fuses. Flashless propellants augmented the efficiency of the guns, as did automatic fuse-setters that improved accuracy and amplified the rate of fire two or three times. Use of electric predictors became fairly common. In 1944, the Germans introduced double fuses, both contact and timed, that boosted the efficacy of guns severalfold. By then, the Allies were customarily installing the U.S. Navy–developed proximity fuses in their shells, a technology the Germans never successfully employed.

For all that, the Germans put to trial several innovative antiaircraft techniques, such as squeeze-bore and sabot mechanisms designed primarily to increase the muzzle velocity of guns. During the course of the war, Germany developed four types of flak rockets, some guided, some not. The effect of flak rockets was in the main psychological, though, since German forces lacked operational proximity fuses, and radio-controlled guidance systems were rudimentary and subject to degradation.

In several urban areas, such as Berlin, Vienna, and the "flak alley" around Köln, Germany constructed large flak towers to serve as gun platforms. Some covered an entire city block and were more than 130 ft high (corresponding in size to a 13-story building) with reinforced concrete walls up to 8 ft thick. Batteries sited on the roofs mounted heavy antiaircraft artillery and multiple-barreled pom-pom cannon in the structures' turreted corners.

As the war progressed and Allied air raids occurred almost daily, German antiaircraft defenses faced challenges in growing measure. The quality of flak personnel plummeted as youngsters, women, disabled veterans, foreigners, and even prisoners of war serviced the artillery. At war's end, nearly half of all German gun crews were auxiliaries or civilians. Ammunition shortages manifested themselves in a big way in 1944, necessitating firing restrictions during air raids. Shortages would eventually reduce firing potential by more than one-half.

Nonetheless, German flak units caused about one-third of Allied aircraft losses and inflicted at least two-thirds of total aircraft damage through 1944. As German fighter protection became weaker, antiaircraft artillery invariably took on a larger role, continuing to impair Allied aircraft and to degrade bombing accuracy. According to U.S. reports, the USAAF lost 18,418 aircraft in European combat, 7,821 of them downed by flak. Follow-on studies credited antiaircraft artillery for as much as 40 percent of bombing errors.

After the June 1944 Allied invasion of Europe, Germany launched its V-1 buzz-bomb campaign in earnest. These low-altitude weapons, flying at nearly 400 mph, were tricky to locate and even harder to down. Fighters had little time to spot and destroy a buzz bomb. Antiaircraft artillery constituted the final line of defense against the V-1s.

Increasing motorization of land forces fostered a need for self-propelled antiaircraft artillery. Although U.S. ground forces used the .50 caliber Browning machine gun in various configurations for basic air defense, these were frequently mounted with the 37 mm antiaircraft gun, so the latter could aim with the Browning's tracer fire. After 1943, the army's chief heavy antiaircraft artillery piece, the 90 mm gun, was often mounted on a multipurpose carriage for antiaircraft or field artillery use. In early 1944, the army adopted the 120 mm antiaircraft stratosphere gun, which was nearly twice the size and weight of the 90 mm fieldpiece.

Beginning in 1940, the U.S. Navy devoted considerable attention to improving its antiaircraft defenses. Experience showed that 20 mm cannon of Swiss design were many times more effective against aircraft than machine guns. By 1945, the navy had deployed about 13,000 20-mm artillery tubes aboard ship and had inflicted nearly one-third of all Japanese aircraft losses with these weapons. In due course, the navy deployed some 5,000 40-mm guns of Swedish design in single, dual, and quad mounts. Also widely used shipboard was the 5-inch/38-caliber dual-purpose—that is, antiaircraft and antiship—gun, and some 3,000 were eventually mounted on ships. Proximity fuses in the 5-inch weapon greatly increased antiaircraft effectiveness.

Throughout the war, technological constraints and manufacturing hindrances beset Japanese antiaircraft-artillery capabilities. In 1941, the Japanese deployed just 300 guns in defense of the home islands, and by 1945, even in the face of the American air onslaught, Japan had only 2,000 guns earmarked for homeland defense. The standard Japanese antiaircraft gun throughout the war was the 75 mm type that first saw service in the 1920s. In the Japanese navy, the 25 mm was the standard light antiaircraft gun, and the 5-inch was the standard heavy. Some 500 heavy artillery pieces were committed to the defense of Tokyo by 1944, but fire control and radar capabilities for most weaponry remained inadequate.

Compared with that of the Germans, Japanese flak was far less effective against Allied air attack. During the entire war, Japanese antiaircraft artillery was credited with destroying just 1,524 American aircraft. Japanese naval vessels, perennially lacking in shipboard antiaircraft defense, suffered accordingly.

In sum, during the war, flak was often quite lethal and cost-effective, downing many enemy aircraft and complicating air missions. It made low-altitude bombing and strafing operations a risky business. Evolving technology—above all, radar—increased gun efficacy exponentially.

David M. Keithly

See also
Braun, Wernher von; Proximity Fuse; Radar; Strategic Bombing; V-1 Buzz Bomb
References
Chamberlain, Peter, and Terry Gander. *Anti-Aircraft Guns of World War II.* New York: Arco, 1976.
Hogg, Ian V. *The Guns of World War Two.* London: MacDonald and Jane's, 1976.
———. *Anti-Aircraft: A History of Air Defense.* London: MacDonald and Jane's, 1978.
Werrell, Kenneth P. Archie. *Flak, AAA, and SAM.* Maxwell Air Force Base, AL: Air University Press, 1988.

Anti-Comintern Pact (25 November 1936)

Formal alliance between Germany and Japan. Signed in Berlin on 25 November 1936, the Anti-Comintern Pact was ostensibly a response to the activities of the Communist International (the Comintern), the Soviet organization that claimed leadership of the world socialist movement. Nominally intended to oppose the existence and expansion of international communism, the agreement was really a diplomatic tool directed at achieving other goals.

German Special Ambassador Plenipotentiary Joachim von Ribbentrop first proposed such an agreement in 1935, but the Foreign Office and the army opposed it. Since World War I, the Germans had worked to develop a close relationship with China. This pact would nullify these efforts, as Japan and China were at loggerheads over the Japanese takeover of Manchuria. Nevertheless, Adolf Hitler's approval ended discussion. Hitler hoped that the pact would pressure Great Britain not to interfere with Germany's military buildup and his plans for eastward expansion. In any case, British leaders were concerned about the escalating Japanese threat to their interests in the Far East.

Developed from conversations between Ribbentrop and Japanese military attaché Major General Hiroshi Ōshima, the pact was Hitler's effort to tie Japan to Germany. Japanese leaders saw it as an important step toward finding an ally in an increasingly hostile world. Alienated from the West by its takeover of Manchuria, Japan was also involved in armed clashes with Soviet forces in the Far East. The Japanese hoped that a pact with Germany would

---

HISTORIOGRAPHICAL CONTROVERSY
⁓Axis Cooperation, Myth and Reality⁓

The United States and Great Britain formed one of the closest and most effective alliances in history during World War II, and both cooperated reasonably well with their other principal ally, the Soviet Union. In sharp contrast, the three major Axis powers—Germany, Italy, and Japan—failed to coordinate their efforts and often failed to communicate their intentions to one another. This lack of cooperation actually mirrored the fractious relationships of their own armed services. The Japanese army and navy refused to share resources, technology, or merchant shipping with each other. The German armed forces also hoarded scarce resources, and the German and Italian air forces only grudgingly supported their navies.

What might better Axis cooperation have accomplished? Obviously, geographic separation and their differing objectives and enemies limited the extent of Axis cooperation, but the three powers might have helped one another much more than they did. Perhaps the major issue was the failure of the three states to develop common goals and objectives. If Japan had joined Germany in a full-scale invasion of the Soviet Union, the Axis powers might have won the war.

Simply communicating their plans and objectives would have made a tremendous difference. Germany never informed Italy in advance of its invasion of France and the Low Countries, nor did Italy inform Germany beforehand of its invasion of Greece. Japan did not inform either of its planned attack on Pearl Harbor. Germany might have positioned U-boats off the American coast to go into action immediately after the United States entered the war. Japanese submarines might have entered the Battle of the Atlantic and made Allied merchant shipping their primary targets.

Even aggressive patrols and military demonstrations along the Manchurian border by Japan's Kwantung Army could have tied down Soviet forces and prevented the transfer of some of the 40 Soviet divisions that spearheaded the 1941 winter counteroffensive. Italy, as a prewar German study suggested, would have helped Germany immeasurably by remaining neutral and serving as a conduit for critical imports. Once it entered the war, however, Adolf Hitler needed to work Italy into his plans and reward its

strengthen its position vis-à-vis the Soviet Union. Thus, the wording of the pact was more important to the Japanese than to the Germans.

On the same day, Germany and Japan signed another agreement providing that in case of an unprovoked attack by the Soviet Union against Germany or Japan, the two nations would consult on what measures to take "to safeguard [their] common interests," and in any case they would do nothing to assist the Soviet Union. They also agreed that neither nation would make any political treaties with the Soviet Union. Germany also recognized Manzhouguo (Manchukuo), the Japanese puppet regime in Manchuria.

Germany later employed the Anti-Comintern Pact as a litmus test to determine the loyalty of minor allies. Italy adhered to the pact on 6 November 1937. The pact was renewed in 1941 with 11 other countries as signatories.

To many observers, the pact symbolized Germany's resurgence as the most powerful country in Europe. The threat of global cooperation between Germany and Japan directly imperiled the overextended empires of France and Great Britain. However, the pact, much like Germany's actual capabilities, was more illusion than reality. Both signatories failed to cooperate, and only rarely did one even inform the other of its intentions. An even greater indication of the pact's worthlessness was Hitler's breaking of its terms when he signed the German-Soviet Non-aggression Pact in August 1939.

C. J. Horn

See also
German-Soviet Non-aggression Pact; Hitler, Adolf; Japanese-Soviet Neutrality Pact; Ōshima Hiroshi; Ribbentrop, Ulrich Friedrich Willy Joachim von; Tripartite Pact
References
Bloch, Michael. *Ribbentrop: A Biography.* New York: Crown Publishers, 1982.
Boyd, Carl. *The Extraordinary Envoy: General Hiroshi Ōshima and Diplomacy in the Third Reich, 1934–1939.* Washington, DC: University Press of America, 1980.
Bullock, Alan. *Hitler and Stalin: Parallel Lives.* New York: Alfred A. Knopf, 1991.
Schroeder, Paul W. *The Axis Alliance and Japanese-American Relations, 1941.* Ithaca, NY: Cornell University Press, 1958.

Antisubmarine Warfare

The effectiveness of submarine attacks made the development of antisubmarine warfare tactics one of the most important challenges for both sides during World War II. At the beginning of the war, both the Allied and Axis powers

efforts. Early and more significant German support of Italy's offensive in North Africa (support, however, that Italy did not want) against Egypt might well have paid handsome dividends, securing the Suez Canal and Middle Eastern oil, as would have greater Luftwaffe support of the Italian navy.

Honest reporting of their military operations would also have assisted the Axis war efforts. The Japanese government informed neither its citizens nor its allies of its defeat at Midway, and Germany continued to expect significant naval victories from Japan. Similarly, the Germans concealed the magnitude of their defeats on the Soviet front, and Japan continued to expect a Soviet collapse long after that possibility had disappeared. All three failed to share intelligence, technology, and experience. Germany would have benefited from Japanese torpedoes and experience in naval combat and aviation, and Japan

from German advances in rocketry, jet aircraft, radar, and armored warfare. Some of this occurred, of course, but nothing that matched the scale of cooperation that developed between the Allied powers.

The months immediately following Japan's entry into the war offered the greatest opportunity for coordinated Axis attacks. Instead of scattering its efforts at divergent points across the Pacific, a Japanese land and naval offensive might well have seized Ceylon and India and from there threatened Egypt and the Persian Gulf while the Afrika Korps drove into Egypt. There existed a real opportunity to overrun the Middle East and India before the United States could build up its military resources in a significant way.

Still, better cooperation would not have solved the mismatch between the Axis powers' goals and capabilities, their overwhelming lack of resources and in-

dustrial capacity next to the Allies, or Japan's vulnerability to submarine attack.

Stephen K. Stein

See also
Atlantic, Battle of the; BARBAROSSA, Operation; Pearl Harbor, Attack on
References
Megargee, Geoffrey P. *Inside Hitler's High Command.* Lawrence: University Press of Kansas, 2000.
Millett, Allan R., and Williamson Murray, eds. *Military Effectiveness: The Second World War.* Vol. 2. Boston: Unwin Hyman, 1988.
Willmott, H. P. *Empires in the Balance: Japanese and Allied Pacific Strategies to April 1942.* Annapolis, MD: Naval Institute Press, 1982.
———. *The Barrier and the Javelin: Japanese and Allied Pacific Strategies, February to June 1942.* Annapolis, MD: Naval Institute Press, 1983.

A TURNING POINT?
⌇Black May⌇

The defeat of German U-boats in the North Atlantic was called by Germany "Black May." The climactic convoy battles of March 1943 had given a first hint that Allied antisubmarine forces were finally gaining the upper hand in the battle for the North Atlantic sea lines of communication. By early 1943, the fully mobilized American shipyards were producing vast numbers of escort vessels in addition to building more merchant ships than were being sunk. Modern long-range naval patrol aircraft such as the B-24 Liberator and escort carrier-based aircraft were closing the dreaded air gap: the last refuge of the wolf packs from Allied air power in the North Atlantic. At the same time, Allied signals intelligence was reading the German U-boat cipher Triton almost continuously and with minimal delay.

On 26 April 1943, the Allies suffered a rare blackout in their ability to read the German cipher, just as 53 U-boats regrouped for an assault on the convoy routes. Miraculously, two eastbound convoys, SC.128 and HX.236, escaped destruction. However, ONS.5, a weather-beaten westbound convoy of 30 merchant ships escorted by seven warships, stumbled into the middle of the wolf packs on 4 May. During the next 48 hours, the U-boats sank 12 ships, but at an unacceptable cost: escort vessels sank six U-boats, and long-range air patrols claimed three others. Radar in aircraft and escort vessels played a decisive role in giving the nu-

merically overmatched escorts a tactical edge in the battle.

Commander of the German U-boat arm Admiral Karl Dönitz was aware of the tilting balance, but he urged his U-boat commanders not to relent. Yet many U-boats failed to reach their areas of operation. The determined antisubmarine offensive in the Bay of Biscay by aircraft of the Royal Air Force Coastal Command destroyed six U-boats during May and forced seven others to return to base.

During the second week of May, the ragged survivors of the North Atlantic wolf packs, which had operated against convoys ONS.5 and SL.128, regrouped and deployed against HX.237 and SC.129. Only three merchantmen were sunk at the expense of the same number of U-boats. In addition to radar, the contribution of the small escort carrier Biter, which had provided air cover for HX.237 and SC.129, was vital in denying the German submarines tactical freedom on the surface near the convoys. When the U-boats renewed their attacks against convoy SC.130 between 15 and 20 May, escort vessels sank two U-boats, and shore-based aircraft claimed three others. SC.130 suffered no casualties. The U-boat offensive failed entirely against HX.239, a convoy with a rather generous organic air cover provided by escort carriers USS Bogue and HMS Archer. Not a single U-boat managed to close with the convoy, and on 23 May one U-boat fell victim to the rockets of one of the Archer's aircraft. The follow-

ing day, Dönitz recognized the futility of the enterprise and canceled all further operations in the North Atlantic. By the third week in May, more than 33 U-boats had been sunk and almost the same number had been damaged, nearly all in convoy battles in the North Atlantic or during transit through the Bay of Biscay.

The month went down in German naval annals as "Black May," with losses reaching 40 U-boats. At the end of May 1943, the British Naval Staff noted with satisfaction the cessation of U-boat activity. SC.130 was the last North Atlantic convoy to be seriously menaced during the war.

Dirk Steffen

See also
Aircraft, Naval; Aircraft Carriers; Antisubmarine Warfare; Atlantic, Battle of the; Aviation, Naval; Bay of Biscay Offensive; Convoys, Allied; Convoys SC.122 and HX.229, Battle of; Dönitz, Karl; Radar; Signals Intelligence; Wolf Pack

References
Blair, Clay. *Hitler's U-Boat War*. Vol. 2, *The Hunted, 1942–1945*. New York: Random House, 1998.
Gannon, Michael. *Black May*. New York: HarperCollins, 1998.
Terraine, John. *The U-Boat Wars, 1916–1945*. New York: G. P. Putnam's Sons, 1989.
Y'Blood, William T. *Hunter-Killer: U.S. Escort Carriers in the Battle of the Atlantic*. Annapolis, MD: Naval Institute Press, 1989.

underestimated the potential impact of submarine warfare. The British were confident that ASDIC (for Allied Submarine Detection Investigating Committee), later known as *sonar* (*so*und *nav*igation *r*anging), would enable them to detect submarines out to a range of several thousand yards and that they would thus be able to sink German submarines at will. Then too, in September 1939 Germany had few submarines. On 1 September 1939, commander of German submarines Kommodore (commodore) Karl Dönitz

had available but 57 submarines, of which 27 were oceangoing types.

Nonetheless, submarines quickly emerged as potent weapons in the European Theater because of the domination of the British surface navy and improvements in both weapons and tactics. During the first two months of the war, U-boats were able to sink 67 Allied naval and merchant vessels. Italian submarines also participated in this effort, in the course of the war sinking a half million tons of Allied Atlantic shipping. Allied losses continued to climb, and at the peak of the Battle of the Atlantic in March 1943, U-boats sank 96 ships in only 20 days. Meanwhile, after overcoming deficiencies in armament and strategy, U.S. Navy submarines extracted a significant toll on Japanese shipping in the Pacific Theater. By the end of the war, U.S. submarines had accounted for 57 percent of all Japanese naval and merchant losses.

Initially, the main tactics and weapons used in antisubmarine efforts by both sides during the war were those that had been developed and honed during World War I. Soon after the outbreak of World War II, the British reintroduced the convoy system. This had proved successful in World War I, and it minimized losses during World War II. For instance, at the outbreak of World War II, ships traveling in convoys between North America and Great Britain suffered only 2 percent losses until the Germans developed improved tactics. The *Rudeltaktik* (wolf tactic, which the Allies referred to as the wolf pack) developed by Dönitz involved simultaneous attacks at night by many submarines. It diminished the effectiveness of the convoy system, which was in any case initially hampered by a lack of escort ships. Not until 1943 could the Allies deploy sufficient numbers of escorts to optimize the convoy system, which worked best with a ratio of at least one escort for every three merchant ships.

One exception to the convoy system in the Atlantic was the use of fast liners to carry troops. Ships such as the *Queen Elizabeth* and *Queen Mary* were able to travel at more than 26 knots and literally outrun U-boats. Throughout the war, the superliners sailed without escorts and ultimately without casualties. Concurrently, in the Pacific, U.S. submarine success was partly attributable to Japan's failure—prompted by its own glaring lack of escort vessels—to use convoys, which left Japanese merchant and naval ships vulnerable to submarine attack. In December 1941, the Japanese had only four Shimushu or Type A–class ships, their only purpose-built escort warships, and they were not equipped with hydrophones until the autumn of 1942, when the Royal Navy had some 2,100 vessels of all types equipped with sonar.

British defenses of the vital Atlantic trade routes were strengthened in May 1941 when the U.S. Navy began escorting convoys between the United States and Iceland. Then, in June 1941, Canada created the Canadian Escort Force for the same purpose. The Royal Canadian Navy (RCN) played a key role in the Battle of the Atlantic. Comprising only 6 destroyers and 5 minesweepers at the beginning of the war, the RCN grew by war's end to include 2 light carriers, 2 light cruisers, 15 destroyers, 60 frigates, 118 corvettes, and many other vessels. Virtually all these ships were committed to the Battle of the Atlantic.

Antisubmarine weapons existed in two broad forms: passive and active. Passive weapons included underwater mines and impediments, such as submarine nets, designed to prevent submarines from traveling in certain areas. Underwater contact mines exploded when they touched a hull; magnetic mines exploded when a ship or submarine was in their vicinity. Mines could be placed at a variety of depths to make them more effective.

To protect their ships against torpedoes, the Allied powers developed several countermeasures. One of the most successful was the "noisemaker." Towed behind a ship, it could disable advanced acoustic torpedoes. Another was the degausser, which discharged an electronic current at regular intervals through a cable around the hull of a ship. The current helped to reduce the ship's magnetic field, reducing its vulnerability to magnetic torpedoes.

Active antisubmarine weapons included depth charges, torpedoes, aerial bombs, and other explosive devices designed to rupture the hull of a submarine and sink it. The depth charge was a waterproof bomb that could be set to explode at a particular depth. The charge did not have to come into contact with a submarine to be effective; its concussion could breach a submarine's hull.

Depth charges improved during the course of the war. Such weapons could be either rolled off the stern of a ship or fired at specific areas. Weapons such as the "hedgehog," when fired from a ship, delivered several smaller charges over a broad area. Depth charges and torpedoes could also be delivered by aircraft. As the war progressed, the crews of Allied planes and ships became more adept at developing patterns to enhance the effectiveness of depth-charge runs.

Key to the success of a surface attack on submarines was the escorting ships' ability to use their superior speed to keep enemy submarines contained within a certain area and then to deliver successive depth-charge attacks. Submarines usually have a smaller turning ratio than escort vessels, so containment of the submarine was especially important to a successful attack.

Antisubmarine weapons were most commonly deployed by escort ships and airplanes. The escorts were usually small, lightly armed, fast craft ranging from destroyers and corvettes to frigates and small motor launches. Some merchant ships were also equipped with depth charges or other antisubmarine weapons. Aircraft proved especially useful in antisubmarine warfare. They could spot submarines from long distances and either attack the submarines themselves or report a submarine's presence to surface units. Aircraft could also use a variety of weapons to attack the submarine. However, because of the Battle of Britain and the subsequent concentration on strategic bombing, British and U.S. air commanders were reluctant to allocate aircraft for antisubmarine roles. Large flying boats and later the long-range Consolidated B-24 Liberator equipped with radar proved critical in closing the mid-Atlantic gap, a wide area in the central Atlantic that had lacked air protection.

In 1943, the German navy began equipping U-boats with significant antiaircraft defenses, including machine guns and rapid-fire 20 mm and 37 mm cannon. These German antiaircraft defenses were subsequently overcome as the Allies began to deploy additional long-range bombers. During one week-long period in the summer of 1943, Allied aircraft sank nine U-boats in the Bay of Biscay alone.

The increased use of aircraft along the coasts of the United States and Great Britain reduced the number of submarine attacks in these regions, but the air gap remained without air protection. To improve the convoys' chances, the British modified ships into escort carriers—merchant or naval ships that had the capability to launch one or more aircraft.

Critical in antisubmarine warfare was the ability to locate the submarine and therefore render its stealth meaningless. In the immediate aftermath of World War I, sonar (known as ASDIC by the British) was developed. Sonar devices sent out sound pulses and then ranged underwater using the echoes. Using detection devices and direction finders, the Allies were able to detect and attack submarines before they came in range of the merchant vessels. Ships could also be fitted with hydrophones or other listening devices that detected the sounds emitted by a submarine. Although the Germans endeavored to develop rubber sheathing for their U-boats, sonar remained the most important detection device in antisubmarine warfare.

Surface radar could also be used to detect submarines, since the subs had to surface periodically to recharge their electric batteries. British Coastal Command aircraft were also equipped with lightweight 10 cm radar developed by the Massachusetts Institute of Technology radiation laboratory; working with Royal Navy corvettes, such aircraft played a key role in the Battle of the Atlantic. Radar enabled Allied aircraft or surface ships to locate Axis submarines and attack them, even at night. The widespread installation of radar in Allied aircraft brought increasing numbers of U-boat "kills." In response, the U-boats began using their own acoustic detection devices, called Biscay crosses, to warn of approaching planes. However, the devices often did not provide the U-boat crews sufficient time to react before an attack.

Even before the United States entered the war, Washington and London had initiated a variety of cooperative programs to protect merchant ships. German successes added urgency to these efforts, which led to establishment of the Anglo-American integrated convoy system. As a result of the Allied Convoy Conference in 1943, lines of control over convoys were split: the United States controlled the Central and South Atlantic, and Canada and Great Britain controlled the northern convoy routes.

In May 1943, U.S. chief of naval operations Admiral Ernest King created the Tenth Fleet. Although it did not have ships attached to it, the Tenth Fleet maintained the submarine tracking room (covertly classified as *unit F-21*), which used radar and sonar reports and cryptologic intelligence—of immense importance in this campaign—to plot the movement of Axis submarines in the Atlantic and Pacific. F-21 coordinated U.S. antisubmarine efforts with the British tracking section at the Admiralty in London and with a much smaller unit attached to the Canadian naval command.

The combination of aircraft, better intelligence, increased use of radar and sonar, and improved coordination and tactics led to massive losses among the German U-boat force. By 1943, Allied antisubmarine efforts were sinking, on average, one dozen U-boats a month. By the summer of 1943, the Battle of the Atlantic was being won. In 1943 and 1944, the Allies sank 478 U-boats, and Allied merchant losses were dramatically reduced.

Aircraft proved vital in antisubmarine warfare; they could deflect German bomber attacks against the Allied convoys and do battle with surfaced submarines. In order to provide fighter protection, the British equipped several merchantmen with a forward catapult that held a modified Hurricane fighter. After launch and intercept, the fighter would try to make landfall or else would land in the water.

A more satisfactory solution was to fit a flight deck to the hull of a merchant ship. The German cargo/passenger ship *Hannover,* taken in March 1940, was converted into the first escort carrier, the *Audacity,* and entered service in June 1941 carrying six fighters. Additional escort carriers soon appeared in the form of U.S.-built conversions in the Avenger-class. They entered service with the Royal Navy in the first half of 1942. Designed to carry 15 aircraft each, the escort carriers proved invaluable. Unlike their British counterparts, U.S. captains of escort carriers (CVEs, "Jeep" carriers) ultimately enjoyed complete freedom of action to mount hunt-and-kill missions. Teams composed of an escort carrier and half a dozen destroyers or new destroyer escorts sank 53 U-boats and captured 1; the teams may have been the single most important U.S. contribution to the war against the U-boats.

German U-boats succeeded in shattering a special convoy designated "TM I" (Tanker, Trinidad-Gibraltar) that sailed from Trinidad for Gibraltar at the end of December 1942 and incurred 77 percent losses. This led British Prime Minister Winston L. S. Churchill and U.S. President Franklin D. Roosevelt to concentrate on the U-boat menace during their meeting at Casablanca in January 1943. Churchill urged that priority be given to the Battle of the Atlantic, and the Allied leaders decided to provide for the effort additional convoy escorts, aircraft assets (including the

VLR Consolidated B-24 Liberator, which was to be based at Newfoundland for the first time to close the Greenland air gap), and escort carriers. Unfortunately, nearly three months passed before these available assets were diverted to the battle.

Carrier-based aircraft were essential in closing the mid-Atlantic gap, and long-range aircraft flying from Britain also were important, although the preoccupation of the Royal Air Force (RAF) with strategic bombing meant that Coastal Command possessed few long-range aircraft. Only grudgingly did Bomber Command's Air Marshal Arthur Harris make such air assets available. The U.S. Consolidated PBY Catalina and PB2Y Coronado and the British Short Sunderland flying boats proved invaluable, as did long-range B-24 Liberator and British Lancaster bombers.

In August 1944, RAF Bomber Command Squadron 617 (the "Dam Busters") mounted attacks with special "tallboy" bombs against the concrete-reinforced U-boat pens of the Bay of Biscay. These raids were highly effective, and in the last year of the war, 57 U-boats were destroyed by bombing, compared with only 5 destroyed by bombers in the previous five years. This shows what might have been accomplished had the bombers been directed against the submarines earlier. Indeed, after March 1943, aircraft were probably the chief factor in the defeat of the U-boats. Between March 1943 and May 1945, a total of 590 U-boats were destroyed, compared with only 194 in the previous three and one-half years of war. Of the 590 destroyed, 290 were by air power, 174 by ships, and the remainder through a combination of the two or from other causes.

A combination of factors brought the Allies victory in the Battle of the Atlantic. The convoy system was important, but so too was technology, primarily the 10 cm radar sets, sonar, improved depth charges, rockets fired from aircraft, and forward-thrown shipborne antisubmarine "Hedgehogs" or "mousetraps" (small depth charges known to the British as squids). The high-intensity Leigh light on aircraft illuminated the sea at night. Radio detection equipment was vital, and long-range aviation helped narrow the so-called "black hole" in the central Atlantic. Intelligence also played a role, chiefly ULTRA intercepts of U-boat communications that guided aircraft to the submarines. The hunter-killer groups operating independently of the convoys also carried the war to the submarines. It is true, however, that Allied and interservice cooperation was far too long in coming.

In the Pacific Campaign, use of submarines turned out to be decisive, but this time it was the Allies—specifically U.S. submarines—that carried the war to the Japanese. Allied success came in part because the Japanese never developed effective antisubmarine techniques. The Japanese also failed to use their own submarines effectively. Although they developed some fine, large, long-range types, the Japanese never really deployed their submarines against Allied merchant ships. The Imperial Japanese Navy subscribed to the doctrine that submarines were an ancillary weapon of the main battle fleet. The ineffectiveness of U.S. submarines early in the Pacific because of a faulty torpedo only reinforced the Japanese attitude that submarines were not a key weapons system. The Japanese often used their own submarines as long-range transports and supply vessels, and some Japanese submarines carried aircraft. In addition, design problems (the Japanese submarines were large and easily detectable) further minimized Japanese submarines' effectiveness.

Because they lacked radar detection and avoidance systems, Japanese submarines were especially vulnerable to antisubmarine efforts. The Japanese only deployed 190 submarines during the course of the war, and the Allies sank 129 of them. For their part, Japanese submarines only sank 184 merchant vessels during the entire war, and they made no effort to attack Allied transport and supply convoys from the mainland United States. The most significant danger to Allied merchant shipping in the Pacific actually came from the handful of German U-boats and raiders that operated in the area or from Japanese air units. In the Pacific Theater, the Allies also successfully employed the antisubmarine tactics developed in the Atlantic Campaign to further minimize merchant losses.

Ineffective Japanese antisubmarine warfare techniques led to the lowest percentage of losses for U.S. submarines of any of the submarine forces of the major powers during the war. It was not until the end of 1943 that the Japanese navy established its first escort squadron and not until 1944 that significant air units began to engage in antisubmarine patrols. It was a case of too little, too late. The first Japanese depth charges, which used a time fuse rather than a pressure-activated detonation device, were also ineffective. More significantly, the Japanese lacked antisubmarine sonar and lightweight radar sets. These considerations and the loss of so many Japanese aircraft in combat reduced the effectiveness of Japan's antisubmarine patrols. Finally, U.S. submarines could detect Japanese radar emissions.

Antisubmarine warfare came into its own in World War II. It was certainly a key factor in the war at sea, at least in the Atlantic Theater.

Thomas Lansford and Spencer C. Tucker

See also

Atlantic, Battle of; Canada, Navy; Casablanca Conference; Churchill, Sir Winston L. S.; Convoy PQ 17; Convoys, Allied; Depth Charges; Dönitz, Karl; Harris, Sir Arthur Travers; Hunter-Killer Groups; King, Ernest Joseph; Mines, Sea; Minesweeping and Minelaying; Naval Warfare; Roosevelt, Franklin D.; Submarines; U.S. Submarine Operations against Japan; Wolf Pack

References

Blair, Clay. *Hitler's U-Boat War.* 2 vols. New York: Random House, 1996, 1998.

Boyd, Carl, and Akihiko Yoshida. *The Japanese Submarine Force and World War II.* Annapolis, MD: Naval Institute Press, 1995.

Hoyt, Edwin P. *The Death of the U-Boats.* New York: McGraw-Hill, 1988.

Milner, Marc. *The U-Boat Hunters: The Royal Canadian Navy and the Offensive against Germany's Submarines.* Annapolis, MD: Naval Institute Press, 1994.

Padfield, Peter. *War beneath the Sea: Submarine Conflict during World War II.* New York: John Wiley, 1995.

Syrett, David. *The Defeat of the German U-Boats: The Battle of the Atlantic.* Columbia: University of South Carolina Press, 1994.

Antitank Guns and Warfare

The evolution of antitank (AT) warfare in World War II was a continual trade-off between technology and tactical doctrine. At the start of the war, most armies believed that the tank itself was the most effective AT weapon. In the earliest days of the fighting, however, it became clear that the smaller-caliber guns on most tanks were ineffective against opposing armor. The light, towed antitank guns that were supposed to be the backup system were even more ineffective. Thus, field artillery firing in the direct-fire mode became the primary antitank system in 1941 and 1942 on the Eastern Front and in North Africa. Field artillery was only able to return to its primary direct-support mission in late 1942 after large numbers of heavier AT guns had been fielded. Infantry armed with AT rifles were supposed to be the third line of defense. These, too, proved mostly worthless and were quickly replaced with projector-type weapons, such as the U.S bazooka, the British PIAT, and the German Panzerfaust.

For a good 10 years before the war, German doctrine recognized that high-velocity, flat-trajectory antiaircraft guns could be used in an antitank role in emergency situations. In North Africa, the Germans quickly discovered that their 88 mm flak guns were devastatingly effective against British tanks. The Soviets, meanwhile, also believed that the enemy's infantry, rather than its tanks, should be the primary target of Soviet tanks. In 1942, therefore, the Soviets revived the German World War I practice and assigned an antitank role to all artillery weapons. By the final two years of the war, Soviet gun production rates widely outmatched that of the Germans, and the balance tipped in favor of the Soviets.

Most armies used field artillery crews to man antitank units. As the war progressed, antitank guns became larger and more powerful, and many were mounted on self-propelled (SP) carriages to give them mobility equal to the tank. The Germans on the Eastern Front pioneered the use of SP antitank guns in an offensive role. The Soviets also developed a wide range of SP weapons. As the war progressed, the distinctions blurred among the Soviet Union's field, assault, and antitank SP guns. Almost all American SP antitank guns were turret-mounted, but the Germans and especially the Soviets favored turretless vehicles. They were simpler and cheaper to build, and the lack of a turret produced a lower profile that made the vehicles smaller targets.

The Soviets spent the first two years of the war on the defensive, and as a result they mastered defensive AT tactics. At Stalingrad, they deployed four sets of antitank belts to a depth of 6.2 miles. Soviet tanks only counterattacked after all forms of their artillery had stopped the German tank attack. The tactics the Soviets developed at Stalingrad were refined and applied with devastating effect later in the Battle of Kursk, the graveyard of the German panzers.

The U.S. Army organized AT guns into tank-destroyer (TD) battalions. In 1942, a TD battalion had three companies of three platoons of four guns each, either towed or self-propelled. American SP tank destroyers did not do well in North Africa. The operational area was too vast for the guns to mass effectively, and the terrain was too open for the SP vehicles to find good defensive hull-down positions. Many American commanders shifted to the British system of towed antitank guns, but these proved far less effective when combat operations later moved to Western Europe. In that more restricted terrain, the towed guns moved too slowly, and they were too close to the ground to shoot over the hedgerows. By July 1944, the U.S. Army started reequipping all TD battalions with SP guns, but some units still had towed guns by the time of the Battle of the Bulge.

As World War II progressed, the balance shifted back and forth between heavier and more powerful AT guns and thicker and heavier tank armor. Tank designers were faced with the challenge of developing tanks with guns powerful enough to defeat enemy armor, yet with armor strong enough to resist the fire from enemy tanks and AT guns. Larger guns produced more recoil, which required a larger and heavier turret. That combined with stronger armor added to the overall weight of the tank, decreasing the tank's mobility and creating a larger target. Most World War II tanks had heavier armor on the front and sides, where the tank was more likely to be attacked.

Tanks can be defeated in differing degrees, with correspondingly different results. In a mobility kill, a tank becomes immobilized because of damage to its treads or drive train. Many mobility kills resulted when a tank hit a mine. An immobilized tank can still fire, but it can no longer maneuver. The advantage from the attacker's standpoint is that the tank becomes more vulnerable to subsequent attack. A firepower kill happens when the tank's main gun system can no longer fire. Although the tank has almost no combat power at that point, it still has the mobility to withdraw from the action, where it can be repaired and placed back into service. A total kill results when the tank is completely destroyed and the crew is killed or severely wounded. In some situations, a trained tank crew may be more difficult to replace than the tank itself.

There are two basic categories of AT projectiles, kinetic energy and chemical energy. A kinetic energy round is a solid-shot projectile that depends on weight and velocity to penetrate and defeat opposing armor. As weight and velocity increase, so does penetrating power. The distance to the target is also a factor. As the round travels farther, its velocity and penetrating power decrease accordingly. The German 88 mm PAK 43 could penetrate 207 mm of armor at a range of 1,640 ft but only 159 mm at a range of 6,562 ft.

The angle of impact also affects a round's penetrating power. At a 30-degree angle of impact, the penetrating power of the PAK 43 at 1,640 ft dropped to 182 mm. Thus, beginning with World War II, most tanks have had sloped armored fronts. The earlier kinetic energy rounds also had a tendency to ricochet off the sloped surfaces. The solution to that problem was a special soft nose cap that allowed the round to stick to the armor surface just long enough for penetration to begin.

Tapering the bore of the gun also could increase the velocity of a kinetic energy round. The squeeze-bore guns fired a round with a plastic driving band that wore away as the round moved forward through the bore. As the bore narrowed, the pressure behind the round increased, which in turn increased muzzle velocity. As the round left the gun's muzzle, the remnants of the driving band fell away. The Germans used this technique on their smaller 42 mm and 75 mm PAK 41 antitank guns, but technical factors limited the effectiveness of the squeeze-bore technique in larger calibers.

Dense and heavy material such as tungsten made the best kinetic-energy rounds. But at 1.4 times the density of steel, a projectile made completely from tungsten would have been too hard and too heavy for the bore of the gun to survive more than a handful of firings. In 1944, the British solved that problem with the introduction of the armor-piercing discarding sabot (APDS) round. A relatively small but heavy main projectile was encased completely in a plastic casing that fell away as soon as the round left the muzzle. This system had the advantage of placing the pressure produced by a large-bore gun behind a smaller projectile. The result was greater velocity and penetrating power. The APDS remains the primary AT round today.

Chemical-energy rounds defeat armor through a blast effect. The effectiveness of the round depends on its size, composition, and physical configuration rather than on its velocity. Chemical energy rounds tend to travel more slowly and have a more arched trajectory than kinetic energy rounds. Thus, their aiming is far more dependent on an accurate estimate of the range to the target.

Chemical-energy projectiles that produce a uniformly distributed blast effect, such as conventional high-explosive (HE) field artillery rounds, were effective against tanks only in the very early days of World War II. But as the war progressed and armor got heavier and stronger, riveted tank hull construction gave way first to welding and then to whole casting. In response, rounds known as hollow-charge or shaped-charge rounds were developed based on the so-called Monroe Effect. In a hollow-charge round, the explosive material is configured in the shape of a recessed cone, with the base of the cone toward the front of the round. The surface of the inverted cone is lined with light retaining metal such as copper. When the round first hits the target, the explosive is detonated from the rear of the round forward. The hollow cone has the effect of focusing the entire force of the blast onto a small spot on the tank's skin exactly opposite the apex of the cone. The result is a very hot and very concentrated jet of gas that punches its way through the tank's armor and sends red-hot fragments into the tank's interior. The tank crew is killed by its own armor. The shaped-charge chemical-energy rounds were designated "high-explosive antitank" (HEAT).

When a HEAT projectile is fired from a conventional gun tube, the stabilizing spin imparted by the bore's rifling tends to degrade the round's penetrating power. That led to the development of fin-stabilized projectiles fired from smooth-bore launchers, such as the bazooka and Panzerfaust. These close-range infantry weapons proved relatively effective. The HEAT warheads did not depend on velocity, so they could be fired from relatively light weapons. HEAT projectiles do depend on warhead weight, however, and in these weapons, that was limited to what an infantryman could carry.

No single system stood out in World War II as the premier tank killer, although certain systems predominated at certain times and in certain theaters. Overall for the war, some 30 percent of British tanks that were knocked out fell victim to antitank guns, 25 percent were knocked out by enemy tanks, 22 percent hit mines, 20 percent fell victim to artillery indirect fire and air attack, and the rest were knocked out by infantry AT weapons. In North Africa, Axis AT guns accounted for 40 percent of the British tanks knocked out, whereas in Italy it was only 16 percent. Throughout the war, German tanks were generally better armed and more powerful than their British and American counterparts. That meant that Allied tanks destroyed far fewer panzers than the other way around.

David T. Zabecki

See also

Ardennes Offensive; Armored Warfare; Artillery Doctrine; Infantry Tactics; Kursk, Battle of; Mines, Land; Stalingrad, Battle of; Tanks, All Powers

References

Bailey, Jonathan B. A. *Field Artillery and Firepower.* 2d ed. Annapolis, MD: Naval Institute Press, 2003.

Gabel, Christopher R. *Seek, Strike, and Destroy: U.S. Army Tank Destroyer Doctrine in World War II.* Ft. Leavenworth, KS: Combat Studies Institute, U.S. Army Command and General Staff College, 1986.

Hogg, Ian V. *German Artillery of World War Two.* Mechanicsburg, PA: Stackpole Books, 1975.

Weeks, John S. *Men against Tanks: A History of Antitank Warfare.* New York: Mason/Charter, 1975.

Antonescu, Ion (1882–1946)

Romanian marshal and dictator. Born in Piteşti on 14 June 1882 to an aristocratic military family, Ion Antonescu graduated from Romanian military schools in Craiova (1902) and Iaşi (1904). A cavalry lieutenant during the 1907 Peasant Revolt, he fought in the Second Balkan War and was an operations officer during World War I. From 1922 to 1927, he was military attaché in Paris, Brussels, and London. He was chief of the Army General Staff in 1933 and 1934.

As with most others among the nationalistic Romanian military elite, Antonescu favored British and French political influence. However, he closely monitored both the Third Reich's ascendancy and the looming Soviet Union in his vigilance regarding Romanian territorial integrity, pragmatically preparing for a German accommodation should such a choice become necessary. As minister of defense, Antonescu became embroiled in and frustrated by the corrupt governing vicissitudes of King Carol II, especially after 1937. Protesting Carol's February 1938 establishment of the Royal Dictatorship and his suppression of the fascistic Legion of Saint Michael (the Iron Guard), Antonescu defended the Iron Guard's leaders in court and was briefly jailed and outposted to Chisinau (Kishinev) near the Soviet border.

Following the Soviet Union's occupation of Bessarabia and the ceding of Transylvania to Hungary in summer 1940, in September Carol was coerced into naming Antonescu head of the troubled government before abdicating under pressure in favor of his son Michael, 19. Antonescu's title, Conducator, was the Romanian equivalent of Duce or

Führer, and he used his broad powers to oust the Iron Guard from government in January 1941. That June, he assigned 14 Romanian divisions to Germany's invasion of the Soviet Union, Operation BARBAROSSA. For reclaiming Romanian lands from the Soviets, Antonescu was proclaimed marshal by figurehead King Michael I on 23 August 1941. Antonescu continued to supply the German war effort with troops (ultimately, Romania lost substantially more men than Italy) in exchange for German military favor, but on the home front he sought to temper his ally's overbearing appetite for Romania's oil and agricultural bounty.

In coming to terms with Romania's "Jewish question," Antonescu—like Benito Mussolini in Italy—preferred his own solution to anything dictated by Berlin, employing policies that (officially) allowed Jews to emigrate in exchange for payment or to face deportation to Romanian-administered work camps in the Ukrainian region of Transnistria. Nonetheless, Antonescu's regime was responsible for the deaths of more than 250,000 Romanian and Ukrainian Jews and Gypsies as a result of its "romanization" policies during 1940–1944, despite its refusal to join Germany's "final solution" outright.

Antonescu was deposed by coup-installed King Michael on 23 August 1944 and was turned over to the occupying Soviet forces. His war crimes show trial, held in Bucharest on 4–17 May 1946, led to the death sentence, and he was executed there on 1 June 1946.

Gordon E. Hogg

See also

BARBAROSSA, Operation; Holocaust, The; Romania, Role in War

References

Hitchins, Keith. *Rumania: 1866–1947.* Oxford and New York: Oxford University Press, 1994.

Temple, Mark. "The Politicization of History: Marshal Antonescu and Romania." *East European Politics and Societies* 10, no. 3 (1996): 457–503.

Treptow, Kurt. *Historical Dictionary of Romania.* Lanham, MD: Scarecrow Press, 1996.

Antonov, Alexei Innokentievich (1896–1962)

Soviet general. Born the son of a tsarist artillery officer in Grodno, Belorussia, on 15 September 1896, Alexei Antonov attended the Pavlovsky Military School in Petrograd. He was commissioned as an ensign in the Russian army in 1916 during World War I and was wounded in the last great Russian offensive of 1917. In 1918, Antonov joined the Red Army and had his first experience with staff work as chief of staff of a brigade in the Russian Civil War. He graduated from the Frunze Military Academy in 1931 and was then posted to the Kharkov Military District. In 1937, he graduated from the General Staff Academy, and from 1938 to 1940 he was a lecturer at the Frunze Military Academy.

Antonov held numerous staff positions during World War II. Following the German invasion of the Soviet Union in June 1941, he was promoted to major general and became chief of staff of the Kiev Military District. He was chief of staff of the Southern Army Group from August 1941 to July 1942. In December 1941, he was promoted to lieutenant general. During 1942, he was chief of staff first of the North Caucasian Army Group, then of the Transcaucasian Army Group. Appointed chief of operations of the General Staff in December 1942, after April 1943 Antonov was also deputy chief of the General Staff and was thus at the center of events for the remainder of the war. Antonov was promoted to general of the army in August 1943, a rank he held for the remaining two decades of his military career.

Because chief of the General Staff Aleksandr Vasilevsky was absent so frequently, Antonov acted in that role much of the time. A meticulous planner, he helped to orchestrate the major Soviet offensives of the war, including Operation BAGRATION, the encirclement of the German salient in Belorussia and East Prussia that brought the Red Army to the river Elbe.

In February 1945, Antonov replaced Vasilevsky as chief of the Soviet General Staff. He was a member of the Soviet delegation to both the Yalta and Potsdam Conferences. Demoted in 1946 to first deputy chief of the General Staff and then to first deputy commander of the Transcaucasus Military District, Antonov became commander of that same military district in 1950. In April 1954, he was again first deputy chief of the General Staff, and in 1955, he also assumed the post of chief of staff of Warsaw Pact forces. He held these posts until his death in Moscow on 16 June 1962.

Spencer C. Tucker

See also
Belorussia Offensive; Potsdam Conference; Vasilevsky, Aleksandr Mikhailovich; Yalta Conference

References
Bialer, Seweryn, ed. *Soviet Military Memoirs of World War II.* New York: Pegasus, 1969.
Woff, Richard. "Alexei Innokentievich Antonov." In Harold Shukman, ed., *Stalin's Generals* 11–23. New York: Grove Press, 1993.

Antwerp, Battle of (4 September–2 October 1944)

Western Front battle for the key Belgian port of Antwerp. Its port facilities mark Antwerp as an important strategic city in Europe. Antwerp is about 54 miles from the open sea connected by the Scheldt River, which is fairly narrow below the city and then broadens into a wide estuary. The southern bank of the estuary is formed by the European mainland. The northern side is formed by the South Beveland Peninsula and Walcheren Island, which is connected to the peninsula by a narrow causeway. The port had 600 hydraulic and electric cranes as well as numerous floating cranes, loading bridges, and floating grain elevators. Its clearance facilities included extensive marshaling yards and excellent linkage with the Belgian network of railroads and navigable waterways. It was essential for the Anglo-American forces to secure Antwerp as a supply port in order to sustain their offensive.

The British Second Army took Brussels on 3 September and then managed to cover the 60 miles to Antwerp on 4 September. The British 11th Armoured Division entered the city to find that the port was relatively intact, largely because of activities of the Belgian Resistance. Commander Major General George Philip Roberts of the 11th Armored Division ordered a pause for two days, neglecting to order his troops to secure the bridges over the Albert Canal on the northern edge of the city. Indeed, the whole XXX Corps then paused for a three-day rest to refit and refuel. Had the bridges been secured on 4 September, the way would have been open to the eastern base of the South Beveland Peninsula some 17 miles distant. This would have trapped the remaining units of Generaloberst (U.S. equiv. full general) Gustav von Zagen's Fifteenth Army of some 100,000 men in a pocket. By 6 September, however, German resistance had rallied to permit the British only a small bridgehead that was subsequently destroyed.

The German Fifteenth Army was sealed off in the Calais-Flanders region in what was known as the "Breskens pocket." On 4 September, von Zagen ordered an evacuation across the estuary, in which the troops were ferried to Walcheren. By the time the evacuation was completed on 23 September, the Germans had managed to extract some 86,000 men, 616 guns, 6,200 vehicles, and 6,000 horses. Had the Beveland Peninsula been cut off, the evacuation would have taken a different route, a 12-hour journey to reach safety, and allowed for more Allied interference.

Field Marshal Bernard Montgomery did not bring the full force of his 21st Army Group to bear on clearing the surrounding countryside to allow traffic on the Scheldt River. Indeed, he did not even order the First Canadian Army to clear the Scheldt estuary until late September, even while that force was still tasked with clearing the Channel ports. Not until 16 October did Montgomery order that the Scheldt be cleared with the utmost vigor, irrespective of casualties. The port itself did not open for traffic until 26 November.

Most scholars believe Montgomery's failure at Antwerp influenced his concern that the maximum amount of force and effort be applied in the subsequent Operation MARKET-GARDEN. The Battle of Antwerp was a lost opportunity for the Allies to open a major port early, trap a large German force, and potentially end the war sooner.

Britton W. MacDonald

See also
MARKET-GARDEN, Operation; Montgomery, Sir Bernard Law; Scheldt, Battles
References
Levine, Alan J. *From the Normandy Beaches to the Baltic Sea: The Northwest Europe Campaign, 1944–1945.* Westport, CT: Praeger, 2000.
Weigley, Russell. *Eisenhower's Lieutenants: The Campaign of France and Germany, 1944–1945.* Bloomington: Indiana University Press, 1981.

Anzio, Battle of (22 January–25 May 1944)

Allied amphibious operation in Italy from January to May 1944. The idea for an invasion of mainland Italy emerged from the British, most notably Prime Minister Winston L. S. Churchill. The Americans opposed the operation for fear that it might weaken preparations for Operation OVERLORD, the cross-Channel invasion of France. At the August 1943 Quebec Conference, the Americans argued that an invasion of southern France should be the main Mediterranean operation. Nevertheless, the Americans agreed to an Italian Campaign in exchange for a firm British commitment to invade Normandy in 1944.

On 3 September 1943, General Bernard Montgomery's Eighth Army landed at the Italian toe, forcing the surrender of the Italian army. Six days later, American forces under Lieutenant General Mark W. Clark landed at Salerno approximately 30 miles south of Naples. General Albert Kesselring retired his German forces to a position north of Naples known as the Gustav Line. This formidable defensive position took advantage of the Apennine Mountains as well as the Garigliano and Rapido Rivers. The line's western end, closer to Rome, was anchored by the impressive mountain abbey of Monte Cassino. Four separate attempts to break the German line failed as the Allies could not fully employ the Germans' overwhelming naval, armor, and air advantages in the rocky terrain of central Italy.

The failure of frontal assaults on the Gustav Line led to Allied plans for an amphibious operation near the town of Anzio on the Tyrrhenian Sea approximately halfway between the Gustav Line and Rome. Anzio had excellent beaches and was near the main highway that connected the Italian capital to the Gustav Line. A successful amphibious attack there could force the Germans to abandon the Gustav Line and surrender Rome. It might also dislodge Germany from all of Italy.

The Anzio assault was British in conception but chiefly American in execution. Most Americans, including operational commander Major General John Lucas, were not optimistic about the assault's chances. Churchill appealed personally to President Franklin D. Roosevelt to keep sufficient shipping in the Mediterranean to make the assault possible and to increase troop strength from 24,000 to 100,000 men. The timing for Anzio had to be moved forward in order that the landing craft might then be sent to England for OVERLORD rehearsals.

Even though Lucas believed his men were not ready, the landing went ahead as scheduled on 22 January 1944. The Americans achieved tactical surprise and met little resistance. By midnight, 36,000 men and 3,200 vehicles were ashore at the cost of only 13 Allied dead.

Because of the hurried and muddled planning, American leaders had only prepared for a fight on the beaches. Once troops were ashore, confusion reigned. The Americans made no effort to seize the Alban Hills overlooking Anzio. Lucas apparently assumed that Clark, once he had broken the Gustav Line, would move north and take the hills. Clark, for his part, seems to have counted on Lucas to seize the hills and thus divert German resources away from the Gustav Line. In any case, the delay allowed Kesselring to move reserves from Rome to the Alban Hills and pin the Americans down without weakening the Gustav Line.

The Germans now had 125,000 men against the 100,000 Americans and British on the Anzio beachhead. The Germans were strong enough to hold the invaders on the beach, but they lacked the artillery or air support needed to destroy the Allied position. Anzio settled into stalemate. By March, the Americans had a new, more aggressive commander in Lieutenant General Lucian Truscott, but Anzio remained a standoff.

On 17 May, Polish and Free French contingents broke the Gustav Line in costly frontal assaults that the Anzio attack was supposed to have rendered unnecessary. These assaults forced German troops at Anzio to relocate to the Caesar Line north of Rome. On 25 May, Allied forces from Anzio and the Gustav Line linked up. They entered Rome on 4 June, just two days before D day.

Critics argue that the Allied campaigns in Italy were an unnecessary sideshow. Defenders claim that Anzio taught the United States and Britain a crucial lesson in amphibious warfare: get off the beaches as quickly as possible and drive inland.

Michael S. Neiberg

U.S. Sherman M4 tanks and a troop-filled truck move forward to a front-line position in the Anzio beachhead area, 23 May 1944. (Hulton Archive)

See also

Amphibious Warfare; Churchill, Sir Winston L. S.; Clark, Mark
 Wayne; Italy Campaign; Kesselring, Albert; Lucas, John Porter;
 Roosevelt, Franklin D.; Salerno; Truscott, Lucian King, Jr.

References

Blumenson, Martin. *General Lucas at Anzio.* Washington, DC: U.S.
 Army Center of Military History, 1990.
———. *Anzio: The Gamble That Failed.* New York: Cooper Square
 Press, 2001.
D'Este, Carlo. *Fatal Decision: Anzio and the Battle for Rome.* London:
 Harper Collins, 1991.
Graham, Dominick, and Shelford Bidwell. *Tug of War: The Battle for
 Italy, 1943–45.* London: Hodder and Stoughton, 1986.

Aosta, Amedeo Umberto, Duke of

See Savoia, Amedeo Umberto di, Duca d'Aosta.

Arakan, First Campaign (October 1942–May 1943)

First British offensive to regain land lost to the Japanese in
Burma. In January 1942, Japanese forces drove into Burma
(Myanmar) from Thailand to sever Allied lines of communication into China, gain a dominant position in Southeast
Asia, and threaten British India. By May, British forces—
along with allied Indian, Burmese, and Chinese units—
were being pushed north and east into China and north and
west into India. In June, the British-controlled forces were
holding along the Indian border forward of Ledo, Imphal,
and Chittagong, where they began to rebuild and refit their
battered forces. In July, commander of the British Eastern
Army Lieutenant General N. M. Irwin began planning for
an offensive operation against Arakan, a northwest coastal
province of Burma bordering southwestern India (now
Bangladesh) and separated from the rest of Burma by
mountainous jungle terrain.

The offensive was to begin in the late fall and was designed to clear elements of Japanese Lieutenant General
Takeuchi Hiroshi's 55th Division from the Mayu Peninsula

and Akyab Island. In December, Major General W. L. Lloyd's 14th Indian Division conducted a two-pronged assault down the peninsula. Initially successful, the British were in striking distance of Akyab when General Iida Shōjirō, commander of the Japanese Fifteenth Army, reinforced and strengthened the defensive positions near Donbaik and Rathedaung. The British then reinforced the stalled 15th Indian Division with five additional infantry brigades and a troop of tanks. The March 1943 assault on Donbaik failed, and the Japanese quickly then began a counteroffensive that drove Japanese forces back up the peninsula. The 55th Division struck from Akyab, while other Japanese units worked their way over the supposedly impassable mountains to hit the British left flank and rear areas during 13–17 March.

In early April, Major General C. E. N. Lomax relieved Lloyd with the mission of stemming the Japanese attack. British Lieutenant General William Slim, commander of XV Corps, and his staff were redeployed from Ranchi to Chittagong, although Slim did not receive command of the operation until mid-April. The 26th Division headquarters deployed to relieve the staff of the 14th Division when ordered. Fighting on the Mayu Peninsula raged as Japanese units took full advantage of their proven jungle warfare tactics to outmaneuver and cut off British units at multiple points. Lomax attempted to entrap the rapidly advancing Japanese forces; however, although his plan was sound, the battle-weary British forces were overcome and were again forced to retreat, having suffered significant losses of transport and equipment. The Japanese reoccupied Arakan on 12 May. British forces were finally able to disengage and establish a stable defensive position near Cox's Bazaar. The first campaign for the Arakan area was over; the British offensive to regain Burmese territory had failed, and the reputation of Japanese forces as unmatched jungle fighters continued to grow.

J. G. D. Babb

See also
Arakan, Second Campaign; Burma Theater; Slim, Sir William Joseph
References
Allen, Louis. *Burma: The Longest War, 1941–1945.* New York: St. Martin's Press, 1984.
Slim, William J. *Defeat into Victory.* London: Macmillan, 1986.

Arakan, Second Campaign (December 1943–July 1944)

Allied Burma Theater Campaign. Arakan is the northwest coastal province of Burma bordering southwestern India (now Bangladesh); it is separated from the rest of Burma by mountainous jungle terrain. In early 1944, Allied forces in the China-Burma-India Theater were preparing to go on the offensive. U.S. Army Lieutenant General Joseph Stilwell, chief of staff of the Nationalist Chinese Army, planned to direct Merrill's Marauders and Chinese forces against Myitkyina in northern Burma, supported by British Brigadier General Orde Wingate's Chindits. At the same time, Lieutenant General William Slim's British forces would attack from Assam to regain control of the Irrawaddy Valley. An Allied attack in the south by the British XV Corps would secure the Arakan region by again moving down the Mayu Peninsula toward Akyab. Similar in design to the 1942–1943 operation, which had ended in a major British defeat, this offensive had a different result.

In late 1943, three divisions of the British XV Corps were ready to move into the Arakan. The 81st West African Division deployed into the Kaladan Valley to the east of the Mayu Peninsula. The 5th and 7th Indian Divisions relieved the 26th Indian Division forward of Chittagong. A brigade of tanks, the 25th Dragoons, moved forward to provide additional offensive punch. The 55th Japanese Infantry Division, supported by units of the Indian National Army, was defending the Arakan. These formations were later reinforced with elements of the 54th Division. The British aim was to move down the coast of Burma, take the island of Akyab, and prepare to continue the offensive, supporting the overall campaign to retake Burma.

In late December 1943, the Second Arakan Campaign began with the 7th Indian Division attacking on the eastern side of the peninsula and the 5th Indian Division attacking in the west to secure the port of Maungdaw. The initial British objective was to secure the Japanese fortifications guarding the Maungdaw-Buthidaung road that crossed the mountainous spine of the peninsula. The British secured land routes, airfields, and coastal ports to support the offensive, as there was little doubt that the Japanese would counterattack. To forestall this, the British 26th and 36th Indian Divisions were alerted for movement to the Arakan.

The British advance was halted by Lieutenant General Hanaya Tadashi's 55th Division, which was dug in along a mountain spur extending west to the sea near Maungdaw. This Japanese position blocked land access to Akyab. For nearly two months, the British tried without success to break the Japanese defenses, which Burma Area Army commander Lieutenant General Kawabe Masakazu reinforced with the 54th Division. In early February 1944, the 55th Division counterattacked. One element attacked to fix the 5th and 7th Indian Divisions in place, while a second smaller force moved against the 81st, and a third force infiltrated into the XV Corps and attacked the rear area. Designed to cut off supplies and destroy the British divisions when they retreated, this was the identical strategy the Japanese had used successfully in the same area a year earlier.

The Japanese plan was stymied when General Slim refused to authorize a withdrawal and the Allied units dug in. Resupply efforts by air were successful, and the units held. The Japanese then found themselves encircled by the Indian 26th and British 36th Divisions, which came forward, while at the same time the two frontline British divisions reestablished contact with the Japanese. Although the 81st Division was not able to hold in Kaladan, in the Mayu area British units went on the offensive.

In fierce fighting, the British XV Corps drove through the Maungdaw position. Fighting continued through May, but with the British about to continue on to Akyab, they were obliged to break off the attack to send reinforcements to the Imphal area. Nonetheless, for the first time in Burma, British forces had met and decisively defeated a major Japanese attack. With victory in the Arakan, the tide had decisively turned in Burma.

J. G. D. Babb

See also
Arakan, First Campaign; Burma Theater; Chindits; Kawabe Masakazu; Merrill, Frank Dow; Myitkyina, Siege of; Slim, Sir William Joseph; Stilwell, Joseph Warren; Wingate, Orde Charles

References
Allen, Louis. *Burma: The Longest War, 1941–1945.* New York: St. Martin's, 1984.
Bidwell, Shelford. *The Chindit War: Stilwell, Wingate, and the Campaign in Burma, 1944.* New York: Macmillan, 1979.
Slim, William J. *Defeat into Victory.* London: Macmillan, 1986.

ARCADIA **Conference (22 December 1941–14 January 1942)**

Post–Pearl Harbor conference, held between U.S. President Franklin D. Roosevelt and British Prime Minister Winston L. S. Churchill and their staffs. This meeting, code-named ARCADIA, was held in Washington, D.C., from 22 December 1941 to 14 January 1942. It came only two weeks after the Japanese attack on Pearl Harbor and U.S. entry into the war. Its purpose was to hammer out joint strategy and cooperative agreements to achieve victory over the Axis powers.

Roosevelt was determined that direction of the Allied war effort would be from the U.S. capital, and the meeting was designed to underscore that end. Churchill saw the meeting as a means of bringing about full U.S. commitment to the war effort. Members of the British delegation entered the talks believing they would show the Americans how things should be run. It did not work out that way. There were sometimes heated exchanges during the meetings. The British delegation was appalled by the lack of organization and procedure on the U.S. side.

The U.S. representatives to the talks sought to establish a council similar to World War I's Supreme Allied War Council with many participants, which the British opposed. At a meeting early Christmas Day, U.S. Army Chief of Staff George C. Marshall made a strong appeal for unity of command of the South Pacific area. The British concurred, but the issue then arose of which entity the American-British-Dutch-Australian commander (General Archibald Wavell) should report to. This led to heated debate and ultimately to the decision that the authority would be the American military chiefs in Washington with representatives of the British chiefs, but leaving the authority of both intact. Roosevelt approved this decision on 1 January, which led to establishment of the Combined Chiefs of Staff, involving the military chiefs from the British and U.S. sides. This also created, without executive order, the Joint Chiefs of Staff, the U.S. component of the Combined Chiefs of Staff. In effect, the Americans had won and the war would be run from Washington.

Toward the end of the conference, Roosevelt and Churchill agreed to set up an agency for munitions allocation with equal bodies in Washington and London. Marshall strongly opposed this, insisting there be only one entity. Roosevelt agreed, and the U.S. position prevailed. The establishment of the Combined Chiefs of Staff marked the beginning of perhaps the closest-ever collaboration between two sovereign nations at war.

The conferees at ARCADIA also discussed the possibility of an invasion of North Africa, General Douglas MacArthur's appeal for assistance to the Philippines, and the issue of Lend-Lease aid to the Soviet Union. The two nations also agreed that U.S. troops would be sent to Iceland and Northern Ireland. The ARCADIA conference also led to agreement on the epochal Declaration of the United Nations, signed on 1 January 1942 by representatives of 26 countries. The declaration called for the overthrow of the Axis powers and peace on the basis of the Atlantic Charter. But perhaps the chief result of ARCADIA was that it ensured the war would be run from Washington rather than London.

Spencer C. Tucker

See also
Churchill, Sir Winston L. S.; Combined Chiefs of Staff; Joint Chiefs of Staff; Lend-Lease; MacArthur, Douglas; Marshall, George Catlett; Philippines, Japanese Capture of; Roosevelt, Franklin D.; United Nations Declaration; Wavell, Sir Archibald Percival

References
Alldritt, Keith. *The Greatest of Friends: Franklin D. Roosevelt and Winston Churchill, 1941–1945.* London: Robert Hale, 1995.
Kimball, Warren F. *Forged in War: Roosevelt, Churchill and the Second World War.* New York: William Morrow, 1997.

Larrabee, Eric. *Commander in Chief: Franklin Delano Roosevelt, His Lieutenants and Their War.* New York: Harper and Row, 1987.

Sainsbury, Keith. *Roosevelt and Churchill at War: The War They Fought and the Peace They Hoped to Make.* Washington Square: New York University Press, 1994.

Ardeatine Massacre (24 March 1944)

Atrocity committed by the Germans in Italy, a reprisal for Italian partisan bombing in Rome. On 23 March 1944, the Communist-led Gruppi Azione Patriotica (GAP, Patriotic Action Group), commanded by Carlo Salinari, exploded a bomb in the Via Rasella in the center of Rome just as a group of 156 Schutzstaffel (SS) policemen were marching by. The survivors of the bomb blast were then attacked with automatic weapons and grenades. Perhaps as many as 42 German policemen were killed outright, as were 10 Italian civilians. Another 60 Germans were badly wounded.

In retaliation, the German High Command in Berlin ordered the immediate execution of 50 Italians for each German killed in the Via Rasella incident. The German commander in chief in Italy, Field Marshal Albert Kesselring, reduced the number to 10 Italians for each German and directed that those to be executed should be prisoners already under sentence of death. Sufficient condemned prisoners were not located, however, and SS-Obersturmbannführer Herbert Kappler, Nazi police chief of Rome, ordered additional arrests. The details of the operation were arranged by SS-Hauptsturmführer Erich Priebke.

In all, 335 Italians, 75 of whom were Jews and most of whom had no connection with the Via Rasella bombing, were taken from various Roman prisons and transported to the caves on the Fosse Ardeatine (Via Ardeatine) in the southern part of Rome near the catacombs of Saint Calixtus. There they were shot to death in groups of five and buried in the caves. Most of the victims were killed by a single shot to the head, but some were no doubt buried alive when the caves were dynamited. Among the Italians executed were several women and two 14-year-old boys.

In postwar trials, Field Marshal Kesselring; Lieutenant General Kurt Maeltzer, German commandant of the city of Rome; and Colonel General Eberhard von Mackensen, German Fourteenth Army commander were all tried and sentenced to death for their parts in the Ardeatine massacre. The sentences of all three were later commuted to terms of imprisonment. Through a quirk in Italian law, Kappler, the principal perpetrator of the massacre, could not be sentenced to death but was imprisoned. He escaped from a prison hospital in 1977 and died in Germany the following year. Priebke was extradited from Argentina to Italy in 1995; he was eventually convicted and was sentenced to life in prison in 1998.

The Ardeatine massacre has become a symbol of German wartime atrocities in Italy, and the historical realities have been obscured by myth and conjecture. For example, the actual number of Germans killed in the Via Rasella and whether or not Adolf Hitler actually issued a Führerbefehl (Führer order) for the reprisal are still unclear. It has also been alleged that the Via Rasella bombing was planned by the Communist-led GAP specifically to provoke a reprisal that would fall most heavily on the many non-Communist antifascists in German prisons. Only three of the Ardeatine victims were Communists, one of whom was Antonello Trombadori, who until 2 February 1944 had commanded the GAP.

Charles R. Shrader

See also
Italy, Home Front; Kesselring, Albert; Mackensen, Eberhard von; Rome, Advance on and Capture of
References
Katz, Robert. *Morte a Roma: Il massacro delle Fosse Ardeatine.* Rome: Editari Riuniti, 1968.
Spataro, Mario. *Dal Caso Preibke al Nazi Gold.* Rome: Edizioni Settimo Sigillo, 2000.
Trevelyan, Raleigh. *Rome '44: The Battle for the Eternal City.* New York: Viking Press, 1982.

Ardennes Offensive (Battle of the Bulge) (16 December 1944–16 January 1945)

Largest land battle on the Western Front during World War II and the largest engagement ever fought by the U.S. Army. In early December 1944, Supreme Allied Commander General Dwight D. Eisenhower planned major offensives in the northern and southern sectors of the Western Front. To ensure sufficient power for these offensives, he left his 80-mile-wide central sector in the Ardennes lightly defended by Major General Troy Middleton's VIII Corps of the 4th, 28th, and 106th Infantry Divisions; the 9th Armored Division (less Combat Command B); and the two-squadron 14th Cavalry Group. The Allies used this area for new commands to gain experience and to train replacements. The rugged Ardennes terrain and presumed light German force gave Eisenhower reason to deploy fewer troops there. Further, the Allies saw no tactical or strategic objectives in the area.

Neither the 9th Armored nor the 106th had experienced combat, and the 28th and 4th were absorbing thousands of replacements after suffering massive casualties in fighting in the Hürtgen Forest. From south to north on the Corps front were the 4th and part of the 9th Armored, the 28th on a 25-mile front, and the 106th holding 1 of almost 16 miles. The 14th Cavalry screened a 5-mile sector between Major General J. Lawton Collins's VII Corps to the south and Major General Leonard T. Gerow's V Corps to the north.

With the Eastern Front largely static and with the Allies gaining ground in the west, German leader Adolf Hitler meanwhile prepared a massive counteroffensive into this lightly defended area to retake the port of Antwerp. He hoped thereby at a minimum to purchase three or four additional months to deal with the advancing Soviets. Field Marshal Gerd von Rundstedt, German commander in the West, thought Hitler's plan too ambitious and tried to dissuade him, as did other high-ranking officers, to no avail. Preparations for the offensive began in September 1944 with strict security and no radio communication. As a consequence, Allied code-breaking did not learn of the German plans. Other information that might have given Allied commanders pause was ignored.

Early on the morning of 16 December, Field Marshal Walther Model's Army Group B mounted the attack. Bad weather prevented Allied air intervention. Attacking German forces included General der Panzertruppen (U.S. equiv. lieutenant general) Hosso-Eccard von Manteufel's Fifth Panzer Army, Generaloberst (U.S. equiv. full general) Josef "Sepp" Dietrich's Sixth Panzer Army, and General der Panzertruppen Erich Brandenburger's Seventh Army. Army Group B numbered 250,000 men, 1,900 artillery pieces, and 970 tanks and assault guns and was supported by 2,000 aircraft.

In the north, the 99th Division of V Corps stopped the 12th, 277th, and 326th Volksgrenadier Divisions (VGD). But the 14th Cavalry was forced back, and elements of the 3rd Parachute Division (Sixth Panzer Army and 18th VGD [Fifth Panzer Army]) made headway against the 106th Division. The 28th's northern regiment, the 112th, held against elements of the 116th Panzer Division and 560th VGD (Fifth Panzer Army). The 110th Infantry Regiment in the center—hit by the 2nd Panzer Lehr Division, elements of the 116th Panzer Division, and the 26th VGD (Seventh Army)—was decimated. Small, isolated fragments of U.S. forces were surrounded and destroyed. In the south, the hard-pressed 109th held back the 352nd VGD and 5th Parachute Division (Seventh Army). Elements of the 9th Armored and 4th Divisions south of the 28th stopped the 276th and 282nd VGD (Seventh Army).

German forces soon created a bulge in the Allied lines, which gave the battle its name. Ultimately it was 50 miles wide and 70 miles deep. Eisenhower correctly assessed the

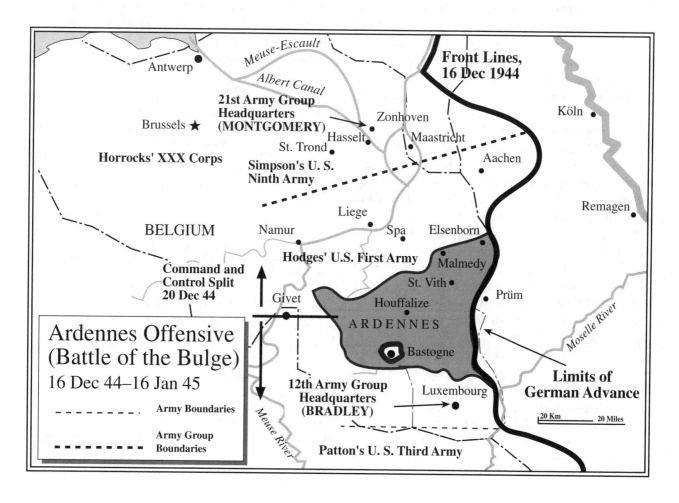

Ardennes Offensive (Battle of the Bulge) 16 Dec 44–16 Jan 45

offensive as a major German effort and immediately ordered the 82nd and 101st Airborne Divisions up from rest areas in France. Traveling by cattle truck, the 101st arrived in the vicinity of the key road hub of Bastogne, Belgium, at midnight on 18 December.

The day of 19 December was pivotal. Eisenhower also sent the 7th and 10th Armored Divisions to support VII Corps. Combat Command R (CCR), 9th Armored Division; Combat Command B (CCB), 10th Armored Division; the 755th Armored Field Artillery Battalion; 705th Tank Destroyer Battalion; and remnants of the 28th Infantry Division joined the 101st. Major General Maxwell D. Taylor, commanding the 101st, was not with the division, which was then commanded by Assistant Division Commander Brigadier General Anthony C. McAuliffe.

Both the 28th and 106th had been destroyed by 19 December, but these two U.S. divisions had irretrievably set back the German timetable. The Germans surrounded and forced the surrender of the 106th's 422nd and 423rd Infantry Regiments, but the 424th extricated itself and withdrew west of the Our River. CCB, 9th Armored Division and the 7th Armored Division under Brigadier General Robert W. Hasbrouk came in on the 424th's north flank. The 112th Infantry of the 28th Division bolstered its south. This diverse force under Hasbrouk defended Saint Vith until 21 December and then withdrew to new positions, which it defended for two more days before withdrawing through elements of the 82nd Airborne and 3rd Armored Divisions.

Also on 19 December, Field Marshal Bernard L. Montgomery, commanding the 21st Army group, on his own initiative deployed his XXX Corps (43rd, 51st, and 53rd Infantry and the Guards Armored Divisions) into positions between Namur and Brussels, blocking further German advance. Meanwhile, the 1st Schutzstaffel (SS) Panzer Division spearhead under Lieutenant Colonel Joachim Peiper was slowed, then halted by U.S. troops.

From 19 December until it was relieved on 26 December, the 101st, aided by armor, artillery, and other miscellaneous units, defended Bastogne against determined attacks by the Panzer Lehr, 26th VGD, and elements of the 15th Panzer Grenadier Division. When called on to surrender, McAuliffe replied, "Nuts!" The U.S. stands at Saint Vith and Bastogne ruined German hope that their counteroffensive would succeed. From 18 December on, German rear areas had been chaotic. The road net, inadequate to support the German offensive, was jammed with traffic, denying the front badly needed reinforcements, supplies, and ammunition.

On 22 December, Major General John Milliken's U.S. III Corps of the 26th and 80th Infantry and 4th Armored Divisions (from Lieutenant General George S. Patton's Third Army) attacked to the north to relieve Bastogne. That same day, too, a thaw set in, slowing tank movements. By 22 December, the Sixth Panzer Army wallowed in mud and rain, the Fifth Panzer Army was hampered by fog and snow, and supply lines were assailed by continuous snow. Clearing weather permitted Allied aircraft to inflict heavy losses (especially on German armor) and to further snarl German traffic and resupply efforts throughout the Bulge. Fighting continued until late January, when the Germans were finally forced back to their original positions.

For the Allies, the Ardennes Campaign was a classic example of a tactical defeat but a strategic victory. The brief delays by the 28th and 106th Divisions, the stands at Saint Vith and Bastogne and on the German flanks, and the snarled traffic in the rear (compounded by Allied air attacks) all bought valuable time. This allowed the Allies to strategically reallocate and realign troops to contain and then destroy the German salient. Both sides sustained heavy casualties in the battle: for the Germans some 100,000 men (almost one-third of those engaged), 700 tanks, and 1,600 aircraft; for the Allies (mostly American, of whom 700,000 were ultimately engaged) 90,000 men, 300 tanks, and 300 aircraft. The difference was that the United States could replace its losses, but Germany could not. Hitler's gamble was an irretrievable disaster. It delayed Eisenhower's campaign by five weeks, but it also devoured already slim German reserves of personnel, tanks, guns, fuel, and ammunition. Germany surrendered four months later.

Uzal W. Ent

See also

Bastogne, Battle for; Brandenberger, Erich; Dietrich, Josef "Sepp"; Eisenhower, Dwight D.; Gerow, Leonard Townsend; Hitler, Adolf; Hürtgen Forest Campaign; Manteuffel, Hasso-Eccard von; McAuliffe, Anthony Clement; Middleton, Troy Houston; Model, Walther; Montgomery, Sir Bernard Law; Peiper, Joachim; Rundstedt, Karl Rudolf Gerd von; Taylor, Maxwell Davenport

References

Cole, Hugh M. *The United States Army in World War II: The European Theater of Operations: The Ardennes: Battle of the Bulge.* Washington, DC: Government Printing Office, 1965.

Eisenhower, John S. D. *The Bitter Woods.* New York: G. P. Putnam's Sons, 1969.

Forty, George. *The Reich's Last Gamble: The Ardennes Offensive: December 1944.* London: Cassell, 2000.

MacDonald, Charles B. *A Time for Trumpets: The Untold Story of the Battle of the Bulge.* New York: William Morrow, 1985.

Arima Masafumi (1895–1944)

Japanese navy admiral. Born in Kagoshima on 25 September 1895, Arima Masafumi joined the Japanese navy in 1915. During the Sino-Japanese War beginning in 1937, he commanded the *Kamikawa-maru*, a transport that had been converted into a seaplane tender, and took part in the operations in southern China. Between 1938 and 1941, Arima had charge of various naval air units.

In October 1942 during the Battle of Santa Cruz, Captain Arima commanded the fleet aircraft carrier *Shōkaku*, flagship of Vice Admiral Nagumo Chūichi's Third Fleet. Although the *Shōkaku* was heavily damaged by U.S. aircraft in the Battle of Santa Cruz, damage control and navigation skills saved the ship. Also in this battle, the *Shōkaku's* aircraft fatally crippled the U.S. aircraft carrier *Hornet,* which was later abandoned and eventually sunk by Japanese destroyers. At the close of the battle, Arima called for continuing air attacks on the remaining U.S. ships, but Nagumo flatly rejected this suggestion. In this sense, Arima was in the same position as Yamaguchi Tamon was at the Battle of Midway.

Following a short stint at the Navy Aviation Department as head of Training Section, in 1943 Arima was promoted to rear admiral, and in the following year he took command of the 26th Air Flotilla based in the Philippines. During the air battle off Taiwan (Formosa) on 15 October 1944, Arima led an attack on U.S. warships. When his "Betty" bomber was hit, Arima ordered the pilot to dive the plane into the U.S. aircraft carrier *Franklin,* but the aircraft missed and was shot down by the U.S. combat air patrol (CAP). To that date, Arima was the highest-ranking Japanese naval officer to carry out a suicide air attack. His dramatic death preceded the first organized kamikaze operation, which took place off Leyte on 25 October. Arima was posthumously promoted to vice admiral.

Tohmatsu Haruo

See also
Kamikaze; Kusaka Ryūosuke; Midway, Battle of; Nagumo Chūichi; Santa Cruz Islands, Battle of; Ugaki Matome; Yamaguchi Tamon

References
Inoguchi Rikihei and Nakajima Tadashi, with Roger Pineau. *The Divine Wind: Japan's Kamikaze Force in World War II.* Annapolis, MD: Naval Institute Press, 1958.

Warner, Denis, and Peggy Warner. *The Sacred Warriors: Japan's Suicide Legions.* New York: Van Nostrand Reinhold, 1982.

Y'Blood, William T. *Red Sun Setting: The Battle of the Philippine Sea.* Annapolis, MD: Naval Institute Press, 1981.

Armaments Production

Armaments production in each combatant nation, like other economic aspects of the war effort, was intimately tied to each nation's decisions about grand strategy and the use of military force. Governments analyzed their economic resources and potential industrial mobilization, and they considered how noneconomic factors such as political tradition, cultural institutions, or the limits of state power would modify or restrict those plans. The resulting policies, which Allan Milward calls *strategic synthesis,* allowed governments to distribute finite resources among the civilian economy, war production, and the armed forces in a more or less rational manner. Put another way, although munitions production was theoretically unlimited, competing demands on resources meant armament creation was often constrained in ways that could not be overcome. The different national limitations on armament expansion help explain why the Allies dominated munitions production during the period 1939–1945.

Limits on armaments production in Nazi Germany were initially political, with the regime explicitly refusing to mobilize the economy too deeply. The Nazis endeavored to prevent a repetition of the experience of World War I, when Imperial Germany suffered political unrest and eventual revolution trying to wage total war. Given Germany's weaker economic position and resources vis-à-vis its opponents, Adolf Hitler deliberately planned to avoid a long war of industrial attrition. Instead, he planned to wage short, intense campaigns with the limited military forces under development since 1936. Hitler's guiding strategic concept was to defeat his enemies quickly and avoid military stalemate on the battlefield. The Italian and Japanese war efforts took a similar approach, mainly owing to their inability to compete with Britain and the United States in war production. Indeed, the small size of the Japanese and Italian economies and the drain on Japan of the Sino-Japanese War precluded a major mobilization effort in any case.

The initial Axis strategies called for a high initial investment in modern military equipment; a readiness to conduct short, opportunistic campaigns; and the careful avoidance of long-term economic mobilization. Unfortunately for the Axis powers, the course of the war quickly rendered these plans obsolete.

The western Allied strategic synthesis was also based on the wartime experience of 1914–1918, although different lessons were drawn from that Pyrrhic victory. Although the war itself was viewed as a political and economic disaster, the concept of mass industrial mobilization was taken for granted. By investing in technologically intensive and financially costly—but manpower-saving—armament programs, the western democracies hoped to avoid the mass bloodletting of World War I. Future wars, their leaders believed, would be won by industrial might invested in such programs as the Maginot Line or four-engine bombers, not by running infantry against enemy trench lines. In contrast to the Axis strategy, the Allied strategy was slow to develop, as it took time to gather resources and mobilize industry for war.

Conversion of a Chevrolet Motor automobile plant in Detroit, Michigan, to armament production: A giant overhead crane moves a 6D Bliss press, weighing 17 tons, from a plant being entirely cleared for outright conversion to armament production. Set up in another of the automobile factory's buildings, this press formed door trim panels for 4 × 4 and 6 × 6 army trucks. (Library of Congress)

As with the western democracies, the Soviet Union also intended to wage machine war on a grand scale, although with a significantly heavier reliance on manpower. Formed out of the experience of the 1919–1920 Russian Civil War, Soviet strategic thinking planned on mass warfare in part because party leaders saw no separation of war, politics, and society. In addition, the policy took advantage of the great resource and manpower reserves available in the Soviet Union. Despite the extreme social and economic disruption caused by industrial and agricultural five-year plans in the 1930s, the experienced and hardened Soviet bureaucracy was confident of a massive industrial response to any future conflict.

Viewed in these terms, there were four main centers of armaments production during World War II: the western democracies (after 1940, only the United States and British Commonwealth), the European Axis (Germany and Italy), the Soviet Union, and Japan. These economic spheres were in no way equal, however; the Axis powers were at a severe disadvantage. In 1938, for example, the Allied gross domestic product (GDP) was 2.4 times the size of the GDPs of Axis nations. This ratio is meaningless, however, if such economic power is not translated into combat-ready munitions.

In 1939–1941, the Axis nations enjoyed a significant armaments advantage, as their rearmament programs had started earlier and had concentrated on frontline aircraft, vehicles, and other equipment. In contrast, the western democracies and the Soviet Union were still heavily engaged in long-range rearmament programs at the outbreak of war. The British and the French were building aircraft factories and capital ships in 1940, for example, while the Russians were still focused on engineering, machine tools, and factory construction. Before the fall of France in June 1940, U.S. armament expenditure was quite low, and the munitions industry was backlogged with European orders for machine tools and aircraft. From an armament perspective, the Allies were trailing behind the Axis in the production of actual combat power despite economic superiority, which partly explains the military success of the German and Japanese offensives through 1941. Allied fortunes were then at a low point as entire countries and colonies fell under Axis control, and the Allied GDP ratio over the Axis fell to 2:1 at the end of the year.

From 1942 on, however, the ratio moved steadily against the Axis powers, particularly as the Allies began coordinating armaments production on a massive scale. During 1942, the United States, Britain, and Canada agreed to pool their resources and allocate the production of munitions on a combined basis. The governing idea was to take advantage of each nation's manufacturing potential, covering any shortfall in other areas through imports from other Allied countries. The British, for example, dedicated a higher proportion of national income to war production than they could normally support (over 54 percent), covering the resulting gap in the civilian economy with imports from North America. Indeed, it was the ability of the western Allies to trade via the world's oceans, despite the challenge by German U-boats, that allowed the combined production process to work.

By 1944, an immense quantitative mobilization drive nearly doubled the 1938 GDP in the United States (with 42 percent of national income dedicated to the war), steadily increasing the Allied production ratio to 3.3:1 over Germany and Italy and to almost 10:1 over Japan. Combat armament production in the United States alone equaled 50 percent of total world munitions output, with the British adding another 15 percent. Although partly a function of mass production methods, another key to Allied success was the advanced level of economic development in Britain and North America. Well-established transport and other advantages gave the western Allied labor force a 1.4:1 productivity advantage over German workers. The combination led to Allied dominance in the output of a whole range of weapons (see Table 1).

In contrast to the western Allies, the Soviet Union struggled against difficult odds. Although the USSR was much larger than Germany in both area and population, Soviet economic production before the war was only equal to that of Germany, primarily owing to more primitive infrastructure and more primitive machine technology. Following a 25 percent collapse in GDP after the German invasion in summer 1941, the Soviets labored under tremendous pressure to match Axis ground armament production. Over a two-year period, almost half the Soviet economy was shifted from civilian to military efforts, with almost 60 percent of national income allocated to the war in 1943. The ability of the Soviet government to mobilize resources and

people proved astonishing, and as noted by Richard Overy, it was this genius for industrial management that allowed the Soviets to pull even with Germany by the end of that year. Despite the accompanying suffering and privation—what Overy called "an exceptional, brutal form of total war"—Soviet workers, helped by Lend-Lease aid from the United States, provided the Red Army with sufficient material to eventually destroy the German armies on the Eastern Front.

Although the German economy was increasingly mobilized for war after 1939, Germany's prewar notion of limited mobilization restricted centralized control of industrial production. Bureaucratic inertia, the resistance of industry to state control, and a dislike of mass production methods placed Germany in a dangerous position by 1941. Hopes for a quick end to the war were finally dashed that winter, and the German government embarked on a more systematic approach to economic mobilization. The ad hoc style of the past was more or less abandoned, although the mobilization program did not truly get under way until after the German defeat at Stalingrad. Between 1943 and 1944, the proportion of Germany's national wealth dedicated to the war effort increased from 52 percent to almost 75 percent, which is revealed in the production figures in Table 1. Despite these gains, however, the smaller European industrial base and difficulties extracting resources from conquered territories meant that German war production could simply not keep pace with the Allies. Germany was beset by enemy armies and heavily bombed from the air, and its economy collapsed in 1945.

In comparison with the larger powers, both the Japanese and the Italians fell woefully short in armaments production. Starting with major disadvantages in resources, transportation, and population, neither country was able to mobilize for a long war of industrial attrition. The disruption of imports, confusion in domestic resource allocations, and the loss of overseas supplies such as fuel, coal, and iron ore led to mobilization failures and declining armaments production. Indeed, labor and resource problems meant Italy was never able to commit more than 23 percent of its GDP to the war effort. Japan fared a little better, dramatically raising the low 1941 ratio (27 percent of GDP) in a massive last-ditch mobilization effort (76 percent of GDP dedicated to military outlays in 1944) before economic collapse helped end the war a year later.

The central core of Allied armaments production superiority was resource and industrial mobilization. Firmly rooted in prewar strategic thinking, the Allies refused to be derailed by Axis success during 1940–1941 and continued to plan for a long war of industrial attrition. Though their efforts were improvised and wasteful, the western Allies

Table 1
Selected Munitions Production of the Great Powers, 1939–1945 (1,000s)

	1939	1940	1941	1942	1943	1944	1945
Tanks and self-propelled guns							
Germany	1.3	2.2	3.8	6.2	10.7	18.3	4.4
Italy	Total production, June 1940–August 1943 = 3.0						
Japan	0.2	1.0	1.0	1.2	0.8	0.4	0.2
United Kingdom	0.9	1.4	4.8	8.6	7.5	4.6	2.1
United States	—	0.4	0.9	27.0	38.5	20.5	12.6
USSR	2.9	2.8	4.8	24.4	24.1	29.0	20.5
Combat aircraft							
Germany	2.3	6.6	8.4	11.6	19.3	34.1	7.2
Italy	1.7	3.3	3.5	2.8	2.0	—	—
Japan	0.7	2.2	3.2	6.3	13.4	21.0	8.3
United Kingdom	1.3	8.6	13.2	17.7	21.2	22.7	9.9
United States	—	—	1.4	24.9	54.1	74.1	37.5
USSR	—	—	8.2	21.7	29.9	33.2	19.1
Guns							
Germany	2.0	6.0	22.0	41.0	74.0	148.0	27.0
Italy	Total production, June 1940–June 1943 = 10.0						
Japan	1.0	3.0	7.0	13.0	28.0	84.0	23.0
United Kingdom	1.0	10.0	33.0	106.0	118.0	93.0	28.0
United States	—	1.8	3.0	188.0	221.0	103.0	34.0
USSR	17.0	15.0	30.0	127.0	130.0	122.0	72.0

— = Data incomplete.

Sources: Harrison, Mark, ed. *The Economics of World War II: Six Great Powers in International Comparison.* New York: Cambridge University Press, 1998; and Overy, Richard. *Why the Allies Won.* New York: W. W. Norton, 1996.

and the Soviet Union gathered resources from around the world, mobilized workers and industrial plant on a massive scale, and achieved a steady increase in armaments production. The Axis powers, smaller in size and resources even at the height of their conquests, could not match this effort, and this failure helped bring about their defeat.

Timothy L. Francis

See also
Blitzkrieg; Home Front *(various nations);* Lend-Lease; Stalingrad, Battle of
References
Harrison, Mark, ed. *The Economics of World War II: Six Great Powers in International Comparison.* Cambridge, UK: Cambridge University Press, 1998.
Milward, Alan. *War, Economy and Society, 1939–1945.* Berkeley: University of California Press, 1979.
Overy, Richard. *Why the Allies Won.* New York: Norton, 1996.

Armored Cars

Four- to six-wheeled ground vehicles protected by a light to moderately thick steel armor skin and armed with weapons ranging from machine guns to a medium gun. Armored cars were used primarily for reconnaissance. They were fast enough to maintain position in front of a body of tanks or mechanized infantry, armored well enough to stop most small-arms fire, and armed well enough to engage hostile infantry and armored cars with a significant chance of success. Virtually all powers in the war used armored cars, but differences may be seen in the designs of cars manufactured by the United States, Great Britain, and Germany.

The United States produced only three armored car designs in any great number: the M8 Scout Car, the M3A1 Scout Car, and the M20 Armored Utility Car. The M8 and M20 were built by Ford, and both used the same basic six-wheeled chassis, armored hull (20 mm of armor, sufficient to stop even a .50 caliber machine gun), Hercules 6-cylinder gasoline engine, and four-man crew. The major difference lay in armament. The M8 had a 37 mm cannon and two machine guns mounted on a turret. The M20 deleted the turret, replacing it with a single machine gun mounted on the turret ring. The M3A1 Scout Car was a four-wheeled design manufactured by White. Slower and having a shorter range than the M8/M20, it was thinly armored (7 mm, sufficient to stop most small arms). It boasted a pair of machine guns, one heavy and one medium.

The British army produced an array of armored car designs. The predominant manufacturers were Associated Equipment Company (AEC), Daimler, Humber, and Morris. These four companies built myriad armored cars of considerable variety, but those of Morris and AEC represent the range of British armored cars.

AEC produced a single design, the AEC Armoured Car, in three models: Marks I, II, and III. These had a common hull armored to early tank standards (57 mm); a four-wheel drive system attached to a 6-cylinder diesel engine, a top speed of 40 mph, and a range of 250 miles. Their chief difference lay in armament. The Mark I carried turreted 2-pounder cannon with coaxial machine gun, the Mark II a turreted 6-pounder with coaxial machine gun, and the Mark III a 75 mm gun with coaxial machine gun.

The Morris Company produced two designs, the Morris Armored Reconnaissance Car and the Morris Light Reconnaissance Car. The Morris Armored Reconnaissance Car went to war with a turreted Boys antitank rifle (.55 caliber bolt-action rifle) and a coaxial machine gun, a thin armored shell (7 mm thick), a 6-cylinder gasoline engine, and the ability to maintain a speed of 45 mph for a range of 240 miles. This armored car had a four-wheel drive train, but unlike most four-wheeled cars, it was also not four-wheeled drive. The Morris Light Reconnaissance Car was slightly superior, possessing 7 mm of additional armor plate and an armament of two machine guns.

Germany also produced a large number of armored car designs built by several firms including Deutsche Werke, Daimler-Benz, Bussing-NAG, and Magirus. However, the 15 vehicles produced by these companies consisted of three basic models. The first, the Sd Kfz 234/2—at nearly 12 tons the largest of German armored cars—could make a top speed of 50 mph on its eight-wheel suspension system and had a range of more than 500 miles. It was heavily armed with a 50 mm tank gun and a coaxial machine gun, but its armor—although heavy for an armored car at 30 mm—left it vulnerable to tanks. The Sd Kfz 231 was of a smaller six-wheeled design and weighed under 6 tons. It was slower, shorter-ranged, more lightly armored (15 mm), and weaker-armed than the 234/2, with a top speed of 38 mph, a range of 250 miles, and an armament of either an M42 ma-

chine gun or a 20 mm cannon. The Sd Kfz 233 was somewhere between the other two armored cars; weighing a bit more than 8 tons, it had a speed of 52 mph and a range of 185 miles. Its armor varied in thickness from 15 mm to 30 mm depending on the amount of supplemental armor welded on. Its most outstanding feature apart from its eight-wheel suspension was the open-topped frame and a 75 mm tank gun with coaxial machine gun behind a thin steel shield.

Three things are clear about armored cars of World War II: there were only so many ways of building a light, fast, wheeled vehicle; most nations produced at least one armored car designed to resemble a wheeled tank; and no matter the manufacturing nation and the components of the particular hull, the objective of the vehicle was the same—to locate enemy forces rather than to engage them in battle.

Harold R. Carfrey

See also
Armored Warfare; Tanks, All Powers
References
Ellis, Chris. *Tanks of World War II*. London: Chancellor Press, 1997.
Foss, Christopher F., ed. *The Encyclopedia of Tanks and Armored Fighting Vehicles*. San Diego, CA: Thunder Bay Press, 2002.
Macksey, Kenneth, and John H. Batchelor. *Tank: A History of the Armoured Fighting Vehicle*. New York: Scribner's, 1970.

Armored Personnel Carriers

German military exercises in 1934 showed that in order to keep up with the now-faster tanks, infantry needed to be motorized. Trucks were sufficiently fast on roads, but they were not at all mobile in open country. Also, troops to be carried needed better protection. Consequently, armored half-tracks and fully tracked vehicles were developed to carry infantry; these came to be known as armored personnel carriers (APCs).

The Germans, with their strategy of rapid deployment of armored and mechanized forces (what came to be called later the blitzkrieg, or lightning war), were the first to develop these kinds of troop carriers with their SdKfz (Sonderkraftfahrzeug, or special motor vehicle) 250 and Hanomag 251 series. Preliminary trials had begun as early as 1926, and in 1939 the German army issued a call for an armored vehicle that could carry half a platoon (four men). Demag built the D7 chassis based on the SdKfz 10, and Buessing-NAG developed an armored body. Production began in June 1941. The SdKfz 250 was 4.77 m long, weighed 6 tons, and could achieve a cross-country speed of up to 37 mph and a road speed of 42 mph. In 1943, the production

A column of half-tracks waits for orders to proceed to a practice engagement at Fort Knox, Kentucky. Later versions were armored and could move 1–4 infantrymen protected from small arms fire and shrapnel. (Library of Congress)

process was simplified, reducing the main armor from 19 complex plates to 9 straight plates. The new version entered production in October 1943. The larger SdKfz 251/1 became the standard vehicle to equip German Armored Infantry Panzergrenadier units and could carry 12 men. It had a cross-country speed of up to 30 mph and a road speed of more than 35 mph; its road range was just under 200 miles.

Both the SdKfz 250 and SdKfz 251 came in various sub-types. The SdKfz 250 had 12 main variants; the 251 had a total of 16. Usually, the vehicles were equipped with one or two machine guns, but some also carried guns or mortars and were used as tank hunters or self-propelled artillery. These half-tracks were produced at least until 1944. In theory, all tank divisions operated together with armored infantry divisions in APCs from the summer of 1942 onward, but the reality was quite different.

Despite having started the trend, the German army was never as mechanized as the American or British forces. The

United States produced the well-known M2 and M3 half-tracks, which were used by all the Allies including the Soviet Union. Although less sophisticated than their German counterparts, these vehicles were produced in much greater numbers. The engine was in the conventional truck position, the transmission being led forward toward the driven front wheels and backward to the track drive wheels through a transfer box. The track suspension had four road wheels, and the tracks had continuous steel bands with metal crosspieces driven by drive wheels that were elevated and to the front.

The M-2 design originated in the four-wheel-drive Scout Car M.3A1 with the rear wheels being substituted through tracks. This led to the Car, Half Track, M-2 which could carry 10 men. It had two machine guns and a 147 hp engine that provided a road speed of 40 mph and cross-country speed of up to 33 mph. It had a 6.35 mm armored hull with 12.72 mm frontal protection. The M-3 was slightly elongated and had room for 13 men. It, too, came with various modifications, such as the antitank gun motor carriage M-3, a personnel carrier that also mounted a 75 mm gun. To meet demand, the International Harvester Company was tasked with producing the M-5 and M-9 series, which were similar to the M-2 and M-3. But even the combined production of the various American factories could not keep up with orders.

During the last stages of the war, self-propelled guns such as the M-7 Priest howitzer motor carriage and the Canadian Ram Mk I (adopted from the U.S. M-3) and the U.S. M-4 Sherman medium tanks were converted to APCs by having their guns or turrets and top decking removed. This meant that the upper bodies of people in the vehicles were visible and vulnerable and that a grenade or shell landing in the open compartment could kill all inside.

The best-known Japanese APCs were the half-tracked Type 1 (known as the Ho-Ha) and the tracked Type 1 (Ho-Ki). The Ho-Ha was similar to the German SdKfz 251 but was somewhat larger. Powered by a 134 hp 6-cylinder engine and weighing 7 tons, it provided room for 15 men protected by armor up to 8 mm thick. The Ho-Ki weighed half a ton less and had 6 mm all-around protection, but it also provided no overhead protection for the rear, troop-carrying compartment. It had a top (road) speed of 25 mph.

During the war, APCs were used extensively in Europe and North Africa. The jungles of the Pacific Theater were less favorable for mechanized combat, so APCs were not used there as much, although the U.S. Marine Corps did employ large numbers of armored amphibious vehicles (known as amphtracs) to deploy troops, equipment, and supplies in Pacific Theater amphibious operations.

Thomas J. Weiler

See also
Armored Cars; Armored Warfare; Tanks, All Powers
References
Chamberlain, Peter, and H. L. Doyle. *Semi-tracked Vehicles of the German Army 1939–1945.* Part 2. Bracknell, UK: Bellona, 1970.
Hunnicut, R. P. *Half-Track: A History of American Semi-Tracked Vehicles.* New York: Presidio Press, 2001.
White, B. T. *Tanks and Other Armored Fighting Vehicles, 1942–1945.* Poole, Dorset, UK: Blandford Press, 1988.

Armored Warfare

Several of the belligerents used both tanks and armored cars in combat in World War I, but it was in World War II that the potential for mobility, firepower, and protection of tanks and other armored fighting vehicles came into its own. In World War I, armored vehicles supported infantry; in World War II, the tank became the centerpiece of armored warfare.

As World War II began, the structure of armored forces depended much on the philosophy driving a country's mechanization efforts. Germany had been particularly active in spite of treaty restrictions. Working secretly with the Soviet Union as early as 1922, Germany led the world in the development of an all-arms armored fighting force, with the role of other weapons subordinated to the requirements of tanks. An important part of emerging German armor doctrine was that offensive tanks should detour around the strong points of enemy defense.

Meanwhile, as late as the end of the 1930s, the British General Staff believed that breakthroughs would be accomplished by infantry supported by tanks and that tank units would be used only to exploit success. In France, although there was a move toward mechanization, most tanks were in separate tank battalions designed to support infantry. In the United States, progress was limited by both budgets and branch jealousy. Tanks were assigned to the infantry, and mechanization of the cavalry was slow. Having learned with the Germans the value of integrated mechanized arms, the Soviet army, initially developing a combined-arms armored force along with Germany, took a giant step backward with Josef Stalin's purge of most senior army officers. When war came, Germany's success in Poland and later in France brought widespread realization of the effectiveness of all-arms armored warfare.

During World War II, armored forces played a role in every theater, but the impact of armored warfare was most evident in Poland in 1939, in France in 1940, on the Eastern Front, in North Africa, and in Western Europe during 1944 and 1945. Difficult terrain limited the importance of armored forces in other theaters.

The German invasion of Poland on 1 September 1939 and its blitzkrieg tactics opened the eyes of the world. Germany attacked with a force of 54 divisions, 6 of them armored and 4 mechanized. With 3,195 tanks, as well as a supporting fleet of 1,538 combat aircraft, in a matter of a few weeks the German army overwhelmed Polish defenses. Learning from operations in Poland, the German army assigned each armored (panzer) division its own air force element. The Germans also learned that truck-mounted infantry could not accompany tanks cross-country or survive even infantry fire. Accompanying infantry required cross-country mobility and some armor protection.

In 1940, save for the Soviet Union, France had the strongest armored force in the world, but France failed to learn from German experience. Most French tanks remained dispersed among infantry formations. The British had created an armored division, but it was never deployed to France, where only one armored brigade joined the British Expeditionary Force (BEF). The Allied defensive strategy in the west was based on an assumption that Germany would attack through the Low Countries, and forces were deployed to meet that expectation. On 10 May 1940, however, Germany struck through the Ardennes toward the Meuse near Sudan, planning to then swing northwest in a wide arc toward the coast.

In spite of the superior armor and firepower of many British and French tanks, the combined-arms attack of the German panzer divisions, well supported by close air support, reached the English Channel by the end of May. By early June, following the evacuation of the BEF and some French forces from Dunkerque, the German army turned its forces south. By the end of June, Germany had defeated France. German armored forces—employed in mass, using surprise, aiming at weak points, and well supported by aircraft—had enjoyed rapid success.

Following the defeat of France, British leaders realized the necessity of building an armored force sufficient to counter German armor, especially as the war had then extended into North Africa when Italy attacked Egypt. British Prime Minister Winston L. S. Churchill directed a British goal of 10 armored divisions by the end of 1941. The government quickly ordered 4,000 tanks from a variety of sources.

The focus of armored warfare next shifted to North Africa, where on 13 September 1940, Italian forces in Libya launched an offensive against British forces in Egypt. The weak British forces, including only one tank battalion and totaling 36,000 men, were pushed back, but the Italian force was exhausted after a 60-mile advance. By December the British were able to launch a successful counterattack, using speed and surprise, with a force that included the 7th Armored Division (only the second to form) and the well-trained Indian 4th Infantry Division. The Italian force was shattered. However, to save his ally from defeat in Libya, Adolf Hitler organized and dispatched the Afrika Korps under Lieutenant General Erwin Rommel. Outmaneuvering the British, Rommel drove them back to Egypt. Through 1941 and most of 1942, the war in the African desert swung back and forth.

German tanks were superior to British tanks, even when the British received tanks from the United States, but British tanks outnumbered German tanks. Rommel also used antitank guns as an integral part of his operations, especially the powerful 88 mm antiaircraft gun in a new role as a highly effective antitank gun. Logistics for both sides were difficult, particularly for Germany and Italy, given Britain's nearly complete control of the Mediterranean. Armored combat in Africa was characterized by rapid movement over long distances and close-in violent fighting when forces met.

Meanwhile, both the Soviet Union and the United States used the experiences of combat in France to rethink their armored forces. The Soviets stopped considering tanks to be useful solely for infantry support, and they started a rapid buildup of armored and mechanized units built on the German pattern. In the United States, the Armored Force was created in July 1940; it placed all armored units under one command. New tanks were designed, and production increased. Two all-arms armored divisions were formed, with three more soon to follow. Ambitious plans of the Armored Force, however, were greatly reduced by the commander of Army Ground Forces Lieutenant General Leslie J. McNair, who believed that infantry and artillery would be the key to success. The army planned for only about 10 percent of its divisions to be armored. Each corps would also have a group of tank battalions for infantry division support.

On 22 June 1941, Germany attacked the Soviet Union. The scale of armored warfare in this theater would dwarf other armored operations. The Germans attacked with 3,200 tanks; the Soviets defended with 20,000. But Germany planned to use the same blitzkrieg tactics of deep armored thrusts that had been successful in France, and it could select the points of attack. Although the attack was led by 25 panzer divisions, it is worth noting that the invading army also included 750,000 horses.

Within weeks, the Soviets had been driven back 200–400 miles; they suffered massive losses as units were surrounded and captured. By mid-July, however, the Soviet defenders began to employ special tactics to repel the invaders. If a German armored spearhead broke through the lines, the Soviets, instead of retreating, closed in on both flanks to try to halt the flow, while other units took up defensive positions to the rear. Large reserve armored units would then attack the German flanks. In addition, the Soviets set up antitank guns and sowed large minefields along expected axes of German advance.

Nevertheless, it was August before the German advance slowed. On 19 November, the Soviets were able to launch a counteroffensive. Inexperienced in the use of mass tank offensive operations, Soviet commanders often failed in their attacks, but by the end of 1941 the Germans were on the defensive. By mid-January 1942, tactical defeats suffered by the Germans threatened to develop into a strategic disaster. Creating and holding a series of strong points, the Germans were able to stabilize the front by March. Several weeks of muddy conditions then held both armies in place. By then, the Soviets had realized any continued offensive would require large massed armored formations, which they created in the form of armored and mechanized corps.

Germany was able to launch offensives in the summers of 1942 and 1943, but the relative strength of the two combatants was changing. On 4 July 1943, German forces, having concentrated most of their Eastern Front armor, attacked the 50-mile-deep Kursk salient, hoping to eliminate it and to cripple Soviet offensive capability. The Soviets were aware of the German plans and prepared a defense in depth marked by an intricate system of minefields and antitank defenses. In the greatest tank battle of all time, the Soviets yielded ground skillfully and launched strong counterattacks. By 23 July, the Soviets had defeated the German offensive.

Each winter, the Soviets countered German attacks with offensives aided by their adaptability to winter and their massive armies. Germany was losing tanks and experienced tank crews at an alarming rate. Meanwhile, the Soviets were able to increase their armor strength substantially because of their own huge ordnance industry and using aid from the United States. From 1942 to 1945, the Soviets manufactured some 30,000 tanks and self-propelled guns, and the U.S. provided 7,056 tanks. The Soviet T-34 medium tank and the IS-2 heavy tank also proved to be more than a match for most German tanks.

Although the Soviets for the most part did not accomplish the breakthroughs typical of German offensives, they were able to conduct a war of attrition. Overall, the Soviet Union, with its unending miles of difficult terrain, its huge population, its massive defense industry, and its terrible winters proved to be too much for the German military machine. By the spring of 1945, the Soviet army had reached the river Elbe and joined hands with U.S. forces.

Meanwhile, U.S. forces were also conducting successful armored operations. Indeed, the U.S. Army was the most highly mechanized military force to that point in history. On 8 November 1942, the United States committed its new Armored Force to battle with successful landings in North Africa. Moving east rapidly, the inexperienced American force was bloodied at the first major battle with the Germans at Kasserine Pass. Recovering, the Americans soon combined with British forces to encircle the Axis forces in Tunis and defeat them there by 13 May 1943. U.S. armor units continued to gain experience in Sicily and Italy, but terrain there made it impractical to use large armored forces. Besides, the Allies now placed their emphasis on building up a force to invade northwestern Europe.

The June 1944 landings on Normandy were accomplished by infantry, although a few tanks rigged as amphibians contributed to the effort. After a firm lodgement had been achieved, large armored forces could be committed. In late July, the highly mobile U.S. Third Army broke out of Normandy. Within a month, the Allies had advanced to the line of the Seine River and liberated Paris. Advancing on a broad front, by mid-September Allied forces had cleared Belgium and northern France. Although the Germans did not offer significant organized resistance, their Panther and Tiger tanks took a toll on the lighter and lesser-gunned—but more numerous—Allied tanks, especially the M-4 Sher-

man medium. Indeed, the United States did not have a heavy tank, the M-26, in combat until early 1945.

In a winter offensive, the Allies attacked the German West Wall on a broad front with the aim of breaking through to the Ruhr industrial district. Gathering his armored forces for a counteroffensive, on 16 December Adolf Hitler surprised the Allies with a mobile attack through the Ardennes. The Germans lacked the means to exploit their initial breakthrough, and within a month, they were stopped. By March 1945, Allied forces had encircled and defeated German forces west of the Rhine and had crossed the river. Capitalizing on its highly mobile armored divisions and on weakening German defense, Allied forces then drove across Germany, which surrendered on 8 May.

Clearly, in the 1930s, Germany had seized the initiative in the development of armored forces and the implementation of armored warfare. Its blitzkrieg tactics were highly successful until attrition and logistics problems began to play a part (particularly on the East European Front) and the Allies caught up in fielding effective armored forces. Whereas the Soviets defeated the German forces by overwhelming them, tactics played a greater part in the West. There the concepts of armored breakthroughs and exploitation were effective, especially in the American Third Army led by Lieutenant General George S. Patton Jr.

Tanks and other armored vehicles were used effectively in other theaters of the war, but in those areas they usually were used as infantry support rather than as highly mobile maneuver forces. Nevertheless, they played an important role in many Pacific campaigns.

From 1939 to 1945, Germany produced some 53,700 tanks, peaking at 22,100 in 1944. During the same period, Japan produced only 4,572, and Italy manufactured 3,054 through August 1943. Great Britain produced 28,296 tanks during the course of the war. The Soviet Union manufactured more tanks than any other power—105,232, more than 40,000 of which were T-34 tank variants. By December 1945, the United States had produced 88,479 tanks in 17 different plants. Production figures for supporting armored vehicle were similarly impressive. Clearly, armored warfare had come of age.

Philip L. Bolté

See also

References

Carruthers, Bob. *German Tanks at War*. London: Cassell and Co., 2000.

Chamberlain, Peter, and Chris Ellis. *Tanks of the World, 1915–1945*. London: Cassell and Co., 1972.

Hofmann, George F., and Donn A. Starry, eds. *Camp Colt to Desert Storm: The History of the U.S. Armored Forces*. Lexington: University Press of Kentucky, 1999.

Mellenthin, Friedrich Wilhelm von. *Panzer Battles*. Norman: University of Oklahoma Press, 1956.

Ogorkiewicz, R. M. *Armoured Forces: A History of Armoured Forces and Their Vehicles*. New York: Arco, 1960.

Piekalkiewicz, Janusz. *Tank War: 1939–1945*. Harrisburg, PA: Historical Times, 1986.

Thomson, Harry C., and Lida Mayo. *United States Army in World War II: The Technical Services, The Ordnance Department: Procurement and Supply*. Washington, DC: Office of the Chief of Military History, 1960.

Arnauld de la Perière, Lothar von (1886–1942)

German navy admiral. Born in Posen (today Poznan, Poland) in 1886, Lothar von Arnauld de la Perière entered the Imperial German Navy in 1903 and was commissioned in 1906. He became a torpedo specialist. Following sea duty, in 1913 Arnaud became adjutant to chief of the naval staff Admiral Hugo von Pohl. He then spent time in Britain acquiring language skills until the outbreak of World War I.

Returning to Germany, Arnauld volunteered for the Imperial Naval Air Service (Zeppelins), but he was recalled by von Pohl. He then volunteered for U-boat service, and on completing submarine school, in October 1915 he took command of the *U-35* based at Pola on the Adriatic. From November 1915 to March 1918, Arnaud completed 14 cruises with the Pola Flotilla. During one cruise alone in 1916, he sank 54 ships totaling more than 90,150 tons. In March 1918, Arnaud took command of the *U-139* in the Atlantic. During his wartime total of 16 patrols, Arnaud sank 196 ships totaling 455,716 tons. This record stands unsurpassed in both world wars and indeed all history.

Retained in the German navy following World War I, Arnauld filled staff billets and commanded the light cruiser *Emden* from 1928 to 1930. He left the navy in 1931 as a captain and subsequently taught at the Turkish Naval Academy from 1932 to 1938. Recalled to the German navy at the start of World War II, Arnauld subsequently served as naval commander in Belgium, the Netherlands, Brittany, and western France. Promoted to vice admiral and named Admiral Southeast, he died in a plane crash at Le Bourget air-

port in Paris on 24 February 1942 en route to take up his new command.

Dana Lombardy and T. P. Schweider

See also

Atlantic, Battle of the; Submarines

References

Grey, Edwin A. *The U-Boat War, 1914–1918*. London: Leo Cooper, 1972.

Miller, David. *U-Boats*. Washington, DC: Brassey's, 2001.

Tarrant, V. E. *The U-Boat Offensive, 1914–1945*. Annapolis, MD: Naval Institute Press, 1989.

Arnim, Hans Jürgen Dieter von (1889–1962)

German army general. Born at Ernsdorf on 4 April 1889, Hans von Arnim was commissioned in the German army in October 1909. During World War I, he saw service on both the Western and Eastern Fronts and won promotion to captain in January 1917.

Arnim continued in the Reichswehr after the war, and in 1935 he took command of the 69th Infantry Regiment. Advanced to Generalmajor (U.S equiv. brigadier general) in January 1938, von Arnim took charge of an Army Service Depot at Schweidnitz in Silesia during 1938 and 1939.

Following the outbreak of World War II, on 12 September 1939 von Arnim took command of the 52nd Infantry Division. He was promoted to Generalleutnant (U.S. equiv. major general) in December 1939. In October 1940, he shifted to head the 17th Panzer Division and led it in Operation BARBAROSSA, the German invasion of the Soviet Union.

Assigned to Major General Heinz Guderian's 2nd Panzer Group, von Arnim proved his mettle as a panzer commander. Seriously wounded near Schklov on 27 June 1941, von Arnim did not return to action until September and participated in the encirclement of Kiev later that month. His forces then took the important railway junction of Bryansk. Shortly after the victory at Bryansk, von Arnim was promoted to General der Panzertruppen (U.S. equiv. lieutenant general) effective in October 1941. He then commanded the XXXIX Motorized Corps, which became a panzer corps in July 1942, and saw action at Tikhvin and Cholm. Arnim was promoted to Generaloberst (U.S. equiv. full general) in December 1942 and assumed command of the Fifth Panzer Army in Tunisia.

Following meetings with Adolf Hitler, Arnim assumed command of Axis forces in Tunisia on 9 December 1942. His performance in this role has drawn criticism from historians. Arnim and Field Marshal Erwin Rommel often worked at cross-purposes, and Arnim failed to take advantage of Rommel's victories at Kasserine and Tebersa. Arnim's own attack by the Fifth Panzer Army in February 1943 toward Medjez el Bat and Beja failed, even though he won a series of tactical victories. Following those events, Arnim received command of Army Group Africa on 9 March 1943.

British forces took Arnim prisoner on 12 May 1943. Incarcerated in an English country house at Hampshire until his release in 1947, Arnim then took up residence in Bad Wildungen, Germany, where he died on 1 September 1962.

Gene Mueller

See also

BARBAROSSA, Operation; Kasserine Pass, Battle of; Kiev Pocket; Rommel, Erwin Johannes Eugen; Tunisia Campaign; Vyazma-Bryansk, Battles for

References

Breuer, William B. *Operation Torch.* New York: St. Martin's Press, 1985.

Mitcham, Samuel W., Jr. "Arnim: General of Panzer Troops Hans-Jürgen von Arnim." In Correlli Barnett, ed., *Hitler's Generals*, 335–358. London: Weidenfeld and Nicolson, 1989.

Arnold, Henry Harley "Hap" (1886–1950)

U.S. Army Air Forces (USAAF) general who led the USAAF and its predecessor, the Army Air Corps, throughout the war. Born on 25 June 1886 in Gladwyne, Pennsylvania, Henry Harley "Hap" Arnold graduated from the U.S. Military Academy in 1907 and was commissioned in the infantry. He transferred into the aeronautical division of the Signal Corps in 1911 and received his pilot's certificate after training with Orville Wright. In 1912, Arnold set a world altitude record and won the first Mackay Trophy for aviation.

During World War I, Arnold served on the army staff in Washington, rising to the rank of colonel and overseeing all aviation training. After the war, Arnold reverted to his permanent rank of captain. During the 1920s, he held a variety of assignments. He supported Colonel William Mitchell at the latter's court-martial, although this was not well received by his superiors. Arnold wrote or cowrote five books on aviation, won a second Mackay Trophy, and continued to rise in the Army Air Corps. He became its assistant chief as a brigadier general in 1935. Three years later he became

General Henry Harley "Hap" Arnold seated at desk in his Munitions Building office. (Photo by U.S. Army Signal Corps, Library of Congress)

chief of the Army Air Corps as a major general after the death of Major General Oscar Westover in a plane crash.

Arnold proved particularly adept at improving the readiness of his service and expanding its resources, even with tight interwar budgets. Promoted to lieutenant general in December 1941, he was designated commanding general of the U.S. Army Air Forces in the March 1942 War Department reorganization, which raised the air arm to equal status with the Army Ground Forces and Army Service Forces. Because the British had a chief of air staff, Arnold was included on the British-American Combined Chiefs of Staff as well as the U.S. Joint Chiefs of Staff. Although he was not a major player in their decisions, he was a loyal supporter of U.S. Army Chief of Staff George C. Marshall, who repaid Arnold after the war by supporting the establishment of an independent U.S. Air Force. Arnold was promoted to general in March 1943 and became one of four five-star generals of the army in December 1944.

During the war, Arnold built an organization that reached a peak of approximately 2.5 million personnel and more than 63,000 aircraft. He was a fine judge of people and selected the best men as his advisers, staff, and field commanders. Arnold also established an emphasis on technological research and development that his service retains today. Although he was not really involved in day-to-day combat operations, his authority to relieve the field commanders who really did run the war gave him leverage to influence their actions. Poor health limited his effectiveness late in the war, especially after a fourth heart attack in January 1945.

Arnold was a proponent of precision bombing, but his pressure for more raids despite bad weather led to increased use of less accurate radar-directed bombardments in Europe, and his demand for increased efficiency in Japan inspired the fire raids there. His main goals were to make the largest possible contribution to winning the war and to ensure that the USAAF received credit for the win through proper publicity.

Although Arnold retired in June 1946, his goal of an independent U.S. air service was realized the next year by his successor, General Carl Spaatz. In May 1949, Arnold was named the first general of the U.S. Air Force. Arnold truly deserves the title "Father of the United States Air Force." He died at Sonoma, California, on 15 January 1950.

Conrad C. Crane

See also
B-29 Raids against Japan; Eaker, Ira Clarence; Marshall, George Catlett; Spaatz, Carl Andrew "Tooey"; United States, Air Force
References
Arnold, Henry H. *Global Mission*. New York: Harper, 1949.
Crane, Conrad C. *Bombs, Cities, and Civilians: American Airpower Strategy in World War II*. Lawrence: University Press of Kansas, 1993.

Coffey, Thomas M. *Hap: The Story of the U.S. Air Force and the Man Who Built It*. New York: Viking, 1982.
Daso, Dik Alan. *Hap Arnold and the Evolution of American Airpower*. Washington, DC: Smithsonian, 2000.

Art and the War

Although imagery of World War II is often thought of in terms of its haunting photographic legacy, thousands of other pictorial records were created by artists who depicted the war as it unfolded around them. Artists served as high-profile correspondents throughout much of the war, vividly documenting its conflicts in drawings, watercolors, and paintings executed on the spot and often under harrowing conditions.

An important precedent for European artists had been set by Pablo Picasso's mural-sized painting, *Guernica* (1937), named after a Basque town bombed by the German Kondor Legion during the Spanish Civil War. In *Guernica*, distended forms and disfigured characters were blown up large and linked to a vast panorama of brutality. The painting, which extended Picasso's fragmented Cubist pictorial language into the political arena, was all the more powerful for its ability to express an idyllic world shattered by the sweeping acts of anonymous warfare.

The warring powers linked art to propagandistic rhetoric. Perhaps the most unusual coupling of art and propaganda can be traced to Adolf Hitler's imagined lineage of the Germanic people from the Greek civilization of antiquity. The revival of severe forms of Greek classicism, along with a "volkish" art and architecture (art and architecture "of the people"), would result in Germany in the most spectacular public rejection of modernism in the twentieth century.

As early as 1933, the Nazi Party had stormed the legendary Bauhaus (academy of arts founded in 1919) in Dessau and padlocked its doors. In 1937, the Nazis ordered museums to be purged of artwork that they considered to have a corrosive effect on the morals of the German people. The targets of Nazi aggression were some of the greatest works of the avant-garde—the lyrical abstractions of Wassily Kandinsky; the raw energetic forms of Ernst Ludwig Kirchner and Die Brucke; the antimilitaristic sentiments and nihilistic acts of George Grosz, Otto Dix, and Berlin Dada. Particularly scorned were the works of Jewish artists who expressed their spirituality in their work, such as Marc Chagall, who had already lived through the Russian pogroms in the century's first decade. Many of the works of the artists in Nazi disfavor were simply destroyed, and 650 were selected from the thousands purged from the museums for a special exhibition *Entartete Kunst (Degenerate Art)* which traveled to a dozen cities in Germany and Austria. In the exhibition, paintings were poorly displayed, often at crooked angles, and sculptures were crowded together in piles; instead of didactic labels, grafitti scrawled on the walls ridiculed the objects and their makers. More than three million people attended this exhibition and a companion to it, *Degenerate Music.*

The U.S. Army Corps of Engineers sent eight artists to document the experiences of American combat troops in Europe. In late 1942, a second War Art Unit was created. A War Art Advisory Committee led by muralist George Biddle and composed of museum directors, curators, and even writer John Steinbeck identified artists for the special unit. Of the 42 individuals selected by the committee, 23 were already on active military duty. Although the first artists were sent to the Pacific Theater, shortly thereafter official artists were deployed to cover the various theaters. By 1943, each branch of the military had assembled its own art unit to commemorate its contribution—by land, air, or sea.

Military artists were first and foremost soldiers who assumed the additional duties of documenting the war's events with the tools of the artist. The images they generated run the gamut from portraying soldiers' and sailors' everyday routines to stirring portrayals of troops in the heat of battle. Such artists participated in the events they recorded, and at times they had to take up weapons with their fellows. When the opportunity arose, they would take out their sketchbooks and drawing instruments to make sketches and jot down notations. Such sketches matured into full drawings or were translated into paint once the combat artists had the opportunity and resources to accomplish it. Soldier-artists also served as illustrators for military publications such as the U.S. Army magazine *Yank,* which was created for the troops. Although civilian artists did not serve in combat, they accompanied the troops on dangerous missions and put their lives in harm's way; at least one civilian artist died when his transport crashed on the way to India.

When a failure by Congress to appropriate funds threatened to eliminate the army's War Art Unit shortly after its inauguration, the contracts of 17 of the 19 civilian artists were taken over by publisher Henry R. Luce's *Life* magazine. The magazine profiled war artists such as Fletcher Martin, Floyd Davis, Tom Lea, Paul Sample, and Rubin Kadish, and photographs of the artists sketching in airplane cockpits or painting on aircraft carriers often appeared next to their works.

Life also ran several contests on the theme of art in the armed services and featured soldiers' work in subsequent multipage spreads. The magazine quickly became the vehicle by which the images moved beyond their original function as reportage to achieve acclaim as works of art in their own right. *Life* sponsored exhibitions of war art at populist venues such as state fairs and at venerable institutions such as the National Gallery in Washington, D.C., and the Metropolitan Museum of Art in New York. It was by examining the objects firsthand—hurried pencil sketches and pen-and-ink scrawls, watercolors and oils put down on wrapping paper and pasteboard from packing boxes—that the public could fully grasp their immediacy, ponder the obstacles the artists had to overcome to record each scene, and be convinced of the soldiers' patriotic duty to make the art.

A second source of funding for the U.S. civilian art contracts came from Abbott Laboratories, a pharmaceutical company in Chicago that provided medical supplies to the troops. The company had an established record of patronage of the arts, and its director of advertising, Charles Downs, realized the power of images to rally the support of the public. Working with the Associated American Artists group in New York, Abbott Laboratories recruited a dozen artists to be sent overseas and successfully lobbied the War Department to provide the artists with the same degree of support given to photographers and filmmakers in terms of housing, transportation, and security clearance. Many of the artists, such as Thomas Hart Benton, Reginald Marsh, and John Stuart Curry, had worked on large-scale mural projects sponsored by the Works Projects Administration during the Great Depression years. Abbott Laboratories commissioned thematic sets of images, oftentimes showcasing their own products, although the stated mission of the project was to create permanent collections that were later donated to the military branches. Abbott also sponsored traveling exhibitions of these works to university galleries and museums across the country.

Although even the Museum of Modern Art in New York complied with the public's appetite for war pictures by sending art supplies to the front and mounting exhibitions from the battlefield, a small but vocal group of artists protested these images as sanitized portrayals of war—or worse, products of the American propaganda machine. Some were critical of the civilian component of the art units and those who traveled as artist-correspondents, charging that they played no direct role in the war effort.

Artists who served in the war designed camouflage patterns or condensed information into strategic charts and maps; their skills directly contributed to the war effort. Some artists objected to the lack of psychological or philosophical commentary in the images themselves, arguing that works of art should offer information beyond that of a photograph and should give a truer sense of the atrocities faced by the soldiers who were battling for freedom. The large community of European exiles gathered in New York

City during the early 1940s created a more ambivalent body of images that speaks of the emotional and psychological complexities of a world at war. Paintings by Max Ernst or the Chilean artist Roberto Matta, often nightmarish plunges into landscapes ruled by irrational forces, were executed in expressionist or surrealist styles.

After the war, U.S. soldiers who had worked in the art units or as artist-correspondents, as well as those who had interest in but no actual background in the arts, were offered the opportunity to pursue formal art training through the GI Bill. It created a generation of college-educated artists who sought to distance themselves from their experiences on the battlefield. Because of the association of conservative pictorial styles with Nazi propaganda and international outrage over Hitler's extreme forms of censorship, postwar art would attempt to break from the past altogether by experimenting with nonobjective styles that would be difficult for any party or platform to co-opt.

Denise Rompilla

See also
Propaganda; Spain, Civil War

References
Barron, Stephanie, and Sabine Eckmann. *Exiles and Emigrés: The Flight of European Artists from Europe.* New York: Harry N. Abrams, 1997.
Barron, Stephanie, and Peter W. Guenther, eds. *Degenerate Art: The Fate of the Avant-garde in Nazi Germany.* New York: Harry N. Abrams, 1991.
Lanker, Brian, and Nicole Newnham. *They Drew Fire: Combat Artists of World War II.* New York: T.V. Books, 2000.

Artillery Doctrine

Artillery and fire-support tactics in World War II owed more to the lessons of World War I than to the theories of mechanized warfare that evolved between the wars. Between 1914 and 1918, artillery went through a series of radical changes, altering forever the face of modern warfare. Most of the artillery innovations of 1914–1918 are still very much with us today, albeit in far more refined technological forms.

Major changes that occurred in World War I had an especially profound influence on the way World War II was fought. The most important change was the perfection of indirect fire, as opposed to direct fire. Indirect fire techniques had been developed before 1914, but during World War I they were standardized and became the norm rather than the exception for artillery combat. Firing an artillery piece by direct fire required the crew to be able to see the target and to aim at it directly, either through open iron or optical sights. Firing using this method limited the range at which guns could engage targets and required the guns to be far forward and exposed to enemy fire. Indirect fire is a system in which a gun can be fired at targets the gun crew cannot see. The gun crew instead aims the piece by sighting on a reference point.

Initially, indirect fire required a forward observer who could see the target and had some means of communication to transmit corrections back to the guns. After the first shot was fired, the observer would make successive corrections until the fall of shot was adjusted onto the target. Near the end of World War I, however, several armies had mastered the technique of firing without observer corrections. Using the correct current weather data and accurate ballistics data about the ammunition and the guns, the necessary adjustments could be mathematically predicted—hence the name *predicted fire* for the technique.

Indirect fire combined with predicted fire had several extremely significant consequences for war fighting. First, it was no longer necessary to physically mass guns on the ground to produce massed fire effects on a target. Guns at diverse points on the battlefield could all fire simultaneously on the same target. The second major consequence was the introduction of depth to combat operations. The ability to engage targets beyond visual range transformed the conducting of warfare from a linear, two-dimensional problem to a three-dimensional problem. The advent of combat aircraft also added significantly to three-dimensional warfare.

These changes came to dominate combat operations in the final years of World War I, but they were not fully developed by the time the war ended. Two major constraining factors were the relatively primitive mobility and communications technologies of the day, which limited the effectiveness of the new fire-support capabilities. Between the wars, the technologies of battlefield transportation and communications made great advances, which contributed significantly to the fact that the stagnation of the trench warfare of World War I was not repeated in World War II.

Germany

Germany led the world in the development of artillery tactics during World War I. Between 1916 and 1918, Colonel Georg Bruchmüller pioneered many of the most important artillery tactical methods: neutralization and suppressive fires, as opposed to simple destructive fires; performance of specific tactical missions by specially trained artillery groups, including infantry support, counterbattery, and deep attack; and fire preparations organized into phases to accomplish specific tactical objectives. In early 1918, Bruchmüller championed the work of Captain Eric Pulkowski, who developed a technique of meteorological corrections—

still in use today, albeit computerized—that made accurate predicted fire both possible and practical.

Ironically, Germany in the interwar years all but abandoned most of the artillery lessons it had taught the rest of the world during World War I. German artillery had been so devastating that the Versailles Treaty only allowed the postwar German army 284 artillery pieces, none larger than 105 mm. As late as 1936, three years after Adolf Hitler came to power, the German army still had only 284 guns. An army not allowed any significant amount of artillery, then, focused on developing alternative tactics centered on the tank, which in theory was supposed to provide its own close fire support. This in turn led the Germans to conclude that even if they had adequate artillery, the guns and especially their ammunition supply would not be able to keep pace with the tanks.

The Germans did recognize that even a massive tank force would sometimes encounter stiff opposition that would slow the momentum of the advance. In such situations, the additional required fire support would come from the air. By 1940, the Germans had developed an impressively sophisticated air-to-ground coordination system that was capable of concentrating as many as 2,700 aircraft over a critical sector. As successful as this system was in France, the Germans did recognize that their panzer forces would still benefit by the addition of highly mobile, organic fire-support assets. At that point they started to develop and field a limited number of self-propelled assault, antitank, and field guns.

The German system of relying primarily on air power for fire support worked fairly well in France. As the war progressed, though, the Germans came to realize that their approach was subject to flaws in three critical areas: mass, weather, and air superiority. When the German army invaded the Soviet Union, the operational theater was so vast and Soviet ground forces were spread so widely that the Luftwaffe could not be overhead everywhere it was needed at one time. The weather in the Soviet Union also severely restricted Luftwaffe operations. But conventional field artillery is practically impervious to weather conditions, and the massively gunned Red Army almost always had adequate fire support. Finally, as the war progressed and attrition sharply affected the Luftwaffe, the Germans lost air superiority. The real importance of the Combined Bomber Offensive mounted by the western Allies was not so much its effect on Germany's industrial base, but rather the steady attrition of Luftwaffe fighters and pilots. By late 1944 and 1945, Germany no longer controlled the air over its own territory, let alone over the battlefields in France or the Eastern Front.

Again abandoning lessons it had taught the world in 1918, the German army of World War II rarely emphasized the massing of artillery above the divisional level. It failed to provide artillery concentrations at the corps, army, or army group levels. The Soviets, though, considered artillery at those levels to be decisive. By 1944, the Germans had come to fully recognize their critical error with respect to artillery, and they desperately tried to recreate the fire-support structure and assets that had served them so well in 1918. By then, however, it was too little, too late.

Japan

The Japanese army believed that the immediate and close support of the infantry attack was the primary mission of field artillery. Secondary artillery missions included destroying the enemy's supporting infantry weapons, destroying obstacles in the way of the infantry advance, and interdicting enemy lines of communication. Counterbattery work had the lowest priority.

The Japanese stressed the importance of keeping their guns well forward, often placing firing positions within a few hundred yards of an enemy's forward positions. Command posts were sited right next to the guns so the battery could be controlled by voice command. But the fire and observation conditions of Asian jungles created special problems for close infantry support. The terrain often made it difficult or impossible to track accurately the positions of the infantry units. The requirement to fire over trees almost always meant that the fall of shot would be too far forward of the infantry. The solution to that problem was to position the guns on the flanks of the attacking infantry.

Under Japanese doctrine, artillery was oriented primarily to the offense. Before an attack, standard Japanese artillery preparation lasted between one and two hours. The preparation was conducted in three phases of roughly equal duration: (1) range adjustment; (2) obstacle destruction; and (3) fire on the enemy's forward positions. As the infantry began its attack, the mission of the artillery shifted to direct support. In defensive situations, the main weight of the Japanese guns would be echeloned 1 to 1.2 miles behind the main line of resistance. As the enemy massed for the attack, the defending artillery would fire a counterpreparation. Once the enemy attack started, the mission of the artillery was to break up the momentum of the assault with a series of standing barrages.

As with the Germans, the Japanese throughout World War II suffered from too little artillery and inadequate organization and control at the higher echelons. Artillery in small units was allocated directly to the tactical-level infantry units, which left almost no fire-support assets for centralized command and control at the divisional level and up. By 1944 the Japanese, too, had come to recognize the gravity of these shortcomings, and they moved to correct the problems. But, as with their German allies, it was too little and too late.

France

The French were slow to modernize their artillery following World War I. Throughout the interwar years, all French tactical thinking was either woefully outdated or too heavily influenced by a defensive orientation. The French believed that massive firepower was the key to victory. They took this idea to its extreme limit and also rejected mobility. They came to regard "weight of metal" as the decisive factor in any defense or attack. This, of course, led to the massive defensive system of the Maginot Line, which sought to replicate on a grand scale the fixed fortifications of Verdun, which had held out in 1916.

The French put all their interwar artillery efforts into artillery in fortresses, largely ignoring mobile field artillery. In the early 1930s, the French did experiment with a mechanized division, but French field artillery was not even motorized until 1934. Throughout the 1920s and 1930s, French tactical doctrine emphasized that the mission of artillery was (1) to destroy any obstacles in the path of the infantry, (2) to accompany the infantry by fire, and (3) to strike at the enemy artillery's capability to hit the friendly infantry. The emphasis on these missions, however, was always within a framework of counterpreparations and defensive fires.

Just prior to the start of World War II, a French artillery preparation had three primary targets: the enemy's infantry, the enemy's known antitank weapons, and the enemy's suspected antitank weapons. Counterbattery fire against the enemy's guns had almost completely fallen out of the French doctrine. The French believed that modern technology and mechanization made counterbattery fires impractical, if not impossible. Finally, the French failed to provide any real doctrine for coordinating artillery with air support and air defense. A result of this failure was that two French divisional artilleries were cut off and then routed at Sedan in May 1940 before the German ground forces had even crossed the Meuse.

United States

As early as the mid-1920s, the U.S. Army started to abandon many of the hard-learned artillery lessons of World War I, and the focus of ground tactics shifted back to an infantry-centered world. Right up to the start of World War II, the U.S. Army neglected the requirements of artillery command and control above the divisional level and almost totally ignored corps-level artillery. What passed for corps-level artillery was little more than a holding pool for units and guns not otherwise assigned to a division. According to the doctrine, corps artillery was supposed to be responsible for counterbattery fire. But even as late as May 1943, the Field Artillery School at Fort Sill, Oklahoma, was still recommending that corps artillery units be parceled out to the divisions during operations.

The U.S. Army, however, did not go quite as far as the British, French, or even the Germans in abandoning the artillery lessons of World War I. The American penchant for technical solutions prevailed, and Fort Sill experimented with various forms of fire control techniques, including aerial observation. By 1934, Fort Sill had developed the first battalion Fire Direction Center, which could simultaneously control and mass the guns of all three of an artillery battalion's batteries. In 1940, Fort Sill introduced the graphical firing table, a specialized artillery slide rule that greatly speeded the calculation of the firing solution. In April 1941, Fort Sill demonstrated for U.S. Army Chief of Staff General George C. Marshall a divisional shoot, controlling and massing against a single target the fires of four separate battalions, totaling 12 batteries.

In the late 1930s, Brigadier General Lesley J. McNair was the assistant school commandant at Fort Sill. McNair had commanded a field artillery brigade in France during World War I. Later, as commander of U.S. Army Ground Forces, he became the chief architect of the U.S. military buildup going into World War II. McNair was a strong believer in flexible massed fires. He championed the development of longer-range guns and supported all initiatives to centralize artillery command and control systems. Under his direction, the number of nondivisional medium and heavy artillery battalions in the U.S. Army nearly doubled between 1942 and 1944.

U.S. Army doctrine in World War II identified two primary field artillery missions: (1) supporting the ground-gaining (infantry, cavalry, armored) units by either neutralizing or destruction fires; and (2) giving depth to combat by counterbattery fire, by fire on enemy reserves, by restricting movement in enemy rear areas, and by disrupting enemy command and control systems.

As the war progressed, the U.S. Army's logistical advantage became increasingly decisive, and the American tactical experience mirrored that of the other Allies. At the corps level, the emphasis increased on command, joint operations, and airpower. Joint operations and airpower were especially important in the Far East, where amphibious operations and jungle terrain made it almost impossible to mass artillery on the ground.

British Commonwealth

The British army had (and still has) a somewhat different approach to artillery command and control. In almost all other armies, the forward observers (FO), who accompanied the infantry and requested—and, if necessary, adjusted—the supporting fires, were junior officers, usually lieutenants. The more senior artillery officers remained in command of the guns or in the command posts of the artillery battalions or the divisional artillery headquarters. The British attached their more senior officers to the command post of the supported maneuver unit. Thus, a British infantry company would have a captain as an FO—or forward observation officer (FOO), as the British called them. The supported infantry battalion commander would have an artillery major as his artillery adviser.

The idea behind the British system is that the senior and more experienced officers would better understand the overall tactical situation. Whereas a lieutenant FO in most armies could only request fires, a British FOO had the authority to order the fires. The British believed this system produced quicker and more responsive fire support. The system depended heavily on radio communication, which was widespread and effective in the British army from 1940 forward.

As with the Germans, the British had rejected most of the artillery lessons of World War I. Great Britain entered World War II with a tactical doctrine that de-emphasized artillery, based on the theory that tanks could operate independently without much support from the other arms. Unlike the Germans, the British did not have an air force structured to provide air-to-ground support for emergencies. Unlike the Luftwaffe, the Royal Air Force before World War II concentrated on building up its bomber forces. The lack of air support for their ground troops cost the British dearly in the campaign for France in 1940.

The British approach to mobile tactics did work well against the Italians at the start of the campaign in North Africa. But once the Germans entered that fight, the British were at a severe disadvantage against the German combined-arms tactics and organizations. Too often, the British tried to attack German positions without adequate artillery preparation and paid a high price. And at the same time, the British had difficulty establishing an effective defense built on fire and maneuver.

What made the British situation even more difficult during the early fighting in North Africa was the fact that they were forced to use most of their field artillery in an antitank role, which left little for infantry support. By 1942, the British were pouring new antitank guns and more field artillery into North Africa, which then allowed them to develop new tactical methods.

General Bernard Montgomery was the primary architect of the new British approach. Montgomery stressed the steady buildup of a superior firepower ratio and the use of artillery to produce shock action in coordination with the other arms. The two main tactical techniques to achieve this were the creeping barrage and the timed concentra-

tion. These techniques had been developed in World War I, but in World War II they were far more sophisticated and effective because of better communications and predicted rather than observed and adjusted fire. At El Alamein, for example, 1,000 British guns produced a massive shock effect by firing more than 1.2 million shells at plotted German targets without having to telegraph the attack by first adjusting the fall of shot. The British also developed a standard fire mission they called the "72-gun battery," which concentrated all the guns of a division on a single target.

Soviet Union

Virtually alone among the world's major armies, the Red Army following World War I intensely studied the artillery lessons of that war and diligently applied them during the interwar years. In the 1920s, Soviet Chief of Artillery Lieutenant General Yuri Shedeyman personally translated from German into Russian the books written by Colonel Georg Bruchmüller about his artillery innovations during World War I. Reflecting their faith in massed firepower, the Soviets by the 1920s had built their army into a combined-arms force with artillery as a major component at all levels.

In 1941, the Soviets initiated a major reorganization of their artillery. The number of guns in a division was reduced by almost two-thirds, but the number of mortars increased by the same proportion. The objective was to make the divisions more mobile. The Soviets grouped their heavier artillery pieces into artillery reserve units, which then could be massed at the decisive point of any battle. Following these reorganizations, Soviet leader Josef Stalin in 1942 directed that artillery should be concentrated to support a breakthrough in a designated sector and that more mobile artillery had to be developed to support the armored units that would exploit the breakthrough.

In late 1942, the Soviets organized their artillery reserve units into artillery divisions. With the exception of one artillery division with which the Germans experimented briefly, the Soviets were the only ones to field such organizations in World War II. By the end of the war, the Red Army had some 90 artillery divisions, about the same number of total divisions in the U.S. Army. In 1943, the Soviets began grouping their artillery divisions into breakthrough artillery corps of two or more artillery divisions and one rocket launcher division. The Soviets believed in holding artillery in reserve—directly the opposite of the American belief that artillery is never held in reserve. At the start of the war, some 8 percent of the Red Army's artillery was in the High Command Artillery Reserve. By the end of the war, this percentage had risen to 35 percent.

On the defensive for the first part of the war, the Soviets drew the following conclusions about fire support in defensive operations: (1) artillery, not aircraft, was the superior form of fire support in the defense, (2) the antitank plan should be the basis for determining the overall deployment of forces, (3) all guns should be capable of direct fire, (4) an artillery reserve was essential, (5) armor should counterattack only after a tank attack had been stopped by artillery, (6) artillery must be sited in depth in prepared positions, and (7) indirect fire was only effective when massed and centrally commanded.

USSR attack doctrine grew out of Soviet experiences launching counterattacks from the defensive. By the time the Red Army went on the offensive in the final years of World War II, its artillery had three primary missions: (1) preparation of the attack; (2) support of the attack, principally through a creeping barrage or fixed concentrations; and (3) accompaniment of the maneuver forces. Accompanying fire was the primary mission of the divisional artillery units, more often than not through close-range direct fire. As a result, divisional artillery units generally suffered 10 times the casualty rates of nondivisional units.

The Soviet system worked for the USSR, but it did have its drawbacks. Operations required a methodical buildup of overwhelming force, which in turn required periods of stability. That meant that operations on the Eastern Front went through cycles of long periods of buildup, followed by brief surges of steamrollerlike momentum. The Soviets ultimately had the manpower and the resources to succeed with this approach on the operational level, but during the interim periods the Germans often were able to achieve stunning tactical successes because of their more flexible organization and doctrine. In the end, however, the Soviets succeeded. In so doing, they proved that conventional artillery—the "god of war," as Stalin called it—was in fact a decisive element at the operational level of war.

David T. Zabecki

See also

Artillery Types; Hitler, Adolf; Infantry Tactics; Maginot Line; Marshall, George Catlett; McNair, Lesley James; Montgomery, Sir Bernard Law; Stalin, Josef

References

Bailey, Jonathan B. A. *Field Artillery and Firepower*. 2d ed. Annapolis, MD: Naval Institute Press, 2003.

Bellamy, Chris. *Red God of War: Soviet Artillery and Rocket Forces*. London: Brassey's, 1986.

Bidwell, Shelford. *Artillery Tactics, 1939–1945*. Warren, MI: Almark, 1976.

Hogg, Ian V. *The Guns: 1939/45*. New York: Ballantine Books, 1970.

Zabecki, David T. *Steel Wind: Colonel Georg Bruchmüller and the Birth of Modern Artillery*. Westport, CT: Praeger, 1994.

Artillery Types

Firepower and maneuver are the two primary elements of land combat power. From the late Middle Ages to the early years of the twentieth century, artillery was the only significant source of land-based firepower. Even after the appearance in World War I of machine guns, tanks, and ground-attack aircraft, artillery still remained the major source of firepower on the battlefield. Throughout history, firepower and mobility technology have been in a constant tug of war with each other. Rarely has one achieved a significant advantage over the other; but whenever that has happened, the results have been devastating.

During World War I, firepower technology far outstripped mobility technology. During the years between the Franco-Prussian War (1870–1871) and the start of World War I in 1914, there was vast technological improvement for artillery and infantry weapons, particularly the machine gun. The result was previously unimaginable levels of battlefield firepower. Battlefield mobility, however, was still primarily a matter of human and animal muscle, as it had been for thousands of years. Thus, firepower had become mechanized by 1914, mobility had not, and the result was trench warfare. By World War II, mobility technology had caught up, and the balance was restored.

Artillery pieces are broadly classified by the ballistic performance of the projectiles they shoot. The three basic categories of cannon, or tube, artillery have not changed in the past 300 years, although individual technologies have advanced considerably. Guns fire projectiles at a very high velocity and on a relatively flat trajectory. They have the greatest range and tend to be the heaviest of artillery pieces. Mortars are generally light weapons that fire a relatively light projectile at low muzzle velocities and short ranges but at high angles of fire—above 45 degrees. Howitzers are extremely versatile weapons, capable of firing at both high and low angles. The muzzle velocity and range of a howitzer are less than those of a gun of comparable size, but a howitzer is far more accurate. A howitzer also can fire a heavier shell than can a gun of the same weight. Most armies in World War II had both guns and howitzers in their arsenals. Although they were technically artillery pieces, mortars were considered infantry weapons by almost all armies.

All forms of artillery through the start of the nineteenth century were the same smooth-bore, muzzle-loading, blackpowder mechanisms that had been in use for hundreds of years. They had poor mobility, and the gun crews engaged their targets by direct fire—that is, the gunner had to see and directly aim at the target, just as if he was firing a large rifle. In the last half of the nineteenth century, artillery made several technological leaps in areas such as improved metallurgical and manufacturing techniques, rifled bores, breech-loading mechanisms, fire-control instruments, and, most importantly, recoil mechanisms.

Modern recoil mechanisms, introduced at the very end of the nineteenth century, allowed the artillery piece to hold its position on the ground as each round was fired. That, in turn, meant that the piece did not have to be reaimed after each round, which produced far more rapid rates of fire. The result was vastly improved accuracy and repeatability, which—combined with modern optics and fire control techniques—made indirect fire possible. Indirect fire is the technique of accurately firing at targets that the gun crew cannot see directly. That important advance extended the effective depth of artillery fire, which in turn led to the very concept of deep battle. The first artillery piece with modern fire control and recoil systems was the French *Canon de 75 mle 1897* (75 mm gun, model 1897), widely known as the "French 75."

Through World War I, all field artillery was horse-drawn. In the interwar years, the horse gave way to the truck as the artillery prime mover in the British and U.S. armies. Many armies, including those of Germany, Japan, Italy, and the USSR, relied heavily on horses until the very end of World War II. Self-propelled (SP) artillery—guns mounted on a wheeled or tracked carriage—also appeared shortly after the end of World War I, when the British Birch Gun was introduced. By the end of World War II, almost all armies had SP guns and howitzers.

According to an old maxim of the British Royal Artillery, the real weapon of the artillery is the projectile—the gun is merely the means of sending a projectile to the target. During World War II the standard artillery projectile was high-explosive (HE), producing both blast and fragmentation effects. The blast was employed primarily against fortifications and fragmentation was used against personnel. Smoke rounds were used to obscure enemy visibility on the battlefield, and illumination rounds were utilized to enhance friendly visibility at night. In the early years of the war, most armies were forced to use their field artillery in an antitank role, which required the guns to fire special armor-piercing (AP) and high-explosive antitank (HEAT) rounds. During World War I, most armies had developed and used a wide array of chemical rounds that produced various combinations of lethal and nonlethal, persistent and nonpersistent effects. Although all sides still had these chemical rounds in their arsenals during World War II, they were not employed.

The fuze is perhaps the most critical element of an artillery round. The point-detonating (PD) fuze triggers the round as soon as it touches the ground, producing a surface burst. Most PD fuzes could be set on "delay" to allow the round to penetrate into the ground and produce a subsur-face burst. The concrete-piercing fuze is a variation of the delay fuze that allows an artillery projectile to burrow into the wall of a bunker or fortification before exploding. The mechanical time fuze was used to produce an air burst, which rained fragments on the target below. This was generally the most effective means of attacking troops in the open. The time fuze, however, required a high degree of skill on the part of the forward observer and the fire direction center personnel to get the time of flight and the height of burst just right. Near the end of World War II, the U.S. Army introduced the proximity fuze, adapted from naval antiaircraft artillery for field artillery work. Also called the variable-time fuze, it contained a small radar transmitter and receiver that produced a perfect 66-ft height of burst every time. The "funny fuze," as Lieutenant General George S. Patton called it, was first used by U.S. artillerymen with devastating effect during the German Ardennes offensive in December 1944.

United States

The U.S. Army classified its field artillery guns and howitzers into three basic categories by weight: light, medium, and heavy. Light guns, used for direct support, were found only in divisional artillery. The airborne divisions and the 10th Mountain Division were armed with the 75 mm M-1A1 pack howitzer. It was designed for easy disassembly, which allowed it to be dropped from the air or transported by six mules. The 75 mm pack howitzer was widely used in Italy and in the jungles of the Pacific, where its transportability was its most important feature.

The workhorse of most infantry divisional artillery was the 105 mm M-2A1 howitzer, the most widely used artillery piece in history. It was accurate and reliable, and it could withstand a great deal of punishment and mishandling. It was first developed in the 1920s as a weapon capable of being towed by a team of six horses, and the design was approved in March 1940.

The M-2A1 was towed by a two-and-a-half ton truck, which also carried the gun's crew and its basic load of ammunition. The armored divisions used the M-2A1's tube and gun carriage on a one of several self-propelled mounts. The standard was the M-7B1, which was mounted on a Sherman tank chassis. In 1945, these guns began to be replaced by the M-37, which was mounted on a Chaffee tank chassis.

In 1943, the army introduced a lightened version of the M-2A1 with a shortened barrel to give airborne units more firepower than the 75 mm pack howitzer delivered. The M-3 howitzer was not a successful design, however. After World War II, the M-2A1 was modified somewhat to become the M-101A1. That version remained in service with the U.S. Army through the Korean and Vietnam Wars. More than 10,200 M-2A1s or M-101A1s were built and supplied to some 45 different armies between 1940 and 1953.

The 155 mm M-1A1 towed howitzer was the standard American medium artillery piece used by the general support battalions of almost all the infantry divisions. It was a successful and popular design, although heavy and somewhat difficult to handle. The cannoneers on the gun crews called these weapons "pigs"—short for pig iron. A self-propelled version of the 155 mm howitzer mounted on a Chaffee tank chassis was designated the M-41, but only about 100 were ever built.

The most widely used American heavy gun was the 155 mm M-1 towed gun, which is not to be confused with the 155 mm M-1A1 towed howitzer. The 155 mm gun was two-and-a-half times as heavy as the 155 mm howitzer and could shoot a shell of the same weight (95 lb) 60 percent farther. The 155 mm gun had a 19-ft barrel and was nicknamed the "long Tom" by all sides. One self-propelled version was the M-12, based on a modified Grant tank chassis. The M-40 version was based on a modified Sherman tank chassis.

The 8-inch M-2 towed howitzer used the same carriage as the 155 mm M-1 towed gun. Whereas the bore sizes of all other U.S. Army artillery pieces were designated in millimeters, this one was designated in inches because it originally was adopted from a U.S. Navy design. Despite its relatively short barrel, the 8 inch had the reputation of being the most accurate artillery piece ever invented. It remained in service in the U.S. Army into the 1960s and in the British Army into the 1970s. After World War II, the U.S. Army also mounted the 8 inch on a self-propelled carriage, and that version remained in service until just after the 1991 Gulf War.

The heaviest U.S. artillery piece was a 240 mm M-1 towed howitzer called the "black dragon." Towed by a 38-ton M-6 tractor, it had surprisingly good mobility for a gun weighing almost 21 tons. Once the gun arrived in a firing position, it took the gun crew about two hours to place the piece into action. The 240 mm howitzer saw extensive service in the Italian Campaign.

France

At the start of the war the French army still had large numbers of the World War I–era 75 mm guns in service. One of them, the French 75, had been the world's first truly modern artillery piece, featuring a hydraulic recoil mechanism and a screw-type breechblock that allowed a high rate of fire. Between the wars, the French had tried to modernize the weapon, updating it with pneumatic tires and a split trail. The Germans captured thousands of these guns from the French in 1940 and incorporated them into lower-priority Wehrmacht units. The Germans also modified the French 75 as an antitank gun for service on the Eastern Front.

In 1939, the French still had more than 1,000 105-mm and 3,000 155-mm World War I–vintage artillery pieces in service. These obsolete weapons were a detriment in 1940. The standard French 105 mm gun was the *Canon de 105 mle 1913 Schneider.* The French also still had in service 450 *Canon de 155 Grand Puissance Filloux* (Can 155 GPF). Despite the age of these weapons from an earlier war, the Germans placed many of the captured weapons into service with their own units—an indicator of Germany's overall weakness in field artillery.

The French did have some small numbers of modern light field guns, including the *Canon de 105 mle 1934-S* the *Canon de 105 court mle 1935-B,* and the *Canon de 105 L mle 1936 Schneider.* Only 159 of the M-1936 guns were in service in 1940. The Germans used those captured pieces primarily for coastal defense. Of even more value to the Germans was the *Can 155 GPF* (the updated version of the *Can 155 GPF-T*), which had a carriage designed for motor transport.

Soviet Union

Unlike most other countries, the Soviets read the lessons of World War I as requiring more artillery rather than less. In 1937, the Red Army had an inventory of 9,200 field and heavy guns, more than twice that of the German army and triple that of the French. When Germany attacked in June 1941, the Soviet artillery arsenal stood at 67,000 tubes (artillery pieces). Throughout the war, Soviet artillery designs were more reliable, durable, and effective than those of virtually all other armies. Soviet army guns generally had longer ranges and greater lethality. The Soviets also developed innovative mass-production techniques that produced large numbers of relatively inexpensive guns. Through their system of design evolution, they repeatedly combined the successful features of various existing designs and could introduce improved models in a very short period of time.

Unlike most other armies, the Soviet army did not put much effort into developing increasingly powerful antitank guns. Soviet field artillery pieces generally fired at a higher velocity than those of most other armies, and experience in the Spanish Civil War convinced the Soviets that if they were provided with the proper ammunition, field guns were the best weapons against tanks. With the USSR's overwhelming tube superiority over Germany, Soviet field guns could be used effectively to mass indirect fires against distant targets and then quickly switch to a direct-fire point defense against tanks when the situation required. In 1941 and 1942, most German tank losses were to fire from towed field guns.

The Red Army suffered huge equipment losses in the early period following the German attack in 1941. In the first five months of the war, the Soviets lost upward of 20,000 guns. But this loss quickly led to a surge in mass production of modern, standardized weapons. The basic divisional support gun was the 76.2 mm M1942 ZIS-3, a long-barreled gun with a split trail. By the end of the war, variants on the same design had been introduced in 85 mm and 100 mm types. With a range of nearly 13 miles, the latter outranged all comparable divisional support guns. The 100 mm version also was mounted on the SU-100 SP assault gun. Soviet medium artillery included the excellent 122 mm M-1931/37 A-19 and the 152 mm M-1937 ML-20 and M-1943 D-1.

Massed artillery was the basis of the defense of Moscow in the winter of 1941. According to Soviet reports, artillery destroyed more than 1,400 German tanks between 16 November and 10 December alone. The Soviets relied on the same tactics in the Battle of Stalingrad. At Kursk on 5 July 1943, the Red Army fired a counterpreparation with 3,000 guns against the assembling German attack force. It was a dramatic demonstration of the power of massed artillery to disrupt an armored attack before it could be launched. As the war wound into its final years and Soviet production continued to swell the Red Army's arsenal, artillery preparations became more and more massive. During the offensive to cross the Vistula and Oder Rivers in January 1945, the Soviets massed 7,600 guns and mortars along the 21-mile breakthrough sector alone, with 33,500 tubes deployed across the entire front.

The Germans were better-armed with artillery than the Soviets in just one area. In 1944, a typical panzer division had some 70 SP guns with calibers up to 150 mm. A Soviet tank corps of the same period had only 20 76-mm SP guns. Despite their overwhelming number of tubes, only about 30 percent of the Soviet guns were larger than 100 mm. The maximum effective range of most of the smaller guns was only about 3.1 miles. Much beyond that range, Soviet gunners had great difficulty supporting the advance of the maneuver units. Thus, the Soviet's large numbers of massed but relatively immobile guns were effective in creating the conditions for successful breakthroughs but ineffective in supporting and sustaining those breakthroughs.

British Commonwealth

By 1939, the British army was the first fully motorized army in the world. All British field guns were towed by a four-wheel-drive truck that also carried the gun crew and the ammunition. The primary British close-support gun was the 25-pounder, which fired a 3.45-inch round. Initially designed in 1930, the 25-pounder had a box trail and an innovative central firing platform that allowed the crew to traverse the gun a full 360 degrees.

The earliest version, the MK-1, was based on the modified carriage of a World War I–vintage gun. The MK-1s saw service in France in 1940. The MK-2, with a carriage specifically designed for the 25-pounder, was introduced in 1940 and saw service in Norway. When firing special armor-piercing ammunition, the 25-pounder was pressed into service as an effective antitank gun during the early years of the war. In 1943, the Australian army introduced a lightweight version of the 25-pounder for jungle operations. The British also mounted it on a Valentine tank chassis to produce a self-propelled version known as "the Bishop." A far more successful design called "the Sexton" mounted the 25-pounder on a Canadian Ram tank. The Royal Artillery also used the American 105 mm M-7 SP howitzer, a system known as "the Priest."

At the start of the war, British medium artillery consisted of World War I–vintage guns, including the 6-inch gun, 6-inch howitzer, and the 60-pounder. These were soon replaced by the 4.5-inch and 5.5-inch guns, which used the same chassis. The 5.5-inch gun was first developed in the 1930s, and its final version was approved in August 1939. It fired a 100 lb shell. The 4.5-inch gun first saw service in North Africa in 1942. Both guns were grouped together in medium field artillery regiments.

Early British heavy artillery also consisted mostly of World War I weapons, including the 8-inch, 9.2-inch, 12-inch, and 18-inch howitzers and 6-inch and 9.2-inch guns. All of these weapons were too heavy and cumbersome for modern mobile warfare, and the British lost most of them in France in 1940. Although the British did start the work to design and develop more modern heavy artillery, they suspended those efforts when the United States entered the war. The British instead adopted the American towed 155 mm gun and towed 8-inch howitzer.

Germany

The Germans had four categories of artillery: the *Kanone* (cannon), the *Haubitze* (field howitzer), the *Moerser* (a heavy howitzer firing at high angle only), and the *Werfer* (mortar). Generically, all artillery pieces were called *Geschuetze* (guns). The three primary calibers of German field artillery were 75 mm, 105 mm, and 150 mm. (The Germans used centimeters to designate their weapons—7.5 cm, 10.5 cm, and 15 cm.) Almost from the start of the war, the Germans recognized that 75 mm guns were ineffective for modern warfare. Those guns, including ones captured from the French, were issued only to low-priority units.

The towed 10.5 cm *leichte Feldhaubitze 18* (le FH 18) was the principal German close-support gun. Designed at the end of World War I, it remained a capable weapon throughout World War II. The main problems were that the Germans never had enough of them, and in almost all units right up until the end of the war they were drawn by horses. On the Eastern Front, the le FH 18 was an effective antitank weapon when armed with the proper ammunition. A self-propelled version for the panzer divisions called the *Wespe* (Wasp) was mounted on a PzKpfw-II tank chassis.

The heavier artillery at the divisional level included a gun (the 10 cm s K 18) and a medium field howitzer (the 15 cm *Schwere Feldhaubitze 18* [s FH 18]). The SP version of the s FH 18, called the *Hummel* (Bumblebee), was mounted on a PzKpfw-IV tank chassis. At the corps and field army echelons, the most common heavy support guns were the 17 cm K 18 gun and the 21 cm *Moerser 18* (Mrs 18) heavy howitzer. Both weapons had a common carriage.

In most World War II armies, the organic fire support for infantry units came from mortars. The Germans did have effective mortars at both company and battalion levels, but on the basis of their experiences from World War I, they also fielded infantry guns right up until the end of the war. The two basic types were the 7.5 cm *leichtes Infantriegeschuetz 18,* designed late in World War I, and the heavier 15 cm *schweres Infantriegeschuetz 33.* The latter was actually too heavy for an infantry gun.

The Germans did produce several SP versions of their field and antitank guns, and they also produced a self-propelled weapon called an assault gun that was more like a turretless tank. Whereas the SP field and antitank guns consisted mostly of standard towed guns mounted on various tank chassis, many of the SP assault guns had no towed equivalent. The 7.5 cm *Sturmkanone 40* (Stu. K. 40) fired a 15 lb shell approximately 4 miles; the 10.5 cm *Sturmhaubitze 42* (Stu. H. 42) fired a 33 lb projectile 4.8 miles; and the 15 cm Stu. H. 43 fired a 95 lb shell only 2.8 miles from a barrel that was only about 6 ft long.

German artillerymen were tactically skilled, and their guns were generally technically advanced. The main problems were that the Germans did not have nearly enough of them, and the mobility of the guns they did have was generally poor. Initially, the Luftwaffe provided the close fire support for the fast-moving panzer divisions on the Eastern Front. But when the Germans found that the Luftwaffe could not be everywhere at once across the vast expanses of the east, especially in bad weather, they found themselves woefully outgunned by the Soviets.

Italy

As with most other European armies, the Italians entered World War II with many obsolescent artillery pieces in service. Italy had, however, started a rearmament program in the 1920s, ahead of most other nations. The Italians entered the war, then, with several modern artillery designs, but none in great numbers. As the war progressed, even the more modern Italian guns quickly became outclassed by British and American guns, whose development had started much later, in the 1930s.

The 75 mm *Cannone da 75/32 modello 37* was initially developed in the 1920s, but it never entered full production. The 75 mm *Obice da 75/18 modello 35* howitzer was another good design, but the Italians only had 68 in service by September 1942. The Italians started the war with more than 900 of the obsolete 149 mm *Cannone da 149/35* in service. Based on a turn-of-the-century design and lacking a modern recoil system, the gun had to be relaid after every round. It was supposed to be replaced in 1940 by the 149 mm *Cannone da 149/40,* but that weapon, too, never went into mass production.

Two of the better Italian designs were kept in production and service by the Germans after Italy surrendered in 1943. By 1942, only 147 of the *Obice da 149/19* howitzers were in service and only 20 of the heavy 210 mm *Obice da 210/22 modello 35,* which was an accurate and mobile piece for its heavy caliber.

Japan

The Japanese came late to artillery. Most Japanese had never seen a cannon before the arrival of Admiral Matthew Perry in 1853. The Japanese army manufactured its first artillery piece only in 1905, and up through World War II almost all Japanese artillery was based on European designs. Japanese guns, however, were lighter, and they had a greater range than comparable European designs of the same caliber. Japanese designers achieved the weight savings at the expense of the strength of the tubes, trails, and especially the recoil systems. As a result, these weapons suffered from an overall lack of ruggedness and high failure rates that proved costly in light of the heavy firing that was necessary during sustained combat.

Throughout the war, the Japanese had both horse-drawn and motorized artillery units. Whereas the U.S. Army and most European armies moved between the wars from 75 mm to 105 mm as the standard caliber for direct support of infantry, the Japanese stayed with 75 mm throughout World War II. The standard divisional support gun was the 75 mm type-90. It was introduced in 1930, but many units entered the war still equipped with the older type-38. The type-90 had a high muzzle velocity, which made it especially effective in an antitank role. The 75 mm type-94 mountain gun was also widely used in the jungle as pack artillery. Weighing just 1,181 lb, it could be carried by 18 men and assembled and laid for firing in about 10 minutes. As with the Germans, the Japanese also had an infantry gun. The 70 mm type-92 battalion gun weighed only 450 lb, but its range was only about one-third that of the type-94 mountain gun.

Japanese general support guns included the 105 mm type-91 howitzer and the 105 mm type-92 gun, introduced in 1931 and 1932 respectively. Both guns fire the same basic projectile, but the far heavier type 92-gun had almost twice the range. With a range of 11.3 miles, the type-92 could throw a 35 lb shell farther than most other artillery pieces of World War II. The Japanese medium artillery battalions were armed with either the 149 mm type-96 howitzer or the 149 mm type-89 gun. Despite weighing almost three times as much as the 105 mm type-92 gun, the 150 mm type-89 gun had a range only 0.9 mile greater. The largest Japanese artillery piece of the war was the 240 mm type-45 howitzer. An elderly pre–World War I design, it was most effective as a coastal defense gun.

With Japan's overwhelming emphasis on the infantry attack, the Japanese entered World War II without adequate industrial resources for large-scale artillery production and maintenance. Their production facilities were not tooled for standardized production and the mass production of interchangeable parts. Thus, the Japanese army was always chronically short of artillery, and it had trouble keeping what it did have in service.

David T. Zabecki

See also

Antiaircraft Artillery and Employment; Artillery Doctrine; Kursk, Battle of; Moscow, Battle of; Patton, George Smith, Jr.; Stalingrad, Battle of; Tanks, All Powers

References

Bailey, Jonathan B. A. *Field Artillery and Fire Power.* 2nd ed. Annapolis, MD: Naval Institute Press, 2003.

Bellamy, Chris. *Red God of War: Soviet Artillery and Rocket Forces.* London: Brassey's, 1986.

Bidwell, Shelford, and Dominick Graham. *Fire-Power: British Army Weapons and Theories of War 1904–1945.* Boston, MA: Allen and Unwin, 1985.

Dastrup, Boyd L. *The Field Artillery: History and Sourcebook.* Westport, CT: Greenwood Press, 1994.

Hogg, Ian V. *The Guns 1939/45.* New York: Ballantine Books, 1970.

———. *British and American Artillery of World War II.* New York: Hippocrene Books, 1978.

———. *The Illustrated Encyclopedia of Artillery.* London: Stanley Paul, 1987.

———. *German Artillery of World War Two.* Mechanicsburg, PA: Stackpole Books, 1997.

McLean, Donald B. *Japanese Artillery: Weapons and Tactics.* Wickenburg, AZ: Normount Technical Publications, 1973.

Zabecki, David T. *Steel Wind: Colonel Georg Bruchmüller and the Birth of Modern Artillery.* Westport, CT: Praeger, 1994.

Aruga Kosaku (1897–1945)

Japanese navy officer. Born 31 August 1897 in Nagano Prefecture, Aruga Kosaku became a career naval officer. He specialized in surface warfare, especially in destroyers. In 1923, Aruga graduated from the advanced course at the Torpedo School, and during the next decade he served in light cruisers. He was promoted to captain in November 1940.

By the beginning of World War II, Aruga was commander of Destroyer Division 4. At the June 1942 Battle of Midway, Aruga's destroyers screened Vice Admiral Nagumo Chūichi's 1st Carrier Striking Force. Two months later, Aruga still commanded Destroyer Division 4 and participated in the Battle of the Eastern Solomons, screening Admiral Abe Hiroaki's Vanguard Group.

In March 1943, Aruga took command of the cruiser *Chokai.* In July 1944, he was appointed head of the Torpedo School. On 25 November 1944, Aruga, now a rear admiral, assumed command of the battleship *Yamato.* Her war record had been undistinguished, and as flagship of the Combined Fleet she had often remained far from the action. The *Yamato* had been damaged by a torpedo from the American submarine *Skate* on 25 December 1943, and her only surface action had been in the battle off Samar in October 1944 against American escort carriers.

On 1 April 1945, U.S. forces landed on Okinawa. Taunted by his army counterpart that the *Yamato* was a floating hotel for idle and inept admirals, commander of the Combined Fleet Admiral Toyoda Soemu drafted orders for Operation ICHI-TEN. The *Yamato* was provided sufficient fuel for a one-way trip to Okinawa. Escorted by one light cruiser and eight destroyers, the *Yamato* was to draw off American carrier planes, leaving the American fleet vulnerable to a mass attack by kamikazes. The *Yamato* would then destroy the American transports off Okinawa and beach herself to serve as an unsinkable fortress. Her crew was then to join the fighting on land.

When the task force commanders learned of the orders, they protested. Although they were willing to die for Japan, they did not believe the plan would produce significant results. They wanted instead to attack U.S. lines of communication. When Second Fleet Commander Vice Admiral Itō Seiichi, who took command of the operation aboard the *Yamato,* refused to change the orders, Aruga and the other commanders accepted their fate. Aruga was overheard to state, "What a glorious way to die!"

The *Yamato* sortied the afternoon of 6 April. Cadets and ill sailors were landed before she left. U.S. forces located the *Yamato* early the next morning and pounded her with waves of carrier planes. She was hit by at least seven bombs and 11–15 torpedoes. When flooding caused a serious list to port, Aruga ordered counterflooding, although many men were trapped below decks. By 2:00 P.M., Aruga realized the end was near. He ordered that Emperor Hirohito's portrait be saved and had himself tied to the compass mounting to avoid surviving the sinking of his ship. At 2:23 P.M., the *Yamato* rolled onto an even keel and exploded. Aruga and Itō were not among the 269 survivors of the *Yamato*'s 2,767-man crew. Aruga was posthumously promoted to vice admiral.

Tim J. Watts

See also

Abe Hiroaki; Eastern Solomons, Battle of the; Kamikaze; Midway, Battle of; Nagumo Chūichi; Okinawa, Invasion of; Toyoda Soemu; *Yamato*; *Yamato*, Suicide Sortie of

References

Dull, Paul S. *A Battle History of the Imperial Japanese Navy (1941–1945).* Annapolis, MD: Naval Institute Press, 1978.

O'Neill, Richard. *Suicide Squads: Axis and Allied Special Attack Weapons of World War II: Their Development and Their Missions.* London: Salamander Books, 1981.

Spurr, Russell. *A Glorious Way to Die: The Kamikaze Mission of the Battleship "Yamato," April 1945.* New York: Newmarket Press, 1981.

Yoshida, Mitsuru. *Requiem for Battleship "Yamato."* Trans. Richard Minear. Seattle: University of Washington Press, 1985.

Asaka Yasuhiko (1887–1981)

Japanese army general and prince. Born 2 October 1887 in Kyoto, Japan, Asaka Yasuhiko was the uncle-in-law of Emperor Hirohito. Commissioned a sublieutenant in the army on graduation from the Military Academy in 1908, Asaka graduated from the Army Staff College in 1914. In the early 1920s, he spent time in France studying the European military establishments.

Asaka was promoted to colonel in 1925 and to major general in 1930 and then taught at the Staff College. In 1933, he received a further promotion to lieutenant general and assumed command of the Imperial Guards Division in 1933. Asaka became a member of the Supreme War Council in 1935. He used his influence as a member of the Imperial Family to further the interests of the military faction in the Japanese government.

As the Sino-Japanese conflict in Manchuria escalated in November 1937, Asaka was assigned the position of deputy commander of the Center China Area Army Group, which was driving on the then–Chinese Nationalist capital of Nanjing (Nanking). The commander, General Matsui Iwane, became ill, and as a result Asaka led the final assault on Nanjing, which ended with the fall of the capital on 13 December 1937. In the ensuing weeks, Japanese troops under Asaka's command committed atrocities on Chinese civilians and soldiers alike. This event, known as the "rape of Nanjing," was reported to the world by foreign correspondents. Asaka returned to Japan

and was promoted to full general in 1939. He held no further field commands.

After the war, Asaka was questioned by U.S. investigators, but as a relative of the emperor he was not charged with war crimes. In his later years, he was well known in Japan for his interest in golf. Asaka died on 13 April 1981 at Atami.

Harold Wise

See also

Hirohito, Emperor of Japan; Nanjing Massacre; Sino-Japanese War

References

Brackman, Arnold C. *The Other Nuremberg.* New York: William Morrow, 1987.

Chang, Iris. *The Rape of Nanking: The Forgotten Holocaust of World War II.* New York: Viking Penguin, 1998.

Yamaoto Masahiro. *Nanking: Anatomy of an Atrocity.* Westport, CT: Praeger, 2000.

Atlantic, Battle of the

The Battle of the Atlantic was the longest campaign of World War II. In it, the German navy tried to sever the Allied sea lines of communication along which supplies necessary to fight the war were sent to Great Britain. To carry out the battle, the Germans employed a few surface raiders, but principally they used U-boats.

At the beginning of the war, the German navy possessed not the 300 U-boats deemed necessary by Kommodore (commodore) Karl Dönitz (he was promoted to rear admiral in October 1939), but 57 boats, of which only 27 were of types that could reach the Atlantic from their home bases. Although an extensive building program was immediately begun, only in the second half of 1941 did U-boat numbers begin to rise.

On the Allied side, British navy leaders were at first confident that their ASDIC (for Allied Submarine Detection Investigating Committee) location device would enable their escort vessels to defend the supply convoys against the submerged attackers, so that shipping losses might be limited until the building of new merchant ships by Britain, Canada, and the United States might settle the balance. However, Dönitz planned to concentrate groups of U-boats (called "wolf packs" by the Allies) against the convoys and to jointly attack them on the surface at night. It took time, however, before the battles of the convoys really began. The Battle of the Atlantic became a running match between numbers of German U-boats and the development of their weapons against the Allied merchant ships, their sea and air escorts (with improving detection equipment), and new weapons.

The Battle of the Atlantic may be subdivided into eight

Officers on the bridge of a U.S. destroyer, escorting a large convoy of ships, keep a sharp lookout for attacking submarines, ca. 1942. (Library of Congress)

phases. During the first of these, from September 1939 to June 1940, a small number of U-boats, seldom more than 10 at a time, made individual cruises west of the British Isles and into the Bay of Biscay to intercept Allied merchant ships. Generally, these operated independently because the convoy system, which the British Admiralty had planned before the war, was slow to take shape. Thus the U-boats found targets, attacking at first according to prize rules by identifying the ship and providing for the safety of its crew. However, when Britain armed its merchant ships, increasingly the German submarines struck without warning. Dönitz's plan to counter the convoy with group or "pack" operations of U-boats—also developed and tested before the war—was put on trial in October and November 1939 and in February 1940. The results confirmed the possibility of vectoring a group of U-boats to a convoy by radio signals from whichever U-boat first sighted the convoy. However, at this time, the insufficient numbers of U-boats available and frequent torpedo failures prevented real successes.

The German conquest of Norway and western France

provided the U-boats with new bases much closer to the main operational area off the Western Approaches and brought about a second phase from July 1940 to May 1941. In this phase, the U-boats, operated in groups or wolf packs, were directed by radio signals from the shore against the convoys, in which was now concentrated most of the maritime traffic to and from Great Britain. Even if the number of U-boats in the operational area still did not rise to more than 10 at a time, a peak of efficacy was attained in terms of the relationship between tonnage sunk and U-boat days at sea. This was made possible partly by the weakness of the convoy escort groups because the Royal Navy held back destroyers to guard against an expected German invasion of Britain. In addition, British merchant shipping losses were greatly augmented during this phase by the operations of German surface warships in the north and central Atlantic; by armed merchant raiders in the Atlantic, Pacific, and Indian Oceans; by the attacks of German long-range bombers against the Western Approaches; and by heavy German air attacks against British harbors. The Germans were also

GREENLAND

Allied Air Cover

Convoy Routes

Murmansk

ICELAND

Reykjavik

Faeroes

Shetland

Narsarssuak

Convoy Routes

Liverpool

U-Boat Hunting Grounds
Sep 1939–May 1940

Goose Bay

Allied Air Cover

St. Johns

Canadian
Coastal Sector

Halifax

New York

Allied Air Cover

Eastern Sea
Frontier

Operation
"DRUMBEAT"

UNITED STATES
(Escort Duties)

GREAT BRITAIN
(Escort Duties)

Gibraltar

U-Boat Hunting Grounds
Apr–Dec 1941

Caribbean Sea
Frontier

Virgin Islands
Martinique
Guadeloupe

Dakar

Freetown

Allied Air Cover

Brazilian
Sector

U-Boat Hunting Grounds
Jan–Jul 1942

Natal

Allied Air Cover

Convoy Routes

The Battle
of the Atlantic

Capetown

— — —   Convoy Routes

‐ ‐ ‐   Escort Duty Divide

———   Limits of Air Cover

– – –   Strategic Defense Sectors

aided by Italian submarines based at Bordeaux and sent into the Atlantic, the numbers of which in early 1941 actually surpassed the number of German U-boats.

In late 1940 and spring 1941, when the danger of an invasion of the British Isles had receded, London released destroyers for antisubmarine operations and redeployed Coastal Command aircraft to support the convoys off the Western Approaches. Thus, in the third phase of the Battle of the Atlantic, from May to December 1941, the U-boats were forced to operate at greater distances from shore. Long lines of U-boats patrolled across the convoy routes in an effort to intercept supply ships. This in turn forced the British in June to begin escorting their convoys along the whole route from Newfoundland to the Western Approaches and—when the U-boats began to cruise off West Africa—the route from Freetown to Gibraltar and the United Kingdom as well.

In March 1941, the Allies captured cipher materials from a German patrol vessel. Then, on 7 May 1941, the Royal Navy succeeded in capturing the German Arctic meteorological vessel *München* and seizing her Enigma machine intact. Settings secured from this encoding machine enabled the Royal Navy to read June U-boat radio traffic practically currently. On 9 May during a convoy battle, the British destroyer *Bulldog* captured the German submarine *U-110* and secured the settings for the high-grade officer-only German naval signals. The capture on 28 June of a second German weather ship, *Lauenburg,* enabled British decryption operations at Bletchley Park (BP) to read July German home-waters radio traffic currently. This led to interception of German supply ships in the Atlantic and cessation of German surface ship operations in the Atlantic. Beginning in August 1941, BP operatives could decrypt signals between the commander of U-boats and his U-boats at sea. The Allies were thus able to reroute convoys and save perhaps 1.5 million gross tons of shipping. During this third phase, the U.S. Atlantic Fleet was first involved in the battle.

The entry of the United States into the war after the Japanese attack on Pearl Harbor ushered in the fourth phase of the battle, presenting the U-boats with a second golden opportunity from January to July 1942. Attacking unescorted individual ships off the U.S. East Coast, in the Gulf of Mexico, and in the Caribbean, German U-boats sank greater tonnages than during any other period of the war.

But sightings and sinkings off the U.S. East Coast dropped off sharply after the introduction of the interlocking convoy system there, and Dönitz found operations by individual U-boats in such distant waters uneconomical. Thus, in July 1942, he switched the U-boats back to the North Atlantic convoy route. This began the fifth phase, which lasted until May 1943. Now came the decisive period of the conflict between the U-boat groups and the convoys with their sea and air escorts. Increasingly, the battle was influenced by technical innovations. Most important in this regard were efforts on both sides in the field of signals intelligence.

On 1 February 1942, the Germans had introduced their new M-4 cipher machine, leading to a blackout in decryption that lasted until the end of December 1942. This accomplishment was of limited influence during the fourth phase, because the German U-boats operated individually according to their given orders, and there was no great signal traffic in the operational areas. And when the convoy battles began again, the Germans could at first decrypt Allied convoy signals.

But when Bletchley Park was able to decrypt German signals anew, rerouting of the convoys again became possible, although this was at first limited by rising numbers of German U-boats in patrol lines. In March 1943, the U-boats achieved their greatest successes against the convoys, and the entire convoy system—the backbone of the Allied strategy against "Fortress Europe"—seemed in jeopardy. Now Allied decryption allowed the dispatch of additional surface and air escorts to support threatened convoys. This development, in connection with the introduction of new weapons and high-frequency direction finding, led to the collapse of the U-boat offensive against the convoys only eight weeks later, in May 1943.

This collapse came as a surprise to Dönitz. Allied success in this regard could be attributed mainly to the provision of centimetric radar equipment for the sea and air escorts and the closing of the air gap in the North Atlantic. In a sixth (intermediate) phase from June to August 1943, the U-boats were sent to distant areas where the antisubmarine forces were weak, while the Allied air forces tried to block the U-boat transit routes across the Bay of Biscay.

The change to a new Allied convoy cipher in June, which the German decryption service could not break, made it more difficult for the U-boats to locate the convoys in what was the seventh phase from September 1943 to June 1944. During this time, the German U-boat command tried to deploy new weapons (acoustic torpedoes and increased anti-aircraft armament) and new equipment (radar warning sets) to force again a decision with the convoys, first in the North Atlantic and then on the Gibraltar routes. After short-lived success, these operations failed and tapered off as the Germans tried to pin down Allied forces until new, revolutionary U-boat types became available for operational deployment.

The final, eighth phase, from June 1944 to May 1945, began with the Allied invasion of Normandy. The U-boats, now equipped with "snorkel" breathing masts, endeavored to carry out attacks against individual supply ships in the shallow waters of the English Channel and in British and Canadian coastal waters. The U-boats' mission was to pin down Allied supply traffic and antisubmarine forces to prevent the deployment of warships in offensive roles against German-occupied areas. But construction of the new U-boats (of which the Allies received information by decrypting reports sent to Tokyo by the Japanese embassy in Berlin) was delayed by the Allied bombing offensive, and the German land defenses collapsed before sufficient numbers of these boats were ready.

The Battle of the Atlantic lasted without interruption for 69 months, during which time German U-boats sank 2,850 Allied and neutral merchant ships, 2,520 of them in the Atlantic and Indian Oceans. The U-boats also sank many warships, from aircraft carriers to destroyers, frigates, corvettes and other antisubmarine vessels. The Germans lost in turn one large battleship, one pocket battleship, some armed merchant raiders, and 650 U-boats, 522 of them in the Atlantic and Indian Oceans.

The Allied victory in the Battle of the Atlantic resulted from the vastly superior resources on the Allied side in shipbuilding and aircraft production (the ability to replace lost ships and aircraft) and from superior antisubmarine detection equipment and weapons. Allied signals intelligence was critical to the victory.

Jürgen Rohwer

See also
Antisubmarine Warfare; Bletchley Park; Depth Charges; Dönitz, Karl; Hunter-Killer Groups; Signals Intelligence; Torpedoes
References
Beesly, Patrick. *Very Special Intelligence: The Story of the Admiralty's Operational Intelligence Centre, 1939–1945.* London: Greenhill Books, 2000.
Blair, Clay. *Hitler's U-Boat War.* Vol. 1, The Hunters, 1939–1942; vol. 2, The Hunted, 1942–1945. New York: Random House, 1996, 1998.
Gardner, W. J. R. *Decoding History: The Battle of the Atlantic and Ultra.* Annapolis, MD: Naval Institute Press, 1999.
Niestlé, Axel. *German U-Boat Losses during World War II: Details of Destruction.* Annapolis, MD: Naval Institute Press, 1998.
Rohwer, Jürgen. *The Critical Convoy Battles of March 1943.* Annapolis, MD: Naval Institute Press, 1977.
———. *Axis Submarine Successes of World War Two: German, Italian and Japanese Submarine Successes, 1939–1945.* London: Greenhill Books, 1999.
Runyan, Timothy J., and Jan M. Copes, eds. *To Die Gallantly: The Battle of the Atlantic.* Boulder, CO: Westview Press 1994.
Sebag-Montefiore, Hugh. *Enigma: The Battle for the Code.* London: Weidenfeld and Nicolson, 2000.
Syrett, David. *The Defeat of the German U-Boats: The Battle of the Atlantic.* Columbia: University of South Carolina Press, 1994.
Wynn, Kenneth. *U-Boat Operations of the Second World War.* Vol 1. Career Histories, U1–U510; vol. 2. Career Histories, U511–UIT25. London: Chatham Publishing, 1998, 1999.

Atlantic Charter (14 August 1941)

First face-to-face meeting between U.S. President Franklin D. Roosevelt and British Prime Minister Winston L. S. Churchill; the basis for the United Nations Declaration. Arranged by Roosevelt, the Atlantic Charter meeting took place in Placentia Bay, Newfoundland. Roosevelt had put out on the presidential yacht *Potomac* under cover of having a vacation, and he then transferred secretly to the cruiser *Augusta.* Churchill traveled across the Atlantic on the battleship *Prince of Wales.* The two leaders and their staffs (including all service chiefs of each side) met aboard these ships beginning on 9 August for four days. Topics of discussion included Lend-Lease aid, common defense issues, and a strong joint policy against Japanese expansion in the Far East. Almost as an afterthought, the meetings produced a press release on 14 August 1941 that came to be known as the Atlantic Charter.

The Atlantic Charter had eight main points: (1) the eschewing by the two heads of government of any territorial aggrandizement for their own countries; (2) opposition to territorial changes without the freely expressed consent of the peoples involved—in other words, self-determination of peoples; (3) the right of all peoples to choose their own forms of government and determination to restore freedom to those peoples who had been deprived of it; (4) free access for all nations to the world's trade raw materials; (5) international cooperation to improve living standards and to ensure economic prosperity and social security; (6) a lasting peace that would allow peoples everywhere to "live out their lives in freedom from fear and want"; (7) freedom of the seas; and (8) disarmament of the aggressor states "pending the establishment of a wider and permanent system of general security."

Although there was no formally signed copy of the Atlantic Charter, just the press release containing the eight guiding principles, these principles had the same appeal as President Woodrow Wilson's Fourteen Points of 1918. Certainly the talks strengthened the bonds between the United States and Britain. Isolationists in the United States denounced the charter for the determination it expressed to bring about "the final destruction of the Nazi tyranny." The government of the Soviet Union later announced its support for the charter's principles, but even at this early stage in the war, there were sharp differences between the Anglo-Saxon powers and the Soviet Union over what the postwar world should look like. Nonetheless, the Atlantic Charter subsequently formed the basis of the United Nations Declaration.

Spencer C. Tucker

See also
Churchill, Sir Winston L. S.; Roosevelt, Franklin D.; United Nations, Declaration

References

Bailey, Thomas A. *A Diplomatic History of the American People.* New York: Appleton-Century-Crofts, 1958.

Larrabee, Eric. *Commander in Chief: Franklin Delano Roosevelt, His Lieutenants and Their War.* New York: Harper and Row, 1987.

Lash, Joseph P. *Roosevelt and Churchill, 1939–1941: The Partnership That Saved the West.* New York: W. W. Norton, 1976.

Meacham, Jon. *Franklin and Winston: An Intimate Portrait of an Epic Friendship.* New York: Random House, 2003.

Sainsbury, Keith. *Churchill and Roosevelt at War: The War They Fought and the Peace They Hoped to Make.* New York: New York University Press, 1994.

Atlantic Wall

German defenses along the European coast, last of the great defensive lines to be built (1941–1944). As German plans to invade Britain faded late in 1940, it became increasingly clear to the German High Command that thousands of miles of European coast had to be defended from Allied invasion. Heavily protected from the beginning were the German submarine bases in France, the occupied Channel Islands, and the Dover-Calais narrow point in the English Channel. Following the June 1941 invasion of Russia and the U.S. entry into the war in December 1941, Germany went on the defensive in the west. Formal work on the Atlantic Wall began in May 1942.

There never was a continuous "wall" per se; that would have been impossible to build or man. What was built was a series of defended zones—artillery and infantry positions overlooking likely invasion beaches and ports. Rivalries and different designs among army and navy units and civilian construction battalions often held up progress, as did strategic arguments about the comparative value of fixed defenses versus mobile reserves. And so did Allied bombardment of transport of construction materials. Nevertheless, the three-year effort by Germany was massive, soaking up huge quantities of men, money, and material.

Thousands of emplacements were built along the coast of France, with lesser facilities in the Low Countries, Denmark, and along the Norwegian coast. Where possible existing fortifications and weapons were used. Highlights of the wall were the often-extensive artillery batteries built into extensive steel-reinforced cement casemates designed to deflect air attacks. A typical position might include four separate 8-inch gun casemates (which, while protecting the gun and its crew, also limited the weapon's field of fire) plus one or more observation and combat-direction posts, all built close to the coastline. The largest positions might feature mobile 14-inch railway-mounted artillery or huge turret-mounted guns. Some of the latter, installed in massive emplacements built near the French coast, could shell England directly across the Channel. Among German defenses were scores of smaller emplacements for machine guns, observation, personnel, command posts, and minefields. Some were camouflaged to look like houses or other structures, and most were built at least partly built into the ground for further protection. A large number of so-called "standard" bunker designs were employed, although each service had its own set of standards. Extensive propaganda made the wall appear impregnable to attack from the sea.

When placed in command of German beach defenses in October 1943, Erwin Rommel made the high-tide mark into the main line of defense, adding obstacles and intervening emplacements covering possible landing points. There were a half million beach obstacles along the English Channel alone, many armed with mines.

In the end the stupendous construction project was largely for naught. Although two-thirds of a planned 15,000 emplacements were completed, few of them fired in anger. D day was hardly hindered by the several emplacements in Normandy (some were shelled from the sea; others were taken by paratroopers or special ranger attacks, as at Point du Hoc), and the rest of the coastal forts were generally captured from behind by advancing Allied forces. Extensive remains of the Atlantic Wall exist to this day.

Christopher H. Sterling

See also

Coast Defense; Fort Drum; Maginot Line; Rommel, Erwin Johannes Eugen; Todt, Fritz

References

Kaufmann, J. E., and J. M. Jurga. "Atlantic Wall." In *Fortress Europe: European Fortifications of World War II*, 381–406. Conshohocken, PA: Combined Publishing, 1999.

Rolf, Rudi. *Atlantic Wall Typology.* Rev. ed. Nieuw Weerdinge, Netherlands: Fortress Books, 1998.

Saunders, Anthony. *Hitler's Atlantic Wall.* Stroud, UK: Sutton Publishing, 2001.

Schmeelke, Karl-Heinz, and Michael Schmeelke. *German Defensive Batteries and Gun Emplacements on the Normandy Beaches.* Atglen, PA: Schiffer, 1995.

Virilio, Paul. *Bunker Archeology.* New York: Princeton Architectural Press, 1994.

Wilt, Alan F. *The Atlantic Wall: Hitler's Defenses in the West, 1941–1944.* Ames: Iowa State University Press, 1975.

Atomic Bomb, Decision to Employ

Although there were extensive consultations about the employment of the atomic bomb, discussions always focused on how to use the new weapon, not whether to use it. The primary aim of Allied decision-makers was to achieve the unconditional surrender of Japan as quickly as possible at the lowest cost in lives, and everyone of importance assumed that if the MANHATTAN Project could produce a workable weapon, that weapon would be expended against an enemy target.

It could be argued that the decision to use the atomic bomb was actually made on 6 December 1941, when the first money was approved to fund its development. At the time, American leaders assumed the new invention would be a legitimate weapon in the war, and they never questioned that assumption afterward.

Although President Franklin D. Roosevelt's key advisers on the project concluded in May 1943 that the first operational bomb should be dropped on Japan, the choice of targets really did not receive systematic attention until two years later. A special Target Committee for the MANHATTAN Project began meeting in April 1945, and by the next month it had selected a shortlist of cities including Kyoto and Hiroshima. On 31 May, a blue-ribbon Interim Committee appointed by Secretary of War Henry L. Stimson began meeting to discuss how best to use the new weapon. A suggestion made at lunch to try a warning and noncombat demonstration was quickly rejected for many practical reasons, and the committee recommended that the bomb be dropped without warning on a target that would make the largest possible psychological impression on as many inhabitants as possible.

Eventually, military planners came up with a target list of Hiroshima, Kokura, Kyoto, and Nigata. Stimson persuaded the planners to substitute Nagasaki for the shrine city of Kyoto and then presented the list to President Harry S Truman in late July. Truman approved the directive without consulting anyone else and wrote in his diary that the bomb would be used between 25 July and 10 August. The new weapon offered the possibility of ending the war sooner, and he had no compelling reason not to employ it. Despite some historians' claims to the contrary, there was no reliable evidence of any imminent Japanese collapse or surrender. Although some leaders did perceive a display of the atomic bomb's power as a potential tool to intimidate the Soviet Union in the future, this was a secondary benefit of its employment and not a factor in operational decisions.

No single government document shows Truman's decision to use the bomb, but there were two relevant military directives from the Joint Chiefs to the U.S. Army Air Forces. The first, to General Henry "Hap" Arnold on 24 July, designated the four possible targets. The next day, a similar order to General Carl Spaatz, who was commanding strategic air forces in the Pacific, added a date: "after about 3 August 1945." That document also directed that other bombs were to be delivered against targets as soon as they were ready. On the basis of these orders, Spaatz selected Hiroshima and then Kokura to be the targets for the first and second atomic missions. (Cloud cover on the day of the second raid caused the shift to the secondary target of Nagasaki.)

Some critics have questioned why there was not more deliberation about whether to use the terrible new weapon. The main concern for decision-makers was to win the war quickly while avoiding a bloody invasion or losing public support for unconditional surrender. Under the conditions in 1945, which had already produced fire raids that had killed far more Japanese civilians than did the attacks on Hiroshima and Nagasaki, no U.S. president or general could have failed to employ the atomic bomb.

Conrad C. Crane

See also

Arnold, Henry Harley "Hap"; B-29 Raids against Japan; Groves, Leslie Richard; Hiroshima, Bombing of; MANHATTAN Project; Nagasaki, Bombing of; Roosevelt, Franklin D.; Spaatz, Carl Andrew "Tooey"; Stimson, Henry Lewis; Tokyo, Bombing of (1945); Truman, Harry S

References

Bernstein, Barton. "The Dropping of the A-Bomb." *Center Magazine* (March-April 1983), 7–15.

Kagan, Donald. "Why America Dropped the Bomb." *Commentary* 100 (September 1995): 17–23.

Merrill, Dennis. *The Decision to Drop the Atomic Bomb on Japan.* Vol. 1, *Documentary History of the Truman Presidency.* Bethesda, MD: University Publications of America, 1995.

Wainsrock, Dennis D. *The Decision to Drop the Atomic Bomb.* Westport, CT: Praeger, 1996.

Walker, J. Samuel. *Prompt and Utter Destruction: Truman and the Use of Atomic Bombs against Japan.* Chapel Hill: University of North Carolina Press, 1997.

ATS

See Great Britain, Auxiliary Territorial Service.

Attlee, Clement Richard (First Earl Attlee and Viscount Prestwood) (1883–1967)

British politician, leader of the Labour Party and deputy leader of the House of Commons, and prime minister. Born 3 January 1883 in the Putney part of London, Clement Attlee was educated at University College, Oxford. He initially practiced law, but after working with the poor in London's East Side, he joined the Labour Party in 1907, living in a settlement house until 1922 (except during World War I). He served as a lecturer at the London School of Economics.

British Labor Party leader Clement Attlee. (Hulton-Deutsch Collection/Corbis)

plans. He was renowned for his ability to remain calm in a crisis, to outline major positions in few words, and to make hard decisions. Pressed by his party, however, he led Labour out of the national coalition in May 1945 after the defeat of Germany (there had not been a general election for a decade). This led to national elections at which Labour won a resounding victory, and Attlee became prime minister on 26 July 1945. He replaced Churchill as the British representative for the remainder of the Potsdam Conference.

Attlee presided until October 1951 over creation of the British welfare state with its nationalization of health services, steel, coal, railways, and civil aviation. He supervised the granting of independence to India and Pakistan on 14 August 1947, a key step in converting the British Empire to the Commonwealth of Nations. On retiring as party leader, he was made an earl in 1955. He spoke often in the House of Lords against Britain becoming part of the Common Market. Attlee died in Westminster, London, on 8 October 1967.

Christopher H. Sterling

See also
Chamberlain, Arthur Neville; Churchill, Sir Winston L. S.; Potsdam Conference
References
Attlee, Clement R. *As It Happened.* London: Heinemann, 1954.
Beckett, Francis. *Clem Attlee: A Biography.* London: Richard Cohen Books, 1997.
Harris, Kenneth. *Attlee.* London: Weidenfeld and Nicolson, 1982.
Pearce, R. D. *Attlee.* Boston: Addison-Wesley Longman, 1997.
Williams, Francis A. *Prime Minister Remembers: The War and Post-War Memoirs of the Rt. Hon. Earl Attlee Based on His Private Papers and on a Series of Recorded Conversations.* London: Heinemann, 1961.

During World War I, Attlee rose to the rank of major and served at Gallipoli and in the Middle East and later on the Western Front.

Elected to Parliament in October 1922, Attlee and held various minor posts in Labour and national governments. He became the head of the Labour Party in 1935 as a compromise candidate, a middle-of-the-road democratic socialist. Attlee and a growing proportion of his party agreed with Winston L. S. Churchill's call for faster rearmament in the face of the threat from Nazi Germany.

Refusing to serve under Neville Chamberlain, Attlee helped to bring about Winston Churchill's government during the crisis of May 1940, when Chamberlain was forced to resign. On 10 May, Churchill named Attlee lord privy seal (he served to 1942) and deputy leader of the House of Commons (effectively deputy prime minister), a position he held from 1942 to 1945. Attlee often chaired cabinet sessions during Churchill's constant travels, and he remained loyal to Churchill throughout the war.

Attlee worked closely with fellow Labourite Aneurin Bevin to develop the 1943 white paper on postwar social

Auboyneau, Philippe Marie Joseph Raymond (1899–1961)

French Navy admiral. Born in Constantinople on 9 November 1899, Philippe Auboyneau graduated from the École Navale in 1918. Between the wars, he attended the French War College and commanded a torpedo boat. He was promoted to commander in December 1939, and when World War II began he was in the Far East serving as French liaison officer to British forces based at Colombo, Ceylon. After Germany invaded France in May 1940, Auboyneau was reassigned to the Mediterranean as liaison officer to British Mediterranean forces under Admiral Sir Andrew Browne Cunningham.

Three months later, Auboyneau chose to follow Brigadier General Charles de Gaulle and joined the Free French in London. There Auboyneau took charge of the 1st Fighting

French Destroyer Division. Promoted to captain in November 1941, in March 1942 he became commander of all Free French naval forces. He headed naval representation on the Council of National Liberation. In November 1942, shortly after the Allied landings in North Africa, Auboyneau moved to Algiers with most of the Free French leaders, becoming deputy chief of the French General Staff. In January 1943, he was promoted to rear admiral. In July 1944, Auboyneau directed the 3rd Cruiser Division in Operation DRAGOON, the Allied invasion of southern France.

Auboyneau was promoted to vice admiral in command of French naval forces in the Far East in September 1945, and he held the position for two years during the Indochina War. In August 1955, he became commander in chief of French naval forces in the Mediterranean based in Algiers. He received promotion to full admiral in December 1957 and directed French naval operations for five years during the Algerian War. Auboyneau retired in December 1960, and he died at Paris on 22 February 1961.

Priscilla Roberts

See also
Cunningham, Sir Andrew Browne; de Gaulle, Charles; DRAGOON, Operation; France, Free French; TORCH, Operation

References
Auphan, Paul, and Jacques Mordal. *The French Navy in World War II.* Trans. A. C. J. Short. Annapolis, MD: Naval Institute Press, 1959.
Gillois, André. *Histoire secrète des Français à Londres de 1940 à 1944.* Paris: Hachette, 1973.
Ordioni, Pierre. *Tout commence à Alger, 1940–1945.* Paris: Éditions Albatros, 1985.
Roskill, Stephen. *The War at Sea.* 3 vols. London: Her Majesty's Stationery Office, 1954–1961.

Auchinleck, Sir Claude John Eyre (1884–1981)

British Army general. Born at Aldershot, England, on 21 June 1884, Claude Auchinleck was known as "the Auk." He graduated from Sandhurst (1902) and saw extensive service in India and Tibet (1904–1912), the Middle East (in often appalling conditions, 1914–1919), and India again (1929–1940), rising to the rank of major general.

Auchinleck returned to England in January 1940, expecting to prepare British units for action in France. Instead, he was sent on 7 May 1940 to command British forces in Narvik in the disastrous Norwegian Campaign, which suffered from lack of air cover and adequate forces and equipment. Just after Britain's evacuation of Norway, on 14 June 1940 Auchinleck took over Southern Command to prepare for a possible German invasion. In this role, he worked effectively to improve the Home Guard. As fears of invasion receded, Auchinleck was promoted to general and sent to India as commander in chief on 21 November 1940 to control pressures for independence while overseeing training of Indian units for Allied use elsewhere.

Auchinleck was called by Winston L. S. Churchill to take the same role in the critical Middle East Theater (21 June 1941), replacing Archibald Wavell. While in Egypt, Auchinleck came under constant pressure from Churchill to undertake aggressive action against Lieutenant General Erwin Rommel's Afrika Korps. He argued, however, that he had to first train his force and overcome the difficulties of having inadequate supplies and armaments. Auchinleck began his offensive, Operation CRUSADER, on Libya in November 1941, but it suffered from the lack of a strong Eighth Army commander in Lieutenant General Alan Cunningham. Auchinleck replaced Cunningham with Major General Neil Ritchie, and for a time the offensive went well. But Rommel struck back, leading to the fall of Tobruk on 21 June 1942, when more than 30,000 men were taken prisoner.

Auchinleck then took direct control of the Eighth Army and stabilized his line at the First Battle of El Alamein later that month, thus saving Egypt. However, Churchill, still impatient for success from a more aggressive commander, relieved him of his command on 5 August 1942. Damning reports from Lieutenant General Bernard Montgomery about Auchinleck surely eased the skids.

Turning down a proffered command in Syria and Iraq, Auchinleck returned to India as commander in chief of the army there (18 June 1943–14 August 1947). Auchinleck was made a field marshal in June 1946, refusing a peerage a year later (he did not wish to be honored for helping to divide India and Pakistan, a result he abhorred). He retired in 1967 to live in Marrakesh, Morocco, and died there on 23 March 1981.

Christopher H. Sterling

See also
Cunningham, Sir Alan Gordon; Norway, German Conquest of; Ritchie, Sir Neil Methuen; Rommel, Erwin Johannes Eugen; Tobruk, Second Battle for, Third Battle of; Wavell, Sir Archibald Percival

References
Connell, John. *Auchinleck: A Biography of Sir Claude Auchinleck.* London: Cassell, 1959.
Greenwood, Alexander. *Field-Marshal Auchinleck.* Durham, UK: Pentland Press, 1991.
Parkinson, Roger. *The Auk: Auchinleck, Victor of Alamein.* London: Grenada, 1977.
Warner, Phillip. *Auchinleck: The Lonely Soldier.* London: Buchan and Enright, 1981.
———. "Auchinleck." In John Keegan, ed., *Churchill's Generals.* New York: Grove Weidenfeld, 1991.

Aung San, U (ca. 1915–1947)

Burmese Army general and nationalist leader. Born in Natmauk in the Magwe district of Myramir (Burma), U Aung San's date of birth is obscure but was possibly 13 February 1915. As a young man, Aung was active in student politics, and in 1936 he and U Nu led a student strike. Aung graduated in 1938 and became involved with the Dohbama Asiayone, a Burmese nationalist organization that sought to obtain independence from Britain. His activities aroused the suspicion of British authorities, who sought to arrest him in 1940.

Aung fled first to China and then to Tokyo, where he arranged with the Japanese to create a military force known as the Burmese Independence Army (BIA) to aid the Japanese in their impending invasion of Burma. During the actual battle, which began with the invasion on 14 December 1941 and continued into the next summer, Aung's BIA provided the Japanese with intelligence and logistical support. Aung received the rank of major general in the Japanese army.

Japanese forces overran Rangoon in March 1942. In August 1943 Japan gave Burma nominal independence, and Aung served in the new government as minister of defense. He soon became disillusioned with the Japanese military government, and in August 1944 he formed the Anti-Fascist League of Burma and secretly worked against the Japanese. On 27 March 1945, as Allied forces advanced into Burma, his army switched sides and joined the British.

Allied forces took Rangoon in June 1945. When the Japanese surrendered in August, Aung began negotiations with the British for Burmese independence, his true goal. This effort culminated in an agreement between British Prime Minister Clement Attlee and Aung San on 27 January 1947 that promised an independent Burma in one year. Facing Communist opposition, Aung's party won a large majority in the April 1947 elections.

On 19 July 1947, Aung was assassinated along with six other political leaders. U Saw, Aung's rival for power, was blamed for the assassination. Aung's daughter, Aung San Suu Kyi, later became a political figure in Burma.

Harold Wise

See also
Attlee, Clement Richard; Burma; China-Burma-India Theater
References
Allen, Louis. *Burma: The Longest War, 1941–1945.* New York: St. Martin's Press, 1984.

Auphan, Paul Gabriel (1894–1982)

French Navy admiral. Born on 4 November 1894 at Alès, Gard, France, Paul Auphan entered the French Naval Academy in 1911. He served in the World War I Dardanelles Campaign and in a submarine. Between the wars he commanded submarines, destroyers, a cruiser, and a naval school ship. He was deputy commander of the Naval Academy at Brest and studied at the Naval War College. He was promoted to rear admiral in March 1931. As a vice admiral in 1936, he commanded the French Mediterranean Squadron (1936–1938) before becoming maritime prefect at Toulon. Known for administrative rather than seagoing skills, in September 1939 Auphan, a protégé of Admiral Jean Darlan, French Navy commander in chief, became naval deputy chief of staff. The day before Franco-German armistice negotiations began in June 1940, Darlan and Auphan promised the British that they would never permit Hitler to control the French fleet, even if this meant scuttling it.

In July 1940 after the armistice, Auphan became director of the French merchant marine. In September 1941, he was named chief of the general naval staff, a position to which in April 1942 he added that of secretary of the navy in the Vichy government. Auphan's defenders later claimed he only accepted these posts to ensure the fleet's continued freedom from German control.

Both before and after the November 1942 Allied invasion of North Africa, Auphan and former French supreme commander General Maxime Weygand pressed Marshal Henri Pétain, head of the Vichy government, to support the Allies openly. After the Allied landings on 8 November 1942, Auphan and Weygand urged Pétain to accept the North African cease-fire with the Allies that Darlan, then in Algiers, had negotiated. At the insistence of collaborationist Vichy French Premier Pierre Laval, Pétain initially condemned Darlan's negotiated cease-fire, but Auphan persuaded Pétain to reverse this stand. On 10 November 1942, Auphan sent a telegram legitimizing Darlan's accord with U.S. Army Lieutenant General Mark W. Clark. Auphan hoped to arrest Laval, but he could not obtain Pétain's authorization and was the only minister to advocate a cease-fire agreement for all North Africa. On 11 November, Auphan ordered Admiral Jean de Laborde at Toulon to destroy the French fleet should German forces threaten the port. With Pétain's approval, on 13 November Auphan cabled Resident General Charles Noguès of Morocco to transfer to Darlan command of all North Africa. On 18 November, Auphan resigned to protest Laval's assumption of full governmental powers.

On 18 August 1944, Pétain empowered Auphan to negotiate the transfer of power to the Free French leader Charles de Gaulle, a development that de Gaulle completely ignored. In September 1944, the new French government revoked Auphan's pension, and in August 1946 the French High Court sentenced him to lifetime imprisonment and forced labor for treason, including for having commanded the Toulon fleet's destruction. Released in January 1955, Auphan was rehabilitated in November 1956. He subsequently published extensively in naval and political history. Auphan died at Versailles (Yvelines) on 6 April 1982.

Priscilla Roberts

See also
Clark, Mark Wayne; Darlan, Jean Louis Xavier François; de Gaulle, Charles; Laval, Pierre; Noguès, Charles August Paul; Pétain, Henri Phillippe; Toulon; Weygand, Maxime

References
Auphan, Paul. *Les Grimaces de l'histoire suivies de l'histoire de mes trahisons*. Paris: Les Iles d'Or, 1951.
———. *Histoire élémentaire de Vichy*. Paris: Éditions France-Empire, 1971.
———. *L'Honneur de servir: mémoires*. Paris: Éditions France-Empire, 1978.
Auphan, Paul, and Jacques Mordal. *The French Navy in World War II*. Trans. A. C. J. Short. Annapolis, MD: Naval Institute Press, 1959.
Paxton, Robert O. *Parades and Politics at Vichy: The French Officer Corps under Marshal Pétain*. Princeton, NJ: Princeton University Press, 1966.

Auschwitz

See Concentration Camps, German.

Australia, Air Force

The Royal Australian Air Force (RAAF) played an important role in the Allied war effort. At the beginning of the conflict, the RAAF was a small, ill-equipped, but well-trained force of 3,489 personnel and 146 mostly obsolete aircraft. These included Anson bombers, flying boats, and the Australian Wirraway, essentially a training aircraft that proved totally inadequate as a fighter. When the war began in September 1939, one squadron was en route to Great Britain to secure new aircraft. The Australian government released this squadron to serve with the Royal Air Force (RAF), which it did for the remainder of the war under the auspices of RAF Coastal Command. In this role, the Australian squadron was responsible for sinking six submarines. Other squadrons served under the RAF in the Middle East and in the Italian Campaigns. Although there were 17 formal RAAF squadrons during the war, Australian pilots served in more than 200 individual Commonwealth squadrons.

To facilitate air training, representatives of the Commonwealth established the Empire Air Training Scheme. This brought potential pilots to Australia for initial training and then sent them to Canada for final flight school and dispatch to Great Britain to serve in the RAF. The RAAF established several flight schools in Australia for a program that eventually trained some 37,000 pilots.

The initial deployment of RAAF assets was to support the war in Europe. The entry of Japan into World War II in December 1941 led to a redeployment of Australian squadrons to the Pacific. Japanese military advances and Japan's air raid on Darwin on 19 February 1942 increased pressure for better air defense over Australia. Beginning in 1942, U.S. air units were dispatched to Australia to bolster the RAAF. On 17 April 1942, all RAAF squadrons in the Pacific were placed under the auspices of Allied Air Forces Headquarters, part of U.S. General Douglas MacArthur's Southwestern Pacific Theater command.

The RAAF participated in almost every major campaign of the Pacific Theater. Four RAAF squadrons, two with Hudson bombers and two flying obsolete Brewster Buffalo fighters, fought in the 1941–1942 Malaya Campaign. Later, elements of these squadrons were withdrawn to the Netherlands Indies and finally back to Australia. Two other RAAF squadrons fought in the Netherlands Indies before being relocated to Australia. RAAF units distinguished themselves in the defense of Milne Bay in September 1942.

Early deficiencies in aircraft were overcome with the addition of P-40 Kittyhawk and Spitfire fighters. The RAAF played an important role in supporting ground operations and in attacking Japanese shipping, including during the Battle of the Bismarck Sea. It also assisted in long-range minelaying operations throughout the war. The RAAF also provided wireless units to its troops who participated in the invasion of the Philippines. By the end of the war, the RAAF numbered 131,662 personnel and 3,187 aircraft.

Thomas Lansford

See also
Air Warfare; Aircraft, Bombers; Aircraft, Fighters; Australia, Role in War; Bismarck Sea, Battle of the; Guadalcanal, Land Battle for; MacArthur, Douglas; Malaya Campaign; Milne Bay, Battle of; New Guinea Campaign; Papua Campaign

References
Firkins, P. *Strike and Return*. Perth, Australia: Westward Publishing, 1985.
Gillison, D. *Royal Australian Air Force, 1939–1942*. Canberra: Australian War Memorial, 1962.

Australia, Army

The Australian Army contributed to Allied successes in North Africa and the Middle East and in the Pacific Theater. During the 1930s, the army had been drastically reduced be-

A member of an Australian tank crew awaits the signal for further attack during fighting at Buna, 1943. (Library of Congress)

cause of financial pressures. The Australian government hoped that in an emergency, it could rely instead on reserve or territorial forces. However, by statute, these forces could not be deployed overseas. On the eve of World War II, the army did expand its reserve component and embark on a program of improving coastal defenses.

When Australia declared war on Germany on 3 September 1939, the army numbered 82,800 men, but this included 80,000 poorly trained volunteer militia. The regular army was basically a small cadre force of officers, noncommissioned officers, and support staff. After New Zealand offered to raise a division to serve with Commonwealth forces in the European Theater, the Australian government announced its intention to do the same, and later it pledged to raise a corps. Given the high casualties sustained by Australian forces in World War I, the government extended conscription only for home defense. This meant that forces would have to be recruited for service abroad. The army grew to four divisions—the 6th, 7th, 8th, and 9th—that were formed into the Second Aus-

tralian Imperial Force (the first having served in World War I). The Imperial Staff decided to send this force to the Middle East for training prior to deployment in France. The first of the Second Australian Imperial Force, the 6th Division, departed Australia in January 1940. Some of the division, which became the nucleus of the 9th Division, went to Britain. In effect, Australia then fielded two separate armies: one in the Middle East and the other for the defense of Australia and its mandate of New Guinea.

With the fall of France in June 1940, the 6th, 7th, and 9th Divisions made up a corps in the Middle East under the command of Lieutenant General Sir Thomas A. Blamey. Recalled to Australia in March 1942, Blamey became both commander of the Australian army and commander of land forces, Southwest Pacific Area.

In North Africa, Australian forces took part in the early victories against Italian forces there. Part of the 6th Division was detached to join the British Expeditionary Force, which had been dispatched to Greece, and it was caught up in the defeats both in Greece and in Crete during the spring of

1941. The 7th Division fought in Syria, and the 9th Division helped defend Tobruk.

Amid increased anxieties about Japanese intentions, additional Australian troops were dispatched to bolster Commonwealth garrisons throughout the Pacific. In August 1941, two brigades of the 8th Division and two squadrons of Royal Australian Air Force aircraft had been sent to reinforce Singapore, where the men were then taken prisoner. With the entry of Japan into the war in December 1941, the Australian government secured the release of two of its divisions from the Middle East. A third division remained there and played a key role in the Allied victory at the Battle of El Alamein in November 1942, after which it, too, returned to the Pacific. In March 1942, much of the 7th Division was redeployed to Columbo. Part of the 7th was also sent to Java in the Netherlands East Indies, where it was captured by Japanese forces. Land forces in Australia itself consisted of an armored division with but few tanks and seven militia divisions. Australia appealed to the United States for military aid, and it also passed legislation that allowed reserve units to be deployed anywhere in the Pacific south of the equator.

In March 1942, the Southwest Pacific Command was formed under General Douglas MacArthur but with General Blamey as commander of land forces. The agreement gave MacArthur complete control of the Australian army, a fact that rankled many Australian officers and politicians—especially as the imperious MacArthur often excluded Australian officers from planning, gave the Australians little credit for their contributions, and generally viewed Australia as a base for American operations. Blamey and MacArthur often disagreed over strategy and over MacArthur's belief that the Australian general was too cautious. MacArthur's forces initially consisted of the seven militia divisions, the 6th and 7th Australian Divisions, and the U.S. 41st Infantry Division in April 1942, followed by the 32nd Infantry Division and other units.

Meanwhile, the main thrust of the Australian land effort centered on the defense of Port Moresby and on a domestic buildup to counter a possible Japanese invasion. From July 1942 to January 1943, the Australians and Americans were locked in combat with the Japanese in Papua and New Guinea. In late August 1942, Japanese forces landed at Milne Bay at the eastern edge of Papua. Australian forces, not greatly superior to the Japanese, contained the landing and forced the Japanese to withdraw. This event, a great psychological lift for the Allies and humiliation for the Japanese, proved that the Allies could defeat the Japanese in jungle warfare.

Although Australia faced significant manpower shortages, its troops continued to support Allied operations in New Guinea, Papua, and Guadalcanal. The Australians were given the task of clearing the Japanese from New Guinea. Australian forces also took part in operations on New Britain and in Borneo in 1945. The Australian army launched its largest amphibious invasion of the war on 1 July 1945 when troops landed at Balikpapan as part of the effort to recapture Brunei. During the war, 691,400 men and 35,800 women served in the Australian army, which suffered (including prisoners of war recovered) 19,351 casualties in the war in Europe and 42,224 in the war in the Pacific. For the two theaters combined, total casualties were 18,713 dead, 22,116 wounded, and 20,746 prisoners of war recovered.

Thomas Lansford and Spencer C. Tucker

See also

Australia, Air Force; Australia, Navy; Australia, Role in War; Blamey, Sir Thomas Albert; Crete, Battle of; El Alamein, Battle of; Guadalcanal, Land Battle of; MacArthur, Douglas; Milne Bay, Battle of; New Britain Island; Solomon Islands, Naval Campaign; Southeast Pacific Theater; Southwest Pacific Theater; Syria; Tobruk, First Battle for, Second Battle for, Third Battle of

References

Day, David. *The Great Betrayal: Britain, Australia and the Onset of the Pacific War, 1939–42.* New York: W. W. Norton, 1989.
———. *Reluctant Nation: Australia and the Allied Defeat of Japan, 1942–45.* New York: Oxford University Press, 1992.
Robertson, John, and John McCarthy. *Australian War Strategy, 1939–1945: A Documentary History.* Brisbane, Australia: University of Queensland Press, 1985.
Thompson, Robert Smith. *Empires on the Pacific: World War II and the Struggle for the Mastery of Asia.* New York: Basic Books, 2001.

Australia, Navy

The Royal Australian Navy (RAN) played an integral part in the Allied war effort in both the Mediterranean and Pacific Theaters. At the beginning of World War II in September 1939, the RAN had declined in strength to two heavy cruisers (the *Australia* and the *Canberra*) mounting 8-inch guns, four light cruisers (the *Adelaide*, the *Hobart*, the *Perth*, and the *Sydney*) mounting 6-inch guns, five old destroyers, and two sloops. Its primary missions were coastal defense and protection of trade.

When the war began, the Australian government immediately started work to build up naval strength. In all, the RAN requisitioned 200 civilian vessels for military use, mainly for coastal defense, transport, and search and rescue missions. Several small vessels were also converted into minesweepers. The government also ordered construction of several warships, including 3 destroyers, 6 frigates, 56 corvettes, and 35 motor launches. By the end of the war, the RAN had 337 vessels in service (and an additional 600 in the naval auxiliary) with 39,650 personnel.

At the beginning of the war, the Australian government sent its five destroyers into the Mediterranean to assist the British there. The *Perth* went to the East Indian station, and the *Australia* and the *Canberra* helped escort Australian troop convoys to Egypt. The RAN also converted three liners into armed merchant cruisers for Royal Navy use, two of them manned by Australian personnel. Two others were commissioned in the RAN. All were sent to the China station. After Italy entered the war, the Australian government sent the *Sydney* to the Mediterranean, where she sank an Italian destroyer and helped to sink an Italian cruiser. In December 1940, the *Sydney* was replaced in the Mediterranean by the *Perth*. Other naval units were also sent, and Australian ships took part in all the big Mediterranean battles, including that in Cape Matapan. Australian ships also participated in the hunt for the German battleship *Bismarck* and performed Atlantic convoy duty. Some 10 percent of the Royal Navy's total antisubmarine ships were from the RAN. Later in the war, eight RAN ships supported the Allied invasion of Sicily in July 1943.

The first real blow to the RAN came in November 1941 when the *Sydney* was sunk off Western Australia by a German armed merchant cruiser. After Japan entered the war in December 1941, nearly all Australian ships were withdrawn to the Pacific Theater either to Singapore or to Australia. The cruiser *Perth* was sunk in the Battle of Sunda Strait in February 1942. The Japanese air raid on Darwin, also in February, and the midget submarine attack in May on Sydney Harbor underscored the need for increased naval strength. By the end of 1942, the Japanese had sunk 30 ships in Australian waters through air, naval, or submarine attack.

For the rest of the war, RAN ships in the Pacific undertook several duties. They engaged in antisubmarine and convoy protection missions and were credited with sinking six Axis submarines and escorting some 1,100 convoys. The RAN also laid some 10,000 defensive mines around Australia and New Zealand and engaged in minesweeping operations throughout the Pacific. RAN ships also fought in the major battles of the theater, including the Battle of the Coral Sea, the Solomon Island Campaign (the cruiser *Canberra* was sunk in the Battle of Savo Island), and the Battle of Leyte Gulf. They also supported operations in Borneo and Burma and the Australian landings at Taraken, Brunei, and Balikpapan in 1945. In all, 45,800 men and 3,100 women served in the Royal Australian Navy during the war.

Thomas Lansford and Spencer C. Tucker

See also

Antisubmarine Warfare; Australia, Role in War; Cape Matapan, Battle of; Convoys, Allied; Crete, Naval Operations off; Darwin, Raid on; Great Britain, Navy; Guadalcanal Naval Campaign; Leyte Gulf, Battle of; Milne Bay; Mines, Sea; Minesweeping and Minelaying; Naval Strengths, Pacific Theater; Savo Island, Battle of; Solomon Islands, Naval Campaign; Sunda Strait, Battle of

References

Day, David. *The Great Betrayal: Britain, Australia and the Onset of the Pacific War, 1939–42.* New York: W. W. Norton, 1989.

———. *Reluctant Nation: Australia and the Allied Defeat of Japan, 1942–45.* New York: Oxford University Press, 1992.

Lockwood, Douglas. *Australia's Pearl Harbour: Darwin, 1942.* Melbourne, Australia: Cassell, 1966.

Thompson, Robert Smith. *Empires on the Pacific: World War II and the Struggle for the Mastery of Asia.* New York: Basic Books, 2001.

Winton, John. *The Forgotten Fleet: The British Navy in the Pacific, 1944–1945.* New York: Coward-McCann, 1969.

Australia, Role in War

Australia played an important role in Allied operations in all theaters of World War II. Although its population was only about 7 million people, Australia covered 3 million square miles of territory and was strategically located in the Southwest Pacific. The war, however, caught Australians unprepared. As with the other Commonwealth nations, Australia followed Britain's lead, and Prime Minister Robert Menzies announced a declaration of war on Germany on 3 September 1939.

The exuberance that had marked the nation's entry into war in 1914 was sadly lacking in 1939. Australians remembered the heavy losses sustained in World War I. Many had suffered in the Great Depression, and ties with Britain had grown weaker. Initially, the nation's war effort was directed at supporting Britain in the European Theater of Operations, but after Japan's entry into the war, Australia became the principal Allied staging point in the Pacific, and during the conflict Australians served in virtually every theater of war.

With 10 percent of its population unemployed, Australia could easily raise men for the war effort, but weapons and equipment were in desperately short supply. In 1939, Australian defense spending was only 1 percent of its gross national product (GNP); not until 1942 did the level of Australian defense spending approach that of the other warring powers. In 1943–1944, Australia was spending 37 percent of GNP on the war effort, in large part from higher taxes and the sale of low-interest government bonds.

During the course of the war, the Australian economy shifted over to military production, and real industrial expansion was achieved. For example, during the war Australia produced 3,486 aircraft. Although new defense spending was concentrated on production of equipment including guns, ammunition, aircraft, and ships, measures were also put in place to increase the reserves. The government introduced conscription, but only for home service, which included assignments to Papua and the mandate of New Guinea. As part of the mobilization for war, industrialist Essington Lewis was placed in charge of the production of munitions, and newspaper publisher Keith Murdoch headed propaganda.

In October 1941, the Labour Party took power; John Curtin was prime minister until his death in July 1945. Labour would govern Australia for the remainder of the war. The generally ambivalent popular attitude toward the war changed when Japan joined the conflict in December 1941. The widespread rapid early Japanese victories raised the possibility that Australia itself might be invaded. This led to more government controls over the economy, including the right for the government to order men and women to work in any occupation. Wages and prices were controlled, and rationing was introduced. The government also increased efforts at civilian defense and the improvement of coastal defenses. An even greater blow for Australians was the February 1942 fall of Singapore and the loss of two brigades of the Australian 8th Division there. The Japanese raid on Darwin later that month—the first time since the arrival of Europeans in Australia that Australians had been killed on their own soil by an invader—caused great anxiety.

Curtin then called for the return of Australian troops and naval assets from the Mediterranean Theater. Gradually most of these forces were released, but British Prime Minister Winston L. S. Churchill was loathe to see so many fine fighting men lost at once from the North African Theater, and he called on Washington to take up the slack. The United States then became Australia's chief ally. Many thousands of U.S. servicemen arrived in Australia (eventually some 10,000 Australian women married U.S. military personnel). This influx required construction of bases and facilities, creating an acute labor shortage and necessitating the discharge of some personnel from the Australia armed forces. Italian prisoners of war were also pressed into labor service.

The labor shortage was also the result of the extensive Australian armaments program, which included an indigenous tank—the excellent medium cruiser Sentinel—that entered production in 1943, and a large shipbuilding program that produced three destroyers and 56 corvettes in addition to some 30,000 small craft and amphibious vehicles. Australian shipyards also repaired or refitted thousands of Australian and Allied ships. To alleviate labor shortages, women's auxiliary units were created for each branch of the military, and large numbers of women went to work in industrial occupations.

In March 1942, the Australian government agreed to the formation of the Southwest Pacific Command with American General Douglas MacArthur as commander in chief and General Sir Thomas Blamey as the commander of land forces. Australia became the principal logistics base for Allied military actions, particularly in the campaigns in New Guinea and the Solomon Islands. The Australian conscripts proved an embarrassment for the government; under pressure from MacArthur, who believed Americans were doing an unfair share of the fighting, the Curtin government secured in February 1943 what became known as the Militia Bill. It permitted deployment of conscripts overseas, although this was to be limited to the Southwest Pacific Area. In August 1943, the Australian Labour Party scored a resounding election victory.

Tensions developed (largely behind the scenes) between MacArthur and the Australian government and armed forces, especially given MacArthur's tendency to take credit himself for any successes and blame others for anything that went wrong. His disparaging attitude toward Australians notwithstanding, Australians distinguished themselves in every theater of war, including North Africa and the Mediterranean and also with the Royal Australian Air Force in Bomber Command. Australian troops scored important successes on the ground in New Guinea and Papua, and they also helped garrison Allied island conquests. In 1945, Australian troops led the invasions of Borneo and Tarakan. They were also in garrison on New Britain Island. The July 1945 invasion of Balikpapan was marked the largest amphibious operation undertaken by Australian forces during the war.

By the end of the fighting, 993,000 Australian men and women had served in the army, air force, and navy, and more than half of them had been deployed overseas. In addition, the nation had suffered 27,073 military dead (including prisoners of war who died in captivity) and 23,467 wounded.

World War II had a profound effect on the Australian nation. During the conflict, Australia established formal diplomatic ties with many more nations, and after the conflict it took pride in its place as a principal Pacific power. The war also enhanced Australian relations with the United States at the expense of existing ties with Great Britain.

Thomas Lansford and Spencer C. Tucker

See also

Australia, Air Force; Australia, Army; Australia, Navy; Blamey, Sir Thomas Albert; Churchill, Sir Winston L. S.; Convoys, Allied; Crete, Battle of; Darwin, Raid on; El Alamein, Battle of; Guadalcanal, Land Battle for; Guadalcanal Naval Campaign; MacArthur, Douglas; Milne Bay, Battle of; New Britain Island; Savo Island, Battle of; Solomon Islands, Naval Campaign; Southeastern Pacific Theater; Southwestern Pacific Theater; Tobruk, First Battle for, Second Battle for, Third Battle of

References

Day, David. *The Great Betrayal: Britain, Australia and the Onset of the Pacific War, 1939–42.* New York: W. W. Norton, 1989.

———. *Reluctant Nation: Australia and the Allied Defeat of Japan, 1942–45.* New York: Oxford University Press, 1992.

Potts, E. Daniel, and Annette Potts. *Yanks Down Under 1941–45: The American Impact on Australia.* New York: Oxford University Press, 1985.

Robertson, John, and John McCarthy. *Australian War Strategy, 1939–1945: A Documentary History.* Brisbane, Australia: University of Queensland Press, 1985.

Thompson, Robert Smith. *Empires on the Pacific: World War II and the Struggle for the Mastery of Asia.* New York: Basic Books, 2001.

Austria

Austria emerged from World War I diminished and impoverished, a shadow of its former self. Once the anchor of the great multinational Hapsburg Empire, the Federal Republic of Austria became a small (32,500-square-mile) state with an overwhelmingly German population of some 7 million people in 1938. Forbidden by the 1919 Treaty of Saint Germain to unite with Germany, Austria was nonetheless drawn inexorably toward its aggressive neighbor. After years of political upheaval and economic hardship, Austrians could not shake the impossible urge to pursue contradictory courses: to foster self-determination and Austrian nationalism and to pursue *Anschluss,* union with Germany (despite the treaty prohibition).

Adolf Hitler's accession to power in 1933 put great pressure on Austria's social, political, and economic stability. Hitler was determined to bring the land of his birth into a greater German Reich. He undoubtedly realized that the annexation of Austria would have international repercussions, and thus he worked to achieve the annexation indirectly. Because the Austrian Nazis took their orders from Hitler, a political victory by that party in Austria would bring about the de facto union of the two states. To achieve this end, Hitler's government began spending considerable sums on propaganda in Austria, including leaflets and radio broadcasts from stations in Bavaria. Berlin also applied major economic pressure, cutting off German tourism (an important source of revenue in Austria) by imposing severe limits on the amount of currency that might be taken out of Germany to that state. Meanwhile, the worldwide economic depression hit the Austrian economy hard.

With armed groups forming in Austria and the threat looming of civil war between the militias of the Christian Socialists and the Social Democrats, Chancellor Engelbert Dollfuss, himself a nominal Christian Socialist, on 12 February 1934 moved against the Social Democrats, outlawing the party, arresting its leaders, and proclaiming martial law. In March the Austrian Parliament—without opportunity to debate and with more than half its members, including Social Democrats, absent—approved a new constitution submitted to it by Dollfuss. It established an authoritarian corporate state that abolished both universal suffrage and political representation of the people.

On 25 July 1934, a small group of Austrian Nazis seized the government radio station and announced that the government had fallen. Another group seized the chancellery, mortally wounding Dollfuss, who had refused to flee, and holding other cabinet ministers captive. The plot was poorly organized, however, and soon collapsed. Within a few days, the Austrian government had put it down without outside assistance, and on 29 July a new cabinet was formed under Kurt Schuschnigg, a Christian Socialist colleague of Dollfuss. A dozen leaders of the putsch were eventually executed, and hundreds more were sentenced to prison.

The events in Austria had repercussions abroad. Italian dictator Benito Mussolini, who considered Austria under his sway, ordered troops to the Brenner Pass. Hitler had initially expressed pleasure at the putsch, but when news arrived of its failure he washed his hands of it. There was in fact little he could have done, as Germany—still largely unarmed—was in no position to oppose Italy. Hitler expressed regret at the Dollfuss murder, recalled his ambassador (who had promised the putschists asylum), and assured the world that Germany had no role in the failed coup. The attempted Nazi takeover of Austria was clearly a setback for Hitler. Nevertheless, the coup attempt had made emphatically clear Austria's dependence on outside support for the maintenance of its independence.

Schuschnigg attempted to continue the Dollfuss agenda, especially the cultivation of relationships with Italy and Hungary. He also endeavored to improve relations with Hitler, but at the same time he contemplated the restoration of the Austrian ruling house of the Hapsburgs, which Hitler vehemently opposed. By 1938, the international situation had dramatically changed for Austria, as Mussolini had become a confederate of Hitler in the Axis alliance. In consequence Schuschnigg, while he pursued an alliance with Czechoslovakia, had little choice but to mend fences with Hitler. On 12 February 1938, he traveled to Berchtesgaden at Hitler's insistence to meet with the German leader. Under heavy pressure, Schuschnigg agreed to appoint Austrian Nazi Arthur Seyss-Inquart as minister of the interior and other Austrian Nazis as ministers of justice and foreign affairs.

On 9 March, however, in an attempt to maintain his nation's independence, Schuschnigg announced a plebiscite on the issue of *Anschluss* to be held in only four days, hoping that the short interval would not allow the Nazis to

Nazi banner with swastika being hung in the plaza in front of the Schloss Esterházy in Eisenstadt, Austria. (Library of Congress)

The consummation of *Anschluss* greatly strengthened Germany's position in Central Europe. Germany was now in direct contact with Italy, Yugoslavia, and Hungary, and it controlled virtually all of the communications of southeastern Europe. Czechoslovakia was almost isolated, and its trade outlets were at the mercy of Germany. Militarily, Germany outflanked the powerful western Czech defenses. It was thus not surprising that, despite Hitler's pledges to respect the territorial integrity of Czechoslovakia, he should next seek to bring that state under his control.

The Austrian army was soon absorbed into the Wehrmacht and the Waffen-Schutzstaffel (Waffen-SS). Austria eventually contributed three army corps and additional military assets (a total of some 800,000 military personnel) to the Axis effort, and the country suffered roughly 400,000 military and civilian casualties during the war.

A great many Austrians enthusiastically supported the Nazi cause. Although Austrians comprised but 6 percent of the population of Hitler's Reich, they furnished 14 percent of SS members and 40 percent of those involved in the Nazi extermination efforts. Anti-Semitism was rife in Austria, and actions against the Jews (who had been prominent in the professions in Vienna, in particular) were applauded by a significant sector of the population, unlike in Berlin.

Austrians who had welcomed the incorporation of their country into the Reich soon discovered to their dismay that German interests dominated much of Austria's economy and that the inhabitants of the Ostmark (as Austria was now known, its medieval name having been revived) were often treated more as a conquered people subject to intense scrutiny and discrimination. This says nothing of the experiences endured by minorities and Jews who came in for special, and horrific, treatment.

Resistance groups formed around the old political factions—socialists, monarchists, nationalists—and soon developed contact with the Allies. In-country resistance and the work of Austrians abroad limited the extent to which Austria remained identified with Nazi Germany. In the 1943 Moscow Declaration, the Allies recognized Austria as the first victim of Hitler's aggression, a view that Austrian politicians did their utmost after the war to nurture.

Austria experienced air attacks beginning in 1943, and the attacks escalated as the Allies moved eastward in 1944. When Germany's military situation crumbled in the spring of 1945, Allied armies converged on Austria. The Red Army entered Austria at the end of March and liberated Vienna in mid-April. At the end of April, a provisional government established under Soviet direction nullified the *Anschluss*. The Allied powers—the Soviet Union, the United States, Britain, and France—each set up occupation zones in Austria and pursued their own interests in the icy atmosphere that fol-

mobilize effectively. Hitler was determined that no plebiscite be held, and on 11 March Seyss-Inquart presented Schuschnigg with an ultimatum, demanding his resignation and postponement of the vote under threat of invasion by German troops, which were already mobilized on the border. Schuschnigg gave in, canceling the plebiscite and resigning. Seyss-Inquart then took power and invited in the German troops (which had actually already crossed the frontier) "to preserve order."

Had it been ordered to fight, the small Austrian army might have given a good account of itself. Germany would have won, of course, but its military was hardly ready for war and a battle might have dispelled some rampant myths about the German military. Indeed, hundreds of German tanks and vehicles of the German Eighth Army broke down on the drive toward Vienna.

On 12 March, Hitler returned to his boyhood home of Linz, Austria, and on the next day Berlin declared Austria to be part of the Reich. On 14 March, perhaps a million Austrians gave Hitler an enthusiastic welcome to Vienna. France and Britain lodged formal protests with Berlin, but that was the extent of their reaction.

lowed Germany's surrender. In October 1945, the Allies formally recognized Austria's provisional government. The Allied military occupation of Austria did not end until the Treaty of Belvedere in 1955.

Jessica Woyan, David Coffey, and Spencer C. Tucker

See also

Croatia; Czechoslovakia; Hungary, Role in War; Moscow Conference; Origins of the War; Poland, Role in War; Schuschnigg, Kurt von; Seyss-Inquart, Arthur; Yugoslavia

References

Bukey, Evan Burr. *Hitler's Austria: Popular Sentiment in the Nazi Era, 1938–1945.* Chapel Hill: University of North Carolina Press, 2000.

Keyserling, Robert H. *Austria in World War II: An Anglo-American Dilemma.* Toronto: McGill-Queens University Press, 1988.

Maass, Walter B. *Assassination in Vienna.* New York: Charles Scribner's Sons, 1972.

Automedon, Sinking of (11 November 1940)

The *Automedon* was a British Blue Funnel cargo ship of 7,528 tons that was sailing from Liverpool to Singapore. Intercepted by the German commerce raider *Atlantis* in the Indian Ocean on 11 November 1940, she was boarded, searched, and then scuttled. In the ship, the Germans discovered a copy of the British War Cabinet minutes for August 1940, which was being conveyed to Singapore. This 87-paragraph document outlined British strategy in the Far East.

The most important part of the document, COS(40)592, was addressed to the British commander in chief in the Far East, Air Marshal Robert Brooke-Popham. It indicated that Britain would not go to war against Japan, even if the Japanese were to invade French Indochina. The document also stated that the British Chiefs of Staff regarded both Thailand and Hong Kong as indefensible against Japanese attack.

Bernhard Rogge, the captain of the *Atlantis,* recognized the significance of these papers and sent them on by ship to Kobe. They were then delivered to German naval attaché in Tokyo Rear Admiral Paul Wenneker, who forwarded them to Berlin. There Adolf Hitler ordered the information passed to the Japanese, and Japanese naval attaché Captain Yokoi Tadao sent a summary of the documents to the Navy Ministry in Tokyo.

On 12 December 1940, Wenneker handed the documents to Vice Admiral Kondō Nobutake, the Japanese navy vice chief of staff. Wenneker also stressed the weak British military posture in Asia and conveyed to Kondō Hitler's suggestion that the Japanese attack Singapore.

There is no doubt that these documents encouraged the Japanese leadership in its decision to advance into Southeast Asia in 1941. They convinced the Japanese naval minister, Admiral Oikawa Koshiro, that Britain would not wage war with Japan over French Indochina.

Kotani Ken

See also

Brooke-Popham, Sir Henry Robert Moore; Commerce Raiders, Surface, German; Hong Kong, Battle of; Kondō Nobutake; Oikawa Koshiro; Pearl Harbor, Attack on; Singapore, Battle for; Yamamoto Isoroku

References

CAB 66/10, Public Record Office, Kew, UK.

Chapman, J. W. M. "Japanese Intelligence 1918–1945." In C. Andrew and J. Noakes, eds., *Intelligence and International Relations 1900–1945.* Exeter, UK: Exeter University Press, 1987.

Elphick, Peter. *Far Eastern File.* London: Hodder and Stoughton, 1997.

Rusbridger, James. "The Sinking of the *Automedon* and the Capture of the *Nankin.*" *Encounter* 375, no. 5 (May 1985): 8–14.

Auxiliary Territorial Services

See Great Britain, Auxiliary Territorial Services.

Auxiliary Vessels

The scope of World War II required huge numbers of auxiliary vessels for combat and support duties. In addition to the construction and conversion of specialist vessels, large numbers of civilian ships were requisitioned. The greatest demand was for coastal patrol, mine warfare, and antisubmarine vessels. Less frequently demanded, although no less important, were aviation ships, hospital ships, harbor craft, floating antiaircraft batteries, and the indispensable support vessel types of the fleet train.

Coastal Patrol Craft, Auxiliary Minesweepers, and Submarine Chasers

As in World War I, fishing fleets provided a cheap and reliable source of vessels and crews for the navies. Fishing vessels were versatile, and with modification they could usually perform patrol, minesweeping, and antisubmarine escort tasks. So successful was the concept of using fishing fleets that the Royal Navy alone ordered the construction of 240 naval trawlers in addition to the nearly 1,000 that it requisitioned during the war.

As the sea frontier of its occupied territories increased throughout the war, Germany too compensated for the

German submarine tender, at Saar, 1937. (Dirk Steffen)

shortfall of purpose-built craft by converting hundreds of national and captured foreign fishing vessels, pilot boats, yachts, harbor craft, and even landing craft into patrollers, auxiliary minesweepers, dispatch vessels, escort vessels, submarine chasers, artillery support ships, and the like. The German navy also built large numbers of commercial-type trawlers, which became known as KFKs (*Kriegsfischkutter*), specifically for military purposes. Finally, the Germans revived the concept of the barrage breaker (*Sperrbrecher*) to counter the growing mine threat against the U-boat bases. Sperrbrechers were medium-sized merchant ships employed for tactical underway mine protection of high-value units. The ships were equipped with bow protection gear and strong magnetic influence gear. Any mine not so swept, such as pressure mines, would ultimately be actuated by the ship itself. To absorb the blast, the ships' holds were lined with sandbags and filled with empty drums or timber to provide additional buoyancy.

Auxiliary Aviation Ships

The increasing demand for aircraft in naval warfare outpaced the capability of many belligerents to respond with new construction of adequate aircraft carriers. Many navies thus relied on seaplane tenders as ersatz carriers. The ma-

jority of those vessels in turn had been converted from civilian vessels or requisitioned from civilian aircraft operators. The Royal Navy in particular had to improvise because of the shortage of escort aircraft carriers (which it introduced in 1941). The Battle of the Atlantic thus witnessed the development of two new types of allied auxiliary aviation vessels: the catapult merchant ship (CAM) and the merchant aircraft carrier (MAC). The former represented a desperate stopgap measure designed to combat the German long-range patrol aircraft, which served as spotters for groups of U-boats and as attack aircraft. CAMs were merchantmen fitted with a single catapult over their forecastle from which a fighter (usually a Hawker Hurricane) could be launched. At the end of the mission, the aircraft was ditched and the pilot had to parachute into the water to be retrieved by a rescue vessel. The concept was superseded by the MACs. These too were regular merchantmen; however, their superstructure and masts had been razed to the weather deck to make way for a flight deck suitable for launching and receiving a small number of aircraft.

The Fleet Train

The vast and highly specialized navies of World War II required an extraordinary amount of support to function and maintain their operational readiness. The fleet train catered to those needs by providing an array of ship types ranging from replenishment ships (tankers and stores ships), tenders, and repair and depot ships to crew-accommodation vessels. Lesser navies, including the German navy, expanded their small prewar core of dedicated support ships by requisitioning merchantmen and converting them into the required support roles. The Germans only used their tankers for underway replenishment of their surface raiders, if in a rather novel fashion as one-stop support ships. The repair and depot ships remained confined to a role of floating base facilities.

Only the U.S. Navy disposed a sophisticated purpose-built fleet train that could deploy to distant waters with the entire fleet. Lacking such, the Royal Navy in 1945 had to rely on the U.S. fleet train. The Japanese navy, although it had a few fleet oilers, never developed a full fleet train team and advanced base force with floating docks, repair ships, and such. The U.S. Navy had designed its fleet train precisely for these operations in order to make up for the interwar limitations on base construction in the Western Pacific. The 13,000-ton Vulcan-class repair ships, for instance, could cope with most emergencies except heavy battle damage. For major repairs, the U.S. Navy commissioned no fewer than 30 forward-area floating docks, including three battleship docks. Since the tankers and stores ships were expected to accompany the fleet even beyond the forward-area bases, underway replenishment capabilities became an integral part of U.S. support ship design. The demand for forward underway replenishment, often at high speeds, ultimately resulted in the development by the U.S. Navy of fast one-stop replenishment ships that could supply consumables, such as oil, aviation fuel, water, ammunition, and stores at once and under way.

Dirk Steffen

See also
Aircraft Carriers; Logistics, Allied; Naval Warfare

References
Gardiner, Robert, ed. *Conway's All the World's Fighting Ships 1922–1946.* London: Conway Maritime Press, 1980.
———. *Conway's History of the Ship: The Eclipse of the Big Gun.* London: Conway Maritime Press, 1992.
Morison, Samuel Eliot. *History of U.S. Naval Operations in World War II.* 15 vols. Boston: Little, Brown, 1947–1962.

AVALANCHE, Operation

See Salerno Invasion.

AVG (American Volunteer Group)

See Flying Tigers.

Aviation, Ground-Attack

Ground-attack aviation is the dedicated use of combat aircraft to attack ground combat units and their supporting echelons on or near the front lines to support friendly ground forces. By the end of World War I, the practice of supporting infantry ground attack with aircraft was gaining acceptance. Air attacks increasingly were employed both in immediate support of ground operations at the front but also upon rear-echelon enemy units.

During the interwar period, military theory and doctrine bifurcated, and two distinct schools of thought developed about the proper use of air power. One school, following the precepts of Italian theorist Guilio Douhet, advocated concentration on strategic bombing by heavy, self-defending "battle planes" on targets far behind the battle lines, with the intent of collapsing an enemy nation's will to continue the fight. Most British and U.S. air power advocates supported this concept.

The second school of thought, generally adhered to by the Soviet Union, France, and Germany, advocated air power in direct support to ground maneuver operations. In this vision of air power, aircraft primarily attacked targets on the front lines or behind the front, which might extend as much as 150 miles. These theorists saw air forces as working in direct support of ground forces, enabling the latter to move farther in the attack or to yield less terrain in the defense.

Each school drove aircraft design in particular directions. Thus, the United States and Great Britain came up with four-engine "strategic" bombers such as the American Boeing B-17 Flying Fortress (Douhet's self-defending "battle plane") and the British Avro Lancaster. The Germans, however, concentrated on fast fighters such as the Me-109 to secure air superiority over the battlefield for fast medium-sized dual-engine bombers such as the Heinkel He-111 and the Dornier Do-17. The Germans, having learned from U.S. Marine Corps operations, also embraced dive-bombing, developing their important single-engine Junkers Ju-87 Stuka, which could deliver its ordnance with great accuracy and proved vital during the war's early campaigns. The Luftwaffe was essentially intended for close air support, geared to ground operations.

The multiple German blitzkriegs against Poland (1939), Norway (1940), and France (1940) demonstrated the great importance of the ground-attack school of thought. Luftwaffe units, working in close coordination with advancing columns of German infantry and armor, were a key element in allowing those columns to cut through opposing forces with seeming ease. We now know that German air-to-ground coordination was far from perfect and that several German troops became casualties of friendly fire.

First with the British in fighting in eastern North Africa and then with the Americans in French North Africa, the western Allies developed their own system of close air support. Almost immediately, the Americans discovered that their own system of command and control for ground-attack operations, developed before the war, was inefficient and could not keep pace with rapidly shifting operations on the ground. Capitalizing on their great strength of being able to adapt to changed circumstances, the Americans jettisoned their own doctrine nearly wholesale and adopted a modified version of the British system. Thereafter their efficiency in ground-attack operations increased markedly.

At the same time, the Soviet air force, which had suffered heavily in the German invasion of the Soviet Union beginning in June 1941, perfected its own system of ground support aviation. The USSR developed some highly successful ground-attack fighters and fighter-bombers in the Yakovlev Yak-4 and especially the Ilyushin Il-2 Sturmovik. Flying low and employing rockets, Sturmoviks were efficient tank killers. Sturmoviks, purpose-built for the ground-attack role, were heavily armored at crucial points to protect against German antiaircraft fire. The Il-2 was perhaps the best ground-attack aircraft of the war. In testimony to its success, the Sturmovik remained in production until 1955; the Soviets produced some 36,000 of them.

Simultaneously, the western Allies began to specialize—in use if not in design—their own aircraft. Both Great Britain and the United States entered the war with credible, if not outstanding, medium bombers such as the North American B-25 Mitchell and the British Bristol Blenheim. The British added other aircraft, including the versatile De Havilland Mosquito, while the Americans produced excellent fighters in the ground-attack role, such as the Vought F4U Corsair, the twin-engine Lockheed P-38 Lightning, the Republic P-47 Thunderbolt, and the North American P-51 Mustang. The P-38, P-47, and P-51 were originally designed as bomber escorts or classic conventional pursuit planes (hence the *P* in the nomenclature). The P-51 Mustang, a superb aircraft, may have been the best all-around fighter of the war, but the P-38 and P-47 each had characteristics that made them more suited to lower-level work and the rigors of close air support. For the Thunderbolt, it was the fact that the aircraft could absorb significant damage and continue flying. Its air-cooled engine was less susceptible to failure from damage than was the Mustang engine, and ground-attack work generally meant taking ground fire while flying at low altitude. The Lightning had twin engines on twin booms with a pod for the pilot slung between them, and it combined decent range with the heavy punch of five .50 caliber machine guns that fired straight ahead from the central pod. (The guns of most conventional aircraft were aimed inward to a single point.) This gave it lethal accuracy; the dual air-cooled engines gave the pilot a decent chance to make it home, even if one engine was shut down. On the British side was the Hawker Typhoon, an underappreciated contender for the title of best ground-attack aircraft of the war.

The air-ground team for the western Allies in the European Theater of Operations truly came into its own in the summer of 1944 during the Allied push across France. The penultimate display of this was the complete linkage between Lieutenant General George S. Patton's Third Army, the widest-ranging and fastest-moving element of the Allied sweep across France, and Major General Elwood "Pete" Queseda's IX Tactical Fighter Command. Patton, with no forces to spare to cover his right flank, committed the security of that increasingly open and vulnerable edge wholly to the air units under Queseda's command.

Ground-attack aviation was also important in the Pacific Theater, although it was perhaps marginally less effective in jungle terrain. U.S. air power proved vital in the struggle for Guadalcanal, for example; both the Japanese and the Americans saw control of Henderson Field as the key to the campaign. Overwhelming air support proved immensely important to Allied forces in the subsequent island-hopping campaigns in the Southwest Pacific along the New Guinea coast and at Bougainville. The introduction of napalm in 1944 gave another potent weapon to close air support fighters such as the F4U Corsair—the combination was used to great effect in the Philippines, the Marianas, and on Okinawa. Ground-attack aviation, which began in World War I, came into its own in World War II.

Robert Bateman

See also
Aircraft, Bombers; Aircraft, Fighters; Blitzkrieg; Bombers; Patton, George Smith, Jr.; Queseda, Elwood Richard "Pete"; Strategic Bombing

References
Boyne, Walter J. *Clash of Wings: World War II in the Air.* New York: Simon and Schuster, 1994.
Buckley, John. *Air Power in the Age of Total War.* London: UCL Press, 1999.
Hallion, Richard P. *Strike from the Sky: The History of Battlefield Air Attack, 1911–1945.* Washington, DC: Smithsonian Institution Press, 1989.
Hughes, Thomas Alexander. *Over Lord: General Pete Quesada and the Triumph of Tactical Air Power in World War II.* New York: Free Press, 1995.
Murray, Williamson. *Luftwaffe.* Baltimore, MD: Nautical and Aviation Publishing, 1985.

Aviation, Naval

On 14 November 1910, flying a Curtiss pusher aircraft, American Eugene B. Ely made the first flight from a ship, the USS *Birmingham*, at Hampton Roads, Virginia. On 18 January 1911, he landed the same Curtiss pusher on the USS *Pennsylvania* in San Francisco Bay for the first landing of a plane on a ship. Britain's Royal Navy later conducted similar tests.

The world's major navies developed four major roles for naval aircraft: reconnaissance, spotting for naval gunnery, attacking enemy fleet and shore installations, and defending the fleet from enemy aircraft. Navies first relied on seaplanes and land-based aircraft, but during World War I Britain began conversion of several ships into aircraft carriers. This undertaking came to include the battle cruisers *Furious, Courageous,* and *Glorious,* all of which served in World War II. The U.S. Navy commissioned its first aircraft carrier, the *Langley,* in 1922; in the same year Japan commissioned its first carrier, the *Hosho.*

Following World War I, the world's navies deployed catapult-launched seaplanes on their battleships and cruisers for reconnaissance and spotting. Many navies considered building aircraft carriers, but only Great Britain, Japan, and the United States built them in significant numbers. During the 1920s and 1930s, aviators in all three of these navies solved the many technical problems of carrier operations despite low budgets, some opposition, and the Washington and London treaties that limited the size, number, and armament of the carriers. Large new aircraft carriers joined the three navies' fleets in the late 1930s and early 1940s.

Each nation developed a force suited to its particular needs. The United States and Japan planned for operations across the vast and relatively empty stretches of the Pacific Ocean, where land air bases would be few. Both nations developed long-range seaplanes, such as the U.S. PBY Catalina, to extend their search range, although only the Japanese navy developed land-based bombers to support its carrier aircraft. Japan also sought to maximize the number of planes on its aircraft carriers. Limited by the size of the carriers' internal hangars, Japan's larger carriers generally carried between 70 and 80 planes. In U.S. carriers planes were parked on the decks, and hangars were used only for repair and maintenance. This enabled the United States to bring as many as 100 planes into battle. The U.S. Navy also took better advantage of folded-wing airplanes to fit large complements on its carriers. Keeping planes on deck also substantially increased the pace of flight operations on the American carriers, allowing planes to be launched at a much higher rate than that from the Japanese or British ships.

Britain planned for war in Europe, where its fleet was likely to confront land-based air power. For that reason, the British favored heavily armored aircraft carriers with armored flight decks capable of withstanding 500-lb bombs. Although this scale of protection reduced the British aircraft complement to half that of comparably sized American aircraft carriers, it paid off repeatedly during the war, when British aircraft carriers survived damage that would likely have sunk a U.S. or Japanese carrier. On 10 January 1941, while protecting a convoy bound from Alexandria to Malta, the *Illustrious* survived hits by 500 lb and 1,000 lb bombs and then survived further damage while under repair at Malta. Later in the war, several British carriers withstood hits from Japanese kamikaze aircraft with minimal damage.

Unlike the case in Japan or the United States, the Royal Air Force, rather than the navy, had authority over naval aviation. This divided leadership slowed innovation, and the Royal Navy entered the war with obsolete aircraft. Typical of this was its Fairey Swordfish biplane torpedo-bomber.

Japan developed its aviators into an elite strike force, selecting only 100 new aviators each year from its rigorous training program. In 1941, they flew the best naval aircraft in the world: the Mitsubishi A6M2 Reisen ("Zero") fighter—so named because it entered service in 1940, the Japanese year 5700, and was henceforth known as the type 0 (Reisen or Zero)—the Aichi D3A "Val" dive-bomber, and the B5N "Kate" torpedo-bomber. These aircraft sacrificed protection for speed and maneuverability, and they considerably outperformed and outranged U.S. naval aircraft. Japanese fleets sent their search planes out to almost 600 miles, compared with 350 miles for the U.S. Navy, and their strike aircraft had a combat radius of 300 miles, compared with 200 miles for most American aircraft.

The Zero established a deadly combat reputation, and Americans flying Grumman F4F Wildcats could only best it with careful tactics and teamwork. The U.S. Douglas SBD Dauntless proved an excellent dive-bomber and served through much of the war, but the obsolete TBD Devastator torpedo-bomber was slow and vulnerable. The U.S. Navy replaced it as soon as it could with the more modern TBF Avenger following the great carrier battles of 1942.

During the first two years of war, aircraft did little to fulfill the promises of prewar aviation advocates. German aircraft rarely hit British warships during the 1940 Norwegian Campaign, and the German battle cruisers *Gneisenau* and *Scharnhorst* sank Britain's aircraft carrier *Glorious* with gunfire. In November 1940, British carrier aircraft surprised Italian battleships docked at Taranto and torpedoed three of them, but this proved little to critics, who argued that battleships at sea would evade bombs and torpedoes and devastate attacking aircraft with their heavy defensive armament.

Critics were also unimpressed by the battering by land-based aircraft that British carriers sustained while escorting

Aerial view of SB2C in upper landing circle showing USS Yorktown, *below, ca. July 1944. (U.S. Navy, National Archives)*

convoys through the Mediterranean. However, carrier aircraft proved critical in bringing the German battleship *Bismarck* to battle. On 16 May 1941, torpedoes dropped by the Swordfish, which had been launched from the *Ark Royal,* jammed the *Bismarck*'s rudder. Yet it required the heavy guns of British battleships to actually sink the ship. Similarly, Japan's brilliantly conceived and executed attack on Pearl Harbor proved only that bases and stationary ships were vulnerable to surprise air attack. Three days later, though, Japanese navy G4M land-based bombers located and sank the newest British battleship, the *Prince of Wales,* and the battle cruiser *Repulse* in an hour-long battle off the coast of Malaya. The British warships shot down only 3 of 129 attacking aircraft. Aircraft would often dominate future sea battles.

Japanese and U.S. aircraft carriers engaged each other in battles in 1942. The first of these, the Battle of the Coral Sea, ended with roughly equal losses for both sides. At Midway, though, Japan lost four carriers and sank only one U.S. carrier, the *Yorktown.* There followed a series of grueling battles around Guadalcanal in which both navies suffered heavily. Aircraft carriers, loaded with fuel and ordnance, proved

particularly vulnerable to even minor damage, and few survived the first year of war in the Pacific. The United States lost five of its seven carriers in these battles, and the sixth suffered heavy damage. Japan suffered similar losses to its carrier fleet; more than 400 of the 765 airmen who attacked Pearl Harbor had died in battle by the end of 1942, in part the consequence of a poor Japanese pilot replacement/training system.

In a desperate effort to replace lost aircraft carriers, the United States and Japan converted light cruisers into small aircraft carriers, such as the U.S. 33-aircraft *Independence,* which joined the fleet in June 1943. Japan also added partial flight decks to two battleships, allowing them to launch but not recover planes, and it converted a Yamato-class battleship to an aircraft carrier, the 64,800-ton *Shinano.* Yet U.S. industry easily won the naval building race. Japan completed three carriers in 1943 and four in 1944–1945; the United States completed 17 of its large Essex-class carriers during the war and more than 60 smaller carriers. By mid-1944, the United States was launching a large aircraft carrier every month.

U.S. carrier operations became increasingly sophisticated after the 1942 battles. Improving radar, which by early

1944 could detect even low-flying aircraft, and new control and communications systems allowed American fighters to intercept attacking aircraft with great success. New ships, increasing antiaircraft armament, and the proximity fuse considerably improved fleet defense. Radar-equipped TBF Avengers proved adept at locating targets at sea and in the air, allowing the U.S. Navy to intercept attacking aircraft at night. Whereas the Japanese navy continued to rely on its prewar aircraft designs, the United States developed several new airplanes, which began joining the fleet in 1943. These included the excellent F6F Hellcat and F4U Corsair, which completely outclassed Japan's Zero in combat.

U.S. aircraft also joined the British Royal Navy—first Wildcats and later Corsairs, Hellcats, and Avengers. By 1943, the United States was supplying most of the Royal Navy's aircraft. U.S. industry also churned out dozens of small escort carriers for both its own navy and the British navy. Carrying two dozen aircraft, these "baby flattops" provided continuous air cover for convoys crossing the Atlantic. Other escort carriers formed the core of antisubmarine hunter-killer groups that prowled the ocean in search of German U-boats and reinforced convoys under attack. Combined with land-based air power, the escort carriers proved the answer to the threat from Germany's U-boats and, in mid-1943, turned the tide of the Battle of the Atlantic. They also provided vital air support for numerous amphibious invasions.

A series of U.S. carrier raids and air offensives further wore down Japanese air strength in the Pacific during 1943. By November, when the United States invaded Tarawa and began its drive across the Central Pacific, 11 U.S. carriers faced only 6 Japanese carriers. U.S. Navy carriers, supported by an enormous fleet train and logistical system, raided throughout the Pacific. They isolated Japanese-held islands before invasion, protected amphibious landings, and provided close air support for the invading soldiers and Marines. American training and combat performance continued to improve, and an excellent submarine and seaplane rescue service saved the lives of many American pilots shot down during these missions.

The Japanese carrier fleet, rebuilt from the 1942 battles and supported by land-based planes, confronted a far larger U.S. fleet in June 1944 in the Battle of the Philippine Sea. The result was the "great Marianas turkey shoot," as the better-trained and better-equipped Americans shot down scores of poorly trained Japanese pilots who failed to press home their attacks and often missed their targets. Japan lost 475 planes and almost as many pilots; the United States lost only 100 planes and 16 pilots. Japanese naval air power never recovered from this defeat.

In the Battle of Leyte Gulf in October 1944, Japan used 1 heavy aircraft carrier and 3 light carriers (with a total of only 116 planes on board) as a diversion to draw away the U.S. battle fleet so Japanese battleships and cruisers could attack the landing beaches. Instead of the superbly trained pilots who attacked Pearl Harbor, Japan relied on the kamikazes, whose suicidal attacks sank dozens of U.S. ships. In the Battle for Okinawa, the kamikazes inflicted more casualties on the U.S. Navy than it had sustained in all of its other wars combined. But the Japanese were unable to stem the U.S. Navy advance across the Pacific. Throughout the Pacific, from the Mariana Islands to the Philippines, Iwo Jima, and Okinawa, U.S. naval aircraft smashed Japanese defenses, destroyed Japanese aircraft, supported invasions, sank Japanese ships, and raided Japanese positions.

By 1945, four British aircraft carriers operated in the Pacific, and these joined more than a dozen American carriers in launching a series of devastating air attacks on Japanese positions in July and August. All told, 1,000 U.S. and 250 British carrier aircraft destroyed more than 3,000 Japanese aircraft in the air and on the ground, adding to the damage B-29 bombers had already inflicted on Japan's home islands. New aircraft carriers continued to join the U.S. fleet, although the first of large 47,000 ton Midway-class battle carriers were not commissioned until September 1945, after the end of the war. Of Japan's carriers, only the old, experimental *Hosho* survived the war. Japan's fortunes in the Pacific war had risen and then sunk with its aircraft carriers.

Stephen K. Stein

See also

Aircraft Carriers; Aircraft, Naval; Air-Sea Rescue; *Bismarck,* Sortie and Sinking of; Cape Esperance, Battle of; Caroline Islands Campaign; Coral Sea, Battle of the; Eastern Solomons, Battle of the; Fletcher, Frank Jack; Gilbert Islands Campaign; Guadalcanal Naval Campaign; Halsey, William Frederick, Jr.; Hunter-Killer Groups; Identification, Friend or Foe; King, Ernest Joseph; Leyte Gulf, Battle of; Mariana Islands, Naval Campaign; Marshall Islands, Naval Campaign; Midway, Battle of; Nagumo Chūichi; Naval Strengths, Pacific Theater; Nimitz, Chester William; Philippine Sea, Battle of the; *Prince of Wales* and *Repulse;* Santa Cruz Islands, Battle of; Sherman, Frederick Carl; Spruance, Raymond Ames; Taranto, Attack on; Truk; Yamamoto Isoroku

References

Hone, Thomas C., Norman Friedman, and Mark D. Mandeles. *American and British Aircraft Carrier Development.* Annapolis, MD: Naval Institute Press, 1999.

Morison, Samuel Eliot. *History of United States Naval Operations in World War II.* 15 vols. Boston: Little, Brown, 1947–1962.

Peattie, Mark R. *Sunburst: The Rise of Japanese Naval Air Power, 1909–1941.* Annapolis, MD: Naval Institute Press, 2001.

Reynolds, Clark. *The Fast Carriers.* Annapolis, MD: Naval Institute Press, 1968, reprinted 1992.

Roskill, Stephen W. *The War at Sea, 1939–1945.* 3 vols. London: Her Majesty's Stationery Office, 1954–61.

Till, Geoffrey. *Air Power and the Royal Navy, 1914–1945.* London: Jane's, 1979.

Avranches, Battle of (7–12 August 1944)

Land battle in France. A town of fewer than 9,000 inhabitants, Avranches is one of the oldest municipalities in Normandy. Situated on a 200-ft bluff at the southwestern base of the Cotentin Peninsula, Avranches overlooks the Bay of Mont Saint-Michel. The Saint-Michel abbey is some eight miles away.

On 31 July 1944, following the breakout of the American First Army from its Normandy bridgehead, Major General John S. Wood's U.S. 4th Armored Division captured Avranches. This forced open a gateway for Lieutenant General George S. Patton's newly activated U.S. Third Army to push west into Brittany or south and east toward the heart of France.

After Patton's advance beyond Avranches to the south revealed the Germans' inability to seal the breach in their line, Kluge would have done well to make a timely general withdrawal to a backup line of defense, possibly at the Seine River. But Adolf Hitler at his command post in distant East Prussia adamantly refused to countenance a retreat. Instead, he demanded a massive offensive west to Avranches. Hitler insisted that such an attack would enable the Germans to reverse the outcome of the entire Normandy Campaign.

General Paul Hausser's Seventh Army, part of Field Marshal Günther von Kluge's German Army Group B, mounted the counterattack. It began on 7 August and was intended to cut off Patton's army from Lieutenant General Courtney H. Hodges's U.S. First Army. Deciphered German radio traffic betrayed the German intentions, and Major General J. Lawton Collins's VII Corps of the First Army deployed to repel the counterattack. Collins noted Hill 317, a commanding elevation near Mortain, a crossroads town nearly 20 miles east of Avranches. Soon the 2nd Battalion of the 120th Infantry Regiment of Major General Leland S. Hobbs's 30th Division held this key position.

Hausser's Seventh Army launched its attack early on 7 August, but the German forces had assembled hastily and did not deploy in the strength that Hitler had desired. Even so, the Germans managed to achieve local surprises and to make forward progress, including the isolation of Hill 317. The hill's defenders held on tenaciously but suffered some 300 casualties during the next few days. Meanwhile, U.S. artillery spotters on the hill called down devastating fire, and Allied air forces dominated the battlefield from above. Heavy fighting engaged all or parts of six American divisions under Collins (north to south): the 9th, 4th, 30th, 1st, and 35th Infantry Divisions and the 2nd Armored Division. The battle lasted until 12 August, but, as early as 8 August, it was clear that the German attack would fail.

A furious Hitler demanded a second and more powerful stroke, which necessarily required some days to organize.

Kluge and his subordinates persuaded him to strike first at Major General Wade Hampton Haislip's XV Corps of Patton's army. Haislip was moving eastward around the Germans' left flank and then northward toward their rear. In the event, the Germans failed to stop Haislip, to launch another attack toward Avranches, and to impede the relentless advance of additional American forces through the Avranches corridor. Thus the principal result of the unsuccessful German counterattack toward Avranches was to place their own forces in a pocket, risking envelopment and destruction.

Richard G. Stone

See also
COBRA, Operation; Collins, Joseph Lawton; Hausser, Paul "Papa"; Hitler, Adolf; Hodges, Courtney Hicks; Kluge, Günther Adolf Ferdinand von; Patton, George Smith, Jr.

References
Blumenson, Martin. *The United States Army in World War II: The European Theater of Operations: Breakout and Pursuit.* Washington, DC: Office of the Chief of Military History, Department of the Army, 1961.
———. *The Battle of the Generals: The Untold Story of the Falaise Pocket: The Campaign That Should Have Won World War II.* New York: William Morrow, 1994.
Collins, J. Lawton. *Lightning Joe: An Autobiography.* Baton Rouge: Louisiana State University Press, 1979.
Reardon, Mark J. *Victory at Mortain: Stopping Hitler's Counteroffensive.* Lawrence: University Press of Kansas, 2002.

"Axis Sally" (Mildred Elizabeth Gillars) (1900–1988)

American-born propaganda broadcaster for the Germans. Born 29 November 1900 in Portland, Maine, Mildred E. Sisk later adopted her stepfather's name, Gillars. She studied drama at Ohio Wesleyan University but left in 1922 without graduating. She moved through a series of jobs, ending up in Germany by September 1934, where she was soon teaching and translating for the Berlitz school in Berlin. She began an affair with Max Otto Koischwitz, another former American, who was broadcasting propaganda for Germany as "Mr. O.K." She later claimed that he pushed her into broadcasting for the Nazi regime.

Gillars was apparently first heard on a German radio station on 6 May 1940 as an announcer on a service directed toward Britain. She soon became the host of entertainment programs. Persuaded and joined by Koischwitz (she later testified), she began regular broadcasts titled *Home Sweet Home* for the German Rundfunk (radio), aimed at U.S. soldiers in North Africa. She used the air names "Midge" and

"Sally" (her American listeners called her "Axis Sally"). She was soon among the highest-paid broadcasters in Germany. In *Midge's Medical Reports,* Gillars featured broadcasts from prisoner-of-war camps, attesting that the camps had high standards of treatment. *Midge at the Mike* offered music and talk for lonesome soldiers interspersed with considerable propaganda. In a particularly chilling broadcast before the D day landings in France, "Vision of Invasion," she claimed thousands would perish.

Koischwitz died in 1944, and Gillars spent the remainder of the war in Berlin. Arrested there by Allied authorities in 1946, she was released and gave an ill-advised press conference explaining her role. That forced Allied action, and she was rearrested and later tried in Washington, D.C. On 10 March 1949, she was found guilty of one of the eight treason counts against her and was sentenced to between 10 and 30 years in prison. She was released on parole on 10 July 1961 from a federal reformatory after serving 12 years. She taught languages and music at a convent in Columbus, Ohio, and died there on 25 June 1988.

Christopher H. Sterling

See also
"Lord Haw-Haw"; Propaganda; "Tokyo Rose"

References
Bergmeier, Horst J. P., and Rainer E. Lotz. *Hitler's Airwaves: The Inside Story of Nazi Radio Broadcasting and Propaganda Swing,* 125–131. New Haven, CT: Yale University Press, 1997.

Edwards, John Carver. "Max Otto Koischwitz, Alias Mr. O.K." In *Berlin Calling: American Broadcasters in Service to the Third Reich,* 56–98. New York: Praeger, 1991.

B

Ba Maw (1893–1977)

Burmese political figure and one of the leaders of Burma's movement to gain independence from Britain, which was achieved soon after World War II. Born in Maubin, Burma, on 8 February 1893 into an aristocratic family, Ba Maw graduated from college in Rangoon in 1913. He also studied abroad at the Universities of Calcutta in India, Cambridge in England, and Bordeaux in France, obtaining both certification as a lawyer in England and a doctorate.

Ba Maw returned to Burma, a British Crown Colony, and began the practice of law, making a mark by defending Saya San, a leader of the Thayawaddy peasant uprising in 1930. In 1933, Ba Maw organized a moderate political party known as Simyetta (People's Party). He became a member of the Legislative Council of Burma and then minister of education for Burma. In April 1937, Ba Maw was appointed the first prime minister of the Burma Crown Colony government when Burma was officially separated from India. Facing radical labor and student unrest, he resigned in March 1939. He then formed a new political alignment, known as the Freedom Bloc, with the Thakin Party and became its chairman. Protesting British policies toward Burma, he quit the legislature in 1940.

Ba Maw was arrested and imprisoned by the British in August 1940 on charges of being in contact with the Japanese and advocating noncollaboration with the British war effort. Escaping from prison in August 1942, Ba Maw came under the protection of Japanese forces advancing to Rangoon. He collaborated with them and was appointed chief of the Burma Central Executive Council established by the Japanese authorities, adopting the title *ahnashin* (lord of authority). When Japan recognized Burma as an independent state in August 1943, Ba Maw became the chief of state of the new Republic of Burma and took the title *adipati* (chief), leading an authoritarian, one-party state.

In November 1943, Ba Maw attended the Greater East Asia Conference in Tokyo with other Asian leaders collaborating with Japan. But the Burmese army, led by Aung San, revolted in March 1945, and when Allied forces defeated the Japanese in Burma the next month, Ba Maw fled to Tokyo via Bangkok. In August 1945, when Japan surrendered, Ba Maw was arrested and interned in Sugamo Prison, Tokyo. Released in July 1946, he returned to Burma and resumed his political activities. He retired from politics in 1962 when the military, led by U Nu, carried out another coup d'état. Ba Maw published his autobiography in 1968. He died in Yangon (Rangoon) on 29 May 1977.

Tobe Ryoichi

See also
Aung San, U; Burma Theater; China-Burma-India Theater
References
Allen, Louis. *Burma: The Longest War, 1941–1945*. New York: St. Martin's Press, 1984.
Ba Maw. *Breakthrough in Burma: Memoirs of a Revolution, 1939–1946*. New Haven, CT: Yale University Press, 1968.

Babi Yar Massacre (29–30 September 1941)

German mass shooting of Soviet Jews outside Kiev, Ukraine. Following the German army's invasion of the Soviet Union on 22 June 1941, four Shutzstaffel Einsatzgruppen (SS mobile killing squads) entered Soviet territory, their task being the physical annihilation of Communist Party functionaries, Red Army commissars, the physically and mentally handicapped, partisans, and Jews.

As the Wehrmacht drove ever deeper into the Soviet Union, the Einsatzgruppen followed, rounding up and slaughtering their intended victims in mass shootings. Consequently, by the time of their disbanding in 1943, when the war on the Eastern Front swung irreversibly in favor of the Red Army, the Einsatzgruppen—with the assistance of the German army and a host of enthusiastic collaborators from the Latvian, Lithuanian, and Ukrainian populations—had committed a multitude of unspeakable atrocities and murdered an estimated 1.5 million Soviet Jews and others.

Among the numerous Einsatzgruppen crimes, the slaughter of Jews at Babi Yar in late September 1941—perpetrated by SS Colonel Paul Blobel's Sonderkommando 4a, a subunit of Otto Rasch's Einsatzgruppe C—was arguably the most notorious. On 19 September 1941, units of the German Army Group South occupied Kiev, the capital of Soviet Ukraine. In the days immediately following, a series of explosions rocked the city, destroying German field headquarters, burning more than one-third of a square mile of the Kiev city center, and leaving some 10,000 residents homeless. Although these explosions were likely the work of the Soviet political police, or NKVD, the Germans saw in them a convenient justification to massacre the city's Jews, a task Blobel's Sonderkommando would have carried out regardless.

After discussions between Blobel, Rasch, and Major General Kurt Eberhard, the German field commander in Kiev, the latter ordered the city's Jews to assemble with their possessions—including money, valuables, and warm clothing—near the Jewish cemetery no later than 7:00 A.M. on Monday, 29 September. The posted order indicated that the Jews were to be resettled and warned that failure to comply would be punishable by death.

Once assembled, Kiev's Jews were marched to Babi Yar, a partially wooded ravine just outside the city. There, the Germans, following the procedure used by Einsatzgruppen since the mass shootings of Soviet Jews began in late June, forced the Jews to strip, dispossessed them of their belongings, and shot them to death in groups of 30 to 40 people. In the course of two gruesome days, Blobel's men, relying exclusively on automatic weapons, murdered 33,771 innocent men, women, and children. Subsequently, they reported that the Jews had offered no resistance and until the last minute had believed they were to be resettled.

During the months that followed the initial Babi Yar massacre, the Germans periodically used the ravine as a murder site, killing several thousand more Jews there, plus an untold number of Gypsies and Soviet prisoners of war. In July 1943, with Soviet forces having seized the military initiative and advancing rapidly, the Germans launched Operation AKTION 1005 to eradicate evidence of their crimes in the Soviet Union. Blobel, who had been released from his duties as commander of Sonderkommando 4a in early 1942 and transferred to Berlin, returned to Kiev, where he oversaw efforts to obliterate traces of the executions at Babi Yar. Throughout August and September, Blobel's men and conscripted concentration camp inmates reopened the mass grave, crushed bones, and cremated the remains of the dead. Despite the Germans' efforts to hide their crimes, significant evidence of the massacres remained and was discovered by Soviet forces following the liberation of Kiev in November 1943.

The Babi Yar massacre of late September 1941 was not the largest German "special action" against the Jews. In October 1941, the Germans and their Romanian allies murdered an estimated 50,000 at Odessa. Nonetheless, more than any other, Babi Yar has come to symbolize an aspect of the Holocaust—mass shootings—that is invariably overshadowed by the horrors of Auschwitz and the other death camps.

Bruce J. DeHart

See also
Holocaust, The; Kiev Pocket; Waffen-SS

References
Berenbaum, Michael, ed. *Witness to the Holocaust: An Illustrated Documented History of the Holocaust in the Words of Its Victims, Perpetrators, and Bystanders.* New York: Harper Collins, 1997.
Krausnick, Helmut, and Hans-Heinrich Wilhelm. *Die Truppe des Weltanschauungskrieges: Die Einsatzgruppen der Sicherheitspolitzei und des SD, 1938–1942.* Stuttgart, Germany: Deutsche Verlags-Anstalt, 1981.
Rhodes, Richard. *Masters of Death: The S.S. Einsatzgruppen and the Invention of the Holocaust.* New York: Vintage, 2002.

"Baby Blitz" (January–May 1944)

German bombing raids against London in 1944. As 1943 drew to a close, the Allies had been achieving great military success against Germany. With British and U.S. bombing raids on German cities increasing in frequency, accuracy, and destructiveness, German leaders were determined to carry out some action to boost civilian morale.

German propagandists turned to *Vergeltung* (retaliation). From January 1943, Minister of Propaganda Joseph Goebbels called on Germans to be patient, as a massive strike to drive Britain from the war was imminent. This blow was to be carried out with Germany's new V-1 and V-2 rockets, but production difficulties forced the Germans to rely on traditional bombers. The bombing plan was drawn up in November by Generalmajor (U.S. equiv. brigadier general) Dietrich Peltz. At Adolf Hitler's direction and beginning in December 1943, the Luftwaffe stationed all available bombers at fields in northern France in preparation for the offensive.

On 21 January 1944, operations commenced when Peltz sent two waves totaling 447 bombers against London. Effective British antiaircraft fire and poor German navigation meant that only a minority of the bombers actually reached their targets. The Germans employed target markers from pathfinder aircraft and dropped a mix of high-explosive and incendiary bombs, but only about 32 tons of bombs actually fell within Greater London. Of 268 tons dropped, most bomb loads were scattered over the English countryside, and 25 bombers were shot down.

On 29 January, the Germans mounted a second attack on London with 285 bombers, mostly Ju-188s and a few Ju-88s. The bombing produced only minimal damage in the London area at a cost of 28 German aircraft shot down.

During February, the Germans sent 1,300 sorties against London. (A sortie is one flight made by one plane.) On 18 February, they managed to drop 175 tons of bombs on the city, and thereafter, 50 percent of the German bombs hit within London. The decreasing size of the German attacking force rendered the greater accuracy less significant, however. By the end of April, when the Germans had to break off the attacks because of prohibitive losses, they had launched a dozen attacks against London, Hull, Bristol, and Portsmouth and dropped a total of some 2,000 tons of bombs at a cost of 329 bombers lost.

Although these attacks, dubbed by the British the "Baby Blitz," involved more aircraft than any other strikes on Britain since 1941, they caused relatively minor damage and few casualties. Indeed, the raids were more costly for German military capabilities than for the British, draining the Luftwaffe of its experienced crews and aircraft and thus of a potentially strong force to oppose Operation OVERLORD. From the end of December 1943 to May 1944, German bomber strength in northern France fell from 695 to 133 aircraft.

William P. McEvoy and Spencer C. Tucker

See also
Aircraft, Bombers; Aircraft, Fighters; Germany, Air Force; Germany, Home Front; Goebbels, Paul Josef; Great Britain, Air Force; OVERLORD, Operation; Propaganda; V-1 Buzz Bomb; V-2 Rocket

References
Killen, John. *A History of the Luftwaffe*. New York: Doubleday, 1968.
Kirwin, Gerald. "Waiting for Retaliation: A Study in Nazi Propaganda Behavior and German Civilian Morale." *Journal of Contemporary History* 16, no. 3 (1981): 565–583.
Murray, Williamson. *Luftwaffe*. Baltimore, MD: Nautical and Aviation Publishing Company of America, 1985.

Bach-Zelewski, Erich von dem (1899–1973)

German Schutzstaffel (SS) general and commander of antipartisan units on the Eastern Front during World War II. Born to a Junker family in Lauenburg, Pomerania, on 1 March 1899, Bach-Zelewski volunteered in 1914 and served in the German army during World War I. In the course of the war, he was awarded the Iron Cross and was promoted to lieutenant. After the armistice, he served in the Freikorps and as a Reichswehr officer until 1924.

In 1930, Bach-Zelewski joined the National Socialist Party and its elite SS, or bodyguard, unit. After 1934, he commanded SS units in East Prussia and Pomerania. In 1939, he was promoted to SS general, and two years later, he was assigned to Army Group Center on the Eastern Front. Bach-Zelewski was largely responsible for masterminding and carrying out the massacre of ethnic and political enemies of the Reich. In July 1941, he took control of 11,000 SS troops, four times the number assigned to the special execution squads (or Einsatzgruppen). Around 6,000 ordinary police were also under his authority. By the end of 1941, Bach-Zelewski commanded over 50,000 men, whose job it was to kill "race enemies," such as Jews, Gypsies, and the mentally and physically disabled.

In June 1943, the SS chief, Heinrich Himmler, appointed Bach-Zelewski as the antipartisan chief on the entire Eastern Front. In the late summer of 1944, he commanded the German units responsible for crushing the Warsaw Rising. Known for his brutality and improvisational skills, he ended the war as a corps commander.

The fact that Bach-Zelewski testified for the prosecution at the Nuremberg war crimes trials and denounced his fellow police chiefs spared him extradition to the Soviet Union. In March 1951, he was condemned by a Munich court to 10 years of special labor, which in practice meant being confined to his home in Franconia. The only individual among the mass murderers who personally took responsibility for his wartime actions, Bach-Zelewski was never prosecuted for his role in the anti-Jewish massacres. Instead, he was tried in 1961 for his participation in the 1934 Blood Purge and sentenced to four and a half years in prison. Indicted again in 1962 for the murder of six communists in 1933, he was tried at Nuremberg and received the unusually harsh sentence of life imprisonment. Neither indictment mentioned his wartime role. Bach-Zelewski died in a prison hospital in Munich on 8 March 1973.

Martin Moll

See also
Bór-Komorowski, Tadeusz; Heydrich, Reinhard Tristan Eugen; Himmler, Heinrich; Holocaust, The; Partisans/Guerrillas; Warsaw Rising

References

Gerlach, Christian. *Kalkulierte Morde: Deutsche Wirtschafts und Vernichtungspolitik in Weissrussland 1941–1944*. Hamburg, Germany: Hamburger Edition, 1999.

Reitlinger, Gerald. *The SS: Alibi of a Nation, 1922–1945*. New York: Viking, 1957.

Bader, Sir Douglas Robert Steuart (1910–1982)

British air force officer and ace pilot in World War II. Born in London on 10 February 1910, Douglas Bader was commissioned in the Royal Air Force (RAF) on graduation from the Royal Air Force Flying School in 1930. After losing both legs in an aircraft accident while performing low-level acrobatics in December 1931, Bader was medically retired with a disability pension on his recuperation in 1933. He then went to work for Shell Petroleum but taught himself how to use his artificial limbs well enough to fly again. In 1939, with war already declared, Bader argued his way back to active duty, flying Hawker Hurricanes. In early 1940, he became a flight commander in a Spitfire squadron.

During the 1940 Battle of Britain, Flight Lieutenant Bader became famous both for the fact that he was a double amputee and because he quickly became an ace. His aggressive flying style and inspired leadership while commander of 242 Squadron, flying Hurricanes in Number 12 Group during the height of the Battle of Britain, came to epitomize British pluck. Dissatisfied with the prescribed tight, "line-astern" formations, Bader insisted, to the point of insubordination, that the RAF conduct attacks in looser formations utilizing all available aircraft. This approach came to be known as the Big Wing concept, identified with Number 12 Group's commander, Air Vice Marshal Sir Trafford L. Leigh-Mallory. By 1941, Bader was promoted to wing commander and took command of Number 11 Wing of three Spitfire squadrons in Sussex.

On 9 August 1941—at the time credited with 22.5 kills, making him one of the highest-scoring British aces—Bader was flying near Le Touquet, France, when he was shot down. Parachuting to safety, he badly damaged one of his artificial legs in the landing. The commander of the unit that had shot him down, Generalmajor (U.S. equiv. brigadier general) Adolf Galland, interceded with Air Marshal Hermann Göring to allow the British to air-drop Bader a replacement leg.

Bader repeatedly attempted to escape imprisonment until he was finally sent to the German maximum-security prisoner-of-war (POW) camp of Colditz Castle, where he spent the remainder of the war. Bader led the Battle of Britain flyby in the postwar victory parade and retired from the RAF in February 1946. His life was the subject of the book *Reach for the Sky* and a movie of the same title. Bader died in London on 5 September 1982.

Robert Bateman and Spencer C. Tucker

See also

Britain, Battle of; Fighter Tactics; Galland, Adolf; Göring, Hermann Wilhelm; Leigh-Mallory, Sir Trafford L.

References

Bader, Douglas. *Fight for the Sky: The Story of the Spitfire and the Hurricane*. Garden City, NY: Doubleday, 1973.

Brickhill, Paul. *Reach for the Sky*. New York: Norton, 1954.

Terraine, John. *A Time for Courage: The Royal Air Force in the European War, 1939–1945*. New York: Macmillan, 1985.

Badoglio, Pietro (1871–1956)

Italian army marshal who helped Italy switch allegience from the Axis to the Allied powers in World War II. Born in Grazzano Monferrato (later renamed Grazzano Badoglio), Italy, on 28 September 1871, Pietro Badoglio entered the Italian military in 1890 as an artillery officer and participated in the campaigns in Abyssinia between 1896 and 1897 and Tripolitania (Libya) from 1911 to 1912. A captain at the beginning of World War I, he rose to lieutenant general in August 1917 and commanded XXVII Corps in the October–November 1917 Battle of Caporetto. His deployment and poor handling of his corps opened a gap in the Italian lines and facilitated the Austro-German advance. Some information on this situation was suppressed, and Badoglio's career did not suffer. Indeed, Badoglio became deputy to the chief of staff of the Italian army, General Armando Diaz.

From November 1919 to February 1921, Badoglio was army chief of staff. In 1924 and 1925, the anti-Fascist Badoglio was ambassador to Brazil, but in May 1925, he returned to Italy as chief of the General Staff and was promoted to field marshal in June 1926.

From 1928 to 1933, Badoglio was governor of Italian North Africa, and during that period, he oversaw the suppression of the Senussi Rebellion. In November 1935, he assumed command of Italian forces in Ethiopia, completing the conquest of that country; he was rewarded with the title of duke of Addis Ababa and named viceroy there in May 1936. In November 1939, Badoglio was again chief of staff of the Italian armed forces, a post he held until he was forced to resign on 4 December 1940 following the failure of Italian forces in Greece.

After Benito Mussolini's arrest in July 1943, King Victor Emmanuel III selected Badoglio as head of the Italian government and commander of the armed forces. Badoglio then dissolved the Fascist Party and many of its institutions, released political prisoners, and failed to enforce the anti-Semitic legislation. He also helped engineer Italy's change from the Axis to the Allied side as a cobelligerent, a move carried out secretly on 3 September 1943. When the German army took over much of Italy, Badoglio, the king, and other members of the government managed to flee Rome on the night of 8–9 September and make their way to Brindisi, where they set up a government in cooperation with the Allies. On 29 September 1943, Badoglio formally surrendered Italy, and on 13 October 1943, Italy declared war on Germany. Following the liberation of Rome, Badoglio stepped down, on 5 June 1944. He died at his family home in Grazzano Badoglio on 1 November 1956.

Spencer C. Tucker

See also

Greece, Campaign (28 October 1940–March 1941; April 1941); Italo-Ethiopian War; Italy, Home Front; Victor Emanuel III, King of Italy

References

Badoglio, Pietro. *Italy in the Second World War: Memories and Documents.* Trans. Muriel Currey. Westport, CT: Greenwood Press, 1948.

Delzell, Charles. *Mussolini's Enemies: The Italian Anti-Fascist Resistance.* Princeton, NJ: Princeton University Press, 1961.

Mack Smith, Denis. *Mussolini's Roman Empire.* New York: Viking, 1976.

Bäer, Heinrich (1913–1957)

German air force officer and World War II ace. Born in Sommerfield, Germany, on 25 March 1913, Heinrich "Pritzel" Bäer joined the Luftwaffe in 1937 and began World War II as an Umteroffizer (U.S. equiv. corporal). Within a year, he had both attained the rank of sergeant and qualified as a noncommissioned fighter pilot. During this time, he was stationed with Jagdgeschwader (Fighter Group) 51.

On 25 September 1939, Bäer scored his first confirmed victory (kill). During the 1940 battle for France, he earned a battlefield commission as a lieutenant. He then fought in the Battle of Britain, raising his total kills to 27.

Transferring to the Soviet Front in 1941, Oberleutnant (U.S. equiv. first lieutenant) Bäer continued to score victories in aerial combat. He obtained 96 kills in this campaign, including 6 against Soviet pilots in a single day. Once shot down behind Soviet lines, Bäer made his way back to German-held territory. He was hospitalized with a spinal injury but rejoined his unit shortly thereafter.

In the spring of 1942, newly appointed Hauptmann (U.S. equiv. major) Bäer was assigned as commander of JG-77 in the North African Campaign, flying from Sicily. In January 1945, Bäer took command of JG-1, a jet fighter training unit. He was then transferred to JG-3, where he scored his two-hundredth career victory. His final assignment of the war was with JV-44, Generalleutnant (U.S. equiv. major general) Adolf Galland's "Expert Squadron." Flying the Me-262 jet, Bäer had 220 career victories in more than 1,000 combat missions. His total of 16 victories in the Me-262 remains the record for a jet aircraft.

Heinrich Bäer completed his military service as a lieutenant colonel. He died in an airplane crash in Brunswick, Germany, while demonstrating the capabilities of a light plane on 28 April 1957.

Kyle D. Haire

See also

Britain, Battle of; Galland, Adolf; Germany, Air Force

References

Angolia, John R. *On the Field of Honor: A History of the Knights Cross Bearers.* Stillwell, KS: Bender Publishers, 1981.

Collier, Basil. *The Battle of Britain.* London: B. T. Batsford, 1962.

Williamson, Gordon. *The Iron Cross: A History, 1813–1957.* New York: Blandford Press, 1984.

Bagramyan (Begramian), Ivan Khristoforovich (1897–1982)

Soviet army general who served as chief of staff of the Southwestern Front. Born in Elizavetpol (now Ganca), in Azerbaijan, on 2 December 1897, Ivan Bagramyan (also widely spelled Bagramian) entered the Imperial Russian Army in 1915 and was a junior lieutenant by 1917. He joined the Red Army in 1920 and the Communist Party only in 1939.

Bagramyan attended the Higher Cavalry School and the Frunze Military Academy. For four years, he was a lecturer at the General Staff Academy. He attained the rank of colonel by 1940, at which time he was posted to the Kiev Special Military District as deputy chief of staff to its commander, General Georgii Zhukov. Bagramyan assisted in preparing a paper for Zhukov entitled "Conducting a Contemporary Offensive Operation," which the general presented at the December meeting of the heads of military districts. The paper helped assure Bagramyan of Zhukov's future support.

At the beginning of the German invasion of the Soviet Union, Bagramyan was operations officer for Marshal Semen Budenny's Southwestern Front. He escaped from the Kiev encirclement and was promoted to major general. In August 1941, Bagramyan became chief of staff to Marshal Semen Timoshenko, commander of the Southwestern and Southern Fronts. Bagramyan orchestrated two Soviet counteroffensives and was promoted to lieutenant general and made chief of staff of an operational group consisting of the Southern, Southwestern, and Bryansk Fronts. In late March 1942, Timoshenko sent Bagramyan to Soviet dictator Josef Stalin to discuss plans for the recapture of Kharkov.

Bagramyan impressed Stalin, and in April, he was promoted to lieutenant general and appointed chief of staff of the Southwestern Front. In May, he was chief of staff of the Direction (Axis) as well. The Soviets recaptured Kharkov, but German forces then threatened to cut them off. Bagramyan sensed the danger, and on 18 May, he urged that the plan be changed; however, Stalin refused to intervene, and three Soviet armies were lost. Stalin made Bagramyan the scapegoat for the disaster, removing him from his post.

In July, a rehabilitated Bagramyan took command of the Sixteenth Army, which he led in the RZHEV-SYCHEV Operation to drive German forces from north of the Volga River and east of the Vazuza River. In February, following the Battle of Stalingrad, the Sixteenth Army was increased to six divisions, two brigades, a tank corps, four tanks brigades, and several artillery regiments. The Sixteenth Army performed well and was renamed the Eleventh Guards Army. It played a major role in the Battle of Kursk. For this success, Bagramyan was promoted to colonel general in July.

Eleventh Guards Army was then redeployed as part of the 2nd Baltic Front in preparation for Operation BAGRATION, the Soviet offensive to destroy German Army Group Center. In November 1943, Stalin promoted Bagramyan to full general in command of the 1st Baltic Front. Bagramyan was the only front commander during the war of non-Slavic origins. On 31 July 1944, his forces reached the Baltic near Riga. In October, Bagramyan was promoted to General of the Army. In January 1945, his forces took Memel, cutting off 20 German divisions. In disfavor for not making as much progress in East Prussia as Stalin expected, Bagramyan found his front downgraded to the Zemland Forces Group.

In April 1945, Bagramyan was appointed commander of the 3rd Belorussian Front, a post he held until its disbandment that August. He had command of the Baltic Military District from 1946 to 1954. One year later, he was promoted to marshal and appointed inspector general of the Ministry of Defense, and from 1956 to 1958, Bagramyan headed the General Staff Academy. Through the decade that followed, he was chief of home front services. Bagramyan died in Moscow on 21 September 1982.

Neville Panthaki and Spencer C. Tucker

See also
BARBAROSSA, Operation; Budenny, Semen Mikhailovich; Kursk, Battle of; Stalin, Josef; Stalingrad, Battle of; Timoshenko, Semen Konstantinovich; Zhukov, Georgii Konstantinovich

References
Bagramyan, Ivan. *Tak Shli My k Pobede*. Moscow: Voenizdat, 1977.
Erickson, John. *The Soviet High Command*. London: Macmillan, 1962.
Jukes, Geoffrey. "Ivan Khristoforovich Bagramyan." In Harold Shukman, ed., *Stalin's Generals*, 25–32. New York: Grove Press, 1993.

Bai Chongxi (Pai Ch'ung-hsi) (1893–1966)

Nationalist Chinese general who was involved in strategic planning during the war years. Born in Guilin (Kweilin), Guangxi (Kwangsi) Province, on 18 March 1983, Bai Chongxi (Pai Ch'ung-his) graduated from the Baoding (Paoting) Military Academy in 1916, serving in his native provincial forces. In December 1924, in cooperation with another Guangxi officer, Li Zongren (Li Tsung-jen), Bai gained control of Guangxi.

Bai joined the Nationalist Party—the Guomindang, or GMD (Kuomintant, or KMT)—in 1925, participating in the Northern Expedition of Jiang Jieshi (Chiang Kai-shek) between 1926 and 1928, while at the same time maintaining his power base in Guangxi. In 1929, Bai and Li, known as the Guangxi clique, rebelled against Jiang for his concentration of power. The resulting struggle ended in stalemate, as national unity seemed more important after the September 1931 Mukden (Shenyang) Incident in Liaoning. In late 1931, Bai and Li rejoined the GMD, working to create a reformist provincial government and resolving their differences with Jiang. In mid-1936, their forces were reorganized as the Nationalist government's Fifth Route Army, with Bai as deputy commander.

In the 1937–1945 Sino-Japanese War, Bai was both deputy chief of staff of the Military Affairs Commission and a member of the National Aeronautical Council, responsible for devising military strategy for the Nanjing (Nanking)-Shanghai area in Jiangsu (Kiangsu) Province. Given the heavy losses sustained by GMD forces during October and November 1937, Bai opposed the stand at Nanjing and argued for keeping Chinese forces intact. Jiang accepted Bai's strategy, known as "trading space for time," and moved the Nationalist government to Chongqing (Chungking), Sichuan (Szechwan) Province.

In Chongqing, Bai continued to participate in strategic planning that led to the first Chinese victory in the Tai'erzhuang (T'ai-erh-chuang) Campaign of March and April 1938 in Jiangsu. In July, Bai commanded the Fifth War Zone, covering Shandong (Shantung) and part of Jiangsu north of the Changjiang (Yangtze) River. In December, Bai personally commanded Chinese forces to halt the Japanese drive on Guangxi. Failing in that goal, he was recalled in January 1939.

Bai remained in Chongqing until the end of the war as deputy joint chief of staff, director of the Military Training Board, and chairman of the Military Inspection Commission. Despite his growing opposition to the Chinese Communists, he strongly supported the "protracted war" theory developed by Mao Zedong (Mao Tse-tung) in 1940 to fight the Japanese.

During the 1946–1949 Chinese Civil War, Bai, first as defense minister and then as director of the Strategic Advisory Commission, grew frustrated by Jiang's refusal to yield any authority and by his military policy related to the civil war, and he resigned in 1948. He returned later that year to command an army group in central China but again disagreed with Jiang's military policies that led to the disastrous defeat of the GMD. At the end of 1949, Bai fled to Taiwan, where he became vice chairman of the Strategy Advisory Committee and a member of the Central Executive Committee of the GMD until his death in Taipei on 2 December 1966.

David M. Bull, Debbie Law, and Spencer C. Tucker

See also
China, Army; China, Civil War in; Jiang Jieshi; Li Zongren; Mao Zedong; Nanjing Massacre; Sino-Japanese War

References
Chassin, Lionel Max. *The Communist Conquest of China: A History of the Civil War, 1945–1949.* Cambridge, MA: Harvard University Press, 1965.

Cheng, Siyuan. *Bai Chongxi Chuan* (The biography of Bai Chongxi). Hong Kong: South China Press, 1989.

Melby, John F. *The Mandate of Heaven: Record of a Civil War, 1945–1949.* London: Chatto and Windus, 1989.

Balbo, Italo (1896–1940)

Italian air marshal who argued against fighting the Allies in World War II. Born in Qartesana, Italy, on 6 June 1896, Italo Balbo joined the army in 1915 when Italy entered World War I and fought as a lieutenant in the Alpini. Balbo joined the Fascist Party in 1921 and was a leader of the 1922 Fascist March on Rome. One of the more brutal commanders of the anti-Socialist Fascist militia, he became a top adviser to Benito Mussolini. After Mussolini became premier, Balbo held various cabinet posts before becoming minister of aviation in 1929, in which position he worked to make Italy a major air power. Balbo personally led a number of transatlantic flights to North and South America that captured public attention in Italy and abroad. But the Italian air force, despite setting numerous air records, was largely a paper tiger and had few modern aircraft.

Promoted to Italy's first air marshal in 1933, Balbo came to be seen as a political threat by Mussolini, who, in January 1934, appointed him governor and commander in chief of Italian forces in Libya. There, Balbo worked against the policy of Italian domination advocated by others, instead favoring a degree of assimilation for the Arab and Berber populations.

Balbo criticized Italy's alliance with Germany. At a Fascist Grand Council meeting on 7 December 1939, he raised the possibility of Italy fighting on the side of France and Britain. He continued to speak out, even to the British ambassador, against Italy going to war with the Allies.

After Italy declared war in June 1940, Balbo accepted command of Italian forces in North Africa. But on 28 June, his plane was shot down near Tobruk by Italian antiaircraft fire, and he was killed. A British air raid had just taken place, and Balbo's plane was downed while attempting to land after it failed to give the proper identification signal. Rumors had it, however, that Mussolini had ordered his death. Il Duce later remarked that Balbo was "the only one capable of killing me."

Spencer C. Tucker

See also
Mussolini, Benito

References
Mack Smith, Denis. *Mussolini's Roman Empire.* New York: Viking, 1976.

Segrè, Claudio G. *Italo Balbo: A Fascist Life.* Berkeley: University of California Press, 1987.

Balck, Hermann (1893–1984)

German general who commanded the Sixth Army at the end of World War II. Born in Danzig-Langfuhr, Prussia, on 7 December 1893, Hermann Balck was the son of William Balck, a World War I division commander and one of Germany's most noted writers on tactics. He entered Hanover Military College in February 1915. During World War I, he served as a mountain infantry officer on the Western, Eastern, Italian, and Balkan Fronts, rising to command a company. He was wounded seven times and was recommended for the Pour le Mérite but never received the award.

Balck remained in the postwar Reichswehr, transferring to the cavalry and becoming an early exponent of mechanization. He twice refused opportunities to be trained as a General Staff officer. Nonetheless, during the 1939 invasion of Poland, he served in Lieutenant General Heinz Guderian's Inspectorate of Mobile Troops, where he was responsible for managing the reconstitution of the German panzer divisions. In late 1939, Balck assumed command as a lieutenant colonel of the 1st Rifle Regiment in the 1st Panzer Division of Guderian's XIX Panzer Corps. On 13 May 1940, Balck's regiment crossed the Meuse River, spearheading Guderian's breakthrough at Sedan.

After the fall of France, German tanks and infantry were task-organized into combined-arms battle groups (Kampfgruppe), largely on Balck's recommendation. This change was a major development in the evolution of combined-arms warfare doctrine. Until then, infantry and armored regiments of a panzer division were committed separately.

Promoted to colonel, Balck served in the April 1941 Greek Campaign as commander of the 3rd Panzer Regiment. After the Germans broke through the Metaxis Line, he commanded the panzer battle group that outflanked the British at Mount Olympus. In November 1941, Balck became inspector of Mobile Troops, the position Guderian had held in 1938. During Operation TAIFUN, the abortive drive on Moscow, he was responsible for managing tank replacements for the panzer divisions.

In May 1942, Balck became the commander of the 11th Panzer Division in the Soviet Union. Promoted to Generalmajor (U.S. equiv. brigadier general) that October, he often commanded from the front, and his principal tactical axiom was "night marches are lifesavers." In December 1942, during the Soviet offensive along the Chir River north of Stalingrad, the 11th Panzer Division crushed a Soviet assault with a series of stunning counterattacks. With Balck issuing only verbal orders over the radio, his division counterattacked in three different directions over a period of four days, destroying a Soviet tank corps and defeating the Fifth Shock Army in the process. The Chir River was perhaps the most brilliantly fought divisional-level battle of World War II.

Promoted to Generalleutnant (U.S. equiv. major general) in January 1943, Balck briefly commanded the XIV Panzer Corps at Salerno in 1943, where he was injured in an airplane crash. He was made General der Panzertruppen (U.S. equiv. lieutenant general) in November 1943 and returned to duty as commander of XLVIII Panzer Corps, heading it during the fierce battles at Kiev, Radomyshl, and Tarnopol in 1944. During those battles, his corps destroyed three Soviet armies. Balck's chief of staff at the XLVIII Panzer Corps was Colonel Friedrich Wilhelm von Mellenthin, who would remain with him for most of the rest of the war. In August 1944, Balck and Mellenthin took over the Fourth Panzer Army. Counterattacking near Baranov, they halted the Soviet offensive in the great bend of the Vistula. For that action, Balck became the nineteenth (out of only twenty-seven) recipient of the Knight's Cross with Oakleaves, Swords, and Diamonds.

In September 1944, Balck assumed command of Army Group G in the west. His mission was to stop Lieutenant General George S. Patton's Third Army and prevent Patton from interfering in the Ardennes Offensive, planned for that December. Late in December, however, Balck was relieved of his command, the victim of political intrigues by Schutzstaffel (SS) chief Heinrich Himmler and Adolf Hitler's periodic witch-hunts. Thanks to the intervention of Guderian, his old mentor, he was reassigned as commander of the reconstituted German Sixth Army, which also had operational control of two Hungarian armies. When the war ended, he kept his troops out of Soviet hands by surrendering them to the U.S. XX Corps in Austria.

Balck remained in captivity until 1947. Throughout that period, he declined to participate in the U.S. Army Historical Division's series of interviews and monographs, although a great many of the other German generals did cooperate. That decision may partially account for Balck's relative obscurity today—and the fact that the U.S. Army's 1950 official history of the Lorraine Campaign tended to dismiss him as a perpetually overoptimistic and swashbuckling martinet. In the late 1970s and early 1980s, however, Balck and Mellenthin did participate in a number of seminars and panel discussions with senior North Atlantic Treaty Organization (NATO) leaders at the U.S. Army War College. In his widely regarded 1956 book, *Panzer Battles,* Mellenthin rejected the portrayal of Balck in the Lorraine Campaign and called him Germany's finest field commander. Balck died in Erbenbach-Rockenau, Germany, on 29 November 1982.

David T. Zabecki

See also
Ardennes Offensive; Armored Warfare; Eastern Front; France, Battle for; Greece Campaign (April 1941); Guderian, Heinz; Himmler, Heinrich; Hitler, Adolf; Lorraine Campaign; Mellenthin, Friedrich Wilhelm von

References
Balck, Hermann. *Ordnung im Chaos: Erinnerungen, 1983–1948.* Osnabrück, Germany: Biblio, 1981.

Guderian, Heinz. *Achtung-Panzer! The Development of Panzer Forces: Their Tactics and Operational Potential.* London: Arms and Armour Press, 1992.

Mellenthin, F. W. von. *Panzer Battles: A Study of the Employment of Armor in the Second World War.* Trans. H. Betzler. Norman: University of Oklahoma Press, 1956.

Balkans Theater

The Balkan Peninsula lies between the Black Sea and the Sea of Marmara to the east, the Mediterranean Sea to the south, the Ionian Sea to the southwest, and the Adriatic Sea to the west. The northern boundary of the Balkans is generally considered to be formed by the Sava and Danube Rivers. In 1939, there were six states south of that line: Albania, Greece, Bulgaria, European Turkey, most of Yugoslavia, and southeastern Romania.

With the exception of Turkey—which remained neutral—the Axis powers of Germany and Italy gained the allegiance of some of the Balkan states and then invaded and conquered the remainder in 1940 and 1941. This move ensured that the Axis powers had control over the eastern side of the Mediterranean, and it provided the security on the southern flank that was a prerequisite to a German invasion of the Soviet Union. With the rapid collapse of France between May and June 1940, Soviet leader Josef Stalin moved swiftly to secure gains promised him under the August 1939 Soviet-German pact. The Red Army occupied Lithuania, Latvia, and Estonia. This development was expected, but Adolf Hitler professed himself surprised by the subsequent Soviet moves in the Balkans.

In late June 1940, Stalin ordered the annexation of the Romanian provinces of Bessarabia and northern Bukovina. Bessarabia had been assigned to the Soviet sphere under the nonaggression pact, but northern Bukovina had not. Also, unlike Bessarabia, Bukovina had never been part of Imperial Russia, and it was the gateway to the Romanian oil fields at Ploesti, vital to the German war machine.

Italy also sought to take advantage of the defeat of France as well as Britain's weakness by opening new fronts in Africa and in Greece. In April 1939, Italian dictator Benito Mussolini had ordered Italian forces to seize Albania. Then, on 28 October 1940, he sent his army into Greece from Albania, without informing Hitler in advance. Hitler most certainly knew of the Italian plans but did not act to restrain his ally, nor did he reproach him. Mussolini's decision, taken on short notice and against the advice of his military leaders, had immense repercussions. Not only did the Greeks contain the Italians, they also drove them back and began their own counterinvasion of Albania. That winter, the campaign became deadlocked, which caused Hitler to consider sending in German troops to rescue the Italians.

Meanwhile, Hitler acted aggressively in the Balkans to counter the Soviet moves and shore up his southern flank before the German invasion of the Soviet Union. In November 1940, he forced both Hungary and Romania to join the Axis powers and accept German troops. Bulgaria followed suit at the beginning of March 1941. Hitler took advantage of irredentist sentiment but also used hardball tactics to secure the allegiance of these countries. He pressured Yugoslavia, and

in late March, under German threats, Prince Regent Paul reluctantly agreed to join the Axis powers.

Early in March 1941, meanwhile, honoring the pledge to defend Greece, British Prime Minister Winston L. S. Churchill dispatched to that country two infantry divisions and an armored brigade. He hoped thereby to forestall a German invasion, but this step also forced the British Middle East commander, General Sir Archibald Wavell, to halt his offensive against the Italians in North Africa.

On March 27, elements in the Yugoslavian army carried out a coup in Belgrade that overthrew Paul and repudiated the German alliance. This move was motivated, above all, by popular sentiment among the Serbs against the alliance. Furious at the turn of events, Hitler ordered German forces to invade Yugoslavia. Marshal Wilhelm List's Twelfth Army and Generaloberst (U.S. equiv. full general) Edwald von Kleist's 1st Panzer Group, positioned in Hungary and Romania for the forthcoming invasion of the Soviet Union, now shifted to southwestern Romania and Bulgaria.

The German invasion of Yugoslavia began on 6 April 1941 with a Luftwaffe attack on Belgrade that claimed 17,000 lives. Eleven German infantry divisions and four tank divisions invaded from the north, east, and southeast. Other Axis troops, including the Third Hungarian Army, took part, but Hungarian Premier Pál Teleki committed suicide rather than dishonor himself by participating in the invasion of neighboring Yugoslavia. The invasion was conducted so swiftly that the million-man Yugoslav army was never completely mobilized. Yugoslavia surrendered unconditionally on 17 April.

Simultaneous with their move into Yugoslavia, the Germans came to the aid of the hard-pressed Italians by invading Greece. This move caught the Greeks with 15 divisions in Albania and only 3 divisions and border forces in Macedonia, where the Germans attacked. Also, the scratch British Expeditionary Force (BEF) in Greece was woefully unprepared to deal with German armor and the Luftwaffe, and between 26 and 30 April, it precipitously evacuated Greece. Many of the roughly 50,000 troops taken off were then landed on Crete. During the evacuation of Greece, British naval units were savaged by the Luftwaffe, with the Royal Navy losing more than two dozen ships to German air attack; many other vessels were badly damaged.

In May 1941, the Germans continued their push south by occupying the island of Crete in the eastern Mediterranean in the first airborne invasion in history. The invasion turned out to be the graveyard of German paratroop forces. Hitler saw the action only as a cover for his planned invasion of the Soviet Union, securing the German southern flank against British air assault and helping to protect the vital oil fields of Ploesti. The German invasion, conducted by parachutists and mountain troops carried to the island by transport aircraft, began on 20 May and was soon decided in favor of the attackers. Again, the Royal Navy suffered heavy losses, although it did turn back a German seaborne landing effort. Churchill's decision to try to hold Crete, unprepared and bereft of Royal Air Force (RAF) fighter support, ignored reality. But Hitler, by his aggressive Balkan moves, barred Soviet expansion there and secured protection against a possible British air attack from the south. These goals accomplished, he was ready to move against the Soviet Union.

From the very beginning of the Axis occupation, the Balkans were a theater for guerrilla warfare until the Red Army invaded in August 1944. In both Greece and Yugoslavia, there were Communist and non-Communist resistance groups, which often fought among themselves as well as against their Greek and Italian occupiers. In Greece, the lead was taken by the National People's Liberation Army (ELAS), which came to be dominated by the Communists, and the National Republican Greek League (EDES). In Yugoslavia, the Chetniks were led by former army officers. Soon, a rival resistance group, known as the Partisans, came to the fore, dominated by the Communists. As in Greece, these two groups would become bitter enemies, even to the point of fighting one another. Ultimately, the British, who oversaw Allied aid to the Yugoslav resistance, decided to back only the Partisans, a decision that helped bring Josip Broz (Tito) to power in Yugoslavia after the war. The Yugoslav resistance largely freed the country from German control.

When Italy left the war in September 1943, Germany had to provide the occupying forces on its own, severely straining resources in men and material. The Allies also conducted a number of commando raids in the Balkans, including the German-occupied islands of the eastern Mediterranean.

In late August 1944, the Red Army's 2nd and 3rd Ukrainian Fronts launched an offensive in Romania against Army Group Südukraine. Romania and Bulgaria soon capitulated and then switched sides, declaring war on Germany. In the case of Romania, these events occurred on 23 August and 4 September, and for Bulgaria, they took place on 25 August and 8 December 1944. In Greece, the Communists made three attempts to seize power: the first came during the 1943–1944 Axis occupation in anticipation of an early end to the war; the second occurred in Athens in December 1944; and the third effort came in the form of a bloody and prolonged civil war from 1946 to 1949. World War II in the Balkans was extremely costly in terms of human casualties, both directly—in actual military losses and civilian casualties resulting from warfare—and indirectly, stemming from shortages of food and other necessities.

In the immediate postwar period, the alignment of the Balkans actually worked out by and large along the lines of the agreement made between Churchill and Stalin at Moscow in October 1944. The Soviet Union dominated Romania and Bulgaria, whereas Greece ended up in the Western camp. Yugoslavia, which was to have been a fifty-fifty arrangement, freed itself from Moscow's grip in 1949.

Thomas J. Weiler and Spencer C. Tucker

See also

Albania, Role in War; Bulgaria, Role in War; Churchill, Sir Winston L. S.; Churchill-Stalin Meeting; Crete, Battle of; Croatia; German-Soviet Non-aggression Pact; Greece Campaign (28 October 1940–March 1941); Greece Campaign (April 1941); Hitler, Adolf; Hungary, Role in War; Kleist, Edwald von; Mussolini, Benito; Romania Campaign; Romania, Role in War; Stalin, Josef; Tito; Turkey; Wavell, Sir Archibald Percival; Yugoslavia Campaign (1941); Yugoslavia Campaign (1944–1945)

References

Beevor, Anthony. *Crete: The Battle and the Resistance.* Boulder, CO: Westview Press, 1994.

Blau, George E. *Invasion Balkans! The German Campaign in the Balkans, Spring 1941.* Shippensburg, PA: Burd Street Press, 1997.

Glenny, Misha. *The Balkans: Nationalism, War, and the Great Powers, 1804–1999.* New York: Viking Penguin, 2000.

Kennedy, Robert M. *Hold the Balkans! German Antiguerrilla Operations in the Balkans, 1941–1944.* Shippensburg, PA: White Mane Press, 2001.

Mazower M. *Inside Hitler's Greece: The Experience of Occupation, 1941–1944.* New Haven, CT: Yale University Press, 1993.

Woodhouse, C. M. *The Struggle for Greece, 1941–1949.* London: Hart-Davis, MacGibbon, 1949.

Balloon Bombs (1944–1945)

Balloon bombs were launched by the Japanese army between November 1944 and July 1945 in Operation FU-GO and carried by the jet stream across the Pacific Ocean, traveling from Japan to North America. The operation was planned by Colonel Kusaba Sueki of the 9th Research Division in reprisal for the Doolittle raid on Tokyo on 18 April 1942. The original plan was to launch the balloon bombs from submarines near the U.S. West Coast, but the Japanese navy refused to provide submarines for such a mission. As a consequence, plans were developed to launch the balloons from Japan.

The balloons were made of paper and *konjak* (a Japanese food made from *taro* paste, used as glue). They were about 30 ft in diameter and were filled with hydrogen. Each balloon carried one 33 lb antipersonnel bomb or two 13.2 lb incendiary bombs.

The balloons flew at a maximum speed of some 120 mph at an altitude of 24,000 to 30,000 ft in a flight that took about 50 hours. During the war, Japan produced 10,000 balloon bombs and launched 9,000 of them against North America, but only about 285 incidents involving them were reported in the United States and Canada. The balloons had no sensor or guidance systems, and once they were released, their flight depended entirely on the jet stream air currents. Therefore, the bombs rarely hit their targets.

In the only reported fatalities from the balloon bombs, one woman and five children were killed while on a picnic in Oregon on 5 May 1945. Some West Coast forest fires were attributed to the balloon bombs, but there is no direct evidence of this. The bombs reached British Columbia in Canada, and Alaska, Oregon, Montana, Washington, California, north Texas, and even Michigan in the United States.

The U.S. government feared that Japan would use the balloons as biological weapons, and it prohibited press reports about them to prevent panic among its citizens. Indeed, the Japanese made preparations for just such an effort, although it was never carried out. The U.S. military, meanwhile, endeavored to locate the balloon launch sites, which were finally identified by analyzing a balloon captured by the U.S. Navy. That the balloons had come across the Pacific from Japan was a considerable surprise.

The Japanese army expended enormous resources in Operation FU-GO. Some 30,000 Japanese soldiers and almost 30,000 civilians were engaged in the operation over a two-year period, and six soldiers were killed in an accident while loading bombs for the balloons.

Kotani Ken

See also

Strategic Bombing; Tokyo, Bombing of (18 April 1942)

References

Mikesh, Robert. *Japan's World War II Balloon Bomb Attacks on North America.* Washington, DC: Smithsonian Institution Press, 1990.

Banten Bay, Battle of (28 February 1942)

Naval battle in the Pacific Theater, also known as the Battle of Sunda Strait. On 27 February 1942, the American-British-Dutch-Australian (ABDA) Command failed to block a Japanese invasion of Java in the Battle of Java Sea, and the surviving ABDA warships retreated to Java. The following day, at around 1:30 P.M., the cruisers USS *Houston* and HMAS *Perth,* together with the destroyer HMNS *Evertsen,* reached Batavia's port of Tanjong Priok. Resupply proved difficult, and only ammunition for the cruisers' secondary guns and 300 tons of fuel, half of the *Perth*'s needs, were secured. Also, the *Houston*'s number 3 turret was damaged, and the crews were exhausted. Nonetheless, the ABDA naval commander, Dutch Admiral Conrad Helfrich, ordered his warships to rendezvous at Tjilatjap on Java's south coast for another sortie against the Japanese.

At 7:00 P.M., the cruisers, commanded by Captain Hec Waller of the *Perth*, steamed west into Sunda Strait but without the *Evertsen*, which was still getting up steam. Two hours earlier, ABDA aircraft had spotted the Japanese approaching Banten Bay, but this information failed to reach ABDA's naval commanders.

At 11:06 P.M., Waller's force encountered the Japanese Western Attack Force near the entrance to Banten Bay. Rear Admiral Kurita Takeo had overall command of the Japanese force covering the invasion. His ships included the heavy cruisers *Suzuya* and *Kumano*, the aircraft carrier *Ryujo*, and destroyers situated about 20 miles north of Banten Bay to protect against an Allied attack from that direction. Just outside the bay were the cruisers *Mogami* and *Mikuma* and a destroyer. Inside the bay were the light cruisers *Natori* and *Yuri*, eight destroyers, and a minelayer protecting 58 Japanese merchantmen that were disembarking troops onto the shore.

Unaware that he was caught between these two Japanese forces, Waller led the *Perth* and *Houston* into the bay to attack the Japanese troop transports. His ships fired at multiple targets while steaming in a 5-mile circle around the bay. Meanwhile, the cruisers of the Japanese covering force came up, which led to some confusion when the two Japanese naval forces fired on each other. In the confusion, the *Houston* and *Perth* were about to escape into the Sunda Strait when a Japanese torpedo struck the latter at 12:05 A.M. Three additional torpedoes finished her off. The *Houston* took a Japanese torpedo hit at 12:15 A.M. but continued to return fire in a gallant effort. Heavy Japanese shelling and additional torpedoes sank the *Houston* by 12:45 A.M.

In the battle, the *Perth* lost 353 crewmen, and of her 320 survivors, 100 died while being held as prisoners of war (POWs). The *Houston* lost 655 crew; of her 368 survivors, 76 died while POWs. Japanese losses, some self-inflicted, included the transports *Sakura Maru*, *Horai Maru*, and *Ryujo Maru* and the minesweeper *W2*, all of which were sunk. The cruiser *Mikuma* and destroyer *Harukaze* were both damaged. Japanese personnel losses are unknown. The Japanese Western Attack Force had crushed Allied opposition and could now expand the beachhead without fear of opposition.

Jonathan "Jack" Ford

See also

Darwin, Raid on; Doorman, Karel Willem Frederik Marie; Java Sea, Battle of the; Kurita Takeo; Lombok, Battle of; Madoera Strait, Battle of; Makassar Strait, Battle of; Menado, Battle of; Netherlands East Indies; Palembang, Battle of; Sunda Strait, Battle of

References

Gill, George Hermon. *Royal Australian Navy, 1942–1945.* Canberra: Australian War Memorial, 1957.

Morison, Samuel Eliot. *History of United States Naval Operations in World War II.* Vol. 3, *The Rising Sun in the Pacific, 1931–April 1942.* Boston: Little, Brown, 1951.

Winslow, Walter G. *The Ghost That Died at Sunda Strait.* Annapolis, MD: Naval Institute Press, 1994.

BARBAROSSA, Operation (22 June 1941)

German invasion of the Soviet Union that opened World War II on the Eastern Front, commencing the largest, most bitterly contested, and bloodiest campaign of the war. Adolf Hitler's objective for Operation BARBAROSSA was simple: he sought to crush the Soviet Union in one swift blow. With the USSR defeated and its vast resources at his disposal, surely Britain would have to sue for peace. So confident was he of victory that he made no effort to coordinate the invasion with his Japanese ally. Hitler predicted a quick victory in a campaign of, at most, three months.

German success hinged on the speed of advance of 154 German and satellite divisions deployed in three army groups: Army Group North in East Prussia, under Field Marshal Wilhelm von Leeb; Army Group Center in northern Poland, commanded by Field Marshal Fedor von Bock; and Army Group South in southern Poland and Romania under Field Marshal Karl Gerd von Rundstedt. Army Group North consisted of 3 panzer, 3 motorized, and 24 infantry divisions supported by the Luftflotte 1 and joined by Finnish forces. Farther north, German General Nikolaus von Falkenhorst's Norway Army would carry out an offensive against Murmansk in order to sever its supply route to Leningrad. Within Army Group Center were 9 panzer, 7 motorized, and 34 infantry divisions, with the Luftflotte 2 in support. Marshal von Rundstedt's Army Group South consisted of 5 panzer, 3 motorized, and 35 infantry divisions, along with 3 Italian divisions, 2 Romanian armies, and Hungarian and Slovak units. Luftflotte 4 provided air support.

Meeting this onslaught were 170 Soviet divisions organized into three "strategic axes" (commanding multiple fronts, the equivalent of army groups)—Northern, Central, and Southern or Ukrainian—that would come to be commanded by Marshals Kliment E. Voroshilov, Semen K. Timoshenko, and Semen M. Budenny, respectively. Voroshilov's fronts were responsible for the defense of Leningrad, Karelia, and the recently acquired Baltic states. Timoshenko's fronts protected the approaches to Smolensk and Moscow. And

Eastern Front 1941

A TURNING POINT?
⌒ German Invasion of the Soviet Union ⌒

On 22 June 1941, the German army began Operation BARBAROSSA, the invasion of the Soviet Union. This event dramatically altered the course of the war. No longer fighting Germany virtually alone, Great Britain now had a formidable ally. Nearly four years later, Soviet troops captured Berlin and Germany was defeated. Was Adolf Hitler's decision to invade the Soviet Union an irrational act? Was BARBAROSSA doomed to failure from the start? Based on the final result, it appears so, but in 1941, many knowledgeable military and political officials believed otherwise.

Even before World War II, Nazi Germany and the Communist Soviet Union were bitter ideological enemies. When the two powers signed the Soviet-German Non-aggression Pact on 23 August 1939, it took most observers by surprise, but this agreement in fact benefited both sides. Germany was free to invade Poland, and the Soviet Union gained both territory and time to rearm. The unexpectedly swift German victory over France in 1940 left Hitler in control of Western Europe. Although Germany lost the Battle of Britain that summer and Hitler indefinitely postponed a sea

invasion of that country (Operation SEA LION) in September, he still had a large, experienced, and undefeated army. In December, Hitler issued Directive No. 21 to "crush Soviet Russia in a quick campaign before the end of the war against England."

In October 1940, Germany's ally Italy invaded Greece. The invasion went poorly, and Britain sent troops to Greece. At the same time, a coup in Yugoslavia led that nation to repudiate its recently signed alliance with Germany. A furious Hitler ordered his army and air force into both Yugoslavia and Greece and then on to Crete.

He next turned his attention to the invasion of the Soviet Union. German overconfidence, based on the quick defeat of France, led Hitler to conclude that the Soviet Union might be defeated in six weeks. Soviet leader Josef Stalin's purges of the officer class and the mediocre performance of the Red Army in the 1940 Russo-Finnish War seemed to support Hitler's conclusion that "all you have to do is kick in the door and the whole rotten structure will crumble to the ground."

BARBAROSSA began late because of Ger-

man delays in assembling the requisite forces for the invasion, the Balkan Campaign, and, above all, inclement weather. The invaders needed a period of dry weather to use their tanks effectively. BARBAROSSA began on 22 June, five weeks after the planned starting date of 15 May. Employing a force of 3.6 million men, nearly 3,000 tanks, and more than 2,700 aircraft, the Germans made dramatic, rapid gains. Early on, the attackers destroyed much of the Red Air Force and then encircled and captured vast Soviet ground formations. A logistical pause of one week in August grew to four weeks, which meant that the German drives on Leningrad and Moscow were seriously impeded by the onset of autumnal rains, mud, and winter weather. In October, the Germans began Operation TAIFUN (TYPHOON) to take Moscow. They never reached the Soviet capital, and in December, Soviet Siberian reinforcements hurled them back. The Germans still held the military initiative, having conquered much of the western Soviet Union and taken 3 million Soviet prisoners of war in little more than six months of fighting. Despite this success, however, they had failed to achieve the quick

those of Budenny guarded the Ukraine. For the most part, these forces were largely unmechanized and were arrayed in three linear defensive echelons, the first as far as 30 miles from the border and the last as much as 180 miles back.

The German plan called for three phases in which they hoped to achieve three broad objectives: the destruction of Soviet armed forces; the capture of political and industrial centers; and the occupation of coal, iron, and agricultural centers in the Ukraine and Caucasus. Phase one called for Nazi ground forces, supported by air, to drive deep into Soviet territory and encircle and destroy Soviet forces west of the Dvina-Dnieper Line while disrupting supply lines and creating maximum chaos. Phase two objectives were the seizure of Leningrad, Moscow, and the Ukraine to prevent political-military direction and economic support to the Red Army. In Phase three, the Wehrmacht was to advance to and hold the Volga-Archangel Line.

Initial Soviet defensive plans differed, but the primary defense in all was to position the bulk of forces along the perceived path of any German attack. The differences in the plans came from disagreements over the exact direction of the assumed main thrust. One concept held that the principal German attack would occur in the north, whereas another prepared for the main attack in the south, into the Ukraine. For whatever reasons, none considered the center of the front toward Moscow as primary. Soviet leader Josef Stalin believed the assault would be launched toward the Ukraine and Caucasus because of the agricultural and mineral resources there. Consequently, final General Staff plans were developed for the Red Army to defend against a southern main thrust.

Whatever the direction of any German attack, Stalin counted on a repeat of the stalemate of the Western Front of 1914 to 1918 or at least a campaign lasting a year or more.

victory that Hitler had sought and instead found themselves bogged down in a long campaign of attrition.

BARBAROSSA may have failed because rainy weather and the need to assemble the resources involved delayed its start by more than a month. Further, the Germans were unprepared for the harsh Russian winter. There are other reasons as well: the Soviet landmass was considerable; the Soviets were able to relocate industry to the east; Soviet resources were vastly superior to those of the Germans in terms of sheer numbers of soldiers, tanks, and aircraft; and German racial policies toward the Soviet population were utterly self-defeating. Repeated poor strategic and operational decisions by Hitler and his generals, massive matériel support from Stalin's Western allies in the form of Lend-Lease assistance, and Soviet pluck and adaptiveness eventually canceled the remarkable early German gains. Despite these advantages, it would take the Red Army nearly three years to liberate what the German armed forces conquered in six months of 1941.

In retrospect, attacking the Soviet Union while Great Britain was undefeated appears to have been a major mistake. There were alternatives. One was to keep up the pressure on Britain via U-boat and aircraft attacks in an attempt to starve that nation into submission. Another was to make a major effort in the Mediterranean Theater. Both Reichsmarschall (Reich Marshal) Hermann Göring, commander of the German air force, and Grand Admiral Erich Raeder, commander of the German navy, argued for a Mediterranean strategy. They presented plans to Hitler for a series of operations to bring Spain into the war on the German side; seize Gibraltar and Malta; and then conquer Egypt, take the Suez Canal, and capture the Middle East oil fields. Thereafter, the Soviet Union could be invaded from the Middle East, if necessary.

Hitler rejected this course of action. Aside from the "nuisance" air attacks of the Blitz and the U-boat campaign in the Battle of the Atlantic, he never maintained the pressure on Britain. He did bolster the Axis effort in North Africa in the creation of the Afrika Korps (Africa Corps), but there, too, he never made a major effort. Even a few additional divisions for General Erwin Rommel might have given the Axis control of the Suez Canal. But instead, Hitler merely found a new way in which to deplete his strength and especially his limited air transport. His concentration on the Soviet Union was based largely on ideological rather than sound strategic reasoning. Ultimately, although Operation BARBAROSSA seriously crippled the Soviet Union, the campaign ended in the defeat of Germany.

Dana Lombardy and T. P. Schweider

See also

Atlantic, Battle of the; BARBAROSSA, Operation; Blitz, The; Göring, Hermann Wilhelm; Hitler, Adolf; Leningrad, Siege of; Moscow, Battle of; Raeder, Erich; Rommel, Erwin Johannes Eugen; SEA LION, Operation; Stalin, Josef

References

Clark, Alan. *Barbarossa.* New York: Penguin, 1966.

Ericson, John. *The Road to Stalingrad.* New York: Harper and Row, 1975.

Fugate, Bryan, and Lev Dvoretsky. *Thunder on the Dnepr: Zhukov-Stalin and the Defeat of Hitler's Blitzkrieg.* Novato, CA: Presidio, 1997.

Isom, Dallas Woodbury. "The Battle of Midway: Why the Japanese Lost." *Naval War College Review* 53, no. 3 (Summer 2000): 60–100.

Magenheimer, Heinz. *Hitler's War: Germany's Key Strategic Decisions, 1940–1945.* London: Cassell, 1998.

Muller, Rolf-Dieter, and Ueberschär, Gerd R. *Hitler's War in the East, 1941–1945: A Critical Assessment.* Providence, RI: Berghahn Books, 2002.

Soviet planning estimated that any war between Germany and the USSR would last a minimum of three years. Critical to ensuring the ability of the Soviet Union to fight a protracted war would be denial of the eastern Ukraine to the Germans, which is why so much Soviet armor was positioned forward in June 1941.

Stalin refused to believe Soviet intelligence reports that German forces were massing on the western approaches to the USSR. He also rejected Western warnings with detailed information of the impending Germany attack. He received a reported 100 Western warnings but dismissed them all as efforts by the Western powers to involve the Soviet Union in the war. The German ambassador to the Soviet Union, Count Friedrich von Schulenberg, who opposed war between Germany and the Soviet Union, even informed an astonished Vladimir Dekanozev, the Soviet ambassador to Germany, that Germany would invade. Reportedly, Stalin informed the Politburo that "disinformation has now reached ambassadorial level."

Although Stalin had utilized the respite of the Soviet-German Non-aggression Pact period to improve war stocks and develop military industries, he ultimately resisted fully mobilizing the Red Army for fear that doing so would provoke Hitler. These factors, plus the self-inflicted decapitation of the Soviet armed forces in the 1937 purges that liquidated 40 to 50 percent of the senior officer corps, left the Red Army unable to prevent the Wehrmacht from achieving tremendous initial victories.

Hitler had ordered that preparations for the invasion of the Soviet Union be complete by May 15, but the assault did not actually occur until June 22, almost the very day that Napoleon Bonaparte had begun his invasion of Russia in 1812. Heavy spring rains in eastern Europe were the most important factor in the delay, as the panzers needed dry, hard ground for an advance across a country with few roads. Also, it took more time than anticipated to assemble the invasion force of more than 3 million men, the largest in history. Motor transport had to be allocated, and the Luftwaffe was also slow to build forward airfields. Moreover, units taking part in the campaign in the Balkans had to be relocated and refitted.

Despite all the German preparations, there was a great disparity in military hardware. The Luftwaffe, still waging operations against Britain and also supporting the Afrika Korps (Africa Corps) in North Africa, was forced to keep 1,150 combat aircraft in these theaters. Thus, only 2,770 combat aircraft were available against the Soviet Union. Arrayed against them were 18,570 Soviet aircraft, 8,154 of which were initially in the west and the bulk of them tactical aircraft of sturdy basic designs, including the excellent Ilyushin Il-2 Shturmovik ground-attack aircraft.

Germany deployed some 6,000 tanks, the Soviets 23,140 (10,394 in the west)—and even in 1941, the Soviets possessed some of the best tanks of the war. Their BT-series and T-26 were superior in armor, firepower, and maneuverability to the German light PzKpfw I and II and could destroy any German tank. Similarly, the Soviet T-34 medium tank and KV-1 heavy tank were superior to the PzKpfw III and IV and indeed any German tank in June 1941.

The German attack began at 3:00 A.M. on 22 June 1941, the longest day of the year, with only two hours of total darkness. Soviet forces were taken completely by surprise. German panzer and mechanized divisions easily broke through the defenses and were deep into Soviet territory by nightfall. Striking Soviet air forces within range, the Luftwaffe, in one day's operation for all practical purposes, gained air supremacy over the operational area. Army Group North took Kaunas in one day and reached the Dvina River after four days, then rolled into Riga on 29 June. Not until they reached new Soviet defensive positions south of Pskov on 8 July did the Germans encounter stiff resistance.

The progress of Army Group South was slowed by numerous natural obstacles, which allowed Soviet forces to withdraw in a more orderly manner and even to counterattack occasionally. The southern army group advanced along three lines: the Lublin-Kovel-Lutsk-Zhitomir-Kiev line; the Przemysl–L'viv (Lvov)–Vinnitsia–Dnieper River line; and a third line from Romania to Odessa and Dnepropetrovsk. Soviet forces avoided German encirclement attempts in this southern zone until Uman, where, in early August, over 100,000 men were encircled and surrendered, along with 300 tanks and 800 pieces of heavy artillery.

The most spectacular results were achieved by Army Group Center. It reached the Dnieper River by 6 July, where it encountered increased Soviet resistance. Before arriving there, however, one column took Vilnius on 24 June and then headed for Minsk, where it joined the second column that had come from Brest-Litovsk. On 27 June, the two columns met to surround a large number of Soviet troops around Grodno and Bialystok, provoking the surrender of 320,000 men, 3,000 tanks, and 2,000 pieces of heavy artillery. Even with stiffening resistance, Soviet forces could not prevent the Germans from crossing the Dnieper on 9 July and seizing Smolensk on 16 July, where they captured another 300,000 prisoners.

Phase one of BARBAROSSA seemed a success. Despite increased resistance, Wehrmacht forces appeared to have open roads to Leningrad, Moscow, and Kiev after capturing nearly a million Soviet troops and killing countless others. Phase two of the German plan, however, proved more difficult to achieve for several reasons. Soviet defenses were stiffening because the initial shock of invasion had worn off and an additional 5 million men in reserve forces had been mobilized and thrown into the breach. In addition, Hitler and his generals had been debating the best course of action for phase two, and the objectives continued to change. The generals believed the army should concentrate on securing Moscow because it was the Soviet capital and a vital communication and industrial center. It offered, they believed, the best chance to destroy the Soviet armies. Hitler, however, at first thought the priority should be the seizure of Leningrad and a linkup with the Finns; then, the Germans and Finns together should clear the Baltic and open a sea line of communications. But by mid-August, Hitler had changed his mind and directed the main effort to focus on the Ukraine and Caucasus in order to gain the resources of those regions, relegating both Leningrad and Moscow to secondary priority. He even directed the other two army groups to yield forces to reinforce Army Group South.

Phase two finally began with an assault on Kiev, which fell to the Germans on 19 September and netted 650,000 additional prisoners. Then, fall rain and mud slowed the German advance in the south. Movement toward Leningrad also slowed, partly because of increased Soviet resistance but also because Hitler conceived a new plan. This plan, known as Operation TAIFUN (Typhoon), called for Leningrad to be encircled, put under siege, and starved into submission; the Crimea, the Donbass, and the Caucasus were to be taken for the coal and oil resources that would be gained for Germany's use.

The new plan accorded the highest priority to the encirclement and capture of Moscow. Previously transferred panzer forces were now to revert to Army Group Center, and operations were to commence on 30 September. In the drive on Moscow, the Germans took Orel on 3 October, and 17 days later, around Vyazma and Bryansk, they captured 665,000 Soviet prisoners. But again, fall rains and mud, increasing Soviet resistance as the Germans neared the capital, and an early drop in temperature to well below zero ground the German advance to a halt.

Some success was had elsewhere. Leningrad was nearly surrounded, and the Crimea was taken along with Odessa, Karkov, and Rostov-on-Don, but these achievements were short-lived when, along the entire front, the Soviets opened their first major counteroffensive in early December 1941.

Because the strategic objective did not change, it can be argued that Operation BARBAROSSA continued for the entire period of Germany's strategic advance, from the surprise attack on 22 June 1941 until the assault that stalled before Moscow in November. However, the commencement of Operation TAIFUN, with its change of operational focus and main objectives, technically ended Operation BARBAROSSA.

Arthur T. Frame

See also

Bock, Fedor von; Budenny, Semen Mikhailovich; Eastern Front; Finnish-Soviet War (Continuation War); German-Soviet Non-aggression Pact; Great Purges; Leeb, Wilhelm Franz Josef Ritter von; Moscow, Battle of; Rundstedt, Karl Rudolf Gerd von; Stalin, Josef; Stalingrad, Battle of; Timoshenko, Semen Konstantinovich; Voroshilov, Kliment Efremovich; Vyazma-Bryansk, Battles for; Zhukov, Georgii Konstantinovich

References

Clark, Alan. *Barbarossa: The Russian-German Conflict, 1941–45.* New York: William Morrow, 1965.

Deutscher, Isaac. *Stalin: A Political Biography.* New York: Oxford University Press, 1969.

Erickson, John. *The Road to Stalingrad: Stalin's War with Germany.* New York: Harper and Row, 1975.

Salisbury, Harrison E. *The Unknown War.* New York: Bantam Books, 1978.

Werth, Alexander. *Russia at War, 1941–1945.* New York: E. P. Dutton, 1964.

Ziemke, Earl F., and Magna E. Bauer. *Moscow to Stalingrad: Decision in the East.* Washington, DC: U.S. Government Printing Office, 1987.

Barbey, Daniel Edward (1889–1969)

U.S. Navy admiral who established the navy's Amphibious Warfare Section and commanded the Amphibious Force, Seventh Fleet. Born on 23 December 1889 at Portland, Oregon, Daniel Barbey graduated from the U.S. Naval Academy in 1912. He served on several ships during World War I and rose to the rank of lieutenant.

Following the war, Barbey was stationed in Wales and Turkey before returning to sea duty in 1922. Between 1928 and 1931, he served as an administrator at the Naval Academy. Promoted to commander in 1933, Barbey held various positions before being assigned to the War Plans Section of the Bureau of Navigation in 1937. There, he worked on developing mobilization strategies. He also became fascinated with amphibious warfare, a subject that had been little studied since World War I. In February 1940, Barbey was promoted to captain and took command of the battleship *New York.*

In January 1941, he became the chief of staff to Rear Admiral Randall Jacobs of the Service Force and Amphibious Force, Atlantic Fleet. He was promoted to rear admiral in June 1942 while on the staff of Chief of Naval Operations Admiral Ernest King. In this capacity, he founded the Amphibious Warfare Section of the U.S. Navy and worked to establish doctrine and tactics, as well as to secure equipment better suited to amphibious operations. Under his leadership, the DUKW amphibious truck was developed, along with other new landing craft designs.

In January 1943, Barbey became commander of the Amphibious Force, Seventh Fleet, setting up his headquarters at Port Stevens, Australia. Working under General Douglas MacArthur from 1943 until the summer of 1945, he commanded 56 amphibious landings in support of various invasions, including those of New Guinea, the Philippines, and Borneo.

Promoted to vice admiral in December 1944, Barbey was the ranking naval subordinate to MacArthur in the southwest Pacific. After the war, he held various positions, including commander of the Seventh Fleet, commander of the Atlantic Amphibious Forces, commander of the Fourth Fleet, and chairman of the Joint Military Board. From March 1947 until September 1950, he commanded U.S. naval forces in the Caribbean. Barbey retired from the navy in June 1951. He died at Bremerton, Washington, on 11 March 1969.

Harold Wise

See also

Amphibious Warfare; King, Ernest Joseph; MacArthur, Douglas; New Guinea Campaign; Philippines, U.S. Recapture of; Southwest Pacific Theater

References

Barbey, Daniel Edward. *MacArthur's Amphibious Navy: Seventh Amphibious Force Operations, 1943–1945.* Annapolis, MD: Naval Institute Press, 1969.

Morison, Samuel Eliot. *History of United States Naval Operations in World War II.* Vol. 8, *New Guinea and the Marianas, March 1944–August 1944.* Boston: Little, Brown, 1953.

———. *History of United States Naval Operations in World War II.* Vol. 13, *The Liberation of the Philippines: Luzon, Minadanao, the Visayas, 1944–1945.* Boston: Little, Brown, 1953.

Barents Sea, Battle of

See Convoy PZQ 17.

Barkhorn, Gerhard (1919–1983)

German air force officer and fighter pilot, the second-highest-scoring ace of World War II, with 301 victories. Born in Königsberg, East Prussia, on 20 March 1919, Gerhard Barkhorn joined the Luftwaffe in March 1938. On completion of his pilot training, he was posted to Staffel 3 (squadron), Jagdgeschwader (fighter wing) 2 (3.JG-2) in October 1939. In August 1940, he was transferred to JG-52 for the Battle of Britain. Barkhorn did not score his first victory until his one hundred and twentieth mission, on 1 July 1941. Within a year, his total stood at 60, and he was awarded the Knight's Cross and, six months later, in January 1943, the Oakleaves. On 23 January 1944, Barkhorn became the first Luftwaffe fighter pilot to have flown 1,000 combat missions and the second to reach 250 victories. For the latter feat, he was awarded the Swords to his Knight's Cross.

During his career, Barkhorn entered combat over 1,100 times. He was shot down nine times, bailed out once, and was wounded twice. On 31 May 1944, with 273 victories, he was well on his way to becoming the leading ace in the Luftwaffe when he was severely wounded in a dogfight. The four months he spent in the hospital allowed another JG-52 ace, Erich Hartmann, to surpass his record. Barkhorn scored his three hundred and first—and final—victory on 5 January 1945.

Barkhorn ended his wartime career as a major flying the Me-262 jet in JV-44, Major General Adolf Galland's "Squadron of Experts." Injuries from a crash landing took Barkhorn out of combat permanently on 21 April 1945. At the end of the war, he surrendered to the Americans and was held prisoner until September 1945.

Barkhorn's postwar career included service in the Federal Republic of Germany's air force from 1956 until his retirement as a major general in 1976. On 6 January 1983, he and his wife, Christl, were involved in a serious automobile accident near Köln (Cologne). Christl died at the scene, and Barkhorn died in the hospital in Köln on 8 January 1983.

M. R. Pierce

See also
Britain, Battle of; Galland, Adolf; Germany, Air Force; Hartmann, Erich Alfred

References
Spick, Mike. *Luftwaffe Fighter Aces: The Jagdflieger and Their Combat Tactics and Techniques.* Mechanicsburg, PA: Stackpole Books, 1996.
Toliver, Raymond F., and Trevor J. Constable. *Fighter Aces of the Luftwaffe.* Fallbrook, CA: Aero, 1977.

Barrage Balloons

Balloons sent aloft to protect against low-level air attack. In 1938, the Royal Air Force (RAF) Balloon Command was established to arrange a system of barrage balloons at strategic sites in Great Britain as antiaircraft devices to guard communities, ports, and industries. Barrage balloons flown from boats prevented aircraft from mining estuaries. Within two years, approximately 6,400 barrage balloons protected Britain, 5,000 of which were in the London area. Air Marshal Sir E. Leslie Gossage directed 52 barrage balloon squadrons, involving 33,000 personnel.

Barrage balloons were designed to prevent low-altitude German air attacks against British factories and other strategic targets. Most of these large, hydrogen-filled, football-shaped balloons were connected to wagons by thick steel cables, which could damage any aircraft that hit them. Camouflage and clouds helped prevent enemy pilots from seeing the barrage balloons.

Mobility was crucial in order to form barriers of barrage balloons. Balloon crews, consisting of members of the Women's Auxiliary Air Force and the RAF Balloon Command, moved barrage balloons as needed and operated winches on the wagons to lower and raise the balloons to designated heights. Some barrage balloons actually reached an altitude of 5,000 feet. Not only did they help prevent German pilots from flying at low altitudes, they also increased the vulnerability of enemy aircraft to antiaircraft weapons, which could be concentrated to fire above their altitudes. During the Blitz, balloon crews devoted night duty to keeping barrage balloons at effective defensive heights and positions. Some 66 German aircraft were lost to collisions with barrage balloon cables.

Smaller barrage balloons were also used to protect shipping, and they floated above Allied ships approaching Normandy for the D day landings. In addition to countering airplanes, barrage balloons were used to protect against attacks by V-1 buzz bombs. In 1944, operators placed a circle of 1,750 barrage balloons in south London, and the balloon cables stopped an estimated 231 V-1s.

The United States employed barrage balloons to help protect vulnerable sites on the U.S. West Coast and the Panama Canal. The Allies also used them in North Africa and in other locations in the Mediterranean. The Germans

U.S. Marine Corps barrage balloons at Parris Island, South Carolina, May 1942. (Library of Congress)

raised barrage balloons over strategic sites in the Reich. Italy and Japan also employed barrage balloons during the war.

A number of the barrage balloons were destroyed by enemy fire or by lightning strikes, and wind and storms often caused balloon damage. Arthur Vestry, a Scottish physicist, devised ways make the balloons lightning-proof, and the Germans sought to develop methods to cut barrage cables without ruining aircraft.

Elizabeth D. Schafer

See also

Antiaircraft Artillery and Equipment; Blitz, The; Britain, Battle of; Camouflage; Great Britain, Home Front; Great Britain, Women's Auxiliary Air Force; Strategic Bombing; V-1 Buzz Bomb; Women in World War II

References

Delderfield, R. F. "A Study in Passive Defence." *Royal Air Force Quarterly* 16, no. 3 (December 1944–September 1945): 167.

Gossage, Leslie. "Balloon Command." *Flying and Popular Aviation* 31, no. 3 (September 1942): 97–100.

Robinson, G. N. *Barrage Balloons.* Maxwell Air Force Base, AL: U.S. Air Force Historical Research Center, 1941.

Turley, R. E. "Barrage Balloons." *Coast Artillery Journal* 85, no. 1 (January-February 1942): 21–22.

Barré, Georges Edmund Lucien (1886–1970)

French Army general who served as the military commander in Tunisia during the war years. Born at Saint-Augnan-sur-Cher on 26 November 1886, Georges Barré graduated from the French Military Academy of St. Cyr in 1912. He then became a colonial officer in Morocco. He distinguished himself in combat in World War I and in subsequent Moroccan pacification efforts. In December 1939, Barré was promoted to brigadier general, and when Germany invaded France in May 1940, he commanded the 7th North African Infantry Division, deployed on the French frontier. Barré's forces fought continuously, sustaining combat casualties of over 30 percent and winning high commendation.

After the June 1940 armistice, Barré was named to head the French delegation to the Italian demilitarization commission on the Libyan frontier. In January 1942, he was promoted to major general and appointed the senior military commander in Tunisia. When British and U.S. forces landed in Africa in November 1942, Barré initially hedged his bets and declared neutrality, his prudence the more advisable because German reinforcements under General

Walter Nehring swiftly arrived in Tunisia, whereas the Allies had not yet landed the 5,000 troops they had originally promised to send there. Barré withdrew his forces into the hills, parleying with the Germans while waiting for Allied forces to arrive to reinforce him. Early in the morning on 19 November 1942, Nehring delivered an ultimatum to Barré, demanding his withdrawal from his stronghold of Medjez-el-Bab within three hours, before dawn. Barré refused, holding the critical redoubt and communications center all day against heavy German air attacks and assaults by the German 5th Parachute Regiment, while the 1st British Parachute Battalion and a U.S. artillery battalion hastily advanced to his support. The French troops finally withdrew under cover of darkness to join with the Free French XIX Corps, fighting hard for the rest of the Tunisia Campaign. In 1943, Barré was promoted to lieutenant general. He retired after the war and died in Paris on 22 January 1970.

Priscilla Roberts

See also
Nehring, Walter Kurt; Tunisia Campaign
References
Barré, Georges. *Tunisie, 1942–1943.* Paris: Berger-Levrault, 1950.
Crémieux-Brilhac, Jean-Louis. *Les Français de l'an 40.* 2 vols. Paris: Gallimard, 1990.
Dessaigne, Francine. *Barré, cet inconnu!* Plougrescant, France: Éditions Confrerie-Castille, 1992.
Jackson, W. G. F. *The Battle for North Africa.* New York: Mason/Charter, 1975.
Paxton, Robert O. *Parades and Politics at Vichy: The French Officer Corps under Marshal Pétain.* Princeton, NJ: Princeton University Press, 1966.

Baruch, Bernard Mannes (1870–1965)

Unofficial U.S. presidential and government adviser before, during, and after World War II. Born in Camden, South Carolina, on 19 August 1870, Bernard Baruch had, before World War I, accumulated a fortune through shrewd stock speculation. A great admirer of U.S. President Woodrow Wilson, Baruch served from 1917 to 1918 as chairman of the War Industries Board, which coordinated the government's industrial procurement for the war effort.

Baruch thereafter became a munificent Democratic contributor who was particularly close to the party's conservative southern power brokers, and a well-oiled publicity machine ably promoted his image as an economic expert ready to serve as an unofficial "adviser to presidents." Baruch maintained close relations with the army, backing the Army Industrial War College, established in 1924, and other efforts at postwar industrial military planning.

Although increasingly unsympathetic to the 1930s New Deal domestic policies of President Franklin D. Roosevelt, the anti-German Baruch largely supported Roosevelt's foreign policies and placed his experience and reputation at the service of the president and the War Department. Baruch successfully suggested that existing American neutrality legislation be modified to enable belligerent nations with the funds and shipping to do so—effectively, Great Britain and its allies—to purchase war supplies in the United States on a "cash-and-carry" basis.

Baruch also advocated major increases in U.S. naval and military strength. As war approached, he supported a comprehensive mobilization of the civilian population and resources, and in the early 1940s, he consistently advocated price stabilization and centralized government direction of all industrial production, proposals that facilitated the creation of the War Production Board in 1943. That organization was headed by Senator James F. Byrnes of North Carolina, an old political associate of Baruch. In February 1944, Baruch and John Hancock, of the investment bank Lehman Brothers, submitted a report on reconversion that recommended the postwar dismantling of government controls and the reversion to job creation through private enterprise. As a postwar adviser on nuclear energy, he advocated policies that effectively ensured that his country would retain its atomic monopoly. Baruch died in New York City on 20 June 1965.

Priscilla Roberts

See also
Byrnes, James Francis; Marshall, George Catlett; Patterson, Robert Porter; Roosevelt, Franklin D.; United States, Home Front
References
Baruch, Bernard M. *The Public Years.* New York: Holt, Rinehart and Winston, 1960.
Hooks, Gregory. *Forging the Military-Industrial Complex: World War II's Battle of the Potomac.* Urbana: University of Illinois Press, 1991.
Schwarz, Jordan A. *The Speculator: Bernard M. Baruch in Washington, 1917–1965.* Chapel Hill: University of North Carolina Press, 1981.

Bastico, Ettore (1876–1972)

Italian army field marshal who was appointed governor of Libya in 1941. Born in Bologna on 9 April 1876, Ettore Bastico joined the army in 1896 and served in the elite Bersaglieri (light infantry). In 1912, he was posted to

Libya, where he took part in pacification operations. Promoted to colonel during World War I and general in 1927, Bastico commanded a division and then a corps during the invasion of Ethiopia. A close friend of Italian dictator Benito Mussolini, Bastico was dispatched to Spain in April 1937 to head the Italian expeditionary force supporting the Nationalist side in the Spanish Civil War. Although he scored one of the few Italian victories at Santander in August, he was relieved of his post in October because of conflicts with the Nationalist leader General Francisco Franco. Nevertheless, in 1938, he received command of Second Army, stationed on the border with Yugoslavia, and in December 1940, he was appointed governor of the Dodecanese Islands.

In July 1941, Bastico became governor of Libya. Although he was, in theory, the superior of the Afrika Korps (Africa Corps) commander Erwin Rommel, he and Rommel immediately developed a contentious relationship over issues involving the command and control of the Axis forces in North Africa. Rommel's repeated rebuffs of Bastico's attempts to rein him in, as well as his increasingly ill disguised contempt for the Italian army, led to a series of heated exchanges between the two, with Rommel referring to Bastico as "Bombastico." Nevertheless, the Axis forces were able to cooperate sufficiently to force the surrender of Tobruk in June 1942. As a result, both Rommel and Bastico were promoted to field marshal.

After the surrender of Tobruk in June 1942, Rommel as usual disregarded Bastico's cautious directives and invaded Egypt. Consequently, the Axis forces became overstretched, thus setting the stage for the decisive British counteroffensive at El Alamein in October 1942. In the wake of the Axis defeat, Bastico was relieved of command in February 1943.

Ettore Bastico retired from the army in 1947. He also wrote a three-volume study of the evolution of warfare. He died in Rome on 2 December 1972.

John M. Jennings

See also
El Alamein, Battle of; Franco, Francisco; Italy, Army; Mussolini, Benito; North Africa Campaign; Rommel, Erwin Johannes Eugene; Spain, Civil War in; Tobruk, First Battle for, Second Battle for, Third Battle of

References
Bastico, Ettore. *L'evolutzione dell'arte della guerra.* 3 vols. Florence, Italy: Casa Editrice Militare Italiana, 1930.
Carver, Michael. *Tobruk.* Philadelphia: Dufour Editions, 1964.
Greene, Jack, and Alessandro Massignani. *Rommel's North African Campaign, September 1940–November 1942.* Conshohocken, PA: Combined Publishing, 1999.
Heckmann, Wolf. *Rommel's War in Africa.* New York: Doubleday, 1981.

Bastogne, Battle for (19 December 1944– 9 January 1945)

Key battle within the German Ardennes Offensive (Battle of the Bulge). Bastogne, Belgium, was an important communications hub; seven main roads, a railroad line, and several minor roads met there. Bastogne and the Ardennes area had been liberated by elements of the U.S. First Army in September 1944. By December, following failed Allied attempts to invade Germany, lines in the west had solidified along the German West Wall (Siegfried Line). As the Allies prepared their next move, Adolf Hitler put in motion a counteroffensive in the Ardennes with the goal of destroying Allied units and recapturing the port of Antwerp. At the very least, Hitler expected to buy time to deal with the Soviets. German success in what was known as Operation WATCH ON THE RHINE depended on total surprise and a rapid capture of Bastogne and the Allied fuel depots and communications routes between it and Saint Vith.

The German offensive, which opened early on 16 December, caught the Americans completely by surprise. General Heinrich von Lüttwitz's XLVII Panzer Corps, the spearhead of the southern German thrust, made for Bastogne, some 20 miles from the German line of attack. The Germans expected to occupy it no later than 18 December, but the poor state of the roads and misinformation provided by Belgians delayed their arrival. Meanwhile, Supreme Allied Commander General Dwight D. Eisenhower correctly concluded that this was a major German offensive rather than a spoiling attack and ordered up reinforcements, including the 101st Airborne Division. Traveling in cattle trucks, the 101st arrived at Bastogne near midnight on the 18 December. The first American units to reach the city, however, were elements of the 10th Armored Division, which had arrived there a few hours earlier.

Major General Fritz Bayerlein's Panzer Lehr Division reached Bastogne just after midnight on 19 December. It attacked immediately, as Bayerlein was aware from radio intercepts that the 101st Airborne was on the way. The Americans beat back the German attack but were under constant German pressure from that point and were completely encircled in a 6-mile-diameter pocket by the evening of 21 December. The Germans now brought up supplies and reinforcements.

On 22 December, four German soldiers, one carrying a white flag, walked toward an American outpost near Bastogne. They carried an ultimatum addressed to "the U.S.A. commander of the encircled city of Bastogne." The message urged Brigadier General Anthony McAuliffe, in command of the division in the absence of Major General Maxwell D. Taylor, to save his troops with an "honorable surrender." McAuliffe's response to the Germans was memorable: "To the German Commander: Nuts. The American commander."

Even though the Germans pressed their offensive all around Bastogne, they failed to take the city. The Allied forces did not break, and Lieutenant General George S. Patton's Third Army was rushing to relieve Bastogne from the south. Patton told an unbelieving Eisenhower that he could wheel his army 90 degrees and strike north into the bulge with three divisions in only two days. He accomplished this feat in one of most memorable mass maneuvers of that or any war.

On 23 December, the weather cleared, freezing the ground and making it passable for armor. Allied planes filled the skies, and transports dropped resupplies to the defenders of Bastogne, then down to only 10 rounds per gun. On Christmas Day, 2nd Armored Division gunners had a "turkey shoot" near the Meuse, destroying 82 German tanks. On 26 December, Lieutenant Colonel Creighton Abrams's 37th Tank Battalion of the 4th Armored Division broke through the German lines, lifting the siege of Bastogne.

The battle now expanded as both sides poured in reinforcements. Fifth Panzer Army made Bastogne its principal effort, as the planned German drive on Antwerp turned into a struggle for Bastogne. Meanwhile, the Americans brought up significant amounts of artillery and armor. Allied aircraft also attacked the German armor without letup, destroying large numbers of tanks. The last major German attack on the city occurred on 4 January. Other smaller attacks took place until 8 January, with the battle ending the next day. The fight for the city had claimed about 2,700 American and 3,000 German casualties; Bastogne itself lost 782 Belgian civilians.

William Head and Spencer C. Tucker

See also
Abrams, Creighton Williams; Ardennes Offensive; Bayerlein, Fritz; Eisenhower, Dwight D.; McAuliffe, Anthony Clement; Patton, George Smith, Jr.; Taylor, Maxwell Davenport

References
Cole, Hugh M. *U.S. Army in World War II, European Theater of Operations—The Ardennes: The Battle of the Bulge.* Washington, DC: Office of the Chief of Military History, Department of the Army, 1965.

Dupuy, Trevor N., David L. Bongard, and Richard C. Anderson Jr. *Hitler's Last Gamble: The Battle of the Bulge, December 1944–January 1945.* New York: Harper Collins, 1994.

Forty, George. *The Reich's Last Gamble: The Ardennes Offensive, December 1944.* London: Cassell, 2000.

MacDonald, Charles B. *A Time for Trumpets: The Untold Story of the Battle of the Bulge.* New York: William Morrow, 1985.

Marshall, S. L. A. *Bastogne: The Story of the First Eight Days.* Washington, DC: Infantry Journal Press, 1946.

Bataan, Battle of (1942)

Key battle of the failed American defense of the Philippine Islands between 1941 and 1942. Bataan is a peninsula on the big island of Luzon; it is some 25 miles long and roughly 20 miles wide and extends south into Manila Bay. The peninsula figured prominently in General Douglas MacArthur's plans for defending the Philippines against a Japanese invasion. The original plan called for U.S. and Philippine forces to withdraw into the Bataan Peninsula and there fight an extended defensive battle until reinforcements arrived from the United States.

MacArthur changed this plan prior to the U.S. entry into the war following the 7 December 1941 attack on Pearl Harbor. He believed that, even with his mobilizing Philippine army and promised reinforcements from the United States, he could defend the entire Philippine Islands against a Japanese invasion. But when elements of Lieutenant General Homma Masaharu's Fourteenth Army landed at Lingayen Gulf on 22 December, it became apparent that MacArthur's new plan would not work. Japanese forces quickly broke through MacArthur's lines north and south of Manila, forcing him to fall back on the original plan but not in orderly fashion. Vast quantities of supplies were lost in the process. By the end of December, more than 67,500 Filipino and 12,500 U.S. troops, as well as 26,000 civilians, were in the Bataan Peninsula. The shortage of supplies put everyone on half rations. Malnutrition, dysentery, and malaria were soon commonplace, with many soldiers unable to fight.

Still, U.S. and Filipino troops put up a stout defense. They lost their main line of defense in late January 1942, but at their secondary line, they stopped Homma's forces by mid-February. The defenders bravely fought on, halting two

Newspapers of 9 April 1942 displayed at a newsstand at a corner drugstore in a Japanese-American neighborhood in Hayward, California, in April 1942, announcing Bataan's fall. (Library of Congress)

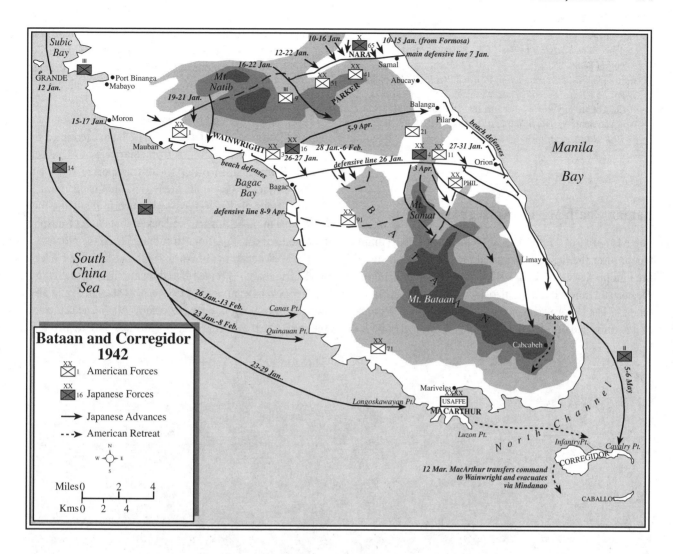

battalion-sized Japanese landings in late January and early February.

Meanwhile, most of Homma's best troops were diverted to the Netherlands East Indies; with more than 2,700 dead, 4,000 wounded, and 13,000 sick, Homma was temporarily unable to mount additional attacks. MacArthur used this pause to shore up his defensive positions, but the realization that no relief force was coming from the United States caused bitter disappointment. The Americans and Filipinos called themselves the "Battling Bastards of Bataan." And in the wake of U.S. defeats at Pearl Harbor, Guam, and Wake Island, as well as the British defeat at Singapore, the resistance that was mounted in Bataan boosted morale on the American home front.

President Franklin D. Roosevelt ordered MacArthur to leave the Philippines on 11 March, and command of U.S.-Filipino forces fell to Major General Jonathan Wainwright. He inherited a hopeless cause. Homma received reinforcements, and his troops finally broke through the American-Filipino lines on 3 April. MacArthur ordered Wainwright not

to surrender, but the U.S. ground forces commander, Major General Edward P. King Jr., realizing that the cause was hopeless, decided to end the fight and capitulated on 9 April.

More than 20,000 Americans and Filipinos perished in the campaign, and roughly 2,000 escaped to the nearby island of Corregidor and fought on until they in turn were forced to surrender on 5 May. The 76,000 prisoners of war of the battle for Bataan—some 64,000 Filipino soldiers and 12,000 Americans—then were forced to endure what came to be known as the Bataan Death March as they were moved into captivity. They had succeeded, however, in delaying the Japanese conquest of the Philippines for 148 days and briefly inspiring the Allied cause during the dark early days of U.S. participation in World War II.

Lance Janda

See also

Bataan Death March; Clark Field, Japanese Raid on; Corregidor, Battle of; Homma Masaharu; Iba Field, Attack on; King, Edward Postell, Jr.; MacArthur, Douglas; Philippines, Japanese Capture of; Wainwright, Jonathan Mayhew

References

Mallonée, Richard. *Battle for Bataan: An Eyewitness Account.* New York: I Books, 2003.

Morton, Louis. *United States Army in World War II: The War in the Pacific—Fall of the Philippines.* Washington, DC: Office of the Chief of Military History, Department of the Army, 1953.

Whitman, John W. *Bataan: Our Last Ditch—The Bataan Campaign, 1942.* New York: Hippocrene Books, 1990.

Bataan Death March (April 1942)

Forced march of 12,000 U.S. soldiers and 64,000 Filipino troops after the Japanese captured the Bataan Peninsula in the Philippines. On 3 April 1942, Japanese General Homma Masaharu launched a new offensive against the Bataan defenders. The U.S. Far Eastern commander, General Douglas MacArthur, had ordered the troops to continue to fight, but six days later, with his men worn down by the strain of constant combat, disease, and starvation, Major General Edward P. King, commander of the forces on Bataan, ordered them to surrender. The troops had been on half rations since January.

Homma had decided that he would hold the prisoners at Camp O'Donnell, 100 miles away. The Japanese forced the prisoners to march 52 miles from Mariveles to San Fernando, Pampanga, in order to be transported by rail to Capas, Tarlac. They would then walk another 8 miles to Camp O'Donnell. King expressed concern about his men being able to make this trip and asked that trucks transport them to their final location. Homma rejected the request.

The trek began on 10 April 1942 and lasted for over a week. The march is remembered for its sheer brutality, but before it even began, each prisoner was searched, and anyone found to possess a Japanese souvenir was executed on the spot. Allied soldiers were, for the most part, denied food

The start of the Bataan Death March. (1945, from a Japanese photograph taken in 1942, Library of Congress)

and water by their guards until the completion of their journey. The only food that some received was a bit of rancid rice. The prisoners of war were given only a few hours of rest each night in crowded conditions. One of the worst forms of punishment inflicted on the captives was known as the sun treatment, in which the prisoner, denied any water, was forced to sit in the scalding Philippine sun without the protection of a helmet. Prisoners were beaten, kicked, and killed for falling behind or violating the smallest rule.

Between 7,000 and 10,000 of the prisoners died before reaching Camp O'Donnell. The Japanese had failed to take into consideration both the poor health of their captives and their numbers. Although a few of the prisoners escaped into the jungle, most were physically unable even to make the attempt. A number were murdered at random by their guards.

Many who survived the march died in the overcrowded, suffocating boxcars on the rail trip to Capas. In the two months after reaching the camp, 1,600 Americans and 16,000 Filipinos died of starvation, disease, and maltreatment. The cruelty of the march became well known, and U.S. commanders used the story of the Bataan Death March to motivate their troops in subsequent fighting against the Japanese.

T. Jason Soderstrum

See also

Bataan, Battle of; Homma Masaharu; King, Edward Postell, Jr.; MacArthur, Douglas; Philippines, Japanese Capture of; Wainwright, Jonathan Mayhew

References

Berry, William A. *Prisoner of the Rising Sun.* Norman: University of Oklahoma Press, 1993.

Bumgarner, John Reed. *Parade of the Dead: A U.S. Army Physician's Memoir of Imprisonment by the Japanese, 1942–1945.* Jefferson, NC: McFarland, 1995.

Falk, Stanley Lawrence. *Bataan: The March of Death.* New York: Norton, 1962.

Hubbard, Preston. *Apocalypse Undone: My Survival of Japanese Imprisonment during World War II.* Nashville, TN: Vanderbilt University Press, 1990.

Young, Donald J. *The Battle of Bataan: A History of the 90-Day Siege and Eventual Surrender of 75,000 Filipino and United States Troops to the Japanese in World War II.* Jefferson, NC: McFarland, 1992.

Batov, Pavel Ivanovich (1897–1985)

Soviet army general who served on the Bryansk Front and in the Battle of Kursk, among many other engagements. Born on 1 June 1897 in the village of Filisovo in the Rybinsk region of Yaroslavl Province, Russia, Pavel Batov entered the army in 1915 during World War I and fought on the Russo-German Front. He won two St. George Crosses and was wounded in combat in 1917. On his recovery, he was assigned to the noncommissioned officer (NCO) school in Petrograd, where he became a convert to Bolshevism. Batov joined the Red Army in August 1918 and fought in the Russian Civil War. Between 1926 and 1927, he attended the Vystrel Officers' School. On graduation, he took command of a battalion of the 1st Moscow Proletarian Rifle Division. He served with this division for nearly nine years, commanding its 3rd Rifle Regiment in 1933. In 1936 and 1937, he served as an adviser to the Republican side in the Spanish Civil War and was twice wounded.

Promoted to brigade commander on his return to the Soviet Union in December 1937, Batov took command of the X Rifle Corps. In early 1938, he assumed command of the III Rifle Corps. At the same time, he served on a special commission to recommend the restructuring of Red Army mechanized and motorized forces. The commission's report, approved in November 1939, unwisely recommended abolishing the army's 4 tank corps and replacing them with 15 smaller motorized divisions.

Batov's III Corps of four divisions participated in the September 1939 Soviet invasion of Poland and in the February–March 1940 phase of the Soviet invasion of Finland. His service in Finland earned him promotion to lieutenant general in June 1940, and soon thereafter, he was named deputy commander of the Transcaucasia Military District.

In June 1941, Batov was summoned to Moscow and given charge of the IX Separate Rifle Corps in the Crimea. No sooner had he taken up his post then the Germans invaded the Soviet Union. In October 1941, Batov became deputy commander of the Fifty-First Special Army. From January to February 1942, he commanded Third Army on the Bryansk Front, and from February to October 1942, he was deputy front commander. He then headed Fourth Tank Army, redesignated Sixty-Fifth Army, in the Stalingrad area. Following the Soviet victory at Stalingrad in January 1943, Batov fought in the Battle of Kursk, the crossing of the Dnieper River, and the drive through Belorussia into East Pomerania and across the Oder River. During the war, Batov was very popular with his men because he was one of the few senior officers who visited the front lines and conversed with the soldiers.

Promoted to colonel general in June 1944, Batov was in the Northern Group of Forces between 1944 and 1948 and was first deputy commanding general of Soviet forces in the occupation of East Germany. Promoted to General of the Army in 1955, he commanded the Carpathian Military District from 1955 and 1958 and participated in suppressing the 1956 Hungarian Revolution. He then commanded the Baltic Military District between 1958 and 1959 and the Southern Group of Forces in 1961 and 1962. He served as chief of staff of Warsaw Pact forces between 1962 and 1965. He them served as inspector general in the Soviet Ministry of Defense until his death in Moscow on 19 April 1985.

Spencer C. Tucker

See also

BARBAROSSA, Operation; Belorussia Offensive; Finnish-Soviet War (Winter War); Kursk, Battle of; Stalingrad, Battle of

References

Bialer, Seweryn, ed. *Stalin and His Generals: Soviet Military Memoirs of World War II*. New York: Pegasus, 1969.

Glantz, David. "Pavel Ivanovich Batov." In Harold Shukman, ed., *Stalin's Generals*, 35–43. New York: Grove Press, 1993.

Battle Cruisers (All Powers)

Large armored cruisers that incorporated the speed and generally the armor of a cruiser but with the armament of a battleship. The original concept for this vessel was the work of the Italian naval constructor Colonel Vittorio Cuniberti in the early twentieth century. The first power to fully endorse Cuniberti's ideas was Great Britain, through the work of First Sea Lord Admiral Sir John Fisher, who viewed the vessel as one capable of performing the duties of cruisers and battleships. Germany and Japan built these vessels in tandem with the British in the years before and during World War I (the United States began six as a result of the 1916 naval building program but finished none). Each country pursued its own designs, the Germans placing more emphasis on armor than their British rivals. In the 1916 Battle of Jutland, poor armor protection contributed to the destruction of three British battle cruisers, whereas the Germans lost only one. The Washington Naval Treaty of 1922 discontinued construction of battle cruisers, and many of the surviving units were scrapped.

By the outbreak of World War II, two nations retained some of their World War I–era battle cruisers. The British maintained the two ships of the Renown-class. As built, the *Renown* and *Repulse* measured 794' (oa) × 90' and displaced 30,835 tons at full load. They were protected by an armor belt with a maximum thickness of 6 inches. They mounted a primary armament of 6 × 15-inch guns as well as 17 × 4-inch guns (following a major refit, the *Renown* substituted 20 × 4.5-inch guns for her 4-inchers). Their engines produced a maximum speed of 30 knots. The British also operated the battle cruiser *Hood,* completed in 1920 to a World War I design, which displaced 45,200 tons fully loaded on a hull that measured 860' (oa) × 104' and was protected by armor with a maximum thickness of 12 inches. She was armed with 8 × 15-inch guns and 12 × 5.5-inch weapons. Her engines could produce a speed of 31 knots. The Japanese also retained their battle cruisers from World War I. These were the four ships of the Kongo-class. They measured 704' (oa) × 92' and originally displaced 32,200 tons fully loaded. The ships were rebuilt between the wars to be both faster and better protected. Belt armor with a maximum thickness of 8 inches protected their hulls. They were armed with 8 × 14-inch guns and 14 × 6-inch weapons and could travel at a maximum speed of 27.5 knots. After reconstruction between 1927 and 1931, these four vessels were reclassified as battleships.

France built two battle cruisers in the interwar period— the two ships of the Dunkerque-class completed in 1937 and 1938. The *Dunkerque* and *Strasbourg* displaced 35,500 tons fully loaded, measured 703'9" (oa) × 102', and were protected by belt armor of a maximum thickness of 9.75 inches. They were armed with 8 × 13-inch and 16 × 5.1-inch guns. Their maximum speed was 29.5 knots.

Finally, the United States ordered six battle cruisers, of the Alaska-class, during World War II but constructed only two. Completed in 1944, the *Alaska* and *Guam* displaced 34,253 tons fully loaded on hulls that measured 808'6" (oa) × 91'1" and were protected by armor 9 inches in thickness. Their armament comprised 9 × 12-inch guns and 12 × 5-inch guns. These ships could steam at a maximum speed of 33 knots.

In World War II, battle cruisers were employed in a variety of duties that included surface action, shore bombardment, antiaircraft fire support to protect aircraft carriers, and occasional service as convoy escorts, in the case of the Allies in the Battle of the Atlantic. The majority of these ships were lost in the war. Surface action claimed the British battle cruiser *Hood* when design deficiencies in its armor resulted in a magazine explosion while the vessel was engaged with the German battleship *Bismarck*. The British vessel *Repulse* succumbed to Japanese air attacks off Malaya. All four of the Japanese battle cruisers were sunk by air, surface, or submarine attacks. Finally, both the French battle cruisers were scuttled to prevent their capture by the Germans.

Only the U.S. Alaska-class ships and the British *Renown* survived the war, but these ships were scrapped after the conflict—the *Renown* in 1948 and the *Alaska* and *Guam* in 1961.

Eric W. Osborne

See also

Atlantic, Battle of the; *Bismarck,* Sortie and Sinking of; Central Pacific Campaign; France, Navy; Great Britain, Navy; Japan, Navy; *Prince of Wales* and *Repulse;* Southeastern Pacific; Southwestern Pacific; United States, Navy

References

Chesneau, Robert, ed. *Conway's All the World's Fighting Ships, 1922–1946*. London: Conway Maritime Press, 1980.

Gibbons, Tony, ed. *The Complete Encyclopedia of Battleships and Battlecruisers: A Technical Directory of All the World's Capital Ships from 1860 to the Present Day*. London: Salamander Books, 1983.

Battle of the Bulge

See Ardennes Offensive.

Battleships

Large, complex war vessels that have the primary mission of establishing control of the seas. Battleships were the toughest warships built. Despite yielding pride of place to the aircraft carrier as the principal sea-control and power-projection warship, battleships remained useful throughout World War II in carrying out a wide array of tasks.

The major naval powers continued to build battleships into World War II. The construction of these capital ships was only arrested under the pressure to construct submarines, antisubmarine warships, landing craft, and aircraft carriers. Italy and Germany launched new battleships as late as 1939 and 1940. Germany's *Bismarck* and *Tirpitz* were 41,700 tons, mounted 8 × 15-inch guns, and were capable of making a speed of 29 knots. Italy's *Vittorio Veneto, Italia, Roma,* and *Impero* (the latter never finished) displaced 40,700 tons, mounted 9 × 15-inch guns, and were capable of 30 knots.

The vulnerability of the battleship to aerial attack was finally demonstrated on 11 November 1940, when three Italian battleships were sunk at anchor in Taranto harbor by elderly British Swordfish torped-bombers from the carrier *Illustrious.* It took only four days, 7 to 10 December 1941, for the Japanese navy to emphasize that the battleship was no longer the capital ship of the world's navies. Building on the Taranto example, Japanese naval airpower practically destroyed the U.S. Navy's Pacific battleship fleet at Pearl Harbor on 7 December 1941. Even after that carnage, there were still those who argued that a well-handled battleship, under way and with good antiaircraft protection, could beat off an aerial assault. They were proven incorrect on 10 December, when the new Royal Navy battleship *Prince of Wales* (36,700 tons, 10 × 14-inch guns, 29 knots) and the elderly battle cruiser *Repulse* (17,300 tons, 6 × 15-inch guns, and 32 knots), under way and defended by an array of antiaircraft guns, were sunk in short order by Japanese naval warplanes.

Yet those four days in December simply confirmed a trend that was already in effect; by that time, no nation was building any new battleships. In November 1941, the Royal Navy had begun the *Vanguard* (44,500 tons, 8 × 15-inch guns, and 30 knots), but this battleship was not completely new, having been constructed to put to use the 15-inch guns and turrets off-loaded from two cruisers that had been converted to aircraft carriers following World War I. The *Vanguard,* leisurely constructed, was not commissioned until 1946, but the French battleship *Jean Bart,* finished in 1955, was the world's last battleship to be completed.

Nonetheless, battleships were still so valued during World War II that all of the capital ships from World War I and the immediate interwar era that had escaped the scrapping frenzy of the 1920s were pressed into combat service. For example, the Royal Navy's Queen Elizabeth–class ships, all but one of which (the *Queen Elizabeth* [27,500 tons, 8 × 15-inch guns, 23 knots]) had fought at Jutland, saw hard service in this new war. Only the Royal Navy, however, could boast of battleships that had fired their main batteries in battleship-to-battleship clashes in both world wars. Most of the later World War I–era battleships that survived into World War II had been extensively modernized in the 1930s to protect them against air and submarine attacks, and in all cases, they were converted to oil-fired propulsion. Although the main armament remained remarkably constant, virtually all World War I–era battleships were extensively rebuilt to afford much greater elevations for the main batteries. In terms of both dollars and time, the cost entailed in rebuilding these vessels usually exceeded the original cost of construction.

Construction of the battleships that served in World War II had, with the exception of the *Vanguard,* been started before their nations had opened hostilities. (The last two units of the U.S. ultimate Iowa-class were indeed started six months after Pearl Harbor, but the *Illinois* and *Kentucky* [48,000 tons, 9 × 16-inch guns, and design speed of 32.5 knots] were never completed.)

Battleship duties in World War II were not all that different from those in World War I: convoy escort and battleship-to-battleship clashes, although shore bombardment received far greater emphasis. As in World War I, there was only one battleship-to-battleship fleet action and but few battleship-to-battleship clashes. Among the latter category, the Royal Navy battle cruiser *Hood* (42,700 tons, 8 × 15-inch guns, 31 knots) and battleships *Barham* (same statistics as the *Queen Elizabeth*) and *Resolution* (28,000 tons, 8 × 15-inch guns, 24 knots) attacked the stationary French *Bretagne* and *Provence* (both 22,200 tons, 10 × 13.4-inch guns, 20 knots), and *Dunkerque* and *Strasbourg* (both 26,500 tons, 8 × 13-inch guns, and 29.5 knots) at Mers-el-Kébir (Oran, Algeria) on 8 July 1940. Their 15-inch shells nearly sank the *Dunkerque* but caused only slight damage to the *Strasbourg.* The *Resolution* also engaged in a gunnery duel with the 95 percent completed *Richelieu* but to no significant effect. The *Prince of Wales, King George V* (same as the *Prince of Wales*), and *Rodney* (33,300 tons, 9 × 16-inch guns, 23 knots) participated in the sinking of the powerful German battleship *Bismarck* in 1941; in November 1942, the U.S. Navy's *Washington* (37,500 tons, 9 × 16-inch guns, 28 knots) sank the

Japanese battleship/battle cruiser *Kirishima* (27,500 tons, 8 × 14-inch guns, 27.5 knots). The *South Dakota* suffered some moderate damage in the same action. Also in November 1942, the *Massachusetts* (38,000 tons, 9 × 16-inch guns, 27.5 knots) hit the uncompleted and anchored French *Jean Bart* (38,500 tons, 8 × 15-inch guns, 32 knots) with five 16-inch shells at Casablanca, and in December 1943, the Royal Navy's new *Duke of York* (same characteristics as the *Prince of Wales*) sank the German *Scharnhorst* (31,900 tons, 9 × 11-inch guns, 32 knots) off North Cape, Norway.

The only battleship fleet action of World War II took place on 25 October 1944, at Surigao Strait, near Leyte, Philippines, when the elderly U.S. battleships *West Virginia* (31,800 tons, 8 × 16-inch guns, 21 knots), *California, Mississippi, Tennessee,* and *Pennsylvania* (all 32,000–32,300 tons, 12 × 14-inch guns, 21 knots), and *Maryland* (31,500 tons, 8 × 16-inch guns, 21 knots), with seven U.S. and one Australian cruisers and a destroyer flotilla, sank the elderly Japanese battleships *Fuso* (30,600 tons, 12 × 14-inch guns, 22.5 knots) by destroyer torpedoes and *Yamashiro* by gunfire and destroyer torpedoes. The *West Virginia* inflicted the most damage, with her 16-inch guns directed by the Mk 8 gunfire control radar.

Surprisingly, the Japanese navy, the killer of battleships, was also the most battleship-minded of any navy engaged in World War II. Although the Japanese built the largest battleships in history (the Yamato-class), both completed units (the *Yamato* and *Musashi* [62,300 tons, 9 × 18.1-inch guns, 27 knots]) were sunk by U.S. naval airpower. Perhaps the most impressive battleships from World War II are those of the U.S. Navy's Iowa-class. These magnificent warships have an unmatched battle history, having fought in World War II, Korea, Vietnam (the *New Jersey* only [48,100 tons, 9 × 16-inch guns, 32.5 knots]), and the Gulf War. All four units easily reached 30-plus knots during their reactivation in the 1980s.

Throughout World War II, the battleships performed magnificently in a shore bombardment role. They also served effectively as antiaircraft platforms for the aircraft carriers and as fast oilers for the destroyers. After the war, U.S. Iowa-class battleships rendered excellent service during the Korean, Vietnam, and Gulf Wars. Eight battleships of World War II remain in existence as museum pieces, and all are American: the *Texas* (27,000 tons, 10 × 14-inch guns, 21 knots), which also served in World War I; the *Massachusetts and North Carolina* (same characteristics as the *Washington*); the *Alabama* (same as the *Massachusetts*); and the *Iowa, New Jersey, Missouri,* and *Wisconsin,* with the *Iowa* and *Wisconsin* (the latter the world's last completed extant battleship) also classed as in reserve (ships that can be recalled to duty).

Stanley Sandler

See also:
Bismarck, Sortie and Sinking of; France, Navy; Germany, Navy; Great Britain, Navy; Italy, Navy; Japan, Navy; United States, Navy; *Yamato*

References
Breyer, Sigfrieg. *Battleships and Battlecruisers, 1905–1970.* Garden City, NY: Doubleday, 1974.
Garzke, William H., Jr., and Robert O. Dulin Jr. *Battleships: Allied Battleships in World War II.* Annapolis, MD: Naval Institute Press, 1980.
———. *Axis and Neutral Battleships in World War II.* Annapolis, MD: Naval Institute Press, 1985.
———. *Battleships: United States Battleships in World War II.* Rev. ed. Annapolis, MD: Naval Institute Press, 1995.
Muir, Malcolm, Jr. *The Iowa Class Battleships.* Poole, UK: Blandford Press, 1987.
Sturton, Ian, ed. *All the World's Battleships: 1906 to the Present.* London: Brassey's, 1996.

Bay of Biscay Offensive (February–August 1943)

Major anti-U-boat operation conducted by the British and American air forces. Beginning in January 1942, Allied maritime patrol aircraft carried out air antisubmarine transit patrols in the Bay of Biscay. The advent of the new 10 cm radar in late 1942 and new methods of operations research encouraged a fresh approach to the flagging campaign there. The revised concept foresaw a continuous barrier patrol of the U-boat transit exit routes from the Bay of Biscay into the Atlantic by a total of 260 aircraft equipped with brand-new ASV Mk. III 10 cm–band radars. Operational command would lie with the Number 19 Group of the Royal Air Force's Coastal Command. Allied projections for success were vague and excessively optimistic, but the planners assumed correctly that it would take the Germans at least four months to respond effectively to the new 10 cm radar.

The actual offensive was preceded by three trial phases: Operations GONDOLA (4–16 February 1943), ENCLOSE I (20–28 March 1943), and ENCLOSE II (5–13 April 1943). Beset by difficulties, such as the withdrawal of the U.S. Army Air Forces' B-24 Liberator bombers, slow delivery of the ASV Mk. III radar, and lack of aircraft, the operations were nonetheless a success in that they demonstrated an increased efficiency in aircraft allocation and in U-boat sightings.

Air Marshal Sir John C. Slessor, head of Coastal Command, decided to launch the full-scale offensive (Operation DERANGE) on 13 April with 131 aircraft. The repeated, accurate night attacks by the Vickers Wellington medium bombers of Number 172 Squadron, then the only Coastal Command aircraft equipped with new ASV Mk. III radars and Leigh Lights, produced instant although unforeseen results. The failure of the German threat receivers to warn the U-boats of the incoming aircraft and the success of two U-boats in shooting down the attacking planes convinced the German U-boat command that the remedy was to give up the night surface transit and to order the U-boats to fight it out with aircraft on the surface during daylight hours.

Coastal Command aircraft wreaked havoc among the grossly overmatched U-boats during those daylight battles. In May alone, six U-boats were destroyed and seven so severely damaged that they had to return to their bases. In turn, the U-boats accounted for only 5 of 21 aircraft lost by the Coastal Command in the Bay of Biscay that month.

The German withdrawal from the North Atlantic convoy routes following the "Black May" of 1943 allowed Slessor to step up the operation with additional air assets. The Germans took to sending the U-boats in groups in order to provide better antiaircraft defense, yet in June, 4 U-boats were lost and 6 others severely damaged. DERANGE peaked in July, when Allied aircraft claimed 16 U-boats—among them 3 valuable Type XIV U-tankers—compelling Grossadmiral (grand admiral) Karl Dönitz to call off a planned operation in the western Atlantic.

German losses in the Bay of Biscay dropped considerably thereafter, but the air patrols remained a formidable obstacle throughout the remainder of the war by forcing the U-boats to remain under water for most of the time during transit. Although the Battle of the Atlantic was ultimately won around the convoys, the Bay of Biscay Offensive contributed to the success by preventing many U-boats from reaching their operational areas in time to saturate convoy defenses as they had done in March 1943.

Dirk Steffen

See also

Aircraft, Bombers; Aircraft, Naval; Antisubmarine Warfare; Atlantic, Battle of the; "Black May"; Dönitz, Karl; Leigh Light; Radar; Slessor, Sir John Cotesworth

References

Blair, Clay. *Hitler's U-Boat War*. Vol. 2, *The Hunted, 1942–1945*. New York: Random House 1998.

Gannon, Michael. *Black May*. New York: Harper Collins, 1998.

Morison, Samuel Eliot. *History of United States Naval Operations in World War II*. Vol. 10, *The Atlantic Battle Won, May 1943–May 1945*. Boston: Little, Brown, 1956.

Roskill, Stephen W. *The War at Sea, 1939–1945*. Vol. 2 and vol. 3, pt. 1. London: Her Majesty's Stationery Office, 1957 and 1960.

Bayerlein, Fritz (1899–1970)

German army general whose various commands included the Panzer Lehr Division. Born in Würzburg, Germany, on 14 January 1899, Fritz Bayerlein joined the German army at age 16 and fought on the Western Front in World War I in the 2nd Jäger Battalion. Bayerlein entered the Reichswehr in 1921 and was commissioned a second lieutenant in January 1922. He held a variety of positions in the interwar years and was a major at the time of the outbreak of the war in September 1939.

During the invasion of Poland, Bayerlein served as a chief of operations of the 10th Panzer Division, part of General of Panzer Troops (U.S. equiv. lieutenant general) Heinz Guderian's XIX Corps. Bayerlein was also operations officer for Panzer Group Guderian in the Battle for France in 1940 and was promoted to lieutenant colonel that September. He continued to serve with Guderian as the operations officer of Guderian's 2nd Panzer Group in the first three months of the invasion of the Soviet Union.

In October 1941, Bayerlein was transferred to North Africa as chief of staff to General Erwin Rommel's Afrika Korps (Africa Corps). He became chief of staff for Panzer Army Afrika in April 1942 and was promoted to colonel. On 30 August, when General Walther Nehring was wounded at the start of the Battle of Alam Halfa, Bayerlein took command of the Afrika Korps. He again led a decimated Afrika Korps during its long retreat after the Battle of El Alamein. Wounded during the last days of the fighting in North Africa, he was evacuated prior to the Axis surrender on 13 May 1943.

Bayerlein was promoted to Generalmajor (U.S. equiv. brigadier general) in July 1943. In October, he took command of the 3rd Panzer Division, beginning his second tour on the Eastern Front. The division distinguished itself in the face of heavy odds, and his breakout of encirclement at Kirovgrad in January 1944 permitted the escape of his own and four other German divisions.

Bayerlein then commanded the newly formed Panzer Lehr Division, which he led from its creation in early 1944 until February 1945. Under Bayerlein, who was promoted to Generalleutnant (U.S. equiv. major general) in May 1944, the division fought in Normandy. The division helped slow the British advance on Caen but was decimated by the massive air attack on 25 July at Saint-Lô in Allied Operation COBRA. Later reconstituted, the division was a unit of the XLVII Panzer Corps of General of Panzer Troops Hasso Manteuffel's Fifth Panzer Army in the attack on Bastogne in December 1944. Bayerlein took command of LIII Corps in February 1945, which included remnants of his old Panzer Lehr Division, and defended the Ruhr pocket until its surrender on 15 April 1945.

Bayerlein was held as a prisoner of war until 1947. Following his release, he wrote about his wartime impressions and experiences in North Africa, in the Soviet Union, and on the Western Front. He also contributed more than 20 studies in the postwar German Military History Program. His postwar reminiscences are insightful historical analyses of Germany's leaders and military campaigns. Bayerlein died in Würzburg on 30 January 1970.

Jon D. Berlin

See also
Afrika Korps; Alam Halfa, Battle of; Ardennes Offensive; Armored Warfare; Bastogne, Battle for; COBRA, Operation; El Alamein, Battle of; Falaise-Argentan Pocket; France, Battle for (1940); Guderian, Heinz; Nehring, Walter Kurt; North Africa Campaign; Rommel, Erwin Johannes Eugen; Ruhr Campaign; Saint-Lô, Battle of; Tunisia Campaign

References
Liddell Hart, Basil H., ed. *The Rommel Papers.* New York: Harcourt, Brace, 1953.
MacDonald, Charles B. *A Time for Trumpets: The Untold Story of the Battle of the Bulge.* New York: William Morrow, 1984.
Mitcham, Samuel W., Jr. *Rommel's Greatest Victory: The Desert Fox and the Fall of Tobruk, Spring 1942.* Novato, CA: Presidio, 1998.
Ritgen, Helmut. *Die Geschichte der Panzer-Lehr Division in Westen: 1944–1945.* Stuttgart, Germany: Motorbuch-Verlag, 1979.

Bayonets

Knife- or daggerlike weapon attached to the muzzle end of a firearm for the purpose of hand-to-hand combat. Developed during the early to middle seventeenth century in Bayonne, France, the bayonet gave a musketeer a means to defend himself during close combat. It eventually rendered obsolete the foot soldiers with pole arms who were employed to protect the musketeers.

The first bayonets were simply inserted into the muzzle of the barrel. This action, however, rendered the firearm useless for its intended purpose. Such "plug" bayonets were replaced with the "socket" style of bayonet that fit over the barrel itself, an invention sometimes attributed to Marquis Sébastien Le Prestre de Vauban. Such bayonets use a metal stud or the front sight to stay aligned. A simple pressure fit or a locking ring keeps the bayonet attached. The blade is offset from the barrel, allowing the firearm to be loaded and fired with the bayonet attached. By the twentieth century, most bayonets were attached, by means of a spring-loaded catch, to a separate lug mounted next to the barrel.

Most early bayonet blades had a triangular cross section. In the early nineteenth century, long sword bayonets with flat, knifelike cross sections made their appearance. By the twentieth century, this style of bayonet was dominant, al-though numerous other shapes, including the cruciform and the spike, could be found.

By World War II, the bayonet was rapidly losing prominence as a fighting weapon. Its length and weight, which had proven cumbersome in the trenches of World War I, also affected the accuracy of the firearm to which it was attached. Furthermore, many bayonets were expensive to produce, ill suited as fighting knives, and of little use to the soldier requiring a utility knife capable of opening cans or hammering tent pegs. More important, however, the increased use of rapid-fire semi- and fully automatic weapons had made close combat an increasingly rare occurrence.

Today's soldier still carries the bayonet, but, incorporating the experiences of World War II and later conflicts, the modern bayonet is short, well balanced, and strong. It is also capable of performing numerous tasks, both as a weapon and as a tool. Throughout history, the bayonet has been used in combat as a weapon of last resort by soldiers of all armies.

Stephen L. Gibbs

See also
Rifles
References
Ammer, Christine. *Fighting Words.* New York: Paragon, 1989.
Janzen, Jerry L. *Bayonets.* Broken Arrow, OK: Cedar Ridge Publications, 1987.
Weeks, John. *Infantry Weapons.* New York: Ballantine Books, 1971.

Beaverbrook, Lord

See Aitken, William Maxwell.

Beck, Ludwig (1880–1944)

German army general who was involved in attempts to overthrow Adolf Hitler. Born in Biebrich, Germany, on 29 June 1880, Ludwig Beck joined the army in 1898 and as a lieutenant attended the Kriegsakademie (War Academy) in Berlin from 1908 to 1911. Promoted to captain in 1913, he qualified as a General Staff officer the same year and served in a variety of staff and command positions during World War I on the Western Front.

Beck continued in the postwar Reichswehr, rising to command of the 1st Cavalry Division. Promoted to General-major (U.S. equiv. brigadier general) in February 1931 and Generalleutnant (U.S. equiv. major general) in December 1932, he was appointed, in October 1933, chief of the Truppenamt (Troop Office), the thinly disguised covert General

Generaloberst Ludwig Beck was chief of staff of the German army before the war. He opposed and deeply despised Nazi leader Adolf Hitler. (Hulton Archive by Getty Images)

Staff prohibited to the Germans under the Versailles Treaty. In 1933, Beck was the primary author of Truppenfuehrung (Unit Command), which remained the principal warfighting manual of the German army until 1945. The body of doctrine in that manual profoundly influenced the conduct of combined-arms warfare for the remainder of the twentieth century.

In March 1935, the Truppenamt was redesignated General Staff of the Army, and in May, Beck was promoted to General der Artillery (U.S. equiv. lieutenant general). He presided over the expansion of the revived General Staff and the development of war plans based on a defensive strategy. His peers considered him a master military planner. He clearly understood that any future war would necessarily become a multifront conflict, which Germany could not win. As late as 1935, however, Beck continued to believe the officer corps of the German army could keep the National Socialists under control. But as Adolf Hitler continued the push to invade Czecho-

slovakia in 1938, Beck opposed him openly, writing a series of memoranda describing the inherent dangers in the policy of aggression.

He attempted to mobilize other generals to oppose Hitler's policies, but he failed to gain the support of the army commander in chief, General Walther von Brauchitsch. In August 1938, Beck retired from the army and was promoted to Generaloberst (U.S. equiv. full general). He then organized a covert opposition group of active and retired officers and other conservatives, maintaining contact with other democratic opposition movements. Beck also contacted London in an attempt to secure British and French support for a coup against Hitler. British Prime Minister Neville Chamberlain declined to support such a move. Shortly before the 1940 invasion of the west, Beck's group tried to warn Belgium.

By 1943, Beck had become convinced that the only way to save Germany was to assassinate Hitler. His group tried several times, culminating in Colonel Claus von Stauffenberg's bomb attempt on 20 July 1944. If Stauffenberg had succeeded, the conspirators planned to use the Home Army to establish martial law, seize the radio stations, and arrest the key Nazi and Schutzstaffel (SS) leaders. As the head of the planned interim government pending free elections, however, Beck refused to agree to the systematic summary execution of party and SS leaders to secure success.

When the conspirators learned that Stauffenberg had failed, Beck nonetheless insisted on continuing the putsch, called Operation VALKYRIE, saying that Germany deserved the attempt. The attempt was unsuccessful. Arrested in the Bendlerstrasse in Berlin, Beck was offered the privilege of shooting himself. When two tries only rendered him unconscious, a sergeant shot Beck in the neck, ending his life on the night of 20–21 July 1944.

Despite being unfairly and inaccurately painted by Heinz Guderian as a rigid and unimaginative opponent of armored warfare, Beck helped rebuild the German military into an efficient war-fighting machine. In his early opposition as a general to Hitler's policy of aggression and in his later active opposition as a private citizen, Ludwig Beck proved that during the Third Reich, true German patriotism was incompatible with Nazism.

David T. Zabecki

See also
Brauchitsch, Heinrich Alfred Hermann Walther von; Germany, Army; Guderian, Heinz; Hitler, Adolf; July Bomb Plot; Stauffenberg, Claus Philip Schenk von
References
Goerlitz, Walter. *History of the German General Staff, 1637–1945.* Trans. Brian Battershaw. New York: Praeger, 1953.
Hoffmann, Peter. *The History of the German Resistance, 1933–1945.* Cambridge, MA: MIT Press, 1977.

O'Neill, Robert. "Fritsch, Beck and the Führer." In Corelli Barnett, ed., *Hitler's Generals*, 19–41. New York: Grove Weidenfeld, 1989.

Zabecki, David T., and Bruce Condell. *On the German Art of War: "Truppenfuehrung."* Boulder, CO: Lynne Rienner, 2001.

Begramian, Ivan Khristoforovich

See Bagramyan, Ivan Khristoforovich.

Belgium, Air Service

Formed in March 1920 as part of the Belgian army, the Belgian air force had fewer than 250 aircraft in May 1940, including 90 fighters, 12 bombers, and 120 reconnaissance aircraft. Of this total, only 50 were relatively modern. Belgium produced some of its own planes, including the Renard R-31 reconnaissance aircraft, but most of its aircraft were acquired from Britain and the United States.

Belgian air bases lacked space to disperse the aircraft, and 53 planes were destroyed on the ground by the Luftwaffe on the morning of 10 May 1940, at the beginning of the German invasion of Belgium. Two days later, the Belgians had only between 70 and 80 aircraft remaining. These planes, along with many Dutch aircraft, were incorporated into British and French units. In addition to providing ground support for Allied units, Belgian bombers also carried out one bombing mission in which two squadrons of nine Battle bombers were sent to destroy bridges across the Albert Canal. Although the strike was successful in hitting the targets, the light bombs the planes carried proved ineffective, and six aircraft were lost. This action was the only independent mission carried out by Belgian aircraft during the campaign. Some Belgian air force units participated in the remainder of the campaign for France, in the Battle of Britain, and in the Western Front Campaign of 1944 and 1945.

Lawton Way

See also
Belgium, Army; Belgium, Role in War; Belgium Campaign; Britain, Battle of

Resources
Gunsburg, Jeffery. *Divided and Conquered: The French High Command and the Defeat of the West, 1940.* Westport, CT: Greenwood Press, 1979.

Mollo, Andrew, Malcolm McGregor, and Pierre Turner. *The Armed Forces of World War II: Uniforms, Insignia, and Organization.* New York: Crown Publishers, 1981.

Belgium, Army

In 1936, Belgium renounced its 1919 treaty of alliance with France and reasserted its traditional neutrality. As a consequence, Belgian forces did not carry out any joint maneuvers with their potential French and British allies before the war.

Belgium mobilized its armed forces beginning on 25 August 1939. With the outbreak of the war, the government immediately reaffirmed the nation's neutrality, retaining the right to strengthen its military to prevent attack. Belgian King Leopold III acted as commander in chief of the armed forces, which consisted of an army of 18 infantry divisions, 2 partly motorized divisions, and 2 motorized cavalry divisions in May 1940. In all, the army numbered some 600,000 men. Although impressive on paper, the army suffered from serious weaknesses. Both its men and officers were poorly trained and equipped. Further, the army had virtually no antiaircraft artillery and only 54 tanks (42 British Carden-Loyd M1934s and 12 French Renault AMC-35s). The navy consisted of only a few small coastal defense vessels.

In hopes of remaining neutral, King Leopold had prevented significant military coordination with the French and British military staffs. Although British and French forces did come to the aid of Belgium when it was invaded by German forces on 10 May 1940, the Germans breached the initial Belgian defensive line along the Albert Canal that same day. King Leopold then withdrew the bulk of his forces to a line east of Brussels. British and French troops reinforced the new line, but the German strike through the Ardennes flanked it. Soon, the Allies were forced to abandon Brussels and the surrounding area.

By 24 May, the Belgian army had regrouped in western Flanders, where it was again supported by both French and British forces. The only major battle of the campaign occurred there, on 24–25 May, with Belgian forces again unable to hold off the superior German forces. On 28 May, King Leopold surrendered his army. In addressing the House of Commons on 4 June concerning the Belgian defeat, British Prime Minister Winston L. S. Churchill said that the surrender was given "suddenly, without prior consultation, with the least possible notice" and that this action had "exposed our whole flank and means of retreat." Although Leopold's decision was definitely not the cause of the German victory, it rendered the British military position untenable and led to the evacuation of the British Expeditionary Force at Dunkerque.

In the 18 days of fighting during the campaign, the Belgian army nonetheless fought bravely, with limited resources. Belgian casualties amounted to some 7,500 killed and 15,850 wounded. An additional 2,000 who had been taken as prisoners of war died in German captivity. Some

Belgian soldiers and airmen managed to escape to Britain, where they formed the Independent Belgian Brigade and operated under the British for the remainder of the war.

Lawton Way

See also
Belgium, Air Service; Belgium Campaign; Belgium, Role in War; Dunkerque, Evacuation of; Leopold III, King of Belgium
References
Bitsch, Marie-Thérèse. *Histoire de la Belgique*. Paris: Hatier, 1992.
Bond, Brian. *France and Belgium, 1939–1940*. London: Davis-Poynter, 1975.
Mollo, Andrew, Malcolm McGregor, and Pierre Turner. *The Armed Forces of World War II: Uniforms, Insignia, and Organization*. New York: Crown Publishers, 1981.

Belgium, Role in the War

At the beginning of World War II in September 1939, Belgium was a constitutional monarchy of some 8.2 million people sharply divided along linguistic lines: the Dutch-speaking Flemish provinces in the north and the French-speaking Walloon area of the south and Flanders. The capital, Brussels, was a Walloon preserve, and French speakers dominated the political, economic, and intellectual life of the nation. In the decades before the war, the Flemish areas were beginning to assert themselves, and a Flemish nationalist party, the Vlammsch National Verbond (VNV) held 17 seats in Parliament.

Belgium followed a neutralist foreign policy. The nation had secured its independence from the Kingdom of the Netherlands in 1830, and its neutrality and territorial integrity had been guaranteed by an international treaty signed by the major powers in 1839. The German government's decision to violate that neutrality in August 1914 at the beginning of World War I brought Britain into the war. Occupied by the German army between 1914 and 1918, Belgium had then allied itself with France. With the increase in tensions in Europe, Belgium again sought refuge in neutrality in 1936. King Leopold III and the tripartite government of the Socialist, Catholic, and Liberal Parties renounced the French alliance. The government, however, proclaimed Belgium's right to maintain a military establishment to protect the nation from attack. This policy of armed neutrality found broad support among the Belgian people.

In September 1939, when World War II began, Belgian Premier Hubert Pierlot, leader of the Catholic Party, reiterated the government's resolve to remain neutral, and the government deployed the army along both the German and French borders. Belgians knew the true threat was from Germany, and the government reinforced the frontier with Germany following invasion alerts in November 1939 and January 1940. In the latter case, a German military aircraft had landed in Belgium by mistake, and its passenger was found to be carrying the entire German plan to invade the west, including Belgium.

The German invasion of 10 May 1940 thus did not catch the Belgian government by surprise, and some limited military plans had been made with Britain and France to prepare for that eventuality. Nonetheless, the Belgian military was quickly overwhelmed by the German troops. Although there had been some coordination with the French and British, there were no prepared positions for the latter, and the military situation rapidly deteriorated. On 25 May, King Leopold and his chief ministers met in Wynendaele and agreed on the need to end the military campaign in their country as quickly as possible. Leopold decided to remain in Belgium and share the fate of his countrypeople, whereas the ministers insisted that the government go to France, with whatever military forces could be withdrawn, to continue the fight against Germany. Both parties did what they believed to be appropriate.

King Leopold surrendered the Belgian army unconditionally on 28 May, without coordinating this decision with the very allies who had come to the rescue of his country. This decision produced an immediate 30-mile gap between the British Expeditionary Force and the North Sea that rendered the British military position untenable and forced its evacuation from the port of Dunkerque. Having taken this decision, Leopold then repaired to his palace at Laeken outside Brussels, where he remained under self-imposed isolation for the next four years before being removed to Germany in June 1944.

Leopold's ministers, meanwhile, fled to France, where they held a session of the Belgian Parliament in Limoges on 31 May and criticized the king's actions. When France itself fell to the German army in late June, the Belgian parliamentary representatives abandoned their effort to support the Allies and sought a rapprochement with the king, which he then rejected. He—and most Belgians, for that matter—believed that the war was, in effect, over and that Germany had won. These parliamentarians then set up a Belgian government-in-exile in London. Belgian soldiers who escaped their country to Britain later formed the Independent Belgian Brigade, which operated under British command. Most of the 100 ships of the Belgian merchant marine evaded capture and, in accordance with a July 1940 agreement, operated under British control.

Following the surrender, German authorities promptly established an occupation government in Belgium. The German enclaves of Eupen, Malmédy, and Saint Vith, assigned to Belgium in the settlement following World War I, were promptly reintegrated into the Reich. A German army administration (Militärverwaltungschef), nominally headed by General Ludwig von Falkenhausen, ruled Belgium. Eggert Reeder, president of the military administration, was the real decision-maker and also oversaw German authorities in Belgium, such as the Schutzstaffel (SS) and the Foreign Ministry. Reeder's priorities included advancing the position of the "Germanic" Flemish population at the expense of the francophone Walloons (in accordance with a July 1940 order from Hitler), ensuring that Belgian industry was harnessed for the war machine of the Reich, and administering Belgium with as little German manpower as possible. On 10 May 1940, the Belgian Parliament had passed a law allowing civil servants to administer the country in the absence of the political leaders, and the senior members of each department, the secrétaires-généraux (principal administrative officers), thus became the administrators of Belgium. Reeder worked through these officials in a system of indirect German rule, and although there were conflicts, the secrétaires-généraux agreed to maintain law and order and the nation's industrial and agricultural production.

Some Belgian elites were able to use this time of turmoil to enhance their own positions. The Comité Galopin, a small group of influential bankers and industrialists, controlled the economy and ensured that Belgium provided Germany with the essential materials it required while maintaining their own interests. Many Belgians suffered terribly during the German occupation, however. The dislocation of the fighting and German requisitions led to a severe food shortage, and perhaps a fifth of the population was starving by the fall of 1940. King Leopold was able to convince the Germans to scale back their requisitions of food. He was also able to win some exemptions for women, war orphans, and children of war prisoners among those Belgians deported from the country to work in the Reich. Resistance to the Germans, only sporadic at first, grew with the addition of the Communists after the German invasion of the Soviet Union and as the overall German military situation deteriorated. Relations between these resistance groups and the government-in-exile in London were sometimes strained.

As in other countries occupied by the Germans, some people collaborated actively and were appointed to positions of influence as a result. The Germans also recruited an SS formation under Léon Degrelle for service on the Eastern Front. For most Belgians, however, the occupation produced a sense of solidarity against the occupier as they struggled to secure food, clothing, and shelter and as they lived with the ever present risk of deportation to work in the Reich.

Belgium remained under German occupation until September 1944, when Allied troops arrived and rapidly liberated the country, with the Belgian Parliament returning to Brussels. The sole feat of resistance by arms was the liberation of the port of Antwerp and the prevention of its destruction by the German military, itself an important step. Some German forces remained on islands at the mouth of the Scheldt River until 28 November 1944, from which they were able to prevent the Allies from using the port. On 16 December, on Hitler's orders, German forces launched what became the Battle of the Ardennes (Battle of the Bulge), the goal of which was to take back Antwerp. During the course of the fighting, the Germans reoccupied part of Belgium, but in January 1945, Allied troops were again able to clear all Belgium of German control.

Belgium was fortunate in that the rapid German advance in 1940 and retreat in 1944 had left its cities and countryside relatively unscathed. Antwerp, the least bomb-damaged port in the Channel area, became a major Allied base in the closing campaigns of the war and was the target of a substantial number of German V-2 rockets in early 1945. The Belgian government took reprisals against collaborators, convicting some 53,000 men and women of assisting the enemy.

Shortly after V-E Day, King Leopold and members of the royal family were freed outside Strobl, Austria, by U.S. troops. The king became the center of political turmoil for having surrendered the army and for his refusal to go abroad with his ministers in order to support a government-in-exile. He was also suspected of having both German sympathies and authoritarian preferences. Then, too, he had compounded his unpopularity by his wartime remarriage to a commoner. Leopold's brother, Prince Charles, the count of Flanders, assumed the title of regent. A referendum in March 1950 gave Leopold a 58 percent favorable vote, but his return led to a major crisis, and he relinquished control of affairs to his son, Baudouin, who became king in 1951.

Lawton Way

See also
Ardennes Offensive; Belgium, Air Service; Belgium, Army; Degrelle, Léon; Dunkerque, Evacuation of; Leopold III, King of Belgium

References
Bond, Brian. *France and Belgium, 1939–1940.* London: Davis-Poynter, 1975.
Conway, Martin. *Collaboration in Belgium: Léon Degrelle and the Rexist Movement.* New Haven, CT: Yale University Press, 1993.
Gunsburg, Jeffery. *Divided and Conquered: The French High Command and the Defeat of the West, 1940.* Westport, CT: Greenwood Press, 1979.
Keyes, Roger S. *Outrageous Fortune: The Tragedy of King Leopold III of the Belgians, 1901–1941.* London: Secker and Warburg, 1985.
Willequet, J. *La Belgique sous la botte: Résistances et collaborations, 1940–1945.* Paris: Éditions Universitaires, 1986.

Belgium Campaign (10–28 May 1940)

A key element of the German invasion of western Europe. Belgium had proclaimed its neutrality and sought to avoid involvement in World War II, but to invade and defeat France swiftly, the Germans needed to secure Belgium. When Germany invaded Poland in September 1939, thereby initiating World War II, Belgium declared a state of armed neutrality. Prime Minister Hubert Pierlot resolved to defend the country against all invaders and deployed the army along both the French and the German borders.

Still, Belgians knew the real danger lay to the east, and they had begun mobilizing their armed forces on 25 August 1939. By May 1940, their country fielded an army of more than 600,000 men organized into 22 divisions: 18 infantry divisions, 2 partially motorized Chasseurs Ardannais divisions, and 2 motorized cavalry divisions. Unfortunately for Belgium, this sizable force was hardly equipped to defeat a German invasion. The Belgians possessed few antiaircraft guns and had only 42 light and 12 medium tanks. Their air service had only 184 operational aircraft. Thus, Belgium had no hope of winning a prolonged land campaign with Germany without outside assistance.

German Colonel General Fedor von Bock's Army Group

B operated against Belgium and the Netherlands. The Germans committed Colonel General Walther von Reichenau's Sixth Army, with 17 infantry and 2 tank divisions, to the initial invasion of Belgium. It was to drive southwest. Meanwhile, General of Artillery (Lieutenant General) Georg von Küchler's Eighteenth Army of 11 divisions (9 infantry and 1 each of cavalry and tanks) was expected to subdue the Netherlands quickly and then drive south to join the fighting in Belgium.

Although Belgian intelligence accurately forecast the German attack that occurred on 10 May 1940, no one anticipated the audacious German attack on the fortress of Eben Emael in the first hours of the fighting. Eben Emael was a series of concrete and steel emplacements north of Liège that guarded bridges over the Albert Canal at Briedgen, Veldwezelt, and Vroenhoven. Garrisoned by more than 700 men, the fortress was crucial to Belgian defensive plans because the only hope of slowing the German panzers lay in keeping them east of the canal. German army planners took special notice of Eben Emael for that very reason, and at 5:25 A.M. on 10 May 1940, they sent 78 specially trained men of the Kock Assault Detachment in gliders to crash-land on top of the fortress. The attackers employed hollow charges to

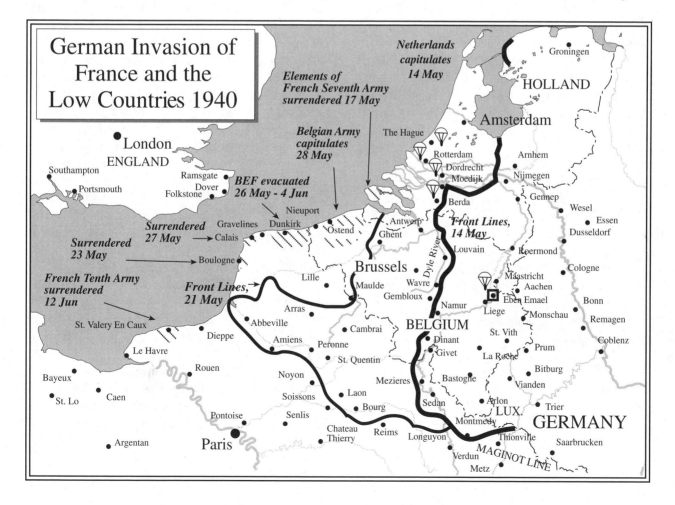

destroy the key gun turrets and bunkers. At the same time, German paratroopers captured the major bridges. Troops of the 223rd Infantry Division followed close behind and took the rest of the Belgian position the next day. In less than 24 hours, the Germans had breached the key Belgian defensive line on the Albert Canal.

Fighting bravely, the Belgians fell back to the Dyle Line east of Brussels, with King Leopold III in personal command. The British and French had planned to send their own forces into Belgium in the event of a German invasion, but there had been little prior coordination between Britain, France, and neutral Belgium. On 12 May, however, elements of the British Expeditionary Force (BEF) and General Georges Blanchard's French First Army began joining the Belgian defenders, and by 15 May, the Allies had some 35 divisions in the Namur-Antwerp area.

As Reichenau's Sixth Army probed the Dyle Line, Georg von Küchler's Eighteenth Army turned south from the Netherlands after the surrender of that country to the Germans on 15 May. This move threatened the Allied left flank. At the same time and to the south, the hammer blow of Colonel General (Karl) Gerd von Rundstedt's Army Group A, heavy in tanks, was driving west and then north through the Ardennes Forest. The overall German plan, Operation SICHELSCHNITT (the cut of the sickle), worked to perfection.

On 25 May, King Leopold III met with his ministers at the chateau of Wynendaele to discuss the possibility of surrender. His ministers wanted to flee to Great Britain and continue the war on the Allied side, but Leopold, despite a pledge to the British and French not to surrender unilaterally, believed that the campaign was lost and that he should end the fighting to save bloodshed and then remain to share the fate of his people. Leopold indeed took this step, surrendering the Belgian armed forces on 28 May. This step exposed the left flank of the British-French line and ended any Allied hopes of holding part of Flanders. British Prime Minister Winston L. S. Churchill then ordered the British navy to evacuate British forces at Dunkerque.

The 18 days of the Belgian Campaign cost the nation some 7,500 troops killed in action and 15,850 wounded. And at least 2,000 Belgian prisoners of war died in German captivity. The country remained under German occupation for the next four years.

Lance Janda and Spencer C. Tucker

See also
Airborne Forces, Axis; Aircraft, Gliders; Belgium, Air Service; Belgium, Navy; Belgium, Role in War; Blanchard, Jean Georges Maurice; Bock, Fedor von; Eben Emael; Küchler, Georg von; Leopold III, King of Belgium; Reichenau, Walther von; Rundstedt, Karl Rudolf Gerd von; SICHELSCHNITT, Operation

References
Deighton, Len. *Blitzkrieg: From the Rise of Hitler to the Fall of Dunkirk.* New York: Alfred A. Knopf, 1980.
Messenger, Charles, and John Keegan, eds. *The Second World War in the West (The History of Warfare).* London: Cassell Academic, 1999.
Mrazek, James E. *The Fall of Eben Emael.* Reprint ed. Presidio, 1999.
Powaski, Ronald E. *Lightning War: Blitzkrieg in the West, 1940.* Indianapolis, IN: John Wiley and Sons, 2002.

Belorussia Offensive (22 June– 29 August 1944)

Massive Soviet offensive in Belorussia, code-named BAGRATION, commencing exactly three years after the German invasion of the USSR. The Soviet offensive, timed in part to meet Soviet leader Josef Stalin's pledge at the Tehran Conference for an operation to prevent the transfer of German forces to the west to meet the Allied invasion of Normandy, resulted in the most calamitous defeat of German forces in the war.

By the beginning of 1944, the Red Army clearly held the initiative on the Eastern Front. The campaign opened in January with offensives at Leningrad and the Ukraine. The Leningrad offensive broke the German siege and ended with Soviet forces on the Estonian border. The Ukrainian offensive ended after nearly all of the Ukraine had been regained and after a southern salient had been created that nearly reached L'viv (Lvov), with the Red Army threatening the borders of Poland and Czechoslovakia. In the process, these offensives destroyed five German armies, causing well over a million German casualties and untold equipment losses, and put pressure on Finland and Romania, Germany's allies.

Because of these successes, particularly in the Ukraine, German leader Adolf Hitler believed the Soviet summer offensive would continue from the Ukraine. The Soviets needed favorable terrain for mechanized operations, and two options seemed the most advantageous for them. First, they could push west from Ukraine and then south, removing Romania and its resources from German reach. Second and most likely they could push west and then north toward the Baltic to cut off both Army Group Center in the Belorussian "bulge" and Army Group North along the Baltic coast. A direct thrust in the north seemed possible but provided less strategic advantage, and an attack into Belorussia against Army Group Center seemed least likely because of the poor road network and the restrictive terrain in the forests and the Pripet marshes.

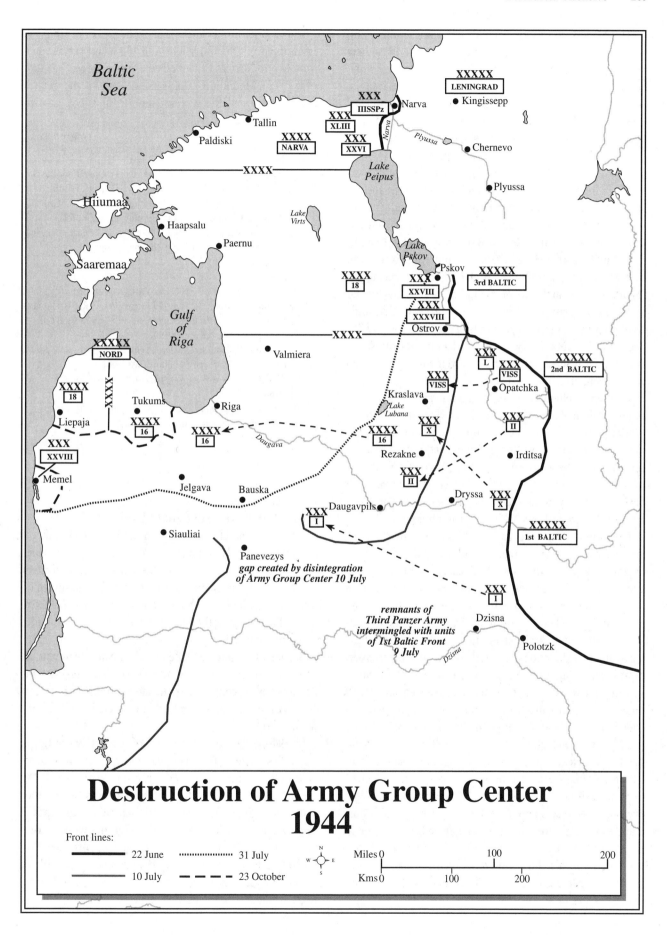

Baltic
Sea

Kingissepp

XXXXX
LENINGRAD

Narva

XXX
IIISSPz

Tallin

XXX
XLIII

Paldiski

XXXX
NARVA

XXX
XXVI

Plyussa

Chernevo

Lake
Peipus

Plyussa

XXXX

Hiiumaa

Lake
Virts

Haapsalu

Lake
Pskov

Saaremaa

Paernu

Pskov

XXXX
18

XXX
XXVIII

XXXXX
3rd BALTIC

Gulf
of
Riga

XXX
XXXVIII

Ostrov

XXXX

XXXXX
NORD

Valmiera

XXX
L

XXXXX
2nd BALTIC

XXXX
18

Tukums

XXX
VISS

Liepaja

Riga

XXX
VISS

Opatchka

XXXX
16

Kraslava

XXX
II

XXXX
16

Daugava

Lake
Lubana

XXX
X

XXX
II

XXXX
16

Irditsa

XXX
XXVIII

Rezakne

Jelgava

Bauska

XXX
II

Memel

Dryssa

XXX
X

Daugavpils

XXX
I

XXXXX
1st BALTIC

Siauliai

Panevezys
gap created by disintegration
of Army Group Center 10 July

XXX
I

remnants of
Third Panzer Army
intermingled with units
of 1st Baltic Front
9 July

Dzisna

Polotzk

Dzisna

Destruction of Army Group Center
1944

Front lines:

——————— 22 June   ················ 31 July

——————— 10 July   – – – – – 23 October

Miles 0   100   200

Kms 0   100   200

The Soviets considered roughly the same options and chose the Belorussian thrust primarily because the others would leave large German forces on the Soviet flanks and because an assault straight into Belorussia would free the Soviet territory that remained occupied. In many respects, Operation BAGRATION was the reverse of Operation BARBAROSSA, fought over many of the same battlefields.

Arrayed against Field Marshal Ernst Busch's Army Group Center were four Soviet fronts (army group equivalents). From north to south were the 1st Baltic Front and the 3rd, 2nd, and 1st Belorussian Fronts, commanded by Generals Ivan Bagramyan, Ivan Chernyakhovsky, Georgii Zakharov, and Konstantin Rokossovsky, respectively. In addition, Soviet leader Josef Stalin appointed two veteran commanders as Stavka (Soviet High Command) special representatives—Marshal Georgii Zhukov overseeing the 1st and 2nd Belorussian Fronts and Marshal Aleksandr Vasilevsky coordinating operations of the 1st Baltic and 3rd Belorussian Fronts. The Soviet fronts counted 168 divisions, plus a large Belorussian partisan movement. Army Group Center numbered only 54 divisions.

German intelligence keyed on identifying main thrusts by the location of Soviet tank armies, of which there were six in 1944. However, Soviet air supremacy and their own shortage of assets denied the Germans long-range aerial reconnaissance. German military intelligence was forced to rely on signals intercepts, and Soviet deception focused on disguising heavy reinforcements moving into Belorussia and tank concentrations behind the front lines.

Operation BAGRATION began on 22 June with Soviet battalion- and company-sized infantry raids along the front probing for weaknesses while several divisions conducted major attacks to seize openings in the line. Between 23 and 28 June, the Red Army broke through German lines in six places and encircled large German forces at Vitebsk and Bobruisk, taking 20,000 prisoners. On 3 July, the Soviets, striking from two directions, entered Minsk, the Belorussian capital, capturing nearly 100,000 Germans east of the city.

After five weeks, the Red Army had advanced almost 360 miles while destroying Army Group Center. The operation ended inside Poland on the Vistula River. Between 23 June to 29 August 1944, along a more than 600-mile-wide front, the Soviets defeated Army Group Center and advanced from 300 to 360 miles. In the process, the Soviets destroyed 17 German divisions and 3 brigades; 50 German divisions lost over half their strength. The German army High Command's official figure of losses was about 300,000 men, or 44 percent of those engaged, but this number may be low. Soviet losses were also high, with more than 178,000 dead and missing (8 percent of the total force involved) and more than 587,000 sick and wounded.

The advance into Belorussia led to advances in other sectors of the front, the Ukraine, and Estonia and Latvia where Army Group North's link to other German forces was temporarily cut. Operation BAGRATION was one of the greatest Soviet victories of the war and one from which German forces could never recover.

Arthur T. Frame

See also

Bagramyan, Ivan Khristoforovich; BARBAROSSA, Operation; Busch, Ernst; Chernyakhovsky, Ivan Danilovich; Eastern Front; Estonia; Kursk, Battle of; Latvia; Lithuania; Moscow, Battle of; Rokossovsky, Konstantin Konstantinovich; Stalin, Josef; Stalingrad, Battle of; Tehran Conference; Vasilevsky, Aleksandr Mikhailovich; Warsaw Rising; Zhukov, Georgii Konstantinovich

References

Connor, William M. "Analysis of Deep Attack Operations: Operation Bagration, Belorussia, 22 June–29 August 1944." Report, Combat Studies Institute, U.S. Army Command and General Staff College, Fort Leavenworth, KS, March 1987.

Glantz, David M., and Harold S. Orenstein, eds. *Belorussia, 1944: The Soviet General Staff Study.* London: Cass, 2001.

Werth, Alexander. *Russia at War, 1941–1945.* New York: E. P. Dutton, 1964.

Zaloga, Steven. *Bagration 1944: The Destruction of Army Group Centre.* London: Osprey Books, 1996.

Belov, Pavel Alekseyevich (1897–1962)

Soviet army general who fought in the Battle of Kursk and the invasion of Poland. Born at Shuya, Russia, on 18 February 1897, Pavel Belov joined the Russian army as a private in 1916 during World War I and rose to noncommissioned officer. In 1919, he joined both the Red Army and the Communist Party. During the Russian Civil War, he commanded a cavalry squadron.

Between 1922 and 1929, Belov led a cavalry regiment. He graduated from the Frunze Military Academy in 1934 and then was deputy commander and later commander of a cavalry division. From 1935 to 1940, he was chief of staff of a cavalry corps.

In 1940, Belov took command of the II Cavalry Corps, later redesignated I Guards Cavalry Corps, which played a major role in halting the German advance on Moscow in December 1941. Promoted to lieutenant general, Belov took command of Sixty-First Army from General M. M. Popov in June 1942 and participated in heavy fighting with the Germans in the Battle of Kursk and also around Voronzeh. Promoted to colonel general in July 1944, Belov fought with his army in the recovery of Ukraine and the invasion of Poland, then participated in the Berlin Offensive.

Following the war, Belov commanded the Southern Ural Military District from 1945 to 1955, then chaired the Voluntary Association for Support of the Army, Air Force, and Navy. He retired in 1960 and died in Moscow on 3 December 1963.

Spencer C. Tucker

See also
Berlin, Land Battle for; Kursk, Battle of; Poland–East Prussia Campaign; Popov, Markian Mikhailovich; Ukraine Campaign

References
Belov, Pavel A. *Za nami Moskva.* Moscow: Voenizdat, 1963.
———. *Istoriia Sotsialisticheskikh Uchenii.* Moscow: Nauka, 1977.
Bialer, Seweryn. *Stalin and His Generals: Soviet Military Memoirs of World War II.* New York: Pegasus, 1969.

Belzec

See Concentration Camps, German.

Beneš, Eduard (1884–1948)

Czech statesman who helped establish the independent state of Czechoslovakia. Born on 28 May 1884 at Kozlany, Bohemia, Eduard Beneš studied at Charles University in Prague, the Sorbonne in Paris, and the University of Dijon, where he earned a doctorate in law in 1908. In 1909, Beneš was appointed professor of economics at the Prague Academy of Commerce, and in 1912, he became a professor of sociology at the University of Prague. There, he met Tomáš G. Masaryk and came to embrace his social and political philosophies. As one of the leaders of the Czech nationalist movement against Austria, Beneš went abroad during World War I, first to Paris, where he worked as a journalist to promote the cause of Czech independence. That same year, he joined the Czechoslovakian National Council, recognized by the Allies in 1918 as the provisional government of Czechoslovakia.

On his return to Prague at the end of the war, Beneš became the first foreign minister of the new state. From 1918 to 1935, he worked to strengthen the security of Czechoslovakia, the cornerstone of which was a 1924 alliance with France. In addition, he worked to cooperate with Romania and Yugoslavia, with the three states signing collective security arrangements that led to the so-called Little Entente. Beneš was also a tireless advocate of the League of Nations, serving as League Council chairman five times. He secured a mutual security pact with the Soviet Union in 1935.

In December 1935, Beneš succeeded Masaryk on the latter's resignation as president of Czechoslovakia. The one intractable problem he could not solve was that of the minorities in his nation. The Czechs were not even a majority of the population of the state, and there were serious problems with the Ukrainians, the Slovaks, and especially the Germans. Adolf Hitler pushed the demands of the latter from relief of grievances into annexation by the Reich of those areas in which Germans were a majority. Beneš and his government went as far as they could without actually ceding territory, but at the September 1938 Munich Conference, the British and French agreed to Hitler's dismemberment of Czechoslovakia. A week later, Beneš resigned and went into exile in France.

Beneš became president of the Czechoslovakian government-in-exile in London in July 1940. He hoped to make his country a bridge between the East and the West, and he signed a 20-year treaty of alliance with the Soviet Union in 1943. He returned to Prague on 16 May 1945, stopping first in Moscow to confer with Josef Stalin.

Beneš was reelected president in 1946, but his hopes of nonalignment ran afoul of the Cold War. The Soviets staged a coup d'état in Prague in February 1948, and Beneš was forced to accept Communist control. Rather than agree to a new constitution that would legalize the Communist seizure of power, he resigned on 7 June 1948. He died in Sezimovo Üsti, Bohemia, on 3 September 1948.

Annette Richardson

See also
Czechoslovakia; Hitler, Adolf; Munich Conference and Preliminaries

References
Beneš, Edvard. *Democracy Today and Tomorrow.* London: Macmillan, 1939.
———. *Edvard Beneš in His Own Words: Threescore Years of a Statesman, Builder and Philosopher.* New York: Czech-American National Alliance, Eastern Division, 1944.
———. *My War Memoirs.* Trans. Paul Selver. Westport, CT: Greenwood Press, 1971.
Lukes, Igor. *Czechoslovakia between Stalin and Hitler: The Diplomacy of Edvard Beneš in the 1930s.* New York: Oxford University Press, 1996.
Taborsky, Edward. *President Edvard Beneš: Between East and West, 1938–1948.* Stanford, CA: Hoover Institution Press, 1981.

Bennett, Donald Clifford Tyndall (1910–1986)

British air force air vice marshal who commanded Number 8 Group. Born in Toowoomba, Queensland, Australia, on 14 September 1910, Donald Bennett enlisted in the Australian air force as a young man, acquiring licenses as a pilot, navigator, wireless operator, and ground engineer. He resigned in 1935 to join British-based Imperial Airways, setting the world's long-distance air record for seaplanes in 1938 in a flight from Dundee, Scotland, to South West Africa.

In 1940, Bennett became flight superintendent of the Atlantic Ferry service, and in the depths of winter, he piloted the first of thousands of American-built airplanes that would be flown to Britain. In 1941, he returned to the Royal Air Force, joining the Air Navigation School, where he began to develop pathfinding techniques for guiding bombers to their targets many hundred miles away. In 1942, he commanded Numbers 77 and 10 Bomber Squadrons at Leeming, Yorkshire. Shot down over Norway during an attack on the German battleship *Tirpitz*, Bennett escaped via Sweden and was awarded the Distinguished Service Order.

Shortly afterward, the British Air Ministry directed Bomber Command to establish a pathfinding force, and Bennett was named commander of Number 8 Group. The Pathfinder Force quickly developed great expertise in identifying and marking targets and effectively orientating bombers toward them. In 1943, Bennett was promoted to air vice marshal, but although many considered his contributions to Bomber Command a major reason for its success, his relations with other bomber group commanders were often strained. In particular, his colleagues resented losing some of their best crewmen to Number 8 Group.

Bennett left the Royal Air Force at the end of the war to become a civil aviation executive. During the 1948–1949 Berlin Airlift, his private commercial aviation firm flew numerous flights to Berlin, 250 of them with Bennett himself piloting an aircraft. For some months in 1945, he held a vacant seat in Parliament as a Liberal, but he lost it in the general elections that same year. He ran unsuccessfully as a Liberal in 1948 and 1950 and then ran again in 1967 as a decidedly reactionary National Party standard-bearer. Bennett died on 15 September 1986 at Wexham Hospital, Buckinghamshire, England.

Priscilla Roberts

See also
Great Britain, Air Force; Pathfinders; Strategic Bombing
References
Bennett, D. C. T. *Pathfinder*. London: Frederick Muller, 1958.
Maynard, John. *Bennett and the Pathfinders*. London: Arms and Armour Press, 1996.
Musgrove, Gordon. *Pathfinder Force: A History of 8 Group*. London: Crecy Books, 1992.
Richards, Denis, and Hilary St. G. Saunders. *The Royal Air Force, 1939–45*. 3 vols. London: Her Majesty's Stationery Office, 1975.

Bennett, Henry Gordon "Cocky" (1887–1962)

Australian army general who served in Singapore during the Japanese invasion. Born in Melbourne, Australia, on 15 April 1887, Henry Bennett was an insurance clerk and Australian reserve officer in the early years of the twentieth century. After World War I began, he joined the Australian Infantry Force in 1914. Bennett served with distinction in the Gallipoli Campaign and on the Western Front, displaying personal courage and winning recognition as an outstanding frontline commander, but he was also known for his frequent complaints, self-promotion, tactlessness, and poor interpersonal skills.

Between the wars, Bennett pursued a successful business career and also rose from colonel to major general in the Australian citizen armed forces. He resented and publicly criticized both permanent regular army officers and British military representatives. Bennett particularly disliked Sir Thomas Blamey, who headed the World War II Australian Infantry Force, occupying a position Bennett coveted.

Despite his seniority, Bennett received no command until September 1940, when he headed the Australian 8th Division. In September 1941, he accompanied his force to Singapore, where his relations with his juniors and with British military officers were predictably inharmonious. When the Japanese invaded in January 1942, Bennett commanded "Westforce" on the peninsula and had some initial successes against the Japanese troops. Withdrawing to Singapore Island, he commanded the Western Area, which bore the brunt of the main Japanese assault on 8 February. After five days of fierce fighting, Bennett and others advised Lieutenant General Sir Arthur Ernest Percival, the British commander, to surrender. When negotiations began, Bennett handed over command of his force to a subordinate, and with other Australian officers, he fled by sampan from Singapore, reaching Melbourne on 2 March.

Bennett received a mixed reception. He was promoted and became commander of III Corps in Perth, but Blamey ensured he received no further field command, and in May 1944, Bennett gave up active duty. Seeking to exonerate himself, he published a highly apologist book stating his case, an effort undercut when General Percival was released by the Japanese at the end of the war in August 1945 and wrote to Blamey condemning Bennett's actions as desertion of his men. A military court of inquiry ruled against Bennett, although a civilian commission exonerated him, a decision that was generally considered politically motivated. In retirement, Bennett cultivated an orchard farm and wrote extensively on military topics. He died at Dural, New South Wales, on 1 August 1962.

Priscilla Roberts

See also
Australia, Air Force; Blamey, Sir Thomas Albert; Percival, Arthur
    Ernest; Singapore, Battle for
References
Bennett, Henry. *Why Singapore Fell.* London: Angus and Robertson,
    1944.
Keogh, E. G. *The South West Pacific, 1941–45.* Melbourne, Australia:
    Grayflower Productions, 1965.
Legg, Frank. *The Gordon Bennett Story.* Sydney, Australia: Angus
    and Robertson, 1965.
Lodge, A. B. *The Fall of General Gordon Bennett.* Boston: Allen and
    Unwin, 1986.
Wigmore, Lionel. *The Japanese Thrust.* Canberra: Australian War
    Memorial, 1957.

Berenguer y Fuste, Dámaso (1873–1953)

Spanish army general who briefly served as minister of war. Born on 4 August 1873 in Cuba, Dámaso Berenguer was educated in a military school for orphans in Spain. He joined the Spanish army in 1889 and fought against rebel forces in Cuba between 1892 and 1898. He then served in North Africa and was promoted to lieutenant colonel in 1909. From 1911 to 1916, he participated in efforts to subdue Moroccan tribesmen and won a series of battles against them. Made a brigadier general in 1913, he was military governor of Malaga in 1916. Two years later, he was promoted to major general and named minister of war. In 1919, Berenguer became the high commissioner in Spanish Morocco, and a year later, he was made count of Xuaen. In 1920, Berenguer sent General Fernandes Silvestre against El Raisuli, a Moroccan warlord controlling Jibala. On 21 July 1921, Silvestre and 12,000 of his men were killed in an ambush, and Berenguer was held partly responsible. Court-martialed in consequence, he was placed on the reserve list in June 1924 but was amnestied a month later.

In 1926, King Alfonso XIII named Berenguer as head of his Military Household. In January 1930, Berenguer was called to head the Spanish government on the ouster of General Miguel Primo de Rivera. He relaxed some of the restraints of the Rivera dictatorship, but, faced with frequent strikes and civil unrest and in poor health, Berenguer resigned in February 1931. Appointed minister of war in March, he served only until Alfonso's departure that April. When the Republicans came to power, Berenguer was arrested and imprisoned (from 1931 to 1939) but released on the Nationalist victory in the Spanish Civil War. Berenguer died in Madrid on 19 May 1953.

Kevin D. Strait

See also
Franco, Francisco
References
Carr, Raymond. *Spain, 1809–1939.* Oxford: Clarendon Press, 1966.
Hills, George. *Franco: The Man and His Nation.* New York:
    Macmillan, 1967.

Bergeret, Jean Marie Joseph (1895–1956)

French army general and air minister in the Vichy government. Born in Gray, Haute Saone, France, on 23 August 1895, Jean Bergeret volunteered for military service at the start of World War I and was selected for special officer training at the French Military Academy of St. Cyr. Immediately after graduation, he saw combat, in which he distinguished himself. Bergeret showed remarkable ability and won rapid promotion. After attending the French War School, he joined the Armée de l'Air, the French military air service, in 1928. He rose to air staff chief of operations and won promotion to brigadier general shortly before the beginning of World War II.

When Germany invaded France in May 1940, the marked French inferiority to Germany in the air caused Bergeret some humiliation. He remained loyal to the Vichy government, heading the commission that negotiated armistice terms with Italy in the summer of 1940. From September 1940 until April 1942, he served as air minister. The return to the government of the collaborationist Pierre Laval, whom Bergeret despised, led him to resign. Bergeret was then appointed inspector of air defenses.

In November 1942, just before the Allied invasion of North Africa, Bergeret joined General Henri Giraud in Algiers, where he became personal assistant and confidential adviser to Admiral Jean Darlan. He was in charge of the latter's headquarters security arrangements when Darlan was assassinated in his office in December 1942. From then until March 1943, Bergeret was deputy high commissioner for North Africa. In October 1943, a Gaullist purge of the National Resistance Council brought Bergeret's arrest and that of several other Vichy supporters, and he was imprisoned until September 1945. Eventually, in November 1948, all charges against him were dropped, although his career was effectively over. Bergeret died in Neuilly, near Paris, on 30 November 1956.

Priscilla Roberts

See also
Darlan, Jean Louis Xavier François; France, Air Force; Giraud, Henri
    Honoré; TORCH, Operation
References
Charbonnières, Guy de Girard de. *Le duel Giraud–de Gaulle.* Paris:
    Plon, 1984.

Macmillan, Harold. *War Diaries: Politics and War in the Mediterranean, January 1943–1945.* New York: St. Martin's Press, 1984.

Ordioni, Pierre. *Tout commence à Alger, 1940–1945.* Paris: Éditions Albatros, 1985.

Paxton, Robert O. *Parades and Politics at Vichy: The French Officer Corps under Marshal Pétain.* Princeton, NJ: Princeton University Press, 1966.

Berlin, Air Battle of (November 1943–March 1944)

Between November 1943 and March 1944, the Royal Air Force (RAF) Bomber Command conducted 16 raids on the German capital in an attempt to defeat Germany by destroying Berlin. This effort was the third in a series of campaigns in 1943, with the first levied against German industrial production in the Ruhr Valley from April to July and the second launched against the city of Hamburg late in July.

The largest city in Germany, Berlin covered nearly 900 square miles. Attacking it not only would strike at the seat of power in the Third Reich but also would cripple a major industrial base for the German armed forces. Factories in Berlin contributed one-third of the Reich's electrical components as well as one-quarter of the army's tanks and half its field artillery.

Bolstered by the success of recent air raids, in particular the attack on Hamburg, Air Chief Marshal Sir Arthur "Bomber" Harris believed he could do the same with Berlin and force a German surrender. If he could get the Americans to join in, he expected losses to be between 400 and 500 aircraft. However, because of its own recent heavy losses over Germany, the U.S. Army Eighth Air Force would not able to participate. Despite this setback, Harris received approval in early November 1943 from Prime Minister Winston L. S. Churchill to begin the bomber offensive. He employed the RAF's new Avro Lancaster heavy bomber, as this four-engine aircraft had the requisite range to strike targets deep in German territory. The first raid, the largest battle Bomber Command had yet fought, occurred on the night of 18–19 November.

Attacking heavily defended Berlin was not an easy task. The city was ringed with a flak belt 40 miles wide and a searchlight band over 60 miles across. The defense centered on 24 128-mm antiaircraft guns grouped in eight-gun batteries on flak towers. Additionally, the city's extensive subway system provided underground shelter for the civilians. Only the Ruhr region was more heavily defended.

The British employed Window—strips of foil dropped from aircraft to jam German radar. To counter this, the Germans organized groups of single-engine fighters to attack the bombers as they were caught in searchlights. The Germans called this new tactic Wilde Sau (Wild Boar), and the technique helped them until they could develop effective radar. By early 1944, German night-fighter aircraft—primarily Ju-88s, FW-190s, and Bf-109s—were successfully employing bomber-intercept tactics with the help of SN2, an aircraft-based, air-to-air radar that would cause Bomber Command's losses to approach 9 percent for a single raid. To make matters worse for the British, many bombs did not come close to their desired targets, as chronically poor weather over Berlin forced pathfinders to mark targets blindly, relying exclusively on H2S radar; this problem was exacerbated by the fact that the number of experienced pathfinder radar operators dwindled as casualties mounted during the campaign.

The Battle of Berlin came to an end in March 1944 when the bombers passed under the control of the Supreme Allied Command to prepare for the Normandy Invasion. During the offensive, Bomber Command flew 9,111 sorties to the "Big City" and dropped 31,000 tons of bombs. Bomber Command lost 497 aircraft—5.5 percent of the force employed—and more than 3,500 British aircrew were killed or captured. On the German side, nearly 10,000 civilians were killed, and 27 percent of the built-up area of Berlin was destroyed. Harris's goal of defeating Germany was not, however, realized.

M. R. Pierce and John D. Plating

See also
Antiaircraft Artillery and Employment; Churchill, Sir Winston L. S.; Fighter Tactics; Germany, Air Force; Göring, Hermann Wilhelm; Hermann, Hans-Joachim; Kammhuber, Josef

References
Cooper, Alan W. *Bombers over Berlin: The RAF Offensive, November 1943–March 1944.* Northhamptonshire, UK: Patrick Stevens, 1985.

Middelbrook, Martin. *The Berlin Raids: RAF Bomber Command, Winter 1943–44.* London: Cassell, 1988.

Neillands, Robin. *The Bomber War: The Allied Air Offensive against Nazi Germany.* New York: Overlook Press, 2001.

Berlin, Land Battle for (31 March–2 May 1945)

Berlin, capital of the Reich, was vital to the German war effort. Adolf Hitler spent little time there during the war, but the city was the administrative center of the new German empire and powerhouse of the war effort, the greatest industrial and commercial city in Europe. Berlin was also a vital communications and transportation hub and a key

HISTORIOGRAPHICAL CONTROVERSY
Eisenhower and Berlin

In the midst of the Cold War, with Germany divided and memories of wartime cooperation between the Western powers and the Soviet Union nearly forgotten, many historians questioned whether Supreme Allied Commander General Dwight D. Eisenhower had been correct in choosing not to race Soviet forces to capture Berlin in April 1945. The detractors argued that conquest of the city by the Western Allies would have provided a useful bargaining chip with the Soviets and might have kept them out of Central Europe and thereby changed the course of history. According to this view, there might have been no Berlin crisis in 1948, no Berlin Wall erected in 1961, and no divided Germany. Proponents of the idea criticized Eisenhower for naively focusing on military goals rather than the more important long-term political and diplomatic aspirations.

Chester Wilmot began the debate in 1952 with *The Struggle for Europe,* in which he argued that British forces could have taken Berlin if Eisenhower had unleashed them in early April 1945. Quite predictably, British Field Marshal Bernard Montgomery echoed similar sentiments in his 1958 memoirs and suggested that Eisenhower had forgotten that winning the war militarily hardly mattered if the Allies lost it politically. John Toland in *The Last Hundred Days* (1965) and Cornelius Ryan in *The Last Battle* (1966) offered similar appraisals, although they added that any drive on Berlin would have en-

countered strenuous resistance in the city's suburbs.

Eisenhower's defenders, by contrast, claimed that no other decision was practical. By late January 1945, Soviet forces were only 35 miles east of Berlin, whereas Eisenhower's armies were hundreds of miles to the west. The Soviets then regrouped and resupplied their forces for two months while the Allies closed from the west, but even in April, the Red Army had much stronger units in proximity to Berlin than either the Americans or the British. Led by Walter Bedell Smith in *Eisenhower's Six Great Decisions* (1956) and supported by Stephen Ambrose in *Eisenhower and Berlin, 1945: The Decision to Halt at the Elbe* (1967), Eisenhower's supporters also argued that he had to worry about the supposed National Redoubt (an imagined German stronghold in the Alps) in southern Germany, the 100,000 casualties that General Omar N. Bradley estimated it would cost to capture the city, and the fact that Allied agreements regarding the postwar division of Germany placed a jointly occupied Berlin well within the Soviet zone of control. How, they asked, could Eisenhower have defended losing 100,000 men for territory he knew the United States would turn over to the Soviet Union as soon as the war ended?

Since the end of the Cold War, the debate has softened considerably, and most historians now view the Soviet capture of Berlin on 2 May 1945 as the logical military conclusion to the war in

Europe. U.S. units may have been only 48 miles from Berlin when Eisenhower finally ordered them to halt on 15 April, but the odds on their seizing the city in force in advance of the Soviets were extremely long. In that sense, a bold U.S. or British dash for Berlin was militarily unnecessary, and in light of Allied agreements regarding the postwar division of Germany, it would have been politically foolhardy as well.

Lance Janda

See also

Berlin, Land Battle for; Bradley, Omar Nelson; Eisenhower, Dwight D.; Hodges, Courtney Hicks; Marshall, George Catlett; Montgomery, Sir Bernard Law; Patton, George Smith, Jr.; Stalin, Josef; Zhukov, Georgii Konstantinovich

References

Ambrose, Stephen. *Eisenhower and Berlin, 1945: The Decision to Halt at the Elbe.* New York: W. W. Norton, 1967.

Montgomery, Bernard. *The Memoirs of Field Marshal the Viscount Montgomery of Alamein.* Cleveland, OH: World, 1958.

Ryan, Cornelius. *The Last Battle.* New York: Simon and Schuster, 1966.

Smith, Walter Bedell. *Eisenhower's Six Great Decisions.* New York: Longman and Green, 1956.

Toland, John. *The Last 100 Days.* New York: Random House, 1965.

Wilmot, Chester. *The Struggle for Europe.* Westport, CT: Greenwood Press, 1952.

production center, particularly for electrical products and armaments.

In August 1940, after the bombing of London, Bomber Command of the Royal Air Force (RAF) raided Berlin, but the city enjoyed a respite thereafter until March 1943; then there was another pause. The battle for the city began in earnest in November 1943 with the first in a long series of punishing Allied air raids, with particularly severe attacks in

March 1944. Somehow, Berliners managed to carry on amid the ruins.

Hitler returned to Berlin from the Alderhorst (Eagle's Nest), his retreat at Ziegenberg, by train on 16 January 1945, and as the war drew to a close, the city became the ultimate prize, at least for the Soviets. Josef Stalin wanted it desperately. So did British Prime Minister Winston L. S. Churchill, but he was overruled by U.S. leaders, who showed little interest in capturing the city, particularly after agreements setting up the postwar occupation placed Berlin deep within the Soviet zone. The supreme commander of Allied forces in the west, General Dwight D. Eisenhower, who was in any case distracted by a phantom Nazi Alpine "National Redoubt," said he had no interest in the capital. High casualty estimates for taking the city (Lieutenant General Omar Bradley posited a cost of 100,000 men) also deterred Eisenhower. Thus, although U.S. forces, including the 82nd Airborne Division, were readied for such an assault, the task was left to the Soviets.

Stalin concealed the U.S. ambivalence concerning Berlin from his front commanders, Generals Ivan S. Konev and Georgii K. Zhukov. By early February, Zhukov's 1st Belorussian Front and Konev's 1st Ukrainian Front had completed the initial phase of their advance into Germany. Zhukov's troops were across the Oder River, 100 miles from Berlin. The Soviets had surrounded large German troop concentrations at Breslau and Posen. Meanwhile, Soviet forces carried out a horrible revenge on eastern Germany, in which tens of thousands of civilians were murdered. Total casualties ranged into the millions.

Zhukov might then have pushed on to the capital in another several weeks had not Stalin ordered a halt, necessary because of logistical problems resulting from the vast distances the Soviet forces had covered to that point. Meanwhile, Konev's forces threatened the German capital from the southeast. In defense of Berlin, Hitler had only the remnants of his Third Panzer and Ninth Armies, now constituting Army Group Vistula. In March, however, he ordered that the city be held "to the last man and the last shot."

On 8 March, alarmed by the American crossing of the Rhine the day before, Stalin summoned Zhukov to Moscow to discuss an offensive against Berlin. The now rapid progress of the Western Allies eastward set off alarm bells in Moscow, and Stavka (the Soviet High Command) rushed plans for an offensive to take the German capital. On 31 March, Stalin ordered the offensive to begin. Zhukov would make the principal drive on Berlin, while Konev supported him on the left flank and Marshal Konstantin Rokossovsky's 2nd Belorussian Front on the lower Oder moved on Zhukov's right flank. Altogether, the three fronts had some 1.5 million troops, 6,250 armored vehicles, and 7,500 aircraft. Opposing them, the German Ninth Army and Third Panzer Army had only 24 understrength divisions, with 754 tanks and few aircraft.

Zhukov's frontal assaults on Berlin's defenses from the east failed. On 18 April, Stalin ordered him to go around Berlin from the north, while Konev encircled the city from the south. Hitler, meanwhile, ordered his Ninth Army to stand fast on the Oder, thus facilitating Konev's move.

On 20 April, Hitler's birthday, Konev's tanks reached Jüterbog, the airfield and key ammunition depot south of Berlin. That same day, Hitler allowed those of his entourage who wished to do so to leave the city. He pledged to stay.

The Soviets completed the encirclement of the city on 25 April. Also on that day, Soviet and U.S. forces met on the Elbe River. Hitler attempted to organize the Ninth Army as a relief force for Berlin, but it, too, was surrounded and soon destroyed. Although Lieutenant General Walther Wenck's Twelfth Army tried to relieve the city from the west, it was too weak to accomplish the task. Meanwhile, the defense of Berlin itself fell to miscellaneous German troops unfortunate enough to be pushed back there and by old men and boys hastily pressed into service for the daunting task. On 30 April, with the defenders' ammunition nearly depleted and the defenses fast crumbling and as Soviet troops took the Reichstag (Parliament) building, Hitler committed suicide. On 2 May, Lieutenant General Hans Krebs, chief of the German General Staff, surrendered Berlin.

Given their country's suffering in the war, Soviet soldiers hardly needed encouragement to destroy the German capital, the symbol of Nazism. They also committed widespread atrocities in the city both during and after its fall. Bradley's estimate of the cost of taking Berlin was, in fact, low. According to one source, the "Berlin Strategic Offensive" from April 16 to May 8, involving the 1st Belorussian, 2nd Belorussian, and 1st Ukrainian Fronts, produced a staggering total of 352,475 Soviet casualties (including 78,291 dead)—an average of 15,325 a day.

What is remarkable is how Berlin came back. It survived the destruction of the war and the building of the Berlin Wall in 1961, which divided the city into east and west portions. Today, it is once again the capital of a united, powerful, but this time peaceful German state.

Spencer C. Tucker

See also

Berlin, Air Battle of; Bradley, Omar Nelson; Churchill, Sir Winston L. S.; Eisenhower, Dwight D.; Konev, Ivan Stepanovich; Krebs, Hans; Rokossovsky, Konstantin Konstantinovich; Stalin, Josef; Zhukov, Georgii Konstantinovich

References

Beevor, Antony. *The Fall of Berlin, 1945.* New York: Viking Penguin, 2002.
Read, Anthony, and David Fisher. *The Fall of Berlin.* New York: W. W. Norton, 1992.
Ryan, Cornelius. *The Last Battle.* New York: Simon and Schuster, 1966.

Bernadotte of Wisborg, Folke (Count) (1895–1948)

Swedish diplomat and Red Cross official who worked on behalf of prisoners of war. Folke Bernadotte was born in Stockholm, Sweden, on 2 January 1895; his father was a brother of King Gustav V. Although hemophilia limited his activities, Bernadotte served in the Swedish army from 1918 to 1930. His skills were diplomatic rather than military, and he also worked closely with the Swedish Red Cross, of which he became a vice president, organizing prisoner-of-war exchanges.

Bernadotte was also a vice president of the Swedish Boy Scouts, and during World War II, he integrated that organization into neutral Sweden's defense network. He traveled extensively on behalf of the Swedish Red Cross, arranging exchanges of thousands of British and German prisoners in 1943 and 1944, and between 1944 and 1945, he concluded an agreement with Germany whereby Scandinavian prisoners would be transferred to the Neuengamme camp near Hamburg.

Bernadotte visited Berlin in February 1945 to finalize the details of this arrangement with Heinrich Himmler, head of the Schutzstaffel (SS). At that time, Himmler expressed interest in negotiating surrender terms with the Western Allies, under which the Germans would spare those Jews still alive in concentration camps in exchange for Allied concessions. (Bernadotte has sometimes been criticized for a lack of concern about rescuing Jews, but this charge is based on a faked letter purportedly sent from him to Himmler.) In April 1945, Himmler met again with Bernadotte, suggesting that Germany would surrender in the west to Britain, France, and the United States, in exchange for their assistance against the Soviet Union in the east. Bernadotte relayed these suggestions to British Prime Minister Winston L. S. Churchill, who passed them on to U.S. President Harry S Truman, only to have them promptly rejected.

Bernadotte became president of the Swedish Red Cross in 1946. In May 1948, the United Nations appointed him to mediate peace in Palestine. Just four months later, however, on 17 September 1948, terrorists from the Jewish Stern Gang assassinated him in Jerusalem.

Priscilla Roberts

See also
Himmler, Heinrich; Prisoners of War; Sweden
References
Bernadotte, Folke. *The Curtain Falls: The Last Days of the Third Reich*. New York: Alfred A. Knopf, 1945.
Toland, John. *The Last 100 Days*. New York: Random House, 1966.

Besson, Antoine Marie Benoit (1876–1969)

French army general under the Vichy regime. Born on 14 September 1876 at Saint Symphonien near Lyons, France, Antoine Besson graduated from the French Military Academy of St. Cyr in 1898. He then joined the 4th Regiment of Zouaves. During World War I, he distinguished himself in fighting on the Western Front, winning numerous decorations and eventually rising to command his regiment.

In July 1937, Besson was promoted to full general, commanding the Sixth Army, and he became a member of France's Supreme War Council. During the German invasion of France in May and June 1940, he commanded the 3rd Army Group (consisting of 3 armies totaling 36 divisions on the extreme right flank of the Allied line) on the Colmar-Mulhouse section of the front, protected by the Jura Mountains and Switzerland. During the German assault, Besson's troops found the overwhelming German air superiority particular demoralizing.

Following the German breakthrough, Besson followed orders and withdrew to the Seine River on 8 June, to positions below the Aisne and the Somme Rivers as far as Neufchâtel. Within a week, as his men retreated in disorder to be isolated on the Loire River, he had become a strong advocate of signing an armistice, preferring that outcome to the continued and senseless slaughter of his forces. Besson spent the remainder of the war as a German prisoner of war, sparing him the opprobrium attached to many Vichy officials. Subsequently, he became director of the French Prisoner of War Service. He died in Paris on 25 July 1969.

Priscilla Roberts

See also
France Campaign
References
Crèmieux-Brilhac, Jean-Louis. *Les Français de l'an 40*. 2 vols. Paris: Gallimard, 1990.
Draper, Theodore. *The Six Weeks' War: France, May 10–June 25, 1940*. New York: Viking, 1964.
Horne, Alistair. *To Lose a Battle: France 1940*. Boston: Little, Brown, 1969.
Spears, Edward L. *Assignment to Catastrophe*. 2 vols. New York: Wynn, 1954–1955.

Béthouart, Marie Émile Antoine (1889–1982)

French army general and briefly head of the French mission in Washington during World War II. Born at Dôle, France, in the Jura Mountains, on 17 December 1889, Émile Béthouart graduated from the French Military Academy of

St. Cyr in 1912. During World War I, he served with Alpine troops and was wounded three times. As French military attaché, he was present when King Alexander of Yugoslavia was assassinated in Marseille, France, in October 1934.

Promoted to brigadier general in April 1940, Béthouart led the Franco-Polish expeditionary force that took part in the Norwegian Campaign of that spring. After France surrendered to Germany in June 1940, he initially remained with Vichy forces and took over the Casablanca Division in southern Morocco. By late 1942, Béthouart was prepared to collaborate with U.S. forces invading North Africa, and he negotiated with American representatives, including U.S. civilian Robert Murphy. Béthouart promised that men under his command would occupy all key points and welcome the invaders. At the last moment in the confused meetings and negotiations, he also informed his superior, Governor-General Charles Noguès, of events. Noguès had earlier warned the Americans that his forces would oppose them, and he ordered Béthouart and a subordinate arrested and tried for treason. Noguès then ordered their execution, a command U.S. Army Major General George S. Patton Jr. was able to countermand following the American landing.

From December 1942, Béthouart headed the French mission in Washington, negotiating large-scale military aid from the United States. Returning to Algiers, he became chief of the National Defense Staff, organizing the French Army of Africa in preparation for the invasion of France. In August 1944, Béthouart commanded I Corps of the First French Army in the invasion of southern France, through the Vosges Mountains into Alsace and across the Rhine as far as the southern bank of the Danube. His men saw particularly heavy action in the Colmar region.

Béthouart subsequently headed French occupation forces in Austria. In 1949, he became a full general. After retiring in 1955, he entered politics and became a senator. Béthouart died in Fréjus in southern France, on 17 October 1982.

Priscilla Roberts

See also
France, Army; Juin, Alphonse Pierre; Noguès, Charles Auguste Paul; North Africa Campaign; Patton, George Smith, Jr.; TORCH, Operation

References
Aglion, Raoul. *De Gaulle et Roosevelt: La France Libre aux États-Unis.* Paris: Plon, 1984.
Béthouart, M. E. *Cinq années d'espérance, 1939–45.* Paris: Plon, 1968.
———. *Dès hécatombes glorieuses au désastre (1914–1940).* Paris: Plon, 1972.
Lemaigre-Dubreuil, Jacques. *Les relations franco-américains et la politique des généraux.* Paris: Publications Elysées, 1949.
Paxton, Robert O. *Parades and Politics at Vichy: The French Officer Corps under Marshal Pétain.* Princeton, NJ: Princeton University Press, 1966.

Bevin, Ernest (1881–1951)

British trade unionist, statesman, and member of the War Cabinet. Born at Winsford, Somerset, England, on 7 March 1881, the illegitimate son of a village midwife, Ernest Bevin became a drayman in Bristol. During a dock strike in 1910, he affiliated the local carters with the Dockers' Union. By 1914, Bevin was a national organizer for the Transport Workers' Federation.

Although noted for his pugnacious personality, Bevin preferred negotiation rather than confrontation with employers. He supported British participation in World War I and later made the massive Transport and General Workers' Union, which he organized in 1921, a restraining force on volatile occasions such as the General Strike of 1926. Bevin deplored the coalition with Conservatives and Liberals formed in 1931 by Labour Prime Minister Ramsay MacDonald, but his equally strong distaste for pacifism and appeasement of the Fascist regimes alienated him from other Labour Party leaders who had also broken with MacDonald. Bevin was finally drawn toward Winston L. S. Churchill's circle of antiappeasers.

When Churchill became prime minister in May 1940, he appointed Bevin minister of labor, bringing him into the War Cabinet the following October. Bevin remained at his post until the Labour Party withdrew from Churchill's wartime coalition in May 1945. Many asserted that no one else could have mobilized the country's manpower and industrial resources as efficiently. With a mixture of coercion and rewards informed by humane common sense, he reluctantly conscripted and deployed workers, including women, where they were most needed. But Bevin also insisted on full rights of collective bargaining with employers and adequate provision for workplace safety and comfort. Work stoppages nearly disappeared. Ministers responsible for production and procurement often challenged him, but skillful use of his near dictatorial powers and the intense personal loyalty he evoked among millions of workers gave him the advantage in political or bureaucratic controversies.

When the British Labour Party took office after Churchill's electoral defeat in July 1945, Bevin became foreign secretary. Until ill health forced his retirement in 1951, he strove to prevent the spread of communism in Western Europe and to build an anti-Soviet alliance that included the United States. Bevin died in London on 14 April 1951.

John A. Hutcheson Jr.

See also
Attlee, Clement Richard; Churchill, Sir Winston L. S.; Great Britain, Home Front

References
Bullock, Alan. *The Life and Times of Ernest Bevin.* 3 vols. New York and London: Norton, 1960–1983.

Calder, Angus. *The People's War: Britain, 1939–1945*. New York: Pantheon, 1969.

Weiler, Peter. *Ernest Bevin*. Manchester, UK: Manchester University Press, 1993.

Bhamo, Siege of (14 November– 15 December 1944)

Key battle in north Burma in late 1944. In August 1944, Allied forces had taken Myitkyina on the China-Burma border. Chinese Generalissimo Jiang Jieshi (Chiang Kai-shek) demanded that Chinese divisions at Myitkyina then be directed south against Bhamo to draw off the Japanese from Lungling. Lieutenant General Joseph W. Stilwell, commander of all U.S. Army forces in the China-Burma-India (CBI) Theater and chief of staff to Jiang, opposed this move on the basis that the troops needed rest, but he also believed the Japanese could hold Bhamo without withdrawing troops from Lungling. In mid-September, Jiang again demanded Stilwell undertake an offensive against Bhamo to take pressure off Lungling; if that did not occur, he said, he would withdraw Y-Force back across the Salween River to protect Kunming. Jiang feared that a Japanese victory at Lungling would be followed by an attack on Kunming.

With the rainy season in north Burma coming to an end and as part of a campaign to take Rangoon, Stilwell ordered a renewal of the offensive. He had five Chinese divisions, the excellent British 36th Division, and the Mars Force of one Chinese and two U.S. regiments. Opposing him was Japanese Lieutenant General Honda Masaki's Thirty-Third Army, consisting of three understrength divisions. Stilwell planned an envelopment to trap the Thirty-Third Army between his force and Y-Force in Yunnan.

The offensive opened on 15 October 1944 with Chinese Lieutenant General Sun Liren (Sun Li-jen) and his First Army, composed of the 30th and 38th Divisions, advancing toward the main elements of Thirty-Third Army at Bhamo as the British 36th Division moved down the Railroad Corridor to protect the flank. At the same time, the bulk of Stilwell's troops would head south from Mogaung, cross the Irrawaddy River near Shwegu, and gain the Burma Road near Lashio.

On 18 October, three days after the offensive began, Stilwell was relieved of command. The charge that the American general had disobeyed orders in failing to advance on Bhamo was part of Jiang's litany of complaints in demanding Stilwell's relief. U.S. Army Lieutenant General Dan I. Sultan, Stilwell's deputy, took over as commander of U.S. and Chinese forces in the South-East Asia Command.

On 6 November, Chinese forces began crossing the Irrawaddy, and a week later, the siege of Bhamo began. It lasted from 14 November to 13 December. Stubborn Japanese defenses there held up the Chinese 30th and 38th Divisions for a month. With further resistance impossible, some 800 Japanese survivors managed to escape at night, rejoining the 56th Division in the mountains between Bhamo and Namkham. The Chinese divisions then began a slow pursuit.

The offensive was abandoned at the end of November, the consequence of a Japanese offensive in China. Jiang decided to withdraw the Chinese 14th and 22nd Divisions from Burma. Both were flown out to stop Japanese drives in south China. This action forced Sultan to abandon Stilwell's plan to encircle the Thirty-Third Army in favor of securing the road east from Bhamo to Namkham.

Steven M. Cunningham

See also
Burma Theater; Honda Masaki; Jiang Jieshi; Stilwell, Joseph Warren; Sultan, Daniel I.; Sun Liren

References
Allen, Louis. *Burma: The Longest War, 1941–45*. New York: St. Martin's Press, 1984.

Owen, Frank. *The Campaign in Burma*. London: Whitefriars Press, 1946.

Tuchman, Barbara. *Sand against the Wind: Stilwell and the American Experience in China, 1911–45*. New York: Macmillan, 1971.

"Big Week" Air Battle (20–25 February 1944)

Name later given by the press to air combat over Germany in Operation ARGUMENT, a series of intensive Allied air strikes at the end of February 1944 against the German aircraft industry's final-assembly plants, ball-bearing factories, and facilities producing aircraft components. The Allies initiated the operation in order to reduce the effectiveness of Luftwaffe fighters against Allied bombers over Germany and to prepare for the invasion of Normandy. Although the Luftwaffe still maintained significant numbers of aircraft, it could not long survive both sustained losses in the air and attacks on its production facilities.

A period of clear weather allowed the Allies to begin the campaign. Bomber Command of the Royal Air Force (RAF) joined in for nighttime raids, but the bulk of the attacks were made by the U.S. Army Air Forces (USAAF) in daylight operations. Between 20 and 25 February 1944, some 1,000 bombers and 900 fighters of the U.S. Eighth Army Air Force carried out 13 major attacks against 15 centers of the German aviation industry. In the last four days of the offensive, Fifteenth Air Force, headquartered at Foggia, Italy, joined in.

As the commander of U.S. Strategic Air Forces in Europe, Lieutenant General Carl Spaatz, had predicted, the German fighters contested the raids. Between 20 and 25 February, the Eighth and Fifteenth Air Forces flew a combined total of 3,800 sorties and dropped almost 10,000 tons of bombs. USAAF losses were heavy, with 226 bombers shot down (6 percent of the force engaged). Fighters from other Allied countries flew 3,673 sorties, with only 28 fighters lost (less than 1 percent). The USAAF claimed more than 600 German fighter aircraft were shot down. In the operation, the P-51 Mustang fighter played a notable role; German fighters were no match for it, especially as many were weighed down by heavy armaments designed to destroy the Allied bombers. In the months ahead, the Allied bombers switched over to a concentration on German oil-production facilities.

German fighter losses for the entire month of February came to 2,121, with another 2,115 destroyed in March. Clearly, the days of the Luftwaffe were numbered. "Big Week" was a major defeat for the Luftwaffe and claimed many of its best pilots. This reduction in German air strength was an essential prelude to the successful Normandy Invasion in June 1944.

Spencer C. Tucker

See also
Spaatz, Carl Andrew "Tooey"; Strategic Bombing

References
Boyne, Walter J. *A Clash of Wings: World War II in the Air.* New York: Simon and Schuster, 1994.
Buckley, John. *Air Power in the Age of Total War.* London: UCL Press, 1999.
Neillands, Robin. *The Bomber War: The Allied Air Offensive against Nazi Germany.* New York: Overlook Press, 2001.

Billotte, Gaston Henri Gustave (1875–1940)

French army general and commander of the 1st Army Group during the battle for France. Born on 10 February 1875 in Sommeval (Aube), near Troyes, France, Gaston Billotte graduated from the French Military Academy of St. Cyr in 1896. Commissioned in the naval infantry, he served in Indochina until 1915, and during World War I, he held a variety of command and staff positions. While leading an infantry division, he was twice gassed.

Billotte returned to Indochina after the war, becoming commander of French forces there in 1930. Seven years later, he was inspector general of colonial troops. Billotte advocated the employment of tanks in the French military, and Charles de Gaulle credited him with the creation of the first two French tank divisions. Just before the outbreak of war in 1939, Billotte took command of 1st Army Group and positioned this unit along the Belgian border around Malmédy. Among its five armies was the British Expeditionary Force (BEF).

Billotte's 1st Army Group played the major role in the battle for France. On the German invasion of the west in May 1940, Billotte moved the bulk of his forces into Belgium in accordance with prearranged plans. The Germans then struck to the south, overrunning Billotte's southernmost army, the Ninth, in the area between Sedan and Givet. On May 14, realizing the threat this posed to his northern forces, Billotte ordered a withdrawal from the Dyle Line to the Escaute River.

On the night of 21 May, Billotte was seriously injured in a car accident after meeting with the new French army commander, General Maxime Weygand. His incapacitation increased confusion in the French army command. Billotte died of his injuries in Ypres on 23 May 1940.

Kevin D. Strait

See also
de Gaulle, Charles; France, Battle for; Weygand, Maxime

References
Beaufre, André. *1940: The Fall of France.* Trans. Desmond Flower. New York: Alfred A. Knopf, 1968.
Chapman, Guy. *Why France Fell: The Defeat of the French Army in 1940.* New York: Holt, Rinehart and Winston, 1969.
Ginsburg, Jeffrey. "The Battle of the Belgian Plain, May 12–14, 1940: The First Great Tank Battle." *Journal of Military History* 56, no. 2 (April 1992): 207–244.
Horne, Alistair. *To Lose a Battle: France, 1940.* Boston: Little, Brown, 1969.

Bismarck, Sortie and Sinking of (May 1941)

The sinking of the *Bismarck* occurred at the height of German battleship operations in the Atlantic Ocean. The commander of the German navy, Grand Admiral Erich Raeder, expected the new battleship *Bismarck,* which was to be available in the spring of 1941, to provide an opportunity to test the navy's "battle group" strategy in support of a war on commerce. Repairs to the battleships *Gneisenau* and *Scharnhorst* forced delays, and the naval command decided to send the *Bismarck* and the heavy cruiser *Prinz Eugen* to sea as soon as possible to attack shipping in the North Atlantic in Operation RHINE EXERCISE. Raeder was determined to demonstrate the value of the battleships to the war effort, and the *Bismarck* was rushed into action with an incomplete antiaircraft control system and equipment scavenged from other ships.

Vice Admiral Günther Lütjens, the fleet commander and task force leader, opposed the "piecemeal approach" and advocated delaying the mission until the other battleships were available, including the *Tirpitz*. His pessimism played a key role in his decisions over the course of the operation.

British intelligence, including ULTRA, alerted the Royal Navy that a major German naval operation was under way, and aircraft spotted the two ships in Bergen on 21 May 1941. The British took countermeasures to patrol the Iceland-Faroes passage and the Denmark Strait to block the German breakout into the Atlantic. On 23 May, the British cruisers *Norfolk* and *Suffolk* spotted the two German raiders in the Denmark Strait. The persistence of the British cruisers in shadowing the German ships led Lütjens to conclude that the British possessed new radar.

Off Iceland at about 5:55 A.M. on 24 May, in the Iceland Battle or the Battle of the Denmark Strait, British Rear Admiral Lancelot E. Holland's battle cruiser *Hood* and battleship *Prince of Wales* engaged the *Bismarck*. The *Hood* was hit in her magazines by the German battleship's fourth salvo and blew up. Only 3 of her 1,419 crewmen survived. The *Prince of Wales* took seven hits (four from the *Bismarck*) and was damaged.

Although the *Bismarck* had received only three hits, the ship was leaking oil, and her speed was also reduced from flooding in the forward compartments. At about 4:00 P.M., Lütjens detached the *Prinz Eugen* in a vain effort to draw the British off while the *Bismarck* made for the French port of Saint-Nazaire to carry out repairs. In the early morning of 25 May, the *Bismarck* managed to elude her pursuers, but Lütjens was unaware of this in spite of reports from Naval Command Group West. When Lütjens broke radio silence, these messages were picked up by Allied high-frequency direction-finding (HF/DF) receivers. Increased German radio traffic along the French coast suggested that the destination of the *Bismarck* was a French port, which was later confirmed by a British intercept of a Luftwaffe signal. The chief British ships that had been chasing the *Bismarck* in the wrong direction now altered course. In the meantime, Force H with the aircraft carrier *Ark Royal* had departed Gibraltar to provide air reconnaissance off the French west coast.

On 26 May, Swordfish torpedo-bombers from the *Ark Royal* and Coastal Command's patrol bomber (PBY) aircraft regained contact with the *Bismarck*. Late in the day, Swordfish from the *Ark Royal* attacked, and a lucky torpedo hit jammed the German battleship's twin rudder system, making her unable to maneuver. With no air cover or help from the U-boats or other ships available, the fatalistic Lütjens, remembering the reaction to the scuttling of the *Graf Spee* and Raeder's orders to fight to the last shell, radioed the hopelessness of the situation.

At 8:45 A.M. on 27 May, the British battleships *King George V* and *Rodney* opened fire. By 10:00, although hit by hundreds of shells, the *Bismarck* remained afloat. As the heavy cruiser *Dorsetshire* closed to fire torpedoes, the Germans scuttled their ship. Three torpedoes then struck, and the *Bismarck* went down. Reports of German submarines in the area halted British efforts to rescue German survivors. Only 110 of the crew of 2,300 survived. Lütjens was not among them.

A furious Adolf Hitler regarded the sinking of the *Bismarck* as a major loss of prestige and ordered that no more battleship operations be undertaken without his permission. The major German ships were now relegated to the defense of Norway, leaving the brunt of Germany's naval war to the U-boats.

Keith W. Bird

See also

Germany, Navy; Lütjens, Günther; Plata, Río de la, Battle of; Raeder, Erich; Signals Intelligence

References

Bercuson, David J., and Holger H. Herwig. *The Destruction of the "Bismarck."* Woodstock, NY, and New York: Overlook Press, 2001.

Burkard, Baron von Müllenheim-Rechberg. *Battleship "Bismarck": A Survivor's Story.* Annapolis, MD: Naval Institute Press, 1990.

Winklareth, Robert J. *"Bismarck" Chase: New Light on a Famous Engagement.* Annapolis, MD: Naval Institute Press, 1998.

Bismarck Sea, Battle of (2–5 March 1943)

Southwestern Pacific naval battle. As General Douglas MacArthur's troops fought to expel the Japanese from New Guinea, it fell to the U.S. Army Air Forces (USAAF) to interdict Japanese resupply efforts. When Lieutenant General George C. Kenney assumed command of Fifth Air Force in the Pacific in August 1942, he found many of his units operating obsolescent aircraft and using ineffective tactics. Kenney quickly devised two important new tactics. First was the development of skip-bombing, in which medium bombers—A-20 Havocs and B-25 Mitchells—attacked Japanese ships from low altitude and literally "skipped" bombs into the sides of their targets. The bombs used time-delayed fuses so that the explosions would occur either within the ships, should they penetrate the hulls, or below their waterlines, as the bombs sank after hitting the hulls. Second, crews installed additional forward-firing .50 caliber machine guns in medium bombers, designed to either sink small vessels or suppress antiaircraft fire. Also, several squadrons of the Royal Australian Air Force were available to supplement the Fifth Air Force.

In January 1943, Allied forces undertook a major offensive along the New Guinea coast. In response, the Japanese sent additional resources via convoys across the Bismarck Sea. On the night of 28 February 1943, a large Japanese force under Rear Admiral Kimura Masatomi, consisting of eight transports and eight destroyers left Rabaul with 6,900 troops of the 51st Division, bound for Lae, New Guinea.

The Japanese recognized the threat posed by Allied airpower, but Lae was too important to lose. Some 100 fighters (40 navy and 60 army) provided air cover for the convoy. Kenney knew of the Japanese activity through signals intelligence and reconnaissance flights. American B-24s first sighted the Japanese formation on 1 March, but eight B-17s sent to attack it failed to locate the Japanese force because of cloud cover. The following day, another B-24 reacquired the target, and eight B-17s attacked with 1,000-pound demolition bombs, sinking one transport and damaging another. Two of the Japanese destroyers rescued approximately 950 men and rushed ahead to Lae, returning to the convoy early the next morning.

On 3 March, the largest Allied air effort yet seen in the theater assembled to attack the Japanese when the convoy came within range of the medium bombers. At 10:00 A.M., B-17s bombed the convoy to disrupt its formation. Shortly thereafter, Australian Beaufighters, followed by heavily armed B-25s and A-20s, attacked the convoy from an altitude of 500 feet or less, while P-38s engaged Japanese escort fighters. Out of 47 bombs dropped by the attackers, 28 reportedly found their targets. Allied aircraft repeated their assault that afternoon but with less success, as the weather began to interfere.

By the end of the day, all of the Japanese transports and three destroyers had sunk. A fourth destroyer was heavily damaged and was sunk by Allied aircraft the next day. The remaining destroyers collected as many survivors as possible and returned to Rabaul. Over the next few days, aircraft and patrol torpedo (PT) boats patrolled the area, strafing and bombing any remaining Japanese: this was to prevent any enemy troops from reaching land, where they would pose a threat because they would not surrender. Additionally, Allied pilots sought retribution against Japanese flyers who had machine-gunned an American crew parachuting from their stricken B-17.

In the battle, the Japanese lost some 60 aircraft, 12 ships, and some 3,700 men. The Allied cost was 3 fighters, 1 B-17, and 1 B-25. MacArthur described the victory as "the decisive aerial engagement" in the Southwest Pacific Theater. After the battle, Japanese transports never again sailed within range of Allied airpower. Without reinforcement, the Japanese lost Lae to Australian troops some seven months later.

Rodney Madison

See also

Aircraft, Bombers; Kenney, George Churchill; Kimura Masatomi; MacArthur, Douglas; New Guinea Campaign; Rabaul; Solomon Islands, Naval Campaign; Southwestern Pacific Theater

References

Craven, Wesley Frank, and James Lea Cate, eds. *The Army Air Forces in World War II.* Vol. 4, *The Pacific: Guadalcanal to Saipan, August 1942 to July 1944.* Washington, DC: Office of Air Force History, 1983.

McAulay, Lex. *Battle of the Bismarck Sea.* New York: St. Martin's Press, 1991.

Morison, Samuel Eliot. *History of United States Naval Operations in World War II.* Vol. 11, *Breaking the Bismarcks Barrier, 22 July 1942–1 May 1944.* Boston: Little, Brown, 1950.

Null, Gary. *The U.S. Army Air Forces in World War II: Weapon of Denial—Air Power and the Battle for New Guinea.* Washington, DC: Air Force History and Museum Programs, 1995.

Bittrich, Wilhelm (1894–1979)

German Waffen-SS general. Born in Wernigerode, Germany, on 26 February 1894, Wilhelm "Willi" Bittrich was a fighter pilot in the Imperial German Air Service during World War I. Following the war, he served with a Freikorps unit, then spent several years as a civilian stockbroker. He joined the Schutzstaffel (SS) in 1932.

During the September 1939 Polish Campaign, Bittrich served as the adjutant on Oberführer Josef "Sepp" Dietrich's Leibstandarte Adolf Hitler, a Waffen-SS regiment. He then fought in the SS-Verfügungs Division (later the 2nd SS Division) in the campaign for France. Promoted to Oberführer, Bittrich took command of SS Regiment Deutschland in the 2nd SS Das Reich Division at the end of 1940. During the German invasion of the Soviet Union, he briefly led that division when its commander was wounded in December 1941. In January 1942, illness forced Bittrich to resign his command.

From 1 May 1942 to 15 February 1943, Bittrich, promoted to SS-Gruppenführer und Generalleutnant der Waffen-SS, was head of the SS Cavalry Brigade, which grew into a full division during that time and saw continuous action on the Eastern Front. Bittrich was then tasked with organizing and commanding what eventually became the Hohenstaufen 9th SS Panzer Division and directed the division in its first combat in the breakout of the Soviet encirclement at Tarnopol in April 1944.

In July 1944, Bittrich was transferred to the Normandy Front in France and appointed commander of II SS Panzer Corps. Remnants of the corps that escaped destruction in the Falaise pocket in August were in an ideal position to deal with the British 1st Airborne Division's attack on Arnhem on 17 September 1944 during Operation MARKET-GARDEN. Bittrich's reaction was decisive: he ordered the 9th SS Panzer Division to contain and attack the 1st British Airborne at Arnhem and the 10th SS Panzer Division to attack the U.S. 82nd Airborne Division at Nijmegen and stop the advancing British XXX Corps. This quick response resulted in the destruction of the British airborne forces at Arnhem, marking the last German battlefield victory of the war.

Bittrich's II SS Panzer Corps participated in the Ardennes Offensive (Battle of the Bulge). In January 1945, the corps was transferred to the Eastern Front but fought its way back to the west before the end of the war. Surrendering to the Americans, Bittrich was turned over to the French, who convicted him of war crimes and imprisoned him until 1954. Bittrich died in Wolfratshausen, Germany, on 19 April 1979.

Dana Lombardy

See also

Ardennes Offensive; Dietrich, Josef "Sepp"; Falaise-Argentan Pocket; MARKET-GARDEN, Operation

References

Angolia, John R. *On the Field of Honor.* San Jose, CA: Bender, 1980.
Ryan, Cornelius. *A Bridge Too Far.* New York: Simon and Schuster, 1979.
Schneider, Jost W. *Their Honor Was Loyalty.* San Jose, CA: Bender, 1977.

"Black May" (May 1943)

Defeat of the German U-boats in the North Atlantic. The climactic convoy battles of March 1943 had given a first hint that Allied antisubmarine forces were finally gaining the upper hand in the battle for the North Atlantic sea lines of communication. By early 1943, the fully mobilized American shipyards were producing vast numbers of escort vessels in addition to building more merchant ships than were being sunk by U-boats. Modern, long-range naval patrol aircraft, such as the B-24 Liberator, and escort carrier–based aircraft were closing the dreaded air gap, the wolf packs' last refuge from Allied airpower in the North Atlantic. At the same time, Allied signals intelligence was reading the German U-boat cipher Triton almost continuously and with minimal delay.

On 26 April, the Allies suffered a rare blackout in their ability to read the German cipher, just as 53 U-boats regrouped for an assault on the convoy routes. Miraculously, two eastbound convoys, SC.128 and HX.236, escaped destruction, but ONS.5, a weather-beaten, westbound slow convoy of 30 merchant ships escorted by 7 warships stumbled into the middle of the wolf packs on 4 May. During the next 48 hours, the U-boats sank 12 ships but at an unacceptable cost: escort vessels sank 6 U-boats, and long-range

air patrols claimed 3 others. Radar in aircraft and escort vessels had played a decisive role in giving the numerically overmatched escorts a tactical edge in the battle.

The commander of the German U-boat arm, Admiral Karl Dönitz, was aware of the tilting balance, but he urged his U-boat commanders not to relent. Yet many of the vessels did not even reach their areas of operations. The determined antisubmarine offensive in the Bay of Biscay by aircraft of the Royal Air Force Coastal Command destroyed 6 U-boats during May and forced 7 others to return to base.

In the second week of May, the ragged survivors of the North Atlantic wolf packs, which had operated against Convoys ONS.5 and SL.128, regrouped and deployed against HX.237 and SC.129. Only 3 merchantmen were sunk, at the expense of the same number of U-boats. In addition to radar, the small escort carrier *Biter,* which had provided air cover for HX.237 as well as for SC.129, was vital in denying the German submarines tactical freedom on the surface near the convoys. When the U-boats renewed their attacks against Convoy SC.130 between 15 and 20 May, escort vessels sank 2 U-boats, and shore-based aircraft claimed 3 others. SC.130 suffered no casualties. The U-boat offensive failed entirely against HX.239, a convoy with a rather generous organic air cover (aircraft attached to the convoy) provided by the escort carriers USS *Bogue* and HMS *Archer.* Not a single U-boat managed to close with the convoy, and on 23 May, a U-boat fell victim to the rockets of one of the *Archer*'s aircraft. The following day, Dönitz recognized the futility of the enterprise and canceled all further operations in the North Atlantic. During the month to that point, more than 33 U-boats had been sunk and almost the same number had been damaged, nearly all of them in convoy battles in the North Atlantic or during transit through the Bay of Biscay. The month went down in German naval annals as "Black May," with the loss of 40 U-boats. At the end of May 1943, the British Naval Staff noted with satisfaction the cessation of U-boat activity. SC.130 was the last North Atlantic convoy to be seriously menaced during the war.

Dirk Steffen

See also

Aircraft, Naval; Aircraft Carrier; Antisubmarine Warfare; Antisubmarine Warfare—A Turning Point? Black May; Atlantic, Battle of the; Aviation, Naval; Bay of Biscay Offensive; Convoys, Allied; Convoys SC.122 and HX.229, Battle of; Dönitz, Karl; Radar; Signals Intelligence; Wolf Pack

References

Blair, Clay. *Hitler's U-Boat War.* Vol. 2, *The Hunted, 1942–1945.* New York: Random House, 1998.
Gannon, Michael. *Black May.* New York: Harper Collins, 1998.
Morison, Samuel Eliot. *History of United States Naval Operations in World War II.* Vol. 10, *The Atlantic Battle Won, May 1943–May 1945.* Boston: Little, Brown, 1956.

Blamey, Sir Thomas Albert (1884–1951)

Australian army general, commander in chief of the Australian army during much of World War II, and the first Australian field marshal. Born on 24 January 1884 in Wagga-Wagga, Australia, Thomas Blamey secured a commission through competitive examination in 1906. He made captain in 1910 and attended staff college in India between 1911 and 1913.

During World War I, Blamey served as a staff officer in Egypt, at Gallipoli, and on the Western Front. He rose to the rank of brigadier general in 1918. Following the war, he served on the Imperial General Staff. In 1925, Blamey retired from the regular army and became chief police commissioner in Victoria, Australia, while remaining a general in the militia.

Blamey resigned his police position in 1936 following a minor scandal in which he lied under oath to protect the reputations of two women who were victims of robbery. Shortly after the beginning of World War II, he rejoined the regular army, was promoted to lieutenant general, and was assigned command of I Corps. Serving in Egypt in 1940 under General Archibald P. Wavell, he oversaw the evacuation of Australian troops from Greece following the German invasion of that country in April 1941. Promoted to full general in September 1941, Blamey became commander in chief of Australian forces in March 1942.

Under orders from General Douglas MacArthur, who was concerned about the Japanese occupation of Buna in Papua and a possible invasion of Australia, Blamey took personal command of the ground forces and led them in the recapture of Buna in January 1943. He also held personal command in September 1943 in a campaign that took the city of Lae and liberated the eastern New Guinea coast. Following these actions, Blamey found himself relegated to a background role as MacArthur assumed more control of Allied armies in the theater.

As the Allies island-hopped closer to Japan, Blamey undertook operations against isolated Japanese troops in islands bypassed by MacArthur. These actions, bereft of significant naval and air support, proved costly and were criticized by many as unnecessary, but Blamey believed that it was in Australia's interest that these occupied islands be freed. At the end of the war, he signed the Japanese surrender document as the Australian representative. Discharged in January 1946, he was promoted to field marshal in June 1950. Blamey died at Melbourne on 27 May 1951.

Harold Wise

See also
Australia, Army; Australia, Role in War; Buna, Battle of; Greece Campaign (April 1941); MacArthur, Douglas; New Guinea Campaign; Papuan Campaign; Wavell, Sir Archibald Percival

References
Gallaway, Jack. *Odd Couple: Blamey and MacArthur at War.* Queensland, Australia: University of Queensland Press, 2000.
Hetherington, John. *The Life of Field Marshal Sir Thomas Blamey.* Melbourne, Australia: Cheshire, 1954.
Horner, David. *Blamey: The Commander in Chief.* Sydney, Australia: Allen and Unwin, 1998.

Blanchard, Jean Georges Maurice (1877–1954)

French army general who briefly assumed command of the 1st Army Group in 1940. Born at Orléans on 9 December 1877, Jean Blanchard graduated from the École Polytechnique in 1899 as an artillery specialist and was commissioned in the artillery. During World War I, he served at the front and on staff assignments, winning two citations for bravery and promotion to major. He was made a brigadier general in 1932 and a major general three years later. In 1938, Blanchard became director of French higher military instruction.

When World War II began, Blanchard took command of the First French Army near Cambrai, France, as part of General Gaston Billotte's 1st Army Group. When Germany invaded on 10 May 1940, Blanchard followed the prearranged French strategic plan, moving his army forward to the Dyle River in support of the Belgians. He had the British Expeditionary Force (BEF) under Lord John Gort on his north flank and General André Corap's Ninth French Army to the south. After advancing approximately 25 miles, Blanchard encountered General Walther von Reichenau's German Sixth Army and was forced to withdraw and join those Allied troops cut off by the German drive down the Somme River to the English Channel.

Following Billotte's death in an automobile accident on 25 May 1940, a shattered Blanchard took over command of the 1st Army Group. British colleagues, such as General Alan Brooke, grimly noted that he was "merely existing and hardly aware of what was going on around him," completely bewildered and incapable of issuing orders. On 29 May, a harassed Brooke even threatened to have Blanchard shot if his orders disrupted Brooke's evacuation plans. On 1 June 1940, Blanchard left Dunkerque for Britain on a French destroyer, and in late August, he was placed on the French army's reserve list. Thereafter, he faded into obscurity, although he was later awarded the Grand Cross of the Legion of Honor. Blanchard died at Neuilly-sur-Seine on 23 November 1954.

Priscilla Roberts

See also

Billotte, Gaston Henri Gustave; Brooke, Sir Alan Francis; Corap, André Georges; Dunkerque, Evacuation of; France, Battle for; Reichenau, Walther von; Vereker, John Standish Surtees Pendergast

References

Alanbrooke, Lord. *War Diaries, 1939–1945.* Ed. Alex Danchev and Daniel Todman. London: Phoenix Press, 2001.

Crémieux-Brilhac, Jean-Louis. *Les Français de l'an 40.* 2 vols. Paris: Gallimard, 1990.

Draper, Theodore. *The Six Weeks' War: France, May 10–June 25, 1940.* New York: Viking, 1964.

Horne, Alistair. *To Lose a Battle: France 1940.* Boston: Little, Brown, 1969.

Spears, Edward L. *Assignment to Catastrophe.* 2 vols. New York: Wynn, 1954–1955.

Blandy, William Henry Purnell (1890–1954)

U.S. Navy admiral who was commander of Cruisers/Destroyers, Pacific Fleet, in 1945. Born in New York City on 28 June 1890, William Blandy graduated at the head of his class from the U.S. Naval Academy in 1913 and began his career on the battleship *Florida.* He participated in the 1914 Veracruz landing and served in convoy duty during World War I.

During the interwar period, Blandy specialized in naval gunnery and ordnance. As head of the Bureau of Ordnance's Gun Section between 1927 and 1929, he contributed to innovations in gun designs. In February 1941, he was chosen over a hundred more senior officers to become chief of the Bureau of Ordnance as a rear admiral. In this post, Blandy was instrumental in the production of new weapons systems, such as the 40 mm Bofors and 20 mm Oerlikon guns, as well as the proximity fuse. He also had to deal with problems such as the malfunctioning Mark XIV torpedoes.

In December 1943, Blandy left administrative work to assume command of Amphibious Group One of the Pacific Fleet, from January 1944 to July 1945. His first combat operation was the Kwajalein invasion in February 1944. Blandy then commanded Task Group (TG) 51.1, the Joint Expeditionary Force Reserve, at Saipan in June 1944. For the attack on the Palau Islands in September 1944, he was in charge of TG 32.2, the Angaur Attack Group.

Blandy's expertise in gunnery and ordnance made him the choice to command Amphibious Support Task Force (TG 52), charged with all prelanding activities, including shore bombardment, minesweeping, and underwater demolition. Blandy was responsible for the preassault operations at Iwo Jima in February 1945. His Amphibious Support Task Force then played a key role in the Okinawa operation in the spring of 1945, where it paved the way for the landings on Kerama Retto and Okinawa itself. Blandy ended the war as commander of Cruisers/Destroyers, Pacific Fleet, from July to November 1945. He was promoted to vice admiral in November 1945.

As the navy's ordnance expert, Blandy commanded the joint army-navy nuclear tests (Operation CROSSROADS) at Bikini Atoll in July 1946. From February 1947 until his retirement three years later, he was commander in chief, Atlantic Fleet. Blandy died in Queens, New York, on 12 January 1954.

Robert Krumel

See also

Antiaircraft Artillery and Employment; Iwo Jima, Battle for; Kwajalein, Battle for; Naval Gunfire, Shore Support; Saipan, Battle of

References

Reynolds, Clark G. *Famous American Admirals.* Annapolis, MD: Naval Institute Press, 2002.

Rowland, Buford, and William H. Boyd. *U.S. Navy Bureau of Ordnance in World War II.* Washington, DC: U.S. Government Printing Offfice, 1953.

Blaskowitz, Johannes Albrecht von (1883–1948)

German army general and commander of the First Army for much of World War II. Born on 10 July 1883 at Peterswalde, East Prussia, Johannes Blaskowitz saw action on both fronts during World War I, rose to the rank of captain, and was awarded the Knight's Cross. He continued in the Reichswehr after the war and was promoted to General der Infanterie (U.S. equiv. lieutenant general) in December 1935. In the next year, he took command of Military District II, and in January 1938, he became the commander of Third Army, leading it into Prague as part of the German absorption of Czechoslovakia in March 1939.

Blaskowitz commanded Eighth Army in the September 1939 German invasion of Poland, with the task of protecting Tenth Army's northern flank during the drive on Warsaw. Following initial German success, the Poles counterattacked on 9 September against the flank of the Eighth Army and managed to destroy one of Blaskowitz's five infantry divisions before they were defeated, with Tenth Army's assistance. The Battle of Kutno was the biggest Polish victory of the campaign.

On 23 October 1939, Blaskowitz was made commander of German forces occupying Poland. An officer of the old school who set high standards for his men, he was shocked by the brutal actions of the Schutzstaffel (SS) against the local population. Blaskowitz went so far as to draw up a memorandum protesting these actions, which earned him Adolf Hitler's distrust.

Blaskowitz briefly commanded Ninth Army in the invasion of France between May and June 1940 and then was the military governor of northern France before being assigned to command the First Army stationed in France in October 1940. Blaskowitz remained in this position until 10 May 1944, when he was assigned command of Army Group G, defending the Mediterranean and South Atlantic French coasts. In Operation DRAGOON in August 1944, the Allies invaded the French Riviera and easily pushed aside Blaskowitz's thinly spread forces. Relieved of his command in September 1944, he returned to command Army Group H in Holland in January 1945, where he demonstrated compassion for the Dutch by permitting them medical supplies and food during the Allied advance.

Captured on 8 May 1945 by Canadian forces, Blaskowitz was charged with war crimes that involved passing along Hitler's order regarding the execution of enemy commandos. Rather than face trial, he committed suicide on 5 February 1948 in Nuremberg, Germany. Some believe he was murdered to prevent him from revealing SS secrets.

Harold Wise

See also

Commando Order; DRAGOON, Operation; Hitler, Adolf; Poland Campaign

References

Giziowski, Richard. *The Enigma of General Blaskowitz.* New York: Hippocrene Books, 1997.

Wilt, Alan F. *The French Riviera Campaign of August 1944.* Cardondale: Southern Illinois University Press, 1981.

Bletchley Park

Secret British decrypting center. Just prior to the beginning of World War II, the British Government Code and Cypher School (GC&CS) purchased a Victorian mansion known as Bletchley Park (BP, also called Station X or War Station), located some 50 miles north of London in Bedfordshire. British code-breakers, some of them veterans of World War I, began moving to Bletchley Park in August 1939. The staff, headed by Alistair Dennison, soon numbered 150 people. Thereafter, BP grew very rapidly. By late 1942, BP personnel numbered around 3,500, a figure that would expand to 10,000 by 1945. BP's overseas stations were the Combined Bureau, Middle East; the Wireless Experimental Centre at Delhi; and the Far East Combined Bureau. Each had its own outposts.

The personnel at Bletchley Park were a mix of mathematicians, cryptographers, engineers, and eccentrics. Among them was Alan Turing, regarded as the father of the modern computer. There were also members of the various British military services, as well as foreign military personnel. At BP, they continued the work begun by the Poles in reading German signals traffic and unlocking the secrets of the German Enigma encoding machine.

To house the growing staff, "temporary" wooden huts were built on the garden grounds. These were numbered, and different types of analysis were conducted in each. Hut 3 decrypted German army and air force codes, Hut 6 focused on German army and air force Enigma cryptanalysis, Hut 4 worked on German naval translating and processing, and Hut 8 handled German navy Enigma cryptanalysis. Others worked on Italian and Japanese codes. The intelligence produced by BP was code-named the ULTRA secret.

By 1940, Bletchley Park had come up with additional devices that, given time, could sort through the possible variations of an encoded text. Careless German practices, mostly in the Luftwaffe, gave the electromechanical devices called "bombes" a head start and greatly shortened the delay between receiving and decoding messages. The changeable settings of the Enigma machine meant that most messages could not be read in real time, but the information was nonetheless invaluable.

The staff at BP was ultimately able to provide an important advantage to the Allies in the war. The Axis powers never learned of the success of the Allied decrypting operations, and the activities at Bletchley Park remained unknown to the public until 1974, when Group Captain F. W. Winterbotham revealed them in his book entitled *The Ultra Secret.*

A. J. L. Waskey

See also

Counterintelligence; Electronic Intelligence; Enigma Machine; Signals Intelligence

References

Friedman, Maurice. *Unraveling Enigma: Winning the Code War at Station X.* South Yorkshire, UK: Leo Cooper, 2001.

Hinsley, F. H., and Alan Stripp. *Code Breakers: The Inside Story of Bletchley Park.* New York: Oxford University Press, 1994.

Lewin, Ronald. *Ultra Goes to War.* New York: McGraw-Hill, 1978.

Winterbotham, F. W. *The Ultra Secret.* New York: Harper and Row, 1974.

Blitz, The (August 1940–May 1941)

English term for Germany's sustained night air attacks on British cities, chiefly London, from August 1940 to mid-May 1941. The term *Blitz* is taken from the German word

Uniformed woman leads group of boys through bomb-damaged residential area in London during the "Blitz," 1941. (Library of Congress)

blitzkrieg (lightning war). Early in the war, the British government undertook preparations to deal with air attacks, especially in London.

The Blitz began as the daylight Battle of Britain, for control of the air over the island, was reaching a climax. The Germans hoped at first to drive the Royal Air Force (RAF) from the skies, and then they sought to destroy the RAF by hitting factories and ground installations; finally, they turned to terrorizing the civilian population by bombing cities. This thrust was, in effect, triggered on the night of 24–25 August when German bombers, which were supposed to target an oil depot at Thameshaven, struck London instead. The German bombers had hardly retired when British Prime Minister Winston L. S. Churchill ordered a retaliatory strike on Berlin. On 5 September, German leader Adolf Hitler issued a directive calling for "disruptive attacks on the population and air defenses of major British cities, including London, by day and night." Such bombing could

not have significant military value and was intended primarily to destroy civilian morale.

On 7 September 1940, the German Luftwaffe carried out a major raid that devastated the London's East End. The bombers returned over the next two days, and more than 1,000 people were killed. From the beginning to the middle of November, London was the target. The intensity of raids varied, but with good weather and a full moon, they were massive. On 15 October, for instance, 538 tons of bombs fell on the city.

British authorities had rejected both the idea of building deep shelters and the concept of using the Underground (subway), for fear of creating a bunker mentality: some actually worried that people would refuse to return to the surface. Londoners forced the issue on 8 September when crowds pushed their way into the subway's Liverpool Street Station for refuge. The authorities capitulated, and by Christmas, 200,000 bunks were available in the Underground, with that many more ready for installation. A decision to build deep shelters was taken in October, but the Blitz was over before the first was completed. Nonetheless, by February 1941, some 92 percent of Londoners could be sheltered in a combination of public and private facilities.

Initially, the shelters were dismal places. Overcrowding was the rule, and sanitation was primitive at best. In mid-November 1940, the government instituted a food train to supply the hungry and thirsty citizens below ground, and communities began developing. People returned to the same shelter night after night and slept in the same bunks. Sing-alongs were organized, and professional entertainment was often provided. The authenticity of this sort of camaraderie has been questioned, and some scholars have referred to the "myth of the Blitz." Certainly, the camaraderie has been exaggerated at times, but Londoners seem to have known that a brave front was expected of them, and they made real efforts to live up to the expectation. The cheerful endurance and determination that was initially claimed and then later rejected as myth was, in fact, real. Of course, it was not universal or without cracks, but Londoners by and large kept daily routines in place with humor and mutual support. Predictions of disruptions proved mostly false. Initial class discontent because working-class areas in the East End were the first targets disappeared as the Germans pounded the rest of the city.

Life was not easy in London during that period. In the first six weeks of major raids, some 16,000 houses were destroyed and another 60,000 badly damaged, with the result that 300,000 people needed places to stay. By the end of the Blitz, one in six Londoners had been rendered homeless. Many historical sites were also damaged, including Buckingham Palace. Most sites, however, survived and proved to be symbols of defiance. The king and queen remained in London, and Big Ben, despite sustaining some damage, struck every hour. London also got some respite as raids were directed against other cities. There was a major attack on Birmingham on 25 October 1940, and on 14 November, the city of Coventry was hit with a level of intensity beyond all previous efforts. Liverpool, Southampton, Birmingham, and Bristol were also struck.

London passed the Christmas of 1940 in comparative tranquility, and precautions were relaxed. Then, on 29 December, the great fire raid came. It was not the biggest raid ever, but the Christmas complacency among Londoners resulted in a slowed response, and enormous damage ensued. After another respite, March and April 1941 saw the skies again filled with German raiders. The worst nights were 16 and 19 April, which left 2,000 people dead and 148,000 homes damaged. Providers such as the Londoners' Meal Service, which was operating 170 canteens, were strained.

Once again, however, there was a relative pause—and again, precautions waned. On 10 May, crowds flooded into London for a football championship match, only to be joined by German raiders. The attack was the worst raid of the war, with more than 3,000 dead or seriously injured, 250,000 books burned at the British Museum, and pilots reporting the glow of fires visible as far away as 160 miles. It was also the last major raid of the Blitz. The British—and Londoners in particular—still had to face occasional raids and the V-1 and V-2 terror weapons at the end of the war, but for the Germans, strategic and tactical plans no longer included massive assaults from the air. Of course, as time passed, their ability to make them also waned.

One of the lessons of the Blitz was that, contrary to German expectations and intent, bombing the civilian population often strengthened its morale and determination, a lesson the Allies themselves failed to learn in their strikes against civilian targets in Germany.

Fred R. van Hartesveldt and Spencer C. Tucker

See also
"Baby Blitz"; Britain, Battle of; Churchill, Sir Winston L. S.; Great Britain, Home Front; Strategic Bombing

References
Calder, Angus. *The Myth of the Blitz*. London: Cape, 1991.
Calder, Angus, and Dorothy Sheridan, eds. *Speak for Yourself: A Mass Observation Anthology*. London: Cape, 1984.
Longmate, Norman. *How We Lived Then*. London: Hutchinson, 1971.
Marwick, Arthur. *The Home Front*. London: Thames and Hudson, 1976.
Ziegler, Philip. *London at War*. New York: Alfred A. Knopf, 1995.

Blitzkrieg

The so-called blitzkrieg (lightning war) doctrine is one of the most enduring myths of World War II. In the early years of the war, however, the swift and stunning German successes in Poland in 1939 and France in 1940 came to be interpreted in the West as the result of some sort of revolutionary new military doctrine that relied on combined-arms operations, with ground and air forces working together as a well-oiled military machine.

Military doctrine has been defined as the fundamental principles by which military forces guide their actions in support of national objectives. But what became known popularly as blitzkrieg was not a set of fundamental principles, nor was it written down as an authoritative document. Rather, the term *blitzkrieg* was created for public consumption. It did appear occasionally in the military literature between 1936 and 1940, but the German writers generally used it in reference to a short war, as opposed to the drawn-out trench warfare of World War I. The term became fixed in the public mind after articles appeared in *Time* magazine, one on 25 September 1939 about Germany's invasion of Poland and another on 27 May 1940 about the fall of France.

Immediately following World War I, the leaders of the much reduced German army studied the causes of the defeat in 1918 and concluded that a lack of traditional mobile, maneuverable forces and tactics had resulted in the war of attrition that eventually doomed Imperial Germany on the battlefield. Unlike the French, who determined that better defenses would be the key to winning the next war and hence built the Maginot Line, the Germans concluded that the next war would be of short duration and won by maneuver warfare in the classical sense.

The German field service regulations of 1921, *Führung und Gefecht der verbundenen Waffen* (Command and Combat of the Combined Arms), together with the updated version of 1934, *Truppenführung* (Unit Command), were infantry-oriented documents that cast tank and air assets strictly in an infantry-support role. Although *Truppenführung*, which remained the official doctrine for the German army through 1945, emphasized traditional German thinking on mobility, it did allow for decentralization of control, and it provided considerable latitude for force structure changes. It was also not tied rigidly to specific operational concepts, to the exclusion of all others. Rather than a inflexible tactical cookbook, the manual was a philosophical treatment of the conduct of operations and leadership.

During the interwar years, the German mobility advocates enthusiastically read the works of the leading mobile warfare theorists of the time, J. F. C. Fuller, Charles de Gaulle, and Basil Liddell Hart. Younger German officers aggressively advanced the argument that a tank force could alter the outcome of battles. Many of the older officers resisted the notion that the tank could be a decisive combat arm, remembering the grave difficulties armored units experienced in World War I.

After Adolf Hitler came to power in Germany in 1933, he quickly made it clear he intended to rearm the nation, and he was interested in the iconoclastic ideas of the younger officers. In June 1934, Colonel Heinz Guderian became the chief of staff of the newly formed Motorized Troop Command. A little more than a year later, the Germans fielded an experimental panzer division. In October 1935, while still only a colonel, Guderian assumed command of one of the three new panzer divisions. He immediately set out to convince the traditionally infantry-oriented German General Staff to accept the concepts of armored warfare. Although Guderian received only limited support from some of his superiors, Hitler encouraged him and his aggressive concepts.

German motorized detachment riding through the remains of a Polish town during the blitzkrieg of September 1939. (Library of Congress)

Meanwhile, the fledgling German air force also underwent important changes. Prior to the German intervention in the Spanish Civil War, most Luftwaffe officers saw airpower in the same terms as their peers in most other air forces of the period. The two most essential missions were conducting long-range strategic bombing and achieving air superiority over the battlefield; the ground-support mission was largely ignored. But the successes of German air-ground operations during the Spanish Civil War convinced a number of high-ranking Luftwaffe officers to reconsider ground support. General Ernst Udet, in charge of Luftwaffe development after 1936, pushed through the development of a dive-bomber, the Ju-87 Stuka. The aircraft was extremely accurate, very mobile, and designed specifically to support ground forces. It became the plane that added the critical air dimension to mobile operations.

The Polish Campaign of 1939 was executed in very short order and had all the outward appearances of a dazzling success of German arms. But the so-called blitzkrieg doctrine was never used in that campaign. Rather than being committed in mass, the panzer units were allocated to the various field armies. The Luftwaffe was primarily concerned with establishing air superiority and striking deep at Polish lines of communications. Tank maintenance was a severe problem, and too often, the German system of resupply was unequal to the required tasks. But in the end, Germany crushed Poland very quickly, and that success obscured the serious operational, tactical, and technical problems the Wehrmacht experienced.

Between the end of the Polish Campaign and the start of the attack in the west against France and Britain in May 1940, the German army made some significant changes. The panzer divisions were organized into corps. The number of tanks in the German army increased only slightly, but the number of tanks per division decreased, and thus, the number of panzer divisions grew. Out of necessity rather than doctrinal design, the panzer divisions became combined-arms units, with a balance between tanks, infantry, artillery, engineers, and other arms. Tactical air, especially the Stuka, became an important element in the combined-arms mix because Germany was woefully short of field artillery.

The Germans did not go into France planning for a rapid and overwhelming victory. But they achieved one because of a combination of luck; better leadership and training; superior concentration of forces; and correspondingly poor French leadership, training, and tactics. At first, the Germans were stunned by their success, but they soon fell victim to their own propaganda and began to believe in the myth of blitzkrieg.

In June 1941, the Germans invaded the Soviet Union, this time anticipating a rapid campaign. They did not mobilize their economy for the invasion, nor did they accumulate the necessary stockpiles or provide adequately for the long lines of communications or winter conditions. Drawing the wrong lessons from the French Campaign, they believed that their use of tactical airpower had been so successful that it more than compensated for their severe shortage of artillery. That approach may have worked against the poorly deployed French and British, but against the artillery-oriented Soviets, it was a recipe for disaster. The Germans learned quickly that the Luftwaffe could not be everywhere at the same time over the vast expanses of the eastern battlefields, especially with the onset of poor weather. The Soviets, with their abundant conventional field artillery, seldom lacked direct fire support.

The term *blitzkrieg* described a set of results, unique to a specific place and a specific time. The coordinated use of mobility, communications, and combined arms was not a revolution in military affairs, as it has often been portrayed, but rather a natural evolution of military doctrine that was clearly identifiable in the closing months of World War I. The myth of blitzkrieg, however, did obscure serious flaws in the German war machine, including supply, transport, maintenance, artillery, and intelligence. That circumstance proved progressively costly to the Germans as the war advanced and the Allies grew stronger and as the mechanized battlefield became increasingly lethal.

David T. Zabecki

See also

de Gaulle, Charles; Fuller, John Frederick Charles; Guderian, Heinz; Hitler, Adolf; Infantry Tactics; Liddell Hart, Sir Basil Henry; Maginot Line; Spain, Civil War in; Udet, Ernst

References

Citino, Robert M. *The Path to Blitzkrieg: Doctrine and Training in the German Army, 1920–1939.* Boulder, CO: Lynne Rienner, 1999.

Corum, James. *The Roots of Blitzkrieg: Hans von Seeckt and German Military Reform.* Lawrence: University Press of Kansas, 1992.

Guderian, Heinz. *Panzer Leader.* New York: E. P. Dutton, 1952.

———. *Achtung—Panzer! The Development of Armoured Forces, Their Tactics and Operational Potential.* London: Arms and Armour Press, 1992.

Zabecki, David T., and Bruce Condell, eds. *On the German Art of War: "Truppenführung."* Boulder, CO: Lynne Rienner, 2001.

Bloch, Claude Charles (1878–1967)

U.S. Navy admiral who served as a commander at Pearl Harbor. Born in Woodbury, Kentucky, on 13 July 1878, Claude Bloch graduated from the U.S. Naval Academy in 1895 and was a cadet at the Battle of Santiago Bay during the 1898 Spanish-American War. He was also part of the international force sent to relieve the foreign legations in Beijing during the 1900 Boxer Uprising. A gunnery specialist, Bloch served in European waters during World War I, commanding a battleship. In 1927, he was chief of the Bureau of Ordnance. During the 1930s, Bloch held several important administrative positions, including budget officer and judge advocate general, and his appearances before congressional committees were widely considered superlative. A staunch advocate of preparedness and a member of the navy "gun club," which emphasized a blue-seas navy based on battleships and cruisers rather than carrier aviation, Bloch supported the fortification of Guam. In 1937, he became commander of the Battle Force, U.S. Fleet, and the following year, he took command of the West Coast–based U.S. Fleet.

In 1940, Bloch became commander of the 14th Naval District, Pearl Harbor, normally an enjoyable preretirement assignment. As a warning gesture to Japan in 1940, however, President Franklin D. Roosevelt transferred the West Coast Fleet, Bloch's former command, from California to Hawaii. Bloch sought to strength Hawaiian defenses, but he encountered much interference and obstruction from the fleet's new commander, Admiral Husband Edward Kimmel. Yet Bloch's own opposition to the installation of antitorpedo nets contributed to the disastrous Japanese attack on Pearl Harbor of 7 December 1941. Although both Kimmel and General Walter Short, the army commander, were removed from their commands, Bloch served out his term until April 1942, when he retired. A congressional inquiry subsequently exonerated him from all responsibility for the Pearl Harbor debacle.

Recalled to Washington in April 1942 to serve on the navy's General Board, he retired in August 1942 at the rank of full admiral. In retirement, he headed the Navy Board for Production Awards until the end of World War II. Bloch died in Washington, D.C., on 6 October 1967.

Priscilla Roberts

See also

Kimmel, Husband Edward; Pearl Harbor, Attack on; Roosevelt, Franklin D.; Short, Walter Campbell

References

Clausen, Henry C., and Bruce Lee. *Pearl Harbor: Final Judgment.* New York: Crown Publishers, 1992.

Conroy, Hilary, and Harry Wray, eds. *Pearl Harbor Reexamined: Prologue to the Pacific War.* Honolulu: University of Hawaii Press, 1990.

Prange, Gordon William, with Donald M. Goldstein and Katherine V. Dillon. *Pearl Harbor: The Verdict of History.* New York: McGraw-Hill, 1986.

Blockade-Running

In the early stage of the war, the main lines of communication between the Axis powers were either over land via the Trans-Siberian Railway or across the sea by surface blockade-runners. Japan used German blockade-runners to send such goods as rubber, cooking oil, lead, tin, and tea to Germany. In return, the ships carried industrial products such as locomotives and machinery and various pieces of technical equipment, scientific instruments, and chemical and pharmaceutical products to Japan. In addition, ships carried supplies and spare parts for German warships in the Far East. Some blockade-runners also supplied German armed merchant cruisers operating in the South Atlantic, Indian Ocean, and Pacific.

After Germany invaded the Soviet Union (Operation BARBAROSSA), the continental line was cut, and only sea routes remained. The blockade-running that began in April 1941 and ended in October 1943 involved a total of 36 ships traveling from Asia to Europe. Six of them were recalled or returned after sustaining damage, and of the 30 that remained, 11 were sunk by Allied forces or were scuttled by

their own crews to prevent capture. Another 2 were accidentally sunk by German submarines, and 1 was seized by a U.S. cruiser. Thus, 16 ships actually completed their voyages and delivered cargo at the port of Bordeaux in German-occupied France.

In the other direction, 23 ships, including 5 fleet supply ships, were sent from Europe to the Far East between September 1941 and April 1943. Of these, 16 reached Asian ports, 5 were sunk or scuttled, and 2 were recalled or returned to port.

Overall, 45.8 percent of the blockade-runners on the Far East route were lost. However, annual ship losses rose dramatically over the course of the war: between April 1941 and October 1942, only 12.1 percent were lost, whereas in 1943, losses rose to 85.7 percent. Of 104,700 tons of materials loaded on the ships, only 26,600 tons reached their destinations. In addition to raw materials and equipment, these ships also transported passengers. Some 900 passengers embarked to travel from the Far East to Europe, but fewer than half of them arrived safely. A total of 136 died when their ships were sunk, and the remainder became prisoners of war or remained in the Far East after their ships turned back.

From early 1944, submarines took over the blockade-runners' mission. Between then and early March 1945, 16 German U-boats sailed to the Far East as combat cargo transporters. But only 8 actually arrived in Far Eastern ports, carrying some 930 tons of cargo. The other 8 boats were lost, most of them to hostile action. Through the end of 1944, only 3 submarines reached Europe, but none got to Germany: the U-843 arrived at Norway but was sunk in the Kattegat Straits; the U-510 and U-861 reached French ports.

Under the code name AQUILA, 5 Italian submarines also participated in blockade-running. Departing France, they carried some 500 tons of supplies for German/Italian submarine bases in the Far East, as well as personnel and cargo for Japan. None of them returned to Europe. The Japanese also sent 5 submarines to Europe to transport German military technology and to exchange personnel. Ultimately, 4 of them reached the Continent, but only 3 returned: 2 to Singapore and 1 to Japan. All these submarines had Japanese and German technicians, liaison officers, and equipment and blueprints of German's newest weapons. Of 89 passengers aboard Axis submarines traveling from Japan, 74 arrived in France; the remainder died when their boats were sunk. A total of 96 passengers sailed in the opposite direction, 64 of them arriving safely; 22 were lost while under way, and 10 others fell into American hands.

Hirama Yoichi

See also
Submarines
References
Boyd, Carl, and Yoshida Akihiko. *The Japanese Submarine Force and World War II*. Annapolis, MD: Naval Institute Press, 2002.
Krug, Hans J., and Yoichi Hirama. *Reluctant Allies: German-Japanese Naval Relations in World War II*. Annapolis, MD: Naval Institute Press, 2002.

Blomberg, Werner von (1878–1946)

German field marshal and minister of war under the Nazi regime. Born in Stargard, Germany, on 2 September 1878, Werner von Blomberg served as a staff officer during World War I. From 1927 to 1929, he headed the Truppenamt, the clandestine staff organization outlawed under the Treaty of Versailles. Blomberg traveled to the Soviet Union to further the secret military cooperation between the two countries, and he was one of the first German generals to support Adolf Hitler. He participated in the Geneva disarmament talks but was recalled at the end of January 1933 to become defense minister (later, war minister) in Hitler's first cabinet. In April, he was made commander in chief of the German armed forces.

An enthusiastic Nazi, Blomberg was a key figure in Hitler's consolidation of power. He pressured the Führer to remove the Sturmabteilungen (SA, or Storm Troops) as a possible threat and supported Hitler in the subsequent June 1934 purge of the Nazi Party (the Blood Purge), after which he issued an order congratulating Hitler, even though two army generals were among the victims. On the death of German President Paul von Hindenburg, Hitler called on Blomberg to swear an oath of allegiance to him personally, which Blomberg in turn imposed on his fellow officers, thereby helping to confirm Hitler's control of the armed forces. (Blomberg was soon known by his fellow officers as the "Rubber Lion.") In gratitude for his support, the Führer promoted Blomberg in April 1936, making him the first field marshal of the Reich.

The relationship between the two men would change, however. After Hitler revealed his expansionist plans in November 1937, Blomberg and army commander General Werner von Fritsch objected, and Hitler determined to remove both men from their posts. The chance to get rid of Blomberg came in January 1938 after he remarried. Both Hitler and Luftwaffe chief Hermann Göring were witnesses to the marriage, but Göring soon learned that Blomberg's new wife had been a prostitute. On 24 January, he shared this information with Hitler, who summoned Blomberg and dismissed him the next day. In his conversation with the Führer, Blomberg suggested that Hitler assume the post of war minister himself, which he did a week later.

Blomberg took no part in the war, but as a prominent German official, he was detained after the war and testified at the war crimes trials in Nuremberg. He died there while still in detention on 14 March 1946.

Robert T. Kaczowka

See also
Fritsch, Werner Thomas von; Germany, Army; Germany, Home Front; Hitler, Adolf
References
Görlitz, Walter. "Blomberg." In Correlli Barnett, ed., *Hitler's Generals*, 129–137. New York: Grove Weidenfeld, 1989.
Mitcham, Samuel W., Jr. *Hitler's Field Marshals and Their Battles*. Chelsea, MI: Scarborough House, 1988.

Blue Division (1941–1943)

Spanish division that fought with the German army against the Soviet Union in World War II. Lieutenant General Augustin Muñoz Grandes commanded the Division Azul (Blue Division) of 18,000 men. The initiative for a Spanish expeditionary force came from Spain's dictator, Francisco Franco, immediately after the German invasion of the Soviet Union in June 1941. The division was assembled in some haste, as Franco feared that the Soviet Union would be defeated before Spain could make a military contribution. Motivations behind the establishment of this force were Franco's staunch anticommunism, his gratitude to Germany for its critical assistance to the Nationalist cause during the Spanish Civil War, and his interest in providing a dumping ground for the Spanish Fascists (Falangists)—hotheads who were advocating social revolution in Spain. Fearful of offending the Allied powers too greatly, Franco styled the division a "volunteer" force. The division's name came from the blue shirts worn by the soldiers, although in the German order of battle, the unit was officially designated the 250th Division.

Adolf Hitler saw the division as a means to bind Spain more closely to the Axis cause. He therefore ordered that it be issued German equipment and transport and even pension payments. The division reached the Eastern Front by early October 1941 and soon proved itself in the difficult fighting before Leningrad, especially in the winter of 1942. Of the 47,000 men who fought as part of the division in its two years at the front, 22,000 became casualties, but forces opposite the Blue Division lost more than 49,000 men, according to Red Army estimates. Hitler called the Spanish soldiers "extraordinarily brave, tough against privations, but wildly undisciplined." Spanish improvisation was a constant irritant to the Germans.

With the Allied invasion of North Africa and the German reversals at Tunis and Stalingrad, Franco recalled the division in October 1943, replacing it with a legion of only 1,500 men. The division failed to achieve its goals of defeating communism, but it had another purpose as well: to demonstrate to Hitler that the Spanish would fight and take casualties in order to forestall any German plans to occupy Spain and seize Gibraltar. Undoubtedly, the Blue Division did impress Hitler on this point and helped to keep Iberia free of fighting in World War II.

Andrew W. Lander

See also

Franco, Francisco; Leningrad, Siege of; Spain, Civil War in; Spain, Role in War

References

Kleinfield, Gerald R., and Lewis A. Tambs. *Hitler's Spanish Legion: The Blue Division in Russia.* Carbondale: Southern Illinois University Press, 1979.

Payne, Stanley G. *Fascism in Spain, 1923–1977.* Madison: University of Wisconsin Press, 1999.

French Premier Léon Blum arriving at 10 Downing Street, London, for talks with Prime Minister Clement Attlee in 1945. (Hulton Archive by Getty Images)

Blum, Léon (1872–1950)

French premier from 1936 to 1937. Born in Paris on 9 April 1872, Léon Blum attended the prestigious École Normale Supérieure. While studying law at the Sorbonne, he was drawn to socialism. After graduating in 1894 with highest honors, he pursued a literary career as a critic. The Dreyfus Affair drew the Jewish Blum into politics, and he joined the French Socialist Party (SFIO) in 1904. Rejected for military service in World War I, he won election to the Chamber of Deputies in 1919. The Socialist-Communist split in 1920 presented him with an enormous challenge as he worked to rebuild the SFIO. Blum came to be considered the leader of his party through his frequent articles in its chief newspaper, *Le Populaire.* Certainly, his doctrines and his quiet, effective leadership were key factors in the party's revival.

The SFIO became the leading party in the Popular Front, which also included the Radicals and Communists. After the Popular Front victory in the spring 1936 elections, Blum became France's first Jewish and first Socialist premier on 4 June 1936. Under his leadership, the government enacted sweeping social legislation, including the nationalization of leading banks and industries and the establishment of a 40-hour workweek and other worker benefits. Unfortunately, these changes came at precisely the time that Germany was cutting worker benefits and straining to rearm.

Blum failed to win centrist and rightist support for his programs, and the flight of capital abroad and foreign reverses, especially the failure to aid the Spanish Republic during the Spanish Civil War (under pressure from London), led to his undoing. Too late, he realized the need for France to rearm. After the Chamber of Deputies refused his request for emergency fiscal powers, he resigned as premier in June 1937, although the SFIO continued in the Popular Front coalition.

Arrested on the orders of the Vichy government following Germany's defeat of France in July 1940, Blum was put on trial in Riom in February 1943, along with other leaders of the Third Republic, and charged with responsibility for the French defeat. His spirited defense embarrassed the Vichy government and helped lead to the suspension of the trial. Taken prisoner by the Gestapo in 1943, he was held in both the Buchenwald and the Dachau concentration camps until his release at the end of World War II.

Blum returned to France as a respected elder statesman. He headed a caretaker government between 1946 and 1947 and secured aid from the United States to assist in the reconstruction of his nation. He then retired permanently to his estate at Jouy-en-Josas, although he continued to write for *Le Populaire.* Blum died there on 30 March 1950.

Annette Richardson

See also
France, Battle for; France, Role in War; France, Vichy

References
Blum, Léon. *For All Mankind*. Trans. W. Pickles. New York: Viking Press, 1946.

Colton, Joel G. *Léon Blum: Humanist in Politics*. New York: Alfred A. Knopf, 1966.

Dalby, Louise Elliott. *Léon Blum: Evolution of a Socialist*. New York: T. Yoseloff, 1963.

Grayson, Jasper Glenn. *The Foreign Policy of Léon Blum and the Popular Front Government in France*. Chapel Hill: University of North Carolina Press, 1962.

Lacouture, Jean. *Léon Blum*. New York: Holmes and Meier, 1982.

Blumentritt, Günther (1892–1967)

German army general and commander of the Fifteenth Army on the Western Front. Born in Munich on 10 February 1892, Günther Blumentritt entered the Germany army in 1911, serving a year as a Fahnenjunker (officer cadet) in the 71st Thüringen Infantry Regiment before matriculating at the Danzig Kriegsakademie (War College) in early 1912. Commissioned in November 1912, Blumentritt served in various regimental staff positions on the Eastern Front during World War I, ending the war as a senior lieutenant. He served briefly in the Thüringen Freikorps in 1919, where he advanced from company commander to corps adjutant. Despite never having held a command in the regular army, his wartime performance was sufficient to gain his entry into the postwar Reichswehr. In November 1919, he took command of a company in the 11th Jäger (light infantry) Regiment.

Blumentritt's postwar career followed a conventional path, with nearly annual rotations between staff and low-level command positions in infantry, cavalry, and artillery units. His star began to rise in the early 1930s, no doubt assisted by his close friendship with two future field marshals—Erich von Manstein and Wilhelm von Leeb. In 1933, Blumentritt became an instructor in tactics at the Officers' Course, Germany's clandestine General Staff or War College (institution forbidden under terms of the Versailles Treaty that ended World War I). He left the War College as an lieutenant colonel and General Staff officer in October 1935.

Most of Blumentritt's subsequent assignments were in staff positions. He was Colonel General (Karl) Gerd von Rundstedt's operations chief for the invasion of Poland and then Colonel General Günther von Kluge's chief of staff for the invasions of France and the Soviet Union. He became chief of staff to Field Marshal von Rundstedt's Army Group D in France in September 1942 but was injured in a railway accident in January 1943 and did not return to service until 10 June 1944, after Allied troops had landed in Normandy.

Blumentritt's association with von Kluge and others involved in efforts to overthrow Adolf Hitler led to his temporary suspension in early September 1944. Later that same month, he was promoted to general of infantry (U.S. equiv. lieutenant general) and given command of XII SS Corps on the Western Front. In January 1945, he took command of Twenty-Fifth Army in Holland, and in March, he assumed command of the First Parachute Army, ending the war in Schleswig-Holstein. He was held until January 1948.

Blumentritt enjoyed a brief postwar career as a commentator on Western Allied strategy, and he wrote extensively. In addition to his memoirs, he wrote a well-received book on von Rundstedt that was translated into English in 1952, and he edited another on the German tactics and operations against the Allies in the fighting in Normandy. Blumentritt died in Munich on 12 October 1967.

Carl O. Schuster

See also
Kluge, Günther Adolf Ferdinand von; Leeb, Wilhelm Franz Josef Ritter von; Manstein, Fritz Erich von; Rundstedt, Karl Rudolf Gerd von

References
Barnett, Correlli. *Hitler's Generals*. London: Orion, 1995.

Blumentritt, Guenther. *Von Rundstedt: Soldier and the Man*. London: Odhams Press, 1952.

Cooper, Mathew. *German Army, 1933–1945*. New York: Bonanza Books, 1984.

Bock, Fedor von (1880–1945)

German army field marshal and commander on the Eastern Front in 1941 and 1942. Born into an old noble Prussian family at Küstrin, Germany, on 3 December 1880, Fedor von Bock joined the army in 1898. During World War I, he became a major and won the Pour le Mérite.

After the war, Bock remained in the army. Adolf Hitler did not purge him, despite his well-known adherence to the former monarchy. Promoted to colonel general, Bock participated in the German invasions of Poland and France as commander of Army Groups North and B, respectively. He was shocked by the Schutzstaffel (SS) treatment of Jews in Poland, but he decided against making an official protest. In July 1940, he was one of 12 new field marshals created by Hitler.

During the invasion of the Soviet Union (Operation BARBAROSSA), Bock's Army Group Center had the task of capturing Moscow. In July 1941, his forces took Minsk, and three weeks later, they reached Smolensk. When Bock was only 225 miles from Moscow, Hitler decided to divert some of his forces to Leningrad and Kiev. Bock was not able to resume his advance before October, and bad weather forced a halt in December 1941. Hitler then dismissed him, but after only a month's rest, he was again sent to the Eastern Front to command Army Group South.

In the 1942 summer offensive, Hitler instructed Bock to destroy Soviet forces west of the Don River, to reach the Volga, and to secure the Caucusus oil fields. Bock enjoyed initial success at Voronezh, but after his progress slowed, Hitler replaced him with General Maximilian von Weichs on 15 July 1942. Bock never returned to command. In 1944, his nephew, Henning von Tresckow, approached him about the possibility of joining the July plot against Hitler. Bock refused as he had in 1941 after being confronted with SS atrocities in the Soviet Union. As an old-style Prussian officer, he was unable to break his oath of office, but he did not pass his knowledge about the plot to overthrow the Führer on to the Gestapo.

Bock continued to press for a return to military service, but his efforts were in vain. He and his wife were killed as the result of an Allied air raid in Schleswig-Holstein on 3 May 1945, during which a fighter pilot fired on their car. Bock died the following day.

Martin Moll

See also
BARBAROSSA, Operation; Eastern Front; Guderian, Heinz; Hitler, Adolf; Minsk, Battle for; Moscow, Battle of; Smolensk, Battle of; Vyazma-Bryansk, Battles for; Weichs zur Glon, Maximilian Maria Joseph von

References
Mitcham, Samuel W., Jr. *Hitler's Field Marshals and Their Battles*. Chelsea, MI: Scarborough House, 1988.
Turney, Alfred W. *Disaster at Moscow: Von Bock's Campaigns, 1941–1942*. London: Cassell, 1971.

BODENPLATTE, Operation (1 January 1945)

Operation BODENPLATTE (BASE PLATE) was the last major effort by the Luftwaffe to check Allied airpower in the west. The commander of German fighter defenses, Major General Adolf Galland, attempted to hoard his fighter force for one concentrated blow against the Allied air forces. However, each time he was able to gather such a force, it was dispersed to other fronts or used piecemeal against waves of attacking Allied bombers. In the fall of 1944, Galland had again assembled a sizable fighter force only to have it decimated during the Battle of the Bulge in December. In desperation, the Luftwaffe High Command directed Major General Dietrich Peltz, commander of II Jagdkorps (Fighter Corps), to execute a surprise attack on Allied bases in Belgium.

The intent of the plan was to buy time for the Luftwaffe to battle the Allied bombers. The Germans hoped to force the Allies to remove their fighters from the Continent, allowing the Luftwaffe an opportunity to regain control of the skies over the front and achieve some advantage against the bombers. The plan envisioned hurling all available aircraft in an early-morning, low-level attack against 16 Allied fighter fields in Belgium. Planning began in strict secrecy in mid-December, with the operation set to take place in the next period of good weather. Weather analysts determined that the conditions would be right on 1 January 1945, and orders were issued accordingly on 31 December.

To maintain operational security, group commanders were not briefed on the details of the plan, and for many, the first news of the upcoming attack came very late on 31 December. By the time orders reached subordinate levels, there was not always sufficient time for proper briefings. In many cases, the briefing consisted of a simple "follow me" direction. Even in the best of circumstances, an operation of this complexity would have been hard to execute, but it was particularly difficult for the poorly trained Luftwaffe pilots at the end of 1944.

Some 800 aircraft took part in the attack. Early on 1 January, the fighters lifted off from fields behind the front. Some experienced night-fighter pilots led the formations to the front lines and then turned back, leaving the other fighters to find their targets and return on their own. An unexpected ground mist delayed some takeoffs, and confused German antiaircraft gunners opened fire on late-arriving aircraft, shooting down a number of them. Some German pilots became lost and attacked the wrong fields. Over some targets areas, the surprise was complete, but at others, the Allies were beginning their own daily air operations and were able to react quickly.

In the final analysis, Operation BODENPLATTE achieved some tactical success but at an unacceptable cost. The Germans destroyed a total of 134 Allied aircraft and damaged an additional 62. The Allies could easily absorb these losses, however, and there was no thought of relocating air operations to Britain. The Luftwaffe lost some 300 aircraft to all causes. More important, 214 Luftwaffe pilots were killed, missing, or captured. This operation marked the end of the road for the German air force, which was largely ineffective for the remainder of the war.

M. R. Pierce

See also
Galland, Adolf; Germany, Air Force; Göring, Hermann Wilhelm
References
Boyne, Walter J. *Clash of Wings: World War II in the Air*. New York: Simon and Schuster, 1994.
Elmhirst, T. W., ed. *The Rise and Fall of the German Air Force, 1933–1945*. New York: St. Martin's Press, 1948.
Gerbig, Werner. *Six Months to Oblivion: The Eclipse of the Luftwaffe Fighter Force*. New York: Hippocrene Books, 1975.

Bohr, Niels Henrik David (1885–1962)

Nobel Prize–winning Danish atomic physicist. Born in Copenhagen on 18 November 1885, Niels Bohr earned a doctorate in physics from Copenhagen University in 1911. He then studied in Britain, at Cambridge and Manchester, under the leading physicists J. J. Thompson and Ernest Rutherford. By 1913, Bohr's work on the development of quantum theory was internationally acclaimed. Returning to Copenhagen, he speedily made that university a leading international center of theoretical physics, attracting distinguished scientists from around the world. In 1922, a Nobel Prize recognized his work on quantum theory and atomic structure.

In 1938 and 1939, Bohr visited the United States, warning American scientists that he believed German experiments proved that the atom could be split and, by implication, that the opponents of Nazi Germany must develop atomic weapons before Germany did so. After Hitler occupied Denmark in 1940, Bohr refused German requests for his scientific collaboration and was active in the anti-Nazi resistance. (In the late 1990s, Michael Frayn's acclaimed play *Copenhagen* provoked a well-publicized historical debate over Bohr's part in dissuading his former student, German scientist Werner Heisenberg, from pressing ahead with a German nuclear bomb project.)

British Secret Service operatives helped Bohr to escape to the United States in 1943, where he joined the MANHATTAN Project's laboratory at Los Alamos, New Mexico, working under its director, his old scientific associate J. Robert Oppenheimer. There, he contributed materially to the secret program developing atomic weapons. With the 1945 atomic explosions over Hiroshima and Nagasaki, Bohr hoped that the bomb's destructive potential might eventually force nations to abandon war as unacceptably devastating, a view that influenced Oppenheimer.

When the war ended, Bohr returned to Copenhagen to resume his scientific work. He campaigned for the open exchange of ideas and people among nations as a means of controlling nuclear weapons. One Soviet general has alleged that Bohr deliberately assisted a Soviet physicist with vital atomic information. Bohr died in Copenhagen on 18 November 1962.

Priscilla Roberts

See also
MANHATTAN Project; Nuclear Weapons; Oppenheimer, Julius Robert

References
Aaserud, Finn. *Redirecting Science: Niels Bohr, Philanthropy, and the Rise of Nuclear Physics.* Cambridge: Cambridge University Press, 1990.
Blaedel, Niels. *Harmony and Unity: The Life of Niels Bohr.* New York: Springer-Verlag, 1988.
French, A. P., and P. J. Kennedy, eds. *Niels Bohr: A Centenary Volume.* Cambridge, MA: Harvard University Press, 1985.
Pais, Abraham. *Niels Bohr's Times: In Physics, Philosophy, and Polity.* New York: Oxford University Press, 1991.
Petruccioli, Sandro. *Atoms, Metaphors, and Paradoxes: Niels Bohr and the Construction of a New Physics.* Cambridge: Cambridge University Press, 1993.

Boisson, Pierre François (1894–1948)

French colonial administrator and governor-general of French West Africa during the Vichy regime. Born at Saint-Launeuch in Brittany, France, on 19 June 1894, Pierre Boisson entered the army at the beginning of World War I in August 1914. He lost a leg in 1916 at the Battle of Verdun. After the war, Boisson joined the French Colonial Service, and in 1936, he was appointed governor-general of French Equatorial Africa, based in Brazzaville, where he was known as a harsh but honest and able administrator.

Following France's armistice with Germany in late June 1940, Boisson at first vehemently demanded that French forces continue fighting, but he was soon won over to the Vichy government when its head of state, Marshal Philippe Pétain, sent him to Dakar as governor-general of French West Africa and high commissioner for French Africa. Ambition persuaded the energetic Boisson to accept the new regime. Arriving in Dakar on 23 July 1940, he banned Germans from the city, but in September 1940, he also defeated an attempt by Free French leader General Charles de Gaulle to take over both Dakar and the French battleship *Richelieu,* which was sheltering there.

After the 8 November 1942 Allied landings in North Africa, Admiral Jean Darlan reached an accord with Lieutenant General Mark Clark, deputy U.S. commander, and ordered Boisson to bring French West Africa into the Allied camp, instructions Boisson took 10 days to obey. Nonetheless, U.S. President Franklin D. Roosevelt rather admired the straightforward Boisson's uncompromising and even-handed style, which, though brutal when necessary, was direct, honest, and effective. Boisson's relations with the Allies were cold but correct, and Roosevelt initially insisted that de Gaulle leave him in his post; only on 1 July 1943, after de Gaulle became head of the Provisional French National Committee, was Boisson dismissed.

Ignoring Roosevelt's protests, de Gaulle ordered Boisson arrested on 15 December 1943. He was then incarcerated for two years without trial and only released on grounds of ill health. In 1948, Boisson was summoned to a trial before the French High Court of Justice, but before proceedings began, he died suddenly, on 20 July, at Châtou, Paris.

Priscilla Roberts

See also

Africa; Clark, Mark Wayne; Dakar, Attack on; Darlan, Jean Louis
Xavier François; de Gaulle, Charles; France, Vichy; Pétain, Henri
Philippe; Roosevelt, Franklin D.

References

Hitchcock, William I. "Pierre Boisson, French West Africa, and the
Postwar Epuration: A Case from the Aix Files." *French Historical
Studies* 24, no. 2 (Spring 2001): 305–341.

Hoisington, W. A., Jr. *The Casablanca Connection: French Colonial
Policy, 1936–1943.* Chapel Hill: University of North Carolina
Press, 1984.

Ordioni, Pierre. *Tout commence à Alger, 1940–1945.* Paris: Éditions
Albatros, 1985.

Paxton, Robert O. *Parades and Politics at Vichy: The French Officer
Corps under Marshal Pétain.* Princeton, NJ: Princeton University
Press, 1966.

conspiring to overthrow the regime, Bonhoeffer was held at
the Tegel, Buchenwald, and Flossenburg concentration
camps. He was hanged at Flossenburg on 9 April 1945.
Many Christians consider him to be a martyr.

A. J. L. Waskey

See also

Canaris, Wilhelm Franz; Counterintelligence; Hitler, Adolf; Religion
and the War; Resistance; Stauffenberg, Claus Philip Schenk von

References

Bethge, Eberhard. *Dietrich Bonhoeffer: A Biography.* Rev. ed.
Minneapolis, MI: Fortress Press, 2000.

Gruchy, John W. de., ed. *The Cambridge Companion to Dietrich
Bonhoeffer.* Cambridge: Cambridge University Press, 1999.

Robertson, Edwin. *The Shame and the Sacrifice: The Life and
Martyrdom of Dietrich Bonhoeffer.* New York: Macmillan, 1988.

Bonhoeffer, Dietrich (1906–1945)

German theologian and Abwehr counterspy. Born on 4 February 1906, in Breslau, Silesia, Dietrich Bonhoeffer was the
son of the prominent neurologist and psychiatrist Karl Bonhoeffer and studied theology at Tübingen, Rome, and Berlin
between 1923 and 1927. From 1930 to 1931, he attended
classes taught by Reinhold Niebuhr at Union Theological
Seminary in New York City. In 1931, Bonhoeffer began
teaching theology at Berlin and was ordained a Lutheran
minister. From July 1933 until April 1935, he served two
German parishes in London.

After Adolf Hitler came to power in 1933, Bonhoeffer rejected his government's efforts to create a united national
Protestant church, the German Christians, that would syn-
thesize National Socialism and Christianity. Instead, he
urged evangelical Christians to join the Confessional
Church, which opposed Nazism. Bonhoeffer returned to
Germany to lead a Confessional Church seminary at Finken-
walde, which was closed by the authorities in October 1937.

In 1938, Bonhoeffer's brother-in-law Hans von
Dohnanyi introduced him to Major General Hans Oster,
Colonel General Ludwig Beck, and Admiral Wilhelm Canaris of the Abwehr. Bonhoeffer then decided to offer active
resistance to the regime, and by 1939, he had become a double agent in Canaris's counterespionage service. As an Abwehr counterspy, he maintained links abroad and held to
his pacifist principles.

In Stockholm in 1943, Bonhoeffer secretly saw Anglican
Bishop George Bell of Chichester, England, for the Abwehr.
This meeting failed to gain Allied support for the German
resistance. Bonhoeffer also participated in Abwehr Operation SEVEN to spirit Jews out of Germany.

Arrested by the Gestapo on 5 April 1943 on charges of

Borghese, Junio Valerio (1906–1974)

Italian navy officer and ardent Fascist. Born on 6 June 1906
at the family estate near Rome, Junio Borghese spent three
years as a student in Britain before entering the Italian
Naval Academy. He graduated in 1928 and was commissioned an ensign. Lieutenant Borghese was commanding a
submarine during the Spanish Civil War when, on 31 August 1937, he mistakenly attacked the British destroyer *Havock* while she was on neutrality patrol, believing she was a
Loyalist vessel. In trying to locate Borghese's submarine, the
Havock employed sonar for the first time in a wartime situation. Neither vessel was damaged in the exchange.

During the early stages of World War II, Borghese's
620-ton submarine *Scire* transported three two-man
"human" or "guided" slow (2–4 knots) torpedoes in the
daring and successful attack at Alexandria on 19 December
1941. The raid sank the battleships *Queen Elizabeth* and
Valiant (which were, however, refloated and repaired) and
damaged a destroyer and an oiler. Although all the vessels
were repaired, these losses severely curtailed British naval
operations in the Mediterranean in the first half of 1942.

Promoted to commander, Borghese was given charge of
the 10th Light Flotilla, known as the "X" MAS (Decima Mas).
Borghese, now called the "Black Prince," conducted other
operations up to the September 1943 armistice that resulted
in total Allied losses of almost 200,000 tons of shipping, although many of the ships were sunk in harbors and were
later raised and repaired.

As a diehard Fascist, Borghese struck an independent
agreement between his "X" MAS unit and the Germans after
the armistice, agreeing to continue the war as an autonomous
force. The unit ultimately numbered some 25,000 men and
operated primarily on land in antipartisan activities,

especially in Italy's border areas with Yugoslavia, Austria, and Switzerland in an attempt to retain those lands as Italian territory. In April 1945, Borghese and his wife, who worked in the office of the secretary of state of the Vatican, were taken by the Americans, who hoped to learn tactics that Borghese and the "x" MAS had employed against Yugoslav partisans.

Held in prison for three years after the war, Borghese was put on trial in Rome in November 1948 on charges of having committed war crimes against the partisans. Acquitted, he was set free in February 1949. He then entered Italian politics on the far right wing. On 7 December 1970, he led an abortive coup against the Italian government. Fleeing to Spain, he died there in mysterious circumstances in Cádiz, on 26 August 1974. One of the most successful Italian naval officers of the war, Borghese was also a modern condottiere.

Jack Greene

See also
Cunningham, Sir Andrew Browne; Frogmen; Italy, Navy; Submarines, Midget

References
Borghese, J. Valerio. *Sea Devils*. Annapolis, MD: Naval Institute Press, 1995.
Greene, Jack, and Alessandro J. Massignani. *The Naval War in the Mediterranean, 1940–1943*. London: Chatham Publishing, 1998.
———. *Valerio Borghese and the X MAS*. New York: Da Capo Press, 2004.
Sadkovich, James J. *The Italian Navy in World War II*. Westport, CT: Greenwood Press, 1994.

Boris III, Tsar of Bulgaria (1894–1943)

King of Bulgaria whose country, though nominally an Axis power, remained autonomous throughout the war years. Boris III was born Boris Klemens Robert Maria Pius Ludwig Stanislaus Xaver, prince of Saxe-Coburg and Gotha, duke of Saxony, and prince of Tirnovo, at the royal palace in Sofia on 30 January 1894. His father was the bombastic and Machiavellian Tsar Ferdinand, who had been ruling since 1887. His mother, Princess Maria Luisa of Bourbon Parma, died while giving birth to his youngest sibling. Boris was educated by palace tutors and married Princess Giovanna of Savoy, daughter of King Victor Emmanuel III of Italy, in 1930. They had two children, Maria Luisa and Crown Prince Simeon.

Boris rose to power following his father's abdication on 3 October 1918, at the end of World War I. Bulgaria was then in desperate straits. The 1919 Treaty of Neuilly involved loss of territory and the payment of reparations. As a consequence of his country's many problems, Boris experienced an exceptionally stormy reign. The 1920s were filled with internal political strife, and economic problems forced Bulgaria to depend on Germany for supplies.

Boris favored a neutralist course for his country. He proved to be an adept diplomat and an intelligent yet cautious leader who was genuinely respected by his people for his skillful handling of the many problems besetting the kingdom. He was an unwilling junior partner in the Axis alliance during World War II. Pressured into joining the alliance by Germany, Boris regained the southern Dobruja region from Romania in 1940, which led to his being known as the "King Unifier" and the "Liberator Tsar."

By 1941, Boris had little choice but to commit to the Axis powers and allow German troops to cross through his country en route to the Soviet Union. Unlike the other Balkan states, Bulgaria remained autonomous during the war. Although it did not invade Yugoslavia or Greece, its troops did garrison parts of Macedonia and western Thrace. In December, Bulgaria declared war on the United States and Britain, but Boris infuriated Adolf Hitler by withholding Bulgarian troops from the war effort and refusing to declare war on the Soviet Union or send Bulgarian Jews to the death camps. His actions helped save 50,000 Jews. Boris and Giovanna also arranged for transit visas permitting thousands of other Jews to go to Palestine.

Boris's continuous obduracy regarding German policies led to a stormy meeting with Hitler at the latter's Wolfsschanze headquarters near Rastenburg on 14 August 1943, in which Boris bluntly said that Bulgaria would follow its own path. He returned to Sofia depressed over the probable eventual fate of his country. Boris died at the royal palace in Sofia two weeks later, on 28 August 1943, most likley from an embolism, although there were suspicions he had been poisoned. A regency then took power on behalf of the underage King Simeon II, who reigned until he was deposed on 9 September 1946.

Annette Richardson

See also
Bulgaria, Role in War

References
Crampton, R. J. *A Concise History of Bulgaria*. Cambridge: Cambridge University Press, 1997.
Groueff, Stephan. *Crown of Thorns: The Reign of King Boris III of Bulgaria, 1918–1943*. Lanham, MD: Madison Books, 1987.
Lalkov, Milcho. *Rulers of Bulgaria*. Sofia: Kibea Publishing, 1997.

Bór-Komorowski, Tadeusz (1895–1966)

Polish army general and commander of the armed underground movement in Poland. Born in Chorobrów, a village in the Brzeżany district of Austrian Poland, on 1 June 1895, Tadeusz Bór-Komorowski joined the Austro-Hungarian army in 1913 and studied at the Military Academy in Vienna. Until 1918, he fought on the Russian and Italian Fronts, attaining the rank of second lieutenant. After 1918, he served in the Polish army, mostly commanding cavalry units, and he was promoted to colonel in 1933.

Komorowski was supervising a cavalry training center in the Polish Corridor (the territory separating East Prussia from the rest of Germany) at the time of the September 1939 German invasion of Poland. Although his unit was forced to surrender at the end of September, Komorowski avoided capture and joined the underground Związek Walki Zbrojnej (ZWZ, Union for Armed Struggle) in Kraków.

In May 1940, the commander in Chief of Polish armed forces in exile, General Władysław Sikorski, sent Komorowski to Warsaw as a brigadier general and deputy commander to General Stefan Rowecki, then leader of the ZWZ. When the Gestapo arrested Rowecki in 1943, Komorowski replaced him, under the pseudonym Bór, as commander of the armed underground movement, which had become the Armia Krajowa (AK, Home Army) in 1942.

On Komorowski's orders, given with the approval of the government-in-exile's delegate in Poland, the Home Army rose against the German occupation in Warsaw on 1 August 1944. Although the Germans were hard-pressed to put down this Polish effort to retake Warsaw, the uprising ended in utter defeat for the Poles after two months of heavy fighting.

After his promotion to commander in chief of the Polish armed forces on 30 September, Komorowski was captured by the Germans in October 1944. Liberated by the U.S. Army on 5 May 1945, he emigrated to London and resigned as commander in chief in 1946. As prime minister of the Polish government-in-exile from 1947 to 1949, Komorowski remained a prominent member of the Polish émigré community until he died in England on 24 August 1966.

Pascal Trees

See also

Anders, Władysław; Poland, Role in War; Rowecki, Stefan; Sikorski, Władysław; Warsaw Rising

References

Bór-Komorowski, Tadeusz. *The Secret Army*. Nashville, TN: Battery Press, 1984.

Korbonski, Stefan. *The Polish Underground State*. New York: Columbia University Press, 1978.

Kunert, Andrzej, comp. *Generał Bór-Komorowski w relacjach i dokumentach* (General Bór-Komorowski based on reports and documents). Warsaw: RYTM, 2000.

Bormann, Martin Ludwig (1900–1945)

German official who was head of the Chancellery and Adolf Hitler's private secretary. Born in Halberstadt, Germany, on 17 June 1900, Martin Bormann served in the German army at the end of World War I. He then joined the Freikorps, but in 1924, he was sentenced to a year in prison for committing a vengeance murder.

After his release, Bormann joined the National Socialist Party and was attached to the Sturmabteilungen (SA, Storm Troops) Supreme Command. From July 1933, he was the chief of staff in the office of Deputy Führer Rudolf Hess. Diligent and efficient, Bormann began his rise to power. He secured Hitler's trust by running his villa, the Berghof, at Berchtesgaden. He then began taking over Hess's duties and made himself indispensable to Hitler.

In May 1941, Hess flew to Scotland. Hitler then abolished the Office of Deputy Führer and renamed it the Party Chancellery, choosing Bormann as its head. In April 1943, Bormann was appointed secretary to the Führer. He wrote down all of Hitler's commands, translating them into firm orders, and he controlled access to the Führer. He proved himself a master of intrigue and manipulation. He was virtually Hitler's deputy and, some would argue, the second most powerful man in the Reich.

Skillfully steering Hitler into approving his own schemes, Bormann acquired the inside track for displacing dangerous rivals. Always a guardian of Nazi orthodoxy, he strengthened the Nazi Party and increased his grip on domestic policy. He advocated radical measures when it came to the treatment of Jews, the conquered peoples, and prisoners of war.

In October 1944, Bormann became executive head of the Volkssturm (militia). He signed Hitler's last will and testament and watched the Führer commit suicide in the Chancellery bunker on 30 April 1945. Bormann then left the bunker. Most likely, he was killed trying to cross the Soviet lines. Doubts, however, persisted, and numerous sightings of Bormann were reported. He was sentenced to death in absentia at the Nuremberg war crimes trials. Bormann was pronounced dead in 1973 after his remains were found in Berlin and identified.

Martin Moll

See also

Germany, Home Front; Hess, Walter Richard Rudolf; Hitler, Adolf; Holocaust, The; International Military Tribunal: The Nuremberg Trials

References

Lang, Jochen von. *Der Sekretär: Martin Bormann—Der Mann, der Hitler beherrschte*. Stuttgart, Germany: Deutsche Verlags-Anstalt, 1977.

McGovern, James. *Martin Bormann*. New York: William Morrow, 1968.

Schmier, Louis E. "Martin Bormann and the Nazi Party, 1941–1945." Ph.D. diss., University of North Carolina, Chapel Hill, 1969.

Trevor-Roper, Hugh R., ed. *Hitlers politisches Testament: Die Bormann-Diktate vom Februar–April 1945*. Hamburg, Germany: Knaus, 1981.

Bose, Subhas Chandra (1897–1945)

Indian nationalist politician and Axis collaborator. Born in the Bengal on 23 January 1897, Bose attended college in India and then went to Cambridge University to prepare for a civil service career. Although he passed the civil service exams in 1920, he instead embarked on a career in nationalist politics. He joined the Indian National Congress and participated in a number of acts of civil disobedience in the 1920s and 1930s, for which he was frequently jailed. In 1938, Bose became the president of the congress. At that point, however, he broke with Mohandas Gandhi and other congress leaders because he advocated the use of violence to expel the British from India.

He was arrested by the British authorities in June 1940, but he managed to escape to Afghanistan and eventually made his way to Germany. Arriving in Berlin in January 1941, Bose, who had developed an admiration for totalitarian political systems, attempted to enlist Nazi support for the creation of a pro-Axis Indian army recruited from among prisoners of war in North Africa. Because of Nazi racial biases, however, Bose was able to raise only a small, token unit.

Hoping to have better luck with Germany's Axis partner, Bose undertook a perilous four-month submarine journey to Japan. After arriving in Tokyo in June 1943, he became the leader of the Indian National Army, a Japanese-sponsored force of approximately 13,000 Indian former prisoners of war. In October 1943, Bose led the Provisional Government of Free India. In that capacity, he made propaganda broadcasts for the Japanese, and in November 1943, he participated in the Greater East Asia Conference, an attempt by Japan to foster Asian solidarity under its leadership. Bose was killed in an airplane crash in Taiwan on 18 August 1945.

John M. Jennings

See also
Gandhi, Mohandas Karamchand; India
References
Fay, Peter Ward. *The Forgotten Army: India's Armed Struggle for Independence, 1942–1945*. Ann Arbor: University of Michigan Press, 1993.

Lebra, Joyce C. *Jungle Alliance: Japan and the Indian National Army*. Singapore: Asia Pacific Press, 1971.

Bottai, Giuseppe (1895–1959)

Italian Fascist journalist, theorist, and cabinet minister. Born in Rome on 3 September 1895, Giuseppe Bottai interrupted his studies there in 1915 to join the Italian army. He served at the front until the end of World War I; thereafter, he finished law school and then embarked on simultaneous careers in politics and literary publishing in 1919.

From 1919, Bottai involved himself with veterans' affairs, also embracing futurism and running successfully for Parliament in 1921. At the same time, he edited or published in *Popolo d'Italia*, *Le Fiamme*, *La Patria*, *Giornale di Roma*, *Gerarchia*, and *Critica Fascista*, which he founded the year after he took part in the Fascist 1922 March on Rome. Bottai used *Critica Fascista* to focus on the technocratic elite within the Fascist movement, as well as a vehicle for his increasingly revisionist interpretation of fascism.

By 1929, Bottai was in the government as minister of corporations, stressing liberal reforms that pleased neither Benito Mussolini nor Italian industrialists skeptical of his technocratic ideas for a planned economy. From 1932, he was without a cabinet portfolio, but four years later, he became minister of national education. Despite his penchant for attempting updated reforms within the Fascist ranks, he busied himself in his new office with some deliberate social engineering. This approach meant fortifying the traditional rural base of Italian fascism through the development of trade schools for lower-middle-class students—thus deflecting them from the higher education path—and leaving unaddressed the handicapping of the social climb for middle- and upper-class offspring (including prominent Jews) who were otherwise bound for the universities. This paradox was characteristic of Bottai's peculiar theories and reforms, and he doggedly hoped for success with his educational and cultural strategies. However, he was thwarted by the arrival of World War II, the demands of which contrasted sharply with the cavalcade of officially imagined improvements he had been concocting for the Fascists' delectation, as well as for their propaganda machine.

On 25 July 1943, Bottai, opposed to the German-Italian alliance, joined Fascist Grand Council colleagues in voting to depose Mussolini, after which he went into hiding. Finally making his way to North Africa, he joined the French Foreign Legion in 1944. Following the general amnesty of November 1947, Bottai returned to Italy from North Africa in August 1948 to reclaim a professorship at the University of Rome and to establish the political review *A.B.C.* in 1953. Giuseppe Bottai died in Rome on 9 January 1959.

Gordon E. Hogg

See also
Italy, Home Front; Mussolini, Benito

References

Cannistraro, Philip V. *Historical Dictionary of Fascist Italy.* Westport, CT: Greenwood Press, 1982.

Koon, Tracy H. *Believe, Obey, Fight: Political Socialization of Youth in Fascist Italy, 1922–1943.* Chapel Hill: University of North Carolina Press, 1985.

Bougainville Campaign (1 November 1943–15 August 1945)

One of the northern Solomon Islands, Bougainville is approximately 130 miles long and 48 miles across at its widest point. The Allies established and held a bridgehead there beginning in November 1943, in order to help neutralize the nearby Japanese base at Rabaul on New Britain Island.

On 1 November 1943, Allied forces, organized into the I Marine Amphibious Corps under Lieutenant General Alexander A. Vandergrift (after 9 November, under Major General Roy S. Geiger), landed at Empress Augusta Bay about midway up the west coast of Bougainville. Japanese Lieutenant General Hyakutake Haruyoshi's Seventeenth Army defended the island. During the next days, in the Battle of Empress Augusta Bay, U.S. Navy forces turned back an attempt by a Japanese task force to attack the landing force, while Allied air units secured aerial supremacy over Bougainville. Later that month, American destroyers intercepted a Japanese task force bringing reinforcements to nearby Buin Island in the Battle of Cape St. George, sinking two Japanese destroyers and a destroyer transport and halting further Japanese shipment of reinforcements to the Solomon Islands.

Initially, Hyakutake, who had 40,000 troops and 20,000 naval personnel, put up little resistance in the belief that the

U.S. Marine Raiders gathered in front of a Japanese dugout on Cape Totkina on Bougainville, Solomon Islands, which they helped to take, January 1944. (National Archives)

U.S. landing was a ruse. Moreover, he was hindered in organizing a counterattack by the island's rugged terrain. During the next weeks, the invading Marines expanded their perimeter to the ridges overlooking the bay and established a strong defensive position while construction units built airfields to assist in the defense of the bridgehead and to attack Rabaul. In December 1943, the Marines were withdrawn, and defense of the bridgehead was entrusted to the U.S. Army XIV Corps, commanded by Major General Oscar W. Griswold.

In March 1944, Hyakutake finally launched a major offensive to destroy the bridgehead, hurling 15,000 men against the 60,000 Americans defenders. Fierce battles took place at the "Creeks" area and Hill 700 in the middle of the perimeter and at Hill 260 on the east side. The American positions were too strong, however, and by the end of the month, the Japanese had been repelled, having lost 5,000 killed and another 5,000 wounded.

By this time, Rabaul had been effectively neutralized, and thereafter, Bougainville, which had provided vital air bases for the victory, became a backwater. The Japanese, cut off from outside aid, were content to be contained, and Griswold saw no need to undertake an offensive against them as long as the bridgehead was secure. U.S. forces engaged only in aggressive patrolling to keep the Japanese off balance. At the end of 1944, the Australian I Corps, commanded by Lieutenant General Sir Stanley Savige, replaced the Americans in the bridgehead. Unlike the Americans, the Australians were not content to be garrison troops, and in early 1945, Savige launched an offensive to wipe out the remaining Japanese. Although they were handicapped by disease, starvation, and supply shortages, the Japanese resisted in sustained fighting until the end of the war, losing 18,000 dead to all causes; the Australians suffered 516 killed and 1,572 wounded. Of the 60,000 Japanese on Bougainville when the Americans landed, only 21,000 remained to surrender in August 1945.

John Kennedy Ohl

See also
Cape St. George, Battle of; Empress Augusta Bay, Battle of; Geiger, Roy Stanley; Griswold, Oscar Woolverton; Hyakutake Haruyashi; Rabaul; Solomon Islands, Naval Campaign; Southeastern Pacific Theater; Vandegrift, Alexander Archer

References
Gailey, Harry A. *Bougainville: The Forgotten Campaign, 1943–1945.* Lexington: University Press of Kentucky, 1991.
Miller, John, Jr. *Cartwheel: The Reduction of Rabaul.* Washington, DC: Office of the Chief of Military History, Department of the Army, 1959.
Morison, Samuel Eliot. *History of United States Naval Operations in World War II.* Vol. 6, *Breaking the Bismarcks Barrier, 22 July 1941–1 May 1944.* Boston: Little, Brown, 1950.
Ohl, John Kennedy. *Minuteman: The Military Career of General Robert S. Beightler.* Boulder, CO: Lynne Rienner, 2001.

Bowhill, Sir Frederick William "Ginger" (1880–1960)

Air chief marshal in the British air force and air officer commanding, Transport Command. Born on 1 September 1880, in Gwalior, India, the son of an army officer, Frederick Bowhill worked in the merchant marine for 16 years. In 1912, he learned to fly, and the following year, he became a flying officer in the Royal Flying Corps, Naval Wing. During World War I, he saw combat attacking submarine bases and zeppelins off the English coast. He also served in Mesopotamia and in the Mediterranean, finishing the war as a wing commander. He remained in the Royal Air Force between the wars, serving in Britain, Egypt, and Iraq and at the Air Ministry in London.

In 1931, he was promoted to air vice marshal and appointed air officer commanding Fighting Area, Air Defence of Great Britain. In August 1937, Bowhill, now knighted and an air marshal, took over Coastal Command, where he remained until June 1941. An innovative leader, he developed systems to control aircraft from the ground that proved invaluable during the Battle of Britain and afterward, urged the use of barrage balloons to protect cities from low-level aerial bombardment, and helped to develop the Women's Auxiliary Air Force. Bowhill's command participated in the rescue of captured British seamen from the German blockade-runner *Altmark* in 1940 and in the destruction of the German battleship *Bismarck* in 1941.

In June 1941, Bowhill moved to Canada to organize and take over from civilian control the Royal Air Force Ferry Command, initially set up in 1940 by a group of Montreal businessmen to transport desperately needed North American–built airplanes to Britain. The assignment demanded tact, charm, and diplomacy, all qualities that Bowhill and his wife exercised in full measure. In 1943, Bowhill became air officer commanding in chief, Transport Command; he remained in this post until the end of the war, retiring four years after the normal retirement age. He subsequently spent two further years in Montreal as the British representative of the provisional International Civil Aviation Organization. Until 1957, Bowhill was also the Ministry of Civil Aviation's chief aeronautical adviser. He died in London on 12 March 1960.

Priscilla Roberts

See also
Barrage Balloons; *Bismarck,* Sortie and Sinking of; Great Britain, Air Force

References
Pollard, A. O. *Leaders of the Royal Air Force.* London: Hutchinson, 1940.
Richards, Denis, and Hilary St. G. Saunders. *The Royal Air Force, 1939–45.* 3 vols. London: Her Majesty's Stationery Office, 1975.

Roskill, Stephen. *The War at Sea*. 3 vols. London: Her Majesty's Stationery Office, 1954–1961.

Terraine, John. *A Time for Courage: The Royal Air Force in the European War, 1939–1945*. New York: Macmillan, 1985.

Boyington, Gregory "Pappy" (1912–1988)

Marine Corps officer and aviator who led the famed Black Sheep Squadron. Born on 4 December 1912, in Coeur d'Alene, Idaho, Gregory Boyington graduated from the University of Washington in 1934 with a degree in aeronautical engineering. Joining the Marine Corps in 1935, he became a naval aviator two years later. Excessive drinking, marital estrangement, financial difficulties, and disrespect for superior officers characterized his next four years of service; nevertheless, he was recognized as an excellent pilot. In late 1941, Boyington volunteered for service with Colonel Claire Chennault's American Volunteer Group (the Flying Tigers) in China.

Flying in defense of Burma and later in China during the spring of 1942, Boyington was credited with two aerial victories, although he maintained that he had downed six Japanese aircraft. Transferred to the South Pacific in early 1943, he was promoted to major and ordered to form a new squadron to take the place of the refitting VMF-214 unit. This new unit, also designated VMF-214 and operating in the Solomon Islands, became legendary as the Black Sheep Squadron.

Between September 1943 and January 1944, the Black Sheep Squadron claimed it destroyed or damaged 197 Japanese aircraft. Boyington, nicknamed "Gramps" by his men and "Pappy" by the press because he was 30 years old, became something of a folk hero in the United States, immortalized in lavish news coverage. He himself downed 22 Japanese aircraft in this period. Combined with his earlier 6 in China and Burma, his 28 aerial victories made him the leading Marine Corps ace of all time.

Boyington was shot down on 3 January 1944 on a fighter sweep over Rabaul after being jumped by more than 20 Japanese aircraft. Picked up by a Japanese submarine, he spent the remainder of the war in prisoner-of-war camps. On his return to the United States in 1945, he was promoted to colonel and awarded the Medal of Honor and the Navy Cross.

Boyington left the service in 1947. He then held a succession of jobs, constantly struggling with alcoholism and marital problems. In 1958, he wrote *Baa Baa, Black Sheep,* detailing his war experiences. In the 1970s, he produced the short-lived television series *Baa Baa Black Sheep,* based loosely on his book. Boyington died in Fresno, California, on 11 January 1988.

Luke B. Kingree

See also
Chennault, Claire Lee; Fighter Tactics; Solomon Islands, Naval Campaign; United States, Marine Corps
References
Boyington, Gregory. *Baa Baa, Black Sheep*. New York: G. P. Putnam, 1958.
Gamble, Bruce. *Black Sheep One: The Life of Gregory "Pappy" Boyington*. Novato, CA: Presidio, 2000.
Walton, Frank E. *Once They Were Eagles*. Lexington: University Press of Kentucky, 1986.

Bradley, Omar Nelson (1893–1981)

U.S. Army general and commander of 12th Army Group. Born in Clark, Missouri, on 12 February 1893, Omar Bradley secured an appointment to the U.S. Military Academy in 1911. He graduated in 1915, a member of what would become known as the "class the stars fell on," and was commissioned a second lieutenant of infantry.

Assigned to the 14th Infantry Regiment in Spokane, Washington, Bradley saw service along the Mexican border during the 1916 crisis that followed Pancho Villa's raid on Columbus, New Mexico. Like his classmate Dwight D. Eisenhower, Bradley missed combat in World War I. During the interwar period, his career followed a familiar pattern, with a number of troop commands interspersed with assignments at various military schools, including West Point. His most significant assignment was as chief of the Weapons Section during Colonel George C. Marshall's tenure as deputy commandant at the Infantry School at Fort Benning, Georgia.

Bradley graduated from the Army War College in 1934. Following service in General Marshall's secretariat of the General Staff between 1939 and 1941, he was promoted to brigadier general in February 1941 and assigned command of the Infantry School. Promotion to major general followed in February 1942, and Bradley successively commanded the 82nd Infantry Division and the 28th National Guard Division. In February 1943, Marshall dispatched him to North Africa, where General Eisenhower assigned him as deputy commander of Lieutenant General George S. Patton's II Corps in the wake of the Kasserine Pass debacle. When Patton assumed command of Seventh Army, Bradley took command of II Corps and led it with great distinction both in Tunisia and in Sicily.

In October 1943, Bradley assumed command of First Army and transferred to England to prepare for the cross-Channel invasion. He commanded U.S. ground forces on D day in Operation OVERLORD and during the ensuing Normandy Campaign. On 26 July, First Army broke the German

General Omar Bradley, ca. 1950. (Library of Congress)

lines outside Saint-Lô in Operation COBRA, Bradley's operational masterpiece. On 1 August 1944, he assumed command of 12th Army Group, which then encompassed General Courtney Hodges's First Army and General George Patton's Third Army.

During the subsequent drive across France, Bradley performed well but not spectacularly. His failure to close the Falaise-Argentan gap reflected poorly on his ability as a strategist and undoubtedly extended the war in the west. When Hitler launched the Ardennes counteroffensive, Bradley was slow to react, but in the subsequent campaign, he renewed Marshall's and Eisenhower's confidence by carefully orchestrating the advance of the American armies on Field Marshal Bernard L. Montgomery's right flank. By war's end, Bradley had clearly emerged as Eisenhower's most trusted military adviser. As 12th Army Group grew to include four separate armies, the largest purely American military force in history, Bradley was promoted to full general in March 1945, on the eve of Germany's capitulation.

Following the war, Bradley headed the Veterans' Admin-

istration, and in February 1948, he succeeded Eisenhower as army chief of staff. In this post, he championed the continued unification of the nation's armed forces. One year later, he became the first chairman of the Joint Chiefs of Staff and was subsequently promoted to the five-star rank of General of the Army in September 1950. During the Korean War, Bradley supported President Harry S Truman's relief of General Douglas MacArthur and opposed expansion of the war. Bradley retired from active military service in August 1953 to become chairman of the board of Bulova Watch Corporation. During the Vietnam War, he served as an adviser to President Lyndon Johnson. Bradley died on 8 April 1981, in Washington, D.C.

Cole C. Kingseed

See also

Ardennes Offensive; COBRA, Operation; Eisenhower, Dwight D.; Falaise-Argentan Pocket; France Campaign; Hodges, Courtney Hicks; Kasserine Pass, Battle of; MacArthur, Douglas; Marshall, George Catlett; Montgomery, Sir Bernard Law; Normandy Invasion and Campaign; North Africa Campaign; OVERLORD, Operation; Patton, George Smith, Jr.; Rhine Crossings; Saint-Lô, Battle of; Sicily, Invasion of; TORCH, Operation; Truman, Harry S; Western European Theater of Operations

References

Bradley, Omar N. *A Soldier's Story*. New York: Henry Holt, 1951.

Bradley, Omar N., and Clay Blair. *A General's Life*. New York: Simon and Schuster, 1983.

Weigley, Russell F. *Eisenhower's Lieutenants*. Bloomington: Indiana University Press, 1981.

Brandenberger, Erich (1892–1955)

German army general and a commander in the invasion of the Soviet Union. Born on 15 July 1892, in Augsburg, Germany, Erich Brandenberger became an officer candidate in July 1911 and was commissioned in the artillery two years later. He fought in World War I and remained on active duty thereafter, primarily in staff positions. He was promoted to lieutenant colonel in July 1934 and to colonel two years later.

Brandenberger was serving as chief of staff of XXIII Corps at the outbreak of war in September 1939. Promoted to Generalmajor (U.S. equiv. brigadier general) in July 1940, he took over the 8th Panzer Division in February 1941. His unit was part of Colonel General Erich Hoepner's 4th Panzer Group of Army Group North at the commencement of Operation BARBAROSSA, the invasion of the Soviet Union. In the first few days of the offensive, Brandenberger's men seized a critical viaduct and then bridges over the Daugava River at Daugavpils.

Promoted to Generalleutnant (U.S. equiv. major general) in August 1942, Brandenberger remained with the 8th

Panzer until January 1943 and was engaged in the effort to relieve the pocket at Velikiye Luki. He was promoted to general of panzer troops in August 1943 and then led the XVII and XXIX Corps on the Eastern Front. The latter was active in the southern Ukraine.

Brandenberger took command of Seventh Army in August 1944 under Field Marshal Walter Model, commander of Army Group B. His delaying tactics in the Hürtgen Forest–Eifel Mountains area slowed the U.S. advance, inflicting heavy casualties on the Americans. His defense of this area assured German control of the northern Eifel area, enabling Hitler to launch the Ardennes Campaign with a secure northern flank. Brandenberger's Seventh Army was the southernmost of the three German armies, and his objective was to secure the southern flank to protect the operations of the Fifth and Sixth Panzer Armies. He enjoyed some initial success, but in the end, he was forced back by the counterattacks of Lieutenant General George S. Patton's Third Army.

Making the most of the meager resources available to him, Brandenberger mounted effective actions against superior numbers of advancing Allied troops for the remainder of the war. Following the Ardennes Campaign, he fought skillful delaying actions west of the Rhine River against the U.S. First and Third Armies, often recommending withdrawal in the face of overwhelming odds. However, as a result of such actions, his relations with Model were strained, and the latter relieved him of command on 20 February 1945. Brandenberger returned to active duty to command the Nineteenth Army on 25 March 1945, against the French First Army in the Black Forest area. The Nineteenth Army was forced back through southern Germany until surrendering on 5 May 1945 near Innsbruck, Austria.

Brandenberger was interviewed by the Americans during his postwar internment and contributed 10 manuscripts for the German Military History Program. He died in Bonn on 21 June 1955.

Jon D. Berlin

See also

Bastogne, Battle for; Dietrich, Josef "Sepp"; Hoepner, Erich; Hürtgen Forest, Campaign; Lorraine Campaign; Manteuffel, Hasso Eccard von; Model, Walther; Palatinate Campaign; Patton, George Smith, Jr.; Rhine Crossings; West Wall, Advance to the

References

MacDonald, Charles B. *The Battle of the Huertgen Forest.* Philadelphia: Lippincott, 1963.
———. *A Time for Trumpets: The Untold Story of the Battle of the Bulge.* New York: William Morrow, 1984.
———. *The Siegfried Line Campaign.* Washington, DC: Center of Military History, U.S. Army, 1993.
Mitcham, Samuel W., Jr. *The Panzer Legions: A Guide to the German Army Tank Divisions of World War II and Their Commanders.* Westport, CT: Greenwood Press, 2001.

Brauchitsch, Heinrich Alfred Hermann Walther von (1881–1948)

German army field marshal who became chief of staff of the army in 1938. Born in Berlin on 4 October 1881, Heinrich Alfred Hermann Walther von Brauchitsch entered the 3rd Guards Field Artillery Regiment in 1901. He was promoted to captain in 1904, and between 1910 and 1912, he studied at the War Academy and served as a General Staff officer in Berlin. During World War I, he continued as a staff officer in several divisions and then a corps.

Brauchitsch remained in the Reichswehr after the war. In 1921, he commanded an artillery battery, and the next year, he served as a staff officer in the Truppenamt (the secret General Staff), organizing maneuvers to test the employment of motorized troops supported by aircraft. In 1925, as a lieutenant colonel, he commanded a battalion of the 6th Artillery Regiment. Following additional staff work, he was promoted to colonel in 1928. Two years later, he was made Generalmajor (U.S. equiv. brigadier general) and became a department head in the Truppenamt. In 1932, he was inspector of artillery, and a year later, he was promoted to Generalleutnant (U.S. equiv. major general) and took command of both the Königsberg Military District and the 1st Division. In 1935, he commanded the I Army Corps at Königsberg, and in April 1936, he was advanced to General der Artillerie (U.S. equiv. lieutenant general). Brauchitsch was responsible for developing the 88 mm gun, one of the best artillery pieces of World War II, as both an antitank and antiaircraft weapon.

In 1938, when General Werner von Fritsch resigned as chief of staff of the army, Adolf Hitler promoted Brauchitsch to Generaloberst (U.S. equiv. full general) and appointed him to succeed Fritsch. He was an enthusiastic National Socialist, but he opposed Hitler's plans for territorial expansion, although not with the passion of his predecessor. Brauchitsch also believed strongly that the military should maintain a neutral stance in politics, and he felt bound by his soldier's oath to obey Hitler as commander in chief.

Brauchitsch coordinated the early German victories in World War II, in Poland, France and the Low Countries, and the Balkans. He opposed the stop order during the campaign for France that allowed the British Expeditionary Force (BEF) to escape at Dunkerque. Hitler raised Brauchitsch to field marshal in July 1940, but the German invasion of the Soviet Union, Operation BARBAROSSA, increased tensions between the two men. The general believed Moscow should be the primary target, whereas the Führer ordered a shift toward Leningrad in the north and the Donets Basin in the south. Brauchitsch also opposed Hitler's stand-fast order calling on the army to hold fast in the face of the Soviet counteroffensive, believing the army should withdraw to more easily defended positions. Ultimately, Hitler went so far as to blame Brauchitsch for the failure of the 1941 offensive in the Soviet Union.

On 9 December 1941, Hitler dismissed the general and assumed the post of commander of the army himself. Brauchitsch retired from the army 10 days later. Listed as a major war criminal and in poor health, he testified at the International War Crimes Tribunal at Nuremberg. He died in a British military hospital at Hamburg-Barmbeck while awaiting trial, on 18 October 1948.

Gene Mueller and Spencer C. Tucker

See also
Dunkerque, Evacuation of; Fritsch, Werner Thomas von; Halder, Franz; Hitler, Adolf; International War Crimes Tribunal: The Nuremberg Trials; Keitel, Wilhelm

References
Bond, Brian. "Brauchitsch: Field Marshal Walter von Brauchitsch." In Correlli Barnett, ed., *Hitler's Generals,* 75–99. New York: Grove Weidenfeld, 1989.
Deist, Wilhelm, ed. *The German Military in the Age of Total War.* Leamington Spa, UK: Berg Publishers, 1985.
Deutsch, Harold C. *Hitler and His Generals: The Hidden Crisis, January–June 1938.* Minneapolis: University of Minnesota Press, 1974.

German physicist and rocket scientist Wernher von Braun, with globe. (Photo taken between 1950 and 1970, Library of Congress)

Braun, Wernher von (1912–1977)

German physicist and rocket scientist who relocated to the United States and helped develop the U.S. space program. Born in Wirsitz, Posen, Germany (now Poland), on 23 March 1912, Wernher von Braun decided as a teenager to become a physicist and pioneer in space rocketry. After graduating from the Berlin Institute of Technology in 1932, he earned a doctorate in physics from the University of Berlin, concentrating on developing liquid-fueled rocket engines.

In 1932, the German military began funding von Braun's work, and after heading a team of 80 engineers building rockets in Kummersdorf, he took over a new, custom-designed facility at Peenemunde in the Baltic, the remoteness of which allowed long-range rocket testing. By 1943, von Braun's team had successfully developed several rockets—the A-2, A-3, and A-4, the last capable of reaching Britain. Von Braun made no secret of his interest in sending rockets to explore space rather than using them as weapons, leading the German Schutstaffel (SS) and Gestapo to arrest him for frivolous indulgence.

In 1943, as an Allied victory seemed increasingly likely, Adolf Hitler ordered von Braun's group to develop the A-4 as a "weapon of vengeance" to shower explosives on Lon-

don. Von Braun's colleagues argued that, without him, they could not accomplish this task, so he was freed. The first operational V-2 ("Vengeance") rocket was launched in September 1944.

In early 1945, fearing for his group members' personal safety and the program's future, von Braun stole a train, forged travel documents, and led his production team to surrender to U.S. military representatives in western Germany. The Americans seized V-2s, spare parts, and scientific documents from the Peenemunde and Nordhausen facilities and gave von Braun and 126 of his scientists visas for the United States. The group initially settled at Fort Bliss, Texas, but transferred to Huntsville, Alabama, in 1950, where they shared their knowledge with American scientists and laid the foundations of the U.S. rocketry and space-exploration programs.

Von Braun's well-publicized suggestions that the United States build a space station and launch manned missions to the moon contributed to the establishment of the National Aeronautics and Space Administration in 1958, Skylab, and the Apollo space program during the 1960s. Von Braun retired in 1972, and he died at Alexandria, Virginia, on 16 June 1977.

Priscilla Roberts

See also

V-2 Rocket

References

Bergaust, Erik. *Wernher von Braun: The Authoritative and Definitive Biographical Profile of the Father of Modern Space Flight.* Washington, DC: National Space Institute, 1976.

Neufeld, Michael J. *The Rocket and the Reich: Peenemunde and the Coming of the Ballistic Missile Era.* Cambridge, MA: Harvard University Press, 1996.

Piszkiewicz, Dennis. *The Nazi Rocketeers: Dreams of Space and Crimes of War.* Westport, CT: Praeger, 1995.

———. *Wernher von Braun: The Man Who Sold the Moon.* Westport, CT: Praeger, 1998.

Rival, Michel. *Les apprentis sorciers: Haber, von Braun, Teller.* Paris: Seuil, 1996.

Stuhlinger, Frederick I. Ordway, III. *Wernher von Braun, Crusader for Space: A Biographical Memoir.* Malabar, FL: Krieger, 1994.

Brazil

The participation of Brazil on the side of the Allies in World War II marked a new chapter in the nation's history. The war severed Brazil's traditional relationships with western European sources of loans and investment capital. As a consequence, even before the United States joined the war, President Getúlio D. Vargas (the Brazilian dictator from 1930 to 1945) entered into an agreement with Washington to lease bases in northeastern Brazil along the air routes to Africa in return for Washington's support for Vargas's project of developing a national iron and steel mill at Volta Redonda. Such a step was unprecedented in Brazilian history and left Vargas open to charges that he had bargained away the national sovereignty.

Brazil did not follow the United States into the war in December 1941. Although the Brazilian government declared its solidarity with the United States, it also maintained diplomatic ties with the Axis states. The pretense of neutrality ended when Brazil severed these diplomatic relations, a step announced at the February 1942 Rio Conference. The fact that this consultative conference was held in Rio de Janeiro was indicative of the strategic importance that the U.S. government attached to Brazil. Following the conference, Brazil received a large quantity of U.S. military supplies, and it allowed the stationing of some U.S. troops on its soil.

Any Brazilian government efforts to avoid outright involvement in the war ended with the sinking of Brazilian merchant ships by German submarines. On 22 August 1942, Brazil declared war on Germany and Italy (it did not declare war on Japan until 5 June 1945), and in return, it received important military and technological aid from the United States.

Brazil proved an important addition to the Allied military effort. The country occupied a strategic position geographically, and bases there would play a significant role in the war against German U-boats in the South Atlantic. Brazil was also a key link in the air route between Florida and the Middle East, and it furnished important raw materials, especially rubber, to the Allied war effort. Brazil was also the only Latin American state, apart from Mexico (with one air squadron), to furnish combat forces.

Under the order of the Brazilian dictator Vargas, Major General João Baptista Mascarenhas de Moraes, commander of the Second Military Region of São Paulo, began organizing the Brazilian Expeditionary Corps (FEB) in late 1943; it was to cooperate with Allied military operations in Europe. In 1944, Brazil shipped this expeditionary force to Italy. It also sent other military elements by air, including doctors and nurses.

The first part of the FEB departed Rio de Janeiro for Naples on 2 July 1944. Other elements followed over the next months, with the fifth and last component arriving in February 1945. The FEB troops were largely untrained and had no combat experience when they arrived in Italy to serve with Lieutenant General Mark Clark's U.S. Fifth Army, but they entered fighting that September and continued in the line until the end of the war. In all, 25,445 Brazilians fought in the Italian theater.

In addition to army personnel, 400 men of the Brazilian air force fought with the 350th Squadron of the U.S. Army Air Forces in Italy. Ships of the Brazilian navy also worked with the U.S. Navy in patrolling the Brazilian coast.

Brazil's cooperation with the Allies in the war affected national development through the growth of important ties between the nation and the United States. The U.S. share in Brazilian trade jumped from 24 percent in 1938 to 55 percent in the early 1940s, and it remained at that level. Further, the war also had been fought in the name of democracy, and in 1945, the Brazilian army overthrew Vargas and his dictatorship in a bloodless putsch.

Jó Klanovicz and Spencer C. Tucker

See also

Cassino/Rapido River, Battles of; Clark, Mark Wayne; Italy Campaign; Latin America and the War

References

Humphreys, R. A. *Latin America and the Second World War.* 2 vols. London: Athlone Press, 1981, 1982.

Lima, Rui. *Senta a pua.* Rio de Janeiro, Brazil: Biblioteca do Exército, 1980.

McCann, Frank D., Jr. *The Brazilian-American Alliance, 1937–1945.* Princeton, NJ: Princeton University Press, 1973.

Moraes, João T. M. de. *A FEB pelo seu comandante.* São Paulo, Brazil: Ipê, 1947.

Silva, Hélio. *O Brasil declara guerra ao eixo.* São Paulo, Brazil: Três, 1998.

Brereton, Lewis Hyde (1890–1967)

U.S. Army Air Forces and U.S. Air Force general who served in numerous theaters and campaigns during World War II. Born on 21 July 1890 in Pittsburgh, Pennsylvania, Lewis Brereton attended St. John's College in Annapolis, Maryland, for two years before entering the U.S. Naval Academy, where he graduated in 1911. He then gave up his ensign's commission to secure a commission as a second lieutenant in the U.S. Army coastal artillery.

In 1912, Brereton transferred to the Aviation Section of the Signal Corps and became a pilot the following year. When the United States entered World War I in April 1917, he was among the first aviators of the American Expeditionary Forces (AEF) in France. As commander of the 12th Aero Squadron between March and October 1918, he shot down four German planes and earned the Distinguished Service Cross.

Following occupation duty in Germany, Brereton served as air attaché in Paris from 1919 to 1922. He next was an instructor at Kelly Field, Texas, and Langley Field, Virginia, and commanded the 2nd Bombardment Group. He graduated from the Command and General Staff School in 1927 and then held a succession of assignments. Promoted to temporary brigadier general in 1940, he commanded the 17th Bombardment Wing at Savannah, Georgia. The next year, he advanced to major general and commanded the Third Air Force at Tampa, Florida.

In November 1941, Brereton took command of the Far Eastern Air Force in the Philippines. General Douglas MacArthur refused him permission to launch an immediate strike on Formosa following the Japanese attack on Pearl Harbor, and as a result, nearly half of his planes were destroyed in the Japanese attack of 8 December 1941. Following the fall of the Philippines, Brereton took command of Tenth Air Force in India.

In June 1942, he went to Cairo to command the Middle East Air Force, later designated the Ninth Air Force. He planned the air strikes against the oil refineries of Ploesti, Romania, in August 1943. One year later, as a lieutenant general, Brereton took command of the First Allied Airborne Army, which participated in Operation MARKET-GARDEN, the unsuccessful Allied invasion of the Netherlands. In December 1944, during the Battle of the Bulge, Brereton's planes dropped supplies to the encircled 101st Airborne Division at Bastogne, Belgium, and in March 1945, they dropped troops near Wesel, Germany, in Operation VARSITY to secure a bridgehead over the Rhine.

After the war, Brereton again commanded the Third Air Force at Tampa, Florida. He transferred to the U.S. Air Force in 1947 and was a member of the Military Liaison Committee of the Atomic Energy Commission before retiring in

1948. Brereton published his memoirs in 1946. He died in Washington, D.C., on 19 July 1967.

Zoltán Somodi

See also
Ardennes Offensive; Clark Field, Japanese Raid on; MacArthur, Douglas; MARKET-GARDEN, Operation; Pearl Harbor, Attack on; Ploesti, Raids on; Rhine Crossings; Strategic Bombing

References
Brereton, Lewis Hyde. *The Brereton Diaries: The War in the Pacific, Middle East and Europe, 3 October 1941–8 May 1945.* New York: William Morrow, 1946.

Craven, Wesley Frank, and James Lea Cate, eds. *The Army Air Forces in World War II: Official History.* 7 vols. Chicago: University of Chicago Press, 1948–1958.

Winton, John. *War in the Pacific: Pearl Harbor to Tokyo Bay.* New York: Mayflower Books, 1978.

Brett, George Howard (1886–1963)

U.S. Army Air Forces general who commanded all air forces in the Southwest Pacific Area (SWPA). Born in Cleveland, Ohio, on 7 February 1886, George Brett graduated from the Virginia Military Institute in 1909 and a year later was commissioned a second lieutenant in the Philippine Scouts. In 1911, Brett received a regular army commission in the cavalry, and in 1916, he became a pursuit pilot in the Signal Corps. During World War I, he served in France and England in logistical assignments.

Between the world wars, Brett graduated from the Command and General Staff School in 1930 and the Army War College in 1936. Promoted to brigadier general in 1939, he served as chief of the Matériel Division at Wright Field, Ohio, from 1939 to 1940. In October 1940, promoted to major general, he was named acting chief of the air corps.

Shortly after the United States entered World War II, he took command of U.S. Army forces in Australia, with responsibility for turning Australia into a support base. For a brief time in early 1942, Brett, who was now a lieutenant general, served as deputy commander of the American-British-Dutch-Australian (ABDA) Command, headquartered on Java in the Netherlands East Indies. Following his return to Australia, Brett became commander of the Fifth Air Force and deputy supreme commander and head of all air forces in the Southwest Pacific Area.

From the outset, Brett's relations with General Douglas MacArthur, commander of SWPA, were strained. MacArthur saw him as too close to Australian politicians, believed he had too many Australians in command and administrative positions, and saw him as responsible for the poor performance of SWPA units in combat. In Brett's defense, it must be pointed out that SWPA suffered from a lack of supplies and trained staff officers and from ill-equipped aircraft. But Brett did not have the confidence of MacArthur, and in the summer of 1942, he was replaced by Major General George Kenney.

In November 1942, Brett became head of the Caribbean Defense Command, a post he held until the end of the war. He retired in March 1946 and died in Winter Park, Florida, on 2 December 1963.

John Kennedy Ohl

See also

Kenney, George Churchill; MacArthur, Douglas; Southwest Pacific Theater

References

Craven, Wesley Frank, and James Lea Cate. *Army Air Forces in World War II.* Vol. 1, *Plans and Early Operations: January 1939 to August 1942.* Chicago: University of Chicago Press, 1948.

Griffith, Thomas E. *MacArthur's Airman: General George C. Kenney and the War in the Southwest Pacific.* Lawrence: University Press of Kansas, 1998.

James, D. Clayton. *The Years of MacArthur.* Vol. 2, *1941–1945.* Boston: Houghton Mifflin, 1975.

Bridgeford, Sir William (1894–1971)

Australian army general who commanded the 3rd Infantry Division in the Bougainville Campaign. Born on 28 July 1894, at Ballarat, Australia, William Bridgeford studied at the Royal Military College, Duntroon. Service in France during World War I earned him a Military Cross. An excellent administrator with an easygoing, genial personality, he served in assorted staff and training positions in the small Australian army between the wars and also took further courses at the Staff College, Quetta, and the Imperial Defence College, London. By the late 1930s, Bridgeford seemed destined for success, but during World War II, he attained advancement and high command more slowly than expected, probably because of personal enmities he aroused during the Greek Campaign.

When World War II began, Bridgeford was military liaison officer in the Australian High Commission in London. In June 1940, he took command of the 25th Australian Infantry Brigade then being formed in Britain. From November 1941 through 1942, he was deputy adjutant and quartermaster general at the headquarters of I Corps in the Middle East. He made valiant efforts to supply operational units during the Greek Campaign, for which he won the Commander Order of the British Empire (CBE).

In 1942, Bridgeford returned to Australia, assuming command of the 3rd Armoured Division in April. From August 1943 to April 1944, his forces participated in the campaign leading to the successful occupation of Madang, New Guinea. Bridgeford then took command of the 3rd Infantry Division, which he led during the 1944–1945 Bougainville Campaign, receiving four mentions for bravery in dispatches.

After the war, Bridgeford became quartermaster general of the Australian Military Forces. From November 1951 to February 1953, he was commander in chief of Commonwealth forces in Korea. Bridgeford retired from the army in 1953. He was the chief executive officer of the 1956 Melbourne Olympic Games and remained strongly interested in sports activities until his death in Brisbane on 21 September 1971.

Priscilla Roberts

See also

Australia, Army; Bougainville Campaign

References

Dexter, David. *The New Guinea Offensives.* Canberra: Australian War Memorial, 1961.

Keogh, E. G. *The South West Pacific, 1941–45.* Melbourne, Australia: Grayflower Productions, 1953.

Long, Gavin. *To Benghazi.* Canberra: Australian War Memorial, 1952.

———. *Greece, Crete and Syria.* Canberra: Australian War Memorial, 1953.

———. *The Final Campaigns.* Canberra: Australian War Memorial, 1963.

Britain, Battle of (10 July–30 September 1940)

A series of individual engagements between the German Luftwaffe and the British Royal Air Force (RAF) between 10 July and 30 September 1940. The battle was first given its name by Prime Minister Winston L. S. Churchill during a speech in the British Parliament on 18 June 1940.

Adolf Hitler assigned the Luftwaffe the task of eliminating the RAF and winning control of the skies over Britain, an essential precondition to the German invasion of England (Operation SEA LION). There were additional reasons for the attack as well. Hitler did not particularly want a war with the British and had publicly appealed for an end to the conflict, only to be rebuffed on each occasion. He nevertheless hoped that if the Luftwaffe were to inflict sufficient damage, the British would be forced to sue for peace. Thus, plans went forward, but Hitler expressly forbade Luftwaffe attacks on civilian targets and on London in particular.

The British frantically worked to prepare for a German invasion, although their army had abandoned most of its

Table 1
Luftwaffe Frontline Attack Aircraft in the Battle of Britain, as of 13 August 1940
(excluding reconnaissance and weather reconnaissance aircraft)

Unit, Commander, and Base Location	Fighter		Dive-Bomber	Bomber		
	Bf-109	Bf-110	Ju-87	Do-17	He-111	Ju-88
Luftflotte 2 Kesselring Brussels	536	119	58	235	207	51
Luftflotte 3 Sperrle Paris	303	112	241	~6	164	216
Luftflotte 5 Stumpff Stavanger	Out of range	32	—	—	61	62

Source: Data from Bungay, Stephen. *The Most Dangerous Enemy: A History of the Battle of Britain.* London: Aurum, 2000.

Table 2
RAF Fighter Command Frontline Day-Fighters and Night-Fighters in the Battle of Britain, as of 1 July 1940

Unit, Commander, and Base Location	Day-Fighter			Night-Fighter
	Hurricane	Spitfire	Defiant	Blenheim
10 Group Brand Box (created from 11 Group, 8 July 1940)	24	20	—	11
11 Group Park Uxbridge	194	72	—	28
12 Group Leigh-Mallory Watnall	72	57	12	20
13 Group Saul Newcastle	58	51	14	10

Source: Data from Bungay, Stephen. *The Most Dangerous Enemy: A History of the Battle of Britain.* London: Aurum, 2000.

equipment in France during the Dunkerque evacuation. They did what they could, removing signposts and such; a blackout had been observed from very early in the war. The Germans were expected to attack in strength by parachute, and there was a certain amount of hysteria about fifth columnists (covert enemy sympathizers) and spies. The British also experimented with means of setting the sea on fire, and Bomber Command secretly trained crews in the use of poison gas.

German plans called for the Luftwaffe to establish air superiority over southern England between 8 August and 15 September. To accomplish this, it had to achieve a highly favorable kill ratio in the air or destroy RAF Fighter Com-

mand's infrastructure on the ground, while keeping a sufficiently large fighter force intact to protect the German invasion fleet. Although leaders of the Luftwaffe were confident of defeating the RAF in the air, they were concerned about attrition among German aircraft.

Reichsmarschall (Reich Marshal) Hermann Göring had three Luftflotten available to prosecute the battle (for summary see Table 1). Luftflotte 2, based in Belgium and commanded by Feldmarschall (field marshal) Albert Kesselring, was the largest with 1,206 aircraft, over half of them fighters. General Hugo Sperrle headed Luftflotte 3, with 1,042 aircraft, in France, and Feldmarschall Hans-Jürgen Stumpff

A TURNING POINT?
⌒Battle of Britain⌒

The Battle of Britain had important ramifications for the course of World War II. The most immediate of those that aided the Allied cause were the dividends that accrued from the fact that Germany had suffered its first major defeat in the war. The British triumph gave hope to the peoples of occupied countries in Europe and helped feed partisan resistance against German occupation forces. More important, this battle helped convince many in the neutral United States to favor offering greater assistance to Britain. Increasing popular support assisted President Franklin D. Roosevelt in securing passage of the March 1941 Lend-Lease Act, which provided vital war supplies to Britain and to other countries fighting the Axis powers.

In military terms, the Battle of Britain had a tremendous impact on Germany's war effort. The Luftwaffe never fully recovered from its losses in the battle, as Britain then surpassed Germany in aircraft production. Also, because Britain remained in the war, Germany now had to spread its military resources even more thinly, including assisting Italy in combatting British forces in the Mediterranean. Rather than the quick conclusion of the war that

German leader Adolf Hitler and commander of the Luftwaffe Reichsmarschall (Reich Marshal) Hermann Göring had believed was inevitable, the Germans faced a protracted conflict that placed great strain on their limited military resources.

This situation became far worse for Germany with the June 1941 commencement of Operation BARBAROSSA, the German invasion of the Soviet Union. The Battle of Britain played a role even before the opening of hostilities between the Germans and the Soviets. Hitler's decision to conquer the Soviet Union was based on his long-held belief in the need to secure Lebensraum (living space) for the German people, but he also expressed the opinion that a German defeat of the Soviet Union would in turn force Great Britain to surrender. Ultimately, BARBAROSSA resulted in a protracted two-front war in Europe. Following the entry of the United States into the conflict as an Allied power, U.S. military might, as well as substantial American material and military resources provided to Britain and the Soviet Union, presented the Germans with a war that they could not win, for Allied resources far surpassed those available to Germany.

The June 1944 Allied landing in Normandy was the final proof of the importance of the Battle of Britain. This amphibious assault on Hitler's Europe was made possible only because Britain remained a secure base for the assembly of the vast armada needed for the operation. In many respects, the 1940 struggle for mastery of the skies over Britain had changed the entire outcome of World War II in Europe.

Eric W. Osborne

See also

BARBAROSSA, Operation; Britain, Battle of; Göring, Hermann Wilhelm; Hitler, Adolf

References

Brown, Peter. *Honour Restored: Dowding, the Battle of Britain, and the Fight for Freedom.* London: Grub Street, 2003.

Clayton, Tim. *Finest Hour: The Battle of Britain.* New York: Simon and Schuster, 2000.

Hough, Richard. *The Battle of Britain.* London: Hodder and Stoughton, 1989.

James, T. C. *The Battle of Britain.* London: Cass, 2000.

Overy, R. J. *The Battle of Britain: The Myth and the Reality.* New York: Norton, 2001.

commanded Luftflotte 5, based in Norway, with only 155 offensive aircraft.

RAF Fighter Command, headed by Air Chief Marshal Hugh Dowding, was organized into four fighter groups with a total of 754 single-seat aircraft (for summary see Table 2). Air Vice Marshal Sir Quintin Brand commanded 10 Group, covering the southwestern United Kingdom. It bordered 11 Group, headed by Air Vice Marshal Keith Park, which was in the southeast and thus likely to bear the brunt of the German attack. Air Vice Marshal Trafford L. Leigh-Mallory commanded 12 Group in the Midlands, and Air Vice Marshal Richard Saul headed 13 Group, covering northern England and Scotland. Of the four group commanders, Keith Park was probably the most capable.

A significant advantage held by Dowding was that his force had the world's only integrated air defense system. Based on the telephone and teleprinter network, Ii was very resilient, merging inputs from radar stations and observer corps, filtering friendly or "doubtful" contacts, and devolving responsibility to group and sector levels. Group headquarters (HQs) allocated raids to sectors, which then scrambled fighters and guided them by radio to intercept the attacking aircraft. The system was the product of years of careful thought, and it enabled Dowding to make the most effective use of his scarce resources. The Luftwaffe was, of course, aware that some sort of fighter-direction system was in use but had no idea of its scope or capabilities.

In terms of aircraft, the German Messerschmitt Bf-109

This picture, taken during the first mass air raid on London, 7 September 1940, describes more than words ever could the scene in London's dock area. Tower Bridge stands out against a background of smoke and fires. (New Times Paris Bureau Collection, USIA, National Archives)

and the British Supermarine Spitfire were quite evenly matched; the British Hurricane had a lower performance but was more maneuverable. Both RAF fighters benefited from the introduction of constant-speed propellers and 100-octane fuel during the battle. The Bf-110 was shown to be inferior to single-engined fighters, and the German Junkers Ju-87 Stuka dive-bomber was so vulnerable that it was withdrawn partway through the Battle of Britain. The RAF, however, had much to learn about fighter tactics. The Luftwaffe was using flexible, open formations that had worked well in Spain and earlier in the war. Many RAF squadrons were still using close formations that allowed little tactical flexibility.

About 80 percent of the RAF pilots were British, and roughly 10 percent were from Commonwealth countries, the bulk of them New Zealanders and Canadians, with some Australians, South Africans, and Rhodesians. In June 1940, 1 Squadron of the Royal Canadian Air Force (RCAF) arrived with its own Hurricanes. Most of the remaining 10 percent were pilots who had escaped from occupied Europe (Poles, Czechs, Belgians, Free French), and complete squadrons of Czechs (the 310 and 312 Squadrons) and Poles (the 302 and 303 Squadrons) were formed as the battle progressed. There were probably about 11 American pilots, but since some of them pretended to be Canadian in order to circumvent U.S. neutrality, it is difficult to be sure.

Beginning on 4 July 1940, a few isolated engagements took place between British and German fighters, and on 10 July, the Germans began the actual battle by mounting their first bombing raid against a convoy in the English Channel. The British had one ship sunk and one Hurricane lost; the

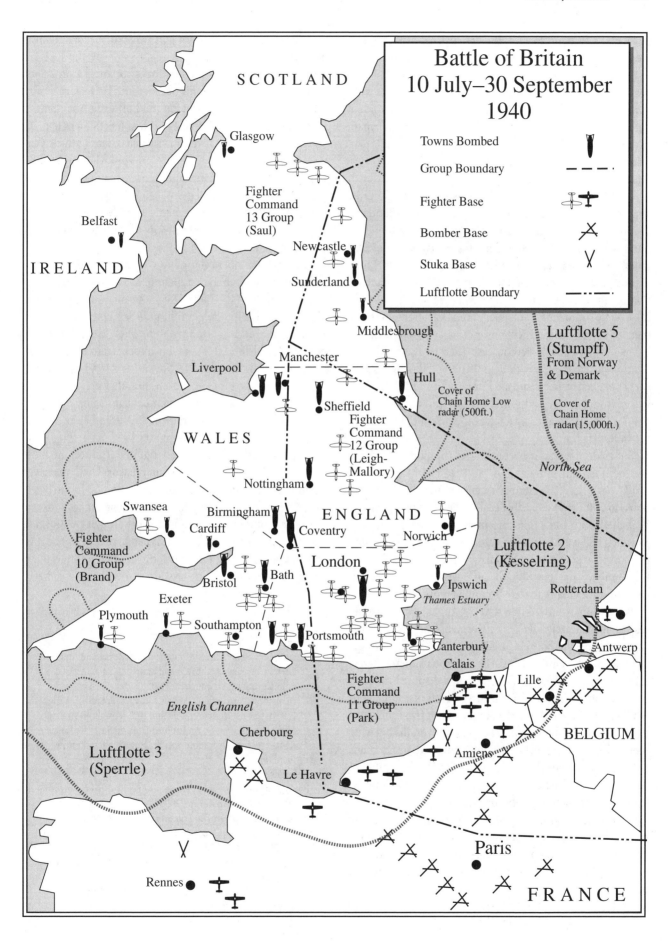

Battle of Britain
10 July–30 September
1940

Towns Bombed

Group Boundary

Fighter Base

Bomber Base

Stuka Base

Luftflotte Boundary

SCOTLAND

Glasgow

Belfast

IRELAND

Fighter
Command
13 Group
(Saul)

Newcastle

Sunderland

Middlesbrough

Manchester

Liverpool

Hull

Sheffield

WALES

Fighter
Command
12 Group
(Leigh-
Mallory)

Nottingham

Swansea

Birmingham

ENGLAND

Cardiff

Coventry

Norwich

London

Fighter
Command
10 Group
(Brand)

Bath

Bristol

Exeter

Plymouth

Southampton

Ipswich

Thames Estuary

Portsmouth

Canterbury

Calais

English Channel

Fighter
Command
11 Group
(Park)

Cherbourg

Luftflotte 3
(Sperrle)

Le Havre

Amiens

BELGIUM

Rennes

Paris

FRANCE

Luftflotte 5
(Stumpff)
From Norway
& Demark

Cover of
Chain Home Low
radar (500ft.)

Cover of
Chain Home
radar(15,000ft.)

North Sea

Luftflotte 2
(Kesselring)

Rotterdam

Antwerp

Lille

Germans lost two Dornier Do-17s, two Bf-109s, and a Messerschmitt Bf-110. Over the next few weeks, the Luftwaffe mounted repeated raids on convoys and coastal targets and attempted to engage British fighters en masse with fighter sweeps, but RAF controllers carefully avoided fighter-versus-fighter combat. Early in the battle, German harbors and shipping became RAF Bomber Command's priority targets; many minelaying and antishipping sorties were made against the massing invasion barges.

On 12 August, the Luftwaffe attacked and temporarily disabled radar stations at Dover, Pevensey, and Rye, and the Ventnor station was out of action for three days, although a dummy signal was sent out while repairs were made. The following day was designated "Alder Tag" (Eagle Day) and marked the beginning of the German attack on Fighter Command. The Germans' plan for multiple raids was handicapped by bad weather and poor communications. Some of their bombers attacked without escorts and were lucky to escape with relatively few losses. There was very heavy fighting on 15 August, with the Luftwaffe flying over 2,000 sorties against airfields and aircraft factories. Luftflotte 5 attacked from Norway for the first and last time and was badly mauled. The Luftwaffe lost a total of 75 aircraft in exchange for 34 RAF fighters.

Both sides inevitably overestimated the amount of damage they were inflicting and overinflated claims for propaganda purposes. The Germans believed that the RAF was down to 300 fighters, partly because they had badly underestimated the production rate of British aircraft. In fact, Dowding still had about 600 fighters. However, the high sortie rate (RAF pilots sometimes flew five missions daily) was beginning to take its toll on the aircrews of both sides, and cases of combat fatigue were becoming more common.

Bad weather between 16 and 19 August offered some respite for the defenders. The Germans then heavily escorted subsequent bombing raids in a bid to wear down the last few British fighters. The RAF's 11 Group suffered determined attacks on several airfields, and a dispute broke out between Park, who used squadron-sized attacks, and Leigh-Mallory, who favored use of a "big wing" of five squadrons to deal a crushing blow to the enemy. However, the big wing took so long to assemble that it only contacted the Germans at full strength on three occasions, and the large number of fighters involved led to exaggerated claims that gave a misleading impression of its effectiveness.

Toward the end of August, Dowding was beginning to run out of pilots, in spite of transfers from other commands and the length of the pilot training course being cut. The Poles of 303 Squadron were declared operational and quickly became the squadron in Fighter Command with the highest kill-to-loss ratio, 14-to-1.

Following the inadvertent jettisoning of German bombs over London and subsequent night raids by the RAF on Berlin, the Luftwaffe shifted its focus to London on 7 September. With hindsight, this decision can be seen as a mistake, but the prevailing view in the Luftwaffe was that the RAF had taken heavy damage and had few fighters left. On 15 September, the Luftwaffe launched a large attack protected by many escorts that were progressively engaged by Park's fighters as the force approached London, where the bombers were confronted by Leigh-Mallory's big wing. Many aircraft were shot down on both sides; the RAF claimed 185 kills, but the Luftwaffe actually lost 56 aircraft against 28 RAF fighters.

On 27 September, Germany's Operation SEA LION was postponed indefinitely. At Benito Mussolini's insistence, however, units of the Italian Regia Aeronautica (the Italian air force) arrived in Belgium in mid-September and began training for attacks in England. They were, however, equipped with obsolete and obsolescent aircraft, and on their only daylight raid, on 11 November 1940, nearly half of the attacking force of two dozen aircraft were shot down, with no loss to the RAF. German daylight raids continued during October but tailed off through November as the emphasis gradually shifted to night attacks.

The Luftwaffe had effectively blunted itself on the most sophisticated air defense system in the world and was never again to be as strong relative to its opponents. In the Battle of Britain, the Luftwaffe had 2,698 experienced aircrew killed or captured, resulting in a shortfall that the German training machine was poorly equipped to make up. The RAF lost 544 fighter pilots and over 1,100 bomber aircrew, but it learned several important lessons and built up a cadre of experienced fighter units.

Andy Blackburn

See also

Aircraft, Bombers; Aircraft, Fighters; Aviation, Ground Attack; Chemical Weapons and Warfare; Churchill, Sir Winston L. S.; Combat Fatigue; Dowding, Sir Hugh Caswall Tremenheere; Dunkerque, Evacuation of; Fighter Tactics; France, Battle for (1940); Göring, Hermann Wilhelm; Hitler, Adolf; Kesselring, Albert; Leigh-Mallory, Sir Trafford L.; Park, Sir Keith Rodney; Radar; SEA LION, Operation; Sperrle, Hugo Walter; Strategic Bombing

References

Bungay, Stephen. *The Most Dangerous Enemy: A History of the Battle of Britain.* London: Aurum, 2000.

Deighton, Len. *Fighter: The True Story of the Battle of Britain.* London: Random House, 1996.

Price, Alfred. *Spitfire Mark I/II Aces, 1939–41.* Oxford: Osprey, 1995.

Ramsey, Winston, ed. *The Battle of Britain Then and Now.* London: After the Battle, 1987.

Townsend, Peter. *Duel of Eagles.* London: Orion, 2000.

Weal, John. *Bf 109D/E Aces, 1939–41.* Oxford: Osprey, 1995.

Brooke, Sir Alan Francis (First Viscount Alanbrooke) (1883–1963)

British army general and chief of the Imperial General Staff from December 1941 to January 1946. Born 23 July 1883 in Bagnères de Bigorre, France, Alan Brooke graduated from the Royal Artillery School at Woolwich and was commissioned in the Royal Artillery in December 1902. He served in Ireland and India in the years before World War I. On World War I's Western Front, he rose from captain to lieutenant colonel. Between the wars, Brooke was an instructor at the Staff College (1923–1926), commandant of the School of Artillery (1929–1932), and inspector of artillery as a major general by 1935. Early on, it was clear his was one of the strongest intellects in the British army.

On the eve of war (31 August 1939), Lord Alanbrooke was appointed commander of II Corps of the British Expeditionary Force (BEF) in France, a position that lasted until his evacuation with many of his troops at the end of May 1940. He briefly returned to France from 12 to 18 June 1940, this time as nominal commander of the BEF. He became commander of the Home Forces on 19 July 1940, working to improve readiness for the expected German invasion.

Brooke was named chief of the Imperial General Staff (CIGS) on 25 December 1941 and held the post until 25 January 1946, serving concurrently (from March 1942) as chairman of the Chiefs of Staff Committee. He was constantly in meetings, including all summit conferences from 1942 through 1945 concerned with the strategic direction of the war. He held off the American desire for a premature cross-Channel invasion while supporting action in North Africa and Italy to spread and destroy German forces prior to an invasion of France.

Brooke's feelings toward Prime Minister Winston L. S. Churchill varied from admiration to exasperation. Churchill's penchant for late-night meetings, his impetuosity or interference in military affairs, and his focus on detail at the expense of broader strategic thinking constantly tried his patience. Brooke's diaries, first published in highly edited fashion in the mid-1950s (and only made available in their full form in 2001), include some of the first postwar criticism of Churchill. Brooke grew to hate the meetings of the Combined Chiefs of Staff for the constant wrangling that arose—especially given his dim view of the strategic thinking of U.S. military leaders, especially Generals George C. Marshall and Dwight D. Eisenhower. A firm supporter of General Bernard Montgomery, he had little patience for those he believed to be of limited abilities.

Promoted to field marshal in January 1944, Brooke was created a baron (becoming Lord Alanbrooke of Brookborough in September 1945) and a viscount (in January 1946)

and was knighted later in 1946. He died on 17 June 1963 at Ferney Close, England.

Christopher H. Sterling

See also

Churchill, Sir Winston L. S.; Eisenhower, Dwight D.; Marshall, George Catlett

References

Bryant, Arthur. *The Turn of the Tide, 1939–43: Based on the Diaries of Field Marshal Viscount Alanbrooke.* London: Collins, 1955.

———. *Victory in the West, 1943–45: Based on the Diaries of Field Marshal Viscount Alanbrooke.* London: Collins, 1957.

Danchev, Alex, and Daniel Todman, eds. *War Diaries, 1939–1945: Field Marshal Lord Alanbrooke.* Berkeley: University of California Press, 2001.

Fraser, David. *Alanbrooke.* London: Collins, 1982.

———. "Alanbrooke." In John Keegan, ed., *Churchill's Generals,* 89–103. New York: Grove Weidenfeld, 1991.

Brooke-Popham, Sir Henry Robert Moore (1878–1953)

Royal Air Force (RAF) chief marshal. Born on 18 September 1878 at Mendlesham, Hartismere, in Suffolk, England, Henry Brooke-Popham entered the army on graduation from Sandhurst in 1898. In 1911, he became a pilot, and he was a major in the Royal Flying Corps in 1914 at the beginning of World War I.

Considered too old to fly missions, Brooke-Popham served as a staff officer on the Western Front. Following the war, as a member of the RAF, he was posted to the Air Ministry and went on to command the RAF Staff College between 1921 and 1926. Promoted to air vice marshal in 1926, he served in various leadership positions in Britain and the Middle East until retiring in 1937 to become the governor of Kenya.

Brooke-Popham returned to active duty in September 1939 at the beginning of World War II. His first assignment was to help organize the British Empire Air Training Scheme in Canada and South Africa, a program that trained pilots from the British dominions. In October 1940, now an air chief marshal, he was appointed British commander in chief of the Far East, responsible for ground and air forces in the British possessions of Burma, Hong Kong, Malaya, and Singapore.

Plagued by organization difficulties, including the lack of a clear chain of command (area naval forces reported to a different commander), Brooke-Popham attempted to balance his military-diplomatic role and bolster British defenses against a possible Japanese attack. However, his ideas, including a proposed British invasion of Thailand, were mostly ignored. British and colonial troops under his command were ill prepared for the Japanese invasion of Malaya in early December 1941, and Brooke-Popham was relieved on 27 December. Many have assigned him the blame for the subsequent loss of Singapore. Brooke-Popham died at Halton, Buckinghamshire, England, on 20 October 1953.

Harold Wise

See also
Malaya Campaign
References
Day, David. *The Great Betrayal: Britain, Australia & the Onset of the Pacific War, 1939–1942.* New York: W. W. Norton, 1988.
Falk, Stanley J. *Seventy Days to Singapore.* New York: G. P. Putnam, 1975.

Browning, Frederick (1896–1965)

British army general and founder of British airborne forces. Born in London on 20 December 1896, Frederick Browning was educated at Eton and the Royal Military Academy, Sandhurst. He joined the British army in France in 1915 and served with the Grenadier Guards. At age 20, he commanded a company, earning the nickname "Boy," which he kept for life. He also won the Distinguished Service Order (DSO) and the French Croix de Guerre.

Browning continued in the British army after World War I and served a tour as adjunct at Sandhurst (between 1924 and 1928). From 1935, he commanded the Grenadier Guards battalion, mostly in ceremonial duties. In 1940, he took command of a brigade. At the end of that year, Browning, a certified pilot, received command of the 1st Airborne Division, which he built from scratch. In October 1941, Major General Browning then organized the Airborne Command, which eventually had 17 brigades. He set high standards for himself and his men in terms of training, fitness, and dress. Marked by strong esprit de corps, the British Airborne Command adopted the red beret and the name "Red Devils."

Elements of Browning's airborne forces participated in the Allied "race for Tunis" in November 1942. Browning then served as airborne adviser to U.S. General Dwight D. Eisenhower in planning the airborne assault on Sicily, although he personally saw no action. Promoted to lieutenant general in January 1944, he took command of the expanded airborne formation, I Airborne Corps, which included the 1st and 6th Airborne Divisions, a Special Air Service (SAS) unit, and, later, the Polish Airborne Brigade. He led I Airborne Corps in the Normandy Invasion.

In August 1944, on the creation of the First Allied Airborne Army, Browning became its deputy commander under U.S. Army Lieutenant General Lewis H. Brereton, although he retained command of I Airborne Corps as well. He played a major role in Operation MARKET-GARDEN, landing at Nijmegen by glider with the U.S. 82nd Airborne Division. He then led the I Airborne Corps in the crossing of the Rhine and the advance to the Baltic.

Following the end of fighting in Europe, Browning was appointed chief of staff of South-East Asia Command under Lord Louis Mountbatten. He returned to Britain in late 1946 and served as secretary to the minister of war. He retired from the army in January 1948 but served as comptroller of Princess (later Queen) Elizabeth's household. Browning died at his estate, Menabilly, near Fowey in Cornway, Britain, on 14 March 1965. He was survived by his wife, the novelist Daphne du Maurier.

John A. Komaromy and Spencer C. Tucker

See also
Brereton, Lewis H.; Eisenhower, Dwight D.; MARKET-GARDEN, Operation; Montgomery, Sir Bernard Law; Mountbatten, Louis Francis Albert Victor Nicholas; Sicily, Invasion of; TORCH, Operation
References
Gregory, Barry. *British Airborne Troops, 1940–45.* New York: Doubleday, 1974.
Norton, Gregory G. *The Red Devils: The Story of the British Airborne Forces.* Harrisburg, PA: Stackpole Books, 1971.

Broz, Josip

See Tito.

B-29 Raids against Japan (June 1944– August 1945)

The attacks on Japan by the B-29 Superfortresses of the Twentieth Air Force, part of the U.S. Army Air Forces (USAAF), began in June 1944 and were key components in the series of shocks that produced the Japanese surrender in August 1945. The bombers burned down cities, mined waterways, destroyed major industrial targets, and eventually dropped two atomic bombs.

Planning for the use of the long-range B-29s against Japan did not begin until early 1943. Operation MATTERHORN, launching these heavy bombers from China, was finally approved at the Cairo Conference in December 1943, and the

Formation of B-29s releasing incendiary bombs over Japan in June 1945. (Library of Congress)

Combined Chiefs of Staff there also supported basing in the Mariana Islands. In April 1944, General Henry "Hap" Arnold established the Twentieth Air Force, to be commanded out of Washington so he could keep the B-29s under his control. The first aircraft were rushed to the Far East that month.

Primary bases for the XX Bomber Command of the Twentieth Air Force were located in India, with forward operating fields in China. Results were disappointing, even after Arnold sent his best problem-solver and combat commander, Major General Curtis LeMay, to take over the troubled unit. Facilities were austere, supply lines were long, crew training was inadequate, and the hastily fielded B-29s suffered from a host of technical problems, especially with their engines. In 10 months of operations, the XX Bomber Command delivered fewer than 1,000 tons of bombs to Japan, all against targets in Kyushu.

The USAAF had greater hopes for the XXI Bomber Command based in the Marianas, which launched its first attack on Japan in late November. This unit had better logistics and more secure airfields, and it was closer to Japan than the XX Bomber Command. Arnold expected Brigadier General Haywood Hansell, one of the architects of precision-bombing doctrine, to exert decisive airpower against Japan's homeland fortress and prove the worth of an independent air service. But Hansell was unable to put his theories into effective practice. In addition to the same problems faced in MATTER-HORN, the XXI Bomber Command ran into a combination of cloud cover and jet stream winds over targets that rendered high-altitude precision bombing almost impossible.

In January 1945, a frustrated Arnold decided to consolidate all B-29s in the Marianas under LeMay, who reorganized the staff, instituted new training, and improved maintenance. After a month of ineffective precision attacks, however, LeMay, on his own initiative, shifted tactics as well. He adopted low-level, night, area, incendiary attacks, designed to cripple key targets by burning down the cities around them and to destroy the Japanese ability and will to carry on the war. The first raid on Tokyo on the night of 9–10 March was a spectacular success militarily, killing more than 90,000 people and incinerating 16 square miles. By the end of the war, B-29s had burned out 178 square miles in some 66 cities and killed many hundreds of thousands of people.

The Superfortresses also performed other missions against the enemy home islands. A psychological warfare campaign to drive panicked civilians out of targeted cities caused over 8 million Japanese to flee to the countryside. Mines dropped in waterways during the last five months of the war sank or damaged over 1 million tons of scarce shipping. And of course, B-29s from the 509th Composite Bomb Group dropped two atomic bombs. Japanese leaders and postwar bombing evaluations acknowledged that the B-29s made a significant contribution to ending the war.

Conrad C. Crane

See also
Aircraft, Bombers; Arnold, Henry Harley "Hap"; Hiroshima, Bombing of; Incendiary Bombs and Bombing; Nagasaki, Bombing of; Strategic Bombing; Tokyo, Bombing of (1945)

References
Crane, Conrad C. *Bombs, Cities, and Civilians: American Airpower Strategy in World War II.* Lawrence: University Press of Kansas, 1993.
Craven, Wesley Frank, and James Lea Cate, eds. *The Army Air Forces in World War II.* 7 vols. Chicago: University of Chicago Press, 1948–1953.
Hansell, Haywood S., Jr. *Strategic Air War against Japan.* Maxwell Air Force Base, AL: Airpower Research Institute, 1980.
Werrell, Kenneth P. *Blankets of Fire: U.S. Bombers over Japan during World War II.* Washington, DC: Smithsonian, 1996.

Buchenwald

See Concentration Camps, German.

Buckner, Simon Bolivar, Jr. (1886–1945)

U.S. Army general and head of the Alaska Defense Command from 1940 to 1944. Born near Munfordville, Kentucky, on 18 July 1886, Simon Buckner Jr. was the son of a Confederate army general and governor of Kentucky. He graduated from the U.S. Military Academy in 1908 and was commissioned a second lieutenant of infantry. Assignment to the Aviation Section of the Signal Corps kept him in the United States during World War I but made him one of the most air-minded of the army's ground officers. Buckner was an instructor in tactics at West Point between 1919 and 1923. He then completed the Advanced Infantry Course. After graduating from the Command and General Staff School in 1925, he continued there as an instructor from 1925 to 1928. He graduated from the Army War College in 1927, where he would also be an instructor between 1929 and 1932. Buckner returned to West Point as an instructor, and from 1933 to 1936, he was commandant of cadets.

Promoted to colonel in 1937, Buckner commanded the 66th Infantry Regiment in 1937 and 1938. He was then on duty with the Civilian Conservation Corps in Alabama between 1938 and 1939, before serving as chief of staff of the 6th Infantry Division in 1939 and 1940. Buckner was

Major General Simon Bolivar Buckner Jr., commanding general of the Alaska Defense Command, at his headquarters in Alaska, awarding the distinguished service medal to Colonel Benjamin B. Talley, engineering officer who planned and supervised the construction of all army installations in Alaska, 1943. (Library of Congress)

promoted to brigadier general to October 1940 and to major general in August 1941. Between 1940 and 1944, he headed the Alaska Defense Command. His primary responsibility was the construction of defense facilities, but units of his command cooperated with the navy in evicting the Japanese from two of the Aleutian Islands, Attu and Kiska.

A month after being promoted to lieutenant general in May 1943, Buckner went to Hawaii to organize the new Tenth Army. He headed an army review panel that investigated the intraservice dispute over Marine Lieutenant General Holland M. Smith's relief of Army Major General Ralph Smith on Saipan. Buckner commanded the main landings on Okinawa in April 1945. Citing logistical difficulties, he rejected navy pleas that he mount a subsidiary landing on the south end of the island.

On 18 June 1945, just three days before organized Japanese resistance ended, Buckner was killed by a coral fragment sent flying by the explosion of a Japanese shell. He was the highest-ranking American officer killed by enemy fire during the war.

Richard G. Stone

See also

Okinawa, Invasion of; Saipan, Battle of; Smith, Holland McTyeire; Smith, Ralph Corbett

References

Appleton, Roy E., et al. *United States Army in World War II: The Pacific Theater of Operations—Okinawa.* Washington, DC: Office of the Chief of Military History, Department of the Army, 1948.

Belote, James H., and William M. Belote. *Typhoon of Steel: The Battle for Okinawa.* New York: Harper and Row, 1969.

Garfield, Bryan. *The Thousand Mile War: World War II in Alaska and the Aleutians.* Garden City, NY: Doubleday, 1969.

Budapest, Battle of (3 November 1944– 13 February 1945)

A long siege that ended with the expulsion of German troops from Budapest by the Soviet army. During this one battle, Soviet forces sustained half of all casualties suffered by them during the campaign in Hungary.

The city of Budapest stretches along both sides of the Danube River and consists of Pest on the east bank and Buda on the west bank. During the siege, there was heavy fighting for virtually every building. Hundreds of thousands of civilians were trapped in the city, unable to leave. They soon were caught in the cross fire without food and bereft of essential services, such as electricity. The siege of Budapest lasted 108 days, and for 52 of those days, the defending Germans were completely surrounded.

In September 1944, Soviet troops invaded Hungary from Romania. The Hungarian government was then desperately trying to leave the war, and on 28 September, representatives of Hungarian Regent Miklós Horthy de Nagybánya were dispatched to Moscow. There, they signed a preliminary armistice agreement on 11 October, which Horthy announced publicly four days later. This step led to the German army's occupation of Budapest. The Germans forced Horthy to appoint Ferenc Szálasi, head of the German Arrow Cross (Fascist) Party, as "Leader of the Nation" by using his son as a hostage.

SS-Obergruppenführer Karl Pfeffer-Wildenbruch commanded the German defense of Budapest. He had at his disposal the 8th and 22nd SS Cavalry Divisions and elements of the 13th Panzer Division, the 60th Panzergrenadier Division, and the 271st Volksgrenadier Division. Some units of the Hungarian army under General Iván Hindy fought alongside the Germans. Altogether, the defenders numbered some 92,000 men. Adolf Hitler ordered that Budapest and Hungary be held at all costs. He needed Hungary for its agriculture and industry but also as a location from which to mount a future counterattack in the Carpathian Basin.

Josef Stalin's goal was to drive Hungary from the Axis alliance and introduce a Soviet-style political and social system as soon as possible. His plan to expand the Soviet sphere of interest was threatened by a British proposal to send forces to the Adriatic in autumn 1944 and from there perhaps move against the Carpathian Basin. Stalin was determined to forestall any British presence in the area, and on 28 October 1944, he ordered the capture of Budapest. He did not anticipate a lengthy battle for the city.

The Soviet 2nd Ukrainian Front (army group), commanded by General of the Army Rodion Y. Malinovsky, and the 3rd Ukrainian Front, commanded by Marshal of the Soviet Union Fedor I. Tolbukhin, now converged on the Hungarian capital. In all, the Soviets committed some 157,000 men, including a Romanian contingent, to the operation. Red Army troops first reached the east bank of the city (Pest) on 3 November 1944, but operations then halted. Following several unsuccessful attempts, Soviet forces completed the encirclement of the city on 25 December. On 1 January 1945, the Soviets took the first buildings in Pest proper, and by 18 January, they had all of Pest under their control. Many civilians and defending army units escaped across the Danube to the Buda side, but before the evacuation was completed, all the bridges over the Danube connecting the two halves of the city were blown. Meanwhile, on 24 December 1944, fighting had begun in Buda on the west bank.

General Pfeffer-Wildenbruch wanted to break out with his forces on 28 December when the Soviet encirclement was still loose, but Hitler strongly opposed this and ordered his troops to stand fast. Hitler did attempt to relieve the German garrison, however. The first effort was made in early January 1945 by SS-Obergruppenführer Herbert Gille's IV SS Panzer Corps from Komárno, about 30 miles west of Budapest, but the attempt was unsuccessful. Gille then tried again from the vicinity of Lake Balaton to the southwest, but got no closer than 15 miles from the city.

Intense fighting continued, meanwhile, between German and Soviet forces in a small area of Buda, only some 3 miles by 4 miles in size. On 11 February 1945, Pfeffer-Wildenbruch authorized his remaining men to break out of the city westward through the Buda Hills to join up with other German troops just outside the Soviet encirclement. Only some 800 of these men succeeded. The Soviets declared Buda secure on 13 February. Pfeffer-Wildenbruch was among those captured and remained a prisoner in the Soviet Union until 1955. The fighting is estimated to have claimed the lives of 60,000 German troops. The Soviets lost 72,000 confirmed dead, with another 80,000 missing. Some 105,000 Hungarians, mostly civilians, were also dead. Among survivors of the siege were some 100,000 Jews who had managed to escape Arrow Cross roundups. The last German army units did not leave Hungary until 4 April 1945.

Anna Boros-McGee and Spencer C. Tucker

See also
Horthy de Nagybánya, Miklós; Malinovsky, Rodion Yakovlevich; Romania, Role in War; Stalin, Josef; Tolbukhin, Fedor Ivanovich; Vörös, János

References
Gasparovich, László. *A rettegés ötven napja: Budapest ostroma és a kitörési kísérlet* (50 days of fear: The siege of Budapest and the attempt to break it). Debrecen, Hungary: Hajj and Fiai, 1999.
Gosztonyi, Péter. "Budapest felszabadítása vagy elfoglalása?" (The liberation or the occupation of Budapest?) *Árgus* 11 (February 2000): 43–44.
Ziemke, Earl F. *Stalingrad to Berlin: The German Defeat in the East.* Washington, DC: Center of Military History, 1984.

Budenny, Semen Mikhailovich (1883–1973)

Marshal of the Soviet Union and commander of the Red Army Cavalry. Born on 25 April 1883 on a farm near Platoskaya, Russia, on the Don River, Semen Budenny entered the tsarist army at age 20 and served as a dragoon in the 1904–1905 Russo-Japanese War. In 1907, he attended cavalry school, graduating with the rank of sergeant. Returning to his regiment, he served as a platoon sergeant during World War I.

In the Russian Civil War in 1918, Budenny joined a partisan cavalry regiment that grew to a brigade and then a division. Given brigade command, he showed great talent as a cavalry commander at the Battle of Tsaritsyn. During the war, Budenny distinguished himself against the best opposing White (counterrevolutionary forces) cavalry generals, and he ended the civil war in command of a cavalry army. Assigned to support the Western Front, he and Kliment Voroshilov—encouraged by political officer Josef Stalin—refused to obey front commander General Mikhail Tukhachevsky's orders, which led to the 1921 defeat of the Red Army in Poland.

Budenny was appointed deputy commander of Cavalry Forces in 1923. When that post was abolished in 1924, Stalin secured Budenny's appointment as inspector of the cavalry. Despite this relatively modest post, he was one of five generals appointed marshal of the Soviet Union in 1935.

During the 1937 military purges, Budenny headed the Moscow Military District and served on the tribunal that condemned his colleagues to death. But poor troop performance during the Finnish-Soviet War (1939–1940, Winter War) exposed Budenny's outdated training views, causing his removal from district command and appointment to the honorific post of deputy defense commissar. He held this post when the Germans attacked in 1941.

Given command of the strategic Southern Axis, Budenny became responsible for Kiev, which Stalin ordered not to be surrendered. When it became apparent that the city would fall, Budenny recommended its abandonment, resulting in his relief and transfer to command the Reserve Front behind Moscow.

Unable to organize an effective defense when the German army launched its advance on Moscow, Budenny was replaced by General Georgii Zhukov. In spring 1942, Budenny took command of the strategic North Caucasus Axis but was relieved after the Germans crushed the Crimean Front and raced into the Caucasus. In January 1943, Stalin appointed Budenny commander of the Red Army Cavalry. He held that post until 1953. Budenny died in Moscow on 26 October 1973.

Arthur T. Frame

See also

BARBAROSSA, Operation; Cavalry, Horse; Eastern Front; Finnish-Soviet War (Winter War); Great Purges; Kiev Pocket, Battle of the; Moscow, Battle of; Stalin, Josef; Tukhachevsky, Mikhail Nikolayevich; Voroshilov, Kliment Efremovich; Zhukov, Georgii Konstantinovich

References

Anfilov, Viktor. "Semen Mikhailovich Budenny." In Harold Shukman, ed., *Stalin's Generals*, 57–66. New York: Grove Press, 1993.

Glantz, David M., and Jonathan M. House. *When Titans Clashed: How the Red Army Stopped Hitler.* Lawrence: University Press of Kansas, 1995.

Bulgaria, Air Service

As a defeated Central Power in World War I, Bulgaria was forbidden under the Treaty of Neuilly to maintain an air force. In 1936, however, it illegally reconstituted its air force with German biplanes, adding Polish fighters and German Messerschmitt Bf-109E fighters after 1938. Simultaneous domestic production at the Bulgarian national aircraft factory, Darjavna Aeroplanna Rabotilnitza (DAR), augmented the force. After Bulgaria's declaration of war on Great Britain and the United States in December 1941, the Royal Bulgarian Air Force was further increased through Germany's contribution of a number of ex-Czechoslovakian aircraft. Bulgaria entered the war with 228 fighters, dive-bombers, and medium bombers of German, Polish, and Czechoslovakian design, together with DAR dive-bombers and reconnaissance aircraft.

The Bulgarian air force was largely inactive until mid-1943, when the U.S. Army Air Forces (USAAF) conducted their first major bombing raid on the Axis-held oil fields of Ploesti, Romania. The Bulgarians' attempt to engage the U.S. B-24 bombers clearly showed that their air arm was hopelessly obsolete. Most of the fighters could not catch the bombers, and Bulgarian aircraft shot down only 2 B-24s. The Germans then provided the Bulgarians with 120 French Dewoitine D.520 fighters and additional Messerschmitt aircraft.

These additional planes did little to improve the effectiveness of the Bulgarian air force. Between December 1943 and January 1944, Allied bombers sortied virtually unmolested over Bulgaria, and their defensive cover of P-38 fighters shot down 39 Bulgarian fighters with negligible losses of their own. Introduction of the superior P-51 Mustang fighter further reduced the effectiveness of Bulgarian air defenses.

After it was invaded and occupied by the Soviet Union in September 1944, Bulgaria switched sides in the war. Royal Bulgarian Air Force units then provided ground support for the Red Army in Yugoslavia and Hungary.

Eric W. Osborne

See also
Aircraft, Bombers; Aircraft, Fighters; Aircraft, Production of;
    Balkans Theater; Bulgaria, Navy; Bulgaria, Role in War; Ploesti,
    Raids on
References
Tarnstrom, Ronald L. *Handbooks of Armed Forces: Balkans, Part II.*
    Lindsborg, KS: Trogen Publications, 1984.

Bulgaria, Navy

Bulgaria has never maintained a large navy, but the diminutive size of its naval force by the late 1930s was also the product of treaty restrictions stemming from the country's defeat in World War I and the difficult economic conditions Bulgaria faced during the interwar years. The core of the navy consisted of four obsolete Drski-class torpedo boats. Launched in 1907, they displaced 98 tons, were capable of 26 knots, and mounted 3×17.7-inch torpedo tubes. The remaining naval unit, the torpedo gunboat *Nadiejda*, was built in 1898 and displaced 715 tons. She was armed with 2×3.9-inch guns and two torpedo tubes and had a maximum speed of 17 knots.

This force was augmented after 1937 when Bulgaria entered into a military assistance agreement with Germany, which eventually yielded five motor torpedo boats of the 1939 Lurssen design. These vessels displaced 57.6 tons at full load and were armed with two torpedo tubes and a 20 mm antiaircraft gun. Their engines could produce a maximum speed of 37.1 knots. On Bulgaria's entry into World War II in March 1941, Germany also supplied three formerly Dutch motor torpedo boats.

The Bulgarian navy saw little action in World War II. Its principal action came in October 1941, when it and the Romanian navy mined Bulgarian coastal waters. Up until the time Bulgaria was driven from the war and occupied by the Soviet army in September 1944, the navy's chief duties were escorting coastal vessels in the Black Sea and patrolling the Danube River.

Eric W. Osborne

See also
Balkans, Theater; Bulgaria, Role in War
References
Chesneau, Roger, ed. *Conway's All the World's Fighting Ships,
    1922–1946.* London: Conway Maritime Press, 1980.
Tarnstrom, Ronald L. *Handbooks of Armed Forces: Balkans, Part II.*
    Lindsborg, KS: Trogen Publications, 1984.

Bulgaria, Role in the War

In 1940, Bulgaria had a population of 6,341,000 people. It was ruled by both a tsar and a popularly elected parliament. Tsar Boris III dominated the nation's foreign policy and was largely responsible for the nation's neutrality on the outbreak of World War II in September 1939. Boris hoped that peace might be quickly achieved in Europe, and he also took note of the fact that although the Bulgarian people were largely pro-Soviet, the officers of the army were pro-German.

The weakness of Boris's policy, however, was the popular desire to attain additional territory in the Balkans. In World War I, Bulgaria had joined the Central Powers in an attempt to recoup territorial losses from the Second Balkan War. The country's defeat in that conflict led to a peace settlement that had further reduced Bulgarian territory. By 1940, the nation remained the only former Central Power that had not regained some of the land lost through the World War I peace treaties. Popular sentiment to redress this situation was high. Germany partially fulfilled these territorial ambitions on 7 September 1940 through the Treaty of Craiova, which granted the area of the southern Dobruja region to Bulgaria.

German interest in Bulgaria was the product of the increased strategic importance of the country. By late 1940, German plans for the invasion of Greece and those for the conquest of the Soviet Union rendered Bulgaria much more significant to the Axis cause. On 1 March 1941, Sofia entered into an agreement whereby Bulgaria joined the Tripartite Powers and allowed German troops to move through Bulgarian territory. Unlike governments in other regions of eastern Europe, however, the government of Bulgaria remained autonomous.

Sofia stayed noncommitted militarily until 13 December, when it declared war on the United States and Great Britain; the country never declared war on the Soviet Union. Bulgaria's military participation in World War II was limited to the Balkans and centered on the acquisition of territory. Bulgarian troops did not take an active part in Germany's invasion and conquest of Yugoslavia or Greece, but the army did occupy both the Yugoslav and Greek portions of Macedonia and most of western Thrace.

Beyond these actions, Bulgaria contributed little to the Axis cause and often opposed German requests in both the military and civilian sectors. Military operations were confined to garrison duties in Macedonia and Thrace, despite Berlin's attempts to persuade Sofia to commit troops against the Soviet Union. Boris and his government also compromised little on the issue of the Jews, who formed about 1 percent of the nation's population. By the end of the war, most of Bulgaria's Jews had escaped extermination, although the government had confined them to labor camps to appease Berlin. Boris's opposition to German authority increased after the defeat of Italy, which led him to seek a withdrawal from the war.

Bulgarian fortunes declined after 28 August 1943 with the death of Tsar Boris III. His successor, Simeon II, was a child, and the regency that governed in his stead was less effective than Boris had been. Political unrest was compounded by popular instability due to declining Axis fortunes and a weakening of the Bulgarian home front. On 19 November 1943, Sofia experienced its first heavy attack by Allied bombers, and by late 1943, food and consumer goods were in short supply.

Support for a coalition known as the Fatherland Front and composed partially of Communists subsequently began to rise, as the Soviet Red Army marched toward Bulgaria's northern border in the spring of 1944. Efforts by Sofia to secure a peace settlement with the Americans or the British failed. Amid mounting Soviet pressure for a Bulgarian declaration of war against Germany, a new government acceded to Soviet demands on 8 September after Moscow had declared war on Bulgaria three days earlier. Red Army troops subsequently occupied the country and appointed members of the Fatherland Front to the government.

The new government, eager to please Moscow, committed 450,000 Bulgarian troops to the Red Army for operations in Yugoslavia and Hungary, at a cost of 32,000 killed and wounded. As operations unfolded, Communist officials in Bulgaria began the process of firmly fixing the country in the Soviet sphere of influence.

Eric W. Osborne

See also
Balkans Theater; Boris III, Tsar of Bulgaria; Bulgaria, Air Service; Bulgaria, Navy; Germany-Soviet Non-aggression Pact
References
Groueff, Stephan. *Crown of Thorns: The Reign of King Boris III of Bulgaria, 1918–1943.* Lanham, MD: Madison Books, 1987.
Miller, Marshall L. *Bulgaria during the Second World War.* Stanford, CA: Stanford University Press, 1975.

Bulge, Battle of the
See Ardennes Offensive.

Bull, Harold Roe (1893–1976)
U.S. Army general who was made deputy chief of staff for operations at Supreme Headquarters, Allied Expeditionary Force (SHAEF) in 1944. Born in Springfield, Massachusetts, on 6 January 1893, Harold "Pink" Bull graduated from the U.S. Military Academy in 1914 and was commissioned into the infantry as a second lieutenant. Bull served in the American Expeditionary Forces (AEF) in France during World War I. He was an instructor at West Point from 1921 to 1924.

Bull graduated from the Command and General Staff School in 1928 and was an instructor at the Infantry School, Fort Benning, Georgia, between 1928 and 1932. He graduated from the Army War College in 1933 and from the Naval War College in 1934. Bull was secretary of the War Department General Staff in 1938 and 1939. Promoted to brigadier general in July 1941, he was assistant divisional commander of the 4th Infantry Division. He then served as assistant chief of staff for operations of the War Department General Staff in 1942. Promoted to major general in March 1942, Bull headed the Replacement and School Command, Army Ground Forces, from 1942 to 1943. In 1943, Army Chief of Staff General George C. Marshall sent him to North Africa as a special observer. Bull returned to the United States in midyear to take command of III Corps but soon was assigned to Britain on the cross-Channel invasion planning staff.

In early 1944, General Dwight D. Eisenhower made Bull his deputy chief of staff for operations at Supreme Headquarters, Allied Expeditionary Force; he served in that position in 1944 and 1945. Eisenhower thought that Bull would be a fine corps commander if he were not so indispensable as a staff officer. In February 1945, he ranked Bull fourteenth among all U.S. officers in the European Theater. Yet Bull was overshadowed by his British deputy, Major General John Whiteley, and in May 1944, the planning function of the operations section went to Whiteley, who was thus more influential in shaping strategy. Bull's job involved preparing situation reports, conducting briefings, and handling relations with operational headquarters, the Allied governments, and the French Resistance. In January 1945, he accompanied Air Chief Marshal Sir Arthur Tedder on a mission to Moscow.

At times a difficult man, Bull found it hard to deviate from an original plan. He was present at General Omar Bradley's command post when news came of the capture of the Remagen Bridge over the Rhine, and he angered Bradley by insisting that the bridgehead had no place in the overall plan for the defeat of Germany.

After the war, Bull was commandant of the National War College. He retired from the army as a lieutenant general in July 1950. Bull died in Washington, D.C., on 1 November 1976.

Richard G. Stone

See also
Bradley, Omar Nelson; Eisenhower, Dwight D.; Marshall, George Catlett; Remagen Bridge; Tedder, Sir Arthur William
References
Bradley, Omar N., and Clay Blair. *A General's Life: An Autobiography of General of the Army Omar N. Bradley.* New York: Simon and Schuster, 1983.
Crosswell, D. K. R. *The Chief of Staff: The Military Career of General Walter Bedell Smith.* Westport, CT: Greenwood Press, 1991.
Pogue, Forrest. *United States Army in World War II: The European Theater of Operations—The Supreme Command.* Washington, DC: Office of the Chief of Military History, Department of the Army, 1954.

The bodies of three U.S. soldiers lying on the beach at Buna, New Guinea, killed in fighting for Buna Gona. (Hulton Archive by Getty Images)

Buna, Battle of (16 November 1942– 22 January 1943)

Key battle in New Guinea in the Kokoda Trail Campaign. In July 1942, Japanese Major General Horii Tomitaro's South Seas Detachment landed at Buna on the northern coast of Papua, New Guinea. During the next weeks, the force moved south on the Kokoda Trail over the Owen Stanley Mountains toward Port Moresby on the southern coast of New Guinea, from which point they could reach Queensland, Australia, by air. Opposed by Australian and local Papuan forces, the Japanese offensive stalled some 30 miles short of Port Moresby, and during September and October, the remaining Japanese retreated back to Buna. There, the Japanese carved out a fortified zone approximately 16 miles long and 7 miles deep. It was manned by 8,000 troops occupying well-camouflaged bunkers and trenches, most in strong points at Gona and Buna villages and Sanananda Point.

Meanwhile, General Douglas MacArthur, commander of the Southwest Pacific Area, was determined to seize Buna as part of the Allied design to neutralize the Japanese base at Rabaul on New Britain Island. During the fall of 1942, troops from the Australian 7th Division and the U.S. 32nd Infantry Division moved by land and airlift to the Buna area. Because of the reluctance of Allied naval commanders to risk exposing their heavy ships to air attack or the treacherous reefs, MacArthur's divisions had no naval gun support and no transports to carry heavy artillery or tanks. Thus, for fire support, these troops had to depend on aircraft, which proved ineffective, and light guns and mortars, the shells of which bounced off the log walls of the Japanese bunkers.

The Allied attack began on 16 November. The Australians made some limited progress in their assaults on Gona and Sanan
anda. But at Buna, the 32nd Infantry Division faced a tactical nightmare and was stopped in its tracks. Lacking sufficient men, forced to cross nearly impassable swamps and jungles, and encountering murderous machine-gun fire, the division made no headway over the next two weeks despite suffering heavy casualties. High humidity and temperatures as well as jungle diseases added to the hardship.

Convinced the troubles at Buna were the result of poor leadership in the 32nd Infantry Division rather than a lack of proper weapons or the strength of the Japanese positions, MacArthur relieved its commander and turned the battle over to the I Corps commander, Major General Robert L. Eichelberger. Many men in the 32nd believed that MacArthur had done little to support them and did not understand the situation at the front. A resourceful commander committed to the welfare of his men, Eichelberger led from the front and came to be regarded as one of the best Allied commanders in the Pacific. He restored Allied morale and improved the logistical situation. In early December, U.S. engineers were able to open an airfield near Buna, significantly improving the Allied supply situation. The Australians moved in some artillery by air, and they also managed to move in light tanks by coastal barges. The tanks, although few in number, proved invaluable. The fighting was bitter, but on 9 December, the Australians took Gona. The more heavily fortified Buna resisted U.S. pressure, but on 14 December, the Americans took Buna Village. By 2 January 1943, all of the Japanese in the

American sector had been eliminated, and on 22 January, the Australians wiped out the last Japanese pocket at Sanananda.

The cost of the Buna operation was high. Almost all of the Japanese defenders were killed, and on the Allied side, the Australians lost 2,000 dead and wounded and the Americans 2,400. Another 2,900 Americans were hospitalized as a result of disease. Yet for the Allies, Buna was a significant victory, for it provided airfields to support additional offenses in New Guinea and also taught valuable lessons about Japanese tactics and jungle fighting.

John Kennedy Ohl

See also

Eichelberger, Robert Lawrence; Horii Tomitaro; Kokoda Trail Campaign; MacArthur, Douglas; New Guinea Campaign; Southwest Pacific Theater

References

Gailey, Harry A. *MacArthur Strikes Back: Decision at Buna—New Guinea, 1942–1943.* New York: Ballantine Books, 2000.

Luvaas, Jay. "Buna, 19 November 1942–2 January 1943: A 'Leavenworth Nightmare.'" In Charles E. Heller and William A. Stofft, eds., *America's First Battles, 1776–1965,* 186–225. Lawrence: University Press of Kansas, 1986.

Mayo, Lida. *Bloody Buna.* Garden City, NY: Doubleday, 1974.

Milner, Samuel. *United States Army in World War II: The Pacific Theater of Operations—Victory in Papua.* Washington, DC: Office of the Chief of Military History, Department of the Army, 1957.

Burke, Arleigh Albert (1901–1996)

U.S. Navy officer and chief of naval operations after World War II. Born on 19 October 1901 near Boulder, Colorado, Arleigh Burke came from a poor family. He graduated from the U.S. Naval Academy in 1923. He also earned a master's degree in engineering from the University of Michigan in 1931. For the next eight years, he held a series of ship assignments and served in the Bureau of Ordnance in Washington.

On the U.S. entry into World War II, Commander Burke was an inspector at the Naval Gun Factory. His attempts to secure a sea billet were not successful until May 1943, when he was promoted to captain and received command of the eight-ship 23rd Destroyer Squadron in the South Pacific. He then saw action in the Solomons and Marianas Campaigns. Burke led 23rd Squadron, known as the "Little Beavers," in the Battle of Empress Augusta Bay in November 1943. In all, 23rd Squadron fought in 22 engagements and sank 1 Japanese cruiser, 9 destroyers, and 1 submarine. It also shot down more than 30 Japanese aircraft. Burke earned the nickname "31 Knot Burke" for his radio message: "Stand aside! I'm coming through at 31 knots."

Known for his innovations as a commander, Burke became chief of staff of 1st Fast Carrier Force, under Vice Admiral Marc Mitscher, in January 1945. He retained that post for the remainder of the war, coordinating carrier strike operations in the Battles of Iwo Jima and Okinawa.

Between 1945 and 1947, Burke was chief of staff of the Atlantic Fleet before serving in the Office of the Chief of Naval Operations and as director of the navy's nuclear weapons program (1947–1949). His high profile in the so-called Admirals' Revolt, in which the navy protested the priority given to the needs of the air force, led the administration of President Harry S Truman to remove him temporarily from the list for promotion to admiral. Burke was duly promoted to rear admiral in July 1950. During the Korean War, he commanded Cruiser Division 5 in Korean waters, and in July 1951, he was named a negotiator for the UN side in armistice talks. In 1952, he became director of the Strategic Plans Division in Washington, D.C. Two years later, he took command of Cruiser Division 6, followed by command of the Destroyer Force, Atlantic Fleet (1954–1955).

In August 1955, Burke was appointed chief of naval operations (CNO), serving an unprecedented three terms. Refusing a fourth term, he retired in August 1961. While CNO, he oversaw the introduction of nuclear-powered ships in the navy as well as the implementation of the Polaris Ballistic Missile Program. After his retirement, Burke was involved in various business enterprises. He died in Bethesda, Maryland, on 1 January 1996. The Arleigh Burke–class of guided-missile destroyers is named for him.

Jason R. Harr

See also

Cape St. George, Battle of; Empress Augusta Bay, Battle of; Iwo Jima, Battle for; Mitscher, Marc Andrew; Okinawa, Invasion of

References

Jones, Ken, and Hubert Kelley Jr. *Admiral Arleigh (31-Knot) Burke: The Story of a Fighting Sailor.* Annapolis, MD: Naval Institute Press, 2001.

Potter, E. B. *Admiral Arleigh Burke.* New York: Random House, 1990.

Burke-Wadsworth Act

See Selective Service Act.

Burma Air Campaign (1941–1942)

By the time the United States entered World War II at the end of 1941, China had been at war for four years. Virtually the only American force fighting the Axis powers anywhere in the world in December 1941 was the American Volunteer Group (AVG), popularly known as the Flying Tigers. Since August 1941, members of the AVG had been training at the British fighter base in Toungoo, Burma.

The Nationalist Chinese government headed by Jiang Jieshi (Chiang Kai-shek) was not only at war with the Japanese but also locked in an uneasy truce with Chinese Communist forces led by Mao Zedong (Mao Tse-tung). By late 1941, Jiang's troops had failed to block the Japanese move toward Burma, threatening the only land supply route into China that ran over the Himalayas, along the hairpin mountain curves of the Burma Road.

As the Japanese advance threatened Burma, the British requested one of the AVG's three squadrons to help defend Rangoon. On 12 December 1941, the AVG 3rd Squadron, commanded by Squadron Leader Arvid Olson, moved south to Rangoon to join units of the Royal Air Force (RAF), while the other two squadrons flew to Kunming in China to cover the terminus of the Burma Road.

The AVG's first combat occurred over Yunnan Province in China on 20 December. The 1st and 2nd Squadrons shot down 9 of 10 Japanese bombers, losing only 1 of their own P-40Bs. On 23 December, the 3rd Squadron and RAF aircraft shot down 6 Japanese bombers and 4 fighters over Rangoon. The RAF lost 5 aircraft in the battle, and the AVG lost 4. On Christmas Day, the Japanese sent 80 bombers over Rangoon in two waves, escorted by 48 fighters. The AVG knocked down 23 without suffering a single loss. The Japanese attacks continued through New Year's Eve. After 11 days of fighting, the AVG had shot down 75 Japanese aircraft, losing only 4 fighters and 2 pilots in the process.

In early January 1942, 8 aircraft from the AVG's 1st Squadron reinforced the 3rd in Rangoon. The rest of the 1st Squadron followed by midmonth. The AVG went on the offensive, attacking Japanese air bases in Thailand. During one raid alone, AVG pilots destroyed more than 60 Japanese aircraft on the ground. On 23 January, the Japanese again hit Rangoon with 72 aircraft. The AVG shot down 21, suffering only a single loss.

The air battles over the Burmese capital continued until 9 March 1942, when the city finally fell to Japanese ground attack. The Japanese captured the remainder of Burma in May, effectively cutting China off from ground access. For most of the rest of the war, the United States supplied China by air from India in the massive airlift that became known as flying "the Hump."

During the 10 weeks the AVG fought in the skies over Rangoon and the Burma Road, it only had between 5 and 20 operational fighters in Burma at any given time. Yet in 31 separate air battles, they destroyed a confirmed total of 217

Japanese aircraft and probably had 43 more kills (victories). In the process, they lost 6 pilots and 16 P-40s. Fighting alongside the AVG, the RAF had 74 confirmed kills and 33 probables, losing 22 Buffaloes and Hurricanes.

David T. Zabecki

See also

Aircraft, Fighters; Burma Air Campaign; Burma Road; Chennault, Claire Lee; Jiang Jieshi; Mao Zedong; Sino-Japanese War

References

Byrd, Martha. *Chennault: Giving Wings to the Tiger.* Tuscaloosa: University of Alabama Press, 1987.

Ford, Daniel. *Flying Tigers: Claire Chennault and the American Volunteer Group.* Washington, DC: Smithsonian Institution Press, 1995.

Greenlaw, Olga. *The Lady and the Tigers: Remembering the Flying Tigers of World War II.* Ed. Daniel Ford. San Jose, CA: Writers Club Press, 2002.

Burma Road

Important route by which the Western Allies sent supplies to China. The Burma Road followed an ancient trail that such legendary warriors and adventurers as Kublai Khan and Marco Polo as well as anonymous spice and tea traders had traveled. In the early twentieth century, Chinese laborers transformed the path into a road. The route was further improved between 1937 and 1938 during the Sino-Japanese War. The completed Burma Road stretched approximately 700 miles from Lashio in Burma, then a British colony, to Kunming, capital of China's southwestern Yunnan Province. Chinese troops shipped military supplies from the Irrawaddy River ports at Rangoon on the railroad to Lashio for transportation to China via the Burma Road. When Japanese forces occupied Indochina and China's coastal areas, the interior Burma route became more heavily traveled.

The narrow, twisting Burma Road crossed through jungle, plateaus, mountainous terrain as high as 11,000 feet above sea level, gorges, rivers, and valleys. Steep grades and plummeting drops challenged those who traveled it.

Allied transportation of military supplies from Burma via the road was disrupted when Japanese forces seized its southern end in April 1942. Hoping to delay a Japanese invasion, Chinese troops destroyed the Salween River Bridge and 25 miles of the adjacent Burma Road passing through the river's canyon. China was now isolated from Allied aid and faced perhaps its gravest crisis of the entire war. The United States responded by initiating cargo flights over the Himalayas; however, the cargo capacity of such flights "over the Hump" was severely limited, and the Western

A look at the Burma Road. (Franklin D. Roosevelt Library (NLFDR))

Allies feared that China might use its lack of military supplies as the excuse to conclude a separate peace with Japan. By September, Allied forces gained control of some of the region, and Colonel Leo Dawson of the U.S. Army Corps of Engineers had command of road reconstruction. He directed a large group of Chinese engineers and approximately 30,000 local laborers.

In December 1942, U.S. combat engineers began building a road from Ledo in Assam, India, to Burma as an alternate route to bypass the Japanese-controlled sections. As of autumn 1943, Major General Lewis A. Pick directed work on the Ledo Road. By the next summer, builders connected the Ledo and Burma Roads at Mongyu, Burma, and military transport expanded. The two roads, known collectively as the Stilwell Road, were 1,079 miles in length.

Ultimately, some 28,000 U.S. and British engineers and 35,000 Burmese, Chinese, and other ethnic laborers surveyed, cleared, cut rock, widened, and repaired the Burma Road and built bridges. They also built a pipeline paralleling the road. Monsoon winds and the rainy season caused muddy conditions, and workers were plagued by red ants and mosquitoes that transmitted malaria. The strenuous work resulted in more than 1,000 deaths.

The previously Japanese-held parts of the Burma Road were reopened by mid-January 1945, with Pick leading a convoy. By August 1945, 120,000 tons of material and 25,000 vehicles had been transported on the Burma Road.

Following World War II and the Chinese Civil War, parts of the Burma Road fell into disrepair. The road was also altered by the building of more direct routes, and in places, it was improved with easier grades. In some spots, it was widened to as many as six lanes.

Elizabeth D. Schafer

See also

Burma Air Campaign; China, Civil War in; China-Burma-India Theater; Engineer Operations; Pick, Lewis Andrew; Stilwell, Joseph Warren

References

Anders, Leslie. *The Ledo Road: General Joseph W. Stilwell's Highway to China.* Norman: University of Oklahoma Press, 1965.

Bowman, Waldo Gleason, Harold W. Richardson, Nathan Abbott Bowers, Edward J. Cleary, and Archie Newton Carter. *Bulldozers Come First: The Story of U.S. War Construction in Foreign Lands.* New York: McGraw-Hill, 1944.

Coe, Douglas. *The Burma Road.* New York: J. Messner, 1946.

Dod, Karl C. *The Corps of Engineers: The War against Japan.* Washington, DC: Office of the Chief of Military History, Department of the Army, 1966.

Fowle, Barry, ed. *Builders and Fighters: U.S. Army Engineers in World War II.* Fort Belvoir, VA: Office of History, U.S. Army Corps of Engineers, 1992.

Burma Theater (1941–1945)

As part of Japan's southern offensive in the aftermath of its 7 December 1941 attack on Pearl Harbor, its forces landed on the Kra isthmus and moved down Malaysia to take the great British naval base of Singapore. Thereafter, Japan repositioned forces used in the attack on Malaysia and moved into Burma to threaten the British in India. The location and topography of Burma helped determine that it would be a minor theater of action in World War II. As with much of Southeast Asia, the country features mountains and rivers running mostly north and south, and thus, it presented difficult topographical barriers for the Japanese forces advancing from east to west and for the British seeking to move from west to east. Terrain, climate, and disease remained formidable obstacles in the China-Burma-India Theater of War (CBI).

Despite these problems, the Japanese sought to secure Burma in order to cut the so-called Burma Road and further the isolation of China and to bring about an end to the Sino-Japanese War, as well as to stir up nationalist opposition to the British in India. The British government, meanwhile, wanted to keep China in the war and contain Japanese military forces sufficiently to the east to prevent them from encouraging Indian nationalist sentiment.

On 8 December 1941, Japanese Lieutenant General Iida Shōjirō sent the 33rd and 55th Divisions that comprised his Fifteenth Army into Thailand. Then, on 20 January 1942, Iida's reinforced divisions, with air support, crossed into Burma, driving west toward Moulmein and Tavoy. The Japanese had some success in mobilizing Burmese nationalists (notably Aung San) to their cause, promising them independence from British rule. Some uprisings occurred against the British.

The British defenders, initially commanded by Lieutenant General Thomas Hutton, believed the difficult terrain would limit the Japanese to roads and cleared areas. The British suffered early and serious defeats because of this mistaken preconception. On 30–31 January 1942, the Japanese drove Hutton's ill-equipped force—equivalent to two understrength divisions of British, Indian, and Burmese troops—from Moulmein, inflicting heavy casualties in the process. The faster-moving Japanese then forded the Salween River and outflanked the British left. In the 18–23 February Battle of the Sittang, they nearly surrounded Hutton's entire force, destroying 12 British battalions and virtually all heavy equipment.

On 5 March 1942, Lieutenant General Sir Harold Alexander arrived in Rangoon and took command from Hutton but without markedly different results. Reinforcements from India restored British strength to two small divisions, but Alexander knew he could not hold back the Japanese, and

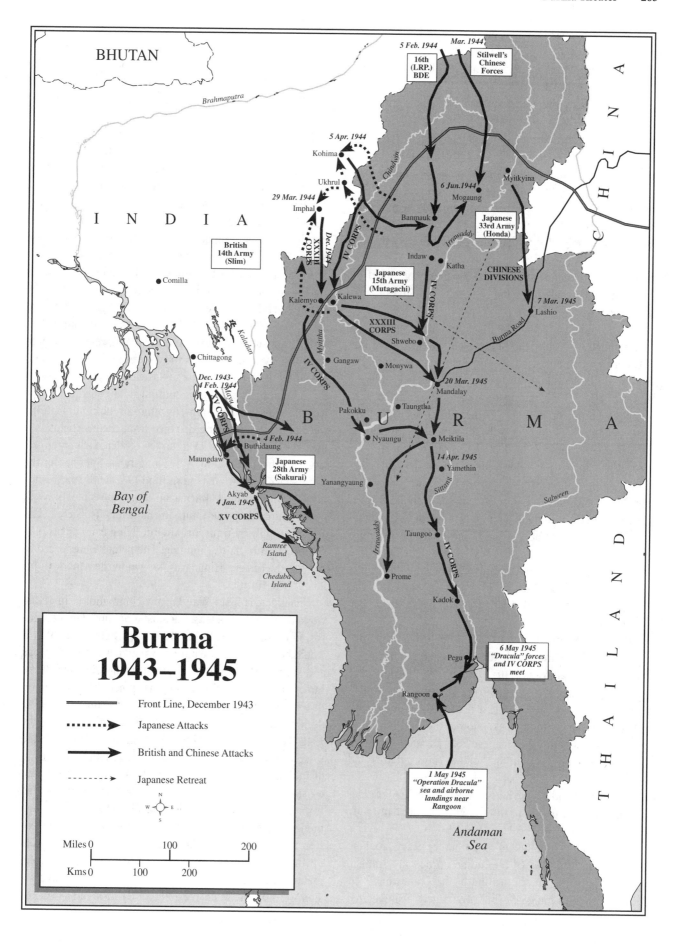

BHUTAN

Brahmaputra

I N D I A

CHINA

5 Feb. 1944

Mar. 1944

16th (LRP.) BDE

Stilwell's Chinese Forces

Kohima

5 Apr. 1944

Myitkyina

Ukhrul

29 Mar. 1944

Imphal

Chindwin

Mogaung

6 Jun.1944

Japanese 33rd Army (Honda)

Banmauk

Irrawaddy

British 14th Army (Slim)

Comilla

Dec.1944

XXXIII CORPS

IV CORPS

Indaw

Katha

CHINESE DIVISIONS

Japanese 15th Army (Mutagachi)

Kalemyo

Kalewa

IV CORPS

7 Mar. 1945

Lashio

Kaladan

XXXIII CORPS

Myittha

Shwebo

Burma Road

Chittagong

Dec. 1943-4 Feb. 1944

IV CORPS

Gangaw

Monywa

Moyu

XV CORPS

20 Mar. 1945

Mandalay

4 Feb. 1944

Buthidaung

Pakokku

Taungtha

B   U   R   M   A

Maungdaw

Japanese 28th Army (Sakurai)

Nyaungu

Meiktila

14 Apr. 1945

Akyab

4 Jan. 1945

XV CORPS

Yanangyaung

Yamethin

Sittang

Salween

Bay of Bengal

Ramree Island

Irrawaddy

Taungoo

IV CORPS

Cheduba Island

Prome

Kadok

Burma
1943–1945

Pegu

6 May 1945 "Dracula" forces and IV CORPS meet

Rangoon

——————— Front Line, December 1943

▪▪▪▪▪▪▶ Japanese Attacks

━━━━━▶ British and Chinese Attacks

╌╌╌╌▶ Japanese Retreat

1 May 1945 "Operation Dracula" sea and airborne landings near Rangoon

N
W   E
S

Andaman Sea

T H A I L A N D

Miles 0   100   200

Kms 0   100   200

on 7 March, after hard fighting, he abandoned Rangoon and vast storehouses of supplies to the advancing Japanese; Alexander himself barely evaded capture. The Japanese occupied Rangoon the next day.

At that point, the understrength Nationalist Chinese Fifth and Sixth Armies, nominally commanded by U.S. Lieutenant General Joseph Stilwell, entered northern Burma along the Burma Road to help the retreating British. The British held the right (southern) side of a rough defensive line across Burma; the two Chinese armies held the center and left. Major General William Slim, who arrived in Burma in mid-March, took command of the Burma Corps, as the British units were titled. Slim turned out to be one of the top field commanders of the war. However, the British continued to move along roads, and the Japanese continued to move through jungle trails and thus were able to outflank and defeat them.

General Iida made plans to attack first at Yenangyaung. He intended to occupy the Chinese Fifth Army, leave the Sixth Army to the east alone, and then mass against the Burma Corps at Yenangyaung to secure the oil fields there.

On 21 March 1942, the Japanese struck the Fifth Army at Toungoo, cutting off the entire Chinese 200th Division. Chinese counterattacks under Stilwell, supported by Slim's British troops, allowed the 200th Division to fight its way free. Allied forces were slowly driven back, however. Although both Chinese armies at times fought well, they and the British did not cooperate effectively. Both sides were then reinforced, leading to a temporary pause in the fighting. The addition of part of the Chinese Fifty-Sixth Army permitted Stilwell to strengthen his defense of the Rangoon-Mandalay Railroad. Slim and Stilwell now laid plans for a counteroffensive, but Iida had also been reinforced, in the form of two additional divisions freed up by the surrender of Singapore.

The Japanese struck first, attacking the Burma Corps, defending Yenangyaung, and holding elsewhere. In the ensuing Battle of Yenangyaung (10–19 April 1942), the Japanese temporarily trapped the 1st Burma Division, but British counterattacks, assisted by pressure from the Chinese 38th Division on the Japanese flank, allowed the 1st Division to escape. At this point, the Japanese 56th Division surprised the Chinese Sixth Army in the Loikaw-Taunggyi area and defeated it. On 29 April, troops of the Japanese 56th Division entered Lashio and cut the Burma Road to China. Alexander now ordered his troops to withdraw across the Irrawaddy River.

General Slim continued to retreat under heavy Japanese pressure until he reached the Indian border and Imphal, with the Japanese pursuit halting at the Chindwin River. Meanwhile, the Chinese Sixth Army largely disintegrated under Japanese attacks, and other Chinese forces withdrew into Yunnan.

The rainy season beginning in May brought a welcome lull in operations for both sides. The Japanese now occupied four-fifths of Burma and needed time to organize their vast gains there and elsewhere, and the British wanted the respite to prepare a defense of eastern India. The cost of the fighting had been high, particularly for the British. A Japanese army of 50,000 men had beaten 40,000 British and Indian troops and inflicted on them some 30,000 casualties. The Japanese had also defeated 95,000 Nationalist Chinese troops, and only Major General Sun Li-jen's 38th Division withdrew as a fighting unit. At the same time, the Japanese had suffered only some 7,000 casualties themselves.

Allied air support had been largely ineffective. Colonel Claire Chennault's American Volunteer Group (AVG, the Flying Tigers) and Royal Air Force (RAF) fighters did what they could, claiming a high kill ratio against Japanese aircraft. But a surprise Japanese raid on Magwe on 21 March 1941 destroyed most British and American planes there and forced the RAF to withdraw to airfields in India. Although the RAF and Flying Tigers continued to try to assist the withdrawing Allied troops, ground-air communications were poor, and the long distance from their airfields and thus the limited time over target rendered their efforts largely ineffective. The arrival of long-range Spitfires for the RAF helped somewhat. And in June 1942, with land resupply to China through Burma no longer possible, Stilwell, now commanding the China-Burma-India Theater, began aerial resupply by transport aircraft flying from airfields in northeastern India to Kunming. The planes were forced to fly over the eastern Himalayas, known to the American pilots as "the Hump."

General Archibald Wavell, now commanding in India, worked to prepare defenses against a possible Japanese invasion of that country from Burma. Wavell realized that it would be a year or more until he would have trained troops and sufficient matériel to assume the offensive, but at the same time, he worried about the effects of inaction on British, Indian, and Burmese morale. As a consequence, he decided to conduct a limited offensive action during the 1942–1943 dry season. Accordingly, in December 1942, the British launched a counterattack by the 14th Indian Division of Indian and British units against Arakan, the northwest coastal province of Burma and an area largely separated from the rest of the country by rugged mountains. Although the Japanese there were badly outnumbered, the 14th Division moved too slowly, allowing the Japanese time to build up their strength and to fortify. Iida rushed in reinforcements, and in March 1943, troops of the Japanese 55th Division went on the offensive and worked their way over the

A Chinese machine gun crew in their gun pit in the Burmese jungle. (Library of Congress)

mountains to hit the British in the flank and force their troops back to India by May. The British had again been proven wrong in their assumption that the Japanese would stick to existing roadways.

Meanwhile, Brigadier General Orde Wingate secured Wavell's approval to try "long-range penetration attacks" with his 77th Indian Brigade, known later as the Chindits (their emblem was a *chinthe,* a mythical Burmese beast resembling a lion, and they operated beyond the Chindwin River). This move was a British effort to try to beat the Japanese at their own game in using infiltration tactics. The Chindits would operate deep behind enemy lines in an effort to damage Japanese communications, destroy supplies, and sow confusion. The force of 3,000 Chindits would rely entirely on aerial resupply for food, clothing, medicines, and arms.

The first Chindit raid began with a crossing of the Chindwin River in February 1943. The force managed to cut sections of the Mandalay-Myitkyina and Mandalay-Lashio railroads, and in mid-March, they crossed the Irrawaddy River. This latter move brought major Japanese reaction, forcing a

Chindit withdrawal in April. Newspapers in the Allied countries claimed a great victory, but in reality, the raid had been a failure militarily. The damage to Japanese troops and positions was slight, and the raiders lost half of their force.

Although the British fared poorly on land, the Royal Navy continued to control the Indian Ocean, which was immensely important for the long supply lines to the Middle East and to the Soviet Union. Meanwhile, to secure the loyalty of Indian nationalists, the British held out the promise of eventual sovereignty after the war. The major Allied problems in the Burma Theater remained the nearly complete lack of cooperation between the British and Chinese strategists, the inability to cope with Japanese tactics, and inadequate resources and supplies for a fighting front far down the Allied priority list.

Stilwell now mounted a drive into northern Burma. In February 1943, he committed the American-trained reconstituted Chinese 38th Division in upper Assam on the Burma-India border, where U.S., Chinese, and Indian engineers were building a road from Ledo. The 38th Division drove the few Japanese from the area. In late October, having secured the reluctant support of General Wavell and the agreement of Chinese Nationalist leader Jiang Jieshi (Chiang Kai-shek) to employ his forces to reopen a land route to China, Stilwell committed the 38th Division south into the Hukawng Valley, where it was resupplied entirely by air. At the same time, the Chinese 22nd Division moved up from Ramgarh to Ledo. Meanwhile, Stilwell pushed construction of the road from Ledo.

In late November, Japanese forces struck the 38th and subjected it to punishing attacks, completely cutting off some of its units. U.S. aerial resupply prevented the Japanese from overrunning the troops, however. At the end of December, Stilwell arrived, along with light artillery, and the Chinese then counterattacked, driving the Japanese from the Hukawng Valley.

During January and February 1944, there was stalemate in the Hukawng Valley. Japanese Major General Tanaka Shinichi's 18th Division halted the advance of the Chinese 38th and 22nd Divisions. The Chinese resumed their advance in late February.

Much of the rest of Burma had remained quiet throughout 1943. In a considerable engineering feat, the Japanese built a 250-mile-long railroad across Burma, in the process employing as slave labor British prisoners captured at Singapore and some American captives. The Japanese utilized the railroad to mass supplies for an attack on eastern India. On 1 August 1943, they also granted Burma its "independence," although this step did not resonate sufficiently with the Japanese-installed Burmese government to enable Japan to exploit fully Burmese rice and petroleum resources.

The Japanese reorganized their forces in Burma, which were under the overall command of the Southern Resources Area commander, Field Marshal Count Terauchi Hisaichi, in Saigon. In March 1943, Lieutenant General Kawabe Masakazu had assumed command from General Iida of the six Japanese divisions in Burma. Kawabe had direct supervision of the two divisions in southwest Burma; the other four Japanese divisions were in the north under Lieutenant General Mutaguchi Renya. Kawabe directed Mutaguchi to invade eastern India with three of his divisions, and toward that end, the Japanese amassed some 100,000 troops. The Japanese intended to seize the Imphal-Kohima Plain of Manipur, the logical British staging area for an invasion of Burma from central India. Their second major goal was to take and hold the rail line into Assam that passed through Manipur. Along it flowed most of the supplies that were ferried into China, as well as those destined for Stilwell's divisions in north Burma.

On the night of 3 February 1944, the Japanese attacked in the south, and once again, they surprised the British with the size and speed of the assault. But the now experienced British and Indian troops held their positions even when surrounded and did not surrender their supply dumps, which the Japanese needed to support their advance. British and U.S. aircraft flew supplies to the defenders in Imphal, and other aircraft strafed the Japanese. General Slim also organized a relief column, drove it to Imphal, and broke the siege after 88 days on 22 June. After desperate fighting by both sides, the Japanese, short of supplies and facing the onset of the monsoon season, called off the attack, and Fifteenth Army began to withdraw.

In October 1943, Vice Admiral Lord Louis Mountbatten had taken up his post as commander of the new South-East Asia Command, although command ambiguities remained. He and Slim agreed that British forces could not do much until the next dry season, although they were willing to organize some spoiling attacks to take pressure off a larger offensive sought by General Stilwell for his Chinese units. Wingate, now a major general and enjoying British Prime Minister Winston L. S. Churchill's full support, planned a second and even more audacious raid for his Chindits that would include three brigades supported logistically by the U.S. Army Air Forces. The operation involved 25,000 men, of whom 3,000 were Americans. Led briefly by Brigadier General Frank Merrill, the U.S. force was known as Merrill's Marauders.

The March 1944 raid began with high promise, but the whole venture was doomed from the start because its success rested on the active participation of Chinese divisions. These forces were being husbanded by Jiang Jieshi, who drove his chief of staff, Stilwell (also commanding all U.S. forces in the CBI), to distraction. In secret instructions to his generals, Jiang sharply limited Chinese military involvement, which in any case proved to be ineffectual. Another factor that contributed to the failure of the raid was the death of Wingate in a plane crash in India on 24 March, whereon Stilwell controlled operations. Wingate and Stilwell were much alike—both eccentric and dynamic—but they seldom disclosed their intentions, and as a result, there were serious failures in planning and staff work. Stilwell, in fact, disliked the British and did not use the Chindits effectively. Nor did he understand the difficulties facing guerrilla forces while dependent on aerial resupply but operating as conventional units.

The Japanese, heavily outnumbered in the air and lacking other modern weapons, fought back with considerable tenacity. Finally, the monsoon rains that began in mid-May slowed the offensive and brought more malaria. By June, the chief Allied enemies were not the Japanese but exhaustion, malnutrition, and disease. Although the raid inflicted 50,000 Japanese casualties against only 17,000 for the

British, Allied forces were obliged to withdraw from Burma in July. Since it was ultimately unsuccessful, the 1944 Burma Campaign has remained a controversial subject. Unfortunately for all involved, it had no practical effect on the outcome of the war.

The lack of Chinese support in this operation displeased U.S. leaders, who had hoped that Nationalist armies would tie down the Japanese forces. Jiang, however, seemed more preoccupied with building up his own strength so that he could do battle with his domestic opposition, the Chinese Communists, after the war. Washington's realization that it could not count on Jiang to fight the Japanese resulted in increased support for forces under Admiral Chester Nimitz in the central Pacific and General Douglas MacArthur in the southwest Pacific.

As the Japanese offensive ended, the Allies began their own offensive in October 1944, with the British largely in support of a Chinese attack. Stilwell employed five American-trained and American-equipped Chinese divisions to take Myitkyana. Opposing them was the Japanese Thirty-Third Army, composed of three depleted divisions commanded by Lieutenant General Honda Masaki. Stilwell hoped to be able to trap the Thirty-Third Army between the five divisions in Burma and the Y-Force in Yunnan. However, Stilwell's poor relationship with Jiang and the situation in China after the Japanese attacked to remove the threat of U.S. strategic bombers there led Jiang to demand that Washington replace Stilwell. This change occurred on 18 October, with Stilwell succeeded by Lieutenant General Daniel Sultan. Jiang's recall of two of the Chinese divisions from Burma to help stop the Japanese offensive in south China brought the Chinese offensive against the Japanese in Burma to a halt in December.

By fall 1944, the Allied position in Burma had improved considerably and the Japanese position had weakened, reflecting the relative fortunes of each side in the larger conflict. General Slim followed up his successful relief of Imphal, and in October, the British crossed the Chindwin River. The new Japanese commander in Burma, Lieutenant General Kimura Heitaro, had 10 divisions. He wanted to let the British advance in the center and outrun their supplies; then, he would counterattack to cut off and surround the British. This approach set the stage for the climactic battles of 1945.

In December 1944, the Allies assumed the offensive in the south (assisted by landing craft no longer needed for the invasions of France), in the center, and from China in the north. The southern advance required crossing many rivers and canals, and the going was naturally rather slow, although the Anglo-Indian forces regained the port of Akyab and Ramree Island as Kimura withdrew. Meanwhile, two Chinese divisions advanced into north Burma, reopened the Burma Road against negligible Japanese resistance, and seized Lashio in early March.

The chief battle took place in central Burma. Slim figured out Kimura's plan, and with great fanfare, he dispatched forces to cross the Irrawaddy River while sending several divisions quietly to the south to outflank the Japanese, cut their line of communications and retreat, and possibly take the entire Japanese force defending central Burma. Advancing on a 140-mile front, the British captured Meiktila on 4 March. They took Mandalay two weeks later, while repulsing a simultaneous Japanese counterattack against Meiktila.

Slim sought to gain Rangoon while the roads and rice paddies were still sunbaked, dry, and hard. On 3 May, a combined amphibious, land, and airborne attack recaptured the capital city, and the fighting largely came to an end. Most Japanese troops fled to neighboring Thailand.

Charles M. Dobbs and Spencer C. Tucker

See also
Airlift; Alexander, Harold Rupert Leofric George; Aung San, U; Burma Air Campaign; Burma Road; Churchill, Sir Winston L. S.; Engineer Operations; Honda Masaki; Hump, The; Iida Shōjirō; Jiang Jieshi; Kawabe Masakazu; Kimura Heitaro; Merrill, Frank Dow; Mountbatten, Louis Francis Albert Victor Nicolas; Mutaguchi Renya; Slim, Sir William Joseph; Stilwell, Joseph Warren; Sultan, Daniel I.; Sun Liren; Tanaka Shinichi; Terauchi Hisaichi; Wingate, Orde Charles

References
Allen, Louis. *Burma: The Longest War, 1941–1945.* New York: St. Martin's Press, 1984.
Bidwell, Shelford. *The Chindit War: Stilwell, Wingate, and the Campaign in Burma, 1944.* New York: Macmillan, 1979.
Callahan, Raymond A. *Burma, 1942–1945.* London: Davis-Poynton, 1978.
Connell, John. *Wavell, Supreme Commander, 1941–1943.* London: Collins, 1969.
Lunt, James D. *"A Hell of a Licking": The Retreat from Burma, 1941–1942.* London: Collins, 1986.
Prefer, Nathan N. *Vinegar Joe's War: Stilwell's Campaigns for Burma.* Novato, CA: Presidio, 2000.

Burns, Eedson Louis Millard (1897–1985)

Canadian army general and commander of the I Canadian Corps in Italy in 1944. Born in Westmount, Quebec, on 17 June 1897, Eedson Burns studied for two years at the Royal Military College at Kingston, Ontario. He served with the engineers and signalers in World War I. He was wounded twice during the conflict, received the Military Cross, and ended the war as the youngest staff captain in the Canadian Expeditionary Force.

Burns remained in the army after the war, and his career

advanced steadily. He studied at the School of Military Engineering at Chatham in 1920, served as an instructor at the Canadian Royal Military College (1924–1926), was assigned to the Geographic Section of the General Staff (1931–1936), and attended the Staff College at Quetta (1928–1929). He was promoted to brevet lieutenant colonel in 1935. Burns was a prolific writer, authoring numerous articles in the *Canadian Defence Quarterly* and H. L. Mencken's *American Mercury*.

When World War II began in Europe, Burns was studying at the Imperial Defence College. He was assigned from there to the General Staff under Brigadier General Henry Crerar at Canadian Military Headquarters, London. When Crerar was posted as chief of the Canadian General Staff, Burns accompanied him as special assistant and then became assistant deputy chief of the General Staff. He was posted as the brigadier general staff with the Canadian Corps in Britain in February 1941. Burns was then promoted to brigadier and took command of a brigade in the 4th Canadian Armoured Division. He then commanded the 2nd Canadian Infantry Division and the 5th Canadian Armoured Division, being promoted to major general in January 1944. He took command of the I Canadian Corps in Italy in March 1944.

Burns's first task was to pierce the Hitler Line across the Liri Valley. The May 1944 attack started out well. But casualties soon began to mount, and movement was hampered both by inexperience at lower levels of command and by traffic jams. Burns received the blame and was rated poorly by Lieutenant General Sir Oliver Leese, commanding the British Eighth Army. Burns's leadership style made his subordinates uncomfortable, including his dismissal of suggestions and use of sarcasm, as well as his preoccupation with trivial matters of troop dress and discipline.

In August and September 1944, the I Canadian Corps played a major role in breaking the Gothic Line, for which Burns received much praise. This success did not save him, however, and when the advance stalled in the mud, the old complaints resurfaced. Lieutenant General Charles Foulkes replaced him in November 1944.

Burns served the rest of the war commanding all Canadian rear-area units with 21st Army Group. After the war, he worked with the Department of Veterans Affairs until 1954, when he took command of the UN Truce Supervisory Organization operating along the Israeli-Arab borders. Burns was promoted to lieutenant general in 1958 and retired the following year. He died at Manotick, Ontario, on 13 September 1985.

Britton W. MacDonald

See also
Crerar, Henry Duncan Graham; Foulkes, Charles C. C.; Italy Campaign; Leese, Sir Oliver William Hargreaves

References
Burns, E. L. M. *General Mud: Memoirs of Two World Wars.* Toronto, Canada: Clarke, Irwin, 1970.
Granatstein, J. L. *The Generals: The Canadian Army's Senior Commanders in the Second World War.* Toronto, Canada: Stoddart, 1993.

Burress, Withers Alexander (1894–1977)

U.S. Army general, in command of VI Corps at the end of World War II. Born in Richmond, Virginia, on 24 November 1894, Withers Burress graduated from the Virginia Military Institute in 1914 and was commissioned in the infantry two years later. In World War I, he served in the 2nd Division in the American Expeditionary Forces. Burress graduated from the Command and General Staff School in 1931 and the Army War College in 1935. An excellent instructor, he served in that capacity at the Infantry School for two years from 1920 and again at the Command and General Staff School from 1931 to 1933. In 1935, he returned to the Virginia Military Institute as a Reserve Officers' Training Corps (ROTC) professor and subsequently commandant. He remained there until 1940, intensifying and improving the training of officer cadets in anticipation of war.

In 1940, Burress joined the G-3 (training) section of the General Staff, with special responsibility for raising and training troops as wartime pressures suddenly caused a huge expansion in the army. From October 1941 to early 1942, Colonel Burress was the assistant commandant of the Infantry School, Fort Benning, Georgia. He was promoted to brigadier general in March and assigned to the Puerto Rican District on its activation in August 1942. After rising to the rank of major general, he commanded and trained the 100th Infantry Division. That division landed at Marseille, France, in October 1944 and fought in the difficult Vosges Mountains Campaign (including the sustained winter siege and assault on the Maginot fortress of Bitche), winning a further spectacular victory at Heilbronn in early 1945 and pressing on to Stuttgart.

From September 1945 to 1946, Burress commanded VI Corps. Always the scholar, he had charge of the Infantry School at Fort Benning from 1948 to 1951; I Corps from 1951 to 1953; and the First Army from 1953 to 1954. He retired as a lieutenant general in 1954. Burress died in Arlington, Virginia, on 13 June 1977.

Priscilla Roberts

See also
United States, Army; Vosges, Advance to

References

Cline, Ray S. *United States Army in World War II: Washington Command Post—The Operations Division.* Washington, DC: U.S. Government Printing Office, 1951.

McDonald, Charles B. *U.S. Army in World War II: European Theater of Operations—The Last Offensive.* Washington, DC: U.S. Government Printing Office, 1973.

Watson, Mark Skinner. *United States Army in World War II: Chief of Staff—Prewar Plans and Preparations.* Washington, DC: U.S. Government Printing Office, 1950.

Busch, Ernst (1885–1945)

German army field marshal who commanded the Sixteenth Army in the invasion of the Soviet Union. Born in Essen-Steele in the Ruhr on 6 July 1885, Ernst Busch graduated from Gross-Lichterfelde Cadet Academy in 1904 and joined the Westphalian 13th Infantry Regiment. Commissioned a second lieutenant in the 57th Infantry Regiment in 1908, he was promoted to first lieutenant and assigned to the War Academy in 1913. Busch spent most of World War I on the Western Front as an infantry commander. Promoted to captain in 1915, he became a battalion commander in the 56th Infantry Regiment and fought in numerous battles, including Verdun. He was awarded the Pour le Mérite for exceptional valor.

Busch was retained in the German army after the war and held staff billets. He was promoted to major in 1925 and lieutenant colonel in 1930. After serving as a battalion commander in the 9th Infantry Regiment, he rose to colonel and assumed command of that regiment in 1932.

Busch became an enthusiastic follower of Adolf Hitler and Nazism. Promoted to Generalmajor (U.S. equiv. brigadier general), he took command of the 23rd Infantry Division in 1935; two years later, he was made a Generalleutnant (U.S. equiv. major general). Busch was rewarded for his unflagging support of Hitler during the 1938 Blomberg-Fritsch crisis by being promoted to General der Infanterie (U.S. equiv. lieutenant general) and given command of VIII Corps.

In the September 1939 invasion of Poland, Busch's VIII Corps formed the left flank of Army Group South, taking Kraków, advancing along the Vistula River, and ending the campaign at L'viv (Lvov). Given command of Sixteenth Army for the 1940 invasion of France and the Low Countries, Busch was assigned to cover the left flank of General of Panzer Troops Heinz Guderian's XIX Motorized Corps. In recognition of his service, he received promotion to Generaloberst (U.S. equiv. full general).

During Operation BARBAROSSA, the German army's invasion of the Soviet Union, Busch's Sixteenth Army covered the right flank of Army Group North on its drive to Leningrad. From 1942 to 1943, his army opposed numerous Soviet attacks and conducted the successful defense and relief of the Kholm and Demyansk pockets. Busch suffered no serious defeats, but after the initial push into the Soviet Union in 1941, he won no major victories.

Promoted to Feldmarschall (field marshal) in February 1943, Busch received command of Army Group Center in October. Eight months later, in Operation BAGRATION, the Soviets destroyed his army group. Relieved of his command on 28 June, Busch was retired but was brought back to command Army Group Northwest in March 1945 to oppose the Allied western advance into Germany. Busch died in British captivity at Aldershot, England, on 17 July 1945.

Dana Lombardy and T. P. Schweider

See also

BARBAROSSA, Operation; Belorussia Offensive; France Campaign; Leningrad, Siege of; Poland Campaign

References

Angolia, John R. *On the Field of Honor.* San Jose, CA: Bender, 1980.

Mitcham, Samuel W. *Crumbling Empire: The German Defeat in the East, 1944.* Westport, CT: Praeger, 2001.

Ziemke, Earl F. *Stalingrad to Berlin: The German Defeat in the East.* Washington, DC: U.S. Government Printing Office, 1966.

Bush, Vannevar (1890–1974)

U.S. scientist who was involved with the MANHATTAN project. Born on 11 March 1890, in Everett, Massachusetts, Vannevar Bush earned both bachelor's and master's degrees in engineering at Tufts College before completing a joint doctorate at the Massachusetts Institute of Technology (MIT) and Harvard University. By 1932, he was dean of engineering at MIT. During World War I, he designed a device utilizing magnetic fields to detect submarines. The navy deemed it worthless for combat, which affected Bush's attitudes regarding the relationship between science and government. He was interested in machinery that would automate thinking, and by 1931, he had built the first electronic analogue computer to solve, at great speed, complex differential equations.

In 1938, Bush was selected as president of the Carnegie Institution in Washington, D.C., his duties including advising the government on scientific research. He also was chairman of the National Advisory Committee for Aeronautics from 1939 to 1941. During World War II, he worked to establish relationships between scientists and government officials regarding research resources, especially those concerning defense work. He emphasized the importance of technological innovation and proficiency to national security.

In June 1940, Bush presented President Franklin D. Roosevelt his ideas about the coordination of military research as a partnership of scientific, industrial, business, and government groups. This approach led to the establishment of the National Defense Research Committee (NDRC), with Bush as its director, in June 1941. In addition, Bush secured congressional funding to create the Office of Scientific Research and Development (OSRD), which then oversaw the NDRC.

An adroit administrator, Bush became involved in significant technological developments, particularly in putting together a team for the MANHATTAN Project as well as improving radar and developing radio-guided bombs. He also recruited civilian scientists to work on military projects. His July 1945 report, "Science: The Endless Frontier," advised President Harry S Truman regarding governmental peacetime development of science and technology. The 1950 National Science Foundation incorporated many of Bush's ideas for postwar science and government cooperation for basic research and education.

In 1945, Bush's *Atlantic Monthly* essay, "As We May Think," discussed the hypothetical "memex," a machine capable of information storage and retrieval with associative linking. This automatic technology would enable humans to augment their memory technically. Computer engineers later stated that Bush's ideas influenced their digital development of hypertext and the Internet. Bush published extensively. He died at Belmont, Massacusetts, on 28 June 1974.

Elizabeth D. Schafer

See also
Engineer Operations; MANHATTAN Project; Radar; Roosevelt, Franklin D.; Truman, Harry S; United States, Home Front

References
Bush, Vannevar. *Modern Arms and Free Men: A Discussion of the Role of Science in Preserving Democracy.* New York: Simon and Schuster, 1949.
———. *Pieces of the Action.* New York: William Morrow, 1970.
Kevles, Daniel K. *The Physicists: The History of a Scientific Community in Modern America.* Cambridge, MA: Harvard University Press, 1995.
Zachary, G. Pascal. *Endless Frontier: Vannevar Bush, Engineer of the American Century.* Cambridge, MA: MIT Press, 1999.

Byrnes, James Francis (1879–1972)

U.S. politician, wartime "assistant president" to Franklin D. Roosevelt, and secretary of state from 1945 to 1947. Born on 2 May 1879, in Charleston, South Carolina, the son of Irish immigrants, James Byrnes studied for the law. After qualifying as a lawyer, he won election to Congress in 1910, and in 1930, he became a senator for North Carolina. A longtime friend of President Roosevelt, Byrnes used his considerable negotiating talents to steer New Deal legislation through Congress from 1933 onward. In 1941, Roosevelt appointed him to the Supreme Court.

Sixteen months later, in 1942, Byrnes left the bench to head the new Office of Economic Stabilization. The following year, he became director of the Office of War Mobilization (from 1944, the Office of War Mobilization and Reconversion). In domestic policy, Byrnes, often called the "assistant president," exercised powers second only to those of Roosevelt himself. Responsible for coordinating all domestic war agencies and federal government departments, he worked closely with both Congress and the bureaucracy to devise the most efficient arrangements to implement the war effort.

Passed over as Roosevelt's vice presidential running mate in 1944, Byrnes, already considered a hard-liner on the Soviet Union, attended the February 1945 Yalta Conference of the "Big Three" Allied leaders. Returning to Washington, he successfully lobbied Congress to support the outcome of Yalta, deliberately glossing over outstanding contentious issues dividing the Soviet Union and its allies. Still disappointed over the 1944 election, he resigned in March 1945.

On Roosevelt's death one month later, Vice President Harry S Truman became president. Truman immediately appointed Byrnes as head of a top-secret committee on the employment of atomic weapons, then in their final stage of development, whose existence Byrnes recommended be kept secret even from U.S. allies until their first use in combat. He believed U.S. possession of the bomb would make Soviet behavior more malleable.

In June 1945, Truman made him secretary of state. Attending the July 1945 Potsdam Conference, Byrnes hoped the speedy employment of atomic weapons against Japan would prevent the Soviet Union from entering the Pacific war and enhancing its influence in Asia. He also helped to reach a compromise agreement on German reparations. Returning to Washington, he took part in drafting the Japanese surrender agreement in August, implicitly agreeing to retain the emperor. As Soviet-U.S. relations became more strained after the war, Byrnes sought for several months to negotiate compromise solutions, traveling extensively to meet with other foreign ministers outside the United States. In early 1946, political complaints that he was too conciliatory led Byrnes to assume a harsher rhetorical stance toward the Soviet Union. Even so, at the end of the year, Truman—increasingly irked by Byrnes's policies, his secretive diplomacy, and his condescending attitude—made George C. Marshall secretary in his stead.

Byrnes returned to South Carolina and wrote his memoirs. In 1948, he broke with Truman over the issue of civil rights; subsequently, he served two terms, from 1951 to 1955, as governor of South Carolina, defending segregationist policies. Byrnes died in Columbia, South Carolina, on 9 April 1972.

Priscilla Roberts

See also

Atomic Bomb, Decision to Employ; Marshall, George Catlett; Potsdam Conference; Roosevelt, Franklin D.; Truman, Harry S; Yalta Conference

References

Byrnes, James F. *Speaking Frankly.* New York: Harper, 1947.

———. *All in One Lifetime.* New York: Harper, 1958.

Messer, Robert F. *The End of an Alliance: James F. Byrnes, Roosevelt, Truman, and the Origins of the Cold War.* Chapel Hill: University of North Carolina Press, 1982.

Morgan, Curtis F. *James F. Byrnes, Lucius Clay, and American Policy in Germany, 1945–1947.* Lewiston, NY: Edwin Mellen Press, 2002.

Robertson, David. *Sly and Able: A Political Biography of James F. Byrnes.* New York: Norton, 1994.

Walker, Richard, and George Curry. *The American Secretaries of State and Their Diplomacy.* Vol. 14, *E. R. Stettinius, Jr., and James F. Byrnes.* New York: Cooper Square, 1965.

C

Cairo Conference (23–26 November and 3–7 December 1943)

Code-named SEXTANT, this two-part conference was held in Cairo, Egypt, to discuss military strategy; the primary participants were U.S. President Franklin D. Roosevelt and British Prime Minister Winston L. S. Churchill. The meetings in Cairo took place before and after a conference bringing together Roosevelt, Churchill, and Soviet leader Josef Stalin at Tehran. The Tehran Conference (code-named EUREKA) proved necessary after Stalin refused to attend SEXTANT because a Chinese delegation, headed by Jiang Jieshi (Chiang Kai-shek), was to participate; since the Soviet Union was not then at war with Japan, Stalin did not want to attend or allow any other Soviet representative to take part in SEXTANT. Churchill had had doubts about a meeting with Jiang, too, for he regarded China as a sideshow until the war in Europe was won, but Roosevelt hoped to see China as a fourth great power after the war. In addition to large U.S., British, and Chinese delegations, Lord Louis Mountbatten, supreme commander of the Allied Southeast Asia Command, attended SEXTANT with his own delegation.

Roosevelt traveled across the Atlantic on the battleship *Iowa* and met with General Dwight D. Eisenhower in Algeria before flying on to Cairo, where he met with Jiang. At the Cairo Conference, Roosevelt, Churchill, and Jiang restated their determination to fight on until the war was won. Jiang pressed for an amphibious operation in the Bay of Bengal to coincide with Chinese participation in the fighting in Burma. Roosevelt initially agreed to this plan but was forced to withdraw his pledge following discussions at Tehran.

The Allied leaders announced in the Cairo Declaration that after the war, Japan would be reduced to the territories it held before World War I. China would regain Manchuria, the Pescadores Islands, and Formosa, and Korea would, "in due course," be restored to independence. In the meantime,

a joint U.S., Chinese, and Soviet trusteeship would hold sway in Korea, an arrangement that might last for 40 years. The mandated Japanese islands would, in all probability, pass to U.S. control, and it was implied that the USSR would regain South Sakhalin Island (lost in the Russo-Japanese War) and secure the Kuriles (which had never been Soviet territory). Stalin also wanted a warm-water port for the Soviet Union, probably at Dairen, Manchuria.

The second part of SEXTANT, which followed the Tehran Conference, included discussions with President Ismet Inönü of Turkey in an effort to draw his country into the war on the Allied side. In addition, Roosevelt informed Churchill of his decision to appoint General Eisenhower to command the Normandy Invasion.

Spencer C. Tucker

See also
Burma Theater; China, Role in War; Churchill, Sir Winston L. S.; Eisenhower, Dwight D.; Jiang Jieshi; Mountbatten, Louis Francis Albert Victor Nicholas; OVERLORD, Operation; Roosevelt, Franklin D.; Tehran Conference; Turkey

References
Larrabee, Eric. *Commander in Chief: Franklin Delano Roosevelt, His Lieutenants & Their War.* New York: Harper and Row, 1987.
Sainsbury, Keith. THE TURNING POINT: ROOSEVELT, STALIN, CHURCHILL, AND CHIANG KAI-SHEK, 1943: THE MOSCOW, CAIRO, AND TEHERAN CONFERENCES. Oxford: Oxford University Press, 1985.
Snell, John L. *Illusion and Necessity: The Diplomacy of Global War, 1939–1945.* Boston: Houghton Mifflin, 1963.

Calabria, Battle of (9 July 1940)

Mediterranean air and naval battle fought between the British and Italians off the Calabrian coast of Italy; the Italians and Germans know it as the Battle of Punta Stilo.

Beginning on the evening of 6 July 1940, the Italians dispatched a large convoy from Naples to Benghazi. At the same time, the British commander in the Mediterranean, Vice Admiral Andrew B. Cunningham, sent two small convoys with numerous civilians on board from Malta to Alexandria. On 7 July, the Italians learned of the British ship movements and immediately sent naval units from several bases to sea. Vice Admiral Inigo Campioni had command, concentrating the ships in the Ionian Sea. Campioni had the modernized but small battleships *Cesare* and *Cavour,* with 12.6-inch guns; 6 heavy and 10 light cruisers; and 41 destroyers and torpedo boats. Also at sea but scattered throughout the Mediterranean were 25 Italian submarines.

Cunningham planned to cover the convoys with his naval force at Alexandria, consisting of the battleships *Warspite, Malaya,* and the unmodernized *Royal Sovereign,* all armed with 15-inch guns; the aircraft carrier *Eagle;* 5 light cruisers; and 23 destroyers. Vice Admiral Sir James Somerville sortied from Gibraltar with Force H as a feint, which resulted in the loss of a destroyer to an Italian submarine and some minor splinter damage from high-altitude bombing.

Following the safe arrival of the Italian convoy at Benghazi, Campioni decided to try to intercept the British convoy and its escorts steaming from Alexandria. He hoped that by the time of the naval encounter, the Italian air force would have been able to damage the British ships as they approached the Italian coast. Indeed, more than 100 Italian aircraft conducted attacks on the British vessels, but the high-level bombing did little damage: all but one bomb missed. The bomb that hit its target damaged the light cruiser *Gloucester,* and a near miss damaged the *Eagle* sufficiently to keep her from participating in the subsequent air attack on Taranto. The Italians planes also carried out several attacks in error on their own warships, again with no result.

Meanwhile, Cunningham was maneuvering to position his own ships so as to block the Italian ships from returning to Taranto. The *Eagle* launched several air attacks. Although not hitting any Italian ships, these attacks disrupted their movement, and British fighters did shoot down and chase off Italian reconnaissance aircraft. As a consequence, by the morning of 9 July, the Italians were not cognizant of the exact location of the British ships, whereas the British had fairly reliable information on the location of the Italian vessels.

The battle opened on the afternoon of 9 July as the two fleets at last came into contact, and it lasted nearly two hours. The fight was initially a long-range cruiser gunnery duel, resulting in no damage to either side, although the British salvo spreads tended to be much tighter than those of the Italians.

As the Italian battleships came into action, they were opposed by Cunningham's flagship, the *Warspite,* the fastest of the three British battleships. In the ensuing action, three British 6-inch-shell hits on the Italian heavy cruiser *Bolzano* and one 15-inch-shell hit on the *Cesare* slowed both and compelled the Italian main force to retire. The fact that three British battleships had outgunned the entire Italian fleet deeply affected Italian tactics.

As the Italian main force pulled back, both sides ordered their destroyers forward. At long range, the Italians fired torpedoes through their smoke screens but registered no hits. The ships in the Italian fleet then retired to their home ports. The Germans later criticized the Italians for not having launched night torpedo attacks with their numerous destroyers.

On 10 July, the *Eagle* mounted an air strike on Augusta, Italy. An Italian destroyer was sunk but was later raised and repaired, and an oiler was damaged. Meanwhile, the British Malta convoys arrived safely at Alexandria.

The Battle of Calabria raised British morale, for the Royal Navy had successfully engaged a numerically superior enemy force close to its own coast. The Italians' failure could be traced to poor coordination between their air and naval assets, although this situation steadily improved in the course of the war. The Italians also came to realize the ineffectiveness of high-altitude bombing against warships maneuvering at high speed and firing back. The Battle of Calabria demonstrated the fallacy of the decision made by Italian dictator Benito Mussolini and his navy to completely embrace land-based aviation at the expense of aircraft carriers. Thereafter, Italian naval leaders were reluctant to commit major naval units beyond the range of their land-based aircraft.

Jack Greene

See also
Campioni, Inigo; Cunningham, Sir Andrew Browne; Mussolini, Benito; Somerville, Sir James Fownes; Taranto, Attack on

References
Greene, Jack, and Alessandro Massignani. *The Naval War in the Mediterranean, 1940–1943.* London: Chatham Publishing, 1998.
Mattesini, Francesco. *La Battaglia di Punta Stilo.* Rome: Ufficio Storico Della Marina, 1990.
Sadkovich, James J. *The Italian Navy in World War II.* Westport, CT: Greenwood Press, 1994.
Smith, Peter C. *Action Imminent.* London: William Kimber, 1980.

Callaghan, Daniel Judson (1890–1942)

U.S. Navy admiral and task force commander in the Pacific Theater. Born on 26 July 1890 in San Francisco, Daniel Callaghan graduated from the U.S. Naval Academy in 1911.

He served chiefly on destroyers, commanding one in 1916 before becoming the engineering officer of a cruiser during the last two years of World War I.

Following that war, Callaghan served on battleships and cruisers as a gunnery and operations officer. Known as an excellent staff officer, he became naval aide to President Franklin D. Roosevelt in July 1938, a post he feared would hamper his chances of becoming an admiral. Callaghan returned to sea duty in the spring of 1941 as the captain of the cruiser *San Francisco,* which was at Pearl Harbor on 7 December 1941 but suffered no damage in the Japanese attack.

In the spring of 1942, Callaghan became chief of staff to the commander of the Southwest Pacific Command, Admiral Robert Ghormley. He helped plan the U.S. landings on Guadalcanal and led the task force providing fire support for that operation in August 1942. He fought with distinction in the Battle of Cape Esperance on 12 October and was promoted to rear admiral. When Admiral William F. Halsey replaced Ghormley on 18 October, Callaghan received command of Task Force 67.4, composed of cruisers and destroyers.

In early November, Callaghan's two cruisers and eight destroyers escorted a U.S. reinforcement convoy to Guadalcanal. When the transports departed to return to Noumea on 12 November, Halsey ordered Callaghan, whose force was now joined by an antiaircraft cruiser and two destroyers under Rear Admiral Norman Scott, to intercept a much more powerful Japanese bombardment force under Vice Admiral Abe Hiroaki, which was also acting as cover for Japanese transports carrying a large troop reinforcement for Guadalcanal. Scott was junior to Callaghan, and the latter assumed command.

Just after midnight on 13 November, Callaghan's ships intercepted Abe's force of 2 battleships, 1 light cruiser, and 14 destroyers off Lunga Point, Guadalcanal, on its way to shell Henderson Field. In a hard-fought, 24-minute action, the Americans sank 2 Japanese destroyers and crippled the battleship *Hiei* (which was later sunk by carrier aircraft), while losing 2 cruisers and 4 destroyers of their own. Abe's task force and that carrying 13,000 Japanese reinforcements to Guadalcanal, which it was designed to mask, both turned back.

Callaghan, dubbed "the Fighting Admiral," was killed by a shell that struck the bridge of the cruiser *San Francisco* during the action. He was awarded the Medal of Honor posthumously.

Harold Wise

See also
Abe Hiroaki; Cape Esperance, Battle of; Ghormley, Robert Lee; Guadalcanal Naval Campaign; Halsey, William Frederick, Jr.; Roosevelt, Franklin D.; Solomon Islands, Naval Campaign

References
Frank, Richard B. *Guadalcanal.* New York: Random House, 1990.
Grace, James W. *The Naval Battle of Guadalcanal: Night Action, 13 November 1942.* Annapolis, MD: Naval Institute Press, 1999.
Hammel, Eric. *Guadalcanal, Decision at Sea: The Naval Battle of Guadalcanal, November 13–15, 1942.* Pacifica, CA: Pacifica Press, 1988.
Morison, Samuel Eliot. *History of United States Naval Operations in World War II.* Vol. 5, *The Struggle for Guadalcanal, August 1942–February 1943.* Boston: Little, Brown, 1949.
Murphy, Francis. *Fighting Admiral: The Story of Dan Callaghan.* New York: Vantage Press, 1952.

Camm, Sir Sydney (1893–1966)

British aircraft designer who specialized in military planes. Born in Windsor, England, on 5 August 1893, Sydney Camm showed a keen interest in aviation at an early age. In 1912, he designed and flew a man-carrying glider. Shortly before the outbreak of World War I, he joined the Martinsyde Aircraft Company as a woodworker. He left Martinsyde in 1923 to be a senior draftsman with the Hawker Engineering Company, rising to chief designer within 2 years. He remained with Hawker for 43 years, where his work emphasized simplicity, symmetry, and lightness.

From 1925 onward, Camm concentrated on military design, working closely with the Royal Air Force (RAF) and producing the Rolls-Royce aircraft engines that were closely integrated into the aircraft. His first big success was the Hawker Hart day-bomber biplane and its variants, of which 3,000 were eventually built. In 1933, Camm moved over to monoplanes, and in 1934, he took on a British Air Ministry order for an eight-gun fighter named the Hurricane. The Royal Air Force's first monoplane fighter aircraft, the Hurricane was fast, maneuverable, and sturdy. A low-wing plane with retractable landing gear and an enclosed cockpit, it was built around the Rolls-Royce Merlin engine. The Hurricane carried eight .303 machine guns and reached a top speed of 315 mph at its first flight in late 1935.

During the Battle of Britain, the Hurricane made up the bulk of Fighter Command's aircraft and bore the brunt of the Luftwaffe onslaught. Though outclassed by the Bf-109, the Hurricane could, in the right hands, hold its own against the German fighter. Later versions were used successfully as fighter-bombers in North Africa. By August 1940, over 2,000 Hurricanes had been delivered to the RAF and were serving in 32 squadrons. During the war, a total of 14,500 Hurricanes were produced, many of which went to the Soviet Union. Camm designed two more fighters for the RAF during World War II, the Typhoon and the Tempest. Both were successful ground-attack aircraft.

Following the war, Camm began designing jet aircraft, including the Hunter and the first operational vertical take-off and landing (VTOL) aircraft, the Harrier. He continued to serve on the board of Hawker Siddeley Aviation until his death in Surrey, England, on 12 March 1966.

M. R. Pierce and Priscilla Roberts

See also
Bader, Sir Douglas Robert Steuart; Britain, Battle of; Dowding, Sir Hugh Caswall Tremenheere; Messerschmitt, Wilhelm "Will" Emil

References
Bader, Douglas. *Fight for the Sky.* Garden City, NY: Doubleday, 1973.
Fozard, John W., ed. *Sydney Camm and the Hurricane: Perspectives on the Master Fighter Designer and His Finest Achievement.* Washington, DC: Smithsonian Institution Press, 1991.
Gallico, Paul. *The Hurricane Story.* Garden City, NY: Doubleday, 1959.
Richards, Denis, and Hilary St. G. Saunders. *The Royal Air Force, 1939–45.* 3 vols. London: Her Majesty's Stationery Office, 1975.

Camouflage

The disguising of military personnel, equipment, or installations. With technical advances in long-range aviation and aerial photography, as well as optical sights for weapons systems, camouflage became a regular feature of World War II. It was applied to individual soldiers, to their equipment (such as tanks and warships), and to industrial facilities and airfields.

Camouflage, also called protective concealment, attempts to disguise an object that is in plain sight in order to hide it from something or someone. If an object cannot be concealed—often something large, such as an airfield or a warship—camouflage may succeed merely by preventing an enemy from identifying the object. Camouflaging is normally accomplished by applying disruptive or blending paint or material to the object.

Modern camouflage techniques can be traced back to the French Army's Camouflage Division, established in 1915, when the army gave artists the responsibility for concealing airfields. The term *camouflage* comes from the French word *camoufler,* meaning "to blind or veil."

During World War II, aircraft were often camouflaged, in direct contrast with the practice in World War I, attributed particularly to Germany, of painting some aircraft in bright colors in order to intimidate opposing aviators. World War II aircraft tended to be painted in graduated color schemes, with darker shades on top growing progressively lighter toward the plane's undersection.

This technique served two purposes. The indistinct boundary between colors aided in obscuring the aircraft's silhouette and shape, leaving an opposing pilot unsure if a superior type of plane was about to be engaged. This scheme also allowed for a degree of camouflage both while the plane was in the air and when it was on the ground, particularly when a lightly painted aircraft belly was viewed against a light sky or when the green aspect of the same airplane parked on a grass field was seen from above.

Airfields themselves were camouflaged to avoid enemy air strikes. An advanced airfield, for example, might be obscured by having camouflage netting extend a wheat field onto one of the runways and having another runway appear as a football field delineated by steel-wool "ditches." Troops might even play sports on the airfield to help deceive enemy reconnaissance.

Although the aim was to avoid detection, obscuring clear identification often might suffice. For instance, the multiangular paint scheme in varying shades of gray that was applied to many naval vessels during the war served to confuse an enemy's determination of the vessels' speed and bearing, rather than to render them invisible. By diminishing torpedo or gunfire accuracy, a ship had a greater chance to avoid being hit.

Army vehicles, routinely painted green, brown, or gray to blend in with fields or urban areas, often had their camouflage augmented by their crews. Camouflage netting was used to break up the distinctive outlines of many vehicles, such that a parked tank might appear like a small tree. Netting, however, worked best with stationary vehicles, artillery pieces, and logistics sites. If used on other equipment or when a vehicle was moving, nets interfered with movement and vision, and they got in the way of effective tank fire.

Deception planners went to great lengths to create mock airfields and ports, complete with phony ships, planes, tanks, and personnel. Camouflage was incorporated into these plans; for example, simulated equipment was camouflaged to make it appear more authentic. Occasionally, such camouflage would intentionally be poorly applied: if it was too effective, the enemy might not have seen the phony equipment at all, negating the deception effort. False sites drew many German air strikes during the 1940 Battle of Britain.

A form of electronic camouflage was required as radar and radio interception expertise advanced. This type of camouflage normally took the form of maintaining radio silence to avoid detection. However, in the absence of stealth technology, it was easier to deceive radars through electronic camouflage than to conceal the target. In 1944, for example, German radars were tricked into believing Calais was the target of Operation OVERLORD when small, towed barges with electronic emitters gave off the radar reflection of approaching 20,000-ton amphibious ships.

British Prime Minister Winston L. S. Churchill, always in-

Not one but two soldiers. The sniper on the left is wearing regular fatigues, and the one on the right is in full battle dress disguised as though he were part of the terrain, ca. 1942. (Library of Congress)

terested in military gadgetry, was a great supporter of camouflage efforts, though his efforts in this field met with varying degrees of success. For instance, attempts to deny the Germans navigation landmarks by concealing inland lakes with coal dust failed: the dust blew to the edges and outlined the lakes, making them even more prominent. Churchill also insisted that factories be concealed with smoke, a technique that depended largely on wind conditions and adversely affected the workers involved. The Germans also frequently used smoke in an effort to obscure the targets of Allied air raids.

As the war progressed, increasingly technical reconnaissance and surveillance efforts and subsequent countermeasures forced intelligence staffs to confirm reports through more than one information source in their attempts to defeat complex camouflage problems.

Robert B. Martyn

See also

Churchill, Sir Winston L. S.; Deception; Photographic
    Reconnaissance

References

Cruickshank, Charles. *Deception in World War II*. New York: Oxford
    University Press, 1979.

Hartcup, Guy. *Camouflage: A History of Concealment and Deception
    in War*. Boston: Houghton Mifflin, 1980.

Campioni, Inigo (1878–1944)

Italian admiral who was executed for treason under Italy's Fascist regime. Born in Viareggio, Italy, on 14 November 1878, Inigo Campioni attended the naval academy at Livorno (Leghorn), graduating in 1896. He fought in the 1911–1912 war with Turkey and served aboard a battleship during much of World War I. At the end of the latter conflict, he was a highly decorated destroyer commander.

In the interwar period, Campioni led naval design programs at the La Spezia weapons laboratory, served as naval attaché in Paris, and held various Naval Supreme Command staff posts. In 1936, he was promoted to full admiral, and two years later, he became vice chief of staff of the Italian navy. In 1939, he was elected to the Italian Senate.

Regarded as his country's most promising naval officer, Campioni was appointed to operational command of Italy's battle fleet at the beginning of World War II. He led the fleet in a number of engagements against the British in the Mediterranean, notably the Battles of Calabria (Punta Stilo) on 9 July 1940 and Cape Teulada (Spartivento) on 27 November 1940. In the latter engagement, Campioni failed to intercept two converging British convoys. His superior naval force was hampered by the British having broken the Italian naval codes, by poor Italian reconnaissance, and by the failure of Italian air cover to materialize for well over an hour after the start of the battle. Campioni was subjected to intense criticism for his lack of aggressiveness, especially on those rare occasions when his fleet outgunned the opponent. On 8 December 1940, he was relieved of operational command and made deputy chief of staff of the Naval Supreme Command.

In July 1941, Campioni was assigned to command Axis occupation forces in the Dodecanese Islands. After Italy's surrender to the Allies on 8 September 1943, he was contacted by the British and urged to resist German attempts to establish control over the Aegean region. Although Italian forces strenuously resisted the German takeover, they were compelled to surrender on 11 September 1943.

The Germans held Campioni prisoner at Schokken (Skoki) in Poland until January 1944, when he was turned over to Benito Mussolini's puppet Italian Social Republic in northern Italy and jailed in Verona. Tried at Parma for treason, Campioni was found guilty and executed there by Fascist authorities on 24 May 1944. In November 1947, the Italian government honored Campioni by posthumously awarding him the Gold Medal for Military Valor.

John P. Vanzo and Gordon E. Hogg

See also

Calabria, Battle of; Italy, Navy

References

Bragadin, Marc'Antonio. *The Italian Navy in World War II.* Menasha, WI: George Banta, 1957.

Dizionario biografico degli Italiani. Vol. 17. Rome: Istituto della Enciclopedia Italiana, 1974.

Greene, Jack, and Alessandro Massignari. *The Naval War in the Mediterranean, 1940–1943.* London: Chatham Publishing, 1998.

Rocca, Gianni. *Fucilate gli ammiragli: La tragedia della Marina Italina nella Seconda Guerra Mondiale.* Milan, Italy: Mondadori, 1990.

Canada, Air Force

Canada had virtually no air force before World War II, but it developed one quickly. When the war began in Europe in September 1939, the Canadian government agreed to help train Royal Air Force (RAF) pilots, leading to the development of the British Commonwealth Air Training Plan. Through it, some 130,000 pilots and aircrew from Canada, Britain, and other Allied nations were trained at Canadian airfields built or enlarged with British and, later, American assistance. The Royal Canadian Air Force (RCAF) itself grew to over 250,000 personnel.

Thousands of Canadian pilots and aircrew served in the RAF, often in fighter or bomber squadrons composed entirely of Canadians. Ultimately, the RCAF sent 48 squadrons and 94,000 personnel overseas. In the European Theater, RCAF squadrons fought in the Battle of Britain, in Malta, in the campaigns of the Western Desert, and over Europe. In the Pacific Theater, two Canadian transport squadrons served in Burma and a squadron of Consolidated PBY Catalina patrol bombers was based at Ceylon. The RCAF also provided air defense for Canada and assisted in the defense of U.S. installations in Alaska.

In June 1941, the RCAF formed its first bomber squadron. Its Number 6 Group of eight squadrons was formed in Britain in January 1943, flying Wellington bombers from Yorkshire and then Lancaster and Halifax bombers. The group flew 41,000 sorties and dropped 126,000 tons of bombs, one-eighth of Bomber Command's total. It suffered 3,500 dead. In all, 17,101 Canadian aircrew died in the war, some 40 percent of Canada's total war dead.

RCAF pilots also played an important role in ferrying American-built aircraft to the British Isles. Air Commodore N. R. Anderson of the RCAF had lobbied for the ferrying of aircraft in April 1940, arguing that it would save valuable shipping space. The idea languished until the British minister of war production, Lord Beaverbrook, gave it his support and insisted on an experimental flight. This flight took place in November 1940, when a group of Hudsons crossed the Atlantic from Newfoundland without loss. Regular transfers continued, slowly at first because of a shortage of pilots and navigators but gaining momentum when increasing numbers of graduates of the Air Training Plan became available. Ultimately, the RCAF delivered more than 9,000 two- and four-engine aircraft to Britain in this manner. Subsequently, the RCAF also supplied Lend-Lease aircraft to the Soviet Union from airfields in northwest Canada. Many of the routes developed in this activity became the first routes of Trans-Canada Airlines after the war.

Terry Shoptaugh

See also

Aircraft, Bombers; Aircraft, Fighters; Aircraft, Naval; Aircraft, Transport; Aitken, William Maxwell; Lend-Lease

References

English, Allan. *The Cream of the Crop: Canadian Air Crew, 1939–1945.* Montreal, Canada: McGill and Queen's University Press, 1996.

Wise, Sydney F. *The Creation of a National Air Force.* Toronto, Canada: University of Toronto Press, 1980.

Canada, Army

Surmounting serious difficulties, Canada raised a substantial army that earned distinction in heavy fighting during World War II. In July 1939, the Permanent Active Militia, as it was then styled, was a minuscule force of 4,261 soldiers. Reserves, most of them untrained, numbered 51,418. But by 1943, a prodigious effort produced six infantry divisions, two armored divisions, two armored brigades, two army artillery groups, an immense logistics organization, and the Canadian Women's Army Corps—a remarkable achievement for a nation of 11.5 million people.

Initially, the Liberal government of Prime Minister Mackenzie King pursued a strategy that emphasized industrial and agricultural production, air and naval forces, and a small expeditionary ground force of two divisions. This strategy reflected the fundamental antagonism between English and Scottish Protestant Canadians and French Roman Catholic Canadians, with the French minority constituting a quarter of the population. Efforts to impose conscription in 1917, during World War I, sparked serious rioting, proved unenforceable in French communities, and pushed Canada to the brink of civil war. Understandably, the Canadian government in World War II was unwilling to risk such a crisis again. The conflict was sharpened by English and Scottish domination of the armed forces and officer corps.

This limited strategy was shattered by the German conquest of France in June 1940. All Canadian resources were mobilized for total war by the sweeping National Resources Mobilization Act of 17 June 1940. But compulsory military service was restricted to service in Canada; overseas service remained voluntary. Three infantry divisions were stationed on the coasts of Canada. Many French Canadians were willing to defend Canada, but few were willing to fight for Great Britain. Four French Canadian infantry regiments did have sufficient volunteers for overseas service, however.

In July 1940, then Major General Henry Crerar assumed the post of chief of the General Staff. A capable administrator, he organized the framework within which a vastly expanded Canadian army swiftly emerged. By December 1940, two Canadian infantry divisions formed the Canadian Corps in England. In June 1943, the Canadian army in England numbered three infantry divisions, two armored divisions, and two armored brigades.

The Canadian army was organized on the British model, and much of its equipment was also British. Rugged and accurate, the 7.7 mm Lee Enfield No. 4 was the standard bolt-action rifle. Adapted by Enfield from a Czech design, the low-recoil and very accurate Bren 7.7 mm light machine gun proved effective. By 1942, 60 percent of all Bren guns were manufactured in Canada. The 87.6 mm howitzer—rugged, easily handled, and versatile—and the 140 mm gun, introduced in 1942, were the major artillery weapons. The Canadians did employ the U.S. M-4 Sherman as their tank.

The Canadian army had to contend with serious difficulties. Undermanning was a constant problem, with Canadian units rarely at their established strength, a consequence of the voluntary system. Training suffered from the rapid pace of expansion and the lack of experience among senior officers. In addition, training in unit-level maneuvers was poor, and the army was slow to develop a common system of tactics.

An early tragedy of the war involved the Canadian garrison in Hong Kong. Caught up in the sweep of the opening Japanese offensive, 1,975 soldiers waged a forlorn defense in December 1941, suffering 800 casualties and the death of their commander. The Canadians also sustained heavy losses in the 19 August 1942 raid on the French seaport of Dieppe. A total of 4,963 Canadians from the 2nd Division took part and encountered well-planned German defenses. Only 2,110 of these men returned to England; 65 percent of the Canadian troops were killed or wounded and/or taken as prisoners.

On 10 July 1943, 1st Canadian Infantry Division and 1st Army Tank Brigade were committed to the invasion of Sicily, operating as part of the British Eighth Army. On 3 September, the Canadians crossed the Straits of Messina to Italy and fought their way up the Adriatic coast. In November, they were joined by the 5th Armoured Division and formed the I Canadian Corps. Initially, the corps was led by General Crerar, but he returned to England and assumed command of First Army in March 1944. The Canadian First Army fought within the framework of 21st Army Group, commanded by Field Marshal Bernard L. Montgomery. The able Lieutenant General E. L. M. Burns then took command of Canadian forces in Italy.

In the heavy and often frustrating fighting of the Italian Campaign, the Canadians acquitted themselves well. In May 1944, Canadian forces in the Liri Valley participated in the Allied offensive that broke through the Gustav Line. In

A Canadian soldier receives attention from a medical orderly next to a burning overturned German tank amid heavy rubble, while Allied forces attempt to trap the German Seventh Army in nearby Falaise, France. (Library of Congress)

August 1944, a Canadian thrust near the Adriatic created an opportunity to move into the Po River valley, but the British moved too slowly, and the chance was lost.

In the Normandy Invasion of 6 June 1944, the Canadian 3rd Infantry Division and 2nd Armoured Brigade landed on Juno beach as part of the British Second Army. Joined by the 2nd Infantry and 4th Armoured Division, they formed the Canadian II Corps on 11 July, commanded by Lieutenant General Guy Simonds. He had led both infantry and armored divisions in Italy. On 23 July 1944, the Canadian First Army was activated, led by General Crerar. It also included British I Corps and the Free Polish 1st Armored Division.

The Battle for Normandy was a crucible of fire for the Canadians. They and the British were deployed in the eastern sector of the beachhead, terrain reasonably favorable for German armored operations. To thwart offensives in this area, most German armor fought the British and Canadians. Canadian forces proved well trained and skilled in combat and played a key role in the defeat of a formidable German opponent. In Lieutenant General Guy Simonds, the Canadian army found an outstanding leader who showed himself to be an innovative and exacting commander. Crerar and Simonds were good partners, with Crerar the manager and Simonds the battlefield leader.

After Normandy, First Army proceeded along the French coast taking seaports. On 4 September 1944, the British 11th Armoured Division captured the vital port of Antwerp, with the Belgian Resistance saving all its port facilities and docks from German destruction. However, Antwerp could only be reached by the 45-mile-long Scheldt estuary, and swift action was imperative to prevent German deployment of defenses along the Scheldt. At this critical juncture, British

Field Marshal Montgomery halted his forces, preferring to concentrate his troops for a thrust into northern Germany, Operation MARKET-GARDEN. This decision gave the Germans time to establish strong defenses along the Scheldt and at its mouth.

After the British defeat at Arnhem in late September, the strategic focus returned to ousting German forces from the Scheldt and opening Antwerp. This daunting task fell heavily on the Canadian First Army. On 26 September, Crerar had departed to England for treatment of complications from dysentery, and Simonds assumed his command.

The Scheldt Campaign was a nightmare, fought on sodden mud flatlands bereft of cover and intersected by canals and dikes ideally suited for defense. Montgomery assigned the Canadians the lowest priority for supplies, and only a direct and explicit order on 9 October from General Dwight D. Eisenhower to clear the Scheldt compelled Montgomery to furnish the Canadians (including their British corps) the supplies they needed. Throughout October, bitter fighting raged as Canadian and British soldiers slowly overcame tenacious German resistance. Amphibious tanks and tracked amphibious landing vehicles proved useful. Equipped for amphibious operations, the 52nd Lowland Scottish Division joined the Canadians in this battle.

The assault on Walcheren Island was the climax of the campaign. Commanding the mouth of the Scheldt estuary, Walcheren's defenses included heavy coastal artillery. Royal Marines and Commandos joined Scots and Canadians to capture Walcheren on 9 November. Minesweepers cleared the channel, and Antwerp was finally opened on 28 November 1944. The Scheldt Campaign cost the Allies 12,873 casualties, half of them Canadian.

In December, a shortage of infantry replacements compelled the Canadian government to extend conscription for overseas service to troops already in home service. This move aroused a furor, but only 16,000 of 63,000 eligible soldiers were sent overseas. When Crerar returned to lead First Army, he was entrusted with an Allied force of 475,000 men dedicated to winning control of the Rhineland. In a series of massive operations in February and March 1945, Crerar demonstrated his skill in logistics. German forces were eliminated between the Maas and Rhine Rivers, a loss of more than 90,000 men. In the closing months of the war, I Canadian Corps was transferred from Italy to the Netherlands and completed the liberation of the latter.

The Canadian army made a substantial contribution to the Allied victory. The men of this overwhelmingly volunteer force had fought with courage and tenacity in many hard battles. But they also paid a heavy price, for 22,917 Canadians were killed and 52,679 wounded.

Sherwood S. Cordier

See also

Canada, Role in the War; Crerar, Henry Duncan Graham; Dieppe Raid; Eisenhower, Dwight D.; Hong Kong, Battle of; Italy Campaign; King, William Lyon Mackenzie; MARKET-GARDEN, Operation; Montgomery, Sir Bernard Law; Normandy Invasion and Campaign; Rhineland Offensive; Scheldt, Battles; Sicily, Invasion of; Simonds, Guy Granville

References

Copp, Terry. *Fields of Fire: The Canadians in Normandy.* Toronto, Canada: University of Toronto Press, 2003.

Copp, Terry, and Robert Vogel. *Maple Leaf Route.* Vol. 1, *Falaise.* Alma, Canada: Maple Leaf Route, 1983.

————. *Maple Leaf Route.* Vol. 4, *Scheldt.* Alma, Canada: Maple Leaf Route, 1985.

Murray, Williamson, and Allan R. Millett. *A War to Be Won: Fighting the Second World War.* Cambridge, MA: Belknap Press, 2000.

Nicholson, G. W. L. *The Canadians in Italy, 1943–1945.* Ottawa: Department of National Defence, 1957.

Stacy, C. P. *Arms, Men and Governments: The War Policies of Canada.* Ottawa: Department of National Defence, 1970.

Canada, Navy

At the outbreak of World War II, the Royal Canadian Navy (RCN) had only 6 destroyers and 5 minesweepers. By 1945, it had grown to include 2 light carriers, 2 light cruisers, 15 destroyers, 60 frigates, 118 corvettes, and many other ships. The third-largest Allied fleet, the Canadian navy mustered a total of 363 vessels, most of which were built in Canadian shipyards. From 3,165 men in 1939, the RCN expanded to 89,000 men and 6,700 women by 1945.

In the gale-swept seas of the North Atlantic, the Canadian fleet played a crucial role in the long struggle against German submarines. Having expanded so rapidly, the RCN suffered from poor training and a dearth of advanced equipment. Early in 1943, Canadian corvettes and frigates were sent to English bases, where they were fitted with new radar, sonar, and high-frequency direction-finding detection gear. In addition, the crews underwent intensive training in anti-submarine tactics and warfare. Of particular value was the Western Approaches Tactical Unit established in Liverpool in February 1942, which trained escort captains and commanders in a common doctrine of convoy defense. Practical training was provided by exercises against Royal Navy submarines. As a result, by mid-1943, the Canadians fought much more effectively in the Atlantic arena.

They organized the massive convoys that set out from Nova Scotia and Newfoundland. As radio interception and the breaking of German codes assumed major roles in the war against the submarines, the RCN Operational Intelligence Centre proved a key Canadian capability. And by 1944, most close escort in the North Atlantic was performed by the Canadian fleet. In all, the RCN provided eight mid-Atlantic support groups and escorted more than 25,000 merchant ships laden with 180 million tons of cargo from North America to Great Britain.

Built to a British design stressing mass production, the Flower-class corvette was the mainstay of the escort fleet. Displacing 1,245 tons at full load, the vessel was armed with a 4-inch gun and 40 (later 70) depth charges. The Flower-class ships proved to be miserable seaboats, however, taking on water and rolling furiously, and at 16.5 knots, they were too slow for offensive operations.

A far more effective escort was the River-class frigate, weighing 1,920 tons at full load. The River-class vessel could make 21 knots and mounted two 4-inch guns, a Hedgehog mortar, and 126 (later 150) depth charges.

The Canadian navy was also active in surface warfare operations. The RCN secured four large British Tribal-class destroyers that proved especially effective in Canadian service. At full load, the Tribals weighed 2,519 tons and easily made 36 knots. Formidably armed in terms of guns, they mounted 6 × 4.7-inch cannon, 2 × 4-inch dual-purpose guns, and 4 × 40-mm antiaircraft weapons. Four torpedo tubes were also fitted. Canadian Tribals saw heavy action, especially in spring 1944 in the English Channel against German destroyers and heavy torpedo boats (900-plus tons). In the course of these battles, the *Athabaskan* was lost on 29 April 1944.

The RCN played a considerable part in the Normandy Invasion. Ten thousand sailors and 109 warships participated in Operation NEPTUNE and landed 45,000 troops on the beaches. The Canadian array included 15 destroyers, 11 frigates, 19 corvettes, 16 minesweepers, and 30 landing craft.

In the course of the war, 2,024 men of the RCN were killed and 24 ships were sunk. At the same time, however, the Canadian navy played an important role in the Allied victory by destroying or capturing 42 surface warships and helping to sink 33 submarines.

Sherwood S. Cordier

See also

Antisubmarine Warfare; Atlantic, Battle of the; Canada, Role in the War; Normandy Invasion and Campaign

References

German, Tony. *The Sea Is at Our Gates: The History of the Canadian Navy.* Toronto, Canada: McClelland and Stewart, 1990.

Milner, Marc. *The North Atlantic Run: The Royal Canadian Navy and the Battle for the Convoys.* Annapolis, MD: Naval Institute Press, 1985.

Worth, Richard. *Fleets of World War II.* Cambridge, MA: Da Capo Press, 2001, pp. 109–112 and 125–126.

Canada, Role in the War

Arguably the greatest contributor, militarily and economically, of the "small" Allied powers in World War II, Canada put 10 percent of its population—slightly over 1 million men and women—into uniform and provided the fourth-largest output of war matériel.

Canada entered the war superficially united, but French Canadian support was lukewarm, and the specter of overseas conscription, which had been so divisive in World War I, loomed. Since Canada's military contribution could not be decisive, conscription remained a political issue, and its potential for wrecking national unity could not be overestimated.

Prewar isolationism had left Canada virtually disarmed, but when Canadian leaders declared war a week after Britain had (a pointed display of their country's status as a completely self-governing dominion), they were confident that a military effort on the scale of World War I would be unnecessary. This time, Ottawa promised to match commitments to resources and make the economic sinews of war, not expeditionary forces, its priority. Predictably, this "limited liabilities" policy did not survive the defeat of France. Thereafter, for Canada, it would be total war.

On the economic front, after some faltering steps, the results were magnificent. Underutilized capacity, the country's bane during the depression, aided the government in its task of mobilizing the war economy. Coming up with the staggering sums to pay for it all proved an equal challenge. American neutrality—and Britain's precarious economic and financial position—greatly complicated Ottawa's task, a situation finally resolved by the Hyde Park agreement signed with the United States in April 1941. By 1944, the gross national product (GNP) had more than doubled, with 50 percent of that figure being war production. Although foodstuffs and vital raw materials such as nickel and aluminum dominated Canada's wartime exports to the United States and Britain, the production of armaments—including close to 1 million motor vehicles—was also very significant. Sound management and the advantages of virtual economic integration with the United States ensured that Canada, alone among the Allies, avoided having to seek Lend-Lease assistance; it even launched its own generous Mutual Assistance Program, with Britain the chief beneficiary.

Given these very significant contributions to the common cause, Canadian officials aspired to play a role in Allied decision making. Canada more than earned its appointment to the Combined Food and Production and Resources Boards in 1943, but when it came to grand military strategy, vague hopes of "sitting at the table" went unfulfilled. Gracefully, if somewhat reluctantly, Ottawa accepted its status as a junior partner.

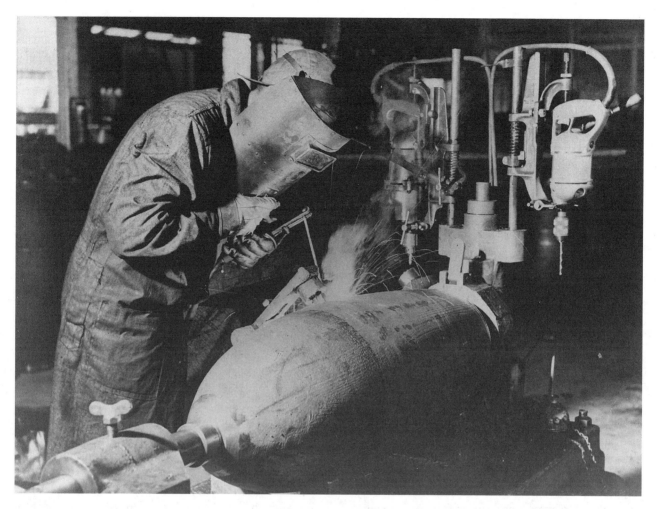

Production of 500-pound bombs in Canada. (Library of Congress)

From the outset, Prime Minister Mackenzie King's focus had been to help Britain, an approach the great majority of Canadians embraced. Doing so necessitated close cooperation—especially economic cooperation—with the United States. The presumption that Canada could serve as a linchpin between Washington and London was a Canadian conceit, although certainly, a neutral United States could materially assist Britain by helping Canada. Once the United States entered the war, however, direct engagement with the British rendered Canada's erstwhile diplomatic role superfluous. For reasons of mutual benefit, Canadian-American ties deepened steadily. As leading Canadian historian J. L. Granatstein has aptly concluded, "Britain's weakness forced Canada into the arms of the United States," but it generally went willingly and certainly profitably. With a war to win, few Canadians worried about the long-term implications of this shift in regard to their sovereignty.

In military terms, Canada boasted the fourth-largest air force and third-largest navy among the Allies by 1945, as well as an expeditionary force of nearly six divisions. In keeping with the country's "Atlanticist" orientation, Ottawa committed virtually the entire force to Europe. It is scarcely an exaggeration to say the Pacific war, save for some panic after Pearl Harbor, hardly touched the Canadian consciousness.

Nationalism dictated that the government follow a "Canadianization" policy whereby the armed forces would, as far as possible, fight in recognizable national units under national command. At the same time, the English Canadian majority's undiminished emotional attachment to Britain, not to mention practical considerations, guaranteed that these forces would operate under overall British command and fight in British campaigns—in other words, the military-political relationship formalized in 1917 and 1918 would continue. Unfortunately, Canadianization would prove a mixed blessing. On one hand, it satisfied (and encouraged) national pride and unquestionably aided the voluntary enlistment system. On the other, the limited availability of experienced Canadian commanders—and, particularly in the Royal Canadian Navy (RCN) and Royal Canadian Air Force (RCAF), the inability of domestic industry to produce technically sophisticated armaments in a timely fashion—exacerbated the enormous growing pains experienced by the rapidly expanding armed forces. Finally, until mid-1943, nationalism also dictated that the army not be split up, a decision that denied the army necessary combat experience.

Canada's military role was that of willing subordinate. Building armed forces in wartime guarantees a steep learning curve, and Canada's experience in the war bears this out. In 1939, the Canadian regular forces numbered 10,000. At peak strength in 1944, 780,000 Canadians were in uniform: 80,000 in the RCN, 210,000 in the RCAF, and the remainder in the army. The achievements of the army in Italy, Normandy, the Scheldt, and the liberation of Holland; of the RCAF's administration of the British Commonwealth Air Training Plan as well as participation in 6 Group and throughout RAF Bomber Command; and of the RCN in convoy operations in the Battle of the Atlantic all materially contributed to the Allied victory, at a cost of 42,000 Canadian dead.

Canada's role in the war, both militarily and economically, was far more significant than non-Canadians have credited over the years. That said, the major impact of Canadian participation was on Canada itself. The war rebuilt the Canadian economy, witnessed the implementation of overdue socioeconomic reforms, and greatly strengthened the sense of nationhood and national self-confidence. Isolationism gave way to internationalism, and the country emerged from the conflict well placed to do more than its share in the immediate postwar years to rebuild and defend Western Europe.

Patrick H. Brennan

See also

Canada, Air Force; Canada, Army; Canada, Navy; King, William Lyon Mackenzie

References

Bercuson, David J. *Maple Leaf against the Axis: Canada's Second World War.* Toronto, Canada: Stoddart, 1995.

Douglas, W. A. B., and Brereton Greenhous. *Out of the Shadows: Canada in the Second World War.* New York: Oxford University Press, 1977.

Granatstein, J. L. *Canada's War: The Politics of the Mackenzie King Government, 1939–45.* Toronto, Canada: Oxford University Press, 1975.

———. *How Britain's Weakness Forced Canada into the Arms of the United States.* Toronto, Canada: University of Toronto Press, 1989.

Smith, Denis. *Diplomacy of Fear: Canada and the Cold War, 1941–1948.* Toronto, Canada: University of Toronto Press, 1988.

Stacey, C. P., and Barbara M. Wilson. *The Half-Million: The Canadians in Britain, 1939–1946.* Toronto, Canada: University of Toronto Press, 1987.

Canaris, Wilhelm Franz (1887–1945)

German navy admiral and head of German military intelligence during World War II. Born in Aplerbeck, Westphalia, Germany, on 1 January 1887, Wilhelm Franz Canaris entered the German navy in 1905. Serving aboard the cruiser *Dresden* off the South American coast at the beginning of World War I, he established an intelligence network to track Allied movements. On 14 March 1915, the British attacked the *Dresden* at Valparaiso, Chile, but Canaris escaped Chilean internment and returned to Europe in October. From November 1915 until October 1916, he was in Spain on an intelligence mission. In April 1918, he became a U-boat commander in the Mediterranean.

After the war, Canaris, an ardent conservative and nationalist, was active in covert operations to rebuild the German military, working in Japan with German designers to build submarines. He then resumed his naval career, increasingly in intelligence activities. Promoted to captain in 1931, he took command of the battleship *Schlesien* the next year. He was named to head military intelligence—the Abwehrabteilung (Abwehr)—in January 1935 and was promoted to Konteradmiral (U.S. equiv. rear admiral) in April. One of his first successes was to convince Adolf Hitler to intervene on the side of the Nationalists in the Spanish Civil War in July 1936.

The Fritsch Affair in 1938, when untruthful allegations of homosexual activities destroyed the career of Colonel General Werner von Fritsch, disillusioned Canaris, and shortly thereafter, the Abwehr became tied to anti-Nazi elements in Germany. Canaris opposed Hitler's policies, predicting they would lead to war and inevitable defeat. Despite the admiral's reticence, Hitler personally liked him, and the Abwehr did provide much useful information, all of which gave Canaris some protection as he aided a limited number of Jews and covertly undermined German attempts to involve Spain in the war. He was promoted to full admiral in January 1940.

Canaris resisted Reinhard Heydrich's efforts to take over the Abwehr, but his position was threatened when Heydrich uncovered evidence that he had committed treason. Heydrich's assassination in May 1942 provided a brief reprieve for the admiral, and it was not until February 1944 that Hitler removed him from his post. Shortly thereafter, he was placed on the navy's inactive list; he lived under a loose but comfortable house arrest at Burg Lauenstein until June, when Hitler recalled him to Berlin as head of mercantile warfare.

Implicated in the July 1944 bomb plot against Hitler (though he did not take an active role), Canaris was arrested afterward. Initially, there was no evidence against him, but discovery of his secret diaries led to his trial and conviction. Canaris was hanged at Flossenbürg Prison on 9 April 1945.

Rodney Madison

See also
Fritsch, Werner Thomas von; Germany, Navy; Heydrich, Reinhard Tristan Eugen; Hitler, Adolf; Resistance

References
Brissaud, André. *Canaris: A Biography of Admiral Canaris, Chief of German Military Intelligence in the Second World War*. Trans. Ian Colvin. New York: Grosset and Dunlap, 1970.
Hohne, Heinz. *Canaris: Hitler's Master Spy*. Trans. J. Maxwell Brownjohn. Garden City, NY: Doubleday, 1979.

Cape Esperance, Battle of (11–12 October 1942)

Second of five surface actions fought off Guadalcanal. The battle occurred 8 miles west-northwest of Savo Island as both U.S. and Japanese forces maneuvered to protect their own reinforcements moving toward Guadalcanal.

Rear Admiral Norman Scott led Task Force 64, consisting of two heavy cruisers, two light cruisers, and five destroyers. Scott's mission was to protect transports carrying the U.S. Army's 164th Infantry Regiment to Guadalcanal by searching for and attacking Japanese ships. Scott's crews had just undergone three hard weeks of night training, and the admiral was fully prepared to engage in a night action, in which the Japanese had hitherto enjoyed superiority. Scott had developed simple tactics and rehearsed them, keeping his crews at station from dusk to dawn. His ships operated in a single column, with destroyers forward and aft of his cruisers.

Japanese Rear Admiral Goto Aritomo commanded a bombardment group, Cruiser Division 6, composed of three heavy cruisers and two destroyers. It protected Rear Admiral Joshima Takagi's two seaplane carriers and six destroyers, transporting some 700 men and artillery belonging to Lieutenant General Hyakutake Haruyashi's Seventeenth Army to Guadalcanal. Goto planned to shell Henderson Field to neutralize the U.S. air threat while Joshima landed the reinforcements off the northwestern cape of Guadalcanal.

American aircraft tracked Goto's force as he approached, although communication fumbles aboard the U.S. ships nearly rendered that advantage moot. Goto and Joshima did not expect opposition, and preoccupied with navigation and preparations for the Henderson Field bombardment, they ignored indications that U.S. vessels were nearby. Lacking radar, the Japanese blundered into the Americans. Their lookouts did spot the American ships and identify them as enemy, but Goto believed they were friendly and flashed recognition signals.

At 11:25 P.M. on 11 October, U.S. radar from the light cruiser *Helena* first picked up the Japanese, but Scott, on the flagship heavy cruiser *San Francisco,* did not learn of this before he ordered his ships to turn at 11:30. Eight minutes later, while his formation was still in some mild disorder from the turn, Scott received his first radar warning. Fortunately for him and the Americans, the turn inadvertently allowed the U.S. ships to cross the T of Goto's approaching ships. The Americans opened fire at 11:46 P.M. at less than 5,000 yards. Surprise was total. Goto believed that Joshima's ships were shooting at him.

American 8-inch, 6-inch, and 5-inch guns pounded the Japanese ships. Among the casualties was Goto, who was mortally wounded. Before his death, he ordered his force to withdraw, and a running gunfire duel followed. The heavy cruiser *Furutaka* and the destroyer *Fubuki* were sent to the bottom. The heavy cruiser *Aoba* was badly damaged and would require four months to repair. In an associated action on 12 October, Henderson Field aircraft sank the destroyers *Murakumo* and *Natsugumo,* which were searching for survivors. On the American side, the destroyer *Duncan* was sunk, the cruiser *Boise* was heavily damaged, the cruiser *Salt Lake City* was lightly damaged, and the destroyer *Farenholt* was damaged. Meanwhile, Henderson Field had been spared Japanese shelling, and American morale soared, especially as some on the U.S. side put Japanese losses at up to three cruisers, five destroyers, and a transport.

Despite their tactical defeat, the Japanese did land their troops and supplies safely, as did the Americans on 13 October. Because Japanese torpedoes had not been successfully employed in the Battle of Cape Esperance, the Americans discounted their effectiveness. U.S. Navy leaders also incorrectly concluded that using the single-column formation and gunfire was the way to fight at night. This approach slighted the destroyers' main battery, the torpedo, and effectively tied the destroyers to the cruisers' apron strings. The Americans deployed this way in another night action on 13 November, much to their chagrin.

John W. Whitman and Spencer C. Tucker

See also
Guadalcanal, Land Battle for; Guadalcanal Naval Campaign; Hyakutake Haruyashi; Radar; Savo Island, Battle of; Solomon Islands, Naval Campaign; Torpedoes

References
Cook, Charles O. *The Battle of Cape Esperance: Strategic Encounter at Guadalcanal*. New York: Crowell, 1968.
Frank, Richard B. *Guadalcanal*. New York: Random House, 1990.
Lacroix, Eric, and Linton Wells II. *Japanese Cruisers of the Pacific War*. Annapolis, MD: Naval Institute Press, 1997.
Morison, Samuel Eliot. *History of United States Naval Operations in World War II*. Vol. 5, The Struggle for Guadalcanal, August 1942–February 1943. Boston: Little, Brown, 1949.
Poor, Henry V. *The Battles of Cape Esperance, 11 October 1942, and Santa Cruz Islands, 26 October 1942*. Washington, DC: Naval Historical Center, Department of the Navy, 1994.

Cape Matapan, Battle of (28 March 1941)

Naval battle between the British and Italians in the eastern Mediterranean Sea. Despite its crippling fuel shortages and at the urging of its German allies, the Italian navy set out on 26 March 1941 to attack British convoys around Crete. Under Vice Admiral Angelo Iachino, the force included the battleship *Vittorio Veneto;* the heavy cruisers *Trieste, Trento, Bolzano, Zara, Fiume,* and *Pola;* the light cruisers *Luigi di Savoia* and *Garibaldi;* and 17 destroyers. On 27 March, combined Royal Navy forces under Vice Admiral Andrew B. Cunningham (Force A) and Vice Admiral Henry D. Pridham-Wippell (Force B), alerted by key radio intercepts to the Italian movements, steamed from Alexandria and the Aegean, respectively, in search of the Italian force.

With neither side entirely certain of the other's precise order of battle or position, despite aerial reconnaissance, elements on each side sighted their opponents south of Crete on the morning of 28 March, and they exchanged fire off the island of Gaudo. When he learned of the presence of an aircraft carrier (the HMS *Formidable*) from his radio decrypters, Iachino reasoned that a more powerful British force lay beyond the several cruisers currently engaged by his flagship, *Vittorio Veneto.* Having lost the advantage of surprise—and now expecting imminent air attacks—he turned the Italian force northwest toward home.

In steady pursuit behind him followed Cunningham's Royal Navy task force, composed of the *Formidable* and the battleships *Warspite, Valiant,* and *Barham,* together with 4 cruisers and 13 destroyers, bolstered by British aircraft operating from nearby shore bases. The Italian force received little useful air cover from its own air force or its German allies and suffered accordingly. Despite withering antiaircraft fire from *Vittorio Veneto* and escorting ships, attacking British planes managed to torpedo the battleship at midafternoon on 28 March.

Cunningham judged that the progress of the Italian force, now drawn in around its wounded flagship, would likely be slow, and he plotted it at about 12 knots. But despite having shipped 4,000 tons of water and making way on only two of four propellers, the *Vittorio Veneto* worked up to a speed of 19 knots and thus moved its formation farther along than expected on the run toward home waters.

With night falling, however, Iachino received the unwelcome news that the heavy cruiser *Pola* had been stopped dead by an aerial torpedo attack. Believing that the British were still some 170 miles astern, he instructed the cruisers *Zara* and *Fiume* (with four destroyers) to turn back and tend to their sister ship. In fact, from a distance of less than 50 miles, Cunningham was closing as fast as his flagship, the old battleship HMS *Warspite,* and her sister ships *Valiant* and *Barham* could make way.

By 8:30 P.M., radar sets aboard the vanguard cruisers *Ajax* and *Orion* had picked up the derelict *Pola,* about 6 miles distant; it was presumed to be the *Vittorio Veneto.* As the main British force drew closer and prepared to attack the *Pola,* an in-line formation of six more unknown ships (the *Zara, Fiume,* and their escorts) was suddenly detected at 10:25 P.M. at 4,000 yards, which shifted the British targeting and drew a wall of concentrated fire from the British battleships' main and secondary batteries at nearly point-blank range. The *Zara* and *Fiume* were reduced to flaming wrecks within several minutes; the *Fiume,* along with the destroyers *Alfieri* and *Carducci,* sank within an hour. The *Zara* and *Pola* remained afloat until early the following morning, finally dispatched by scuttling charges and by torpedoes from British destroyers. Some 40 miles ahead, the main body of the Italian force pressed onward, arriving in Taranto on the afternoon of 29 March after evading the renewed chase given by Cunningham.

Using radar, which the Italians still lacked, and vastly superior air cover to great advantage, Cunningham had, in the Battle of Cape Matapan, established Royal Navy primacy in the Mediterranean. The loss of five valuable warships and 2,300 lives would call Iachino's judgment into question, and the Italian navy would not again venture from its harbors in force until the first Battle of Sirte Gulf in December 1941.

Gordon E. Hogg and Charles R. Shrader

See also
Battleships; Cunningham, Sir Andrew Browne; Great Britain, Navy; Iachino, Angelo; Italy, Navy; Radar; Sirte, First Battle of

References
Giorgerini, Giorgio. *Da Matapan al Golfo Persico.* Milan, Italy: Mondadori, 1989.
Greene, Jack, and Alessandro Massignani. *The Naval War in the Mediterranean, 1940–1943.* London: Chatham, 1998.
Pack, S. W. C. *Night Action off Cape Matapan.* Annapolis, MD: Naval Institute Press, 1972.
Stephen, Martin. *Sea Battles in Close-Up: World War 2.* Annapolis, MD: Naval Institute Press, 1991.

Cape St. George, Battle of (25 November 1943)

Naval battle in the Pacific Theater. This final surface action in the Solomons area was brought on by Japan's attempt to reinforce its garrison at Buka in northern Bougainville on the night of 24–25 November 1943. The transport group under Captain Kagawa Kiyoto was made up of three destroyer-transports: the *Amagiri, Uzuki,* and *Yugiri*—with the destroyers *Onami* and *Makinami* as escorts.

The Allies had long been reading the Japanese naval

code, however, and Captain Arleigh Burke and the 23rd Destroyer Squadron of five destroyers arrived just after midnight and took up station athwart the direct Buka-Rabaul route to intercept the Japanese on their return trip. The night was dark, with low-hanging clouds that produced occasional rainsqualls. The sea was calm.

Burke's plan was for his division—the *Charles F. Ausburne* (flag), *Claxton,* and *Dyson*—to launch a torpedo attack while Commander B. L. Austin's division of the *Converse* and *Spence* covered with its guns; then the two squadrons would reverse roles. The action unfolded nearly as Burke had hoped. At 1:40 A.M. on 25 November, the two unsuspecting Japanese escorts appeared, and Burke, closing the range quickly, launched 15 torpedoes at 1:56, then turned hard right to avoid any Japanese torpedoes coming his way. None did. Both Japanese escorting destroyers were mortally stricken. The *Onami* went down quickly; the *Makinami* somehow managed to stay afloat until the *Converse* and *Spence* could sink her with gunfire.

Burke then set out in pursuit of the three transports that had turned north and were trying to make good their escape to Rabaul. In the running fight, the Japanese spread out. Burke went after the *Yugiri* and at 3:28 A.M. sank her with gunfire.

Burke continued the chase until 4:04 A.M., and then, with only two hours of darkness remaining to shield him from the Japanese air bases at Rabaul, he turned for home. He had fought a near perfect action, sinking three enemy destroyers at no cost except for the oil and munitions expended. For the Japanese, however, the battle rang down the curtain on the costly war of attrition they had tried to wage in the Solomons. Their misfortunes continued; in mid-May, they lost the submarines *I-176* and *I-16* while they were attempting to supply the Buka garrison.

Ronnie Day

See also
Bougainville Campaign; Empress Augusta Bay, Battle of
References
Morison, Samuel Eliot. *History of United States Naval Operations in World War II.* Vol. 6, *Breaking the Bismarcks Barrier, 22 July 1942–1 May 1944.* Boston: Little, Brown, 1960.
Potter, E. B. *Admiral Arleigh Burke.* New York: Random House, 1990.

Capra, Frank (1897–1991)

Hollywood filmmaker who produced a series of inspirational movies during the war years. Born on 19 May 1897, at Bisaquino, Sicily, Frank Capra immigrated to the United States with his family in 1903. After a stint in the army during World War I, he made a career as a director, emphasizing stories of ordinary Americans who overcame corruption, greed, or cynicism. His films included *Mr. Deeds Goes to Town* (1936), *Mr. Smith Goes to Washington* (1939), and *Meet John Doe* (1941).

When the United States entered World War II, Capra was making *Arsenic and Old Lace.* Putting the project on hold until 1944, he rejoined the army as a major and was assigned to the Morale Branch in February 1942. The army's chief of staff, General George C. Marshall, ordered Capra to "make a series of documented, factual-information films—the first in our history—that will explain to our boys in the Army why we are fighting, and the principles for which we are fighting." After studying Leni Riefenstahl's *Triumph of the Will* and other German propaganda films, Capra produced a series of seven movies entitled *Why We Fight.* The first of these documentaries was released in October 1942. The films were shown not only to the troops but also in war plants starting in April 1943 and then to the general public by the end of May 1943. They were designed to be educational, inspirational, and recreational. Each examined what was seen as a totalitarian conspiracy to take over the free world.

After the last of these movies, subtitled *War Comes to America,* was released in 1945, Capra returned to civilian life to form Liberty Films. He continued to make movies until 1961. Capra died in La Quinta, California, on 3 September 1991.

T. Jason Soderstrum

See also
Art and the War; Film and the War; Marshall, George Catlett; Propaganda; Riefenstahl, Leni
References
Capra, Frank. *The Name above the Title: An Autobiography.* New York: Belvedere, 1982.
Glatzer, Richard, and John Raeburn. *Frank Capra: The Man and His Films.* Ann Arbor: University of Michigan Press, 1975.
Maland, Charles J. *Frank Capra.* Boston: Twayne Publishers, 1980.

Carlson, Evans Fordyce (1896–1947)

U.S. Marine Corps general and leader of the famous Carlson's Raiders. Born in Sidney, New York, on 26 February 1896, Evans Carlson enlisted in the army at 16 in 1912 and served in the Philippines and Hawaii from 1912 to 1915 before being discharged. He was recalled a year later for service on the Mexican border. During World War I, he was a captain on the staff of General John J. Pershing, commander of the American Expeditionary Forces, in France.

Dissatisfied in civilian life after the war, Carlson joined the Marines as a private in 1922. Intelligence duty with the 4th Marines Regiment in Shanghai from 1927 to 1929 sparked his deep fascination with China. After two years spent fighting Sandinista guerrillas in Nicaragua, Carlson returned to Beijing in 1933. In 1935, Captain Carlson began a friendly relationship with President Franklin D. Roosevelt while serving as second in command of the Marine detachment at the president's Warm Springs, Georgia, retreat.

When the Sino-Japanese War commenced in July 1937, Carlson returned for a third time to China, and he frequently wrote to Roosevelt regarding Chinese military and political affairs. He traveled extensively on officially sanctioned journeys with Chinese Communists, admiring the cooperation, simplicity, camaraderie, and fundamental democracy evident among officers and troops alike. He resigned in 1939 to write more freely about China's determined resistance in numerous articles and particularly in a book entitled *Twin Stars of China* (1940). Despite being charged with naïveté, he extolled the People's Army while optimistically foreseeing genuine cooperation between Guomindang (Nationalist) and Communist Chinese.

Joining the Marine Reserves as a major, Carlson was called to active duty in April 1941 and was soon promoted to lieutenant colonel. He commanded the experimental 2nd Marine Raider Battalion, known as Carlson's Raiders, and emulated People's Army principles of cooperation, self-reliance, and guerrilla tactics. (The unit's catchphrase, *gung ho*, approximates a Chinese term meaning "work together.") Carlson's Raiders slipped ashore from submarines at Makin Atoll, in the Gilberts, on 17 August 1942 (with the president's son, James Roosevelt, as executive officer) to destroy communications and gather intelligence. The raid boosted home front morale, but although it was moderately successful, 30 of 200 men perished, including 9 who were stranded during exfiltration and later beheaded by their Japanese captors. Subsequently, Carlson's Raiders repeatedly engaged the Japanese on Guadalcanal during long-range patrols, killing nearly 500 enemy troops while suffering only 16 deaths among the Marines.

Slowed by malaria, Carlson served as an adviser on Hollywood's popular 1943 account of the Makin raid, appropriately titled *Gung Ho*. He later returned to the Pacific—but as an observer rather than a unit commander. Serious wounds received at Saipan while rescuing a fallen enlisted man forced his retirement, with promotion to brigadier general.

In his last campaign, he vigorously and publicly opposed aiding the Nationalists in China's civil war up until he succumbed to heart disease in Portland, Oregon, on 27 May 1947. Some portrayed Carlson as a romantic or a Christian Socialist. Senator Joseph McCarthy branded him "the Red General," but Marine Corps Commandant David Shoup remarked, "He may have been Red, but he wasn't yellow."

Mark F. Wilkinson

See also
Guadalcanal, Land Battle for; Makin Island Raid; Saipan, Battle of; Sino-Japanese War; Southwest Pacific Theater

References
Blankfort, Michael. *The Big Yankee: The Life of Evans Carlson of the Raiders.* Boston: Little, Brown. 1947.

Frank, Benis M., and Henry I. Shaw Jr. *Victory and Occupation: History of U.S. Marine Corps Operations in World War II.* Vol. 5. Washington, DC: Historical Branch, G-3 Division, Headquarters, U.S. Marine Corps, 1968.

Frank, Richard B. *Guadalcanal: The Definitive Account of the Landmark Battle.* New York: Penguin, 1990.

Shewmaker, Kenneth. *Americans and Chinese Communists, 1927–1945: A Persuading Encounter.* Ithaca, NY: Cornell University Press, 1971.

Smith, George W. *Carlson's Raiders: The Daring Assault on Makin.* Novato, CA: Presidio, 2001.

Zimmerman, Phyllis A. *The First "Gung Ho" Marine: Evans F. Carlson of the Raiders.* Novato, CA: Presidio, 2004.

Carol II, King of Romania (1893–1953)

Romanian monarch who reigned from 1930 to 1940. Born on 15 October 1893 at Sinaia, Romania, Carol was the eldest child of Ferdinand I of Romania and Princess Marie of Great Britain. Carol's upbringing was controlled by his great-uncle Carol I of Romania, who encouraged his fixation on German militarism, including service in a German army regiment in Potsdam. Carol toured the front in the Second Balkan War but took little part in World War I, save as a diplomatic envoy to Russia in January 1917. He provoked scandal by deserting and eloping with "Zizi" Lambrino in September 1918, although the marriage was later annulled by the Orthodox Church.

During the early 1920s, Carol appeared to have reformed, marrying Helen of Greece in March 1921 and fathering a son, Michael. However, he associated himself with a single political party, the National Peasants, and he played little role in running the country, apart from founding the Romanian Boy Scouts. Before long, he met a divorcée, Elena Lupescu, for whom he abandoned his marriage in August 1925 and went into exile in Paris, formally renouncing the throne in favor of his son. His father, Ferdinand, died in 1927, and in May of the following year, Carol attempted a coup but was thwarted by British intelligence. On 6 June

Carol II, King of Romania, in full regalia. (Library of Congress)

1930, he successfully returned to Bucharest and disbanded the regency to seize the throne from his son.

Carol's reign was disastrous for Romania. He alienated the upper classes by persecuting the surviving members of his family, exiling his siblings Nicholas and Ilena and his ex-wife Helen, allowing his mistress Lupescu to choose his advisers, and encouraging political gridlock by playing off one political party against the other.

Carol II allowed Corneliu Zelea-Codreanu's Iron Guard to encourage fascism, at least until it began attacks on Lupescu, who was Jewish. His subsequent 1933 banning of the Iron Guard led to the assassination of two prime ministers. To restore order after the national elections in February 1938 failed to establish a political majority for any party, Carol II declared himself dictator and named the Orthodox patriarch Miron Christea as his prime minister. Carol was unable to protect Romania from the effects of the German-Soviet Non-aggression Pact of August 1939 and was forced to cede part of Transylvania to Hungary, Bessarabia to the Soviet Union, and the southern Dobruja region to Bulgaria.

Carol II fled the country with Lupescu and the royal art collection in September 1940, leaving his son, Michael, as king, under the control of General Ion Antonescu. He spent the rest of his life in exile in Brazil and Portugal. He married Lupescu in 1952 and died in Estoril, Portugal, on 4 April 1953.

Margaret Sankey

See also
Antonescu, Ion; Romania, Role in War
References
Bolitho, Hector. *Roumania under King Carol.* New York: Longmans, Green, 1940.
Easterman, Alexander Levvey. *King Carol, Hitler and Lupescu.* London: V. Gollancz, 1942.
Quinlan, Paul D. *The Playboy King: Carol II of Romania.* Westport, CT: Greenwood Press, 1995.

Caroline Islands Campaign
(15 February–25 November 1944)

A series of air attacks, naval bombardments, and amphibious assaults during the U.S. Navy's 1944 drive across the Central Pacific. A chain of 680 islands, islets, and atolls stretching across the Pacific between the Marianas and New Guinea, the Caroline Islands were part of the German Empire prior to World War I. In the peace settlement following the war, the victorious powers gave Japan the Marshall Islands and all of the Marianas save Guam.

These acquisitions dramatically increased Japanese power in the Pacific and created a potential major problem for the United States, as the Carolines straddled the sea-lanes between Hawaii and both the Philippines and China. Indeed, Japanese control of the Carolines caused so much concern that it spurred development of the amphibious warfare doctrine of the U.S. Marine Corps during the interwar period, a process that accelerated after Japan fortified Ponape, Truk, Yap, and Peleliu in the 1930s.

Following the entry of the United States into World War II in 1941, Japanese units in the Solomons and Gilberts were gradually destroyed or isolated by U.S. forces pushing across the Central Pacific. Kwajalein Atoll fell on 7 February 1944, and U.S. Fifth Fleet forces under Admiral Raymond A. Spruance accelerated preparations to capture Eniwetok Atoll as part of an overall plan approved by the Combined Chiefs of Staff in December 1943. The plan called for the seizure of key islands in the Marianas as bases to support a strategic bombing campaign against Japan and for selected attacks to support the South Pacific forces of General Douglas MacArthur.

To cover the Eniwetok landings, however, certain bases in the Carolines first had to be neutralized. Between 15 and 26 February 1944, B-24 Liberator bombers from Major General

Japanese Nakajima B6N Tenzan ("Jill" in the Allied code name) flying through hail of AA fire to attack the USS Yorktown *during the U.S. Navy raid on Truk in the Caroline Islands. (Official U.S. Navy photo, Library of Congress)*

Willis H. Hale's Seventh Army Air Force struck Ponape. The Eniwetok landings took place on 17 February, and on that day and the next, aircraft carriers from Vice Admiral Marc A. Mitscher's Task Force 58 launched more than 30 raids on Truk, which served as the major forward Japanese fleet anchorage and base in the Central Pacific. Each of the raids included at least 150 planes, and together, they destroyed more than 250 Japanese aircraft and some 200,000 tons of ships, including 2 light cruisers, 1 destroyer, 2 submarine tenders, 1 aircraft ferry, 6 tankers, and 17 merchant ships.

Eniwetok fell on 22 February, and Mitscher's airmen carried out more attacks on Truk on 29 and 30 April. Those attacks, combined with significant shore bombardment by Spruance's battleships, destroyed another 100 Japanese planes. The cumulative effect was so great that the Joint Chiefs of Staff (JCS) chose to bypass Truk and move westward, isolating the substantial Japanese garrison there.

Between June and August, U.S. forces fought the Battle of the Philippine Sea and seized Saipan, Tinian, and Guam in the Marianas, then continued west to attack the Philippines. To cover the initial Philippine landings on Mindanao and Morotai, U.S. planners intended to capture both Peleliu and Yap in the Carolines for use as air bases and forward staging areas. Those plans changed, however, following the September 1944 raids on the Philippines by Mitscher's Task Force 38 of Admiral William F. Halsey's Third Fleet. Halsey found Japanese defenses so weak that he recommended bypassing Morotai, Mindanao, Yap, and Peleliu and moving ahead with the attack on Leyte in October. The JCS agreed but decided to launch the landings on Peleliu and Morotai anyway because the troops for those attacks were already embarked.

Morotai fell on 15 September, the same day that Marines of the 1st Division landed on Peleliu and began one of the most grueling and perhaps unnecessary campaigns of the war. For the first time, the Japanese chose not to defend the beaches of an island under assault. Instead, the 5,300 defenders burrowed into the coral and prepared a main line of defense well inland. They counterattacked frequently; made use of underground tunnels, bunkers, and caves; and fought a battle of attrition in heat that sometimes reached more than 120 degrees. By the time the Peleliu Campaign ended on 25 November, more than 1,950 U.S. troops had been killed, and a regiment of the Army's 81st Division had been brought in as reinforcements. Whether the island needed to be taken and whether it materially aided the capture of the Philippines is extremely doubtful.

And yet, if Peleliu was a mistake, U.S. forces compensated by performing brilliantly throughout the rest of the Carolines. A regimental combat team of the 81st Division took Ulithi Atoll on 23 September, and in less than two weeks, the U.S. Navy was utilizing its splendid large anchorage for attacks against Formosa. The rest of the 81st Division took Angaur (in Palau, near Peleliu) from 1,600 Japanese defenders on 23 October, and with that, the Caroline Campaign came to a close.

Although no decisive battles were fought during the campaign, it was a vital stepping stone toward victory in the Battle of the Philippine Sea and in the conquest of the Marianas and the Philippines. Ulithi became the major U.S. forward fleet anchorage for the duration of the war and played a critical role in the eventual defeat of Japan. Moreover, the strategy of island-hopping reached maturity in the Carolines, as did the evolution of the U.S. Navy's fast-attack carrier groups and the concept of refueling and replenishing at sea. In these and other subtle ways, the campaign played an integral if underappreciated role in the final outcome of the war. One measure of the success of the U.S. strategy may be found in the experience of the British naval squadron that returned to raid Truk in June 1945. By then, that island had been so pummeled by U.S. attacks and its garrison so emaciated by isolation and lack of supplies that the British had no targets worthy of the name. Truk was little more than a prison for its defenders.

Lance Janda

See also

Amphibious Warfare; Central Pacific Campaign; Eniwetok, Capture of; Halsey, William Frederick, Jr.; Kwajalein, Battle for; MacArthur, Douglas; Mitscher, Marc Andrew; Naval Gunfire, Shore Support; Nimitz, Chester William; Peleliu, Battle of; Philippine Sea, Battle of the; Spruance, Raymond Ames; Truk

References

Gailey, Harry A. *Peleliu, 1944*. Annapolis, MD: Nautical and Aviation Publishing, 1983.
Gayle, Gordon D. *Bloody Beaches: The Marines at Peleliu*. Washington, DC: Marine Corps Historical Center, 1996.
Morison, Samuel E. *History of United States Naval Operations in World War II*. Vol. 7, *Aleutians, Gilberts and Marshalls, June 1942–April 1944*. Boston: Little, Brown, 1951.
———. *History of United States Naval Operations in World War II*. Vol. 8, *New Guinea and the Marianas, March 1944–August 1944*. Boston: Little, Brown, 1955.
———. *History of United States Naval Operations in World War II*. Vol. 12, *Leyte, June 1944–January 1945*. Boston: Little, Brown, 1958.

Carpet Bombing

The tactical application of strategic area bombing, originally used to direct a "carpet" of bombs to obliterate a target. Carpet bombing was first employed by the Germans at Guernica in April 1937 during the Spanish Civil War, in what they called "a controlled vivisectional experiment in modern bombing tactics."

By 1944, Allied carpet bombing involved heavy bombers dropping thousands of tons of relatively small bombs in an effective preparatory assault prior to a land attack. In this sense, the tactic was first utilized against Monte Cassino, Italy, on 15 February 1944. Waves of heavy and medium bombers dropped 435.5 tons of high explosives and reduced the local abbey to ruins. Ironically, the Germans, who had not previously garrisoned the abbey, now moved into the rubble and strengthened their defensive lines.

Following the June 1944 Normandy Invasion, Allied planners envisioned using fleets of bombers to blow holes in the German defenses, through which Allied armor and mechanized forces could then pour. The British tried using heavy bombers in close-air support during Operation CHARNWOOD in early July. The attempt failed largely because of poor target selection and the fact that the bombing ended hours before the British ground attack, allowing the Germans to reorganize their defense. In Operation GOODWOOD in mid-July 1944, British and American bombers tried again. After the carpet bombing, Allied ground forces met with initial success, but they foundered against a German antitank gun line that had not been a major target during the bombardment.

Operation COBRA on 24–25 July 1944 was another such effort and the most significant example of carpet bombing. U.S. bombers dropped 4,169 tons of bombs on the Saint-Lô area as part of the effort to support the breakout from Normandy. The bombers struck a box that was 7,000 yards wide and 2,000 yards deep. During the first day, many of the bombs fell short, hitting U.S. frontline troops and inflicting hundreds of friendly casualties. Among the dead was Lieutenant General Lesley J. McNair, chief of staff of Army Ground Forces. The second day's attacks were highly successful, helping Lieutenant General Omar N. Bradley's forces to break out from the bocage, or hedgerow, country.

The use of strategic bombers for tactical missions such as carpet bombing met with strong resistance from leaders of the U.S. Army Air Forces (USAAF), who believed that army ground commanders were misusing airpower. They argued that the effects achieved at the tactical level were slight compared to those that could be achieved at the strategic level. However, the lack of priority afforded to tactical-strike support and interdiction finally forced the hand of the ground commanders. Beginning in April 1944 and lasting until September, General Dwight D. Eisenhower was given the authority to control the use of the USAAF's strategic bombers.

Although the sight of an armada of bombers was awe-inspiring and the simultaneous impact of hundreds of bombs was similar to an earthquake, the actual effect on tactical operations was mixed. The bombers lacked precision, and their bombs produced craters and rubble that impeded a rapid advance by attacking forces. The destruction of Caen in July 1944, for instance, was so complete that wheeled and tracked vehicles could not make it through the bombed areas. Although carpet bombing in support of offensive operations raised the morale of attacking ground troops, it was a poor substitute for effective tactical air support.

C. J. Horn

See also
Aircraft, Bombers; Aviation, Ground-Attack; Brereton Lewis Hyde; Cassino/Rapido River, Battles of; COBRA, Operation; Collins, Joseph Lawton; GOODWOOD, Operation; McNair, Lesley James; Quesada, Elwood Richard "Pete"; Strategic Bombing

References
Crane, Conrad. *Bombs, Cities, and Civilians: American Airpower Strategy in World War II.* Lawrence: University Press of Kansas, 1993.
Craven, W. F., and J. L. Cates. *The Army Air Forces in World War II.* Chicago: University of Chicago Press, 1949.
Freeman, Roger A. *The Fighting Eighth.* London: Cassell, 2000.

Carrier Raids, U.S. (January–March 1942)

The series of offensive strikes initiated by U.S. naval forces of the Pacific Fleet almost immediately after the Japanese surprise attack on its base at Pearl Harbor. Despite the slim resources available following the Pearl Harbor attack, the newly appointed commander in chief of the Pacific Fleet, Admiral Chester W. Nimitz, and the commander in chief of the U.S. Fleet, Admiral Ernest J. King, agreed that a passive defense was out of the question. King directed Nimitz to guard the important Hawaii–Midway–Johnston Island triangle in the eastern Pacific and to protect the vital sea line of communications from Hawaii via Line Islands, Samoa, and Fiji to New Zealand and Australia.

Almost immediately, Nimitz began to plan for carrier raids against Japanese holdings in the Gilbert and Marshall Islands in an effort to take some pressure off the American-British-Dutch-Australian Command (ABDACOM, more commonly known as ABDA), whose area included Burma, Malaya, the Dutch East Indies, western New Guinea, northern Australia, and, nominally, the Philippines. In planning the raids, Admiral Nimitz found his thinking in opposition to that of many of his senior subordinates in the Pacific Fleet, who considered the use of carrier forces against heavily defended land bases much too risky unless complete surprise could be assured. Siding with Nimitz, however, was Vice Admiral William F. "Bull" Halsey, the fleet's senior carrier admiral, who offered to lead the attacks.

The first offensive raid was planned against the Japanese outpost on Wake Island at the end of January 1942. Vice Admiral Wilson E. Brown's Task Force 11, formed around the carrier *Lexington,* was assigned the mission until the Japanese torpedoed the oiler attached to his group and the mission was scrubbed. On 25 January, Admiral Halsey's Task Force 8, centered on the carrier *Enterprise,* raided Japanese bases at Kwajalein, Wotje, and Taroa in the northern Marshall Islands while Task Force 17, formed around the carrier *Yorktown* and commanded by Rear Admiral Frank Jack Fletcher, struck at bases in the southern Marshalls. Although they were mere pinpricks in terms of the damage and delay they caused the Japanese offensive, the raids raised morale in the fleet and provided the carrier air groups with valuable practice.

On 24 February 1942, Halsey's task force, now redesignated Task Force 16, sailed back into the fight with a raid on Wake Island. From there, he moved on to strike Marcus Island, barely 1,000 miles from the Japanese home islands. At the same time, Admiral Brown's Task Force 11 was sent south to attack the recently captured Japanese base at Rabaul on the island of New Britain, northeast of New Guinea. While still at a considerable distance from Rabaul, Brown's task force was spotted by Japanese air patrols and subsequently attacked by Japanese bombers without fighter protection. In the ensuing fight, the *Lexington*'s fighters nearly wiped out the attacking bombers, while only sustaining light losses themselves.

Brown withdrew temporarily and requested support in the attack on Rabaul from Nimitz and was quickly joined by Fletcher's task force. By the time it arrived, however, more lucrative targets appeared nearer at hand when, on 8 March, the Japanese landed forces at Lae and Salamaua on the eastern peninsula of New Guinea. Sailing into the Gulf of Papua on the opposite side of the peninsula on 10 March, Brown and Fletcher launched 104 aircraft and sent them over the rugged Owen Stanley Mountains. The aircraft emerged undetected to find unprotected Japanese ships unloading troops and supplies at the two locations. The attacking Americans sank a large minesweeper, a transport, and a converted light cruiser. Nine other ships were damaged before they could escape to the open sea. Only one U.S. plane and one aviator were lost. This attack was the greatest U.S. naval success in the war to that point, but even more important, it convinced the Japanese that successful operations against New Guinea would require the protection of aircraft carriers.

Although the actual destruction of Japanese assets was minimal, these carrier raids led the Japanese High Command to make several momentous decisions. The Naval General Staff feared that Australia would become a major base from which Allied counteroffensives could be launched and decided that it should be attacked and seized. The Army General Staff, staggered by the great distances involved in the attack, countered with a proposal to capture Port Moresby in southeastern New Guinea and use it for attacks on northern Australia to check Allied advances from that direction. This decision led to the Battle of the Coral Sea in May 1942.

The most dramatic American carrier operation early in the war came on 18 April 1942, when 16 U.S. Army Air Forces (USAAF) B-25 bombers lifted off the deck of the carrier *Hornet*, part of Halsey's Task Force 16, and attacked Tokyo, Nagoya, Osaka, and Kobe. Known as the Doolittle raid for the commander of the B-25s, Lieutenant Colonel James H. Doolittle, the attack did little physical damage but caused psychological shock among the Japanese leadership.

Jarred by these raids, members of the Imperial Naval Staff concluded that something had to be done about the American carrier threat. As a result, they suspended operations in the southeastern region (the Bismarcks, Solomons, eastern New Guinea, Papua, New Caledonia, Fiji, and Samoa), pulled air assets back to defend the Japanese home islands, and threw their support to the Combined Fleet's Admiral Yamamoto Isoroku's previously unpopular plan to seize the island of Midway.

Arthur T. Frame

See also
Aircraft Carriers; Coral Sea, Battle of the; Doolittle, James Harold "Jimmy"; Fletcher, Frank Jack; Halsey, William Frederick, Jr.; King, Ernest Joseph; Nimitz, Chester William; Pearl Harbor, Attack on; Tokyo, Bombing of (18 April 1942); Yamamoto Isoroku

References
Bradley, John H. *The Second World War: Asia and the Pacific.* Wayne, NJ: Avery, 1984.
Lundstrom, John B. *The First Team: Pacific Naval Air Combat from Pearl Harbor to Midway.* Annapolis, MD: Naval Institute Press, 1984.
Morison, Samuel E. *History of United States Naval Operations in World War II.* Vol. 3, *The Rising Sun in the Pacific, 1931–April 1942.* Boston: Little, Brown, 1948.
Prange, Gordon W. *Miracle at Midway.* New York: Penguin, 1983.
Spector, Ronald H. *Eagle against the Sun: The American War with Japan.* New York: Vintage Books, 1985.

Carton de Wiart, Sir Adrian (1880–1963)

British army general who was a divisional commander and head of Britain's military missions in Poland and Yugoslavia. Born on 5 May 1880, in Brussels, Belgium, Adrian Carton de Wiart briefly attended Oxford University before joining the British army. With his reckless style of leadership, he was wounded in nearly every campaign in which he was a participant. He saw action in the 1899–1902 Boer War and in India. In November 1914, he lost an eye while fighting in Somaliland, and in May 1915, he lost a hand in the Second Battle of Ypres, an action for which he was awarded the Victoria Cross. One year later, he was promoted to brigadier general and became friends with Winston L. S. Churchill.

In February 1919, Carton de Wiart arrived in Poland as head of the British Military Mission and observed the Russo-Polish War. In 1924, he retired from the British army and settled in Poland. Just prior to the beginning of World War II, he was recalled to British army service and made head of the British Military Mission to Poland. After that country's collapse in the German invasion of September 1939, he escaped via Romania. In his memoirs, Carton de Wiart stated that the campaign left him with an appreciation for the speed of mechanized warfare, the effect of airpower, and the peril posed by fifth columnists.

In November 1939, Carton de Wiart was appointed to command 61st Division, and in April 1940, he took over the Central Norwegian Expeditionary Force, tasked with securing Trondheim. Heavy air raids by the Luftwaffe prevented success, and Carton de Wiart and his troops were evacuated by the Royal Navy in early May. Afterward, he commanded the 61st Division while it trained and garrisoned Northern Ireland.

In April 1941, Carton de Wiart became head of the British Military Mission to Yugoslavia. On the way to his post, his aircraft was shot down, and he was captured by the Italians. He spent the next two years as a prisoner of war, plotting his escape. He and Lieutenant General Richard O'Connor broke out in March 1943 and enjoyed eight days of freedom before being recaptured. He was repatriated to Britain in August on the conclusion of the Italian armistice.

In October 1943, Prime Minister Churchill appointed Carton de Wiart as British representative to the Kuomintang's Generalissimo Jiang Jieshi (Chiang Kai-shek) and as liaison between Jiang and Lord Louis Mountbatten. Carton de Wiart retired in 1946 and published his memoirs, *Happy Odyssey,* four years later. He died in County Cork, Ireland, on 5 June 1963.

Mitchell McNaylor and Spencer C. Tucker

See also

China-Burma-India Theater; Churchill, Sir Winston L. S.; Jiang Jieshi; Mountbatten, Louis Francis Albert Victor Nicholas; Norway, German Conquest of; O'Connor, Richard Nugent; Poland Campaign

References

Carton de Wiart, Sir Adrian. *Happy Odyssey.* Foreword by Winston S. Churchill. London: Jonathan Cape, 1950.

Sheffield, G. D. "Carton de Wiart and Spears." In John Keegan, ed., *Churchill's Generals,* 323–349. New York: Grove Weidenfeld, 1991.

Casablanca Conference (14–24 January 1943)

Important U.S.-British strategic planning conference held in Morocco. Following the successful Allied landings in North Africa and the breakout of the British Eighth Army at El Alamein, British Prime Minister Winston L. S. Churchill and U.S. President Franklin D. Roosevelt and the Combined Chiefs of Staff met at Casablanca, Morocco, between 14 and 24 January 1943. Soviet leader Josef Stalin was invited but declined to attend, citing the pressure of military operations.

The principal topic of discussion at the conference—which was code-named SYMBOL and took place in a hotel complex in Anfa, a suburb of Casablanca—was strategic military options once North Africa had been cleared of Axis troops. The British, who arrived at the meetings far better prepared than the Americans, made a strong case for invasions of Sicily and then the Italian peninsula. The Americans, who preferred concentration on a cross-Channel inva-

The unconditional surrender announcement at the Casablanca Conference at Casablanca, French Morocco, Africa. President Franklin Roosevelt, with Prime Minister Winston Churchill at his side, addressing the assembled war correspondents. (Library of Congress)

HISTORIOGRAPHICAL CONTROVERSY
Unconditional Surrender—A Hindrance to Allied Victory?

On 16 January 1943, at the close of the Casablanca Conference, U.S. President Franklin D. Roosevelt informed the press that peace would be achieved only with the total elimination of German and Japanese military power, which would necessitate the unconditional surrender of Germany, Italy, and Japan. Roosevelt was thinking of the end of World War I, when an armistice concluded hostilities, allowing German leaders to say that their nation had not been defeated militarily. The British—and Prime Minister Winston L. S. Churchill, in particular—did not appear comfortable with Roosevelt's remarks, although Churchill immediately announced his support publicly. He later said that he would not have used those words. He remained convinced that such an absolute and categorical expression of policy would stiffen Axis resolve. Certainly, the Allied demand for unconditional surrender became a handy propaganda instrument for the Axis powers.

Over the years, some have argued that the insistence on unconditional surrender actually prolonged the war. B. H. Liddell Hart, for example, asserted that the demand for unconditional surrender strengthened German resolve and was skillfully exploited by Joseph Goebbels's Propaganda Ministry, especially when it could be coupled with alleged scenarios such as the "Morgenthau Plan" to convert postwar Germany into a primarily agricultural and pastoral country. According to Liddell Hart, implacable German resistance in the last two years of the war was, in part, the consequence of the unconditional surrender policy.

Albert Speer, Germany's minister of armaments, lent credence to the argument that demands for unconditional surrender hardened German resistance. He suggested that Adolf Hitler entertained no illusions about the seriousness of the Allied position on Germany's surrender and that the Führer realized the Nazis had burned all their diplomatic bridges. He repeatedly told his cohorts that there was no turning back. This information implies that the Germans might otherwise have overthrown the Hitler regime, but it is doubtful that many Germans would have been attracted to this course by Allied assurances of moderation. Hugh R. Trevor-Roper dismissed the controversy as "much ado about nothing." Terms could only be made with holders of power or alternative power brokers. Some German military leaders might have been ready to bargain with the Allies, but conditions that included abolition of the Wehrmacht would probably not have been acceptable to them. In fact, German military opposition to Hitler failed, and the German democratic opposition was badly fragmented and often a will-o'-the-wisp. To be sure, Allied leaders were in concurrence on the point that the war would have to end with Axis surrender. Historian Gerhard Weinberg noted that the difference between surrender and unconditional surrender was merely a matter of nuance.

The demand for unconditional surrender had another advantage for the Western leaders. Both the British and U.S. governments sought to assure the Soviet Union that they were in the conflict for the duration and hence would not consider an arrangement with the Germans at Moscow's expense. In emphasizing the diplomatic aspects of the unconditional surrender policy, Vojtech Mastny suggested that the latter was, in part, intended to reassure the Kremlin. Stalin displayed substantial skepticism, in public at least, about the British and American determination to remain in the war and assumed that, given the chance, they would negotiate with Germany behind his back. After all, he himself had approached the Germans on several occasions about a deal. Until the winter of 1943, Stalin portrayed the war as an exclusively Russian-German conflict that, by implication, could be settled in a mutually advantageous manner between two belligerents.

David M. Keithly

See also

Casablanca Conference; Churchill, Sir Winston L. S.; Hitler, Adolf; Roosevelt, Franklin D.; Speer, Albert; Stalin, Josef

References

Cave Brown, Anthony. *Bodyguard of Lies.* Vol. 1. New York: Harper and Row, 1975.

Liddell Hart, Basil H. *History of the Second World War.* New York: Perigee Books, 1982.

Speer, Albert. *Inside the Third Reich.* New York: Avon Books, 1971.

Trevor-Roper, H. R. *The Last Days of Hitler.* New York: Macmillan, 1962.

Weinberg, Gerhard L. *A World at Arms: A Global History of World War II.* New York: Cambridge University Press, 1994.

sion of France, reluctantly acceded. "We came, we listened, and we were conquered," remarked Major General Albert Wedemeyer, one U.S. attendee.

The Allied leaders at Casablanca took another important step in deciding to launch a combined bomber offensive against Germany. On the day the conference opened, the sur-

vivors of a special convoy from Trinidad arrived at Gibraltar. The convoy's devastating losses to German U-boats—77 percent—forced the two Allied leaders to assign priority to winning the Battle of the Atlantic. They agreed to divert to that struggle additional convoy escorts, escort carriers, and aircraft assets (including the VLR [very long range]

Consolidated B-24 Liberator, which would, for the first time, be based at Newfoundland to close the Greenland air gap).

But the Casablanca Conference is chiefly remembered for Roosevelt's surprise announcement that the Allies would insist on "unconditional surrender." Churchill, who had not been informed that the announcement would be made, nonetheless immediately supported it. Some have charged that this decision needlessly prolonged the war by preventing negotiations with factions in the German resistance to Adolf Hitler that might have led them to topple his regime. Certainly, the declaration was a windfall for the German propaganda machine. In making the announcement, Roosevelt had in mind World War I and the way the German Right had utilized the November 1918 armistice to spread the myth that Germany had not been defeated militarily. That outcome had been a powerful assist in Hitler's rise to power.

Another aspect of the Casablanca Conference concerned relations with the French. General Charles de Gaulle, leader of the Free French, was not informed of the meeting beforehand; Churchill simply ordered him to Morocco, which was then still a French protectorate. Roosevelt and Churchill pushed de Gaulle into a partnership with General Henri Giraud, who had been spirited out of France by submarine. De Gaulle, already upset because Britain had undermined the French position in Syria and Lebanon, was eventually able to elbow the politically inept and equally stubborn Giraud into the shadows. However, the whole affair affected de Gaulle's attitude toward Britain and the United States.

Spencer C. Tucker

See also
Churchill, Sir Winston L. S.; Combined Chiefs of Staff; de Gaulle, Charles; El Alamein, Battle of; Giraud, Henri Honoré; Roosevelt, Franklin D.; Strategic Bombing; TORCH, Operation; Wedemeyer, Albert Coady

References
Berthon, Simon. *Allies at War: The Bitter Rivalry among Churchill, Roosevelt, and de Gaulle.* New York: Carroll and Graf, 2001.
Kersaudy, François. *Churchill and De Gaulle.* New York: Atheneum, 1982.
Larabee, Eric. *Commander in Chief: Franklin Delano Roosevelt, His Lieutenants & Their War.* New York: Harper and Row, 1987.
Viorst, Milton. *Hostile Allies: FDR and De Gaulle.* New York: Macmillan, 1965.

Cash-and-Carry (November 1939)

U.S. program to allow states that were victims of aggression to purchase arms to fight the Axis powers. In July 1936, civil war broke out in Spain, and a year later, the Sino-Japanese War began. Then, in May 1937, the U.S. Congress passed the Neutrality Act, which committed the nation to "permanent neutrality." The act revamped existing neutrality legislation to include a prohibition on the sale of arms or munitions to either side in a civil war as well as a declared war between states. Travel by U.S. citizens on belligerent ships was made illegal, no longer just cautioned against as something undertaken at the passenger's risk. Well aware of the financial impact of trade, Congress provided that the president would draw up a list of certain strategic raw materials, such as oil, that were to be paid for on delivery and then transported on ships belonging to the belligerent power. Thus was born the phrase *cash-and-carry*. These provisions were to last for two years.

In September 1939, Germany invaded Poland, beginning World War II. Public sentiment in the United States demanded that the country stay out of the conflict, but it also generally favored assistance to the states fighting Germany and Japan. In any case, the cash-and-carry provisions of the 1937 act had expired in May 1939, with the consequence that U.S. merchant vessels were free to sail into the war zones, albeit with the possibility that they would be sunk and the United States drawn into war. At the same time, the Western democracies could not purchase arms in the United States.

On 27 October 1939, the U.S. Senate voted 63 to 31 to repeal the embargo on arms to belligerents, and a week later, the House of Representatives followed suit, with a majority of 61 votes. Under the November 1939 act, cash-and-carry remained in effect. The United States could sell war materials to belligerents provided that they could pay cash for the goods and transport them in their own vessels. This act was, in fact, a compromise: the noninterventionists yielded on the arms embargo in order to secure the provision preventing U.S. ships from sailing into the war zones, and the repealists accepted the latter in order to secure an end to the ban on arms sales.

The terms of the act were intentionally crafted to favor the Atlantic sea powers that possessed merchant and naval forces to transport the material. To remain within the legal bounds of American neutrality, cash-and-carry was extended to all belligerents, both Axis and Allied, that could meet the specific requirements of the act. Japan was thus able to take advantage of its provisions—until the U.S. government embargoed war goods and froze Japanese assets in 1941, precipitating Tokyo's decision to launch an attack on the United States.

British Prime Minister Neville Chamberlain informed U.S. President Franklin D. Roosevelt that he thought the November 1939 act would have a "devastating effect upon German morale," but that was hardly the case, as U.S. factories were only just beginning to produce quantities of weapons. The act also opened up the dilemma of how to allot the few weapons that were being produced. U.S. rearmament was barely under way at that point, and the armed services would have to compete with the Western democracies for American weapons. Many Americans also opposed the act because it provided assistance to the Soviet Union, and the legislation became an issue in the 1940 presidential campaign.

James T. Carroll and Spencer C. Tucker

See also

Armaments Production; Chamberlain, Arthur Neville; Roosevelt, Franklin D.; United States, Home Front

References

Kennedy, David. *Freedom from Fear: The American People in Depression and War, 1929–1945.* New York: Oxford University Press, 1999.

Lash, Joseph P. *Roosevelt and Churchill, 1939–1941: The Partnership That Saved the West.* New York: W. W. Norton, 1976.

Cassino/Rapido River, Battles of (1944)

A series of engagements between the Allies and Germans for control of Monte Cassino, a massif strategically located at the entrance of the Liri Valley in Italy. The site of a Benedictine abbey established in A.D.529, Monte Cassino formed an important part of the German Gustav Line, a set of defensive positions stretching across the Italian peninsula and blocking the Allied approach to Rome.

Following up on the Allied success on Sicily in July and August 1943 (Operation HUSKY), the American Fifth Army landed at Salerno, a city on the western coast of Italy, on 9 September 1943 (Operation AVALANCHE) and began to push north. With rugged mountain ranges, heavy rains, and stiff German resistance barring the advance, Allied progress was slow. In late 1943, having broken through the Volturno Line (a German defensive line anchored on the Volturno River), the Allies found themselves up against the Gustav Line. To force the German commander, Field Marshal Albert Kesselring, to fight in two directions (west and south), the Fifth Army's commander, Lieutenant General Mark Clark, planned Operation SHINGLE, an amphibious landing at Anzio/Nettuno, north of and behind the Gustav Line. By landing at Anzio/Nettuno with a corps, Clark believed it would be possible to turn Colonel General Heinrich von Vietinghoff's Tenth Army out of the Gustav Line, thus opening the Liri Valley and the routes to Rome.

To prepare for the landing of Major General John Lucas's American VI Corps and its subsequent linkup with Fifth Army, Clark ordered attacks by the British X Corps and the U.S. II Corps. In order to seize key heights to protect the southern flank of II Corps as it began its attack up the Liri Valley, Lieutenant General Richard McCreery's X Corps assaulted across the Garigliano River on 17 January 1944. Failing to cross the river, the British attacked once more two

days later but did not achieve their objectives. As a result, Major General Geoffrey Keyes's II Corps would assault across the Rapido River with its left flank exposed.

Keyes's plan to attack across the Rapido River and into the Liri Valley was simple. The 36th Infantry Division would move forward, with two regiments abreast, roughly 3 miles downstream from the town of Cassino; the 34th Infantry Division would attack with three regiments abreast north of Cassino. Beginning their strike on 20 January, the Americans immediately encountered stiff resistance from General der Panzertruppen (U.S. equiv. lieutenant general) Fridolin von Senger und Etterlin's German XIV Corps.

Throughout the night of 20 January, the Americans struggled to find their way through minefields, cross the river in rubber rafts and canvas boats, and erect footbridges. Sunrise the next morning exposed the Americans to accurate German artillery and rocket fire. Concerned with his losses, the 36th Infantry Division commander, Major General Fred Walker, prevailed on Keyes to delay a renewed effort until after dark. Attacking again on the evening of 21 January, the 36th Infantry Division suffered heavy losses without establishing a lodgment on the far side of the Rapido. Against Keyes's wishes, Clark authorized Walker to halt the attack on the morning of 22 January.

With the 36th Infantry Division stalled, Clark now intended to envelop Cassino from the north. Attacking on 25 January with the 34th Infantry Division and units of General Alphonse Juin's French Expeditionary Corps, the Allies soon ground to a halt. Once again, the soggy ground, a strong current, and determined German resistance frustrated Clark's efforts to capture Cassino. Over the next several days, the 34th Infantry Division, including the Nisei 100th Infantry Battalion, inched its way up and over the heights north of Cassino but was unable to capture the abbey or the town. By 11 February, the II Corps attack was spent, and the task for opening the Liri Valley fell to Lieutenant General Bernard Freyberg's New Zealand II Corps.

Believing the only way to capture Cassino was to eliminate the abbey from the commanding heights above the town, Freyberg received permission to bomb it, and on 15 February, waves of bombers dropped 435.5 tons of high explosives, reducing the abbey to ruins. Although the Germans had not previously garrisoned the abbey, its destruction allowed them to position troops amid the rubble and to strengthen their lines. Launching Operation AVENGER on 15 February, Freyberg's subordinates, facing the same problems as the Americans had earlier, fought with little success to capture Monte Cassino. Frustrated by his lack of progress, Freyberg ordered a halt to AVENGER after three days of fighting.

Freyberg set the next attack for 24 February. Called Operation DICKENS, the attack comprised two infantry divisions and a tank regiment. Believing a direct approach would prove more effective, Freyberg planned to attack frontally into the town of Cassino, but heavy rains delayed the operation until 15 March. Following the Italian Campaign's first massive carpet bombing, Freyberg's troops engaged in heavy fighting within the town and on the surrounding heights. For the next 10 days, II New Zealand Corps fought in close combat amid the ruins of Cassino with little effect. Because Freyberg failed to commit his reserves in a decisive manner, his conduct of the operation resulted in the heavy casualties he had hoped to avoid. By 24 March, the II New Zealand Corps attacks had halted, with the Germans still in possession of portions of Cassino and the abbey's ruins.

By mid-April, the Polish II Corps, commanded by Lieutenant General Władysław Anders, began to move into the line opposite Cassino. As part of an Allied deception plan, activity along the Gustav Line almost completely ceased. On 11 May, the Allies attacked with Fifth Army and the British Eighth Army, and although the offensive caught the Germans by surprise, casualties among the Poles were still high. Fifth Army's progress south of Cassino in the Liri Valley, however, rendered Monte Cassino unimportant to the Germans' defense. On the evening of 17 May, the defenders withdrew, and the next day, the Polish II Corps occupied Monte Cassino, completing a four-month battle for the heights. Casualties for the Allies numbered some 120,000; the Germans suffered almost 130,000.

David M. Toczek

See also

Anders, Władysław; Anzio, Battle of; Clark, Mark Wayne; Freyberg, Bernard Cyril; Italy Campaign; Japanese Americans; Juin, Alphonse Pierre; Kesselring, Albert; Keyes, Geoffrey; Lucas, John Porter; McCreery, Sir Richard Loudon; Senger und Etterlin, Fridolin Rudolf von; Sicily, Invasion of; Vietinghoff gennant Scheel, Heinrich Gottfried von; Wilson, Henry Maitland

References

Blumenson, Martin. *U.S. Army in World War: European Theater of Operations—Salerno to Cassino.* Washington, DC: Office of the Chief of Military History, Department of the Army, 1969.

———. *Bloody River: The Real Tragedy of the Rapido.* Boston: Houghton Mifflin, 1970.

Ellis, John. *Cassino, the Hollow Victory: The Battle for Rome, January–June 1944.* New York: McGraw-Hill, 1984.

Piekalkiewicz, Janusz. *Cassino: Anatomy of the Battle.* Harrisburg, PA: Historical Times, 1988.

Casualties

World War II exacted a heavy toll on the combatant nations and the world community as a whole. Although figures vary widely based on the source employed, perhaps 50 million servicemen and civilians were killed in the course of the conflict. World War II is thus the most destructive war in human history (see Table 1).

In terms of combat losses for the principal Allied powers, the Soviet Union had 8,668,400 military personnel killed. The majority of these were in the army, as the Soviets bore the brunt of the fighting on land against Germany. By the end of the war, the Chinese had 1,324,516 soldiers killed, a number of whom became casualties as early as the 1937 Japanese invasion. The United States, Great Britain, and France suffered far fewer losses, although in relative terms, given their smaller populations, the impact was still high. Of these powers, Great Britain's armed forces had 397,762 men killed. This figure includes losses incurred by imperial and Commonwealth forces: Canada sustained 37,476 deaths, India 24,338, Australia 23,365, New Zealand 10,033, and South Africa 6,840. The United States suffered 292,129 battle deaths, and the French lost 213,324 servicemen. The latter figure includes Free French forces.

Smaller Allied powers also lost heavily in comparison to their populations. Poland had 320,000 killed, and Greece lost 73,700. The Netherlands lost 6,238 servicemen. Belgium's armed forces lost 7,760 men. The dead of Norway totaled 4,780, and Denmark's losses were 4,339, a figure that includes merchant sailors in the service of other Allied navies.

The principal Axis powers had significantly fewer casualties than did the Soviet Union, but their populations were also much smaller. Germany, which waged a two-front war, suffered the most, with 2,049,872 dead. Japan sustained 1,506,000 deaths, and Italy lost 259,732 men. This number includes some 17,500 men killed in battle after that nation declared itself a cobelligerent of the Allies.

The other Axis powers endured heavy losses as well. Romania suffered greatly with 300,000 deaths, most of these incurred while the country was an Axis power but a small number being deaths suffered after it joined the Allies late in the war. Hungary lost 147,435 men, and Finland's dead numbered 79,047 soldiers, sailors, and airmen. Bulgaria, initially an Axis power, suffered 10,000 deaths, with some of these individuals being in the service of the Allies late in the war.

Civilian deaths greatly increased the human toll, as the age of total warfare embraced the civilian sector, too. Including battle deaths, total Soviet deaths in the war may have reached 27 million. Germany was second in terms of civilian losses. Most of these were the result of Allied bombing raids, which claimed the lives of some 410,000 civilians. Air attacks on the home fronts of other nations also carried a heavy cost. In Japan, about 500,000 people lost their lives, whereas Great Britain suffered 92,673 deaths.

Table 1
Casualty Figures for World War II

	Battle Deaths	Wounded	Missing in Action	Civilian Dead
Allied Powers				
Australia	23,365	39,803	32,393	—
Belgium	7,760	14,000	—	76,000
Canada	37,476	53,174	10,888	—
China	1,324,516	1,762,006	115,248	1,000,000
Denmark	4,339	—	—	1,800
France	213,324	400,000	—	350,000
Great Britain	397,762	348,403	90,188	92,673
Greece	73,700	47,000	—	325,000
India	24,338	64,354	91,243	—
Netherlands	6,238	2,860	—	200,000
New Zealand	10,033	19,314	10,582	—
Norway	4,780	—	—	7,000
Poland	320,000	530,000	420,760	3,000,000
South Africa	6,840	14,363	16,430	—
Soviet Union	8,668,400	14,685,593	4,559,000	14,012,000
United States	292,129	670,846	139,709	6,000
Axis Powers				
Bulgaria	10,000	21,878	—	10,000
Finland	79,047	50,000	—	11,000
Germany	2,049,872	4,879,875	1,902,704	410,000
Hungary	147,435	89,000	170,000	285,000
Italy	259,732	77,494	350,000	146,000
Japan	1,506,000	500,000	810,000	500,000
Romania	300,000	—	100,000	200,000

Note: Dashes indicate figure is unknown.

Sources: Data from Bullock, Alan, *Hitler and Stalin: Parallel Lives,* New York: Alfred A. Knopf, 1992; Dupuy, Richard Ernest, *World War II: A Compact History,* New York: Hawthorn Books, 1969; Keegan, John, *The Second World War,* New York: Penguin, 1989; Keegan, John, ed., *The Times Atlas of the Second World War,* New York: Harper and Row, 1989; Krivosheev, G. F., *Soviet Casualties and Combat Losses in the Twentieth Century,* London: Greenhill Books, 1993; and Sorge, Martin K., *The Other Price of Hitler's War: German Military and Civilian Losses Resulting from World War II,* New York: Greenwood, 1986.

Adding to civilian figures were atrocities committed against civilians. Chief among these was the Holocaust, the German campaign to exterminate Europe's Jewish population. The Holocaust claimed an estimated 6 million Jews. Half of this number were Polish citizens, and some 1.2 million came from the Soviet Union. Hungary's figure for Jewish deaths was 450,000, and Romania's total reached 300,000. The Baltic states lost 228,000 of their citizens. Germany itself sent 210,000 of its own people to their deaths.

The aftermath of World War II claimed additional victims. Some of these losses were the result of efforts by the Soviet Union and other Eastern and Central European governments to drive out their German minorities. Perhaps 2 million of the 14 million ethnic Germans who had been living in Eastern Europe died in the course of this expulsion. The final legacy of the war was an estimated 11 million people displaced by the conflict, some of whom perished from simple lack of food or shelter.

In addition to the death totals, large numbers of people were wounded, many of them seriously. These casualties, too, imposed a heavy financial toll on all combatant states after the war. Finally, it should be noted that death tolls in the war would have been much higher save for new miracle drugs and blood plasma.

Eric W. Osborne

See also
Holocaust, The; Military Medicine
References
Dupuy, Richard Ernest. *World War II: A Compact History*. New York: Hawthorn Books, 1969.
Keegan, John. *The Second World War*. New York: Penguin, 1989.
Krivosheev, G. F. *Soviet Casualties and Combat Losses in the Twentieth Century*. London: Greenhill Books, 1993.
Sorge, Martin K. *The Other Price of Hitler's War: German Military and Civilian Losses Resulting from World War II*. New York: Greenwood, 1986.

CATAPULT, Operation (July 1940)

Operation carried out by the British navy, beginning on 3 July 1940, to neutralize, seize, and if necessary destroy French navy warships, which the British feared would fall into German hands. In 1940, the French navy was the second most powerful in Europe and had many modern warships. With the defeat of France and the German capture of its Atlantic ports, a number of French warships ended up in British harbors; by 3 July, these included the old battleships *Courbet* and *Paris,* a super destroyer leader, two destroyers, six torpedo boats (called light destroyers by the French), and numerous other small warships. Many more vessels remained in French ports, however.

When the French entered into armistice talks with the Germans, Prime Minister Winston L. S. Churchill and the War Cabinet became concerned over the final disposition of the French fleet. Although the French navy commander, Admiral Jean Darlan, had promised the British government that France would scuttle the fleet rather than see it fall into German hands, Britain's leaders were not certain that would be the case. And with the threat of a German invasion of Britain looming, Churchill was determined to secure the French fleet. Such a dramatic action on the part of his nation would also demonstrate to the Americans that Britain was determined to continue in the war.

The armistice terms did indeed allow the French government to retain control of the fleet, but it was to be disarmed, mostly at the French navy base of Toulon and also at colonial French ports. At that time, a majority of the French ships were in North Africa, at the ports of Mers-el-Kébir, Oran, Algiers, Bizerte, Alexandria, or elsewhere overseas. The almost completed and powerful battleships *Richelieu* and *Jean Bart* had escaped France and were at Dakar and Casablanca, respectively. At Mers-el-Kébir, there were the two fast battleships *Dunkerque* and *Strasbourg;* the two older, modernized battleships *Provence* and *Bretagne;* the seaplane tender *Commandant Teste;* and some large destroyers and miscellaneous warships. Oran served as base to seven destroyers, and Algiers had six modern light cruisers.

Over some opposition and at Churchill's insistence, the War Cabinet approved Operation CATAPULT to carry out the "simultaneous seizure, control or effective disablement or destruction of all the accessible French Fleet." French naval commanders were offered a series of options: they could join Britain and continue the fight, they could sail their ships to a neutral port and be disarmed there, or they could scuttle their ships. If French commanders rejected these options, the British naval commanders were under orders to open fire and sink the French ships themselves.

The plan, which unfolded on 3 July, met with considerable success in those areas under British control. At Portsmouth, the British seized the old French battleship *Courbet,* along with other small vessels. At Plymouth, they secured the battleship *Paris,* two destroyers, a torpedo boat, and three sloops. There, also, they took the *Surcouf,* the world's largest submarine. Three submarines and other craft were secured from the ports of Falmouth and Dundee. In their home ports, the British secured almost 200 small warships, including minesweepers, tugs, submarine chasers, and trawlers. The vessels were taken at a cost of three sailors killed, two British and one French. Later, 3,000 of the ships' 12,000 officers and sailors joined the Free French. Also seized were French merchant ships and their crews.

CATAPULT was also successful in the West Indies. Prolonged talks involving the British, French, and Americans led to the internment of the aircraft carrier *Béarn* and two light cruisers at Martinique. At Alexandria, Vice Admiral Sir Andrew Cunningham negotiated with Vice Admiral René Émile Godfroy, who commanded a French squadron consisting of the rebuilt World War I–era battleship *Lorraine;* the heavy cruisers *Duquesne, Tourville,* and *Suffren;* the light cruiser *Duguay-Trouin;* three destroyers; and one submarine. In deft negotiations, Cunningham managed to secure an agreement that the French ships would be disarmed and their fuel emptied. Some of the sailors were also repatriated to France.

The operation was not so effective farther west in the Mediterranean. At Mers-el-Kébir, the French refused to yield and fought a battle with Vice Admiral James Somerville's newly formed Force H from Gibraltar. In the action, the French battleship *Bretagne* blew up and sank. The *Provence* was also badly damaged and beached herself; the battleship *Dunkerque* ran aground. In this battle, 1,297 French seamen died; another 351 were wounded. Later, on 5 July, the *Strasbourg, Commandant Teste,* and a few destroyers broke free and escaped. There was also fighting at Dakar, where a small British squadron built around the tiny aircraft carrier *Hermes* damaged the battleship *Richelieu* on 8 July.

Because of CATAPULT, the Vichy French government severed diplomatic relations with Britain. The German government also lifted demobilization requirements for the French fleet and elements of its air force, and the French then mounted several largely ineffectual air strikes against Gibraltar. On 26 July, London declared a blockade of metropolitan France and French North Africa, although it was never heavily enforced.

Those who had opposed CATAPULT believed it would drive a wedge between the two former allies; they also expected France to honor its pledge to Britain to scuttle the fleet if necessary. In these beliefs, they were quite correct. Despite their sharp animosity toward Britain for launching CATAPULT—an animosity that lingers to this day—the French honored their pledge. In November 1942, following the Allied landings in North Africa (Operation TORCH), the French scuttled their ships when the Germans tried to secure them at Toulon. Operation CATAPULT was one of the most tragic aspects of the war.

Jack Greene

See also

Churchill, Sir Winston L. S.; Cunningham, Sir Andrew Browne; Dakar, Attack on; Darlan, Jean Louis Xavier François; Godfroy, René Émile; Mers-el-Kébir; Somerville, Sir James Fownes; TORCH, Operation

References

Huan, Claude. *Mers-El Kébir: La rupture franco-britannique.* Paris: Economica, 1994.

Marder, Arthur. *From the Dardanelles to Oran: Studies of the Royal Navy in War and Peace, 1915–1940.* Oxford: Oxford University Press, 1974.

Tute, Warren. *The Deadly Stroke.* New York: Coward, McCann and Geoghegan, 1973.

Catholic Church and the War

The Catholic Church's record in World War II, particularly its assistance to Jews and resistance to the Holocaust or lack thereof, has generated intense controversy. Individual Catholics certainly acted with considerable bravery in opposing Nazi agendas. Archbishop Galen of Münster condemned Germany's euthanasia program in 1941, which led Adolf Hitler to suspend mass killings (although so-called mercy killings continued on a smaller scale). Other Catholics hid Jews and served bravely in the Resistance in France or as chaplains at the front (more than 3,000 in the U.S. Army alone). Yet the Vatican refused to issue official statements condemning the Holocaust. Meanwhile, in an exercise in bad timing, the Vatican extended diplomatic relations to Japan early in 1942, at the high tide of Japanese aggression in Asia and the Pacific.

In part, nationalist loyalties constrained the Vatican and proved more powerful, if not more resilient, than supranational Catholicism. In the Nazi puppet state of Croatia, Franciscan monks and ultranationalist priests lent their moral authority to the murder of tens of thousands of Jews and Orthodox Serbians in 1941. A few bloodthirsty priests even joined in the killing. Meanwhile, anti-Bolshevism drove many European priests to support the Nazi "crusade" against the Soviet Union, and traditional expressions of biblical anti-Semitism and consistent opposition to Zionism tended to inhibit sympathy for Jews.

Ultimately, Pope Pius XII was responsible for exercising and enforcing the church's moral authority, and evidence indicates he was a Germanophile. As a cardinal, he had negotiated the 1933 concordat between the Vatican and Nazi Germany that gave the Holy See tighter control over independent-minded German Catholics. It also gave Hitler important international recognition and a freer hand in Germany, as it led to the dissolution of Germany's Catholic Center Party.

In the invasion of Poland in September 1939, the Nazis revealed their murderous nature. Polish priests were either murdered or deported to concentration camps. In the Warthegau region alone, the Nazis killed more than 300 priests. Apparently concluding that official condemnations would goad the Nazis to further excesses, Pius XII remained silent. And after failing to protest the mass murders of priests, it was not surprising that the pope, who knew of the mass murders of the Jews by mid-1942, nevertheless refused to condemn these crimes officially.

Pius XII was too cautious, and his well-intentioned attempts at behind-the-scenes diplomacy proved ineffectual. Critics have cited his reluctance to identify the Jews as victims (he preferred the pusillanimous term *unfortunate people*) to suggest that he was an uncaring anti-Semite. Such accusations are unjust, however. Guided more by concerns about the preservation of the church hierarchy and the physical survival of Rome, Pius XII failed to lead morally and speak authoritatively. Exaggerated caution, not anti-Semitism, accounted for his reluctance to remonstrate against Nazi war crimes.

In March 1998, John Paul II issued a document entitled "We Remember: A Reflection on the Shoah." Although it called for Catholics to repent if they had known about the Holocaust yet failed to act, this document absolved Pius XII of blame and praised him for resolute diplomacy that reputedly led to the salvation of hundreds of thousands of Jews. Controversy nevertheless continues today on whether Pius XII should be beatified and made a saint or vilified as "Hitler's pope." Yet a middle ground does exist between hagiographers, on the one hand, and scandalous and carping caricaturists, on the other.

William J. Astore

See also

Chaplains; Charities; Holocaust, The; Pius XII, Pope; Religion and the War

References

Cornwell, John. *Hitler's Pope: The Secret History of Pius XII.* New York: Viking, 1999.

Crosby, Donald F. *Battlefield Chaplains: Catholic Priests in World War II.* Lawrence: University Press of Kansas, 1994.

Goldhagen, Daniel Jonah. *A Moral Reckoning: The Role of the Catholic Church in the Holocaust and Its Unfulfilled Duty of Repair.* New York: Alfred A. Knopf, 2002.

Lewy, Guenter. *The Catholic Church and Nazi Germany.* New York: McGraw-Hill, 1964.

Phayer, Michael. *The Catholic Church and the Holocaust, 1930–1965.* Bloomington: Indiana University Press, 2000.

Catroux, Georges Albert Julien (1877–1969)

Free French general and colonial administrator. Born on 29 January 1877, at Limoges, France, Georges Catroux was the son of a general and spent much of his youth in the Middle East. He graduated from the French Military Academy of St. Cyr in 1898, joined the French Foreign Legion, and served in North Africa. During World War I, Catroux was wounded and captured on the Western Front while commanding a company of Algerian *tirailleurs* (riflemen). Between the wars, he returned to colonial service, becoming a full general and commanding XIII Corps in Algeria in 1938. In 1939, Catroux's advocacy of sweeping military reforms led the chief of staff, General Maurice Gamelin, to place him on the reserve list.

In August 1939, Catroux, known for his relatively liberal views regarding colonialism, was sent to Indochina as governor-general. He was one of only two overseas commanders who rejected the June 1940 armistice with Germany. Following the French military defeat, Catroux also came under intense Japanese pressure for base rights in northern Indochina, which the Vichy government conceded in late August 1940 in exchange for Japanese recognition of French sovereignty over the colony. Ordered back to France on 26 July 1940, he led an unsuccessful colonial anti-Vichy revolt, before joining Charles de Gaulle's Free French forces in London in September.

When British forces took Vichy-held Syria in June 1941, Catroux immediately became the Free French delegate general for the mandates of Syria and Lebanon and promised the areas postwar independence, pledges that de Gaulle declined to endorse. Deeply involved in the complicated maneuverings between Vichy and Free French representatives in Algiers after the November 1942 Allied landings, in which

the Free French eventually prevailed, Catroux was designated to establish control over all French colonial forces. Although he stalwartly supported de Gaulle, he lamented his leader's ferocious quarrels with the British. In June 1943, Catroux became commissioner for Muslim affairs throughout the French colonies. Appointed governor of Algeria in June 1944, he began extending French citizenship to Algerian Muslims. In September, he was named French minister for North Africa.

After the war, Catroux spent the years between 1945 and 1948 as the French ambassador to Moscow, and in 1954, he presided over France's inquiry into the loss of Indochina. In 1956, he became governor-general of Algeria but resigned after four days when reactionary European colonists objected to his presumed proindependence views. A de Gaulle confidant during the general's 1953–1958 exile, Catroux chaired the court-martial in 1961 that condemned those French generals who rebelled against de Gaulle's instructions to cease hostilities in Algeria. Catroux died in Paris on 21 December 1969.

Priscilla Roberts

See also

de Gaulle, Charles; France, Free French; Gamelin, Maurice Gustave; North Africa Campaign

References

Gillois, André. *Histoire secrète des Français à Londres de 1940 à 1944.* Paris: Hachette, 1973.

Kersaudy, François. *Churchill and de Gaulle.* New York: Atheneum, 1981.

Ordioni, Pierre. *Tout commence à Alger, 1940–1945.* Paris: Éditions Albatros, 1985.

Caucasus Campaign (22 July 1942–February 1943)

German campaign, dubbed Operation EDELWEISS, to capture the rich Caspian oil fields. Although the offensive was unsuccessful, the territory taken in this operation represented the farthest points to the east and south reached by the German army during the war.

The great German summer offensive, Operation BLAU (BLUE), opened on 28 June. General Erich von Manstein had argued for a concentration in the center of the front. He believed that Soviet leader Josef Stalin would commit all available resources to save Moscow and that this approach offered the best chance of destroying the Red Army; it would also result in a more compact front. Adolf Hitler rejected this sound approach and instead divided his resources. In the north, he would push to take Leningrad, still under siege, and link up with the Finns. But the main effort would be Operation BLAU to the south, in which the Caucasus oil fields located near the cities of Baku, Maikop, and Grozny would be the ultimate prize. Securing these areas would severely cripple Soviet military operations, while at the same time aiding those of Germany.

Hitler ordered Field Marshal Fedor von Bock's Army Group South to move east from around Kursk and take Voronezh, which fell to the Germans on 6 July. Hitler then reorganized his southern forces into Army Groups A and B. Field Marshal Siegmund List commanded Army Group A, the southern formation; General Maximilian von Weichs had charge of the northern formation, Army Group B.

Hitler's original plan was for Army Groups A and B to cooperate in a great effort to secure the Don and Donets Valleys and capture the cities of Rostov and Stalingrad. The two could then move southeast to take the oil fields. The Germans expected to be aided in their efforts there by the fact that most of the region was inhabited by non-Russian nationalities, such as the Chechens, whose loyalty to the Soviet government was suspect.

On 13 July, Hitler ordered a change of plans, now demanding that Stalingrad, a major industrial center and key crossing point on the Volga River, and the Caucasus be captured simultaneously. This demand placed further strains on already inadequate German resources, especially logistical support. The twin objectives also meant that a gap would inevitably appear between the two German army groups, enabling most Soviet troops caught in the Don River bend to escape eastward.

On 22 July, Army Group A's First Panzer and Seventeenth Armies assaulted Rostov. Within two days, they had captured the city. A few days later, the Germans established a bridgehead across the Don River at Bataysk, and Hitler then issued Führer Directive 45, initiating EDELWEISS. He believed that the Red Army was close to defeat and that the advance into the Caucasus should proceed without waiting until the Don was cleared and Stalingrad had fallen. The operation would be a case of strategic overreach.

Securing the mountain passes of the Caucasus region between the Black and Caspian Seas was crucial in any operation to take the oil fields. To accomplish this task, Army Group A had special troops trained for Alpine operations, including Seventeenth Army's XLIX Mountain Corps. Supporting Army Group A's eastern flank was Army Group B's Fourth Panzer Army.

At the end of July, List had at his disposal 10 infantry divisions as well as 3 Panzer and 2 motorized divisions, along with a half dozen Romanian and Slovak divisions. Hitler expected List to conquer an area the size of France with this force. Despite these scant German and allied forces, the Soviets had only scattered units available to oppose the German advance. On 28 July, the Soviets created the North Caucasus Front, commanded by Marshal Semen Budenny, and Stalin ordered his forces to stand in place and not retreat. But even reprisals failed to stem the Soviet withdrawal before Army Group A's rapid advance, which had all the characteristics of a blitzkrieg. Indeed, the chief obstacles to the German advance were logistical, created by the vast distances involved and terrain problems. The Germans used aerial resupply where possible and also horses and camels to press their advance.

By 9 August, the 5th SS Panzer Division had taken the first of the Caucasus oil fields at Maykop. To the west, infantry and mountain formations of the Seventeenth Army had made slower progress, but on 9 August, they took Krasnodar, capital of the rich agricultural Kuban region. They then moved in a broad advance into the Caucasus Mountains, with the goal of taking the Black Sea ports of Novorossiysk, Tuapse, and Sukhumi. Soviet forces, meanwhile, continued to fall back into the Caucasus. As Budenny's North Caucasus Front prepared to defend the Black Sea ports, the Soviets sabotaged the oil fields, removing much of the equipment and destroying the wellheads. So successful was this effort that there would be no significant oil production from the region until after the war.

By the end of August, the German advance had slowed to a crawl. For the Seventeenth Army, the problems were terrain and a stiffening Soviet resistance. Bitter fighting occurred in Novorossiysk, beginning on 18 August when the Germans threw six divisions against the city. It fell on 6 September, although the Soviets managed to evacuate their defending marine infantry by sea.

To the east, the advance of the First Panzer Army, pushing toward the oil fields at Grozny, also slowed. Problems there were largely logistical, with a serious shortage of fuel impeding forward movement. In addition, Hitler was gradually siphoning off First Army's strength, including two divisions, some of its artillery, and most of its air support (diverted north to the cauldron of Stalingrad). Weather now became a factor, with the first snowfall in the mountains on 12 September. Displeased with the progress of his forces in the Caucasus and despite List's objections, Hitler assumed personal control of Army Group A on 10 September and sacked List.

Hitler's plan was far too ambitious for the assets committed. The weather had become a critical concern, as did continuing German logistical problems. The Soviets, meanwhile, were able to feed additional resources into the fight. On 14 October, the Germans suspended offensive operations in the Caucasus, except for the Seventeenth Army efforts on the Terek River and around Tuapse. The Germans

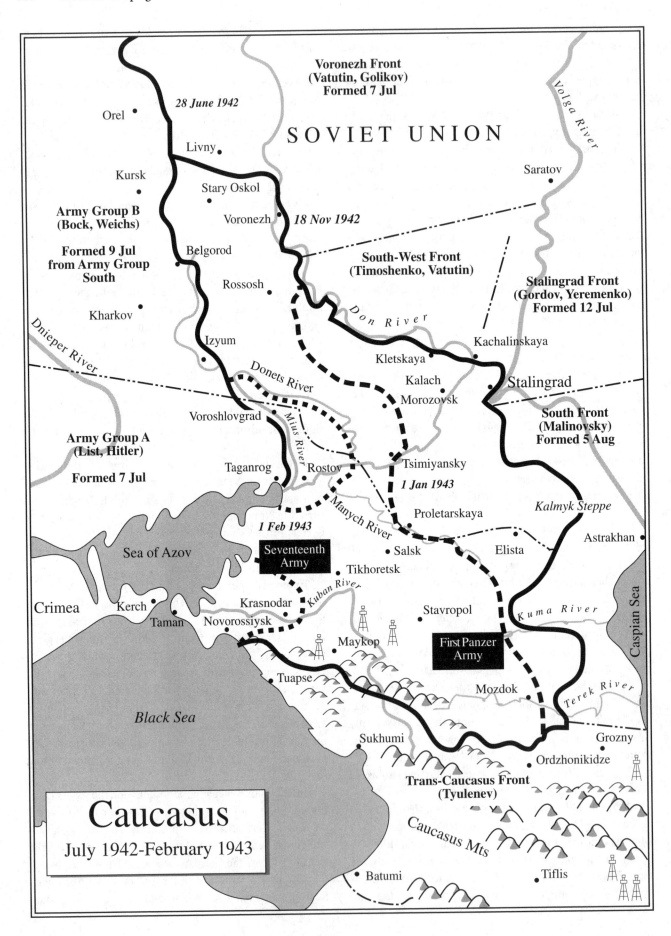

Voronezh Front
(Vatutin, Golikov)
Formed 7 Jul

28 June 1942

Orel

Livny

SOVIET UNION

Kursk

Stary Oskol

Saratov

Army Group B
(Bock, Weichs)

Voronezh

18 Nov 1942

Belgorod

Formed 9 Jul
from Army Group
South

Rossosh

Don River

South-West Front
(Timoshenko, Vatutin)

Stalingrad Front
(Gordov, Yeremenko)
Formed 12 Jul

Kharkov

Izyum

Kachalinskaya

Dnieper River

Donets River

Kletskaya

Kalach

Stalingrad

Mius River

Morozovsk

Voroshlovgrad

Army Group A
(List, Hitler)

Taganrog

Rostov

Tsimiyansky

South Front
(Malinovsky)
Formed 5 Aug

Formed 7 Jul

1 Jan 1943

Manych River

Proletarskaya

Kalmyk Steppe

1 Feb 1943

Sea of Azov

Seventeenth
Army

Salsk

Elista

Astrakhan

Tikhoretsk

Crimea

Kerch

Krasnodar

Kuban River

Stavropol

Kuma River

Caspian Sea

Taman

Novorossiysk

Maykop

First Panzer
Army

Black Sea

Tuapse

Mozdok

Terek River

Sukhumi

Grozny

Ordzhonikidze

Trans-Caucasus Front
(Tyulenev)

Caucasus

July 1942–February 1943

Caucasus Mts

Batumi

Tiflis

took Tuapse several days later but then called a halt to offensive operations on 4 November.

Events at Stalingrad now took precedence. By the end of November, Soviets forces had encircled the German Sixth Army at Stalingrad, and Soviet successes there placed the Axis forces in the Caucasus in an untenable situation. Then, on 29 November, the Soviet Transcaucasus Front launched an offensive of its own along the Terek. The Germans repulsed this attack, but on 22 December, German forces began a withdrawal from positions along the Terek River. At the end of December, with the situation to the north growing more precarious daily, Hitler reluctantly ordered Army Group A to withdraw. This movement began in early January, with Soviet forces unable seriously to disrupt it. By early February, German forces had withdrawn to the Taman Peninsula, from which Hitler hoped to renew his Caucasus offensive in the spring. In October 1943, however, German forces there were withdrawn across Kerch Strait into the Crimea.

Germany's Caucasus Campaign turned out to be a costly and unsuccessful gamble. Ultimately, by splitting his resources between Stalingrad and the Caucasus, Hitler got neither.

Michael Share and Spencer C. Tucker

See also
Bock, Fedor von; Budenny, Semen Mikhailovich; Crimea Campaign; Hitler, Adolf; List, Siegmund Wilhelm Walter; Paulus, Friedrich; Sevastopol, Battle for; Stalin, Josef; Stalingrad, Battle of; Weichs zur Glon, Maximilian Maria Joseph von

References
Erickson, John. *The Road to Stalingrad.* London: Weidenfeld and Nicolson, 1975.
Glantz, David M., and Jonathan M. House. *When Titans Clashed: How the Red Army Stopped Hitler.* Lawrence: University Press of Kansas, 1995.
Seaton, Albert. *The Russo-German War, 1941–1945.* New York: Praeger, 1971.
Werth, Alexander. *Russia at War, 1941–1945.* New York: Carroll and Graf, 1964.

forestall developments in naval aviation, and to assert the peculiar ethos of the harbor-bound "fleet in being" as a passive naval deterrent—and preservative.

France had long been the Italian navy's presumptive regional rival, but from March 1935, Admiral Cavagnari began to focus on Great Britain as a more likely Mediterranean threat. He proposed developing a large Italian counterfleet to deal with that threat, although Mussolini refused to consider the concept. The Italian navy embarked on more modest building and rebuilding projects focused on capital ships, but as late as 1938, it had no plans for an aircraft carrier, despite the manifest lack of cooperation between the navy and air force. Also, the May 1939 Friedrichshaven summit confirming the Pact of Steel left Cavagnari skeptical of the practical benefits of a naval alliance with Germany.

The coming of war in June 1940 nonetheless found Italy with a navy that was well positioned to disrupt British movements in the Mediterranean. Cavagnari, however, did not deploy his forces decisively, which effectively gave an initially weaker Royal Navy opportunities to regroup and build to strength.

The 11 November 1940 torpedo attack on the Italian fleet at Taranto by Royal Navy carrier aircraft clearly demonstrated the power of naval aviation, and it crippled not only the Italian navy but also the credibility of the "fleet in being" imperative. Mussolini relieved Cavagnari of his dual command in December 1940, and the admiral soon went into retirement. He died in Rome on 2 November 1966.

Gordon E. Hogg

See also
Italy, Navy; Mussolini, Benito; Taranto, Attack on

References
Bragadin, Marc'Antonio. *The Italian Navy in World War II.* Annapolis, MD: Naval Institute Press, 1957.
Mallett, Robert. *The Italian Navy and Fascist Expansionism, 1935–1940.* London: Cass, 1998.

Cavagnari, Domenico (1876–1966)

Italian navy admiral who was given a dual command by Benito Mussolini but relieved of it early in the war. Born on 20 July 1876, at Genoa, Italy, Domenico Cavagnari graduated from the Italian Naval Academy in 1895 and served as a destroyer captain in World War I. In 1933, Mussolini named him both undersecretary of the navy and naval chief of staff, offices that, over time, Cavagnari would use to position the navy more favorably with the Fascist regime, to

Cavallero, Ugo (Conte) (1880–1943)

Italian army marshal, industrialist, and government figure under Benito Mussolini's regime. Born at Castello Monferrato, Italy, on 20 September 1880, Ugo Cavallero was commissioned an infantry lieutenant in 1900. He became a gunnery instructor in 1906 and graduated from the War College at Turin in 1911. As a captain, he fought in Libya during the 1912–1913 war with the Ottoman Empire. He served largely at the staff level during World War I, reaching the rank of brigadier general in 1918.

Cavallero also sought advancement in industry, assuming the directorship of the Pirelli Works in 1920. Five years later, he was called on by Italian Premier Mussolini to serve as undersecretary of war. In that capacity, he awarded Pietro Badoglio the highest posts in the Italian army before souring on him and stripping him of his powers in 1927 and then publicly snubbing him in 1928—a scandal that cost Cavallero his own powerful post. Again finding a lucrative refuge in industry, he assumed the presidency of the Ansaldo arms and shipbuilding conglomerate, devoting himself to updating and improving its output. Ironically, the Italian navy's 1933 protests that a new cruiser was receiving substandard armor plate and machinery obliged Cavallero to resign in disgrace, although proof of his complicity in the scandal was never established.

Next joining the Italian delegation to the 1932–1934 Geneva arms conference, Cavallero commanded Italian forces in East Africa in 1937 but resigned in spring 1939 after a dispute with his superior, the duke of Aosta. That June, Cavallero began shaping the Pact of Steel with Germany, conveying to Berlin Mussolini's wish to delay war until 1943, when Italy might be fully armed. In December 1940, he succeeded Badoglio as military chief of staff, and he struggled to maintain the tenuous Italian Balkan Front even as Mussolini demanded a (doomed) March 1941 offensive. Cavallero cleaned house at the War Ministry beginning in May 1941; his reforms of the three military branches came amid increased German strategic control of the Italian war effort and were hampered by Il Duce's habitual interference. Elevated in rank to marshal in July 1942, Cavallero was thwarted in his plans for an assault on Malta by German demands for Italian forces on the Soviet Front. Until January 1943, he attempted to evacuate Libya while deflecting the criticism of, among others, Mussolini, who dismissed him from office on 6 February 1943.

Arrested and imprisoned by Badoglio after Mussolini was removed on 25 July 1943, Cavallero tried to link himself with anti-Duce conspirators. After the 8 September armistice, Field Marshal Albert Kesselring, the German commander in Italy and a personal friend to Cavallero, released him and offered him military command of the new Fascist Italian Social Republic. Cavallero was discovered dead of an apparently self-inflicted pistol wound at Kesselring's headquarters in Frascati, outside Rome, on 14 September 1943.

Gordon E. Hogg

See also
Badoglio, Pietro; Italy, Role in War; Kesselring, Albert; Malta; Mussolini, Benito; Savoia, Amedeo Umberto di
References
Cannistraro, Philip V. *Historical Dictionary of Fascist Italy.* Westport, CT: Greenwood Press, 1982.

Dizionario biografico degli Italiani. Vol. 22. Rome: Istituto della Enciclopedia Italiana, 1974.
Knox, MacGregor. *Hitler's Italian Allies: Royal Armed Forces, Fascist Regime, and the War of 1940–43.* New York: Cambridge University Press, 2000.

Cavalry, Horse

After their domestication, horses served as mounts for countless soldiers over the centuries. Associated with gallantry and courage, they were valued as cavalry mounts for their speed and ability to cover rough ground that was inaccessible to vehicles. Cavalry troops rode into battle; dragoons were mounted infantrymen who used the horses for transportation to battle and then fought dismounted. Not until the 1911–1912 Italo-Turkish War did mechanized vehicles began to replace horses. Although limited in number in comparison with previous conflicts, cavalry troops fought during World War II on both the Allied and Axis sides.

Britain and the United States did not utilize cavalry to any appreciable extent, but other Allied countries deployed horse cavalry because they could not afford sufficient mechanized equipment. Cavalry supplemented motorized vehicles. Especially on the Eastern Front, horses proved to be capable transportation and combat mounts that could overcome difficult conditions and the lack of paved roads. Poland, the Soviet Union, Germany, Italy, China, Japan, and Hungary all employed horse cavalry units in the war.

Cavalry charges sometimes enabled soldiers to take enemy troops by surprise, and they provided shock value. Mounted raids permitted soldiers to seize property and destroy military supplies and encampments. Horses also provided a means for scouts to conduct reconnaissance. But modern weapons with high-volume firepower were serious obstacles for the vulnerable unarmored cavalry; also, procuring forage and veterinary care for their horses were problems for all cavalry forces.

Poland maintained cavalry reconnaissance units and brigades. In September 1939, it had 41 cavalry regiments, of which only 3 were mechanized. Armed with guns and anti-tank rifles, the Polish cavalry confronted German tanks. At Morka, for example, the Wolynska Cavalry Brigade engaged the 4th Panzer Division for three days and disabled 80 German tanks and armored vehicles before retiring. World War II myths include tales that Polish cavalry armed with lances charged German tanks, and Italian newspapers printed stories about a Polish cavalry attack that did not occur and was actually German propaganda. Some notable authentic cavalry charges of the war included the 1 September 1939 engagement between German lancers and Polish troops at the

Ulatkowka River and the 12 August 1942 Italian charge at Chebotarevsky in the Soviet Union. Most World War II cavalrymen, however, were really dragoons who fought dismounted.

Germany fielded five cavalry divisions in 1940. In addition, the Germans assigned reconnaissance cavalry squadrons to infantry divisions and stationed a cavalry brigade in East Prussia. The German 1st Cavalry Division covered some 1,200 miles in the Battle for France. France also had horse cavalry that endeavored to stop the German advance. The German army then expanded its cavalry strength and capabilities for Operation BARBAROSSA, the invasion of the Soviet Union.

The Red Army employed some 1.2 million horses to support its cavalry, artillery, and supply needs. At the time of the June 1941 German invasion, the Soviets had reduced their 7 cavalry corps and 32 cavalry divisions of 1937 to 4 corps and 12 divisions, of which 4 were mountain cavalry. One of the last significant cavalry charges on the Eastern Front occurred in November 1941 outside Musino, near Moscow, when the 44th Mongolian Cavalry Division attacked the Germans. The defenders used machine-gun fire to kill many of the attacking troops and an estimated 2,000 horses in only 10 minutes. No Germans died in the battle.

The Soviets supplemented their mounted forces with artillery. Given the primitive Soviet transportation system and the weather that turned tracks into seas of mud, horses were often more effective at transport than vehicles. Guerrillas in Ukraine also utilized horses to raid the Germans, and a number of these fighters, including Cossacks and Kalmucks who were highly skilled horsemen well familiar with local conditions, actually fought the Soviets, even after the end of World War II. When the XV (SS) Cossack Cavalry Corps surrendered to the British and were turned over to the Soviets in 1945, the troops were either executed outright or sent to labor camps in Siberia.

The British army deployed the 1st Cavalry Division, as well as the Royal Dragoons and Royal Scots Greys, both of which were mechanized in 1941. The Cheshire Yeomanry and Queen's Own Yorkshire Dragoons fought Vichy French troops in Syria in 1941 before becoming mechanized. The final horse cavalry charge in British history occurred on 21 March 1942, at Toungoo, Burma. Captain Arthur Sandeman commanded the Central India Horse of the Burma Frontier Force. Mounted on mostly Burmese ponies, his column of primarily Sikh horsemen spotted Japanese troops constructing trenches and defenses. Sandeman and his men mistook the Japanese for Chinese soldiers and approached them. Too late, they realized their mistake. Sandeman, an old-fashioned officer who preferred horses to machines, then waved his sword to lead a charge and was killed. Some

of his men followed him, but many retreated to a nearby airfield.

The U.S. Army also had horse cavalry units at the start of the war, although half of its 17 cavalry regiments were dismounted by 1941. Most were mechanized, although some fought as infantry. On 1 April 1941, the army activated the 2nd Cavalry Division at Fort Riley, Kansas. Almost 6,000 cavalry horses were stationed at Fort Riley early in the war, but by the end of 1942, all U.S. cavalry regiments had been mechanized. They nonetheless retained emblems and traditions of the horse cavalry.

The U.S. 26th Cavalry Regiment served in the Philippines, arriving there in December 1941 to counter invading Japanese troops. The American cavalry successfully deterred Japanese tanks and led a counterattack so that U.S. and Filipino troops could withdraw into the Bataan Peninsula. Because the Allied forces were short of food, the cavalry horses were subsequently killed for meat. The 26th Cavalry was then mechanized and fought until the 9 April 1942 surrender to the Japanese.

Major General Lucian K. Truscott Jr. formed the 3rd Provisional Reconnaissance Troop Mounted in Italy in 1943. The horses of this unit proved useful for traveling in the mountains during the fighting there. Lieutenant General George S. Patton Jr. emphasized that "as good as U.S. armor was, the war could still have used some horses. If we'd had a brigade or a division of horse cavalry in Sicily and Italy the bag of Germans would certainly have been bigger."

The National Defense Act of 1947 officially ended mounted units in the U.S. military. In post–World War II military actions, cavalry horses seemed obsolete except in parts of the Third World where deep snow and mountainous conditions hindered movement by vehicle. Modern cavalry is primarily known as mechanized, armored, or air cavalry.

Elizabeth D. Schafer

See also

Animals; Armored Warfare; BARBAROSSA, Operation; China-Burma-India Theater; Germany, Army; Italy Campaign; Partisans/Guerrillas; Patton, George Smith, Jr.; Philippines, Japanese Capture of; Poland, Army; Poland Campaign; Soviet Union, Army; Tanks, All Powers; Truscott, Lucian King, Jr.

References

Brereton, John M. *The Horse in War*. New York: Arco, 1976.

Ellis, John. *Cavalry: The History of Mounted Warfare*. New York: G. P. Putnam, 1978.

Lunt, James D. *Charge to Glory! A Garland of Cavalry Exploits*. London: Heinemann, 1960.

Piekalkiewicz, Janusz. *The Cavalry of World War II*. Harrisburg, PA: Historical Times, 1979.

Rogers, Colonel H. C. B. *The Mounted Troops of the British Army, 1066–1945*. London: Seeley Service, 1959.

Rudnicki, K. S. *The Last of the War Horses*. London: Bachman and Turner, 1974.

Truscott, Lucian K., Jr. *The Twilight of the U.S. Cavalry: Life in the Old Army, 1917–1942.* Edited and with Preface by Lucian K. Truscott III and Foreword by Edward M. Coffman. Lawrence: University Press of Kansas, 1989.

Urwin, Gregory J. W. *United States Cavalry: An Illustrated History.* Dorset, UK: Blandford Press, 1983.

CBI

See China-Burma-India Theater.

Censorship

The practice of suppressing and/or manipulating information and news, often by a government agency. Every nation involved in World War II applied censorship to some degree. But exactly what was censored and how it was censored varied from country to country. Totalitarian Germany and the Soviet Union generally manipulated the news by completely controlling the newspapers and radio stations: citizens normally knew only what their governments decided they should know. German Minister of Propaganda Joseph Goebbels, for example, rigidly controlled the flow of news to the German people. The governments of Italy and Japan held similar powers and used them frequently, but there were also surprising instances when newspapers were able to criticize those governments without severe repercussions. Still, the Japanese people at large knew nothing about their navy's great defeat in the June 1942 Battle of Midway. In Great Britain, the wartime government preferred to enforce censorship through prior restraint by creating a detailed censorship code and having government employees enforce it by carefully reviewing the contents of all news before it could be published or broadcast. Most of the Commonwealth nations followed suit, creating censorship codes and enforcing them as Britain did.

The U.S. system of wartime censorship also employed written censorship codes, but the government enforced these codes in a less intrusive way. This unique system of "voluntary self-censorship" was created just after Pearl Harbor. President Franklin D. Roosevelt decided that American censorship should begin with separate spheres for military information and domestic news. Thus, the U.S. Army and Navy kept control of their information by such traditional expedients as editing the mail of military personnel (the extent varied widely from unit to unit) and issuing very general press releases. In the field, the army and navy required American correspondents to agree to specific rules or be banned from combat theaters. Military censors also reviewed the copy written by correspondents, which had to be approved before it could be transmitted to their home offices.

For the most part, correspondents accepted military censorship without protest. At one point, virtually the entire press corps in Sicily voluntarily suppressed the story about Lieutenant General George S. Patton slapping two soldiers. Writer John Steinbeck, who spent about five months in Europe as a war correspondent, remembered that he and his colleagues censored themselves more vigorously than did the military censors.

For domestic news, Roosevelt created the Office of Censorship. This body was similar to the Creel Committee of World War I, which had developed a general censorship code that the media then pledged to follow. However, knowing how American reporters and editors had resented George Creel's heavy-handed approach, Roosevelt shrewdly selected Byron Price, lead editor of the Associated Press, to head his new office. Price, in consultation with a censorship operating board composed of representatives of several federal agencies, handled the press fairly by applying the new censorship codes for the press and for radio news in a consistent manner.

Neither of the codes was very long, and the details were deliberately somewhat vague. Price preferred to ask editors to guide their own actions by asking themselves, "Is this information I would like to have if I were the enemy?" This appeal to patriotism worked well, for throughout the war, editors tended to censor their agencies' stories so heavily that Price's staff and the volunteer monitors who reviewed local newspaper stories for the office often suggested that deleted information could be returned to the text.

The most serious challenge to censorship came in June 1942, when Stanley Johnston, a reporter for the *Chicago Tribune,* gained access to a confidential navy communiqué based on the navy's ability to read Japan's naval codes. From this information, Johnston wrote a story revealing that the U.S. Navy had advance information about the Japanese attack on Midway. This scoop, which the *Chicago Tribune* published without submitting it to Price's censors, threatened to expose U.S. code-breaking operations. Outraged at the harm this could have done to the war in the Pacific, the Department of Justice prepared a case against the newspaper for violating the Espionage Act. In the end, however, the government dropped the matter, partly because the story had not contravened the existing censorship code but largely because a public trial would only further jeopardize the code-breaking secret. Fortunately for the Allies, the Japanese apparently were not aware of the story.

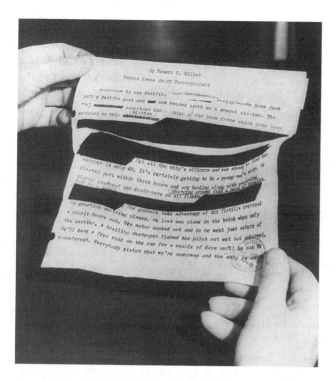

Page of notebook of Robert C. Miller, United Press correspondent, which had parts blacked out when passing through Naval censorship, 1942. (Library of Congress)

The censorship code was then revised and reissued with greater restrictions. The main impact of the incident seems to have made most editors even more cooperative in censoring their own stories. By 1944, a few reporters had picked up gleanings about the purpose of the top-secret MANHATTAN Project, yet all of them kept quiet about the knowledge that America was building an atomic bomb. The fact that one of these reporters was the notorious whistle-blower Drew Pearson only underscores how readily the media accepted the need for wartime censorship.

Throughout the war, most of the Office of Censorship's 15,000 employees were not battling with the press but instead were monitoring the vast amount of mail, cables, and telephone calls that went overseas, seeking to keep information from falling into the wrong hands. As had the media, American citizens accepted this censorship without great protest. Indeed, few Americans seemed to complain about censorship at all, which was very different from the way they groused about rationing, taxes, shortages, or many of the other restrictions that the war had placed on their freedoms.

Even after 1945, there was remarkably little criticism of wartime censorship, in marked contrast to the complaints that followed the war in Britain and elsewhere. These attitudes shed light on popular American views of the emergency in the early months after Pearl Harbor. They also suggest that Byron Price had been right when he told President Roosevelt that he would get more cooperation from Americans by asking them to help him rather than telling them what to do.

Terry Shoptaugh

See also

Goebbels, Paul Josef; Journalism and the War; MANHATTAN Project; Midway, Battle of; Patton, George Smith, Jr.; Roosevelt, Franklin D.

References

Steinbeck, John. *Once There Was a War*. New York: Viking, 1958.

Summers, Robert, ed. *Wartime Censorship of Press and Radio*. New York: H. W. Wilson, 1942.

Sweeney, Michael. *Secrets of Victory: The Office of Censorship and the American Press and Radio in World War II*. Chapel Hill: University of North Carolina Press, 2001.

Central Pacific Campaign

The U.S. Navy's overarching strategy for defeating the Japanese by making a thrust through the Central Pacific had its roots in a long-standing concept for a maritime war with Japan. War Plan Orange dated to 1898, and though modified many times, the basic scheme remained consistent. Plan Orange called for marshaling the main battle fleet in the eastern Pacific, then steaming to the Philippines, where a decisive Mahanian-style battle fleet engagement would occur. Simultaneously, the navy would relieve the beleaguered Philippine army garrison. Faced with catastrophic defeat and total American command of the sea, Japan would presumably surrender.

The successful Japanese strike on Pearl Harbor completely disrupted Plan Orange and the Central Pacific thrust. With all Pacific Fleet battleships sunk or damaged and only five aircraft carriers available in the Pacific, the navy was in no condition to execute Plan Orange, defeat the Imperial Japanese Navy in a decisive battle for command of the sea, or even reinforce or evacuate the Philippine defenders. Consequently, for almost two years, the navy engaged in peripheral operations against the Japanese defensive perimeter, supporting the Marines and the army in the Solomon Islands and New Guinea and repelling Japanese main strike forces at the Battles of the Coral Sea and Midway.

By mid-1943, with Essex-class fleet carriers coming on line from the "two ocean" Naval Expansion Act of 1940 and fast battleships of the North Carolina– and South Dakota–classes for antiaircraft support and shore bombardment, the commander in chief of the Pacific Fleet, Admiral Chester Nimitz, stood ready to launch the Central Pacific assault against the Japanese Empire.

The dual-pronged Pacific strategy that emerged in 1943 represented a compromise between the services. The ABC Conference (between Britain, Canada, and the United States in March 1941) established Pacific operational areas, which the Joint Chiefs of Staff reconfirmed in March 1942. The agreement gave the navy operational control over the Central and South Pacific areas; the army had responsibility for the southwest Pacific. The army area commander, General Douglas MacArthur, advocated an advance up the New Guinea coast along the New Guinea–Mindanao axis to isolate the Japanese base at Rabaul and drive to the Philippines. The navy, meanwhile, pressed for a Central Pacific thrust. In March 1943, the Joint Chiefs agreed on a compromise plan whereby both services would advance along their preferred routes while simultaneously supporting each other. The results of this dual-pronged strategy formed from compromise were devastating for Imperial Japan.

To face two simultaneous threats, the Japanese, unable to concentrate against a single-threat axis, had to stretch their air, naval, and ground forces perilously thin. By adopting a "leap-frogging" operational mode in both the Central and southwest Pacific, U.S. forces could attack strategic points, such as islands with airfields, while simply bypassing and isolating large Japanese garrisons, such as Truk and Rabaul. These latter then withered on the vine.

Another component of the Central Pacific strategy was the submarine offensive against Japanese shipping. This offensive further reduced Japan's capability to reinforce and sustain isolated garrisons as U.S. forces advanced key island by key island, beginning with Operation GALVANIC against the Gilbert Islands in November 1943. In the interwar years, the Marine Corps had made great strides in amphibious operations, and Guadalcanal had been a useful test of amphibious doctrine. Nimitz and his chief of staff, Vice Admiral Raymond Spruance, had originally conceived of the first thrust going against the Marshall Islands; however, the Gilberts were closer to Hawaii and within range of land-based air cover.

The Central Pacific thrust offered a number of advantages. The many islands and atolls provided a target-rich environment that prevented the Japanese from determining the precise route of advance and forced them to defend all points. The size of the islands and atolls discouraged the establishment of large garrisons. The long distances between islands mitigated mutual support, and American carrier airpower inhibited supply and reinforcement. Further, the line of communications from Pearl Harbor and the mainland United States would be shorter than that to the southwest Pacific. The Central Pacific also offered a more healthful climate than the jungles of New Guinea. And an advance through the Central Pacific would cut off and isolate Japanese forces in the South Pacific.

There were, of course, some disadvantages to a Central Pacific thrust. These included the requirement for overwhelming naval and air superiority, which could not be achieved until late 1943 and necessitated the defeat of the main Japanese battle fleet (which occurred in the Battle of Midway). The U.S. plan would also rely on successful amphibious operations, which had not been totally proven.

Operation GALVANIC commenced in late autumn 1943 with landings on Tarawa Atoll (the primary objective being Betio, with its airfield) and Makin Atoll. The joint army, navy, and marine force employed overpowering numbers, with more than 200 ships and 35,000 troops under Rear Admiral Richmond K. Turner, commander of V Amphibious Force. Task Forces 52 and 53 assaulted the atolls on 20 November 1943. Six fleet carriers and five light carriers, escorted by six battleships, provided overwhelming firepower, naval gunfire support, and air cover. Additionally, several hundred army, navy, and marine aircraft participated from the base at Ellice Island. Despite Japanese air attacks from the Marshalls, the air threat proved negligible. On Tarawa, strong fortifications, bunkers, hidden obstacles, and barbed wire slowed the advance—a prelude to future Japanese defensive schemes—and with orders to fight to the last man, the garrison staunchly resisted. Very few Japanese survived, another indicator of the bitter struggle unfolding in the Central Pacific Campaign. U.S. forces suffered a 17 percent casualty rate and encountered other problems as well, including faulty beach and surf intelligence, the inability of landing craft to negotiate shallow atoll waters, inadequate landing craft, too little advance shore bombardment, and poor communications. The Gilberts experience provided many valuable lessons for the U.S. Navy and Marines on how to conduct future operations.

The Marshall Islands were next. Despite a dearth of transports, Operation FLINTLOCK finally commenced on 31 January 1944. Eniwetok and Kwajalein (the world's largest coral atoll) succumbed to overwhelming force and the pounding from Vice Admiral Marc Mitscher's Fast Carrier Task Force 58. The Americans had learned from the Gilberts experience, and casualties among the assaulting forces were much lighter. With the capture of the Marshalls by March, 10 weeks ahead of the established timetable, the navy bypassed several heavily fortified Japanese-held islands and turned its attention to the Mariana Archipelago.

The assault on the Marianas, Operation FORAGER, aimed at taking Guam, Saipan, and Tinian Islands. From these bases, the Japanese home islands would be within striking distance of the B-29 Superfortress heavy bombers. The assault on Saipan commenced on 13 June 1944, with landings on 16 June. Determined to halt the advance by interdicting the supporting naval forces, Vice Admiral Ozawa Jisaburo mounted an assault on the Americans in the Battle of the Philippine Sea. However, the assault, which commenced on 19 June, turned into disaster as the better-trained and better-equipped U.S. Navy pilots decimated the inexperienced Japanese airmen in what came to be called the "great Marianas turkey shoot." Ozawa lost 325 of 375 attacking aircraft; Japanese naval airpower disappeared in a day, never to play any significant role in the war thereafter except in desperate suicide attacks in the last months.

Saipan was taken by 13 July. The Marines landed on Tinian on 24 July and secured it on 2 August. Guam, the last of the major islands, was struck on 21 July and was finally declared secured on 10 August.

With the loss of the Marianas, the Japanese defensive perimeter had been decisively breached. U.S. strategic bombing of the Japanese home islands now began in earnest and ended in the atomic bomb attacks launched from Tinian a year later. From the Marianas, the two prongs of the Pacific strategy came together again with the invasion of the Philippines in October 1944.

Tenacious Japanese defenders and their fortifications did cause heavy American casualties, and the difficulties inherent in staging such massive invasion efforts presented formidable challenges to U.S. operations. Nonetheless, the Central Pacific Campaign succeeded decisively. The Imperial Japanese Navy's hitherto deadly air arm had been utterly destroyed, and the stage was set for the final Allied thrust through the Philippines, Iwo Jima, and Okinawa and on toward the Japanese home islands.

Stanley D. M. Carpenter

See also

Amphibious Warfare; Gilbert Islands Campaign; Guadalcanal Naval Campaign; Guam, Battle for; Iwo Jima, Battle for; Kwajalein, Battle for; MacArthur, Douglas; Makin Island, Battle of; Mariana Islands, Naval Campaign; Marshall Islands, Naval Campaign; Mitscher, Marc Andrew; Naval Strengths, Pacific Theater; New Guinea Campaign; Nimitz, Chester William; Ozawa Jisaburo; Philippines, U.S. Recapture of; Rainbow Plans; Saipan, Battle of; Southwest Pacific Theater; Tarawa, Battle of; Tinian, U.S. Invasion of; Two-Ocean Navy Program

References

Dull, Paul S. *A Battle History of the Imperial Japanese Navy, 1941–45.* Annapolis, MD: Naval Institute Press, 1978.

Harries, Meirion, and Susie Harries. *Soldiers of the Sun: The Rise and Fall of the Imperial Japanese Army.* New York: Random House, 1991.

Morison, Samuel Eliot. *History of United States Naval Operations in World War II.* Vol. 8, *New Guinea and the Marianas, March 1944–August 1944.* Boston: Little, Brown, 1948.

Spector, Ronald H. *Eagle against the Sun: The American War with Japan.* New York: Free Press, 1985.

Van de Vat, Dan. *The Pacific Campaign: The U.S.-Japanese Naval War, 1941–1945.* New York: Touchstone, 1991.

Century Group

See Fight for Freedom.

Cephalonia Island

Scene of a German atrocity in 1943. Cephalonia Island (variously spelled as Cephallonia, Cefallonia, Kefalonia, Kefallonia, and Kefallinia), about 200 miles from Italy, is the largest of the Ionian Islands west of Greece. Located at the mouth of the Gulf of Corinth, it lies across a strait from the island of Ithaca. Beginning in April 1941, the Italians occupied the island and informed the Greek inhabitants that they were now Italian citizens.

In May 1943, the Italian Acqui 33rd Infantry Division arrived on Cephalonia. Its commander, Division General Antonio Gandin, was fluent in German, a veteran of the Soviet Front (1941–1942), known to a number of German generals, and a recipient of the Iron Cross. The 33rd Division was composed of about 11,500 enlisted men and officers and was centered on two infantry regiments (the 17th and 317th), an artillery regiment (the 33rd), the 27th Blackshirt Legion and the 19th Blackshirt Battalion, and various support units. In addition, the Italians had some naval coastal batteries, a few torpedo boats, and two aircraft.

Allied gains in 1943 led the Germans to consider the possibility that the Italians would opt out of the war, whereon the Germans decided to reinforce their token garrison on Cephalonia. Between 5 and 6 July, Lieutenant Colonel Hans Barge's 966th Grenadier Regiment arrived, along with a battery of self-propelled guns and nine tanks. This addition brought the German strength to a total of 1,800 men. Shortly thereafter, on 25 July, Mussolini's government collapsed. The Italians on Cephalonia, however, were ignorant of the plans of the Italian War Office and of the possibility of conflict with the Germans.

On the evening of 8 September 1943, Marshal Pietro Badoglio, with the agreement of King Victor Emmanuel, ordered Italian troops to cease all hostilities against Anglo-American forces. Badoglio also ordered that Italian forces should respond with "maximum decision" to any offensive action from "[any] direction whatsoever." The Germans, meanwhile, chose to treat Italians who resisted their authority as mutineers, or *francs-tireurs.*

On 11 September, the Germans on Cephalonia gave Gandin an ultimatum to surrender his weapons. While he was attempting to delay a decision, word came that Italian forces on Corfu were fighting the Germans and that, elsewhere, the Germans were sending the Italians who surrendered to internment camps, despite promises they would be repatriated. On 13 September, the Germans attempted to re-inforce their garrison on Cephalonia, but the Italians opened fire on the two barges carrying troops and supplies and sank both. The next day, Colonel Barge hand-delivered to Gandin an order demanding the Italians turn over their weapons, issued by Lieutenant General Hubert Lanz, commanding the German XXII Mountain Corps. That same day, troops of the 1st Alpine Division under the command of Major von Hirschfeld landed on the island.

Meanwhile, the Italian War Office, now located at Brindisi, ordered the 33rd Division to fight the Germans. Gandin then issued orders to attack the German positions on the island on 15 September if they did not surrender. On that day, German aircraft attacked the Italian positions, and the Italians in turn took 400 German troops as prisoners. Intense fighting continued until 22 September. During that time, the British and Americans, whether from ignorance or from distrust of the Italians, had forbidden the Italian navy or air force to aid Italian troops fighting in Greece. With their ammunition exhausted and having sustained some 1,300 casualties, the Italians surrendered. Almost simultaneously, the Italian War Office announced that help was on the way, but it was too late.

Men of the German XXII Mountain Corps had received a special Führer Order to execute all the Italian soldiers who had fought on Cephalonia. Many who surrendered were shot in their positions, and a group of Bavarian soldiers who protested this action were threatened with summary execution themselves. Large numbers of Italian troops were slain where they were taken; the remainder were transported to the town of San Teodoro and held in the town hall. General Gandin was shot first, but before the bullets hit his body, he threw his Iron Cross into the dirt. His staff and then all the officers were executed, followed by the noncommissioned officers, the enlisted men, and even the medical personnel. The officers' bodies were then weighted and dumped into the sea by navy men who were, in turn, shot. In all, about 4,750 Italians were summarily executed. The only ones spared were the military chaplains, who would later provide many of the details of the massacre. About 1,200 Italians, led by Captain Renzo Appollonio, joined with some Greek partisans and escaped to the mainland.

A group of about 4,000 who had surrendered their arms without fighting were imprisoned in barracks on the island. In October, they were put onto three ships sailing for Greece, but the ships hit mines shortly out of port. Those who did not drown were machine-gunned by the Germans. In all, 390 Italian officers and 9,640 enlisted men perished at the hands of the Germans. In 1948, the Military Tribunal at Nuremberg sentenced General Lanz to 12 years of imprisonment. He was released in 1954.

In the year 2000, Universal Studios released *Captain Corelli's Mandolin,* a romantic story of the Italian occupation and the 33rd Division's destruction. The film was based on Louis de Bernières's novel of the same name.

A. J. L. Waskey

See also
Badoglio, Pietro; International Military Tribunal: The Nuremberg Trials; Victor Emanuel III, King of Italy

References
D'Angelo, Rudy. "Cefalonia—1943: Massacre of the Royal Italian ACQUI Division." *Military Advisor* 8, no. 2 (Spring 1997): 14–17.
Formato, Romualdo. *L'eccidio Cefalonia.* Milan, Italy: U. Mursia, 1968.
Harris, Andy. *Captain Corelli's Island: Cephallonia.* London: Pavillion Books, 2000.
Lamb, Richard. *War in Italy, 1943–1945: A Brutal Story.* New York: St. Martin's Press, 1993.

Chaffee, Adna Romanza, Jr. (1884–1941)

U.S. Army general, regarded as the father of the armored branch. Born in Junction City, Kansas, on 23 September 1884, the son of the second chief of staff of the U.S. Army, Adna Chaffee graduated from the U.S. Military Academy in 1906.

Chaffee was commissioned in the cavalry and served with the 15th Cavalry Regiment in Cuba until 1907. Between 1907 and 1911, he was assigned to the Mounted Services School at Fort Riley, Kansas. There, he commanded the mounted detachment supporting students and staff at the Army War College. After attending the French Cavalry School at Saumur (1911–1912), Chaffee returned to teaching at Fort Riley. In 1914 and 1915, he served with the 7th Cavalry Regiment in the Philippines. Chaffee was then assigned to West Point, where he was senior cavalry instructor for the Tactical Department until 1917.

Following the U.S. entry into World War I, Chaffee attended the staff school at Langres, France, and then was an instructor there. Thereafter, he was assigned as a staff officer with the 81st Division and fought with it in the St.-Mihiel and Meuse-Argonne offensives. He ended the war as a temporary colonel.

Following occupation duty in Germany as a staff officer of III Corps, Chaffee reverted to his permanent rank of captain in 1919. He was then an instructor at the Command and General Staff School at Fort Leavenworth, Kansas. He was promoted to major in 1920. After various assignments, he served as the G-3 of the 1st Cavalry Division at Fort Bliss, Texas, between 1921 and 1924. Chaffee graduated from the Army War College in 1925, and from then until 1927, he commanded a squadron of the 3rd Cavalry Regiment. He next served on the War Department General Staff. Promoted to lieutenant colonel in 1929, he was charged with developing mechanized and armored forces for the army. A staunch supporter of mechanized warfare, Chaffee was probably the leading proponent of a separate armored force. In 1931, he joined the new 1st Cavalry Regiment (Mechanized) at Fort Knox, Kentucky, as its executive officer.

Between 1934 and 1938, Chaffee was chief of the Budget and Legislative Planning Branch of the War Department. He then returned to Fort Knox to command the 1st Cavalry Regiment. In November 1938, he was promoted to brigadier general and received command of the 7th Mechanized Brigade, which he led during the maneuvers at Plattsburgh, New York, in 1939 and in Louisiana in 1940, both of which had significant impact on U.S. Army mechanized doctrine.

Chaffee received command of the new Armored Force in June 1940 and thus had charge of the development of the 1st and 2nd Armored Divisions. In October 1940, he took command of the I Armored Corps as a major general, but by that point, he was already ill from cancer. The disease took his life in Boston, Massachusetts, on 22 August 1941. In 1945, the army named its new light tank, the M-24, in his honor.

Mark A. Buhl

See also
Armored Warfare; Tanks, All Powers
References
Gillie, Mildred H. *Forging the Thunderbolt: A History of the Development of the Armored Force.* Harrisonburg, PA: Military Service Publishing, 1947.
Johnson, David E. *Fast Tanks and Heavy Bombers: Innovations in the U.S. Army, 1917–1945.* Ithaca, NY: Cornell University Press, 1998.

Neville Chamberlain served as prime minister of Great Britain during 1937–1940. He is most remembered for his pursuit of appeasement. (Hilton Archive by Getty Images)

Chamberlain, Arthur Neville (1869–1940)

British politician, leader of the Conservative Party, and prime minister from 1937 to 1940. The son of a distinguished political family, Neville Chamberlain was born on 18 March 1869 in Birmingham, England, and graduated from Mason College, Birmingham. He administered a family plantation in the Bahamas and later ran a metals business, becoming lord mayor of Birmingham in 1915. He was elected to Parliament in December 1918 and achieved cabinet rank quickly, serving as minister of health (1923, 1924–1929, and 1931) and becoming an important reformer in that post. After serving as chancellor of the exchequer (1923–1924, 1931–1937), he was clearly in line to be prime minister.

Chamberlain assumed that post on the retirement of Stanley Baldwin on 28 May 1937. Intellectually arrogant and convinced his opinions were correct in all things, he rarely sought advice from a generally weak cabinet, listening only to his confidant, Sir Horace Wilson. He was woefully ignorant of foreign affairs, and his policy through most of the 1930s was to cut defense spending while appeasing those who appeared to pose threats. In April 1938, he abandoned Royal Navy bases in Ireland. Until his final weeks in office, however, he enjoyed strong support in Parliament and from the establishment British press.

Chamberlain is remembered most for his dogged efforts to appease Adolf Hitler in order to avoid war, culminating in the shameful Munich Agreement of 30 September 1938, which gave the Sudeten portion of Czechoslovakia to Germany (without any Czech participation in the decision) to avert a threatened German invasion. At home, Chamberlain was widely praised for bringing "peace in our time." He ignored the tiny parliamentary minority led by Winston L. S. Churchill, who argued that Britain had to rearm. And he virtually forced Anthony Eden to resign as foreign secretary on 19 February 1938 when they disagreed about discussions with the Italian government. He only reluctantly repudiated appeasement when Germany occupied the remainder of Czechoslovakia on 10 March 1939.

Finally pushed hard by members of his own cabinet, Chamberlain issued an ultimatum to Hitler after Germany's invasion of Poland on 1 September 1939. Receiving no answer, he took his nation to war two days later and directed Britain's effort for the first eight months of the conflict. His War Cabinet now included Churchill, back as first lord of the Admiralty. Although much of the period passed as the so-called Phony War, April and May 1940 saw Germany's disastrous invasion and occupation of Norway and Denmark and its invasion of the Low Countries and France.

By then, Chamberlain had lost his support in the House of Commons, and after several days of emotional debate, he was replaced by Churchill on 10 May 1940, with a multiparty national government. Chamberlain became lord president of the council (he remained head of the party) and a member of the War Cabinet until 30 September 1940, when he resigned due to ill health. He died of cancer on 9 November 1940, in Heckfield, England.

Christopher H. Sterling

See also
Churchill, Sir Winston L. S.; Eden, Sir Robert Anthony; Hitler, Adolf; Munich Conference and Preliminaries; Mussolini, Benito; Origins of the War

References
Dilks, David. *Neville Chamberlain.* Vol. 1, *Pioneering and Reform, 1869–1929.* Cambridge: Cambridge University Press, 1984.
Dutton, David. *Neville Chamberlain.* London: Arnold, 2001.
Fuchser, Larry William. *Neville Chamberlain and Appeasement: A Study in the Politics of History.* New York: Norton, 1982.
Macleod, Iain. *Neville Chamberlain.* London: Muller, 1961.
McDonough, Frank. *Neville Chamberlain, Appeasement & the Road to War.* Manchester, UK: Manchester University Press, 1998.
Parker, R. A. C. *Chamberlain and Appeasement: British Policy and the Coming of the Second World War.* New York: St. Martin's Press, 1993.

Chang, Fa-k'uel
See Zang Fakul.

Chang Hsüeh-liang
See Zhang Xueliang.

Chang-Ku-feng
See Zhanggufeng.

Channel Dash (11–13 February 1942)

Passage of the German battleships *Scharnhorst* and *Gneisenau* and the heavy cruiser *Prinz Eugen* through the English Channel from Brest, France, to Wilhelmshaven, Germany, in February 1942. In March 1941, the *Scharnhorst* and *Gneisenau* had arrived at Brest, on the French Atlantic coast, after a commerce-raiding voyage, and they were joined by the *Prinz Eugen* in June 1941. Though vulnerable to British bombing, the ships constituted a standing threat to Allied convoys in the Atlantic. However, by late 1941, Adolf Hitler was convinced that the British were planning to invade Norway, and against the advice of his naval commanders, he demanded that the *Scharnhorst, Gneisenau,* and *Prinz Eugen* return to Germany for deployment in Norwegian waters.

In early 1942, when British intelligence strongly suggested a possible German breakout and passage through the Straits of Dover, preparations for aerial and naval attacks, already under way for nearly a year, were accelerated. The British assumed that the German ships would transit the narrowest part of the Channel at night, but the Germans planned Operation CERBERUS to conceal the ships' departure from Brest and to run the straits in daylight, counting on surprise to prevent a timely British concentration of adequate resistance.

Exceptional cooperation between German naval and air commands combined with failures in British technology and communications to bring the Germans almost complete success. At 10:45 P.M. on 11 February, the three big ships and an escort of six destroyers, with Vice Admiral Otto Ciliax commanding, cleared Brest harbor. Not until 11:09 A.M. on 12 February, when the Germans were less than an hour from the straits and had been reinforced by torpedo boat squadrons from French ports, did the British identify the ships. By noon, the German vessels were in the Dover narrows, and although attacked by British coastal artillery, torpedo boats, and the Fleet Air Arm, they passed through unscathed. Later attacks along the Belgian and Dutch coasts by destroyers and by Royal Air Force fighters and bombers were no more successful. Although the *Gneisenau* struck one mine and the *Scharnhorst* hit two (the second one seriously slowing her and separating her from the rest of the flotilla), all the German ships were safely in the Elbe estuary by 10:30 A.M. on 13 February.

Amid German euphoria and British humiliation, thoughtful minds on both sides realized that this German tactical success in the Channel represented a self-inflicted strategic defeat in the Atlantic. Even the sense of victory was short-lived, for the mine damage to the *Scharnhorst* took six months to repair, the *Prinz Eugen* was torpedoed on 23 February by a British submarine in the North Sea, and the *Gneisenau* was irreparably damaged during air raids on Kiel on 26 and 27 February.

John A. Hutcheson Jr.

See also
Germany, Navy; Great Britain, Navy; Naval Warfare

References
Barnett, Correlli. *Engage the Enemy More Closely: The Royal Navy in the Second World War.* New York: W. W. Norton, 1991.

Kemp, Peter. *The Escape of the "Scharnhorst" and "Gneisenau."* Annapolis, MD: Naval Institute Press, 1975.

Robertson, Terence. *Channel Dash.* New York: E. P. Dutton, 1958.

Van der Vat, Dan. *The Atlantic Campaign: World War II's Great Struggle at Sea.* New York: Harper and Row, 1988.

Chaplains

Throughout the history of warfare, nations and their leaders have relied on the spiritual and emotional support of military chaplains of various denominations and spiritual traditions to attend to the needs of their fighting men. In some cases, military chaplains are commissioned officers in a branch of the military; in others, they are appointed by the leaders of their respective religious denominations.

All of the major nations relied on the services of chaplains. Great Britain and the Commonwealth nations commissioned chaplains from all denominations and gave them wide latitude in their responsibilities to ensure that the spiritual and emotional needs of their soldiers were met. The Church of England and Roman Catholic dioceses provided the largest number of chaplains to the British military. The Soviet government put aside its opposition to the Russian Orthodox Church in the great "patriotic war": it reopened churches and released priests and bishops from long prison sentences to bolster the morale of the Soviet people. Russian Orthodox priests also accompanied the Red Army throughout the war. Military chaplains in Germany and Italy were unique because of their close connection with the state. For example, German chaplains were required to pray for the fatherland and the Führer at their religious services. The Italian army enjoyed the spiritual support of a wide range of Catholic chaplains from a number of dioceses and religious orders as well as the assistance of local clergy, since a vast majority of the Italian army served in Italy.

In the United States during World War II, chaplains from all of the major religious groups—Protestant, Catholic, Jewish, and Latter Day Saints—served the 12 million men and women of the armed services without regard to the religious affiliation of the supplicant. A total of 8,100 chaplains served in the U.S. military during the war in all theaters of operation as well as on the home front. The requirements for the chaplaincy were straightforward: a certificate of ordination, two years of successful ministerial experience, and endorsement from the individual's denomination.

Chaplain candidates temporarily vacated their obedience to their religious bodies and were subject to the discipline and orders of their military superiors. In place of boot camp, the candidates were enrolled in Chaplain School (two weeks for the navy and four weeks for the army), where they were indoctrinated in armed forces law, drills, customs, and, most important, interdenominational cooperation. Those chaplains assigned to specialized units (such as paratroopers) were required to undergo the same training as the men they were serving, and many volunteered for these rigorous assignments. The Geneva Convention defined chaplains as noncombatants, and close attention was paid to ensuring that their roles were not compromised in combat situations.

Although the official functions of military chaplains included conducting religious services, preaching, encouraging those who were experiencing difficulties, and writing families of those lost in battle, many received medals and distinctions for valor. Two chaplains (a Protestant and a Catholic) on the battleship *Oklahoma* at Pearl Harbor were the first to die in battle, on 7 December 1941. A total of 77 U.S. chaplains died during World War II, and chaplains received 2,453 medals for valor. The most highly decorated military chaplain was Catholic Chaplain Albert Hoffman, who lost a leg while serving with the army in Italy, and perhaps the most famous act of courage occurred on the deck of the U.S. Army transport *Dorchester* on 3 February 1943, when four chaplains (two Protestants, one Catholic, and one Jew) gave their life vests to others and went down with the ship.

In carrying out their duties, military chaplains of the belligerent nations demonstrated both compassion and personal bravery. Their services were much appreciated by the men to whom they ministered, frequently in difficult circumstances. The chaplains themselves often referred to their years in the military during World War II as the most rewarding of their ministries.

James T. Carroll

See also

Catholic Church and the War; Religion and the War

References

Crosby, Donald. *Battlefield Chaplains: Catholic Priests in World War Two.* Lawrence: University Press of Kansas, 1994.

Kurzman, Dan. *No Greater Glory: The Four Immortal Chaplains and the Sinking of the "Dorchester" in World War II.* New York: Random House, 2004.

Stroup, Russell Cartright. *Letters from the Pacific: A Combat Chaplain in World War II.* Ed. Richard C. Austin. Columbia: University of Missouri Press, 2000.

Charities

Private or quasi-private organizations created to provide aid to both civilians and military personnel during the war. At the beginning of World War II, the British and French instituted a naval blockade of Germany, halting the shipment of food, among other items. This policy often hurt innocents, as it contributed to hunger and even starvation in some places. A number of people in Britain opposed this policy and formed the national Famine Relief Committee at Oxford, which eventually became Oxfam.

At the beginning of World War II, Canadian charities mobilized to lobby the government regarding the Canadian Patriotic Fund Bill and the War Charities Bill, which were, essentially, improved versions of World War I legislation. To coordinate voluntary assistance, the Canadians created the Department of National War Services.

As American charities mobilized, President Franklin D. Roosevelt, aware that multiple war-relief appeals might discourage donations, issued an order in mid-September 1939 that required all war-relief organizations to secure certificates of registration from the Department of State. Among American charities, the Community Chests (successors of the Community War Chests of World War I and predecessors of today's United Way) joined with many relief agencies—including the United States Committee for the Care of European Children, the Volunteer Bureaus, and the Junior Leagues—to meet wartime needs. U.S. charities often helped European refugees to survive while they waited for visas and steamship tickets to the United States or elsewhere.

On 16 September 1940, the United States instituted its first peacetime conscription. To aid military personnel, the Navy Relief Society and the Army Relief Society were formed by the military itself. On 11 March 1941, Congress passed Lend-Lease legislation: as well as weapons, this aid included billions of dollars in food and nonmilitary assistance to nations fighting the Axis powers. That same year, the Young Men's Christian Association (YMCA), Young Women's Christian Association (YWCA), National Catholic Community Service, Salvation Army, Jewish Welfare Board, and National Traveler's Aid Association formed the United Service Organizations (USO). At President Roosevelt's request, the USO operated the military services' huts and canteens.

In 1942, there was widespread starvation in Greece, caused, in large part, by the German seizure of Greek food supplies. An estimated 500,000 Greeks starved to death in the war years. The Oxford Famine Relief Committee, well connected to the exiled Greek government, promoted international aid. Wheat from Canada, purchased by relief agencies, was allowed through the British blockade to Turkey in Swedish ships flying the Red Cross flag. The Germans allowed the wheat into Greece, in ships flying Turkey's Red Crescent insignia. Spain also received food shipments from charities.

In 1943, Russian War Relief was organized as an agency of the National War Fund, with much of the aid coming from the United States. Also in 1943, many American agencies formed the United Relief organization, with the Red Feather as its symbol.

In Germany, the Nazis ran their own annual charity once a year. Known as Winterhilfe (Winter Help), it was the official private charitable organization of the Nazis. Those who refused to contribute were often denounced and sometimes threatened. In China, many organizations were involved in relief work, including members of the Friends Society, Mennonites, and Brethren. The Red Cross was also active in relief work in Portugal, aiding refugees and handling tons of packages for prisoners of war; however, the relief work was hampered by the lack of provisions in the Geneva Convention to cover civilian relief.

In February 1944, Washington took the lead in moving from a policy of blockade to controlled relief. Dislocations at the end of the war increased the need for relief. By 27 November 1945, a consortium of 22 American charities united to created the Cooperative for American Remittances to Europe (CARE) to handle postwar charity. The new UN organization was also actively involved in this effort through the United Nations Educational, Scientific and Cultural Organization (UNESCO), created in late 1945.

A. J. L. Waskey

See also
Bernadotte of Wisborg, Folke; China, Role in the War; Greece, Role in the War; Portugal; Roosevelt, Franklin D.

References
Black, Maggie. *Cause of Our Time: Oxfam, The First Fifty Years.* Oxford: Oxford University Press, 1993.
Curti, Merle. *American Philanthropy Abroad: A History.* New Brunswick, NJ: Rutgers University Press, 1963.
Mazower, Mark. *Inside Hitler's Greece: The Experience of Occupation, 1941–1944.* New Haven, CT: Yale University Press, 1997.
People and Events: A History of the United Way. Alexandria, VA: United Way of America, 1977.

Chelmo

See Concentration Camps, German.

Chemical Weapons and Warfare

Poison gas had been utilized with considerable effect by the major belligerents in World War I. In the course of the conflict, the combatants had deployed about 113,000 tons of chemicals, and some estimates indicate over 1 million soldiers were injured by poison gas during the war, 10 percent of them fatally.

In the interwar period, the major powers discussed outlawing the use of poison gas, but they also continued to produce it. Prior to World War II, more than 40 nations signed the Geneva Protocol of 1925 banning the offensive use of chemical weapons in warfare. All of the main combatants in World War II save the United States and Japan ratified the protocol, which went into force in August 1928. Although the United States had first proposed the treaty, isolationist sentiment blocked its ratification in the Senate. Japan feared giving away any advantage in case of a conflict with the far more populous China. The signatory powers, however, reserved the right to utilize chemical weapons in a retaliatory attack and to employ them against a country that had not signed the protocol.

Chemical weapons are categorized by their effects on human beings, animals, and plants. Lung irritants, such as phosgene, make victims choke or suffocate, with symptoms usually delayed for several hours after contact. Vesicants, such as mustard gas, cause the skin to blister and the eyes to swell, sometimes with loss of sight. The symptoms of vesicants can be delayed up to 48 hours. Lacrimators are tear gases, such as chloracetophenone and brombenzylcyanide, which irritate the eyes and cause difficulty with breathing.

The warring powers also produced irritant smoke (such as sneezing gases or adamsite), screening smokes, and incendiaries. A new and very deadly chemical agent, nerve gas, was developed during the war. Nerve gases take effect quickly, producing symptoms in 10 to 30 minutes, depending on whether they are inhaled or absorbed through the skin.

Chemical weapons can be launched in a variety of forms: through shells and bombs that explode and disperse the chemicals into the air in drops or small particles, from containers with vaporized solids that infiltrate the air as a smoke, and through liquids released from airplanes as drops or mist. Chemical weapons can be more useful than conventional weapons, since their effects are longer lasting, sometimes persisting for days or weeks. The most desirable chemical agents have many of the same characteristics in common. They are effective in small concentrations, difficult to protect against, quickly and cheaply manufactured, made from easily obtainable raw materials, heavier than air, easily and safely transportable, effective against multiple parts of the body, and not easily detectable.

Three of the most common means used to deploy chemical agents by the end of World War I were the portable gas cylinder, the Livens Projector, and the chemical mortar. But these delivery systems were obsolete by the time of World War II, given the greater mobility of infantry troops. Accordingly, the size of chemical mortars was increased as was their range (to 1,400 yards), and the Livens Projector was replaced by 100 mm caliber, mobile rocket launchers. During the interwar years, governments also experimented with using airplanes to deliver chemical weapons, through cluster bombs and spraying. By the time World War II began, aerial bombardment with chemical weapons was the most common deployment mechanism. It is also possible to deploy chemical weapons, particularly mustard gas, in land mines and grenades. German leaders debated the feasibility of combining missiles and chemical weapons, but production of such mechanisms did not occur.

In stark contrast to the situation in World War I, chemical weapons were used only sparingly in World War II. The major powers were reluctant to employ them. This was, in part, because they were convinced that their opponents had extensive stockpiles of poison gases and because their own populations were not adequately prepared to withstand a retaliatory attack. They also did not wish to be the first to violate the Geneva Protocol. Several key leaders were hesitant to authorize the use of chemical weapons. Adolf Hitler, who had been gassed at Ypres in 1918, had a strong aversion to the use of gas as an offensive weapon, and President Franklin D. Roosevelt also opposed the use of chemical weapons. For the European powers in particular, the threat of retribution against cities and large-scale civilian suffering was a major deterrent. The shipping of chemical weapons and equipping friendly troops for chemical attacks also presented logistical difficulties. Lastly, fighting in World War II, marked as it was by rapid movement, was dramatically different from the trench warfare of the previous conflict. Early in the war, the Axis powers scored a succession of quick victories and did not need to resort to poison gas.

The fate of the SS *John Harvey* illustrated the difficulty of shipping poison gas. The ship sailed from the United States to Italy in 1943, carrying 2,000 bombs loaded with mustard gas. Each bomb held 60 to 70 pounds of the gas. The ship docked at Bari on 28 November 1943. Four days later, German aircraft attacked the port. Their 20-minute assault sank 17 ships and badly damaged 8 others. Racked by explosions, the *John Harvey* sank, and some of the mustard gas in the bombs in her hold was released. It mixed with the oil and smoke and rolled across the water. More than 1,000 Allied soldiers and Italian civilians died as a result, and hundreds were blinded, some permanently. The death rate was particularly high because no one knew of the cargo until several weeks had passed.

Yet such difficulties did not preclude the use of poison gas in the war. The Italians, for example, utilized mustard gas and tear gas grenades in their 1935–1936 conquest of Ethiopia. They employed it to protect their flanks by saturating the ground on either side of the advancing columns. They also targeted Ethiopian communications centers and employed mustard gas against Ethiopian military personnel. In fact, the Italians deployed more than 700 tons of gas against the local population, either as bombs (each container contained about 44 pounds) or sprayed from aircraft. Their use of chemical weapons was indiscriminate, targeting both military and civilian areas. One-third of all Ethiopian military casualties in this conflict resulted from exposure to chemical agents.

The Italian decision to employ chemical weapons on a large scale in Ethiopia prompted other nations to renew their production of such weapons and to plan for protecting their armed forces and civilian populations. France began production at a phosgene facility at Clamency in 1936. The U.S. government reopened mustard gas and phosgene plants in New Jersey the following year. The Soviet Union opened three new chemical weapons production plants. And in November 1938, after the Munich Conference, the British government issued tens of thousands of gas masks to civilians and mandated a minimum level of production of 300 tons of mustard gas per week, with 2,000 tons held in reserve.

At the beginning of World War II, Germany held a commanding lead in the stockpiling of chemical weapons, but its government officials did not know this. German stockpiles in 1939 are estimated at 10,000 tons, as compared with 500 tons in Great Britain, 1,000 tons in the United States, and 2,000 tons in Japan.

During World War II in the European Theater, chemical weapons were never deliberately employed on a large scale. In June 1940, British Prime Minister Winston L. S. Churchill discussed with his cabinet the idea of using poison gas to repel a German invasion of either Great Britain or Ireland. Although many of the senior military staff opposed this notion, the cabinet approved it. The British government also considered the use of poison gas to combat the German V-1 and V-2 rockets later in the war. By 1944, Germany's production capacity was 10,000 tons of poison gas per month; in addition, myriad delivery systems were available, including grenades filled with hydrogen cyanide and machine guns capable of firing bullets faced with tabun or sarin. The Luftwaffe had more than 480,000 gas bombs, ranging in size from 33 to 1,650 pounds.

In the Pacific Theater, the Japanese were also involved in massive production of poison gas and had been since the later portion of World War I. By 1937, Japan was daily producing up to 2 tons of lewisite, a virulent form of mustard gas. In their invasion and occupation of China from 1937 to 1945, the Japanese employed a wide variety of poison gases, including phosgene, hydrogen cyanide, mustard gas, and Lewisite. Since the Chinese population, both military and civilian, was completely unprotected against chemical warfare, the effects were devastating.

The Japanese deployed the chemicals weapons by aerial bombardment and artillery shells. They also designed rockets capable of holding 10.5 quarts of a chemical agent and traveling up to 2 miles; flamethrowers that propelled hydrogen cyanide; and a handheld antitank weapon that employed hydrogen cyanide. The Japanese also utilized gas grenades during the Imphal Campaign in 1944. The United States considered using poison gas during the invasion of Iwo Jima and the proposed invasion of the Japanese home islands, but the former was never ordered and the latter proved unnecessary.

The deadliest form of chemical warfare at that time, nerve gas, was never used in battle. A German scientist, Gerhard Schrader, employed by I. G. Farben in 1936, discovered tabun while he was trying to create a more powerful insecticide. Tabun can be absorbed directly into the body and is colorless and odorless. It stops the nervous system from producing a key enzyme, acetylcholinesterase, that allows contracting muscles to relax. If this enzyme is not active, important muscles, such as the heart, contract and begin to spasm. As all the body's muscles contract, the person suffocates. Tabun is 100 to 1,000 times more deadly than chlorine gas and 10 to 100 times more deadly than mustard or phosgene gas. Later, Schrader discovered a second and even more toxic nerve gas, which he named sarin. It is almost 10 times more lethal than tabun. In 1944, a still more deadly nerve gas, soman, was discovered, but it was never mass-produced during the war. Great Britain also manufactured sarin and soman.

Germany's leaders chose not to deploy tabun, since they lacked the ability to protect their own population against this nerve gas and no known antidote existed. The Germans did test their nerve gases on unwilling inmates of concentration and prisoner-of-war camps. At the Natzweiler concentration camp, tests with both mustard and phosgene gases were also conducted on unwilling prisoners. Germany moved its storage of nerve gas in 1944 in anticipation of Allied advances in the west, but their production facility in Silesia fell into Soviet hands.

The German government also used a poison gas, namely, Zyklon B, against prisoners in concentration camps and in its killing centers in Poland. Zyklon B was developed in the 1930s by Deesch, a subsidiary of I. G. Farben that was experimenting with more powerful insecticides. Zyklon B, also known as Prussic acid, is hydrogen cyanide—a powerful, toxic, volatile, and colorless liquid. In order to transport the gas, it was absorbed by wood circles or small cubes because of its great volatility.

Zyklon B was dropped into gas chambers and caused suffocation, as well as feelings of fear and dizziness and vomiting. The Germans constructed gas chambers to use Zyklon B in their camps at Auschwitz, Buchenwald, Sachsenhausen, Neuengamme, Majdanek, Mauthausen, Stutthof, Lüblin, Gross-Rosen, Ravensbrück, and Treblinka. In Auschwitz alone, more than 2.5 million people were murdered through the use of Zyklon B between May 1940 and December 1943. At other concentration camps and killing centers, prisoners were killed by carbon monoxide poisoning.

By 1945, the major combatants as a group had stockpiled more than 500,000 tons of chemical weapons, led by the United States with 110,000 tons. This amount was five times the total amount of gas employed in World War I. Although poison gases were never used in large-scale attacks during World War II, the threat was present throughout the conflict. Given their deadly nature, the updated deployment systems, and the large stockpiles, chemical weapons could have played an enormous role in World War II.

Laura J. Hilton

See also

Concentration Camps, German; Holocaust, The; Imphal and Kohima, Sieges of; Incendiary Bombs and Bombing; Strategic Bombing

References

Clarke, Robin. *The Silent Weapons.* New York: David McKay, 1968.

Cookson, John, and Judith Nottingham. *A Survey of Chemical and Biological Warfare.* New York: Monthly Review Press, 1969.

Harris, Robert, and Jeremy Paxman. *A Higher Form of Killing.* New York: Hill and Wang, 1982.

International Institute for Peace and Conflict Resolution. *The Problem of Chemical and Biological Warfare.* Vol. 1, The Rise of CB Weapons. Uppsala, Sweden: Almquist and Wiksell, 1971.

Price, Richard M. *The Chemical Weapons Taboo.* Ithaca, NY: Cornell University Press, 1997.

Spiers, Edward. *Chemical Warfare.* Urbana: University of Illinois Press, 1986.

Ch'en Ch'eng

See Chen Cheng.

Chen Cheng (Ch'en Ch'eng) (1898–1965)

Chinese Nationalist general who commanded the Chinese Expeditionary Army and served as war minister. Born in Qingtian (Ch'ingt'ien), Zhejiang (Chekiang) Province, on 4 January 1898, Chen Cheng (Ch'en Ch'eng) enrolled at the Baoding (Paoting) Military Academy in 1919 and graduated in 1922. He then served both in his native province and in Guangdong (Kwangtung) Province. In 1924, Chen became an artillery in-structor in the Huangpu (Whampoa) Military Academy, where he joined the Nationalist Party—the Guomindang, or GMD (Kuomintang, or KMT)—and developed a close relationship with Jiang Jieshi (Chiang Kai-shek). He then held a number of command posts in the Eastern and Northern Expeditions between 1925 and 1928, as well as the antiwarlord and anti–Chinese Communist "extermination campaigns" of the early 1930s. Chen became commander in chief of the Fourth Group Army, a position second only to Jiang's, in early 1937.

After the Sino-Japanese War began in July 1937, Chen took command of the Fifteenth Group Army and became deputy commander of the Fourth Reserve Army; that November, he was also made commander in chief of the Third War Area of Zhejiang and southern Jiangsu (Kiangsu), defending both Shanghai and Nanjing (Nanking). When both cities fell at year's end, Chen went to Wuhan, Hubei (Hupeh), assuming the post of defense commander in chief in January 1938. He was concurrently commander of the newly created Ninth War Area of southern Hubei, northern Jiangsu, and Hunan in June and governor of Hunan in July. After Wuhan's fall in late October 1938 in the First Battle of Changsha in Hunan, Chen moved to Chongqing (Chungking) in Sichuan (Szechwan), where he was responsible for guerrilla and corps training. In October 1939, he became commander of the Sixth War Area, comprising the areas west of Hunan including eastern and southern Hubei and eastern Sichuan. From May 1940, he held back the Japanese advance to Chongqing at Yichang (Ichang), Hubei.

In February 1943, Chen was also made commander of the Chinese Expeditionary Army, responsible for preparing the joint Anglo-American-Chinese Burma Campaign launched the next year (he was succeeded in this post by Wei Lihuang [Wei Li-huang] in October). After the Japanese launched their Operation ICHI-Gō against Henan (Honan) in April 1944, Chen became commander of the enlarged First War Area of Hebei, northern Shandong (Shantung), Henan, Anhui (Anhwei), and Shaanxi (Shensi). When the Japanese advanced into Guangxi (Kwangsi), Guizhou (Kewichow), and Yunnan at the end of the year, Chen left the battlefield and, as war minister, concentrated on modernizing GMD forces, employing U.S. technical and material assistance.

After the beginning of the Chinese Civil War, Chen became director of the Northeastern Headquarters in August 1947. He resigned in January 1948 on the grounds of illness, and his position was taken by Wei. In October, Chen fled to Taiwan, where he assumed the governorship, preparing the GMD retreat from the mainland. In 1954, he was elected vice president of the Republic of China. Chen died in Taipei on 5 March 1965.

Debbie Law

See also

China, Army; China, Civil War in; ICHI-Gō Campaign; Jiang Jieshi; Sino-Japanese War; Wei Lihuang

References

Chi, Hsi-sheng. *Nationalist China at War: Military Defeats and Political Collapse, 1937–45.* Ann Arbor: University of Michigan Press, 1982.

Fang, Zhilin. *Chen Cheng Dazhuan* (The great biography of Chen Cheng). Taipei: Jinfeng, 1995.

Levine, Steven I. *Anvil of Victory: The Communist Revolution in Manchuria, 1945–1948.* New York: Columbia University Press, 1987.

Sun, Zhaiwei. *Jiang Jieshi De Chongjiang Chen Cheng* (Jiang Jieshi's favorite general: Chen Cheng). Zhengzhou, China: Henan Renmin Chubanshe, 1990.

Ch'en I

See Chen Yi.

Ch'en Yi

See Chen Yi.

Chen Yi (Ch'en Yi/Ch'en I) (1901–1972)

Chinese military leader and People's Republic of China marshal. Born in Lezhi (Lochih), Sichuan (Szechuan) Province, to a well-to-do family on 16 August 1901, Chen Yi (Ch'en Yi/Ch'en I) studied at both Shanghai University and Beijing (Peking) College of Law and Commerce before traveling to France in 1919 on a work-study program. During his stay in France, he met Zhou Enlai (Chou En-lai) and became politically active. In 1921, he was deported from France for involvement in protests by Chinese exchange students. On his return to China, Chen joined the Nationalist Party—the Guomindang, or GMD (Kuomintang, or KMT)—in 1921 and the Communist Party in 1923, which were then loosely allied in the struggle to reunify China. Following study at the Sino-French University of Beijing between 1923 and 1925, Chen became a political instructor at the Huangpu (Whampoa) Military Academy in 1925. He then served on the staff of General Ye Ting's (Yeh T'ing) 24th Division at the beginning of the Northern Expedition, the Nationalist-led reunification campaign launched in the summer of 1926.

In 1927, the alliance between the Communists and Nationalists collapsed, and civil war ensued. Chen participated in the abortive Communist Nanchang Uprising of Jiangxi (Kiangsi) Province in August 1927. In January 1929, he joined Zhu De (Chu Teh) in the Communist enclave of Jiangxi and commanded the 12th Division of the Red IV Corps fighting Nationalist forces under Jiang Jieshi (Chiang Kai-shek). He did not join Mao Zedong (Mao Tse-tung) in the epic Long March of 1934 and 1935 but instead stayed behind to organize guerrilla forces in south-central China, which eventually became part of the New Fourth Army.

Following the outbreak of war with Japan in 1937, he fought with the New Fourth Army against the Japanese along the Changjiang (Yangtze) River. After the Japanese inflicted a sharp defeat on the New Fourth Army in January 1941, Chen, who had been a sector commander, took command of the entire army. From that point until 1945, his New Fourth Army greatly expanded the area of Communist control in central China by conducting a highly effective guerrilla campaign characterized by rapid maneuver.

After Japan's surrender, Chen was formally assigned command of the New Fourth Army. In the 1946–1949 Chinese Civil War, he encircled the Nationalist 2nd and 7th Army Groups, destroying them in the Huai-Hai Campaign between November 1948 and January 1949; after that, he advanced to take Nanjing (Nanking) in Jiangsu (Kiangsu) Province in April and both Wuhan in Hubei (Hupeh) Province and Shanghai in Jiangsu Province in May. Chen was then mayor of Shanghai and commander of the East China Military Region (1949–1956) and vice premier (1956). He was promoted to marshal of the People's Liberation Army in 1955 and served as China's foreign minister from 1956 to 1968. Attacked by Red Guards during the Cultural Revolution, he died in Beijing on 6 January 1972.

John M. Jennings

See also

China, Civil War in; China, Role in War; Jiang Jieshi; Mao Zedong; Zhou Enlai; Zhu De

References

Whitson, William W. *The Chinese High Command: A History of Communist Military Politics, 1927–1971.* New York: Macmillan, 1973.

Wilson, Dick. *The Long March, 1935: The Epic of Chinese Communism's Survival.* New York: Viking, 1971.

Chennault, Claire Lee (1893–1958)

U.S. Army Air Forces general and leader of the Flying Tigers. Born in Commerce, Texas, on 6 September 1893, Claire Chennault was raised in rural Louisiana. He taught English and business at a number of southern colleges until August 1917, when he became a second lieutenant in the army reserve. He remained in the United States during World War I, transferring to the Signal Corps and completing pilot training in 1920.

An accomplished airman, Chennault then held a number of assignments, among them command of the 19th Pursuit Squadron in Hawaii between 1923 and 1926. He developed into an outspoken advocate of fighter aircraft in a period when prevailing military thought subscribed to the doctrines espoused by Italian airpower theorist Giulio Douhet and their underlying assumption that "the bomber will always get through." While serving as an instructor at the Air Corps Tactical School in 1935, Chennault wrote *The Role of Defensive Pursuit,* an important but controversial book at the time because it pointed out the need for fighter aircraft. In 1937, the army removed him from flying status because of a serious hearing loss and forced him into medical retirement as a captain.

In May 1937, Chennault went to China as aviation adviser to the Nationalist government of Jiang Jieshi (Chiang Kai-shek). When the Japanese attacked China that September, he became a colonel in the Chinese air force and began testing his tactical theories. In late 1940, Chennault was allowed to recruit American military pilots for service in China, despite the strong opposition of the State, War, and Navy Departments. His American Volunteer Group (AVG), popularly known as the Flying Tigers, consisted of some 200 ground crew and 100 pilots flying semiobsolete Curtiss P-40B fighters. The AVG entered combat for the first time on 20 December 1941. By the time the unit disbanded in July 1942, it claimed 296 Japanese aircraft shot down, with only 12 of its own planes and 4 of its pilots lost.

In April 1942, Chennault was recalled to active duty with the U.S. Army as a colonel. A few months later, he was promoted to brigadier general and put in command of the newly formed China Air Task Force (CATF), a subordinate command of the U.S. Tenth Air Force in India. In March 1943, the CATF became the Fourteenth Air Force, with Chennault promoted to major general.

The CATF and the Fourteenth Air Force were economy-of-force organizations in a tertiary theater and therefore always operated on a shoestring. Utilizing Chennault's theories, however, both organizations achieved combat effectiveness far out of proportion to their size and resources. By 1945, the Fourteenth Air Force had destroyed some 2,600 Japanese aircraft and thousands of tons of supplies.

During his time in China, Chennault conducted a long-running and public feud with Lieutenant General Joseph Stilwell, the equally stubborn and irascible U.S. commander of the China-Burma-India Theater. Chennault engineered Jiang's demand for Stilwell's recall, but Chennault himself was removed from command and forced into retirement for a second time on 1 August 1945.

After the war, Chennault remained in China. He established and operated the Civil Air Transport (CAT) airline, which supported Jiang's Nationalist government in its civil war with Mao Zedong (Mao Tse-tung) and his Communists forces. In 1950, Chennault sold his interest in CAT to the Central Intelligence Agency, but he remained the chairman of the airline's board until 1955. He died at Walter Reed Army Hospital in Washington, D.C., on 27 July 1958. Only days before his death, Chennault was promoted to lieutenant general.

David T. Zabecki

See also
China, Civil War in; China-Burma-India Theater; Jiang Jieshi; Mao Zedong; Stilwell, Joseph Warren

References
Byrd, Martha. *Chennault: Giving Wings to the Tiger.* Tuscaloosa: University of Alabama Press, 1987.
Chennault, Claire Lee. *Way of a Fighter.* New York: G. P. Putnam, 1949.
Ford, Daniel. *Flying Tigers: Claire Chennault and the American Volunteer Group.* Washington, DC: Smithsonian Institution Press, 1991.
Samson, Jack. *Chennault.* New York: Doubleday, 1987.

Cherbourg, Capture of (June 1944)

The capture of the French port city of Cherbourg, on the northern shore of Cotentin Peninsula, was vital to the Allied buildup for the Normandy breakout. On 7 June 1944, Major General J. Lawton Collins's VII Corps attacked westward from the Utah Beach lodgment across the Cotentin Peninsula to isolate the port of Cherbourg. On 18 June, VII Corps succeeded in cutting completely across the peninsula and isolating parts of four German divisions in the Cherbourg pocket commanded by Generalleutnant (U.S. equiv. major general) Karl Wilhelm von Schlieben.

With VIII Corps holding the southern shoulder of the Allied success, VII Corps advanced northward on Cherbourg starting on 19 June. That same day, a strong storm hit Normandy. Three days later, when the storm lifted, the artificial harbor (Mulberry A) at Omaha Beach had been destroyed, which made the capture of Cherbourg even more urgent. When Collins launched VII Corps with three divisions abreast, the German defenses along the eastern shore of the peninsula were outflanked, and Schlieben had no choice but to fall back into the Cherbourg defenses that circled the city along high ground. By 21 June, VII Corps invested the defenses, and the fall of the city was imminent.

Bomb damage in Cherbourg, France, on its liberation in late June 1944. (National Archives)

On 22 June, the Allies launched heavy air attacks to open the final phase of the battle. Collins ordered the main attacks in the center and left, conducted by the 79th and 9th Divisions, while the 4th Division supported in the east. On 22 June, Adolf Hitler ordered Schlieben to fight to the last and leave nothing but ruins for the Allies. VII Corps made a steady advance on 22–23 June and reached Cherbourg's outer suburbs of Octeville and Tourlaville, which were taken on 24 June. The air attacks made an impact on German morale, and on 25 June, a naval task force headed by three battleships supported the final attack on Cherbourg proper with naval gunfire.

The 4th and 9th Divisions seized their objectives inside the city by nightfall on 25 June. The 79th Division had a more difficult fight around Fort du Roule, which finally fell on 26 June. Schlieben made his final radio message that afternoon and was captured shortly thereafter; he refused to order a general surrender of forces.

Organized German resistance ended on 27 June, but fighting continued as VII Corps reduced several strong points that had been previously bypassed, including Cap de la Hague at the northwest corner of the peninsula, the port

facilities themselves, and other resistance pockets on the Cotentin Peninsula. The harbor strong points, under heavy dive-bomber attack, held out until 29 June, and when the 9th Division seized Cap de la Hague on 30 June, the campaign was concluded.

The heavy fighting to take Cherbourg severely damaged the port facilities. VII Corps found landing berths blocked by sunken ships, the harbor mined, the breakwater ripped open, and dock facilities demolished. Three weeks passed before the docks were able to receive cargo, and it was several months before shipments could be received in quantity—a serious blow to Allied logistical planning.

Thomas D. Veve

See also

Collins, Joseph Lawton; Hitler, Adolf; Mulberries; Normandy Invasion and Campaign

References

Breuer, William B. *Hitler's Fortress Cherbourg: The Conquest of a Bastion.* New York: Stein and Day, 1984.

Harrison, Gordon A. *United States Army in World War II: The European Theater of Operations—Cross Channel Attack.* Washington, DC: Office of the Chief of Military History, 1951.

Chernyakhovsky, Ivan Danilovich (1906–1945)

Soviet army general and the youngest Soviet front commander of World War II. Born in Uman in Ukraine on 29 June 1906, Ivan Chernyakhovsky joined the Red Army in 1924 and the Communist Party in 1928, when he was commissioned. He held a variety of assignments before the war. He graduated from Kiev Artillery School in 1928 and the Mechanization and Motorization Academy in the late 1930s. By 1940, he was a colonel commanding the 28th Tank Division in the Baltic Special Military District.

Following the June 1941 German invasion of the Soviet Union, Chernyakhovsky fought with his division as a part of XVIII Tank Corps on the Leningrad Front until July 1942. After being promoted to Generalmajor (U.S. equiv. brigadier general) and then Generalleutnant (U.S. equiv. major general), he commanded Sixtieth Army and took part in the Kursk Offensive of 1943. He was promoted to Generaloberst (U.S. equiv. full general) in March 1944. Marshal Georgii Zhukov recommended him to command the Western Front, which he took over in April 1944 just before it was renamed the 3rd Belorussian Front.

In the Belorussian Offensive, Chernyakhovsky's command participated in the taking of Minsk; moved through Latvia and took Vilna; and drove into East Prussia, eventually taking Königsberg (now Kalinin). Promoted to General of the Army in June 1944 just days before his thirty-eighth birthday, Chernyakhovsky was one of the finest Soviet front commanders. Unusual for senior Soviet commanders of the war, he was a Jew and had joined the army after the civil war and never attended the Frunze Military Academy. Chernyakhovsky did not live to see the capture of Königsberg: he was mortally wounded by artillery fire at Melzak, Poland, and died on 18 February 1945.

Spencer C. Tucker

See also
Kursk, Battle of; Leningrad, Siege of; Zhukov, Georgii Konstantinovich
References
Bialer, Seweryn. *Stalin and His Generals: Soviet Military Memoirs of World War II.* New York: Pegasus, 1969.
Shukman, Harold, ed. *Stalin's Generals.* New York: Grove Press, 1993.

Cherwell, Lord

See Lindemann, Frederick Alexander.

Cheshire, Geoffrey Leonard (1917–1992)

Royal Air Force (RAF) officer and pioneer of the "master bomber" technique. Born at Chester, England, on 7 September 1917, Geoffrey Cheshire was educated at Oxford University and joined the Air Squadron there in 1936. He was commissioned in the Royal Air Force Volunteer Reserve in 1937, and when war became imminent, he accepted a regular commission and was assigned to bombers.

Cheshire began his first combat tour in June 1940, with 102 Squadron. Completing his first tour, he immediately accepted a second, with 35 Squadron. After a short stint as an instructor pilot, during which he wrote *Bomber Pilot,* Cheshire returned for a third operational tour, as wing commander of 76 Squadron. His bombing missions took him over the heavily defended Ruhr region, Berlin, and Bremen. Finishing his third tour, Group Captain Cheshire became a deputy base commander in March 1943.

Cheshire was unhappy when he was not flying and relinquished his rank to return to flying duties for a fourth time, in October 1943, as wing commander of Guy Gibson's 617 Squadron. There, he pioneered the "master bomber" technique, in which a low-flying Mosquito bomber flew ahead of and below the main attack force to mark targets with incendiaries. This placed the marking aircraft, which Cheshire regularly flew, into the teeth of the fiercest enemy fire, at altitudes as low as 200 feet. While commanding 617 Squadron, he led every raid using the master bomber procedure, including the 24–25 April 1944 raid against Munich. In this action, his Mosquito was pushed perilously close to its maximum fuel range at an altitude of 700 feet over the city's heavy air defenses, and it was exposed to 12 straight minutes of enemy fire during the withdrawal. Cheshire also flew important missions in support of the Normandy bombing campaign and against the Le Havre E-boat pens.

Cheshire won his Victoria Cross, awarded 8 September 1944, for flying an incredible 100 missions over German-held territory between 1940 and 1944. His citation prominently mentions the Munich raid. Retiring from the RAF in December 1945, he founded Cheshire Foundation Homes in 1948, a worldwide organization that provides housing and services to disabled persons. Created Baron Cheshire of Woodall in 1991, he died in Cavendish, Suffolk, England, on 31 July 1992.

Thomas D. Veve

See also
Aircraft, Bombers; Bader, Sir Douglas Robert Steuart; Gibson, Guy Penrose; Great Britain, Air Force; Harris, Sir Arthur Travers
References
Braddon, Russell. *New Wings for a Warrior: The Story of Group-Captain Leonard Cheshire, V.C., D.S.O., D.F.C.* New York: Rinehart, 1954.
Cheshire, Leonard. *Bomber Pilot.* London: White Lion Publishers, 1973.
Laffin, John. *British VCs of World War 2: A Study in Heroism.* Gloucester, UK: Sutton Publishing, 1997.
Morris, Richard. *Cheshire: The Biography of Leonard Cheshire, VC, OM.* New York: Viking, 2000.
Turner, John Frayn. *VCs of the Air.* Shrewsbury, UK: Airlife Publishing, 1993.

Chevallerie, Kurt von der (1891–1945)

German army general who participated in Operation BAR-BAROSSA. Born on 23 December 1891 in Berlin to a family of Huguenot origin, Kurt von der Chaevallerie was commissioned in the army as a lieutenant in August 1911. His first assignment was with the 5th Guards Grenadier Regiment in Berlin-Spandau. Decorated for valor in World War I, he remained on duty with the 4th Infantry Regiment after the war.

During the interwar period, Chevallerie held a variety of infantry command assignments and staff posts. He commanded the 83rd Infantry Division as a Generalmajor (U.S. equiv. brigadier general) at the outbreak of World War II. Promoted to Generalleutnant (U.S. equiv. major general), he commanded the 99th Light Division in Operation BAR-BAROSSA, the invasion of the Soviet Union. He took command of LIX Army Corps in December 1941 and was promoted to General der Infanterie (U.S. equiv. lieutenant general). In January 1942, Chevallerie's forces sealed a dangerous gap between Velikiye Luki and Rzhev, preventing a Soviet breakthrough. He was also involved in the effort to rescue the surrounded garrison at Velikiye Luki in January 1943.

At the time of the Normandy Invasion, Chevallerie commanded First Army, part of Army Group G under Generaloberst (U.S. equiv. full general) Johannes von Blaskowitz. Chevallerie's duties were to defend southwest France and the Bay of Biscay areas. He had about 100,000 men but few first-rate combat soldiers. Most of his men were garrison or coastal defense troops fit mainly for occupation duties or limited defensive missions. Chevallerie eventually wound up defending the Paris-Orléans gap area south of Paris. He was unable to accomplish the impossible and halt the Allied advance, so Adolf Hitler removed him from command and placed him on the command reserve list, where he remained for the rest of the war.

Chevallerie disappeared in the Soviet assault on and capture of Kolberg on 18 March 1945. He may have died either in the city or in Soviet captivity shortly after. His younger brother was Generalleutnant (U.S. equiv. major general) Helmut von der Chevallerie, who commanded the 11th Panzer Division and then the 273rd Reserve Panzer Division.

Jon D. Berlin

See also
BARBAROSSA, Operation; Blaskowitz, Johannes Albrecht von; France Campaign; Rundstedt, Karl Rudolf Gerd von

References
Carell, Paul. *Hitler Moves East, 1941–1943*. Boston: Little, Brown, 1965.
———. *Scorched Earth: The Russian-German War, 1943–1944*. Boston: Little, Brown, 1972.
Mitcham, Samuel W., Jr. *Retreat to the Reich: The German Defeat in France 1944*. Westport, CT: Praeger, 2000.
Ziemke, Earl F. *Stalingrad to Berlin: The German Defeat in the East.* Washington, DC: U.S. Government Printing Office, 1968.

Chiang Kai-shek

See Jiang Jieshi.

Children and the War

During World War II, millions of men and women around the world served in the armed forces of their respective nations. Millions of others contributed to the war effort by maintaining vital services and laboring in war-related industries. And children went to war as well. Even those far removed from the fighting were affected by the war. They collected scrap metal and other materials that would be vital to the war effort, participated in austerity programs, left school to work on farms, grew vegetables in urban plots, and suffered from the same shortages and wartime prohibitions as did their parents.

In many lands, children experienced the horrors of war firsthand, both as combatants and victims. Children were the most vulnerable part of the population, and many

Chinese soldier, age 10, with heavy pack, who is a member of a Chinese division boarding planes at the North Airstrip, Myitkyina, Burma, bound for China, 5 December 1944. (National Archives)

English children in a bomb dugout. (British Information Service, Library of Congress)

perished from starvation, malnutrition, or disease. Others fell victim to Nazi Germany's euthanasia programs. Some 1.2 million Jewish children throughout Europe died in the Holocaust.

Many children perished as a direct result of Soviet policies as well. Polish authorities estimated that about 140,000 Polish children were uprooted from their homes in the Soviet-occupied portion of Poland. Of these, perhaps 40,000 simply disappeared. In the Far East, Chinese children suffered along with their parents in the Japanese reprisal campaigns. Children were also the innocent victims of the indiscriminate bombing of cities conducted by both sides, beginning with German air attacks on Warsaw and ending with the atomic bombs dropped by the United States on Hiroshima and Nagasaki. To avoid such bombings, many children in most nations under air attack were sent into the countryside to live with relatives or even with strangers. A number were also sent abroad, separated from their parents for years and, in many cases, forever; examples include the British children sent to North America and the Finnish children sent to Sweden.

In the Soviet Union, children helped patrol their neighborhoods at night to make certain that blackouts were being enforced. They filled sandbags and water buckets to prepare against incendiary bomb attacks and were enlisted to help in constructing antitank defenses before Moscow in the summer of 1941. Children were also actual combatants. They fought with partisan units in the Soviet Union and in Yugoslavia, among other nations. They also helped collect intelligence on Axis occupying forces. And in the last desperate fighting of World War II in Europe, Adolf Hitler pressed many young German boys into the army.

After the war, conditions were desperate in many parts of the world. In Vietnam, perhaps a million people perished in famine, including many children. Conditions were equally desperate in other states. Large numbers of people were displaced by the war, left homeless and hungry. There were perhaps 13 million abandoned European children at the end of World War II. Poland claimed a million orphans and France 250,000.

Adults were changed by the war, but so were the children who survived it. As they aged, their childhood experiences remained a reference point for their adult lives and served as a benchmark with which to measure future generations.

John Morello and Spencer C. Tucker

See also
Hiroshima, Bombing of; Holocaust, The; Nagasaki, Bombing of; Strategic Bombing

References
Dwork, Deborah. *Children with a Star: Jewish Children in Nazi Europe.* New Haven, CT: Yale University Press, 1991.
Halls, W. D. *The Youth of Vichy France.* Oxford: Oxford University Press, 1981.
Macardle, Dorothy. *Children of Europe: A Study of the Children of Liberated Countries—Their War-Time Experiences, Their Reactions, and Their Needs, with a Note on Germany.* Boston: Beacon Press, 1949.
Sosnowski, Kiryl. *The Tragedy of Children under Nazi Rule.* New York: Howard Fertig, 1983.
Werner, Emmy E. *Through the Eyes of Innocents: Children Witness World War II.* Boulder, CO: Westview Press, 2000.

China, Air Force

In December 1941, at the beginning of the Pacific war, the Nationalist China Air Force (CAF) had already been at war with Japan for almost four years. Beginning in 1932, trainers, pilots, and aircraft from the United States, Italy, Germany, and the Soviet Union had all played a part in building the Nationalist Chinese air element and the small air arms of several Chinese warlords. In July 1937, the CAF had three air groups, with a mix of U.S. and Italian fighters and bombers. Fewer than 100 of the more than 600 aircraft in the Chinese inventory were combat ready, however, and pilots had varying levels of competence and experience. Available forces immediately went into action to support the Nationalist army units in their defense of Shanghai, Jiangsu (Kiangsu) Province, in early August and to assist in the fighting withdrawal of Chinese forces into central China. From 1937 until the German invasion of the USSR in June 1941, the Soviets were the major supplier of aircraft, pilots, and trainers to China. The CAF was decimated in the late 1930s by the well-trained and well-equipped Japanese forces.

In April 1937, retired U.S. Army Air Corps officer Claire Chennault arrived in China to serve as an aviation adviser to the Nationalist government of Jiang Jieshi (Chiang Kai-shek). Chennault organized and led the American Volunteer Group (AVG) of the CAF, known as the Flying Tigers. In September 1941, Washington dispatched the American Military Mission to China (AMMISCA) to "advise and assist" in rebuilding the Nationalist forces. Providing aircraft to the CAF and its AVG was a high priority, and the creation of a Chinese military capable of taking the war to the Japanese was the mission of Lieutenant General Joseph Stilwell. Prior to the general's arrival in Asia in March 1942, Washington had decided to try to build up and maintain a CAF of 500 operational aircraft, including the Lockheed P-38 Lightning; the Curtiss P-40 Warhawk; the Republic P-43 Lancer; the Vultee P-66 Vanguard; and later, the North American P-51 Mustang fighters and the North American B-25 Mitchell and Consolidated B-24 Liberator bombers. With the closing of the land line of communication through Burma, the United States also promised the Chinese Curtiss C-46 Commando and C-47 Skytrain transport aircraft. From 1941 to V-J Day, Washington allocated 1,568 U.S. aircraft for China.

When the line of communication with Burma closed, everything had to be flown over "the Hump" (the Himalayas) to bases in southwestern China. Chennault, who rose to major general commanding the U.S. Fourteenth Air Force in March 1943, wanted to concentrate air assets on the destruction of Japanese air forces in China and build a bomber force capable of hitting critical targets in eastern China and the Japanese home islands. The United States also continued training the CAF and supplying equipment and aircraft to it and to its logistic arm, the China National Aviation Corporation. However, the U.S. Tenth and Fourteenth Air Forces required most aircraft delivered to the China-Burma-India Theater simply to keep the air bridge open and to support Allied offensives in Burma.

At the end of the war, U.S. aircraft were transferred to the CAF. When the Chinese Civil War began, Jiang's Nationalist forces had a competent air arm of nearly 500 aircraft and more than 5,000 trained pilots, aircrew, and maintenance personnel.

J. G. D. Babb

See also
Aircraft, Bombers; Aircraft, Fighters; Aircraft, Transport; Chennault, Claire Lee; China, Army; Flying Tigers; Hump, The; Jiang Jieshi; Lend-Lease; Sino-Japanese War; Stilwell, Joseph Warren

References
Hotz, Robert, ed. *Way of a Fighter: The Memoirs of Claire Lee Chennault.* New York: G. P. Putnam, 1949.

Liu, F. F. *A Military History of Modern China, 1924–1949.* Princeton, NJ: Princeton University Press, 1956.

Romanus, Charles F., and Riley Sunderland. *Stilwell's Mission to China.* Washington, DC: U.S. Government Printing Office, 1987.

China, Army

The armed forces of China before and during World War II reflected the deep political divisions of that nation. Each major faction maintained its own military organization. In addition to conventional forces controlled by the principal political factions in the country, various warlords had their own regional forces, the loyalties of which shifted according to the circumstances of the moment. Alongside these, at the local level, village defense forces struggled to protect their inhabitants against bandit gangs that roamed large stretches of the countryside.

Civil war between the Nationalists and Communists and the Nationalists and warlords had been raging intermit-

tently in China since 1927. Following the Japanese takeover of Manchuria and incursions into north China, these two factions arranged an uneasy truce, but underlying the Chinese military effort during the war was the realization of the prominent role played by the military in Chinese politics. Then too, by the end of 1942, Chinese leaders, including Nationalist leader Jiang Jieshi (Chiang Kai-shek) and Communist leader Mao Zedong (Mao Tse-tung), believed that the United States and its allies would defeat Japan. Given this belief and their own ardent conviction that a powerful military establishment would be essential in winning the postwar political struggle for power that was bound to follow, they planned (or rather, did not plan) their military moves accordingly. This approach meant, for the most part, avoiding contact with powerful Japanese forces, much to the exasperation of such individuals as Jiang's army commander, U.S. Army Lieutenant General Joseph W. Stilwell.

The Nationalist Army
The army had always been central to the power of the Nationalist Party—the Guomindang, or GMD (Kuomintang, or KMT). The National Military Council (NMC) controlled the military establishment; Jiang was its chairman, with complete power over the NMC, and as such, he directed all Nationalist military forces. At the beginning of the war, these numbered about 1.5 million men.

In the 1930s, the German government had sent military advisers to China to help train the Nationalist Army. In consequence, the Nationalist Central Armies were patterned more or less along German lines. Throughout the period, these were the best trained of the Nationalist forces, although still inferior to Japanese or Western forces. At the beginning of the Sino-Japanese War in 1937, the Central Armies numbered about 300,000 men. Included in this body was "the Generalissimo's Own," a force of some 80,000 men: armed with German weapons, it was the elite force of Jiang's military establishment. In addition to these relatively well-trained formations, there were some 1.2 million men in other units of indifferent training and capability. Though Nationalist senior leaders were often corrupt and not well educated, the middle ranks—trained at the Huangpu (Whampoa) Military Academy in Guangzhou (Canton), Guangdong (Kwangtung) Province—were capable. Most Nationalist soldiers, however, were conscripts, dragooned into service, and of low quality.

In the summer of 1941, the United States extended Lend-Lease aid to the Nationalist government, although the bulk of the early assistance went toward improving transport to China over the Burma Road from India. This route was cut off when the Japanese invaded Burma in force in early 1942, and it was not reopened until 1945. In the meantime, much

Camouflaged Chinese soldiers repel a charge by Japanese troops along the Salween River near Burma, ca. June 1943. (Franklin D. Roosevelt Library (NLFDR)

of the U.S. military aid to China was flown in over the Himalayas ("the Hump"). Tonnages by air gradually increased, but heated arguments occurred over the allocation of these still inadequate resources. Not until January 1945 was the Ledo Road (later known as the Stilwell Road) opened to China.

By the end of the war, the Nationalist Army numbered some 300 divisions. Although each supposedly had 10,000 men, some were seriously undermanned. Much military assistance, in the pipeline, continued to flow into China after the war, and the bulk of this ended up in Nationalist hands. The result was an army that was large in size and relatively well equipped but of limited capability and with indifferent leadership and inadequate training.

Chinese Communist Army

According to the agreement whereby the Nationalists and

Communists would make common cause against the Japanese, Chinese Communist forces in north China came to be designated the Eighth Route Army, authorized to a strength of three divisions. In 1938, the Nationalists also authorized formation of the smaller New Fourth Army in the lower Changjiang (Yangtze) River region.

The Chinese Communists refused to allow any Nationalist political authority in areas they controlled and denied the Nationalist side their military resources. Communist military forces were controlled by the Military Affairs Committee, which was responsible to the Communist Party Central Committee. Through the war, Mao chaired this committee.

Although the Communists' equipment was not on a par with that available to the Nationalists, their military leadership and training were both superior, and their morale was significantly higher. Unlike the Nationalist forces, in which many of the men taken into the service were removed to other areas and forcibly kept there, Communist forces remained in their own areas and were seen by the people as a positive force, even helping them with crops and looking after their welfare.

Meanwhile, Communist forces grew far beyond the numbers authorized by the Nationalists, although little expansion occurred after midwar, both because the Communists endeavored to improve the quality of their forces and because of Japanese "pacification" campaigns and Nationalist military actions. Nonetheless, at the end of the war, Mao could claim an army of about 1 million men, with reserves and local-level militia forces numbering an additional 2 million.

Collaborationist Armed Forces

The Japanese also organized collaborationist armed forces in the areas of China occupied by their troops. These highly unreliable forces were drawn from a variety of sources under a wide range of motivations. Some local commanders obeyed whichever side seemed ascendant at the moment. Nominally at least, many of these forces belonged to the Nationalist side. In the early 1940s, collaborationist forces might have numbered some 900,000 men.

Nationalist forces suffered most heavily in the first year of fighting the Japanese, especially in three months of struggle for Shanghai and the subsequent effort to defend Nanjing (Nanking) in Jiangsu (Kiangsu) Province. The Chinese lost perhaps a million dead, wounded, or missing in the first year of the war alone. The Nationalists then withdrew into the interior, relocating the capital to Chongqing (Chungking) in Sichuan (Szechwan). The Chinese then transformed the war into a struggle of attrition, which Japanese forces, despite their superior mobility, could not win.

Although the Communist forces conducted operations against the Japanese rear areas and some large-scale conventional offensives, the brunt of the fighting that then occurred was borne by the Nationalist Army and warlord forces loyal to Jiang. In the eight years of fighting through 1945, the Nationalists suffered more than 3 million casualties, while inflicting up to 2 million casualties on the Japanese. They were never able to gain a decisive victory over their antagonist, but the Chinese tied down significant numbers of Japanese forces until the end of the war.

In January 1941, the Chinese united front was severely damaged when the Nationalists attacked the Communist New Fourth Army. Open war now broke out between the Nationalists and the Communists. The fighting in China was henceforth a three-way contest. The Nationalists were no longer able to launch major offensives against the Japanese, but they were in a relatively secure position in central China. The Communists had also been weakened in fighting

against the Nationalists and the Japanese, but they maintained control of large areas in north-central China. The Japanese, with a great expenditure of troops and material, were only in control of the line of communications and were dangerously overextended in China even as they widened the war by attacking the United States.

Aside from grudgingly providing a small portion of their troops to General Stilwell to assist in the Allied recapture of Burma, Nationalist forces did not conduct any major actions from 1942 until forced to defend against Japan's August 1944 ICHI-Gō Offensive. That offensive was precipitated by the establishment of U.S. air bases from which the United States could conduct strategic bombing raids on the Japanese home islands. The real battles for the Nationalist and Communist forces came in 1945 over Manchuria and marked the beginning of the Chinese Civil War.

J. G. D. Babb and Spencer C. Tucker

See also

China, Air Force; China, Navy; Hump, The; ICHI-Gō Campaign; Jiang Jieshi; Lend-Lease; Mao Zedong; Shanghai, Battle of; Sino-Japanese War; Stilwell, Joseph Warren

References

Eastman, Lloyd E. *Seeds of Destruction: Nationalist China in War and Revolution, 1937–1949*. Stanford, CA: Stanford University Press, 1984.

Harries, Meirion, and Susie Harries. *Soldiers of the Sun: The Rise and Fall of the Imperial Japanese Army*. New York: Random House, 1991.

Wilson, Dick. *When Tigers Fight: The Story of the Sino-Japanese War, 1937–1945*. New York: Penguin, 1982.

China, Civil War in (1945–1949)

Internecine conflict between China's governing Nationalist Party—the Guomindang, or GMD (Kuomintang, or KMT)—and supporters of the Chinese Communist Party (CCP), which began immediately after World War II and brought the establishment of the People's Republic of China (PRC).

The roots of the Chinese Civil War went back as far as the late 1920s. After the foundation of the CCP in 1921, the Soviet Comintern (Communist International) advised its members to collaborate with other political groups supporting the Chinese Revolution, especially the GMD. The Guomindang had been founded by Sun Yixian (Sun Yat-sen), the revered revolutionary leader who was elected provisional president of the new Republic of China in 1911. After Sun's death in 1925, military leader Jiang Jieshi (Chiang Kai-shek) won power within the GMD and began to eliminate all potential rivals. In 1926, Jiang, alarmed by abortive but bloody Communist uprisings in several industrial cities, began to purge Communist Party members from the Guomindang institutions in which they had previously been prominent and to suppress them elsewhere. In mid-1927, he made the Communist base in Jiangxi (Kiangsi) Province of south-central China the new target of the Northern Expedition he had launched the previous year against northern warlords, and he suppressed several further Communist insurrections.

Led by Mao Zedong (Mao Tse-tung) and fortified by several former GMD military units whose commanders defected to the Communists, this rural base developed into the Jiangxi Soviet Republic, whose military forces numbered 200,000 by 1933. Chinese Communists also mounted several further urban and rural insurrections, and Jiang regarded them as the greatest threat to his government—even more serious a threat than the Japanese troops who established the client state of Manzhouguo (Manchukuo) in Manchuria in 1932 and who constantly sought to enhance Japan's influence in north China. Between 1930 and 1934, Jiang waged annual campaigns against the Ruijin (Juichin) base in Jiangxi. In the last of these campaigns, he succeeded in forcing Communist supporters to retreat 6,000 miles to the remote northwestern province of Shaanxi (Shensi) in the famous Long March.

In 1935 and 1936, Jiang ordered troops commanded by his loyal ally, Manchurian warlord Zhang Xueliang (Chang Hsüeh-liang), to attack and, he hoped, eliminate the few thousand remaining Communists. The soldiers rejected his orders, arguing that all Chinese should unite to fight the Japanese, not each other. In the December 1936 Xi'an (Sian) Incident, Zhang kidnaped Jiang and forced him to form a united anti-Japanese front with the Communists. The GMD-CCP relationship remained strained, as Communists developed their own military forces—the Eighth Route Army, commanded by Zhu De (Chu Teh), and the New Fourth Army, under Lin Biao (Lin Piao)—and retained control of northern Shaanxi.

The following year, a minor clash between Chinese and Japanese troops at the Lugouqiao (Lukouch'iao) Marco Polo Bridge, near Beijing (Peking) in Hebei (Hopeh) Province, quickly escalated into full-scale warfare between the two countries. Over the following 18 months, Jiang gradually retreated to Chongqing (Chungking) in the far southwestern province of Sichuan (Szechwan), abandoning northern and eastern China to protracted Japanese occupation. The Communists controlled northwestern China. For three months in late 1940, the Communists launched the "Hundred Regiments" Campaign against Japan, but their eventual defeat by the better-equipped Japanese convinced them to switch to tactics of establishing guerrilla bases behind Japanese

lines in north and central China. This policy provoked ferocious Japanese reprisals against Communists and civilians alike, but it proved effective in disrupting Japanese control and in enhancing both the Communists' reputation as dedicated opponents of Japanese rule and their postwar political position. It did not suffice, however, to defeat Japanese rule.

By 1940, Mao was already making plans for a postwar Communist government of China. By this time, both sides anticipated a fierce postwar struggle for power and sought to position themselves advantageously for it. In late 1941, GMD forces attacked and defeated the Communist New Fourth Army in the lower Changjiang (Yangtze) Valley, an episode marking the fundamental breakdown of CCP-GMD collaboration, though an uneasy alliance continued until 1944. GMD forces possessed superior equipment and funding, but Jiang's abandonment of much of China to Japanese rule and his reliance on a protracted strategy of attrition, together with the corruption that characterized many top officials of his regime, eroded his hold on popular loyalties. Communist morale was high: their idealistic rhetoric, the spartan living conditions at their Yan'an (Yenan) base in Shaanxi, their attractive and charismatic leaders, and their dangerous though small-scale partisan operations all caught the popular imagination and impressed many visiting Western journalists and officials.

The war ended in August 1945 with Japanese occupation forces still in place throughout China. CCP membership had reached 1.2 million people, plus military forces of 900,000, and the Communists controlled an area whose population numbered 90 million. In Manchuria, despite Jiang's objections, entering Soviet forces facilitated the surrender of Japanese troops and equipment to Communist units. U.S. leaders, especially Ambassador Patrick J. Hurley in late 1945, sought to strengthen Jiang's regime; to promote reform from within; and to encourage Nationalist-Communist reconciliation and the formation of a coalition government in which Communists would have some influence, albeit as junior partners.

The most sustained such effort was the 13-month (December 1945–January 1947) mission to China of the former U.S. Army chief of staff, General George C. Marshall. In January 1946, he arranged a temporary cease-fire in the developing civil war; it was broken later that spring when, as Soviet units withdrew, GMD forces attacked Chinese Communist troops in Manchuria, winning control of that region in late May. That same month, the Communists rechristened their military forces the People's Liberation Army (PLA). It proved impossible to devise any further agreements acceptable to both sides.

Full-scale civil war resumed on 26 June 1946, when Nationalist units launched an offensive against Communist-held areas in Hubei (Hupeh) and Henan (Honan) Provinces. The United States continued to provide massive loans and quantities of military hardware to the GMD government but prudently refused to commit American troops. As the Cold War rapidly developed, Soviet and American officials clearly backed different parties in the evolving Chinese Civil War, but neither was prepared to run great risks to assist its favored candidate.

By 1947, as inflation and corruption both ran rampant, Chinese businesspeople and the middle class began to desert the GMD, and many fled overseas. As they had against the Japanese, the Communists frequently employed guerrilla tactics against Nationalist forces. Their introduction of land reform persuaded many peasants to support them. These tactics supplemented the full-scale military campaigns they soon had the strength to launch. In mid-May 1947, Lin and the New Fourth Army opened a major offensive in northeastern China, and six weeks later, another large army, commanded by Liu Bocheng (Liu Po-ch'eng), moved southwest across the Huang He (Hwang Ho) (known to Westerners as the Yellow River) into Shandong (Shantung) Province. In September 1948, Lin began a massive campaign in Manchuria, capturing Shenyang (Mukden) in Liaoniang Province in November shortly after 300,000 GMD troops surrendered to him. In north-central China, the Communist Huai River Campaign ended victoriously on 10 January 1949 after PLA troops surrounded 66 regiments, representing one-third of the existing GMD military forces. In January 1949, the GMD government fled to Taiwan, and that same month, Beijing, China's symbolic capital, fell to Lin's troops. The southern city of Guangzhou (Canton) in Guangdong (Kwangtung) fell the following October, as Communist forces gradually consolidated their hold over the entire country. On 1 October 1949, Mao proclaimed the new People's Republic of China.

The Chinese Civil War and American support of the GMD government—which, even after its move to Taiwan, continued until the 1970s—left a lasting legacy of distrust and suspicion that divided the United States and mainland China for several decades. American officials viewed the establishment in China of a Communist government sympathetic to the Soviet Union as a major Cold War defeat, a perception enhanced by China's November 1950 intervention in the Korean War. For at least two decades, Chinese leaders in turn regarded the United States as their country's most significant international adversary, a perspective that only began to change after President Richard Nixon moved to reopen relations with China in the early 1970s.

Priscilla Roberts

See also

Chen Yi; Chennault, Claire Lee; China, Army; China, Role in War; Jiang Jieshi; Lin Biao; Mao Zedong; Marco Polo Bridge, Battle of; Marshall, George Catlett; Zhou Enlai; Zhu De

References

Dreyer, Edward L. *China at War, 1901–1949*. New York: Longman, 1995.

Eastman, Lloyd E., ed. *The Nationalist Era in China, 1927–1949*. Cambridge, MA: Harvard University Press, 1991.

Fairbank, John K., and Albert Feuerwerker, eds. *The Cambridge History of China*. Vol. 13, Republican China, 1912–1949, Part 2. Cambridge: Cambridge University Press, 1986.

Liu, F. F. *The Military History of Modern China, 1924–1949*. Princeton, NJ: Princeton University Press, 1956.

Westad, Odd Arne. *Cold War and Revolution: Soviet-American Rivalry and the Origins of the Chinese Civil War, 1944–1946*. New York: Columbia University Press, 1993.

———. *Decisive Encounters: The Chinese Civil War, 1946–1950*. Stanford, CA: Stanford University Press, 2003.

China, Eastern Campaign (April–November 1944)

Japanese offensive in China during World War II. In late 1943, the Japanese High Command decided to launch its first major offensive in China since 1939. There were several goals. One was to seize the airfields in eastern China that were being used by the U.S. Fourteenth Air Force to attack shipping on the Changjiang (Yangtze) River and along the China coast, especially since these airfields potentially could be used by long-range Boeing B-29 bombers against the Japanese homeland. A second goal was to capture the Hunan-Kwangsi, Canton-Hankow, and Peking-Hankow railroad lines in order to secure the land transportation link between the Japanese stronghold in northern China and Japanese forces in Southeast Asia. A third goal was to destroy several large bodies of Chinese Nationalist troops and further the deterioration of the regime of Nationalist Generalissimo Chiang Kai-shek, perhaps even to the point of collapse.

The offensive, code-named ICHI-Gō (Operation NUMBER ONE), began on 17 April 1944 when 100,000 troops from the North China Area Army pushed south along the Peking-Hankow railroad. Spearheaded by tanks, the Japanese easily brushed aside the poorly equipped Chinese, many of whom were provincial troops commanded by generals who once had been opponents of Chiang. By June, the Japanese had gained control of the railroad and dispersed more than 300,000 Chinese, at a loss of 1,000 of their own dead. Having long experienced onerous taxation, conscription, and mismanagement by Chiang's regime, many peasants aided the Japanese and even attacked groups of retreating Chinese.

The second phase of the campaign began at the end of May when 250,000 troops from the China Expeditionary Army moved south across the Changjiang River. Over the next weeks, despite heavy bombing by Fourteenth Air Force pilots, the advancing Japanese seized the vital rail centers of Changa-sha and, after a fierce 47-day siege, Heng-yang. Following a lull in which they regrouped their forces into the Sixth Area Army, the Japanese resumed the offensive in late August. By the end of November, they had forced the evacuation of many Allied airfields and joined up with other units that had driven north from Canton and Indochina to complete the corridor between northern China and Southeast Asia. The Japanese successes sent a wave of panic through Nationalist China, and for a time, Allied leaders feared the Japanese would drive to the west and take Chungking, the Nationalist capital. The Japanese, however, had no plans to advance to Chungking. Their supply line was overextended, and they were increasingly concerned about a possible U.S. threat to the China coast.

Their 1944 Eastern Campaign was a major victory for the Japanese. They occupied an area inhabited by 100 million people and took control of most of the Nationalists' granary and industrial base, devastating their economy. In addition, the Japanese gained the railroad connection they had sought, inflicted 700,000 casualties on the Chinese, and weakened the U.S. air war in China. Even more important for the long term, the campaign demonstrated the weaknesses of Chiang's ability to wage war, costing him badly needed popular support in his ongoing struggle with the Chinese Communists.

John Kennedy Ohl

See also
Chennault, Claire Lee; China, Role in War; ICHI-GŌ Campaign; Jiang Jieshi; Sino-Japanese War

References
Eastman, Lloyd D. *Seeds of Destruction: Nationalist China in War and Revolution, 1937–1949.* Stanford, CA: Stanford University Press, 1984.
Romanus, Charles P., and Riley Sunderland. *United States Army in World War II: China-Burma-India Theater.* 3 vols. Washington, DC: U.S. Government Printing Office, 1952–1958.
Wilson, Dick. *When Tigers Fight: The Story of the Sino-Japanese War, 1937–1945.* New York: Viking, 1982.

China, Navy

In the 1920s, Germany assisted the Nationalist government of China in establishing a naval academy at Mamei in Fujian (Fukien) Province, and in 1927, the Nationalist leaders also set up the Chinese Naval General Headquarters. However,

the vast bulk of resources went into the army and air forces. When war with Japan began in July 1937, the Nationalist navy consisted of a few old gunboats, some small coastal vessels, and river craft. The navy also maintained a few naval stations inland on the major rivers and a facility that manufactured mines and naval explosives.

The Japanese quickly destroyed the larger Chinese naval craft during and after the August 1937 Battle of Shanghai in Jiangsu (Kiangsu) Province. Nonetheless, throughout the war, elements of the Chinese navy conducted sabotage attacks against Japanese ships and shore bases in China.

In early 1942, the U.S. Navy sent to China a small detachment known as the Sino-American Cooperative Organization (SACO) or the "Rice Paddy Navy," under the joint command of Nationalist General Dai Li (Tai Li) and U.S. Navy Captain Milton E. "Mary" Miles. Its mission was to establish and man weather stations and communications facilities, gather intelligence, and conduct sabotage and guerrilla operations in the coastal areas and along the inland rivers of China. In 1943, Miles was promoted to commodore and assigned as commander, Naval Group China.

At the end of the war, there was a significant interservice battle over the type of navy China should maintain, who would control it, and how it would be equipped. Disputes slowed the effort to build a postwar Nationalist navy. In any case, however, Nationalist leaders did not see maritime forces as critical in the coming battle with the Communists.

J. G. D. Babb

See also
China, Air Force; China, Army; Dai Li

References
Liu, F. F. *A Military History of Modern China, 1924–1949.* Princeton, NJ: Princeton University Press, 1956.
Miles, Milton E. *A Different Kind of War: The Little Known Story of the Combined Guerrilla Forces Created in China by the U.S. Navy and the Chinese during World War II.* New York: Doubleday, 1967.
Tolley, Kemp. *Yangtze Patrol: The U.S. Navy in China.* Annapolis, MD: Naval Institute Press, 1971.

China, Role in War

China, one of the four major Allied powers of World War II, fought Japan alone for four years and throughout the war tied down over a million Japanese troops. The war strengthened the position of the Chinese Communists and helped to precipitate the eventual downfall of the governing Nationalist Party—the Guomindang, or GMD (Kuomintang, or KMT)—of President Jiang Jieshi (Chiang Kai-shek).

For China, war began in July 1937, when long-standing hostilities with Japan, provoked by the latter country's effective annexation of Manchuria in 1931 and a continuing series of territorial, economic, and political incursions in other areas, caused a small skirmish near the Lugouqiao (Lukouch'iao) Marco Polo Bridge, close to Beijing (Peking) in Hebei (Hopeh) Province, to escalate into full-scale warfare. The Chinese invariably called the conflict "the War of Resistance against Japanese Aggression." Until December 1941, when China formally declared war on Japan and thereby aligned itself with the Western Allies after the Japanese attack on Pearl Harbor, Japan dismissively referred to the Chinese conflict as the "China Incident"; after that date, it became part of the "Greater East Asia War."

For much of the 1930s, the Chinese Nationalist government effectively acquiesced in Japanese demands. Although President Jiang believed that war with Japan would probably become inevitable in time, he sought to defer this until, with the help of German military advisers, he had successfully modernized China's armed forces. In the early 1930s, his first priority was to eliminate the GMD's major political rival—the Chinese Communist Party (CCP) led by the charismatic and innovative Mao Zedong (Mao Tse-tung), against whose forces Jiang mounted annual campaigns every year from 1930 to 1935. Only after December 1936—when another leading Chinese politician, the Manchurian warlord Zhang Xueliang (Chang Hsüeh-liang), captured Jiang and made his release conditional on the formation of a united Nationalist-Communist anti-Japanese front—did Jiang reluctantly and temporarily renounce his deeply rooted anti-Communist hostility.

The two camps never trusted each other, and political factionalism within the GMD also continued throughout the war, hampering Jiang's freedom of action and his ability to wage effective warfare against Japanese forces. Communist and GMD forces remained essentially separate, mounting independent operations. From late 1938 onward, the GMD government, headed by Jiang and based in Chongqing (Chungking) in Sichuan (Szechwan) Province, controlled southwest China. The Communists held sway over northwest China from their base in Yan'an (Yenan) in Shaanxi (Shensi) Province.

In its early stages, China's war with Japan was one of rapid movement and military disaster. In late July 1937, Japanese troops took over the entire Beijing-Tianjin (Tientsin) area of north China. They inflicted a series of major defeats on Jiang's military, wiping out most of his modernized units and, over the following 18 months, successively taking Shanghai and Nanjing (Nanking), Guangzhou (Canton), and Wuhan, China's provisional capital after Nanjing fell. Chinese troops had occasional triumphs—notably,

the April 1938 Battle of Taierzhuang (Hsieh Chan T'ai-Erh-Chuang)—but these were rarely followed up. Japanese leaders assumed Jiang would sue for peace before the end of 1938, but to their frustration, he refused to do so.

Jiang adopted a strategy of "trading space for time," based on the assumption that by retreating, the Chinese could force the Japanese to overextend themselves, making them vulnerable to a lengthy war of attrition. This prediction proved substantially correct, as by 1940, Japanese forces were bogged down in an inconclusive war in mainland China, occupying vast tracts of territory without fully controlling them. Even so and despite the scorched-earth policy Jiang followed, the regions he ceded to Japanese rule—from March 1940 exercised through the puppet regime of renegade Chinese politician Wang Jingwei (Wang Ching-wei)—included most of China's leading cities, its major industrial areas, and its most fertile and densely populated agricultural regions. Jiang's early, dogged resistance to Japanese invasion won him great national prestige, but his subsequent protracted abandonment of most of northern and eastern China to Japanese occupation eventually damaged his standing and weakened his authority.

From 1931 onward, Jiang sought assistance against Japan from Western powers and the League of Nations, but effectual aid was rarely forthcoming. The league restricted itself to nonrecognition of Manzhouguo (Manchukuo) and moral condemnation of Japan's policies, together with the imposition of limited economic sanctions on Japan—restrictions that only some of its member states observed. In 1938, the U.S. government extended limited economic assistance to China, making a loan against its tung oil supplies.

By the late 1930s, the growing demands of Germany and Italy in Europe preoccupied most Western nations, and the Sino-Japanese War remained a distant sideshow, albeit one with implications for the European powers' colonial positions in Asia. In summer 1940, the German conquest of most of western Europe brought Japanese demands that Britain, France, and the Netherlands forbid the sale or transit of war supplies to China through their Asian colonies; France's Vichy government was also forced to open air bases in Indochina to Japanese warplanes. In autumn 1940, Japan formally joined Germany and Italy in the Tripartite Alliance of the Axis powers. These actions brought additional U.S. economic and military assistance for China, including the dispatch of American warplanes, and in 1941, President Franklin D. Roosevelt drastically tightened economic sanctions on Japan and repeatedly demanded the withdrawal of Japanese troops from China.

When Japan attacked American forces at Pearl Harbor on 7 December 1941, simultaneously declaring war on Great Britain and swiftly annexing British, Dutch, and American territories in East and Southeast Asia, China finally formally declared war on Japan. Jiang was named supreme commander of the Allied China Theater, receiving substantial amounts of military aid under the American Lend-Lease program. Even so—and despite his Western-educated wife's skillful dissemination in the United States of an image of China as a heroic, democratic, and modernizing state—Jiang's relations with other Allied leaders were poor.

Jiang's single-minded focus on Chinese interests, regardless of the impact on the broader Allied coalition, annoyed Roosevelt and British Prime Minister Winston L. S. Churchill. Nonetheless, it sometimes paid dividends. At the 1943 Cairo Conference, Allied leaders agreed that China should regain all territories annexed by Japan since 1895. Jiang also sought to end foreign extraterritorial privileges and concessions in China and, less successfully, to regain the British colony of Hong Kong. And at the autumn 1944 Dumbarton Oaks meeting, China was one of the five great powers awarded permanent Security Council seats in the new United Nations. At the February 1945 Yalta Conference, however, Roosevelt, Churchill, and Soviet leader Josef Stalin agreed (in Jiang's absence) that, in return for joining the war against Japan from which it had remained aloof, the Soviet Union should regain the special rights tsarist Russia had exercised in Manchuria before 1905.

The continuing Chinese inability or reluctance to mount an aggressive campaign against the Japanese occupiers irritated British and American officials, especially U.S. Lieutenant General Joseph W. Stilwell, American commander of the China-Burma-India Theater and Jiang's chief of staff. Stilwell hoped to modernize the Chinese army and lead it in such a venture—an undertaking Jiang opposed as impractical, probably motivated in part by fears that this would weaken his own control of the Chinese military and his postwar position vis-à-vis the Chinese Communists. Over Jiang's opposition, Stilwell also sought to supply weapons to all anti-Japanese forces in China, including the Communists. Ultimately, at Jiang's insistence, Roosevelt withdrew Stilwell in 1944. Many Allied officials and journalists also deplored the pervasive corruption of the Nationalist regime that Jiang, though personally honest, tolerated.

Such shortcomings among the Nationalists enhanced the image of the Chinese Communists. Since 1937, they had supposedly been Jiang's partners against Japan, even though both the Nationalists and Communists believed that civil war was ultimately inevitable and sought to strengthen themselves for the anticipated confrontation. The Communists' Eighth Route Army, created in 1937, and the New Fourth Army built up by Lin Biao (Lin Piao) fought largely behind Japanese lines in central China and the northern Hebei and Shanxi (Shensi) Provinces, working closely with local guerrilla and partisan forces and building up bases that would potentially enhance the postwar Communist position. Communist forces adopted this strategy after their defeat in the "Hundred Regiments" Campaign of August to November 1940, in which Japanese rail and road networks in north China were attacked. CCP-GMD cooperation largely ceased after the 1941 New Fourth Army Incident, when Nationalist troops attacked and defeated that unit in the lower Chanjiang (Yangtze) Valley.

Despite the Chinese Communists' undoubted ruthlessness, their reputation far surpassed that of the Guomindang government. Idealistic young students and intellectuals flocked to join the Communists. Their selfless dedication and austere lifestyle and the charm and ability of their top leaders, especially Zhou Enlai (Chou En-lai), later China's premier, impressed Western journalists and officials who visited their Yan'an base, including the young diplomats of the 1944 U.S. "Dixie Mission." Nonetheless, despite their disillusionment with GMD leaders, senior American officials never endorsed the Chinese Communists.

When the war ended in August 1945, Japanese troops were still in occupation throughout China. In Manchuria, despite objections from Jiang, Soviet forces turned over to Communist Chinese units arms and equipment captured from the Japanese. American leaders, especially Ambassador Patrick J. Hurley in late 1945, were concerned about Communist inroads in China and sought to strengthen Jiang's regime, to promote reform, and to encourage GMD-CCP reconciliation and the formation of a coalition government in which Communists would have limited influence. Between December 1945 and January 1947, the former U.S. Army chief of staff, General George C. Marshall, was in China endeavoring to secure an accommodation between the two sides. In January 1946, he arranged a temporary cease-fire, but it was broken later that spring when, as Soviet forces withdrew, GMD forces attacked Chinese Communist troops in Manchuria. No further agreement acceptable to both sides could be brokered, and civil war continued until the Communists secured military victory. The GMD government retreated to the island of Taiwan, and on 1 October 1949, Mao proclaimed the new People's Republic of China. From then onward, China would play a major role in the Cold War that succeeded and grew out of World War II.

Priscilla Roberts

See also

Burma Theater; Cairo Conference; Chennault, Claire Lee; China, Civil War in; China-Burma-India Theater; Churchill, Sir Winston L. S.; Japan, Role in the War; Jiang Jieshi; Lend-Lease; Lin Biao; Mao Zedong; Marco Polo Bridge, Battle of; Marshall, George Catlett; Sino-Japanese War; Stilwell, Joseph Warren; Yalta Conference; Zhou Enlai

References

Boyle, J. H. *China and Japan at War, 1937–1945: The Politics of Collaboration.* Stanford, CA: Stanford University Press, 1972.

Eastman, Lloyd E. *Seeds of Destruction: Nationalist China in War and Revolution, 1937–1945.* Stanford, CA: Stanford University Press, 1984.

———, ed. *The Nationalist Era in China, 1927–1949.* Cambridge, MA: Harvard University Press, 1991.

Fairbank, John K., and Albert Feuerwerker, eds. *The Cambridge History of China.* Vol. 13, *Republican China, 1912–1949, Part 2.* Cambridge: Cambridge University Press, 1986.

Hsü, Immanuel C. *The Rise of Modern China.* 6th ed. New York: Oxford University Press, 2000.

Morley, J. W., ed. *The China Quagmire: Japan's Expansion on the Asian Continent, 1933–1941.* New York: Columbia University Press, 1983.

Schaller, Michael. *The U.S. Crusade in China, 1938–1945.* New York: Columbia University Press, 1979.

Spence, Jonathan. *The Search for Modern China.* 2nd ed. New York: Norton, 1999.

Tuchman, Barbara. *Stilwell and the American Experience in China, 1911–1945.* New York: Macmillan, 1970.

Van der Ven, Hans J. *War and Nationalism in China, 1925–1945.* New York: Routledge-Curzon, 2003.

China-Burma-India (CBI) Theater

General geographic reference for the immersion of East Asia, Southeast Asia, and South Asia in the war against Japan. China-Burma-India (CBI) also refers to an Allied military command structure in the Pacific Theater that was established early in the war. At the December 1941 ARCADIA Conference in Quebec, British Prime Minister Winston L. S. Churchill and U.S. President Franklin D. Roosevelt agreed to set up the American-British-Dutch-Australian Command (ABDA) under General Sir Archibald Wavell in India. Separate from but nominally equal to the ABDA was the China Theater under Generalissimo Jiang Jieshi (Chiang Kai-shek) as supreme commander, in recognition of China's role in fighting Japan since at least the start of the Sino-Japanese War in 1937. Lieutenant General Joseph Stilwell, who had more experience in China than any other senior U.S. Army officer and spoke Chinese fluently, became the senior Allied officer in the region. His two titles were "commanding general of the United States Army Forces in the Chinese Theater of Operations, Burma, and India" and "chief of staff to the Supreme Commander of the Chinese Theater" (Jiang Jieshi). The chain of command was confusing because American forces in China came under the authority of Wavell's ABDA Command. Wavell also commanded forces in Burma, whereas Stilwell was to have direct command of Chinese forces committed to Burma (initially, three armies of up to 100,000 men). From the beginning, Stilwell and Jiang did not get along, and Stilwell was repeatedly handicapped by Jiang's interference in military matters.

In February, following the loss of most of the Netherlands East Indies, the ABDA Command was done away with. From that point forward, the Pacific became an American responsibility, with the British assuming authority from Singapore to Suez. Jiang continued to control the China Theater, and Wavell, headquartered in India, had authority over India and Burma. At the same time, Stilwell formed a new headquarters, the American Armed Forces: China, Burma, and India. The command included the small prewar U.S. military advisory group and Major General Claire Chennault's American Volunteer Group (AVG, known as the Flying Tigers), later a part of Tenth Army Air Force.

This command structure continued until the August 1943 Quebec Conference, when Churchill and Roosevelt agreed on the establishment of the more integrated South-East Asia Command (SEAC), with British Admiral Lord Louis Mountbatten as commander and Stilwell as his deputy. Operations in Burma were separated from those in India, now under command of General Claude Auchinleck, commander in chief there since June 1943.

Designed to improve Allied military operations in the region, the new command structure did not achieve that end. Conflicts and different goals remained, with Jiang being the chief problem in Allied cooperation. But the British and Americans also had different priorities. The British were mainly concerned with the defense of India and preventing the Japanese military from exerting an influence on growing Indian nationalism. London saw defeating the Japanese in Burma as the chief means to bring about that end, rather than as a means to channel supplies to China. British military efforts in Burma would thus ebb and flow. The United States was primarily interested in building up China's military strength, and Burma would be a chief route for these supplies to reach China; indeed, President Roosevelt saw China taking its rightful place as a major world power at war's end. U.S. military planners also saw China as a potential location for heavy bombers to be used in the strategic bombing of Japan. These conflicting views were exacerbated by the personalities involved. Stilwell continued to feud with Jiang, and he also held that the British were more interested in defending their Asian empire than in fighting Japan. Stilwell wanted to recover Burma, and he worked hard to improve the fighting ability of those Chinese army units he could influence. The only way to get substantial military heavy equipment to China—which was essential if its fighting ability was to improve dramatically—was by way of Burma, and so construction of the so-called Ledo Road there became imperative. In the meantime, the United States undertook a massive logistical air supply operation to

China from bases in India over "the Hump" of the Himalaya Mountains, the highest in the world. The ubiquitous C-47 (DC-3) aircraft was the workhorse for much of this campaign.

Construction of the 478-mile-long Ledo Road to connect the old Burma Road from Ledo, India, to Bhama, Burma, took 25 months. The new road ran through jungles, over mountains, and across 10 rivers. U.S. Army Brigadier General Lewis A. Pick had charge of this vast project, one of the major engineering accomplishments of the war.

Meanwhile, Jiang refused to yield operational command of the growing Chinese military establishment to General Stilwell. Jiang saw the Chinese forces as much as a means to defeat the Communists in China after the war as to destroy the Japanese forces in the current conflict. Stilwell fervently believed that, properly trained and equipped, Chinese soldiers could be the equal of any in the world, but all of his efforts to eradicate corruption, weed out ineffective leaders, and end political interference in the Chinese military were rebuffed by Jiang. The Chinese Nationalist leader repeatedly promised reforms but delivered only sufficient compliance to keep up the flow of U.S. military aid.

General Chennault and airpower advocates believed that Japan might be bombed into submission from bases in eastern China. Stilwell dismissed such views and pointed out that the Japanese could simply carry out an offensive to wipe out the bases. Nonetheless, the first production B-29 Superfortresses were sent to China from India, and an ambitious base-construction program was undertaken. Although a few air bombing missions were carried out, the Japanese responded by mounting a great ground offensive, the ICHI-GŌ Campaign, in mid-1944, during which all the bases were captured without significant Chinese ground resistance. The B-29s were shifted from CBI to the Marianas in the Central Pacific. Roosevelt now applied heavy pressure on Jiang to carry out the reforms advocated by Stilwell and place an American general, preferably Stilwell, in command of the Chinese army. Frustrated by its inability to turn China into a major theater of war, the United States increasingly used its massive naval strength to invest in the highly productive "leap-frogging" strategy of securing important islands as stepping stones toward Japan across the Central Pacific. As a result, China was more and more marginalized and downgraded to a minor theater of war, chiefly important for its role in tying down a million Japanese troops.

Stilwell, now at wit's end, reached an impasse with Jiang and was recalled to Washington in October 1944. He was replaced by U.S. Army Major General Albert Wedemeyer, a far more tractable individual bent on getting along with Jiang. The demands for reforms in the Chinese military came to an end. In effect, CBI ended in October 1944 when it was di-

vided into two spheres of command, India-Burma and China. Stilwell's deputy, General Daniel L. Sultan, became the commander of U.S. forces in India-Burma and directed the Allied military effort in northern Burma.

The CBI featured unique air, guerrilla, and logistical operations. Among innovative military and air tactics originating in the CBI was the establishment of Long-Range Penetration Groups, more popularly known as Wingate's Chindits and Merrill's Maurauders. Utilizing air assets, British and U.S. commanders projected ground troops far behind Japanese lines, their communication and supply provided by air. Here and elsewhere, guerrilla operations were developed and intelligence and insurgency operations carried out. William Donovan and the Office of Strategic Services were active in the theater.

Finally, the CBI was a major scene of postwar confrontation. Early in the war, Japan had conquered and overrun much of China and most of the European and U.S. colonies in the Pacific. The arrival of Japanese forces in Indochina was a great blow to French influence, and the defeat of the British at Singapore had an even more powerful impact on British prestige. President Roosevelt envisioned the end of colonization after the war, but with the arrival of the Soviet threat, new U.S. President Harry S Truman was less sympathetic. Although the Philippines, India, Burma, and some other states gained independence just after the war, the process of decolonization was actually delayed in some areas, resulting in costly wars in the Netherlands East Indies and French Indochina. As for China, American efforts by Roosevelt's inept ambassador to China, Patrick J. Hurley, to mediate between the Chinese Nationalists and Communists came to naught; that vast country soon disintegrated into civil war. The United States, which had already committed to Jiang, found itself unable to adopt a neutral stance and paid the price in influence when the civil war ended in a Communist victory in 1949.

Eugene L. Rasor and Spencer C. Tucker

See also

Auchinleck, Sir Claude John Eyre; Burma Air Campaign; Burma Road; Burma Theater; China, Role in War; Chindits; Donovan, William Joseph; Hump, The; Jiang Jieshi; Mountbatten, Louis Francis Albert Victor Nicholas; Office of Strategic Services; Singapore, Battle for; Sino-Japanese War; Stilwell, Joseph Warren; Wavell, Sir Archibald Percival; Wedemeyer, Albert Coady

References

Ienaga, Saburo. *The Pacific War: World War II and the Japanese, 1931–1945.* Oxford: Blackwell, 1968.

Levine, Alan J. *The Pacific War: Japan versus the Allies.* Westport, CT: Praeger, 1995.

Rasor, Eugene L. *The China-Burma-India Campaign, 1931–1949: Historiography and Annotated Bibliography.* Westport, CT: Greenwood Press, 1998.

Romanus, Charles P., and Riley Sunderland. *United States Army in World War II: China-Burma-India Theater.* 3 vols. Washington, DC: U.S. Government Printing Office, 1952–1958.

Schaller, Michael. *The U.S. Crusade in China, 1938–1945.* New York: Columbia University Press, 1979.

Spector, Ronald H. *Eagle against the Sun: The American War with Japan.* New York: Free Press, 1984.

Thorne, Christopher G. *The Approach of War, 1938–1939.* New York: St. Martin's Press, 1967.

———. *Allies of a Kind: The United States, Britain, and the War against Japan, 1941–1945.* New York: Oxford University Press, 1978.

———. *The Issue of War: States, Societies, and the Far Eastern Conflict of 1941–1945.* New York: Oxford University Press, 1985.

Tuchman, Barbara. *Stilwell and the American Experience in China, 1911–1945.* New York: Macmillan, 1970.

Chindits

Name applied to irregular forces raised by British Brigadier General Orde Wingate for special operations in Burma in 1943 and 1944. The term, selected by Wingate himself, was derived from the Burmese word *Chinthé,* the name of a mythical, griffinlike creature, stone effigies of which guard the entrance to Burmese temples.

In early 1942, Wingate was transferred to India at the request of General Archibald Wavell, who commanded Allied forces in the Far East. Wavell had known Wingate since service in Palestine and respected his innovative thinking, especially in the use of irregular forces. Wingate was tasked to apply this ability against the Japanese in Burma, who had seemed invincible up to that time. To accomplish this

Chindits (members of General Orde Wingate's Allied commando force) moving through jungle in Burma. (Hulton Archive by Getty Images)

mission, he developed the concept of long-range penetration operations, which consisted of semi-independent guerrilla forces operating deep in the rear of Japanese forces. These forces would be resupplied by air.

Under cover as 77th Brigade, Wingate formed what he called the "Chindits" out of disparate elements of Gurkhas, the Burma Rifles, and British units, and he conducted strenuous training in central India through 1942. On 16 February 1943, this force of about 3,000 men with 1,000 pack animals crossed the Chindwin River into northern Burma, thereby launching the first Chindit operation (Operation LONGCLOTH). The force was organized into six columns, the nucleus of each being an infantry company, and given the objectives of disrupting communications (notably, by cutting the Myitkyina-Mandalay railway line) and creating general havoc through ambushes and other small-unit operations. LONGCLOTH, which ended in late April, achieved mixed success and took heavy casualties. Only 70 percent of those who had crossed the Chindwin in February returned, and of these, only about 28 percent would be fit for future active service.

Nevertheless, in a theater where all had been doom and gloom previously, the campaign's limited achievements were widely heralded. British Prime Minister Winston L. S. Churchill, in particular, seized on the publicity and promised Wingate his personal support for future operations, even taking him along to the Quebec (QUADRANT) Conference in August 1943. Plans now commenced for a larger, more ambitious campaign. Using the cover of 3rd Indian Division, six brigades and a U.S. air contingent were trained for an operation that was to be coordinated with a push south from northern Assam by a joint Sino-American force under General Joseph Stilwell. Wingate expanded his concept to include "strongholds," semipermanent bases from which operations could be conducted. Each was to be built around an airstrip and include other support facilities.

On 5 March 1944, the second Chindit operation (Operation THURSDAY) began. One brigade having already begun to move by foot into the area of operations the previous month, two additional brigades, preceded by glider-borne pathfinder teams, were flown into strongholds deep inside Burma. The remaining brigades were held in reserve. Once again, there were some successes. The railway line was again interrupted, the town of Mogaung was briefly captured, and the Japanese response appeared generally confused. Unfortunately, Wingate was killed in a plane crash on 24 March. Without his inspired, if unorthodox, leadership, the operation slowly began to lose momentum. Eventually, it would collapse from both exhaustion and outside intervention.

In early April, the Chindits were put under Stilwell's operational control. Stilwell distrusted the Chindit concept (and the British), and despite their specialized training, the Chindits were turned into regular infantry formations. In August, they were withdrawn from combat and at the beginning of 1945 disbanded.

In concrete terms, the achievements of the Chindits seemed small and their cost-effectiveness questionable. However, Japanese Fifteenth Army commander General Mutaguchi Renya would write after the war that Chindit operations, especially Operation THURSDAY, were an important reason why his forces were unable to invade India. In any case, the Chindits served as a morale booster at a critical time and were a pioneering concept for special operations brought to fruition by a determined and imaginative Wingate in the face of significant opposition.

George M. Brooke III

See also

Burma Theater; Churchill, Sir Winston L. S.; Mountbatten, Louis Francis Albert Victor Nicholas; Mutaguchi Renya; Slim, Sir William Joseph; Stilwell, Joseph Warren; Wavell, Sir Archibald Percival; Wingate, Orde Charles

References

Bidwell, Shelford. *The Chindit War.* London: Hodder and Stoughton, 1979.

Bierman, John, and Colin Smith. *Fire in the Night: Wingate of Burma, Ethiopia, and Zion.* New York: Random House, 1995.

Calvert, Michael. *Prisoners of Hope.* Rev. ed. London: Les Cooper, 1971.

Thompson, Julian. *War behind Enemy Lines.* London: IWM/Sidgwick and Jackson, 1998.

Cho Isamu (1895–1945)

Japanese army general who committed suicide at Okinawa. Born in Fukuoka, Japan, on 19 January 1895, Cho Isamu graduated from the Military Academy in 1916. Promoted to captain in 1925, he graduated from the Army War College three years later. He was appointed a member of the Chinese Section of the Army General Staff in 1929 and was advanced to major in 1931. Cho was so bold that he planned a coup d'état with his superior, Lieutenant Colonel Hashimoto Kingoro, in March 1932. The attempt failed, but he was not punished.

In August 1937, Cho joined the Army Expeditionary Force in Shanghai as chief of the intelligence staff. He participated in the fighting for Nanjing (Nanking) and was one of the instigators of the atrocities there in December 1937, known as the Nanjing Massacre. Cho was appointed commander of the 74th Infantry Regiment in March 1938 and fought against the Soviet forces at Changkufeng in July 1938. As chief of staff of the 26th Division, he persuaded the governor-general of French Indochina, General Georges Catroux, to admit Japanese occupation troops there in September 1940.

Cho was promoted to major general in October 1944 and appointed chief of staff of Thirty-Second Army, commanded by Lieutenant General Ushijima Mitsuru, in the defense of Okinawa against the U.S. invasion of that island in April 1945. When the Americans smashed the Japanese defense line, Cho and Ushijima committed suicide on 23 June 1945.

Kotani Ken

See also
Catroux, Georges Albert Julien; French Indochina; Hashimoto Kingoro; Nanjing Massacre; Okinawa, Invasion of; Ushijima Mitsuru

References
Gow, Ian. *Okinawa: Gateway to Japan.* Garden City, NY: Doubleday, 1985.
Komatsu Shigero. *Okinawa Ni Shisu: Dai 32 Gun Shireikan Ushijima Mitsuru No Shogai* (Death in Okinawa: The life of the Thirty-Second Army commander Mitsuru Ushijima). Tokyo: Kojinsha, 2001.
Yamamoto Masahiro. *Nanking, Anatomy of an Atrocity.* Westport, CT: Praeger, 2000.

Choltitz, Dietrich von (1894–1966)

German army general who commanded the Greater Paris area in 1944. Born on 9 November 1894, in Wiesegräflich, Upper Silesia, Germany, Dietrich von Choltitz was a fourth-generation professional soldier. A page in the Saxon court, he was educated at various cadet schools and began his military career as a senior officer cadet in the 107th Infantry Regiment in 1914; he fought in that unit during World War I as a company commander and adjutant. Choltitz served in the cavalry in the 1920s and early 1930s and then transferred to the air-transportable 16th Infantry Regiment of the 22nd Infantry—later, air-landing—Division. He was promoted to major in 1937 and to lieutenant colonel in April 1938. He took command of the 3rd Battalion of the 16th Regiment on 1 September 1939 and the entire regiment 10 days later.

Choltitz's regiment fought in Poland in September 1939, and he was with the element that attacked Rotterdam in May 1940. He was promoted to colonel in April 1941. His regiment participated as a part of the Eleventh Army of Army Group South in Operation BARBAROSSA, the invasion of the Soviet Union, in actions along the Prut, Dniester, and Bug Rivers and in the assault on the fortress of Sevastopol in the autumn of 1941, where it suffered heavy losses. Choltitz was involved in the summer 1942 assault on the fortress and on 28 June 1942 his men crossed North Bay in rubber boats

and helped lead a surprise attack in the rear of the fortress city, which surrendered on 2 July 1942.

Choltitz took command of the 260th Infantry Division in August 1942. He remained engaged in southern Russia and held a variety of positions, some of them only briefly. He was deputy commander of the crack XLVIII Panzer Corps in November 1942, acting commander of XVII Corps (December 1942–March 1943), commander of the 11th Panzer Division (March–May 1943), and again acting commander again of the XLVIII Panzer Corps (May–August 1943).

On 12 June 1944, General der Artillerie (U.S. equiv. lieutenant general) Erich Marcks, commanding the LXXXIV Corps of Colonel General Friedrich Dollman's Seventh Army in the Cotentin Peninsula of Normandy, was mortally wounded in an attack by an Allied fighter bomber. On 15 June, Choltitz arrived to replace Marcks. Units of the command were hard hit by the Saint-Lô carpet bombing of 25 July 1944, and much of the command was destroyed. Choltitz made maximum use of the limited resources at hand to slow the American advance. Field Marshal Günther von Kluge, however, unjustly sacked him on 28 July 1944 for the Normandy debacle.

Adolf Hitler promptly reassigned Choltitz, promoting him to General der Infanterie (U.S. equiv. lieutenant general) and appointing him commander of the Greater Paris area on 7 August 1944. Choltitz had few available resources to stop the advance of the Western Allies, however, and he resolutely refused to allow aircraft and artillery attacks in defense of Paris. Receiving orders from Hitler on 23 August to begin demolishing parts of the city, he refused and ensured a relatively orderly turnover of the city, with little damage to its public buildings and monuments, via negotiations with the French Resistance. Swedish Consul General Raoul Nordling served as one intermediary. Choltitz formally surrendered on 25 August 1944 and became a prisoner of war. Three days later, Field Marshal Walther Model asked the president of the Reich Military Tribunal to open criminal charges against Choltitz.

While in captivity, Choltitz contributed two monographs to the German Military History Program. Following his release in April 1947, he retired in Baden-Baden. Choltitz wrote a short monograph entitled *Brennt Paris?* (Is Paris Burning?), published in 1950. He also published his memoirs, *Soldat unter Soldaten* (Soldier among Soldiers), in 1951. Choltitz died in Baden-Baden on 5 November 1966, probably better remembered in France than in Germany.

Jon D. Berlin

See also
Cherbourg, Capture of; COBRA, Operation; Dollman, Friedrich; France Campaign; Guderian, Heinz; Kluge, Günter Adolf Ferdinand von; Manstein, Fritz Erich von; Model, Walther; Paris, Liberation of; Saint-Lô, Battle of; Sevastopol, Battle for

References

Carell, Paul. *Hitler Moves East, 1941–1943.* Boston: Little, Brown, 1964.

Choltitz, Dietrich von. *Soldat unter Soldaten.* Konstanz: Europa Verlag, 1951.

Mitcham, Samuel W., Jr. *Retreat to the Reich: The German Defeat in France, 1944.* Westport, CT: Praeger, 2000.

———. *The Panzer Legions: A Guide to the German Army Tank Divisions of World War II and Their Commanders.* Westport, CT: Greenwood Press, 2001.

Chou En-lai

See Zhou Enlai.

Christian X, King of Denmark (1870–1947)

King of Denmark who rallied the Danish people after the Germans invaded their country. Born on 26 September 1870, near Copenhagen, Christian X was the son of King Frederick VIII of Denmark and Princess Louise of Sweden. The prince was tutored within the palace and received military training. He married Alexandrine of Mecklenburg-Schwerin in 1898. On the death of his father, he inherited the throne on 13 May 1912.

King Christian X enforced Denmark's neutrality throughout World War I. He took in numerous Romanov relatives fleeing the Russian revolutions, including his aunt, the Dowager Tsarina Maria Feodorovna. During the 1930s, the king promoted national unity and became the first European ruler to visit a Jewish synagogue. Denmark's nonaggression pact with Germany seemed to assure peace, so Christian X was taken by surprise when Germany invaded his country on the morning of 9 April 1940. The king instructed his forces to surrender and appealed to his subjects to behave correctly so as to give the Germans no pretext for further violence. Under house arrest, he became a rallying symbol for the Danes, noted for the daily horseback rides he took alone. His position was a difficult one, as he refused to allow Danish Nazis into the government but did allow Schutzstaffel (SS) recruitment and agree to have a pro-German prime minister. In 1941, Adolf Hitler interpreted Christian X's cool response to birthday greetings as a pretext for forcing Denmark to sign the Anti-Comintern Pact on 23 November. The king became even more important as a resistance symbol in 1943, when the Germans assumed control of the government over royal and cabinet protest. Guarded only by the Copenhagen police and confined to a wheelchair after a riding accident, the elderly king was beloved by his people, and his popularity gave rise to two apocryphal legends: that he offered to wear a yellow star if Danish Jews had to do so and that he challenged

Christian X, King of Denmark. (Library of Congress)

German soldiers to shoot him for taking down a Nazi flag flying over Copenhagen.

After the liberation of Denmark in May 1945, the king asked for dispensation to avoid signing death sentences for collaborators but retained the ability to pardon them. He also exiled members of his family who had shown marked sympathy to the Germans during the occupation. Christian X died in Copenhagen on 20 April 1947.

Margaret Sankey

See also

Denmark Campaign; Denmark, Role in War

References

Petrow, Richard. *The Bitter Years: The Invasion and Occupation of Denmark and Norway, April 1940–May 1945.* New York: William Morrow, 1974.

Van der Kiste, John. *Northern Crowns: The Kings of Modern Scandinavia.* Stroud, UK: Sutton, 1996.

Werner, Emmy E. *A Conspiracy of Decency.* Boulder, CO: Westview Press, 2002.

Christie, John Walter (1865–1944)

U.S. inventor and tank designer. Born in River Edge, New Jersey, on 6 May 1865, J. Walter Christie went to work at the

Delamater Iron Works in New York City at age 16. After attending evening classes at Cooper Union, he became a consulting engineer for several steamship lines. Around 1900, he developed a ring-turning lathe that resulted in a stronger turret track for naval guns.

Christie then entered the automobile industry, building his own cars and testing them in speedway races. Among his designs was a front-wheel-drive car. He also invented a steam-engine, piston-packing ring that was used in ferryboat engines. In 1912, Christie began manufacturing wheeled tractors to pull fire-fighting equipment, selling several hundred to New York City alone.

In 1916, Christie designed a four-wheel-drive truck for use by the military in the rugged terrain of the southwestern United States in the event of trouble with Mexico. That year, the army contracted with his Front Drive Motor Company for a motor carriage for a self-propelled, 3-inch gun. During World War I, Christie became interested in tank design. The first of some 15 designs for the army was for a "convertible," self-propelled, 8-inch gun that could operate either on tracks (for cross-country mobility) or at a higher speed on its own road wheels. It was produced as a single prototype in 1921 but failed to meet army design specifications, beginning what would be an acrimonious relationship between Christie and the Ordnance Department.

This experience led Christie to design the first American postwar tank, the 3-man, 13.5 ton Medium Tank M1919, with a removable track that could be stored around the tank hull during road operations. The M1928 was powered by a Liberty aircraft engine and had both great speed and a revolutionary suspension system of large, weight-bearing wheels on torsion bars. The army ordered five M1928s. This vehicle was highly influential in tank design abroad, first in the USSR and then in Britain. The Soviets acquired two copies and used the M1928 as the basis for their BT-series. Their T-34 tank, which employed the Christie suspension system, may have been the best tank of World War II.

The U.S. Army purchased three M1931 (U.S. designation, T-3) Christie tanks, and the Soviets bought two. The vehicle was armed with both a 37 mm gun and a machine gun. Christie's M1932 employed light-weight materials and had a forward-facing propeller so that it could be dropped from a low-flying aircraft, fly, and hit the ground running. It could make road speeds of 36 mph on tracks or 65 mph on wheels, enabling it to leap a 20-foot gap from a 45-degree ramp. It was also sold to the Soviets. Christie's M1936, a 6 ton, 2 man tank, was capable of cross-country speeds of up to 60 mph. In Britain, it evolved into the first Cruiser tank.

For the United States, Christie also designed turret tracks for battleships, as well as gun mounts and carriages. His amphibious platform for a 75 mm gun, begun in 1921, led to the first amphibious tank. Never fully appreciated in his own country, in part because of his acerbic and combative personality, Christie died penniless and embittered in Falls Church, Virginia, on 11 January 1944.

Robert Bateman and Spencer C. Tucker

See also
Tanks, All Powers
References
Hofmann, George F. "Christie's Last Hurrah." *Armor* (November-December 1991): 14–19.
———. "Army Doctrine and the Christie Tank: Failing to Exploit the Operational Level of War." In George C. Hofmann and Donn A. Starry, eds., *Camp Colt to Desert Storm: The History of U.S. Armored Forces*, 92–143. Lexington: University Press of Kentucky, 1999.

Christie, Ralph Waldo (1893–1987)

U.S. Navy admiral and commander of submarines in the South Pacific. Born at Somerville, Massachusetts, on 30 August 1893, Ralph Christie graduated from the U.S. Naval Academy in 1915. Eight years later, he obtained a master of science degree from the Massachusetts Institute of Technology (MIT). On entering the navy, Christie specialized in the submarine service and torpedoes, commanding individual submarines in 1919, 1920, 1923, and 1924 and pursuing research at MIT that contributed to the development of the trouble-prone magnetic torpedo exploder.

From 1939 to 1940, Christie commanded Submarine Division 15, before moving to Brisbane, Australia, to take over Submarine Squadron 20, which he commanded from late 1940 to 1942. In November 1942, Christie was promoted to rear admiral, and in April 1943, he became commander of submarines in the South Pacific, operating out of Perth and Fremantle in Western Australia. Christie's forces made extensive use of ULTRA and MAGIC intelligence material, gathered from code-breaking and radio direction–finding technology used against Japanese vessels, and succeeded in interdicting Japan's capacity to control its conquered Pacific territories and maintain an operational seagoing navy. Despite Christie's obvious talents and achievements as a submarine commander, he clashed repeatedly with the Seventh Fleet commander, Admiral Thomas Kinkaid, over management of his force; among other things, Christie pushed for decorations for his men and had a habit of awarding them at dockside. Another problem was the number of casualties that resulted from his aggressive tactics. These difficulties caused Kinkaid to replace him in February 1945.

Christie's subsequent commands included the Puget Sound Navy Yard, between 1945 and 1948, and the U.S.

naval forces based in the Philippines. He retired in August 1949 as a vice admiral. Christie died in Honolulu, Hawaii, on 19 December 1987.

Priscilla Roberts

See also
Kinkaid, Thomas Cassin; Submarines; Torpedoes; United States, Navy
References
Blair, Clay, Jr. *Silent Victory: The U.S. Submarine War against Japan.* Philadelphia and New York: Lippincott, 1975.
Hoyt, Edwin P. *How They Won the War in the Pacific: Nimitz and His Admirals.* New York: Weybright and Talley, 1970.
Wheeler, Gerald E. *Kinkaid of the Seventh Fleet: A Biography of Admiral Thomas C. Kinkaid, U.S. Navy.* Washington, DC: Naval Historical Center, Department of the Navy, 1995.

Chu The

See Zhu De.

Chuikov, Vasily Ivanovich (1900–1982)

Marshal of the Soviet Union who took the surrender of Germany's Berlin garrison in 1945. Born in the village of Serebryanye Prudy in the Moscow region on 12 February 1900, Vasily Chuikov left home and became a mechanic at age 14. He joined the Red Army four years later. By 1919, he had risen to command a regiment, and during the Russian Civil War, he fought in Siberia and in the western Ukraine. He also fought in the 1920 Russo-Polish War. Chuikov graduated from the Frunze Military Academy in 1925 and was assigned to China two years later, fighting in the battle for the Chinese Eastern Railroad in 1929. He served in the Special Red Banner Far Eastern Army until 1932 and managed to survive the purge of the officers in the Far East in the late 1930s.

Chuikov served in the Soviet invasions of Poland (1939) and Finland (1939–1940), commanding Fourth and Ninth Armies, respectively. He was promoted to lieutenant general in June 1940 and returned to China for a third tour, serving as a military attaché beginning in December 1940. But he was recalled in March 1942 to become deputy commander and then commander of the newly formed Sixty-Fourth Army (22 July 1942). A protégé of Georgii Zhukov, Chuikov then took command of Sixty-Second Army on the west bank of the Volga at Stalingrad, which he defended at tremendous cost. His determination was a major factor in enabling the Soviets to hold until they could mount a counteroffensive.

Assigned to the Southwestern Front in March 1943, the Sixty-Second Army was redesignated the Eighth Guards Army. Chuikov led his troops in spearheading the liberation of Ukraine and Belorussia from German forces and was pro-

moted to colonel general in October 1943. In mid-1944, Eighth Guards Army was transferred to Konstantin Rokossovsky's 1st Belorussian Front. The unit then distinguished itself in operations in eastern Poland, taking Lublin and Lodz. The Vistula-Oder operation between January and February 1945 opened the way to Berlin, and Chuikov's tanks spearheaded the final assault on Berlin in a front-wide night attack; on 2 May 1945, Chuikov's headquarters took the surrender of the German Berlin garrison on behalf of the Red Army High Command.

Chuikov was promoted to General of the Army after V-E Day and served as deputy commander and then commander of Soviet occupation forces in eastern Germany (1946–1953). Promoted to marshal of the Soviet Union in 1955, he served as commander of the Kiev Military District (1953–1960) and as commander of Soviet Ground Forces (1960–1964). He was chief of civil defense from 1961 to 1972, after which he served in the general inspectorate of the Ministry of Defense. Chuikov died in Moscow on 18 March 1981.

Claude R. Sasso

See also
Berlin, Land Battle for; Krebs, Hans; Rokossovsky, Konstantin Konstantinovich; Sokolovsky, Vasily Danilovich; Zhukov, Georgii Konstantinovich
References
Chuikov, V. I. *The End of the Third Reich.* Moscow: Progress Publishers, 1978.
Chuikov, V. I., and V. Ryabov. *The Great Patriotic War.* Moscow: Planeta Publishers, 1985.
Sasso, Claude R. "Soviet Night Operations in World War II." Leavenworth Papers, no. 6. Fort Leavenworth, KS, U.S. Army Command and General Staff College, 1982.
Woff, Richard. "Vasily Ivanovich Chuikov." In Harold Shukman, ed., *Stalin's Generals*, 67–74. New York: Grove Press, 1993.
Zhukov, Georgii K. *Reminiscences and Reflections.* 2 vols. Moscow: Progress Publishers, 1974.

Churchill, Sir Winston L. S. (1874–1965)

British political leader, cabinet minister, and prime minister and minister of defense, from 1940 to 1945. Born at Blenheim Palace, Oxfordshire, on 30 November 1874, Winston Leonard Spencer Churchill was the eldest son of Lord Randolph Churchill, third son of the duke of Marlborough and a rising Conservative politician, and his wife, Jennie Jerome, an American heiress. Educated at Harrow and the Royal Military Academy, Sandhurst, from 1895 to 1899, Churchill held a commission in the British army. He visited Cuba on leave and saw active service on the Afghan frontier and in the Sudan, where he took part in the Battle of Omdurman. Captured by South African forces in 1899 while reporting on the Boer War as a journalist, he made a dramatic escape from Pretoria and went to Durban, winning early popular fame.

Churchill emulated his father—who attained the position of chancellor of the exchequer before resignation, illness, and premature death cut short his political career—by entering politics in 1900 as a Unionist member of Parliament. In 1904, his party's partial conversion to protectionism caused him to join the Liberals, who made him president of the Board of Trade (1908–1910) and home secretary (1910–1911) after they returned to power.

As first lord of the Admiralty (1911–1915), Churchill enthusiastically backed the campaign of First Sea Lord John "Jackie" Fisher to modernize the British navy with faster battleships and more efficient administration. One of the few initial cabinet supporters of British intervention in World War I, Churchill soon took the blame for the disastrous 1915 Dardanelles expedition against Turkey, which prompted his resignation. He spent the six months up to May 1916 on active service on the Western Front but regained high political office in July 1917, when Prime Minister David Lloyd George made him minister of munitions in his coalition government.

In December 1918, Churchill moved to the War Office, where he unsuccessfully advocated forceful Allied action against Russia, in the hope of eliminating that country's new Bolshevik government. In late 1920, he became colonial secretary. Two years after Lloyd George's 1922 defeat, Churchill returned to the Conservatives, who made him chancellor of the exchequer in November 1924, a post he held for five years. He reluctantly acquiesced in Britain's return to the gold standard, and his determination to suppress the 1926 General Strike won him the lasting enmity of much of the labor movement.

By 1928, Churchill believed that the postwar peace settlement represented only a truce between wars, a view forcefully set forth in his book *The Aftermath* (1928). When Labour won the 1929 election, Churchill lost office, but he soon began campaigning eloquently for a major British rearmament initiative, especially the massive enhancement of British airpower, to enable the country to face a revived Italian or German military threat. From 1932 onward, he sounded this theme eloquently in Parliament, but Conservative leaders remained unsympathetic to his pleas. Throughout the 1930s, although Churchill held no cabinet position, he nonetheless continued to the campaign for rearmament. He also became perhaps the most visible and vocal critic of the appeasement policies of the successive governments of Prime Ministers Stanley Baldwin and Neville Chamberlain, who effectively tolerated German rearmament, Chancellor Adolf Hitler's deliberate contravention of the provisions of the Treaty of Versailles,

Prime Minister Winston Churchill of Great Britain, giving victory sign. (The Illustrated London News Picture Library)

and Germany's and Italy's territorial demands on their neighbors.

When Britain declared war on Germany in September 1939, Churchill resumed his old position as first lord of the Admiralty. Despite the German attacks on the British aircraft carrier *Courageous* and the battleship *Royal Oak,* as well as the responsibility he himself bore for the Allied disaster in Norway during April and May 1940, he succeeded Chamberlain as prime minister on 10 May 1940, the day Germany launched an invasion of France and the Low Countries. Over the next three months, repeated disasters afflicted Britain, as German troops rapidly overran the Low Countries and France, forcing the British Expeditionary Force to withdraw in disarray that June from the Dunkerque beaches of northern France, abandoning most of its equipment. Throughout the summer of 1940, during the Battle of Britain, German airplanes fiercely attacked British air bases, an apparent prelude to a full-scale cross-Channel invasion.

Churchill responded vigorously to crisis. Although he was 65, he still possessed abundant and unflagging energy; his vitality was fueled by his habit of an afternoon siesta, after which he normally worked until two or three the next morning. His fondness for sometimes fanciful and questionable strategic plans often exasperated his closest advisers, as did his attachment to romantic individual ventures—such as those launched by the Special Operations Executive intelligence agency, whose creation he backed enthusiastically. Even so, Churchill was an outstanding war leader. On taking office, he delivered a series of rousing and eloquent speeches, affirming Britain's determination to continue fighting even without allies and voicing his conviction of ultimate triumph. Churchill also followed a demanding schedule of morale-boosting personal visits to British cities, factories, bomb targets, and military installations, which he continued throughout the war.

Besides rallying the British people to endure military defeat in France and the bombing campaign Germany soon launched against Britain's industrial cities, Churchill's speeches, which caught the international imagination, were designed to convince the political leaders and people of the United States—the only quarter from which Britain might anticipate effective assistance—of his country's commitment to the war. U.S. President Franklin D. Roosevelt responded by negotiating the "destroyers-for-bases" deal of August 1940, whereby the United States transferred 50 World War I–vintage destroyers to Britain in exchange for naval basing rights in British Caribbean Islands and North America.

Since the war began, Britain had purchased war supplies in the United States on a "cash-and-carry" basis. By December 1940, British resources were running low, and Churchill addressed a letter to Roosevelt, who had just won reelection, requesting that he provide more extensive U.S. aid to Britain. Roosevelt responded by devising the Lease-Lend Act that was passed by Congress the following spring, which authorized the president to provide assistance to countries at war whose endeavors enhanced U.S. national security. In August 1941, Churchill and Roosevelt met for the first time at sea, in Placentia Bay off the Newfoundland coast, and agreed to endorse a common set of liberal war aims—the Atlantic Charter—and to coordinate their two countries' military strategies. Churchill also agreed to allow British scientists to pool their expertise in nuclear physics with their American counterparts in the MANHATTAN Project, a largely U.S.-financed effort to built an atomic bomb; the project reached fruition in summer 1945.

Churchill was relieved by Japan's December 1941 attack on the American naval base of Pearl Harbor, Hawaii, and the subsequent German and Italian declarations of war on the United States because these actions finally brought the United States fully into the war and, from his perspective, guaranteed an ultimate Allied victory. In the interim, as

1942 progressed, he needed all his talents to sustain British resolution through various disasters, including Japan's conquest of Hong Kong, Malaya, Singapore, and Burma and British defeats in North Africa.

After Germany invaded the USSR in June 1941, Churchill also welcomed the Soviet Union as an ally, though his relations with Soviet leader Josef Stalin were never as close as those with Roosevelt. Churchill made repeated visits to the United States and met Roosevelt at other venues. In addition, all three leaders gathered at major international summit conferences at Tehran in November 1943 and Yalta in February 1945, and Churchill also met Stalin separately on several occasions. He traveled abroad more than any of the other Allied leaders, often at substantial personal risk.

Stalin resented the Anglo-American failure to open a second front in Europe until June 1944, a decision due in considerable part to Churchill's fear that, if Britain and the United States launched an invasion of western Europe too soon, the campaign would degenerate into bloody trench warfare resembling that between 1914 and 1918. Meeting Roosevelt in May 1943 in Washington, he finally succumbed to American pressure to open the second front the following summer. Churchill also resented intensifying U.S. pressure for the phasing out of British colonial rule, a prospect made increasingly probable by Britain's growing international weakness.

As the war proceeded and Soviet forces began to push back German troops, Churchill feared that the Soviet Union would dominate postwar Eastern Europe. Soviet support for Communist guerrillas in occupied countries and for the Soviet-backed Lublin government in Poland reinforced his apprehensions. In October 1944, he negotiated an informal agreement with Stalin whereby the two leaders delineated their countries' respective spheres of influence in Eastern Europe. At the February 1945 Yalta Conference, Churchill and Roosevelt both acquiesced in effective Soviet domination of most of that region. The three leaders also agreed to divide Germany into three separate occupation zones, to be administered by their occupying military forces but ultimately to be reunited as one state. In April 1945, Churchill unavailingly urged American military commanders to disregard their existing understandings with Soviet forces and take Berlin, the symbolically important German capital. Despite the creation of the United Nations in 1945, Churchill hoped that close Anglo-American understanding would be the bedrock of the international world order, a perspective intensified by his continuing fears of Germany.

In July 1945, the British electorate voted Churchill out of office while he was attending a meeting at Potsdam, replacing his administration with a reformist Labour government. Churchill was still, however, honored as "the greatest living Englishman" and the war's most towering figure. He used his prestige to rally American elite and public opinion in favor of taking a stronger line against Soviet expansionism in Europe and elsewhere, a position he advanced to enormous publicity in his famous March 1946 "Iron Curtain" speech at Fulton, Missouri. Churchill's six best-selling volumes of memoirs, *The Second World War,* presented a somewhat roseate view of Anglo-American wartime cooperation, and they were carefully designed to promote the continuing alliance between the two countries, which had become his most cherished objective. From 1951 to 1955, Churchill served again as Conservative prime minister. Declining health eventually forced him to resign from office. A House of Commons man to the core, he consistently refused the peerage to which his services entitled him. Churchill died in London on 24 January 1965. For many, his death marked the symbolic final passing of Great Britain's imperial age. Churchill received the first state funeral for any British commoner since the death of the duke of Wellington over a century before. An idiosyncratic political maverick whose pre-1939 record was, at best, mixed, Churchill rose to the occasion to become the greatest British war leader since the earl of Chatham in the eighteenth century.

Priscilla Roberts

See also
Atlantic Charter; Britain, Battle of; Cash-and-Carry; Chamberlain, Arthur Neville; Churchill-Stalin Meeting; Cold War, Origins and Early Course of; Destroyers-Bases Deal; Dunkerque, Evacuation of; Great Britain, Home Front; Hitler, Adolf; Lend-Lease; MANHATTAN Project; Moscow Conference; Placentia Bay; Quebec Conference (1943); Quebec Conference (1944); Roosevelt, Franklin D.; Special Operations Executive; Stalin, Josef; Tehran Conference; Yalta Conference

References
Gilbert, Martin S. *Winston S. Churchill.* 8 vols. New York: Random House, 1966–1988.

Jablonsky, David. *Churchill and Hitler: Essays on the Political-Military Direction of Total War.* Portland, OR: Cass, 1994.

Jenkins, Roy. *Churchill.* London: Macmillan, 2001.

Kimball, Warren F., ed. *Churchill and Roosevelt: The Complete Correspondence.* Princeton, NJ: Princeton University Press, 1984.

Larres, Klaus. *Churchill's Cold War: The Politics of Personal Diplomacy.* New Haven, CT: Yale University Press, 2002.

Lash, Joseph P. *Roosevelt and Churchill, 1939–1941: The Partnership That Saved the West.* New York: W. W. Norton, 1976.

Lukacs, John. *Churchill: Visionary, Statesman, Historian.* New Haven, CT: Yale University Press, 2002.

Ramsden, John. *Man of the Century: Winston Churchill and His Legend since 1945.* New York: Harper Collins, 2002.

Stafford, David. *Roosevelt and Churchill: Men of Secrets.* London: Little, Brown, 1999.

Churchill-Stalin Meeting (TOLSTOY, 9–10 October 1944)

Meeting in Moscow that determined spheres of influence in eastern Europe. Concerned particularly about issues involving postwar Poland, Greece, and the Balkans, Winston L. S. Churchill originated this meeting, code-named TOLSTOY. Josef Stalin would not travel from the Soviet Union, so on 27 September 1944, Churchill asked him to receive a small British delegation to discuss these and related issues, including the entry of the Soviet Union into the war against Japan.

Facing imminent national U.S. elections, President Franklin D. Roosevelt could not attend. (Churchill had just seen him in Quebec but informed him about this proposal only two days *after* sending his note to Stalin.) Roosevelt saw the meeting as a preliminary for the forthcoming summit at Yalta and asked that U.S. Ambassador Averell Harriman observe, although in the end, Harriman was not present for some crucial two-man talks.

Stalin agreed to the meeting, and Churchill, Foreign Minister Anthony Eden, and Chief of the Imperial General Staff General Alan Brooke flew to Moscow, where they stayed from 9 to 18 October 1944. British Ambassador Clark Kerr also joined the delegation.

Churchill's primary concern was to gain freedom of action in the difficult Greek political situation, which teetered on civil war. This he proceeded to get. During dinner conversation with Stalin, he produced a half sheet of paper (terming it a "naughty document") and wrote out proposed spheres of postwar influence: Romania, 90 percent Soviet; Greece, 90 percent British; Yugoslavia and Hungary, both to be evenly divided between the USSR and the Western Allies; and Bulgaria, 75 percent Soviet. Stalin checked and approved the page and gave it back to Churchill. Though the numbers may seem somewhat arbitrary at first glance (with the exception of those for Greece, where the issue was very much in doubt), they merely reflected the reality of a surging Red Army and understated it in regard to both Yugoslavia and Hungary. Although Soviet Foreign Minister Vyacheslav Molotov and Eden dickered about some of the percentages the next day, nothing was changed. All parties present concurred that they were guidelines for discussion and nothing more.

Churchill and Stalin agreed to put off decisions about Poland until Roosevelt could be present. Still, there was considerable argument over the "London" versus "Lublin" Poles and how they might share power after the war. The head of the London Poles, Stanislaw Mikołajczyk, joined the conference briefly but disagreed with Lublin's representatives and with most of what was proposed as to border adjustments and governance.

Extensive discussions of military plans also took place, and regular reports were sent to Roosevelt in Washington by Churchill and Harriman and to the War Cabinet in London by Churchill. The meeting laid some of the groundwork for the subsequent Yalta Conference, but it also cleared the way for firm British action in Athens in December 1944, designed to put down Greek Communist guerrillas. The Soviets, true to the TOLSTOY discussions, did not intervene.

Christopher H. Sterling

See also
Brooke, Sir Alan Francis; Churchill, Sir Winston L. S.; Eden, Sir Robert Anthony; Harriman, William Averell; Mikołajczyk, Stanislaw; Molotov, Vyacheslav Mikhailovich; Quebec Conference (1944); Roosevelt, Franklin D.; Stalin, Josef; Yalta Conference

References
Barker, Elisabeth. *Churchill and Eden at War.* New York: St. Martin's Press, 1978, pp. 272–285.
Carlton, David. *Churchill and the Soviet Union.* Manchester, UK: Manchester University Press, 2000.
Feis, Herbert. *Churchill, Roosevelt, Stalin: The War They Waged and the Peace They Sought—A Diplomatic History of World War II.* Princeton, NJ: Princeton University Press, 1957.
Gilbert, Martin. *Winston S. Churchill.* Vol. 7, *Road to Victory, 1941–1945.* Boston: Houghton Mifflin, 1986, pp. 989–1010.

Chynoweth, Bradford Grethen (1890–1985)

U.S. Army general who argued for the independent deployment of tanks. Born in Fort Warren, Wyoming, on 20 July 1890, Bradford Chynoweth graduated from the U.S. Military Academy in 1912 and was commissioned a second lieutenant in the Corps of Engineers. He served through World War I, rising to the rank of temporary lieutenant colonel. Reverting to his permanent rank of captain after the war and despairing of his chances at promotion in the postwar military, he left the army in 1919.

Bored by civilian life, Chynoweth rejoined the army in November 1920 as a major of infantry. He was a close friend of Captain Dwight D. Eisenhower and Major George S. Patton Jr. Chynoweth contributed steadily to the professional discourse of the era, writing articles for a number of professional journals. In the *Cavalry Journal,* he argued strongly for tanks as a new combat arm.

Chynoweth served on the Infantry Board at Fort Benning, Georgia, when Colonel George C. Marshall was director of the Infantry School there. His strongest supporter was his brother-in-law and author of the army's capstone doctrinal publication, the *Field Service Regulations* (1923)—

Major George A. Lynch. Chynoweth attended both the Command and General Staff School (1927–1928) and the Army War College (1931–1932). Following an assignment with the army's G-3 (Training) section, he served three years as a senior instructor with the 44th Division of the New Jersey National Guard.

Appointed military attaché in London in the spring of 1939, he soon fell out with U.S. Ambassador Joseph Kennedy Sr. over his own prediction that Germany would attack France and that, subsequently, the Germans would bomb London from the air. Kennedy did not trust Chynoweth and demanded and secured his recall. Given his choice of postings by his brother-in-law (now a major general and chief of infantry), Chynoweth took command of a tank battalion with the 66th Infantry Regiment. He served with the 66th between October 1939 and July 1940 and with the 53rd Infantry Regiment between July 1940 and November 1941.

During the 1941 maneuvers, Chynoweth finally had the chance to demonstrate his theories about mobile warfare, which he did with considerable success. However, he also ran afoul of a commander, who recommended that he be removed from the army, but Chynoweth was subsequently exonerated.

Colonel Chynoweth continued to argue for the independent employment of tanks. Assigned to the Philippines in the fall of 1941, he took command of the defenses on Cebu and the Visayan Islands. From there, he waged a masterful defense throughout the winter of 1941–1942, and he was prepared to retire to the interior of the islands where he had stockpiled materials when he was ordered by his superiors to surrender.

Chynoweth spent the remainder of the war as a prisoner of the Japanese. Only on his repatriation in 1945 did he learn that just prior to his capture, he had been promoted to brigadier general. He retired in October 1947, pursued graduate studies at the University of California, Berkeley, and wrote his memoirs (*Bellamy Park*). Chynoweth died at the Presidio in San Francisco on 8 February 1985.

Robert Bateman, George F. Hofmann, and Uzal W. Ent

See also
Armored Warfare; Eisenhower, Dwight D.; Marshall, George Catlett; Patton, George Smith, Jr.; Philippines, Japanese Capture of
References
Chynoweth, Bradford Grethen. *Bellamy Park.* Hicksville, PA: Exposition Press, 1975.
Hofmann, George F., and Donn A. Starry, eds. *Camp Colt to Desert Storm: The History of the U.S. Armored Forces.* Lexington: University Press of Kentucky, 1999.
Johnson, David E. *Fast Tanks and Heavy Bombers: Innovation in the U.S. Army, 1917–1945.* Ithaca, NY: Cornell University Press, 1998.

Ciano, Galeazzo (Conte di Cortellazo) (1903–1944)

Italian diplomat and foreign minister under Benito Mussolini. Born at Livorno (Leghorn), Italy, on 18 March 1903, Galeazzo Ciano was the son of World War I naval hero Admiral Costanzo Ciano. Dabbling in theatrical criticism and journalism and earning a law degree by 1925, he was propelled by his father (by then a prominent Fascist) into the foreign service of Italy's new regime. Posted to South America and then Asia, the young socialite found diplomatic life and its connections most agreeable, particularly when his 1929 posting to the Holy See returned him to Rome, where he met and married (in April 1930) Edda Mussolini, Il Duce's daughter.

In June 1933, Ciano was the delegate to the World Monetary and Economic Conference in London, and by June 1935, he was made minister for press and propaganda, a position he left two months later to lead a bomber squadron in the Ethiopian War. Less than a month after Ciano's return to Italy, on 9 June 1936, Mussolini appointed him foreign minister, a move that made both men targets of disapproval from near and far. Loyal Fascists decried the elevation of an opportunistic nepotist, whereas the diplomatic corps in Italy and beyond expected only the worst from a ministry formed in Ciano's dillentantish image.

Ciano's foreign ministry undertook a mix of standard Fascist foreign policy initiatives (such as Italy's withdrawal from the League of Nations, Balkan incursions, and military intervention in the Spanish Civil War) with proposals for regional alliances that sought to curb Germany's hegemony by linking Italy with, variously, Austria, Czechoslovakia, Hungary, and Yugoslavia. Ciano's diaries reveal his antipathy for Germany and detail his September 1939 forging of a "nonbelligerency" policy designed to forestall Italy's entry into the war.

With the Italian declaration of war on 10 June 1940, Ciano resumed bomber pilot duty over Greece, repatriating in April 1941 to find his minister's portfolio reduced to mere courier status. Eventually, he was fired in a February 1943 cabinet shift, and after participating in the Fascist Grand Council's no-confidence vote on Mussolini's rule on 25 July 1943, he unsuccessfully sought asylum in Spain. Cynically (or guilelessly) arranging his family's passage to Germany instead that August, Ciano, not surprisingly, was made a prisoner of Il Duce's new Italian Social Republic after the September 1943 armistice. Receiving no mercy from Mussolini despite Edda Ciano's pleas, he was tried and condemned on a charge of treason and was executed by a firing squad at Verona on 11 January 1944.

Gordon E. Hogg

Galeazzo Ciano, son-in-law of Benito Mussolini and author of an important World War II diary. (Hulton Archive by Getty Images)

See also
Greece Campaign (28 October 1940–March 1941); Italy, Home Front; Mussolini, Benito
References
Ciano, Galeazzo. *Diario, 1937–1943*. Milan, Italy: Rizzoli, 1980.
Moseley, Ray. *Mussolini's Shadow: The Double Life of Count Galeazzo Ciano*. New Haven, CT: Yale University Press, 1999.

Clark, Mark Wayne (1896–1984)

U.S. Army general who received the surrender of German forces in Italy. Born at Madison Barracks, New York, on 1 May 1896, Clark graduated from the U.S. Military Academy in 1917 and was wounded during action in France in 1918. He graduated from the Infantry School in 1925, the Command and General Staff School in 1935, and the Army War College in 1937.

Made a brigadier general in August 1941, Clark was working on army expansion when the war began. He was

Lieutenant General Mark Clark, commander of the U.S. Fifth Army in Italy. (Library of Congress)

Army to escape encirclement and reach the Gothic Line to the north.

As the cross-Channel invasion of France became the chief focus of Allied efforts in Europe, the Italian theater gradually became secondary. In December 1944, Clark succeeded Sir Harold Alexander as commander of the multinational 15th Army Group, and in March 1945, he became the U.S. Army's youngest full general. He led the Allied offensive that breached the Gothic Line, crossed the Po River, and entered Austria just as the war in Europe ended. On 4 May 1945, he personally received the surrender of all German forces in Italy.

After the war, Clark commanded U.S. occupation forces in Austria (1945–1947), Sixth Army (1947–1949), and Army Field Forces (1949–1952). He succeeded General Matthew Ridgway as commander of U.S. forces in the Far East and of United Nations Forces in Korea (May 1952–October 1953) and chafed at restrictions placed on his command. Clark wrote two memoirs, *Calculated Risk* (1950) and *From the Danube to the Yalu* (1954). On his retirement from the army in 1954, he served as president of The Citadel (1954–1960). He died in Charleston, South Carolina, on 17 April 1984.

Thomas D. Veve

See also
Alexander, Sir Harold Rupert Leofric George; Anzio Beachhead; Cassino/Rapido River, Battles of; Darlan, Jean Louis Xavier François; Eisenhower, Dwight D.; Italy Campaign; Ridgway, Matthew Bunker; Salerno Invasion; TORCH, Operation; Wolff, Karl

References
Blumenson, Martin. *United States Army in World War II: The Mediterranean Theater of Operations—Salerno to Cassino.* Washington, DC: Office of the Chief of Military History, U.S. Army, 1969.
———. *Mark Clark.* New York: Congdon and Weed, 1984.
Clark, Mark W. *Calculated Risk.* New York: Harper, 1950.

promoted to major general as chief of staff of Army Ground Forces the following April. He rose to lieutenant general in November 1942 and was named deputy supreme commander for the Allied invasion of North Africa, Operation TORCH, under Lieutenant General Dwight D. Eisenhower. Clark met secretly with Vichy French officials in October 1942 prior to the Allied invasion to seek their cooperation, and he negotiated a cease-fire with the French authorities two days after the landings.

Given command of Fifth Army, Clark led the invading U.S. troops at Salerno, Italy, in September 1943. However, Fifth Army's slow advance up the western side of the Italian peninsula led to harsh criticism of Clark's abilities. His troops suffered heavy casualties in the attempt to penetrate the Gustav Line, and the bombing of the monastery on Monte Cassino plagued his reputation; heavy casualties at the Rapido River prompted a Senate investigation. The Anzio landings in January 1944 did little to speed up Fifth Army's advance, and the assault failed to lead, as was hoped, to a quick capture of Rome. Fifth Army finally liberated Rome on 4 June 1944, but Clark was roundly criticized for his determination that U.S. troops be the first to liberate the Eternal City, which allowed the German Tenth

Clark Field, Japanese Raid on (8 December 1941)

Devastating Japanese air attack in the Philippines. To secure the lines of communication between the oil-rich Netherlands East Indies and the home islands, the Japanese planned to seize the Philippine Islands. The first step in that process was the elimination of U.S. airpower.

American planners had long recognized the vulnerability of the Philippines to Japanese attack. In July 1941, President Franklin F. Roosevelt named General Douglas MacArthur commander of United States Army Forces in the Far East (USAFFE). His air commander was Major General Lewis

Brereton. By the fall of 1941, Brereton had priority in aircraft deliveries, and in early December, the Far East Air Force (FEAF) possessed 35 Boeing B-17s Flying Fortresses, more than 100 modern Curtiss P-40 Warhawk fighters, and some 135 older aircraft.

At 2:40 A.M. on 8 December 1941 (7 December on Hawaii time), the U.S. Navy's Asiatic Fleet Headquarters in Manila learned of the attack on Pearl Harbor but then had trouble informing MacArthur. An hour later, MacArthur's chief of staff, Brigadier General Richard Sutherland, heard a commercial broadcast reporting the attack and woke the general. Official word from the War Department did not arrive until 5:30 A.M. Brereton placed his aircraft on standby and requested permission from MacArthur to strike Takao harbor, Formosa, to destroy Japanese warships and shipping gathering there for the invasion of the Philippines. MacArthur refused permission, and Sutherland denied Brereton access to MacArthur.

At 9:20 A.M., Japanese army aircraft bombed Baguio, the Philippine summer capital north of Clark Field. Fog on Formosa, however, delayed the Japanese navy raid on the Clark and Iba airfields. At 11:30 A.M., reports of incoming aircraft reached FEAF headquarters. Clark Field received a warning, but it was not passed to V Bomber Command. Although the Americans had one radar station operating and nearly 10 hours had elapsed since the attack on Pearl Harbor, the Japanese caught most of Clark's aircraft on the ground, launching 53 bombers and 44 Zero fighters at the airfield. All the attacks on Luzon cost the Japanese only 7 fighters lost. The Americans lost 18 B-17s; 35 P-35s and P-40s; and another 25 to 30 B-10s, B-18s, and observation aircraft. The FEAF ceased to exist as a meaningful force on the first day of the war.

Blame for the American disaster has never been suitably determined. Complacency played a role, as American strategists discounted the technical achievements and fighting ability of the Japanese. Brereton wrote that had permission been granted to attack Formosa, his Clark Field bombers would not have been caught on the ground. Sutherland blamed Brereton for not dispersing all his B-17s to the south (only half had been sent there) as ordered prior to 8 December, whereas MacArthur held the War Department responsible for not strengthening the defense of the Philippines soon enough. Nonetheless, although army and navy commanders at Pearl Harbor were removed following the Japanese attack there, MacArthur retained his post in the Philippines.

Rodney Madison

See also
Brereton, Lewis Hyde; Iba Field, Attack on; Japan, Air Forces; MacArthur, Douglas; Pearl Harbor, Attack on; Philippines, Japanese Capture of; Roosevelt, Franklin D.; United States, Army Air Forces

References
Bartsch, William H. *Doomed at the Start: American Pursuit Pilots in the Philippines.* College Station: Texas A&M Press, 1992.
———. *December 8, 1941: MacArthur's Pearl Harbor.* College Station: Texas A&M Press, 2003.
Craven, Wesley Frank, and James Lea Cate, eds. *The Army Air Forces in World War II.* Vol. 1, *Plans and Early Operations, January 1939 to August 1942.* Washington, DC: Office of Air Force History, 1983.
James, D. Clayton. "The Other Pearl Harbor." *MHQ: The Quarterly Journal of Military History* 7 (Winter 1994): 22–29.
Morton, Louis. *The United States Army in World War II: The War in the Pacific—The Fall of the Philippines.* Washington, DC: Center of Military History, U.S. Army, 1989.

Clay, Lucius DuBignon (1897–1978)

U.S. Army general who served as military governor in Germany. Born on 23 April 1897 at Marietta, Georgia, Lucius Clay graduated from the U.S. Military Academy in 1918 as an army engineer. He was an instructor at West Point between 1924 and 1928. He also served on General Douglas MacArthur's staff (1937); had charge of the construction of the Red River Dam near Denison, Texas (1938–1940); and headed the Civil Aeronautics Authority Defense Airport Program (1940–1941). In the latter position, he oversaw the expansion and improvement of 277 airports and the construction of 197 new ones.

In March 1942, Clay was promoted to brigadier general (the youngest in the army) and appointed assistant chief of staff for matériel. Rising to major general that December, he oversaw both military procurement and production. In November 1944, General Dwight D. Eisenhower called him to Europe to take on the herculean task of rejuvenating for Allied supply the French port of Cherbourg, which the Germans had destroyed. On leave from the army, he was next deputy chief of the Office of War Mobilization and Reconversion in Washington (December 1944 to April 1945).

Clay returned to Europe at the end of the war as a lieutenant general and Eisenhower's civilian affairs deputy, and in March 1947, he became U.S. military governor in Germany. In that position, he played a key role in rebuilding western Germany. When the Soviet Union imposed a blockade of Berlin in 1948, Clay recommended the Western Allies attempt an airlift, which President Harry S Truman approved. Days after the blockade ended in May 1949, Clay retired. He was one of the few occupying generals to have a street named after him (Clay Allee in Berlin). Clay was then chairman of the board of the Continental Can Corporation, although he carried out several special governmental assignments as well. He died in Chatham, Massachusetts, on 16 April 1978.

T. Jason Soderstrum

See also
Eisenhower, Dwight D.; MacArthur, Douglas
References
Backer, John H. *Winds of History: The German Years of Lucius DuBignon Clay.* New York: Van Nostrand Reinhold, 1983.
Clay, Lucius DuBignon. *Decision in Germany.* Garden City, NY: Doubleday, 1950.
Smith, Jean Edward. *Lucius D. Clay: An American Life.* New York: Henry Holt, 1990.

CO

See Conscientious Objector.

Coast Defense

Fortifying important harbors to protect against attack from the sea. During World War II, most fighting nations developed new harbor fortifications or manned ones developed before the war, though very few of these locations saw action.

Most major American port cities (including those in Panama and the Philippines) were protected by coastal forts, many of which originally dated from the turn of the century and were thus on caretaker status as obsolete when the war began. In the continental United States, more than 30 new batteries designed to a common standard and with greater ranges were constructed before and during the war. These installations were chiefly shielded twin batteries of 6-inch guns as well as a few heavily casemated 16-inch batteries, the largest coastal defenses ever installed. A number of existing batteries were also casemated to protect against possible air attack. Older weapons from other batteries were often sent to other nations, such as Brazil and Canada, to bolster their coast defense. Fully manned in the opening months of the war, batteries were increasingly placed on caretaker status, and new construction (of more than 100 batteries) was halted by 1944.

Only the American-built harbor forts at Manila—most constructed early in the century—actually saw action, as Japanese forces advanced down the Bataan Peninsula between December 1941 and May 1942. U.S. mortar and gun batteries on Corregidor and other harbor islands and the twin turrets of Fort Drum in Manila Bay dueled with Japanese artillery, ships, and aircraft until the final American surrender in April and May. The forces at Drum prevented Japan's use of Manila Bay and also kept the Japanese from flanking the Bataan defenses by sea. Hawaii (Oahu), already extensively armed, was further fortified with naval turrets,

including two removed from the sunken battleship *Arizona,* but none of its batteries saw action in the war.

In Canada, the key ports on the Atlantic (Halifax and Sydney, Nova Scotia) and the Pacific (Vancouver and Victoria) had been fortified earlier, usually with British 9.2-inch and smaller artillery in open emplacements. Several were upgraded with new guns and communications links. Although all of the Canadian forts were manned in support of convoy and military shipping, none saw action.

Major British harbors had been fortified at least since the mid-nineteenth century. Although some new emplacements were constructed, chiefly along the coast facing the mainland, British batteries were largely holdovers from the turn of the century and World War I. With Britain facing invasion in 1940, a host of emergency batteries were hastily built using cast-off 4-inch and 6-inch naval weapons. Pillboxes and other armored positions festooned coast and countryside. Sizable antiaircraft "sea forts" were built in the Thames and Mersey estuaries in 1942 and 1943 and were quite effective. Huge 14-inch and 15-inch guns emplaced near Dover controlled the Channel and could bombard Atlantic Wall defenses along the French coast. Unfortunately, British coastal batteries at Hong Kong (in 1941) and Singapore (in 1942) did little to slow the Japanese advances.

Coastal defense was extensively developed by the Axis powers, most specifically by the massive German Atlantic Wall. The Italian ports of Genoa and Venice were heavily defended with batteries, and the Germans added more after 1943. Few of these saw action, as Allied forces typically went around them or took them from behind. Japan rapidly fortified Pacific islands taken over in 1941 and 1942, and most of these facilities saw active combat, as did some of the extensive facilities protecting the Japanese home islands.

Christopher H. Sterling

See also
Atlantic Wall; Fort Drum; Hong Kong, Battle of; Maginot Line; Phillipines, Japanese Capture of; Singapore, Battle for
References
Berhow, Mark A. *American Seacoast Defenses: A Reference Guide.* Bel Air, MD: Coast Defense Study Group Press, 1999.
Hogg, Ian V. *Coast Defences of England and Wales, 1856–1956.* Newton Abbot, UK: David and Charles, 1974.
Lazzarini, Furio, and Carlo Alfredo Clerici. *The "Amalfi" Battery and Venice's Coast Fortifications during the Two World Wars.* Parma, Italy: Albertelli Editore, 1997.
Lewis, Emanuel Raymond. *Seacoast Fortifications of the United States: An Introductory History.* Washington, DC: Smithsonian Institution Press, 1970.
McGovern, Terrance C. "Manila Bay: The American Harbour Defences." *Fort* 23 (1995): 65–110.
———. "The American Harbour Defences of the Panama Canal." *Fort* 26 (1998): 3–119.

Nicholson, General Sir Cameron. *The History of Coast Artillery in the British Army.* London: Royal Artillery Institution, 1959.
Survey of Japanese Seacoast Artillery. Tokyo: U.S. Army Seacoast Artillery Research Board, 1946.

COBRA, Operation (25–31 July 1944)

U.S. Army breakout from the Normandy Peninsula in July 1944. The success of the Allied invasion of 6 June 1944 dissipated to frustration when the tenacious German defense of the Cotentin Peninsula stifled efforts to expand beyond the initial beachheads. The supreme commander of the Allied Expeditionary Forces, General Dwight D. Eisenhower, had grown impatient with the disrupted timetable as General Sir Bernard L. Montgomery failed to take Caen and Lieutenant General Omar N. Bradley's First U.S. Army remained stalled in the bocage, or hedgerow, country. To break the deadlock, two offensive plans were developed. Operation GOODWOOD, led by British Lieutenant General Miles C. Dempsey, would fix the German attention on British forces as they moved to capture Caen. Meanwhile, Bradley developed Operation COBRA, a mobile ground attack to break out of the Cotentin Peninsula, drive west into Brittany, and culminate in a wide sweep to the southeast to stretch German defenses to the breaking point.

Tactical command for COBRA fell to aggressive VII Corps commander Major General J. Lawton Collins. Collins would have six divisions and almost 100,000 men for the attack. The plan hinged on a concentrated strike by heavy bombers to destroy a significant portion of the German lines. After the bombardment, an overwhelming ground attack by the U.S. 9th, 4th, and 30th Infantry Divisions would penetrate the disrupted German defenses and hold open a corridor for the exploiting mobile divisions. Opposing Collins was the German LXXXIV Corps, which had experienced heavy fighting and had many understrength units, such as the Panzer Lehr Division, which could muster only 3,200 troops along a 3-mile front.

A key element in the COBRA plan was to locate a point of penetration where there were sufficient parallel roads in the direction of the attack to allow follow-on forces into the breach. The most controversial aspect of the operation was the "carpet bombing" by strategic bombers. Bradley designated a rectangular target box 2,500 yards wide and over 7,000 yards long, and his IX Tactical Air commander, Major General Elwood "Pete" Quesada, met with Air Chief Marshal Sir Trafford Leigh-Mallory to coordinate the air attack. However, the competing needs for dropping maximum bomb tonnage, maintaining tactical positions for the infantry, and placing 1,500 bombers in the milewide corridor in a single hour could not be entirely reconciled.

COBRA was scheduled for 24 July, but overcast skies led Leigh-Mallory to call off the carpet bombing. Unfortunately, Eighth Air Force bombers were already in flight, and they approached the target from a perpendicular direction, causing bombs to fall short of the target and into the 30th Infantry Division, killing 25 and wounding 131. The attack postponed and the surprise lost, an infuriated Bradley was told that another attack would follow the next day.

On 25 July, bombers dropped 4,400 tons of bombs. The Germans, alerted from the previous attack, had dug in. Despite this, the Panzer Lehr Division was left in shambles, with 70 percent of its soldiers suffering shock and several battalion command posts destroyed. The Americans, in exposed positions and ready to move, suffered in "shorts" (bombs that fell short of their targets, landing on friendly forces) another 111 men killed, almost 500 wounded, and psychological trauma for 200 more. Among the U.S. dead was Lieutenant General Lesley J. McNair, commander of Army Ground Forces, who was visiting the front to observe the attack.

In spite of this tragedy, VII Corps immediately attacked, although strong pockets of German resistance limited the advance to only a mile or two. The next day, Collins made a bold decision to commit his armored and motorized forces, even though no U.S. unit had reached its planned objectives. The disrupted German command-and-control network failed to react when U.S. armored divisions sliced through the lines on 26 July. The next day, Collins's mobile units exploited their success deeper into the German rear areas, which led Bradley to order VIII Corps through the breach to seize Avranches.

According to the plan, once forces moved toward Brittany, the Third U.S. Army, commanded by Lieutenant General George S. Patton Jr., would be activated. To facilitate this transition, Bradley gave Patton immediate command of the VIII Corps, which he drove hard to capture Avranches on 31 July and mark the end of COBRA. In just six days, the entire German Front collapsed, enabling the Allies to carry out their own operational blitzkrieg deep into France.

Steven J. Rauch

See also

Bradley, Omar Nelson; Carpet Bombing; Collins, Joseph Lawton; Dempsey, Miles Christopher; France Campaign; GOODWOOD, Operation; Leigh-Mallory, Sir Trafford L.; McNair, Lesley James; Patton, George Smith, Jr.; Quesada, Elwood Richard "Pete"

References

Blumenson, Martin. *Breakout and Pursuit.* Washington, DC: Center of Military History, 1961.
Carafano, James J. *After D-Day: Operation Cobra and the Normandy Breakout.* Boulder, CO: Lynne Rienner, 2000.

Cochran, Jacqueline (ca. 1906–1980)

American aviatrix who commanded the Women Airforce Service Pilots (WASP). Abandoned at birth, Jackie Cochran was born sometime between 1905 and 1908 near Muscogee, Florida. Growing up with a foster family in extreme poverty in Florida and Georgia, she received only two years of formal education. She worked at a variety of jobs in various settings, from cotton mills to beauty parlors. In 1932, Cochran earned her pilot's license, and in 1934, she won her first air race. She married Keith Odom, a wealthy businessman, in 1936. Two years later, Cochran was the first woman to win the Bendix Trophy and was recognized as the leading female pilot in the world.

When the United States entered World War II, Cochran attempted to change the U.S. Army Air Corps policy of not allowing women pilots to fly its planes. Seeing that the matter was hopeless, she took a group of women pilots to England to fly with the Royal Air Force's Air Transport Auxiliary. During her absence, the Air Transport Command organized the Women's Auxiliary Ferrying Squadron (WAFS), a civilian command for women to ferry aircraft throughout the contiguous United States. Nancy Harkness Love took command of the unit.

Cochran returned to the United States, angry that the WAFS had been formed without her. As a peace offering, the chief of staff of the U.S. Army Air Forces (USAAF), General Henry H. Arnold, authorized Cochran to organize, in November 1942, the Women's Flying Training Detachment (WFTD) to train future ferry pilots. In August 1943, the two women's groups were merged under Cochran's command and renamed the Women's Air Force Service Pilots. Seeing this as a chance for women to prove themselves as military pilots, Cochran pushed for missions beyond simple ferrying. In addition to ferrying every type of military aircraft in the U.S. inventory, the WASPs performed flight checks, towed antiaircraft targets, trained male pilots, and worked as test pilots.

Despite Cochran's efforts to secure military status for the unit—and Arnold's support for that designation—Congress failed to approve it, and the women remained civilians throughout the war and did not secure veteran's status until 1978. In 1945, Cochran was awarded the Distinguished Service Medal.

Following the war, Cochran continued to fly. In 1953, she became the first woman to break the sound barrier, and she also campaigned for female astronauts. In 1960, she was the first woman to launch from and land on an aircraft carrier. Awarded the Legion of Merit by the U.S. Air Force in 1970, she was the first woman enshrined in the Aviation Hall of Fame, in 1971. By the time of her death in Indio, California,

on 9 August 1980, Cochran held more aviation records and "firsts" than any other aviator.

Pamela Feltus

See also
Arnold, Henry Harley "Hap"; United States, Women Airforce Service Pilots

References
Cochran, Jacqueline, with Mayann Bucknum Brinley. *Jackie Cochran*. New York: Bantam Books, 1987.
Cochran, Jacqueline, with Floyd Odum. *The Stars at Noon*. Boston: Little, Brown, 1954.
Merryman, Molly. *Clipped Wings: The Rise and Fall of the Women Airforce Service Pilots of World War II*. New York: New York University Press, 2001.

Cockleshell Heroes (6–12 December 1942)

British commandos who, on 11–12 December 1942, attacked German ships in the Gironde River at Bordeaux, France. The commandos had been organized under the cover name of Boom Patrol Detachment. Following intensive training, they set sail to execute Operation FRANKTON (popularly known as Operation COCKLESHELL). The plan had been developed at the headquarters of Rear Admiral Lord Louis Mountbatten, chief of combined operations. It called for the launching of six two-man, collapsible canoes on a moonless night off the Gironde estuary, in an effort to destroy up to 12 German merchant ships. December had been chosen because the longer nights of winter would give greater cover to the raiders.

On the night of 6 December, the party of 12 Royal Marines under Major Herbert G. "Blondie" Hasler arrived in the Bay of Biscay off the Gironde on board the British submarine *Tuna*. Their mission was to paddle the canoes, known as Cockle Mark IIs, nearly 100 miles from their launch point up the Gironde to Bordeaux and there destroy the German merchant ships with mines. The commandos were then to make their way home via Spain on foot.

Bad weather delayed the commando launch until the night of 7 December, and an even more serious setback occurred when one canoe was damaged in launching and had to be scrubbed. The remaining five successfully launched and then set out for the mouth of the Gironde. Then one of the boats capsized, and its two men were drowned: just four canoes and eight men remained. The Gironde's tidal races caused another canoe to become separated. It was spotted by Germans ashore, and its crewmen were captured. Although the two men were in uniform, they were brutally interrogated (they revealed nothing) and were executed at

Bordeaux early on 13 December by a firing squad acting under Hitler's infamous Commando Order.

Another canoe sank after hitting an underwater obstacle as it neared Bordeaux. While making their way to Spain, the two men from this boat were betrayed to the Gestapo at La Reole. Taken to Paris, they were executed there on or about 23 March 1943.

The men in last two canoes—the first containing Hasler and Marine William Sparks and the second with Corporal A. F. Laver and Marine W. H. Mills—paddled the 91 miles to Bordeaux at night (going ashore and sleeping in the day) in cold and wet conditions. Finally reaching their target, they set time-delay limpet mines on four cargo ships and a small tanker during the night of 11–12 December. When the mines exploded the next morning, the ships flooded and sank; a minesweeping vessel was also badly damaged. None of the ships again saw service in the war.

After setting the mines, Hasler, Sparks, Laver, and Mills paddled to the riverbank, scuttled their canoes, and split up to attempt the trip to Spain and safety. Laver and Mills made for Ruffec but were betrayed to the Germans by French police at Montieu. They were shot in Paris on or about 23 March 1943.

Hasler and Sparks walked 100 miles northeast to make contact with the French Resistance at Ruffec. From there, Resistance members led them across France to the Spanish border, then they made their way to Gibraltar. They were the only Royal Marines to survive the operation, arriving in Britain in April 1943. Hasler was awarded the Distinguished Service Order (DSO) and Sparks the Distinguished Service Medal (DSM). The story was commemorated in a 1955 film entitled *The Cockleshell Heroes*.

A. J. L. Waskey

See also

Commando Order; Commandos/Rangers; Mountbatten, Louis Francis Albert Victor Nicholas

References

Phillips, C. E. Lucas. *Cockleshell Heroes*. London: Heinemann, 1956.
Southby-Tailyour, Ewen. *Blondie: A Life of Herbert George Hasler—Cockleshell Hero, Navigator and Inventor Extraordinary*. London: Leo Cooper, 1998.
Sparks, William, and Michael Munn. *The Last of the Cockleshell Heroes: A World War Two Memoir*. 3rd ed. London: Leo Cooper, 1995.

Cold War, Origins and Early Course of

Even before World War II ended in Europe, there were ominous signs portending future difficult relations between the Soviet Union and the United States. In what Washington and London regarded as a clear violation of their pledges at Yalta, the Soviets refused to allow the establishment of genuinely democratic governments in Poland and in other parts of eastern and central Europe liberated by the Red Army. There was also sharp disagreement between the Western Allied powers and the Soviet Union over the occupation and future governance of Germany and Japan. From these uneasy beginnings, the "Cold War" (the phrase was coined by Truman administration adviser Bernard Baruch in 1947) began soon after the end of World War II. The Cold War was the single most momentous development of the postwar world, and it dominated international relations around the globe for nearly half a century.

The Cold War's roots can be traced back to the years before World War II. Following the Bolshevik seizure of power in Russia in November 1917, the Western Allies, including the United States, had supported the White forces that sought to overthrow the new regime. They and Japan even dispatched expeditionary forces to Russia. Although these troops were soon withdrawn, much ill will had been sown. On its side, Moscow did its best to undermine democratic governments and bring about Communist revolutions in Germany, Hungary, and elsewhere.

The Soviet Union remained largely an outlaw state, and in the 1930s, international events occurred largely as if it did not exist. The mistrust between the West and the Soviets prevented the formation of an effective coalition against Germany before the outbreak of World War II. Soviet dictator Josef Stalin had no love for either the Fascist or the Western nations, and he was prepared to deal with whichever side could offer him the most. Soviet security, rather than ideology, was his motivation.

The Western governments were dismayed when, on 23 August 1939, the Soviet and German governments signed a nonaggression pact in Moscow that allowed German leader Adolf Hitler to begin World War II without fear of Soviet intervention. Stalin, for his part, gained space (which France and Britain had been unwilling to grant) and time with which to rebuild his military, which he had devastated in the Great Purges of the late 1930s. The Western governments were even more dismayed when they learned of secret protocols in the pact that awarded eastern Poland and the Baltic states to the Soviet Union. Between September 1939 and June 1941, Germany gained much from the agreement with the Soviet Union. The secret provisions also included a trade agreement that was of the greatest advantage to Germany in fighting Britain and France.

Nonetheless, immediately following the German invasion of the Soviet Union in June 1941, Stalin called on Britain to open a "second front" in order to draw off some of the German ground and air forces overrunning the western part of his country. From June 1941, Germany consistently committed three-quarters or more of its ground strength on the Eastern Front. Stalin claimed to be deeply frustrated and suspicious that the Western Allies were so slow to invade Europe and instead fought only on the periphery—first in an invasion of French North Africa in November 1942, then Sicily in July 1943, and finally Italy in September 1943—with the invasion of France not occurring until June 1944. Stalin claimed his Western allies were content to watch from the sidelines as the USSR "fought to the last Russian." Throughout the war, he took massive amounts of Lend-Lease aid, but he never came to trust the United States and Britain as much as he had trusted Hitler; indeed, he regarded the leaders of these Western powers with the deepest suspicion.

Distrust deepened over the postwar fate of Poland. Twice in the twentieth century, Poland had served as an invasion route to Soviet territory, and Stalin was determined to secure Soviet hegemony over that country. He demanded the eastern half of prewar Poland, which had, in any case, been awarded to Russia by the Curzon Commission set up by the Paris Peace Conference following World War I (the so-called Curzon Line). He also recognized an exile regime of pro-Soviet Poles, known as the Lublin government, rather than the legitimate Polish government-in-exile in Britain, called the London Poles. Stalin was well aware of the weaknesses and vulnerability of his own society. As the West had used the new states of eastern Europe as a *cordon sanitaire* (buffer zone) after World War I to prevent the spread of Bolshevism, so Stalin was determined to use the Soviet occupation of these same states as a buffer against the Western powers and the spread of their ideas into his empire.

British Prime Minister Winston L. S. Churchill was comfortable with the world of power politics and was more willing to bargain with the Soviet Union, trading primacy in one country for that in another. But domestic politics and international diplomacy mixed uneasily in the United States, and the Roosevelt administration was influenced by the votes of millions of Polish Americans. Indeed, U.S. President Harry S Truman, who took office in April on Franklin D. Roosevelt's death, informed Soviet Foreign Minister Vyacheslav Molotov that Poland had become a symbol of American foreign policy. Stalin refused to see the logic in this approach, protesting that he had not insisted on the postwar fate of North Africa or Belgium—why, then, should America insist on the postwar fate of Poland? Although Stalin did agree to broadly "representative governments" and "free and unfettered elections" in the case of Poland and other states in Eastern and Central Europe, such phrases were merely window dressing that could be interpreted as the Soviets wished.

The real stumbling block was the future of Germany. At the Potsdam Conference in July 1945, Stalin spelled out the heavy reparations he expected to extract from Germany. He was also determined that Germany would never again threaten the Soviet Union. His wartime partners in the West were concerned about destabilizing the most powerful economy in Europe and about having to pay the cost of the reparations themselves, albeit indirectly. They wanted a unified Germany with a true democratic government. Meanwhile, since the Allies could not agree on the amount of reparations, the Soviets began dismantling factories and portable items in their occupation zone and shipping them back to the Soviet Union.

There were divisive Asian issues as well. At Yalta, Stalin had agreed to join the war against Japan two to three months after the end of the war in Europe. In return, the Soviet Union was to receive south Sakhalin Island and the Kuriles (which had never been Soviet territory). At Potsdam, Stalin reiterated his pledge of Soviet intervention in the war against Japan, but he sought a zone of occupation in Japan proper, which Truman refused. The Red Army subsequently overran Manchuria and occupied the northern half of the Korean Peninsula (agreed to by the Allies for the purposes of taking the Japanese surrender, which U.S. forces took in southern Korea). But the government established in North Korea, led by veteran Communist Kim Il-sung, refused to allow free elections and rebuffed efforts to reunify the two Koreas.

In Manchuria, Soviet forces stripped the province of its industry, sending the factories back to the USSR. Some Western observers were also convinced the Soviet Union was supporting the Communist guerrillas of Mao Zedong (Mao Tse-tung) in the resumption of the Chinese Civil War, although that was, in fact, not the case. Soviet troops did turn over much captured Japanese equipment to Mao's forces.

In February 1946 from Moscow, U.S. Chargé d'Affaires George Kennan sent to his superiors in Washington what became known as the "Long Telegram" (of 8,000 words), explaining the factors behind the conduct for Soviet foreign policy. Kennan urged that the United States should seek to "contain" the Soviet Union from further expansion. Soon thereafter, on 5 March 1946, Churchill, by then the former British prime minister, spoke at Westminster College in Fulton, Missouri, and declared that "from Stettin in the Baltic to Trieste in the Adriatic, an iron curtain has descended across the continent." Churchill called for Anglo-American cooperation to withstand Soviet expansionism, but his appeal failed to draw a U.S. policy response.

In early 1947, the British government informed a surprised Truman administration that it was no longer able to bear the burden of shoring up the Greek and Turkish governments. Truman stepped into the breach, and on 12 March, he asked the U.S. Congress for $400 million to help the Greek government resist communist guerrillas and the Turkish government to withstand Soviet pressure to secure unfettered access through the Dardanelles. Truman's call for U.S. aid to free peoples seeking to resist outside or internal pressures came to be known as the Truman Doctrine.

At the same time, the economic situation in Europe continued to deteriorate. Europe had not recovered from the devastation of the war, and the harsh 1946–1947 winter was particularly damaging. Relief costs, borne chiefly by the United States, were high, and there appeared to be no end in sight. On 3 June 1947, in a speech at Harvard University, Secretary of State George C. Marshall described the difficult situation and made clear that the United States had much to lose if the European economy collapsed. He called on Congress to fund a vast economic aid package, based on recovery plans submitted by the European governments. This program became known as the Marshall Plan. Immensely successful, it helped Europe recover, improved the ability of Western European countries to resist communism, and, not incidentally, helped the American economy prosper. The plan was deliberately designed to force European cooperation, and the Soviet Union rejected this program; it refused to participate and denied permission for its Eastern European satellites as well. The Soviet Union would form its own feeble counterpart, the Molotov Plan. Clearly, two mutually antagonistic blocs were forming.

Meanwhile, with the Allies unable to cooperate, the situation in Germany worsened. To cut financial costs, the British and American governments combined their occupation zones economically in what became known as Bizonia (the French later merged their zone, making it Trizonia). Also, because a common currency for all four zones was merely underwriting the Soviets, the three Western governments moved to establish a separate occupation currency. They also promised free elections. The Soviets viewed these moves as threatening and walked out of the Allied Control Council meeting in early 1948. In April, claiming technical reasons, they temporarily closed surface access routes to the western occupation zones in Berlin to military traffic. When this did not result in a change of Anglo-American policy toward Germany, the Soviets instituted a complete blockade of surface access routes into the city. The Truman administration responded with the Berlin Airlift and flew in not only food and medical supplies, for example, but also fuel to heat homes and factories. In May 1949, the Soviets ended the blockade, but the division of Germany into eastern and western halves seemed complete.

As the Berlin blockade drew to a close, the final chapter was taking place in the long Chinese Civil War. The uneasy wartime truce between the Nationalist Party—the Guomindang, or GMD (Kuomintang, or KMT)—and the Communists was broken in 1947 when Nationalist leader Jiang Jieshi (Chiang Kai-shek) attempted to secure Manchuria. Despite massive amounts of U.S. aid, the Nationalists were defeated and fled to Taiwan (Formosa) in 1949 as Communist leader Mao Zedong (Mao Tse-tung) announced the establishment of the People's Republic of China on 1 October 1949. The situation also seemed to worsen when the Soviet Union detonated an atomic device in August 1949, ending the U.S. nuclear monopoly.

Then, on June 25, 1950, the Cold War turned hot as North Korean forces, supported by the Soviet Union and China, invaded South Korea. The Truman administration responded. In what Truman said was the most difficult decision he had to make as president, he authorized U.S. forces to intervene. At that point, the Cold War became enshrined in American foreign policy, and in November 1950, the Truman administration approved a national security policy statement (NSC 68/4) calling for a real policy of containment. Opposing what it perceived to be Soviet expansionism and aggression became a defining characteristic of U.S. foreign policy until the collapse of the Soviet Union in 1991.

Charles M. Dobbs and Spencer C. Tucker

See also

Baruch, Bernard Mannes; Churchill, Sir Winston L. S.; German-Soviet Non-aggression Pact; Germany, Occupation of; Hitler, Adolf; Japan, Occupation of; Jiang Jieshi; Mao Zedong; Marshall, George Catlett; Molotov, Vyacheslav Mikhailovich; Potsdam Conference; Roosevelt, Franklin D.; Stalin, Josef; Truman, Harry S; Yalta Conference

References

Byrnes, James F. *Speaking Frankly.* New York: Harper and Brothers, 1947.

Dobbs, Charles M. *The Unwanted Symbol: American Foreign Policy, the Cold War, and Korea, 1945–1950.* Kent, OH: Kent State University Press, 1981.

Feis, Herbert. *Between War and Peace: The Potsdam Conference.* Princeton, NJ: Princeton University Press, 1957.

Fontaine, Andre. *History of the Cold War, 1917–1966.* 2 vols. New York: Pantheon, 1968.

Gaddis, John L. *We Now Know: Rethinking Cold War History.* New York: Oxford University Press, 1997.

Kennan, George F. *Memoirs, 1925–1950.* Boston: Little, Brown, 1967.

Kuniholm, Bruce R. *The Origins of the Cold War: Great Power Conflict and Diplomacy in Iran, Turkey and Greece.* Princeton, NJ: Princeton University Press, 1994.

Seton-Watson, Hugh. *Neither War nor Peace: The Struggle for Power in the Postwar World.* New York: Praeger, 1960.

Thomas, Hugh. *Armed Truce: The Beginnings of the Cold War, 1945–1946.* New York: Atheneum, 1987.

Yergin, Daniel H. *Shattered Peace: The Origins of the Cold War.* New York: Penguin, 1990.

Collaboration

Literally "cooperation" or "unity of effort" but interpreted during World War II to mean working actively with the enemy, implying treasonable activity. The issue is a complex one, for collaboration could run from selling the occupier agricultural produce to rounding up Jews and actively assisting in the prosecution of military activities. Collaboration could be military, political, economic, social, or cultural. In any case, such activities implied treason (in varying degree, of course) on the part of the collaborator. One point that must be made, however, is that one side's "collaborator" was the other side's "ally," "loyalist," or "assistant." Collaboration with enemy occupying forces occurred on both sides during the war.

Western and Northern Europe

France presents a complicated picture. Following their defeat of France, the Germans dictated armistice terms that saw them occupy about two-thirds of the country to the north and west. The French were allowed to establish an "independent" government in the remainder of the country, with its capital at Vichy. The term *collaboration* was actually first used in the course of a meeting between Vichy head of state Marshal Henri Philippe Pétain and German leader Adolf Hitler at Montoire-sur-Loire on 24 October 1940. Pétain and his supporters concluded that Germany had won the war and that, for the foreseeable future, that nation would dominate the Continent. The marshal therefore informed the French people that he accepted "in principle" the idea of "collaboration" with Germany.

Despite Pétain's pronouncement, the French population was bitterly divided, and a small minority at first rallied to the Resistance led by young Brigadier General Charles de Gaulle in London (he had been condemned to death in absentia by the Vichy government as a traitor). Germany had very direct sources of pressure on Vichy, including heavy "administration costs" that amounted to more than 60 percent of French national income, control over traffic across the armistice demarcation line, possession of a million French prisoners of war (POWs), and exploitation of the press.

Following the Allied invasion of French North Africa, the Germans occupied the remainder of France. While de Gaulle established his position in North Africa and the French Empire in general, Vichy Premier Pierre Laval became increasingly open about collaborating with Germany within continental France, including active participation in the rounding up and deportation of Jews and the hunting down of partisans by the Milice, the 30,000-man-strong Vichy militia force. Meanwhile, as the fortunes of war shifted, de Gaulle's influence in France grew.

Certainly, a large number of French men and women collaborated with the Nazi regime, and many made sizable fortunes in the process. In addition, little was done after the war to punish such war profiteers. The carefully nurtured myth in postwar France of a nation of resisters was totally false, although thousands of French men and women did risk their all for the Allied cause.

Occupation arrangements varied in other western European countries. Belgium experienced a rather harsh German military rule, whereas the Netherlands and Norway had civil administrations, and Denmark was able to retain sovereignty until August 1943. After the war, the Belgian government punished, in varying degree, some 53,000 men and women adjudged to have collaborated with the German occupiers.

Vidkun Quisling of Norway was one of the most notorious collaborators, his name becoming synonymous with the term *traitor*. In February 1942, Quisling became minister president of Norway, but his effort to Nazify his country was ardently resisted by most of the population. Anton Mussert was his Dutch counterpart and founder of the Netherlands Nazi Party. The party membership was 30,000 at the start of the war, increasing to a peak of 50,000.

Eastern Europe

Although Poles prided themselves after the war on offering little collaboration with the hated German and Soviet occupiers, collaboration did take place in their country. In the General Government set up by the Germans, units of Polish police operated under German command, as did Jewish police in the ghettos established by the Germans. Even during the Holocaust, the Germans discovered those individuals who would collaborate in the concentration camps—the Kapos, or trusties, who worked for the German guards in the Sonderkommando. When Soviet forces invaded eastern Poland, they mobilized large numbers of Poles to fight for them against Germany; many Poles regarded these soldiers as collaborators.

In the rest of central and eastern Europe, experiences varied. Bulgaria, nominally an Axis power, hardly participated in the war. Its government did send troops to occupy Thrace and Macedonia in Greece, but it steadfastly rejected Hitler's demands that it dispatch troops to the Eastern Front. Hungary and Romania both supplied troops for the German invasion of the Soviet Union, suffering heavy losses in the process. They also actively participated in rounding up Jews to be sent to the extermination camps. In both Greece and Yugoslavia, there was active resistance to the Germans, although the government of newly independent Croatia, carved from Yugoslavia, was highly supportive of Berlin and its policies.

German Führer, Adolf Hitler (center left) *and Italian Dictator, Benito Mussolini* (center right). *(Library of Congress)*

The Soviet Union

Many inhabitants of the eastern portions of the Soviet Union, such as the Baltic states and Ukraine, openly welcomed the German army as their liberator and collaborated fully with it, until they discovered that German occupation policies were even more repressive than Soviet rule had been. In 1943 alone, as Soviet troops moved westward, the Soviet secret police, or NKVD, arrested more than 931,000 people for questioning. Hundreds of thousands of Soviet minorities—most notably the Crimean Tartars but also Turks and Chechens, among others—were simply deported en masse to the eastern USSR as a consequence of their wartime collaboration with the Germans. General Andrei Vlasov, a Hero of the Soviet Union, agreed to head the German-sponsored Russian Liberation Army, although Hitler refused to allow it any real function. Hundreds of thousands of Soviet prisoners worked in the German army in nonmilitary roles, as cooks, drivers, and the like. Much of their motivation came from the simple desire to stay alive, as millions of Soviet soldiers perished from starvation in German POW camps.

One tragic episode following the war resulted from the decision by the Western powers to hand over to the USSR millions of Soviet citizens, many of whom had lived in the West for decades and had played no wartime collaborative role. Nonetheless, they were shipped off to work at hard labor in the gulags.

Far East

In the Far East, Japan's occupation of its conquered territories was generally quite harsh. Paradoxically, as the war dragged on, Japan encouraged independence from colonial rule in some areas, especially in those lands that had been European or U.S. colonies. A notable example of the latter was the Netherlands East Indies, where indigenous peoples were treated comparatively well, in contrast to Europeans, and where the postwar independence movement was effectively encouraged. There as elsewhere, there was considerable popular support for Tokyo's efforts to eliminate the influence of the European colonial masters. One component of the Japanese theme of a "Greater East Asia Co-prosperity

Sphere" was to grant independence to Asian states. But the phrase *Asia for the Asians* actually meant that Asian peoples were to be subordinate to Japan.

In French Indochina, the Japanese allowed the French colonial administration to remain in place for purposes of expediency, for Indochina could thus be held with fewer Japanese troops. In March 1945, however, with the war almost certainly lost for Japan, the French plotted to liberate Indochina themselves. The Japanese then took control and granted Vietnam its "independence." The Vietminh, diehard Vietnamese nationalists led by Ho Chi Minh, rejected collaboration, fought both the French and the Japanese, and appealed to Washington for support.

Much to the surprise of the Japanese, most Filipinos remained loyal to the United States. But under heavy Japanese pressure, the Philippine government did accept the principle of collaboration and even declared war on the United States. Following the liberation of the islands, however, few Filipino collaborators were punished, and the Philippines received independence. Burma had its share of collaborators. A number of Burmese regarded the Japanese as liberators, and the Burmese Independence Army actively fought on their side.

Throughout its long occupation of much of China, Japan sought collaborators. Wang Jingwei (Ching-wei), a founding father of the Nationalist Party, grew disillusioned with Nationalist leader Jiang Jieshi (Chiang Kai-shek) and his failure to make peace with the Japanese. In March 1940, the Japanese installed Wang as head of the puppet Reorganized Nationalist Government in Nanjing (Nanking). However, Wang's hopes of presenting himself as a credible alternative to Jiang were dashed on the rocks of Japanese military domination. Wang died in Japan in November 1944 while undergoing medical treatment.

After the Allied victories in Europe and the Pacific in spring 1945, collaborators were variously punished. Many individuals were simply executed on the spot by soldiers and civilians. In France, women who had fraternized with the Germans had their heads shaved, among other indignities. Some key political leaders, such as Quisling, were tried and executed. In France, the aged Marshal Pétain was tried and sentenced to death, but de Gaulle remitted that sentence in recognition of his World War I services, and the marshal spent the remainder of his life in prison.

Arthur I. Cyr and Spencer C. Tucker

See also

China, Role in War; Churchill, Sir Winston L. S.; Concentration Camps, German; Conscript Labor; de Gaulle, Charles; France, Role in War; France, Vichy; Hitler, Adolf; Ho Chi Minh; Holocaust, The; Jiang Jieshi; Laval, Pierre; Partisans/Guerrillas; Pétain, Henri Philippe; Quisling, Vidkun Abraham Lauritz Jonsson; Resistance; Vlasov, Andrei Andreyevich; Wang Jingwei

References

Bennett, Rab. *Under the Shadow of the Swastika—The Moral Dilemmas of Resistance and Collaboration in Hitler's Europe.* New York: New York University Press, 1999.

Calvocoressi, Peter, and Guy Wint. *Total War: The Story of World War II.* New York: Pantheon/Random House, 1972.

Ehrlich, Blake. *Resistance: France, 1940–1945.* Boston and Toronto, Canada: Little, Brown, 1965.

Littlejohn, David. *The Patriotic Traitors: The History of Collaboration in German-Occupied Europe, 1940–45.* Garden City, NY: Doubleday, 1972.

Steinberg, David. *Philippine Collaboration in World War II.* Ann Arbor: University of Michigan Press, 1967.

Collins, Joseph Lawton (1896–1987)

U.S. Army general who executed Operation COBRA. Born on 1 May 1896 in New Orleans, Louisiana, Joseph Collins graduated from the U.S. Military Academy in 1917. Although he did not take part in combat in World War I, he commanded a battalion during the occupation of Germany between 1919 and 1921.

Collins was then an instructor at West Point (1921–1925) and at the Infantry School at Fort Benning, Georgia (1925–1931). He also served in the Philippines and was an instructor at the Army War College (1938–1941). Shortly after the Japanese attack on Pearl Harbor, Colonel Collins was named chief of staff of the Hawaiian Department and made a brigadier general. In May 1942, he was promoted to major general and took command of the 25th Division, which relieved the 1st Marine Division on Guadalcanal in December 1942. Collins earned the nickname "Lightning Joe" from his men for his aggressiveness on Guadalcanal.

Collins then led the 25th Division during the successful operations on New Georgia in the summer of 1943. Transferring to Europe in January 1944, he received command of VII Corps, the post he held for the remainder of the war. On D day, spearheaded by its 4th Division, VII Corps landed on Utah Beach. It seized the vital port of Cherbourg on 27 June. VII Corps is probably best remembered for Operation COBRA, the breakout from the Normandy beachhead at Saint-Lô on 25 July, an operation largely planned by Lieutenant General Omar N. Bradley but executed by Collins. VII Corps then repelled the German counterattack at Mortain, which led to the creation of the Falaise-Argentan pocket.

Collins led VII Corps at Aachen; at the Battle of the Bulge, where the corps held the northern shoulder of the bulge; at Cologne; in the Ruhr pocket; and, as the war ended, in the Harz Mountains. In April 1945, he was promoted to lieutenant general. One of the war's best corps commanders,

Collins is remembered as an officer who led from the front and enjoyed the full confidence of General Dwight D. Eisenhower and Omar Bradley.

Collins served as vice chief of staff of the army from 1947 to 1949. Promoted to full general, he was the U.S. Army chief of staff from 1949 to 1953 and special representative to the Republic of Vietnam between 1954 and 1955. Collins retired from the army in March 1956. He died in Washington, D.C., on 12 September 1987.

Thomas D. Veve

See also
Ardennes Offensive; Bradley, Omar Nelson; Cherbourg, Capture of; COBRA, Operation; Eisenhower, Dwight D.; Falaise-Argentan Pocket; Guadalcanal, Land Battle for; New Georgia, Battle of; Normandy Invasion and Campaign; OVERLORD, Operation; Pearl Harbor, Attack on; Rhine Crossings; Ruhr Campaign; Saint-Lô, Battle of

References
Collins, J. Lawton. *Lightning Joe: An Autobiography.* Baton Rouge: Louisiana State University Press, 1979.
Weigley, Russell F. *Eisenhower's Lieutenants.* Bloomington: Indiana University Press, 1981.

Collishaw, Raymond (1893–1976)

Canadian fighter pilot and senior Royal Air Force officer who took command of 14 Group, Fighter Command in 1942. Born on 22 November 1893 in Nanaimo, British Columbia, Raymond Collishaw became a seaman in the Canadian Fisheries Protection Service after leaving school and then joined the Royal Naval Air Service in January 1916. After training, he was assigned to Number 3 Wing, a long-range bomber unit in France. In February 1917, he was posted to Number 3 (Naval) Squadron and began his successful career as a fighter pilot. He moved to Number 10 (Naval) Squadron in April, flying Sopwith Triplanes, and brought his personal score of enemy aircraft shot down to 38 by 28 July, when he returned to Canada on leave. He went back to France to command Number 13 (Naval) Squadron and was credited with 59 enemy aircraft shot down by the end of World War I.

Collishaw remained with the new Royal Air Force after the war. He saw action in south Russia in 1919, then served in a variety of home and overseas stations in the years before World War II. In 1940, he was in command of 202 Group, the Royal Air Force units in the western desert of Egypt, when war with Italy began on 10 June. Collishaw's theater commander, Air Chief Marshal Sir Arthur Longmore, ordered him to keep his aggressive tendencies in check, largely because of immediate difficulties of supply.

But as reinforcements arrived, Collishaw was able to extend air operations against the Italians.

In December 1940, preparations began for a full-scale land offensive into Libya. Collishaw's air units commenced a wide-ranging offensive to set the stage and provided close support for Lieutenant General Sir Richard O'Connor's spectacularly successful advance and destruction of Italian forces under Marshal Rodolfo Graziani. This success was quickly reversed as the British sent troops and aircraft to Greece and German forces under Generalleutnant (U.S. equiv. major general) Erwin Rommel commenced operations in Africa. Collishaw's air forces provided support as the British retreated and then again stabilized their situation on the Egyptian border.

Collishaw returned to Britain on the staff of Headquarters, Fighter Command in August 1941, then took command of 14 Group, Fighter Command on 21 March 1942. He retired as an air vice marshal in 1943 and remained in England until the end of the war, when he returned to Vancouver. In Canada, he set up several very successful mining-exploration operations. Collishaw died in West Vancouver on 28 September 1976.

Paul E. Fontenoy

See also
Graziani, Rodolfo; Greece Campaign (28 October 1940–March 1941; April 1941); North Africa Campaign; O'Connor, Sir Richard Nugent; Rommel, Erwin Johannes Eugen

References
Collishaw, Raymond. *Air Command, a Fighter Pilot's Story.* London: W. Kimber, 1973.
Playfair, I. S. O., et al. *The Mediterranean and Middle East.* Vols. 1–3. London: Her Majesty's Stationery Office, 1954–1960.
Richards, Denis, and Hilary St. G. Saunders. *Royal Air Force, 1939–1945.* London: Her Majesty's Stationery Office, 1953–1954.

Colmar Pocket, Battle for the (20 January–9 February 1945)

Colmar pocket was the German bridgehead west of the Rhine River and south of the city of Strasbourg, held by Colonel General Friedrich Wiese's Nineteenth Army of eight divisions (some 50,000 men). On 7 January 1945, the Germans launched a major attack out of the Colmar pocket, gaining very little ground. But the Allies wanted to remove the pocket, and the task was assigned to General Jean de Lattre de Tassigny's First French Army of 6th Army Group.

On 20 January, de Lattre's troops attacked the Colmar pocket. The French I Corps led off by attacking the southern flank. On the night of 22–23 January, II Corps assaulted the northern flank. The objective was to envelop the pocket by

Two smiling French soldiers fill the hands of American soldiers with candy, in Rouffach, France, after the closing of the Colmar pocket, 5 February 1945. (Still Picture Records LICON, Special Media Archives Services Division (NWCS-S), National Archives)

converging on Neuf-Brisach and the Rhine Bridge at Breisach. Deep snow along with German mines, machine guns, tanks, and artillery kept the attacks from gaining much ground.

The U.S. 3rd Infantry Division, which was attached to the French, then crossed the Fecht and Ill Rivers. The Germans counterattacked, but the 3rd held them off and reinforced its bridgehead. Severe shortages of French troops led to the eventual attachment to the operation of the entire U.S. XXI Corps, composed of the 3rd, 28th, and 75th Infantry Divisions. Major General Frank Milburn commanded XXI Corps.

Milburn's XXI Corps took over the right of the French II Corps zone and the main effort to envelop the Colmar pocket from the north. The II Corps guarded its left, clearing that area to the Rhine.

The attack continued. The 28th Division arrived at Colmar on 2 February, and the 75th entered the outskirts of Neuf-Brisach in the rear of the pocket. The U.S. 12th Armored Division was then added to the attack. On 3 February, it drove south through the 28th. Pockets of German resistance held up one arm of the attack, but the other, driving down the main road, captured Rouffach on 5 February. Other task forces surrounded the town and met the 4th Moroccan Division from the I Corps. This maneuver split the pocket.

On 5 February, leading elements of the U.S. 3rd Division arrived outside the walled town of Neuf-Brisach. Early the next morning, as the Americans prepared to attack the city, they encountered a Frenchman who took them to a 60-foot tunnel that led into the town from the dry moat. An American platoon entered through this tunnel and found only 76 German soldiers, who surrendered without a fight. Before leaving the town, their officers had told them to fight to the finish.

French forces finished off the pocket on 9 February. In the entire operation, the Allies had sustained about 18,000 casualties and the Germans between 22,000 and 36,000. Only the 708th Volksgrenadier Division, evacuating the pocket on 3 February, escaped reasonably intact. The German 2nd Mountain Division had 1,000 battle casualties and 4,700 men taken as prisoners. Only 500 members of the German 198th Infantry Division and 400 men of the German 338th Infantry Division managed to escape. The Germans also abandoned 55 armored vehicles and 66 field pieces.

Uzal W. Ent

See also
Alsace Campaign; Lattre de Tassigny, Jean Joseph Marie Gabriel de
References
Eisenhower, David. *Eisenhower at War, 1943–1945.* New York: New Vantage Press, 1987.
Weigley, Russell F. *Eisenhower's Lieutenants: The Campaigns of France and Germany, 1944–1945.* Bloomington: Indiana University Press, 1981.

Combat Fatigue

Combat fatigue—also known as battle fatigue, war neurosis, exhaustion, or shell shock—is a variable group of symptoms including excessive fatigue, an exaggerated startle response, tremors, violence, nightmares, delusions, hallucinations, withdrawal, and catatonia. Herodotus described combat-induced mental illness in the Athenian army during the Battle of Marathon in 490 B.C., but the diagnosis was relatively infrequent prior to the twentieth century. The Russians established the first military psychiatric service during the Russo-Japanese War. The problem became widespread in World War I, during which it was termed *shell shock* under the mistaken theory that explosive concussions caused small brain hemorrhages leading to cerebral dysfunction. By World War II, it was widely understood that the symptoms were psychiatric in nature, were similar to traumatic neuroses seen in the civilian population, and were not caused by identifiable anatomic brain damage.

In spite of an early British emphasis on battlefield psychiatry and an American attempt to exclude men with psychiatric illness from military service, mental illness remained a major cause of combat disability, with about 30 percent of Allied combat zone casualties being psychiatric. Although physicians in World War I had learned that treatment close to the front lines made it possible to return a number of psychiatrically disabled soldiers to combat, the

lesson was forgotten. Early in World War II, patients with combat fatigue were routinely evacuated to rehabilitation hospitals, and most were discharged. As manpower became scarce, more of these men were placed in pioneer or labor details in the rear area, but few returned to combat.

Captain Frederick R. Hanson, an American neurologist and neurosurgeon who had joined the Canadian army early in the war and participated in the landing at Dieppe, transferred to the U.S. Army and developed what became a successful and widely employed treatment for what the British now termed *exhaustion* or *combat fatigue.* The essential parts of the regimen included sedation, brief periods of rest, and treatment in a facility close to the front, where the patients and staff continued to wear combat clothing. Hanson realized that treating these patients as if they were mentally ill and physically separating them from their units made it unlikely that they would return to duty. Using his treatment protocols, the British and American armies were able to return 70 to 80 percent of combat fatigue victims to their units, and only 15 to 20 percent of patients requiring evacuation to the zone of the interior were psychiatric.

Shortly after the Italian invasion, the U.S. Army established the post of division psychiatrist, and Hanson produced a manual for internists so nonpsychiatrists could use his methods. As the war went on, Allied military psychiatrists became convinced that no soldier was immune from combat fatigue. They hypothesized that any man subject to continuous combat for a long enough time would become nonfunctional and estimated that 200 days of constant action was about the maximum a soldier could be expected to tolerate. The British adopted a system of unit rotation to give their men regular periods of rest and were able to stretch the tolerable period to close to 400 days, but the Americans, except in the U.S. Army Air Forces, adopted a more haphazard approach of rotating individuals with the longest periods of service rather than entire units. It was not until later wars that regular unit rotation became standard.

Military physicians, mindful of the heavy clinical and financial burden of long-term psychiatric illness after World War I, correctly warned that the true cost of combat fatigue would not become evident until after the soldiers returned to civilian life.

Jack McCallum

See also
Military Medicine
References
Cowdrey, Albert E. *Fighting for Life: American Military Medicine in World War II.* New York: Free Press, 1994.
Slight, David. "Psychiatry and the War." In William H. Taliaferro, ed., *Medicine and the War,* 150–171. Chicago: University of Chicago Press, 1944.

Combined Chiefs of Staff

Ad hoc organization, composed of the British and American military chiefs of staff, that coordinated combined strategic planning and conduct of World War II. The ground work for military collaboration developed at least a year and a half before the United States was drawn into the war. The U.S. Navy Department established a permanent observer mission in London to discuss naval cooperation and information exchange. U.S. Army observers only went to London on special missions until the War Department set up permanent liaison in the spring of 1941. In early 1941, agreements called for the exchange of military missions, and the British established its Joint Staff Mission, representing the British chiefs.

The Combined Chiefs of Staff (CCS) was formally established by the two powers in January 1942 shortly after the ARCADIA Conference made the Anglo-American alliance a fact. The organization was to consist of the British chiefs of staff and the their opposite numbers in the United States. But since there were no opposite numbers established in the United States at that point, the U.S. Joint Chiefs of Staff (JCS) was formed, consisting of the army chief of staff, General George C. Marshall; the deputy army chief of staff for air and commanding general of the army air forces, Lieutenant General Henry H. Arnold; the chief of naval operations, Admiral Harold R. Stark, and the commander in chief of the U.S. Fleet, Admiral Ernest J. King. In March 1942, Stark's and King's positions were combined under King, and Stark went on to command U.S. Naval Forces in Europe, headquartered in London. In July, President Franklin D. Roosevelt, acting in his capacity as commander in chief of the armed forces, brought out of retirement the former chief of naval operations, Admiral William D. Leahy, and appointed him chief of staff to the president.

The British Chiefs of Staff (BCS) organization included the chief of the Imperial General Staff, General Sir Alan Brooke; the first sea lord, Admiral Sir Dudley Pound; and the chief of the air staff, Air Chief Marshal Sir Charles Portal. These men met with their American counterparts only at infrequent military-political conferences, but in the interim, they were represented at the permanent body in Washington by the Joint Staff Mission. The original members of the that mission were Lieutenant General Sir Colville Wemyss, Admiral Sir Charles Little, and Air Marshal A. T. Harris. In addition, Field Marshal Sir John Dill sat as a member of the Combined Chiefs representing Prime Minister Winston L. S. Churchill.

The CCS were to formulate and execute policies and plans related to the strategic conduct of the war, to include war requirements, allocation of munitions, and transportation requirements. Combined planning was done by the staffs of the JCS and BCS, the Joint Planning Staff—patterned after the British design—and the Joint Planners.

Actual planning of the respective national staffs would work its way through the JCS or BCS for coordination by the Combined Planners, the CCS planning staff, which was more a coordinating than an originating body. This system worked surprisingly well during the war, as the United States and Britain closely integrated their war efforts.

Arthur T. Frame

See also

ARCADIA Conference; Arnold, Henry Harley "Hap"; Brooke, Sir Alan Francis; Dill, Sir John Greer; Joint Chiefs of Staff; King, Ernest Joseph; Leahy, William Daniel; Marshall, George Catlett; Portal, Sir Charles Frederick Algernon; Pound, Sir Alfred Dudley Pickman Rogers; Stark, Harold Raynsford "Betty"; Tehran Conference

References

Blumenson, Martin. *United States Army in World War II: European Theater of Operations—Breakout and Pursuit.* Washington, DC: Center of Military History, 1984.

Harrison, Gordon A. *United States Army in World War II: European Theater of Operations—Cross-Channel Attack.* Washington, DC: Center of Military History, 1951.

Matloff, Maurice. *United States Army in World War II: The War Department—Strategic Planning for Coalition Warfare, 1943–1944.* Washington, DC: Center of Military History, 1959.

Commando Order (18 October 1942)

Order issued by German leader Adolf Hitler to counter British commando raids. On 18 October 1942, Hitler issued order 003833/42g.Kdos.OWK/Wst, known historically as the Commando Order. In addition to this order, a directive from army headquarters (Number 551781/42G.K) stated that only commanders of units involved were to see the Commando Order. The order was issued in 12 copies only, and headquarters required that in no circumstances was it to fall into Allied hands and that both documents were to be destroyed immediately following their reading and comprehension.

Hitler claimed that the Allied commando raids were a violation of the Geneva Convention, and he ordered, "From now on all enemies on so-called commando missions in Europe or Africa challenged by German troops, even if they are in uniform, whether armed or unarmed, in battle or in flight, are to be slaughtered to the last man." In his supplementary directive, he explained to his commanders the reason for the order. Because of Allied successes, Hitler noted,

I have been compelled to issue strict orders for the destruction of enemy sabotage troops and to declare noncompliance with these orders severely punishable. . . . It must be made clear to the enemy that all sabotage troops will be exterminated, without exception, to the last man.

This means that their chance of escaping with their lives is nil. . . . Under no circumstances can [they] expect to be treated according to the rule of the Geneva Convention. . . . . If it should become necessary for reasons of interrogation to initially spare one man or two, then they are to be shot immediately after interrogation.

Despite Hitler's order, Allied commando raids persisted until the end of the war.

Berryman E. Woodruff IV

See also

Churchill, Sir Winston L. S.; Hitler, Adolf; Mountbatten, Louis Francis Albert Victor Nicholas

References

Fergusson, Bernard. *The Watery Maze: The Story of Combined Operations.* New York: Holt, Rinehart and Winston, 1961.

Shirer, William L. *The Rise and Fall of the Third Reich: A History of Nazi Germany.* New York: Simon and Schuster, 1960.

Commandos/Rangers

Specialized, highly skilled, elite troops. Rangers were often the first to fight, and generally conducted raids and other specialized tasks, frequently in advance of an amphibious assault. But because of their training, commando troops were often employed in patrolling and sniping after a landing and on occasion served as bodyguards for prominent figures. All rangers and commandos were trained in infantry skills as well as close-quarter battle techniques. They were adept with rifles, knives, grenades, and blunt instruments. Their fitness was paramount, and they were conditioned through long training to make their way across many miles of terrain to reach their objectives. They were self-reliant, resourceful, and aggressive.

Britain formed its first commandos in southern England in June 1940, just after the evacuation of the British Expeditionary Force from France. A designated British commando unit was the equivalent of a battalion and consisted of 10 troops of 50 men each. On formation and during their initial training, the first commando troops were given a ration allowance and billeted in local houses, where they were responsible for their own discipline and were made to rely on their initiative and self-motivation. In October 1940, Number 3 Commando, with a total of 475 officers and men, moved to the Combined Training Centre at Inverary in Scotland. Other commando units were also forming at the time.

The first British commando operation took place in March 1941 against German installations on the Lofoten Islands of Norway. Later commandos raided South Vaagso, also in Nor-

way, and they conducted operations against the Channel Islands, were landed by submarine off Sicily before Operation HUSKY, and were responsible for many other operations against German coastal installations. Commandos were again in the forefront of the landings in France in Normandy in June 1944, and they took on an infantry role as they advanced inland, despite the fact that commando troops were not line infantry but special forces. On 6 June 1944, commandos mounted an attack on the German battery at Merville overlooking the invasion beaches; the battery was destroyed.

When the United States entered World War II, Brigadier General Lucian Truscott, U.S. Army liaison to the British General Staff, convinced Army Chief of Staff General George C. Marshall of the need for an American commando unit. On 26 May 1942, the army authorized formation of the 1st Ranger Battalion, which was activated on 19 June. During the war, the United States formed six ranger battalions. The first through fifth served in the North African and European Theaters, whereas the sixth served in the Pacific.

For training, the U.S. 1st Ranger Battalion was sent to the British Army Command's Training Centre in Scotland. For several weeks, the American rangers were tested to their limits by the Commando Centre trainers. Eighty-five percent of those who began the course graduated.

On 19 August 1942, 50 American rangers were added to a British and Canadian commando raid on the French port city of Dieppe. Three rangers died and five were captured, but the Americans won high praise for their efforts. Rangers subsequently took part in raids on Norway while attached to British commandos units. They also fought in Sicily and participated in the landings in Italy at Salerno and Anzio. As raiding forces, they were only lightly equipped, but they were subsequently employed as infantry troops nonetheless. The 1st and 3rd Battalions led the attack on Cisterna but were almost wiped out. The remaining 4th Battalion took heavy casualties while trying to rescue the first two. Of 1,500 men in the three battalions, only 449 remained.

During the Allied invasion of France, the U.S. 2nd Ranger Battalion landed on the west flank of Omaha Beach with A Company of the 116th Infantry Regiment and moved up to the village of Vierville-sur-Mer to secure the coastal road to Pointe du Hoc, destroying the German positions and radar station along the way. Meanwhile, the 5th Ranger Battalion received the important task of disabling a battery of six 15 cm German coastal artillery pieces at Pointe du Hoc. These guns would be capable of hitting almost any Allied ship supporting the U.S. landing. The rangers successfully scaled the cliffs, but much to their surprise, they found that the German artillery had already been removed from Pointe du Hoc. The rangers then pushed inland, destroying some of the pieces behind the beaches.

British commandos who landed in Normandy on 6 June set out to capture a German gun site protected by snipers. (Hulton Archive by Getty Images)

A joint U.S.-Canadian brigade-sized unit, known as the First Special Service Force, also took part in the Aleutian Campaign, in the fighting in Italy, and in the August 1944 landings in southern France. In subsequent European fighting, rangers continued to lead the way and were some of the first units to counter the German Ardennes Offensive in December 1944. In 1945, ranger units established bridgeheads across the Rhine River into the heart of Germany.

Elite formations also served in the Pacific Theater. During the Quebec Conference of August 1943, U.S. President Franklin D. Roosevelt and British Prime Minister Winston L. S. Churchill agreed to have a U.S. ground unit spearhead the Chinese army with a long-range penetration mission behind Japanese lines in Burma. Its goal would be to destroy Japanese communications and supply lines and to play havoc with Japanese forces while an attempt was made to reopen the Burma Road.

A presidential call for volunteers for "a dangerous and hazardous mission" elicited some 2,900 volunteers. Officially designated as the 5307th Composite Unit (Provisional)—code-named GALAHAD—the unit later became popularly known as Merrill's Marauders after its commander, Brigadier General Frank Merrill. Organized into combat teams, two to each battalion, the Marauder volunteers came from various theaters of operation. Some came from stateside cadres; some from the jungles of Panama and Trinidad; and the remainder were veterans of campaigns in Guadalcanal, New Georgia, and New Guinea. In India, some Signal Corps and Air Corps personnel were added, as well as pack troops with mules.

Following training, undertaken in great secrecy in the jungles of India, about 600 men were detached as a rear-echelon headquarters to remain in India to handle the soon to be vital airdrop link between the six Marauder combat teams (400 men to a team) and the Air Transport Command. In units designated by color-coded names—Red, White, Blue, Green, Orange, and Khaki—the remaining 2,400 Marauders began their march up the Ledo Road and over the outlying ranges of the Himalaya Mountains into Burma.

The Marauders, with no tanks or heavy artillery support, moved overland some 1,000 miles through extremely dense and almost impenetrable jungles and came out with glory. In 5 major and 30 minor engagements, they defeated units of the veteran Japanese 18th Division, the conquerors of Singapore and Malaya who vastly outnumbered them. Moving in the rear of the main Japanese forces, they disrupted supply and communication lines and climaxed their operations with the capture of Myitkyina Airfield, the only all-weather airfield in Burma. The unit was consolidated with the 475th Infantry on 10 August 1944.

The 6th Ranger Battalion was activated at Port Moresby, New Guinea, in September 1944. Commanded by Colonel Henry "Hank" Mucci, it was the first American force to return to the Philippines. Its mission was to destroy Japanese coastal defense guns, radio, and radar stations on the islands of Dinegat and Suluan off Leyte. Landing three days in advance of the main Sixth Army invasion force on 17–18 October 1944, the 6th Battalion swiftly killed or captured some of the Japanese defenders and destroyed all their communications. The unit took part in the U.S. landings on Luzon, and several behind-the-lines patrols, penetrations, and small unit raids served to prime the rangers for what was to become universally known as one of the most daring raids in U.S. military history.

On 30 January 1945 in the Cabanatuan raid—led in person by Colonel Mucci—C Company, supported by a platoon from F Company, struck 30 miles behind Japanese lines to rescue some 500 emaciated and sickly prisoners of war, many of them survivors of the Bataan Death March. The rangers, aided by Filipino guerrillas, killed over 200 members of the Japanese garrison, evaded two Japanese regiments, and reached the safety of American lines the following day. Intelligence reports had indicated the Japanese were planning to kill the prisoners as they withdrew toward Manila. Effective reconnaissance work by Filipino scouts contributed to the success of the raid.

Later commanded by Colonel Robert Garrett, the 6th Battalion played an important role in the capture of Manila and Appari. At the end of the war, it was preparing to take part in the invasion of Japan. The unit received the Presidential Unit Citation and the Philippine Presidential Citation. It was inactivated on 30 December 1945, in Kyoto, Japan. It and other elite units from the World War II era gave rise to the special forces of today's military establishments.

David Westwood

See also

Airborne Forces, Allied; Airborne Forces, Axis; Ardennes Offensive; Churchill, Sir Winston L. S.; Cockleshell Heroes; Commando Order; Dieppe Raid; Makin Island Raid; Marshall, George Catlett; Merrill, Frank Dow; Myitkyina, Siege of; Normandy Invasion and Campaign; Philippines, U.S. Recapture of; Rhine Crossings; Roosevelt, Franklin D.; Sicily, Invasion of; Truscott, Lucian King, Jr.

References

Durnford-Slater, John. *Commando.* London: Greenhill Books, 2002.
Lane, Ronald L. *Rudder's Rangers.* Manassas, VA: Ranger Associates, 1979.

Commerce Raiders, Surface, German

Germany entered World War II with a navy ill equipped for waging war against a major naval power. The head of the German navy, Grand Admiral Erich Raeder, supported by Adolf Hitler, had planned to build a powerful surface fleet of capital ships to challenge Britain and the United States for world naval mastery. War came too early for this "Z Plan," however.

When the war began in September 1939, Raeder recognized that his navy was inadequate for the task ahead, stating that it "would be able to do little more than show that it could die courageously." Lacking the ability to challenge the British and French in a general engagement, the German navy fell back on the experience of World War I as Raeder sought to wage a war to destroy British commerce. He recognized that surface raiders patrolling the oceans and sinking ships in an irregular manner could in no way serve as a distant blockade of Great Britain. Instead, he hoped that they would force the dispersion of Allied naval forces from more important theaters and wear down a large part of the Allied naval strength through the need to escort convoys and form task groups to hunt down elusive raiders.

Raeder had sent the pocket battleships *Deutschland* and *Admiral Graf Spee* to sea in mid-August 1939. However, valuable time was lost, as Hitler's reluctance to make the first hostile move against Britain meant that the ships were not authorized to begin operations until 26 September. The two German capital ships initially met Raeder's expectations, sinking numerous merchant ships and by October forcing the Allies to employ a force of 3 carriers, 3 battleships, and 15 cruisers in task groups to hunt for—or to provide strengthened convoy escorts against—these two German ships. The threat did not last long, however, because Germany's strategic position prior to June 1940 precluded easy transit and resupply of the ships. In November 1939, the *Deutschland* returned to Germany, and the *Graf Spee* met its demise in the Río de la Plata in South America in December 1939.

The loss of the scuttled *Graf Spee,* major surface ship losses suffered in the April 1940 Norway Campaign, and the sinking of battleship *Bismarck* in May 1941 all led Hitler to place restrictions on the use of his capital ships, so that by 1943, they rarely ventured to sea.

Beginning in 1940, the Germans relied on another type of ship, the armed merchant cruiser (AMC), for commerce raiding. They eventually fielded nine AMCs, known in German as *Hilfskreuzers.* Made to look innocuous, the AMCs were capable of rapidly changing their profile to confuse prey and hunter alike; in essence, they were stealth ships. Freighters best served this purpose, as they possessed the holds needed to store supplies for long cruises and could mount 6 × 150-cm guns.

From 1940 through early 1943, a total of nine armed merchant raiders operated at sea, mainly in distant waters where many unescorted merchant vessels belonging to the Allies were still to be found. The German AMCs initially proved elusive, and by the end of 1940, they had sunk 54 Allied vessels totaling 366,644 tons; they also forced the British to devote a larger portion of their naval assets to the effort to hunt them down. However, as the war dragged on, Allied intercepts of German radio communications led to the sinking of four of the AMCs as well as some of their supply ships. The other five AMCs reached German-controlled ports but could not slip back out through the Allied blockade.

The German AMCs sank 846,321 tons of shipping, a major return for what was, after all, a relatively minor investment. This figure represented 7.5 percent of all the tonnage sunk by Germany in the war. The impact of the AMCs cannot be quantified by this statistic alone, however. These nine ships also disrupted shipping timetables, forced longer voyages, and delayed the arrival of desperately needed Allied war matériel. The capture of the British cargo ship *Automoden* by the AMC *Atlantis,* with the seizure of important British government papers, dealt a serious blow to Britain's position in the Far East.

A voyage that might normally have taken only two weeks may have extended into months because of a raider's activities. Beyond that, the secondary and tertiary effects, combined with the efforts to eliminate the AMCs, produced results well out of proportion to the time, money, and manpower that Germany put into the program. However, as in World War I, the German navy could not take advantage of their impact, and by the spring of 1943, no more AMCs were at sea.

C. J. Horn

See also
Atlantic, Battle of the; *Automedon,* Sinking of; Dönitz, Karl; Hitler, Adolf; Plata, Río de la, Battle of; Raeder, Erich; Z Plan

References
Bekker, Cajus. *Hitler's Naval War.* New York: Zebra Books, 1974.
Mohr, Ulrich, and A. V. Sellwood. *Sea Raider Atlantis.* Los Angeles, CA: Pinnacle Books, 1955.
Muggenthaler, August Karl. *German Raiders of World War II.* Englewood Cliffs, NJ: Prentice-Hall, 1977.

Commissar Order (13 May 1941)

Order issued to the German army by Adolf Hitler on 6 June 1941, two weeks before the start of Operation BARBAROSSA, the German invasion of the Soviet Union. In early March 1941, Hitler addressed his generals and informed them of what would later be known as the "Commissar Order." It called on the German military to execute any captured Soviet commissars, the Communist Party officials assigned to military units. This order contravened all international conventions governing the treatment of prisoners of war. In remarks to his commanders, Hitler justified his order on the grounds that the commissars were "the bearers of ideologies directly opposed to National Socialism." He also said that German soldiers guilty of breaking international law would be "excused." Although Field Marshal Erich von Manstein and some other German generals refused to obey the order, it was widely carried out.

Craig S. Hamilton

See also
BARBAROSSA, Operation; Commando Order; Hitler, Adolf; International Military Tribunal: The Nuremberg Trials; Manstein, Fritz Erich von

References
Bartov, Omer. *The Eastern Front, 1941–1945: German Troops and the Barbarisation of Warfare.* New York: St. Martin's Press, 1986.
Cecil, Robert. *Hitler's Decision to Invade Russia, 1941.* New York: David McKay, 1975.
Koch, H. W. *Aspects of the Third Reich.* New York: St. Martin's Press, 1985.
Shirer, William. *The Rise and Fall of the Third Reich.* New York: Simon and Schuster, 1960.

Committee to Defend America by Aiding the Allies (1940–1941)

The most prominent pro-Allied lobbying organization in the United States prior to American intervention in World War II. Established in May 1940 at the prompting of President Franklin D. Roosevelt, the Committee to Defend

America (CDA) was a private organization dedicated to assisting Britain and France by providing American support, both moral and material. The committee developed from an earlier 1939 lobbying group that had helped to bring about changes in American neutrality legislation permitting Allied purchases in the United States. Headed by William Allen White, a prominent Kansas journalist, the CDA's organizing committee included Clark Eichelberger and Frank Boudreau, Thomas W. Lamont, and Frederic R. Coudert. White requested 650 prominent Americans to join and form local committee chapters, and eventually, around 600 such groups existed nationwide, their estimated membership totaling between 6,000 and 20,000 people.

Some CDA members favored outright intervention in the war, but publicly, the organization sought only to aid the Allies, short of going to war—a circumspect stance that was made particularly politic in the bitterly fought 1940 presidential election, in which foreign affairs and peace were major issues. As interventionists became more prominent within the organization, White resigned in January 1941, and in November, Eichelberger succeeded him.

Supposedly "one step ahead" of the Roosevelt administration, CDA leaders worked closely with pro-Allied officials, including Roosevelt, Secretary of War Henry Lewis Stimson, and Secretary of the Navy Frank Knox. Indeed, measures that CDA representatives proposed to the government—for example, increased American naval protection for convoys bound for Britain, enhanced material aid, and extended wartime protective zones—often originated within the administration. These tactics enabled the government to claim it was responding to popular pressure. CDA officials also rallied popular and congressional support for government initiatives, including the 1940 destroyers-for-bases deal with Britain, the introduction of Selective Service conscription, and 1941 Lend-Lease legislation. By mid-1941, with the election past, Roosevelt increasingly took executive action on foreign issues, which decreased the CDA's significance. After Pearl Harbor, the CDA disbanded. Eichelberger and other CDA activists subsequently campaigned prominently for the creation of the United Nations.

Priscilla Roberts

See also
Destroyers-Bases Deal; Fight for Freedom; Lend-Lease; Roosevelt, Franklin D.; Selective Service Act; Stimson, Henry Lewis
References
Johnson, Walter. *The Battle against Isolation.* Chicago: University of Chicago Press, 1944.
Namikas, Lise. "The Committee to Defend America and the Debate between Internationalists and Interventionists, 1939–1941." *The Historian* 61, no. 4 (Summer 1999): 843–864.

COMPASS, Operation (7 December 1940– 7 February 1941)

British campaign against Italian forces in North Africa. On 13 September 1940, three months after Italy entered World War II, Italian dictator Benito Mussolini ordered the commander of Italian forces in Libya, Marshal Rodolfo Graziani, to invade Egypt with General Mario Berti's Tenth Army. Graziani's nine ill-equipped divisions of 250,000 men vastly outnumbered the 36,000 British, New Zealand, and Indian troops of Lieutenant General Richard O'Connor's Western Desert Force (WDF) in Egypt. But Graziani made no attempt to advance after crossing the Egyptian-Libyan border and instead settled in a chain of fortified camps around Sidi Barrani. The British commander in chief, General Archibald Wavell, therefore conceived a plan to throw Graziani off balance while he dealt with the Italians in East Africa. Because of a shortage of transport in particular, Wavell envisaged not a sustained offensive but a swift, large-scale raid lasting no more than five days.

Operation COMPASS began on 7 December with a two-day, 70-mile march by British forces across the desert. After passing through a gap between the Italian camps, Major General Noel Beresford-Peirse's 4th Indian Division stormed Nibeiwa camp from the rear, with 50 Matilda infantry tanks of the 7th Royal Tank Regiment at the spearhead. The British surprised the Italian garrison and took 4,000 prisoners, almost without loss.

British forces also stormed Tummar East and West camps that same day, and overran the camps around Sidi Barrani the next day. On the third day, Major General Michael Creagh's 7th Armoured Division—the famous Desert Rats—swept westward to the coast beyond Buq Buq and cut the Italian line of retreat. In three days, the British captured 40,000 Italian troops and 400 guns; the remnants of the Italian army took refuge in Bardia, the first town inside Libya, and were rapidly surrounded.

These astonishing results were unforeseen and caused immense problems. The Indian 4th Division was recalled for dispatch to Sudan, as previously planned, leading to the unusual spectacle of British troops withdrawing eastward just as the Italians fled west. The Australian 6th Division, commanded by Major General Iven Mackay, was transferred from Palestine, but the shortage of trucks and the need to feed and evacuate huge numbers of prisoners led to a three-week delay before the operation could be resumed. The ingenious development of field supply dumps in the desert alleviated the problems of transporting supplies across long distances, but the operation's success was only possible because of the capture of large numbers of Italian trucks.

Generale di Corpo (U.S. equiv. lieutenant general) d'Armata Annibale "Electric Whiskers" Bergonzoli signaled to

Mussolini, "In Bardia we are and here we stay." The Australian infantry, supported by British battleship gunfire support, began the assault on 3 January 1941. After three days, the Italian garrison of 45,000 men surrendered, with 462 guns and 129 tanks. The Matilda tanks, which were almost invulnerable to the Italian guns, were again the key to the rapid success, and the Australian commander claimed that each tank was worth an entire infantry battalion.

Even before the fighting concluded, 7th Armoured Division drove west to encircle and isolate Tobruk, which was attacked on 21 January. Although just 16 of the precious Matildas were still running, they once again made the vital penetration, and the fortress fell the next day, yielding 30,000 Italian prisoners, 236 guns, and 87 tanks.

Tobruk's large port allowed supplies to be delivered by sea direct from Alexandria, and O'Connor intended to allow XIII Corps, as the WDF was known from 1 January 1941, to recuperate. On 3 February, however, intelligence revealed that the Italians were preparing to abandon Cyrenaica and withdraw beyond the El Algheila bottleneck. O'Connor immediately planned a daring initiative and sent his depleted tanks from Mechili across almost 100 miles of the roughest country in North Africa in just 33 hours to cut off the fleeing Italians at Beda Fomm late on 5 February. In a fitting climax, the miniscule British force of no more than 3,000 men and 39 Cruiser tanks held off Italian attempts to break out until the morning of 7 February when, completely demoralized, 20,000 Italians surrendered, with 216 guns and 120 tanks.

In a scant 10 weeks, the Commonwealth force of two divisions advanced more than 700 miles and captured 130,000 Italian prisoners, more than 380 tanks, 845 guns, and well over 3,000 vehicles at the relatively slight cost of 500 killed, 1,373 wounded, and 55 missing. O'Connor far exceeded all expectations, but he was confident that he could continue his advance to Tripoli and completely clear Africa of all Italian forces. Historians have since argued that a golden opportunity to finish the war in Africa was wasted, but recent research has shown that, without an operational port at Benghazi to maintain an advance, supply difficulties would have proven impossible. Nevertheless, British Prime Minister Winston L. S. Churchill had already directed Wavell to halt the advance at Benghazi in favor of the campaign in Greece and leave only a minimum force to hold Cyrenaica against the recently arrived German general Erwin Rommel.

Paul H. Collier

See also
Churchill, Sir Winston L. S.; Egypt; Graziani, Rodolfo; Mussolini, Benito; North Africa Campaign; O'Connor, Richard Nugent; Rommel, Erwin Johannes Eugen; Wavell, Sir Archibald Percival

References
Baynes, John. *The Forgotten Victor: General Sir Richard O'Connor.* London: Brassey's, 1989.
Collier, Paul. "The Capture of Tripoli in 1941: 'Open Sesame' or Tactical Folly?" *War and Society* 20, no. 1 (May 2002): 81–97.
Pitt, Barrie. *The Crucible of War: Western Desert, 1941.* London: Jonathan Cape, 1980.

Concentration Camps, German (1933–1945)

Concentration camps are most often associated with Nazi Germany, but the modern concentration camp is generally thought to have originated with Spanish General Valeriano Weyler y Nicolau in 1896 during the Cuban insurrection against Spain. Weyler sought to concentrate the civilian population near army installations, isolating these *reconcentrados* from the guerrillas. In Cuba at that time—and also in the Philippines during the 1899–1902 Philippine-American War and in South Africa during the 1899–1902 Boer War—large numbers of civilians died in such camps as a consequence of overcrowding, disease, and inadequate supplies.

During World War II, Germany established a number of different types of concentration camps. They may be grouped as penal, transit, labor, or extermination centers. Most served more than one purpose; that is, they were typically both penal and labor. But all of the camps saw brutality and merciless loss of life, whether as the result of disease, starvation, torture, exposure to the elements, forced labor, medical experiments, or outright execution. All major camps had subcamps that were sources of slave labor. Collectively, the camps numbered in the thousands.

The Nazis opened their first concentration camp at Dachau, near Munich, in March 1933, only two months after Adolf Hitler came to power. This camp was the model for the many others to follow. It operated continuously until April 1945, when the U.S. Army liberated the inmates. Originally intended for the temporary detention of political prisoners, the camps became permanent institutions manned by the Schutzstaffel (SS) Totenkopfverbande (Death's Head detachments). In these camps, the more sadistic guards, of whom there was no shortage in the SS, were more or less free to inflict indescribable cruelties on the inmates without fear of disciplinary action. The camp system gradually evolved from penal camps to the infamous death mills of Auschwitz, Belzec, Chelmno, Maidanek, Sobibor, and Treblinka.

At first, the camps housed political enemies. Foremost

were Communists and Social Democrats. Jews were initially targeted insofar as they belonged to these other groups, but they were considered "spoilers of German blood" and quickly became the primary victims. In time, Gypsies, Jehovah's Witnesses, homosexuals, and the mentally ill all fell prey to the Nazis and their collaborators. By 1939, seven large camps existed, with numerous subcamps. These seven large camps were Dachau, Sachsenhausen, Buchenwald, Neuengamme, Flossenbürg, Mauthausen, and Ravensbrück. As the war spread, forced labor became more and more a part of war production, and prisoner exploitation expanded. In the end, the camps stretched from the Pyrenees to eastern Europe, and literally millions of people had perished in then. Some camps, notably Drancy in France and Westerbork in the Netherlands, were primarily transit facilities, where Jews were herded together for onward shipment via railroad to the dreadful death mills.

No one will ever know just how much the people in the surrounding communities knew about the internal workings of the camps, but the Nazis had accomplices wherever camps existed. There were penal, work, or transit camps in all countries occupied by or allied with Germany. In western and eastern Europe, including the Baltic states, indigenous troops augmented the SS in the camps. In southern Europe, local forces operated their own camps or executed their victims rather than ship them to the death mills of eastern Europe. One glaring case was the Jasenovac camp operated by the Nazi puppet of Croatia. There, the Croatian Fascists, the Ustaše, killed tens of thousands of Serbs, Jews, Gypsies, and political enemies.

All the camps were very much alike. In them, the guards did whatever they could to strip every bit of human dignity from the inmates. Those who could do so were forced to work at hard manual labor 11 to 12 hours a day. Those who could not were encouraged to die. The sign over the camp gate reading *Arbeit macht Frei* (work brings freedom) meant the work of slave labor and freedom only in the release of death.

On arrival at a concentration camp, men and women were segregated and taken off for "medical inspection." There, they were forced to strip naked and were deloused. Heads were shorn, the hair retained to use for manufacturing mattresses and upholstering furniture. Following a cursory medical inspection, those pronounced fit to work were given clothes, had numbers tattooed on their arms, and were assigned to barracks where they would exist until they became too weak to work any longer. Those judged unfit to work were taken off in another direction to be executed.

For those who passed the medical inspection, life in the camp was defined by deliberate degradation, with every effort expended to break them physically, mentally, and morally. Barracks were so overcrowded that there often was not enough room for everyone to lie down at once. Buckets were frequently the only sanitary facilities provided, and there were never enough of these. Barracks were unheated, and in many, there was no cover provided, even in winter.

At dawn each morning, men and women lined up in front of their respective barracks for roll call, standing in their thin rags even in winter. This dreaded *zahlappell* (roll call) occurred at 3:00 A.M. and was repeated 5:00 P.M. It lasted for hours each time, until the guards could make an official and complete count. Every form of disease was present in the camps, with little or no medical treatment provided. Nourishment was totally inadequate. Breakfast usually consisted of a cup of ersatz coffee and a small portion of stale or moldy bread. Lunch was typically a cup of poorly fortified soup. And dinner routinely consisted of a small serving of bread, perhaps some potatoes or cabbage, and putrid tea.

Punishment in the camps was frequent and brutal, and it often occurred without justification: it had to be especially horrific if it was to exceed the brutality of daily life in the camps. Regulations in some camps required that beating with an axe handle was to be restricted to 25 blows at a time and that a week had to pass before a second beating could be given, but the guards seem not to have paid much attention to such rules. Often, the inmates were assembled to witness punishments and executions, and prisoners were sometimes placed in solitary confinement in total darkness in cells where they could neither stand nor sit nor lie for days or weeks. At Buchenwald, Belsen, and elsewhere, medical experiments were carried out on unwilling victims, who, if they survived, were often maimed for life. Such experiments investigated, among other things, the effects of rapid compression and decompression, how much cold and exposure a person could stand before he died, and how best to revive a victim of freezing.

A number of German industries—such as I. G. Farben, the giant chemical firm that also manufactured the Zyklon B gas employed in the death camps—were attracted to Auschwitz and other camps with the promise of cheap slave labor. At Auschwitz, I. G. Farben built an enormous factory to process synthetic oil and rubber in order to take advantage of the slave labor available. This facility was the largest plant in the entire I. G. system, and it was built largely by slave labor. Work was physically exhausting, and beatings for any breach of the rules were common. I.G. claimed it provided a "special diet" for its workers, which nonetheless resulted in a weight loss of six to nine pounds a week for the prisoners. Death usually came after three months. As an I. G. physician's report noted, "The prisoners were condemned to burn up their own body weight while working and, providing no infection occurred, finally died of exhaustion." Slave labor

Inmates of the Ampfing concentration camp in Germany liberated by U.S. Third Army Signal Corps. (U.S. Army, Library of Congress)

became a consumable raw material. At least 25,000 people were worked to death at I. G. Auschwitz.

All inmates had to wear insignia (colored triangles) revealing the reason for their incarceration. There were variations, but typically, Jews wore two superimposed triangles that formed a yellow star. Common criminals wore green. Political prisoners had red. Persons considered asocial (e.g., Gypsies and vagrants) wore black. Homosexuals wore pink and Jehovah's Witnesses purple.

Prisoners had to observe a definite hierarchy of prisoner officials, as well as the SS guards. The average prisoner had to answer to fellow prisoners at work or in the barracks. The most despised fellow prisoner was the Kapo, typically a heavy-handed supervisor willing to beat prisoners for the slightest infraction. The prisoners' work assignments and records were in the hands of other prisoners known as scribes and elders. These prisoner officials could make an inmate's life miserable—or even end it. Likewise, they could make life somewhat easier, and it often behooved ordinary prisoners to make note of this situation. Prisoner officials received better treatment in exchange for their cooperation. But comforts were rare indeed for the victims of this brutal process. The Nazi concentration camp system took the lives of millions and was the principal instrument of the Holocaust.

Dewey A. Browder

See also

Allied Military Tribunals after the War; Croatia; Eichmann, Karl Adolf; France, Vichy; Germany, Home Front; Heydrich, Reinhard Tristan Eugen; Himmler, Heinrich; Hitler, Adolf; Holocaust, The; International Military Tribunal: The Nuremberg Trials; Jewish Resistance; Latvia; Lithuania; Poland, Role in War; Prisoners of War; Wannsee Conference

References

Bauer, Yehuda. *A History of the Holocaust.* New York: Franklin Watts, 1982.

Sofsky, Wolfgang. *The Order of Terror: The Concentration Camp.* Trans. William Templer. Princeton, NJ: Princeton University Press, 1997.

U.S. Holocaust Memorial Museum. *Historical Atlas of the Holocaust.* New York: Macmillan, 1996.

Coningham, Sir Arthur "Mary" (1895–1948)

Royal Air Force (RAF) air marshal and pioneer in the use of tactical air support. Born in Brisbane, Australia, on 19 January 1895, Arthur Coningham served in the New Zealand army in World War I until discharged for health reasons in April 1916. He then joined the British Royal Flying Corps and became a pilot, acquiring the nickname of "Mary," de-

rived from "Maori." Following the war, Coningham remained in the newly formed Royal Air Force. He served in both Iraq and Egypt and taught at the RAF college, among other assignments.

At the beginning of World War II, Coningham was promoted to air commodore and given command of Number 4 Group, composed of long-range night-bombers based in Yorkshire. Coningham was convinced of the necessity of close-air support, which he was able to demonstrate on his promotion in July 1941 to air vice marshal and assignment to North Africa as commander of the Western Desert Air Force. There, he became one of the pioneers of tactical air support, which his units provided for the British Eighth Army on the ground. Coningham improved coordination between air and ground forces, and his aircraft played an important role in the British victory in the Battle of El Alamein (October–November 1942).

Coningham had charge of air support in other key Allied operations. He commanded the First Tactical Air Force during the invasion of Sicily (July–August 1943) and subsequent action in Italy. Transferred to command of Second Tactical Air Force in January 1944, he worked to plan air support for the Normandy Invasion that June. During the invasion itself and continuing until the end of the war in Europe, he earned high praise from Allied ground commanders.

At the end of the war, Coningham commanded the RAF Flying Training Centre. Knighted and promoted to full air marshal in 1946, he nonetheless was forced to retire in August 1947, having had little service with the air staff: he had spent his entire career as an active pilot. Coningham died on 30 January 1948 in a passenger plane crash in the Atlantic Ocean.

Harold Wise

See also

Aviation, Ground-Attack; El Alamein, Battle of; Great Britain, Air Force; Normandy Invasion and Campaign; Sicily, Invasion of; Tedder, Sir Arthur William

References

Orange, Vincent. *Coningham: A Biography of Air Marshal Sir Arthur Coningham.* Washington, DC: Center for Air Force History, 1992.

Richards, Denis, and Hilary S. Saunders. *Royal Air Force, 1939–1945: Official History.* 3 vols. London: Her Majesty's Stationery Office, 1953–1954.

Terraine, John. *A Time for Courage: The Royal Air Force in the European War, 1939–1945.* New York: Macmillan, 1985.

Conolly, Richard Lansing (1892–1962)

U.S. Navy admiral who commanded forces in almost all of the largest amphibious operations of the war. Born in Waukegan, Illinois, on 26 April 1892, Richard Conolly was commissioned in the navy on his graduation from the U.S. Naval Academy in 1914. He served in destroyers in the Atlantic, winning the Navy Cross for his part in rescuing a transport vessel damaged by a German submarine attack. Between the wars, Conolly earned a master of science degree at Columbia University, served as an instructor at the Naval Academy, and captained several destroyers.

From 1939 to 1942, Conolly served in the Pacific Theater, successively commanding 6th and 7th Destroyer Squadrons and providing the destroyer screen for the April 1942 raid on Tokyo. Promoted to rear admiral in July 1942, he spent several months on the staff of the chief of naval operations and commander in chief of the U.S. Fleet, Admiral Ernest J. King.

From March to October 1943, Conolly served with the Atlantic Fleet Amphibious Force and took part in the invasions of Sicily, where he earned the nickname "Close-in Conolly" for the naval fire support his ships provided the ground forces. That September, he commanded the amphibious component that landed the British 46th Division at Salerno, Italy. Again, he used his destroyers and cruisers to provide close gunfire support.

Conolly then transferred to the Pacific, using his amphibious landing expertise in operations at Kwajalein, Wake, and Marcus Islands. In 1944 and 1945, he commanded Group 3 of the Pacific Fleet Amphibious Force, leading the July 1944 landing on Guam and the January 1945 landing on Lingayen Gulf (Leyte), and Okinawa. He participated in six of the seven largest amphibious operations of World War II, missing only Normandy.

Conolly was the U.S. naval representative at the 1946 Paris Peace Conference. Promoted to full admiral, he subsequently commanded the Twelfth Fleet for four months and then U.S. Naval Forces, Eastern Atlantic and Mediterranean Fleet from 1947 to 1950. He then spent three years at Newport, Rhode Island, as president of the Naval War College. Conolly retired in November 1953 to become president of Long Island University, where he remained until he and his wife died in a commercial air crash at La Guardia Airport in New York, on 1 March 1962.

Priscilla Roberts

See also

Guam, Battle for; King, Ernest Joseph; Kwajalein, Battle for; Leyte, Landings on and Capture of; Okinawa, Invasion of; Sicily, Invasion of; Tokyo, Bombing of (1942)

References

Barbey, Daniel E. *MacArthur's Amphibious Navy: Seventh Amphibious Force Operations, 1943–45.* Annapolis, MD: Naval Institute Press, 1969.

Hoyt, Edwin P. *How They Won the War in the Pacific: Nimitz and His Admirals.* New York: Weybright and Talley, 1970.

Morison, Samuel Eliot. *History of United States Naval Operations in World War II.* Vol. 7, *Aleutians, Gilberts and Marshalls, June 1942–April 1944.* Boston: Little, Brown, 1951.

———. *History of United States Naval Operations in World War II.* Vol. 8, *New Guinea and the Marianas, March 1944–August 1944.* Boston: Little, Brown, 1953.

Conscientious Objector (CO)

An individual who seeks exemption from military service based on matters of conscience; in this regard, the conscientious objector (CO) differs from the "draft dodger." The first COs were members of small Protestant religious denominations, notably the Mennonites. Although their members were not forced to bear arms, even by Germany and Russia, such groups were generally taxed or required to perform alternative service. During World War I, a number of the democratic nations made provisions for conscientious objection. In Britain, preference was accorded on religious grounds, but CO status was also extended to those who opposed the war on political and ethical grounds. This generous government view was, however, often tempered by local boards, which chose to interpret the law more narrowly.

Perhaps surprisingly, given the rampant pacifism of the 1920s that followed the great bloodletting of World War I, COs were too few in number in World War II to have any impact on the war effort of their respective countries. The Axis states refused to recognize CO status, as did the Soviet Union and many others of the warring states.

Conscientious objector status was most honored in North America, Australia, New Zealand, the United Kingdom, the Netherlands, and the Scandinavian states. In the United Kingdom during World War II, CO status was granted on a more fair basis than it had been in World War I. Unconditional exemptions were granted to 6.1 percent of COs there, and alternate service was allowed in civilian jobs. Fewer than 10 percent of British COs were jailed, compared to 33 percent in World War I. The United Kingdom had 60,000 COs, or 1.2 percent of the number drafted, compared with 0.125 percent in World War I.

The United States also widened its interpretation of CO status in World War II. At the time Congress was about to vote on the Selective Service Act in 1940, there was uncertainty about how the draft would treat men who wanted to be exempted from military service on grounds of conscientious objection. A third of all Americans had indicated in polls that they favored either jailing COs or forcing them to fight in combat units, but Congress instead adopted a plan conceived by religious groups and known as Civilian Public Service (CPS).

The exact details of the CPS program were not worked out until early 1942, but it put COs to work on a variety of domestic tasks. Representatives of the Society of Friends (Quakers), the Brethren, and the Mennonites supervised those in CPS, and the costs of the program were paid by these three church organizations at the rate of $35 per month for each CO. CPS members sometimes received a few dollars a month for expenses from church groups but were otherwise not paid. Those seeking to obtain CO status had to file a special document, Form 47, along with their draft information. Local draft boards could and often did reject these requests, but an appeals procedure existed for such cases.

In all, about 37,000 American men obtained CO status. Most were Quakers, Mennonites, and Brethren. There were also Jehovah's Witnesses, socialists, communists, and others who professed pacifism. An additional 6,000 men who either did not receive CO status or turned it down were prosecuted for refusing to be inducted into the military and served some time in prison.

In many parts of the country, COs took up tasks that previously were assigned to members of the New Deal's Civilian Conservation Corps, such as reforestation, road building, and repairing drought damage. Other COs performed excellent service in mental hospitals. A few volunteered as guinea pigs for medical research, and some valuable advances in battling malaria and other tropical diseases came from these experiments. Although Major General Louis Hershey, head of the Selective Service, testified before Congress that, overall, COs were making valuable contributions in the nation, they generally were not welcome in most localities.

Some COs did enter the military and served overseas in noncombat roles, including the dangerous job of combat medic. Among them was Desmond Doss, a CO who declined a chance to be in the CPS program and entered the U.S. Army as a medic. Private First Class Doss landed on Okinawa with the 77th Infantry Division. There, on 2 May 1945, he pulled as many as 70 wounded soldiers off an escarpment while under heavy fire, for which he was awarded the Medal of Honor.

After the war ended, COs returned to civilian life, and their wartime status was generally forgotten. The CPS program, however, served as the model for subsequent objector programs during the Korean and Vietnam conflicts.

Terry Shoptaugh and Spencer C. Tucker

See also
Hershey, Louis Blaine; Okinawa, Battle of; United States, Home Front

References
Eller, Cynthia. *Conscientious Objectors and the Second World War.* New York: Praeger, 1991.
Gara, Larry, and Lenna Mae Gara. *A Few Small Candles: War Resisters of World War II Tell Their Stories.* Kent, OH: Kent State University Press, 1999.

Conscript Labor

The practice of forcing captive people to provide labor was widespread during World War II. The Axis powers utilized forced labor on a scale that dwarfed in size and severity that employed by the Allies. German practices and policies are the most extensively documented. Ironically, early in the war, Germany complained forcefully about Soviet labor practices regarding prisoners of war (POWs). Among other things, Moscow was accused of not adhering to the 1929 Geneva Convention, an accord that detailed the requirements for fair and humane treatment of war prisoners. No doubt, the Soviets were guilty of brutal and exploitative behavior early in the war; that was certainly the case later. However and with further irony, Soviet armies at the time had been ordered formally to respect the convention, and Stalin's government had, through Sweden's good offices, requested that Germany do the same. Moreover, despite their protestations over Soviet policies, the Germans starved and worked to death millions of Soviet POWs after June 1941. In May 1944, a German government report indicated that of 5,160,000 POWs from the Soviet Union, only slightly more than 1 million survived. At the time, there were approximately 5 million conscripted foreign workers in Germany.

As war losses and production pressures grew, Germany increasingly turned to forced labor to address these problems. The Nazi occupation regime in Poland, under Schutzstaffel (SS) police official Hans Frank, provided the model for the rest of the Reich. Frank had virtually absolute powers, although his formal title was head of government and not head of state. Decrees and rules made Jews and all other Poles subject to arbitrary conscription for work.

Such policies were subsequently copied in the Baltic states and occupied Soviet territory. Masses of people were rounded up and sent to Germany as laborers, regardless of age or state of health. The indiscriminate approach quickly created new problems. By 1942, an estimated 100,000 such conscripts had been sent back home because they were too old or sick to be useful as labor. The trains used for this transport, as with the Jews in the Holocaust, diverted scant transportation assets from strictly military use.

The response by the regime in Berlin was to increase the comprehensiveness and severity of the conscription process. By the end of the war, the minimum age for laborers had been reduced to 10 years. As Germany began to suffer military reversals in the Soviet Union, pressures grew for additional manpower for the front, and this soon created direct competition with the military. In the autumn of 1942, SS Chief Heinrich Himmler reached an agreement with Minister of Justice Otto Thierack and Minister of Armaments Albert Speer whereby concentration camp inmates and prisoners of war would be released for factory work in return for allocation of an agreed percentage of their output of weapons to the SS. This agreement provided explicitly that any person identified by the Nazi regime as "antisocial" could be worked to death.

In March 1942, stricter and more detailed controls were added to the forced labor program. Fritz Sauckel was appointed plenipotentiary for the deployment of labor, with great power over German and foreign workers. The geographic reach of the program was extended, with forced conscription now used in western and southeastern Europe as well as in the east. In the Soviet Union, however, skilled workers tended to retreat with the Red Army forces rather than wait for the occupiers. In western Europe, existing factories were already supplying the German war effort.

German policies reflected not the implementation of any detailed plan but the increasing pressures of the war. By May 1943, Sauckel's sustained and brutal approach had yielded approximately 2 million additional foreign workers, and the total labor force employed in Germany had been increased by just under 2 million, despite growing military manpower pressures at the fighting fronts. Yet clearly, the expansion rate could not be maintained. By that time, Poland had been effectively drained of useful labor. Southeastern Europe had a large population, but a significant percentage of the people there were needed for existing agricultural industry, which was, in turn, vital to feeding the populations in Germany and the other occupied territories.

Such pressures only mounted over time. By 1943, Soviet military offensives had reduced the number of workers available to the Reich. Western European production facilities were becoming even more important as the Allied bombing effort took a toll on German factories. In desperation, German authorities began to bypass local governments and other established authorities in the drive to find laborers for the war production machinery. In a telling example, 1,000 French police in Marseille were forced into transport vans while they were out on a practice exercise. Yet there was never a truly comprehensive recruitment of available workers, as ideology vetoed some ready and skilled conscription, most notably the Jews. Still, all occupied states were required to send laborers to work in the Reich, often in horrific conditions. France alone sent 2.5 million of its citizens to work in Germany, and 200,000 did not return home after the war.

The Nazis initially failed to make use of one ready labor source—women. Nazi doctrine dictated that a woman's place was in the home, focused on reproduction. In 1942, despite extensive military engagements in the Soviet Union and North Africa, 189,000 fewer women were employed in the German workforce than in 1939. As early as 1942, Speer had recommended that women be recruited for industry,

but Adolf Hitler would have none of it. Not until 1943 were women between the ages of 17 and 45 required to register for work. Later, the upper age was raised to 50. By 1944, German women actually outnumbered men in the labor force.

Conscript workers ultimately provided a very large component of the overall German workforce during the war. The total by 1944 had reached approximately 7 million people. They accounted for roughly one-fifth of the entire workforce during World War II in Germany. As the needs of the war became more urgent and as military defeats grew, the German Reich policy of forced labor in occupied territories was overshadowed by the steadily more brutal repression, persecution, and extermination of European Jews. Ghettos, notably in Poland and Lithuania, were organized to segregate the Jewish population and also provide a structure of highly exploited labor. The populations were divided into relatively small groups, though often numbering more than 100 people, under the authority of a leader selected by the German occupiers.

In theory, the residents were to receive free board and lodging in exchange for work. In practice, people ranging from mere children to the elderly were worked to exhaustion, illness, and often death, in an environment in which ration cards were often not honored, shops frequently had no goods, and German authorities continued to steal from those whose homes and other possessions outside the ghetto had already been looted. Black markets grew, along with increasingly severe public health problems.

By 1942, the Nazi regime was totally committed to the "final solution"—the complete extermination of the Jews of Europe. The pace of genocide gathered momentum, centered in concentration camps built to accomplish that purpose. Only a minority of influential Germans argued, without success, the fundamental irrationality of depriving the Reich of labor, much of it highly skilled, at a time when shortages of manpower were growing ever more severe. In this sense, Hitler's genocide policy combined self-destructive irrationality with immorality on a massive scale.

Meanwhile, in the Pacific Theater, Japanese approaches to forced labor approximately reflected the harshness of Germany. The population of Korea, which had been a colony of Tokyo for a half century, endured particularly harsh treatment, broadly comparable to that experienced by Poland's people. Koreans were conscripted wholesale, the men for particularly grueling and unpleasant physical labor, the women often forced into prostitution for the Japanese military. In this particular case, Tokyo seems to have made special efforts to employ conscripted labor as a means to degrade a very old national opponent. In China and in Asia generally, Japan carried out brutal labor policies, along with widespread atrocities. Japanese behavior in China and elsewhere generally mirrored Nazi excesses throughout Europe, though unlike the Germans, the Japanese did not have a compulsion to provide detailed documentary records.

The treatment of prisoners of war raised distinctive issues. In theory, POWs were protected by specific provisions in the Geneva Convention of 1929. These provisions implemented the general declarations of the Hague Conventions of 1899 and 1907, as well as very long established customs, or at least intentions, of using restraint in dealing with military prisoners. Under the Geneva Convention, prisoners of war were to be removed promptly from the battle area and provided medical care. Also, the International Red Cross was to be permitted to inspect POW facilities. Officer prisoners were not to be employed as laborers, and noncommissioned officer prisoners were to handle only supervisory tasks.

The well-known Japanese rejection of the legitimacy of military surrender led to particularly harsh treatment of their captives—American as well as British and other European military and civilian personnel seized during the months of early Japanese ground successes in the Philippines, Malaya, and other places. Japan had not signed the Geneva Convention on the treatment of prisoners, and the fate of captives often depended on the attitudes and whims of local commanders. Japan's desperate need for manpower to use in construction and other tasks alleviated the harshness of treatment meted out to prisoners to some extent. The Japanese even established some minimum compensation for POW laborers, then took back a portion for postal savings accounts to finance their war effort. Prisoners removed to Japan often fared better than those elsewhere in the Pacific, receiving better food, greater security, and some positive contacts with the civilian population—if, that is, their unmarked "hell ships" were not sunk by Allied submarines en route to the Japanese home islands.

In Europe, the treatment of American and British prisoners of war generally was better than that accorded other nationalities in eastern Europe and their comrades in the Pacific, though conditions were still harsh. The fate of Soviet and other soldiers captured in the fighting on the Eastern Front often was simple summary execution. By one accepted estimate, more than 80 percent of Red Army troops captured under the Wehrmacht did not survive captivity. In contrast, there are documented examples of German officers endeavoring to treat their Western Front prisoners in a relatively humane manner, and consequently, these Allied POWs had a far higher rate of survival. Such contrasting fates directly reflected Nazi ideology, which held that Anglo-Saxons were Aryans whereas Slavic peoples were viewed as subhuman.

Yet this situation should not be overstated. Allied POWs taken on the Western Front in Europe were still used as laborers for especially gruesome tasks, including removing corpses. There are documented instances of Allied bomber crews being forced to bail out of crippled aircraft and then immediately murdered by outraged German soldiers and civilians on the ground (it should be noted this also happened on Malta to German and Italian aircrews). The same sentiments fueled a willingness to exploit American and other prisoners of war as forced laborers. Yet, at the same time, American officers in prison camps on more than one occasion expressed concern about undue fraternization with the German captors and warned the men under their command to keep their distance. Likewise, Allied officers in these camps regularly protested the treatment of prisoners, including the forced labor regimes.

The Allies made plans to deal with the problem of refugees, including forced laborers, after the war. In November 1943, representatives of 45 nations, the United States among them, established the United Nations Relief and Rehabilitation Administration (UNRRA) as the official agency to handle the situation. At the time, estimates of the likely number of refugees at the conclusion of the war ranged up to 21 million. After the German surrender in May 1945, a range of structures, including former concentration camps and military barracks, were used for a comprehensive relief effort that continued until 1947. On 1 July of that year, the Provisional Committee of the International Refugee Organization (IRO) took over responsibility from the UNRRA for approximately 700,000 people remaining in its care.

Following the war also, the newly formed United Nations gave sustained attention to defining and implementing standards for humane treatment of war prisoners and labor. This dimension of the work required directly reflected the horrific legacy of World War II.

Arthur I. Cyr

See also

Catholic Church and the War; Charities; Eichmann, Karl Adolf; Himmler, Heinrich; Holocaust, The; Prisoners of War; Religion and the War; Rosenberg, Alfred; Saukel, Fritz; Speer, Albert; Unit 731, Japanese Army

References

Astor, Gerald. *Crisis in the Pacific.* New York: Donald I. Fine Books, 1996.

Burleigh, Michael. *The Third Reich: A New History.* New York: Hill and Wang, 2000.

Foot, M. R. D. *Resistance: European Resistance to Nazism, 1940–45.* New York: McGraw-Hill, 1977.

Homze, Edward L. *Foreign Labor in Nazi Germany.* Princeton, NJ: Princeton University Press, 1967.

Jackson, Julian. *France: The Dark Years, 1940–1941.* New York: Oxford University Press, 2001.

Continuation War

See Finnish-Soviet War (25 June 1941–4 September 1944).

Convoy PQ 17 (27 June–7 July 1943)

Disastrous Allied Arctic convoy to Murmansk in the USSR. From August 1941 through May 1945, the Western Allies sent some 4 million tons of supplies to the northern Soviet Union via the Arctic. A total of 811 ships in convoy sailed east, of which 58 were sunk. A large percentage of these losses occurred in one convoy, PQ 17. It sailed from Iceland on 27 June 1942, with 36 merchantmen protected by 4 corvettes, 2 antiaircraft ships, and 4 antisubmarine trawlers. At the same time, eastbound Convoy QP 13, made up of 35 merchantmen, sailed from Kola Inlet. British Rear Admiral L. H. K. Hamilton commanded a covering force to protect both convoys, consisting of 2 British and 2 U.S. heavy cruisers, plus 1 British and 2 American destroyers. En route, British Commander J. E. Broome joined them with 6 destroyers to provide additional protection. Distant cover was provided by the Home Fleet under Admiral Sir John Tovey. He commanded a mixed British and U.S. force, consisting of 2 battleships, 1 aircraft carrier, 2 cruisers, and 14 destroyers.

Tovey was under strict orders to steer clear of the German airfields in northern Norway, where the Luftwaffe had massed 103 bombers, 42 torpedo-bombers, 20 dive-bombers, and 89 reconnaissance aircraft to block any convoy's passage. The Germans also had 10 U-boats on station, so their tactical reconnaissance advantage was formidable. The Allies hoped to trump this with strategic intelligence gleaned through ULTRA decrypts; however, a change in German Enigma cipher settings on 3 July led to an intelligence blackout. Political pressure from Washington and Moscow compelled leaders to insist that the convoy proceed, and it sailed blindly into a German trap.

The British first sea lord, Admiral of the Fleet Sir Dudley Pound, agonized over the choices of action available to him. He could not recall the convoy, and he would not allow the Home Fleet to close with it and risk an overwhelming German air and submarine attack. Allied intelligence also assumed that German navy surface units in Norway would attempt an attack. These forces consisted of the battleship *Tirpitz,* the pocket battleships *Scheer* and *Lützow,* the heavy cruiser *Hipper,* 10 fleet destroyers, and 2 oceangoing torpedo boats.

Even before PQ 17 sailed, Pound informed Tovey that if he believed a German surface attack was imminent, he would order the convoy to scatter. Tovey pointed out in no uncertain terms to Pound that this was contrary to all recent British experience. In any case, at 9:00 P.M. on 4 July, Pound, incorrectly assuming that the Germans' big ships were on their way to intercept the convoy and would reach it early the next day, began sending signals ordering PQ 17 to scatter and its cruisers and fleet destroyers to withdraw toward the Home Fleet, as they were too weak to face the German squadron that he believed to be at sea. Although scattering was the logical precaution when a convoy was under surface attack, it was a suicidal move when made against aircraft and submarines.

Of the 34 merchant ships still with the convoy when the order to scatter was given, only 13 reached Murmansk. The Allies had suffered one of their worst maritime defeats of the war, the tragedy of which was deepened by the fact that it need not have happened. Convoys to Murmansk were then suspended for the summer, as perpetual Arctic daylight and German strength made them untenable.

James Levy

See also

Convoys, Allied; Pound, Sir Alfred Dudley Pickman Rogers; Tovey, John Cronyn

References

Kemp, Peter. *Convoy! Drama in Arctic Waters.* London: Arms and Armour Press, 1993.

Roskill, S. W. *White Ensign: The British Navy at Way, 1939–1945.* Annapolis, MD: Naval Institute Press, 1960.

Woodman, Richard. *Arctic Convoys.* London: John Murray.

Convoys, Allied

Organized groups of merchant vessels escorted by warships to defend against Axis attack. As a result of its experience in the latter stages of World War I, Britain was quick to set up the convoying of merchant vessels at the beginning of World War II. There was some initial hesitation because of the feared detrimental effect convoys could have on the efficient employment of shipping, but that would change after the liner *Athena* was torpedoed and sunk on 3 September 1939, indicating that Germany had commenced an unrestricted campaign of submarine warfare against merchant vessels. The first convoy—eight tankers sailing from Gibraltar to the Persian Gulf via the Cape of Good Hope—actually departed on 2 September with a cruiser escort for fear of a possible Italian entry into the war. Regular east coast convoys between the Firth of Forth and the River Thames started on 6 September, as did outbound transatlantic convoys from Liverpool two days later.

Operational convoys were set up to cover the movement of merchant vessels chartered by the government to transport and supply the British Expeditionary Force (BEF) across the English Channel. Subsequent convoys carried troops to Norway and supported operations in North Africa, the Mediterranean, the Middle East, the Far East, and all the other theaters of operations.

A special category of convoys included the series that carried cargo and war materials to the Soviet Union and the smaller series that ran to resupply the island of Malta. These operations were unusual in that, in addition to the strong naval close escorts that normally covered convoys, they often also featured substantial distant cover by heavy units of the main fleet. Between August 1941 and May 1945, 42 convoys were undertaken to the northern USSR, and there were 36 return convoys. A total of 835 ships sailed outbound, losing 60 of their number; 710 returned, with a loss of 37 ships. The Malta convoys included a series of major fleet operations from both the eastern and western ends of the Mediterranean to assist the passage of supplies for the island. Between November 1940 and August 1942, 82 merchant ships took part in these convoys, of which 29 were sunk, and there were substantial losses among their naval escorts as well.

Trade convoys were required for regular commercial traffic on those passages most at risk of air or submarine attack. The initial series operated along the east coast, from London down the English Channel, and outbound from the west coast across the Atlantic and to Gibraltar. The east coast convoys and those to Gibraltar were escorted throughout their passage, whereas escorts accompanied those outbound into the Atlantic only until they were just beyond the expected operating area of German submarines. At that point, the convoy dispersed, each ship proceeding individually to its destination. Depending on their destination, some vessels might detach from an outbound convoy prior to its dispersal. Inbound convoys assembled at Halifax, Gibraltar, Freetown, and—for a short period—at Kingston, Jamaica. These convoys were escorted by cruiser or armed merchant cruisers until they reached the limit of U-boat operations, where antisubmarine escorts took over. A heavily escorted convoy series also operated between Scotland and Bergen, Norway, commencing in November 1939.

The end of the so-called Phony War in May 1940, with the invasion of France and the Low Countries, brought major changes to the convoy system. The German attack on

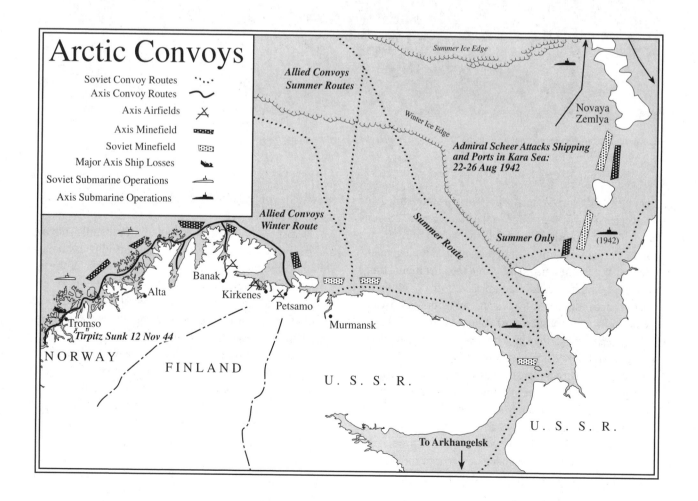

Convoy of Allied trucks moving through the ruins of Valognes, France, 1944. (Library of Congress)

Denmark and Norway in April 1940 abruptly ended the Norwegian convoys, and the collapse of France in June brought even more substantial changes. From French bases, German aircraft operated against shipping in the Channel and far into the Atlantic, and the operational range of the U-boats increased dramatically. Convoys along the Channel accommodated local traffic only, and all oceanic traffic from the east coast now sailed north around Scotland. A series of interlocking convoys running both clockwise and counterclockwise provided escort for all coastal shipping. To accommodate the need for more transatlantic convoys, a second series of slower convoys originating from Sydney, Cape Breton, Nova Scotia, was initiated. The increased threat of attack led to the provision of escort throughout the voyage for all convoys to and from Freetown. Finally, Italy's simultaneous entry into the war terminated all commercial traffic in the Mediterranean save

for very heavily escorted operational convoys to carry supplies into Malta.

The dispersal point for westbound transatlantic convoys and the pickup point for escort groups meeting eastbound shipping gradually moved westward as the range of the escorts was increased. In mid-1941, the United States imposed its "neutrality zone" on the western Atlantic and began escorting British convoys in conjunction with Royal Canadian Navy escorts, operating from Argentia in Newfoundland. North Atlantic convoys now were escorted throughout their passage by antisubmarine vessels.

The German declaration of war on the United States on 10 December 1941 brought a major westward expansion of U-boat operations against shipping. A disastrous period followed while the U.S. Navy struggled to secure the escorts and crews required to convoy the enormous volume of merchant traffic along the East Coast of the United States; it also struggled with the very concept of convoy itself. Nevertheless, by mid-1942, an elaborate and comprehensive system of interlocking convoy routes and sailings was established for the East Coast of North America and in the Caribbean. As the commander of German submarines Admiral Karl Dönitz became aware that the convoy system had been extended to a specific area, he shifted U-boat operations to another area where unescorted traffic still operated. Consequently, the scope of the U.S. Navy's convoy system gradually expanded to encompass almost all traffic between Rio de Janeiro and Halifax.

Landing operations in North Africa and the Mediterranean brought about some changes. Apart from the significant number of operational troop convoys, the opening of the Mediterranean introduced a series of convoy routes within that sea, and a British shortage of fuel oil also led to a series of fast tanker convoys between the Caribbean and the United Kingdom. In 1944, Allied military successes in France began to allow a gradual reduction in the scope of convoy. The reduction occurred because U-boats were forced to make more extended passages to their patrol areas as their home ports moved farther from the Atlantic and because German aircraft no longer had quick access to British coastal waters. All these trade convoys sailed at regular intervals, regardless of the number of ships waiting at the departure port. Changes in the interval or convoy cycle could be made but only after careful consideration of the impact on the efficiency of the limited escort force and on trade patterns.

Efficient use of both escorts and shipping required that the employment of convoy be extended or contracted in response to perceived threat levels. Because the U-boats' maximum surface speed was about 16 knots in ideal conditions and much less in the open ocean, ships capable of 15 knots or more sailed independently. Between November 1940 and June 1941, this minimum was lowered arbitrarily to 13 knots, and losses among vessels sailing independently almost tripled; the upper speed limit was then reinstated. For oceanic convoys, a minimum speed of 7.5 knots soon became the norm, with slower vessels obliged to proceed independently. Ships in coastal convoys, however, could be appreciably slower.

To make the danger zone as a convoy passed a submarine as small as possible, the standard convoy formation, except while transiting cleared channels through minefields, was always a broad front. The most common formation had from 6 to 12 columns in the convoy, each with up to 6 ships. Some of the very large convoys that ran during the spring of 1944, when a shortage of escorts forced planners to consolidate convoys, had as many as 19 columns with 9 or 10 ships each, but this was far in excess of the normal size. Ships in

each column steamed at 400-yard intervals until mid-1943, when the growing number of less experienced captains forced an increase to 600 or even 800 yards. Columns were initially spaced 600 yards apart during daylight and 1,000 yards apart at night, but scientific analysis determined that the wider spacing was preferable from a "hit statistic" perspective, and later convoys standardized on the broader spacing. Early in the war, smaller convoys of no more than 35 ships were considered easier to protect, but again, analysis demonstrated that larger convoys made more efficient use of available escorts, so the convoy size increased to 60 ships or more.

Convoy most certainly diminished the efficient use of shipping assets to some extent, and the simultaneous arrival of large numbers of vessels caused significant bottlenecks in the unloading process. Nevertheless, there can be no doubt as to the efficacy of convoy in protecting merchant vessels from attack during World War II, as the dramatic reduction of sinkings after the introduction of convoy on the East Coast of the United States demonstrated.

Paul E. Fontenoy

See also
Aircraft Carriers; Antisubmarine Warfare; Atlantic, Battle of the; Depth Charges; Dönitz, Karl; Germany, Air Force; Germany, Navy; Great Britain, Air Force; Great Britain, Navy; Hunter-Killer Groups; Leigh Light; Liberty Ships; Sonar; United States, Army Air Forces; United States, Coast Guard; United States, Navy; Walker, Frederick John; Wolf Pack

References
Grove, Eric J. *Defeat of the Enemy Attack on Shipping, 1939–1945.* London: Naval Records Society, 1998.
Hague, Arnold. *The Allied Convoy System, 1939–1945: Its Organization, Defence and Operation.* Annapolis, MD: Naval Institute Press, 2000.
Morison, Samuel Eliot. *History of United States Naval Operations in World War II.* Vol. 1, *The Battle of the Atlantic, 1939–1943.* Boston: Little, Brown, 1947.
———. *History of United States Naval Operations in World War II.* Vol. 10, *The Battle of the Atlantic Won, May 1943–May 1945.* Boston: Little, Brown, 1956.
Roskill, S. W. *The War at Sea.* 3 vols. London: Her Majesty's Stationery Office, 1956–1961.

Convoys, Axis

When war began in September 1939, Germany essentially abandoned any attempt to maintain its oceanic trade. Those vessels beyond easy reach of the homeland endeavored to reach neutral ports, where they were interned, and closer vessels broke for home, with the navy providing cover for those carrying important cargoes.

Norwegian and Swedish ore traffic was the most important sector in Germany's European trade, and securing it became the principal focus of the navy's trade protection efforts throughout the war. After the successful German invasion of Norway, the navy introduced the convoy of merchant shipping along the Norwegian coast late in 1940. Convoys generally were small—three to six ships—and escorted by a few torpedo boats, trawlers, and light craft. British submarines and aircraft were the principal threats. As the war progressed and British air attacks became more effective, the Germans added defensive coastal antiaircraft batteries and antiaircraft escorts. In addition to ever increasing strikes by shore-based Royal Air Force Coastal Command aircraft, the Royal Navy mounted periodic carrier strikes against German coastal shipping in 1942 and 1943, culminating over the next two years with more concentrated assaults using escort carriers that came close to paralyzing this traffic.

When war with the Soviet Union began, the Soviet navy's Northern Fleet submarines initiated attacks on German shipping around northern Norway and were soon joined by British submarines operating from Kola Bay. Joint operations continued until 1944, when the British crews were sent home and the submarines were turned over to the Soviet navy. Substantial numbers of Soviet naval aircraft also joined the attack against German convoys from 1943. This assault against the northern Norwegian convoys cost the Germans some 500,000 tons of shipping, a relatively small amount considering annual traffic was well in excess of 6 million tons.

War with the Soviet Union also brought the threat of attack on the Swedish ore traffic, primarily by Soviet submarines at first. The Germans endeavored to keep shipping within Swedish territorial waters as far as possible, escorting vessels for the final leg of their passage behind the protection of defensive minefields and net barriers. During 1942 and 1943, Soviet submarines succeeded in sinking only about 20 ships for a total of some 40,000 tons of shipping, out of over 1,900 vessels in convoy representing well over 5.6 million tons of shipping. During 1944, the Soviet army's advances and the defeat of Finland meant that aircraft played a greater role in antishipping operations, but German losses remained relatively light. The collapse of German positions on the Baltic coast early in 1945 required the evacuation by sea of more than 2 million troops and others. Despite some spectacular successes (the sinking of the *Wilhelm Gustloff* and *General Steuben* with but 1,200 survivors from the more than 9,000 passengers aboard, for example), Soviet attacks were remarkably ineffective; the Germans lost only about 20 ships with a total of some 100,000 tons of shipping.

The Italian navy began convoying traffic carrying supplies to its forces in Libya almost as soon as it entered the war, for British submarines and aircraft immediately began an interdiction campaign. The navy's responsibilities expanded as Italy undertook campaigns in Yugoslavia and Greece in 1941 and increased still further when Germany took on a larger role in the Balkans and North Africa. During 1941, Italy also began convoying shipping along the Libyan coast. Italian convoys generally were small—three to six merchant vessels, with two or three escorting destroyers or torpedo boats. As British surface forces operating from Malta began attacking Libya-bound shipping, the Italian navy had to deploy heavier covering forces, often including cruisers and eventually battleships, to support particularly valuable convoys. In this struggle over shipping, the British possessed two great advantages: radar, which vastly enhanced the night-attack capabilities of its aircraft and surface ships, and signals intelligence, especially ULTRA, which consistently gave them advance convoy routing information.

Axis fortunes in this campaign fluctuated greatly. From mid-1941, Axis forces in North Africa required approximately 100,000 tons of supplies each month. But in March 1942, for example, only 47,588 tons got through, whereas in April, 150,389, tons arrived. Overall, the Italian navy succeeded in bringing about 80 percent of all convoyed shipping through to its destination.

Despite its direct experience of successful convoy operations by its destroyers in the Mediterranean during World War I, the Imperial Japanese Navy was very slow to introduce convoying of merchant shipping after the Pacific war began. The navy possessed very few suitable escort vessels at the outbreak of war, which reflected the overwhelming emphasis it placed on planning for the decisive fleet action that was the centerpiece of its operational strategy. Japan's response to the burgeoning unrestricted submarine campaign conducted by the United States against its shipping was to increase aggressive surface and air patrols and continue to eschew defensive convoy of its traffic. Not until the later part of 1944, by which date its merchant fleet had been devastated by American submarines, did the navy begin limited convoy, especially of the crucial tankers carrying fuel from the Dutch East Indies, but by then it was too late.

Paul E. Fontenoy

See also
Antisubmarine Warfare; Germany, Navy; Italy, Navy; Japan, Navy; Signals Intelligence; *Wilhelm Gustloff*
References
Goulter, Christina J. A. *Forgotten Offensive: Royal Air Force Coastal Command's Anti-shipping Campaign, 1940–1945*. London: Cass, 1995.

Levine, Alan J. *The War against Rommel's Supply Lines, 1942–1943.* Westport, CT: Greenwood Press, 1999.

Parillo, Mark P. *The Japanese Merchant Marine in World War II.* Annapolis, MD: Naval Institute Press, 1993.

Polmar, Norman, and Jurrien Noot. *Submarines of the Russian and Soviet Navies, 1718–1990.* Annapolis, MD: Naval Institute Press, 1991.

Convoys SC.122 and HX.229, Battle of (14–20 March 1943)

Largest North Atlantic convoy battle of World War II. March 1943 was the high-water mark of the German U-boat campaign against Allied convoys in the North Atlantic. Between 10 and 20 March, Allied signals intelligence suffered a temporary blackout in its operations against the German U-boat cipher Triton. At the same time, the German signals intelligence service was able to decipher the rerouting instructions for two eastbound convoys: SC.122 and HX.229.

The German U-boat command had an unprecedented concentration of U-boats in the North Atlantic at that time, and on 14 March, it set about forming three large packs from boats that had been operating against the convoys SC.121 and HX.228. Groups Raubgraf (8 boats) and Stürmer (18 boats) were to operate against SC.122, and group Dränger (11 boats) was deployed against HX.229.

On 16 March, the first U-boat made contact with HX.229. Both convoys were sailing close to each other, and HX.229 was closing on the slower SC.122, which had already passed the Raubgraf patrol line undetected. The Raubgraf boats, as well as 11 boats of the Stürmer group, were thus deployed against HX.229 in the mistaken belief that it was SC.122. Inadequately defended by only 2 destroyers and 2 corvettes, HX.229 suffered a heavy mauling by the packs during the night of 16–17 March. The same night, U-boats of the Stürmer group made contact with SC.122. Realizing that the two convoys were about to merge, the German U-boat command committed the remainder of its 40 available U-boats within range to the battle. Throughout 17 March, long-range B-24 Liberator bombers from Iceland and SC.122 escorts with high-frequency direction-finding (HF/DF) equipment succeeded in fending off the contact-keeping boats. Only 1 U-boat managed to close for an attack, sinking 2 ships out of SC.122 on that day.

On 18 March, air cover provided by the Liberators of the Number 120 Squadron again prevented 21 of the 30 U-boats deployed against HX.229 from reaching the scene, and again, only 1 U-boat succeeded in closing for a daylight attack. A reinforcement of the surface escort group prevented serious losses during the night of 18–19 March, in which the U-boats claimed only 2 further ships before intensified air cover, now flying out of the British Isles, forced them to desist. Two U-boats were damaged and 1 was sunk before Grossadmiral (grand admiral) Karl Dönitz called off the operation on 20 March.

The tally of 21 Allied ships sunk, totaling 141,000 tons of shipping, as well as 1 destroyer lost during this largest convoy battle of the war was impressive, yet it was also deceptive. It had been achieved primarily because the sheer numbers of U-boats had saturated the convoy defenses. Nevertheless, only 16 of the 40 U-boats deployed against both convoys had actually been able to make contact, and owing to the diligence of the convoys' hard-pressed air and sea escorts, only 9 succeeded in torpedoing ships. Of the 39 U-boats that survived the battle, 16 subsequently required more than 40 days of maintenance due to damage sustained during the battle. Committing virtually all available North Atlantic boats to four convoys—SC.121, SC.122, HX.228, and HX.229—also meant that the other four eastbound North Atlantic convoys in March 1943 made their passage entirely unmolested.

Dirk Steffen

See also
Aircraft Carrier; Aircraft, Naval; Antisubmarine Warfare; Atlantic, Battle of the; Aviation, Naval; Bay of Biscay Offensive; Convoys, Allied; Dönitz, Karl; Radar; Signals Intelligence; Wolf Pack

References
Blair, Clay. *Hitler's U-Boat War: The Hunted, 1942–1945.* New York. Random House, 1998.

Boog, Horst, Werner Rahn, and Reinhard Stumpf. *Der Globale Krieg: Die Ausweitung zum Weltkrieg und der Wechsel der Initiative.* Vol. 6 in the series *Das Deutsche Reich und der Zweite Weltkrieg,* ed. Militärgeschichtliches Forschungsamt. Stuttgart, Germany: Deutsche Verlags-Anstalt, 1990.

Roskill, S. W. *White Ensign: The British Navy at Way, 1939–1945.* Annapolis, MD: Naval Institute Press, 1960.

Coral Sea, Battle of the (7–8 May 1942)

World War II battle fought by U.S. Pacific Fleet and Japanese carrier forces as the United States attempted to prevent a Japanese landing at Port Moresby on New Guinea. The Battle of the Coral Sea was the first naval engagement in history in which two fleets fought without opposing surface ships making visual contact.

Following their successful attack on Pearl Harbor and early military triumphs, Japanese leaders were reluctant to continue with their original strategy of shifting to a defensive posture. They feared the adverse impact this might exert on their forces' fighting spirit and believed that it would work to Japan's disadvantage by allowing the Western powers time to regain their strength.

Japanese naval leaders in particular were anxious to occupy the Hawaiian Islands and Australia, the two chief points from which U.S. forces might mount offensive operations. U.S. carriers were operating out of Pearl Harbor, still the headquarters of the U.S. Pacific Fleet. If Japanese forces could take the Hawaiian Islands, it would be virtually impossible for the U.S. Navy to conduct long-range Pacific naval operations. Also, securing the islands to the north and east of Australia—the Solomons, New Caledonia, and Samoa—would enable the Japanese to establish bases to cut the Allied lifeline from the United States to Australia. Japanese long-range bombers would then be able to strike targets in Australia itself, preparatory to an invasion and occupation of that continent.

The Japanese army was not enthusiastic about either proposal. Most of its assets were tied down in China, and the Guandong (Kwantung) Army continued to garrison

Manchuria. Invading Australia and occupying even the populated areas would require significant military resources that the army could not spare. The Army Ministry and General Staff in Tokyo therefore advocated holding the gains already achieved in the southern advance and shifting resources to China. The army formally vetoed the navy plan in early April 1942, but in effect, it was dead by the end of January. Japanese navy leaders hoped, however, that a success either eastward toward Pearl Harbor or southwest toward Australia might overcome army opposition.

Admiral Yamamoto Isoroku and the Combined Fleet Staff favored taking Midway Island, 1,100 miles west of Pearl Harbor, as a preliminary step before invading Hawaii. Yamamoto expected this move would provoke a strong U.S. naval reaction, enabling him to set a trap for and destroy the U.S. aircraft carriers. The Japanese Naval Staff, however, preferred the southeasterly drive to isolate Australia. By the end of March, the Japanese had already advanced from Rabaul into the Solomon Islands and along the northern

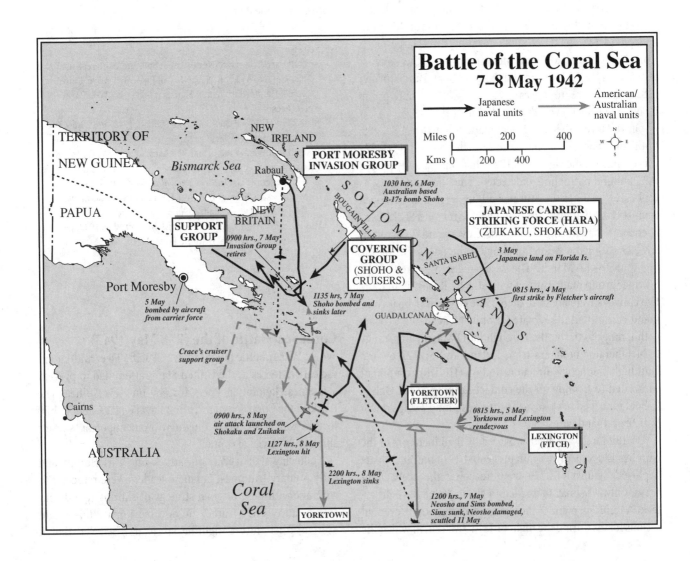

The Battle of the Coral Sea—fires rage on the Carrier Lexington. *(Library of Congress)*

coast of New Guinea. The Japanese Imperial General Staff searched for a strategy to follow up their successes. Initially, the Naval General Staff favored assaulting Australia, fearing an Allied buildup there could lead to a counteroffensive against the Japanese defensive perimeter. The army rejected an Australian operation because of long distances, insufficient troops, and inadequate transportation. In January 1942, both agreed on a less demanding joint invasion of Lae and Salamaua in New Guinea; the seizure of Tulagi in the Solomons; and the capture of the Australian base of Port Moresby in Papua, New Guinea.

On 8 March 1942, American carriers, sent to beleaguer the Japanese base at Rabaul northeast of New Guinea, interdicted Japanese landing operations at Lae and Salamaua on the Papuan peninsula of eastern New Guinea. Two carrier task forces, one built around the carrier *Lexington* under Vice Admiral Wilson E. Brown and Rear Admiral Frank Jack Fletcher's task force centered on the carrier *Yorktown*, sailed into the Gulf of Papua on the opposite side of the peninsula.

Together, on the morning of 10 March, they sent 104 aircraft across the high Owen Stanley Mountains to emerge undetected and find Japanese ships discharging troops and supplies at the two villages. The attacking American aircraft sank three Japanese ships, including the converted light cruiser *Kongo Maru,* at a cost of only one plane and one aviator lost.

The action caught the Japanese operational commander, Vice Admiral Inouye Shigeyoshi, by surprise and convinced him that conquest of New Guinea would have to be postponed until he could secure fleet carriers for protection. That opportunity came only after the return of the carriers from the Japanese raids into the Indian Ocean.

In early April 1942, the attention of the Imperial Naval General Staff was on southeast operations (seizure of strategic points in New Guinea, New Caledonia, the Fiji Islands, and Samoa) to isolate Australia. However, the April 1942 (Doolittle) raid on Tokyo refocused their attention on the destruction of the U.S. carriers and forced an earlier date for the Tulagi and Port Moresby operations, with the New Caledonia, Fiji, and Samoa operations to follow after Midway.

Admiral Inouye, commanding the Fourth Fleet and Operation MO, as it was designated, broke his forces into five groups: two invasion groups to land army and naval forces at Tulagi and Port Moresby; a support group to establish a seaplane base in the Louisiade Archipelago off New Guinea; a small covering group with the light carrier *Shoho*; and the main striking force of two fleet carriers, *Shokaku* and *Zuikaku*, plus escorts. This striking force, commanded by Vice Admiral Takagi Takeo, was to support both landings and protect the entire force from American carriers.

At Pearl Harbor, Admiral Chester W. Nimitz, commander of the U.S. Pacific Fleet, determined from intercepts that the Japanese would probably attack Port Moresby on 3 May, and on 29 April, he ordered Rear Admiral Frank Jack Fletcher, commanding the *Yorktown* group, to operate in the vicinity of the Coral Sea beginning on 1 May. Rear Admiral Aubrey Fitch's *Lexington* group and the American-British-Dutch-Australian Command (ABDACOM) combined naval force of two Australian cruisers, the American heavy cruiser *Chicago*, and two U.S. destroyers under Rear Admiral John Crace, of the Royal Navy, were also placed under Fletcher's tactical command. The two carrier groups and Crace's force formed Task Force 17 (TF 17) when they rendezvoused on 1 May some 250 miles off the New Hebrides. While the *Lexington*'s group refueled, Fletcher sailed the *Yorktown*'s group north on 2 May to reconnoiter, having received reports of approaching Japanese naval forces.

On 3 May, the Japanese Tulagi invasion group began landing forces without opposition. Learning of the landings, Fletcher decided to strike Tulagi the next morning without waiting for the *Lexington* to join him. He sent his fleet oiler and its escorts to inform Fitch and Crace of his change of plans and to order them to join him 300 miles south of Guadalcanal on 5 May. The *Yorktown* then closed on Tulagi undetected on 4 May and launched three air strikes that met little resistance. Admiral Takagi's carrier striking force had been delayed and was nowhere near Tulagi. Inexperienced as they were, the American attackers were ineffective, only damaging a destroyer to the point that she had to beached and sinking three small minesweepers and four landing barges. They also shot up some grounded aircraft. However, even this small success was enough to send the rest of the Tulagi force steaming back to Rabaul.

Withdrawing southward, Fletcher rejoined Fitch and Crace as scheduled on 5 May. TF 17 then moved northwest, expecting to catch Japanese forces as they emerged from the Jomard Passage into the Coral Sea. Although sightings were made by both sides on 6 May, essentially ineffective reconnaissance led to little significant action by either.

Before dawn on 7 May, the opposing fleet carriers passed within 70 miles of each other. At dawn, both sides sent out search planes over the Coral Sea. The Japanese sighting of an American "carrier and cruiser" led to the sinking of the destroyer *Sims* and the severe mauling of the oiler *Neosho*. At about the same time, an American scout reported two Japanese carriers north of the Louisiades. After the *Lexington* and *Yorktown* launched their aircraft, Fletcher discovered that his forces had been sighted by a Japanese scout plane. The action prompted by the American sighting turned out to be a wild goose chase, but the *Lexington* and *Yorktown* pilots stumbled on the light carrier *Shoho* and sank her.

Early the next morning, the two carrier forces found each other. The American planes concentrated their attack on the fleet carrier *Shokaku* but hit her with just three bombs, causing only modest damage. The fleet carrier *Zuikaku* escaped attack by hiding in a rainsquall. The *Shokaku*'s damage was sufficient to prevent launch-and-recovery operations, and when the Americans withdrew, she turned north toward Japan.

Meanwhile, planes from the *Shokaku* and *Zuikaku* found the *Lexington* and *Yorktown*. Diving out of the sun, torpedo planes hit the *Lexington* twice on the port side, and dive-bombers scored two minor hits. The *Yorktown* was hit by only one bomb, which did no major damage. Confident they had sunk the *Saratoga*, the *Lexington*'s sister ship, and the *Yorktown,* the Japanese pilots withdrew. Neither ship sank, however, until gasoline vapors aboard the *Lexington* reignited fires that eventually became uncontrollable; as a result, she was abandoned, with Fletcher ordering her scuttled by torpedoes from a nearby destroyer.

Both sides hailed their achievements in the Coral Sea and scored themselves a win. Tactically, the Japanese came out ahead. The Americans were hurt most by the loss of the *Lexington,* one of its largest carriers, whereas the Japanese lost only the light carrier *Shoho* and suffered severe damage to the large carrier *Shokaku*. However, though the Japanese scored a tactical win, the Americans had finally blunted a Japanese offensive thrust, preventing the occupation of Port Moresby and thus winning the strategic victory. In addition, significant losses in aircraft, aircrew, and repairs to the *Shokaku* prevented both Japanese carriers from taking part in the critical Battle of Midway a month later.

Arthur T. Frame

See also

Aircraft Carriers; Carrier Raids, U.S.; Doolittle, James Harold "Jimmy"; Fletcher, Frank Jack; Halsey, William Frederick, Jr.; Inouye Shigeyoshi; King, Ernest Joseph; Nimitz, Chester William; Takagi Takeo; Tokyo, Bombing of (1942); Yamamoto Isoroku

References

Dull, Paul S. *A Battle History of the Imperial Japanese Navy, 1941–1945.* Annapolis, MD: Naval Institute Press, 1978.

Hoyt, Edwin P. *Blue Skies and Blood: The Battle of the Coral Sea.* New York: S. Eriksson, 1975.

Lundstrom, John. *The First Team: Pacific Naval Air Combat from Pearl Harbor to Midway.* Annapolis, MD: Naval Institute Press, 1990.

Millet, Bernard. *The Battle of the Coral Sea.* Annapolis, MD: Naval Institute Press, 1974.

Morison, Samuel Eliot. *History of United States Naval Operations in World War II.* Vol. 4, *Coral Sea, Midway and Submarine Actions, May 1942–August 1942.* Boston: Little, Brown, 1949.

Prange, Gordon W. *Miracle at Midway.* New York: Penguin, 1983.

Spector, Ronald H. *Eagle against the Sun: The American War with Japan.* New York: Vintage Books, 1985.

Corap, André Georges (1879–1953)

French army general and commander of the Ninth French Army who was blamed for a German breakthrough in May 1940. Born at Pont Andemer, France, on 15 June 1878, André Corap entered the French army in 1898 on graduation from the French Military Academy of St. Cyr. He fought in World War I and earned distinction in the 1920–1926 Rif Rebellion in Morocco, where he captured the rebel leader Abd-el-Krim in 1926. Ten years later, Corap became a regimental commander in Morocco.

With the onset of World War II in September 1939 and the mobilization of French forces, Corap was appointed to command the 2nd Military Region of Amiens and the Ninth French Army. His sector of the northeastern front was particularly poorly fortified, and he had far fewer divisions than his counterparts behind the Maginot Line. When German forces invaded on 10 May 1940, in accordance with the prescribed Dyle plan, Corap immediately wheeled his troops north to take up positions north of the Meuse River between Namur and Flize, just to the west of Sedan. His forces arrived on 11–12 May to find that two German panzer corps, under German Generals Hermann Hoth and Georg Hans Reinhardt, had anticipated them. Badly mauled by frontal attacks from these troops and under heavy assault, the Ninth Army virtually disintegrated when its right flank came under heavy attack after the collapse of General Charles Huntziger's Second French Army, around Sedan. Only a few units held together and fell back to reserve positions during the night of 14–15 May.

General Alphonse Georges, commander in chief of French northeastern forces, held Corap responsible for the German breakthrough, and on 15 May, Georges insisted that Corap exchange commands with General Henri Giraud, who

headed the Seventh Army. Corap only held this post for four days before Defense Minister Édouard Daladier removed him. On 21 May, Prime Minister Paul Reynaud publicly held Corap responsible for the disaster on the Meuse frontier, implying that he might be tried for treason. This move seems to have been a desperate search for a scapegoat. Ironically, Huntziger, who bore at least as much blame as Corap, received a promotion and later became minister of war in the Vichy French government.

After the armistice, Corap accompanied the Vichy government to Bordeaux in a vain effort to clear his name. Subsequent revelations at the 1941 Riom trial largely exonerated him, but he held himself aloof from further debate, retiring to his home at Fontainebleau, where he died on 15 August 1953.

Priscilla Roberts

See also

Daladier, Édouard; France, Battle for; Georges, Alphonse Joseph; Giraud, Henri Honoré; Hoth, Hermann; Huntziger, Charles León Clément; Maginot Line; Reinhardt, Georg Hans; Reynaud, Paul

References

Allard, Paul. *L'énigme de la Meuse: La vérité sur l'affaire Corap.* Paris: Éditions de France, 1941.

Crémieux-Brilhac, Jean-Louis. *Les Français de l'an 40.* 2 vols. Paris: Gallimard, 1990.

Draper, Theodore. *The Six Weeks' War: France May 10–June 25, 1940.* New York: Viking, 1964.

Horne, Alistair. *To Lose a Battle: France 1940.* Boston: Little, Brown, 1969.

Shirer, William. *The Collapse of the Fourth French Republic.* New York: Simon and Schuster, 1989.

Corregidor, Battle of (April–May 1942)

Known officially as Fort Mills, Corregidor was the final bastion of U.S. and Filipino forces in the Philippines. The largest of the islands off the entrance to Manila Bay at 2.74 square miles, Corregidor is shaped like a tadpole. The island's chief installations included the post headquarters, a huge barracks, and coastal batteries. Contained within the tail of the island was a vast underground network known as Malinta Tunnel, which measured 1,400 feet in length and 30 feet in width, with 25 400-foot laterals branching from it. The tunnel was the administrative and operational heart of the island fortress. Kindley Airfield was situated on the extremity of the tail on the second-highest point of the island. The island also had batteries with an array of 18 12-inch and 10-inch coastal guns and 24 12-inch mortars, plus antiaircraft guns and machine-gun positions. Almost all of the armament on the island was obsolete in 1942, but as long as

Surrender of American troops at Corregidor, Philippine Islands, May 1942. (Still Picture Records LICON, Special Media Archives Services Division (NWCS-S), National Archives)

the troops on Corregidor held the island, they could effectively keep the Japanese fleet from using Manila Bay. This was the basic mission of the troops on Corregidor in War Plan Orange.

On the departure of General Douglas MacArthur and his staff to Australia, Major General Jonathan M. Wainwright assumed command of these forces from 12 March 1942. The Japanese had bombed and shelled the island constantly since February, but they did so with growing intensity starting in April. For 27 days, from 9 April to 6 May, the Japanese daily increased the shelling. By 5 May, the beach defenses had been destroyed, the huge seacoast guns had been silenced, and the antiaircraft batteries had been reduced to scrap. All wire communication had been destroyed, and every attempt to restore it was in vain. Even the geography of Corregidor had changed; the island lay scorched, leafless, and covered in the dust of thousands of explosions.

By the beginning of May, the 9,400 men on Corregidor knew a Japanese attack was imminent. The island's defenders had sustained 600 casualties since 9 April, and those men who had not been injured were beginning to succumb to malnutrition and malaria. General Wainwright wrote on 4 May that there was only enough water to last for four days and that the fortress' power supply would only hold out for one week at most.

Late in the night of 5 May, the long-awaited Japanese attack began, following a particularly intense artillery bombardment directed against the tail end of the island. Shortly before 10:00 P.M., as Japanese landing craft steamed toward the eastern end of the island, an order went out for all able-bodied troops to resist the landing.

The fight for Corregidor lasted only 10 hours. Japanese troops cut across the island, then turned west toward Malinta Tunnel. Most of the fighting during the night and the early morning of 6 May took place at Battery Denver, on a ridge near the east entrance of the tunnel. U.S. troops, including coast artillerymen and a battalion of 500 sailors, fought bravely. At 8:00 A.M., after the Japanese had taken tanks and artillery ashore for a frontal assault, General Wainwright committed the last of his reserves on the island. The final blow to the defenders came when the Japanese sent three tanks into the action. The first sight of armor panicked the defenders and caused some to flee from the lines.

By 10:00 A.M., the situation was critical, with the defenders having no means of stopping the Japanese tanks. Already, 600 to 800 U.S. troops had been killed and another 1,000 wounded. Every reserve had been thrown into the battle, and the Japanese had destroyed all defensive artillery. The Japanese were planning to mount an attack on the other side of the island and would reach Malinta Tunnel, with its 1,000 wounded, in a few hours. Fearing a slaughter, Wainwright decided to surrender. By 12:00 noon on 6 May, all weaponry larger then .45 caliber had been destroyed; all codes, radio equipment, and classified materials had been burned; and the surrender message had been broadcast to the Japanese. The U.S. flag was lowered and burned, and a white flag was hoisted. Wainwright then communicated to President Franklin D. Roosevelt that he had made the decision to surrender. It had taken the Japanese five months to seize the island, instead of the two months they had originally estimated. U.S. forces retook Corregidor in February 1945.

Frank Slavin III

See also
Bataan, Battle of; Fort Drum; MacArthur, Douglas; Philippines, Japanese Conquest of; Wainwright, Jonathan Mayhew
References
James, D. Clayton. *The Years of MacArthur.* Vol. 2, *1941–1945.* Boston: Houghton Mifflin, 1970.
Morton, Louis. "Bataan Diary of Major Achille C. Tisdelle." *Military Affairs* 11, no. 3. (Autumn 1947): 130–148.
———. *United States Army in World War II: The War in the Pacific—The Fall of the Philippines.* Washington, DC: Office of the Chief of Military History, Department of the Army, 1952.

Corsica, Recapture of (8 September–4 October 1943)

French Mediterranean island occupied by Italian forces on 11 November 1942. Free French leader General Charles de Gaulle was determined to retake Corsica, and the Allies soon began sending French and U.S. Office of Strategic Services (OSS) operatives to the island by submarine. In late August 1943, at de Gaulle's behest, General Alphonse Juin drew up invasion plans. Assuming that the Italians would remain neutral, Juin planned a force of two divisions to carry out simultaneous east and west landings to cut the island's two main coastal roads. On 8 September 1942, the armistice with Italy was announced. By that date, elements of the French troops were ready to deploy, but they lacked the sealift required for the men and their supplies. Nonetheless, de Gaulle was determined to proceed on a reduced scale if need be to liberate Corsica by force of French arms.

Generalleutnant (U.S. equiv. major general) Fridolin von Senger und Etterlin commanded German forces on Sardinia and Corsica. On 11 September, following the Italian surrender to the Allies, Adolf Hitler ordered Senger to transfer the 90th Panzer Division from Sardinia to join the Schutzstaffel (SS) brigade already on Corsica. The first French element, a battalion, landed at Ajaccio on 12 September. Although Italian Major General Giovanni Magli said that his men would fight the French, that arrangement did not last long. Soon, much of his VII Corps garrison of four divisions, as well as thousands of local maquis resistance fighters, were engaging the Germans. Meanwhile, the French steadily built up their resources on the island; two Free French cruisers and two destroyers, as well as torpedo boats and submarines, participated in the lift of men and supplies. Commodore W. G. Agnew's British 12 Cruiser Squadron provided cover. Ultimately, the French landed some 6,800 men, 30 tanks, and 20 artillery pieces on the island.

On 15 September, Hitler ordered the evacuation of Corsica, which took place through the port of Bastia, which the

Germans had taken by force from its Italian defenders two days earlier. The Germans completed their withdrawal from the island on 4 October, wrecking harbor facilities as they departed. Although they were able to remove most of their troops and 3,200 vehicles, the Allies sank 17,000 tons of German shipping; the Germans also had 55 transport aircraft destroyed, most of them on the ground, and they abandoned substantial quantities of equipment. De Gaulle traveled to Ajacco on 8 October and addressed the people in the town hall square the next day. The numbers of military dead in the Allied reoccupation of Corsica came to about 450 Germans, 637 Italians, 75 French and Moroccans, and 170 maquis.

Spencer C. Tucker

See also

de Gaulle, Charles; Juin, Alphonse Pierre; Maquis; Senger und Etterlin, Fridolin Rudolf von

References

Auphan, Paul, and Jacques Mordal. *The French Navy in World War II.* Annapolis, MD: Naval Institute Press, 1959.

de Gaulle, Charles. *The Complete War Memoirs of Charles de Gaulle, 1940–1946.* Trans. Jonathan Griffin and Richard Howard. New York: Simon and Schuster, 1960.

Molony, C. J. C., et al. *History of the Second World War Series: The Mediterranean and Middle East.* Vol. 5. London: Her Majesty's Stationery Office, 1973.

Cota, Norman Daniel "Dutch" (1893–1971)

U.S. Army general who was highly decorated for his leadership on Omaha Beach on 6 June 1944. Born in Chelsea, Massachusetts, on 30 May 1893, Norman "Dutch" Cota graduated from the U.S. Military Academy in 1917 and was commissioned in the infantry with the 22nd Regiment. He was an instructor at West Point between 1918 and 1920. Cota transferred to the Finance Department in 1920 and was the finance officer of West Point until 1924, when he transferred back to the infantry. Cota graduated from the Infantry School, Fort Benning, Georgia, in 1925 and served in the Hawaiian Department. He graduated from the Command and General Staff School in 1931, was an instructor at the Infantry School in 1932 and 1933, graduated from the Army War College in 1936, and was an instructor at the Command and General Staff School from 1938 to 1940.

Cota had charge of plans and trained in the 1st Infantry Division from March 1941; he was its chief of staff from 1942 to February 1943, taking part in the capture of Oran during Operation TORCH, the invasion of French North Africa in November 1942. Promoted to brigadier general in Febru-

ary 1943, he became U.S. adviser to the Combined Operations branch of the European Theater of Operations. Later that year, he was assistant commander of the 29th Infantry Division.

On 6 June 1944, Cota landed with his division on Omaha Beach, Normandy. Several of the men in his landing craft (an LCVP, or landing craft vehicle and personnel) were killed by German fire as soon as the ramp went down, and Cota was the only general officer on the beach that day. With American forces almost pushed back into the sea, he was an inspiring presence. Realizing that the men were doomed if they remained on the beach, he exposed himself to German fire as he repeatedly led small parties forward. Many historians credit him with almost single-handedly preventing a disaster on Omaha that day. Cota later received the Distinguished Service Cross for his actions. Wounded at Saint-Lô, he spent two weeks in the division hospital.

On 13 August 1944, he took command of the 28th Infantry Division, which he led through Paris in a liberation parade in August 1944, part of a show of force in support of General Charles de Gaulle to prevent a possible Communist takeover. Cota was promoted to major general in September 1944.

On 2 November, the 28th Infantry Division began an attack to capture the town of Schmidt in the heart of the Hürtgen Forest, as part of the Siegfried Line Campaign. The plan of attack was a recipe for disaster, with all three regiments of the division attacking in diverging directions; it had been imposed on the division by staff officers at V Corps. Cota protested his orders to both V Corps commander Major General Leonard Gerow and First Army commander Lieutenant General Courtney Hodges but was ordered to execute the plan. Over the next nine days, the 28th Infantry Division suffered more than 6,000 casualties. Near the end of the battle, Cota himself collapsed under the pressure of what was happening to his division.

If not for his performance on Omaha Beach, Cota almost certainly would have been relieved of his command after this debacle; as it was, Schmidt cast a long shadow over him. The 28th Division was pulled out of the line and sent south to a quiet sector in Belgium to reconstitute. On 16 December, it was manning the sector of the line known as Skyline Drive when the Germans launched the Ardennes Offensive. Although the already weak 28th Division was mauled during the German attack, it did not break. Rather, it conducted a tenacious and effective fighting withdrawal that contributed in no small part to disrupting the German timetable for the offensive. Cota returned to the United States in August 1945 to prepare for the invasion of Japan and retired from the army as a major general in 1946. He died in Wichita, Kansas, on 4 October 1971.

David T. Zabecki

See also

de Gaulle, Charles; Gerow, Leonard Townsend; Hodges, Courtney
Hicks; Hürtgen Forest Campaign; Normandy Invasion and
Campaign; TORCH, Operation

References

Ambrose, Stephen E. *D-Day, June 6, 1944: The Climactic Battle of
World War II.* New York: Simon and Schuster, 1994.

MacDonald, Charles B. *A Time for Trumpets: The Untold Story of the
Battle of the Bulge.* New York: William Morrow, 1985.

Miller, Robert A. *Division Commander: A Biography of Major General
Norman D. Cota.* Spartanburg, SC: Reprint Publishers, 1989.

Counterintelligence

Organized activities initiated to counter an opponent's intelligence operations. Counterintelligence operations may include blocking an enemy's sources of information, deceiving the enemy, and working to prevent enemy sabotage and the gathering of intelligence information.

When World War II began, electronic warfare had matured considerably since the end of World War I. In 1939, unlike in 1914, many nations had functioning cryptological departments, and virtually all nations during the war broke codes of the other side. Circumstances in 1939 varied widely, however. Great Britain, for example, had a solid organization, centered on the Government Code and Cypher School at Bletchley Park. Such operations played key roles in counterintelligence on both sides.

Communications technology did not solve all counterintelligence issues, as the British discovered soon after the fall of France in 1940 when an influx of refugees from the Continent began arriving on their shores. Before long, an average of 700 aliens were entering the country per month, and the Travel Section of MI-5 (Security Service) knew that each person needed to be interrogated so that spies could be identified before they could do much harm. A pedestrian approach was required. Near the Clapham Junction Railway Station was the empty Royal Victoria Patriotic School (RVPS), built to educate the children of Crimean War veterans. The students of RVPS and the nearby Emanuel School, an old and excellent London public school, had been evacuated to the country for the duration of the war. The RVPS, later known as the London Reception Center (LRC), became MI-5's principal interrogating facility. Some 33,000 aliens were inspected at LRC during the war, but only three enemy agents were passed through undetected. The agent at large for the longest period, from November 1940 to April 1941, was Dutch parachutist Englebertus Fukken. He was found dead in a Cambridgeshire air-raid shelter, a suicide. In the early days, a proven German agent might be hanged at the RVPS,

next to the faculty common room. Eventually, after 27 July 1940, those aliens held at the LRC were sent to Ham in west London for further study and interrogation. Under the command of Colonel R. W. G. "Tin Eye" Stephens, Camp 020 was the interrogation center of last resort. It should be remembered that 020 functioned in 1940 under fear of the planned German invasion of the British Isles, Operation SEA LION.

As the war progressed, more and more German agents arrived, not via the refugee route but by parachute or coastal landing at night from German small craft or even U-boats. On capture—and MI-5 was good at that—these persons could not claim to be refugees. Some did not wait for apprehension but turned themselves in and volunteered to work for the Allies. Under the chairmanship of Sir John Masterman, an Oxford don who had the distinction of spending all of World War I interned in Germany, the XX (Doublecross) Committee came into being to develop a deception plan to utilize these possible double agents. Composed of representatives of MI-5, MI-6 (Secret Intelligence Service), the Special Operations Executive (SOE), and other organizations, the committee set up a phony radio situation that fed doctored information mixed with some real facts back to German controllers. The ruse became more successful than most members of the XX Committee ever thought it would or could be.

The Germans were also active in counterintelligence operations, one of which worked specifically against SOE. ENGLANDSPIEL was a German operation set up in the Netherlands by Major Herman Giske of the Abwehr and Colonel Josef Schreide of the Reichssicherheithauptamt (RSHA, the Reich Main Security Office) to break up British espionage rings in Holland. The Abwehr, the military secret service under Admiral Wilhelm Canaris, contained many anti-Nazi elements. The RSHA, which was anything but anti-Nazi, was under Schutzstaffel (SS) chief Heinrich Himmler. The two organizations did not greatly appreciate each other. ENGLANDSPIEL worked something like the XX Committee in reverse. The Germans "turned" several SOE parachutists who then asked SOE to send monetary, material, and human assistance to the espionage rings in Holland. That the British did. ENGLANDSPIEL lasted until two agents escaped from Haaren Prison and made their way to Switzerland; they then exposed the German operation. The operation had ended by the beginning of April 1944, but it had been quite successful. The British carried out 190 aircraft drops of people and equipment. Of 54 captured agents, 47 were executed. The Germans took 3,000 Sten guns, 5,000 revolvers, 2,000 hand grenades, 500,000 rounds of ammunition, 75 radio transmitters, and 500,000 Dutch guilders. ENGLANDSPIEL was probably the greatest Allied espionage defeat of World War II.

Mention must also be made of the Germans' deception plan for Operation BARBAROSSA, their 22 June 1941 attack on the Soviet Union. For such a momentous military action, there was virtually no attempt at deception. The Abwehr and other organizations merely stated that the transfer of troops from west to east was (1) intended to aid Italy's faltering campaign against the Greeks, and (2) a deception for British consumption designed to signal that Operation SEA LION had been abandoned. Soviet leader Josef Stalin received as many as 100 warnings and ignored all of them, dismissing them as deliberate Allied disinformation.

The Western Allies also had a great success in Operation MINCEMEAT, their unique deception campaign preceding the Sicily landings in July 1943. This operation was developed to convince the Germans that the Greek islands and Sardinia were the next Allied targets after North Africa, instead of the more logical Sicily. Lieutenant Commander Ewen Montagu (1901–1985), British navy liaison to the XX Committee, proposed disguising a dead body as a British officer and floating it ashore in Spain, with appropriate evidence on the body. The corpse selected was that of a man (as yet unidentified) who had died of pneumonia, which produced symptoms similar to a death by drowning. The plan worked to perfection, causing the Germans to shift their assets to Greece and Sardinia. In 1953, Montagu revealed the whole saga in his book *The Man Who Never Was*, a best-seller later made into a successful motion picture.

The most significant Allied deception of the entire war was Operation FORTITUDE, which had two aspects. FORTITUDE NORTH was designed to convince Adolf Hitler that the Allies were planning to invade Norway from Scotland. FORTITUDE SOUTH was to convince Hitler that the main Allied invasion of France would come through the Pas de Calais area. By October 1943, the Germans had seriously begun to strengthen their West Wall defenses, and the Pas de Calais was the shortest route across the English Channel. The Allies wanted as many German divisions as possible around the Pas de Calais and in Norway, to be kept there as long as possible so that they themselves might consolidate their lodgment in Normandy. The Allies therefore created a fictitious army and "stationed" it in southeastern England. Identified as the 1st Army Group (FUSAG), it was equipped with every material object Shepperton Movie Studios could devise, including inflatable rubber tanks, trucks, artillery, and landing craft, all suitably camouflaged. Movie-type sets abounded, and an oil storage facility and large dock were built near Dover. As the crowning touch, U.S. Lieutenant General George S. Patton, whom the Germans expected to command any Allied invasion of the Continent, was placed in command.

Although the primary emphasis on the bogus performances was the Pas de Calais, Norway got its share of the focus as well. The British Fourth Army, commanded by General Sir Andrew Thorne, was a force of 350,000 fictitious

soldiers "assembled" in Scotland. It, too, had the false rubber and cardboard creations that characterized the operation in the south. The British increased aerial reconnaissance of the Norwegian coast, released portions of the Grand Fleet from Scapa Flow for a cruise along the Norwegian coast, and made electric plaintext and coded inquiries about bridges and snow levels in Norway. FORTITUDE NORTH ultimately tied down some 400,000 German troops.

German controllers contacted their spies in Britain, not realizing that all were under XX Committee control. The Germans naturally wanted their agents to ferret out any information available about the expected invasion of the Continent. Their two best people—Dusko Popov, code-named TRICYCLE, and Juan Pujol, code-named GARBO—had been under XX Committee control for some time, and they simply substantiated, if not enhanced, the deception. GARBO's material was directly accessed by Hitler's personal intelligence staff, and the agent actually received medals from both sides during the war.

Meanwhile, the SOE and its U.S. counterpart, the Office of Strategic Services (OSS), as well as French partisans scheduled various tasks for D day: a bridge blowing, railway cuttings, pylon and wire destruction, and more. The deception plan worked out better than expected. Hitler held German units in place along the Pas de Calais. Indeed, some were still there a month after the Normandy landings.

Ernest M. Teagarden

See also
BARBAROSSA, Operation; Bletchley Park; Camouflage; Canaris, Wilhelm Franz; Churchill, Sir Winston L. S.; Coral Sea, Battle of the; Deception; Electronic Intelligence; Enigma Machine; FORTITUDE, North and South, Operations; Himmler, Heinrich; Jiang Jieshi; MANHATTAN Project; Maquis; Midway, Battle of; MINCEMEAT, Operation; Nimitz, Chester William; Normandy Invasion and Campaign; Office of Strategic Services; OVERLORD, Operation; Partisans/Guerrillas; Patton, George Smith, Jr.; SEA LION, Operation; Signals Intelligence; Special Operations Executive; Stalin, Josef; Stimson, Henry Lewis; Turing, Alan Mathison; Yamamoto Isoroku

References
Howard, Michael. *Strategic Deception in the Second World War.* New York: W. W. Norton, 1995.
Kahn, David. *The Codebreakers.* London: Weidenfeld and Nicolson, 1967.
Montagu, Ewen. *The Man Who Never Was.* London: Evans Brothers, 1953.
Prados, John. *Combined Fleet Decoded.* Annapolis, MD: Naval Institute Press, 1995.
Richelson, Jeffrey T. *A Century of Spies.* New York: Oxford University Press, 1995.
Smith, Michael. *The Emperor's Codes.* New York: Arcade, 2001.
Waller, John H. *The Unseen War in Europe.* New York: Random House, 1996.
Yardley, Herbert O. *The American Black Chamber.* New York: Ballantine Books, 1981.

Crace, Sir John Gregory (1887–1968)

British navy admiral who commanded a U.S.-Australian task force in the Battle of the Coral Sea. Born on 6 February 1887, at Gungahleen, New South Wales, Australia, John Crace joined the Royal Navy in 1902 as a colonial cadet at the midshipman training college at Devon, Britain. In World War I, he saw service at sea as a torpedo lieutenant.

After the war, Crace specialized in torpedoes. Following various assignments that included sea service, he became assistant to the second sea lord in 1937. A rear admiral when World War II began, he was assigned to command the Australian Squadron, in effect becoming the commander of the Royal Australian Navy (RAN). The RAN was subordinate to the British Admiralty, and Crace considered asking for another more responsible position in the Royal Navy.

After the United States entered the war, the U.S. Navy assumed overall Allied command of the South Pacific, and Crace took command of the mixed U.S.-Australian cruiser Task Force 44. In May 1942, the Allies became aware that the Japanese were preparing to invade Port Moresby, New Guinea. Along with two U.S. carrier task forces, Crace and his squadron set out to intercept the Japanese invasion force, which reconnaissance aircraft had reported as headed for the Jomard Passage. In the early afternoon of 7 May, Japanese medium bombers and torpedo-bombers attacked Crace's ships, but skillful maneuvering averted major damage at the hands of the Japanese and also from U.S. B-17s, which mistakenly attacked the friendly force.

The presence of Crace's ships and mistaken Japanese impressions as to the size of his unit led the invasion force headed for Port Moresby to turn back. Crace's ships played no other role in the Battle of the Coral Sea. They remained in the Jomard Passage for another two days, until being notified of the overall course of the battle. They then headed south and returned to Australia.

Crace received high marks from the Americans both as a seaman and as a commander of a joint force. He retired from the navy in 1942 and died in Liss, Hampshire, England, on 11 May 1968.

Harold Wise

See also
Coral Sea, Battle of the
References
Hoyt, Edwin P. *Blue Skies and Blood: The Battle of the Coral Sea.* New York: S. Eriksson, 1975.
Morison, Samuel Eliot. *History of United States Naval Operations in World War II.* Vol. 4, *Coral Sea, Midway and Submarine Actions, May 1942–August 1942.* Boston: Little, Brown, 1947.

Crerar, Henry Duncan Graham (1888–1965)

Canadian general and commander of the First Canadian Army in northwest Europe between 1944 and 1945. Born on 28 April 1888, at Hamilton, Ontario, Henry Crerar served with distinction in the artillery during World War I, ending the war as counterbattery staff officer for the Canadian Corps. During the interwar years, he remained in the small Permanent Force (regular army), primarily in staff appointments, and attended both the British Staff College (1923–1924) and Imperial Defence College (1934–1935).

A brigadier at the war's outset, Crerar was promoted to major general in January 1940 and appointed chief of the Canadian General Staff six months later. In that capacity, he played a central role in dispatching two ill-trained Canadian battalions to Hong Kong—and Japanese captivity—in 1941, but he also built up a solid training establishment. Crerar, promoted to lieutenant general in November 1941, was ambitious, ruthless, and jealous of rivals. Posted overseas to command I Canadian Corps that year, he spent much of his time intriguing against Lieutenant General Andrew McNaughton and had a major role in planning the disastrous Dieppe raid. He subsequently commanded I Canadian Corps in Italy from November 1943 until he was recalled to England in March 1944 to lead the First Canadian Army in the Normandy Invasion. With that appointment, Harry Crerar had reached the pinnacle for a Canadian officer.

Although historians have acknowledged his obvious administrative abilities, the excessively cautious and uninspiring Crerar was, at best, a pedestrian field commander. Field Marshal Bernard Montgomery, under whose command he served in the campaign in northwest Europe, had little confidence in him. His bitter rivalry with the abler Lieutenant General Guy Simonds was unjustified on any military grounds, and there is little doubt, for this and other reasons, that the latter would have replaced him had the war continued much longer. Operation VERITABLE, the assault on the Reichswald region in Germany in February 1945, was Crerar's battlefield masterpiece, characterized by thorough preparation and the accumulation of vast resources.

Crerar deserves much credit for effectively representing Canadian interests in Allied councils and for building an overseas headquarters. He retired from the army in 1946 and died in Ottawa on 1 April 1965.

Patrick H. Brennan

See also
Canada, Army; Dieppe Raid; Falaise-Argentan Pocket; Foulkes, Charles C. C.; Hong Kong, Battle of; McNaughton, Andrew George Latta; Montgomery, Sir Bernard Law; Normandy Invasion and Campaign; Rhineland Offensive; Simonds, Guy Granville

References

English, J. A. *Failure in High Command: The Canadian Army and the Normandy Campaign.* Ottawa: Golden Dog Press, 1995.

Granatstein, J. L. *The Generals: The Canadian Army's Senior Commanders in the Second World War.* Toronto, Canada: Stoddart, 1993.

Crete, Battle of (May 1941)

Largest airborne assault of the war up to May 1941. This German victory, however, also marked the end of major German airborne operations. Between 20 and 26 April 1941, British forces evacuated Greece. Crete had become a vital British base for logistical use, and many of the troops evacuated from Greece were landed there.

This fact alone would have made the island a target for the Germans, but there were other good reasons for a Ger-

man assault. Crete was a key to the Aegean Sea. It could be used as an air base for attacking British positions in North Africa and for protecting Axis Mediterranean shipping, especially oil supplies. It might even become a stepping stone on the route to the Suez Canal. More important, Adolf Hitler saw its capture as necessary to secure his vital southern flank against air attack (especially on the oil fields of Ploesti) before he launched Operation BARBAROSSA, the invasion of the Soviet Union.

British Major General Bernard Freyberg commanded the British corps on Crete, centered on the 2nd New Zealand Division. The Allied garrison numbered some 27,550 men and was, in fact, a mixed group of British, Australian, New Zealander, and Greek forces. Most had only recently arrived, and the defenders were hardly a cohesive force. Equipment—even basic weaponry—was in short supply. Air support was provided by several dozen aircraft only. Unlike the Germans, the British did not have air bases within fighter range of the island, which left the Luftwaffe free to

Lord Louis Mountbatten waves to the crews of the remaining ships of the fifth flotilla from the bridge of the Kipling *as she enters Alexandra Harbor the day after the Battle of Crete. (Hulton Archive by Getty Images)*

operate virtually unopposed, especially since the defenders had few antiaircraft guns.

The German plan for the invasion, code-named Operation MERKUR (MERCURY), centered on parachute drops on the three main airfields of Máleme, Hēráklion, and Rétimo. The Germans planned to hold these and local beaches, especially Suda Bay, until reinforced. Freyberg had been alerted by ULTRA intercepts as to the German invasion plans, and he established defensive positions at these obvious targets, but lack of transport meant his divided forces could not provide support for one another. The ULTRA information also worked against the defenders, as Freyberg did not know that the naval assault was only a small one, easily turned back by the Royal Navy, and he therefore allocated considerable assets to protect against that threat—assets that would have been used to far better purpose to defend the vital airfields.

On 20 May 1941, the Germans launched MERKUR. The operation ultimately involved some 22,000 soldiers—paratroops and mountain forces—and was supported by more than 500 combat aircraft, 700 transport planes, and 80 gliders. The Royal Navy halted the seaborne invasion. Airborne forces at Rétimo were crushed by the few tanks available to the British, and the landings at Hēráklion were also defeated. The key to the battle, however, proved to be at Máleme and nearby Canea and Suda.

Luftwaffe bombing at Máleme was particularly effective, and the attackers arrived before the defenders had regained their equilibrium. The British were also surprised by the use of gliders, which landed significant numbers of troops. The fighting was desperate and in some doubt for a time, but the Germans were able to bring in just enough resources to beat off the British counterattacks; the Luftwaffe then ferried in additional supplies to the German troops. Suda Bay became untenable for the British, and the Germans began to land reinforcements. On 24 May, Freyberg informed London that German seaborne landings could not be stopped without completely unacceptable naval losses that would put the entire eastern Mediterranean at risk. Three days later, with the Germans expanding their area of control and Italian troops landing at Sitia on the eastern end of the island, the British ordered an evacuation.

The Royal Navy was able to evacuate almost 18,000 men, at a cost of 2,011 casualties. In naval operations around Crete, however, the Royal Navy lost three cruisers and six destroyers and had a number of additional ships significantly damaged, including an aircraft carrier. Allied personnel losses were 1,742 dead, 2,225 wounded, and 11,370 captured. The Germans won a victory but at high cost. They lost 220 aircraft and had another 150 damaged, and their casualties totaled some 6,700 (3,300 dead), although certain British sources reported much higher totals.

The German attack on Crete was audacious and innovative. Hitler, however, refused pleas by Generalleutnant (U.S. equiv. major general) Kurt Student that the airborne forces next assault Malta; indeed, he removed Student from command of operations on Crete during the battle. In effect, the Battle of Crete was Germany's last real airborne operation of the war, for the German forces that participated were used as elite infantry thereafter. Ironically, the Allies then embraced paratroop operations.

Fred R. van Hartesveldt

See also

Airborne Forces, Axis; BARBAROSSA, Operation; Crete, Naval Operations off; Freyberg, Bernard Cyril; Löhr, Alexander; Parachute Infantry; Student, Kurt

References

Bennett, Ralph F. *Ultra and Mediterranean Strategy, 1941–1945.* New York: William Morrow, 1989.

Freyberg, Paul. *Bernard Freyberg, VC.* London: Hodder and Stoughton, 1991.

Kiriakopoulos, G. C. *Ten Days to Destiny: The Battle for Crete, 1941.* Brookline, MA: Hellenic College Press, 1997.

MacDonald, Callum. *The Lost Battle: Crete 1941.* New York: Free Press, 1993.

Simpson, Tory. *Operation Mercury, the Battle for Crete, 1941.* London: Hodder and Stoughton, 1981.

Crete, Naval Operations Off (21 May– 1 June 1941)

British naval activity first to defend and then to evacuate the island of Crete. After the British Expeditionary Force (BEF) was defeated and subsequently evacuated from Greece between 24 and 30 April 1941, many of these troops were then relocated to the Greek island of Crete. Adolf Hitler's decision to send forces to conquer the island in order to shore up his southern flank prior to invading the Soviet Union led to an epic confrontation between airpower and seapower.

Allied radio intercepts and ULTRA intelligence revealed the broad outlines of the German plan, which consisted of airborne assaults and a sea invasion. They did not reveal the relative strength of these attacks, however. Particularly serious for the British forces was the lack of air assets. By 18 May, German air attacks on Crete had left the defenders with only a dozen aircraft, and Britain's one aircraft carrier, the *Formidable*, began the battle with only four serviceable planes. While patrolling the island to prevent a German seaborne landing, Royal Navy sailors, exhausted from their role in the evacuation from Greece, were exposed to the full weight of the Luftwaffe's 700 combat aircraft operating from bases in Greece, as well as occasional Italian air strikes.

The German assault on Crete, Operation MERKUR (MERCURY) began on 20 May. German air superiority forced the Royal Navy's warships to retire south of Crete during the day, and the defenders rarely managed to put more than a dozen planes in the air at any one time. Long-range bombing of the Luftwaffe's bases in Greece by British aircraft based in Malta and Egypt failed to affect German air operations in any material way.

On the night of 21–22 May, British warships intercepted two lightly escorted troop convoys, each composed of 20 small, overloaded coastal vessels packed with troops and escorted by a single Italian torpedo boat. In one-sided engagements, British cruisers and destroyers sank 10 ships in one convoy and 2 in the other. Only the British squadron's need to retire south before daybreak to protect it from Axis air attack saved the second convoy from total destruction. The surviving ships of both convoys returned to Greece. Some 400 German soldiers were lost in this effort, and Germany thereafter relied entirely on air supply and reinforcement in its invasion.

Despite the best efforts of the Royal Navy and the defenders on the ground, it became impossible to defend the island once German troops had captured Máleme Airfield. On 26 May, with the situation hopeless, island commander Major General Bernard Freyberg ordered an evacuation. Once again, the Royal Navy rushed to rescue Commonwealth and Allied soldiers (wags said that BEF stood for "Back Every Fortnight").

The long distances involved and the Luftwaffe's complete control of the air made the evacuation particularly difficult, but the British commander in the Mediterranean, Admiral Andrew B. Cunningham, ordered his ships to continue the evacuation regardless of cost. Despite constant German air attack, they managed to evacuate almost 18,000 of Crete's 32,000 defenders, but the Royal Navy suffered very high losses itself in the process. In the weeklong operation, German air attacks sank three cruisers, six destroyers, and several smaller vessels and inflicted serious damage on the *Formidable*, the battleships *Barham* and *Warspite*, three cruisers, and numerous other warships. Few British warships escaped without damage, and some 2,000 British sailors died, along with a similar number of evacuated soldiers. In the course of the fight, many ships completely exhausted their antiaircraft ammunition. The Luftwaffe lost only a few dozen aircraft.

Stephen K. Stein

See also
Crete, Battle of; Cunningham, Sir Andrew Browne; Freyberg, Bernard Cyril; Great Britain, Navy; Hitler, Adolf

References
MacDonald, Callum. *The Lost Battle: Crete 1941*. New York: Free Press, 1993.

Pack, S. W. C. *The Battle for Crete*. Annapolis, MD: Naval Institute Press, 1973.
Roskill, Stephen W. *The War at Sea, 1939–1945*. Vol. 1. London: Her Majesty's Stationery Office, 1954.
Spector, Ronald. *At War at Sea*. New York: Viking, 2001.
Thomas, David. *Crete 1941: The Battle at Sea*. London: New English Library, 1975.

Crimea Campaign (April–May 1944)

Two-month campaign in April and May 1944 that resulted in the Soviet liberation of the Crimean Peninsula, an area that dominates the northern Black Sea and is connected with Ukraine by the 4-mile-wide Perekop isthmus. As Soviet operations around Kursk drew to an end, Generals of the Army Fedor I. Tolbukhin and Rodion Malinovsky received instructions to prepare an offensive for mid-August 1943 to clear the Donets Basin region of German troops.

By the winter of 1943, German Army Groups South and A (together numbering 93 divisions) still held a line along the Dnieper River. The German Seventeenth Army held the Crimea but had been isolated from other Wehrmacht units north of it since October. The isolation of the Seventeenth Army was accomplished by Major General Nikolai I. Trufarov as commander of the Soviet Fifty-First Army of Tolbukhin's 4th Ukrainian Front, which was at Perekop and along the Sivash, and General of the Army Andrei Yeremenko's Independent Coastal Army in Kerch. Indeed, the plight of German forces in the south was such that Army Groups South and A had to be reformed. On 5 April 1944, they were redesignated as Army Groups North Ukraine and South Ukraine, respectively.

Malinovsky's 3rd Ukrainian Front recaptured Nikolaiev on 28 March and then drove toward Odessa, which it retook on 10 April. Meanwhile, on 22 March, Romanian dictator General Ion Antonescu had flown to Berlin in an effort to persuade Adolf Hitler to allow his Romanian forces to withdraw from the Crimea. As might have been expected, the mission was futile. Hitler was determined to hold the Crimea, for in Soviet hands, it would serve as a base from which Soviet aircraft could attack the Romanian oil fields at Ploesti.

Tolbukhin's 4th Ukrainian Front was assigned the task of destroying Colonel General Erwin Jänecke's Seventeenth Army, a mixed force of 11 German and Romanian divisions, totaling some 150,000 men. In March, Tolbukhin had been summoned to meet with Soviet dictator Josef Stalin and the chief of the General Staff, Marshal Aleksandr Vasilevsky, to discuss the plan. The Crimean operation would involve the 4th Ukrainian Front, the Independent Coastal Army, the

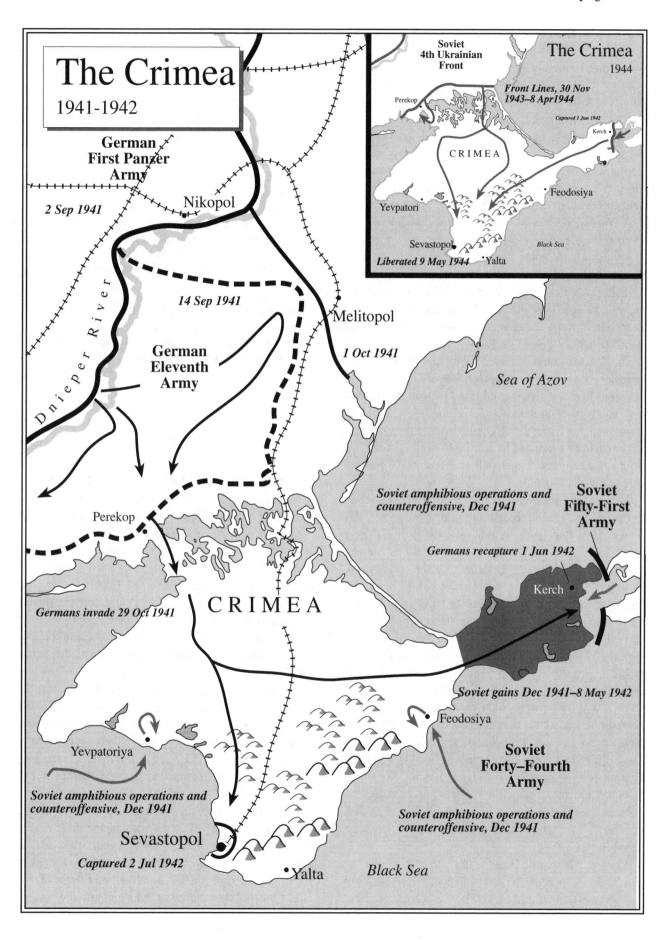

The Crimea
1941-1942

German First Panzer Army

2 Sep 1941

Nikopol

Dnieper River

14 Sep 1941

German Eleventh Army

Melitopol

1 Oct 1941

Sea of Azov

Perekop

Germans invade 29 Oct 1941

C R I M E A

Soviet amphibious operations and counteroffensive, Dec 1941

Soviet Fifty-First Army

Germans recapture 1 Jun 1942

Kerch

Soviet gains Dec 1941–8 May 1942

Feodosiya

Soviet Forty–Fourth Army

Soviet amphibious operations and counteroffensive, Dec 1941

Yevpatoriya

Soviet amphibious operations and counteroffensive, Dec 1941

Sevastopol

Captured 2 Jul 1942

Yalta

Black Sea

The Crimea
1944

Soviet 4th Ukrainian Front

Perekop

Front Lines, 30 Nov 1943–8 Apr 1944

Captured 1 Jun 1942

Kerch

C R I M E A

Yevpatori

Feodosiya

Sevastopol

Black Sea

Yalta

Liberated 9 May 1944

Azov Flotilla, and the Black Sea Fleet. Tolbukhin would attack across the Perekop isthmus and through the Sivash lagoon using Lieutenant General Georgii F. Zakharov's Second Guards Army and Lieutenant General Iakov G. Kreizer's Fifty-First Army. Follow-up attacks would target Simferopol and Sevastopol. Simultaneously, General Yeremenko would establish a bridgehead on the Kerch Peninsula and block the German escape route as well as German attempts to reinforce against Tolbukhin. Colonel General T. T. Khryukin's Eighth Air Army would support Tolbukhin, and Colonel General Konstantin A. Vershinin's Fourth Air Army would back Yeremenko. In all, the operation would involve 450,000 Soviet personnel.

On 8 April, Tolbukhin's artillery opened the attack at Perekop, followed by an artillery barrage at Sivash. Soviet engineers, working waist-deep in icy water, constructed a pontoon bridge. The next day, Yeremenko attacked from Kerch. On 11 April, Soviet forces reached the railroad junction at Dzhankoy, behind the Perekop isthmus.

On 12 April, Jänecke ordered his divisions to retreat toward Sevastopol from two prepared lines of defense stretching some 20 miles. This step occurred without Hitler's formal approval. Jänecke's forces reached Sevastopol in surprisingly good order, and he hoped to hold there until his forces could be evacuated by sea. By 13 April, Tolbukhin's troops had captured Simferopol, and Yeremenko had secured Feodosia and Yalta.

In the meantime, from 18 April, the Soviets built up their forces and artillery in preparation to storm the fortress defenses of Sevastopol, which stretched some 25 miles. These preparations were completed by 5 May, the starting date of the final battle to liberate the Crimea. At the end of April, Hitler had decided that Sevastopol had to be held, but its defenses were much weaker than they had been in 1941 when the Germans had attacked there. Also, Jänecke had only five weak divisions and little equipment. Because of Jänecke's repeated requests that his forces be evacuated, Hitler replaced him on 2 May with General der Infanterie (U.S. equiv. lieutenant general) Karl Allmendinger.

On 5 May, the Soviet Second Guards Army attacked from north of Sevastopol via the Belbel Valley. This attack was, however, diversionary; the main Soviet attack occurred on 7 May, pitting the Fifty-First Army and the Independent Coastal Army against Sapun Ridge separating Sevastopol from the Inkerman Valley. Soviet forces broke through the German lines, forcing the defenders from the old English cemetery. The Germans then retreated to the Chersonese subpeninsula.

Only on 9 May, with both the city and harbor in Soviet hands, did Hitler authorize an evacuation. The remnants of the German-Romanian force attempted to hold a dock at Kherson. However, any German hopes for a final evacuation by sea were dashed by Soviet air and naval operations. Consequently, on 13 May, the remaining Axis troops surrendered to the Red Army. Soviet authorities put total German losses in the Crimea Campaign at 50,000 killed (most all of them Germans) and 61,000 taken prisoner (30,000 of them at Chersonese). The Germans admitted to having 60,000 men lost; regardless, another German army had been destroyed.

Neville Panthaki

See also

Amphibious Warfare; Antonescu, Ion; Hitler, Adolf; Malinovsky, Rodion Yakovlevich; Petrov, Ivan Yefimovich; Ploesti, Raids on; Sevastopol, Battle for; Stalin, Josef; Tolbukhin, Fedor Ivanovich; Vasilevsky, Aleksandr Mikhailovich; Yeremenko, Andrei Ivanovich

References

Erickson, John. *The Road to Berlin*. New Haven, CT: Yale University Press, 1984.

Manstein, Erich von. *Lost Victories*. Ed. and trans. Anthony G. Powell. Chicago: Henry Regnery, 1958.

Werth, Alexander. *Russia at War, 1941–1945*. New York: E. P. Dutton, 1964.

Cripps, Sir Richard Stafford (1889–1952)

British politician and minister of aircraft production. Born in London on 24 April 1889, Richard Stafford Cripps was educated at both Winchester and Oxford University. He studied chemistry and then law, becoming a lawyer in 1913.

Physically unfit for military service, Cripps drove an ambulance in France during World War I. In 1918, he returned to the legal profession, in which he made a fortune. During the depression, he began to shed his Christian Socialist views and move toward Marxism. He also became involved in Labour Party politics and was elected to Parliament in 1931. Cripps was briefly solicitor general before refusing to serve in the National Government of 1931. Over time, he became more involved in left-wing causes and increasingly opposed to fascism. In 1939, he and Aneurin Bevan were expelled from the Labour Party because their demands for a popular front were regarded as excessively procommunist. Cripps remained in Parliament as an independent through the war.

In 1940, Prime Minister Winston L. S. Churchill sought to encourage Soviet entry in the war. Hoping that Cripps's left-wing reputation would give him some leverage in Moscow, Churchill appointed him ambassador to the Soviet Union. The experiment failed, however, and Cripps was recalled. Churchill then moved to bring him into the government, and in February 1942, Cripps became lord privy seal and leader of the House of Commons. That summer, he was sent to India to offer that country dominion status in hopes of rallying its people against Japan. But divisions in India were too great for this approach to be effective, and Cripps returned to London. His dissatisfaction with the British war effort and with Churchill in particular led to his removal from the War Cabinet in October 1942, but the next month, he was appointed minister of aircraft production, a post he held for the remainder of the war.

In July 1945, Cripps was readmitted to the Labour Party and was appointed president of the Board of Trade. In 1947, he became chancellor of the exchequer in the new Labour government. Through moral suasion, he mounted an austerity campaign, even convincing unions to accept a voluntary wage freeze. His dominance was challenged in September 1949 when he devalued the pound, and just a year later, exhausted and ill, he resigned. Cripps died in Zurich, Switzerland, on 21 April 1952.

Fred R. van Hartesveldt

See also
Aitken, William Maxwell; Churchill, Sir Winston L. S.; Dowding, Sir Hugh Caswall Tremenheere; India

References
Burgess, Simon. *Stafford Cripps: A Political Life.* London: Orion, 1999.
Cook, Colin A. *The Life of Richard Stafford Cripps.* London: Hodder and Stoughton, 1957.
Estorich, Eric. *Stafford Cripps: Master Statesman.* New York: Day, 1949.
Gorodetsky, Gabriel. *Stafford Cripps' Mission to Moscow, 1940–42.* Cambridge: Cambridge University Press, 1984.

Croatia

The peace treaties ending World War I created the Kingdom of the Serbs, Croats, and Slovenes, soon known as Yugoslavia. Ethnic diversity in the new country, which had a substantial Muslim population, led to instability and strife. Serbia, around which the new nation was formed, had been on the Allied side in the war; Croatia had been part of the old Austro-Hungarian Empire, and Croats had fought for the Central Powers. Although both peoples were Slavs, there were significant differences between them: Croatians, for example, used the Roman alphabet and were Roman Catholic, whereas Serbs utilized the Cyrillic alphabet and were Orthodox Christians.

With some justification, Croats in particular believed themselves discriminated against in the new Serb-dominated state, which imposed political, social, and eco-

nomic restrictions on Croatia. In response to these policies, Croats formed a separatist group known as the Ustae, which was supported by fascist Italy. Many Croats were pro-German and pro-Italian.

Croatians generally supported the Yugoslav government's initial 25 March 1941 decision, admittedly taken under heavy German pressure, to join the Axis alliance in World War II. The coup in Belgrade two days later that reversed this course alienated many Croats, and when the German Second Army and Italian Second Army marched into Slovenia and Croatia on 6 April, they received an enthusiastic welcome from many inhabitants. Croat units in the Yugoslav army mutinied, and on 10 April, Ustae activists proclaimed an independent Croatia and began negotiations with the Germans. Italy and Hungary each annexed parts of Croatia; what remained was combined with Bosnia-Herzegovina to form the Independent State of Croatia, or Nezavisna drzava Hrvatska (NDH), with Ante Pavelic as president. Croatia adhered to the Tripartite Pact in June 1941.

The fascist leaders of the NDH supported a policy of ethnic cleansing; the Ustaše forcibly converted to Roman Catholicism tens of thousands of Orthodox Serbs and Jews, and Orthodox Serbs were subject to racial laws. Serbs had to wear blue armbands with the letter P for *Pravoslav* (Orthodox) before they were deported to death camps. The Catholic Church, led by Archbishop Alojzije Stepinac, acquiesced in this and refused to speak out against the murder of Serbs, Jews, and Gypsies (Roma). These groups faced execution at concentration camps, of which the most infamous was Jasenovac, or they were transported to German death camps such as Auschwitz and Bergen-Belsen. Of an estimated 40,000 Croatian Jews, 32,000 died. Of the other groups, 26,000 Romani and between 330,000 and 390,000 Serbs were executed. There are no reliable estimates as to the number of Muslims killed.

Croat army forces defended the new state's borders and assisted the Germans and Italians in securing the Balkans. Some Croat units were even deployed to defend Nazi-occupied France. Although there were antifascist groups in the Independent State of Croatia, such as the Council for the National Liberation of Croatia (ZAVNOH), these groups were largely ineffective. Many Croats did join the Partisans, led by Tito (Josip Broz), to fight the Axis occupiers.

At the end of the war, as Tito's Partisans pushed north, NDH forces and fascist Croats fled to Austria. What remained of the NDH army surrendered in May 1945. British military authorities returned many NDH officials and soldiers hiding in Austria to Yugoslavia. Croatia was then reintegrated into a communist Yugoslavia. Tito had his vengeance on the Croats. Within weeks of the war's end, the

Partisans executed, without trial, perhaps a quarter million people who had sided with the Germans, most of them Croats.

Robert W. Duvall

See also
Tito; Yugoslavia

References
Macan, Trpimir, Josip Šentija, and Ivo Banac. *A Short History of Croatia.* Zagreb: The Bridge, 1992.
Tanner, Marcus. *Croatia: A Nation Forged in War.* New Haven, CT: Yale University Press, 1998.

CROSSBOW, Operation (October–December 1943)

Code name for Anglo-American air operations against the German long-range weapons program. British intelligence knew about German attempts to create a long-range military rocket within months of the war's beginning. In April 1943, Duncan Sandys, a member of Britain's War Cabinet, conducted a study of German weapons research and declared the rocket program constituted a serious threat. Discovering more about these new "V," or "Vengeance," weapons became a priority. Approximately 40 percent of all Allied reconnaissance flights from Britain between 1 May 1943 and 31 March 1944 sought information concerning Germany's V programs. The Royal Air Force soon began operations against such targets.

Two main types of V weapons were developed by Germany. First was the V-1, commonly referred to as the buzz bomb, the "flying bomb," or the "doodlebug." This was an unmanned flying bomb powered by a pulse-jet engine and developed by the German air force. Initially, V-1s were to be launched from fixed sites, but as those sites came under Allied attack, the Germans developed simpler, prefabricated launch rails that could be set up faster than the Allies could find and destroy them. The second type was the V-2, a rocket that reached the edge of the earth's atmosphere and flew at supersonic speeds. Developed by the German army, the V-2 was much more difficult for the Allies to attack because it used a mobile launching platform mounted on a truck. On the night of 17–18 August 1943, 597 RAF bombers left Britain to strike Peenemünde, the center of German rocket research on the Baltic coast. Over 700 people died in the attack, although most were forced laborers.

In November 1943, the CROSSBOW committee formally came into existence to coordinate all information concerning Germany's missile program as well as implement appropriate countermeasures. The most important CROSSBOW sites were the launch complexes for V weapons located in northern France. There were two kinds of sites under construction. First were seven "large sites," massive concrete bunkers for the storage and assembly of V-1s and V-2s. Second were numerous "ski sites," so called because of the large, curved structures designed to launch V-1s. American tests indicated the most effective assaults against these sites were made from minimal altitude using fighter-bombers. British commanders, however, had little faith in the American tests and insisted that heavy bombers should continue to be used against CROSSBOW targets, despite the growing diversion of resources from the combined bomber offensive and preparations for the Allied invasion of France. The dispute was never satisfactorily resolved.

On 12 June 1944, the first V-1s struck Britain. Initially, Allied commanders did not divert resources from OVERLORD, the invasion of France, to attack the V-1 launch sites, but within two weeks, the number of V-1s reaching Britain forced a response. On average, 97 V-1s struck Britain daily between 12 and 26 June 1944. The largest attack was on the night of 15–16 June, when 151 flying bombs reached Britain, of which 73 struck London. By 15 July, 2,579 V-1s had struck Britain, 1,280 of which fell within the London area.

As a result, the supreme commander of the Allied Expeditionary Forces, General Dwight Eisenhower, gave priority to CROSSBOW sites above all other targets, excepting "the urgent requirements of the battle." During the next two months, operations against these sites consumed half the energies of Bomber Command, and some 3,000 Allied aircrew were lost in Operation CROSSBOW. At its peak, the defense of the British Isles against the V-1s included an antiaircraft belt along the coast of 1,000 guns using the new proximity fuze, more than 2,000 barrage balloons, and 21 fighter squadrons.

By September 1944, the Allied advance in France had pushed the Germans beyond the range from which V-1s could reach Britain. But after a brief respite, attacks continued from the Netherlands, either launched in midair by obsolescent bombers or from newly constructed launch rails. The last V-1 reached England on 28 March 1945. One day earlier, the last V-2 had struck Britain. Casualties from the V-1 amounted to 6,139 killed and 17,239 seriously wounded; the V-2 accounted for 2,885 deaths and 6,268 seriously wounded.

Rodney Madison

See also
Peenemünde; Peenemünde, Raid; V-1 Buzz Bomb; V-2 Rocket

References
Craven, Wesley Frank, and James Lea Cate, eds. *The Army Air Forces in World War II.* Vol. 3, *Europe: Argument to V-E Day, January 1944 to May 1945.* Washington, DC: Office of Air Force History, 1983.

McGovern, James. *Crossbow and Overcast.* New York: William Morrow, 1964.

Saunders, Hilary St. George. *Royal Air Force, 1939–1945.* Vol. 3, *The Fight Is Won.* London: Her Majesty's Stationery Office, 1954.

Cruisers

Class of warships that in the World War II era possessed moderate armor and armament and were capable of high speed. These vessels were the successors of the eighteenth-century frigates in the age of sail. Frigates were primarily employed as reconnaissance ships for the main battle fleet. They also served in commerce protection, commerce raiding, surface combat against enemy vessels of similar strength, and blockades. Technological innovations in the mid-nineteenth century, such as steam power and iron armor, led to the development of the first modern cruiser, the U.S. Navy's *Wampanoag,* commissioned in 1867. By World War I, the major naval powers of the world had produced six different types of cruisers, charged with the tasks formerly assigned to frigates. They also were given a new task that resulted from technological change—protecting the capital ships of the fleet from torpedo attack. These warships were primarily armored cruisers, protected cruisers, light cruisers, and scouts. Also in production was the battle cruiser—a warship that incorporated battleship armament on a cruiser-sized hull and was capable of high speed. This vessel, however, was viewed largely as a capital ship rather than a cruiser. The final type was the armed merchant cruiser, a civilian-owned merchant ship or passenger liner converted to carry weapons in time of war.

In the years immediately following World War I, most of the armored, protected, and scout cruisers were considered obsolete and scrapped. The major maritime powers, primarily Great Britain, also largely discarded battle cruisers because their light armor did not adequately protect them against heavily armed enemy warships. Britain kept three (the *Hood, Renown,* and *Repulse;* the *Tiger* was discarded in 1930), whereas Japan had four Kongo-class ships.

The interwar years produced many of the cruisers that participated in World War II. Military and diplomatic developments directly affected their design, although technologically, they were almost the same as those of World War I. Many naval officials viewed the continued construction of cruisers as a dubious endeavor, partly because of the increasing ability of aircraft to perform reconnaissance, the primary duty of cruisers up to that time. Construction, however, did not diminish, as the major maritime powers still desired a warship that was capable of protecting trade routes and providing support for amphibious operations—a relatively new role that had surfaced in World War I. These vessels also proliferated as part of a new, worldwide naval arms race.

Following World War I, the great powers attempted through international agreements to prevent an arms race in warships, which many politicians believed had been a factor in the tensions that had led to war. The resulting 1922 Washington Naval Conference produced the situation that diplomats had sought to avoid when it placed restrictions on the tonnage of cruisers but not on the numbers allowed to each naval power. The nations that signed the 1922 agreement tried to correct this problem at the 1930 London Conference, which separated cruisers into two basic types: those mounting 8-inch guns and those with 6-inch or smaller guns. Building ratios between the signatory powers based on total tonnage of cruisers restricted the numbers of each type, and a clause from the Washington Treaty, stating that no warship could displace more than 10,000 tons or carry guns larger than 8 inches, governed their size. Even so, cruisers continued to be the largest surface warships built, as restrictions on battleship construction that had been set out at the Washington Naval Conference remained in place.

The 8-inch-gunned cruisers, known as "heavy cruisers," were built primarily in the years before the 1930 London Conference because most of the world's major maritime powers had already built up to the tonnage limit set for these ships by the Washington agreement. Although the United States and France managed to produce some vessels that were well-balanced designs, the majority were generally unsatisfactory, as armor was sacrificed in order to meet the 10,000-ton restriction of the Washington Treaty. An example of this imbalance was the American heavy cruiser *Portland.* This vessel measured 610' × 66', displaced 10,258 tons, and mounted a primary armament of 9 × 8-inch guns. She had a maximum speed of 32.5 knots, but the ship's armor protection consisted of a belt only 2.5 inches thick and an armored deck that was 2.5 inches deep. This armor was generally effective only against opposing destroyers armed with 5-inch guns. Larger shells could easily penetrate the protection.

Japan and Italy, each of which had signed one or both of the treaties, built heavy cruisers that solved this problem of protection through subverting the terms of the agreements. Germany, which was restricted by the Treaty of Versailles, also built heavy cruisers that violated its agreement: the heavy cruisers of the Prinz Eugen–class and the more powerful Deutschland-class. The latter class of ships mounted 6 × 11-inch guns and displaced 11,700 tons, in contravention of the 10,000-ton limit set out in the treaty.

The naval powers also produced large numbers of 6-inch-gunned, light cruisers, particularly after the 1930

London Conference as each built up to the construction limit for the type. Many of these vessels also suffered from inadequate armor protection as a result of the restrictions of the naval treaties. An example was the British light cruiser *Arethusa,* which measured 506' × 51' and displaced 5,270 tons. She mounted 6 × 6-inch guns and was protected primarily by an armored belt with a maximum thickness of 3 inches that only covered her machinery and ammunition spaces.

These vessels were charged with the same duties as the cruisers of the World War I era, with the notable exception of reconnaissance, as airplanes now fulfilled that role. For the cruisers, reconnaissance duty was replaced by a new task, resulting from the threat posed by airplanes to surface warships. Most interwar cruisers, particularly light cruisers, were built with large batteries of antiaircraft guns to protect battleships and aircraft carriers against enemy aerial attack. Some light cruiser designs were also purpose-built for this specific role. In 1937, Great Britain built the first units of the Dido-class, which became known as antiaircraft cruisers. These vessels mounted 10 × 5.25-inch guns in dual-purpose turrets that could either be trained on surface targets or elevated to an extreme angle for use against aircraft.

By the beginning of 1940, four months after the start of World War II, interwar cruiser construction, in combination with some battle cruisers retained from World War I, had created a large world cruiser force. Great Britain maintained 3 battle cruisers, 18 heavy cruisers, and 50 light cruisers; the United States had 18 heavy and 19 light cruisers; Japan operated 4 battle cruisers (by then rebuilt and reclassified as battleships), 28 heavy cruisers, and 38 light cruisers; Italy had 7 heavy cruisers and 12 light cruisers; France maintained 2 battle cruisers, 10 heavy cruisers, and 7 light cruisers; Germany operated 2 battle cruisers, 6 heavy cruisers, and 6 light cruisers; and the Soviet Union possessed 9 light cruisers. These numbers were augmented by wartime construction.

Cruisers in World War II fulfilled all of the roles that naval officials in the interwar years believed to be important. These ships were particularly valuable on the outbreak of the war in Europe in September 1939. The German navy, being much smaller than it had been in World War I, was not powerful enough to face the British Royal Navy in open combat. As a result, it was given the task of waging a commerce war on Great Britain's overseas trade routes in an effort to deny that country war materials and supplies. British cruisers were consequently used to protect against these raiders. This situation resulted in the 13 December 1939 Battle of Río de la Plata (River Plate), the first naval engagement between German and Allied warships in the conflict. The battle pitted the German pocket battleship *Admiral Graf Spee* against one British heavy cruiser and two light cruisers.

As a result of the encounter, the German vessel retreated to Montevideo, Uruguay, where its commander scuttled his ship rather than renew battle. British cruisers also served in the 1941 hunt for the German battleship *Bismarck* and heavy cruiser *Prinz Eugen,* which had been dispatched into the Atlantic to prey on shipping. Although commerce warfare by surface warships declined somewhat after the sinking of the *Bismarck* due to Adolf Hitler's loss of confidence in the navy, British cruisers continued to guard merchant convoys in the Atlantic Ocean against the occasional sortie of German warships.

In June 1940, with Italy's entry into the war, this duty expanded to the Mediterranean. British cruisers guarded against Italian cruisers attempting to disrupt supply lines that led through the Mediterranean Sea to the British home islands. Allied cruisers also performed commerce protection duties in the Arctic Ocean following Germany's invasion of the Soviet Union in 1941. Armed merchant cruisers on the Allied side were involved in blockade duty as well from the opening days of the war in the Atlantic. However, this effort was not very effective because after occupying Norway and France in 1940, the Germans had access to goods beyond those from the Soviet Union.

Cruisers also provided gunfire support for amphibious invasions not only in the Atlantic, Mediterranean, and Arctic Theaters but also in the Pacific Ocean, following the U.S. entry into the war in December 1941. Germany employed cruisers in the 1940 invasion of Norway, and the Allies utilized them during the 1942 amphibious assault in North Africa and the invasions of Sicily and Italy in 1943. They were also used to bombard and to direct fire during the 1944 invasion of Normandy, France, in Operation OVERLORD. The role of cruisers in supporting amphibious invasions proved particularly important in the Pacific, where mostly American cruisers bombarded Japanese island possessions in preparation for the landing of amphibious forces.

Arguably the greatest use of cruisers in the Pacific Theater was in their new role as antiaircraft protection for battleships and aircraft carriers. Throughout the conflict, cruisers received upgrades to their antiaircraft weaponry, as a response to the extreme threat of air attack. New antiaircraft light cruisers augmented this force. Allied cruisers provided vital cover in operations across the Pacific Theater: in the 1945 battle for Okinawa, for instance, cruisers formed part of the defensive screen to prevent Japanese suicide aircraft, known as kamikazes, from crashing into Allied ships.

The valuable duties performed by cruisers in World War II resulted in a heavy toll of ships sunk. Japan lost 39 light and heavy cruisers. Great Britain had 27 vessels sunk, and Italy and the United States lost 13 and 12, respectively. France lost 10 cruisers, the majority scuttled in order to prevent their capture by the Germans following the surrender of France in 1940. And the Germans lost 7 cruisers, the majority of these sunk early in the war in commerce raiding or during the invasion of Norway.

Eric W. Osborne

See also

Atlantic, Battle of the; Battle Cruisers; *Bismarck,* Sortie and Sinking of; Caroline Islands Campaign; Central Pacific Campaign; Destroyers; Gilbert Islands Campaign; Guadalcanal Naval Campaign; *Indianapolis,* U.S. Cruiser, Sinking of; Kamikaze; Leyte, Landings on and Capture of; Mariana Islands, Naval Campaign; Marshall Islands, Naval Campaign; Narvik, Naval Battles of; North Cape, Battle of; OVERLORD, Operation; Plata, Río de la, Battle of; *Rawalpindi,* Loss of; Solomon Islands, Naval Campaign; Southeast Pacific Theater; Southwest Pacific Theater

References

Chesneau, Roger, ed. *Conway's All the World's Fighting Ships, 1922–1946.* London: Conway Maritime Press, 1980.

George, James L. *The History of Warships: From Ancient Times to the Twenty-First Century.* Annapolis, MD: Naval Institute Press, 1998.

Preston, Anthony. *Cruisers.* London: Hamlyn, 1983.

Spector, Ronald H. *Eagle against the Sun: The American War with Japan.* New York: Free Press, 1985.

Van der Vat, Dan. *The Atlantic Campaign: World War II's Great Struggle at Sea.* New York: Harper and Row, 1988.

CRUSADER, Operation (18 November– 30 December 1941)

The failure of Operations BREVITY and BATTLEAXE, the British efforts in Libya during the summer of 1941 to relieve the siege of Tobruk, spurred British Prime Minister Winston L. S. Churchill's determination to gain a decisive victory over General Erwin Rommel in North Africa. Disregarding advice to improve the defense of the Far East, particularly the British garrison in Singapore, Churchill rushed reinforcements to Egypt.

By November 1941, Lieutenant General Alan Cunningham's Eighth Army was significantly stronger than Rommel's Panzer Gruppe Afrika in every category. It had more than 700 tanks plus 500 in reserve and in shipment, as compared with Rommel's 174 German and 146 obsolete Italian tanks; it also had almost 700 aircraft, against 120 German and 200 Italian aircraft on Rommel's side. Moreover, Rommel had not received any German reinforcements, and the Italian infantry divisions that had been transferred to Africa lacked any inherent transport of their own, which seriously restricted their movement in desert conditions. Rommel had, however, received large numbers of 50 mm antitank guns, which significantly improved his antitank capability. He had carefully husbanded all his supplies and planned to

launch another offensive to capture Tobruk, but he was preempted by General Claude Auchinleck, commander in chief for the Middle East, who launched Operation CRUSADER on 18 November.

Auchinleck planned for Lieutenant General A. R. Godwin-Austin's XIII Corps to pin down the Axis outposts on the Egyptian frontier at Bardia and Sollum, while Lieutenant General Willoughby Norrie's XXX Corps, comprising the mobile armored regiments, would sweep south of these fortified positions through the desert "to seek and destroy" Rommel's armored force. Auchinleck firmly believed that the backbone of Rommel's army had to be destroyed before Eighth Army linked up with the Tobruk garrison, which itself would break out from the fortress. From the outset, therefore, the two corps would be operating independently.

A huge storm the night before the attack turned the desert into a quagmire and grounded Luftwaffe reconnaissance flights. The element of surprise was soon wasted, however, as the British attack became disjointed and the armored brigades became involved in piecemeal battles. The majority of the fighting took place around the escarpment of Sidi Rezegh, with the Italian-built road on which Rommel's supplies were transported at the bottom and a German airfield on top. But in a repeat of the summer offensives, the British again failed to combine their armor in a concentrated blow.

The first phase of the battle, from 18 to 23 November, saw hard, confused fighting in which British and German tank formations were habitually intermingled in the highly fluid battle and often found themselves behind what would have been the enemy's lines if they had existed. Events culminated on Sunday, 23 November, aptly known in the German calendar as Totensonntag, or "Sunday of the Dead"—the name by which the Germans remember this battle. Up until that day, Rommel's skillful tactics had decimated the attacking British force, which had just 70 tanks remaining in the end. But in a concentrated attack launched by Rommel on 23 November, he lost 70 of his remaining 160 tanks.

At the end of this phase of the battle, Rommel believed that the British armor had been smashed and was spread in disorganized chaos across the desert. But despite the fact that he was thus far victorious on the battlefield, he knew that the British were able to sustain greater losses because they had a large reserve from which they could replenish their strength. He therefore decided to exploit the British confusion by striking at their vulnerability—their supplies and lines of communication. By launching a lightning thrust to the frontier, he also planned to strike at the morale and the confidence of the British troops and their commanders, as he had successfully done in the past.

Generalleutnant (U.S. equiv. major general) Ludwig Cruewell, commander of Deutsches Afrika Korps,

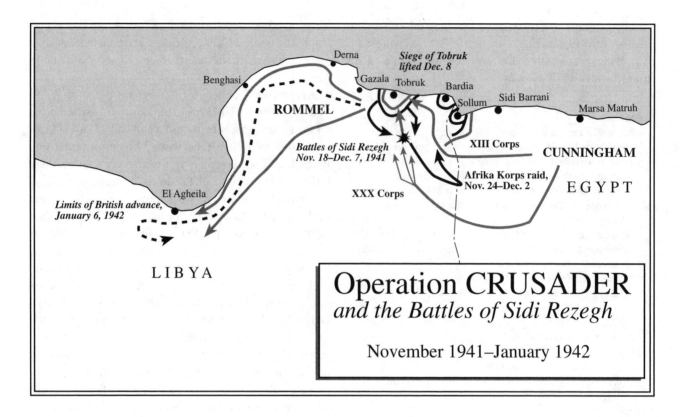

Operation CRUSADER
and the Battles of Sidi Rezegh

November 1941–January 1942

suggested that it would be better to reorganize and salvage the vast stocks of German and British matériel abandoned on the battlefield. But on 24 November, ignoring this sound advice, Rommel personally led the deep thrust with the mobile 15th, 21st, and Ariete Armored Divisions to the frontier and into the rear of the Eighth Army; he hoped this action would cause panic, result in the capture British supplies, and relieve his garrisons on the border. Rommel's "dash for the wire" very nearly succeeded, as he almost overran the two main British supply dumps and created a stampede among the British. Cunningham pessimistically sought permission to withdraw from the battle, but Auchinleck held command with a firm grip and replaced him as commander of Eighth Army with Major General Neil Ritchie on 26 November.

Rommel managed to link up again with his forces surrounding Tobruk, and he inflicted additional heavy losses on XIII Corps, which itself had advanced in an attempt to relieve Tobruk. But his losses and the strain on his supplies became too great, and on 7 December, he began to withdraw. Ultimately, he had to abandon his garrisons in the frontier outposts at Bardia and Sollum, with the loss of 14,000 troops, yet he withdrew with as much skill as he had shown on the battlefield and escaped, with his army still intact, from Cyrenaica back to El Algheila, where he had started nine months earlier.

For the first time in the war, the British had defeated the German army. They achieved much success in the battle, finally raising the siege of Tobruk and inflicting 33,000 casualties at a cost of only 18,000 British and Commonwealth casualties. But most of the Axis losses were Italian troops or German administrative staff who surrendered in mid-January in the border posts, whereas the British casualties were predominantly highly experienced, desert veterans who could not be easily replaced. Moreover, the British had failed in their principal objective of destroying Rommel's armored forces, and he was again recuperating on secure supply lines while the British attempted to prepare for the next offensive over extremely long lines of communication.

The concurrent resurgence of Axis naval power in the central Mediterranean enabled the Italians to send more supplies and reinforcements to Rommel. With additional tanks and fuel, he launched an attack on 21 January 1942, and the next day, his force, which now included more Italian divisions, was renamed Panzer Armee Afrika. Rommel's probing raid again precipitated a hasty British withdrawal, and he recaptured Benghazi, but his forces were still too weak to advance beyond the British defensive positions on the Gazala Line, which ran from Gazala (35 miles west of Tobruk) and 50 miles southward into the desert to Bir Hacheim. There, both sides paused, recuperating and preparing for the next round of the "Benghazi Handicap" in the North African Campaign.

Paul H. Collier

See also

Afrika Korps; Auchinleck, Sir Claude John Eyre; Churchill, Sir
Winston L. S.; Cunningham, Sir Alan Gordon; Dorman-Smith,
Eric "Chink"; Egypt; Gott, William Henry Ewart "Strafer"; North
Africa Campaign; Ritchie, Sir Neil Methuen; Rommel, Erwin
Johannes Eugen; Tobruk, Second Battle for

References

Gudmundsson, Bruce L., ed. *Inside the Afrika Korps*. London:
Greenhill, 1999.

Heckman, Wolf. *Rommel's War in Africa*. New York: Smithmark,
1995.

Humble, Richard. *Crusader*. London: Leo Cooper, 1987.

Jackson, W. G. F. *The North African Campaign, 1940–43*. London:
Batsford, 1975.

Liddell Hart, B. H., ed. *The Rommel Papers*. London: Collins, 1953.

Moorehead, Alan. *Desert War: The North African Campaign,
1940–1943*. London: Cassell, 2000.

Pitt, Barrie. *The Crucible of War: Western Desert, 1941*. London:
Jonathan Cape, 1980.

Crutchley, Sir Victor Alexander Charles
(1893–1986)

Royal Navy admiral whose forces participated in major actions in the Pacific, including the disastrous Battle of Savo
Island. Born on 2 November 1893 in London, Victor Crutchley served at sea in World War I and won the Victoria Cross
for heroism during the British action at Ostend, Belgium, in
May 1918. He commanded the light cruiser *Diomede* between 1935 and 1936 and was captain of the battleship *Warspite* from 1937 to 1940, seeing action during the Norwegian
Campaign. On 13 April 1940, he led the *Warspite* and several
destroyers into Narvik harbor and sank every German ship
there.

Crutchley then commanded the Royal Navy barracks at
Devonport before being transferred to the Pacific as a rear
admiral in June 1942 to take charge of a squadron of Australian and U.S. ships that had recently participated in the
Battle of the Coral Sea. His forces assisted with the U.S. invasion of Guadalcanal on 7 August 1942. However, Crutchley's dispositions contributed to the subsequent Japanese
victory in the 8–9 August Battle of Savo Island, which saw
one Australian and three U.S. cruisers sunk, with no Japanese losses. Crutchley avoided official censure for the defeat
and went on to participate in further operations in the Pacific, mostly in support of various amphibious landings.
Promoted to vice admiral, he was made the commander at
Gibraltar in 1945 and remained in that post until his retirement two years later. Crutchley died in Nettlecombe, Dorset,
England, on 24 January 1986.

Harold Wise

See also

Guadalcanal Naval Campaign; Narvik, Naval Battles of; Savo Island,
Battle of

References

Loxton, Bruce, with Chris Coulthard-Clark. *The Shame of Savo:
Anatomy of a Naval Disaster*. Annapolis, MD: Naval Institute
Press, 1997.

Morison, Samuel Eliot. *History of United States Naval Operations in
World War II*. Vol. 5, *The Struggle for Guadalcanal, August
1942–February 1943*. Boston: Little, Brown, 1949.

Pitt, Barrie. *Zeebrugge: St. George's Day, 1918*. London: Cassell, 1958.

Roskill, Stephen W. *The War at Sea, 1939–1945: Official History*. Vol.
1. London: Her Majesty's Stationery Office, 1954.

Cunningham, Sir Alan Gordon
(1887–1983)

British army general who served as a commander in Operation CRUSADER. Born on 1 May 1887 in Dublin, Alan Cunningham was the younger brother of a future admiral, Andrew Browne Cunningham. He was commissioned in the
army on graduation from Sandhurst in 1906. Decorated for
his service in World War I as a member of the Royal Horse
Artillery, Cunningham was a General Staff officer at the
Straits Settlements in Southeast Asia between 1919 and
1921. As a brigadier general, he commanded the 1st Division of the Royal Artillery from December 1937 until September 1938, when he took command of the 5th Antiaircraft
Division.

For most of 1940, Cunningham commanded, in succession, the 66th, 9th, and 51st Infantry Divisions in Britain before assuming command of forces in Kenya in October. He
was assigned the task of conquering Italian Somalia from
the south with his 11th and 12th African Divisions and the
1st South African Division. Cunningham invaded Somalia in
January, taking Kismayu on 14 February and Mogadishu on
25 February 1941. He then drove northward to Harar and on
to the capital of Addis Ababa, which fell on 6 April. Cooper-
ating with General William Platt's forces from the Sudan, he
pinned the Italian forces at Amba Alagi and forced their surrender. The campaign was a great success for Cunningham,
who was then transferred to command the British Eighth
Army in Egypt on 10 September 1941.

Beginning on 18 November, Eighth Army launched Operation CRUSADER, General Claude Auchinleck's offensive to
relieve the siege of Tobruk. With scant time to prepare and
as a stranger to armored warfare, Cunningham found himself outmaneuvered by the Afrika Korps (Africa Corps)
commander, General Erwin Rommel, at Sidi Rezegh, 20
miles from Tobruk. In what became known as the Battle of

Totensonntag, British forces suffered heavy losses, and Cunningham himself was forced to evacuate by plane. On 26 November, Auchinleck relieved him and replaced him with General Neil M. Ritchie.

Cunningham then commanded the Staff College at Camberley (1942–1943) and the Eastern Command (1944–1945). Promoted to full general, he retired in October 1946. Between 1945 and 1948, he served as the last British high commissioner to Palestine and Transjordan. Knighted on his return to Britain, Cunningham died on 30 January 1983.

Harold Wise

See also

Auchinleck, Sir Claude John Eyre; North Africa Campaign; Ritchie, Sir Neil Methuen; Rommel, Erwin Johannes Eugen; Somalia; Tobruk, Second Battle for

References

Barnett, Correlli. *The Desert Generals.* New York: Viking, 1961.

Churchill, Winston. *The Second World War.* Vol. 3, *The Grand Alliance.* Boston: Houghton Mifflin, 1950.

Cunningham, Sir Andrew Browne (First Viscount Cunningham of Hyndhope) (1883–1963)

British Admiral of the Fleet and first sea lord from 1943 through 1945. Born in Dublin on 7 January 1883, Andrew Cunningham enrolled at Stubbington House near Portsmouth to prepare for entry into the Royal Navy. Rated a midshipman in 1898, he saw action with the Naval Brigade in the 1899–1902 South African War. Although he later served in a variety of warships, he was happiest in destroyers and torpedo boats. In 1911, Cunningham took command of the destroyer *Scorpion,* remaining with her until early 1918 and spending most of World War I in the Mediterranean, the theater that became inseparably identified with his career. Promoted to captain in 1920, he thereafter held staff positions in the Baltic, Mediterranean, and West Indies. After being made rear admiral in 1934, he commanded the destroyer flotilla in the British Mediterranean Fleet from 1934 to 1936. He then commanded the battle cruisers squadron and was second in command of the Mediterranean Fleet in 1937 and 1938. From September 1938 until June 1939, he was deputy naval chief of staff. Promoted to vice admiral and universally called "ABC," Cunningham became commander of the Mediterranean Fleet in June 1939.

The collapse of France militarily and Italy's entry as an Axis belligerent in June 1940 prompted his first significant actions in World War II—the peaceful neutralization of the French fleet at Alexandria and an engagement with the Italians on 9 July 1940 off Calabria; in the latter, he pursued a powerful force returning from North Africa into Italian home waters, damaging its flagship. Four months later, on 11 November 1940, with his fleet strengthened by the addition of the carrier *Illustrious,* Cunningham launched a night air attack on the Italian base at Taranto, sinking three battleships, two of which were later raised and repaired. On 28 March 1941, he fought the Italians off Cape Matapan, sinking three heavy cruisers and two destroyers and damaging a battleship. Soon afterward, however, British armies in Greece and Crete required evacuation, and Cunningham's full support of them brought severe losses to his ships from German air attacks.

In June 1942, Cunningham became the Admiralty's representative to the Combined Chiefs of Staff in Washington. Promoted to Admiral of the Fleet, he became Allied naval commander in chief in the Mediterranean in October 1942. Cunningham oversaw Operation TORCH, the Allied landings in North Africa in November 1942, and the Allied assaults on Sicily in April 1943 and at Salerno five months later, followed by Italy's surrender and internment of the Italian fleet at Malta.

When First Sea Lord Sir Dudley Pound died in October 1943, Cunningham succeeded him, serving in the post for the rest of the war. Often at odds with Prime Minister Winston L. S. Churchill, he also faced growing American naval dominance and a very different war in the Pacific. Ennobled in September 1945, he retired in June 1946, recognized as one of the last British admirals in the Nelson tradition. Cunningham died in London on 12 June 1963.

John A. Hutcheson Jr.

See also

Calabria, Battle of; Cape Matapan, Battle of; Crete, Naval Operations off; Great Britain, Navy; Italy, Navy; Pound, Sir Alfred Dudley Pickman Rogers; Salerno Invasion; Sicily, Invasion of; Taranto, Attack on; TORCH, Operation

References

Barnett, Correlli. *Engage the Enemy More Closely: The Royal Navy in the Second World War.* New York: Norton, 1991.

Cunningham, Andrew Browne. *A Sailor's Odyssey: The Autobiography of Admiral of the Fleet Viscount Cunningham of Hyndhope.* New York: Dutton, 1951.

Grove, Eric J. "Andrew Browne Cunningham: The Best Man of the Lot." In Jack Sweetman, ed., *The Great Admirals: Command at Sea, 1587–1945,* 418–441. Annapolis, MD: Naval Institute Press, 1997.

Pack, S. W. C. *Cunningham the Commander.* London: Batsford, 1974.

Winton, John. "Admiral of the Fleet Viscount Cunningham of Hyndhope." In Stephen Howarth, ed., *Men of War: Great Naval Leaders of World War II,* 207–226. New York: St. Martin's Press, 1992.

Cunningham, Sir John Henry Dacres (1885–1962)

British navy admiral who was commander in chief and Allied naval commander in the Mediterranean. Born on 13 April 1885, at Demerara, British Guiana, John Cunningham joined the British navy in 1900 and specialized in navigation. During World War I, he served in the West Indies, in the Mediterranean, and with the Grand Fleet. In 1916, he survived the sinking of the battleship *Russell,* struck by a mine in the waters off Malta. Between the wars, Cunningham, promoted to captain in 1924, held a variety of staff and seagoing positions, acquiring an intimate knowledge of Mediterranean waters while serving there during the Abyssinian crisis. In 1938, he became fifth sea lord and chief of naval air services. He was promoted to vice admiral in 1939.

In 1940, his squadron took part in the Norway Campaign and the ill-fated Anglo-French expedition to Dakar. In early 1941, Cunningham was appointed fourth sea lord, responsible for supplies and transport—a vital position in which he remained for two years, winning a knighthood in 1941. In June 1943, he became commander in chief of the Levant, one of the two Mediterranean commands; later that year, he was made commander in chief and Allied naval commander of both commands, directing British, U.S., French, and Greek vessels. Cunningham's forces were responsible for amphibious assaults at Anzio and in the south of France (Operation DRAGOON).

In May 1946, Cunningham took over as first sea lord from Lord Cunningham of Hyndhope, thereby becoming the first navigation officer to attain the navy's highest position. (The two men were not related.) As part of the British postwar economy drive, he supervised drastic cuts in the wartime fleet, including the scrapping of many serviceable vessels. In January 1948, he was promoted to Admiral of the Fleet, retiring in September 1948 to become chairman of the Iraq Petroleum Company, where he remained for ten years. He died in London, on 13 December 1962.

Priscilla Roberts

See also
Anzio, Battle of; Cunningham, Sir Andrew Browne; Dakar, Attack on; DRAGOON, Operation; Norway, German Conquest of
References
Chatterton, Edward K., and Kenneth Edwards. *The Royal Navy: From September 1939 to September 1945.* 5 vols. London: His Majesty's Stationery Office, 1942–1947.
Jones, Matthew. *Britain, the United States, and the Mediterranean War, 1942–1944.* New York: St. Martin's Press, 1996.
Roskill, Stephen. *The War at Sea.* 3 vols. London: Her Majesty's Stationery Office, 1954–1961.

Cunningham, Winfield S. (1900–1986)

U.S. Navy officer in command of the naval air station on Wake Island. Born in Rockfield, Wisconsin, on 16 February 1900, Winfield Cunningham entered the U.S. Naval Academy in 1916. His class graduated in 1919 because of World War I, and Cunningham was commissioned an ensign. He then held a variety of sea assignments. In 1924, he was accepted for flight training. His aviation career began in scout planes and culminated with command of VF 5 (Fighting Five) Squadron aboard the carrier *Yorktown.*

On 28 November 1941, Commander Cunningham took command of the naval air station under construction at Wake Island in the Pacific. His command consisted of 500 Marines from the 1st Defense Battalion, 12 F-4F Wildcat aircraft of Marine fighter squadron VMF 211, and various support personnel. There were also more than 1,100 civilian contractors assisting in the construction.

The Japanese attacked Wake Island beginning on 8 December (7 December in Hawaii). For 15 days, the defenders held them off, but eventually, faced with overwhelming odds and concerned over the fate of the civilians on the island, Cunningham was forced to surrender. He and his command spent the next four years in Japanese captivity. During this time, Cunningham attempted to escape twice.

In 1946, Cunningham took command of the seaplane tender *Curtiss.* From June 1947 until his retirement from the navy as a rear admiral in June 1950, he commanded the Naval Technical Training Center, Memphis, Tennessee. Cunningham died on 3 March 1986 in Memphis.

M. R. Pierce

See also
Wake Island, Battle for
References
Cressman, Robert J. *The Battle for Wake Island: A Magnificent Fight.* Annapolis, MD: Naval Institute Press, 1995.
Cunningham, Winfield S., and Lydel Sims. *Wake Island Command.* Boston: Little, Brown, 1961.
Schultz, Duane. *Wake Island: The Heroic, Gallant Fight.* New York: St. Martin's Press, 1978.

Currie, Lauchlin (1902–1993)

Adviser to President Franklin D. Roosevelt. Born 8 October 1902 in West Dublin, Nova Scotia, Canada, Lauchlin Currie studied at the London School of Economics and Harvard, where he taught for several years. He moved to Washington in 1934 to work at the U.S. Treasury and Federal Reserve Board and was Roosevelt's White House adviser on economic affairs from 1939 to 1945.

Sent to Chongqing (Chungking) in January 1941, Currie

met there with Chinese leaders. He recommended that China be added to the Lend-Lease program, despite the fact that Generalissimo Jiang Jieshi (Chiang Kai-shek) was more interested in building up his strength vis-à-vis the Communists than in fighting the Japanese. He helped set up the American Volunteer Group (the Flying Tigers) under Claire Chennault as well as a training program in the United States for Chinese pilots, and he expanded the China National Aviation Corporation.

Currie's paper to the Joint War Board in May 1941 on Chinese aircraft requirements stressed the role a Chinese air force could play in defending Singapore, the Burma Road, and the Philippines against Japanese attack and also pointed out China's potential for bombing Japan itself. Currie recommended Owen Lattimore as political adviser to Jiang and argued against concessions to Japan.

In 1942, when British Prime Minister Winston L. S. Churchill diverted supplies from China to North Africa and Jiang threatened to discontinue war with Japan, Roosevelt dispatched Currie to Chongqing to soothe the generalissimo and to patch up strained relations between Jiang and his chief of staff, U.S. Lieutenant General Joseph W. Stilwell. Currie recommended Stilwell's recall, but this action was delayed until 1944. By 1943, when he moved to the Foreign Economic Administration, Currie had come to share Churchill's view of China as a relatively unimportant theater. In early 1945, he headed the Allied delegation to Bern to persuade the Swiss to block Nazi bank balances and halt the flow of German supplies through Switzerland to Italy.

Part of Currie's work involved negotiating with the Soviets on wartime and postwar loan agreements and other matters. When his name appeared in partially decrypted Soviet cables between Moscow and Washington—the so-called Venona Papers—some believed Currie was a Soviet agent. He appeared before the House Committee on Unamerican Activities (HUAC) in August 1948 to deny these allegations. Although no charges resulted, U.S. authorities refused to renew Currie's passport in 1954 because he had taken up residence in Colombia following his appointment as the head of a World Bank mission there between 1949 and 1950 and his subsequent marriage to a Colombian. In 1958, he became a Colombian citizen. Currie taught in the United States and Canada as a visiting professor from 1966 to 1971, but he was active in Colombia as that government's most important economic adviser until his death in Bogota on 23 December 1993.

Roger Sandilands

See also
Chennault, Claire Lee; China, Role in War; Flying Tigers; Lend-Lease; Roosevelt, Franklin D; Stilwell, Joseph Warren; Switzerland; Tobruk: Second Battle for, Third Battle of

References
Sandilands, Roger J. *The Life and Political Economy of Lauchlin Currie: New Dealer, Presidential Adviser, and Development Economist.* Durham, NC: Duke University Press, 1990.
Schaller, Michael. *The U.S. Crusade in China.* New York: Columbia University Press, 1979.

Curtin, John Joseph (1885–1945)

Australian politician and prime minister from 1941 to 1945. Born at Creswick, Victoria, Australia, on 8 January 1885, John Joseph Curtin became a printer and trade union activist. During World War I, he was imprisoned for his activities as secretary of the Anti-conscription League. In 1917, Curtin switched to journalism, editing the Perth-based weekly *Westralian Worker.* Eleven years later, he was elected as the Labour member of Parliament for the seat of Fremantle, a position he held with only one break, between 1931 and 1934, until his death; he also became head of the Labour Party in 1935.

In the internationally crisis-ridden late 1930s, Curtin's party split over foreign policy, but he favored extensive rearmament and moving closer to the United States for protection. When World War II began, he refused to join the coalition government headed by Sir Robert Menzies but pledged his party's support for war. On 3 October 1941, Curtin became prime minister; he remained in that post until his death almost four years later. He emphasized his country's growing autonomy from Britain by making a separate Australian declaration of war on Japan following that country's attack on Pearl Harbor. Curtin infuriated both Winston L. S. Churchill and Franklin D. Roosevelt by refusing to allow Australian troops returning from the Middle East to divert to Burma. He called for greater Australian reliance on the United States and, from spring 1942, worked closely with the U.S. commander in the South Pacific, General Douglas MacArthur, in demanding more British and U.S. resources for the Pacific Theater. Curtin nonetheless resented Australia's exclusion from many critical wartime decisions, and he sought to develop a Commonwealth secretariat. A heavy smoker, Curtin died of lung congestion at Canberra, Australia, on 5 July 1945.

Priscilla Roberts

See also
Australia, Role in War; Churchill, Sir Winston L. S.; MacArthur, Douglas; Menzies, Robert; Roosevelt, Franklin D.

References
Curtin, John. *In His Own Words: John Curtin's Speeches and Writings.* Ed. David Black. Bentley, Australia: Paradigm Books, Curtin University, 1995.
Day, David. *John Curtin: A Life.* New York: Harper Collins, 1999.

Ross, Lloyd. *John Curtin: A Biography.* South Melbourne, Australia: Macmillan, 1977.

Smith, Frederick T. *Backroom Briefings: John Curtin's War.* Ed. Clem Lloyd and Richard Hall. Canberra: National Library of Australia, 1997.

Czechoslovakia

In 1938, the Republic of Czechoslovakia had the highest standard of living and was the only democracy in central Europe. It also had an intractable minorities problem that made it vulnerable to neighboring states, especially Germany. Czechoslovakia numbered about 15 million people in all, but only about 7 million—not even a majority of the population—were Czechs. Three million were Germans, 2.5 million were Slovaks, and 1 million were Hungarians. In addition, there were about a half million Ukrainians living in Ruthenia and also a number of Poles.

Czechoslovakia had been formed at the end of World War I from a union of Bohemia and Moravia, which had long been part of Austria, and Slovakia, which had been part of Hungary. The 1919 Paris Peace Conference awarded it Ruthenia, in order to provide a land connection with Romania. With Romania and Yugoslavia, Czechoslovakia formed the so-called Little Entente. In addition, the Czechs had a firm alliance with France as well as one of Europe's most important arms-manufacturing centers in the Skoda Works at Pilsen, and it had an excellent, 400,000-man army. These facts, however, counted for little when the French and British, under heavy pressure from German leader Adolf Hitler at the September 1938 Munich Conference, forced the Czech government headed by President Eduard Beneš to yield the Sudetenland, with a largely German population, to Germany. This area contained the natural defenses of the new state. Hungary and Poland also seized territory.

Then, on 15 March 1939, Hitler broke his pledge to respect what remained of Czechoslovakia and gathered the remainder of the state into the Reich. Acquiring it was a tremendous boost to the Germans militarily, for thirty-five highly trained and well-equipped Czech divisions disappeared from the anti-Hitler order of battle. Hitler had also eliminated the threat from what he had referred to as "that damned airfield," and the output of the Skoda arms complex would now supply the Reich's legions. In Bohemia and Moravia, the Wehrmacht absorbed 1,582 aircraft, 2,000 artillery pieces, and sufficient equipment to arm 20 divisions. Indeed, any increase in armaments that Britain and France achieved by March 1939 was more than counterbalanced by German gains in Czechoslovakia. There, the Germans secured nearly a third of the tanks they deployed in the west in spring 1940, and between August 1938 and September 1939, Skoda produced nearly as many arms as all British arms factories combined.

The Germans organized their new acquisition as the Protectorate of Bohemia-Moravia. The Slovak lands became the Republic of Slovakia, a vassal state of Germany ruled by the Slovak People's Party, which was headed by Roman Catholic priest Monseigneur Jozef Tiso. Slovakia had declared its independence from the remainder of Czechoslovakia on 14 March. The eastern province of Ruthenia (Trans-Carpatho-Ukraine) was ceded to Hungary.

The Germans immediately disbanded the Czech military, allowing President Emile Hácha only a small ceremonial guard. Although long-term German plans for the protectorate included the removal of the Slavic population and its replacement by Germans, initial German occupation policies were much more lenient than in the remainder of central and eastern Europe, inspired by the goal of exploiting Czech industry and resources without inciting revolt. The initial occupation period was peaceful. This fact is explained by several factors: the area's proximity to the Reich proper, disillusionment with the West following the Munich Agreement, lenient German policies, and the lack of coordinated Czech resistance. Student protests against German rule in October 1939 on the anniversary of the independence of Czechoslovakia did, however, bring closure of the universities and the execution of nine students.

On 16 April 1940, Baron Konstantin Hermann Karl Neurath became Reich protector of Bohemia-Moravia, after the departure of the military governor, Generaloberst (U.S. equiv. full general) Johannes von Blaskowitz. However, Berlin became dissatisfied with Neurath's lack of harsh measures to curb protests, and on 27 September 1941, he was replaced by the head of the Reich Security Office, Reinhard Heydrich. The latter declared martial law and carried out a series of arrests that destroyed the leadership of the student protesters and other Czech national opposition.

On 27 March 1942, a group of British-trained Czech commandos ambushed Heydrich's car in Prague and mortally wounded him; he died on 4 June. The Gestapo then instituted a wave of terror during a period of martial law that lasted until July and included the destruction of the villages of Lidice and Lezaky and the deaths of most of their inhabitants. On 20 August 1943, Wilhelm Frick was appointed Reich protector. However, Hans Frank, Reich minister of state for Bohemia and Moravia, exercised real authority. The level of active Czech resistance remained relatively low and consisted chiefly of providing intelligence information.

President Beneš had gone abroad in October 1938, and he established a Czech government-in-exile, first in Paris

German troops entering Waldhaeusl in Czechoslovakia, 3 October 1938. (Hulton Archive)

and then in London. In the summer of 1942, he secured official British and Free French repudiation of the 1938 Munich Agreement. But Beneš stressed accommodation with the Soviet Union, and he traveled to Moscow to sign a formal treaty of alliance with the Soviets on 18 July 1941. He sought a democratic, independent Czechoslovakia that would be a bridge between East and West.

During the war, the Czech government-in-exile contributed an armored brigade to the Allied cause—some 5,000 men who fought with British forces in the Normandy Campaign. Czech pilots participated in the 1940 Battle of Britain, and four Czech squadrons (three fighter and one bomber) served with the Royal Air Force during the war. Czech military units were also formed on Soviet territory, including, by the summer of 1943, the 1st Czechoslovak Parachute Brigade of some 2,500 men. The 2nd Czechoslovak Parachute Brigade was formed in 1944, and it participated in an uprising in Slovakia against the government

there in August 1944. Czech military units in the Soviet Union ultimately established the I Czechoslovakian Corps, which distinguished itself in the fighting to cross the Carpathian Mountains. The Soviets also formed the 1st Czechoslovakian Fighter Regiment, which evolved into the 1st Czechoslovakian Air Division by the end of the war.

On 5 May 1945, a general uprising occurred in Bohemia and Moravia against the Germans, centered on a rising in the city of Prague as Soviet Marshal Ivan Konev's 1st Ukrainian Front approached from the east and U.S. Lieutenant General George S. Patton's Third Army drove on the capital from the west. The Czech government-in-exile appealed to Supreme Commander of Allied Expeditionary Forces General Dwight D. Eisenhower for assistance, but he refused to allow Patton to intercede. The Germans reinforced with two divisions, but they had no tanks or artillery and were halted by General Andrei Vlasov's 1st Division, which had deserted from the Germans. On 9 May, Vlasov's troops cleared the remaining Germans from Prague, taking some 10,000 prisoners. The next day, Konev's troops entered the city. The Germans formally surrendered on 11 May. During the war, an estimated 350,000 people in the protectorate died as a result of the German occupation.

Meanwhile, Tiso's Slovak People's Party ruled Slovakia. Tiso's wartime independent Slovak government was dominated by fascist, anti-Czech, anti-Semitic elements, represented by personalities such as Karol Sidor and Alexander Mach, who were supported by a paramilitary organization known as the Hlinka Guards. The war stimulated economic growth in Slovakia, and on 24 November 1940, Slovakia signed the Anti-Comintern and Tripartite Pacts. Its military commitment to the Axis was two divisions, comprising some 50,000 men. Slovakia adopted a resettlement program for its Jewish population in August 1940, and it enacted a Nuremberg-type Jewish code on 10 September 1941. An uprising by Slovaks against the Tiso government was crushed by German military intervention in the form of 40,000 troops by October, the Soviets being unable to provide military assistance to the resistance. At the end of the war, Tiso's government retreated with German forces into Austria in April 1945, and Tiso surrendered there to U.S. forces on 8 May 1945. Beneš's cherished hopes of an independent democratic Czechoslovakia after the war were not realized. In 1948, the Communists seized power in the country.

Neville Panthaki and Spencer C. Tucker

See also

Beneš, Eduard; Blaskowitz, Johannes von; Collaboration; Eisenhower, Dwight D.; Frick, Wilhelm; Heydrich, Reinhard Tristan Eugen; Konev, Ivan Stepanovich; Lidice Massacre; Munich Conference; Neurath, Konstantin Hermann Karl; Partisans/Guerrillas; Patton, George Smith, Jr.; Resistance; Tiso, Josef; Vlasov, Andrei Andreyevich

References

Dolezal, Jiri. *Czechoslovakia's Fight: Documents on the Resistance Movement of the Czechoslovak People, 1938–1945.* Prague: Publishing House of the Czechoslovak Academy of Sciences, 1964.

Korbel, J. *Twentieth-Century Czechoslovakia: The Meanings of Its History.* New York: Columbia University Press, 1977.

Mamatey, V., and R. Luza, eds. *A History of the Czechoslovak Republic, 1918–1948.* Princeton, NJ: Princeton University Press, 1973.

Mastny, Vojtech. *The Czechs under Nazi Rule: The Failure of National Resistance, 1949–1942.* New York: Columbia University Press, 1987.

Prazmovska, Anita. *Eastern Europe and the Origins of the Second World War.* New York: St. Martin's Press, 2000.